# What's New in This Edition

Previous editions of *PowerBuilder Unleashed* dealt with the features of the then-current versions of PowerBuilder, versions 4.0 through 6.0. This edition has been reworked to cover the new features and products available in PowerBuilder 7.0. Some of these new features include

- The new PowerBuilder development environment

- The Web DataWindow

- Enhanced component-generation features

- Enhanced support for transaction servers

- Enhanced Internet capabilities

- Integration with Enterprise Application Studio (EAS)

In addition, the examples and descriptions from the previous editions have been reworked. This means even more in-depth and advanced concepts for you to use.

We have also enhanced some chapters to address such issues as

- PowerBuilder and the UML

- New PowerBuilder controls

- Expanded PFC functionality

Above all, we hope that this edition of *PowerBuilder Unleashed* will be your definitive reference guide for your PowerBuilder development efforts.

# PowerBuilder 7.0
### Third Edition

*Simon J.A. Herbert*
*Simon Gallagher*
*Joe Quick*
*Ken Reppart*

## SAMS

A Division of Macmillan USA
201 West 103rd Street
Indianapolis, Indiana 46290

# Unleashed

# PowerBuilder 7.0 Unleashed, Third Edition

International Standard Book Number: 0-672-31782-6

Library of Congress Catalog Card Number: 99-64777

Printed in the United States of America

First Printing: November 1999

01  00  99     4  3  2  1

## Trademarks

All terms mentioned in this book that are known to be trademarks or service marks have been appropriately capitalized. Sams Publishing cannot attest to the accuracy of this information. Use of a term in this book should not be regarded as affecting the validity of any trademark or service mark.

PowerBuilder is a trademark of Sybase, Inc.

This publication was produced using the Advent **3B2** Publishing System.

## Warning and Disclaimer

**EXECUTIVE EDITOR**
*Rosemarie Graham*

**ACQUISITIONS EDITOR**
*Shelley Johnston*

**DEVELOPMENT EDITOR**
*Susan Shaw Dunn*

**MANAGING EDITOR**
*Charlotte Clapp*

**PROJECT EDITOR**
*George E. Nedeff*

**COPY EDITOR**
*Geneil Breeze*

**INDEXER**
*Chris Barrick*

**PROOFREADERS**
*Maryann Steinhart*
*Mary Ellen Stephenson*
*Tony Reitz*

**TECHNICAL EDITORS**
*Kevin Thompson*
*David Ray*
*Joel Pearson*
*Harris R. "Beau" Lynch III*

**MEDIA DEVELOPER**
*Jason Haines*

**INTERIOR DESIGN**
*Gary Adair*

**COVER DESIGN**
*Aren Howell*

**COPY WRITER**
*Eric Borgert*

**3B2 DESIGN**
*Scott Cook*

**3B2 LAYOUT**
*Susan Geiselman*
*Daniela Raderstorf*

# Overview

# Table of Contents

## PART III DESIGN TO DEPLOYMENT

### 17 Application Development and PowerBuilder 655

### 18 Analysis, Design, and Implementation 671

## PART VII    APPENDIXES

### A    PowerBuilder Resources    1225

### B    PowerBuilder Data Types    1231

### C    Investigating Exported Code    1235

### D    Getting Certified in PowerBuilder    1255

# About the Authors

**Simon J.A. Herbert** graduated in 1991 from the University of Notre Dame with a bachelor of arts degree in economics and computer applications. He is an engineer manager at Praxis Solutions, an Indianapolis-based software process engineering company. Simon is a Certified PowerBuilder Developer Associate and has taught as a Certified PowerBuilder Instructor (versions 3.0 to 6.0). He is also a Microsoft Certified Professional and Certified Trainer in Visual Basic.

Simon has been developing custom business applications for the past eight years. These applications encompass numerous different business systems, including insurance, sales, order entry, pharmaceutical clinical trials, financials, and Web-based training development. These systems were developed using Visual Basic, Access, InterDev, and PowerBuilder running against a variety of different DBMSs (Sybase, MS SQL Server, and Oracle). Simon's current focus is on helping define and use repeatable processes in the creation of software by implementing techniques such as use cases and the UML.

You can reach Simon on the Internet at herbs@iquest.net and explore his Web pages at http://members.iquest.net/~herbs/.

**Simon Gallagher** graduated in 1991 from the University of Kent at Canterbury, England, with a first-class bachelor of science with honors degree in computer science. He is now an independent consultant and part-time instructor based in Indianapolis. Simon is also a Certified PowerBuilder Associate since version 3.0 and is still hoping—although now it seems against all hope—to find time to become a Certified PowerBuilder Professional. He is also a Microsoft Certified Professional, Microsoft Certified Trainer in SQL Server, and a Microsoft Certified System Engineer.

Simon has been programming in PowerBuilder since version 2.0 and has successfully fielded a number of different applications, ranging from a property tax reporting system to an order-entry system. He has been involved with a number of different hardware platforms and operating systems, and has a broad knowledge of databases and development languages. As part of the PowerBuilder 2.0 project team, he worked to help debug the first Informix 5.0 DBMS interface for PowerBuilder.

You can reach Simon on the Internet at raven@iquest.net and explore his Web pages at http://members.iquest.net/~raven/raven.html.

**Joe Quick** graduated in 1992 from Indiana University in Bloomington, Indiana, with a bachelor's degree in computer information systems within the School of Business. Now a consultant with Professional Data Dimensions, Inc., Joe has been developing in PowerBuilder since version 3.0 and has worked on a number of applications across multiple business sectors including manufacturing, clinical pharmacology, and life re-insurance. You can reach Joe via email at jquick@iquest.net.

**Ken Reppart** graduated in 1995 from Taylor University with a bachelor of science degree in political science/systems. Since then, he has done client/server development on a number of development platforms, including PowerBuilder, Visual Basic, and Microsoft Office. Ken has had the opportunity to develop applications in several industries, including finance, manufacturing, insurance, education, and semiconductors. He sometimes resides in Indianapolis and works as a client/server consultant.

Ken's professional interests include software engineering, object-oriented programming, and program visualization. He is currently researching the visualization of database structures using multidimensional graphing techniques. You can reach Ken at kenneth@reppart.org, or visit his Web site at http://www.reppart.org/members/kenneth.

# Dedication

*To my son, Malcolm; my wife, Rebecca; and our new son, Devon, for being my inspiration and for keeping life in perspective. Also, to my parents, Ann and Alan Herbert, for their guidance, love, and support.*

—Simon J.A. Herbert

*To my parents, Paul and Hilary, for their intelligence, gentleness, sense of humor, support, patience, and understanding that have been so inspirational in my life. And to my grandparents, Cyril and Joy Lowther and George and Audrey Gallagher, who have been so supportive and loving over the years. Last but never least, to Andrea, my wife and constant companion in life's little journey. Woof! (A dedication to Ulric, my dog, in terms he would understand!) This book is for all of you who have been a guiding light and influence in my life.*

—Simon Gallagher

*To my wife, Michelle, and my beautiful daughter, Bailey, for their patience, support, and inspiration throughout not only this task, but also my life as a whole. Also, to my parents, Mike and Terry, for instilling a strong work ethic and the desire to tackle new challenges.*

—Joe Quick

*To my wonderful family, for inspiring me to be my best and for always supporting and loving me. For my mother, without whom I would have surely gotten lost along the way.*

—Ken Reppart

# Acknowledgments

This book is the combined effort of a number of people, and we would like to take this opportunity to thank Shelley Johnston, our acquisitions editor, and Susan Dunn, the development editor, for their help, guidance, and patience through the process of writing this book.

Thanks to all those who have sent encouraging emails for all the editions, and many thanks for keeping our spirits up while writing this new edition.

Many thanks to all of those who have contacted us to point out the odd problem that made it past us and for other useful suggestions on the previous editions. They have been greatly appreciated, and we have tried to act on many of the suggestions—please don't hesitate to drop us an email. Thanks to all the people involved at Sams Publishing. Thanks to our technical editors Kevin Thompson, David Ray, Joel Pearson, and Beau Lynch for catching our stupid mistakes.

Many thanks to our co-workers and friends for their assistance, knowledge, encouragement, and keeping track of the Mood-O-Meter.

The most special thanks come from all four authors to our families, near and far, who have been supportive of our efforts.

—Simon, Simon, Joe, & Ken

In addition to the individuals already noted, I would like to thank a few more people. First, I wouldn't have had the motivation or patience to attempt any book without the love and support of my family. Rebecca, thanks for your encouragement, for giving me the time to work, and for letting me vent. A huge thanks also goes to my oldest son, Malcolm, for your smile, providing much-needed distractions, and making the pressure bearable. Rebecca, Malcolm, and Devon, thanks for reminding me of what's really important.

To the rest of my family, the Herberts, Josons, Higgins, Kruses, and Warfields, thank you for all your encouragement. Also, many thanks go to my friends at and out of work for providing me with ideas and keeping me sane (company salute for you, Terry). To Ken, Joe, and Simon for being great guys to work with and great friends.

—Simon J.A. Herbert

Many thanks go to my mother, Hilary, for her impromptu transatlantic French lesson (see if you can find where that is in the book!).

Special thanks to Ulric (my 3-year-old collie) for being a late-night (early-morning) writing companion.

To Mike Mangin, Lance Gordon, and Sherri Anderson for their always-down-to-earth views on PowerBuilder development—thanks for keeping my feet on the right path when it was required. Many thanks to Dennis Prothero for allowing me to be part of his development team and for his contribution to Chapter 18.

*—Simon Gallagher*

In addition to the already mentioned individuals, I would like to thank a few more people. I wouldn't have been able to accomplish this task without the love and support of my family. Michelle, thank you for the time and understanding. To my daughter, Bailey, you give not only perspective on life but inspiration as well.

To both of my families, the Quicks and the Gundlachs (Gun-Locks), for the love and support that have always been endless. Also, to my fellow developers on Release 1: the Phantom Menace, Tony Reid, Tony O'Neill (the test freak), Dave Hill, Anil Dantes, and Brad Miller. The distractions, ribbing, and humor were priceless. Finally, to the Takamine guitar company for producing such a wonderful, mind-clearing distraction when I just couldn't look at another word.

*—Joe Quick*

Thanks to everyone who helped me with the two long-distance moves I undertook during the writing of this book. Special thanks to Holly for helping keep me on track and being there when I needed someone to talk to. Additional thanks to Steven, Robert and Heidi, Jen, the whole café crew, and all those who have challenged, encouraged, and supported me over the years.

*—Ken Reppart*

# Tell Us What You Think!

As the reader of this book, *you* are our most important critic and commentator. We value your opinion and want to know what we're doing right, what we could do better, what areas you'd like to see us publish in, and any other words of wisdom you're willing to pass our way.

As an associate publisher for Sams, I welcome your comments. You can fax, email, or write me directly to let me know what you did or didn't like about this book—as well as what we can do to make our books stronger.

*Please note that I cannot help you with technical problems related to the topic of this book, and that due to the high volume of mail I receive, I might not be able to reply to every message.*

When you write, please be sure to include this book's title and authors as well as your name and phone or fax number. I will carefully review your comments and share them with the authors and editors who worked on the book.

Fax:      317-581-4770

Email:    office_sams@mcp.com

Mail:     Michael Stephens, Associate Publisher
          Sams Publishing
          201 West 103rd Street
          Indianapolis, IN 46290 USA

# Introduction

Since 1994 there has been a steady succession of PowerBuilder books, ranging from beginner-oriented books to more advanced volumes. Many of them, however, fail to provide much in-depth knowledge. In 1995, the first edition of *PowerBuilder Unleashed* was released with the aim of providing an all-encompassing book, one that would really allow you to unleash the power in PowerBuilder.

*PowerBuilder Unleashed* was written not as a tutorial or a replacement for the PowerBuilder manuals but as a complement to them. It provides a depth of knowledge based on real-world experience not found in most other books, and we hope you will turn to this book as your central repository of information about PowerBuilder.

This book doesn't spend time creating a fanciful application that is of little real use to people; it does, however, show many advanced concepts and include a number of reusable objects that can be incorporated into your existing framework. If you don't have a framework yet, these can be used to start building the foundations for one. Sample code from relevant chapters has been made available on the CD-ROM included with this book, and you should find some of it sufficiently useful to drop it into your existing framework or class library.

We recognize that some beginning and intermediate developers learn quickly, and some of the early chapters were written with you in mind. These chapters help bridge the gap for all PowerBuilder developers and include information for those of you who consider yourselves at an advanced level. While we were writing this book, we all managed to surprise each other with little pieces of information that you might have expected seasoned developers to know.

Throughout this book you will encounter a small variety of naming and coding standards. We didn't want to constrain ourselves to any one particular style because so many different standards are in use. The code you will see uses the standards that we use in our everyday application development; you might want to adopt some or all of the standards used.

A great deal of thought, time, and effort has been poured into making this the best book we could produce. *PowerBuilder Unleashed* addresses the advanced concepts the Power-Builder community is crying out for. We hope this will be the reference and guide you turn to first while you are developing your PowerBuilder applications.

PowerBuilder 7.0 has incorporated some significant changes and is still changing, which means we were discovering new features after this book was submitted for editing. We have managed to include all the new features that we learned about during the review stage.

One last thing before you delve into this book: If you find any discrepancies, bugs, or outright lies, we want to know. You can send your findings to us, either in care of Sams Publishing or to the Internet accounts listed in the author biographies. The feedback from the previous editions has been very positive, and we hope to hear more about your PowerBuilding experiences.

Happy reading, and may you expand your knowledge.

# PowerBuilder 7.0 New Features

**CHAPTER 1**

PowerBuilder 7.0 delivers a brand new look and feel to the development environment. In keeping up with changing times, Sybase has enhanced its IDE to provide a more flexible tool to help you with software creation. With the new look, PowerBuilder 7.0 has incorporated new technology for the Internet, components, and n-tier software solutions. These enhancements coincide with the release and consequent integration with Sybase's Enterprise Application Studio (EAS) version 3.0.

This chapter provides a brief overview of the new PowerBuilder features as they relate to particular areas, and tells you where to look in the book for more details.

# Developer Productivity

It's hard not to notice the radical changes to the development environment when you first open PowerBuilder 7.0. Until now, developers have been using basically the same interface for a number of years. Although the new interface takes some time to get used to, much of the interface has been created with developer ease-of-use and speed in mind.

PowerBuilder 7.0 productivity features include the following:

- Pane technology—The multiple pane/view technology introduced with the Power-Builder 6.0 debugger has become the standard for most of 7.0's IDE. This allows for complete customization of the development environment.

- AutoScript—The PowerBuilder 7.0 script editor automatically displays a list of possible ways to complete a statement that you're entering. This includes functions, events, properties, variables, and controls.

- Object-centric development—All objects are accessed in the same manner and have a greater consistency in the development environment for the different objects.

- Help integration—PowerBuilder has increased developers' ability to implement custom help solutions into their applications.

- New controls—PowerBuilder 7.0 offers several new window controls to enhance the look and feel of your applications.

- Developer-defined shortcut keys—You can now define your own keyboard shortcuts for most tasks that you want to accomplish.

- Enhanced ease-of-use features—These features include such functionality as a true Explorer-style Library painter, multilevel Undo/Redo, and expanded Recently Used lists for objects, applications, and connections.

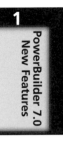

- New wizards—PowerBuilder 7.0 includes several wizards to help you create applications, components, and objects.

- To-do list—This is a system- and developer-generated list of tasks that still need to be completed.

For more information on the new interface, see Chapter 2, "PowerBuilder 7.0 Development Environment."

# Internet

With PowerBuilder 7.0, Sybase has continued to expand and refine its Internet capabilities. These advances integrate with the tool suite provided in Sybase's Enterprise Application Studio. PowerBuilder 7.0's new Internet features include the following:

- By providing the Web DataWindow (also called the HTML DataWindow), PowerBuilder 7.0 gives you the power of the DataWindow using HTML and JavaScript that's generated for you.

- With the ActiveX DataWindow, developers can use existing DataWindows in an Internet Explorer browser.

- Support for JPEG and GIF (including animated GIFs) by all controls that allow images.

- Enhanced table support.

- Integration with the EA Server's Web capabilities.

Along with these Internet-specific features are a number of component-generation enhancements that you can use when developing Internet applications in PowerBuilder. For more information on PowerBuilder's Internet features, see Chapter 29, "PowerBuilder and the Internet," and Chapter 30, "Developing Internet Applications with PowerBuilder."

# Distributed Computing

To supplement the Internet features and EAS, PowerBuilder continues its dedication to the distributed environment. New features for PowerBuilder 7.0 include the following:

- EAS components—PowerBuilder 7.0 components (native code) can be executed within EA Server.

- MTS components—You can generate COM components with PowerBuilder to be deployed to Microsoft Transaction Server (MTS).

- Component code validation—When deploying a PowerBuilder custom class user object as a component, PowerBuilder can provide a warning of invalid code for the selected deployment environment (Jaguar or COM).

- Integrations wizards—Wizards have been added to help you create and deploy components to EA Server and MTS.

- Enhanced component control—You control your component's instance pooling and transactions.

- Error logging—You can log errors for MTS and EA Server.

- Resultset support—Components can use two new types, `ResultSet` and `ADOResultSet`, to return database resultsets from components.

For information on these new features, together with the rest of the functionality of Distributed PowerBuilder, see Chapter 28, "Developing Distributed PowerBuilder Applications."

# Database Connectivity

PowerBuilder 7.0 supports the following new or enhanced database connectivity features:

- JDS and JDM (Sun and Microsoft) JDBC database interface support

- OLE DB interfaces for OLE DB API compliant DBMS (such as Microsoft SQL Server)

- Oracle 8.0.04 and 8.0.05 database interfaces

- Sybase Open Client database interface for use with PowerBuilder n-tier application deployed to Jaguar CTS

- Informix 9. *x* database interface

- Enhancements for new functionality to the Sybase Open Client interface for use with Adaptive Server Enterprise (ASE) 11.5

- Updated ODBC driver for Sybase Adaptive Server Anywhere version 6.0

- Support for DirectConnect Transaction Router Service via the Sybase DirectConnect interface to DB2/MVS databases

For more information on the new database connectivity features in PowerBuilder 7.0, see Chapter 3, "Database Management Systems."

# Component Creation

PowerBuilder 6.0 introduced the Component Factory, Sybase's object-generator technology, which allows developers to generate different component models by using existing PowerBuilder knowledge. PowerBuilder 7.0 has expanded this functionality to enhance distributed application development including the Internet. In addition to your standard PowerBuilder executable application components, the 7.0 component features allow you to create

- Jaguar components/proxies

- COM/MTS components

- Java proxies

- PowerBuilder proxies

- OLE Automation servers

This technology allows PowerBuilder developers to extend their knowledge to create different deployment options. Chapter 20, "Application and Component Implementation, Creation, and Distribution," covers the generation of these components.

# EAS Integration

PowerBuilder 7.0 fits into Sybase's Enterprise Application Studio very nicely. This ties to Sybase's strategy of creating an Integrated Application Environment (IAE) to create, deploy, and manage client/server and distributed applications. PowerBuilder 7.0 can deploy native PB code to EA Server directly from the development environment. These native PowerBuilder components can be debugged remotely, and included is the capability for Live Editing for testing these components. The tight integration with PowerBuilder and the rest of EAS provides a powerful environment for creating and deploying client/server, distributed, and Internet applications.

These interactions with EAS are discussed in several places in PowerBuilder 7.0. The integration of the tools is mentioned throughout the book.

# Summary

In creating version 7.0 of PowerBuilder, Sybase has continued to listen to the needs of the development community and to follow the direction of current technology. PowerBuilder has revamped its development environment interface and expanded its distributed application and Internet capabilities. With this new release, PowerBuilder looks to ensure its place as a leader in the application-development tools market.

# PowerBuilder 7.0 Development Environment

If you've developed in prior versions of PowerBuilder, your first reaction when opening the 7.0 development environment might be to ask, "What happened?" The second question might be, "What do I do?". This chapter addresses your interface questions.

In PowerBuilder 6.0, Sybase completely reworked the Debugger's interface to include its Pane/View metaphor. This was to get developers used to the radical change that the development environment was about to undertake. As you can see, the development environment has been completely rewritten in PowerBuilder 7.0 to provide a more flexible and powerful environment. In this chapter, you see how to use the Pane/View metaphor and the common views you will find throughout the various object painters.

# Working with Objects

Before you can even use a pane or view to develop your application, you first have to be able to create your objects. In prior versions, this was done by selecting the appropriate object painter icon on the PowerBar and specifying whether you wanted to create a new object, inherit an object, or open an existing object. This would be fine except that the painter icons are no longer on the PowerBar.

Sybase has implemented *object-centric development*. The access path to all objects is the same through the PowerBar. Figure 2.1 shows the new PowerBar.

The first three icons on the PowerBar are used to create, inherit, and open the different PowerBuilder objects. If you click the New PowerBar icon, you see the New dialog, which contains six tab pages. The following identifies the tab pages and describes the options on them.

**FIGURE 2.1**
*The 7.0
PowerBar.*

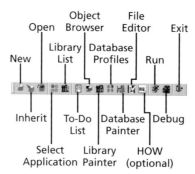

| Tab Name | Description |
| --- | --- |
| Start Wizard | Lets you create new PowerBuilder applications, new PowerBuilder applications based on a template, new Jaguar components, new COM/MTS components, and new OLE Automation servers. It also includes the Migration Assistant for migrating existing PowerBuilder applications to 7.0. |
| Object | Lets you create all the standard PowerBuilder objects (user objects, windows, menus, structures, functions) and provides four wizards to help you create Connection objects (to a database or transaction server), Jaguar components, COM/MTS components, and OLE Automation servers. |
| DataWindow | Lets you create any of the 11 styles of the DataWindow object. |
| Database | Allows you to access the Database Painter, create new query objects, and create new pipeline objects. |
| Project Allows | you to use wizards or manually create project objects for PowerBuilder executables, proxy objects, Jaguar proxy objects, Jaguar components, COM/MTS components, OLE Automation servers, Java proxies, and applications that use Web.PB. |
| Tool | Allows you to access the Library painter, PowerBuilder's file editor, the Debugger, the DataWindow Syntax tool, the Application Profiler, and the PFC Extender. |

**2**

**PowerBuilder 7.0 Development Environment**

Select the tab you want, double-click the icon you want to use, and you are on your way.

If you want to inherit a window, menu, or user object or open an existing object, you will use essentially the same interface. Clicking either the Inherit or Open icon on the PowerBar opens a dialog like the one shown in Figure 2.2.

**FIGURE 2.2**

*The Open dialog.*

To use the Inherit or the Open dialog, select the kind of object you want to work with (for example, a window) from the Object Type list box at the bottom of the dialog. All objects of the selected type will be listed near the top of the dialog. If you have multiple libraries in your application's library search path, selecting a different library in the Application Libraries list will change the objects displayed in the list box. After you find the object you want to work with, select it and click OK. This takes you into the painter for the selected object type.

**Tip**

You can select multiple libraries at once in the Application Libraries list box by Ctrl+clicking or Shift+clicking.

Although each object has different functionality, some elements remain the same across all object painters. The rest of this chapter focuses on these common features. The other chapters in this book focus on those interface components specific to the different painters.

# Panes and Views

When a painter opens, it displays a series of windows, referred to as *panes* (see Figure 2.3). Each pane enables you to look at a different aspect of the object you're working with.

Having multiple panes open at once reduces the number of modal dialogs that you need to work with in PowerBuilder.

**FIGURE 2.3**
*The Window painter.*

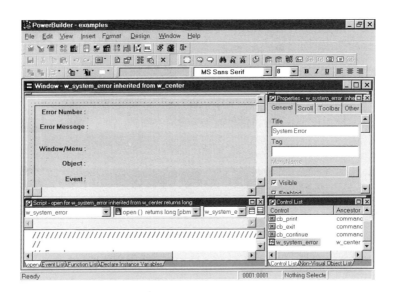

First you must familiarize yourself with the way in which you can configure the development environment to your liking. The goal of the new interface is to provide more functionality and give you full control over what information is viewed and the way in which it's viewed.

## What You Can View

Each pane displays different information that you can use. PowerBuilder provides a default layout for each painter, but you can change that layout to suit whatever task you're performing. To access the different views available to you in a particular painter, look at the View menu. When you select a view, the painter opens a separate pane in which to display that information.

## The Anatomy of a Pane Window

You can view each piece of information in an individual pane, or you can stack the panes and create a tab interface within a pane. When you begin using the new interface, it might be difficult at first to keep track of the different panes and what each one represents. You can specify whether each pane should have a title bar, depending on your comfort level with the painter.

By default, some of the views don't display any title bars. If you move your mouse to the top of a pane, the title bar appears with a description of the pane. The title bar allows you to maximize the pane and close it via the standard title bar buttons. In a pane has been maximized, clicking the Restore button will return the pane to its original size in relation to the other panes. In addition to using these buttons, you can click the thumbtack in the upper-left corner of the title bar in each pane; this "pushes in" the thumbtack so that the title bar remains in view. When the title bar is displayed, you can right-click it and toggle the view between being docked or floating. A floating view makes the view a pop-up window so that it sits on top of all other views.

> **Tip**
>
> It's a good idea to use these title bars until you have a chance to customize your layout. When you are comfortable with the views, you can remove the title bars to increase your workspace.

You can use the handle (a small rectangle with a blue line in it) to "carry" the pane to a new location. When you position your mouse over the handle, the mouse pointer changes to an arrow with a small rectangle. You can click the handle and drag the pane to a new location.

Pane movement is probably the most difficult process to get used to. You can use the pane handle to drop the pane in numerous locations. The basic movements are similar to the movements you can make with any PowerBuilder toolbars—to the top, bottom, left, or right. The only twist is that the options for placement depend on which other panes are open. If you have four panes open, you can specify whether the pane you're moving will be sized to the full screen or relative to a pane. Suppose that you want to move a pane to the right side of the screen. You can place the pane along the full length of the screen, or next to another pane.

Another option for pane placement is on top of another pane. When this is done, the dragged pane is merged with the target pane, and each view is displayed as a tab.

If you want to take a tab from an existing pane and view it as a standalone pane, choose the desired object from the View menu to open a new pane. You now have the same information being displayed twice: once as an individual pane and once as a tab in a pane. To remove the tab page, select the tab, right-click it, and choose Close from the pop-up menu.

## Saving Layouts

After you open all the views that you need and size them appropriately, you can save your layout by choosing Options from the Design menu. On the Options property sheet, click the Layout tab. If you want to save your current layout, select the item from the displayed list that says (Current) and click the Save As button. You can then enter a name for the new layout.

PowerBuilder allows you to create as many views as you want. To switch between views, just go to the Layout tab, select the view you want, and click OK. If you want to return to the default PowerBuilder layout, click the Default button on the Layout tab. This feature lets you customize the painters to the different tasks you're performing.

# Common Views

Although each painter will have views that aren't used anywhere else in PowerBuilder, a number of common views are used across several painters.

## Layout View

Layout view (see Figure 2.4) displays a graphical representation of the object you're working with. In Layout view, you can add, move, and delete controls and control the design of the graphical aspect of the object.

**FIGURE 2.4**
*Layout view.*

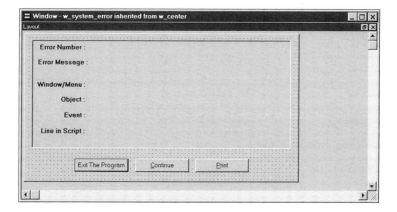

PowerBuilder 7.0 has multiple-level Undo/Redo. This means that if you change the location of several objects in Layout view, PowerBuilder keeps track of them, and you can actually step back more than one level.

## Properties View

Instead of the modal property sheet found in the past few versions of PowerBuilder, you now have a Properties view (see Figure 2.5). The displayed properties are for the object you're working on or for any selected controls. The Properties view dynamically changes what's displayed when you select a different object. The selection of an object can be done by using the Layout, Control List, or Non-Visual Object List views.

**FIGURE 2.5**

*Properties view.*

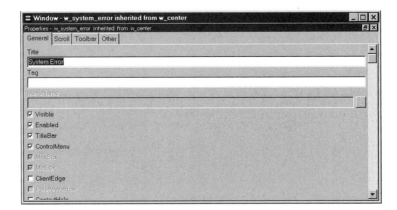

### Tip

If you select more than one object at the same time, PowerBuilder displays the properties common to all selected objects.

If you right-click the Properties view, you can change how the property labels appear on the view. You can choose for the labels to be on the top of the property or on the left side of the property.

### Note

The property names listed on the property sheet are the exact names that you will use to reference the properties in your code.

> **Tip**
>
> If you're working with an object that has many design-time properties, placing the labels on the left allows you to reduce the amount of scrolling that needs to be done.

## Control List View

Control List view displays all visual controls on the object you're working with. When you select one or more controls in the list, they are also selected in Layout view, and their common properties are displayed in Properties view. If you double-click an object in Control List view, Script view is displayed for the specific object.

## Non-Visual Object List View

The Non-Visual Object List view looks similar to Control List view. It shows a list of the nonvisual objects inserted into the object.

## Script View

Before you can master the PowerScript language (covered in Chapter 7, "The PowerScript Language"), you need a place to write your code. Because PowerBuilder is event-driven, your code will be dispersed across events for the different objects that make up your PowerBuilder application. Scripts can be written for many PowerBuilder objects: the application object, windows, window controls, menus, user objects, and functions. It doesn't matter whether the script you're writing is for a menu's `Clicked` event or a DataWindow control's `Constructor` event—the interface will be the same. The Script view is the editor you use throughout PowerBuilder to enter PowerScript statements.

> **Tip**
>
> To easily work with Script view, maximize it unless you have your resolution set to at least 1024 × 768 pixels.

As well as writing scripts for objects, you often need to write user-defined functions and events to incorporate all the business rules and commonly used procedures. Script view is the underlying foundation for the creating both.

# Script View Navigation

If you're coding the first script for your object, PowerBuilder places you in the most commonly used or default event for that object (for example, the Clicked event for a command button). The Script view title bar identifies the object and the event that causes the script to execute.

It's likely that you will want to code a script for a different event for the same object. To do so, click the Event drop-down list box located at the top of the view and select the desired event.

You can also activate the list by pressing Ctrl+2. The arrow keys enable movement up and down through the list. Pressing Enter when your choice is highlighted takes you to the script for the event, and pressing Esc closes the drop-down list. Script view indicates whether code is written for an event by placing a picture of a sheet of paper with lines on it next to the event name. The icon will appear up to three different ways:

- *All white* indicates that there is script written for an event for the current object only.

- *All purple* means the current object is inherited; it indicates that script has been written in an event for the ancestor.

- *Half white/half purple*, as you might expect, means that there is script written in the current descendant and in the ancestor.

For more information on accessing the script, see the later section "Script Inheritance."

# Script View Properties

You can customize the Script view. Choose Options from the Design menu to open the Options property sheet. The property sheet for the Script view lets you specify general settings, the font used, syntax color specifications, and the drop-downs available.

## The Script Tab Page

Use the Script tab page to specify general settings for the Script view's behavior. You can define for auto-indentation how many spaces you want to equal one tab (the default is three). It also contains the Enable Auto Indenting check box, which enables/disables PowerBuilder's capability to automatically perform indentation on flow-of-control statements. For example, without this option set, on a Choose...Case statement, you would specify the test expression to be evaluated by the statement, press Enter, press Tab, and then place the first Case statement. With Auto Indent, you don't need to press Tab because PowerBuilder recognizes the flow-of-control statement and indents for you.

As well as providing the auto-indentation settings, the Script tab page has several options that you can turn on or off. The Allow Dashes in Identifiers check box, when checked, allows you to create variable names containing dashes. The other four check boxes indicate what types of warnings and messages the script compiler displays: compiler and database warnings and obsolete and informational messages.

## The Font Tab Page

The Font tab page allows you to specify the font used in Script view. You can specify not only the font but also the font style, size, strikeout, underlining, and the text and background colors. After you make your selections, click OK to close the property sheet or the Apply button to automatically apply your changes but not close the property sheet.

**Note**

The property settings for Script view are global; they are applied to all scripts for all applications.

## The Coloring Tab Page

One other feature that makes coding for PowerBuilder developers easier is a color-coded script editor. Depending on the settings you specify on the Coloring tab page, PowerBuilder uses different colors to indicate keywords, comments, data types, and so on.

The Coloring tab page allows you to turn off the color coding by deselecting the Enable Syntax Coloring check box. If it's checked, though, you have 15 different types of PowerScript statements, such as enumerated data types and keywords, that you can specify to be colored differently. For each specified PowerScript statement, you can set the text color and the background color. This is useful because you can now differentiate comments, keywords, errors, and data types just based on their colors.

**Tip**

One use of a color-enabled editor is to make comments appear as very light gray so that they blend into the background and allow you to see the actual code statements.

## The AutoScript Tab Page

The AutoScript tab page specifies how new function behaves. AutoScript helps you write your application's code. When you pause while typing code into Script view, PowerBuilder displays a pop-up window with a list of variables, functions, and properties. The first item in the list that matches what you've typed is selected. Double-clicking an item in the list pastes it into your code (this can also be done by pressing Enter and then Tab). You can include local variables, class variables, and class functions in the list that appears.

If you don't want the pop-up window to always appear when you pause, you can choose the Activate Only Immediately After a Dot option. This means that the pop-up window will appear only after you type a period into Script view.

After you specify all the preferences for Script view, click OK or Apply to have the changes made to your scripting environment.

# The PainterBar Script Icons

To help you write scripts for your application, the PainterBar contains several options to provide standard text editor functionality (for example, Cut, Copy, and Paste) as well as some shortcuts useful in writing code.

## Pasting Variables

A common need when writing code is the capability to enter specified application component names (method arguments, global variables, instance variables, PowerBuilder object names, shared variables, or window names) into your script. PowerBuilder 7.0 includes six toolbar icons for displaying lists of those application components so that you can paste them into your script.

When you click an icon on the PainterBar, a drop-down list appears with all applicable values. By clicking an item that appears in the drop-down list, you paste the item name into your script where the cursor is positioned. This saves you from having to type the name or remember a multitude of object names.

### Note

The use of these drop-downs points out one of the many reasons it's important to give your objects and controls meaningful names rather than accept the defaults. It's difficult to remember the difference between `cbx_1` and `cbx_22` from a drop-down list, but you can easily remember `cb_insert` and `cb_delete`. For information on naming conventions, see Chapter 18, "Analysis, Design, and Implementation."

The Paste list boxes can also be accessed by right-clicking Script view, selecting Paste Special, and then selecting the desired component type.

---

**Caution**

In the Windows environment, when you use the drop-down lists to paste information into your script, PowerBuilder copies the selected object or variable to the Windows Clipboard. Therefore, anything that has been previously copied to the Windows Clipboard is destroyed.

---

## Text Manipulation

Because Script view is essentially a text editor, it provides the standard Windows capability to undo changes, cut, copy, paste, erase/clear, and select all text. These text-manipulation options are also available on the Edit menu.

---

**Note**

Script view has two useful features: draggable text and multilayer undo. You can select text, click it (without releasing the mouse button), and drag it to a new location. By holding down the Ctrl key while using the same process, you can copy the selected text.

---

## Adding Comments

Also located on the PainterBar are two icons that provide the capability to comment out and uncomment selected text. The comment icon uses the single-line comment ( / / ) for all lines selected as opposed to the multiline comment ( /*). This provides a quick method of commenting out large blocks of code.

All the PainterBar icons discussed thus far help manipulate the text that you've typed into Script view. Wouldn't it be useful to have a development tool that helps write the code? Script view provides this capability with four more PainterBar icons. The Paste Function, Paste SQL, Paste Statement, and Object Browser icons increase productivity and reduce the need for memorization of exact syntax by using a graphical interface to assist in code generation.

## Pasting Functions

The Paste Function toolbar icon displays a pop-up menu that lets you chose all the built-in PowerBuilder functions, user-defined global functions, and global external functions. From the list, you can select one that opens a drop-down list in Script view. From the list, you can select a function and paste it into your script. The only detractions to using this method are that only the function name is pasted into your script (instead of the full function syntax) and it takes some length of time before the dialog opens. You must access online help to find the syntax for the pasted function.

## The Paste SQL Option

The Paste SQL icon provides a method for graphically creating cursor, noncursor, and stored procedure SQL statements. Clicking the PainterBar icon displays a pop-up menu that allows you to specify the type of SQL statement you want to create. When the SQL statement is coded to your satisfaction, it's pasted into the Script view. For detailed information on Paste SQL's capabilities, see Chapter 4, "SQL and PowerBuilder."

## Pasting Statements

To insert the syntax for PowerScript statements such as `If...Then`, `For...Next`, and `Choose Case`, click the Paste Statement icon on the PainterBar. Like the other Paste options, you are presented with a pop-up menu that allows you to select the desired flow-of-control statement.

Select the statement type that you want to paste into your script. The statement's framework is then inserted after the cursor in your script. You must then modify the statement to suit your particular business logic. For example, if you can't remember the exact syntax for the `Choose Case Else` statement, select it from the Paste Statement pop-up, and you will see the following appear in your script:

```
CHOOSE CASE /*expression*/
    CASE /*item*/
        /*statementblock*/
    CASE ELSE
        /*statementblock*/
END CHOOSE
```

## The Object Browser

You access the Object Browser from the PowerBar by using the icon of the glasses in front of two cubes (which hasn't changed much from version 6.5). The Object Browser gives extra development assistance by allowing you to paste any attribute, object, variable, or function into your application. This tool can be useful when you consider that the PowerScript language contains more than 400 different functions. In addition to each function, multiple objects and controls have attributes you must learn. It becomes increasingly difficult to remember object names, attributes, and functions as your application continues to grow. The Object Browser provides a means to reduce the amount of information you must memorize (and that you have to type into your event script).

The Object Browser enables you to view all objects and the properties, functions, global variables, instance variables, names, shared variables, and structures associated with them (see Figure 2.6). It's a pop-up window, so it always appears on top of whatever painter you're working with in PowerBuilder. This increases the browser's functionality considerably as you use it to view object information without having to constantly open and close it. The browser also allows you to open your PowerBuilder application's objects from within it (by right-clicking the object name in the browser window and selecting Edit from the pop-up menu).

**FIGURE 2.6**

*The Object Browser.*

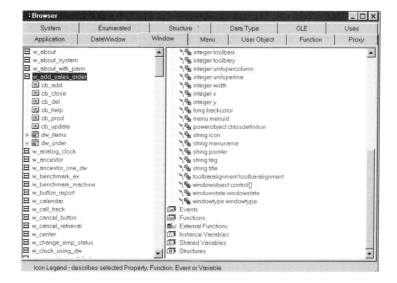

The Object Browser uses several tab pages to access each different type of object you can have in your application. In most of the tab pages, the Object Browser is divided into two list boxes. The list box on the left indicates all objects in your application that are of the object type selected (you get this information by clicking a tab). The list box on the right displays detailed information or categories about the selected object, such as properties, events, functions, variables, and structures.

For each category, the Browser indicates the inheritance and access designation. (In Figure 2.6, the arrow next to a property indicates that it's inherited.) The squares next to a property indicate scope, access designation, and read and write access by using different numbers of squares and coloration. Although you can memorize what each graphical representation means, it's considerably easier to view the legend at the bottom of the Object Browser.

> **Note**
>
> You can control whether you view the Object Browser legend and inherited properties, events, and functions by right-clicking the right half of the browser. This displays a pop-up menu with the options Show Inherited and Show Legend.

You can also view the object inheritance tree in your application by right-clicking and selecting Show Hierarchy. If you want additional information about the selected item, right-click the item and select Help to open to the appropriate PowerBuilder help page.

After selecting the desired attribute or function, right-click it and select Copy to have the information copied to the Clipboard. After doing this, you can position your cursor in your script and paste the copied information into your script.

To reference controls in a window, select Window as the object type, which then lists all window objects in the current application (the Show Hierarchy option must be off). Locate the desired window and double-click the object's name. This expands the list, with the window name followed by the name of the controls that appear on the window. You can use the same method for user objects and to reference the menu-item hierarchy (see Figure 2.7).

The Object Browser is also the best place to find all the valid enumerated data types. If you select an object type as Enumerated, the browser shows all of PowerBuilder's enumerated data types and the possible values for each.

The browser also allows you to create a rich text format (RTF) document that displays the selected object and the corresponding category details (see Figure 2.8). You do this by selecting Document from the pop-up menu. From the Document window, you can export the RTF document to a file, copy it to the Clipboard, or print it.

## Searching and Replacing

You can search for specified text and replace text in Script view. The Find, Find Next, and Replace options can be accessed from the Edit menu or from the three PainterBar icons containing binoculars. The Find option opens the Find Text dialog, which allows you to incorporate case matching, expressions, searching forward and back, and wrapping the search when the beginning or end is reached. Find Next lets you continue your search on the specified text. In addition to a search facility, you can use the Replace Text dialog, which is useful for making variable name changes throughout a script. Changes can be made all at once or can be verified before each replacement is made.

**FIGURE 2.7**
*An expanded menu hierarchy using the Object Browser.*

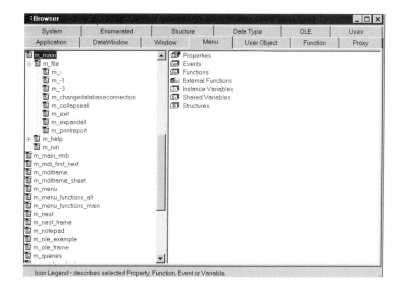

**2**
PowerBuilder 7.0
Development
Environment

**FIGURE 2.8**
*The Document window.*

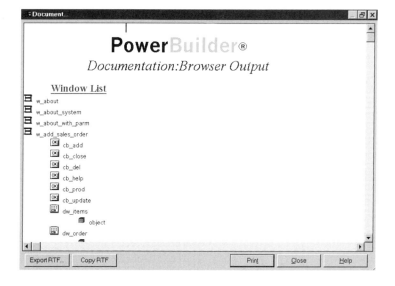

An additional option under the Edit menu only is Go To. This option opens a large submenu, which lets you quickly navigate to a specific line number, event, function, control, or variable.

> **Note**
>
> While you are in Script view, PowerBuilder displays a position counter in the status bar. This counter indicates the line where the cursor is positioned and the number of positions from the far-left side of the painter. The line counter enables easy movement to a particular line number. An asterisk also appears if PowerBuilder has detected any change to the script.

## Compiling the Script

Script view automatically compiles any code when you click the Close icon or select a different script or object. If you prefer to have the code compile as it's coded, press Ctrl+L, select the Compile PainterBar icon, or choose Compile from the Edit menu. If the script compiles cleanly, PowerBuilder lets you move on and work on something else. If the code syntax isn't correct, the Script view displays an error code and a message stating what the problem is (see Figure 2.9).

**FIGURE 2.9**
*The compile error message window.*

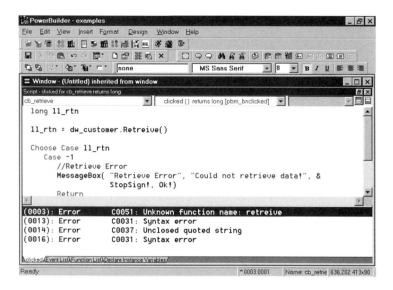

The error message at the bottom of Script view provides the line number on which the error occurred, the PowerScript error code, and the PowerScript error message. To correct the problem, you must first go to the line in error. You could start at the beginning and count lines, but that might get tedious if the script is more than 10 lines long. The row number and column number are also displayed in the MicroHelp area of the status bar in the bottom-right corner. The best method to jump to the line in error is to click the error message for the error you want to fix; the cursor will move to that line number.

After jumping to the erroneous line, you need to determine which error occurred and what fix is required. If the problem is with the syntax of a PowerScript statement or function, position the cursor within the keyword and press Shift+F1. Context-sensitive help will be displayed for the PowerScript statement.

A common (and unhelpful) error message, `Error C0031: Syntax error`, indicates only that PowerBuilder has found an error; it doesn't give a clear indication of where the problem might be. Often, the culprit causing the error is a missing keyword or punctuation mark.

Occasionally, the syntax error message points to the number of a line with no code. This situation frequently occurs when you're using a flow-of-control statement such as an `If...Then` statement with the `End If` not coded or an embedded SQL statement without the semicolon terminator.

If a compile error occurs, your first reaction probably is to move on and deal with the compile error later. No problem, right? Wrong! Remember, PowerBuilder won't let you save the object until the problem is resolved. If you're going to leave the problem until later, select the lines of code causing the error (or, even easier, use the Select All PainterBar icon) and click the Comment icon on the PainterBar. You can then save the object and return later to uncomment the erroneous code and fix the problem.

You can also capture compiler warnings, database warnings, informational messages, and obsolete syntax messages by selecting the corresponding menu items under the Script tab page (accessed from the Options menu's Design option). All messages display in the same window as the compile errors, but unlike with compile errors, you're not forced to address a warning message to leave the Script view or save the object. With the database warnings, PowerBuilder actually validates embedded SQL against the current database (see Chapter 5, "Databases and the Database Painter"), which may or may not be the intended database and might not have had the referenced database objects created in it yet. The obsolete syntax message is useful if you're migrating an existing application or are used to coding in earlier versions of PowerBuilder. You should aim to fix this last type of errors because Sybase might stop supporting some function names and syntax that have been carried through from previous versions.

2

PowerBuilder 7.0
Development
Environment

**Note**

A useful new feature of PowerBuilder 7.0 is the capability to hide and show any error messages you receive. In prior versions, there was no way to remove the error message window unless you fixed all the errors or commented everything out and compiled. PowerBuilder 7.0 provides an icon in the upper-right corner of Script view that toggles the display of the error window. This gives you additional space to work in when fixing errors.

## Keyboard Command Reference

For you keyboard enthusiasts, Table 2.1 is a list of valid keystrokes that can be used while in the Script view.

TABLE 2.1    Keyboard Commands That Can Be Used in the PowerScript Painter

| Keyboard Shortcut | Action |
| --- | --- |
| Ctrl+$n$ ($n$=1 through 3) | Script view drop-down list boxes |
| Ctrl+F4 | Close painter |
| Ctrl+A | Select all |
| Ctrl+C | Copy |
| Ctrl+F | Find text |
| Ctrl+G | Find next text |
| Ctrl+H | Replace text |
| Ctrl+L | Compile script |
| Ctrl+Q | Exit PowerBuilder |
| Ctrl+V | Paste |
| Ctrl+X | Cut |
| Ctrl+Y | Redo |
| Ctrl+Z | Undo |
| Ctrl+left arrow | Skip previous word |
| Ctrl+right arrow | Skip next word |
| Shift+F6 | Text editor |
| Shift+F1 | Context-sensitive help for selected function |

If a keyboard shortcut that you want isn't there, PowerBuilder 7.0 lets you create your own keyboard shortcuts.

# Script Inheritance

The Edit menu deserves additional attention with respect to the Window, Menu, and User Object painters. If inheritance is being used, the Edit menu enables a special menu item, Extend Ancestor Script. Its options are used to determine how PowerBuilder handles any scripts written for each event in the ancestor object. If an event contains code in the event for the ancestor, the Page icon in the Select Event drop-down list box will be purple. If the icon is half purple and half white, the event contains code in the ancestor and descendant objects' scripts for that event.

To view an ancestor script, first select the desired script in the descendant object. When this event is displayed in Script view, the farthest right drop-down list at the top of Script view will be enabled. This list contains the names of all ancestor objects for the current object you're editing. To view a specific ancestor's script, select the ancestor object name from the list, and PowerBuilder will display the code to you in Script view.

For more discussion on inheritance, see Chapter 10, "Windows and the Window Painter."

# Declaring Variables

PowerBuilder 7.0 gives you a new way to declare global, instance, and shared variables. Regardless of whether the scope of a variable is global, shared, or instance, the same interface is used to declare it.

From Script view, select the option (Declare) from the leftmost drop-down list at the top. To specify the scope of the variable, use the drop-down list immediately to the right of the (Declare) option.

After you specify the scope, you can type the data type(s) and variable name(s) into Script view.

## Tip

PowerBuilder 7.0 allows you to dynamically add properties to your objects' property sheets by including additional syntax to variable declarations. These property sheet additions are then realized in the object descendants. This additional functionality is provided by using the `descriptor` syntax that's inserted after the variable name. The `descriptor` command is followed by a string containing a series of commands referred to as the `pb_format`. The string specifies the property data type, where to add the variable on the property sheet, the order of the property within the sheet, the interface style of the property (check box, slider, single-line edit, and s soforth), and the label associated with the property. An example of this is

```
boolean ib_security descriptor "pb_format"="DataType=boolean~t" + &
        "Group=General~tOrder=0~tStyle=Checkbox~tLabel=Security"
```

The details of the `descriptor` syntax can be found in a white paper titled "PowerBuilder 7.0 Documentation for Advanced Users" on the Sybase Developer Network at `http:\\sdn.sybase.com`. Use this syntax at your own risk; it is unsupported and could be removed at any time.

You can also use the Paste SQL PainterBar icon to generate SQL `DECLARE` statements for cursors and stored procedures, which are then pasted in the Declare section of the Script view. The cursor declaration takes you into the SQL painter; the stored procedure declaration takes you into the Select Procedure dialog (see Chapter 4, "SQL and PowerBuilder").

## Declaring Global and Local External Functions

The Global External Functions and Local External Functions options work in the same manner as the declaring variables. After choosing (`Declare`) and the type of external function you want, you can write your dynamic link library (DLL) function call syntax in Script view. You make API calls to the Windows SDK and third-party vendor DLLs via this method. For more information on the calling syntax, see Chapter 36, "API Calls."

## User Events

When you initially write scripts for various PowerBuilder objects, you have a set list of events for each given object. You can, however, specify additional events for a window, for window controls, or for a user object by capturing the underlying Windows messages. You can also create custom events that Windows doesn't trigger automatically but that you can manually trigger via your code.

When defining a new user event, first select in Script view the object for which you want the event defined. The second drop-down next to the object name shows those events defined for the object. If you want to see the declaration of the event (the corresponding Windows messages captured to trigger the events), click the Show/Hide Prototype icon in the top-right corner of Script view.

The declarations of the predefined PowerBuilder events are disabled because you can't alter them. They do show you the event ID (which maps to a Windows message), event name, return type, and any event arguments.

To declare your own user event, scroll to the top of the list of events and select the (`New Event`) item. If the event prototype section of Script view wasn't previously displayed,

PowerBuilder automatically displays the event prototype with no values specified (see Figure 2.10).

FIGURE 2.10

*A user event declaration.*

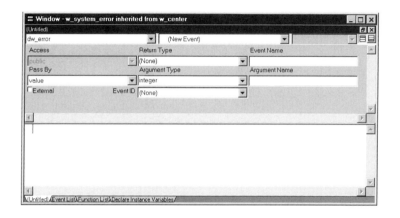

The Event Name text box specifies the name of the event. This is the name that appears in the Event drop-down list box with all the currently defined events and is used to refer to the event. The one naming standard for user-defined events is to begin the event name with ue_ followed by a descriptive name (for example, ue_keypressed). You can use the Event ID drop-down list to select the event ID assigned to the event name. You can enter the event ID by scrolling to the event ID you want in the Event ID drop-down.

### Tip

The new event names are placed alphabetically in the Select Event drop-down. If you name your user events beginning with ue_, all your defined events will be placed in the list. This makes it easier to document and maintain your application.

The list of event IDs corresponds to specific Windows messages. No PowerBuilder manual offers definitions of these IDs, but the names are similar to the Windows message names (for example, pbm_mousemove maps to the Windows message wm_mousemove). These event IDs define what are referred to as *object events*. Some events also have event arguments also displayed in the event prototype.

In addition to the PowerBuilder object events you can define, you can create a user event that you can trigger manually and that Windows doesn't trigger. There are two methods of doing this. The first method was the only means available in versions before 5.0: You declare a user event and specify one of the 75 custom user event IDs that PowerBuilder provides. Those event IDs all begin with pbm_custom and remain in the product for backward compatibility. It's mentioned here because you may see some older applications with this still used.

For all the predefined PowerBuilder event IDs, the arguments are already defined and can't be modified. These arguments can be directly referenced in your script, thus removing the need to check the WordParm and LongParm attributes of the Message object.

In addition to being able to create the aforementioned object and user events, you also can create custom events. Custom events are effectively functions and are treated similarly by PowerBuilder. These events aren't associated with any PowerBuilder event IDs. They allow you to define the arguments and return a value from the new event.

To create your own custom event and specify the argument's passed and return value, type an event name and leave the event ID drop-down list set to (None).

Within the event prototype, you can specify as many arguments as you want by right-clicking the prototype section and selecting Add Parameter, which inserts a new line for the event prototype. For the new argument, you specify the argument name, any valid PowerBuilder data type for the argument, and whether the argument is passed by reference or by value. If you want to delete an argument, select the desired argument and select Delete Parameter from the pop-up menu. In addition to arguments, you can also specify a return value data type for the event. For information on how to call the new event and pass arguments, see Chapter 7, "The PowerScript Language."

> **Note**
>
> If you want the event to be used as part of a component you're building, select the External check box.

After a user event is defined, clicking in the Script view or selecting another event adds the event name to the drop-down list of events. If you select the new event name from the Event drop-down list, you can begin coding your script.

After you define all your events, you might need to code the script to execute them (for user and custom events). User events can be executed by using TriggerEvent() or

`PostEvent()`. The custom events have their own syntax for passing arguments; see Chapter 7 for descriptions of each method.

If a desired Windows message isn't located in the list of PowerBuilder event IDs, PowerBuilder defines an event for you that's known as the `Other` event. These unmapped Windows messages trigger the `Other` event for the particular object. Through PowerScript code and use of the `Message` object, the Windows message can be trapped, and appropriate actions can be coded.

> **Note**
>
> Because the `Other` event is triggered for all unmapped Windows messages, writing substantial script for this event can slow the application's performance.

# Context-Sensitive Help

To ease in your learning and understanding of the PowerScript language, PowerBuilder has incorporated context-sensitive help into the Script view. To invoke help for a particular PowerScript statement, place th cursor within the PowerScript function name or keyword and press Shift+F1. An alternative method for getting context-sensitive help is to right-click the desired PowerScript statement and select Help from the pop-up menu.

# Creating Functions

Although the PowerScript language provides many functions to accomplish various tasks, most applications need to perform additional processing that PowerBuilder doesn't supply. Functions and subroutines enable the creation of modularized and reusable code. Functions and subroutines are created by using the Function painter and can be defined on an object or a global level.

## Functions Versus Subroutines

The only difference between a function and a subroutine is that a function always returns a value of a specific data type (for example, an integer). Subroutines, on the other hand, don't return values and therefore have no return type.

An important but occasionally confusing point is that subroutines and functions are both created in the Function painter. For each subroutine or function, some common components must be specified in its definition: the function/subroutine name, any arguments to be passed, whether the arguments are passed by reference or by value, access designation (only for object-level functions), and the data type of the return value (for functions only).

## Access Privileges

You can specify three access privileges for an object-level function or subroutine: public, private, and protected. The access privileges determine from where a function can be called.

A designation of *public*, valid for global and object-level functions, means that the function can be called from any script in the application. *Private* means that the function can be called only from scripts in the object in which it was declared. *Protected* is an extension of private in that, in addition to being called from the object in which it was declared, the function can be called from the object's descendants.

## Arguments

Arguments can be any valid data type or class within PowerBuilder—they include all standard and enumerated data types, variables, controls (such as a DataWindow control), objects (such as windows), specific objects (w_order_detail, for example), and arrays of all the above. You can specify as many arguments as you need.

Arguments can be passed by reference, by value, or as read-only. In passing an argument by reference, PowerBuilder is actually passing the argument's memory location. This enables the function or subroutine to modify the argument's value. If an argument is passed by value, PowerBuilder passes a copy of the argument's current value. The argument can be changed by the function or subroutine, but the change won't be reflected in the script that executed the function.

An example of passing by reference versus by value is demonstrated in the following code:

```
Int A, B, C
A=2
B=3
C=f_calculate (A, B)
```

The function f_calculate() takes two arguments, X and Y. The return type is an Integer. The body of the text increments X and Y each by 1 and returns the value of X multiplied by Y:

```
//Args: X - Integer
//      Y - Integer
//Returns an Integer
X++
Y++
Return X * Y
```

To understand how passing by reference and by value affects the values of A, B, and C, see Table 2.2.

TABLE 2.2    Passing Values by Reference Versus by Value

| X *by Val* Variable | X *by Ref* Y *by Val* | X *by Val* Y *by Ref* | Y *by Ref* |
|---|---|---|---|
| A | 2 | 3 | 2 |
| B | 3 | 4 | 4 |
| C | 12 | 12 | 12 |

A read-only argument passes the memory location of the argument, but the called function can't change the argument.

## Return Values

The last component of the function declaration is to specify the return type. Because a subroutine doesn't return a value, select (None) from the drop-down list box for the return type. If you're planning to specify a return type, you must include the keyword Return followed by an expression of the correct data type in the body of the function script. If Return is omitted, PowerBuilder displays a compile error requesting that a Return statement be coded.

> **Note**
>
> When using conditional logic and returning values based on those conditions, be sure to include a Return statement for each condition. Omission of a Return statement won't be flagged as a compile error as long as one Return statement exists within the function script. Therefore, at runtime you will get an application error when the function tries to exit without a Return. To ensure that this doesn't happen, assign a value to a variable and place a Return statement at the end of the function. You are then always passing back a default value if you forget to code the Return in your script.

## Global Functions

You can access a function object from the Object tab after clicking the New icon on the PowerBar. The New Function painter is basically the Script view, and the Prototype section is the main tool you use to create or declare a function or subroutine.

The first step is to name the function or subroutine. Global function names begin with f_ followed by a descriptive name of the processing. Access designation for global functions is always public. The Return Type drop-down list box shows all the valid return types and the (None) specification for a subroutine. After you decide which arguments are needed for the function, use the Add, Insert, and Delete Parameter pop-up menu items to provide the appropriate number of arguments. Naming standards for arguments are the same as for other variables, with the addition of adding a_ or arg_ to the front. After declaring the argument name, choose from the list of argument types and whether the arguments should be passed by reference or by value.

The Script view within the Function painter acts the same in almost every way as it does with object events. Global functions are best suited to processing that spans multiple objects. For that reason, global functions can't be encapsulated into one object and therefore are saved as separate objects in your PowerBuilder library.

> **Tip**
>
> If your application needs to create functions that span multiple objects, you can encapsulate them into a custom class user object rather than create separate global functions.

### Object-Level Functions

In contrast to global functions, object-level functions and subroutines are encapsulated and stored within the object for which they are declared (for example, stored with a window's definition). Local functions can be written for the application object, windows, menus, and user objects. Declaring an object-level function is much the same as declaring a user event.

Object-level functions are defined by selecting the option, (Functions), from the leftmost drop-down list in Script view. When you choose this option, the function prototype is displayed, which allows you to specify the function name, access designation, arguments, and return value(s).

## Event List View

Event List view displays the event signature for all system and user-defined events for the currently selected object. If the event has a script written for it, an icon appears to the left of the event name. The icon's colors work the same as in Script view to indicate the existence of an ancestor and/or descendant script. Double-clicking an event in the list opens Script view at the chosen event.

# Function List View

Much like Event List view, Function List view displays the full function signature for all system and user-defined object functions. An icon appears next to the function name to indicate the existence of a script. The icon's coloration has a different meaning with functions than for events, however. When the icon next to a function is half purple/half white, it means that the ancestor function is overridden instead of extended. Double-clicking a user-defined function opens it in the Script view.

# Structure View

You use a structure to create a collection of one or more related variables. You might be familiar with structures from other languages, where they're known as *structs*, *user types*, or *records*. Creating a structure instead of using the separate entities gives you a high-level reference to these related variables. A common use for structures is to pass multiple values between objects (see Chapter 7, "The PowerScript Language"). Structure view enables the creation of a new data type or structure class. You then use the structure class to create structure instances for use in PowerBuilder scripts.

## Global Structures

You can access the Structure painter (see Figure 2.11) by clicking New on the PowerBar, selecting the Object tab, and clicking the Structure icon . In the first column, you enter the names of each variable or field within the structure. Use the second column to specify the data type of each field. The data type can be any standard or enumerated data type, another structure, or a class. Variables can be inserted and deleted by using the new PainterBar icons.

FIGURE 2.11

*The Structure painter.*

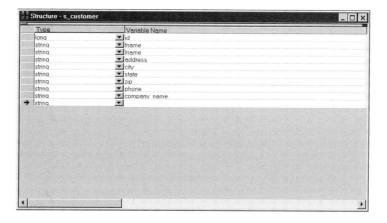

After you declare all the variables, click the Save PainterBar icon, which prompts you to specify a name. Global structure names begin with s_ followed by a descriptive name. A global structure is saved as a separate object in your PowerBuilder library.

## Object-Level Structures

Structures can be declared for the application object, windows, menus, and user objects. As with object-level functions, object-level structures are defined by choosing Structure View from the View menu. The interface is the same for object-level and global structures. Object-level structures are saved with the object for which they were defined and therefore aren't a separate object in your PowerBuilder library.

## Structure List View

Structure List view simply lists all object-level structures that have been defined for the object you're now working on. Double-clicking the structure's name in the list opens the structure in Structure view.

# Select Application

In previous versions of PowerBuilder, if you wanted to change the application that you were using, you had to go to the Application painter or the Library painter. This is no longer the case in PowerBuilder 7.0. To change from one application to another, click the Select Application icon on the PowerBar. The Select Application dialog (see Figure 2.12) opens.

**FIGURE 2.12**

*The Select Application dialog.*

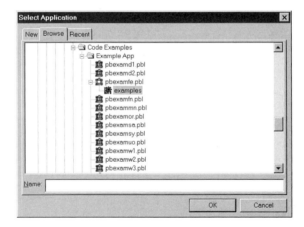

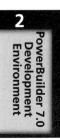

From this window, you can create a new application (standard PowerBuilder, Jaguar, COM/ MTS, or OLE Automation), migrate an existing application, browse your computer and network drives for an existing application, or select from an application that you've recently used.

# Library Search Path

Similar to the change made for selecting applications is the capability to change your application's library search path. Before PowerBuilder 7.0, you could do this only in the Application painter. Now clicking the Library List icon on the PowerBar opens the Library List dialog (see Figure 2.13). From this dialog, you can type in the full path to the libraries you want to include in your application's search path. An easier way to specify the libraries that comprise your application is to click the Browse button and use the Select Library dialog to locate the desired PowerBuilder Library (.pbl) files.

**FIGURE 2.13**
*The Library List dialog.*

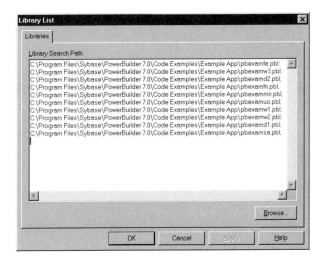

# To-Do Lists

New to PowerBuilder 7.0 is the concept of a To-Do List (see Figure 2.14). A To-Do List is nothing more than a text list of items that you need to complete for your current application.

**FIGURE 2.14**

*A PowerBuilder
To-Do List.*

The items in your list can be created on of two ways: manually by yourself or generated by a PowerBuilder wizard. In addition to straight text reminders, you can create a to-do item that's linked to a particular PowerBuilder object. When the item is double-clicked, PowerBuilder opens the specified object/script. The To-Do List items are stored by application in the Windows Registry.

To manually edit the list, right-click it to open a pop-up menu. From this menu, you can choose to add, delete, and edit to-do items as well as check/uncheck an item as completed. You can also check an item as complete by clicking the column on the left side of the To-Do List. One pop-up menu option is to add a link to a particular object in your application. To do this, open the object to which you want to create a link. From the object's painter, open the To-Do List, bring up the pop-up menu, and click Add Link. You can then enter any text message defining the activity you need to complete; PowerBuilder automatically generates the link to the object.

**Tip**

To transport your personal To-Do List from one computer to another, right-click the list and choose Export to save the list as a text file. Then, on the other computer, select Import to bring your list into PowerBuilder.

# Running/Previewing Objects

Most times when you want to test your application, you use the Run icon on the PowerBar. Sometimes, however, you might want to just run or preview an object (for example, a window or DataWindow) by itself. To do this, choose Run/Preview from the File menu. This opens the Run/Preview dialog, which asks you to specify the object you want to run or preview. Select the desired object and click OK. PowerBuilder then runs that object apart from the rest of the application.

# Most Recently Used Options

On the File menu, PowerBuilder keeps track of the most recently used objects, applications, and connections. The object list can contain up to the last eight objects accessed. The application list displays the last eight PowerBuilder applications accessed. Finally, the connection list displays up to the last five database connections used. You can increase the number of objects and applications displayed up to 36 and the number of connections up to 10 by choosing System Options from the Window menu and filling in the corresponding text boxes.

# Keyboard Shortcuts

Although PowerBuilder includes a number of keyboard shortcuts to keep you from having to jump back and forth to the mouse, some areas aren't covered. If you are a keyboard enthusiast, this new feature is for you. PowerBuilder 7.0 lets you define your own keyboard shortcut for any existing menu item.

To create a new keyboard shortcut, choose Keyboard Shortcuts from the Window menu. The Keyboard Shortcuts dialog appears, displaying the menu bar items for the current menu (see Figure 2.15). Each menu can be expanded to show its menu items. The first thing to do is locate the menu item for which you want to create the shortcut and select it. In the Press Keys for Shortcut text box, press the keys that you want to associate with the menu item. If the keyboard shortcut is already in use, PowerBuilder displays a message indicating the shortcut is in use and by what menu item. You also can remove and reset menu items by using the appropriate buttons on the dialog.

**FIGURE 2.15**

*The Keyboard Shortcuts dialog.*

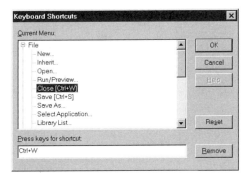

# Summary

The new PowerBuilder 7.0 interface has been dramatically reworked to provide developers with total control over the development environment. The PowerBuilder environment aids developers by providing an easy-to-use interface equipped with tools that decrease the amount of time spent coding. In addition to helping developer productivity, the changes help PowerBuilder maintain its competitiveness as an application development tool.

# Database Management Systems

CHAPTER 3

In response to the pressure of end users who want accessible data, the client/server platform has become the dominant computing architecture of the 1990s. Corporate departments have felt the need to develop applications for their own specialized purposes, whereas organizations need information systems to support the overall business system. The client/server platform allows the distribution of components across a network to create a flexible architecture that meets departmental needs as well as organizational needs. This architecture enables companies to use various database management systems, network protocols, and end-user tools together effectively.

The database management system (DBMS) enables shared access to data within a database. The DBMS maintains the database's security, integrity, and reliability. Deciding on a development tool is important, but just as important is the choice of DBMS. When you make that choice, you need to consider a number of points, including scalability, platforms support, and technical support.

PowerBuilder can use two interface types to access your DBMS of choice: standard database interfaces (ODBC, JDBC, and OLE DB) or a native database interface.

The standard database interface uses a standard-compliant driver (ODBC and JDBC) or a data provider (OLE DB) to translate calls to the DBMS's standard API.

A native database interface communicates directly with the DBMS's standard API. PowerBuilder provides native connections to a number of DBMSs. To connect to a specific DBMS, four components need to be installed (see Figure 3.1):

- The Sybase-supplied database interface usually consists of a single dynamic link library (DLL). The DLL's name should be PB*xxx*70.DLL, where *xxx* is a three-character description of the DBMS. For example, PBMSS70.DLL is the Microsoft SQL Server database interface.

- The DBMS vendor-supplied client software provides the API with which the Sybase DLL interacts. For example, NTWDBLIB.DLL is the 32-bit MS SQL Server-specific DLL.

- The database network support files vary depending on the type of network in which the DBMS server is located. For example, for 32-bit MS SQL Server listening on Named Pipes, the database network file is DBNMPNTW.DLL.

- The (optional) gateway software allows access to heterogeneous data sources that are otherwise directly inaccessible.

The installation of each layer is too varied to be described here, but each software piece comes with adequate instructions.

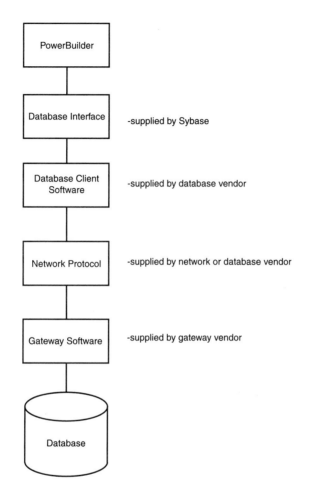

**FIGURE 3.1**
*Components required to connect to a DBMS.*

PowerBuilder

Database Interface          -supplied by Sybase

Database Client Software    -supplied by database vendor

Network Protocol            -supplied by network or database vendor

Gateway Software            -supplied by gateway vendor

Database

3

Database Management Systems

---

**Tip**

Each layer might support only a certain version of one or another of the additional layers. Your best bet is to get the most up-to-date version of all the drivers. You should, however, always make backup copies of older drivers when you upgrade.

---

PowerBuilder supports database access through four different driver types: native (which communicate to the native drivers of the DBMS), ODBC, OLE DB (the new database access architecture Microsoft is pushing to replace ODBC), and JDBC (Java connectors). The PowerBuilder native drivers directly support the following DBMSs:

- Sybase Adaptive Server Enterprise 11.5

- Oracle versions 7.3, 8.0.3, 8.0.4, and 8.0.5

- Informix versions 6. $x$, 7. $x$, and 9. $x$

- Microsoft SQL Server 6. $x$ and 7. $x$

- Sybase Adaptive Server Anywhere 6.0

- Direct Connect Interface for Access services and TRS databases

PowerBuilder supplies the following ODBC drivers:

| | |
|---|---|
| Btrieve | Paradox |
| DB2 | SQLBase |
| DBASE | Microsoft SQL Server |
| Informix 5. $x$, 6. $x$, 7. $x$, and 9. $x$ | Sybase SQL Server |
| OpenIngres 1.2 and 2.0 | Text |
| Oracle 7. $x$ and 8. $x$ | Excel5 |
| Progress 7.3 and 8. $x$ | |

The supplied JDBC drivers work with the Microsoft or Sun virtual machines. Sybase also supplies PowerBuilder and Intersolv OLE DB providers.

**Note**

PowerBuilder's Professional and Desktop editions include only the ODBC interfaces.

The following native database interfaces are no longer supported in PowerBuilder 7.0:

- Informix INET 5 (IN5)

- Microsoft SQL Server 4.x DB-Lib (SYB)

- Oracle 7.1 (O71) and Oracle 7.2 (O72)

- Sybase Net-Gateway for DB2 (NET)

- Sybase InformationConnect DB2 Gateway (MDI)

- Sybase SQL Server DB-Lib (SYT)

PowerBuilder 7.0 also no longer supports the INTERSOLV Excel 4.0, INTERSOLV Paradox 4.0, and INTERSOLV Scalable SQL ODBC drivers.

> **Note**
>
> Before looking at the features of your particular DBMS, you need to understand isolation levels. The names as well as the precise meaning of *isolation levels* vary greatly among DBMSs. An isolation level specifies the degree to which one transaction operation is visible to another concurrent transaction and determines how the DBMS isolates and/or locks data from other processes.

# Informix

The Informix Dynamic database server from Informix Software, Inc. comes in two different packages: Informix-SE and Informix-OnLine.

Informix Dynamic Server is available for UNIX and Windows NT and is designed for small to midrange applications. It's sold as the low-maintenance, high-reliability solution for small businesses or self-contained departments that don't have vast database-administration expertise.

## Connecting PowerBuilder to Informix Databases

The Informix database interface goes through Informix API to make connections to the database. This means you must have the appropriate Informix-supplied drivers installed to use the interface: Informix ESQL version 7.2 for Informix 7. *x* and version 9.1 for Informix 9. *x*.

Table 3.1 shows the information for the required profile settings.

**3**

Database Management Systems

**TABLE 3.1**   Informix Profile Settings

| Profile Setting | Profile Value |
| --- | --- |
| DBMS | IN7 or IN9 tells PowerBuilder which database interface—PBIN770.DLL or PBIN970.DLL—to use. |
| UserID | The user account name on the host computer running the Informix database server. |
| DBPass | The password required to connect to your database. |
| Database | The name of the database to access. |
| ServerName | The server name in the following format: *host_name@server_name*, where *host_name* is the name of the host computer, and *server_name* is the name of the server with the Informix database you're connecting to. |

TABLE 3.1   Informix Profile Settings

| Profile Setting | Profile Value |
| --- | --- |
| AutoCommit | This controls whether PowerBuilder works inside or outside the scope of a transaction. Values are TRUE and FALSE (default). |
| DBParm | DBMS-specific connection parameters: |

| | | |
| --- | --- | --- |
| | Lock | Specifies the transaction isolation level: 'Dirty read' (read pages now being modified), 'Committed read' (read only committed changes), 'Cursor stability' , and 'Repeatable read' (guarantees that a page read multiple times within a transaction has the same values). |
| | Scroll | Specifies a *scroll cursor* that allows you to fetch the next row, previous row, first row, or last row when pulling data out of a table. Values are 0 (default—don't use scroll) and 1. |
| | DisableBind | Specifies whether to carry out input parameter binding. Values are 0 (default—enabled) and 1. |
| | INET_DBPATH | Specifies the Informix DBPATH setting that identifies a list of directories that contain Informix databases. This is valid only with the Sybase Informix interface on Windows. |
| | INET_PROTOCOL | Specifies the network protocol to communicate with the server. This is valid only with the Sybase Informix interface on Windows. |
| | INET_SERVICE | Specifies the name of the service that the Informix server is using to listen on. This is valid only with the Sybase Informix interface on Windows. |

To have the PowerBuilder repository tables created correctly, make sure that the first person to connect to the database has sufficient authority to create tables and grant permissions to PUBLIC.

# Microsoft SQL Server

Microsoft SQL Server 6. *x* and 7. *x* are high-performance relational database management systems that operate entirely within Microsoft's Windows NT operating system. SQL Server for Windows NT provides a database engine that can be used for small to large systems development and combines high availability, security, transaction processing, fault tolerance, server-side data integrity, remote stored procedures, connectivity services, and an integrated enterprise-wide server administration tool. MS SQL Server also provides tight integration with OLE object technology and Visual Basic.

Microsoft continues to extend its product and now has improved ANSI SQL support, including declarative referential integrity and server cursor support. Since splitting with Sybase on the joint development of the SQL Server product, Microsoft has also introduced its own set of enhancements to Transact-SQL and the engine. For example, MS SQL Server 7 now supports full (SELECT, INSERT, UPDATE, and DELETE) row-level locking.

# Connecting PowerBuilder to MS SQL Server Databases

The Sybase MS SQL Server database interface lets you access versions 6. *x* and 7. *x*. Table 3.2 shows the information for the required profile settings.

TABLE 3.2    Microsoft SQL Server Profile Settings

| Profile Setting | Profile Value | |
|---|---|---|
| DBMS | MSS tells PowerBuilder to use PBMSS70.DLL. | |
| Database | The database you want to use. | |
| LogId | The login account for the SQL Server. Alternatively, if the server accepts trusted connections and you can make a trusted connection, you can leave this blank. | |
| LogPass | The password associated with the LogId specified. Again, if a trusted connection is being made, the LogId is ignored. | |
| ServerName | The name of the computer running the database server. | |
| AutoCommit | This controls whether PowerBuilder works inside or outside the scope of a transaction. Values are TRUE and FALSE (default). | |
| DBParm | DBMS-specific connection parameters: | |
| | Language | Specifies the language you want to use when displaying error messages and date formats. This must be set up on the server first. |
| | Lock | Specifies the transaction isolation level: 'RU', read uncommitted (read pages now being modified); 'RC', read committed (read only committed changes); 'RR', repeatable read (guarantees that a page read multiple times within a transaction has the same values); and 'TS', serializable (prevents other transactions from modifying pages that have already been read). |
| | Log | Specifies whether updates of text and image data should be logged in the SQL Server transaction log. Values are 0 (don't log) and 1 (do log, the default). |
| | SystemProcs | Specifies whether system stored procedures and user-defined stored procedures are shown within various PowerBuilder painters. Values are 0 and 1 (default is to show both). |

**3**

Database
Management
Systems

**TABLE 3.2** Microsoft SQL Server Profile Settings

| Profile Setting | Profile Value | |
| --- | --- | --- |
| | DateTimeAllowed | Controls whether columns having a DateTime data type can be used as unique key columns in WHERE clauses for updates and deletes. Values are 0, prohibit (default), and 1, allow. |
| | MaxConnect | Allows you to control how many simultaneous connections can be made to a database. The default is 25. |
| | OptSelectBlob | Allows you to optimize SELECTBLOB processing in a DataWindow object. The default, 0, is to not optimize SELECTBLOB processing, causing PowerBuilder to open a second database connection to process the SELECTBLOB request. If you set this property to 1, PowerBuilder uses the initial database connection to process the SELECTBLOB. This setting should be used when you're not selecting BLOB (binary large object) or binary data for retrieval in a DataWindow object. |
| | PBCatalogOwner | Specifies the non-default owner for the tables in the Sybase repository. |
| | Async | Allows synchronous operations to occur on the database server. Values are 0 (synchronous, the default) and 1 (asynchronous operation). |
| | DBGetTime | Specifies the number of seconds PowerBuilder should wait for a response from the DBMS when you retrieve rows and the Async parameter is set to 1. |
| | CursorLock | Specifies locking options for cursors; used with the Release and CursorScroll parameters. Values are 'Lock' (lock rows as they're fetched), 'Opt' (default is don't lock rows and check updates against time stamps or previous known values), 'OptVal' (don't lock rows and check updates against previous known values), and 'ReadOnly' (no updates allowed through cursor). |

**TABLE 3.2**  Microsoft SQL Server Profile Settings

| Profile Setting | Profile Value | |
|---|---|---|
| | CursorScroll | Sets scrolling options for cursors. Values are `'Forward'` (cursor moves only forward through resultset), `'KeySet'` (keys are saved for the entire resultset and as the cursor scrolls through the resultset, the keys in the keyset are used to retrieve the current values for each row), `'Dynamic'` (default—only the current row information is stored), and `'Insensitive'` (all the data that makes the resultset is saved and used to provide the request row information). |
| | StaticBind | Controls whether PowerBuilder gets a resultset description from the DBMS before retrieving data. Values are `1` (disabled, the default) and `0` (get description). |
| | DBTextLimit | Controls the maximum length of a text field to be returned without treating the text as a BLOB data type. Values are `0` (returns maximum text length) to `32,763` bytes. The maximum text length is the lesser of the `DBTextLimit` value and the setting for the SQL Server global variable `@@textsize`. |
| | AppName | Specifies the application name you want to use when connecting. |
| | Host | Specifies the workstation name when connecting. This can be any value you want but is usually used to indicate the client's machine. |
| | PacketSize | Specifies the packet size in bytes that you want the server to set for transferring data to and from PowerBuilder. Values must be a multiple of 512; the default is `512` bytes. |
| | Secure | Specifies whether you want to use Windows NT integrated login security and a secure (trusted) connection to the SQL server. Values are `0` (use standard security, the default) and `1` (integrated security). |

Unlike other Sybase database interfaces, the SQL Server database interface doesn't require you to install the Sybase stored procedures used for gathering table information. The Sybase SQL Server database interface uses SQL Server's own catalog stored procedures to get information about tables and columns.

# Oracle

Oracle Corporation's database supports mission-critical applications. It's portable to a wide range of hardware and operating system platforms, from desktop systems to mainframes and supercomputers. These platforms include UNIX, VMS, MVS, VM, HP MPE/XL, Siemens, ICL, OS/2, Macintosh, Windows 95/98/NT, and Novell NetWare. Hardware architectures supported include Symmetric Multiprocessors, Clustered Multiprocessors, Massively Parallel Processors, and Loosely Coupled Multiprocessors. These kinds of choices allow complete freedom in selecting a suitable database server platform to meet current and future needs without affecting existing applications.

## Connecting PowerBuilder to Oracle Databases

Connecting to an Oracle server is certainly one of the more complex processes of installation you will run into, more so than any other DBMS. Because supporting Oracle databases isn't easy, Sybase supplies four different Oracle database interfaces, one for each version of Oracle. Each interface uses different Sybase DLLs and shared libraries, accesses different versions of Oracle, and is supplied on different operating system platforms.

The Oracle 7.3 driver requires SQL*Net version 2.3 or higher, Oracle 8.0 requires Net8 version 8.0.3, and Oracle 8.0.4 requires Net8 version 8.0.4. Table 3.3 shows the information for the required parts of the profile settings.

**TABLE 3.3**  Oracle Profile Settings

| Profile Setting | Profile Value |
| --- | --- |
| DBMS | 073 (Oracle version 7.3), OR8 (Oracle 8.0), or 084 (Oracle 8.0.4) tells PowerBuilder which DLL to use to connect: O73 loads PBO7370.DLL, OR8 loads PBOR870.DLL, and O84 loads PB08470.DLL. |
| ServerName | The Oracle server connect string. The syntax depends on the version of the Oracle client interface. For Net8 8.0.3 or higher, the syntax is *OracleServiceName*; for SQL*Net 2. *x*, the syntax is @TNS:*OracleServiceName*. |
| LogID | The login ID for the database server. |
| LogPass | The password required to connect to the server. |
| DBParm | DBMS-specific connection parameters: |
| | ThreadSafe  Determines whether the Oracle 7.3 thread-safe client libraries are used when accessing the server. The default, 'No', is recommended when building nondistributed applications. |

**TABLE 3.3**   Oracle Profile Settings

| Profile Setting | Profile Value | |
|---|---|---|
| | PBDBMS | Determines how PowerBuilder uses Oracle stored procedures as data sources for DataWindow objects. This depends on the version of your Oracle database and how you specify the PBDBMS setting (see note following this table). |
| | MixedCase | Determines whether connections to the database are to be case-sensitive (1) or case-insensitive (0, the default). |
| | PBCatalogOwner | Specifies the non-default owner for the tables in the Sybase repository. |
| | TableCriteria | Enables you to specify criteria to limit the tables and views listed in the Select Tables dialog. |
| | Async | Allow synchronous operations to occur on the database server. Values are 0 (synchronous, the default) and 1 (asynchronous operation). |
| | DBGetTime | Specifies the number of seconds PowerBuilder should wait for a response from the DBMS when you retrieve rows and the Async parameter is set to 1. |
| | Block | Determines the number of rows that a DataWindow object or report can fetch from the database at one time. The value is between 1 and 1000, where 1 turns blocking off. |
| | CacheName | Allows you to specify a Jaguar connection cache by name. This parameter is used only when you deploy a custom class user object as a Jaguar component. |
| | GetConnectionOption | Controls the behavior of Jaguar if all connections in a cache are being used. The default, JAG_CM_FORCE, allocates and opens a new connection that's deallocated when the connection is closed. JAG_CM_NOWAIT causes an error to be raised if no connection can be made. JAG_CM_WAIT causes the component to pause until a connection is available. |

**3**

Database Management Systems

**TABLE 3.3**  Oracle Profile Settings

| Profile Setting | Profile Value |
| --- | --- |
| ReleaseConnectionOption | Controls the behavior of Jaguar when control of a connection is released. The default, JAG_CM_UNUSED, causes connections taken from a cache to be placed back and connections created outside a cache to be destroyed. JAG_CM_DROP forces the connection to be destroyed; if the connection was originally from a cache, a new connection is created to replace it. |
| UserContextObject | Specifies whether control of a transaction should be made by using the TransactionServer transaction service context object. |
| SQLCache | Specifies the number of SQL statements that PowerBuilder should cache. Default is 0. |
| DisableBind | Specifies whether to carry out input parameter binding. Values are 0 (enabled, the default) and 1 (disabled). |
| StaticBind | Controls whether PowerBuilder gets a resultset description from the DBMS before retrieving data. Values are 1 (disabled, the default) and 0 (get description). |
| DelimitIdentifier | Encloses the names of tables, columns, indexes, and constraints in double quotation marks when it generates SQL statements. Values are 'Yes' and 'No'. |
| Date | Specifies a date data type, which PowerBuilder uses when it builds SQL UPDATE statements. The syntax is: ' ""Sybase_date_format"" ' The spaces and single quotation marks must appear as shown. |
| DateTime | Works the same as Date, but also includes a time. |
| Time | Works the same as Date, except that it's just a Time value. |
| DecimalSeparator | Specifies the non-default decimal separator setting used by the back-end DBMS. Default value is '.'. |
| FormatArgsAsExp | Determines if a DataWindow or report retrieval argument of a decimal data type exceeds 12 digits and converts the argument to scientific (exponential) notation. The default is 'Yes', convert the value. |

> ### Note
>
> As indicated in Table 3.3, the version of Oracle database you're using and how you specify the PBDBMS setting can determine how PowerBuilder uses Oracle stored procedures as data sources for DataWindow objects.
>
> DataWindow/Report
>
> | Oracle Version | Data Source | PBDBMS Setting |
> | --- | --- | --- |
> | 7.2 or higher (default) | Stored procedure that has a resultset as an IN OUT parameter | 0 |
> | 7.x | Stored procedure that uses PBDBMS.Put_Line function calls to build the SQL SELECT statement | 1 |

# Sybase Adaptive Server Enterprise and Sybase SQL Server

The Sybase family of database products consists of a number of components used to provide security and support for large database system development on UNIX or Windows NT platforms. The family name for Sybase Database Servers before version 11.5 is Sybase SQL Server; for versions 11.5 and higher, it's Sybase Adaptive Server Enterprise. All Sybase System 11 and higher products are built on the Open Client and Open Server Architecture foundation and share the same interfaces. Modularizing the software into clients, servers, and interfaces enables the integration of the framework with different data sources, applications, and services.

# Connecting PowerBuilder Sybase Databases

The Sybase database interface lets you access Systems 10 and higher by using the CT-LIB API (SYC). When using PowerBuilder with Jaguar, you must use a different version of the CT-Lib software—the SYJ database interface rather than SYC. However, this is only a runtime setting; you must still use the SYC interface in the PowerBuilder development environment. If you're deploying to a UNIX client, Sybase provides the SYD Sybase Adaptive Server Enterprise distributed application interface. This interface works with the thread-safe libraries that are part of the Sybase Open Client Version 11.1.1 or higher.

Table 3.4 shows the information for the required parts of the profile settings.

**TABLE 3.4** Sybase Server Profile Settings

| Profile Setting | Profile Value | |
| --- | --- | --- |
| DBMS | SYC tells PowerBuilder to use PBSYC70.DLL; SYJ tells PowerBuilder to use PBSYJ70.DLL; SYD tells PowerBuilder to use the appropriate interface for the UNIX flavor it's running on. | |
| Database | The database you want to use. | |
| LogId | The login account for the SQL server. | |
| LogPass | The password associated with the LogId specified. | |
| ServerName | The name of the computer running the database server. This name must match exactly (including case) the server name specified in the SQL.INI file (for Windows) or Interfaces file (for Macintosh and UNIX). | |
| AutoCommit | This controls whether PowerBuilder works inside or outside the scope of a transaction. Values are TRUE and FALSE (default). | |
| DBParm | DBMS-specific connection parameters. Note that Sybase has many DBParm options; only some are listed here: | |
| | Release | Specifies whether to use Sybase Open Client Client-Library (CT-Lib) 10. *x* or 11. *x* behavior. Values are '10.x', '11', or '11.5'. |
| | PWDialog | Specifies whether PowerBuilder displays a password expired dialog as necessary during a connection. Values are '0' (don't show dialog, the default) and '1' (do show). |

TABLE **3.4**   Sybase Server Profile Settings

| Profile Setting | Profile Value | |
| --- | --- | --- |
| | Language | Specifies the language you want to use when displaying error messages and date formats. This must be set up on the server first. |
| | CharSet | Specifies the character set you want the Sybase Open Client software to use. |
| | Locale | Specifies the locale name that you want the Sybase Open Client software to use. The default locale is defined in the LOCALES.DAT file. |
| | UTF8 | Specifies whether the database server has standard ANSI or UTF8 installed as its default character set. |
| | Lock | Specifies transaction isolation level: '0', read uncommitted (read pages now being modified); '1', read committed (read only committed changes, the default); and '3', serializable (prevents other transactions from modifying pages that have already been read). |
| | Log | Specifies whether updates of text and image data should be logged in the SQL Server transaction log. Values are 0 (don't log), and 1 (do log, the default). |
| | SystemProcs | Specifies whether system stored procedures and user-defined stored procedures are shown within various PowerBuilder painters. Values are 0 and 1 (show both, the default). |
| | PBCatalogOwner | Specifies the non-default owner for the tables in the Sybase repository. |
| | TableCriteria | Enables you to specify criteria to limit the tables and views listed in the Select Tables dialog. |
| | Async | Allows synchronous operations to occur on the database server. Values are 0 (synchronous, the default) and 1 (asynchronous operation). |

**3**

Database
Management
Systems

**TABLE 3.4** Sybase Server Profile Settings

| Profile Setting | Profile Value | |
|---|---|---|
| | DBGetTime | Specifies the number of seconds PowerBuilder should wait for a response from the DBMS when you retrieve rows and Async is set to 1. |
| | CursorUpdate | Specifies whether cursors are declared read-only or updatable. Values are '0' (read-only, the default) and '1' (updatable). |
| | Block | Determines the number of rows that a cursor can fetch from the database at one time. The value is the number of rows, with 100 as the default. |
| | StaticBind | Controls whether PowerBuilder gets a resultset description from the DBMS before retrieving data. Values are 1 (disabled, the default) and 0 (get description). |
| | DelimitIdentifier | Encloses the names of tables, columns, indexes, and constraints in double quotation marks when it generates SQL statements. Values are 'Yes' and 'No'. |
| | AppName | Specifies the application name you want to use when connecting. |
| | Host | Specifies the workstation name when connecting. |
| | PacketSize | Specifies the packet size in bytes that you want the server to set for transferring data to and from PowerBuilder. Values must be a multiple of 512; the default is 512 bytes. |
| | PWEncypt | Whether Open Client should automatically encrypt your password when connecting to the database server. Values are 'Yes' (default) and 'No'. |

Sybase also includes a number of security and directory service settings that can be specified in the DBParm attribute. You should refer to the Sybase driver information that comes from Sybase.

To have the PowerBuilder repository tables created correctly, make sure that the first person to connect to the database has sufficient authority to create tables and grant permissions to PUBLIC.

# Connecting PowerBuilder to Adaptive Server Anywhere

Sybase Adaptive Server Anywhere is a complete client/server DBMS that ships with PowerBuilder. Many PowerBuilder developers are familiar with this standalone database but don't realize that Adaptive Server Anywhere also has a multiuser SQL network server. The standalone is packaged with PowerBuilder; the multiuser server version can be purchased for a relatively low cost, depending on the number of user connections required.

Use Sybase SQL Anywhere as an example of a connection to an ODBC data source. Connection to other ODBC data sources use the same settings.

> **Note**
>
> With the 6.0 version of PowerBuilder, Sybase introduced Sybase Adaptive Server Anywhere for UNIX platforms. This allows for instant database connectivity straight out of the box.

Table 3.5 shows the required profile settings. Not all ODBC drivers and/or back-end DBMSs support the features listed.

**3**

Database Management Systems

TABLE **3.5**  ODBC Profile Settings

| Profile Setting | Profile Value |
|---|---|
| DBMS | ODBC |
| Database | The database you want to use. |
| AutoCommit | This controls whether PowerBuilder works within the scope of a transaction. Values are TRUE and FALSE (default). This option is available *only* if the driver and back-end DBMS support this feature. |
| DBParm | DBMS-specific connection parameters: |
| | ConnectString  Specifies the parameters required to connect to the data source. The syntax is<br>'DSN = *data_source_name*; {UID = *user_ID*;<br>PWD = *password*;<br>*other_required_parameters*}' |

**TABLE 3.5** ODBC Profile Settings

| Profile Setting | Profile Value | |
|---|---|---|
| | MsgTerse | Controls whether ODBC error messages show the SQLSTATE prefix. Values are 'Yes' and 'No' (default). |
| | PBCatalogOwner | Specifies the non-default owner for the tables in the Sybase repository. |
| | TableCriteria | Enables you to specify criteria to limit the tables and views listed in the Select Tables dialog. |
| | Async | Allows synchronous operations to occur on the database server. Values are 0 (synchronous, the default) and 1 (asynchronous operation). |
| | DBGetTime | Specifies the number of seconds PowerBuilder should wait for a response from the DBMS when you retrieve rows and Async is set to 1. |
| | Block | Determines the number of rows that a DataWindow object or report can fetch from the database at one time. The value is from 1 and 1000, where 1 turns blocking off. |
| | InsertBlock | Specifies the number of rows that you want the Data Pipeline in PowerBuilder to insert at one time. Values are 1 to 100, with the default as 100. |
| | SQLCache | Specifies the number of SQL statements that PowerBuilder should cache. The default is 0. |
| | CursorLib | Specifies the cursor library to use: 'ODBC_Cur_Lib' (ODBC Version 2.0 cursor library), 'If_Needed' (ODBC Version 2.0 cursor library if ODBC driver doesn't support cursors), and 'Driver_Cursors' (default is use data source's native cursor support). |

TABLE 3.5   ODBC Profile Settings

| Profile Setting | Profile Value | |
|---|---|---|
| | CursorLock | Specifies locking options for cursors: `'Lock'` (lock rows as they're fetched), `'Opt'` (don't lock rows and check updates against time stamps or previous known values), `'OptVal'` (don't lock rows and check updates against previous known values), and `'ReadOnly'` (no updates allowed through cursor). |
| | CursorScroll | Sets scrolling options for cursors: `'Forward'` (cursor moves only forward through resultset), `'Keyset'` (keys are saved for the entire resultset, and as the cursor scrolls through the resultset, the keys in the keyset are used to retrieve the current values for each row), `'Dynamic'` (default; only the current row information is stored), and `'Static'` (all the data that makes the resultset is saved and is used to provide the request row information). |
| | PBUseProcOwner | Controls whether a stored-procedure based `DataWindow` should prefix the procedure name with the owner. |
| | DisableBind | Controls whether to carry out input parameter binding. Values are `0` (enabled, the default) and `1`. |
| | StaticBind | Controls whether PowerBuilder gets a resultset description from the DBMS before retrieving data. Values are `1` (disabled, the default) and `0` (get description). |
| | DelimitIdentifier | Encloses the names of tables, columns, indexes, and constraints in double quotation marks when it generates SQL statements. Values are `'Yes'` and `'No'`. |
| | IdentifierQuoteChar | Specifies the single quotation mark you want PowerBuilder to delimit the names of identifiers with. |
| | Date | Specifies a `date` data type that PowerBuilder uses when it builds SQL `UPDATE` statements. The syntax is `' ""Sybase_date_format"" '` The spaces and single quotes must appear as shown. |

TABLE 3.5 ODBC Profile Settings

| Profile Setting | Profile Value | |
| --- | --- | --- |
| | DateTime | Works the same as Date, but also includes a time. |
| | Time | Works the same as Date, except that it's just a time value. |
| | DecimalSeparator | Specifies the non-default decimal separator setting used by the back-end DBMS. The default value is '.'. |
| | FormatArgsAsExp | Converts a DataWindow or report retrieval argument of a decimal data type exceeding 12 digits to scientific (exponential) notation. The default is 'Yes'. |
| | PacketSize | Specifies the network packet size in bytes. |
| | LoginTimeOut | Specifies the number of seconds the ODBC driver should wait for a login request to an ODBC data source. The default is 15 seconds. |

The ODBC driver also includes a ConnectOption setting that can be specified in the DBParm attribute. Refer to the ODBC driver information that comes from Sybase for the available settings.

## Other ODBC Data Sources

With PowerBuilder, you can access many other ODBC data sources by using ODBC-compliant drivers. Which ODBC data sources (other than Sybase Adaptive Server Anywhere) can be accessed by using PowerBuilder depends on the platform:

| Platform | Access Other ODBC Data Sources? |
| --- | --- |
| Windows | Yes |
| UNIX | Only the INTERSOLV ODBC drivers supplied by Sybase are supported. You can't use ODBC drivers obtained from other vendors. |

To find out more about your own specific DBMS connection settings, set your browser to `http://sybooks.sybase.com:80/onlinebooks/group-pb/pbg0700e/connpb/`.

# Using the Database Profile Dialog Window

Database profiles allow you to store the parameter settings for your database connections under a specific name for the development environment. Each profile is stored in the initialization file for PowerBuilder:

| Platform | Filename | Location |
| --- | --- | --- |
| Windows | PB.INI | PowerBuilder product directory |
| UNIX | .pb.ini (hidden) | $HOME directory |

By using one of these stored profiles, you can easily switch between different databases and DBMSs and, using a new feature, export and import them for sharing with other developers in your group.

The Database Profiles dialog greatly helps you create and maintain PowerBuilder database profiles. As Figure 3.2 shows, a tree-view window lists all currently installed database interfaces and profiles created for each of them.

**FIGURE 3.2**

*The Database Profiles window.*

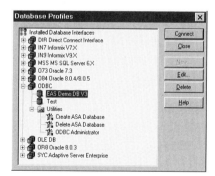

## Managing a Database Profile

Choosing either the New or Edit button from the Database Profiles dialog opens a DBMS-specific Database Profile Setup dialog. Each DBMS shares a common set of five tabbed pages: Connection, System, Transaction, Syntax, and Preview. Some DBMSs have additional pages. For example, Microsoft SQL Server has an additional Network page (see Figure 3.3).

**FIGURE 3.3**
*Database Profile
Setup dialog for
MS SQL Server.*

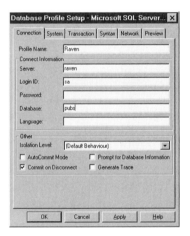

These DBMS-specific dialogs facilitate your formulating the DBParm settings. Choices are made through drop-down lists and check boxes, so you don't have to remember the exact syntax. After you make all your selections, you can choose the Preview tab to view and copy the connection syntax you've just specified (see Figure 3.4).

## Sharing Database Profiles

A new feature within the Database Profiles dialog helps you share database connection information among a development group or create an INI file with connection information for your deployed application. By right-clicking a database interface entry, you can choose to import or export a profile. Within the export window, you can select multiple entries to be written to the one INI file. However, you can import only one INI file at a time, with the information being written into the PB.INI file.

**FIGURE 3.4**
*The Preview page.*

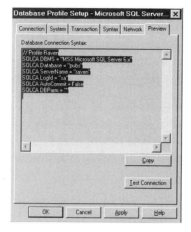

## Database Utilities

To give you a central point from which you can access a particular DBMS's tools, Sybase has added the capability to tie these tools into the Database Profiles dialog. Sybase has already tied in some utilities for a few DBMS interfaces: ODBC, Oracle 7.3, and OLE DB.

Sybase's idea was to provide access to all the utilities necessary for configuring and testing the client side of a database connection. To use a utility, simply double-click the entry in the profile window. You can add utilities by right-clicking the Utilities folder under the appropriate DBMS interface and choosing Add utility from the pop-up menu. This in turn opens a dialog prompting you for the executable's name and location.

# Database Design

The database is the central point of any data-based system, and the amount of time invested in the creation of a quality database design greatly determines the quality and success of the system as a whole. Database design can be broken into four parts:

1. Normalizing and finalizing table relationships.
2. Identifying entity, data, and relational integrity.
3. Creating the data's physical schema.
4. Creating database objects (triggers, stored procedures, and indexes).

Developing the physical schema uses the products of the data analysis to indicate the tables, columns, and relationships among tables. Columns are assigned data types and possibly even extended attributes, such as the edit style, initial value, validation, display format, and so on. For a more complete description of the extended attributes, refer to Chapter 5, "Databases and the Database Painter."

Table relationships as well as the primary and foreign keys are also defined, and the data analysis determines most of the table relationships and how they are to be implemented. You can, and should, use a normalization technique to optimize the entities and the relationships between them.

## Normalization

During the data-modeling phase, you use a formal technique known as *normalization* to eliminate certain types of undesirable dependencies among entities. This technique also highlights the constraints and dependencies in the data and aids the data modelers in understanding the actual nature of the data.

By normalizing the database design, you can reduce the amount of stored redundant data, thus easing data maintenance, reducing storage requirements, and dramatically improving data integrity. With normalization, data integrity is easier to enforce because the data resides in only one place in the database. As you will see in the examples used to illustrate the normal forms later in this chapter, the size of the records for entities is reduced with normalization as well. For such DBMSs as Sybase's or Microsoft's SQL Server, the smaller the row size, the more data can be stored per data page, again improving storage requirements and I/O processing because fewer pages need to be read.

But this process has some drawbacks. Because you're breaking up attributes and placing them into separate entities, you have to perform joins between those entities to access a complete record of information. As such, you're accessing data pages for multiple entities and receive a hit in your I/O activities as well as CPU resources because the server has to determine the best method of retrieving the requested information. Techniques to address each of these drawbacks are beyond the scope of this book but can be found in any DBMS-specific book.

> **Note**
>
> Sams offers a number of books in its *Unleashed* series that address individual DBMSs which provide this kind of information—for example, *Microsoft SQL Server Unleashed*, *Oracle Unleashed*, and *SQL Unleashed*.

The higher normal forms that can be reached—typically 3NF and higher—produce well-designed databases with high levels of data independence. Entities in the database model are described as having a certain normal form if they satisfy particular criteria. Each level of the normal forms builds on the previous level.

The five levels of data normalization are as follows:

- Eliminate repeating groups (1NF, or first normal form)

- Eliminate redundant data (2NF, or second normal form)

- Eliminate columns not dependent on a key (3NF, or third normal form)

- Isolate independent multiple relationships (4NF, or fourth normal form)

- Isolate semantically related multiple relationships (5NF, or fifth normal form)

# First Normal Form

To eliminate repeating groups, create a separate entity for each group of related attributes and assign to this new entity a primary key and a foreign key to link it back to the parent entity.

---

**Note**

Sometimes you *won't* want to eliminate a repeating group, which can make this rule difficult to apply. If you have a finite number, usually small, of repeating values that you need to access as side-by-side columns rather than as rows, leave them in the parent. For example, consider that for each order you track up to four service representatives. Depending on how those pieces of data are entered and reported determines whether they stay in the parent or receive their own entity.

---

# Second Normal Form

To eliminate redundant data, you need to create separate entities for attributes that don't fully depend on the entire primary key of the entity.

# Third Normal Form

To eliminate non-key columns that aren't mutually independent, create separate entities for these attributes.

Third normal form is adequate for most database situations but can't adequately handle the case in which an entity has two or more candidate keys that are composite and have at least one common attribute. To compensate for this situation, a modified form of third normal form was introduced by two well-known database theorists and is known as *Boyce Codd Normal Form* (BCNF).

Some data models might require use of two additional, higher normal forms to produce a better-designed database model:

- *Fourth normal form*is concerned with isolating independent multiple relationships. Basically, an entity can't have more than one one-to-many (1:n) or many-to-many (n:m) relationship that's not directly related to another relationship.

- *Fifth normal form*concentrates on isolating semantically related multiple relationships. You might want to separate many-to-many relationships that are logically grouped; you would use fifth normal form to do so.

> **Tip**
>
> To arrive at a 3NF database design, a simple rule is, "Each attribute must be a fact about the key, the whole key, and nothing but the key." (Wiorkowski and Kull, *DB2 Design & Development Guide*.)

As stated previously, third normal form is adequate for most databases, but some require further normalization. At this point in the normalization process, you have a functioning database schema; all you need is a system to access it. You must now use the requirements gathered in the analysis phase to create a design that can be developed for implementation. This additional step creates a database design that's usually one step back from the final level of normalization. This process is called *denormalization*.

## Denormalization

Denormalization takes the actual use of the tables and data into consideration to break some normalization rules to provide for duplicate or unrelated attributes in some entities. This has the advantage of minimizing joins and helping resolve some aggregate values that incur a large penalty to calculate. It also might require less storage space when you compare the additional column sizes against the overhead of a separate table and associated indexes.

> **Note**
>
> If you take Sybase/Microsoft SQL Server for an example and repeat three four-character columns in one table, the amount of additional storage required is 12 bytes. However, if the columns were in their own tables, you would have the storage requirements of a primary key, part of which would be a foreign key to the parent table, together with the four-character column for each row. For example, if the primary key of the parent were an eight-character column, the overall storage requirements to store the three rows would be 36 bytes.

But denormalization is usually done for data-access reasons and not for data modifications, so you should weigh the pros and cons for each and what the focus of the database is to be—query or data entry.

# Summary

This chapter covered all the leading database-management systems that PowerBuilder supports through native drivers, along with the ODBC driver that allows access to other DBMSs for which native drivers aren't provided. Each table listed the required and available settings that are made to a transaction object to connect to each server. You saw the new database profiles window that makes setting up and maintaining database connections much less painful. Finally, you saw the process for normalizing and denormalizing a database so that you can make best use of the DBMS you choose to use.

**3**

Database Management Systems

# SQL and PowerBuilder

**CHAPTER 4**

After you create the database with tables and views based on the conceptual schema, the next step is to communicate with the database system to manipulate or modify the data. Each database management system (DBMS) has its own *Data Manipulation Language* (DML), but all DMLs are based on a single language—*Structured Query Language* (SQL), pronounced "sequel" or "S-Q-L."

The precursor to today's SQL was originated by Dr. E.F. Codd in the 1970s as a means of accessing his new concept: relational databases. The first implemented version of the query language theorized by Codd was developed by D.D. Chamberlin in 1976 and was known as Sequel. SQL was first adopted for IBM's System R project, a research prototype that was to yield SQL/DS and DB2 and has since been approved as the official relational query language standard by the American National Standards Institute (ANSI). SQL can be found in many different forms throughout PowerBuilder, from the most obvious (embedded SQL) to the least obvious (DataWindows).

There are three main types of SQL statements. The most common is the *query*, a request for information. Next are the statements for *data modification* (the adding, deleting, or updating of data). The last type covers the administration of the system and transactions (for example, creating tables, granting security permissions, and committing and rolling back transactions).

Before diving into SQL's mysteries, you need to understand a number of terms. Database tables can be called *entities*, *tables*, or *relations*. Tables contain *rows*, or *records* of data, and describe one occurrence of that entity. Within each row are a number of *attributes*, *fields*, or *columns*. The usage of each term is related to the area of description. When discussing a conceptual data model, use the terms *entities*, *attributes*, and *relationships*; when using DMLs, however, the correct terms are *tables* and *columns*.

SQL is based on *tuples* (record occurrences) and tuple-oriented relational calculus. This means that when two tables are joined, a multiplication effect occurs. For example, table A has 10 records and table B has 20 records. If the two tables are simply joined (that is, without a WHERE clause), the result consists of 200 records; each record from table A joins with each record from table B. This is important because the multiplication factor can cause novice SQL programmers some problems when join conditions aren't quite correct. This also means that you need to adjust your mind-set. Rather than deal with a procedural language or method to solve problems, you need to think relationally, and you need to remember that you can now operate collectively on sets of data.

This chapter details aspects of SQL from the basics of the SELECT statement through advanced SQL constructs. The Sybase demonstration database (EASDemoDB.db) that comes with PowerBuilder is used to illustrate SQL examples. Some additional examples are written to use the pubs database that comes with Microsoft and Sybase SQL Server.

# Working with SQL

Before seeing how to incorporate SQL into PowerBuilder applications, first examine the different kinds of SQL statements available. The following sections describe the SELECT, INSERT, UPDATE, and DELETE statements and how they're constructed and used.

## Understanding Queries

The basis of a query is the SELECT statement. You will find a number of variations and limitations among the various DBMSs you will encounter, but in its simplest form, it's structured as follows:

```
SELECT target list
FROM list of relations
```

*target list* is a projection (the columns to be used instead of the columns that won't be used) of a subset of the columns from one or more tables, or, put simply, the names of the values to retrieve. A *join* links the rows of two or more tables to provide the relations of a query.

This is the most common form of a query:

```
SELECT target list
FROM list of relations
WHERE conditions
```

The values of certain columns (usually primary or foreign keys) are compared in the *conditions* clause. This provides a link between two tables and a method to restrict the resulting rows from a table. Sometimes this linkage is automatically carried out by the DBMS if the columns are key values. Sybase Adaptive Server Anywhere is an example of this automatic linkage, which helps reduce the complexity of the WHERE clause. The syntax used in Sybase SQL Anywhere requires you to specify a NATURAL or KEY JOIN in the FROM clause of a query. You can find more information on this feature by exploring the Sybase SQL Anywhere documentation that comes with PowerBuilder.

To retrieve attributes emp_lname and city from a single relation employee with no selection criteria, thus returning all rows in the table, the WHERE clause is omitted and the statement appears as follows:

```
SELECT emp_lname, city
FROM employee;
```

These might be the results from running this query (in the Database Administration painter):

**4**

**SQL and PowerBuilder**

```
Last Name          City
Whitney            Needham
Cobb               Waltham
Chin               Atlanta
Jordan             Winchester
Breault            Milton
```

You can place selections (or restrictions) on this query within the WHERE clause. For example, to list just the employees from California, the query becomes

```
SELECT emp_fname, city
FROM    employee
WHERE   state = 'CA';
```

> **Caution**
>
> Users of Sybase Adaptive Server Anywhere *must* use a single quotation mark (')
> instead of a double quotation mark (") in the preceding and following examples.
> In fact, according to ANSI syntax, you use double quotation marks to delimit
> keywords (*quoted identifiers*) and single quotation marks to delimit string
> constants.

However, to create a link between multiple relations, another WHERE clause is added:

```
SELECT employee.city, customer.city
FROM    employee, customer, sales_order
WHERE   employee.emp_id = sales_order.sales_rep AND
        sales_order.cust_id = customer.id;
```

The results of this query follow, but note that if you run this query against the demo database, you get a succession of the same first city for just one employee (because there are multiple entries of an employee in the sales_order table):

```
City            City
Atlanta         Raleigh
Atlanta         South Laguna
Atlanta         Bohemia
Atlanta         Winnipeg
Atlanta         Lakewood
```

In this example, two columns of the same name (City) are retrieved. Also note that the table name prefixes the column name to inform the DBMS from which tables to pull the values and in what order. This is called *aliasing*, and you can alias tables and columns in this manner. Also note that three tables are involved in the join, and the WHERE clause has now become a compound statement. Multiple conditions are related using AND or OR and enable the construction of complex truth conditions.

## Understanding NULLs

SQL is based on three-state logic: TRUE, FALSE, and Unknown. The unknown value is represented by RDBMSs as NULL, and you have to be as aware of NULLs in your SQL as you are in your PowerScript. NULLs are used to represent a missing or unknown value, or to indicate that a value for that column in a record isn't applicable. The NULL value isn't the empty string or a zero; it's the absence of a value. Like PowerBuilder, the DBMS provides a means to check the equality of a value to NULL because a NULL is never equal to anything, including itself. So, for example, the following query produces some unexpected results:

```
SELECT emp_lname
FROM   employee
WHERE  city = 'Indianapolis' OR
NOT    city = 'Indianapolis';
```

This query doesn't return all employees. If some employees' cities have NULL values, their records won't appear in the resultset. To check whether a column equals NULL, use the special phrase IS NULL . Using any other operator gives a FALSE value if used against a NULL value, and the join will fail. A negation of the WHERE clause doesn't solve the problem (as can be demonstrated by running the previous query), because three-valued logic  (TRUE, FALSE, and Unknown), not two-valued logic (just TRUE and FALSE), is in operation. Therefore, NOT Unknown  values are also Unknown (at least in SQL!). The correct syntax for the sample query is this:

```
SELECT emp_lname
FROM   employee
WHERE  city = 'Indianapolis' OR
NOT    city = 'Indianapolis' OR
       city IS NULL;
```

**4**

**SQL and PowerBuilder**

### Note

Obviously, you wouldn't code a query to return all employees in this way; this is shown only to illustrate the correct way to handle NULL values. Also notice that you get the same number of results in the demo database because there are no NULL city values.

If you want to default NULL to a usable value—say, for the purpose of grouping your resultset—use the ISNULL() function. ISNULL() takes two parameters: the column or expression you suspect might be NULL and the value to which you want it to default if the column or expression is NULL. For example,

```
SELECT emp_lname
FROM    employee
WHERE   ISNULL (salary, 0) = 0;
```

returns all employees who have a zero salary, together with all employees who have yet to be assigned a salary (new hires) and therefore have a NULL salary amount.

> **Note**
>
> As noted earlier, not all DBMSs support the same syntax. For instance, Oracle uses an NVL() function instead of ISNULL() (for example, NVL(salary, 0) ).

## The SELECT Statement

Because each DBMS has its own variations, what follows is a generalization of the complete SQL SELECT statement:

```
SELECT { DISTINCT } select_list
FROM [ table_list ¦ view_list ]
WHERE search_conditions
GROUP BY non_aggregate_expressions
HAVING search_conditions
ORDER BY column_list { [ ASC ¦ DESC ] }
```

The DISTINCT keyword removes duplicate rows from the resultset. A row is considered *duplicate* if all values in the select list completely match those of another row. NULL values are considered to be equal for the DISTINCT keyword. Most systems include the opposite keyword ALL in their syntax, which explicitly asks for all rows. This is the default behavior of a query; the keyword is included only for backward compatibility with earlier versions of SQL.

## The Retrieval List

*select_list* contains a comma-separated list of columns, constants, expressions, or an asterisk (representing all columns). *Expressions* are functions, subqueries, arithmetic operators, or any combination of columns, constants, and expressions. The asterisk selects all columns in all tables but can also be qualified with a table name to select all the columns in only that table.

## The WHERE Clause

The WHERE clause can include the standard comparison operators (such as =, >, <, and !=), ranges (BETWEEN), lists (IN), pattern matches (LIKE), and the unknown value operator (IS NULL ). Each condition can be combined by using the standard logical operators (AND, OR) and also nested within parentheses. The DBMS most often makes the appropriate data conversion when comparing values of varying data types. Here's an example:

```
WHERE date_entered = '12/06/69'
```

> **Note**
>
> This example works against a SQL Server environment, but against Sybase Adaptive Server Anywhere you're required to phrase it as '1969-12-06'. Other databases may require other specific formats to work, and you should refer to the appropriate DBMS SQL book.

The NOT keyword can be applied before any operators to negate the expression. For example, the following returns all employees that didn't start in 1986:

```
SELECT emp_lname
FROM   employee
WHERE  start_date NOT BETWEEN '86/1/1' AND '86/12/31';
```

## Joins

Three main types of join conditions are used in the WHERE clause: the inner join, the outer join, and the self-join.

An *inner join* links two tables on matching column names by using the equality operator (=), such as

```
SELECT employee.emp_fname
FROM   employee, department
WHERE  employee.dept_id = department.dept_id;
```

An *outer join* returns all rows from an outer table, with any values taken from the inner table being NULL if no join condition exists. The construction of an outer join varies from one DBMS to another, although the tendency is to conform to ANSI SQL standards; with SQL Server the syntax is *= and =* specified in the WHERE clause, whereas ANSI syntax

**4**

**SQL and PowerBuilder**

uses LEFT ¦ RIGHT ¦ FULL OUTER JOIN in the FROM clause. For example, to list all the department names with everyone in that department and to allow for cases in which no one belongs to a department (such as a new department), the query against SQL Server might be

```
SELECT dept_name, emp_lname, emp_fname
FROM    department d, employee e
WHERE   d.dept_id *= e.dept_id;
```

or specified using ANSI syntax

```
SELECT dept_name, emp_lname, emp_fname
FROM    department LEFT OUTER JOIN employee
ON      department.dept_id = employee.dept_id;
```

Some DBMSs place restrictions on outer joins that prevent other joins on either (or both) inner and outer tables; SQL Server restricts regular joins on the inner table.

Another type of join is the *self-join*, when values are compared within a table column. Constructing this type of join requires *table aliasing*—renaming a table within the SELECT. Here's an example:

```
SELECT DISTINCT e1.emp_fname, e1.emp_lname, e1.zip_code
FROM    employee e1, employee e2
WHERE   e1.state = 'MA' AND
        e1.zip_code = e2.zip_code AND
        e1.emp_id <> e2.emp_id
ORDER BY e1.zip_code;
```

This returns all employees from Massachusetts who live in the same ZIP code. DISTINCT eliminates the duplicate records found due to the self-join. The not-equality operation on the employee_id removes any self-matches (to give only a list of multiple employees who live in the same area, therefore eliminating any employees who are the only ones in a specific ZIP code).

## Subqueries

A *subquery* is a SELECT that exists within another statement (for example, SELECT, INSERT, UPDATE, or DELETE) and provides one or more rows to be used in the outer statement's evaluation. A subquery is used for three main purposes:

- To generate a list for use with the IN operator

- To generate a single value

- With the EXISTS, ANY, and ALL operators

The two subquery types are single-column single-value and single-column multivalue. The first subquery type can be used anywhere an expression can be used, whereas the subqueries that return multiple rows can be used only in the WHERE clause with the operators EXISTS or IN.

Single-value subqueries can be expressions in the select list or even in the HAVING clause; they provide a clean way of carrying out additional checks and/or restrictions on the data to be included in the results. You can construct a wide variety of subqueries, and, depending on the database, you might be able to use other operators (such as ANY, ALL, and SOME in Sybase Adaptive Server Anywhere).

## Single-Value Subqueries

A single-value subquery, as its name suggests, has sufficient restrictions placed on it so that only one row with only one value (column, expression, or constant) is returned. In the following example, even though the query itself returns more than one row, each subquery produces just a single value:

```
SELECT id,
       line_id,
       quantity,
        (SELECT SUM(quantity)
         FROM sales_order_items),
       total,
       ship_date
FROM
       sales_order_items
WHERE  prod_id =
        (SELECT id
         FROM product
         WHERE name = 'shorts');
```

This example illustrates two subqueries: one in the select list and one in the WHERE clause. If the subquery in the WHERE clause returns more than one row, you get a runtime error. The first subquery guarantees a single value thanks to the aggregate function you're using and because there's no GROUP BY clause. This subquery doesn't return any really useful information, just the total quantity within the table.

## Correlated Subqueries

A subquery that depends on the outer query for values is known as a *correlated* subquery. The subquery is executed repeatedly, once for each row selected by the outer query, and can't be resolved independently:

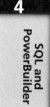

**4**

SQL and
PowerBuilder

```
SELECT emp_fname, emp_lname
FROM    employee e1
WHERE   city =
     (SELECT city
       FROM employee e2
       WHERE e2.emp_id = e1.manager_id );
```

This query returns all employees who live in the same city as their managers. The subquery depends on the outer query supplying the `manager_id` for each row. The equality operator can be used because there's only one manager per employee.

Now look at the example introduced in the preceding "Single-Value Subqueries" section. What might be more interesting than the total table quantity is the quantity for each order. To provide this information, use a correlated subquery as follows:

```
SELECT id, line_id, quantity,  (SELECT SUM(quantity)
    FROM sales_order_items soi2
    WHERE soi2.id = soi1.id) total, ship_date
FROM    sales_order_items soi1
WHERE   prod_id =
     (SELECT id
       FROM product
       WHERE name = 'shorts' );
```

## Subqueries with IN

A subquery is used with the IN keyword to produce a set of values against which a value or column can be compared to check whether it's a member. The IN keyword indicates membership inclusion; NOT IN indicates membership exclusion. Here's an example:

```
SELECT id, line_id
FROM    sales_order_items
WHERE   prod_id IN  (300, 301, 302, 303);
```

The following query is a check for what sales order items have been entered for out-of-stock products:

```
SELECT id, line_id
FROM    sales_order_items
WHERE   prod_id IN
     (SELECT id
       FROM product
       WHERE quantity = 0);
```

## Subqueries with EXISTS

A parent query can use a subquery with EXISTS to test for the existence of rows. It is typically constructed using a correlated subquery.

This example returns all products that have sold more than 40 items in a single sale:

```
SELECT name
FROM    product
WHERE  EXISTS
    (SELECT id
      FROM sales_order_items
      WHERE sales_order_items.prod_id = product.id AND
      quantity > 40);
```

The actual data returned by the subquery is ignored. All you're checking for is the existence of at least one record; it's purely a Boolean check.

# Aggregate Functions

Each DBMS provides its own set of aggregate functions, but a number of them are common: COUNT(), SUM(), AVG(), MAX(), and MIN(). Additional functions might be within your specific DBMS (for example, Sybase Adaptive Server Anywhere also provides a LIST() function). These common functions are detailed as follows:

| Aggregate Function | Result |
| --- | --- |
| AVG([DISTINCT] expression) | Produces an average of the numeric values in the expression |
| COUNT([DISTINCT] expression ¦ *) | Returns the number of records that fall within the expression |
| MAX(expression) | Gives the highest value of the expression |
| MIN(expression) | Gives the lowest value of the expression |
| SUM([DISTINCT] expression) | Totals the numeric value in the expression |

Note that SUM() and AVG() work only on numeric values.

## The GROUP BY and HAVING Clauses

Aggregate functions return summary results and are usually used with the GROUP BY and HAVING clauses. GROUP BY collects the data into related groups. For example, the following returns one record for each product with the total number of sales:

```
SELECT id, SUM (quantity)
FROM    sales_order_items
GROUP BY id;
```

Leaving off the GROUP BY clause generates a database error informing you that the nonaggregate columns must be included in a GROUP BY clause. This is an enforced syntax constraint; *all* nonaggregate columns appearing in the select list *must* be specified in a GROUP BY clause.

The HAVING clause sets conditions on which groups appear in the resultset and is comparable to the WHERE clause, except that it works only on aggregate expressions. For example, the following returns a list of all products, the number of orders for each, and the total quantity ordered for each product that has sold more than 4,000 items:

```
SELECT DISTINCT name, COUNT (product.id),
    SUM (sales_order_items.quantity)
FROM    sales_order_items, product
WHERE sales_order_items.prod_id = product.id
GROUP BY name
HAVING SUM (sales_order_items.quantity) > 4000;
```

Another example is useful in determining the presence of duplicate data within a table:

```
SELECT emp_fname, emp_lname
FROM    employee
GROUP BY emp_fname, emp_lname
HAVING COUNT(*) > 1;
```

## The ORDER BY Clause

The last clause of a SELECT is ORDER BY , which sorts values in ascending (ASC) or descending (DESC) order. If multiple columns are listed, the results are sorted in column order, left to right. The sort order that your DBMS imposes affects the results of an ORDER BY . This might mean uppercase values appear before lowercase, or numbers appear after alphabetic characters. If the ORDER BY is left off a query, the DBMS usually returns rows in the physical order in which they exist in the table (for example, a table with a clustered index returns rows in the index key sequence).

## The INSERT Statement

The INSERT statement is used to enter new rows into a table. In most DBMSs, you also can use INSERT, with UPDATE and DELETE, against database views, usually with certain restrictions. One common restriction to using these commands against a view is that they can affect only one table of the view at any one time. So to insert values into a two-table view, you're required to issue two INSERT statements. Each DBMS imposes a different set of restrictions on what operations can be carried out against a view. The syntax for an INSERT is as follows:

```
INSERT [INTO] {table_name | view_name}
    [(column_list)]
{VALUES  (constant_expressions) | select_statement }
```

*column_list* can be any number of columns from the table but must include columns that are specified as NOT NULL , don't have a default bound to them, and aren't server generated (for example, time stamps or identity). Neglect to do this and you will get an error telling you that the offending column can't be NULL. The VALUES clause requires a list of constants that are of the same data type as those listed in *column_list*. This clause can be replaced by a SELECT statement that returns any number of rows with a column list that matches that of the INSERT. The *column_list* of the INSERT isn't required if all the columns are to receive values, but it's advisable to list the columns anyway. If the table structure were to change (for example, if a column were added) and you hadn't coded the SELECT statement to return the additional information, the INSERT could fail, depending on that column's specification (for example, NOT NULL ). You're also taking a leap in the dark by not explicitly specifying the order of the columns because you're relying on the physical ordering of the receiving columns. Following are examples of both kinds of INSERT:

```
INSERT INTO authors
    (name, book)
VALUES
    ('Gallagher', 'PowerBuilder 7.0 Unleashed');

INSERT INTO authors
    (name, book)
SELECT name, book
FROM    new_authors
WHERE   name LIKE 'G%';
```

By using a SELECT as part of the INSERT, you can even populate a table based on itself. An INSERT of data must conform to any rules or triggers that might be defined on the table and columns.

## The UPDATE Statement

The UPDATE statement modifies existing rows of data. This is its syntax:

```
UPDATE {table_name | view_name}
SET column = {expression | NULL | (select_statement)}
  [,column = {expression | NULL | (select_statement)}]
[FROM {table_list | view_list}]
[WHERE search_conditions]
```

**4**

**SQL and PowerBuilder**

The SET clause specifies the column to be modified and the value or expression to be used as the new data. The expression can't be an aggregate function, but might be an aggregate result returned by a SELECT on the condition that only one value is returned. If the sub-SELECT returns more than one row, an error occurs stating that a subquery returned more than one row. If the query uses tables specified in the UPDATE, the statement is known as a *correlated update*.

The FROM clause permits the expression to use columns from other tables, and the WHERE clause controls which rows the UPDATE affects. If you omit the WHERE clause from an UPDATE statement, all rows in the table are affected. Some examples are as follows:

```
// Set all author royalty values to zero

UPDATE authors
SET    current_month_royalties = 0;

// Set the sales of authors with Gallagher as their name to 100,000
// ....we can all dream can't we? :)

UPDATE authors
SET    sales = 100000
WHERE  name = 'Gallagher';

// Update the quantity sold and date modified with data
// from the sales table

UPDATE authors
SET    sales = authors.sales + sales.quantity,
       change_date = GetDate()
FROM   authors, sales
WHERE  authors.author_id = sales.author_id;

// Carry out same modification except for authors that had a last
// shipment before the last day in the sales table
UPDATE authors
SET    sales = authors.sales + sales.quantity,
       change_date = GETDATE()
FROM   authors, sales
WHERE  authors.author_id = sales.author_id AND
       authors.last_shipped <  (SELECT MAX (ship_date)
FROM   sales);
```

As with the INSERT statement, new values must conform to the table's triggers and the column's rules.

# The DELETE Statement

The last data-manipulation statement is the most destructive—DELETE. This is the syntax:

```
DELETE
FROM [table_name ¦ view_name]
{WHERE search_conditions}
```

The WHERE clause restricts the rows affected by DELETE, just as it does with the other statements. DELETE must pass any triggers attached to the affected table. After DELETE is issued, there is no way to recover the records affected other than to cause an explicit ROLLBACK or if a trigger fails (which does its own ROLLBACK).

# Good SQL Practices

Now for a few practice exercises to help with the readability of the SQL you write and to provide a better interface to canned queries, stored procedures, and views.

Capitalize the SQL statements to make them stand out from column names, table names, and other expressions, as shown in the many code examples in this chapter.

Wherever a computed value or expression is returned, it's considered good manners to give it a name related to the value. For example, the following SELECT returns a salesperson and the number of items sold:

```
SELECT  employee.emp_lname, COUNT(*)
FROM    employee, sales_order
WHERE   employee.emp_id = sales_order.sales_rep
GROUP BY employee.emp_lname
ORDER BY COUNT(*);
```

These are the results for this query:

```
emp_lname      Count(*)
Kelly          47
Dill           50
Poitras        52
 .
 .
 .
Clark          57
Overbey        114
```

As you will see next, if the SELECT is modified to alias the columns, the meaning of the query is much clearer, and if you alias the tables, the join conditions don't look as awkward. It's advantageous to use table aliases with large statements that join and select columns from many tables. The overall size of the statement is much smaller, which reduces network traffic somewhat, but the main benefit is that it aids in the readability and therefore maintainability.

For example, the following query is the same as the previous query except that it names the two returned values and aliases the tables used:

```
SELECT e.emp_lname LastName, COUNT(*) TotalSales
FROM    employee e, sales_order s
WHERE   e.emp_id = s.sales_rep
GROUP BY LastName
ORDER BY TotalSales;
```

This query produces the same results, but the computed column is now named as follows:

```
LastName       TotalSales
Kelly          47
Dill           50
Poitras        52
 .
 .
Clark          57
Overbey        114
```

Always list the columns that you will use repeatedly in a SELECT or an INSERT statement rather than rely on * or implicit column order. The column names, order, and even existence might vary without the SELECT or INSERT being appropriately modified, and you can get unexpected results by relying on the column order and existence.

# SQL Within PowerBuilder

The SQL statements just described can be embedded directly into your PowerScript and will perform in the same manner as they would from the Database painter. However, embedded SQL enables you to include PowerScript variables in various areas of the commands, whereas you can't include them if you work from the Database painter.

The SELECT statement gains an INTO clause that enables the specification of bind or host variables for the placement of the results. *Bind variables* are PowerScript variables prefixed by a colon (:) that are treated the same as any other column or value by the SQL.

All embedded SQL is terminated by a semicolon (;), the same as when executing SQL from within the Database painter. This means that you don't need to—in fact, PowerBuilder won't allow you to—use the line-continuation character (&) if your SQL extends over many lines. You just keep going and terminate the statement on the last line with a semicolon.

Therefore, the following query

```
SELECT  COUNT (books), SUM (sales)
INTO    :ll_TotalBooks, :ldc_Sales
FROM    authors
WHERE   name = :ls_Name
HAVING SUM (sales) > 15000;
```

uses the PowerScript variable ls_Name to find the appropriate author and then the variables ll_TotalBooks and ldc_Sales to hold the values returned. ls_Name restricts the query to returning just one row; otherwise, a database error occurs on subsequent SQL commands because additional rows in the resultset are still waiting to be fetched. If no rows are found, you get a zero or NULL value in the PowerBuilder variables (this is DBMS specific).

> **Note**
>
> In the [DataBase] section of your PB.INI is the entry TerminatorCharacter=;. This enables you to change the terminator character, but only for the Database painter. The ; must still be used for all embedded SQL.

## Transaction Objects

PowerBuilder controls embedded SQL and DataWindows through *transaction objects*, of which the SQLCA is the default and globally available transaction object. The SQLCA (SQL Communications Area) is a nonvisual object that contains relevant information on a connection to the database. The first ten attributes contain information necessary to connect, and the last five are used to receive information from the DBMS on the last operation executed. The default transaction object contains the attributes listed in Table 4.1.

**4**

**SQL and PowerBuilder**

**TABLE 4.1**   Attributes of the Default Transaction Object

| Attribute Name | Data Type | Description |
|---|---|---|
| DBMS | String | The name of the database vendor |
| DataBase | String | The name of the database |
| UserId | String | The username to connect by |
| DBParm | String | Specific to the DBMS |
| DBPass | String | The password to be used with the user ID |
| Lock | String | The isolation level |
| LogId | String | The username to connect by |
| LogPass | String | The password to be used with the log ID |
| ServerName | String | The database server name |
| AutoCommit | Boolean | The automatic commit indicator: |

TABLE **4.1**  Attributes of the Default Transaction Object

| Attribute Name | Data Type | Description |
|---|---|---|
| | | TRUE—Commit automatically after every action |
| | | FALSE—Don't commit automatically (the default) |
| SQLCode | Long | The success or failure code of the last operation: |
| | | 0—Success |
| | | 100—No results |
| | | 1—Error |
| SQLNRows | Long | The number of rows affected |
| SQLDBCode | Long | The database vendor's error code |
| SQLErrText | String | The database vendor's error message |
| SQLReturnData | String | Specific to the database vendor |
| ClassDefinition | PowerObject | Class information about the object |

Not all of the first ten attributes need to be given a value. For example, Sybase Adaptive Server Anywhere requires only the DBMS and DBParm attributes to be filled. DBParm holds the relevant data source name and login information, instead of LogPass, LogId, and the similarly related attributes such as database and server names. For native database interfaces, DBParm specifies DBMS-specific options. (See the online help under DBParm for more information.)

The AutoCommit attribute must be set to TRUE to create temporary tables or for any other database statements that require execution outside a PowerBuilder-controlled transaction. This is to ensure database consistency during execution and to improve database performance. The AutoCommit attribute affects only INFORMIX, Microsoft SQL Server, ODBC (if driver and back-end DBMS support this feature), SQL Server 4. *x*, Sybase InformationCONNECT DB2 Gateway interface, and Sybase SQL Server System 10 and System 11 database management systems. If the InformationCONNECT DB2 Gateway is being used and is configured for long transactions, changing AutoCommit has no effect. If the gateway is configured for short transactions, setting AutoCommit to FALSE changes the gateway configuration to support long transactions.

The DBMS fills SQLNRows, which varies in meaning from vendor to vendor but is usually checked after DELETE, UPDATE, or INSERT to ensure that the correct number of records were affected. SQLCode is usually sufficient to check after executing a SELECT command.

Situations will arise that require an additional connection to the database, such as a need to issue UPDATE, SELECT, or DELETE inside an open cursor that's already using the SQLCA. You create it by declaring a variable of type Transaction and assigning it the SQLCA attributes. A straight assignment can't be made because this then becomes a pointer to the SQLCA and that already has an open connection! After you populate the new transaction object, it needs to be connected to the database. For example, you might expect the following to work, but it doesn't:

```
Transaction trCursor
trCursor = CREATE transaction
trCursor = SQLCA
```

You will instead have to use the following:

```
Transaction trCursor
trCursor = CREATE transaction
trCursor.DBMS = SQLCA.DBMS
trCursor.Database = SQLCA.Database
// Etc. for the remaining transaction object attributes
```

As you learn in Chapter 7, "The Powerscript Language," it's important to destroy anything you create. With this in mind, you should issue a DESTROY trCursor just before the previous cursor leaves scope.

## Connecting and Disconnecting

After the transaction object is populated, the next step is to connect it to the database. You most often do this in the startup of an application, either in the application's Open event or a login window. In this syntax,

```
CONNECT [USING transaction_object];
```

the transaction object is the default (SQLCA) or one that you've previously defined and initialized.

> **Tip**
>
> It's good practice to explicitly state that the transaction object to be used is the SQLCA when doing a CONNECT, even though the USING clause is optional. This improves your code's readability and gives novice programmers a clearer understanding of what's happening. It's also a good habit to get into because if you ever omit a transaction object that you've created, it can be difficult to track down the problem.

**4**

**SQL and PowerBuilder**

To drop the connection to the database, a similar statement is used:

```
DISCONNECT [USING transaction_object];
```

Again in this case, the transaction object is the SQLCA or one you've declared. Remember that the USING clause is optional for the SQLCA, but it's best to specify it explicitly.

# Logical Units of Work

Interaction with a DBMS is broken down into *logical units of work* (LUWs), or transactions. Transaction processing by the DBMS ensures that when a transaction is completed, all changes are reflected in the database, or that if the transaction fails, the changes are rolled back or undone to the point where the transaction started.

The classic example used to describe units of work is a bank account fund transfer: If a clerk makes a debit to an account and for some reason the debit process fails (say the database connection is lost), the actual debit of funds that took place is undone. Without a logical unit of work, the account could be left with a debited balance, but the clerk couldn't be sure that the transaction had been completed and that other possibly affected tables were appropriately updated.

PowerBuilder provides two commands to carry out transaction processing: COMMIT and ROLLBACK. The syntax for these is as follows:

```
COMMIT [USING transaction_object];

ROLLBACK [USING transaction_object];
```

The transaction object is again optional, but it's advised even if it is the SQLCA and required if using a programmer-defined transaction. COMMIT tells the DBMS to accept all changes and to go ahead and make them permanent, whereas ROLLBACK indicates that any changes since the last COMMIT should be undone.

PowerBuilder uses the COMMIT and ROLLBACK statements as the basis of database transactions, which, as you will see later, isn't always a good thing. When a DISCONNECT is issued, an automatic COMMIT is executed. You might want to code the COMMIT yourself or even issue a ROLLBACK in case Sybase decides that this is a bug rather than a feature.

The DBParm value called CommitOnDisconnect can be set to 'Yes' or 'No' to control whether a COMMIT or ROLLBACK is issued on a disconnection.

Using the PowerBuilder transaction-management statements means that transactions can't be nested as they can be natively with some DBMSs.

# Checking for SQL Failures

To check for the failure of an embedded SQL statement, consult SQLCA.SQLCode. If the SQLCode is 0, the previous command succeeded, and a COMMIT should be issued. (To free DBMS resources, such as locks and buffers, a COMMIT should be issued after a SELECT that has used any lock-holding mechanism.) If the code is -1, the SQL failed, and a ROLLBACK should be issued, which again frees DBMS resources and leaves the application in a state to continue processing the next transaction. Here's an example:

```
UPDATE employee
SET    emp_fname = "Simon"
WHERE  emp_id = 95
USING  SQLCA;
If SQLCA.SQLCode = 0 Then
    COMMIT USING SQLCA;
Else
    ls_Error = SQLCA.SQLErrText
    ROLLBACK USING SQLCA;
    MessageBox ("Update Failure", ls_Error)
End If
```

Occasionally, the developer checks the SQLCode for the value 100. This value signifies that no data was returned as a result of the previous statement and is checked after a singleton SELECT or a FETCH. FETCH statements usually occur in loops; the indicator for the end of the resultset is a SQLCode value of 100.

**Note**

A *singleton* SELECT returns only one record of information.

The specific DBMS error code and error message are taken from the transaction object attributes SQL DBCode and SQL ErrText, respectively. These two values are the ones usually reported in any error-message dialog.

**4**

**SQL and PowerBuilder**

**Tip**

In most systems, the DBMS error code is checked against a hard-coded list or another database table to replace SQL ErrText with a more user-friendly message. Of course, if the error message indicates a lost or not-connected transaction, the error script that generates the new message must be able to handle this situation. This is usually done by hard-coding the connection error messages into the script while leaving the rest of the messages in a database table.

## DECLARE and FETCH

In embedded SQL, which produces multiple-row resultsets, or in a stored procedure that requires execution, you use a different set of statements. The object used for traversing a multirow resultset is called a *cursor* and provides a movable, single-row view of the results (the resultset).

## The DECLARE Statement

The DECLARE statement is comparable to a variable declaration, and as such it isn't executed—it's used only to prepare the transaction object.

> **Note**
>
> You can declare the same cursor only once in the same script. If you have a declared cursor that's outside the local scope, the same scope rules that apply to standard variables (for example, String or Integer) also apply to cursor declarations.

This is the syntax to declare a cursor using a SELECT:

```
DECLARE cursor_name CURSOR FOR select_statement
{USING transaction_object};
```

In the following example, note the use of a bind variable in the WHERE clause:

```
DECLARE employee_data CURSOR FOR
SELECT   emp_fname, emp_lname
FROM     employee
WHERE    birth_date < :ldtm_CutOff
USING    SQLCA;
```

For a stored procedure, the syntax is similar:

```
DECLARE procedure_name PROCEDURE FOR database_procedure_name
@parmameter1 = value1, @ parameter2 = value2,...
{USING transaction_object};
```

Here's an example:

```
DECLARE employee_data CURSOR FOR
sp_employee_by_birth_date @cut_off = :ldtm_CutOff
USING SQLCA;
```

The actual stored procedure would be written as

```
CREATE PROCEDURE sp_employee_by_birth_date @cut_off DATETIME
AS
SELECT *
FROM employee
WHERE birth_date <= @cut_off;
```

SQL Server and Sybase stored procedures support the use of OUT to denote a parameter used as an output from the procedure. Some DBMSs require you to specify the resultset if one is generated by the stored procedure (for example, Sybase Adaptive Server Anywhere's RESULT clause in the stored procedure declaration). This is the syntax for OUT:

```
DECLARE procedure_name PROCEDURE FOR database_procedure_name
@parmameter1 = value1, @ parameter2 = value2 OUT,...
{USING transaction_object};
```

Although the DECLARE statement is only a declaration, it's part of a specific order of SQL statements and must be terminated with a ;. There's no need to check (indeed, no point in checking) the SQLCode because a DECLARE is simply that—a declaration, not an action.

## Using OPEN, EXECUTE, and FETCH

When the SQL statement is declared, the next step is to execute it. For declared cursors, the OPEN statement is used:

```
OPEN cursor_name;
```

For declared procedures, the EXECUTE command is used:

```
EXECUTE procedure_name;
```

The SQLCode of the transaction object, defined in the DECLARE, should be checked for SQL failure after an OPEN or an EXECUTE. If the OPEN or EXECUTE is successful and a result is generated, the data cursor is placed before the first row of the resultset. The FETCH statement is used to step to the first row and then subsequent rows, and it does the actual retrieval of the data into host variables. If the OPEN or EXECUTE fails, you should close the cursor and process the error. This is the syntax for the FETCH:

```
FETCH cursor_name ¦ procedure_name INTO host_variable_list;
```

Some DBMSs permit the use of FETCH FIRST , FETCH PRIOR , implicit FETCH NEXT , and FETCH LAST , which (as their names imply) fetch the first row, the previous to current row, the next row, and the last row, respectively. If no direction is indicated, PowerBuilder assumes FETCH NEXT . The FETCH statement is normally used inside a loop to collect the data into other PowerBuilder structures, such as arrays or even DataWindows. When a FETCH is issued against the resultset and the last record is already retrieved, `SQLCode` takes the value `100`, indicating that there are no more result rows. Here's an example:

```
li_Count = 0
Do
li_Count ++
FETCH employee_data INTO :ls_FirstName[ li_Count],
    :ls_LastName[ li_Count];
Loop While SQLCA.SQLCode = 0
```

To finish the processing of the cursor or procedure and to release client and server resources, a `CLOSE` statement is executed:

```
CLOSE cursor_name ¦ procedure_name;
```

`SQLCode` should be checked after this statement, although a failure at this stage probably indicates wider server problems.

> **Caution**
>
> Be careful not to place a `COMMIT` or `ROLLBACK` within an open cursor or stored procedure that's returning multiple rows. It will close the cursor or procedure.

# Dynamic SQL

Now that you've mastered the basic syntax of embedded SQL, you can explore dynamic SQL. *Dynamic SQL* enables the execution of database commands that aren't supported directly as embedded SQL, such as *Database Description Language* (DDL), `CREATE TABLE` and `DROP TABLE` , or SQL in which parameters or results are unknown at the time of development.

Dynamic SQL can be categorized into four types:

- No resultset or input parameters
- No resultset but requires parameters
- Known resultset and input parameters
- Unknown results and parameters at development time

PowerBuilder supports only the main SQL statements  (`SELECT`, `INSERT`, `UPDATE`, and `DELETE`) with its transaction statements  (`CONNECT`, `DISCONNECT`, `COMMIT`, and `ROLLBACK`), because these are common in all databases. To execute SQL syntax specific to a database, you have to resort to one of the forms of dynamic SQL.

# Type 1

This type of dynamic SQL is often used to execute DDL and other database-specific code. This is the syntax:

```
EXECUTE IMMEDIATE sql_statement { USING transaction_object };
```

For example, to drop a table, use this:

```
EXECUTE IMMEDIATE "DROP TABLE employee" USING SQLCA;
```

# Type 2

The second type is used for SQL statements that require one or more parameters that are unknown at development time and don't return resultsets. It's also used for DDL statements that require runtime-defined parameters. Here are the syntax and sequence:

```
PREPARE dynamic_staging_area FROM sql_statement {USING transaction_object};
EXECUTE dynamic_staging_area USING parameters;
```

The Type 2 syntax uses one of the other SQL objects defined in PowerBuilder—the *SQL dynamic Staging Area* (SQLSA), which stores SQL in preparation for later execution. The SQL is stored with the number of parameters and the transaction object to be used. The SQLSA's attributes are protected and can't be accessed at runtime. As with the SQLCA, the SQLSA is a default object instantiated from the DynamicStagingArea class, and user-defined classes or variables can be used in its place.

The PREPARE statement is used to prepare the SQLSA for execution of the SQL statement. Within the PREPARE statement's SQL, the ? character indicates the placement of all PowerBuilder variables to be supplied during execution. These characters are called *placeholders*. When the SQL statement is executed, the ? characters are replaced by the values signified by EXECUTE's USING clause. These values can be PowerBuilder variables or object attributes. The order of the placeholders and the order of the EXECUTE parameter list must be the same. Here's an example:

```
PREPARE SQLSA FROM
"UPDATE employee SET termination_date = GETDATE() WHERE emp_id = ?"
USING SQLCA;
EXECUTE SQLSA USING :ll_EmployeeId;
```

Another example looks like this:

```
PREPARE SQLSA FROM
"INSERT INTO employee( emp_id, manager_id ) VALUES( ?, ?)"
```

```
USING SQLCA;
EXECUTE SQLSA USING :ll_NewEmployeeId, :sle_assigned_manager_id.text;
```

Type 2 syntax can be reduced to Type 1 syntax by using string concatenation to put the parameters into the SQL statement. However, most uses of Type 2 have the statement declared outside a script's local scope. This allows the SQL statement to be prepared once and used multiple times. The execution of the code is faster, but you can obviously have only one statement prepared to run at any one time (unless you're using variables declared as type SQLSA and preparing the statements for these instead of the SQLSA).

# Type 3

The third type of dynamic SQL is probably the most frequently used after Type 1. The SQL statement produces a known resultset for a known number of parameters. These are the syntax and statement order:

```
DECLARE cursor_name DYNAMIC CURSOR FOR dynamic_staging_area;

PREPARE dynamic_staging_area FROM sql_statement
{ USING transaction_object };

OPEN DYNAMIC cursor_name { USING parameter_list };

FETCH cursor_name INTO host_variable_list;

CLOSE cursor_name;
```

For a stored procedure, the syntax uses different DECLARE syntax and an EXECUTE statement instead of an OPEN:

```
DECLARE procedure_name DYNAMIC PROCEDURE FOR dynamic_staging_area;

PREPARE dynamic_staging_area FROM sql_statement
{ USING transaction_object };
EXECUTE DYNAMIC procedure_name { USING parameter_list };

FETCH procedure_name INTO host_variable_list;

CLOSE procedure_name;
```

A popular use for the Type 3 syntax is populating an internal table or drop-down list boxes (DDLBs) with data from a database table. You can perform the same functionality with a DataWindow, but you might not want the overhead of this object. The dynamic SQL is written as a function, either global or attached to a specific object (as a user object). The following example is of a function attached to a DDLB user object that takes a SQL

SELECT string as a parameter that it uses in the PREPARE. During the FETCH cycle it issues AddItem() calls to fill the list box. Listing 4.1 shows the code.

**LISTING 4.1** Sample Code for Type 3 Dynamic SQL

```
String ls_Value
DECLARE listbox_values DYNAMIC CURSOR FOR SQLSA;
PREPARE SQLSA FROM :as_Select USING SQLCA;
OPEN DYNAMIC listbox_values;

If SQLCA.SQLCode < 0 Then
    MessageBox ("DataBase Error", &
        "Unable to open dynamic cursor in PopulateList function " + &
        SQLCA.SQLErrText)
    Return SQLCA.SQLCode
End If

This.SetRedraw( FALSE)
This.Reset()

Do While SQLCA.SQLCode = 0
    FETCH listbox_values INTO :ls_Value;
    If SQLCA.SQLCode = 0 Then
        This.Additem( Trim( ls_Value))
    ElseIf SQLCA.SQLCode < 0 Then
        MessageBox( "DataBase Error", &
            "Unable to fetch row from table specified" + &
            SQLCA.SQLErrText)
    End If
Loop

This.SetRedraw (TRUE)
CLOSE listbox_values;
```

When the FETCH reaches the end of the resultset, the SQLCA.SQLCode becomes 100 and the loop is left. The redraw for the list box or drop-down list box object is turned off so that the object doesn't flicker onscreen each time the AddItem() method is called.

# Type 4

The fourth type of dynamic SQL is the most complicated because it's coded with no knowledge of the input parameters or the return resultset. The *SQL dynamic Description Area* (SQLDA) is used to hold information about the parameters and resultset columns, and like the SQLCA and SQLSA it's the default object instantiated from a system class—in this case, the DynamicDescriptionArea class. The following attributes are available for investigation after a statement is described in the SQLDA:

| Attribute Name | Description |
| --- | --- |
| NumInputs | The number of input parameters |
| InParmType | An array of the input parameter data types |
| NumOutputs | The number of output parameters |
| OutParmType | An array of the output parameter data types |

The input parameters are specified in the DECLARE statement in the same manner as before—by using the ? character. The actual values are set with the SetDynamicParm() function, which takes the index position of the parameter and the value. The value can be of Integer, Long, Real, Double, Decimal, String, Boolean, Unsigned Integer, Unsigned Long, Date, Time, or DateTime data type. The appropriate data type is stored in the InParmType array, and the value is stored in a data type-specific array. After execution, the resultset is gathered value by value, using one of the following functions:

| Function Name | Used For |
| --- | --- |
| GetDynamicNumber() | TypeInteger!, TypeDecimal!, TypeDouble!, TypeLong!, TypeReal!, TypeBoolean!, TypeUnsignedInteger!, TypeUnsignedLong! |
| GetDynamicString() | TypeString! |
| GetDynamicDate() | TypeDate! |
| GetDynamicTime() | TypeTime! |
| GetDynamicDateTime() | TypeDateTime! |

These are the syntax and statement order for Type 4 dynamic SQL:

```
DECLARE cursor_name ¦ procedure_name DYNAMIC CURSOR ¦ PROCEDURE
FOR dynamic_staging_area;

PREPARE dynamic_staging_area FROM sql_statement
{ USING transaction_object };

DESCRIBE dynamic_staging_area INTO dynamic_description_area;

OPEN DYNAMIC cursor_name USING DESCRIPTOR dynamic_description_area;

EXECUTE DYNAMIC procedure_name USING DESCRIPTOR dynamic_description_area;
```

```
FETCH cursor_name ¦ procedure_name
USING DESCRIPTOR dynamic_description_area;

CLOSE cursor_name ¦ procedure_name;
```

The order of the statements is critical. Successive statements depend on the completion of the previous ones.

After the FETCH occurs, a Choose...Case statement is usually entered to determine the data type and then extract the value (see Listing 4.2).

**LISTING 4.2** An Example of Type 4 Dynamic SQL

```
Long ll_ValueCount = 0
DECLARE customer_data DYNAMIC CURSOR FOR SQLSA;
PREPARE SQLSA FROM "SELECT company_name FROM customer WHERE state = ?"
USING SQLCA;
DESCRIBE SQLSA INTO SQLDA;
SetDynamicParm( SQLDA, 1, "IN")

OPEN DYNAMIC customer_data USING DESCRIPTOR SQLDA;
If SQLCA.SQLCode <> 0 Then
    MessageBox( "Database Error", "Unable to open dynamic cursor.")
    Return
End If

FETCH customer_data USING DESCRIPTOR SQLDA;
If SQLCA.SQLCode = 100 Then
    MessageBox( "Select Error", "Unable to retrieve data.")
    CLOSE customer_data;
    Return
End If

Do
    ll_ValueCount ++
    Choose Case SQLDA.OutParmType[ ll_ValueCount]
        Case TypeLong!
            ll_Value = SQLDA.GetDynamicNumber( ll_ValueCount)
            //Process value
        Case TypeString!
            ls_Value = SQLDA.GetDynamicString( ll_ValueCount)
            //Process value
    End Choose
```

**4**

**SQL and PowerBuilder**

**LISTING 4.2** CONTINUED

```
Loop While ll_ValueCount <> SQLDA.NumOutPuts
CLOSE customer_data;
```

Error checking should be carried out after the OPEN or EXECUTE, FETCH, and CLOSE statements. It wasn't included in the example so that the dynamic SQL syntax and statement flow would be more obvious. The application or user usually prepares the dynamic SELECT statement at runtime.

As an alternative to using dynamic SQL Type 4, you can use a dynamically created DataWindow to achieve the same effect. Be aware, however, that accessing the retrieved columns with the dynamic DataWindow requires additional processing because you are required to check the data type of the column (because you have to use the Type 4 syntax) before you can extract a piece of data.

# Pasting SQL Statements

So that the syntax of the embedded SQL statements doesn't need to be fully memorized, PowerBuilder provides a SQL Statement painter. This is accessed from the PowerScript painter toolbar or the Edit menu.

> **Note**
>
> Generally, it's more time consuming to paint the statements than to directly type them. The various painter windows are typically only of any use during the initial stages of a project before you become familiar with the syntax of stored procedures and the other SQL statements. It's useful to know these painters are there to fall back on when your memory fails or while you're starting out.

You can create three types of SQL statements: cursors, non-cursors, and procedures. The non-cursor statements are composed of the singleton SELECT (returns only one row), INSERT, UPDATE, and DELETE. The following sections use SELECT to introduce the SQL painter and then introduce just the differences for the subsequent statement types.

## Pasting a SELECT

If you choose to paste a SELECT statement, a dialog lists the available tables in the current database (see Figure 4.1). Make your selection by clicking the table name (you can select multiple tables if a join is required) and then clicking the Open button.

FIGURE **4.1**

*The Select Tables dialog.*

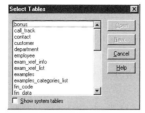

PowerBuilder queries its own system tables for extended information on the tables selected and displays each table in a child window, showing the column names, labels, data types, and extended comments (see Figure 4.2). The attributes displayed in the child windows are controlled from the Design menu or by right-clicking the background of the SQL Select painter.

FIGURE **4.2**

*Table child windows.*

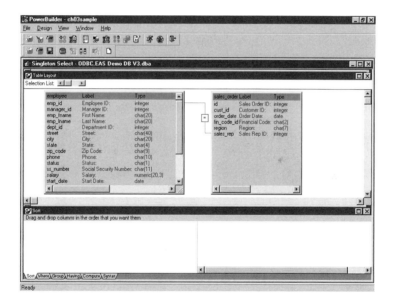

In addition to the opened child windows, access is now granted to the painter toolbar and the tab control at the bottom of the SQL painter main window. In Figure 4.2, two selected tables are connected by key values; PowerBuilder automatically draws the relationship and defaults the operator to equality. Clicking the box that contains the equal sign opens the Join painter (see Figure 4.3), which enables you to alter the joining condition. Starting with PowerBuilder 4.0, the specification of outer joins was simplified considerably. Rather than have you figure out which side of a relationship is outer or on which side of an operator another character appears (SQL Server can use *= and =* to signify outer joins),

PowerBuilder displays the join condition in plain English that's context sensitive to the tables involved in the join.

**FIGURE 4.3**
*The Join painter.*

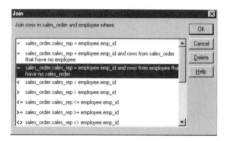

The Where tab specifies additional WHERE conditions (see Figure 4.4). Clicking the first column displays a drop-down list of all the columns. The next column lists standard operators, and the third column is the value to use in the comparison. If another column, function, or other value is to be used, you can type it in or use a pop-up menu. The last column lists the logical operators to join multiple conditions.

**FIGURE 4.4**
*The Where tab.*

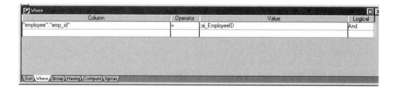

The pop-up menu, accessed by right-clicking and available on the Value column, provides six options and can be used in the Having and Compute tabs:

- *Columns* lists all columns available from the tables now selected.

- *Functions* lists the functions supported by the current DBMS.

- *Arguments* lists all the objects and their attributes accessible from the script that the SQL will be pasted into.

- *Value* becomes active as soon as a column is specified and can be used to provide a list of distinct values from the actual database table.

- *Select* opens another instance of the query painter so that you can define a subquery.

- *Clear* clears the current text from the field.

The next step is to select which columns are to be returned. Do this by clicking the appropriate column names from the table child windows. As you select the columns, they appear at the top of the window to the right of the Selection List horizontal scrollbar (see Figure 4.5). You can alter the column order after selection by clicking the boxed column names that have appeared and dragging left or right. If the column doesn't appear in the list, the Selection List scrollbar can be used to move through the columns until it appears.

**FIGURE 4.5**
*The selection list.*

To add aggregate or other database functions, select the Compute tab. This opens a notes area in which you can enter the function. If a different tab is selected or Enter is pressed, the Compute column appears at the end of the selection list.

The COUNT(cust_id) column is added to the SELECT via the Compute tab. Now you must specify a GROUP BY to return the data correctly. The Group tab lists all columns from all selected tables. To generate a grouping, drag the columns from the left side to the right side (see Figure 4.6).

**FIGURE 4.6**
*The Group tab.*

As mentioned at the beginning of this chapter, a HAVING clause is sometimes used to place conditions on the groups of data to be returned. You enter the HAVING clause by using the Having tab, which displays the same grid as the Where tab (see Figure 4.7). The HAVING clause is constructed in the same way as a WHERE.

**FIGURE 4.7**
*The Having tab.*

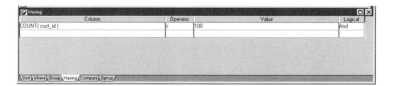

**4**

**SQL and PowerBuilder**

Use the Sort tab to specify an ordering of the values. As with specifying the grouping requirements, sorting also involves dragging the columns from left to right (see Figure 4.8), with the first column on the right being the first column sorted on, and so on down the list. Choose an ascending or descending sort by using the check box to the side of the column name.

**FIGURE 4.8**

*The Sort tab.*

The last operation before returning to the Script painter is to specify the PowerBuilder variables into which the SELECT will return data. Open the Into Variables dialog (see Figure 4.9) from the toolbar (a red arrow pointing away from a grid) or from the Design menu.

**FIGURE 4.9**

*The Into Vari-
ables dialog.*

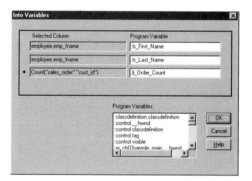

The lower area of the dialog lists the currently defined application variables accessible from the script into which the SQL statement will be pasted. (Local variables don't appear.) You can make your selections from this list or enter them manually into the program variable field next to each column name. If you haven't yet declared the variables, you can still type them in at this point because no error checking or compilation is carried out.

After you construct the SELECT and click the Return button or select the menu option, the complete SQL syntax is pasted into the script at the current cursor position (see Figure 4.10).

**FIGURE 4.10**

*The pasted*
SELECT *statement.*

```
≡ Window - w_ch03sample_main inherited from window
Script - open for w_ch03sample_main returns long
w_ch03sample_main                    ▼    open ( ) returns long [pbm_open]          ▼

    SELECT "employee"."emp_fname",
           "employee"."emp_lname",
           Count("sales_order"."cust_id")
      INTO :ls_First_Name,
           :ls_Last_Name,
           :li_Order_Count
      FROM {oj "employee" LEFT OUTER JOIN "sales_order"
        ON "employee"."emp_id" = "sales_order"."sales_rep"}
     WHERE "employee"."emp_id" = :ai_EmployeeID
  GROUP BY "employee"."emp_lname"
    HAVING ( COUNT( cust_id ) < 100 )

  ORDER BY "employee"."emp_lname" ASC,
           "employee"."emp_fname" ASC  ;
```

## Pasting an INSERT

Choosing INSERT from the Paste SQL menu displays the Table Selection dialog as you saw with the SELECT, except that only one table can be selected. The Insert Column Values dialog appears automatically after you choose a table (see Figure 4.11). This dialog is split into four main areas:

- The top area is editable and shows the columns to be used in the statement with the constants or PowerBuilder variables to be used to specify the values.

- The list box in the lower middle represents the table for which the statement is being generated. This is where you select the columns to be included in the INSERT. PowerBuilder selects all the columns by default.

- To the lower right is the list of accessible program variables. As you did with the Into Variables dialog for the SELECT, you can enter variables that have yet to be declared.

- Along the lower left of the dialog are Null, Select, and Clear buttons. Null inserts the appropriate NULL specification into the current cursor position in the column value field. Clear resets all the column values. Select enables the construction of a SELECT as the source of the values and opens the same painter used for the SELECT specified at the start of this section.

After you specify a SELECT and fill in and disable the column values for the INSERT, you can make changes only through the Select painter (Figure 4.12 shows the Insert Column Values dialog completed for a SELECT). The SELECT resultset must exactly match the one specified for the INSERT.

When the INSERT is defined, it's pasted back into the script by using any methods described for the SELECT.

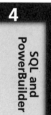

**4**

**SQL and PowerBuilder**

**FIGURE 4.11**

*The Insert
Column Values
dialog.*

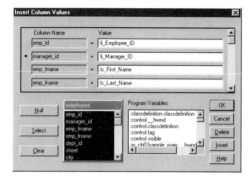

**FIGURE 4.12**

*A completed
Insert Column
Values dialog.*

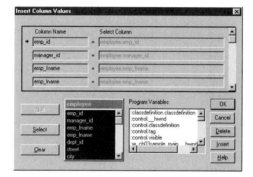

## Pasting an UPDATE

Declaring an UPDATE statement follows much the same process as declaring an INSERT. After you understand and master the basic painter layout, you can generate the statements quickly. As with an INSERT, only one table can be selected, after which the Update Column Values dialog appears (see Figure 4.13). By default, PowerBuilder doesn't select any columns for the table. When you select a column, it appears in the list at the top of the dialog with a field that specifies the value to be assigned. This value can be a PowerBuilder variable (from the list or directly entered) or a constant.

You can specify a WHERE clause by selecting the Where tab. The finished UPDATE is then pasted back into the Script painter.

## Pasting a DELETE

The DELETE statement is the easiest of all the statements to create because it requires only the selection of a single table and (optionally) specifying a WHERE clause.

FIGURE **4.13**
*The Update Column Values dialog.*

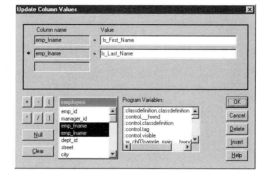

# Cursor Painting

You define the four types of cursor statements by using steps similar to those in the previous sections. You use the same dialogs to declare a cursor as you used for the singleton SELECT, except that when the declaration is finished, a dialog prompts for the name of the cursor (see Figure 4.14). The completed statement is then pasted back into the Script painter.

FIGURE **4.14**
*The Save Declare Cursor dialog.*

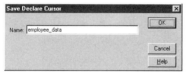

When you declare a FETCH on a cursor, a dialog appears, which enables you to select from a set of predefined cursors (see Figure 4.15). These cursors must be declared in one global, shared, or instance variable section. Locally declared cursors aren't listed. The lower section of the dialog shows the source for the currently highlighted cursor.

FIGURE **4.15**
*The Select Declared Cursor dialog.*

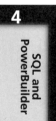

After the cursor is selected, the Into Variables dialog automatically appears (see Figure 4.16) so that you can define the INTO variables. The INTO variables section lets you define a maximum of only 25 variables; for that reason, the cursor source appears in the lower-left corner of the dialog to provide a preview of the expected results.

**FIGURE 4.16**

*The Into Variables dialog.*

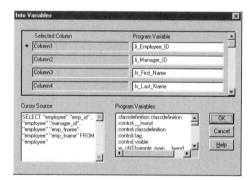

**Note**

For FETCH statements manually coded into PowerScript, there's no limit on the number of INTO variables.

The resulting code is then pasted back into the Script painter, but unless the cursor resultset isn't known or isn't immediately accessible, it takes considerably more time to paint the statement than it takes to code it directly.

## The UPDATE WHERE CURRENT OF Statement

To modify the data that you're accessing through a cursor, you can use the UPDATE WHERE CURRENT OF statement. To paint an UPDATE that acts on a cursor, select Cursor Update from the Paste SQL toolbar button. As with the FETCH, a list of the available cursors is displayed with the selected cursor source. When a cursor is selected, a second dialog appears (see Figure 4.17), in which you can define the update column values.

The Update Column Values dialog works exactly the same way in this situation as it does for the FETCH. Leaving this dialog pastes the statement into the Script painter.

**FIGURE 4.17**
*The Update
Column Values
dialog.*

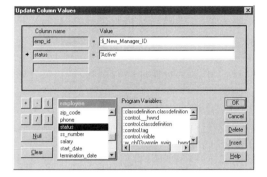

## The DELETE WHERE CURRENT OF Statement

In addition to the UPDATE statement that acts on the current record of a cursor, there's also a statement that allows you to delete the record.

To paint a DELETE that acts on a cursor, click the Paste SQL button on the toolbar and select Cursor Delete from the popup menu. As with the FETCH and UPDATE statements, a list of the available cursors is displayed with the selected cursor source. When a cursor is selected, the dialog closes and leaves a screen empty of everything but the Syntax tab. The only options are to select a different cursor or return to the Script painter.

### DECLARE PROCEDUREs

Painting stored procedure DECLAREs and FETCHes is similar to painting the earlier cursor statements. Selecting Procedure Declare displays a dialog of stored procedures in the current database (see Figure 4.18) with the source of the current selection listed in the bottom pane.

**FIGURE 4.18**
*The Select Proce-
dure dialog.*

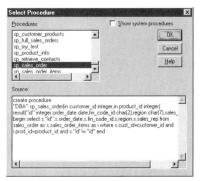

4

SQL and
PowerBuilder

The Parameters dialog appears next, with PowerBuilder automatically prompting you to fill in the parameters that require values (see Figure 4.19). When you try to leave the dialog, you're prompted for a name (see Figure 4.20) before PowerBuilder will paste the statement into the Script painter.

**FIGURE 4.19**

*The Parameters dialog.*

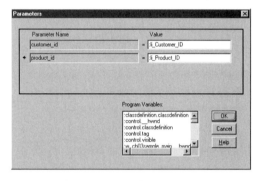

**FIGURE 4.20**

*The Save Declare Procedure dialog.*

## The FETCH FROM PRODEDURE Statement

The Procedure Fetch procedure is identical to using FETCH from a cursor (see Figure 4.21), except that in the parameter specification window it maintains the parameter awareness demonstrated during the DECLARE (see Figure 4.22). As with the FETCH, it's generally more time consuming to generate the syntax than to enter it directly.

**FIGURE 4.21**

*The Select Declared Procedure dialog.*

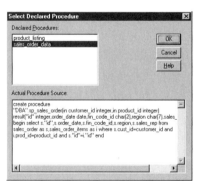

FIGURE 4.22
*The Into Variables dialog.*

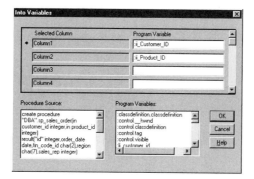

# Advanced Concepts

This section explores some tricks of using SQL to carry out complex tasks and some tips on how to write good client/server applications.

## Logical Units of Work, Revisited

An important consideration in application development is effective transaction management, which is essential to maximizing concurrency and ensuring consistency.

When a PowerBuilder CONNECT is issued, a transaction is started; work is carried out, and COMMITs and ROLLBACKs are executed. After each COMMIT and ROLLBACK, the old transaction is closed and a new transaction begins. This might sound like an acceptable situation, but most DBMSs have a problem with long-running transactions. In this discussion, the SQL Server DBMS is used as an example, but the concepts and problems may apply to any other DBMSs as well, unless special transaction logging is available for a DBMS.

A running PowerBuilder application always has an open transaction. For example, a user logs in to the application and retrieves some data into a DataWindow. Any read locks the DBMS has on the data won't be released until a COMMIT, ROLLBACK, or DISCONNECT is issued. These locks have been held intentionally with a special keyword (in SQL Server, it's HOLDLOCK). Also, because most novice PowerBuilder developers issue only COMMITs and ROLLBACKs after data-modification statements, this transaction stays open until the user actually does a data modification. This may be for an excessive amount of time. That's why Sybase states that a COMMIT or ROLLBACK should be issued after every piece of SQL or every instance of DataWindow access, to free any server resources that might have been consumed, *and* to close and reopen the transaction.

4

SQL and
PowerBuilder

> **Note**
>
> This isn't the case for DataWindows set up to use the `SetTrans()` function instead of `SetTransObject()`. For a discussion of the differences, see Chapter 14, "DataWindow Scripting."

With a typical production system, the *transaction log* (a constant record of all modification actions carried out in the database that's used in database recovery procedures) is automatically or manually dumped a couple times per day. When a transaction log is dumped, the DBMS removes all records up to the last one that's still active. If the application detailed previously is left on all day and is used only for read-only queries, the transaction started when the PowerBuilder CONNECT was issued will be open all day. Any attempts to dump or truncate the log will have no effect, and the log will eventually fill up, causing database-wide problems.

The solution is to take transaction management away from PowerBuilder and manage it more effectively. I say *effectively* because if you continue to use the default setup and actually issue a COMMIT or ROLLBACK after a data retrieval, you still have an open transaction. All you managed to do was move down the log a little. For better management, set the AutoCommit attribute of the transaction object to TRUE and then when a unit of work (that is, a modification) begins, the developer needs to explicitly tell the SQL server. This is achieved by using Type 1 dynamic SQL and issuing an EXECUTE IMMEDIATE for BEGIN TRANSACTION and then an EXECUTE IMMEDIATE for either ROLLBACK TRANSACTION or COMMIT TRANSACTION at the end of the unit of work.

Notice that you now don't need to worry about any queries and can make all your transactions as short as possible. For example, to update a DataWindow, the code becomes the following (note that error checking for the embedded SQL is ignored only for clarity):

```
EXECUTE IMMEDIATE "BEGIN TRANSACTION" USING SQLCA;

If dw_1.Update() = -1 Then
    EXECUTE IMMEDIATE "ROLLBACK TRANSACTION" USING SQLCA;
Else
    EXECUTE IMMEDIATE "COMMIT TRANSACTION" USING SQLCA;
End If
```

By controlling when a transaction is active, better performance can be expected from the server and the Database painter. Therefore, try to code for concise transactions and make sure that you finish a transaction before giving control back to a user. For example, don't begin a transaction, save some data, and then prompt the user that an error occurred during the save without first rolling back the transaction. Be aware, though, that issuing a ROLLBACK destroys the contents of the SQLCA that pertains to the error that occurred, so make a copy of the information before issuing that command. This makes transaction processing the short-lived process that it's supposed to be. You can easily build this functionality into a user-defined transaction object (see Chapter 26, "Building User Objects").

It might be tempting to try to flip the value of the AutoCommit attribute or just place COMMITs after every SELECT, but both options have hidden side effects. Changing the value of AutoCommit to TRUE automatically issues a COMMIT, and when set to FALSE it automatically issues a BEGIN TRANSACTION. A COMMIT after a SELECT finishes the current transaction but unfortunately also starts a new one.

**Note**

Remember that only INFORMIX, Microsoft SQL Server, ODBC (if driver and back-end DBMS support this feature), Sybase InformationCONNECT DB2 Gateway interface, and Sybase SQL Server System 10 and System 11 database management systems are affected by the AutoCommit attribute.

# Using Stored Procedures

If your DBMS supports stored procedures, you can usually extract information by using one of three mechanisms. In fact, you might be able to use all three at one time. The rest of this discussion focuses on the SQL Server DBMS, although the concepts are similar for other DBMSs.

**Note**

For information on placing stored procedures within user objects for encapsulation purposes, see the "Transaction Objects and RPCFUNC" section in Chapter 13, "The User Object Painter."

Stored procedures can return data in any or all of the following ways:

- *As a return value.* By using the RETURN statement in the stored procedure, you can pass back a single numeric value. This is exactly the same as the PowerScript Return statement.

- *As an output parameter.* Using the OUTPUT keyword after a stored procedure's argument, when defining it in the database, allows data to be returned via the argument.

- *As a resultset of the stored procedure.* A statement in the stored procedure is a SELECT statement that returns data, usually the last statement. With some DBMSs you can return multiple resultsets, where the last statement isn't the only SELECT statement within the stored procedure. You can use only one result of a stored procedure as the source for a DataWindow.

The DECLARE, EXECUTE, FETCH, and CLOSE statements introduced earlier in this chapter are used to access the different returned information.

## Accessing a Return Value

To use a return value passed back by a stored procedure, you must first alter the declaration for the stored procedure. The DECLARE statement now becomes this:

```
DECLARE ProcedureName PROCEDURE
FOR @ ReturnValue = DBProcedureName USING SQLCA;
```

The name you give to *ReturnValue* is irrelevant; PowerBuilder is using it purely as a placeholder for its own internal use.

> ### Caution
>
> If you're using the Microsoft SQL Server 6. *x* driver when calling stored procedures, place the keyword EXECUTE before the procedure name. Otherwise, you get a no row found error on any subsequent FETCH statements.

You then use the FETCH command to retrieve the returned value. A combined example is shown in the section "Accessing Returned Data from a Stored Procedure."

## Accessing an OUTPUT Variable

To specify a parameter or multiple parameters that will be used to return values by the stored procedure, you need to modify the DECLARE statement so that it looks like this:

```
DECLARE ProcedureName PROCEDURE
FOR DBProcedureName    @InParameter = : PBVariable1,
                       @OutParameter = : PBVariable2 OUTPUT
USING SQLCA;
```

Again, the names you give *InParameter* and *OutParameter* are irrelevant, but it's a good practice to give them the same or similar names as the actual stored procedures. The bindings to PowerBuilder variables are used only to pass values to the stored procedure during the EXECUTE; you must still use the FETCH command to access the values.

## Accessing Returned Data from a Stored Procedure

The first task is to retrieve all the rows for the resultset or resultsets returned by the stored procedure. If there are none, you just code for the return value and/or output parameters.

The resultset of a stored procedure is retrieved by executing a loop and carrying out a FETCH until no rows are left. At the end of each resultset, the SQLCA.SQLCode becomes 100.

The values for a RETURN or an OUTPUT parameter are retrieved after the last row of the last resultset of the stored procedure using a FETCH statement. The RETURN value is first and then any OUTPUT parameters:

```
FETCH ProcedureName INTO
:ReturnValue, : OutParameter1, : OutParameter2, .. : OutParameterN;
```

To demonstrate how this works, consider the following stored procedure with a return value and two parameters (one defined as an OUTPUT) that produces two resultsets of differing sizes and columns:

```
CREATE PROCEDURE sp_results_demo @InParmInt Int, @OutParmInt Int OUTPUT
AS
BEGIN
    SELECT 1, 2, 3, 4
    SELECT uid, id
    FROM sysobjects
    WHERE type = 'U'
    SELECT @OutParmInt = 69
    RETURN 16
END
```

This simple stored procedure demonstrates each feature. The PowerScript you would use to access each returned value is simple:

```
Long ll_ReturnValue, ll_Parm1, ll_Parm2, ll_Result1, ll_Result2,
Long ll_Result3, ll_Result4, ll_Result5, ll_Result6

DECLARE results_demo PROCEDURE FOR
        @return = sp_results_demo
        @InParmInt = :ll_Parm1,
        @OutParmInt = :ll_Parm2 OUTPUT
USING SQLCA;
```

4

SQL and
PowerBuilder

```
EXECUTE results_demo;
//
// Retrieve the values for the first result set

Do While SQLCA.SQLCode = 0
    FETCH results_demo INTO :ll_Result1, :ll_Result2, :ll_Result3,
        :ll_Result4;
Loop


// Setup to retrieve the values for the second result set.
// NOTE: The SQLCA.SQLCode will be 100 before this next line executes.
//       Therefore preload the first row, if there is one.
FETCH results_demo INTO :ll_Result5, :ll_Result6;
Do While SQLCA.SQLCode = 0
    FETCH results_demo INTO :ll_Result5, :ll_Result6;
Loop


// Capture the return value, and output parameter value

FETCH results_demo INTO :ll_ReturnValue, :ll_Parm2;
CLOSE results_demo;
```

When you try to compile this PowerScript, the PowerBuilder compiler may give you some compilation warnings concerning the return value. You can safely ignore any such warning, and you won't be prompted again.

> **Note**
>
> If you're trying to use output parameters with a SQL Server DBMS and keep getting the SQLDBCode 179 and the error message `Can't use the OUTPUT option when passing a constant to a stored procedure`, set your transaction objects `UserId` property to an empty string. You must do this before connecting the transaction.

## Optimizing Queries

Each DBMS claims to have the best query optimizer—the one that outperforms all competitors in terms of speed. The performance of SQL, however, depends on the developer. Of course, the optimizer can make a poorly written query run at an acceptable speed, but is that really the point? SQL should be written with the best possible performance and optimization built in. Developers wouldn't intentionally write inefficient program code and shouldn't do it with SQL either.

Before learning about some of the techniques, first explore the steps involved in processing a SQL statement:

- *Parsing* verifies the SQL to make sure that it's syntactically correct and creates a query tree; this step is also known as *query detachment*. A *query tree* is an internal representation of the original query, decomposed into a sequence of subqueries involving a single relation or two relations. The target lists of the queries either are used in subsequent queries or are part of the target list of the original query. With the latest versions of DBMSs, parallel query processing is a major enhancement, and these smaller queries can sometimes be carried out at the same time.

- In the *normalization* phase, the query tree is manipulated by using a set of database-independent rules to remove redundancy.

- *Optimization* is where the vendor's optimizer varies from the rest of the pack. By using a number of rules, the optimizer looks at each clause in the query tree to optimize joins to limit the amount of data scanned. As you will see next, not all SQL operators (notably, <>) allow a query to be optimized.

- The optimizer generates an *execution plan*. This plan determines which indexes, if any, are used to retrieve the data. Associated with each index and processing clause is a cost. If the cost is too high, the optimizer generally performs a full-table scan rather than use the index to go directly to the desired records. This means that the DBMS reads each data page of a table from start to end. Careful consideration of the indexes on a table is an important stage of your database design and implementation duties.

- By the *physical access* stage, the optimizer has looked at a number of query trees and has come up with a *query plan*, which is used by the DBMS to access the necessary data pages, collect the intermediate results, and package them for transport to the client.

You can improve the performance of the query optimizer by using the following techniques:

- A query optimizer depends on indexed columns to make the best choice. When an index is created, statistics on the data distribution are stored by the DBMS. To try to force the use of an index, name an indexed column in the WHERE clause.

- Generally, the left-hand rule is applied for composite indexes, so use the leftmost column from the index to improve the chances of index usage. For example, if a table has an index of id, lname, fname, you need to use any of the following combinations: id, lname, fname; id, lname; or id. Other combinations won't use the index.

**4**

**SQL and PowerBuilder**

- When examining a WHERE clause, the optimizer places penalties against conditions making use of NOT, NOT IN, !=, or OR. Using these conditions will likely cause SQL Server to ignore any indexes and perform a full-table scan. Where possible, try to reverse the logic to use IN, =, and AND to get an index to be used.

- The optimizer generally doesn't undertake algebraic logic on WHERE conditions. For example, age > 100 / 5 runs faster than age * 5 > 100 because it can use an index to pull values greater than 20, rather than have to pull each age and multiply it by 5.

- When possible, place as many restrictions as you can on each table so that joins are made by using a smaller subset of the data than if no restrictions were imposed.

- If the tables involved in the join are different sizes, try to select a column from the smaller of the tables. This aids the optimizer by reducing the potential resultset.

- Don't perform unnecessary sorting or grouping. These operations require time and resources on top of that required by the query to just locate and collect the data.

- If appropriate, use a temporary table for intermediate results. Because you can create indexes on temporary tables, you can make a performance gain when dealing with a large resultset. Just remember to create the index after inserting all the data. Selective use of a temporary table with large queries allows the query as a whole to be broken down into smaller and better-optimized steps.

- Sybase Adaptive Server Anywhere allows the explicit specification of a row return percentage with each condition. For example, if a > condition is used, the optimizer deduces that about 25 percent of the rows match; if the result is closer to 1 percent, the query performs poorly. If it's known that the results are more likely to be 1 percent, they can be specified in the condition. For example, sales > 10000, 1.

- Sybase Adaptive Server Anywhere's optimizer is self-tuning on equality constraints, and a query that's run a second time is optimized differently and might perform better. The optimizer learns from any mistakes it makes in the execution estimate and stores the results in the database.

Occasionally, PowerBuilder uses a series of SQL statements to carry out a task, such as initializing a window. When possible, these should be collected together and, as the DBMS permits, made into a stored procedure. Because execution of the statements is now made with only one call and the results are returned in one go, network, client, and server usage is greatly reduced.

One last place to look for a performance gain—especially when retrieving large resultsets—is the network. By adjusting the packet size used by the network protocol, you can get more data transferred per packet. You need to change this on both the server and client machine protocol setups.

These tips aren't meant to encompass every DBMS, but are tricks that might be useful in the DBMS you're using. The best place to look for specific tips is in a DBMS-specific book or in one of the reference books supplied with the DBMS.

# Useful Queries

As part of any data migration or SQL debugging, you inevitably will encounter the need to carry out some kind of analysis or check on data and tables. The following sections describe some of the more useful queries that you can use and manipulate to track down even the most elusive data or SQL problem.

## Table Comparison

To compare the data values in one table with those in a second, you can use either of two methods. The simplest to write and understand uses the NOT EXISTS operator. Suppose that you just loaded an updated employee list into employee_load. This table looks identical to the original employee table. This approach doesn't require any indexes on the temporary load table. The query would look something like this:

```
SELECT emp_id, emp_fname, emp_lname
FROM    employee_load
WHERE   emp_id NOT EXISTS
    (SELECT emp_id
     FROM    employee);
```

You could then capture the returned ID into another table, which you can then use in a join to add the new employees to the original employee table.

The second approach is conceptually a little more complex and uses the outer join. By joining the employee and employee_load tables in an outer join, you can collect a list of all employee IDs in the two tables. However, due to the way you join the two tables, new employees show up with a NULL for the employee employee ID value. This would be the code:

```
INSERT INTO new_ids (el_emp_id, e_emp_id)
SELECT el.emp_id, e.emp_id
FROM employee_load el LEFT OUTER JOIN employee e;
```

You can then run a second query on the values in new_ids to determine the new employee IDs:

```
SELECT el_emp_id
FROM new_ids
WHERE e_emp_id IS NULL;
```

This second method may seem like additional work, but it actually performs the same function with fewer I/O requests (logical or physical) because the DBMS doesn't have to run comparisons over the whole range of the subquery.

## False WHERE Conditions

As part of a table-to-table copy, you often need to query the table for its column list. Every DBMS allows you to query tables for their structure in different ways, but most often the resulting information requires extensive editing to provide the comma-separated column list you are after. The following SELECT generates a heading list; you can quickly use Ctrl+right arrow to go through the list, placing commas where needed.

```
SELECT *
FROM table_name
WHERE 0 = 1;
```

## Finding Duplicate Values

Occasionally, things take a turn for the worse and you load the same or similar data into a table while you have the indexes removed. In fact, it's highly recommended when importing large amounts of data that you first remove triggers and indexes from a table, and then reapply the same functionality after the load. After you determine that there are duplicate records, usually on the failure of your primary key rebuild, you need to track down the culprits and transfer the affected records to a temporary table. After you save the affected records, you can delete them from the primary table. The query to find the duplicate data is similar to the following:

```
SELECT emp_id
FROM employee
GROUP BY emp_id
HAVING COUNT (emp_id) > 1;
```

Obviously, a number of other techniques and queries make up your repertoire of data massage tools, and this chapter covers only the most commonly used ones. You will learn about the others with practice and need. Just remember to record them for your future use, as well as for those who follow in your steps to support a system with such requirements.

> **Tip**
>
> Check out the SQL Section of Simon Gallagher's Web page at
> `http://members.iquest.net/~raven/raven.html` for other tips and tricks with SQL.

# Data Type Choices

One major stumbling block during application development is the correct matching of database and PowerBuilder data types. Table 4.2 shows the PowerBuilder data types and the supported data types of Sybase Adaptive Server Anywhere and Microsoft SQL Server.

TABLE **4.2**  PowerBuilder-to-DBMS Data Type Matching

| Data Type | PowerBuilder | Sybase ASA | SQL Server 4.21 |
| --- | --- | --- | --- |
| Double | 2.2e–308 to 1.7e308 | same | 1.79e–308 to 1.79e308 |
| Integer | –32768 to 32767 | 2e31–1 to –2e31 | 2e31–1 to –2e31 |
| Long | 2e31–1 to –2e31 | N/A | N/A |
| Real | 1.17e–38 to 3.4e38 | same | 3.4e–38 to 3.4e38 |
| String | 65536 | 32767 | 8000 |

As you can see in Table 4.2, PowerBuilder and the DBMSs support a wide variety of accuracies and sizes—even two of the major PowerBuilder-supported DBMSs have this variety! You need to be careful to match up the expected maximum sizes of fields. You also need to be aware that if a PowerBuilder Long data type is used, it's actually referencing a DBMS Integer data type.

PowerBuilder won't report any problems it encounters with placing values into data types that have a lesser accuracy. For example, placing a SQL Server integer value of 40,000 into a PowerBuilder variable that's also an integer actually results in the variable holding the value -25,535. This is because the value *overflows* the variable size, loops off the positive end, and starts back at the largest negative number. With strings, a size difference isn't as noticeable because the value is truncated to fit into the available space.

If an application is to be run against multiple DBMSs, the lowest common size should be used when determining the data types of tables and of PowerBuilder variables.

# Primary Key Generation

Not all tables have a single column or multiple columns (a compound key) that make a unique key into the table, so a system-defined key needs to be generated and assigned to a record. System-generated codes that have no real meaning are commonly known as *surrogate keys*. There's some controversy over the use of surrogate keys—E.F. Codd being one of the many antagonists—but these are more a conceptual problem than a practical one. You can generate such keys in several different ways, and indeed some database management systems include facilities such as a special data type to save you from any extra work:

- Use a key lookup table, which is a single table that consists of two columns, a table name, and the last key used. When a new key is required, the table is locked to prevent another user from generating a key at the same time. The value is incremented and saved to a variable. This requires that all tables have the same data type as a key—usually an Integer. Sometimes an upper and lower boundary are specified to roll over a sequence. This is often used when the sequence number is combined with other values. The following steps lock and update the table:

  1. Begin a transaction that can be rolled back if any part fails.
  2. Issue an update that increments the key value by 1. This read locks the table against any other user.
  3. Select the new key value back into a variable.

- On a success, commit the transaction; on a failure of the UPDATE or SELECT, roll it back.

- Use the MAX() aggregate function and increment the value by 1 within a SELECT that holds a lock on the table using HOLDLOCK (this isn't supported by some DBMSs). This requires an index on the column to produce acceptable speed. The SELECT should be part of the data INSERT.

- Some DBMSs support server-generated values, such as SQL Server's timestamp and identity. These produce automatic values that can be used for primary keys, although timestamp is definitely *not* recommended because it changes every time the record is modified. It is always a unique value, but it plays havoc with any foreign keys!

- Use a DBMS or client random-number generator. If the data fails to save, simply generate a new number; as long as the collisions are few and far between, it produces good performance (but also nonsequential keys).

There are a number of additional ways to generate sequence numbers, but they tend to be DBMS-specific. The most commonly used, and widely accepted, method is the key lookup (or sequence table).

# Troubleshooting SQL in PowerBuilder

PowerBuilder includes a feature that enables the capture of database commands. For native database drivers, the Database Trace tool records all the internal commands performed during a connection. The trace can be done during development or at runtime and is written out to a log file called PBTRACE.LOG (in the Windows directory). The trace file documents the following information:

- Connection parameters

- Execution time (measured only in a granularity of 55ms)

- Internal commands issued by PowerBuilder, such as SQL preparation and execution, getting table and column descriptions, binding variables, and disconnecting from the database

This is the format of the trace file:

```
COMMAND:  (time)
{additional_information}
```

COMMAND is the command executed (for example, PREPARE, FETCH NEXT , DISCONNECT); (*time*) is the execution time in milliseconds; and *additional_information* is optional text describing the command. If the execution time appears as 0, the execution actually took between 0ms and 54ms to complete. Here's an example of a trace:

```
LOGIN: (1154 MilliSeconds)
CONNECT TO trace Sybase:
USERID=gallagher_simon
DATA=oe_010
LOGID=gallagher_simon
LOCK=RL
DBPARM=appname='PB App',host='RAVEN-PB',dbgettime='20',async='1'
SERVER=falcon (0 MilliSeconds)
PREPARE: (0 MilliSeconds)
PREPARE:
SELECT DISTINCT  maintenance_tables.table_name
FROM maintenance_tables
ORDER BY maintenance_tables.table_name          ASC   (55 MilliSeconds)
DESCRIBE: (0 MilliSeconds)
name=table_name,len=31,type=CHAR,pbt1,dbt1,ct0,dec0
BIND SELECT OUTPUT BUFFER (DataWindow): (0 MilliSeconds)
name=table_name,len=31,type=CHAR,pbt1,dbt1,ct0,dec0
```

```
EXECUTE: (0 MilliSeconds)
FETCH NEXT: (0 MilliSeconds)
table_name=payment_terms
FETCH NEXT: (0 MilliSeconds)
table_name=product_classes
FETCH NEXT: (0 MilliSeconds)
table_name=resin_codes
FETCH NEXT: (0 MilliSeconds)
table_name=unit_of_measures
FETCH NEXT: (0 MilliSeconds)
Error 1 (rc 100)
COMMIT: (55 MilliSeconds)
DISCONNECT: (0 MilliSeconds)
SHUTDOWN DATABASE INTERFACE: (0 MilliSeconds)
```

This trace shows a successful connect, the selection of four pieces of data from a table, and then a disconnect.

To begin a trace on a connection, the keyword trace is placed at the start of the transaction object's DBMS attribute (that is, SQLCA.DBMS = "trace Sybase" ). The trace is halted by disconnecting from the current database or connecting to another database.

To trace an ODBC data source, you use the same method as for the other databases. With versions of PowerBuilder prior to 6.0, you had to use the ODBC Driver Manager Trace to record information on ODBC API calls. The default log name, PBSQL.LOG, can be user specified with a change to the entry in the [PBCONNECTOPTIONS] section of PBODB070.INI:

```
[PBCONNECTOPTIONS]
PBTrace='ON'
PBTraceFile=C:\PB7\PBSQL.LOG
```

Changing the PBTrace entry is the only way to start ('ON') and stop ('OFF') the trace file from being generated. The trace file produced is more complex than the trace generated for native drivers:

```
SQLDriverConnect(hdbc53CF0000, hwnd369C,
"DSN=Powersoft Demo DB;UID=dba;PWD=***",-3,szConnStrOut,513,
➥pcbConnStrOut,1);
SQLGetInfo(hdbc53CF0000, 6, rgbInfoValue, 512, pcbInfoValue);
SQLGetInfo(hdbc53CF0000, 2, rgbInfoValue, 512, pcbInfoValue);
.
SQLGetInfo(hdbc53CF0000, 46, rgbInfoValue, 2, pcbInfoValue);
SQLGetConnectOption(hdbc53CF0000, 102, pvParam);
SQLGetInfo(hdbc53CF0000, 8, rgbInfoValue, 4, pcbInfoValue);
```

```
SQLAllocStmt(hdbc53CF0000, phstmt56F70000);
SQLGetTypeInfo(hstmt56F70000, 0);
SQLBindCol(hstmt56F70000, 1, 1, rgbValue, 129, pcbValue);
.
SQLFetch(hstmt56F70000);
.
SQLFreeStmt(hstmt56F70000, 1);
SQLAllocStmt(hdbc53CF0000, phstmt56F70000);
SQLTables(hstmt56F70000, "(null)", 0, "dba", 3, "pbcattbl", -3,
➡"(null)", 0);
SQLFetch(hstmt56F70000);
.
SQLDescribeCol(hstmt56EF0000, 20, szColName, 129, pcbColName, pfSqlType,
pcbColDef, pibScale, pfNullable);
SQLBindCol(hstmt56EF0000, 1, 8, rgbValue, 40, pcbValue);
.
SQLBindCol(hstmt56EF0000, 6, 1, rgbValue, 41, pcbValue);
.
SQLBindCol(hstmt56EF0000, 20, 1, rgbValue, 2, pcbValue);
SQLFetch(hstmt56EF0000);
SQLFetch(hstmt56EF0000);
.
SQLFetch(hstmt56EF0000);
SQLFreeStmt(hstmt56EF0000, 1);
SQLDisconnect(hdbc53CF0000);
SQLFreeConnect(hdbc53CF0000);
SQLFreeEnv(henv552F0000);
```

4

SQL and
PowerBuilder

## Note

This (partial) log shows how much more verbose ODBC is during its interaction with a data source. The listing was edited from a file size of 26KB down to the lines you see here, and all this code does is bring up the table list in the Database painter, select the employee table, and pull up data manipulation. The data source ODBC documentation is required to interpret the ODBC API calls.

To aid in the debugging of embedded SQL at runtime as well as during development, embedded SQL should always be followed by a SQLCode check. The only pieces of SQL that don't require a check are the PREPARE and DECLARE statements.

# Advanced SQL

This section covers SQL code, solving some trickier query problems: rotating data, hierarchy navigation, wildcards as data, and pseudo IF statements.

## Rotating Data

Sometimes a series of data needs to be represented as a single line. One approach is borrowed from matrix mathematics (and was described by Steve Roti in the August 1990 issue of *DBMS* magazine). A *pivot*, or rotating matrix, is used to multiply (or, in SQL, to join) the set of data that's to be compressed. For example, if some data needs to be combined to give a weekly total for each week for a number of weeks, the pivot table would be built as follows:

```
Day  Mon  Tue  Wed  Thu  Fri  Sat  Sun
Mon   1    0    0    0    0    0    0
Tue   0    1    0    0    0    0    0
Wed   0    0    1    0    0    0    0
Thu   0    0    0    1    0    0    0
Fri   0    0    0    0    1    0    0
Sat   0    0    0    0    0    1    0
Sun   0    0    0    0    0    0    1
```

The data table is structured like this:

```
Week        Day         Amount
1           Mon         230
1           Mon         320
2           Mon         10
1           Tue         20
2           Tue         50
```

The following SELECT statement then multiplies (joins) this matrix with the data table:

```
SELECT week, Mon = SUM (data * Mon), Tue = SUM  (data * Tue) ...
FROM    weekly_data, pivot
WHERE   weekly_data.day = pivot.day
GROUP BY week;
```

to give the following results:

```
Week        Mon      Tue      Wed      ...
1                    550      20
2                    10       50
```

# Hierarchy Expansion

A common problem encountered in manufacturing applications is *parts explosion*, or the expansion of a hierarchy. The following information and code are based on an example found in the *Transact-SQL* reference manual that comes with Microsoft's SQL Server, but it's widely applicable because it contains the most elementary Transact-SQL statements that should be found in other DBMS scripting languages.

Assume that an employee table contains a circular relationship. A manager is an employee and has employees underneath him; that group also includes managers with employees under them, and so on:

| ManagerName | EmployeeName |
|-------------|--------------|
| Simon | Kurt |
| Simon | Joe |
| Joe | Ken |
| Kurt | Jim |
| Ken | Chris |

This gives the following hierarchy:

```
Simon
    Kurt
        Jim
    Joe
        Ken
            Chris
```

The following code expands the hierarchy down to any depth and uses a temporary table as a stack to hold intermediate results. The variable @current defines the value at which to start expansion (that is, Simon):

```
INSERT INTO #stack values (@current, 1)
SELECT @level = 1
WHILE @level > 0
BEGIN
    IF EXISTS  (SELECT * FROM #stack WHERE level = @level )
    BEGIN
        SELECT @current = item
        FROM    #stack
        WHERE   level = @level
        SELECT @line = SPACE (@level - 1) + @current
        PRINT @line
        DELETE FROM #stack
        WHERE level = @level AND item = @current
```

```
        INSERT #stack
        SELECT EmployeeLastName, @level + 1
        FROM employee
        WHERE ManagerLastName = @current
        IF @@rowcount > 0
            SELECT @level = @level + 1
    END
ELSE
    SELECT @level = @level - 1
END;
```

This example uses the PRINT function to display the information onscreen but can easily be modified to store the information and level to another temporary table. This can then be used to return the data via a SELECT at the end of the code. This information could then be used to populate a DataWindow that has been set up to display hierarchical information.

## Wildcard Tables

An interesting feature of SQL is its capability to store data that contains wildcards and then, during a join, use a wildcard to match multiple values. For example, if a certain type of report needs to be generated per account group, this might be the code table:

| Account_Type | Report_Type |
| --- | --- |
| 425% | 1 |
| 5432.% | 1 |
| 65% | 2 |

This table is then joined to the main data table using a LIKE to determine which account numbers are required for a given report type. For example, if the data table opars_data looked like this:

| Account_Number | Beg_Balance | End_Balance |
| --- | --- | --- |
| 4256.1 | 1000 | 0 |
| 5432.2 | 10000 | 3455 |
| 5431.2 | 60000 | 63455 |
| 6534.6 | 324253 | 232111 |
| 6634.6 | 89754 | 459873 |

you could issue the following statement to generate a list of data from the opars_data table for a report type of 1:

```
SELECT od.*
FROM   opars_data od, code_table ct
WHERE  od.account_number like ct.account_type AND
ct.report_type = 1;
```

The resulting rows from the `opars_data` table would be account numbers 4256.1 and 5432.2.

# Pseudo IF

A useful trick is to emulate a simple `IF` statement within a query. This is often used in SQL import procedures to convert from one data value and data type to another while preserving the meaning. For example, the column "completed" in the raw data is either a C or a blank. The actual table structure makes use of a bitfield; it stores a C as a 1 and a blank as a 0. The following code was written to use SQL Server functions but should be easily convertible to any DBMS that provides comparable functions:

```
SUBSTRING( "01", 1 + ISNULL( DATALENGTH( RTRIM( completed) ), 0), 1)
```

> **Tip**
>
> If your database is ANSI SQL-92–compliant, it will support the CASE expression that's allowed anywhere a regular expression is used. This allows you to create complex IF conditions easily.

This statement first trims off all spaces, leaving an empty string for the case of an empty completed column value. The `DATALENGTH` function returns the length of the string; if the string is `NULL`, a `NULL` is returned. In case of a `NULL` value, the `ISNULL` function is used to turn the `NULL` into a 0. The length of the string is added to 1 to give the starting position in the code string to extract. The `SUBSTRING` function then removes the single character at the specified starting position. The return value from the `SUBSTRING` would then be put through a `CONVERT` function to arrive at the desired numeric value. This statement can be combined into the `SELECT` column list as just another expression. The SQL code is identical to the following PowerScript:

```
If ls_Completed = "C" Then
    li_Completed = 1
Else
    li_Completed = 0
End If
```

Longer codes can be placed into the code string. For example, if the completed column were converted to YES and NO, the code string would become " NO YES ", and the `SUBSTRING` would be set to select three characters out of the string. The starting position for the `SUBSTRING` would be calculated as three times the `DATALENGTH` plus 1:

```
SUBSTRING( "NO YES", 1 + 3 *
            ISNULL (DATALENGTH (RTRIM (completed) ), 0), 3)
```

You can use additional methods to implement decision-making processes in your SQL. For example, another method uses the `CHARINDEX()` SQL function, which takes two parameters: the string you want to search for and the string you want to search. It then returns the position within the second string at which the first occurs. You can use this to turn the return value into a Boolean 1 or 0.

For example, consider trying to conditionally summate a single column based on another value. In the following SQL code, `department_group` is a single-character column, so you can easily pattern match and multiply the counter column by the return value. This gives a conditional value for each record you're operating on, which is then correctly summed:

```
SELECT
    SUM (counter2_elapsed * CHARINDEX ('C', department_group)) converted,

SUM (counter2_elapsed * CHARINDEX ('P', department_group)) printed
FROM summary_production
```

You might be lucky enough to get away with this, but you might have to perform some additional manipulation of the `CHARINDEX()` return value to get a 1 or 0 value.

> **Tip**
>
> Remember that you can use similar techniques in the expressions you can code for DataWindows.

# Summary

This chapter covered the basic SQL statements (`SELECT`, `INSERT`, `UPDATE`, and `DELETE`) and showed you how they can be combined to undertake complex tasks. You learned about how PowerBuilder uses SQL, the process of using simple SQL statements in PowerScript, and how to dynamically construct and execute such SQL at runtime. Transaction management was introduced and further expanded on. Tracing problems for native and ODBC interfaces were covered, and you received some suggestions for where and when to generate error messages.

# Databases and the Database Painter

**CHAPTER 5**

A *database* is a means of organizing a collection of related data and objects to facilitate the searching, sorting, and manipulation of data. Some objects that exist within a database are

- Tables
- Columns
- Indexes
- Constraints (primary and foreign keys)
- Views
- Stored procedures
- Users and groups

To save developers from having to jump out of PowerBuilder to create and maintain these kinds of objects, Sybase provides the Database painter. This allows developers—if they have appropriate rights—to administer databases from within PowerBuilder via a common interface regardless of the target DBMS.

Four panes are accessed from within the Database painter: Objects, Object Layout, Properties, and ISQL. The Data Pipeline painter is also accessible from the toolbar (discussed in detail in Chapter 32, "Data Pipelining").

# Database Objects

The following sections look conceptually at the database objects that you can create and maintain. The rest of this chapter discusses the actual panes and views you use to create and maintain these database objects.

## Tables

A *table* is a collection of related columns/fields and is made up of a number of rows/records. The columns that make up a table have a name, data type, nullability property, and constraints. *Nullability* is whether the column accepts a NULL as a valid value. The opposite is NOT NULL , which requires a value to be specified. Chapter 4, "SQL and PowerBuilder," discusses how to determine tables and their columns.

## Indexes

An *index* provides fast access during data retrieval. Just as in a book, an index is used to go directly to the desired information. If there's no index, the whole table must be searched to find the desired information.

The two index types are *clustered* and *non-clustered*. A clustered index physically orders the data in the sequence of the index; you therefore can have only one clustered index per table. A non-clustered index stores key values for every row, and you can have more than one non-clustered index per table.

## Views

*Views* are ways of looking at data in one or more tables and exist as independent objects. They're based on a SELECT statement and simplify access to a number of tables by making them look like a single table. Views are also useful for security reasons because they can limit access to certain columns.

# Using the Database Painter

The place to work with a relational database from within PowerBuilder is the Database painter, which you open by clicking the Database painter icon (with the two overlapping cylinders) on the PowerBar. After you click the icon, PowerBuilder attempts to connect to the current database profile.

If the current database profile requires you to log on to the database, PowerBuilder displays a dialog in which you can enter your user ID and password.

## Database Profiles

By default, PowerBuilder connects you to the Sybase Adaptive Server Anywhere demo database. To establish a connection to your own database, you need to establish a database profile. In version 6.0, PowerBuilder changed the Database Profiles dialog so that it's easier to use and keep track of all your setups. Version 7.0 adds even more functionality to the Database Profile dialog. For more information on connecting to your particular database, see Chapter 3, "Database Management Systems."

## Working with Database Objects

After you create your database profile and a successful connection is made, PowerBuilder displays the Database painter workspace (see Figure 5.1), which shows a list of the available database interfaces with the current connection expanded to show the top level of options.

If you want to view any system tables in your database or the PowerBuilder repository tables, right-click the Tables folder and choose Show System Tables to refresh the list with the additional table names.

**FIGURE 5.1**

*The Database painter workspace.*

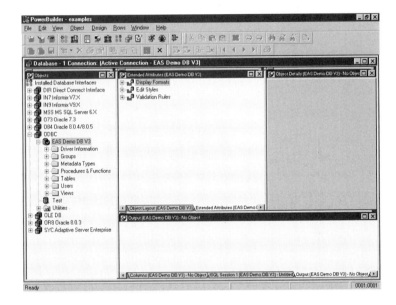

When all the desired tables are displayed, specify the tables that you want to work with by dragging the table's name over to the work area to the immediate right. You can also open tables by right-clicking the table name and choosing Add to Layout from the pop-up menu. As you choose the tables you want to view, PowerBuilder displays a graphical representation of each table in the Object Layout pane (see Figure 5.2).

**FIGURE 5.2**

*The Object Layout pane.*

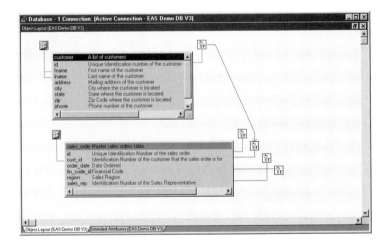

By default, PowerBuilder displays the table name, the column names, comments about both, index keys, and any primary and foreign keys (these are part of the mechanism for setting up referential integrity). To control which information displays for the table view, right-click in the painter workspace (not on any database objects) and toggle on or off the pop-up menu options: Show Comments, Show Index Keys, and Show Referential Integrity. You can also have PowerBuilder arrange the tables in the workspace.

> **Tip**
>
> You want to get as much space as possible for your working area. To do this, use the Maximize and Restore buttons on the pane's title bar.

The other way to arrange tables in the painter is to click the table name and drag the table to the desired location. To resize each table, position the mouse pointer on the edge of the table and then click and drag. You can also move the indexes, primary keys, and foreign keys by simply clicking and dragging them.

At this point, you can view column names and the basic relationships between tables. If you want to find out more of the details of a particular item (table, column, key, and so on), the easiest method is to double-click the item. Depending on what's clicked, PowerBuilder displays different information.

> **Tip**
>
> The Database painter gives you multiple ways to access the same information via the PainterBar, pop-up menus, double-clicking, and the menus. This is a great opportunity to experiment with the different access methods and find which works best for you.

# Working with Tables

In previous versions of PowerBuilder, you had to access a separate painter, the Table painter, to create or alter tables. With version 7.0, table modifications are carried out in another pane of the Database painter. The Table pane's purpose is to allow you to view, modify, and create a table's definition. The Table pane, therefore, can be used as an Alter Table painter for existing tables or a Create Table painter for new tables. Either way, the basic interface is the same (see Figure 5.3).

**FIGURE 5.3**

*The Table pane.*

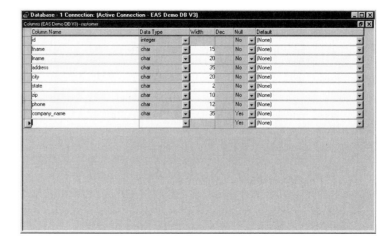

You can get to the Table pane from the Database painter in several ways. If you want to create a new table, right-click the Table folder in the Objects pane and choose New Table. To modify a table, right-click an actual table and choose Alter Table or New...Column from its pop-up menu.

To create a new table, you're required to specify a table name (when you save), the individual column names, and their corresponding data types and sizes. You also can specify the fonts for the table, table comments, primary and foreign keys, and column extended attributes.

In essence, all the Table pane does is create the underlying SQL statements, capturing any graphical changes you make in the interface. To view the SQL that PowerBuilder creates, right-click the background of the Table pane and choose Export Syntax from the pop-up menu. One benefit of the SQL Syntax view is that it lets you save the SQL statement to a file by choosing Save or Save As from the File menu.

When creating a table, you first enter all the necessary information such as the column names, data types, and NULL values for it. After that, to create the table, you choose Save or Save As from the File menu or click the Save icon (the disk) on the PainterBar.

If you're working with an existing table, you can append columns only to the end of the column list, but you can delete them from anywhere in the list (depending on your DBMS). Some DBMSs allow you to increase the number of characters for a column and whether it allows NULL values. Typically, appended columns must allow NULL values because the NULL option is disabled for the columns. The reason is that the new columns won't have any data in them when the table is altered.

After you complete all modifications, PowerBuilder generates the ALTER TABLE SQL statement and sends it to the database when you click Save.

## Table Properties

In addition to the column definitions for a table, the table definition consists of table and column properties. The properties or extended attributes for a column are shown on the right side of the Database painter; you can modify/insert them at any time. (For more information on column properties, see the later section "Column Properties.") You can view a table's properties by choosing Properties from the pop-up menu when you right-click it, or if you double-click a selected table. Either method populates the Table property pane (see Figure 5.4).

**FIGURE 5.4**

*Table properties.*

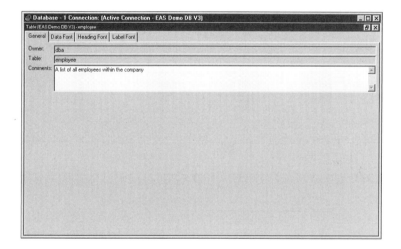

The Table property pane allows you to specify comments and font defaults for data, headings, and labels for a table.

The General tab, shown in Figure 5.4, displays the table owner, the table name, and any comments. The comments can be entered or changed at any time, but the owner and table name can be entered only when the table is created.

The font tabs (see Figure 5.5) for data, headings, and labels enable you to specify the default font, font style, size, and effects for when a column from the table is placed on a DataWindow object. The Data Font specifications are used for column objects, the Heading Font options for column headings, and the Label Font choices for column labels.

5

Databases and
the Database
Painter

**FIGURE 5.5**

*The Data Font tab page.*

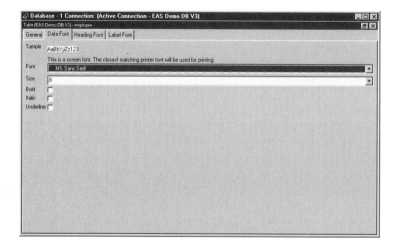

---

**Tip**

As with any font you use, make sure that the fonts are available on your client's machine. If the font isn't found, its display on the user's machine is determined by the closest font the operating system can find.

---

The Primary Key tab page (see Figure 5.6) allows you to specify one or more columns that uniquely identify a single row within a table. To open this pane, double-click an existing primary key icon for a selected table or choose New...Primary Key from a selected table's pop-up menu.

To create a primary key, select one or more columns from the column list. If a primary key isn't created, PowerBuilder renders the table as read-only from within the development environment.

---

**Caution**

Unlike previous versions of PowerBuilder and any decent database tool, you now can't specify the order that the columns appear in the index.

---

**FIGURE 5.6**

*The Primary Key tab page.*

The Foreign Key tab page (see Figure 5.7) lists any foreign keys defined for the table and allows you to create, modify, and delete foreign keys. A foreign key is used to establish a relationship between tables; both primary and foreign keys are used to enforce referential integrity between tables. They're used to ensure that valid values are entered into the tables. Right-clicking the Foreign Keys subfolder under a selected table or on a table in the Object Layout pane also opens the Foreign Key Definition properties.

**FIGURE 5.7**

*The General tab page of the Foreign Key pane.*

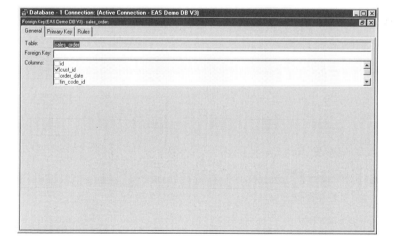

> **Note**
>
> You can also open these properties for existing keys by double-clicking the
> Foreign Key icon in the Object Layout pane.

When you define a foreign key, you specify the relationship between the table now being
worked on and another in the database. In Figure 5.7, a new foreign key is being defined to
establish a relationship between the `sales_order` table and the `customer` table. The key,
`ky_so_customer`, relates the `sales_order` and `customer` tables via the `cust_id` column
(specified on the second tab). This ensures that a row can't be inserted into the
`sales_order` table without the `cust_id` existing in the `customer` table.

As well as defining the relationship, you need to define what happens if a row in the
primary table (on the Rules tab in Figure 5.8), the `customer` table, is deleted. Your options
are to disallow the deletion, perform a cascading delete (thereby deleting all orders for a
customer), or set the `cust_id` column's value to NULL in the `sales_order` table.

**FIGURE 5.8**

*The Foreign Key
Rules definition
tab page.*

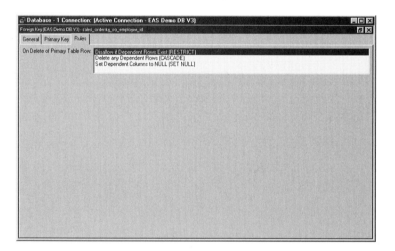

In the same way that you create primary or foreign key indexes, you can create, edit, and
delete additional indexes. Editing or creating a new index opens the Create Index property
pane (see Figure 5.9).

**FIGURE 5.9**

*The General tab page of the Create Index pane.*

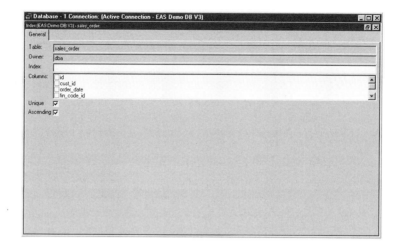

In the Create Index tab page, you can specify the index name, whether it's a unique index, ascending or descending, and the columns to be included in the index. Because an index can't be directly altered, it must be deleted and then re-created to be modified. Using the Indexes pane, PowerBuilder does this for you.

After you specify all the properties for a table, click Save on the toolbar, and PowerBuilder generates the necessary SQL to incorporate your changes.

# Column Properties

You can create or modify the column properties or extended attributes at any time in the Database painter. The extended attributes are used to promote standardization and increase developer productivity when creating DataWindow objects; these properties are stored in the extended attributes repository (PowerBuilder system tables), formerly known as the Powersoft repository, on your database and include the following:

| Extended Attribute | Description |
| --- | --- |
| Comment | Description of the column |
| Header | Default header for the column |
| Label | Default label for the column |
| Display Format | Format of the data when displayed |
| Height, width | Default height and width for the column |
| Initial value | Default initial value for the column |
| Justify | Default alignment justification for the column |

| Extended Attribute | Description |
| --- | --- |
| Validation rule | Default criteria for validation of entered values |
| Edit style | Format of the column during user interaction |

For more information about the extended attribute repository and how to create display formats, edit styles, and validation rules, see the later sections "The Extended Attribute Repository" and "Displaying, Editing, and Validating Data."

> **Note**
>
> The column extended attributes can also be created by right-clicking a column name in the Database painter and selecting Properties.

# Creating Views

As mentioned at the beginning of the chapter, views simplify access to a number of tables by making them look like a single table. To create a view from the Database painter, click the Create View icon on the PainterBar or Select New View from the pop-up menu when you right-click the Views folder. This opens the SQL Select painter, which allows you to graphically design the view definition. (For more information on how to use the SQL painter, see Chapter 4.) After you specify the view definition, close the SQL Select painter. PowerBuilder returns you to the Database painter and displays your view in the painter workspace.

# Dropping Objects

To drop a database object (table, index, key, and so on) in the Database painter, do one of the following: select the object and click the Drop icon (the eraser) on the PainterBar, select Delete from the Object menu, or right-click the object and select Drop from the pop-up menu.

# Logging SQL

When modifying your database, you might want to log the SQL statement you generate. This can be done several ways in the Database painter. You can record all SQL generated in the Database painter for reuse at a later date or for documentation.

To begin the logging process, choose Start Log from the Design menu. The Activity Log tab page of the bottom-most pane comes to the front; you can maximize this to get a better view.

To stop logging, choose Stop Log from the Design menu or right-click in the Activity Log pane and choose Stop Log from the pop-up menu. If the Database painter isn't closed and the log is reopened, any new activities are appended after the information now existing in the log. If you want to save the log to a file, choose Save Log As from the File menu. You can clear the log by choosing Reset View from the pane's pop-up menu.

Another way to gather information from the Database painter is to export an object's syntax to a file. To do this, right-click a selected object and choose Export Syntax, or choose the same option from the Object menu. This opens the DBMS dialog, requesting the desired DBMS. The exporting process requires that PowerBuilder have the proper database interface installed. If you select the ODBC DBMS, PowerBuilder prompts you for the name of a data source. The object's syntax is then written to the log pane.

# The Data Manipulation Pane

The Data Manipulation pane is useful for retrieving and manipulating data from the database. It can be used to create, delete, or modify rows and save the changes back to the database. In essence, the Data Manipulation pane is nothing more than a DataWindow. You can choose to view your data by using one of three presentation styles: grid, tabular, or freeform (you learn more about these in Chapter 6, "The DataWindow Painter").

To access the Data Manipulation pane, select the table whose data you want to view and click one of the three Data Manipulation icons on the PainterBar, choose Data from the Object menu, or choose the Edit Data option from the table's pop-up menu. Each option allows you to specify in which format (grid, tabular, or freeform) you want the data displayed. When the Data Manipulation pane is populated, PowerBuilder retrieves all rows and all columns for the selected table (see Figure 5.10).

During the retrieval, the PainterBar's Retrieve icon changes to a red hand to indicate that you can cancel the retrieval by clicking the icon. When the retrieve is completed, the hand changes back to the Retrieve icon.

**Note**

Many of the icons are available as options on the Rows menu as well.

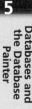

**FIGURE 5.10**

*The Data Manip-
ulation pane.*

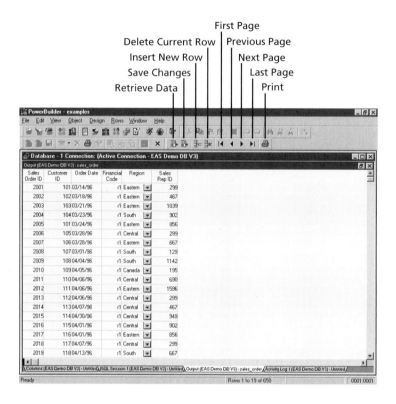

From the Rows menu you can filter and sort your data on the client. Filtering your data requires that you apply a Boolean expression against the rows to determine which rows are displayed. Sorting consists of selecting columns and/or expressions to determine how the rows are sorted.

You can also import data from an external source into the Data Manipulation pane. You do this by choosing Import from the Rows menu, which opens a dialog asking you to specify the name of a tab-separated text file or dBASE II or III file. After you specify the file, PowerBuilder loads the data and displays it in the pane. If an error is encountered, PowerBuilder asks whether you want to continue to import the rest of the data.

In addition to importing data, you can save table information to various file formats. When you choose Save Rows As from the Rows menu, you can specify a file type for saving, such as Text, CSV, SQL Syntax, HTML Table, Excel, or PS Report.

If you made any changes but didn't save them, PowerBuilder asks whether you want to save your changes to the database.

# The Database Administration Pane

The Database Administration pane, the tab page titled ISQL Session (see Figure 5.11), allows you to have an interactive SQL environment within PowerBuilder so that you can execute any SQL statement supported by your DBMS.

**FIGURE 5.11**
*The Database Administration pane.*

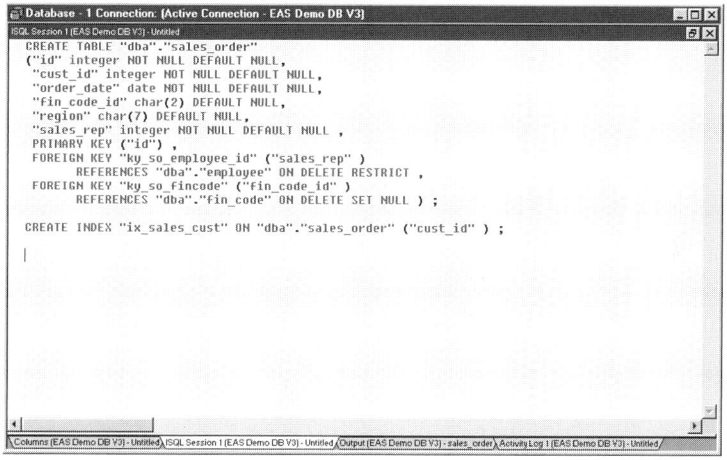
Database - 1 Connection: [Active Connection - EAS Demo DB V3]
ISQL Session 1 (EAS Demo DB V3) - Untitled
CREATE TABLE "dba"."sales_order"
("id" integer NOT NULL DEFAULT NULL,
"cust_id" integer NOT NULL DEFAULT NULL,
"order_date" date NOT NULL DEFAULT NULL,
"fin_code_id" char(2) DEFAULT NULL,
"region" char(7) DEFAULT NULL,
"sales_rep" integer NOT NULL DEFAULT NULL ,
PRIMARY KEY ("id") ,
FOREIGN KEY "ky_so_employee_id" ("sales_rep" )
REFERENCES "dba"."employee" ON DELETE RESTRICT ,
FOREIGN KEY "ky_so_fincode" ("fin_code_id" )
REFERENCES "dba"."fin_code" ON DELETE SET NULL ) ;
CREATE INDEX "ix_sales_cust" ON "dba"."sales_order" ("cust_id" ) ;
Columns (EAS Demo DB V3) - Untitled
ISQL Session 1 (EAS Demo DB V3) - Untitled
Output (EAS Demo DB V3) - sales_order
Activity Log 1 (EAS Demo DB V3) - Untitled

For the most part, the Database Administration pane behaves just like the PowerScript painter or any standard text editor. The toolbar buttons and menu items match the PowerScript painter (discussed in Chapter 7, "The PowerScript Language").

You can type any SQL statements in the pane and then execute them. PowerBuilder requires you to use the termination character (;) after your SQL statement, just like in PowerScript.

> **Note**
>
> You can change the termination character in the Database painter options. For more information, see the next section, "Database Painter Options."

You can build your SQL statements in one of three ways:

- Enter the statement into the workspace via the keyboard

- Paste the statement by using the Paste SQL button

- Open a SQL script file

If you don't know the exact SQL syntax you want to execute, the Paste SQL option allows you to graphically create SQL SELECT, INSERT, UPDATE, and DELETE statements.

Click the Paste SQL icon on the PainterBar or choose Paste SQL from the Edit menu to open the SQL Statement Type dialog (see Figure 5.12). After double-clicking a SQL statement type, PowerBuilder enters the SQL painter, which allows you to graphically build the desired SQL. (For more information on the SQL painter, see Chapter 4.)

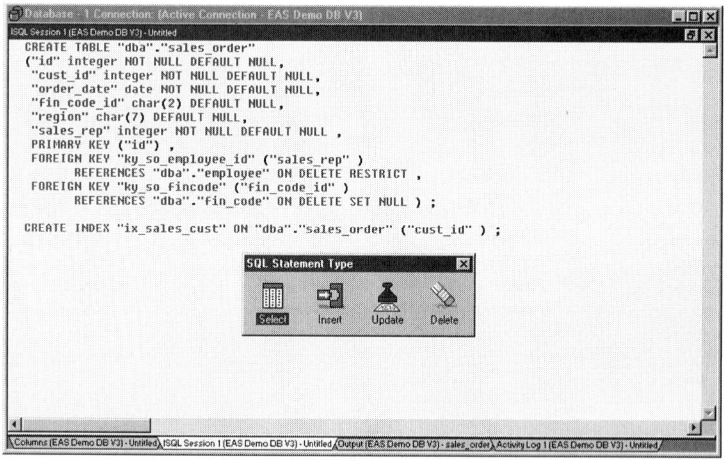

**FIGURE 5.12**

*The SQL State-ment Type dialog.*

When you close the SQL painter, PowerBuilder generates the SQL statement and pastes it into the Data Administration pane. You can also import existing SQL from a file into the Data Administration painter by choosing Import from the File menu.

To execute your SQL, click the Execute icon on the PainterBar, choose Execute SQL from the Design menu, or press Ctrl+L. The SQL is then sent to the database.

# Database Painter Options

PowerBuilder lets you customize the way in which the Database painter behaves and appears. Choose Options from the Design menu to open the Database Preferences dialog (see Figure 5.13). This dialog is divided into six tab pages: General, Object Colors, Script, Font, Coloring, and Layout.

**FIGURE 5.13**
*The Database Preferences dialog.*

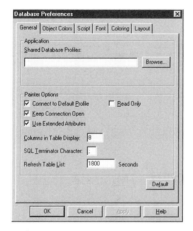

The General tab page lets you specify the following:

| Property | Description |
| --- | --- |
| Shared Database Profile | Specifies the name of an INI file that contains shared database profiles |
| Connect to Default Profile | Specifies whether the Database painter connects to the database upon opening (enabled by default) |
| Keep Connection Open | Specifies whether PowerBuilder keeps your connection to the database open throughout your PowerBuilder session or opens and closes the connection when a painter needs database access (the default is to maintain the connection) |
| Use Extended Attributes | Specifies whether PowerBuilder creates and uses the Extended Attribute System Tables (enabled by default) |
| Read Only | Specifies whether you can modify the repository tables (off by default) |

| Property | Description |
|---|---|
| Columns in Table Display | Specifies the number of columns listed when a table is displayed in the Database painter (default is 8). |
| SQL Terminator Character | Specifies the SQL termination character used in the Database Administration painter (default is ;). |
| Refresh Table List | Specifies the number of seconds that must pass before the Select Tables list is refreshed from the database (default is 1800). |

The Object Colors tab page allows you to set the colors used to display object information in the Database painter. You can set colors for Background, Table Header, Table Header Text, Columns, Columns Text, Columns Comment Text, Index Key Line, Primary Key Line, and Foreign Key Line. These modifications also affect other painters that display database information. To reset the colors to their original PowerBuilder installation values, click the Default button.

# The Extended Attribute Repository

PowerBuilder tracks information on database tables within a set of five tables known as the Extended Attribute System Tables (formerly known as the Powersoft repository). This repository allows the collection and maintenance of extended column attributes: edit masks, display formats, and validation rules.

These five PowerBuilder system tables are found in each database used by PowerBuilder and are referred to as the repository:

| System Table | Application Information for the Database |
|---|---|
| PBCatCol | Information about each table column |
| PBCatEdt | Edit styles |
| PBCatFmt | Display formats |
| PBCatTbl | Tables information |
| PBCatVld | Validation rules |

**Note**

PowerBuilder updates these five tables accordingly whenever the tables, columns, or extended attributes are altered. This is done *only* if the changes are made from within PowerBuilder.

For cases when you're using additional tools outside PowerBuilder, you need to update the repository (choose Synch Extended Attributes from the Design menu). This should be the only direct interaction you have with the repository tables; do *not* try to modify them directly through the Data Manipulation pane.

> **Note**
>
> Certain third-party tools also provide an interface to these tables—for example, Erwin/ERX for PowerBuilder and PowerDesigner—and allow you to create and maintain column labels, headings, edit styles, display formats, and validation rules.

The PBCatTbl table contains table information used in PowerBuilder, such as display fonts and comments. The index for this table is based on pbt_tnam (the column with the table name) and pbt_ownr (the table's owner).

The PBCatCol table contains information on table columns and their extended attributes. The table name and owner columns are pbc_tnam and pbc_ownr, respectively. The index, as for the PBCatTbl table, is based on these two columns, with the addition of pbc_cnam (the name of the column). Each column in the table can be used to join with the three remaining repository tables (PBCatFmt, PBCatVld, and PBCatEdt) through three individual columns:

| | |
|---|---|
| pbc_mask | The display format name from the PBCatFmt table |
| pbc_ptrn | The validation rule name from the PBCatVld table |
| pbc_edit | The edit style name and sequence number from the PBCatEdt table |

The last three repository tables contain the most powerful of the extended attributes:

- The PBCatFmt table contains all the display formats available in the current database. The pbf_name is the name of the display format.

- The PBCatVld table contains all the validation rules for the database table columns. The validation rule names are in the pbv_name column.

- The PBCatEdttable has the edit styles for the database; pbe_name and pbe_seqn designate the key for this table. pbe_name is the edit style name, and pbe_seqn is the sequence number if edit types require more than one row.

# Displaying, Editing, and Validating Data

The extended attributes previously mentioned are used to control the displaying, editing, and validating of data within DataWindows. You store these attributes in the repository and then bind the required characteristics to table columns through other parts of the repository.

> **Note**
>
> Each column in a table can have only one edit style, one display format, and one validation rule.

For a further explanation of how these attributes are used in the DataWindow, refer to Chapter 6 and Chapter 14, "DataWindow Scripting."

> **Note**
>
> Sybase appears to be in the process of removing the modal dialogs from the majority of PowerBuilder. However, the Edit Style, Format, and Rules are split between dialog and pane interfaces. Version 7.0 must have caught them in between changes!

You maintain these three extended attributes by selecting the appropriate Edit Styles, Display Formats, or Validation Rules from the Extended Attributes pane Design menu (see Figure 5.14). You can access this pane by clicking the Extended Attributes tab page in the center pane, or by choosing Extended Attributes from the View menu.

Any changes you make to these three extended attributes do not affect any current column assignments or existing DataWindows.

FIGURE 5.14

*The Edit Styles, Display Formats, and Validation Rules list.*

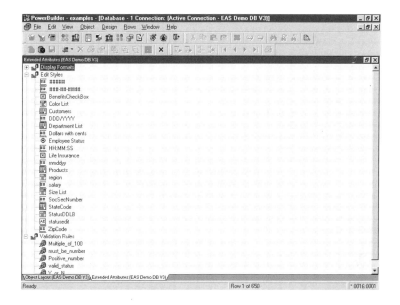

## Tip

Part of the Advanced PowerBuilder Utilities that Sybase used to provide was a program called the DataWindow Extended Attribute Synchronizer (DWEAS). This program synchronized existing DataWindows with the attributes in the Power-Builder repository tables. Because DWEAS is no longer provided with Power-Builder, Sybase doesn't support or maintain it. The source code, however, can be found on the Sybase Developer Network Web site at http://sdn.sybase.com/sdn.

When these three attributes are defined and associated with a column, they become the column's default for that particular attribute each time it's painted on a DataWindow object. These can be overridden in the DataWindow painter.

## Creating and Maintaining Edit Styles

*Edit Styles* specify the mechanism by which column data is entered by the user and presented by the DataWindow:

| Edit Style | Description |
|---|---|
| DropDownListBox | Users select or enter a value. |
| DropDownDataWindow | Users select a value from another DataWindow object. |

| Edit Style | Description |
|---|---|
| CheckBox | Value can be yes, no, or sometimes a third state. For example, yes, no, and maybe could be modeled using a check box. |
| RadioButton | Users select a series of mutually exclusive options. |
| EditMask | Specifies allowable characters that users can enter. |
| Edit | Enables users to enter a value. |

Figure 5.15 is a DataWindow example showing all six edit styles.

**FIGURE 5.15**

*The DataWindow example of the six edit styles.*

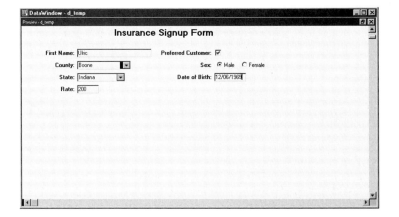

When you choose an existing edit style or choose to create a new one, you're presented with the Edit Styles dialog, which allows you to create and modify edit styles. When you select New or Edit, you are presented with the Style dialog, which has a different appearance for each edit style. For a new edit style, the window initially displays the `Edit` edit style.

## The `Edit` Edit Style

The `Edit` edit style is the default when you create new edit styles. Figure 5.16 shows its dialog.

Most of the options are self-explanatory; following are explanations of some of the others:

- The Limit text box allows you set the upper limit of the number of characters to be accepted. A value of 0 allows any number of characters.

FIGURE **5.16**

*The* Edit *edit style's dialog.*

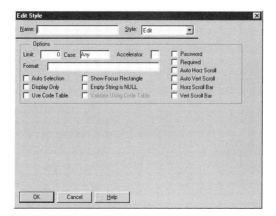

- Accelerator allows you to specify a single character that, when the user presses Alt and that key, sets the focus into the field. You need to indicate the accelerator by altering the static text object that you place alongside the edit field. This is *not* done for you.

- Use Code Table with the area at the bottom of the dialog (shown when you select this option) allows you to set up a list of values that have a display value that maps to a data value. This allows the user to enter a single letter and have PowerBuilder display a longer string. This occurs not only during data entry but also after the data is retrieved from the database.

**Note**

Because code tables are case sensitive, the data values in the code table must exactly match the DataWindow's data. If the data values match, the display value is displayed; if not, the actual value retrieved is displayed.

This option can be used with the Validate Using Code Table option to allow users to enter only values listed in the code table. The data value *must* conform to the data type of the column that uses it.

**Tip**

You can use the special value of Null! to indicate that a null value is the data value for a certain display value.

- The Format text box allows you to enter a display format to use when displaying data. This is most often used with numeric or date/time data.

- By specifying that Empty String is NULL, you tell PowerBuilder to send a NULL value to the database if no value is entered.

- Password makes any data entered into the field appear as a number of asterisk characters.

## The EditMask Edit Style

The EditMask edit style allows you to restrict users' entry of data to a defined format. The dialog (see Figure 5.17) shows you the available mask characters and a test area where you can try entering data against the mask you've created.

**FIGURE 5.17**

*The* EditMask *edit style's dialog.*

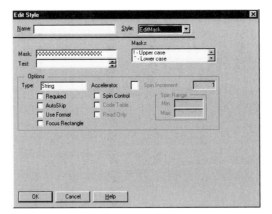

The mask characters are as follows:

- ! makes any alpha character entered uppercase. Numeric and alpha characters are acceptable.

- ^ makes any alpha character entered lowercase. Numeric and alpha characters are acceptable.

- # means that only a numeric character is accepted.

- a means that any alphanumeric character is accepted. No punctuation characters are allowed.

- x means that any character is allowed.

Any other character entered appears as is in the edit mask, so that an edit mask of (###)###-#### appears onscreen initially as ( ) - .

Other options available for EditMask edit styles are as follows:

- Because the edit mask details the exact number of characters users will enter, PowerBuilder can detect when all the data is entered. With the AutoSkip option set, PowerBuilder moves focus to the next field automatically.

- The Spin Control setting displays two spin buttons on the field that can be used to spin through numeric or date values. When you select a spin control, you have access to the Spin Increment and Spin Range fields to control its action.

## The CheckBox Edit Style

If you need to restrict users to a choice of one or two values, use the CheckBox edit style. This style requires users to set the data for the column via a check box control. Figure 5.18 shows the dialog for this edit style.

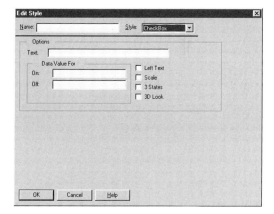

**FIGURE 5.18**
*The CheckBox edit style's dialog.*

You specify a data value for the on or checked state, and a data value for the off or unchecked state. If you turn on the 3 States option, you can also specify a third, Other state (this is less commonly used). The options for Other are

- Scale causes the check box to resize along with the column size within the DataWindow.

**5**

Databases and
the Database
Painter

- By setting Left Text, you can make the label appear on the left of the check box. By default, it appears on the right side.

- 3D Look directs PowerBuilder to display the check box in a 3D style. The default is a flat, 2D appearance.

## The `RadioButtons` Edit Style

The `RadioButtons` edit style is used when users must select from a list of mutually exclusive values. Figure 5.19 shows the dialog for this edit style; it's mainly concerned with the code table area where you specify the display and data values to be used to create the radio buttons.

**FIGURE 5.19**
*The*
`RadioButtons`
*edit style's*
*dialog.*

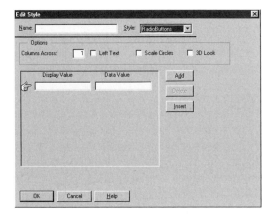

The options available for modifying the edit style are

- The Columns Across option allows you to control how the radio buttons appear. By default, the value is set to 1 and the radio buttons appear vertically.

- The Left Text, Scale Circles, and 3D Look options act just like they do for the `CheckBox` edit style.

## The `DropDownListBox` Edit Style

The `DropDownListBox` edit style appears as a drop-down or regular list box and is based around the code table that again is the center of this dialog (see Figure 5.20).

The values you enter into the code table area actually appear in the list of the edit field when shown in the DataWindow. Other settings are as follows:

FIGURE **5.20**

*The* DropDown-
ListBox *edit
style's dialog.*

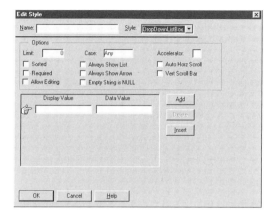

- You can cause the data values to be sorted by setting the Sorted option.

- Allow Editing changes the edit field to allow users to enter/change the data value.

- Always Show List makes the data value always appear below the edit field.

- Always Show Arrow places a drop-down arrow next to the edit field. With this option disabled, users must click the edit field to drop the list down.

- You can cause a vertical scrollbar to appear next to the list by turning on Vert Scroll Bar.

- To allow users to enter more data than can be seen in the edit field, turn on Auto Horz Scroll.

## The DropDownDataWindow Edit Style

The list displayed in the DropDownListBox edit style is static. To provide a dynamic list, you use the DropDownDataWindow edit style, whose dialog is shown in Figure 5.21.

The presentation of this edit style is similar to that of the drop-down list box except that the values come from the database via another DataWindow. Which DataWindow to use as the provider of the data and display values is specified in the DataWindow text box. The DataWindow text box is actually a drop-down list of all available DataWindows in your current application search path. After you select a DataWindow, choose a column for the display value and a column for the data value.

**Tip**

For this purpose, you usually create DataWindows based on database code tables and retrieve only two columns.

**5**

Databases and
the Database
Painter

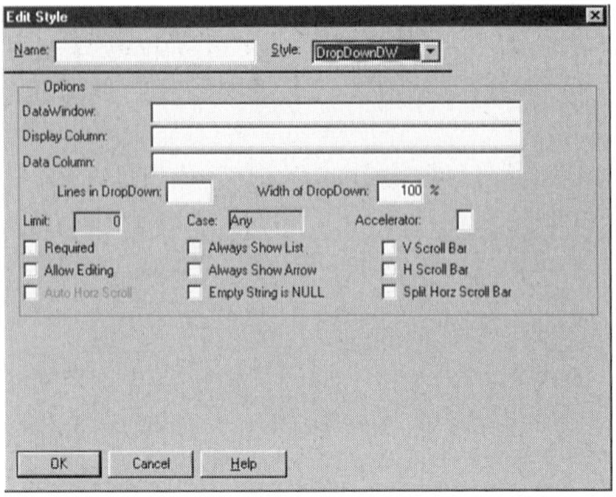

**FIGURE 5.21**
*The* DropDown-
DataWindow *edit*
*style's dialog.*

Two options this style has in addition to those already discussed for the other edit styles are

- The number you put in the Lines in DropDown text box specifies the maximum height of the list portion of the edit style.

- The Width of DropDown option allows you to specify a percentage of the DataWindow column width to display the drop-down list as. Usually this value is larger than 100 percent to allow the list to show more information.

For more discussion on drop-down DataWindows, see Chapter 16, "Advanced DataWindow Techniques II."

# Creating and Maintaining Display Formats

*Display formats* allow you to control the presentation of data in an edit field of a DataWindow. They're applied for display purposes and aren't visible in the current edit field but are applied after focus leaves the field.

When you edit an existing format or choose to create a new format, the Display Format pane opens, allowing you to create and edit display formats (see Figure 5.22).

When you select New from the pop-up menu or double-click an existing format to edit, you are presented with the Display Format Definition pane, where you create your format based on one of five data types: Number, String, Date, Time, or DateTime. Display formats can also be based on the following four sections (which ones are used depends on the data type):

- Positive or General format

- Negative values

**FIGURE 5.22**

*The Display Format pane.*

- Zero values

- Null values

Each section is separated by a semicolon (;). Here is an example:

`$#,##0.00;[RED]($#,##0.00);ZERO VALUE;NULL VALUE`

---

**Tip**

To prevent a zero value from displaying anything, use the format `#,###0;;; .` (Notice that you should also place a space after the last semicolon.)

---

Notice how you can place a string value to display in place of the data value. Keywords also are delimited with square brackets. In the preceding example, the keyword `[RED]` is used to make all negative numbers appear in red. Examples of other colors are `[BLACK]`, `[BLUE]`, and `[GREEN]`. Alternatively, you can specify a color by using a single value that represents the RGB value—for example, `[65536 * blue + 256 * green + red]`, where `blue`, `green`, and `red` are replaced with values between `0` and `255`.

## Numeric Display Formats

When creating a display format for numeric values, you can create a display format for each section: positive, negative, zero, or null. The two numeric-value placeholders that can be used in the display format are

**5**

**Databases and the Database Painter**

- 0 to indicate that a zero should be displayed at the position in the format

- # to indicate that a numeric value should be displayed at that position in the format

Numeric display formats also use other characters that can be used in the format: decimal points, dollar signs, parentheses, percent signs, and spaces.

Some examples of numeric display formats and what they display for various values are as follows:

| Display Format | 6000 | -6 | .6 | 0 |
|---|---|---|---|---|
| [General] | 6000 | -6 | .6 | 0 |
| #,##0 | 6,000 | -6 | 1 | 0 |
| #,##0.00 | 6,000.00 | -6.00 | 0.60 | 0.00 |
| #,##0;(#,##0) | 6,000 | (6) | 1 | 0 |
| 0% | 6000000% | -600% | 60% | 0% |
| 0.00 | 6000.00 | -6.00 | 0.60 | 0.00 |
| 0;0; (ZERO VALUE) | 6000 | -6 | 1 | ZERO VALUE |

As you can see, the percentage (%) character causes the value to be treated as a percentage value and as such is multiplied by 100.

## String Display Formats

When creating a display format for string values, you can create a display format for two sections: general and null.

The single placeholder is @, which matches any single character at that position in the format. Any other character in the format appears in the display.

Some examples of numeric display formats and what they display for various values are as follows:

| Display Format | Simon | Raven | Herb |
|---|---|---|---|
| [General] | Simon | Raven | Herb |
| @@@@ | Simo | Rave | Herb |
| @@-@@-@@ | Si-mo-n | Ra-ve-n | He-rb |
| Hi @@@@@ | Hi Simon | Hi Raven | Hi Herb |

# Date Display Formats

For date values, you can create display formats for two of the sections: general and null. You create the display formats from the following characters:

| Character | Description |
|-----------|-------------|
| d | Day number |
| dd | Day number, with leading zeros if applicable |
| ddd | Day name abbreviation |
| dddd | Full day name |
| m | Month number |
| mm | Month number, with leading zeros if applicable |
| mmm | Month name abbreviation |
| mmmm | Full month name |
| yy | Two-digit year number |
| yyyy | Four-digit year number |

The keywords [General] and [ShortDate] indicate that the short date format description defined in the Microsoft Control Panel for the current machine is to be used for the date display format. The keyword [LongDate] indicates that the long date display description defined in the Microsoft Control Panel is to be used.

Here are some examples of date formats:

| Date Display Format | For Saturday, December 6, 1969 |
|---------------------|-------------------------------|
| mm/dd/yyyy | 12/06/1969 |
| mmmm dd yyyy | December 06 1969 |
| mmm-dd-yy | Dec-06-69 |
| mmmm d, yyyy | December 6, 1969 |
| dddd, mm dd | Saturday, Dec 06 |

# Time Display Formats

For time values, you can create display formats for two of the sections: general and null. You create the display formats from the following characters:

| Character | Description |
|-----------|-------------|
| A/P | A or P, as applicable |
| a/p | a or p, as applicable |
| AM/PM | AM or PM, as applicable |

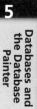

| am/pm | am or pm, as applicable |
|-------|-------------------------|
| h | Hour |
| hh | Hour, with leading zeros if applicable |
| m | Minutes |
| mm | Minutes, with leading zeros if applicable |
| s | Seconds |
| ss | Seconds, with leading zeros if applicable |
| ffffff | Microseconds |

The keyword [Time] indicates that the time format description defined in the Microsoft Control Panel should be used for the time display format.

Here are some examples of time formats:

| *Time Display Format* | *For 12:34:56:123456 AM* |
|----------------------|--------------------------|
| h:mm AM/PM | 12:34 AM |
| h:mm:ss AM/PM | 12:34:56 AM |
| h:mm:ss:fff AM/PM | 12:34:56:123 AM |
| h:mm:ss:ffffff am/pm | 12:34:56:123456 am |

You can combine the display formats for date and time to provide display formats for date/time data.

# Creating and Maintaining Validation Rules

*Validation rules* check the data entered by a user against particular criteria. A validation rule is defined as a Boolean expression. This return value determines whether the ItemError event of a DataWindow is fired on a failed rule. Figure 5.23 shows the standard message box that appears on a failed validation.

**FIGURE 5.23**

*The failed valida-*
*tion message box.*

If you choose an existing rule or create a new rule, the Validation Rules pane displays and allows you to create and edit validation rules. When you're creating a new validation rule (see Figure 5.24), you first state what sort of data type you will be operating against. This really doesn't have any effect except to disable the Match button for anything other than strings.

**FIGURE 5.24**

*The new Valida-*
*tion Rule pane.*

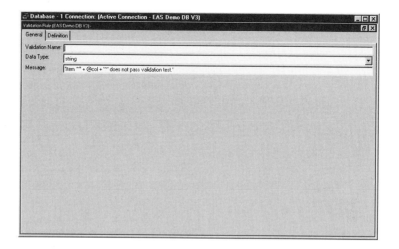

In the Rule Definition area (see Figure 5.25), you create your Boolean expression by using functions (selectable from the list) and the column value. A placeholder indicates the column value because you haven't actually said which column. You paste in the placeholder by clicking the @col button. The placeholder is substituted for the value entered at runtime. The expression can be composed of any valid PowerScript expressions, PowerBuilder functions, and user-defined global functions.

**FIGURE 5.25**

*The Match Pat-*
*tern dialog.*

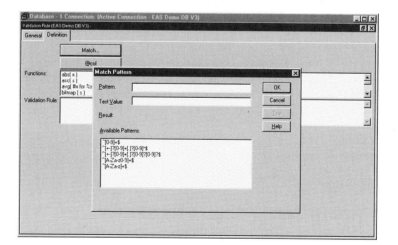

The Match button is used only with string values and opens the Match Pattern dialog. In this dialog, you can create a new match pattern or select one of the predefined match patterns. To test the pattern, enter a value in the test box and click the Test button. PowerBuilder evaluates the value based on your match pattern and determines whether the test value is valid. Clicking OK pastes the pattern onto the Definition tab page.

Within the Message single-line text box on the General tab page you can customize the error message that appears when the validation rule fails. PowerBuilder creates a default one for you:

```
'Item ~'' + @col + '~' does not pass validation test.'
```

Here are examples of validation rules:

```
Not IsNull( @col) And @col <> 0
```

```
@col = 'O' OR @col = 'C' OR @col = 'H'
```

The first example checks that the value entered isn't a NULL or a zero. The second example checks that the value entered is of a certain list of values: O, C, or H.

# Summary

This chapter demonstrated the power of the Database painter to maintain table and column definitions. In addition to database maintenance, the Database painter provides PowerBuilder developers the capability to generate extended column attributes for use with DataWindows and facilities to view and add data and execute interactive SQL statements.

# The DataWindow Painter

**CHAPTER 6**

One reason PowerBuilder is among the strongest application development software packages on the market is the DataWindow. A DataWindow enables you to present data in several different styles for data entry or reporting. It's a unique object that retains knowledge of the data being viewed, and it's therefore a powerful means of providing an application with a high degree of database transaction processing.

This chapter explores what a DataWindow object is, potential data sources, the different presentation styles, enhancing and changing your DataWindow objects, and associating a DataWindow object with a DataWindow control.

# The DataWindow Object

With the plethora of application development software packages available these days, there are numerous ways to retrieve and display data. Unfortunately, these packages are concerned only with developing an easy method to access data and neglect the presentation of the data, or vice versa. PowerBuilder includes a unique object that combines the best of both worlds. A DataWindow object incorporates two major components: data intelligence and a number of different user presentations.

A DataWindow object stores considerable information about the data it's displaying. Obviously, the most important data information is the source of the data. A DataWindow object can display data from a number of sources: a relational database, text or dBASE files (with .TXT or .DBF extensions), or user input. In addition to knowing the data source, a DataWindow object tracks when data has been changed, whether the data is of the correct data type, whether the data is required, whether the data is displayed in a specified format, what method the data is entered in, and whether the data passes any specified validation rules. A DataWindow object automatically performs each test and makes sure that all data passes the tests.

Many developers would be happy to stop with the data intelligence component, but the people who created PowerBuilder also provided an environment to create a wide range of user interfaces. The DataWindow painter presents many predefined presentation styles that generate default formats for your data. These styles include composite, freeform, graphs, grids, labels, group reports, tabular, N-Up, rich text, OLE 2.0, and crosstabs. Within each style, PowerBuilder provides standard report bands (header, detail, footer, summary, and group headers and footers), display formats, sorting, grouping, and combination presentation styles (such as a spreadsheet user interface with an associated graph).

# Creating a DataWindow Object

To open the DataWindow painter, simply click the New icon on the PowerBar. In the New object dialog (see Figure 6.1), select the DataWindow tab.

**FIGURE 6.1**

*The New Data-
Window dialog.*

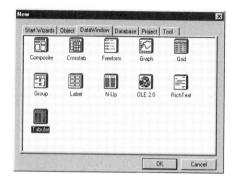

Creating a new DataWindow requires you to specify four main areas: the presentation style, data source, generation options, and Preview When Built check box. The whole process is controlled by the New DataWindow Wizard, which steps you through all the options possible during the construction of a DataWindow. The wizard allows you to go backward and forward through the pages of the wizard, and will occasionally open additional dialogs and painters to gather specific information. Let's look at each part of building a DataWindow.

## DataWindow Presentation Styles

You've seen that the DataWindow object can retrieve data from many different sources (the most common is a relational database). After you determine where the data will be coming from (you should know this location long before you get to this point), the next step is to choose how the information is displayed to users. Will it be a graph or a spreadsheet? Is it to be used to display summary or detail information? PowerBuilder supplies 11 different presentation styles to assist in developing an attractive and intuitive user interface.

### The Tabular Style

The tabular presentation style is a common data layout that displays headings across the top of the page and the data in columns under the headings (see Figure 6.2).

The tabular presentation style is useful for displaying high-level or summary information. From this summary data, the application code allows users to access the detailed records for the summary row.

**Figure 6.2**

*An example of the
tabular presenta-
tion style.*

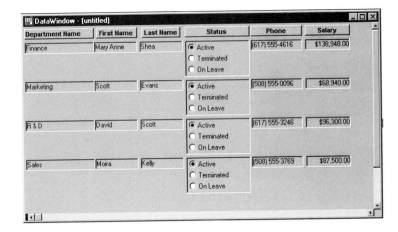

## The Grid Style

Similar to the tabular presentation style is the grid style, which displays headings along the top and columns under the headings but also includes lines separating the columns. The grid style looks and acts much like the standard spreadsheet software packages (for example, Microsoft Excel and Lotus 1-2-3), as shown in Figure 6.3.

The grid style also provides the capability to resize the column widths and row heights, reposition the order of the columns, and split scroll. All this is available at runtime and can be done without any coding.

**Figure 6.3**

*An example of the
grid presentation
style.*

| Customer ID | First Name | Last Name | Address | City | State |
|---|---|---|---|---|---|
| 101 | Michaels | Devlin | 3114 Pioneer Avenue | Rutherford | NJ |
| 102 | Beth | Reiser | 1033 Whippany Road | New York | NY |
| 103 | Erin | Niedringhaus | 1990 Windsor Street | Paoli | PA |
| 104 | Meghan | Mason | 550 Dundas Street East | Knoxville | TN |
| 105 | Laura | McCarthy | 1210 Highway 36 | Carmel | IN |
| 106 | Paul | Phillips | 2000 Cherry Creek N. Dr. | Middletown | CT |
| 107 | Kelly | Colburn | 18131 Vallco Parkway | Raleigh | NC |
| 108 | Matthew | Goforth | 11801 Wayzata Blvd. | Chattanooga | TN |
| 109 | Jessie | Gagliardo | 2800 Park Avenue | Hull | PQ |
| 110 | Michael | Agliori | 13705 North Glebe Road | Columbus | OH |
| 111 | Dylan | Ricci | 14700 Prosperity Avenue | Syracuse | NY |
| 112 | Shawn | McDonough | 15175 S Main Street | Brooklyn Park | MN |
| 113 | Samuel | Kaiser | 404 Bristol Street | Minneapolis | MN |

> **Note**
>
> With a grid presentation, you are locked into the grid format and can't drag the DataWindow objects to a new location to create a different presentation (for example, converting a tabular to a freeform style). You can, however, drag objects to reorder them.

## The Group Style

The group presentation style also extends the definition of the tabular presentation style. The group style does what the name suggests—it logically groups the data according to a specified column (for example, a list of customers in a particular region, with the region specified as the group field). Every time the value for the region changes, the DataWindow enables you to specify some type of calculation (for example, a count of customers or a summary of sales) before it displays the next value (see Figure 6.4).

**FIGURE 6.4**

*An example of the group presentation style.*

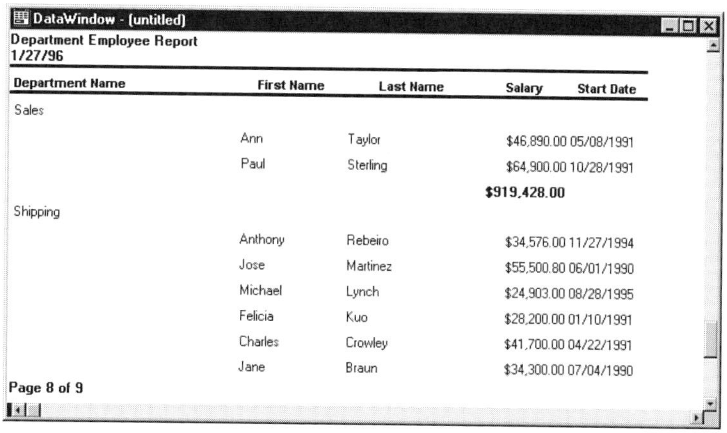

With the group presentation style, only one level of grouping can be specified initially (however, the group can be a compound group). A compound group consists of two or more columns specified for a single group. After the resultset is defined (see the later section "DataWindow Data Sources"), PowerBuilder opens the Set Report Definition page (see Figure 6.5).

**FIGURE 6.5**
*The Set Report Definition page.*

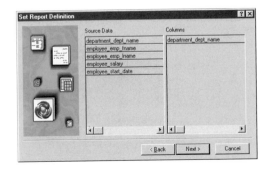

On the Set Report Definition page, specify on which columns to base the group. To select a column, just drag the column from the Source Data list box and drop it into the Columns list box. After you click the Next button, the Set Group Page Data page opens, so that you can specify whether a new page is generated every time the group column's value changes and whether the page number is reset on a group break. There's also a field to specify a page header, which it places in the header band of the DataWindow object.

The default page header is the name of the first selected table specified in the data source and placed before the word "Report." Many times this is a perfectly acceptable title, but, if it's not, you can edit the title in the Page Header multiline edit.

Note that this presentation creates only one group. Because more are often desired, see the later section "Groups" to learn how to create multiple grouping layers.

## The Freeform Style

The styles discussed so far are typically used for displaying multiple rows at one time. In the case of detail-level data, you might want to edit one row at a time. To achieve that functionality, the freeform presentation style provides a format for single-row editing. Instead of the headings-over-columns layout, the freeform style places labels to the left of the associated column (see Figure 6.6).

## The Label Style

If you need to generate labels (mailing, disk, and so on), the label presentation style is an easy way to create them (see Figure 6.7). PowerBuilder supports almost 100 different label types and forms so that the DataWindow objects can be specified to match your label sheets. You can even further tweak the settings from the defaults specified for the label type you pick.

After you select the label presentation style, you are asked to choose a predefined label, and then the Set Label Specifications page opens (see Figure 6.8).

6

The DataWindow Painter

**FIGURE 6.6**

*An example of the freeform presentation style.*

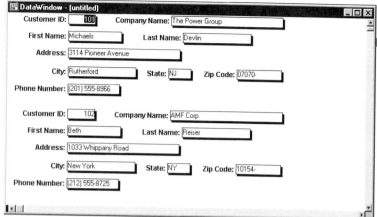

**FIGURE 6.7**

*An example of the label presentation style.*

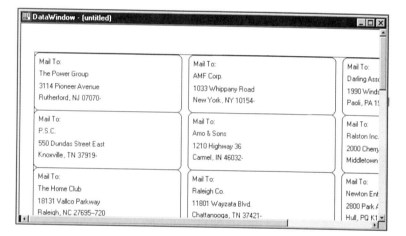

**FIGURE 6.8**

*The Set Label Specifications page.*

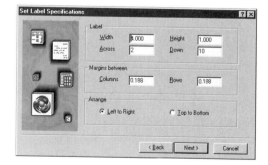

On this and subsequent pages, you can specify the label form on which you want to print your labels, change the height and width of each label, the number of labels across and down a page, whether the label paper is in continuous or single sheets, the page margins, the margins between label columns and rows, and whether you want the labels to print from left to right or from top to bottom.

If you need to change the definition after the labels are created, you can do this from the General tab page of the DataWindow's property sheet.

## The N-Up Style

At first glance, the N-Up presentation style appears to be an excellent style for displaying two or more columns on a page. Although you can display the data in a multicolumn layout, the data reads from left to right across the columns instead of down the columns (see Figure 6.9).

**FIGURE 6.9**

*An example of the N-Up presentation style.*

After you specify the data source, the DataWindow painter opens the Set Number of Rows per Band page, which asks how many columns you want created in the detail band (2 is the default).

Most people expect the data to read down each column before moving to the next column of information (as in a newspaper or telephone directory). PowerBuilder, however, goes against this and goes from the left side to the right side before moving down to the next line. Because of this, the N-Up presentation style isn't used as often as you might expect, except to build a calendar report or when the sort order isn't important. If you need to create a newspaper-style report, the DataWindow painter enables you to do so using a different property, as you see later in the section "Printing."

**Note**

In versions of PowerBuilder before 6.0, if one row was selected, all rows on the same line were also selected. As of version 6.0, only the specified row is highlighted, not the whole line.

## The Crosstab Style

The crosstab presentation style is popular with users who need to analyze data. A crosstab allows users to view summary data as opposed to multiple rows and columns. An easy way to define a crosstab is to specify an example. In a sales application, for example, you can summarize the year's sales for each particular product (see Figure 6.10).

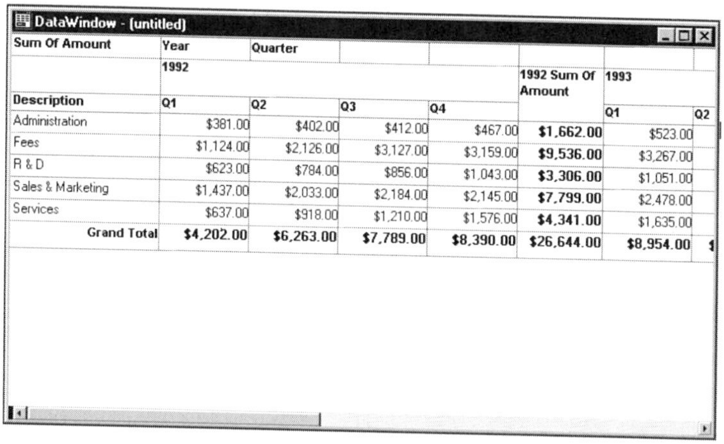


| Sum Of Amount | Year | Quarter | | | | | |
|---|---|---|---|---|---|---|---|
| | 1992 | | | | 1992 Sum Of Amount | 1993 | |
| Description | Q1 | Q2 | Q3 | Q4 | | Q1 | Q2 |
| Administration | $381.00 | $402.00 | $412.00 | $467.00 | **$1,662.00** | $523.00 | |
| Fees | $1,124.00 | $2,126.00 | $3,127.00 | $3,159.00 | **$9,536.00** | $3,267.00 | |
| R & D | $623.00 | $784.00 | $856.00 | $1,043.00 | **$3,306.00** | $1,051.00 | |
| Sales & Marketing | $1,437.00 | $2,033.00 | $2,184.00 | $2,145.00 | **$7,799.00** | $2,478.00 | |
| Services | $637.00 | $918.00 | $1,210.00 | $1,576.00 | **$4,341.00** | $1,635.00 | |
| **Grand Total** | **$4,202.00** | **$6,263.00** | **$7,789.00** | **$8,390.00** | **$26,644.00** | **$8,954.00** | |

**FIGURE 6.10**
*An example of the crosstab presentation style.*

After you select the crosstab presentation style and the data source information, the Define Crosstab Rows, Columns, Values page opens (see Figure 6.11).

Click and drag the source data to the appropriate location. The column (or columns) you want displayed along the top of the crosstab table should be dragged to the Column's list box (in this case, year). The same holds true for the data to be displayed on each row (that is, product description). Finally, the data you want to perform the calculation on (usually a summary or count) should be dragged to the Values list box. The Rebuild Columns at Runtime check box tells PowerBuilder whether to re-create the crosstab headings at runtime or use the headings that you specify at design time (in case the runtime headings are nondescriptive).

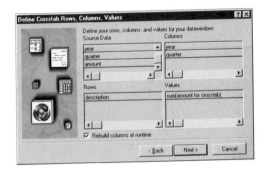

**FIGURE 6.11**

*The Define Crosstab Rows, Columns, Values page.*

If you don't like the default calculation for the value (or the row or column), double-click the calculation to open the Modify Expression dialog (see Figure 6.12).

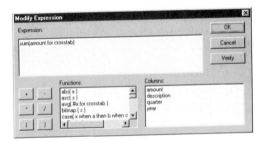

**FIGURE 6.12**

*The Modify Expression dialog.*

In this dialog, you can change the computed expression that appears at the junction of the specified row and column. To change the definition from the DataWindow design, right-click the design and select Crosstab from the pop-up menu.

## The Graph Style

The graph presentation style enables you to display the data using a wide range of different graph types (3D pie, bar, scatter, area, and so on). Figure 6.13 shows an example of a 3D pie graph.

When a data source has been defined, the Define Graph Data page opens, requesting additional information (see Figure 6.14).

With the graph presentation style, all rows are included. (Graphs can be defined in another DataWindow and thus include a subset of the rows, as you'll see later in this chapter.) The Category refers to the X axis or the major independent divisions of the data. These divisions are also known as *datapoints*. The Value refers to the Y axis or the dependent data. An optional Series adds another layer of depth to a graph and refers to a set of datapoints. When this information has been specified, PowerBuilder generates the default column graph (which can be changed later). For an in-depth look at graphing, see Chapter 31, "Graphing."

**FIGURE 6.13**

*An example of the graph presentation style.*

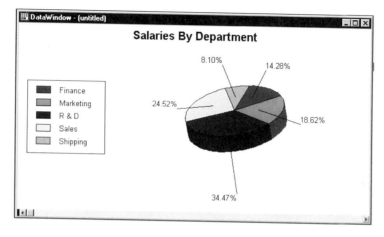

**FIGURE 6.14**

*The Define Graph Data page.*

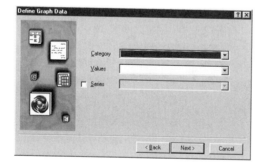

# The Composite Style

The composite style differs from the rest of the presentation styles in its source of data. Notice that when you select the composite style, you're not prompted for the DataWindow data source because the composite presentation consists of multiple, predefined DataWindow objects. After you click OK, you are presented with the Choose Nested DataWindows for Composite page (see Figure 6.15), which contains a list of all the DataWindow objects found in your current application library list.

**FIGURE 6.15**

*The Choose
Nested Data-
Windows for
Composite page.*

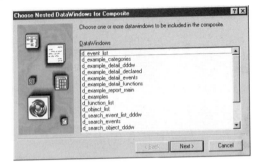

**Note**

The specified DataWindows can't be edited using the composite presentation style.

When all the DataWindows have been selected, PowerBuilder places each one in the painter as a bar and labels each with the name of the DataWindow object. These selected DataWindow objects can't be modified from within the composite style (you must bring up each individual DataWindow to make modifications). Why is this a useful presentation style? In previous releases of PowerBuilder, it was difficult to print multiple DataWindows on the same page without writing some tricky code. Also, it provides an easy method of grouping reports for users, even if the reports aren't directly related.

## The Rich Text Style

The rich text presentation style allows you to place data columns in a rich text document, thus removing much of the need to interact with a word processor outside PowerBuilder.

After you specify your data source, the Specify RichText Settings page opens (see Figure 6.16). In this page, you define how the rich text dialog will appear. The initial text for the document can be from one of two sources: an existing RTF document or the default (which is empty). After you decide what the text will be, a few additional options affect the appearance and how users interact with the document.

The document can include paragraph formatting such as displaying markers for carriage returns, tabs, and spaces. You can also specify which rich text bars are shown: the toolbar, tab bar, and ruler. As with most DataWindows, you can also specify the general background color and the color of each input field.

**FIGURE 6.16**
*The Specify Rich-Text Settings page.*

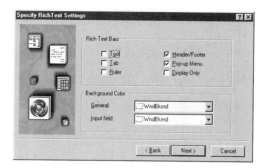

When the rich text DataWindow presentation is opened, the columns appear with their corresponding labels defined in the data repository in the database. The columns appear within braces. You can then treat the DataWindow as you would any document in a word processor and type in the desired text information. To place a column in the text, click the Column toolbar icon, which opens the Select Column dialog, allowing you to specify a particular column. After the layout is defined, the rich text DataWindow is treated like any other, with data retrieved and allowing you to step through the data a row at a time. Users can interact with the text (provided that it's not display only) to make modifications to the text, alignment, font, and so on, as they would in other mail merge applications.

The rich text presentation allows you to include headers and footers, have automatic word wrapping, include a pop-up menu (which includes Properties, Insert File, Cut, Copy, Paste, and Clear), and specify whether the whole DataWindow is read-only. These are modified through the property dialog for the DataWindow opened from the pop-up menu in the Design pane.

Several functions are specifically for use with the Rich Text Edit (RTE) presentation style. The functions are similar to those used for the Rich Text Edit control in the Window painter. For more details, see Chapter 11, "Advanced Controls."

## The OLE Presentation Style

The OLE 2.0 presentation style allows you to incorporate data with an OLE Version 2.0-compliant application. With this presentation, you can embed or link applications—such as an Excel spreadsheet, a Word document, or a graph—that use the data retrieved via the DataWindow (see Figure 6.17).

The first two option pages in the wizard are important for defining the OLE interaction. The first page allows you to specify the data source for the OLE object; you have the same options available here as for other DataWindow styles: Quick Select, Select, Query, and Stored Procedure.

FIGURE **6.17**

*The OLE 2.0 pre-
sentation style.*

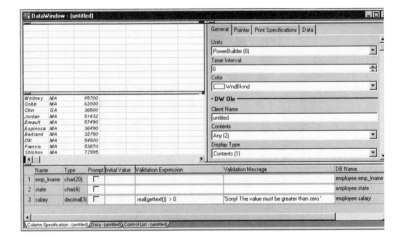

Next you are presented with the Specify OLE Data page (see Figure 6.18). This page
defines how the retrieved data is to interact with the OLE server. If you want data to be
grouped, click the desired columns and drag them to the Group By list box. With one or
more columns specified in the Group By list box, any columns dragged to the target data
are incorporated into a computed column (string columns are counted, and numerics are
summed). If no grouping is to be performed, drag the desired columns to the Target Data
list box, which then displays the actual column values from the database (no computations
are performed in the Target Data list box, unlike when grouping is performed).

FIGURE **6.18**

*The Specify OLE
Data page.*

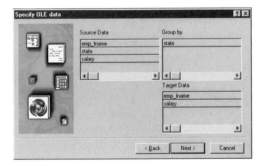

After you finish the DataWindow specification, PowerBuilder opens the DataWindow
painter and prompts you with the Insert Object dialog (see Figure 6.19).

FIGURE 6.19
*The Insert Object dialog.*

Using the different tab pages, you can specify how your OLE object is to be created: as a new object or from an existing object, or with a control (an OCX) inserted. You can also specify whether the object is embedded or linked, and whether it's displayed as an icon.

After you specify the OLE object source, the DataWindow design is displayed with the OLE object server environment activated in-place.

On the Options tab page of the property pane, you can specify how the server is activated, the display type, the client name, the object contents, and how the link is updated. When the OLE definition is complete, the DataWindow retrieves the data and supplies it to the OLE server to manipulate as specified. For more details on OLE, see Chapter 37, "Active X and OLE."

# DataWindow Data Sources

You can select from five data sources for a DataWindow object. These are methods for specifying how PowerBuilder obtains the data you want to display to your users. The five data source choices are Quick Select, SQL Select, Query, External, and Stored Procedure.

## Quick Select

The Quick Select data source generates a SQL statement against one or more tables sharing a key relationship. You typically would use Quick Select if you wanted to retrieve data from a single table and potentially retrieve additional information from related tables. After the tables are selected, you can also specify sorting and WHERE clause criteria to limit the amount of data retrieved.

When you choose Quick Select, PowerBuilder displays the Quick Select dialog (see Figure 6.20).

**FIGURE 6.20**

*The Quick Select dialog.*

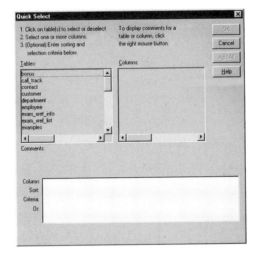

All the tables that exist in the database you are now connected to are listed in the Tables list box in the dialog. Search the list to locate the table from which you want to obtain data. When you select a table (for example, `employee`), all the columns for that table are displayed (see Figure 6.21).

**FIGURE 6.21**

*The list of columns for the `employee` table.*

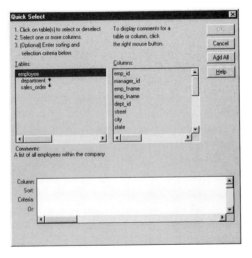

Also notice that if there are any foreign-key relationships to or from the selected table, those related tables are listed in the Tables list box (in Figure 6.21, they are the `sales_order` and `department` tables). The type of relationship is specified by the arrow located next to the table name. For example, the arrow pointing down next to the `sales_order` table means that a column in the `employee` table is a primary key in `sales_order`. When the arrow points up, it indicates that the selected table's primary key is a foreign key in another table. You can select any of these related tables, which in turn show their columns and any relationships.

When all tables have been selected, you can select column names from the Columns list box. If you make a mistake in selecting columns or tables, just deselect the column or table name. To return to the initial list of tables in your database, deselect the table listed at the top of the Tables list box. Selecting columns from the Columns list box causes the columns to appear in the selected columns box at the bottom of the dialog. If you want to retrieve all the columns, click the Add All button.

Beneath each selected column, you can specify sort criteria and selection criteria. To specify sorting, click the Sort row under the column on which you want the sort performed. A drop-down list box appears, enabling you to choose Ascending, Descending, or not sorted (the default). To specify selection criteria, type an expression under the column you want to have limited. If a column has a drop-down list box or drop-down DataWindow edit style defined on the database (refer to Chapter 5, "Databases and the Database Painter"), the drop-down list can be used to select a value in the Criteria rows. Criteria specified on the same row generate a logical AND in the SQL WHERE clause. Criteria specified on different rows generate a logical OR in the WHERE clause (see Figure 6.22).

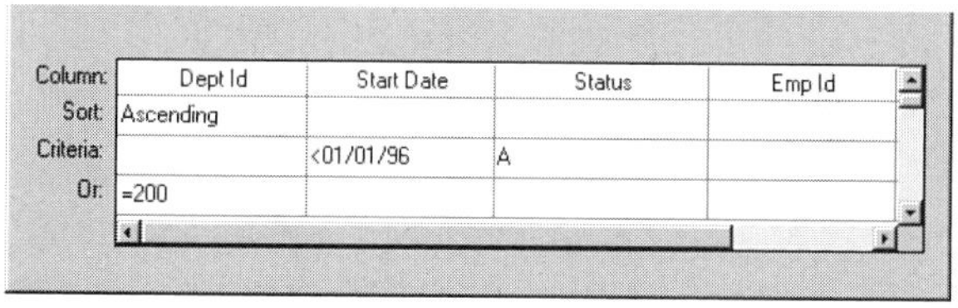

**FIGURE 6.22**

*The selected columns list, with* WHERE *criteria specified.*

| Column: | Dept Id | Start Date | Status | Emp Id |
|---------|---------|------------|--------|--------|
| Sort: | Ascending | | | |
| Criteria: | | <01/01/96 | A | |
| Or: | =200 | | | |

The criteria generated in Figure 6.22 would be as follows:

```
WHERE (start_date < '01/01/96' AND status = 'A') OR
      (dept_id = 200)
```

The order in which the columns are selected is the way PowerBuilder arranges the columns on the DataWindow. If you don't like the current order, you can click a column and drag it to the desired position. After you specify all the information you want, click OK, and the wizard redisplays and changes any of the default colors that you want. Click Next again and PowerBuilder prompts you with a summary. If you need to make any changes, use the Back button. When you are happy with the specifications for the new DataWindow, click the Finish button, and PowerBuilder generates the SELECT statement and default user interface for your DataWindow object (see Figure 6.23).

FIGURE **6.23**
*The default Data-
Window presen-
tation (tabular).*

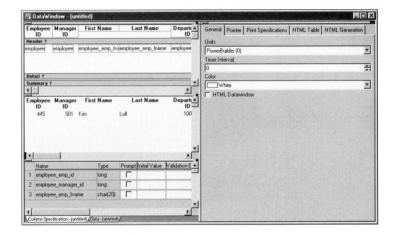

If you decide later that you want to update the SQL statement (that is, add or delete a column or change a logical AND to an OR), click the Data Source button on the DataWindow PainterBar or select Data Source from the Design menu.

Instead of the Quick Select dialog appearing again, PowerBuilder takes you into a new interface called the SQL Select painter, which is also the second data source in the Choose Data Source page of the New DataWindow Wizard.

## The SQL Select Painter

The SQL Select painter is another method you can use to graphically generate a SQL statement to retrieve data from an RDBMS. The SQL Select painter is used in several different places in PowerBuilder and is the most frequently used data source for a DataWindow object. Figure 6.24 shows the SQL Select painter.

The SQL Select painter displays the available tables from which you can retrieve data. The tables that display are those that exist in the database to which you were most recently connected in the Database painter. Select the table(s) from which you want to retrieve data and click the Open button. To select a column, click the column name in the table list, and it will be placed in the Selection List at the top of the painter.

At the bottom of the SQL Select painter is the SQL toolbox. The SQL toolbox consists of a series of tabbed pages that enable you to specify the different clauses of a SELECT statement (for example, HAVING and WHERE). Using the SQL Select painter is covered in detail in Chapter 4, "SQL and PowerBuilder."

In addition to the procedures outlined in Chapter 4, other features of the SQL Select painter are active in the DataWindow painter.

**FIGURE 6.24**
*The SQL Select painter.*

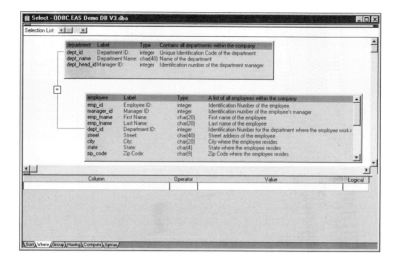

If you feel more comfortable typing the SQL statement as opposed to graphically creating it, select Convert to Syntax from the Design menu. You can toggle back and forth between the Syntax and Graphical modes so that you can work in the mode where you are the most comfortable.

---

**Note**

If you make significant changes while in Syntax mode, PowerBuilder might not be able to convert back to the Graphical mode.

---

The other important component of the SQL Select painter that DataWindows use heavily is retrieval arguments. From the Design menu, select Retrieval Arguments to open the Specify Retrieval Arguments dialog (see Figure 6.25).

A retrieval argument is a variable that you can reference in the WHERE clause of your SELECT statement; it will be given a value at runtime. In the Specify Retrieval Arguments dialog, specify the name of the variable and the data type. If the field is a numeric data type, the data type of the retrieval argument is Number. You can specify as many retrieval arguments as you need. When all retrieval arguments have been defined, click OK. If you try to leave the SQL Select painter at this point, you get a message stating that the retrieval arguments haven't been referenced.

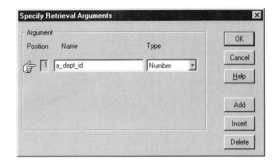

**FIGURE 6.25**
*The Specify Retrieval Arguments dialog.*

A retrieval argument can be referenced in the WHERE and HAVING clauses and in computed columns. The most common place is in the WHERE clause. For example, rather than specify the WHERE clause order_no = 12345, you could use a retrieval argument (defined as a_order_no number) and then construct the clause as WHERE order_no = :a_order_no. When the DataWindow is previewed, you are prompted to specify a value for the retrieval argument. To place the retrieval argument in the WHERE clause, click the Where tab. Next, select the column name from the list box in the Column column, specify an operator and then right-click the Value column. From the pop-up menu, select Arguments, which opens a dialog listing all the defined retrieval arguments. Select the retrieval argument you want and click the Paste button.

> **Tip**
>
> If you want to use array type arguments, include them in the WHERE clause using the IN operator. When you execute a retrieval against the DataWindow, PowerBuilder turns the array into a comma-separated list.

After you specify all the information you want to be in the SQL SELECT statement, click the Return icon on the PainterBar to return to the wizard or you can select Close from the File menu.

## Query Object

The Query data source uses a predefined PowerBuilder query object. A query object consists of a SQL SELECT statement generated in the Query painter. The Query painter interface is, in essence, the SQL Select painter. The difference is that the query object is saved as a separate object into a library. Query objects are useful if you have a SELECT statement that needs to be used as a source for multiple DataWindow objects. This way, you don't have to keep reconstructing the SQL for every DataWindow (which is particularly useful for complex SELECT statements).

> **Tip**
>
> If you're going to share data across your DataWindows, query objects ensure that you start with the same query for each DataWindow.

When you select the Query data source, PowerBuilder prompts you with the Select Query page where you enter, or browse to, the query object you've saved in a library in your library search path.

After initially choosing a query object, you can modify the SQL statement just like the Quick Select and SQL Select data sources. Any changes you make to the SQL statement aren't reflected in the query object.

> **Note**
>
> After a DataWindow specifies a query object as a data source, any changes made to the query object aren't reflected in the DataWindow.

## External Data Source

The External data source is the catchall for those data sources not accessible via the other four data sources (that is, external to a database). This includes such things as embedded SQL, user input, and remote procedure calls (RPC). Instead of the standard relational/SQL-driven data sources you've seen so far, the External data source, when chosen, prompts you for a resultset description (see Figure 6.26).

Click the Add button for each distinct field that you want to be a part of the DataWindow. Specify a field name, the data type, and the length of the field (if applicable). The order in which the fields are typed is important because this is the order in which PowerBuilder creates the user interface (the top field is the farthest to the left, the second field is second from the left, and so on). With the External data source, additional code must be written to populate the DataWindow (for example, direct syntax, SetItem(), or any File or Import function).

**FIGURE 6.26**
*The Define Result
Set page of the
New DataWindow
Wizard.*

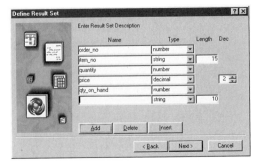

## Stored Procedures

The Stored Procedure data source might not be available to you when you create a new
DataWindow object. The Stored Procedure data source appears only when the DBMS
you're using supports stored procedures (for example, SQL Server). A *stored procedure* is
precompiled SQL that resides in the DBMS. Stored procedures are useful if you have a
long-running or complex SQL statement or series of statements. When you select this data
source, the Select Stored Procedure page appears (see Figure 6.27).

**FIGURE 6.27**
*The Select Stored
Procedure page.*

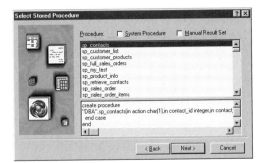

By default, the page shows only the stored procedures that have been created for the
specified database. If you want to display system-stored procedures, click the System
Procedure check box. The Manual Result Set check box specifies whether you want
PowerBuilder to generate the resultset description based on the last SELECT statement found
in the stored procedure or whether you want to do it yourself. If you are unsure about what
each stored procedure is doing, you can see the SQL statements used to generate the stored
procedure at the bottom of the page.

If you decide to define the resultset manually, the Define Stored Procedure Result Set page opens (which operates the same as the wizard page shown in Figure 6.26). As with the External data source option, you specify the fields, data types, and lengths of those fields that the stored procedure will be returning. Because stored procedures can become complex, you might need to specify additional information.

To access any additional conditions for the stored procedure call, you have to wait until PowerBuilder generates the DataWindow. Right-click in the Column Specification pane and select Stored Procedure to open the Modify Stored Procedure Data Source dialog (see Figure 6.28). In this dialog, you can choose a different resultset from the stored procedure.

**FIGURE 6.28**
*The Modify
Stored Procedure
Data Source
dialog.*

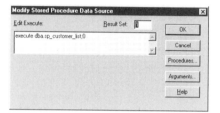

Some DBMSs allow a stored procedure to return information not just through a single result at the end of the procedure but also through any number of completely different resultsets. By using the field in this dialog, you can specify the exact resultset that PowerBuilder should accept for the DataWindow. This is the location to specify the arguments that you need to pass to the stored procedure. First specify them by using the Arguments button and then incorporate them into the stored procedure call shown in the main page.

# A Sample DataWindow

Let's continue with the creation of a tabular DataWindow and see some additional functionality the DataWindow painter provides.

After you specify the tabular presentation and the data source, the default tabular DataWindow design is created (see Figure 6.29).

Notice that the order of the columns (from left to right) corresponds to the order of the fields specified in the data source resultset.

## Report-Level Formatting

If you aren't familiar with standard report-writing software, the design of a DataWindow might be a bit frightening. The design of a DataWindow is broken up into a number of areas referred to as *bands* (similar to many standard reporting software packages). Figure 6.30 shows the bands of the DataWindow object.

**FIGURE 6.29**

*The default tabular DataWindow design.*

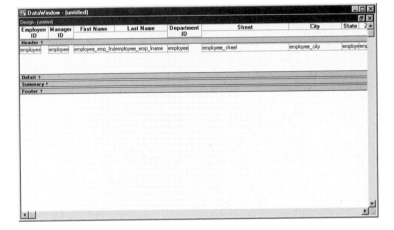

**FIGURE 6.30**

*DataWindow bands.*

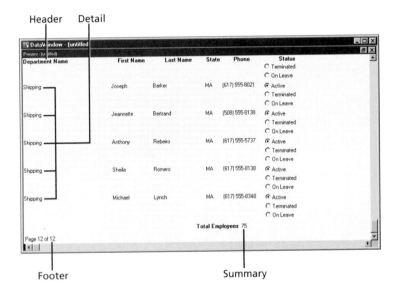

In Design mode (shown in Figure 6.29), each band is indicated by a gray bar below it that holds the name of the band and an arrow pointing to it (for example, Header). The header, detail, footer, and summary bands appear for each DataWindow (except for the graph and label presentation styles, for which the bands don't apply). The typical uses for each are as follows:

- *Header* appears at the top of every page and is used to display titles and column headings.

- *Detail* contains the body of the DataWindow object. Displays rows of data and associated labels. The detail band repeats as many times as necessary within the constraints of the DataWindow object's height.

- *Footer* appears at the bottom of each page and is used to display text and page numbers.

- *Summary* appears on the last page of the DataWindow object and is used to display totals and summaries for the entire DataWindow object.

In addition to the standard four report bands, a DataWindow object can contain bands such as group headers and group trailers. These bands appear only if you create one or more groups for your DataWindow object (by using the group presentation style or specifying your own group).

Each band can be resized to accommodate any layout you want. To resize, just click the gray bar associated with the band you want to resize, and drag.

Remember, though, that any additional whitespace you leave at the top and bottom areas of the band appears in the DataWindow during execution.

## Changing Colors and Borders

Because the default color scheme might not look exactly as you had hoped it would, you might find that you often have to change the look and feel of your DataWindow object.

To change the background color of the whole DataWindow object, select the color you want from the color drop-down list on the General tab; this color is applied to the rest of the report. Notice that on the same tab page you can also specify the units of measurement used in the DataWindow and the timer interval if you're using the DataWindow's internal timer. The Pointer tab is used to specify the pointer that appears in the DataWindow (the default is an arrow). In addition to being able to set the color and the pointer for the whole report, you can specify the same information for each individual report band (right-click the gray band marker and select Properties, or more simply just click to select the band).

After you specify the color of the report and the report bands, it might be necessary to change the appearance of the columns and headings. To accomplish this, click the desired column and the Properties pane will display that column's properties. On the Font tab (see Figure 6.31), you can select the background or text color and the font and font's style.

**FIGURE 6.31**

*The Column
Object property
sheet's Font tab.*

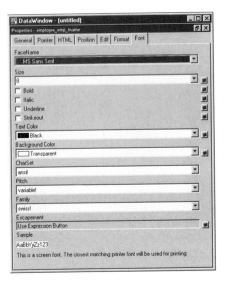

In addition to changing the text and column colors, you can change the border of the column by selecting the General tab and accessing the Border drop-down list box. The valid options are None, Underline, Box, Resize, Shadow Box, 3D Raised, and 3D Lowered. For columns on a tabular presentation, 3D Lowered is a popular choice. You can do the same thing for the headings; 3D Raised is common for headings.

> ## Tip
>
> You might experience some paint problems when you migrate applications written in older versions to the latest version. They include the following:
>
> - For grid-style DataWindows, the process has been modified to ensure that the cell borders stay within the boundaries of each cell.
>
> - When viewing a DataWindow or in Print Preview mode, the border correctly sizes up and down when zooming.
>
> - When printing a DataWindow in previous versions, border pixel sizes weren't being correctly sent to the printer. This has been corrected to improve border display.

Changing properties via property sheets one object at a time can be tedious and time-consuming. You can use a couple methods to simplify this process. Rather than open the property sheet for every column and heading, you can select all the headings or all the columns and format them all at the same time. To select multiple objects in the DataWindow, click one object, hold down the Ctrl key, and click all the other objects you want to select. You can also click the left mouse button on a blank space on the report and drag the pointer. Doing this creates a lasso that selects all objects touched by or within the rectangle created by the lasso. A third method is through the Edit menu: Click the Select cascading menu. This enables you to select everything in the DataWindow; everything to the right, left, above, or below a selected object; all columns; or all text (that is, headings and labels). This is a powerful method of selecting objects and can save you a lot of time during development.

### Note

A feature that greatly assists in the resizing of objects is AutoScrolling. You are no longer required to size an object, stop, move the scrollbars, and continue sizing an object. Movement of objects and their edges isn't restricted to the visible screen.

After you select all the objects you want to modify, you are ready to apply the format changes. Use the drop-down toolbars for the border and the colors (see Figure 6.32).

**FIGURE 6.32**
*The border and color drop-down toolbars.*

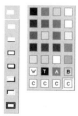

The second method to simplify the color and border designation is found on the Generation tab on the DataWindow Options dialog (see Figure 6.33).

FIGURE **6.33**
*The Generation
tab.*

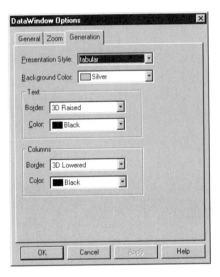

The DataWindow Options dialog—opened by choosing Options from the Design menu—allows you to specify the default colors and background styles for the whole report, text, and columns. These options are on the Generation tab. If you constantly use the same formatting for a particular presentation style, you can save your settings as a default for future DataWindows. This must be specified on the Select Color and Border Settings page of the New DataWindow Wizard.

## Previewing the DataWindow

If you selected the Retrieve on Preview check box in the New DataWindow Wizard, the DataWindow automatically executes the SQL statement and displays the tabular DataWindow, complete with data. If you specified one or more retrieval arguments in your SQL statement, PowerBuilder prompts you for them now. Even if you didn't ask for the preview, the lower pane in the DataWindow painter displays how the DataWindow would look at runtime, just without data. If no data is found to satisfy your request, or if you are using an External data source, no data is displayed.

Starting with PowerBuilder 7.0's use of panes, you get to see the runtime representation along with the design area. As you make changes to the data fields, they are immediately reflected in the Preview pane. This makes for an easy and efficient method of enhancing your DataWindow's look and feel.

You can control the Preview mode by using a different area of the PainterBar (see Figure 6.34).

**FIGURE 6.34**

*The PainterBar for Preview mode.*

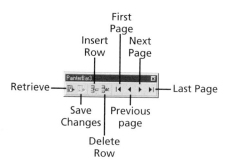

Data is retrieved into the Preview pane automatically only once, when the painter is first entered. If you want to re-retrieve data from the database, click the icon on the PainterBar that shows an arrow pointing toward a DataWindow. The SQL statement is executed, and the Retrieve toolbar icon changes to a red hand. Clicking the red hand cancels the retrieval of data.

If you're creating an editable DataWindow, you can now modify the data. To do so, click a column and change it. To insert a new row, click the Insert Row icon (the one displaying a series of rows with a new row being inserted). This inserts a blank row above the current row (where your cursor is). To delete an existing row, click the icon with the picture of a row with a red X. If you try to exit the DataWindow, PowerBuilder prompts you to save the changes back to the database. You can also update the database by selecting the Save Changes icon on the PainterBar (a red arrow pointing away from the DataWindow). The DataWindow generates the appropriate SQL to insert, update, and delete rows in the database. For more information on how PowerBuilder does this, see the later section "Update Characteristics."

The next four PainterBar icons are used for movement through the resultset displayed in the DataWindow. They enable you to move to the first record, the preceding page (a page is defined as what can be viewed onscreen), the next page, and the last record.

# Sizing, Aligning, and Spacing

After previewing the DataWindow, you might decide that the columns don't look exactly as you had hoped they would. Some columns might be truncated, large gaps might appear between columns, or maybe columns and their corresponding headings aren't lined up correctly.

Just as in the Window painter, the DataWindow painter lets you change the size, alignment, and spacing of all objects in the current DataWindow.

To make any changes to an object, you must first select it. As you've already seen, there are many different ways to select several objects. For alignment, sizing, and spacing, the order in which the objects are selected is extremely important. Therefore, don't use the lasso select to select all your fields because you can't be sure of the order in which PowerBuilder will decide to select them. You must first select a single object; then you can use the lasso.

To align objects in the same band or across different bands, select the object with which you want all other objects to be aligned. After you do this, hold down the Ctrl key and manually select each additional object by clicking it (or, because you've already selected one object, you can use the lasso select for all other objects). You can also choose the Select option from the Edit menu if you need to select a large number of fields. When all desired fields have been selected, choose Align Objects from the Format menu. A cascading menu appears, with pictures specifying how the selected objects will be lined up: on the left, in the center vertically, on the right, on the top, in the center horizontally, or on the bottom. The selected objects jump to their new position in alignment with the first selected object. If you accidentally choose the wrong option, select Undo from the Edit menu, which returns the selected objects to their original positions.

To size an individual object, select the desired object and move the mouse pointer to the edge of the object so that the pointer changes to the double-arrowed line. Click and drag the object's edge to the desired size. If you can't see the edge of an object because a border specification is None, turn on the Show Edges option by selecting Options from the Design menu and clicking the General tab page. To make two or more objects the same size, select one object that has the size (height and width) that you want the other objects to have. Then, using the selection method you prefer, select the other DataWindow objects. From the Format menu, click the Size Objects option to open the cascading menu. The three options in the Size Objects menu are sized according to the first selected object's width, to its height, or to both height and width.

To ensure that the spacing between objects is consistent, position two objects with the desired spacing between them. Select these two objects and then select any objects to which you want to copy the spacing. From the Format menu, choose Space Objects to open the cascading menu, which enables you to specify that the spacing be copied horizontally or vertically. Remember, the spacing is based on the space between the first two objects selected.

Aligning, sizing, and spacing columns can also be accomplished using the drop-down toolbar (see Figure 6.35).

**FIGURE 6.35**
*The alignment, spacing, and sizing drop-down toolbar.*

## Keyboard Shortcuts

Table 6.1 shows the keyboard shortcuts available in the DataWindow painter.

**TABLE 6.1** Keyboard Shortcuts Available in the DataWindow Painter

| *Keyboard Command* | *Description* |
|---|---|
| *Selecting Objects* | |
| Ctrl+up arrow | Select above |
| Ctrl+down arrow | Select below |
| Ctrl+left arrow | Select left |
| Ctrl+right arrow | Select right |
| Ctrl+A | Select all |
| *Text Functions* | |
| Ctrl+B | Bold |
| Ctrl+I | Italic |
| Ctrl+U | Underline |

At any time, you can modify the keyboard shortcuts for any menu items by choosing Keyboard Shortcuts from the Window menu.

## Grid, Ruler, and Zoom

To assist you in arranging columns, headings, and any other objects on the DataWindow, the DataWindow painter provides some additional features: the grid, the ruler, and Zoom.

The grid displays in the DataWindow workspace and enables you to position objects more easily. The ruler appears on the left and top of the painter and helps to position objects in relation to inches. To turn on the grid or ruler, select Options from the Design menu, which brings up the DataWindow Options property sheet discussed in the section "Changing Colors and Borders."

To set the grid and ruler, select the General tab (see Figure 6.36).

**FIGURE 6.36**
*The General tab.*

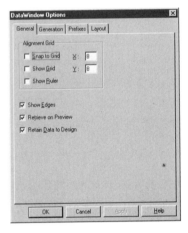

---

**Tip**

The default size of the grid is 8 × 8 pixels. For most practical purposes, this is too large; make it 4 × 4 instead.

---

Another option on the General tab is Snap to Grid. When this option is activated, objects in the DataWindow automatically align themselves with the grid when they are moved or placed on the DataWindow. The Show Ruler option displays a ruler vertically and horizontally, which is useful for determining margins.

The Zoom option under the Design menu enables you to change the scale of the DataWindow workspace so that you can see more of the object or view more detail. The capability to zoom is useful for a couple reasons. If you have a large DataWindow object, you can reduce the workspace scale to view more of the object. Conversely, you can enlarge the workspace to see the DataWindow in more detail. Zoom is view-only (you can't make changes to the DataWindow) and doesn't affect the actual size of the DataWindow object. Zoom is also available in the Preview pane.

# Display Formats, Edit Styles, and Validation Rules

When you previewed the DataWindow object, several of the columns had different formatting (for example, drop-down list boxes, radio buttons, and edit masks). In addition to the data appearing differently, some columns displayed an error message if incorrect data was entered. Where did the formatting and validation rules come from? Why is this consistent across all the DataWindow objects that reference these columns? If you recall, in the Database painter (see Chapter 5), you specified extended attributes for some columns in the database. All this information is stored in the data repository and is used in all subsequent DataWindow objects that reference the columns.

**Note**

In addition to display formats, edit styles, and validation rules being specified in the data repository, some additional extended attributes are used: justification, height, width, header, and label. These can be modified to be the defaults so that manual manipulation doesn't have to be performed each time a column is placed on a DataWindow object.

Let's look at using existing display formats, edit styles, and validation rules—modifying them and creating new ones.

## Display Formats

A *display format* controls how a DataWindow is presented to users. When users click in a field with a display format, the display format disappears. Display formats keep unnecessary formatting from being stored in the database and taking up valuable space. They are useful for columns that users can't modify.

To use a display format, open the Column Object property sheet and click the Format tab (see Figure 6.37).

**FIGURE 6.37**
*The Format tab.*

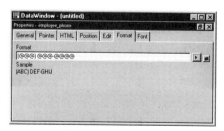

If display formats exist for the data type of the column (for example, String), they can be accessed by using the button to the right of the format entry field. To apply an existing format, click this button and then select the format name. So that you can see what a value will look like with the display format applied to it, PowerBuilder shows a value of the correct data type in the Sample area below the Format single-line edit. For more information on creating a display format, see Chapter 5.

## Edit Styles

Like a display format, an *edit style* changes the way the data is presented to users. Unlike a display format, though, an edit style doesn't disappear when the column has focus. An edit style affects the way users interact with the data. There are six different edit styles: Edit, EditMask, RadioButtons, CheckBox, DropDownListBox, and DropDownDataWindow. To select an edit style, open the Column Object property sheet and click the Edit tab.

**Tip**

You can also center a check box within a column. After selecting the CheckBox edit style, choose Center from the Alignment drop-down list box on the General tab page. This will occur only when there's no text specified for the CheckBox edit style.

If an edit style was assigned to the column in the Database painter, the style name is the selected name in the Name drop-down list box. To select another existing edit format from the data repository, select its name from the drop-down list box. If none of the existing edit styles fit your application's requirements, you can modify an existing edit style or create a new one.

To modify an existing edit style, select a style name from the list box, which then repopulates the Edit tab and allows you to choose the options you require.

**Note**

As soon as you modify an existing style, the edit style name disappears from the Name drop-down list box. This is because you've defined a new style (the edit style defined on the database isn't changed).

The other option is to create a new edit style from scratch. To learn how to create the different edit styles, see Chapter 5.

**Note**

PowerBuilder 6.0 changed the way in which a DataWindow displays when a column has a DropDownDataWindow edit style and a display format. When the column doesn't have focus, the Display format of the parent DataWindow is used. When the column has focus, the data is displayed (and not the Display format).

One edit style is available only in the DataWindow painter, Display as Picture, which is covered next.

## The Display as Picture Style

One additional edit style not available in the Database painter is the Display as Picture style. This style enables you to display pictures instead of text in the DataWindow column. The database column stores the name of a graphics file (Bitmap, Jpeg, GIF, RLE, or Windows Metafile) to be displayed. When data is retrieved into the DataWindow, PowerBuilder searches for the corresponding graphics file and displays the picture in the column instead of the filename. The graphics file doesn't need to be accessible at design time. At runtime, PowerBuilder searches the user's DOS search path to locate the appropriate file. To use the Display as Picture style, click the check box on the General tab of the Column Object property sheet.

# Validation Rules

A column on the DataWindow object can have a validation rule associated with it that ensures that the information users are typing is valid. As with the display formats and edit styles, validation can be defined in the Database painter and extended to apply to the column on the DataWindow. To access a column's validation rules, select the Column Specification pane (see Figure 6.38).

On this pane, you can specify a number of different expressions that contain column names, arithmetic operators, function names, and the like. The validation rule must evaluate to a Boolean value (TRUE or FALSE). If the data being entered for the column doesn't pass the validation rule specified, the error message defined in the Error Message Expression single-line edit is displayed. (See Chapter 9, "Application Objects and the Application Painter," to find out how to set the title bar of the error message window.)

**FIGURE 6.38**

*The Column Specification pane.*

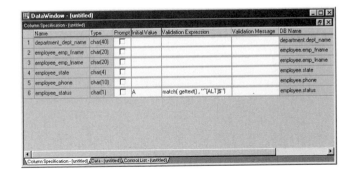

In addition to typing in an expression for the validation rule, you can specify a global user-defined function to perform validation as long as it returns TRUE or FALSE. A global function for a validation rule is useful for performing functions not supported on the Validation tab, such as embedded SQL. For more information on creating validation rules, see Chapter 5.

# Adding and Deleting Columns

After a DataWindow object is created, you might find that you want to add a column to the DataWindow or delete a column from it.

If a column isn't now specified as part of the data source, the first step in adding a column is to add it to the data source specification. To do so, click the icon on the PainterBar with SQL on it or select Data Source from the Design menu. This takes you into the appropriate data source definition painter (the SQL Select painter, the Stored Procedure Wizard page, or the Modify Result Set Description page). When the new column has been added to the resultset, return to the Design mode of the DataWindow object. The new column is placed after the last column on the right in the detail band. Notice that no header or label is placed on the DataWindow with the column.

If a column is being retrieved and is no longer needed, it should be removed from the resultset specification in the same way that a column is added. Ensuring that unnecessary data isn't retrieved helps to increase your application's performance.

So far, you've examined adding and removing a column from the data source. Sometimes you might want to add or keep a column from appearing in the DataWindow but still retrieve the value into memory. An example of when you would retrieve a field and not display it is in the case of a key field. If a table contains a key field that's not deemed useful information to users (for example, a customer ID), that column doesn't need to be shown. If the column is important because it uniquely identifies a row in the DataWindow, however, it should continue to be retrieved. To remove a column, select the column and press the Delete key or select Clear from the column's pop-up menu.

Another common situation is to accidentally delete or remove a column and then find out you need it in the DataWindow. You can add the column back in by clicking the Add Column icon in the object's drop-down toolbar on the PainterBar.

After clicking this icon, click in the DataWindow in the location where you want to place the column. Clicking a report band opens the Select Column dialog (see Figure 6.39).

**FIGURE 6.39**

*The Select Column dialog.*

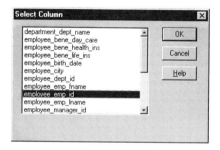

The list box displays all columns specified in the resultset definition for your DataWindow. Select the column that you want to place on the DataWindow object and then click OK to place it in the report band.

---

**Tip**

Although you can add more columns to a DataWindow object by using computed columns, if you want users to be able to enter values that you might not be saving, you can add dummy values to the resultset of the DataWindow SELECT (for example, 0 for a Numeric value and "" for a String value). Pad the string with spaces to the required size. Some databases, such as SQL Server, might require you to use a conversion function to get the right size and data type (for example, CONVERT( CHAR(5), "" ) ).

---

# Tab Order

Just as in the Window painter, a DataWindow object has a tab order that controls how you move about the screen when you press the Tab key. There's a difference between the Window painter tab order and that of the DataWindow painter. In the Window painter, a tab order of 0 means that a control was skipped when users pressed the Tab key. The control can still be clicked and used. In the DataWindow painter, a tab order of 0 not only disables that control in the tab sequence, but it also doesn't allow users to access the column at all.

Use this feature when you want to prevent your users from being able to update or edit a column (this is particularly useful for key columns).

To set the tab order, select Tab Order from the Format menu or click the icon on the PainterBar. As you would be in the Window painter, you are now in Tab mode (see Figure 6.40).

**FIGURE 6.40**

*Tab mode in the DataWindow painter.*

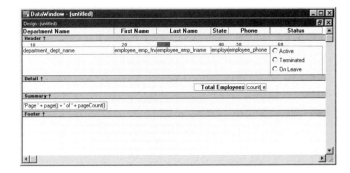

The tab order is specified by the red numbers over each column in the resultset. Only data columns can be included in the tab sequence (notice that computed columns, text objects, and so on have no red number labels). To modify the tab order, click the red numbers and type the new order sequence (from 0 to 999). PowerBuilder renumbers the tab order in increments of 10. To turn off the Tab mode, choose the Tab Order menu item again.

> **Note**
>
> If the DataWindow is a join between two or more tables, the default tab order on all columns is 0 because a DataWindow object can update only one table. To learn how to specify how the DataWindow updates, see the later section "Update Characteristics."

> **Note**
>
> If a column's capability to be edited changes based on a user's security, the preferred method to render a column uneditable is by using the Protect attribute, which preserves the tab order.

# Groups

You've seen how to easily create a DataWindow with one group on it using the Group presentation style. At times, you might want to create a DataWindow with more than one group. Select Create Group from the Rows menu, which opens the Specify Group Columns dialog (see Figure 6.41).

**FIGURE 6.41**

*The Specify Group Columns dialog.*

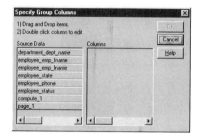

You can specify one or more columns as a group by clicking the column name in the Source Data list box and dragging it to the Columns list box, just as you would for the Group presentation style. Two options that appear on the band's property sheet—and not within the dialog—are New Page on Group Break and Reset Page Number on Group Break. If you want each group to appear alone on one or more pages, click in the New Page on Group Break check box. If you want the page numbers to be reset when this break occurs, select the second check box (this should be used only with the New Page on Group Break check box).

**Note**

To have grouping work effectively, you can include an ORDER BY clause for the grouped column in your SQL statement or for the DataWindow. This ensures that the data is sorted before the grouping takes place. If this isn't done, the resulting report might contain multiple breaks for the same value.

The Group Sort area on the property sheet is used to specify how the groups will be sorted based on any computed columns in the group trailer. For example, if a group break was specified for the department_name column and a computed column counting the number of employees was placed in the group trailer band, the Sort Group tab could be used to indicate that the order of the groups should be based on the computed column. Therefore, you could have the department with the greatest number of employees listed first, followed by the one with the second-highest number of employees, and so on. The other two tabs

(General and Pointer) are used to further define the appearance and behavior of the group header band, such as its height, color, and mouse pointer.

[ic:version]In versions before 7.0, expressions for objects and bands could be accessed in the property sheet on the Expressions tab. Starting with version 7.0, you access expressions through the small button at the side of certain properties (it looks like a red = with a line through it). This button allows you to specify an expression for that property. This means that you now have direct access to a number of properties previously accessed through the old tab. Attribute expression values are discussed in more detail later in the section "Object Attributes."

After a new group is created, you can create a second group by selecting the Create Group menu item again. The DataWindow painter sequentially numbers the groups as they're created. When you create an additional group, don't be alarmed to see that in the Specify Group Columns dialog your previous groups aren't listed in the Columns list box. If at any point you want to modify the definition of a group that you've created, choose Edit Group from the Rows menu and select the number of the group in question. If you aren't sure of a group's number, look on the associated bands, which are numbered.

These bands, in their initial state, have no information in them. Unlike in the Group presentation style, creating a group from within the DataWindow painter doesn't create any computed columns in the group footer bands (see the later section "Computed Columns"). You must do this, as well as move the columns into the respective bands, manually.

If at some point you decide that a group is no longer needed, you can select Delete Group from the Rows menu.

### Caution

If you have any objects in the group header or footer when you specify Delete Group, they're deleted also. Therefore, if you want to continue to display any of this information, you must move it to another report band before the deletion. If you forget, you must re-create the objects.

### Tip

If you enter data programmatically into a DataWindow with one or more groups defined, the additions aren't automatically incorporated into the presentation in the group calculations. To have the grouping recalculated, call the function

`GroupCalc()`. You might also have to call the `Resort()` function if your display relies on a certain data sequence.

## Suppressing Repeating Values

Instead of creating a group report that still gives the appearance of grouping, try the Suppress Repeating Values option. For example, you might have a report that doesn't need to perform any calculation when a new group is processed, but a certain column value is repeated over and over (see the second department column in Figure 6.42).

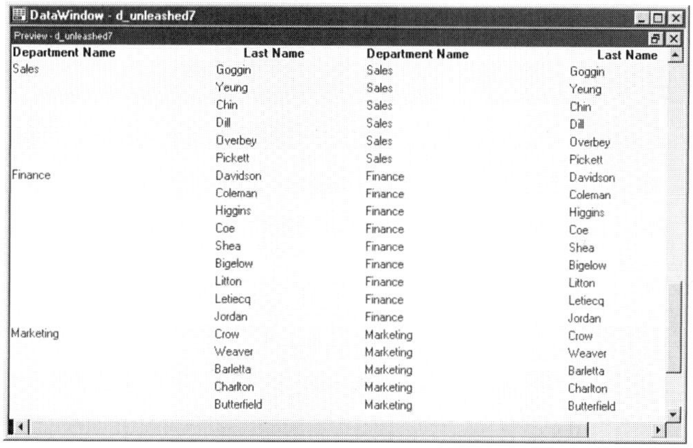

**FIGURE 6.42**
*The DataWindow object showing suppressed and unsuppressed repeating value (department name).*

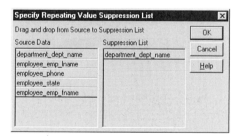

The second department name column in Figure 6.42 is repeated for each row. To prevent this from happening, choose Suppress Repeating Values from the Rows menu, which opens the Specify Repeating Value Suppression List dialog (see Figure 6.43).

**FIGURE 6.43**
*The Specify Repeating Value Suppression List dialog.*

Again, a drag-and-drop interface enables you to specify those columns for which you don't want the values to be repeated for every row. In this example, you would want to click `dept_name` in the Source Data list box and drag it over to the Suppression List area. You can do this for as many columns as you want. This example would result in the first Department Name column within the DataWindow shown in Figure 6.42. As for a group break, the data should be sorted on those columns for which the value is to be suppressed.

## Sliding Columns

To remove spaces between columns, open the Column Object property sheet and select the Position tab. Specify one of the available Slide options: Left, All Above, or Directly Above. Suppose that you're creating mailing labels with first name, last name, address1, address2, city, state, and zip. The size of the name and city fields will vary, and there might be no value specified for address2. If sliding columns weren't used, there would be gaps between the fields, creating an unattractive label. Figure 6.44 shows two labels, the first with no sliding and the second with sliding.

**FIGURE 6.44**

*The mailing label on the left shows no column sliding. The mailing label on the right shows the same columns with Slide Left turned on.*

```
Mail To:

The Power Group

3114 Pioneer Avenue

Rutherford        NJ      07070-
```

```
Mail To:

The Power Group

3114 Pioneer Avenue

Rutherford, NJ 07070-
```

If you specify sliding columns, you can clean up the unnecessary spaces between the columns. For the last name, state, and zip, you would choose Slide Left from the Position tab page. This forces the specified columns to slide to the left and removes the gaps between the columns. To correct the address problem, on the City, State, and Zip columns, select Slide/Directly Above to make all three slide up when nothing is specified in the Address2 column. For the Address2 column, you must turn on the option Autosize Height from the Position tab page. This causes the Address2 column to collapse if no data is in it. If you don't specify Autosize Height, the DataWindow object maintains the size of the Address2 column even if it's empty.

**Note**

If column borders are overlapping, columns will slide beneath each other and look nasty. Unfortunately, this also sometimes occurs when the borders don't overlap. The best way to correct this is to delete the offending columns and then add them back to the DataWindow and reset the slide properties.

# DataWindow Enhancements

In addition to all the formatting you've seen so far (for example, edit styles and colors), several supplementary objects can be placed on a DataWindow to enhance its functionality and interface. These objects include static text, computed columns, bitmap images, graphs, graphics objects, nested reports, and OLE objects. These objects are accessed from a drop-down toolbar (see Figure 6.45) or from the Objects menu.

**FIGURE 6.45**
*The object drop-down toolbar.*

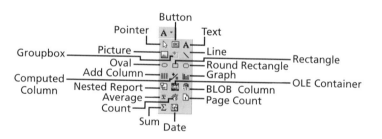

# Static Text Objects

By default, PowerBuilder places some static text fields on DataWindow objects, such as headings and labels. Additional static text fields can be placed on the DataWindow object to enhance the user presentation.

If a new column is added to a report band, a label or heading isn't created for the column. Therefore, you must create one. Another use for static text objects is report headings. To add a text object to a DataWindow, click the Text icon on the drop-down toolbar and click somewhere in the DataWindow object to place the text. After the text is placed on the DataWindow, you can manipulate it to match the formatting of the other fields.

> **Note**
>
> To copy the format of an existing text object or column, select the object before placing the new text or column in the DataWindow. Any text object or column placed into the DataWindow object automatically assumes the formatting of the previously selected object (this doesn't include the border style, however).

To modify the information in the text (that is, change the font, the justification, or the verbiage in the text object), you can use the StyleBar located at the top of the DataWindow painter (see Figure 6.46).

**FIGURE 6.46**

*The StyleBar.*

On the StyleBar, you can change the default text value of text to something a little more meaningful. Click in the single-line edit on the left side of the StyleBar to change the text. If you want the text to span more than one line, all you need to do is resize the object so that the desired text is forced to the next line. If you need to force text to the next line (if you can't position the values as desired), use the ASCII characters for a carriage return (~r) and new line (~n).

> **Tip**
>
> The easiest way to change the text for applicable objects is to simply select the text and then type the new words.

In addition to changing the text value on the StyleBar, you can also change the font type; the font size; whether the font is bold, italicized, or underlined; and the alignment of the text (left, centered, right, or justified).

## Computed Columns

Earlier in this chapter, you saw a reference to creating computed columns in the DataWindow object resultset. Computed columns are calculated on the server and are static until the data is retrieved again. In addition to the columns specified in the resultset for your DataWindow, you can add client-side computed columns. Similar to the server-side computed columns, these columns are used to perform calculations. These computed columns are different from the calculated columns defined in the SQL Select painter because they aren't static fields. The values in a computed column change as the data displayed in the DataWindow object is changed.

The decision to use a client-side column versus a server-side column depends on the functionality of the DataWindow and the type of calculation. If you anticipate that users will be able to change data and will expect to see the changes reflected in the computed column, use a client-side computed column.

To create a computed column on your DataWindow, click the Computed Column icon on the drop-down toolbar. Next, determine where on the DataWindow you want to place the computed column and click that report band. This opens the Modify Expression dialog where you can enter the computation. The Computed Object property sheet appears as soon as you close the dialog (see Figure 6.47).

**FIGURE 6.47**
*The Computed Object property sheet.*

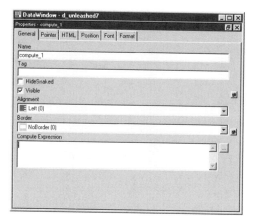

Where you place the computed column depends on what you want that particular field to accomplish. If you want the computed column to appear for every row in the resultset, place the column in the detail band. To show summary statistics for a group, place the column in the group header or footer. Any summarization that you want for the whole report should be placed in the summary band, and, if it's to be repeated on each page, use the header and footer bands.

In the Computed Object property pane, specify a name for the computed column on the General tab page. This enables you to reference the column in your scripts and in other computed columns and to sort on the column. At the bottom of the tab page is a multiline edit box where you write the column expression. The expression can consist of the other columns being retrieved, other computed columns, PowerScript operators, and PowerScript DataWindow functions.

To place a column or function in the expression box, click the button with an ellipsis (...) to open the Modify Expression dialog. Select the desired function name in the Functions list or the desired column in the Columns list. The function and column are pasted into the Expression box. When a function is pasted into the Expression box, the arguments that the function is expecting (if any) are highlighted (see Figure 6.48).

**FIGURE 6.48**

*The Modify Expression dialog using the* Sum() *function.*

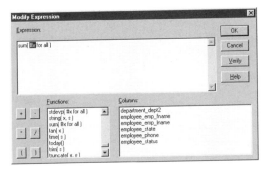

The required data type is designated by the character specified in the argument list (for example, s = String, x = Number, and b = Boolean). When all arguments and functions have been specified for the column, click the Verify button to determine whether the expression is valid. PowerBuilder kindly tells you that the expression is invalid and might give some hint as to what's wrong (for example, Function is expecting a string value ). If you don't know a function or the syntax, you can look in the online help to find all the functions listed in the Functions list box. After the expression is verified successfully, click OK to return to the General tab page. The rest of the Computed Object property sheet allows you to define the font, position, pointer, format, and attribute expressions for the new column just as you would for any other DataWindow column. To modify a computed column definition, select the column and from the General tab page in the Property pane, you can directly edit the expression or use the ... button to reopen the Modify Expression dialog.

**Tip**

A common need for a computed column that's not an obvious calculation is creating a total for that column based on specific criteria. For example, an application needs to compute the total number of active customers (indicated by the value A for the column status). The computed column would be `sum(if(status = 'A', 1, 0) for all)`. A value of 1 is generated for each row with an active status, and then each row with a value of 1 is included in the sum to give a total count.

As well as allowing you to create your own computed columns, PowerBuilder provides many commonly used computed columns to save you the time and effort of having to redefine the field every time you need it. These columns are available as icons on the PainterBar and by choosing Control from the Insert menu (as you will soon see).

To add the page number to the bottom of each page, click the Page Computed Field icon on the drop-down toolbar, or from the Insert menu choose Control and then Page[ ] of [ ]. Then click the footer band. The page number computed column generates the expression

```
'Page ' + page() + ' of ' + pageCount()
```

Another predefined computed field is the current date. This field is usually placed in the header or the footer band. To place it on the DataWindow, click the Today's Date icon on the drop-down toolbar or from the Insert menu choose Control and then `Today()`. Then click the appropriate band. The computed column definition consists of the PowerScript function `Today()`.

The Sum computed field enables you to summarize a detail band column containing a number or amount (for example, salary). To create a summary column, you must first select the field in the detail band that you want to summarize. Click the Sum icon on the drop-down toolbar or choose Control and then Sum from the Insert menu.

If your DataWindow object contains group bands, the computed column sums by group and is placed in the group footer band. If it doesn't, the column calculates the sum for the whole report in the summary band.

Working under the same principle as the summary computed column, you also can create computed columns that determine the average value of a column or count the number of occurrences of an item. To create either column, you must choose Control from the Insert menu or click the Average or Count icon on the drop-down toolbar.

## Pictures

Another object that can be added for display purposes only is a picture object. The picture object is often used to show a company logo in the background of a report. To place a picture on your DataWindow object, click the Picture drop-down toolbar icon and click the band in which you want the picture to appear. This brings up the Select Picture dialog. After you select your image, it is drawn in the Design and Preview panes, and the Picture Object property sheet is shown (see Figure 6.49).

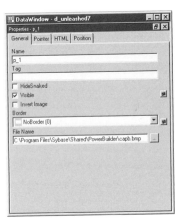

**FIGURE 6.49**

*The Picture Object property sheet.*

The picture you want included in your DataWindow is specified in the File Name single-line edit box. You can specify five different types of graphics files: BMP, RLE, WMF, GIF, and JPEG. If you don't know the directory and filename of the graphics file you want to display, click the browse button (with the ...) to locate the desired file.

On the General tab, you can give the picture object a name (so you can reference the object in your code), and you can select whether you want a border around the image and whether you want the image inverted. The Invert Image check box reverses the colors of the graphics file (that is, it creates a negative image).

To make a picture object display in its original size, right-click the object and select Original Size from the pop-up menu. At any time, you still can increase and decrease the size of the picture by using the mouse.

The problem that now exists is how to get the picture object to not overlay your columns and headings. To do this, place the picture object in the background layer of the DataWindow. PowerBuilder provides a series of layers that control which objects can be placed on top of other objects.

# Layers

The DataWindow object has three levels of depth, or *layers*: the background, the band, and the foreground (see Figure 6.50).

FIGURE **6.50**
*DataWindow layers.*

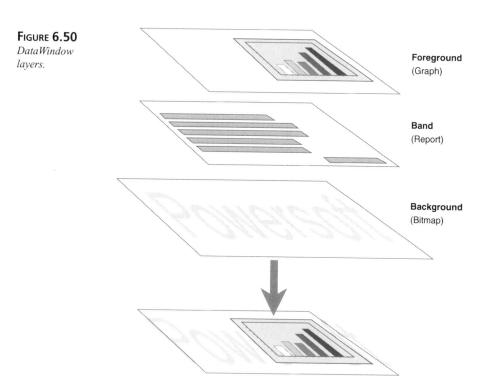

**Foreground**
(Graph)

**Band**
(Report)

**Background**
(Bitmap)

The background layer is usually used for placing picture objects (for example, a company logo). The band layer contains the report itself (this is the default location for almost all objects, except graphs). The foreground layer is most often used for objects that are for display purposes rather than for printing. The most common example of an object that resides in the foreground is a graph (see the next section for more information on graphs).

If an object is created in the band layer and you want it to appear in the foreground or background, open the object's property sheet and select the Position tab page. Within the Layer drop-down list box are the options to specify a DataWindow object in the foreground, band, or background layer. Select the appropriate layer and rearrange the DataWindow to appear as desired (for example, if a picture is sent to the background layer, all other objects can be placed on top of it).

**Note**

A common use of the background layer is to place drawing objects behind columns so that the columns appear to be grouped together. This is a problem when you're using a nested report. Because the nested report resizes depending on the data retrieved, it will dynamically change in size, and the drawing objects don't automatically move with it.

# Graphs

In addition to the Graph presentation style, you also can add a graph to any existing DataWindow object (see Figure 6.51).

**FIGURE 6.51**

*A tabular Data-Window object with a graph object in the foreground layer.*

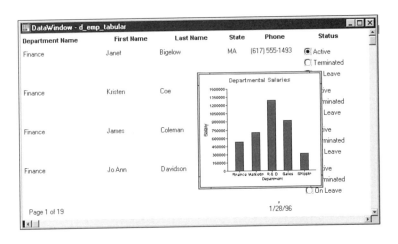

To add a graph, create your base DataWindow object and then click the Graph drop-down toolbar icon or choose Control and then Graph from the Insert menu. Click where you want the graph to appear, which opens the Graph Data dialog (see Figure 6.52).

After you close the dialog, the graph is added to the DataWindow, and the General tab page of the graph's Property pane is shown. This is the same property sheet used in the graph presentation style. From the Rows drop-down list box on the Data tab, specify which rows the graph corresponds to: All (all rows in the DataWindow object) or Page (all rows on the current page). Specify the Category, Value, and optional Series, and click OK. PowerBuilder then creates the default column chart. The graph can be modified just as in the Graph presentation style (for more information on graphing, see Chapter 31.

FIGURE 6.52
*The Graph Data
dialog.*

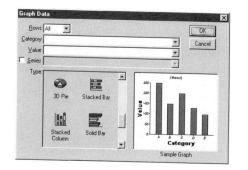

To provide a more friendly interface, you can allow users to move the graph and still view the underlying report. To incorporate this functionality, open the property sheet and select the Position tab. Be sure that the graph is in the foreground layer and select Moveable and Resizable. Users now can click the report, drag it to a new location, and resize the graph to make it larger or smaller.

# Drawing Objects

Several objects exist in the DataWindow painter that simply add artistic value to the DataWindow object. These are rectangles, lines, ovals, and round rectangles. None of these objects has any major significance to the DataWindow, but they are useful for grouping different parts of the report logically. You can also use static text objects for drawing purposes. For example, a 3D raised or lowered text object with no text is useful for grouping objects because it gives you border effects without having to use the line objects.

# GroupBox Objects

The GroupBox object behaves the same as its control counterpart in that it's a frame used to logically group related information and it provides a label to describe the related data. The GroupBox will slide similarly to other drawing objects and can be created or destroyed with the Modify() function.

# Nested Reports

In addition to placing nested graphs, you can also place (or nest) an entire report on a DataWindow object (see Figure 6.53).

To place a nested report on your existing DataWindow object, click the Nested Report icon on the drop-down toolbar or choose Control and then Report from the Insert menu.

A nested report simply consists of another DataWindow object. The report can be dropped in any band of the DataWindow object. After you click the location for the nested report, the Select Report dialog opens, and you can choose the DataWindow object you want.

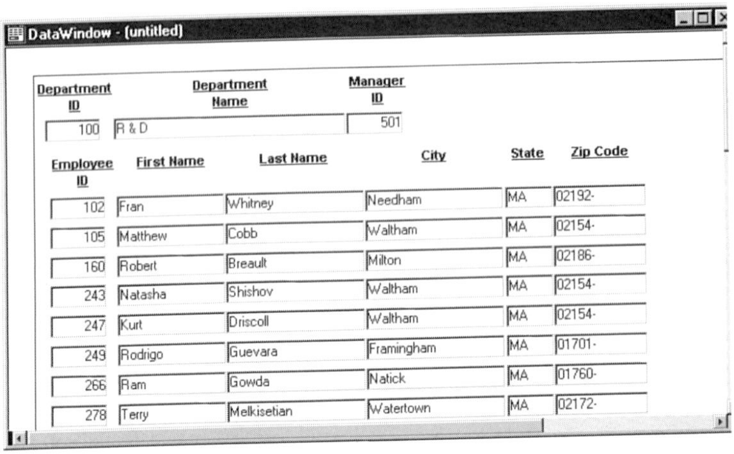

**FIGURE 6.53**

*A nested report.*

In the Design pane, the nested DataWindow appears as a blank box with the DataWindow object's name on it. This box can be moved and resized to appear exactly as you want it. As the name implies, you're creating a nested report. This means that neither the newly created DataWindow object nor the one just dropped on your DataWindow is editable. Therefore, a nested report is for view-only purposes.

Initially, each report retrieves and displays its data independently of the other DataWindow. Although this might be acceptable in some cases, more often than not you will want to establish a relationship between the two reports. Create the association between the two reports by using retrieval arguments or specific criteria.

To associate the reports using retrieval arguments, the nested report must have one or more retrieval arguments defined. The data from the base report is then used to feed data to the retrieval arguments. After defining the retrieval arguments in the nested report (refer to the earlier section "The SQL Select Painter"), select the nested report to display the properties, and the Arguments information will appear on the General tab (see Figure 6.54). (Note that if no retrieval arguments are specified for the nested report, this information won't display within the Property pane.)

This area lists all the retrieval arguments in the nested report and their corresponding data types. The last column asks for an expression that you want the retrieval argument to equal. You can type something in, like a column name or a constant value, or click the ... button to open the (by now familiar) Modify Expression dialog.

You can create any expression in this dialog using column names, functions, and arithmetic operators. Most likely, you will choose a column name from the base report. When this is done, the two reports will be in sync.

**FIGURE 6.54**

*The Argument properties.*

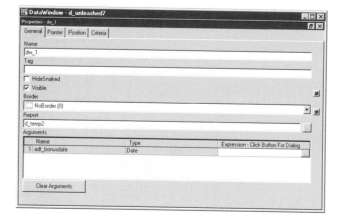

The other way to associate the two reports is to use criteria. To accomplish this, select the Criteria tab and then choose the ... button to display the Specify Retrieval Criteria dialog (see Figure 6.55).

**FIGURE 6.55**

*The Specify Retrieval Criteria dialog.*

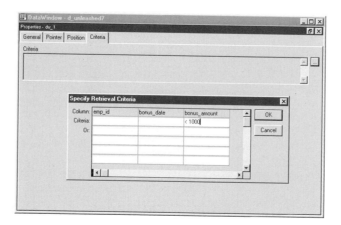

This dialog behaves the same as the Quick Select data source. Criteria specified on the same line are joined by an AND operator, and criteria on different lines are joined by an OR. This is useful if the DataWindows being used don't have retrieval arguments defined. PowerBuilder then retrieves the data according to the specifications in the tab.

A similar process holds true with nested reports placed onto a Composite DataWindow presentation. Even though Composite DataWindows don't have a data source option as do other presentation styles, you can still define retrieval arguments for them. You do this by using the Property pane for the DataWindow object and defining the arguments in the lower area of the pane. Retrieval arguments can be defined here just as in the SQL painter, and you will be prompted for a value when you retrieve for the DataWindow. After one or more retrieval arguments are defined, you can reference the arguments in each nested report on each of their General tabs (refer to Figure 6.54).

## OLE Objects

Another object that you can place on a DataWindow object is the OLE object. *Object linking and embedding* (OLE) is a Windows technology for interprocess communication (IPC) between Windows applications. OLE enables two Windows applications to talk to each other and integrate with one another (for example, using Excel to perform calculations and pass data to your PowerBuilder application). The DataWindow painter supports OLE Version 2.0.

To create an OLE database column on your DataWindow, choose Control and then OLE Database BLOB from the Insert menu or click the BLOB Column icon on the drop-down toolbar and click the DataWindow to place the OLE column. The Database Binary/Text Large Object (BLOB) dialog opens the OLE class description (see Figure 6.56), requesting that you specify information about the database column to which the OLE object is saved.

**FIGURE 6.56**
*The Database Binary/Text Large Object dialog.*

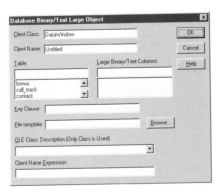

You can also add an OLE container object to your DataWindow presentation by clicking the OLE Container icon on the object drop-down toolbar or choosing Control and then OLE Object from the Insert menu. This opens the Insert Object property sheet, which allows you to specify an OLE server object that's embedded or linked into your DataWindow object. (For a more in-depth look at OLE, see Chapter 37, "ActiveX and OLE.")

# The Button Object

PowerBuilder 6.0 introduced to the DataWindow painter what InfoMaker has had for a while in its Forms painter: a button object. The button object can be a standard command button or a picture button. After placing the button object in one of the bands (most likely the header band), the button's Property pane (see Figure 6.57) can be used to specify the details of the button object.

FIGURE 6.57
*The Button Object property pane.*

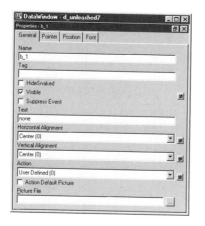

As with a standard button control, you can specify a name for the button and the Text property to appear on the button. You can also specify where the Text property appears by using the Vertical and Horizontal Alignment options. The Vertical Alignment options are to have the button text placed at the top, bottom, or center of the button. You can also specify whether the button displays multiple lines of text with this property. The Horizontal Alignment options are what you would expect: Left, Right, and Center. These are useful if you want to use a picture on your button so that the text can appear underneath or above the picture.

To specify a picture, you can choose your own picture by clicking the Browse button (with the ...) and selecting a graphics filename or typing the name directly into the Picture File edit box on the General tab. You can change the size of the picture by changing the size of the button or by using the Original Size option available from the button's pop-up menu. You can also specify that the button use the default picture that PowerBuilder associates with a button action. To do this, check the Action Default Picture check box.

This brings us to the most important part of the button object, which is the functionality it performs. You have one of two choices. You can select one of the predefined actions from the Action drop-down list box or leave it as its default, User Defined. The predefined actions for the button object are as follows:

- *Append Row* adds a row as the last row in the DataWindow.

- *Cancel* cancels a retrieve in progress that was started as Retrieve with Yield.

- *Delete Row* deletes the current row if the button isn't in the detail band. If the button is in the detail band, the row with which the button is associated is deleted.

- *Filter* opens the Filter dialog.

- *Insert Row* inserts a row directly above the current row if the button isn't in the detail band. If the button is in the detail band, a row is inserted above the row on which the button was clicked.

- *Page First* scrolls to the first page.

- *Page Last* scrolls to the last page.

- *Page Next* scrolls to the next page

- *Page Prior* scrolls to the preceding page.

- *Preview* toggles the DataWindow between Print Preview mode and Preview mode.

- *Preview with Rulers* toggles the rulers on and off in Print Preview mode.

- *Print* sends the DataWindow to the printer.

- *Query Clear* clears any criteria and sort specifications set previously in Query mode and Query Sort mode.

- *Query Mode* displays the DataWindow in Query mode.

- *Query Sort* displays the DataWindow in Query mode with sorting capabilities.

- *Retrieve* retrieves data into the DataWindow.

- *Retrieve (Yield)* retrieves data into the DataWindow with the capability to cancel the retrieval process.

- *Save Rows As* opens the Save As dialog.

- *Sort* opens the Sort dialog.

- *Update* saves changes to the database. If the changes are successful, a COMMIT is performed; otherwise, a ROLLBACK is performed.

The other option is to leave User Defined for the Action drop-down list box, which triggers the ButtonClicking and ButtonClicked events for the corresponding DataWindow control. In these events, you can write your own specific code. For more information on these events, see Chapter 14, "DataWindow Scripting."

The last option on the General tab for the button object is whether you suppress the ButtonClicking and ButtonClicked event processing. If the Suppress Event check box is clicked, PowerBuilder executes the action specified in the Action drop-down list box. If the check box isn't checked, the ButtonClicking event is triggered. If this event returns a 0, the button action is executed. After this action is executed, the ButtonClicked event is triggered. If the ButtonClicking event returns 1, this prevents the button action from executing and the ButtonClicked event from firing.

The button object allows you to implement much of the common functionality used in a DataWindow within the DataWindow object. The added plus is that it requires no additional coding effort. This can be used in a traditional client/server application and considerably extends the functionality of the DataWindow as a component. For more information on PowerBuilder and the Internet, see Chapter 29, "PowerBuilder and the Internet."

# Object Attributes

You've seen that several different objects can be placed on a DataWindow object (for example, headings, columns, and pictures). Each object has attributes you can modify at design time or at runtime. These attributes used to be accessed through a separate dialog in previous versions. Starting with PowerBuilder 7.0, all of these are accessible from within one of the tab pages within an object's property pane.

You can create an expression for certain attributes by clicking the small button with a picture of a red not equal to symbol (no expression defined) or a green equal sign (expression already defined) to manipulate the values assigned to that attribute. For example, a salary column might have the following expression associated with it for the Color attribute:

```
if(salary > 50000, 255, 0)
```

This expression evaluates the value of the salary column to see whether it's greater than 50,000. If the expression is TRUE, the color of the text for the column is red (RGB value of 255); otherwise, the color is black (RGB value of 0). This would be defined on the Font tab page for the Text Color property.

Another common use of the expressions is to change the column object's Color, Visible, and Protect properties based on security settings. You can retrieve user security information into a DataWindow column or have a computed column that calls a global function that returns a user's security. Based on the value of that column, you can change whether users can modify the data, read the data, or not see that data at all.

Numerous tasks can be carried out with a minimal amount of code by using object expressions within a DataWindow. For example, consider protecting the key columns of a DataWindow for existing rows but allowing values to be entered for new rows. Sounds like a lot of code would be required spread around various controls and events of your application? Actually, it can be done using one expression entered for each key column. On the General tab page, click the Expression button for the Protect property and enter the following piece of code:

```
if(IsRowNew(), 0, 1)
```

All other attributes can also have their values modified as the result of an expression. In some cases, specifying an expression at design time achieves the desired result. Unfortunately, this isn't always the case. You might need to dynamically set the expression to modify an attribute of an object on the DataWindow. This is accomplished by using the direct access syntax or the PowerScript function `Modify()` (see Chapter 15, "Advanced DataWindow Techniques I," on how to use both methods).

# Column Specifications

In the lower area of the painter is the Column Specifications property pane (see Figure 6.58).

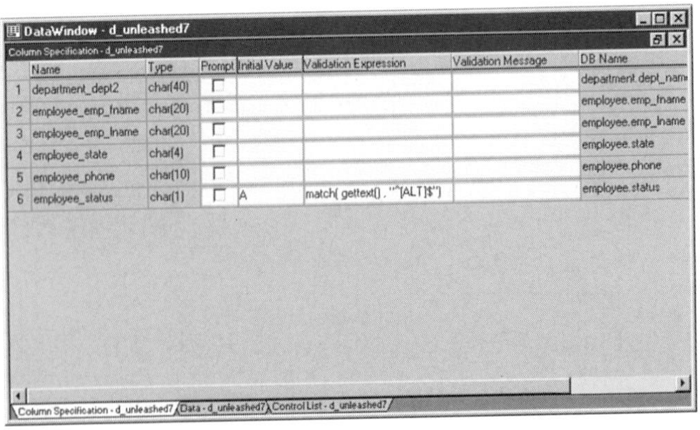

**FIGURE 6.58**

*The Column Specifications property pane.*

This pane displays information about the columns specified in the DataWindow resultset. It lists the names of the objects in the DataWindow; their data types, initial values, validation rules, and validation messages; and the corresponding database column name. Not all fields are specified or need to be. This provides a quick and easy way to add or change validation information and initial values. The validation rules and the initial values will default from the PowerBuilder repository tables situated on the database (if specified) and can then be changed.

# Row Manipulation

After you add all the objects you need to your DataWindow object and have customized their appearance, you can use some additional functions that enable you to manipulate the rows retrieved from the data source. From within the DataWindow painter, you can perform sorting and filtering, import and export data, prompt users to specify retrieval criteria, retrieve data only as you need it, and update specifications.

## Sorting

Sorting can be performed on the client side or the server side. On the server, the sorting is specified by the ORDER BY clause in a SQL SELECT statement. The sorting is handled by the DBMS, and the resultset is returned sorted to the DataWindow.

An alternative to using the ORDER BY clause is to carry out the sorting within the DataWindow object. Sorting on the client is often desirable because it simply re-sorts the data in memory as opposed to issuing another SELECT statement against the database, which could be expensive and an unnecessary waste of resources. Determining where the processing should occur is often dictated by the requirements of the system, the hardware available for server and client, and the server load. You should perform testing to determine whether one location provides better performance than the other. The most frequent location of sorting is within the client itself, to remove the load from the server. Why have the power of a PC on the desktop if it will be used just for displaying data instead of manipulating it?

Specifying sort criteria on the client can be done in Design and Preview modes in the DataWindow painter. In both cases, select Sort from the Rows menu. This opens the Specify Sort Columns dialog (see Figure 6.59).

**FIGURE 6.59**

*The Specify Sort Columns dialog.*

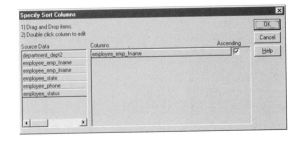

To specify sorting on one or more columns, click the column name in the Source Data list box and drag and drop it into the Columns list box. To specify an ascending sort, make sure that the Ascending check box is checked. When the columns have been placed in the Columns list box, you can change the order by clicking and dragging the columns within the list box. To remove a column from the sort order, just click and drag it outside the Columns list box.

In addition to sorting based on a column, the sort criteria can also be based on an expression. To sort on an expression, double-click a column that has been placed in the Columns list box. This opens the Modify Expression dialog.

Although it's nice that you can specify sorting in the DataWindow painter, it's more likely to be users who want to change the sorting of the data. The same process can be performed at runtime if you use the SetSort() and Sort() functions. See Chapter 16, "Advanced DataWindow Techniques II," for more information on these functions.

## Filtering

Similar in concept to performing a client-side sort, the DataWindow object also enables you to do client-side filtering. A *filter* is an expression that evaluates to a Boolean value (TRUE or FALSE) and is used to limit the data users see. You can, and should, limit the data from the server using the WHERE or HAVING clauses in your SELECT statement. But if users want to continually change the data displayed, constantly sending new queries to the database wouldn't be effective or efficient. Instead, it might make more sense to retrieve all the required data into memory and enable users to filter out the data they don't want to see. Doing this reduces network traffic in the long run with a one-time performance hit and gives your users more flexibility.

To create a filter in the DataWindow painter, select Filter from the Rows menu in Design or Preview mode. This opens the Specify Filter dialog (see Figure 6.60).

The Specify Filter dialog is similar to many other dialogs you've already seen that are used to create expressions. The expression, as previously mentioned, must evaluate to TRUE or FALSE. The expression can consist of columns, relational operators, functions, and values.

**FIGURE 6.60**
*The Specify Filter dialog.*

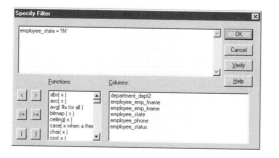

The expressions can be connected using the AND and OR operators and can also contain NOT for negating expressions. Use parentheses judiciously to specify which expression is evaluated first. In addition to using the functions specified in the Specify Filter dialog, you can also use an application global function. After the expression is written, click the Verify button to check whether the expression is valid.

The filtered out data is still in memory (see Chapter 14 for more information on DataWindow buffers) and can be redisplayed to users if you redefine or remove the filter expression. Just as sorting can be done at runtime, so can filtering, if you use the SetFilter() and Filter() functions. See Chapter 16 for more information on these functions.

## Importing and Exporting Data

You can import data to and export data from a DataWindow object. To import data, select Import from the Rows menu in Preview mode in the DataWindow painter. The Select Import File dialog asks you for the name of a tab-separated text file or a dBASE II or III (.DBF) file. If the file layout matches the columns specified for the DataWindow, the data is imported into the DataWindow layout. If the columns don't match, PowerBuilder displays a message box indicating the mismatch and asks whether you want to continue inserting rows from the file. After the import is completed, you must click the Save Changes to Database icon on the PainterBar to save the data back into the current database.

To export data, select Save Rows As from the File menu while in Preview mode. This opens the Save As dialog (see Figure 6.61), which has a drop-down list box that provides many different file formats in which the data can be saved (for example, as an Excel spreadsheet, a SQL statement, or a tab-separated text file).

**FIGURE 6.61**
*The Save As dialog.*

> ### Tip
>
> A helpful format for saving is as an HTML table. This is useful when you're creating a Web page using data because PowerBuilder generates the table tags (<TABLE></TABLE>) and the corresponding detail tags utilizing the DataWindow data.

See Chapter 14 for a full description of the file formats and the SaveAs() function, which lets you display the Save As dialog at runtime.

## Prompting for Criteria

Similarly to specifying a retrieval argument, prompting for criteria enables the selection of data to be more dynamic because users can specify selection criteria. To implement selection criteria, select Column Specification view. This view shows a list of the columns in your DataWindow object.

Select those columns for which you want users to be able to specify additional selection criteria by using the Prompt check box. When you preview the DataWindow or specify the Retrieve() function, the Specify Retrieval Criteria dialog opens (see Figure 6.62).

The Specify Retrieval Criteria dialog works similarly to the Quick Select data source. The column names that you selected in the Prompt For Criteria dialog appear along the top of this dialog. Under any of the columns, users can specify criteria to limit the data retrieved from the database. Any typed-in criteria is used in the SQL statement's WHERE clause.

**FIGURE 6.62**

*The Specify Retrieval Criteria dialog.*

> ## Caution
>
> When using Prompt For Criteria, don't specify a WHERE clause on the data source. This is because anything specified in the Specify Retrieval Criteria dialog is added with a logical AND into your WHERE clause; thus, you could end up with conflicting retrieval criteria and have peculiar results.

To specify criteria, type your criteria on the rows beneath the column names. If criteria are typed on the same line, they're joined by a logical AND. If the criteria are on different lines, they're joined by a logical OR. When criteria have been specified, click OK to execute the SQL SELECT statement with the new WHERE clause. Note that if no criteria are specified, the SELECT statement runs like a standard DataWindow retrieval.

# Retrieving Rows as Needed

You've just seen that, by specifying WHERE clauses and prompting users for additional criteria, you can limit the amount of data being retrieved from the database. It's generally a good idea to limit what's retrieved to reduce long-running queries that consume resources and, worse yet, frustrate users because they have to wait to see the data.

> ## Tip
>
> Remember that filters apply after the data is retrieved from the database, so you still get all the data passed from the server to the client machine.

You have several options to prevent a SELECT statement from running too long and retrieving excessive amounts of data. A simple option is to choose Retrieve Options and then Retrieve, Rows As Needed from the Rows menu. This option retrieves only as many rows as are necessary to display data in the DataWindow; therefore, PowerBuilder needs to retrieve only a small number of rows, and control is returned to users much more quickly.

As users scroll through the data using a resultset cursor, PowerBuilder continues to retrieve the data necessary for display purposes until the end of the result is reached.

Although this is a good option because it provides the appearance of increased performance, it does have its drawbacks. Because PowerBuilder is getting data as it needs it, it's maintaining a connection and, therefore, holding resources on the server. This may result in a locking scheme that's detrimental to the performance of other users. Also, if you're using aggregate functions in any computed fields on the DataWindow, such as Avg() and Sum(), Retrieve Rows As Needed is overridden.

PowerBuilder can retrieve rows to disk, meaning that you can write rows out as they're retrieved to a temporary file on the hard drive to free up your client's memory. The benefit of this option is that it increases the number of rows that can be retrieved from the database. Although this might be useful, you suffer a performance hit because PowerBuilder has to read and write to the hard drive to access the data during the retrieval and any client-side aggregate functions such as filtering and sorting.

# Update Characteristics

One reason the DataWindow object is so powerful is the ease of modifying the database. After you modify data, insert new rows, and delete rows, all you need to do is call the Update() function. This generates the necessary SQL statements (INSERT, UPDATE, and DELETE) and sends them to the database.

For DataWindow objects that have one table as a data source, PowerBuilder uses defaults for how the SQL statements are to be created. Many times this is satisfactory, but sometimes you might want to change the defaults. How you change the update options depends on your application's needs for concurrency and data integrity.

When more than one table is specified in the data source, you must specify how the DataWindow object is going to perform updates to the database. You must specify that updates are in fact allowed, which table is the destination, and which columns are needed to carry out updates.

To change how updates are performed for the DataWindow object, select Update Properties from the Rows menu, which opens the Specify Update Properties dialog (see Figure 6.63).

When you first create the DataWindow, PowerBuilder decides whether the DataWindow object is updatable. It bases its decision on whether the data is coming from one or more tables and whether the primary keys are being retrieved. The Allow Updates check box in this dialog indicates whether you can update the DataWindow object.

**FIGURE 6.63**

*The Specify Update Properties dialog.*

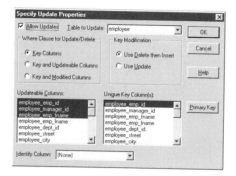

Notice that the list box next to the Allow Updates check box says Table to Update. This means that only one table can be updated in a DataWindow via this method (to see how to update multiple tables on a DataWindow object, see Chapter 14,). If your resultset pulls data from multiple tables, PowerBuilder automatically specifies the DataWindow as not updatable and sets the tab order of all columns to 0 when it's first created.

After checking the Allow Updates check box, select the table that you want the DataWindow to update from the Table to Update drop-down list box.

The next step is to identify which columns on the DataWindow can be updated. Click the columns you want to be able to update in the Updateable Columns list box. Remember, if you have more than one table in your data source, you can update columns in only one of those tables, although all column names appear in the list.

---

**Note**

If you choose a column from a different table that's not valid in the table to be updated, PowerBuilder will generate a runtime error when trying to execute the data modification SQL. This is because it will have included the column and its data value as part of the SQL.

---

After you select which columns you want to update, use the Unique Key Column(s) list box to select the columns that make a row unique. If the primary keys have been specified in your SQL Selection List, you can click the Primary Key button, which checks the specified update table and selects those primary key columns for you.

# Identity

Another option on the Specify Update Properties dialog is the Identity Column drop-down list box. This list box is used to specify sequence number generation for the column specified in the drop-down list (usually the key column). This option applies only to DBMSs that support sequence number generation (also known as *autoincrement columns*).

> **Caution**
>
> If you specify a column as an identity column, don't select it as an updatable column. Otherwise, any UPDATES you perform to the database will fail.

After a new row is saved to the database, PowerBuilder acquires the new value assigned to the identity column and updates the appropriate column in the DataWindow for you.

# Optimistic Locking

There are two ways to update data that users have displayed and modified. The first requires you to lock the data record(s) for the duration of the users' interaction with them. This method requires the acquisition of exclusive database locks to be held until the end of the transaction and can severely affect other users' use of the database tables involved. The second, most common, method uses *optimistic locking*, which does not actually acquires or hold onto any locks for the duration of the time users have the data. Rather it determines at the time of the data modification whether a change has been made by someone else during the time another user was working with the data. The following sections show how optimistic locking can be applied to DataWindow updates.

The Where Clause for Update/Delete group box contains three radio buttons that tell PowerBuilder how to build the WHERE clause in the UPDATE and DELETE SQL statements. The three buttons provide different options for maintaining data integrity and provide a different option from database locking. Rather than lock a row or page (depending on the database-locking granularity), when a row is selected and preventing other users from retrieving the row, you can provide integrity protection via the DataWindow object. The three options are Key Columns, Key and Updateable Columns, and Key and Modified Columns.

# Key Columns

If you specify Key Columns, the DataWindow uses only the key columns specified in the Unique Key Column(s) list box. This option is often used with single-user applications. When PowerBuilder generates an UPDATE or a DELETE statement, it compares the value of the originally retrieved key column for a row, against the value of the key column of that row in the database. If the two values are equal, the update or delete is successful.

Suppose that Simon and Ulric retrieved the following row from the customer table, where Customer_ID is the primary key, and the name, status, and region are updatable:

```
Customer ID: 110
Customer Name: Andrea Gallagher
Status: Preferred
Region: Midwest
```

If Ulric changed the region from Midwest to Southeast, the following UPDATE statement would be generated using key columns:

```
UPDATE customer
SET region = "Southeast"
WHERE customer_id = 110
```

This UPDATE statement will be successful. There will be a problem if Simon also makes changes to the row (for example, changes the region to Northwest); however, Ulric's changes would be overwritten because the key column hasn't been changed. Therefore, in this example, you have high concurrency (both users could access and change the data), but your data integrity is poor.

# Key and Updatable Columns

When the Key and Updateable Columns option is specified, PowerBuilder creates UPDATE and DELETE statements that compare the originally retrieved value for the key columns and the originally retrieved value of any column specified as updatable against the same values in the database. If the values are equal, the update or delete takes place. This is the preferred method because it provides high data integrity.

**Tip**

If you have any approximate numeric data types (real, float, and so on) in the list of updatable columns, then you may have to choose the Key Columns option. This is because of potential rounding problems between PowerBuilder and the DBMS where the same row can't be found due to a mismatch on what PowerBuilder and the DBMS think the value of the approximate number is.

Using the same example, Ulric's change to the region generates the following SQL statement:

```
UPDATE customer
SET region = "Southeast"
WHERE customer_id = 110
AND name = "Andrea Gallagher"
AND status = "Preferred"
AND region = "Midwest"
```

Ulric's update would be successful. If Simon again made his change to the region and tried to update, the update would fail because the WHERE clause didn't change, but the value of the region in the database is now Southeast instead of Midwest. Data integrity is much higher using key and updatable columns even though concurrency is lower. *Concurrency*, in this instance, means that two or more users can access and modify the data simultaneously.

## Key and Modified Columns

When the Key and Modified Columns option is specified, PowerBuilder creates UPDATE and DELETE statements that compare the originally retrieved value for the key columns and the originally retrieved value of any updatable column that was modified against the same values in the database. If the values are equal, the update or delete takes place. This method is a trade-off between key columns and key and updatable columns.

Using the same example, if Simon and Ulric make changes to the same column (for example, region), the end result is the same: The first update will be successful, and the second will fail. However, if the two users modified different columns, then the update would be successful even though the data for the record had already been changed by another user (the region is different). Therefore, the data integrity is lower, but the concurrency is higher. This option is used when it's okay for two users to modify the same row simultaneously as long as they're changing different pieces of data. This method allows you to change differing values simultaneously (such as Key Column), but provides for some security by not allowing the same value to be changed by two different users (Key Column and Updateable.)

**Note**

When there's an *update collision* (when users have retrieved the same record, one user updates a value, and then another also tries to), you need to code your application to respond appropriately to the situation. PowerBuilder provides the

`ReselectRow()` function, which will refresh a specified DataWindow row with the latest values from the database.

# Time Stamps

If your DBMS supports time stamps, you can maximize data integrity by including the time stamp in your resultset for the DataWindow object. PowerBuilder automatically includes the time stamp in the WHERE clause for your updates and deletes and doesn't display it in the Updateable Columns list. Oracle handles time stamps entirely on the server; no extra work is required in the DataWindow.

This option allows you to leave the default at Key Columns and to reap the benefit of a much smaller SQL statement(s) being sent from PowerBuilder to the DBMS.

# Key Modification

The last component to stipulate in the Specify Update Properties dialog is how modification will take place if users change the value of a key column (the key column or columns must be specified as updatable). The two options are Use Delete then Insert and Use Update.

The first option deletes the row and then inserts a new one using the new key value. This option increases the number of reorganizations needed on the database and also has some potential problems. If a primary key is a foreign key in another table and is specified to use a cascading delete, you probably don't want to use Use Delete then Insert unless the trigger also handles reinserting all the appropriate child data.

**Caution**

Along with possibly triggering cascading deletes, the Use Delete then Insert option has a huge "gotcha" if you retrieve only some of a table's columns. Suppose that only 5 of 20 columns from a table are retrieved and a change is made to the primary key value. Using the Use Delete then Insert option causes the whole row to be deleted and any data in the 15 unretrieved columns to be lost.

The second option, Use Update, updates the key value in the row (only some DBMSs allow key column updates). The new key value is included in the update along with the rest of the data. This prevents the problem with the foreign keys and cascading deletes.

> **Note**
>
> Changing Primary Key values for a table is generally a bad idea and isn't recommended.

## Stored Procedure Updates

A feature of DBMSs that developers have used in the past is that of carrying out all data modifications through stored procedures. This has the advantages of extra security, speed, and carrying out additional business rule checks. It did, however, require a lot of additional coding. New to PowerBuilder 7.0 is the capability to specify stored procedures to be used for `Inserts`, `Updates`, and `Deletes` instead of PowerBuilder having to dynamically generate the requisite SQL statements.

By selecting the Stored Procedure Update menu option under the Rows menu, you open the specification dialog (see Figure 6.64).

FIGURE 6.64
*The Stored Pro-
cedure Update
dialog.*

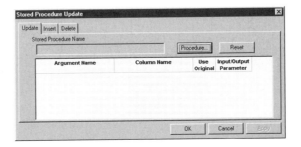

The dialog has a tab for each data modification statement: Update, Insert, and Delete. By using the browse button (with the ...), you can select the desired stored procedure for each action. After the stored procedure is selected, PowerBuilder populates the arguments area. For each argument, you need to specify the following additional information:

- *Column Name* is the name of the DataWindow column that will supply a value for the argument.

- *Use Original* indicates whether the value supplied to the argument is the original as retrieved or the new value as modified by the user. By constructing your stored procedures appropriately, you can carry out the same functionality as described in the earlier section, "Optimistic Locking."

- *Input/Output Parameter* allows you to specify one of three values that indicate the direction the data is to flow between PowerBuilder and the stored procedure:

| | |
|---|---|
| Input | The value is supplied to the stored procedure. |
| Output | The value is supplied to PowerBuilder from the procedure. |
| Input/Output | The value is supplied to the procedure and then overwritten by a new value. |

If you're using Identity values in the database table, you need to use Output or Input/Output parameters so that the stored procedure can pass back the new values.

# Printing

You can set many options to print a DataWindow object. In Design mode, select the Print Specifications tab on the DataWindow Object Property pane (see Figure 6.65).

**FIGURE 6.65**
*The Print Specifications tab.*

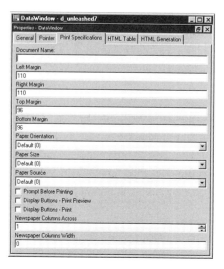

Document Name is the name that appears in the print queue when the DataWindow is printed. The margins (in PowerBuilder units) can be changed for left, right, top, and bottom. The paper orientation, size, and source can also be specified. When checked, the Prompt Before Printing check box displays the Printer Setup dialog before printing begins.

In the bottom section of the Print Specifications tab, you can specify a newspaper-column effect. If you want a report with two columns that read top-to-bottom rather than left-to-right (opposite of the N-Up presentation style), specify 2 in the Newspaper Columns Across single-line edit box and the column width in the Newspaper Columns Width single-line edit box. In addition to specifying this information to get the newspaper columns, you will probably want to use the HideSnaked check box on the General tab page for the Column Object property sheet. (HideSnaked should be used on objects such as column headings and page numbers so that they are printed only once per page and not on every newspaper column on the same page.)

You also can specify whether any button objects on the DataWindow object are printed or viewed in Print Preview mode. This allows you to have the full functionality of the buttons but maintain the richness of your report.

If you are in the Design pane and choose Print from the File menu, the design of the DataWindow object is printed. Several additional printing options appear under the File menu when the Preview pane is selected. In this pane, Print sends the DataWindow object, complete with data, to the printer. If you would rather view the DataWindow object first, select Run/Preview from the File menu and then after selecting the DataWindow, you can choose the Print Preview option from the File menu. When in Print Preview mode, you can select Print Preview Rulers, which places horizontal and vertical rulers on the edges of the DataWindow to help with alignment and spacing. Print Preview Zoom enables you to zoom in or out to view the DataWindow up close or from a distance. For more details on DataWindow printing techniques, see Chapter 16.

> **Note**
>
> PowerBuilder can display scrollbars in Print Preview mode, which is useful when dealing with DataWindows on the Internet. When dragged, the thumb on the scrollbar (the gray square) also displays the current page number, and the screen is refreshed when the thumb is released.

# DataWindow Objects Versus DataWindow Controls

Now that you've created your DataWindow object, you need to place a DataWindow control on a window in the Window painter and associate the DataWindow object with the control. This can be done at design time in the Window painter (see Chapter 10, "Windows and the Window Painter"), or at runtime by setting the `DataObject` attribute of the DataWindow control. The purpose of the DataWindow control is to act as a frame or viewport into the data that the DataWindow object retrieves. To learn more details about how the two link together, see Chapter 14.

# DataWindows and the Internet

Previous versions of PowerBuilder gave developers a limited capability to work DataWindows into their Internet strategy. PowerBuilder 7.0 gives you a DataWindow property, HTML DataWindow, that controls the HTML generated for a DataWindow. By setting this property on, the HTML will use JavaScript to provide update and interactivity functionality.

To control the functionality introduced into the generated HTML, you can set various options on the HTML Generation tab page (see Figure 6.66) for the DataWindow.

**FIGURE 6.66**
*The HTML Gen-eration tab page.*

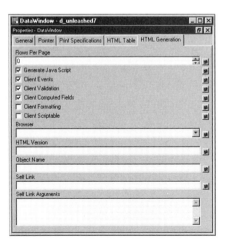

However, certain features available in normal DataWindow use can't be rendered into HTML. These include

- Graph, OLE, and rich text presentation styles and controls

- Aggregate functions used within expressions

- Resizable and movable controls

- Sliding of objects to fill empty space

- Autosizing of object or band, height or width

- EditMasks for column data entry

For additional discussion of these features, see Part V, "Application Partitioning and the Internet," which contains chapters dedicated to PowerBuilder's Internet features.

# Summary

In this chapter, you saw how to create PowerBuilder's most powerful object, the DataWindow object. A DataWindow object has a wide range of presentation styles to choose from to provide an attractive and appropriate user interface. In addition to providing different ways to display data, the DataWindow object can pull information from several different sources.

The DataWindow painter provides a means to create an interface that enables easy access to data (particularly data in a relational database). The DataWindow manages the data and generates all the necessary SQL statements to apply a user's changes to the database. In addition to supplying a method to update a database, the DataWindow painter can be used to create complex reports and graphs as well.

# The PowerScript Language

This chapter introduces you to basic and advanced PowerScript concepts and syntax, object-oriented concepts and the syntax and methods available to implement them, and additional features such as error handling and file processing.

PowerScript, the language used by PowerBuilder, is written using a collection of statements, commands, and functions, with user-defined functions and embedded SQL statements. You write PowerScript for the object events whose actions you want to direct when users trigger them. For example, if you want to close a window when users click a certain command button, you code the appropriate PowerScript statements in the button's `Clicked` event.

# Objects

A PowerBuilder *object* is an application component that has a number of characteristics called *attributes* and behaviors known as *methods* (the collective name for events and functions).

PowerBuilder has many types of objects: applications, windows, menus, global functions, structures, nonvisual user objects, queries, pipelines, and even projects. Within windows and visual user objects, you can place an additional type of object—a control. Each object has a different number of attributes, events, and functions.

## Attributes

An object's *attributes* describe how the object looks (for example, whether it's visible and the color of the text) and the position in which it appears. Some attributes enable or disable certain object behaviors, such as allowing it to be dynamically resized by users. Most of an object's attributes can be set when the object is created and can also be dynamically changed at runtime by using PowerScript.

To access an object's attributes in PowerScript, you use a *dot notation*. The syntax for dot notation is `object`.*attribute*; you can extend off the left side as many objects as you need to point to the correct object/attribute. For example, to access a command button (`cb_close`) within a window (`w_connect`) from a different window, the syntax would be

```
w_connect.cb_close.Enabled = TRUE
```

# PowerScript Basic Concepts

This might seem like an odd section to include in an advanced book; it's really intended for accomplished beginners to intermediate-level developers, and even those who are studying for CPD tests. This short section speeds through the basic ground rules and topics for PowerScript.

## Identifiers

An *identifier*, which can be anything from an object to a variable, must start with a letter and can include the following characters:

- Dash (-)

- Underscore (_)

- Dollar sign ($)

- Pound sign (#)

- Percent sign (%)

The identifier can be up to 99 characters long. PowerBuilder's documentation states a limit of 40, but if you're really desperate for a descriptive name, knock yourself out and go all the way to 99!

That PowerBuilder allows a dash in an identifier is strange, and to prevent yourself from making errors in your expressions, you will want to exercise your right to turn off this feature. In the [pb] section of the PB.INI file is the entry DashesInIdentifiers; to turn off the feature, set this entry equal to 0.

> **Caution**
>
> By default, PowerBuilder uses dashes in the identifiers for separator lines in the Menu painter. If you turn off the dashes in identifiers, you can't save a menu until you rename each separator.

## Labels

A *label* is an identifier followed by a colon (:); it enables you to branch to a certain point within a script and is used with the GOTO statement. You can place any number of labels within a script, although each must be unique. You can't jump to a label in a different script—only to one in the current local scope. For example, to jump to a central point of error handling, you could code the following statements after a SQL statement:

```
If SQLCA.SQLCode <> 0 Then
    Error.Line = 12
    Goto DBError
End If
//
// More of the script here ....
//
Return

DBError:
    error.Object = this.ClassName()
    error.Number = SQLCA.SQLDBCode
    error.Text = SQLCA.SQLErrText
    SQLCA.RollbackTran()
    Open( w_error)
```

### Note

Some developers consider GOTO statements to be "evil" and to be avoided at all costs, but consider that the low-level machine code commands continually branch to implement the desired logic. If you don't use an excessive number of labels—say, no more than three or four—and they are well named and documented in the code, don't hesitate to use a label and GOTO to make your code more concise. If you consider the situation presented in the code example, you would have to code similar statements after each embedded SQL statement rather than the two lines that set the line number and jump. Not only does your code become more concise, but you also have fewer places where you need to make code changes if they're required.

One important statement to remember is Return. It appears in the preceding code example just before the label to prevent the code from "dropping through" into the conditional code. A Return statement immediately terminates script execution and returns to whatever script called the current code. Occasionally you might have to use a GOTO and associated label to leap around areas of code that are reached with other GOTO statements; this might be grounds for reconsidering your logic structure.

# Operators

An *operator* symbolizes the operation performed on one or two operands. PowerScript has four types of operators: arithmetic, relational, logical, and concatenation.

## Arithmetic Operators

*Arithmetic operators* are used for mathematical calculations. Table 7.1 lists the base arithmetic operators and gives an example of each.

**TABLE 7.1**  Base Arithmetic Operators

| Operator | Meaning | Example | Description |
|---|---|---|---|
| + | Addition | n1 = n1 + n2 | Adds n2 to n1 |
| - | Subtraction | n1 = n1 - n2 | Subtracts n2 from n1 |
| - | Negative | n1 = -n1 | Changes the sign of n1—either from negative to positive or vice versa |
| * | Multiplication | n1 = n1 * n2 | Multiplies n1 by n2 |
| / | Division | n1 = n1 / n2 | Divides n1 by n2 |
| ^ | Exponentiation | n1 = n1 ^ n2 | Raises n1 to the n2th power |

Table 7.2 shows the extended arithmetic operators. These operators act on only one operand, and you can't combine them with other operators.

**TABLE 7.2**  Extended Arithmetic Operators

| Operator | Meaning | Example | Description |
|---|---|---|---|
| ++ | Increment | n1 ++ | Increments n1 by 1 |
| - | Decrement | n1 - | Decrements n1 by 1 |
| += | Plus Equals | n1 += n2 | Adds n2 to n1 |
| -= | Minus Equals | n1 -= n2 | Subtracts n2 from n1 |
| *= | Times Equals | n1 *= n2 | Multiplies n1 by n2 |
| /= | Divide Equals | n1 /= n2 | Divides n1 by n2 |
| ^= | Power Equals | n1 ^= n2 | Raises n1 to the n2th power |

**Note**

If you have the `DashesInIdentifiers` option turned on, you must place spaces around the subtraction (-), negative (-), and decrement (- -) operators. Otherwise, PowerBuilder produces an error when compiling the script because it interprets the expression as an undeclared variable.

As with all arithmetic operations, certain types of operations cause runtime errors to occur: attempting to divide by a zero value, causing a Double or a Real data type to overflow, or raising a negative value to a non-integer power. Overflowed integer values cause the resulting value to wrap around to the other end of the range (for example, 32767 + 1 results in the value -32768).

> **Caution**
>
> Overflowing decimals in versions of PowerBuilder prior to 6.0 have a much stranger effect—the resulting value becomes -(Null). This can't be detected with IsNull(), and any expressions that use this value might also result in -(Null) or some other unexpected value.

## Relational Operators

*Relational operators* make a comparison between two operands (which don't have to be numeric). The result of this evaluation can be TRUE, FALSE, or NULL. Table 7.3 lists the relational operators.

**TABLE 7.3**   The Relational Operators

| Operator | Meaning |
|----------|---------|
| = | Equals |
| > | Greater than |
| < | Less than |
| <> | Not equal |
| >= | Greater than or equal to |
| <= | Less than or equal to |

If you're comparing strings, the comparison is case and length sensitive. So, to ensure string matches, you might want to use the Upper() or Lower() function with RightTrim(), LeftTrim(), or Trim().

> **Note**
>
> If you're a C programmer, be aware that the evaluation of an If expression using relational or logical operators in PowerBuilder isn't the same as in C. Each expression is evaluated, and not just up to the point in the expression where it fails (known as *short-circuiting*). Therefore, consider using a Choose...Case construct to evaluate complex, interdependent conditions.

## Logical Operators

*Logical operators* are used to form Boolean expressions, which are expressions that evaluate to TRUE or FALSE. Table 7.4 lists the logical operators and gives an example of each.

TABLE 7.4    The Logical Operators

| Operator | Meaning | Example |
|----------|---------|---------|
| NOT | Logical negation | this.Checked = NOT this.Checked |
|  |  | If NOT ln_Active Then of_Activate() |
| AND | Logical and | If ln_Value > 1 AND ln_Value < 9 Then |
| OR | Logical or | If ln_Value = 1 OR ln_Value = 9 Then |

> **Note**
>
> Unless you're building a simple expression, it always makes good sense to enclose related parts within parentheses. This way, other developers can understand the expression more easily without having to figure out the order of operator precedence.

## The Concatenation Operator

The *concatenation operator* (+) joins the contents of two String or BLOB variables. Both variables must be of the same data type. Here's an example:

```
String ls_String1, ls_String2, ls_String3

ls_String1 = "First"
ls_String2 = "Second"

// ls_String3 now contains: "First Second"
ls_String3 = ls_String1 + ls_String2
```

## Operator Precedence in Expressions

In mathematics, the operators used in expressions are evaluated in a particular order of precedence. You commonly use parentheses to group expressions to aid readability and expected results. Nested groups are evaluated from the inside out. Operators with the same precedence are evaluated from left to right. Table 7.5 lists the operators in descending order of precedence.

**7**

**The PowerScript Language**

**TABLE 7.5**  Descending Order of Operator Precedence

| Operator | Meaning |
| --- | --- |
| +, - | Unary plus and unary minus |
| ^ | Exponentiation |
| *, / | Multiplication and division |
| +, - | Addition, subtraction, and concatenation |
| =, >, <, >=,=<, <> | Relational operators |
| NOT | Negation |
| AND | Logical and |
| OR | Logical or |

# ASCII Characters

PowerBuilder enables you to use special ASCII characters in your strings. The most commonly used ones allow you to force new lines, include tabs, and include quotation marks in a string that's already using the same quotation-mark type (see the next note). The tilde (~) is used in PowerBuilder to introduce special characters. Table 7.6 lists how to specify ASCII characters in PowerBuilder. You usually use these characters when you create display strings for message boxes or write out values to a file.

**TABLE 7.6**  ASCII Characters Available in PowerBuilder

| String | Resulting ASCII Character |
| --- | --- |
| ~n | New line |
| ~t | Tab |
| ~v | Vertical tab |
| ~r | Carriage return |
| ~f | Form feed |
| ~b | Backspace |
| ~" | Double quote |
| ~' | Single quote |
| ~~ | Tilde |
| ~000 to ~255 | ASCII character with the stated decimal value |
| ~h01 to ~hFF | ASCII character with the stated hexadecimal value |
| ~o000 to ~o377 | ASCII character with the stated octal value |

> **Note**
>
> Another way to assign a double (") or single (') quotation mark to a variable is to embed it within the opposite kind of quotation marks (for example, `ls_Single = "'"` and `lc_Double = '"'`).

# Continuing Strings

The continuation character (&) is used to extend not only statements but also strings over multiple lines. You can place the & character at the end of a string without closing quotation marks and then continue the string onto the next line. However, be aware that any spaces and tabs appearing before the & and at the start of the additional lines are also included. Unless you don't care about the extra space (for example, in a Modify() function call), close the string and use the concatenation operator (+). The following is an example of continuing a string:

```
String ls_sample
ls_sample = "This is a sample of using a continuation" + &
            "with the concatenation character"
```

# Standard Data Types

The standard data types available in PowerBuilder are common across many different programming languages and database servers, but you should carefully match Power-Builder's data type definition with that of the intended target or source because it might not be implemented in the same way. A good example of this difference in definitions can be seen by comparing integer data types between Microsoft SQL Server and PowerBuilder.

In SQL Server, an integer is defined as a 32-bit signed value ranging from -2,147,483,648 to +2,147,483,647. In PowerBuilder, an integer is defined as a 16-bit signed value ranging from -32,768 to +32,767. SQL Server's integer definition actually matches that of the PowerBuilder Long data type. Take great care when you match PowerBuilder variables to those of a database. Table 7.7 lists all the standard data types and their definitions and gives an example of each.

**TABLE 7.7**  PowerBuilder Standard Data Types

| Data Type | Definition | Example |
|---|---|---|
| BLOB | Binary large object; used to store large amounts of data | A bitmap |
| Boolean | A truth value (TRUE or FALSE) | FALSE |
| Character or Char | A single ASCII character | A |
| Date | The date, consisting of the full year, the number of the month, and the day | 1969-06-13 |
| DateTime | The date and time combined into a single data type | 1991-03-26 12:10 |
| Decimal or Dec | Signed decimal numbers with up to 18 digits of precision | 3463346.5247 |
| Double | A signed floating-point number with 15 digits of precision and a range from 2.2E-308 to 1.7E+308 | 6.342E+3 |

**TABLE 7.7**  PowerBuilder Standard Data Types

| Data Type | Definition | Example |
|---|---|---|
| Integer or Int | A 16-bit signed number with a range of -32,768 to +32,767 | 7,533 |
| Long | A 32-bit signed number with a range of -2,147,483,648 to +2,147,483,647 | 4,699,247 |
| Real | A signed floating-point number with six digits of precision and a range from 1.17E-38 to 3.4E+38 | 3.6E+7 |
| String | Any ASCII characters with a variable length of 0 to either 59,999 (16-bit) or as large as your system can provide (32-bit) | "Ulric" |
| Time | A time value in 24-hour format: hour, minute, second, and fractions of a second (up to six digits) | 19:18:29.435214 |
| UnsignedInteger, UnsignedInt,or Uint | A 16-bit unsigned number with a range of 0 to 65,535 | 6,324 |
| UnsignedLong or Ulong | A 32-bit unsigned number with a range of 0 to 4,294,967,295 | 43,234,540 |

## Data Type Conversions

PowerBuilder provides a number of data type conversion functions (see Table 7.8) that allow you to change easily from one data type to another.

**TABLE 7.8**  PowerBuilder Conversion Functions

| Data Type | Definition |
|---|---|
| Char | Convert a BLOB, an Integer, or a String to a Char |
| Dec | Convert a String to a Decimal |
| Double | Convert a String to a Double |
| Integer | Convert a String to an Integer |
| Long | Convert a String to a Long |
| Real | Convert a String to a Real |
| Date | Obtain the Date portion of a DateTime value |
| DateTime | Convert a Date and a Time to a DateTime value |
| String | Convert a BLOB, a Date, a DateTime, a numeric, or a Time to String |
| Time | Obtain the Time portion of a DateTime value |

# Strings and Characters

*Characters* are single ASCII elements, and *strings* are collections of zero or more characters, and you can build strings up to a size of 2,147,483,647 characters! If you assign a string value to a character variable, only the first ASCII value is stored. The special characters listed earlier in the section "ASCII Characters," can be assigned to character variables by using an implicit string-to-character conversion. For example, to assign the representation of a tab, the statement is

```
cTabCharacter = "~t"
```

Arrays of characters can also be assigned to string variables, and they obey the following rules:

- You can directly copy a string to an unbounded character array.

- A string that you copy to a bounded array will be truncated to the array's upper boundary.

- If the string is shorter than the upper boundary, the unused elements are initialized to empty strings.

Character arrays can be converted back to strings by assignment to a variable of type String. Characters are copied until an empty character (equal to ' ') is found.

All PowerBuilder functions accept strings and characters or character arrays.

## Dynamic Variable Assignment

You can initialize variables with a value when they're declared. The value set can be a constant value or the result of an expression. If you make an assignment during a variable's declaration, the value set is determined at compile time, not during runtime execution. For example, the following code sets the variable to the time the application was compiled; the variable won't be updated each time this code is called:

```
String ls_Time = String( Now())
```

The only obvious use for this kind of initialization is if you want to capture the time that an application is compiled for auditing or other purposes.

### Note

If you try to assign to a variable dynamically from the attribute of an object, you will get an error.

## Arrays

You use an *array* to collect related pieces of information of the same data type under one name. Each element in an array has a unique index to distinguish it from the others. There are two types of arrays: multidimensional arrays must have a fixed size, whereas single-dimensional arrays can be a fixed size or an unbounded size.

You declare an array by stating the data type of the elements, the name of the variable, and then the size of the array (which is enclosed in square brackets).

## Single-Dimensional Arrays

A *single-dimensional array* is a collection of related items and is declared by using a single size or the To statement to specify a range. Think of this type of array as a filing cabinet and of the array elements as folders in that cabinet. Here are two examples:

```
String ls_This_Is_An_Array[ 30]
Integer li_Another_Array[ 10 To 20]
```

The first example declares an array of 30 strings, with indexes from 1 to 30. The second example declares an array of 11 integers, with indexes starting at 10 and going up to and including 20. Both examples are of fixed size, and any index reference outside the valid range produces a runtime error.

The To notation overrides the default start index of 1 and requires that the first number specified be less than the second number of the range. Negative index ranges are also valid, as are indexes that begin with a negative number and end with a positive number. Following are some examples, all of which define arrays of 21 elements:

```
String ls_Array1[ -10 To 10]
Integer ai_Array2[ -21 To -1]
Real lr_Array3[ 0 To 20]
```

### Working with Unbounded Arrays

*Unbounded* or *variable-size arrays* are single-dimensional arrays for which no index boundaries are defined; PowerBuilder controls their memory requirements and usage at runtime. An unbounded array starts at index 1, which can't be changed. The upper boundary is controlled by the largest index assignment that has been made at the point where you check the boundary. When an unbounded array is first created, the upper index is 0, and the lower is 1. For example, a declaration for an array containing any number of integers is as follows:

```
Integer li_Array4[]
```

Following the declaration of such an array, any index reference over 1 is fully valid. However, the manner in which PowerBuilder assigns memory to the unbounded array is worth noting:

```
li_Array4[ 200] = 100
li_Array4[ 250] = 50
li_Array4[ 350] = 25
li_Array4[ 299] = 12
```

The first use of the array causes PowerBuilder to create a 200-element array, of which it initializes the first 199 elements to the default integer value of 0 and then assigns the value 100 to the 200th element. The second assignment to the array causes an additional 50 elements to be created and added to the array; these are initialized to 0 except for element 250, which takes the value 50. The third assignment causes an additional 100 elements to be added; they're initialized to 0 except for element 350, which takes the value 25. The last assignment doesn't cause any additional memory allocations because it's referencing an already-created element.

Keep in mind the manner in which PowerBuilder creates memory for the unbounded arrays. Any usage of an unbounded array is optimally written if it starts at the largest value and works backward. Each time PowerBuilder is required to allocate more memory, it must deal with the operating system, making it a time-expensive operation. Therefore, causing the maximum size of the array to be created once produces faster execution. This isn't always possible, but it's worth considering if the array can be populated in reverse.

**7**

**The PowerScript Language**

> **Note**
>
> Accessing an element of an unbounded array that's outside the current range causes a runtime error. Of course, the upper boundary might change as execution commences, so that the following code gives an error:
>
> ```
> Integer li_Array4[]
> li_Array4[100] = 10
> If li_Array4[ 101] = 10 Then
> End If
> ```

## Determining Array Boundaries

Two PowerBuilder functions are available for determining the upper and lower boundaries of arrays: UpperBound() and LowerBound(). LowerBound() always returns 1 for unbounded arrays. UpperBound() is usually used before iterating through the array, but a common misuse of this function is to place it in the loop condition:

```
For li_Count = 1 To UpperBound( li_Array4)
    // Do some processing
Next
```

Sybase states that the UpperBound() function is expensive to execute; because any function calls in a loop condition are executed each time, this code calls UpperBound() for every element. To use this function correctly, assign the value to a variable first, like this:

```
li_NumberOfElements = UpperBound( li_Array4)
For li_Count = 1 To li_NumberOfElements
    // Do some processing
Next
```

## Initializing Arrays

Arrays can be assigned values during their declaration, similarly to other data types, and the same declaration syntax can be used after the declaration line, if required. The initialization values must be of the same data type as the array, and for a fixed-size array, they must be a value for each index element. The syntax is a comma-separated list enclosed by braces. Here's an example:

```
Real li_Array5[ 5] = { 1.2, 2.1, 3.2, 2.3, 4.3 }
```

The following is also valid:

```
Real li_Array5[ 5]
li_Array5 = { 1.2, 2.1, 3.2, 2.3, 4.3 }
```

Unbounded arrays can also be initialized similarly, which also sets the initial number of elements for those arrays.

---

**Tip**

A quick and elegant way to reinitialize an array back to default values is to declare another array of the same data type and index boundaries and then assign the new array to the old array. Here's an example:

```
Real lr_CleanArray[6]
// An array ar_ValuesIn is passed as an argument to this function
ar_ValuesIn = lr_CleanArray
```

The disadvantage to this method is the extra memory taken by the second array, but this usually outweighs the time taken to iterate through the original array to reset each element.

# Multidimensional Arrays

*Multidimensional* arrays can be only of fixed size and will contain more than one dimension in the declaration. For example, to model points in 3D space, an array could be created to hold the X, Y, and Z coordinates. Here's an example:

```
Real lr_Points[ 100, 100, 100]
```

The `lr_Points` array consists of $100 \times 100 \times 100$ (or 1 million) elements. The rules for declaring the range for single-dimensional arrays also apply to multidimensional arrays. The following are all valid declarations:

```
Real lr_Axis[ -10 To 10, 20]
Integer li_CoOrds[ 2, 0 To 200, -1 To 3]
String ls_Drawer[ 0 To 100, 0 To 100]
```

Multidimensional arrays can't be initialized. The number and size of a dimension is limited only by available memory. To access elements, specify the dimensional indexes in a comma-separated list, as in the following:

```
lr_Axis[ 4, 5] = 43.5
li_CoOrds[ 1, 43, 2] = 69
ls_Drawer[ 34, 54] = "Gibson"
```

# Arrays in Function Parameters

An array can be declared for a function argument but not for the return value. The argument declaration is modified to include the square brackets and the upper boundary for a fixed-size array. Unbounded arrays can also be declared for function arguments. Although arrays can't be defined for the return value, an argument can be declared as a pass-by-reference argument for the purposes of returning an array. In fact, you should always pass arrays by reference so that PowerBuilder doesn't copy the entire array.

Arrays can also be passed into parameterized events (see the later section "Additional Calling Methods"). The arrays are treated and declared in the same manner as for functions, as discussed in the preceding paragraph.

# Checking Array Equality

To check the equality of array elements to some fixed list, you must use another array variable. Beginning with PowerBuilder 6.0, a compilation error is generated rather than a runtime error if you try to use an array list in a logical expression that checks equality (=) or inequality (<>).

The error PowerBuilder produces is IDS_CM_CO187, Illegal Use of an Arraylist. They can only be used to initialize arrays . The following code produces an error:

```
Integer anArray[3] = {1, 2, 3}

If anArray = {1, 2, 3} Then
    // equality happens!
End if
```

The correct way to check the equality is as follows:

```
Integer li_Array[3] = { 1, 2, 3 }
Integer li_Args[3] = { 2, 3, 4 }

If li_Args = li_Array Then
    // We have equality
End If
```

## NULL **Values**

A NULL value, as you saw in Chapter 4, "SQL and PowerBuilder," can be tricky to deal with in the SQL language. The same is also true in PowerScript.

NULL is an undefined and unknown value. PowerScript variables can become NULL if they're retrieved from a database by using the PowerScript function SetNull() or by calling a PowerScript function or external function that returns handle information to an object.

> **Note**
>
> Beginning with PowerBuilder 6.0, a compiler error is generated if you try to call the SetNull() function on an array or an autoinstantiate argument (including structures). The message depends on the argument; it will be one of the following:
>
> ```
> "The argument to SetNull cannot be an array.", or
> "The argument to SetNull cannot be an autoinstantiate or structure,"
> ```

As does SQL, PowerScript provides a function for testing for a NULL value. IsNull() returns a Boolean value that's TRUE if the value being tested is NULL and FALSE otherwise.

To check that a returned object handle isn't a reference to a NULL object, you use the IsValid() function. For example, to see whether an object is now selected, use the following:

```
GraphicObject lgo_Control
lgo_Control = GetFocus()
If IsValid (lgo_Control) Then
   MessageBox( "Focus", "Something has focus")
Else
   MessageBox( "Focus", "Nothing has focus!")
End If
```

Also be careful when you add two variables, whether they are Integer, String, or any other data type. If one of them is a NULL, the result will be a NULL.

The SetNull() function lets you set PowerScript variables to a NULL value. Be sure to cast the NULL into a variable of the correct data type if you're going to place it in a DataWindow column or use it elsewhere. A NULL integer isn't interchangeable with a NULL string, and even though the DataWindow SetItem() function lets you specify a string variable set to NULL to be placed into an integer column, the actual modification will fail with no error.

# Placement of Script

To get full use of object-oriented programming, code your objects with complete encapsulation as the goal. This is not always feasible or desired, however, so, along with your naming conventions and other standards, you must decide on placement of script.

Some developers code everything into a window's events or functions and call them from within the other controls on the window. What we've tended to do is code object-specific functionality in the object itself and then place the actual business and calculation processes in window functions. With the popularity for distributed applications, the desire to push this business logic and calculations to nonvisual user objects has become more of the norm. Again, the PFC has begun separating much of this logic, made it generic, and placed it in nonvisuals that can be instantiated and referenced whenever the desire is there.

# Classes and Objects

Classes and objects are related but separate concepts. Objects are the instantiated form (the terms *object* and *instance* are interchangeable) of a class, and classes can have zero or more instances. An *object* is a package of related functions and data that has a state, a behavior, and an identity; a *class* is simply a template from which particular instances can be created.

All windows that you create in PowerBuilder are in the class Window. Objects/instances are the actual physical representation of a class and are what you create and destroy.

PowerBuilder defines each class—system classes as well as the classes you create—as a data type and structures them as a class hierarchy.

By using objects the Object Browser, accessible from the PowerBar (see Figure 7.1), you can set the specific class type that you want to zoom in on.

**FIGURE 7.1**

*The Object Browser.*

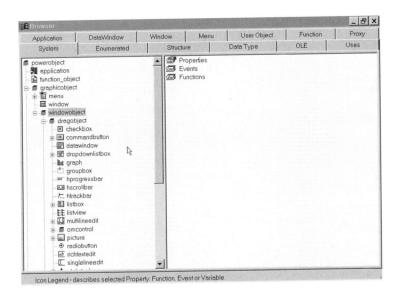

## Creating and Destroying Classes

You use the Create statement to generate an instance of an object class. The only classes you need to use this statement for are nonvisual user objects, such as the standard classes (for example, Transaction and Error), or pop-up menus. Visual user objects and windows should be created by using the appropriate Open() functions. You must instantiate an object variable by using the Create statement before you can have any access to the object's attributes or methods. For example, to create a local version of the Error object, the code is

```
Error eMyError
```

```
eMyError = Create Error
eMyError.Line = 1
```

Here, the object variable is eMyError, and the object class is Error.

> **Caution**
>
> If you use `Create` to make a nonvisual instance of a window class, the `Open` event isn't triggered. In fact, none of the events that relate to a visible window are triggered because the graphical component of the window is never created.

When you use the `Create` statement, PowerBuilder allocates memory for the object; this memory remains in use until it's freed via the `Destroy` statement. For example, at the end of the script started in the previous example, the code required is

```
Destroy eMyError
```

The control property arrays (see Chapter 10, "Windows and the Window Painter") of windows and tab controls are updated with new entries whenever you use PowerScript functions to dynamically create and add visual user objects or tab pages to those objects at runtime.

## Creating Objects Dynamically

In previous versions of PowerBuilder, you could use the `Create` statement to dynamically create user objects. You were, however, limited to creating objects of a stated type. Here's an example:

```
"u_n_application g_App
```

```
g_App = Create u_n_application
```

This was extended in PowerBuilder 5.0 to allow you to define the object type using an expression. This is the syntax:

```
ObjectVariable = Create Using Expression
```

This way, you can decide about what object to create at runtime. *Expression*'s value can be one of the following:

- A String variable

- An Any variable containing a String

- A function that returns a String

- A function that returns an Any (which must be a String at runtime)

You should declare the data type of *ObjectVariable* to be some base class on which you can make generic calls based on the expected values of *Expression*. For example, if you want to carry out a sequence of steps without regard for DBMS specifics, you could use the following code:

```
u_n_transaction lnvo_Tran

lnvo_Tran = Create Using as_TransactionClass

lnvo_Tran.MakeConnection()

lnvo_Tran.BeginTran()

If lnvo_Tran.ProcessValues() Then
  lnvo_Tran.CommitTran()
Else
  lnvo_Tran.RollbackTran()
End If

lnvo_Tran.CloseConnection()

Destroy lnvo_Tran
```

All the methods used are declared in the base class u_n_transaction as virtual functions and then overridden and defined within each descendant class (for example, in u_n_sqlserver_transaction). The descendant class would be passed in the argument as_TransactionClass. For example, if the preceding code were written as a function, you would call it by using this:

```
f_special_database_process( "u_n_sqlserver_transaction")
```

## Garbage Collection

*Garbage collection* is PowerBuilder's removal of unreferenced and orphaned objects from memory. As objects are used (referenced) by your code, PowerBuilder counts each occurrence. When the code that references the object passes out of scope, PowerBuilder decrements the usage count; when that count reaches zero, it knows the object and class can be cleared from memory. This process ensures more efficient memory usage by making space available for new objects to be created without having to resort to disk-based virtual memory.

Before version 6.0, PowerBuilder struggled to implement thorough garbage collection. Garbage collection was implemented much more completely in Version 6.0. PowerBuilder even tries to identify unused objects with circular references—that is, objects that point at themselves, which obviously give you a usage count of one.

As part of this improved garbage collection, Sybase introduced three functions that you can use to modify the period that collection occurs or to force an immediate clean:

- `GarbageCollect()` forces immediate garbage collection, at which point Power-Builder attempts to identify unused objects and then delete the unused objects and classes.

- `GarbageCollectGetTimeLimit()` gets the current minimum period between garbage-collection passes.

- `GarbageCollectSetTimeLimit()` allows you to set the minimum interval between garbage-collection passes; garbage-collection passes won't happen before this interval expires. Setting the minimum interval to a large number can effectively disable garbage collection. If garbage collection is disabled, unused classes won't be flushed out of the class cache.

> **Note**
>
> Garbage collection is *not* a reason to stop using the DESTROY function. Continue to manage the lifetime of your objects as you've done before for maximum efficiency and control.

# Using Object Pointers

To further illustrate that objects can be declared as variables (which are, in fact, pointers to an object), this section examines how to implement a doubly linked list in PowerBuilder.

If you haven't heard of a linked list, let alone a doubly linked list, here's a brief description. A *linked list* represents data values that aren't necessarily stored sequentially. Access to data is made through *links* stored with each data value that point to the next data value in the list. For a *doubly linked list*, the data value is also associated with a pointer to the previous data value. The collection of data and pointer(s) is called an *atom*. Linked lists are used frequently in such languages as C, C++, and Pascal to store related data values.

The atom is implemented as a custom class user object that contains three instance variables: `Any aData`, `u_n_atom ptrNext`, and `u_n_atom ptrPrevious`. The aData variable stores the actual data value. The two pointers, `ptrNext` and `ptrPrevious`, are defined as being of the same type as the user object they are in.

**Note**

You need to save the user object before you can declare the two pointer variables.

To implement a doubly linked list, you provide a custom class user object: u_n_doubly_linked_list. This object maintains a pointer to the head (first item) and tail (last item) of the list by using two instance variables:

- Public ProtectedWrite u_n_atom ptrHead

- Public ProtectedWrite u_n_atom ptrTail

These variables are protected from outside modification but are made available for other objects to traverse the list.

Two functions are provided to add and remove atoms from the list. The function for adding an atom (see Listing 7.1) creates the atom and then makes the appropriate pointer assignments to link it into the list. This function simply appends to the end of the list, which is defined by the ptrTail variable. You can easily enhance this function to allow a new atom to be inserted after a specified atom. This function has only one special case, which is when the first atom is added. This case is checked by looking at the value of ptrHead to see whether it's valid.

**LISTING 7.1** The AddAtom() Method for u_n_doubly_linked_list

```
// Parameters:
//        ReadOnly Any     a_aData

u_n_atom Atom

Atom = Create u_n_atom

If IsValid( Atom) Then
   Atom.aData = a_aData

   If Not IsValid( ptrHead) Then
      ptrHead = Atom
   Else
      ptrTail.ptrNext = Atom
      Atom.ptrPrevious = ptrTail
   End If
```

**LISTING 7.1** CONTINUED

```
    ptrTail = Atom
End If


Return Atom
```

As mentioned previously, the AddAtom() function only appends to the list. To see more complex operations on the linked list structure, look at the DeleteAtom() function (see Listing 7.2), which destroys a specified atom and reassigns the pointers for related atoms. If there's another atom after the one to be deleted, it's assigned as the next atom of the previous atom, and vice versa. There are then two special cases to catch: If you've just deleted the head item or tail item from the list, you need to update the appropriate pointers.

**LISTING 7.2** The DeleteAtom() Method for u_n_doubly_linked_list

```
// Parameters:
//          By Reference u_n_atom      a_unAtom
u_n_atom ptrPrevious, ptrNext

If Not IsValid( ptrHead) Then
    // Empty List
    Return FALSE
End If


ptrPrevious = a_unAtom.ptrPrevious
ptrNext = a_unAtom.ptrNext

If IsValid( ptrNext) Then
    // Point from the atom after the one to be deleted to
    // the atom previous
ptrNext.ptrPrevious = ptrPrevious
End If


If IsValid( ptrPrevious) Then
    // Point from the atom previous to the one being deleted to the
    // atom after
ptrPrevious.ptrNext = ptrNext
End If


If a_unAtom = ptrTail And IsValid( ptrPrevious) Then
    // Move the tail pointer to the previous atom if there is one
    ptrTail = ptrPrevious
End If
```

**LISTING 7.2** CONTINUED

```
If a_unAtom = ptrHead And IsValid( ptrNext) Then
    // Move the head pointer to the next atom if there is one
    ptrHead = ptrNext
End If

Destroy a_unAtom

Return TRUE
```

PowerBuilder automatically handles empty lists because the `ptrHead` and `ptrTail` variables both become invalid; you can check against just one of them by using `IsValid()`.

The `u_n_doubly_linked_list` user object can be set up to be auto-instantiating, and the following examples assume a variable `unDll` of this user object type that's already instantiated. A pointer to a position within the list, `ptrCurrentAtom`, is also used and is declared of type `u_n_atom`.

The code to add a value to the list is simply

```
ptrCurrentAtom = unDll.AddAtom( "SimonG")
```

This code can be issued multiple times to add multiple atoms to the list. Because the data type of the linked list is Any, you can store anything you want in the list. This is much more versatile than linked lists in C or Pascal, which can store only one data type (for single-value atoms).

To remove the current atom from the list, you would use this code:

```
If IsValid( ptrCurrentAtom) Then
    unDll.DeleteAtom( ptrCurrentAtom)
End If
```

To navigate through the list, you can start at the head or tail end, using the appropriate variable. For example, to go to the previous atom from the current one, this would be the code:

```
If IsValid( unDll.ptrHead) Then
    If Not IsValid( ptrCurrentAtom) Then
        ptrCurrentAtom = unDll.ptrHead
    ElseIf IsValid( ptrCurrentAtom.ptrPrevious) Then
        ptrCurrentAtom = ptrCurrentAtom.ptrPrevious
    End If
Else
    MessageBox( "Linked List", "You are already on the first atom in the list!")
```

```
End If
```

```
//Extract the data value - in this case assume numeric
lValue = Long (ptrCurrentAtom.aData)
```

You can traverse in the other direction simply by changing the `ptrPrevious` references to `ptrNext`.

# Class and Instance Pools

PowerBuilder maintains three separate memory pools to track class, instance, and Windows manifestation information.

The first time you instantiate a particular class, the class definition is loaded into the class pool, and then an instance is created in the instance pool. Subsequent instantiations of that object take their definition straight from the class pool. Depending on how you instantiate the object, a pointer to the instance will be in global memory or at the scope level of the variable used. PowerBuilder then uses an additional pool, the Window object pool, to hold information about the actual Window objects manifestation. This last pool is used only for visible classes such as windows, menus, and user objects.

> **Note**
>
> The way the class pool works is somewhat of a mystery, and Sybase has said that the current operation might well change in future releases. Now, when you close a visual object or destroy a nonvisual object (NVO), the memory for the instance is freed immediately. The class information (mostly the methods) goes away at some random (for all practical purposes) time in the future if there are no other instances. It's possible, however, that the class definition will remain in memory until the application terminates. Only autoinstantiated classes are freed immediately when there are no references.

Consider opening two instances of a window, `w_sheet`, by using two local variables and another window, `w_about`, that you open directly:

```
w_sheet lw_Instance, lw_Instance2
```

```
Open( w_about)
//
Open( lw_Instance, "w_sheet")
Open( lw_Instance2, "w_sheet")
```

As you know, this script opens three windows. Now explore what happens in the class and instance pools, and in global and local memory:

1. If this is the first time the class w_about is opened, the class definition is loaded into the class pool.

2. An instance of the class is created in the instance pool.

3. An entry is made into the global memory area of the application that points to the instance. PowerBuilder checks this when you directly open a window to see whether it's already instantiated.

4. The w_sheet class definition is loaded into the class pool.

5. An instance of w_sheet is created in the instance pool.

6. The local variable lw_Instance now points to the instance just created.

7. Another instance of w_sheet is created in the instance pool.

8. The local variable lw_Instance2 points to this instance.

You can see this more easily in Figure 7.2, which shows the two pools and two memory areas.

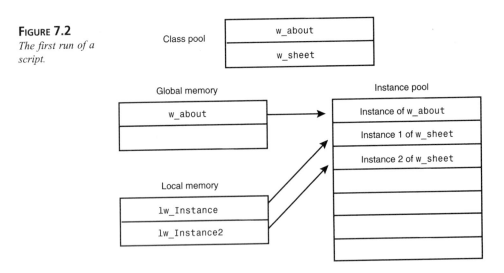

**FIGURE 7.2**
*The first run of a script.*

During the second run of the same script, a slightly different set of operations takes place:

1. The w_about class is already loaded and there's a global memory pointer to an instance of the class, so nothing further is done for the Open (w_about) statement.

2. An instance of w_sheet is created in the instance pool.

3. The local variable lw_Instance points to the instance just created.

4. Another instance of `w_sheet` is created in the instance pool.

5. The local variable `lw_Instance2` points to this instance.

This can be seen more easily in Figure 7.3, which shows the final state of the two pools and two memory areas.

**FIGURE 7.3**
*The second run of the script.*

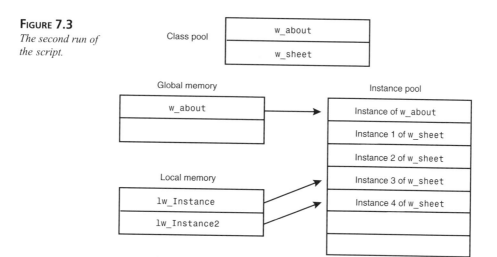

This mechanism for creating class instances is an important concept and allows you to anticipate heavy-use class hierarchies that you might want to preload at the start of the application.

> **Note**
>
> PowerBuilder handles DataWindows differently because DataWindow objects don't have associated scripts, object references, and so on. During runtime execution, a DataWindow engine that handles all service requests manages DataWindows. The engine creates a template of what the DataWindow will look like, an instance of the DataWindow, and a graphical manifestation. If another instance of a DataWindow is requested, the engine creates another template, instance, and graphical manifestation. Storage for these templates and instances is managed on an as-needed basis, not by using the pools previously discussed.

# Variables

You define variables for use within your scripts. They're made up of a type, a scope, a data type, and an initial value. Variables can be declared by using a simple data type (for example, String or Integer), as an object (for example, window, w_about, or cb_connect), or as a structure (for example, Message or s_my_vals). The following sections show the different scopes at which you can declare variables and what access restrictions can be placed on them.

## Object Access Levels

Object-level variables and functions can have their accessibility restricted to allow you to build more encapsulated objects. The three settings are Public, Protected, and Private, in descending order of accessibility. Instance variables for an object can use these keywords in their declaration. If no access is specified, Public is the default, but you will usually include a Public section to make your intentions clear for other developers. Here's an example:

```
Public:
    Integer ii_Count
Protected:
    String is_Title
Private:
    Time itm_Now
```

The object-level function-declaration window provides a drop-down list with the three access levels; Public is the default value.

The Public access level allows the function or variable to be used and changed from anywhere in an application. All global functions and variables are at the Public access level, and this can't be changed.

Protected variables and functions can be used only within the class that declared them and any of its descendants. No access is allowed from outside the class.

The highest level of restriction is Private. Only scripts in the class that declares the function or variable can access them. Access from outside the class, including all its descendants, isn't allowed.

When you're creating highly encapsulated objects, you will make the most use of the Private and Protected levels and provide access to certain variables through Public-level functions. These allow you to completely control any modifications to a variable (for example, to disallow certain values or to trigger particular processing if the variable is set to a certain value).

---

### Caution

Beginning with version 6.0, the visibility of structures local to an object changed from `Private` to `Protected` to allow descendants to also use the structure definition. Before version 6.0, you couldn't use an ancestor's structure unless an instance variable of that type was defined.

---

Four additional access levels can be used only with an instance variable: `ProtectedRead`, `PrivateRead`, `ProtectedWrite`, and `PrivateWrite`. These are used optionally to control the read and write access for variables.

To further restrict which scripts can read a variable's value, use the `ProtectedRead` and `PrivateRead` keywords. With `ProtectedRead`, only scripts for the object that the variable is declared in and any descendant objects can read the variable. For `PrivateRead`, only the object that declared the variable can read from it. These access levels mesh with the overall access levels as follows:

- If the variable's scope is `Public`, use `ProtectedRead` or `PrivateRead`.

- If the variable's scope is `Protected`, only `PrivateRead` can be used. The variable is already implicitly `ProtectedRead`.

- If the variable's scope is `Private`, neither can be used. The variable is already implicitly `PrivateRead`.

If the read access of a variable isn't defined, any script in the variable's scope can read its value.

The write access of a variable can also be further restricted by using the `ProtectedWrite` and `PrivateWrite` keywords. With `ProtectedWrite`, only scripts for the object that the variable is declared in and any descendant objects can change the variable's value. For `PrivateWrite`, only the object that declared the variable can change its value. As with the read restrictions, these access levels also mesh with the overall access levels as follows:

- If the variable's scope is `Public`, you can use `ProtectedWrite` or `PrivateWrite`.

- If the variable's scope is `Protected`, only `PrivateWrite` can be used. The variable is already implicitly `ProtectedWrite`.

- If the variable's scope is `Private`, neither access level can be used. The variable is already implicitly `PrivateWrite`.

If the write access of a variable isn't defined, any script in the variable's scope can change its value.

# Variable Scope

You can define a variable to have one of four different scopes: global, shared, instance, and local. Scope dictates how the variable must be accessed, when it can be accessed, and which variable takes precedence if it's declared within different scopes.

# Global Variables

Global variables are defined to be accessible applicationwide and are stored in the actual application object. As you would with any other programming language, you should minimize the number of global variables in use; otherwise, anywhere in any script a variable could be modified that would make debugging a trickier proposition. Global variables also use a piece of memory for the duration of the application's execution. They are initialized when the application is first opened.

> **Tip**
>
> If you haven't decided on naming conventions for the scope of your variables and run into a situation where you have a local variable declared with the same name as a global variable, there's an easy way to use both. To refer to a global variable that's "hidden" by a local or shared variable, prefix the variable name with the global scope operator (::).

# Instance Variables

Instance variables are defined in an object (application, window, user object, or menu) and are therefore directly accessible anywhere within that object. They are also available, depending on the access level, to outside objects by using dot notation. Instance variables effectively become attributes of the object on which they're defined, and are initialized when the object is created by the application. When the object is destroyed, the instance variables are destroyed with it.

The value of an instance variable isn't shared between two instances of the same class.

**Note**

Remember that multiple occurrences of the same window are called *instances* of the window; don't confuse this with instance variables.

# Shared Variables

Shared variables are defined in the same type of objects as instance variables, but shared variables are associated with the actual class definition, not with the object instances. This means that all instances of the same class share the same variable.

Shared variables always have a `Private` access level that can't be changed because they can be accessed only in the class in which they're defined.

A shared variable is initialized the first time an object of that class is created. When you then destroy the object, the shared variable retains the last value it was set to so that when you create another instance of the object, the shared variable will again hold the last value it was set to. If you have multiple instances of the same object created at the same time, they all access the same variable.

**Tip**

You can use the persistence property of shared variables to hold on to information between different creations of the same window. Suppose that you have a pop-up window that displays status information for another window. In the pop-up's `Open` event, set the window's X and Y attributes to the values of two shared variables. Then, in the pop-up's `Close` event, save the current X and Y attributes of the window to these variables. After you initialize the shared variables to a starting position, the window remembers where it was last positioned for the duration of the application's run. Remember that the memory used by shared variables remains until the application closes, so carefully consider how you use them.

## Local Variables

Local variables are defined at script level. They can be used only within that script and are destroyed at the end of the script. Local variables are used as a scratch pad for holding intermediate data values. They are the most commonly used variable types in scripts that you write.

Local variables can be defined anywhere within your script, even within conditional code blocks. A local variable is still usable outside the block in which it's defined, so unless it really will be used *only* in that block, declare it at the top of the script.

## Order of Precedence

If during the execution of a script PowerBuilder finds an unqualified reference to a variable, it searches for the location of the variable using the following search order:

- Local variables
- Shared variables
- Global variables
- Instance variables

If PowerBuilder can't find the variable at any of these levels, it searches up the object's inheritance chain, looking at the instance variables.

## Controlling Variable Access

When developing applications, you need to analyze all your variables and determine the scope and access level of each. You need to determine when and how all the objects will access and/or modify these variables. By using the techniques discussed in the previous sections, you have several choices.

Suppose that you have the class object uo_order_nos that provides a publicly accessible variable, is_OrderNo. In PowerBuilder, you can achieve this setup in three ways:

- Declare a public variable that can be read from and written to without any control.

- Declare the variable as private and then provide an of_get function and an of_set function that you must use to access the variable's value. All object-oriented purists insist that this mechanism be used because it provides a means to control access and modifications to the variable. Sybase has implemented this mechanism in the PowerBuilder Foundation Class.

- Implement the second type by using the as-yet-unsupported `Indirect` syntax, which allows you to use the `of_get` and `of_set` functions without explicitly calling them.

The `Indirect` syntax is as follows:

```
Indirect DataTypePropertyName{ SetFunction( *value), GetFunction()}
```

`DataType` is the actual data type of the property you want to create. `PropertyName` is the name that external scripts will reference. `SetFunction` and `GetFunction` are the names of the methods you will supply that PowerBuilder will use whenever an external script attempts to read from or write to the property.

As the syntax suggests, this creates a bit of trickery and redirects references to what appears to be the variable through some access functions to the real object. The syntax is declared as `Public`, and the actual variable is declared as `Private`. To understand this better, look at the actual syntax required to make this work.

Consider the string property `is_OrderNo`, which holds specific information for a particular class user object to which you want to control access. The following code would be placed in the `Declare Instance Variables` section of the class user object:

```
Public:
  Indirect String is_OrderNoPub{ of_SetOrderNo( *value), of_GetOrderNo()}

Private:
  String is_OrderNo
```

This declares the actual variable, `is_OrderNo`, and the publicly accessible property, `is_OrderNoPub`. The final step is to provide the two object-level functions specified.

This would be the code for the set function `of_SetOrderNo()`, where `as_Value` is a string argument defined for the function:

```
is_OrderNo = as_Value
```

This would be the code for the get function `of_GetOrderNo()`:

```
Return is_OrderNo
```

You can add as many additional checks and restrictions as you want in these two functions; just remember that they will be called every time that particular property is accessed.

You can use this syntax anywhere you can define an instance scope variable. It makes less sense in anything other than a class user object, however, because the controls in other objects (for example, a window) can still access a private scope variable.

It's a good bet that the syntax will remain close to what it is now in future releases of PowerBuilder that support this functionality. This is because the proxy objects used in distributed PowerBuilder use this syntax as well. Sybase would have to migrate any existing proxy objects if it were to change this syntax.

> **Caution**
>
> Remember that this is unsupported syntax; Sybase won't provide any technical support on problems you might encounter due to it. Sybase also reserves the right to change the syntax and availability of this at any time.

# Constants

PowerBuilder allows you to declare variables as constants. Any variable declaration that can be given an initial value in its declaration can be turned into a constant with the addition of the keyword Constant. You can't modify the value of a constant after its declaration, however. Here's an example:

```
Constant Integer ORDER_HEADER = 1
```

> **Tip**
>
> You might want to use the same convention used here, of using all uppercase for constant variable names to help distinguish them from other variables.

Within all your scripts, you can use the constants you've declared without having to remember which value meant what. As you can see in the following example, your code becomes a great deal more readable, and because you declare the constant in one place, maintaining its value is simple:

```
If ii_Area = ORDER_HEADER Then
   ii_Area = PRINTING
End If
```

These proper constants eliminate the overhead associated with the pseudo constants that developers used in previous versions, by using either global variables or class user objects. The value of the constant is substituted at compile time wherever the constant is referenced.

Constants also correctly state their access properties within the Object Browser—that the object is readable but not writable, for example.

---

**Note**

You can't make multiple declarations on one line. For example, the following one-line declaration declares only one constant, ORDER_HEADER. CUSTOMER_DIMEN-SIONS and PRINTING are declared as normal integers and can be modified:

```
Constant Integer ORDER_HEADER = 1, CUSTOMER_DIMENSIONS = 2, PRINTING = 3
```

You have to split the constants into single-line declarations:

```
Constant Integer ORDER_HEADER = 1
Constant Integer CUSTOMER_DIMENSIONS = 2
Constant Integer PRINTING = 3
```

---

# Functions

You use PowerScript to write global and object-level functions, which use many of the statements and system functions provided by PowerBuilder.

PowerBuilder has a wide range of functions with most of them acting against particular objects and controls. The following sections introduce some of the system functions available.

## GetParent()

The GetParent() function is used to acquire the parent of a specified object and can be used against any visual object (PowerObject class descendant). The syntax is

```
ObjectName.GetParent()
```

where *ObjectName* indicates the window, user object, or menu item that you want to get the parent object of. The function returns a value of type PowerObject. Often you simply use Parent and ParentWindow to access the immediate parent object, but sometimes you need to traverse the parent chain to access the overall parent and its attributes.

---

**Note**

You might think the return type of PowerObject is a little strange when dealing with only visual objects and that a return type of GraphicObject would make more sense. The function was implemented this way because of inheritance constraints encountered by Sybase.

For example, a control in a tab page that is itself a child of a tab control would need to execute a call to GetParent() to obtain the tab control:

```
// Event script within the control sitting in the tab page
Tab ltb_Tab

ltb_Tab = Parent.GetParent()
ltb_Tab.SelectTab( 1)
```

**Tip**

You don't need to check the return value of the GetParent() function because every object has a parent of one kind or another (even if it's the Windows desktop).

This might lead you to create statements within a user object based on a tab page that needs to interact with the window it's on, like this:

```
PowerObject lpo_Parent, lpo_ParentParent, lpo_ParentParentParent
//
// lpo_Parent is the Tab page
lpo_Parent = this.GetParent()
// lpo_ParentParent is the tab control
lpo_ParentParent = lpo_Parent.GetParent()
// lpo_ParentParentParent is the window
lpo_ParentParentParent = lpo_ParentParent.GetParent()
```

However, because a well-encapsulated object can't rely on this kind of structure, you need a different approach. For example, what if the tab control was itself a user object of some kind? The preceding code wouldn't carry out the action you need it to. The following code is more appropriate:

```
PowerObject lpo_Parent, lpo_ParentParent, lpo_ParentParentParent
//
// lpo_Parent is the Tab page
lpo_Parent = this.GetParent()

Do while Lower(lpo_Parent.ClassName()) <> "window!"
```

```
    lpo_Parent = lpo_Parent.GetParent()
Loop
```

## Reverse()

The Reverse() function is a string-manipulation function that provides the capability to reverse a string. Here's an example:

```
String ls_Test = "George"

ls_Test = Reverse( ls_Test)
// Now ls_Test contains "egroeG"
```

This function, as well as IsHebrew() and IsArabic(), is useful in creating internationally sensitive applications.

## The Function Search Chain

When you call a PowerScript function that's not qualified with an object name, PowerBuilder searches for the function in the following order:

- Global external function
- Global function object
- Local external function
- Object-level function
- System function

As you can see from this search chain, you can override PowerBuilder's system functions with your own. Obviously, to speed up the execution of your function calls you should qualify them, where possible, with the object name. It's interesting to note that global functions are executed faster (for unqualified function calls) than object-level functions, although you might expect the reverse.

# The Message Object

The basis of Microsoft's Windows system and other GUI environments is the capture and reaction to system or user events. Most Windows messages are mapped to PowerBuilder events, but occasionally you will have a message that needs to be trapped that isn't mapped.

In those cases, the Message object is used to determine the message ID and optional parameters. The code to make this event trap is placed in a special event found in objects: the Other event. Use the Other event carefully, however, because it adversely affects performance by sending *every* unmapped message to that event.

You also can use the Message object to pass additional parameters on the open or close of a window by using the OpenWithParm(), OpenSheetWithParm(), OpenUserObjectWithParm(), or CloseWithReturn() function.

The TriggerEvent() and PostEvent() functions take optional parameters that the Message object stores (these are introduced in the next section, "Events").

The Message object has nine properties (see Table 7.9). The first four directly map to the Microsoft message structure, the next three are used to pass PowerBuilder data type parameters during an open or close of a window, and the last two communicate to PowerBuilder that the event was handled.

**TABLE 7.9** The Message Object Properties

| Attribute | Data Type | Description |
|---|---|---|
| Handle | Integer | The control/window handle |
| Number | Integer | The (Microsoft Windows) event ID |
| WordParm | UnsignedInt | The word parameter of the Windows message |
| LongParm | Long | The long parameter of the Windows message |
| DoubleParm | Double | A number or numeric variable |
| ClassDefinition | PowerObject | A PowerObject containing information about the object or control |
| StringParm | String | A string or string variable |
| PowerObjectParm | PowerObject | Any PowerBuilder object |
| Processed | Boolean | Part of the script to indicate that the event was processed |
| ReturnValue | Long | The value to return to Windows if it's processed |

If the Processed attribute isn't set to TRUE, default Windows event processes will be executed.

To find the appropriate Windows message ID, you need to consult a Windows API book or have a copy of a Windows C/C++ compiler that provides a copy of WINDOWS.H. The code required to trap a Windows message in the Other event is straightforward as long as you have the correct message ID (and have converted it from hexadecimal to decimal if the value is taken from WINDOWS.H).

For example, to detect when the application goes into an idle state, you would place the following script in the Other event:

```
If Message.Number = 289 Then
```

```
// WM_ENTERIDLE 0x0121
// Do some processing
Message.Processed = TRUE
End If
```

> **Note**
>
> The `Other` event is fired whenever there is a message sent to the window. This is extremely inefficient and not useful because you now can create and define your own user events. For instance, the preceding example can use the `Idle()` event of the application to carry out the same functionality.

You could use a constant in the comparison to make it more readable and eliminate the need for the comment.

# Events

Events are triggered when actions are performed against an object. The script that you write for an event determines what processing takes place in response. PowerBuilder provides a number of default event handlers for the more commonly called events. For example, when you open a window, PowerBuilder handles the creation and screen painting of all the window's controls. An event originates either from the user performing an action or from the execution of a PowerScript statement. Events caused by PowerScript statements can occur at one of two times: immediately or when a request is placed in the Windows event queue that will be executed after the current processing is complete.

You can also use events to allow objects to be loosely coupled with other objects. This means that you can attempt to execute events that an object might have without causing an error if they don't exist; this allows you to generalize code, thus making it more reusable.

As you already know, some PowerScript statements, such as `MessageBox()` and `this.X = 1200`, cause events to be triggered. These are always processed before anything further in the processing queue takes place. To directly control the origination of events, use the two PowerBuilder functions `TriggerEvent()` and `PostEvent()`, or trigger the event with dot notation. Both functions can be used to originate events in an application object, providing that it has at least one open window; otherwise, there's no event queue to post to.

The event types available in PowerBuilder are

- Predefined object events already mapped to `pbm_` event IDs

- User-definable object events that you map to `pbm_` event IDs

- Custom object events that you map with the `pbm_custom` IDs

- Custom object events with multiple parameters and a definable return type

The first two event types provide the relevant parameters for the event. The custom object events (`pbm_custom`) still provide only the `WordParm` and `LongParm` parameters. The final type allows you to define as many arguments as you want, just as you do in function definition, as well as define a return value. This gives you the flexibility of a function while at the same time providing the capability to extend and override ancestor scripts.

In the next sections, you see how to call each type. Remember that the first three are still triggered the same way, but the final type requires a different syntax.

## TriggerEvent()

When you require an event to be executed before continuing with the remainder of a script, you need to use the `TriggerEvent()` function. This function bypasses the object's current event queue and processes the event immediately. The syntax for this function is

```
ObjectName.TriggerEvent( Event {, WordParm, LongParm })
```

*Event* can be a string that identifies a user event or a value of the `TrigEvent` enumerated data type. The optional *WordParm* and *LongParm*, both of the Long data type, are used to pass values to events. These two values are stored in the `Message` object's *WordParm* and *LongParm* attributes and can be retrieved in the event triggered.

The *LongParm* parameter can also be used to pass a single string value to the event. Within the triggered event this string can be retrieved by using the `String()` function. For example, in the calling event, the code might be

```
cb_ok.TriggerEvent( Clicked!, 0, "DO IT")
```

The `Clicked` event for the object `cb_ok` command button would then include the following code:

```
string ls_StringPassed

ls_StringPassed = String( Message.LongParm, "address")
// Other event code
```

> **Caution**
>
> If you're going to use these two parameters, you should retrieve them from the `Message` object at the earliest opportunity in the triggered event. The `Message` object is used continuously by PowerBuilder in the processing of events, and the contents might have changed if you take your time getting to them.

If you want to use the *LongParm* parameter, remember that because both parameters are required, you must set *WordParm* to a value, usually 0.

The `TriggerEvent()` function returns 1 if it's successful and the event script is run, or -1 if the event isn't valid for *ObjectName* or if no script exists for that event. This obviously keeps you from returning any information directly using `TriggerEvent()`. The attributes of `Message` can't be used to return information from the called event because they're cleared out at the end of that event's script processing.

> **Note**
>
> To extend the standard `Message` object, use your own user object to include some additional fields that will allow you to return information. See Chapter 26, "Building User Objects," for more information.

# PostEvent()

To cause the origination of an event after all currently queued events are completed, use the `PostEvent()` function. The `TriggerEvent()` function causes the desired event to be executed synchronously with the calling script, but `PostEvent()` causes the event to be processed asynchronously. This causes posted events to be processed in the order in which they're posted. The syntax for this function is

```
ObjectName.PostEvent( Event{, WordParm, LongParm } )
```

The parameters are the same as for the `TriggerEvent()` function.

That the events happen in the order in which they're issued can lead to some strange happenings when you've posted some events and caused others to be triggered. The triggered events will occur before the posted ones, and you aren't guaranteed the order in which an event will be processed when you post it. For example, a posted event earlier in the queue may cause additional events to be triggered, which might cause some unexpected side effects.

# Additional Calling Methods

PowerBuilder provides a more robust method for calling both functions and events (in other words, the methods of an object). This also provides Sybase with the means to support parameters for events more elegantly than through trying to extend the existing TriggerEvent() and PostEvent() functions. Sybase didn't stop at just adding the parameterized event mechanism but also allows dynamic binding and the capability to post functions. This is the new method syntax:

```
[Trigger ¦ Post] [Static ¦ Dynamic] [Function ¦ Event] MethodName( [ Arguments])
```

> **Note**
>
> The keywords Trigger, Static, and Function are the defaults for this syntax, but you are advised to explicitly state Trigger and Function to make your code more readable.

The only keywords in this syntax that you should be unfamiliar with are Static and Dynamic. The Dynamic keyword allows you to write a call for a method that might not currently exist but will be available at runtime. PowerBuilder does a runtime search for the function and produces an error if it can't locate it. For example, if you have a base class user object but define only certain methods in descendant class objects, you would use the Dynamic keyword:

```
// uo_1 is an ancestor class object that does not have a uf_calculate()
// function. This script can be called with either uo_2 or uo_3, both
// are descendants and do have a uf_calculate() function.
uo_1 luo_Object
Integer li_Value

luo_Object = Create Using as_ObjectClass

li_Value = luo_Object.Dynamic uf_calculate()
```

You would receive a compilation error in the PowerScript editor if you didn't use the Dynamic keyword because the data type of luo_Object is uo_1, which doesn't have a uf_calculate() function. However, the class that luo_Object will be at runtime does have this function.

The keywords can appear in any order. This is the calling syntax for dot notation calls:

```
ObjectName.[ Keywords] MethodName( [ Arguments])
```

In this case, *Keywords* is a combination of `Trigger`, `Static`, and so on.

## The `Trigger` Event and the `Trigger` Function

To call parameterized methods synchronously, you must use the following syntax:

```
ObjectName.Trigger Event EventName( { Parameter1, Parameter2, ..})
```

*EventName* is the name specified in the Events prototype of the object *ObjectName*. Notice the spacing between `Trigger`, `Event`, and *EventName*. These commands must be separated from each other; otherwise, PowerBuilder misinterprets the line as an invalid attribute of the object.

As an example of the new syntax, consider triggering an event on a single-line edit field, `ValidateItem`, that expects two strings. The event script takes these two values, compares them with the value in its `Text` attribute, and returns a Boolean response. The code in the `ValidateItem` event would be

```
// Where as_Value1 and as_Value2 are the parameters defined for the event
If this.text = as_Value1 Or this.text = as_Value2 Then
   Return TRUE
End If


Return FALSE
```

The calling script would look like this:

```
Boolean lb_Return

lb_Return = sle_order_no.Trigger Event ValidateItem( "1059", "1050")

If lb_Return Then
   // Acceptance processing
Else
   // Some other processing
End If
```

As you can see from these scripts, it looks as though you've suddenly gained a lot of programming power. That's not completely so in this case. The event call is *tightly coupled*, meaning that the event `ValidateItem` must exist in the object `sle_order_no` and must take two parameters. In this case, the event is actually little more than a normal function. You will get a compilation error (`C0051: Unknown function name:` ) if you try to call the `ValidateItem` event for an object that doesn't have it defined.

> **Note**
>
> With the introduction of event parameters, you might get informational messages indicating that parameters are now hiding a global, shared, or instance variable. That's why using variable-scope prefixes is a good idea. In the preceding example, event arguments are prefixed with `as-`.

As you can see, the area between object-level functions and the object's events has become a little blurred. Which method, function, or event you use to implement a given piece of functionality is left to your own preference. These are the key differences between events and functions:

- Calling a nonexistent function at runtime produces an error. Calling a nonexistent event simply yields a return value of `-1`.

- Events can extend ancestor processing. Functions override their ancestor's processing, although you can call the ancestor by using the `Super` keyword.

- Events have public accessibility that can't be changed. Object-level functions have a definable access level.

> **Note**
>
> It's up to 50 percent faster to run simple 5,000- and 10,000-iteration loops to call the same functionality in an event than in a function. This is true even with fully qualified function calls.

The same syntax for triggering a parameterized event can also be used to trigger functions; the only benefit to this that we've found is a slight performance gain (the 10,000-iteration loop takes 9 seconds rather than 10 seconds). The syntax is

```
ObjectName.Trigger Function FunctionName( {Parameter1, Parameter2, ..})
```

You might be asking yourself, "What use is a parameterized event to me?" The speed gain is worth it, even if it's not always measurable. In earlier versions, one real benefit came with the capability to post this event into the message queue for later processing; however, with the capability to post functions, that benefit is neutralized. (You learn more about this in the next section.) Probably the best feature of parameterized events is the encapsulation they allow you to achieve with objects. Rather than declare a window function to carry out some processing, you can now collect this functionality with the object that it affects or uses.

> **Note**
>
> If you're using an inherited parameterized event, each level of the event uses the initial value of the arguments. Modifications you make to a parameter value in one level aren't reflected at the other levels of the inheritance chain for the event.

## The `Post` Event and the `Post` Function

There's also a syntax that mirrors the `PostEvent()` function and allows the posting of parameterized events (and even functions) to the event queue for asynchronous execution:

```
ObjectName.Post Event EventName( { Parameter1, Parameter2, ..})
```

The parameters are the same as for `Trigger Event`, and the syntax is identical except for the keyword change from `Trigger` to `Post`. Again, the event call is tightly coupled to the object that you're posting to.

The blurring between object-level functions and the object's events continues with the capability to post functions into the processing queue. This is done with the syntax

```
ObjectName.Post Function FunctionName( { Parameter1, Parameter2, ..})
```

The only restrictions on posting events and functions is that they can't return a value. In fact, PowerBuilder won't allow you to compile the script containing such a call.

## Chaining Calls

This syntax can be extended even further by chaining together multiple calls using the dot notation. With chaining, the return value of the function or event becomes the object for the next call, and so on. Each call must return an object except the last one, which can return anything. This is the syntax:

```
Function1ReturnsObject().Function2ReturnsObject().Function3ReturnsAnything()
```

The following conditions and restrictions apply to the keywords:

- A posted method must be the last method in a chain of calls.

- You can't assign the returned value of a posted method call or pass it as an argument.

- If you post an object function that's not available at runtime, you will get a runtime error.

- The DYNAMIC keyword can be used only with functions.

- You must use the REF keyword before any argument that's passed by reference in a call using DYNAMIC.

- The DYNAMIC keyword can be specified only once in a statement and carries over to additional calls for that statement.

As you might imagine, you can concoct some pretty hairy calling sequences, and you should fully comment about what a chained call is meant to be doing. Also note that because you've chained calls together, you can't test for the failure of a single call before attempting the next. If you need to (and it's usually a good idea to), check the return value of a call. Before making further calls, break the statement into its constituent pieces.

To illustrate the new syntax, here are some examples together with comments of what each call is achieving:

```
// Posting a call to a global function
Post f_calculate_weight(ar_TarePercent, ai_Quantity)
//
// Making a call to a dynamic function of a user object
uo_bag_calcs.Dynamic uf_bag_width( Ref ar_Width, ai_Length, ls_ProductCode)
//
// Assigning a variable to the return of a chained call
ai_Length = uo_bag_calcs.uf_return_bag( ls_ProductCode).uf_bag_length()
```

## The Send() System Function

Two additional ways to send event messages to objects involve using the Send() and Post() functions. Use these two functions if you want to originate an event for an object over which PowerBuilder doesn't have direct control (for example, another Windows application or an external user object).

The syntax for the Send() function, which is comparable to the TriggerEvent() function in its execution, is

```
Send( Handle, Message#, WordParm, LongParm)
```

The *Handle* parameter is the Windows handle to the object to which you want to send a message. The message ID is passed in the *Message#* parameter as an unsigned integer. The *WordParm* and *LongParm* parameters are used in the same manner as for the TriggerEvent() and PostEvent() functions.

For example, if you wanted to change the text of a window, in this case controlled by PowerBuilder, the code would be

```
Send( Handle( w_frame), 12, 0, "This is the new window title")
```

To change the title of a window that's outside PowerBuilder, you first need to acquire its Windows handle by using the Windows FindWindow()API function. For example, you could alter an open Windows calculator window title using the following code:

```
uInt hWnd

hWnd = FindWindow( "scicalc", "calculator")

Send( hWnd, 12, 0, "This is the new window title")
```

## The Post() System Function

The corresponding function to PostEvent() is the Post() function. The syntax is

```
Post( Handle, Message#, WordParm, LongParm)
```

The parameters are the same as for the functions mentioned previously.

## Accessing Ancestor Event Return Values

Occasionally you need to carry out processing at a descendant level of an event that depends on an ancestor script's return value. Before PowerBuilder 6.0, the code required to get the return values from the ancestor scripts was somewhat taxing; it often required overriding the ancestor and then manually calling the ancestor script via code. PowerBuilder 6.0's addition of the AncestorReturnValue local variable makes it much easier by giving you a direct reference to the return value of the direct ancestor script. AncestorReturnValue is declared automatically and assigned the value the ancestor event returned, and the data type always matches that of the event's return type. AncestorReturnValue is available in your descendant script in either of the following cases (both require that the event return a value):

- When you extend an event script in a descendant (the desired way to implement this logic)

- When you override an ancestor script but use the CALL syntax to process the ancestor script (the old method to get hold of the return value of the ancestor script)

The following code shows how you would access an ancestor return value before the advent of the `AncestorReturnValue` variable:

```
// Top of descendant event script - which we have to override
Integer li_AncestorValue

li_AncestorValue = Call Super::MyEvent

If li_AncestorValue = 1 Then
    // Do something
End If
```

With `AncestorReturnValue`, you can rewrite this descendant event script as follows:

```
// Top of descendant event script - which we can leave as extended
If AncestorReturnValue = 1 Then
    // Do something
End If
```

Or, if you really do need to override the descendant script, as this:

```
//
// Some other descendant processing first - event is overriden
//
Call Super::Clicked

If AncestorReturnValue = 1 Then
    // Do something
End If
```

**Caution**

When migrating an application created before PowerBuilder 6.0, `AncestorReturnValue` is generated automatically in any script that extends an event or uses the CALL syntax. This means that a compiler error occurs if you have any variables declared as `AncestorReturnValue`. If you do, rename them *before* trying to migrate. If you implement variable scope and data type prefixes for variables, this won't be an issue.

# Pronouns

PowerBuilder uses four *pronouns*. These four reserved words (`This`, `Parent`, `Parent-Window`, and `Super`) have special meanings that depend on where they're used. Pronouns are used extensively when building objects for inheritance or when building them to be encapsulated (which is the aim of every object). Just like in English, pronouns are used to provide a generic reference to an object, and in PowerBuilder they make your code more reusable.

## This

The pronoun `This` is used in PowerScript to generically reference the object for which the script is written so that you can write code without tying the script to a specific object name. For example, `This.width = This.width * 2` has the same functionality as `cb_delete_row.width = cb_delete_row.width * 2`, except that if the button is renamed, the first piece of code would still work, but the second would require updating to the new button name.

`This` should be used in place of all object self-references (usually attribute access) within the object's scripts. The pronoun can also be used in function call arguments in place of the object's name, as long as the argument isn't being passed by reference (although you can pass it as a `ReadOnly` argument). For example, the following code sample calls a window function for the object `w_frame` and passes itself as an argument:

```
w_frame.RegisterMe( This)
```

> **Note**
>
> Most objects have a reference passed by value when the argument type is by value. The exceptions to this are structures and auto-instantiating objects, which have their contents passed by value. If an object is passed by reference, `This` is a reference to the passing variable.

## Parent

Nearly every object in PowerBuilder—and for that matter, in Windows itself—has a parent. To reference an object's owner, use the `Parent` reserved word. The meaning of `Parent` changes depending on where it's used: in an object on a window, in an object in a custom user object, or in a menu item.

When used in a window control, `Parent` refers to the window. The most common use is in a Close button, where it's used to make the code generic. The following two examples are functionally the same, but the first is generic and makes the object a good candidate for reuse:

```
Close( Parent)
Close( w_script_window )
```

Inside a custom user object, any control that uses `Parent` in fact references the user object itself, not the window on which the user object is placed. This permits controls in the user object to change the parent without mentioning the parent's name. The parent user object's name most likely will be different on each window on which it's placed, so you can't write generic functions without the use of `Parent`. To access the user object's parent object, you can use the `GetParent()` function. You might have to make successive calls until you reach the window or the user object you want. Of course, this allows you access only to the attributes and methods defined for the `PowerObject` class. Sometimes you might want to restrict the kind of object your user object can be placed on and set this instance variable to the appropriate class data type.

---

**Tip**

If you use a standard visual user object for every control used in an application, you can place a `WindowParent()` method on each control that checks to see whether `GetParent()` returns an object of the `window` class and, if it doesn't, returns a call to that object's `WindowParent()` function. The PowerBuilder Foundation Class (PFC) leverages this logic throughout and is discussed in greater detail in Chapter 25, "The PFC." Even if you aren't using the PFC in your application, you may want to look at the code to get an idea about how you might be able to use this logic.

---

When used within a menu item, `Parent` references the menu item on the next level up. The parent depends on the level of cascading. (See Chapter 12, "Menus and the Menu Painter," for a discussion about cascading menu items.)

## ParentWindow

The reserved word `ParentWindow` is used only in menus. `ParentWindow` refers to the window to which the menu is attached and can be used anywhere in the menu. For example, under the menu item `m_close`, the code might be

```
Close (ParentWindow)
```

`ParentWindow` refers to the window the menu is assigned to at runtime. Although this doesn't preclude the hard-coding of a specific window name, a single menu might be associated with multiple windows. This is especially true when you're coding an MDI application because most window sheets usually share a single menu.

## Super

The `Super` pronoun, used only when dealing with inheritance, refers to the ancestor from a descendant object. The name of the ancestor object can be explicitly stated but is more commonly (and more clearly) referred to in generic terms as `Super`.

`Super` can be used with the `CALL` statement to cause execution of ancestor events from a descendant object. This would be used in events that have overridden their ancestors but conditionally need to call the ancestors script for some processing. The syntax for `CALL` is

```
CALL AncestorObject {'ControlName}::Event{ ( Argumentlist ) }
```

*AncestorObject* is the descendant's ancestor object; you can replace it with the `Super` keyword. The optional *ControlName* specifies the name of the control in an ancestor window or a custom user object that you want to trigger the event specified by *Event*. If the event takes parameters, you need to supply the expected arguments. In this case, *AncestorObject* needs to specify a window or user object. Here's an example:

```
CALL Super::Show
```

It also can be used directly to access an ancestor function that has been overridden by the descendant:

```
Super::wf_function( arg1, arg2)
```

By using the `CALL` statement, you can cause the execution of the ancestor script anywhere in your descendant script. Execution of the descendant then continues after the ancestor script is finished. This allows you to carry out descendant processing before allowing the ancestor script to execute. Unfortunately, you don't have access to the local variables in the ancestor script, and you have to use larger scope variables to pass information backward and forward.

The `CALL` syntax includes the capability to post ancestor functions, events, and the capture of return values. The syntax for this form is

```
{Object.} Ancestor :: { FunctionorEvent}{TriggerorPost} Name ({ Argumentlist})
```

where *FunctionorEvent* is the name of the function or event you're calling, and *TriggerorPost* is of the keyword TRIGGER or POST, indicating the call type. An example of a call using this syntax is

```
ls_ReturnValue = Super::TRIGGER wf_function (arg1, arg2)
```

# Statements

PowerScript provides a number of statements that range from control-of-flow to halting the application. The following sections detail the more complex of these; it's assumed that you are familiar with basic coding concepts and syntax.

## Choose...Case

We included this control-of-flow statement to describe a particular usage style that not many people seem to be aware of but has some powerful, practical applications.

The following is an example of a Choose...Case control structure that uses a Boolean test to check whether a certain key was pressed:

```
Choose Case TRUE
    Case KeyDown( KeyPageUp! )
        wf_SynchPageUp( )
    Case KeyDown( KeyPageDown! )
        wf_SynchPageDown( )
    Case KeyDown( KeyUpArrow! )
        wf_SynchUpArrow( )
    Case KeyDown( KeyDownArrow! )
        wf_SynchDownArrow( )
End Choose
```

> **Note**
>
> One major benefit of using Choose...Case is that when the condition is met, it doesn't check any further values. This works similarly to an If...Then...ElseIf statement; however, it's much more readable.
>
> One common mistake among developers is the use of If...Then statements in the ItemChanged event when checking for the column that has changed. Implementing the Choose...Case logic should help optimize your code and avoid any incorrect logic branching that might inadvertently occur with If...Then statements.

## HALT and Return

The HALT statement immediately terminates an application. You can optionally use the keyword CLOSE with HALT to cause the Close event of the application object to be executed before finishing. The normal use for this statement is to stop an application after a serious error that can't be recovered from or after a security violation occurs (for example, on a login screen).

The Return statement halts the current execution of a script as though the script had completed, so that the application waits for further user interaction or returns to the calling script. This statement is used in functions to send a value back to a calling script.

**Caution**

Beginning with PowerBuilder 6.0, if you attempt to return an expression from a subroutine, an error will be generated where there was previously a warning.

# PowerBuilder Units

All sizes in PowerBuilder are measured in PowerBuilder units, or PBUs. The only exceptions to this are the Window painter and DataWindow painter grid sizes, which are measured in pixels. Sybase provides this unit of measure so that your application looks similar running on a VGA, EGA, or SVGA monitor.

Before PowerBuilder 6.0, Sybase used the same technique that Windows uses, which is based on the system font (where sizes are defined in terms of one quarter of the character width and one eighth of the character height). PowerBuilder units, however, are defined in terms of *logical inches*. The size of a logical inch is defined by the operating system as a specific number of pixels.

You don't need to worry about this unless you're making external function calls that require position or size information about a PowerBuilder object, in which case you need to convert to the expected measurement units. Two PowerScript functions are provided to carry out conversions between PBUs and *pels* (picture elements or pixels).

## UnitsToPixels()

The UnitsToPixels() function is used to convert PBUs to pels in the horizontal or vertical direction:

```
UnitsToPixels( Units, ValueDirection)
```

The *Units* parameter is an integer PBU value that will be converted to pels. The *ValueDirection* parameter is of the `ConvertType` enumerated data type and indicates which axis the value belongs on. The valid values for *ValueDirection* are `XUnitsTo-Pixels!` and `YUnitsToPixels!`. The function's return value is the converted value in pels.

### PixelsToUnits()

The `PixelsToUnits()` function is used to convert pels to PBUs in the horizontal or vertical direction:

```
PixelsToUnits( Pixels, ValueDirection)
```

The *Pixels* parameter is an integer pel value that will be converted to PBUs. The *ValueDirection* parameter is of the `ConvertType` enumerated data type and indicates which axis the value belongs on. The valid values for *ValueDirection* are `XPixelsToUnits!` and `YPixelsToUnits!`. The function's return value is the converted value in PBUs.

The `PixelsToUnits()` function—useful when you're accessing the screen size attributes from the `Environment` object—allows you to correctly center a window within the display (see Appendix E).

# File Functions

PowerBuilder provides a number of functions to read and write text and BLOBs (binary large objects) to files. Additional functions provide other ways to manipulate files as well as provide a user interface for specifying filenames.

## File-Access Modes

Files can be read or written to through one of two methods: line mode or stream mode. When reading in line mode, characters are transferred until a carriage return (CR), line feed (LF), or end of file (EOF) is encountered. Writing in line mode causes a carriage return and a line feed to be appended to each line of text written. Stream-mode reading transfers up to 32,765 bytes from a file or until an EOF is found. Writing in stream mode enables up to 32,765 bytes (characters) to be written at a time and doesn't append CR or LF characters.

## Opening a File

When PowerBuilder opens a file, it assigns a unique number to each request, and your PowerScript uses this value in all file operations to indicate the required open file. This value is an integer and is returned from the FileOpen() function on a successful open. -1 is returned on a failure to open.

---

**Note**

You won't receive a return of -1 if the file doesn't exist when you're opening it to write. PowerBuilder creates a new file if the one specified can't be found.

---

The syntax of the FileOpen() function is

```
FileOpen(FileName{,FileMode{,FileAccess{,FileLock{,WriteMode{,   &
                                            Creator,FileType}}}}})
```

FileOpen() uses the following arguments:

- *FileName* is either the complete path to the file or a filename that exists in the machine's search path.

- *FileMode* is the mode discussed in the preceding section and can be either of the two enumerated types: LineMode! or StreamMode!. PowerBuilder uses LineMode! by default if no file mode is specified.

- *FileAccess* is the reason the file is being opened, either to read or write. The enumerated types Read! and Write! are used, with Read! being the default.

- *FileLock* determines whether other users can access the file being operated on and, if so, what kind of access they have. This enumerated type will be one of LockRead-Write!, LockRead!, LockWrite!, or Shared!. LockReadWrite!, the default, permits access to only the user who opened the file. LockRead! gives other users write access but not read access. LockWrite! gives other users read-only access. Shared! permits everyone to read and write. The behavior of this parameter depends on the network you're using.

- *WriteMode* determines whether the file is appended to or overwritten if the file being opened for writing already exists. The enumerated types Append! and Replace! are used, with Append! being the default. *WriteMode* is ignored when you're opening for read.

- *Creator* applies only on the Macintosh and is a four-character, case-sensitive string that specifies the creator of the file. If you don't specify a value, the file's creator is set to ttxt (for TeachText or SimpleText).

- *FileType* is a four-character string indicating the file's type. If you specify a *Creator*, you must also specify a file type. If you don't specify a value, the file's type is set to TEXT.

The following examples illustrate some of these settings and their use on different platforms:

```
Integer li_FileNo
//
// Use default arguments: LineMode!, Read!, LockReadWrite! to read
// a file from the current working directory
li_FileNo = FileOpen("PBU7.TXT")
//
// Open the file PBU7.TXT for writing in stream mode.
// Any existing information is overwritten.
li_FileNo = FileOpen("C:\DOCS\PBU7.TXT",StreamMode!,Write!,LockWrite!,Replace!)
//
// For file access on a Macintosh this would be
li_FileNo = FileOpen("HD:Docs:PowerBuilder Unleashed 7 Intro", &
                     StreamMode!, Write!, LockWrite!, Replace!)
//
// For file access on Unix this would be
li_FileNo = FileOpen("/home/docs/pbu7.txt",StreamMode!,Write!, LockWrite!, &
Replace!)
```

## Closing an Open File

As with database connections, an open file also needs to be closed. The FileClose() function closes the specified file and restores full access to other users. The syntax is

```
FileClose (FileNumber)
```

*FileNumber*, the same integer value returned from FileOpen(), is used in all file operations to distinguish among multiple open files.

## Reading from a File

After you open a file, you can read information from it for use in an application by using the FileRead() function. Its syntax is

```
FileRead (FileNumber, StringOrBlobVariable)
```

*FileNumber* is the integer value returned from the FileOpen() function call. *StringOrBlobVariable* is used to hold the characters or bytes read from the file.

FileRead() returns one of four values:

- -100 if an EOF is encountered

- -1 if an error occurs

- 0 if CR or LF is the first information read (LineMode! access only)

- The number of characters or bytes read into the variable

If the file mode is LineMode!, FileRead() reads characters until a CR, LF, or EOF is found. The end-of-line characters are skipped, and PowerBuilder positions the file pointer at the start of the next line.

If the file mode is StreamMode!, FileRead() reads to the end of the file or the next 32,765 characters or bytes, whichever occurs first. If the file is longer than 32,765 bytes, FileRead() positions the pointer after each read operation so that it's ready to read the next section of information.

The following example opens a file on the G: drive called test.out for reading and locks out all other access to it. The FileRead() is used in a loop condition to read lines into a string array.

```
Integer li_File, li_Count = 0
String ls_FileLines[]

li_File = FileOpen( "G:\test.out", LineMode!, Read!, LockReadWrite!)
Do
   li_Count ++
Loop While FileRead( li_File, ls_FileLines[ li_Count]) > 0
FileClose( li_File)
```

**Note**

This example specifies all parameters, even if they are the default, to make the code more obvious. Write mode isn't specified because this is a read.

# Writing to a File

To write information to a file, use the `FileWrite()` function. `FileWrite()` returns the number of characters or bytes written to the file, or `-1` if an error occurs. Its syntax is

```
FileWrite( FileNumber, StringOrBlobVariable)
```

If the write mode is `Append!`, the file pointer is initially set to the end of the file and is repositioned to the new end of file after each `FileWrite()`. If the file mode is `LineMode!`, `FileWrite()` writes a CR and an LF after the last character of the line. The file pointer is set after these.

If the write mode is `Replace!`, the file pointer is set to the start of the file. After each `FileWrite()` call, the pointer is positioned after the last write.

> **Note**
>
> Because `FileWrite()` can write a maximum of only 32,766 bytes at a time, if the length of the variable exceeds 32,765 (including the string terminator character), `FileWrite()` writes only the first 32,765 characters and returns `32,765`.

Here's an example:

```
Integer li_File, li_Count = 0, li_Loop
String ls_FileLines[]

// Fill the string array with test data
For li_Loop = 1 To 10
   ls_FileLines[ li_Loop] = "Jeff, Natalie, Tyler, Kennedi"
Next

li_File = FileOpen ("G:\test.out", LineMode!, Write!, LockReadWrite!, Append!)
For li_Count = 1 To 10
   FileWrite( li_File, ls_FileLines[ li_Count])
Next
FileClose (li_File)
```

A couple of other ways to read and write information from a PowerBuilder application are specific to DataWindows and are discussed in Chapter 15, "Advanced DataWindow Techniques I," and Chapter 16, "Advanced DataWindow Techniques II."

## Using Windows Dialogs

Windows provides two dialogs that give users access to a number of controls to specify the exact directory and filename for the desired file. You access these dialogs via the `GetFileOpenName()` and `GetFileSaveName()` functions.

Use `GetFileOpenName()` to obtain a valid filename and path for an existing file (see Figure 7.4). The syntax for this function is

```
GetFileOpenName( Title, PathName, FileName {, Extension {, Filter}})
```

`GetFileOpenName()` doesn't open the file the user selects; you must still code a `FileOpen()` call.

**FIGURE 7.4**
*The Select File dialog.*

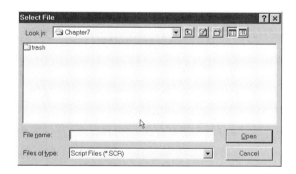

`GetFileOpenName()` uses the following arguments:

- *Title* is a string that you want to appear as the title for the dialog.

- *PathName* holds the full path and filename returned from the dialog.

- *FileName* holds just the filename (and extension) returned from the dialog.

- *Extension* is a string of up to three characters that's used as the default file extension. The default is no extension.

- *Filter* contains a string describing the files to include in the files of type list box and the file mask to associate with it. This argument limits the type of files displayed in the list box. For example, to list only Script Files (*.SCR), the string literal passed as the filter would be

    ```
    "Script Files (*.SCR),*.SCR"
    ```

- To specify multiple filters, use a comma after each set, like so:

    ```
    "Script Files (*.SCR),*.SCR,Data Files (*.DAT),*.DAT"
    ```

The `GetFileOpenName()` function returns one of three integer values:

- 1 on a success

- 0 if the user clicks Cancel (or if for some reason Windows cancels the dialog)

- -1 if an error occurs

An example of a complete call to `GetFileOpenName()` is as follows:

```
nFile = GetFileOpenName( "Select File", ls_FullPath, ls_File, "SCR",  &
                "Script Files (*.SCR),*.SCR,Data Files (*.DAT),*.DAT")

If nFile = 1 Then FileOpen( ls_FullPath)
```

If users try to enter a file that doesn't currently exist, a message box appears (see Figure 7.5).

`GetFileSaveName()` uses the same dialog shown in Figure 7.4 to obtain a filename and path for the save destination. The syntax for this function is

```
GetFileSaveName( Title, PathName, FileName {, Extension {, Filter}})
```

The parameters and action of the dialog are the same as for the `GetFileOpenName()` function, with one difference: Even a nonexistent file can be specified because the file and

**FIGURE 7.5**

*A message box appears when you try to select an invalid file.*

path being built are to be saved to and not read from.

# Checking for File Existence

Occasionally you need to verify a file's existence. For this task, you use the `FileExists()` function:

```
FileExists (FileName)
```

*FileName* is a fully qualified path and filename, or just a filename if the check is being made against the machine's search path, and the function returns TRUE or FALSE. Here are two examples:

```
FileExists( "PB.INI")
FileExists( "WIN.INI")
```

Both examples will return TRUE if the directories \PB *x* and \WINDOWS exist on the machine running the application, and if they're both included in the machine's PATH.

**Note**

The search path might vary from one machine to another, so using fully qualified filenames is advisable. The path is searched in order, so you might find a file in a different directory than the one you were expecting.

**Tip**

You can place PowerBuilder in a loop to wait for the appearance of a certain file. When you execute a Run() command in PowerBuilder, processing continues immediately without waiting for the executable or batch file to finish. However, if you modify the batch file or executable to create a temporary file at the end of the batch, PowerBuilder can check for this file before continuing. A DOS executable can be run from a BAT file to get the same functionality, if required.

# Deleting a File

To delete a file, use the FileDelete() function:

```
FileDelete( FileName)
```

*FileName* can be fully qualified or just the name. It's highly advisable that you specify the full path when deleting a file, for obvious reasons. The function returns TRUE or FALSE on successful deletion of the file.

# Finding the Length of a File

To find the length of a file, use the FileLength() function:

```
FileLength( FileName)
```

This function returns a Long that's the length (in bytes) of the file. If the file doesn't exist, -1 is returned. The following example returns the length of the file BAILEY_JADE.TXT in the current directory:

```
FileLength( "BAILEY_JADE.TXT")
```

FileLength() is usually called around a FileOpen() call to check the number of characters that can be expected from a FileRead().

> **Note**
>
> If the file is being shared on a network, you must call FileLength() before FileOpen(); otherwise, a sharing violation occurs.

## Positioning Within a File

You can move the file pointer backward and forward within a file to specify the point at which the next read or write begins. The syntax is

```
FileSeek( FileNumber, Position, Origin)
```

FileSeek() uses the following arguments:

- *FileNumber* specifies the integer file number returned from FileOpen().

- *Position* is a Long that specifies the new position relative to the *Origin*.

- *Origin* is a SeekType enumerated data type that specifies a position in the file. The values are FromBeginning! (the default), FromCurrent!, and FromEnd!.

The FileSeek() function returns a Long that's the file pointer position after the seek is completed or a -1 if the file doesn't exist. The following example moves the file pointer 95 bytes in from the start of the file:

```
Integer li_File

li_File = FileOpen( "BAILEY_JADE.txt")
FileSeek( li_File, 95, FromBeginning!)
```

> **Note**
>
> Immediately after a FileOpen(), the positions of FromBeginning! and FromCurrent! are the same.

# The Error Object

The Error object contains all relevant information about an error situation needed for reporting to the user. Sybase only shows the use of the Error object with the SystemError event, but there's no reason not to use this structure for passing error information in the rest of the application's events. Table 7.10 lists the attributes of the Error object.

**TABLE 7.10** The `Error` Object's Attributes

| *Attribute* | *Data Type* | *Description* |
|---|---|---|
| ClassDefinition | PowerObject | Class definition information of the object or control |
| Number | Integer | The error number |
| Text | String | The error message text |
| WindowMenu | String | The window or menu where the error occurred |
| Object | String | The object where the error occurred |
| ObjectEvent | String | The event where the error occurred |
| Line | Integer | The line where the error occurred |

A number of errors can occur at the time of an application's execution. The errors listed in Table 7.11 cause the `SystemError` event to be called.

**TABLE 7.11** System Errors that Can Be Trapped in the `SystemError` Event

| Error.Number | Error.Text |
|---|---|
| 1 | Divide by zero |
| 2 | Null object reference |
| 3 | Array boundary exceeded |
| 4 | Enumerated value is out of range for function |
| 5 | Negative value encountered in function |
| 6 | Invalid DataWindow row/column specified |
| 7 | Unresolvable external when linking reference |
| 8 | Reference of array with NULL subscript |
| 9 | DLL function not found in current application |
| 10 | Unsupported argument type in DLL function |
| 12 | DataWindow column type doesn't match GetItem type |
| 13 | Unresolved attribute reference |
| 14 | Error opening DLL library for external function |
| 15 | Error calling external function |
| 16 | Maximum string size exceeded |
| 17 | DataWindow referenced in DataWindow object doesn't exist |
| 18 | Function doesn't return value |
| 19 | Can't convert *name* in Any variable to *name* |
| 20 | Database command hasn't been successfully prepared |
| 21 | Bad runtime function reference |
| 22 | Unknown object type |
| 23 | Can't assign object of type *name* to variable of type *name* |
| 24 | Function call doesn't match its definition |
| 25 | Double or real expression has overflowed |
| 26 | Field *name* assignment not supported |
| 27 | Can't take a negative to a non-integer power |

**TABLE 7.11**  System Errors that Can Be Trapped in the `SystemError` Event

| Error.Number | Error.Text |
|---|---|
| 28 | VBX Error: *name* |
| 30 | Doesn't support external object data type *name* |
| 31 | External object data type *name* not supported |
| 32 | *Name* not found calling external function *name* |
| 33 | Invalid parameter type calling external object function *name* |
| 34 | Incorrect number of parameters calling external object function *name* |
| 35 | Error calling external object attribute *name* |
| 36 | *Name* not found accessing external object attribute *name* |
| 37 | Type mismatch accessing external object attribute *name* |
| 38 | Incorrect number of subscripts accessing external object attribute *name* |
| 39 | Error accessing external object attribute *name* |
| 40 | Mismatched Any data types in expression |
| 41 | Illegal Any data types in expression |
| 42 | Specified argument type differs from required argument type at runtime in DLL function *name* |

If the `SystemError` event hasn't been overridden, PowerBuilder displays a standard message box with an OK button that details the specifics of the error (see Figure 7.6).

Ten errors don't cause the `SystemError` event to be triggered; instead, they cause the application to be terminated immediately (see Table 7.12).

**TABLE 7.12**  Errors that Don't Trigger the `SystemError` Event

| Error.Number | Error.Text |
|---|---|
| 50 | Application reference couldn't be resolved |
| 51 | Failure loading dynamic library |
| 52 | Missing ancestor object *name* |

**FIGURE 7.6**

*Application Execution Error message box for PowerBuilder.*

**TABLE 7.12**  Errors that Don't Trigger the `SystemError` Event

| Error.Number | Error.Text |
|---|---|
| 53 | Missing ancestor object *name* in *name* |

**TABLE 7.12** Errors that Don't Trigger the `SystemError` Event

| Error.Number | Error.Text |
|---|---|
| 54 | Conflicting ancestor object *name* in *name* and *name* |
| 55 | Window close occurred processing yield function |
| 56 | Database interface doesn't support remote procedure calls |
| 57 | Database Interface doesn't support array variables (function *name*) |
| 58 | Blob variable for *name* can't be empty |
| 59 | Maximum size exceeded |

The `SignalError()` function triggers the `SystemError` event programmatically. This is used in the case of errors severe enough to halt the application (for example, the database connection was lost and the server went down). If `SystemError` isn't coded to respond to the error value passed in via the `SignalError()` call, the message is ignored.

`SignalError()` allows you to populate the `Error` object with an error number and text. Its syntax is

```
SignalError( [ number, text])
```

Of more use before calling `SignalError()` or even before calling your own error handler is the `PopulateError()` function. This function populates most of the `Error` object for you and requires you only to specify the error number and error text. This obviously makes trapping errors in your code so much easier and more precise; before PowerBuilder 6.0, you had to count your own line numbers into the script and pull the object's class name, among other things.

To provide a consistent interface to an error situation, many applications use a single window to display and handle the problem. The `Error` object is often used to pass to the window information from the script in which the error occurred. Here's an example:

```
If SQLCA.SQLCode = -1 Then
    PopulateError(SQLCA.SQLDBCode, SQLCA.SQLErrText)
    Open( w_error)
End If
```

The window—in this case, w_error (see Figure 7.7)—then takes the values from the `Error` object in the `Open` event and places them into the appropriate single- and multiline edit controls. w_error allows users to halt the application or try to recover from the error and return to the calling code. To disable the Halt command button, pass in a negative line number; this forces users to return to the calling code because the only enabled button is Recover and Return. You can disable the Quit the Application button if the calling script determines that there's a recoverable option to the situation, a need to disconnect other database connections, or a need to free up some memory usage before halting the application.

After error processing is captured in a single area, other processing can also be carried out. The sample window shown in Figure 7.7 is MAPI enabled and will create and send an email message to a specified user. This functionality is invaluable during user acceptance testing and final deployment to catch any small problems that only end users ever encounter. Another enhancement is that you can code in understandable English so that

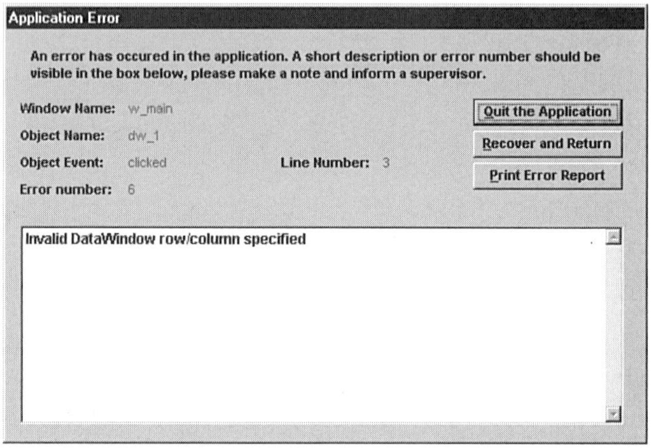

**FIGURE 7.7**

*An example of an error window.*

users can understand many of the cryptic database errors. You would do this with a Choose...Case on the DBMS to provide a more generic (and therefore reusable) error window.

Only two other events specifically trap error events— DBError and ItemError, found only in the DataWindow control. These events are discussed fully in Chapter 14, "DataWindow Scripting."

# Summary

In this chapter, the basic concepts used in PowerBuilder and its programming language, PowerScript, are defined as well as more advanced topics such as events and messages, file functions, and error handling.

# The Library Painter

## IN THIS CHAPTER

As you already know, when you create a new application object, you can also create a PowerBuilder library file with the extension .PBL (pronounced "pibble"). Any other objects you create for your application are also stored in a PBL. A common scenario for an application is to have your objects stored across multiple PBLs. Because library files are a repository for all your objects, you need some method of managing these libraries and the objects contained in them. You do this by using the Library painter.

Because libraries are integral to any PowerBuilder application, you should follow some structure guidelines to get optimum performance out of them. This chapter looks at some library file guidelines and then explores how to manipulate your library files and PowerBuilder objects with the new and improved PowerBuilder 7.0 Library painter. Major enhancements have been made to help make object and library management much easier.

When creating your application, decide where the PowerBuilder library files should reside, for performance as well as source management. The following sections provide some guidelines to help increase the performance and ease of use of your library files.

# Library Placement

Before you begin any development, it's important to decide where to store the actual PBLs (that is, in what drive and directory). There are some special considerations when creating a project that involves multiple developers.

Speed is important to any application. Placing your PBLs locally (on your machine) increases the speed with which your application runs. With a single-developer application, this isn't a problem because the lone developer is the only one who requires access to the objects. With a project involving multiple developers, file location becomes more of an issue. If everyone kept a copy of the libraries locally, no one would have the most recent changes, and developers could overlay each other's work. Even if developers were careful and communicated with one another, they still would have to copy their objects manually to each of the other machines to keep themselves in sync. This doesn't seem like a productive solution, however. To work effectively with multideveloper projects, you have a couple of options:

- Place the libraries on a network drive and have everyone share those libraries. Although this is the most popular method of sharing libraries, it can cause issues when the network is large and slow, thus leading to inefficient use of costly developer time as well as frustration among developers.

- Use a robust source control application, such as Rational's ClearCase, which allows for the management of change within a multideveloper project and still lets you work on local PBLs. This is covered more in Chapter 22, "Application Maintenance and Upgrades."

Table 8.1 shows a standard configuration of a directory structure on a network drive (in this case, n:\) using the first option. (This could also be used on a local drive for a single-developer application.)

**TABLE 8.1**  The Project Directory Structure

| Directory | How the Directory Is Used |
|-----------|---------------------------|
| N:\PROJECTS | Holds common objects for multiple applications (for example, ancestors, user objects, functions) |
| \PROJECT_NAME | High-level reference directory for the following subdirectories: |
| \VERSION | Current version number of PROJECT_NAME. |
| \DEV | PBLs containing objects being developed. |
| \TEST | PBLs containing completed objects that are ready for integration testing. Changes aren't made to this directory. |
| \PROD | Production files for the current version of the application. Contains PBLs, PBDs, PBRs, EXEs, and any other miscellaneous files needed. Developers don't have access to this directory. |

If each developer uses the PBLs located in the DEV directory to make changes, all code is maintained in one place. Unfortunately, this can severely affect the speed of execution and testing due to additional network traffic. To avoid this problem, each developer should maintain a PBL on his own workstation to hold objects on which he is now working.

**8**

**The Library Painter**

**Note**

You might get the message `Save Failed - Probable file I/O Error` when you try to save an object. This typically is because someone else is accessing the library you're writing to or running the application. You can fix this by making sure that the network recognizes the library files as shared files.

You can use the library search path to list a developer's personal development PBL first and then include all the networked PBLs. This is possible because the library search path is stored in each developer's PB.INI file. By placing the test PBL at the top of the library search path, you ensure that PowerBuilder uses your copy of the object and not one found in the network PBLs.

> **Note**
>
> The library search path is important to tuning the performance of your PowerBuilder application. Frequently used objects should be placed near the top so that PowerBuilder doesn't have to search through multiple PBLs to find the requested object. For more information, see Chapter 9, "Application Objects and the Application Painter," and Chapter 20, "Application and Component Implementation, Creation, and Distribution."

# Source Management

The directory structure outlined in Table 8.1 is useful when you need to maintain multiple PowerBuilder library files, but it's also useful for managing source code. As you've seen, the directory structure breaks down each project by version number, and within that version are copies of development, test, and eventual production versions of the PBLs. This structure, or one similar to it, is commonly used across all client/server application-development projects.

Although library placement in the different directories is useful for determining a project's different phases and maintaining source code, it doesn't prevent developers from overlaying each other's code in the DEV directory. To prevent accidental modifications to a particular object, you should have three things in place: communication between team members, version control management, and a mechanism to track work in progress.

Communication between members of the development team is crucial for the success of any application. Information about who is working on each portion of an application should be readily accessible. Unassigned and undefined tasks are the areas in which potential problems can arise. You can avoid many of these problems with a good plan for application version control, ranging from using a directory structure like the one previously described or purchasing a specific software package such as PVCS or ClearCase. Sybase also has its own source-management package, ObjectCycle, for use with PowerBuilder. (For more information on ObjectCycle, see Chapter 22.)

In addition to communication, there should be a mechanism to track whether work is being done on a particular object. PowerBuilder provides a simple interface to check objects in and out to prevent a developer from modifying the same object on which another developer is working. For example, using the standard project directory structure, a developer would check out an object from a public library (DEV) and copy it to a local work library. The test library would be placed at the top of the library search path, and changes would be made to the checked-out object. After all changes were made, the developer would then check the object back in. If another developer tried to access the object while it was checked out, PowerBuilder would display a message indicating the name of the developer who had checked out the object. You learn more about the check-in/check-out facility later in this chapter.

# Library Guidelines

Several guidelines are recommended for use with PowerBuilder library files, both for tuning and ease of use. These guidelines include library organization, library size, and library optimization.

After you have a structure in place for storing your libraries, you also want to decide how to divide the objects logically in your application. In a small application, it's common to have one PBL that contains all the objects for the application. In a large application, however, having a single, large PBL containing all objects can be confusing and inefficient. The two common organization schemes for libraries are by object type and by application functionality.

Organizing your application by object type means that you maintain separate PBLs for the different object types. Suppose that one PBL contains all window objects, a second PBL contains menus, a third contains structures and functions, a fourth has all DataWindow objects, and the last contains the application and project objects. With this method, you know which objects are located in each library.

The downside to this method is that some PBLs could become very large (for example, the window library) and subsequently become difficult to manage. Keep PBL files less than 1MB in size. As the number of objects stored in the PBL increases, so do the sizes of your library files. As this happens, PowerBuilder must access the disk drive for longer periods of time as it moves through the PBL file to satisfy a request for an object. Also, if the number of objects increases to more than 40 or 50 in one library file, the Library painter and the list boxes that display objects in a library (for example, the Select Window dialog) become difficult to work with because you're always scrolling up and down.

An alternative to organizing libraries by object type is organizing by application functionality. One PBL might contain all objects common to the whole application (for example, user objects and the logon window). Another PBL might contain objects for daily sales calculations, and another the quarterly forecast objects. This is the method Sybase has taken for distributing its objects in the PowerBuilder Foundation Class. Although this method can decrease the number of entries in a library file, it can also affect the number of library files. Having too many library files can make them difficult to keep track of and can appear cluttered, and PowerBuilder would have to search through many different libraries to find an object, which can negatively affect performance.

Because both organization methods have their faults, you can use a combination of the two. Separate your objects by higher-level business functionality, and within that functionality divide the PBLs into groups of different objects. One drawback with combining methods, however, is that unless you have support for long filenames, the library names become cryptic and confusing.

> **Tip**
>
> To get the highest performance out of your libraries, optimize them frequently. Just like your hard drive, library files can become fragmented over time, thus increasing the time needed to access objects in each library. Use the Library menu's Optimize option in the Library painter to reorganize your PBLs so that PowerBuilder runs more efficiently.

After you determine the best structure for your library files, you need a tool to manage the library files—the Library painter.

# Using the Library Painter

To access the Library painter, click its icon on the PowerBar or press Shift+F10.

PowerBuilder 7.0 has introduced an exciting new interface for the Library painter. It implemented new and exciting ways to manage, move, and manipulate the objects used in your PowerBuilder applications. This section describes this new interface and points out many of the most exciting features

PowerBuilder 7.0's new interface for the Library painter is similar in look and feel to Windows 95/98 Explorer. The painter displays a tree view directory on the left to list all the available drives, the available directories, the libraries located in the directories, and the objects in the libraries (see Figure 8.1). The Library painter also contains a list view on the right, which behaves like the list view in Windows Explorer. It lists the directories, objects, and—if My Computer (or whatever you've named your computer) is selected on the left side—the drives available.

**FIGURE 8.1**

*The new PowerBuilder 7.0 Library painter.*

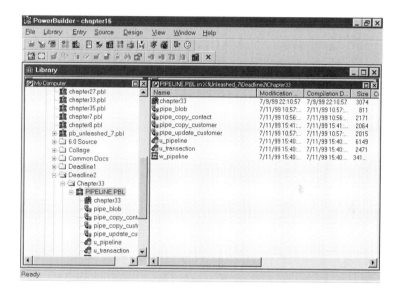

Unlike the Library painter in the past, the current application doesn't always default the to the current view. The painter defaults to the last directory that you were viewing in the tree view. If the tree view isn't currently on the current application, click the Display Current Library toolbar button or choose Current Library from the View menu.

Another new feature is the ability to control the items listed in the tree or list view by setting the root. Choose Set Root from the pop-up menu on the tree or list view, or from the View menu. This allows you to select one of five options (see Figure 8.2) that determines the root directory of the active view:

- My Computer sets the active view to all the directories mapped to your system.

- Library List sets the active view to the current application's library list.

- Directory lets you specify a directory you want to view in the current view.

- Library allows you to select a library that may or may not be the current library list.

- Current Selection limits the active view to see only the items in the currently selected item.

**FIGURE 8.2**
*The Set Root dialog.*

After you select the desired root directory, notice that the View menu lists an option beginning with Back to plus a file or pathname. If you choose this option, you then see an option beginning with Forward to plus the file or pathname. This works similar to the Explorer back and forward icons.

For the directories that contain PBLs, the painter displays the library icon followed by the library filename. The object name and an icon to the right indicating the object type identify each object. Table 8.2 displays the icons and the corresponding object types.

**TABLE 8.2   Library Painter Object Icons**

| Icon | Object Type | Icon | Object Type |
|------|-------------|------|-------------|
| | Application | | Proxy |
| | Data Pipeline | | Query |
| | DataWindow | | Structure |
| | Function | | User Object |
| | Menu | | Window |
| | Project | | |

By default, PowerBuilder displays all objects contained in a particular PBL and all the object information. You can easily modify what's displayed by using the Options dialog (choose Options from the Design menu).

You can specify the last modification date, last compilation date, comments, and compiled object size information display on the General tab page (see Figure 8.3). This page also allows you to choose whether informational and obsolete compiler messages are displayed, whether backups of library files are created when you optimize the library, and whether you're prompted on any delete action.

**FIGURE 8.3**
*The General tab page.*

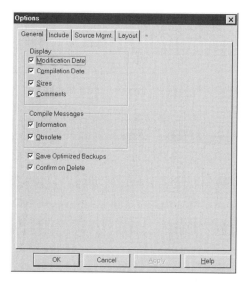

> **Note**
>
> PowerBuilder 7.0 removed the Check Out Status check box on the General tab page. Checked-out objects are now displayed differently than the other objects, as discussed later in this chapter.

The Include page (see Figure 8.4) allows you to specify what PowerBuilder objects you want to see. With this page you can specify the object types you want to view as well as place a mask on the object names you want to view. For example, if you type *ar* in the Name edit box, the only objects that display are those with ar somewhere in the object name. The criteria you specify for the painter are saved for the next time you use the painter.

> **Note**
>
> PowerBuilder 7.0 now lets you specify object types by right-clicking any library and selecting or deselecting any objects in the list. Remember, the list you specify cascades to all libraries.

FIGURE **8.4**

*The Include tab
page.*

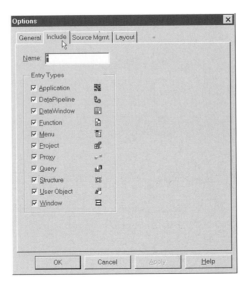

With the Source Mgmt. page, you can further specify how PowerBuilder interacts with your source management software (see Figure 8.5). To specify whether all actions performed on your source code are logged, select the Log All Source Management Activity check box and specify the desired name and location for the log file, and whether you want the activity from your current PowerBuilder session to be appended to file or overwrite existing transactions. If you select overwrite, PowerBuilder prompts you each time you go into the Library painter, asking whether you want to overwrite the log file. The Source Mgmt. page also allows you to require that developers specify comments about the changes made when an object is checked back into a PBL.

**Note**

The Library painter's source management capabilities are due to PowerBuilder's implementation of the SCC API, a standard version-control interface based on Microsoft's Common Source Code Control Interface Specification.

These are the basic components and methods of movement in the Library painter. Now look at some of the different functionalities provided by the Library painter.

**Figure 8.5**
*The Source Mgmt. tab page.*

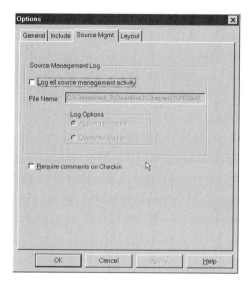

## Maintaining Libraries

As you saw earlier, you should follow a number of guidelines for better performance as well as ease of use. To successfully implement these guidelines, you need to know how to create, delete, and optimize your libraries.

### Creating a Library

Most people are familiar with creating a library in the Application painter. The only problem with this method, however, is that you're required to create an application object at the same time. In the Library painter, you can create a new PBL by choosing Create from the Library menu or by clicking the Create Library icon on the PainterBar (see Figure 8.6). Doing so causes the Create Library dialog to open.

**Figure 8.6**
*The Library painter Painter-Bar.*

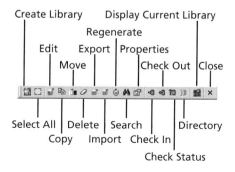

**8**

The Library Painter

After you specify the new name for your library, click the Save button to open the library's Properties sheet, in which you can add comments about the library file's purpose (see Figure 8.7). You also can access this property sheet by choosing Properties from the Library menu or by right-clicking the library file and choosing Properties.

**FIGURE 8.7**

*The library's Properties sheet.*

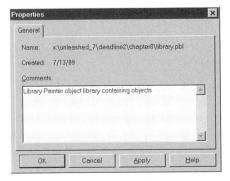

## Deleting a Library

During the course of your application's development, you might need to delete one or more library files. Choose Delete from the Library menu or from the library's pop-up menu. Doing so brings up a message box that asks for a delete confirmation. If you prefer not to be prompted for deletion of your libraries or any objects, you can specify this by clicking the check box on the General tab page of the Options dialog (refer to Figure 8.3).

> **Caution**
>
> Deleting a library deletes the physical file and all objects contained in the file. The library file can't be retrieved via PowerBuilder. Having said this, you may still attempt to recover the deleted library using any file recovery that your operating system supports or any third-party recovery software

## Library Optimization

Because objects are constantly inserted, deleted, and updated in your library files, the library file is constantly fragmented. A fragmented library has areas of unused space and objects that aren't stored contiguously to your hard drive. Fragmentation can have an adverse effect on performance. In addition to the areas of unused space, PowerBuilder sometimes creates something known as a *dead object*—one specified for deletion within

PowerBuilder but for some reason still physically exists in the library. By optimizing your libraries regularly, you can remove the fragmentation and dead objects.

To optimize a library, choose Optimize from the Library menu or from the pop-up menu. To have PowerBuilder create a backup of your library before performing optimization, choose Save Optimized Backups from the General tab page on the Options dialog. PowerBuilder then creates a copy of your library file with the extension .BAK in the same directory as the library selected to be optimized.

## Maintaining Entries

After you create a new library file, you often need to copy or move objects from one library to the new one. You may also need to delete an object from a PBL, which must be done through the Library painter.

### Caution

PowerBuilder 7.0 has taken away the ability to select objects across multiple libraries. You can no longer select all the objects for your application and perform a single action on them.

When the desired objects are selected in the tree or list view, choose Copy from the Entry menu, click the Copy icon on the PainterBar, press Ctrl+C, or choose Copy from the pop-up menu. This opens the Select Library dialog, which asks for the name of the destination library.

Similar to copying objects is the process of moving entries from one library to another. When you specify that you want to move an object, PowerBuilder copies the object to the destination library and then deletes it from the source library. To move one or more entries, select the desired objects and choose Move from the Entry menu, press Ctrl+M, click the Move icon on the PainterBar, or choose Move from the object's pop-up menu. Choosing Move opens a dialog identical to the one used for copying objects.

### Note

When copying and moving objects in PowerBuilder 7.0, you are now prompted to confirm the overriding of objects of the same name in the destination library.

The one missing piece that has caused PowerBuilder developers to scratch their collective heads has finally been implemented in the Library painter. PowerBuilder now supports dragging and dropping of PowerBuilder objects between libraries. If you select an object or group of objects, you can drag and drop it or them on another library, whether or not that library is in the library list. If you want to move the object(s) completely out of the current library and into a different library, drag while pressing the Shift key. It's been a long wait, but I think that the benefits of drag-and-drop functionality will make us forget our years of frustration.

If you've erroneously copied or moved an object or just have an extra object hanging around, the only way to delete that object is through the Library painter. Select the object(s) and choose one of the options PowerBuilder gives you to delete objects. You are prompted to confirm deletions if you have the Confirm on Delete option checked on the Options dialog's General tab page.

> **Note**
>
> PowerBuilder 7.0 now allows you to select the Yes to All button on the deletion confirmation dialog, and you won't be prompted for deletion confirmation for the subsequent objects. If you click just the Yes button, you are continually prompted for deletion confirmation for any subsequent objects. Remember, this functionality isn't available to any prior versions of PowerBuilder.

In addition to copying, moving, and deleting objects, you can also view an object's general property information (see Figure 8.8). Select the desired object and choose Properties from the Entry menu or pop-up menu. Although most of the information on the property sheet is read-only, you can modify the comments for the object.

## Searching Objects

It's often necessary to search through an object or multiple objects for a specific function name, variable, or whatever. You usually need this functionality when you are in the Script view. Unfortunately, PowerBuilder allows you to search only through the displayed script. The Library painter allows you to look for a search string across multiple objects.

To browse for a specified string, select one or more objects and then click the Search icon on the PainterBar, or choose Search from the Entry menu or the pop-up menu. In the Search Library Entries dialog (see Figure 8.9), specify the desired string to search for in the Search For text box (the string can't contain any wildcards or placeholders). If you want to match upper- and lowercase, select the Match Upper/Lowercase check box. When you've specified the desired string, you can select which parts of objects are to be searched (properties, scripts, and variables) and what information you want displayed if a match is found. After you specify everything, click OK to process your search. If any matches are found for the search criteria, the Matching Library Entries dialog appears (see Figure 8.10).

**FIGURE 8.8**
*The object Properties sheet.*

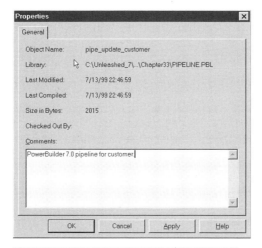

**FIGURE 8.9**
*The Search Library Entries dialog.*

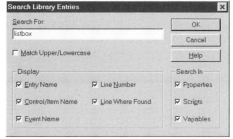

**FIGURE 8.10**
*The Matching Library Entries dialog.*

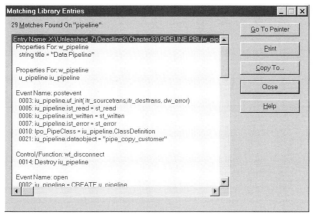

What's specified in the Search Library Entries dialog affects what's displayed in the search results. If you leave the defaults (everything chosen), you will see the entry name, the event/attribute/variable, and the usage of the search string. PowerBuilder lets you perform several functions from the Matching Library Entries dialog:

- If you double-click an entry or click the Go To Painter button, PowerBuilder launches the entry's painter and opens the object. New to PowerBuilder 7.0, the appropriate script where the match was found will now be opened.

- Clicking the Print button sends the search results list from the Matching Library Entries dialog to the printer.

- The Copy To button allows you to specify the name of a text file to which to save the search results.

## Exporting and Importing Entries

By exporting and importing library entries, you can convert your PowerBuilder objects to an ASCII file format and vice versa. This can be useful for viewing object syntax as well as for modifying the object's definition. To learn how to read the exported code syntax, see Appendix C, "Investigating Exported Code."

### Exporting

Exporting an object to a file takes the source code definition of your PowerBuilder object (event scripts and object attributes) and creates an ASCII file. To export an object, select it and click the Export icon on the PainterBar or choose Export from the Entry menu or the pop-up menu. This opens the Export Library Entry dialog (see Figure 8.11).

**FIGURE 8.11**
*The Export Library Entry dialog.*

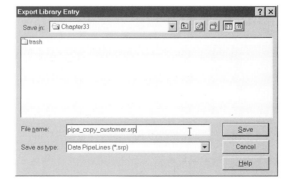

PowerBuilder provides a default name for the exported object based on the object's name. The extension for the objects is .SR *x*, where *x* represents the object type (in this example, a w for a Window object).

> **Note**
>
> If you're running on a platform that doesn't support universal naming conventions (UNCs), the object name is truncated to comply with the local naming conventions.

The exported file can then be pulled up, viewed, and/or modified in any text editor, such as the File Editor that comes with PowerBuilder. Although modifying an exported file typically isn't recommended, sometimes you might need to do so.

## Importing

If you have an exported file in ASCII format, you can import the file to convert the source code back into a compiled PowerBuilder object. To import an ASCII file, click the Import icon on the PainterBar or choose Import from the Entry menu. The Select Import Files dialog (see Figure 8.12) looks for files with the extension .SR*.

**FIGURE 8.12**
*The Select Import Files dialog.*

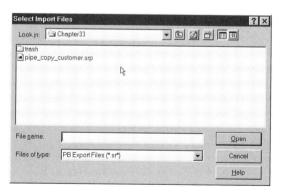

After selecting the desired text file, you're prompted with the Import File Into Library Entry dialog (see Figure 8.13). Select the destination library for the imported object and click OK.

**FIGURE 8.13**

*The Import File Into Library Entry dialog.*

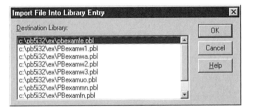

## Caution

If an object with the same name already exists in the destination library, the import overwrites the existing object with the new object. *PowerBuilder doesn't notify you of this.* If the import fails, the original object is deleted.

## Regeneration

A PowerBuilder library file contains an object's compiled version and the source code. *Regeneration* is the process of deleting the existing compiled object and recompiling the source code. Many times you will need to regenerate your library objects (for example, when you migrate your application from one PowerBuilder version to another). Another, more common, case is when you're using inheritance: If a modification is made to an ancestor object, you should regenerate the ancestor and all descendants to ensure that all changes are propagated through the inheritance tree. The Object Browser enables you to easily regenerate descendants of an altered ancestor object.

## Note

Regeneration ensures that descendant objects are updated. The regeneration works the same way for inherited menus and user objects as it does for inherited windows.

To regenerate your objects, select the objects you want and click the Regenerate icon on the PainterBar or choose Regenerate from the Entry menu or from the pop-up menu.

One difficulty of regenerating with inheritance is remembering all the objects involved. An easy way around this is to use the Object Browser and its regeneration capabilities. You can use the Object Browser not only to view your application's objects (see Chapter 2, "PowerBuilder 7.0 Development Environment," for more details), but also to view the class hierarchies of PowerBuilder's system classes, menus, user objects, and windows.

To open the Object Browser, choose Browse Objects from the Window menu. The Object Browser displays the Application tab page as the default. Four tab pages allow you to view a class or object hierarchy: Menu, System, User Object, and Window. Click the System tab, right-click, and select Show Hierarchy to view the system class hierarchy (see Figure 8.14).

**FIGURE 8.14**
*The Object Browser.*

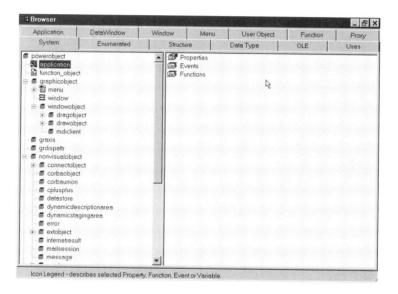

From the three object tabs, you can regenerate the objects and their descendants. This is easier than regenerating each object individually because you can regenerate all objects in an inheritance tree in one go. Select the ancestor object, right-click, and select Regenerate to regenerate the ancestor object and all its descendants.

# Printing

From within the Library painter, you can create several different printouts. You can print a library directory of the objects that it contains and print out object details. To print a library directory, select a library and choose Print Directory from the Library menu or from the pop-up menu. The printout shows all the objects in the library, the size, the modification date, and comments.

To print out the object details, select the object(s) and choose the Print menu item from the Entry menu or from the pop-up menu. The Print Options dialog opens (see Figure 8.15).

**FIGURE 8.15**
*The Print Options dialog.*

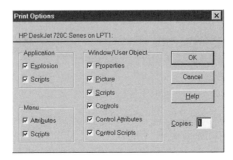

Clicking OK generates a report with the specified options. The objects selected when you choose from the menu dictate what information is printed. As you can see, you can print properties, scripts, control details, and so on.

# Source Management

Any application development should include a plan for source management. PowerBuilder helps you control access to your library entries to ensure that only one developer is working on a library entry at any given time. To best implement this, use a centralized test library to contain the completed objects. Each developer should maintain individual libraries that are used to make changes to copies of the original objects.

Objects can be extracted and inserted from the test library via the Library painter's check-out and check-in facilities. When an object is checked out, only the developer who checked it out can modify or change the object; it can't be modified in the public test library or checked out by another developer. Only after the object is checked back in can modifications be made to it by others.

## Checking Out an Object

When an object is checked out of a library, only the developer who checked it out can modify it. After the object is modified and tested, the developer checks it back into the public test library.

During the check-out process, PowerBuilder copies the selected object to a specified destination library (typically, the developer's private library). PowerBuilder stores—with the checked-out object—information about where the object was taken from and who checked it out. It then sets the status of the object to checked out. This status prevents the original object from being altered and allows only the working copy to be modified.

To check out an object, select the desired object and click the Check Out PainterBar icon or select Check Out from the Source menu or the pop-up menu.

If this is the first time you've checked out an object, PowerBuilder prompts you to enter a user ID (see Figure 8.16). The user ID is stored in the [Library] section of your PB.INI file. You're asked only once to specify a user ID, and you have to manually change the PB.INI file to make any alterations to the ID.

**FIGURE 8.16**

*The Set Current User ID dialog.*

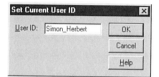

After you enter the User ID, the Check Out Library Entries dialog opens (see Figure 8.17). Specify the destination library and click Open. If the entry isn't already checked out, PowerBuilder creates a working copy in the destination library. If the entry is checked out, PowerBuilder displays a message indicating that the object is checked out and by whom and asks whether you want to continue (in which case PowerBuilder opens a read-only copy of the object for you).

**FIGURE 8.17**

*The Check Out Library Entries dialog.*

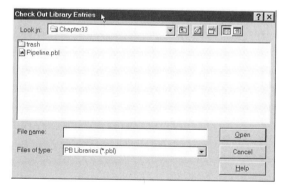

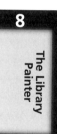

To find out the check-out status of an entry, click the Check Status icon on the PainterBar or select View Check Out Status from the Source menu. The View Entries Check Out Status dialog appears (see Figure 8.18). This dialog can be used to display all checked-out objects as well as print a list of the checked-out objects.

**FIGURE 8.18**

*The View Entries Check Out Status dialog.*

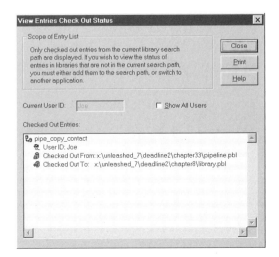

> **Note**
>
> Keep in mind some implications of checking out objects. Because checked-out objects are locked, they can't be moved to a different library because a move deletes the entry from the originating library. These objects can be copied, but the copy won't retain the check-out status.

[ic:version] in PB 7.0]Figure 8.19 shows the new way in which an object has been checked out. It now indicates the status by indenting the object and placing the icon to the left of the object. As you can see, both the original and working copies of the object are indicated by the new style in the tree view; the list view displays them without indentation.

## Checking In an Object

After checking out and modifying an object, you are ready to check it back into the public test library. When you check in an object, the original copy is replaced with the working copy. The checked-out object is copied over the original object and then deletes the working copy in the development library.

To check in the working copy, click the Check In icon on the PainterBar or choose Check In from the Source menu. Multiple objects can be checked out and in at the same time.

**FIGURE 8.19**

*New indention style check-out indicators.*

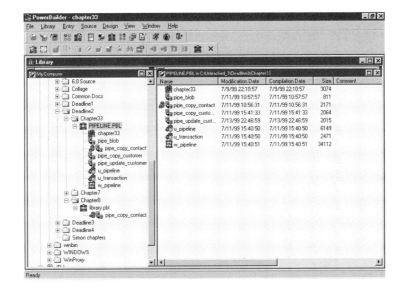

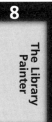

**8**

The Library Painter

> **Note**
>
> You can create a new PBL and copy objects to it to remove their check-out status if something goes wrong during a check in. Of course, this can be frustrating in a multideveloper system because everyone has to check his objects back in first.

## Clearing the Check-Out Status

If for some reason you no longer want to use the checked-out copy, you can clear the check-out status and delete the object from your private development library. To clear the check-out status, choose Clear Check Out Status from the Source menu. PowerBuilder asks whether you want to clear the check-out status of the library entry; click OK. PowerBuilder then asks whether you want to delete the library entry's working copy. Click Yes to delete it or No to leave the copy.

The Library painter shouldn't be relied on as a version-control system because it's only as effective as the techniques and standards followed by the development team. PowerBuilder provides an interface for an external version-control system, such as PVCS or ClearCase; the options for interacting with such a system are provided in the Source menu.

# Creating Dynamic Libraries

With the Library painter, you can create PowerBuilder dynamic libraries (PBDs or DLLs). To create a dynamic library, choose Build Runtime Library from the Library menu or from the pop-up that appears when you right-click a library name. The Build Runtime Library dialog opens (see Figure 8.20).

**FIGURE 8.20**

*The Build Runtime Library dialog.*

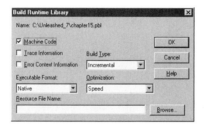

You can specify whether the dynamic library will be P-code or machine code and whether it will contain debug information by using the Trace and Error Context Information check boxes. You can specify the optimization type: No Optimization, Space, or Speed. You also can specify a resource file in the Resource File Name text box if needed. Click OK for PowerBuilder to create the dynamic library. It will have the same name as the source library, but with a .PBD extension for a P-code dynamic library and .DLL for a machine code library.

You can find further discussion of the advantages of using dynamic libraries in Chapter 20, "Application and Component Implementation, Creation, and Distribution."

# Application Migration

When you move from a prior release of PowerBuilder to Version 7.0, you must migrate all your applications. The migration process takes place in the Library painter. If you try to open an application object created in an earlier release in the Application painter, PowerBuilder opens the Library painter and the Migrate Application dialog (see Figure 8.21).

You can also open the Migrate Application dialog by choosing Migrate from the Design menu. From this dialog, you can specify what type of error messages are processed. PowerBuilder captures syntax errors, but it can also display informational messages and obsolete syntax messages. PowerBuilder allows you to specify a library search path for the selected application object. Click the Browse button to open the Select Library dialog. In this dialog, you can select any PBLs you want to include in the search path.

8

The Library Painter

**FIGURE 8.21**

*The Migrate Application dialog.*

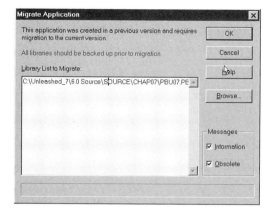

**Tip**

If you mistype or leave out a library name for your application's library search path, regeneration of your objects is unsuccessful and your application migration will fail. PowerBuilder doesn't give you the opportunity to reenter the library search path, so the solution is to modify the search path in your PB.INI file for the specific application. After you change this, try to migrate again.

PowerBuilder 7.0 runs the migration process in what Sybase refers to as *batch mode*. This means that PowerBuilder tries to migrate all objects and displays any messages after all objects are processed. This is useful in that you don't have to review each message as it's processed. Before migration occurs, PowerBuilder indicates that you should perform a backup of any libraries before proceeding with migration.

Any errors are displayed in a Compiler Errors dialog (see Figure 8.22). This dialog displays the erroneous object, event, and line number(s). The message type is indicated next to the actual error message. These messages can be sent to the printer or the Clipboard, or can be written to a text file. If the migration process encounters an error (non-informational and obsolete), migration of that object doesn't occur and the problem must be corrected in the older version of PowerBuilder before the object can be used in 7.0. Those objects can also be exported from within 7.0, modified, and reimported if you know what needs to be changed.

**FIGURE 8.22**

*The Compiler
Errors dialog.*

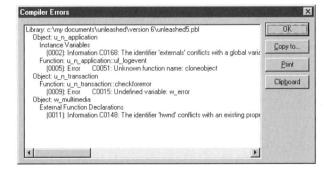

> ### Tip
>
> When you choose New from the PowerBar or the File menu, a Migration Assistant in the Start Wizards tab page helps you locate any obsolete syntax.

# Library Functions Used in PowerScript

You can incorporate a number of PowerScript functions into your application to access library files: LibraryCreate(), LibraryDelete(), LibraryDirectory(), LibraryExport(), and LibraryImport().

The LibraryCreate()function creates an empty PowerBuilder library. The syntax for this function is

```
LibraryCreate (LibraryName {, Comments})
```

The *LibraryName* is the name of the library you want to create. The library is created in the current directory if a path isn't included. If no extension is specified, the .PBL extension is added for you. The *Comments* argument is used to create a description entry for the library. The function returns 1 if it succeeds, -1 if an error occurs.

A LibraryDelete()deletes an entire library file or a DataWindow object from a library. The syntax is

```
LibraryDelete (LibraryName {, ObjectName, ObjectType})
```

The *LibraryName* is the name of the library file. To delete a DataWindow object instead of the library, you must include the *ObjectName* parameter (a string containing the DataWindow object name) as well as *ObjectType*. The *ObjectType* is of enumerated data type `LibImportType` (this now supports only the `ImportDataWindow!` value). The function returns 1 if it succeeds, -1 if an error occurs.

The `LibraryDirectory()` function returns a list of the objects contained in a PowerBuilder library. The list contains the name, date and time of the last modification, and any comments for each object. The list can be restricted to a particular object type if required. The syntax is

`LibraryDirectory (LibraryName, ObjectType)`

The *ObjectType* argument is of the enumerated data type `LibDirType` and identifies the type of objects to be included in the list. Table 8.3 lists the possible values and their descriptions.

**TABLE 8.3** `LibDirType` Values and Descriptions

| Value | Object Type | Value | Object Type |
|---|---|---|---|
| DirAll! | All objects | DirProject! | Project |
| DirApplication! | Application | DirQuery! | Query |
| DirDataWindow! | DataWindow | DirStructure! | Structure |
| DirFunction! | Function | DirUserObject! | User |
| DirMenu! | Menu | DirWindow! | Window |
| DirPipeline! | Pipeline | | |

The function returns a string containing a tab-delimited list with each object, with multiple objects separated by the ASCII value for a new line (~n). Here's an example:

`w_customer_detail~t1/2/96 17:58:04~tCustomer detail list`

The general format is

`object_name ~t date/time modified ~t comments ~n`

The `LibraryExport()` function is used to export an object from a library to a text file. The syntax is

`LibraryExport (LibraryName, ObjectName, ObjectType)`

The *ObjectType* is of the enumerated data type `LibExportType`, which identifies the object type to be exported. Table 8.4 lists the possible values and their descriptions.

**TABLE 8.4** `LibExportType` Values and Descriptions

| Value | Object | Value | Object |
|---|---|---|---|
| ExportApplication! | Application | ExportUserObject! | User |
| ExportDataWindow! | DataWindow | ExportWindow! | Window |
| ExportFunction! | Function | ExportPipeline! | Pipeline |
| ExportMenu! | Menu | ExportProject! | Project |
| ExportStructure! | Structure | ExportQuery! | Query |

The function returns a string containing the syntax of the object if the operation succeeds. This syntax is the same as the syntax generated when the object is exported from within the Library painter. The only difference is that this function doesn't include an export header. An empty string (`""`) is returned if an error occurs.

The `LibraryImport()` function imports objects into a library. Now, only DataWindow objects are supported. The syntax for this function is

```
LibraryImport (LibraryName, ObjectName, ObjectType, Syntax, Errors
    {,Comments})
```

The `ObjectType` parameter is of the `LibImportType` enumerated data type, and now supports only `ImportDataWindow!`. The `Syntax` parameter is a string containing the syntax of the DataWindow object to import. The `Errors` parameter is a string variable that's filled with a description of any errors that occur. `Comments` is an optional string that's used as the comment for the library entry. The function returns 1 for success, -1 if an error occurs. This function is particularly useful for dynamically created DataWindows.

# Summary

As you've seen, the improvements to the Library painter implemented in PowerBuilder 7.0 should help make working with your objects easier. The Library painter allows you to manage libraries and their entities to improve performance and accessibility. With the Library painter, you can create, delete, and optimize your PowerBuilder libraries. The entities of the libraries can be manipulated as well.

You learned that the check-out and check-in facilities provide a useful interface that's designed to protect the development environment. Finally, you were introduced to several PowerScript functions that can be implemented into your application to interface with your application library files.

# Application Objects and the Application Painter

**CHAPTER 9**

When working with any development tool, you need a context to work within and, more importantly, a place to start the application. For you, the PowerBuilder developer, the application object defines the framework in which you begin to create your application.

This chapter defines what an application object is and how to change each object component through the Application painter. It examines the attributes, events, methods, and uses of the application object. This chapter also examines some processing that can be incorporated into a nonvisual user object for use with the application object.

# What's an Application Object?

An *application object* is a nonvisual object that maintains high-level information about your application and is the entry point into your application. What's meant by *high-level information*? The main components stored with the application object are as follows:

| | |
|---|---|
| Default font specifications | Application functions |
| The application icon | Application instance variables |
| Default global class variables | Global external functions |
| Global variables | Application structures |

Whenever an application is executed (at runtime or design time), the application object is first object loaded, and the Open event of the application object is the first script executed. If the script is empty, your application does absolutely nothing, and PowerBuilder prompts you to write a script for the Open event. Therefore, this script must tell PowerBuilder what to do—for example, open the first window (which is explored later in the section "The Open Event").

# Application Painter Basics

To access the Application painter, click the New toolbar button to open a dialog containing all the objects that can be created. Under the Start Wizards tab, you can select the Application or Template Application icon.

To create a new application object, double-click the Application icon. The Specify New Application and Library dialog appears (see Figure 9.1), prompting you to specify the name of the application and the location and name of the new library file (PBL). The application object name has the same restrictions as any other object or variable name (up to 40 characters, no embedded spaces, and so on). After you enter those two pieces of information, click the Finish button. PowerBuilder creates the file and the new application object within.

FIGURE **9.1**

*The Specify New Application and Library dialog.*

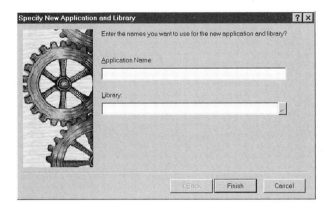

If you have no other painters open in PowerBuilder, you won't notice anything happening after the dialog closes. Rest assured that your file and application have been created. If you now open the Library painter, you can find your library file and application object at the location you created them on your file system. Within the Library painter, you can add descriptive text in the Comments list box to provide additional information about the application (typically a high-level business description).

Selecting the Template Application icon from the Specify New Application and Library dialog opens a new dialog that steps you through providing the following information:

- Application object name and location of library file.

- The type of application you want to create: MDI Application with MicroHelp, SDI Application, or PFC-based application.

- The Library Search Path. If you selected a PFC-based application previously, you need to add the PFC libraries at this point.

- For MDI (multiple-document interface) applications, you are presented with questions relating to the object names for the MDI Frame, MDI Frame Menu, Base Sheet Window, Sheet Menu, Sheet Manager Service, About Window, and Toolbar Window. Optionally, you can create up to three sheet windows, specifying the object names and window titles.

  For SDI (single-document interface) applications, you are presented with questions relating to the object names for the Main Window, Main Menu, and About Window.

- What the application will be connecting to: SQL Database, Jaguar connection, or none.

- For a SQL Database connection, you are prompted with a list of existing Database Profiles.

For a Jaguar connection, you need to specify the server, port, login, and passwords required for it.

- The location of the connection information: INI File, Registry, or controlled by a Script in your application.

Next is the build screen. Clicking the Finish button generates the library file and all the objects you've requested.

The application template method is a quick way to generate a prototype and learn how to create, for example, an MDI application, in PowerBuilder. The template creates: An MDI frame with MicroHelp, a generic sheet, a window for manipulating the toolbars, an About window, a menu for the frame, and an inherited menu for the sheet. This provides a useful framework for beginning developers. If you have more experience, the application template has some useful functionality that can be incorporated into your objects.

If you want to modify the template that PowerBuilder generates, you can change the definition of the default objects. Sybase cleverly implemented template generation. In the PowerBuilder directory, locate a file named PBGEN070.DLL. Make a copy of the file to PBGEN070.PBL and look at the PBL in the Library painter. Surprise! There are the objects PowerBuilder uses to create its default Application template (see Figure 9.2).

**FIGURE 9.2**

*The PBGEN070.PBL object listing in the Library painter.*

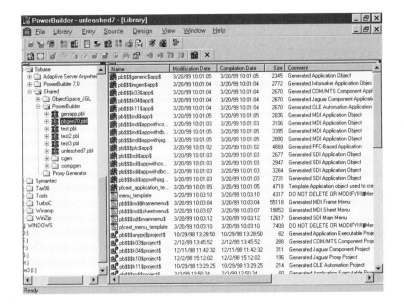

You can modify the default PowerBuilder template objects when you have the PBL form. You can modify the default objects to incorporate additional scripts, functions, and variables, but you won't be able to incorporate any new objects. When you're happy with the objects, you simply rename your template PBL back to PBGEN070.DLL. You now have your own custom application template. (Notice that the window, `pb$$$mdi$toolbars$`, includes a nice interface to include in an MDI application.)

> **Tip**
>
> You should make a backup copy of PBGEN070.DLL before replacing it, just in case you break something with your modifications!

To open an existing application object, you have three options: find the application object by using the Library painter and double-click to open it, use the new version 7.0 feature under the File menu where PowerBuilder maintains a list of recently accessed applications, or use the Select Application item under the File menu. The default is up to eight, but this can be changed under the System Options dialog (accessed from the Window menu) to a maximum of 36. Either brings up the Application painter, as shown in Figure 9.3.

**FIGURE 9.3**
*The Application painter.*

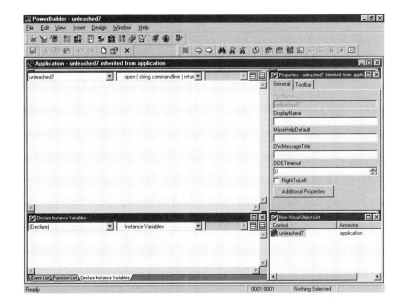

**Note**

You can change the application object only when no other painters are open in PowerBuilder.

The title bar of the Application painter contains the name of the current application. The same holds true for PowerBuilder's title bar. For example, the title in the figure is *PowerBuilder - unleashed7* (*unleashed7* is the name of the currently open application). Each application maintains a list of PowerBuilder library files (PBLs) from which objects can be read and modified. This is important because it defines the scope of objects accessible from other painters. You can open and edit only objects that are within the list of PBLs defined by your application object, and you can have only one application open at a time in PowerBuilder.

## The Library Search Path

The *library search path* is one of the most important aspects of the application object because it defines which objects can be accessed for the current application object. An application comprises multiple objects (windows, menus, and so on) that can be stored in one or several PowerBuilder libraries. The library search path defines a list of libraries from which PowerBuilder can pull objects to be used in the application.

The library search path works in the same way as the DOS search path. If PowerBuilder can't find an object referenced in the first library, it searches through the library list until the specified object is found. Because PowerBuilder starts at the top and works down, it's recommended that you list the libraries with the more frequently used objects near the top to increase performance.

There are three common reasons to set up a library search path:

- You can have quick and easy access to a library that contains objects used across all applications in a company (for example, a logon window or user objects).

- Each developer can maintain a private test library containing checked-out copies of objects being modified. By placing the test library at the top of the list, all objects the developer is modifying in the test library are used instead of any other versions.

- Multiple library files are used to logically arrange the objects that comprise your application. For an in-depth look at how to arrange your objects in your libraries, see Chapter 8, "The Library Painter."

To define the library search path, choose Library List from the File menu or click the Library List toolbar button. In the Library List dialog (see Figure 9.4), you can specify which libraries—local or networked—you want to include.

FIGURE **9.4**
*The Library List dialog.*

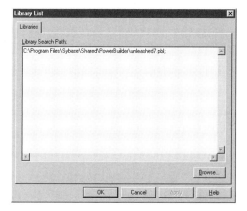

To add a library to the search path, click the Browse button, locate the library's directory, and select the library's name to paste it in the search path list box. (To select multiple libraries in the Library List dialog, hold down the Ctrl or Shift key.) If you prefer to manually type in the library names, use Enter to move to a new line. To remove a library name from the search path, select the PBL name in the edit box and press Delete.

**Note**

The library search path is maintained for each developer using the application, so it must be set up for each developer individually for the application to function correctly. This also allows for the use of the private test library mentioned previously. The library search path is stored in the [Application] section of your PB.INI file. The search path can be modified there as well as in the Preferences painter.

9

Application
Objects and the
Application
Painter

# Components of the Application Object

When you have the application object open in the painter, you are ready to set the default information about your application: application icon, default fonts, and default global variables. To access these attributes, click the Additional Properties button in the Properties pane to open the Application property sheet (see Figure 9.5).

**FIGURE 9.5**

*The Application property sheet.*

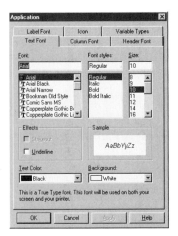

## Setting the Default Fonts

Within the Application painter you can specify the default fonts and text colors, sizes, and styles for the application. You can apply different settings to all text, columns, headings, and labels that appear in your application. By enabling you to choose this information at a high level, PowerBuilder reduces the need for you to set the font properties every time you create a new object (such as a window). What you set at this time will be the standard font used throughout the application.

To change the default fonts, select the appropriate tab page for the object for which you want to set a default. The tab page interface is the same for text, columns, headings, and labels. The only difference is that you can change only the text and background colors on the Text Font tab page.

> **Note**
>
> After an object is created, it no longer has any knowledge of the default fonts. In other words, no link is maintained for the fonts after an object is created, so changing the default font on the application object after objects are already created doesn't affect the created objects.

# The Application Icon

The application icon represents the application when you set up a new item on the Windows Start menu. To select an icon for your application, click the Icon tab. You can choose from the handful of stock icons that PowerBuilder supplies or specify your own .ICO file.

The icon file you choose is also used as the default icon for all windows in that application. Whenever a window is minimized in the application, the application object icon is the default. You can override this in the Window painter (see Chapter 10, "Windows and the Window Painter").

# Default Global Variables

PowerBuilder enables you to use your own customized versions of the default global objects (SQLCA, SQLDA, SQLSA, Error, and Message). First, you must create a standard class user object inherited from one of the aforementioned global objects. (For more information on how to create user objects, see Chapter 13, "The User Object Painter.") After you create the user objects for the global variable you want to change, click the Variable Types tab (see Figure 9.6).

You can change the names of the default objects (for example, Transaction or Error) to the names of the user objects you've created. If you specify a new object associated with the default global variable, PowerBuilder automatically creates an instance of your standard class user object for use within your application. Thus, you can have a customized error object with built-in error routines or SQLCA that contain methods to log you in to your database and trap any errors.

9

Application Objects and the Application Painter

FIGURE **9.6**

*The Variable
Types tab page.*

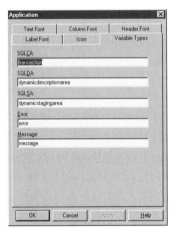

# Application Object Attributes

Within the property sheet, you have easy access to each application object's attributes. These were attributes that had to be accessed using standard dot notation, which is introduced in Chapter 7, "The PowerScript Language," in previous versions of PowerBuilder.

## AppName and DisplayName

The AppName attribute contains the name of the application object. The DisplayName is an alternative name for your application that's easier for end users to read. For example, when using OLE, any dialogs displaying the application's name would use DisplayName. If nothing is specified, DisplayName defaults to AppName.

> **Note**
>
> The AppName is read-only at design time and runtime. Assigning a value to this attribute in your script generates a compile error.

## MicroHelpDefault

The MicroHelpDefault sets the default text of the status bar (or, as the status bar is known in PowerBuilder, MicroHelp). The PowerBuilder (and MDI standard) default is Ready.

## DWMessageTitle

You use the `DWMessageTitle` attribute to change the default title of DataWindow message boxes that display at runtime. For example, rather than use the system default title for a column validation rule error, place the application name in the title to provide a cleaner interface.

## DDETimeOut

The `DDETimeOut` indicates the number of seconds PowerBuilder (as the client) waits to get a response from a DDE server before giving up on communicating. The default response time is 10 seconds.

## RightToLeft

You use `RightToLeft` to display text characters from right to left. This is important in multilingual applications that read from the right of the screen to the left.

# Toolbar Attributes

On the Toolbar page, you have access to each of the following toolbar attributes.

### ToolbarFrameTitle

The `ToolbarFrameTitle` specifies the title bar of your application's MDI frame toolbar when it's floating. The default is `FrameBar`.

### ToolbarSheetTitle

The `ToolbarSheetTitle` attribute works in the same way as the `ToolbarFrameTitle` attribute. The only difference is that the title of the floating toolbar is different from the frame toolbar for the sheet.

### ToolbarPopMenuText

If you've ever wanted to change the text that displays in the toolbar pop-up menu for an MDI application, `ToolbarPopMenuText` is the attribute for you. If you prefer to change the standard menu text from `Left`, `Top`, `Right`, and so on, set `ToolbarPopMenuText` equal to `Move toolbar to the Left`, `Move toolbar to the Top`, and the like. This changes the text attributes of the toolbar but not the functionality. This is particularly useful for applications to be released in a foreign language. For more information, see Chapter 12, "Menus and the Menu Painter."

### ToolbarUserControl

If you don't like giving your users any more flexibility than is necessary, set ToolbarUserControl to FALSE. Doing so disables the pop-up menu on the toolbar in an MDI application and disables the capability to drag the toolbars to different locations.

### ToolbarText and ToolbarTips

The ToolbarTextspecifies whether the toolbar icons are increased in size to display descriptive text on the buttons. It must be TRUE or FALSE. The ToolbarTips specifies whether PowerTips display when the mouse is over a toolbar icon. (Note that ToolbarText must be equal to FALSE for PowerTips to display.)

# Application Object Events

The application object has six system events in which you can code scripts: Open, Close, Idle, SystemError, ConnectionBegin, and ConnectionEnd. You can, of course, add events of your own devising. Within the Application painter, the main pane is that for event scripts.

## The Open Event

Every application has a script for the Open event. When an application is run (at design time or runtime), the first thing to be executed is an Open event. If nothing is coded, PowerBuilder pops up a message box stating that you must place code in the Open event. Since version 5.0, the Open event has an argument called commandline. This is used in place of CommandParm(), which retrieves any information typed on a command line when executing the application's executable. Common uses for the Open event are to create global objects (such as an application manager), populate transaction objects, connect to a database, and open the first window. Within PFC-based applications, the application events are usually coded with one-line redirectors, which pass the arguments from the application object's event to the application manager objects event that contains the actual functionality.

## The Close Event

The Close event is triggered when the user shuts down the application (that is, closes the last window or MDI frame). Some common uses are to disconnect from the database and provide any necessary cleanup of any objects created via PowerScript. It's a good idea to check a flag variable in your script to see whether the application still has a database connection active. If it does, roll back any open transaction, disconnect from the database, and destroy any globally defined objects you might have created (for example, user-defined transaction objects). If the disconnect is unsuccessful, consider writing the database error code and message to a log file or, even better, send an email message that states the problem to the database administrator. If the database is down, it's possible that the network is down, too, so you won't be able to send an email. Therefore, it might be a good idea to implement both solutions!

## The `Idle` Event

The `Idle` event is triggered when the `Idle()` function is explicitly called with an idle time in an object script. The `Idle()` function specifies the number of seconds of inactivity that must pass before the `Idle` event is triggered. After the number of seconds specified by the function elapses with no mouse or keyboard activity, the `Idle` event is triggered. For example, in the `Open` event, coding `Idle(300)` causes the `Idle` event to trigger after 5 minutes (300 seconds) of inactivity.

You use the `Idle` event for several reasons. For an application containing secure data, the `Idle` event can trigger a password-protected screen saver. Another use is for a kiosk that provides a demonstration—if no one touches the keyboard or mouse for more than a few minutes, the `Idle` event kicks in to stop the demonstration or send it to a welcome window. The `Restart()` function can be coded in the `Idle` event, which then restarts the application from the beginning.

## The `SystemError` Event

The `SystemError`event is used to trap severe runtime errors. Two common reasons for this event being triggered are if you refer to an object that doesn't exist or if an error occurs while you're trying to communicate with a DLL. Typically, the `SystemError` event consists of a `Choose...Case` statement that evaluates the `Number` attribute of the `Error` object. For more in-depth information about this event and the `Error` object, see Chapter 7.

## The `ConnectionBegin` Event

The `ConnectionBegin`event is triggered when a client application tries to connect to a server application through the PowerBuilder distributed processing environment. The `ConnectionBegin` occurs only in the server application. For more information on distributed PowerBuilder, see Chapter 28, "Developing Distributed PowerBuilder Applications."

## The `ConnectionEnd` Event

The `ConnectionEnd` is triggered in a distributed processing environment when a client application attempts to terminate a connection to a server application. The `ConnectionEnd` occurs only in the server application. For more information on distributed PowerBuilder, see Chapter 28.

# Global Variables and Global External Functions

*Global variables* can be accessed from any script for any object within an application. *Global external functions* are calls to function libraries that are stored in dynamic link libraries (DLLs). To create or modify these, you use the lower pane within the Application painter.

All global variables and global external function declarations are stored within the application object. This isn't overly exciting or surprising by itself, but it brings up an important point. You shouldn't have more than one application object per application or per library. This is important when migrating applications from previous releases of PowerBuilder. If you have one object (such as a window) referencing a global variable in application A and another object referencing another global variable in application B, a problem can occur. In migration, you must choose which application object you want to migrate, because only one application object is migrated at a time. If you have objects in your library that are accessing global variables in the unmigrated application object, you will receive multiple errors, and migration of those objects will fail.

# Application Object Methods

The application object has eight methods or functions associated with it: `ClassName()`, `GetContextService()`, `GetParent()`, `PostEvent()`, `SetLibraryList()`, `SetTransPool()`, `TriggerEvent()`, and `TypeOf()`.

The `PostEvent()` and `TriggerEvent()` execute events and are covered in depth in Chapter 7. The `ClassName()` function returns the name of the application object, and `TypeOf()` returns the enumerated data type of the application object, `Application!`. These two functions are available to most PowerBuilder objects and aren't used frequently with the application object. The `SetTransPool()` is used with distributed PowerBuilder and is covered in Chapter 28.

## Dynamic Library Lists

The last function, `SetLibraryList()`, is unique to the application object. It's used to change the list of dynamic library files in the library search path. This function works only when the application is being run outside the PowerBuilder development environment. The

`SetLibraryList()` function accepts a comma-separated list of filenames and uses this list to search for specified objects. You would use this to increase performance for different users. If user A used your application for editing purposes and user B used the same application for reporting, it would make sense to place the library containing the objects for editing before the library containing the reporting object for user A. The opposite would be true for user B. By switching the library order in the search path, the performance will be better for both users because the library that's needed the most is found first in the search path. This is also intended for use with cross-platform support. You might have a PBL that contains objects for use with Windows and another PBL for use with a UNIX variant, for example. At runtime, you can point to the appropriate PBL, depending on the operating system.

If you needed to implement this functionality, you could hard-code the dynamic library list into your application. A better approach would be to create a function in a custom class user object that's instantiated in your application object. This would provide the same logic that could be reused for all applications. For more information on an application user object, see Chapter 26, "Building User Objects."

One way to implement the dynamic modification of the library search path would be to read in values from an application's INI file with the following structure:

```
[LibraryList]
NumberOfLibraries = Number of PBDs to be in the search path
Library1 = The first PBD to be in the search path
.

.

LibraryN = The last PBD to be in the search path where[]= LibNum
```

The idea is that only the INI file needs to be changed and that the code can remain generic. There would be as many library entries (`LibraryN`) specified as the number indicated by `NumberOfLibraries`. Each group of end users would maintain a different INI file with a different PBD list order and cause the application to transform itself automatically.

> **Note**
>
> The dynamic library modification has been implemented so far by reading an INI file, which doesn't work on all platforms. An alternative way to maintain this list would be to place it in a table in your database and then, based on the user's security, read the table and assign the appropriate PBD order to the application.

However the PBD list is maintained, you can use the user object function in Listing 9.1 to dynamically build the library search path. This function cycles through the INI file and creates the library list. The application user object has an instance variable, i_application, of type Application that's initialized to the current application object.

**LISTING 9.1** The Public Subroutine of `SetLibraryList()` in **n_cst_unleashed_appmanager**

```
Integer li_libnum, li_count
String ls_liblist, ls_appname


ls_appname = i_application.AppName
li_libnum = ProfileInt(ls_appname + ".ini", "LibraryList", &
                                   "NumberOfLibraries", 0)
For li_count = 1 to li_libnum
   Choose Case li_count
      Case 1    //For the first entry in the list
         ls_liblist = ProfileString(ls_appname + ".ini", "LibraryList", &
                                        "Library1", "")

      Case Else //For all other entries
         ls_liblist = ls_liblist + ", " + ProfileString(ls_appname + &
                     ".ini", "LibraryList", "Library" + &

String(li_count), "")
   End Choose
Next
```

The of SetLibraryList() can be called from the Open event of your application object so that the more commonly used PBDs are placed at the top of the library search path.

Another function often used with the application object is GetApplication(). This function returns a handle of data type Application to your script so that you can reference the application object without having to hard-code the application name into your script. Here's an example:

```
application    i_application

i_application = GetApplication()
i_application.DDETimeOut = 30
```

# Summary

One of the first things you do when developing a PowerBuilder application is create an application object. Every PowerBuilder application must have one because it's the entry point into the application. Without this object, PowerBuilder will do absolutely nothing. The application object also stores high-level information about the application and provides a point of reference for all other objects. The application object is often an underused object in PowerBuilder and can give you the ability to prevent long-running transactions and dynamically change your library search path.

9

Application
Objects and the
Application
Painter

**CHAPTER 10**

# Windows and the Window Painter

The Window object is the primary graphical user interface for an application and consists of attributes, events, and controls. Depending on the operating system you're developing for, windows have several different styles and associated characteristics. This chapter concentrates on the Windows environment and some window coding techniques that you can use in your applications.

# Application Styles

There are two standard ways to construct PowerBuilder applications: as a single-document interface (SDI) or a multiple-document interface (MDI). You can also build a combination of both by incorporating styles from one to the other. Try to conform with the operating system standards that you're developing for.

SDI applications can be likened to text-based programs where there's a completely controlled flow of windows. The name comes from users being able to interact with only one window at a time. Users are limited to a fixed number of choices on each window.

MDI applications require much more thought to program because users can interact with multiple windows (referred to as *sheets*) at any one time. This kind of interface is more intuitive to the way users work, allowing them to open windows to carry out quick modifications or lookups while keeping their main piece of work visible and accessible. Sheets are usually related in functionality and depend on no set sequence of actions for processing.

The main advantage of MDI over SDI application styles is that they are more consistent in their presentation of a user interface. SDI applications tend to have distinct personalities and are therefore more difficult for end users to become familiar with quickly. An excellent example of the contrasts between MDI and SDI can be seen by looking at Word and Excel, and then at the Notepad and Control Panel applications. Both MDI applications, Word and Excel, use the same user interface paradigms, whereas Notepad and the Control Panel are completely different types of SDI applications.

# Modal and Modeless Windows

A window is modal if it requires users to interact with it before allowing them access to other windows of the application. *Modal windows* force users to make a decision before the application can continue. This is called *application modal*. Another version of modal windows, called *system modal*, requires user interaction before anything further in Windows can occur. An example is the Windows System Error window.

A *modeless window* is a dialog that enables access to the application while asking for user interaction. An example of this type of window is a floating toolbar window.

Most windows, or sheets, are nonmodal and don't force users to interact with them.

# Window Types

When you create each window object, you set a style that determines how it will appear to users (for example, whether it has a thick border or can float outside its parent window). PowerBuilder has six distinct types of window objects:

| | |
|---|---|
| Main | Response |
| Pop-up | MDI frame |
| Child MDI | frame with MicroHelp |

## Main Windows

Main windows are independent of all other windows, allowing them to overlap and be overlapped with other windows. Main windows optionally have a menu and a control menu, and can be minimized, maximized, or resized. They always have borders.

The main window type is used in one of two roles, depending on the type of application you're developing. In an SDI application, main windows are used for the first window that you open; from this point, you will usually use the other window types. All the windows you will be opening as sheets (most of the windows used within an MDI application) will be of the main type. Some inexperienced developers use the child type for sheets, which means that you can't attach a menu to the window.

The main type is a generic window (also the default type), which is what most of an application's windows are.

## Pop-Up Windows

A pop-up window provides supporting information to another window. A pop-up window overlaps its parent and can be displayed outside the parent window. It maintains a close relationship with its parent, and will minimize and close with the parent. A pop-up window optionally has a menu, control menu, and border, and can be minimized, maximized, or resized.

You can specify a different parent for the pop-up from the window that's opening it by using a different format for the Open() function (introduced later in the chapter).

Pop-up windows are put to various uses, from find windows to help cue cards. You also can use a pop-up as a progress window. Usually, a great deal of processing occurs in several places in an application: during a save or load, printing complex reports, or undertaking calculations. Some of these processes are good candidates for showing a progress status to users, thus giving them something to watch and helping reduce user-perceived response time. The pop-up style allows placement of the window over the parent while allowing the parent to keep executing. A progress window can easily be created with a pop-up style window and the new progress bar objects. For more information on these controls, see Chapter 11, "Advanced Controls."

# Child Windows

Child windows, as their name implies, are always opened from another window, either a main or a pop-up. A child window exists only within the area of its parent and is clipped to the parent (you can't move it outside this area). Maximizing the window takes up the entire parent area; when you minimize it, it becomes an icon on the bottom edge of the parent. Child windows maintain a strict relationship with their parent and will move, minimize, and close with the parent. Child windows optionally have a control menu and a border and can be minimized, maximized, or resized. A child window is never considered to be an active window and can't have a menu-bar menu assigned to it.

> **Note**
>
> A child window's position is always relative to its parent, not to the screen.

Child windows are rarely used; if you want this kind of functionality, you will usually use an MDI frame and sheets, in which window management is automatic.

# Response Windows

Response windows force users to answer a question before the application will continue. In other words, they are application-modal windows. The window overlaps all the application's open windows, can't be minimized or maximized, and optionally has a control menu.

## About Windows

The infamous About box, or credit window, is an integral part of every application and allows the development team a moment of fame and glory (or should that be infamy and ignominy?).

This is where you can take advantage of the fact that functions called as an initialization for a variable are executed one time during compilation (see Chapter 7, "The PowerScript Language," for more information). You assign a string variable in the `Constructor` event of a static text object to the value of `Today()` concatenated with `Now()`, and then set the object's text value to the date and time the executable (or PBD/DLL) was compiled. You can do it just to show end users that developers usually work long hours and compile at something close to midnight!

**Note**

If you're using PBD/DLLs, you will probably want to do the assignment inside the application object and then make it globally accessible.

## Message Boxes

By using the PowerScript function `MessageBox()`, you can open predefined application-modal windows. They allow you to set the window's title and text and select from a list of command buttons and pictures to customize the window. This is the syntax for the function:

```
MessageBox( Title, Text{, Icon{, Button{, Default}}})
```

The *Title* parameter is the text that appears in the window's title. The *Text* parameter is what will be displayed in the window, and this can be a string, a number, or a Boolean value.

**Note**

If a string argument in the function call is NULL, the window won't open.

**Tip**

Rather than pass a string value for the *Text* argument, you can pass a Boolean or a number. PowerBuilder automatically converts this for you and displays it in the window. This trick is useful during debugging, when you want to display the value of a variable.

**10**

**Windows and the Window Painter**

The *Icon* parameter determines what picture shows on the left side of the window and is a value of the Icon enumerated data type, the valid values of which are Information! (the default), StopSign!, Exclamation!, Question!, and None!. The *Button* parameter is of enumerated data type Button and is used to control which type of buttons display in the window. The valid values for Button are Ok! (the default), OkCancel!, YesNo!, YesNoCancel!, RetryCancel!, and AbortRetryIgnore!. The *Default* parameter is used to set the button that will be the default (responds to the Enter key), and this defaults to the first button.

MessageBox() returns the number of the selected button, or -1 if an error occurs. The buttons are numbered sequentially from left to right in the order listed in the enumerated data type.

### Caution

Because the generated message box is an application-modal window, be careful where you use it. Using MessageBox() in the Modified,GetFocus, LoseFocus, Item-FocusChanged, ItemChanged, Activate, and Deactivate events will cause problems in your application because of the occurring focus changes.

The MessageBox() function also can cause strange behavior if it's used after a PrintOpen() call. For more information, see Chapter 14, "DataWindow Scripting."

## Message Box Manager

An ideal way to manage messages, warnings, and errors for applications—especially when you start to field more than one—is to place them into a central database table. You can then write a reusable function or nonvisual user object that interprets a request and retrieves and displays the correct message in the desired style. This makes your application messages more consistent between applications. The Error service in the PowerBuilder Foundation Class (PFC) is built around this concept.

# MDI Frame Windows

The MDI frame window is the basis of an MDI application in that it defines the working area for the whole application and is the overall manager for open sheets. The frame *must* have a menu associated with it, can optionally have a control menu, and can be minimized, maximized, or resized.

MDI frames can also be set to include a MicroHelp area, which appears as a frame area at the bottom edge of the window and displays application information. This is actually a special part of the MDI window, rather than a property for the window. You can interact with this area only by using the SetMicroHelp() function, which takes a single argument, the text to display.

An MDI application has six key components, as shown in Figure 10.1.

**FIGURE 10.1**

*Key components in an MDI application.*

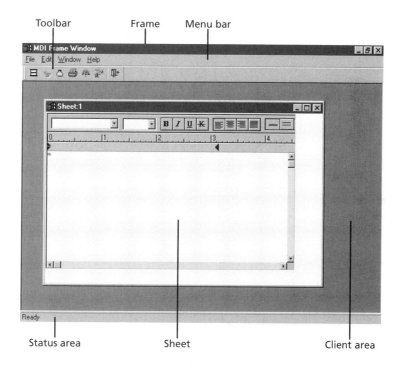

Sheets in an MDI frame can exist only in the client area, and a sheet is active only when the frame is. Sheet windows are considered active only in the context of the frame. In nearly all respects, sheets act like the child window type.

## The Client Area

The client area is specified by a special control, called mdi_1, in the frame window. The client area rarely has any other controls placed on it, but when it does, the MDI frame is said to be *customized*. When you customize, you must programmatically alter the size of the mdi_1 control to fit inside the area on the frame that has been left free (not in use by other controls). You must place code in the Resize event of the frame to handle this.

**Note**

If you don't resize the `mdi_1` control and then try to open any sheets, you won't be able to see them.

For example, if you customized the frame by adding a row of command buttons along the top edge, the `Resize` script would look something like this:

```
Uint uiX, uiY, uiW, uiH

uiX = WorkspaceX()
uiY = cb_1.Y + cb_1.Height
uiW = WorkspaceWidth()
uiH = WorkspaceHeight() - uiY - mdi_1.MicroHelpHeight
mdi_1.Move( uiX, uiY)
mdi_1.Resize( uiW, uiH)
```

In a standard frame, PowerBuilder automatically manages sizing the `mdi_1` control.

## MicroHelp

MicroHelp displays information for the application. This information can be set with a function or automatically by PowerBuilder.

Menu items can have text that's shown in the MicroHelp as users pass the mouse pointer over them. This provides a longer description of the menu item's purpose. To set the MicroHelp text from within your code, use the `SetMicroHelp()` function, which takes one parameter—the text you want displayed.

Most developers use the `Tag` attribute of window controls to hold similar information and then place a call to the function with `w_frame.SetMicroHelp( This.Tag)` . This call is usually made in the object's `GetFocus` event. See the later section "Tag Values" for a discussion on tag values.

## Menus

There are two common styles of providing menus for MDI sheets: sharing a single menu between the frame and each sheet or providing menus for the frame and each individual sheet. You can, of course, mix the two styles.

**Note**

If a sheet that doesn't have an associated menu is opened, the frame menu becomes the active menu.

Menus are an integral part of an MDI application and are used to carry out actions and navigate through the application screens. You should be aware of some issues in the interaction between menu objects and sheets. Chapter 12, "Menus and the Menu Painter," provides a detailed discussion of menus in MDI applications.

You may have noticed that most Windows applications have a Window menu. The items listed on this drop-down menu allow users to perform various actions on opened MDI sheets, from arranging open sheets to lining up iconized sheets along the bottom edge of the frame. These actions are all carried out with one function, `ArrangeSheets()`. This function can be used only on MDI sheets and has the following syntax:

```
MDIFrameWindow.ArrangeSheets( ArrangeType)
```

The *ArrangeType* parameter is of the ArrangeTypes enumerated data type and can take these values:

| Value | Description |
|---|---|
| Cascade! | Overlap the open sheets so that the title bars are all visible. |
| Layer! | Completely overlap the open sheets one on top of the other. |
| Tile! | Arrange open sheets in a tile pattern, from left to right. |
| TileHorizontal! | Arrange open sheets so that they are top to bottom. |
| Icons! | Arrange just minimized sheets along the frame's bottom. |

All but the last value also arrange minimized sheets along the frame's bottom in addition to their other actions.

## Toolbars

A number of attributes on MDI frame windows relate to the display of toolbars:

| Attribute | Description |
|---|---|
| ToolbarVisible | Whether the toolbar is visible on the frame |
| ToolbarHeight | The height of the floating toolbar |
| ToolbarWidth | The width of the floating toolbar |
| ToolbarX | The X location of the floating toolbar from the frame |

| *Attribute* | *Description* |
| --- | --- |
| ToolbarY | The Y location of the floating toolbar from the frame |
| ToolbarAlignment | Where the toolbar is attached, or whether it's floating |

Each attribute except ToolbarAlignment is a Number, String, or Boolean value. ToolbarAlignment accepts values from the enumerated data type of the same name. The acceptable values are AlignAtBottom!, AlignAtLeft!, AlignAtRight!, AlignAtTop!, and Floating!.

Another item that you will find on the previously mentioned Window menu opens a dialog that gives access to some of these toolbar attributes. The application template that PowerBuilder generates for you comes with such a window, or you can create your own. Toolbars are covered in more detail in Chapter 12.

## MDI Sheets

When you open a window as a sheet with the OpenSheet() function, regardless of the window's style, it opens as a sheet with its control menu, minimize, maximize, resize, title bar, and even the visibility attributes overridden. Depending on the parameters you pass OpenSheet(), the size and location of the window might also be overridden.

Any alterations you want to make to a sheet's appearance must be done after it's opened. You may decide to create a sheet manager that can handle these kinds of modifications. You see how to do this with some simple calls in Chapter 36, "API Calls."

## Window Instances

Each PowerBuilder object belongs to, or defines, a particular class (or, if you are a little unsure on the subject of classes, a data type). You can declare variables using the name of any of these classes, which is how you can create multiple instances of a window. As with the more normal data types (such as String), the window is declared in a script as follows:

```
w_parent lw_Parent
```

The variable lw_Parent is an instance of the class w_parent. After you instantiate the variable with an Open() window function, you can use this variable to access properties and functions for the window.

The only problem with class instances is in accessing a particular instance. Because there's no global handle to reference a window instance, you must decide whether you need to manage the instances yourself. (Methods for this are discussed in the next section.)

If you don't create a variable of the window class and instantiate it with an Open() function, but directly specify the window class in the call, you're using the global class reference. This means that any subsequent calls to Open() with that window class won't open an additional window but rather set the focus to the already opened window, at least until it's closed, at which point you can reopen it with an `Open()` call.

# MDI-Specific Functions

One of the most important functions of an MDI application is the control of the open sheets. Most sheet management that you want in an MDI is automatic; to carry out additional work, you often need to maintain information on the open sheets. You can take two approaches to managing your MDI sheets.

In the first approach, you can track each sheet as you open it and close it, usually through an MDI sheet manager object.

> **Tip**
>
> You would build the MDI sheet manager as a custom class user object (otherwise referred to as a *nonvisual user object*, or NVO) and make it an instance variable of the frame window. The PFC contains its own sheet manager, `n_cst_winsrv_-sheetmanager`.

There are two methods of opening instances that such a manager can use:

- Using an array for holding instances of the same window class. For example, an array declared of type `w_sheet` (declared at the appropriate scope) would be used in the following code to open three sheets:

```
OpenSheet( aw_Sheet[1], w_frame)
OpenSheet( aw_Sheet[2], w_frame)
OpenSheet( aw_Sheet[3], w_frame)
```

  Access to these open sheets can now be made by using the pointer value in the array at the appropriate index.

- Opening instances of the same window class or of different windows that are descendants of a base class. You can do this if you won't be using individual window class attributes and functions or if you've defined the functionality (via virtual functions or public and protected variable declarations) in the base class. The following code opens three instances of different window classes that have all been inherited from the base class `w_sheet`:

```
Integer li_Index
String as_WindowClass[3] = { "w_sheet1", "w_sheet2", "w_sheet3" }
```

```
w_sheet aw_Sheet[3]

For li_Index = 1 To 3
  OpenSheet( aw_Sheet[ li_Index], as_WindowClass[ li_Index], w_frame)
Next
```

Both of these methods require you to manage the arrays. For example, what happens when a window is closed? Do you blank out the index and reuse it, or do you just keep expanding at the end of the array for each sheet?

In the second approach, you can open and close sheets without tracking them and resort to using the MDI sheet functions that PowerBuilder provides. This is referred to as a *reusable reference variable*.

One of the most frequently used functions in an MDI application is GetActiveSheet(), which returns a handle to the currently active sheet, if there is one. The syntax for the function is

```
mdiFrameWindow.GetActiveSheet()
```

Always use the IsValid() function to check the returned handle from this function to ensure that a handle to a sheet was actually returned. GetActiveSheet() is sometimes combined with GetNextSheet() to "walk" through the open sheets. More frequently, GetFirstSheet() is combined with GetNextSheet(), as follows:

```
Window lw_Instance

lw_Instance = w_frame.GetFirstSheet()
Do While IsValid( lw_Instance)
   // Carry out something against sheet.
   lw_Instance = w_frame.GetNextSheet( lw_Instance)
Loop
```

The approach you choose depends much on the type of application you're developing and what operations you want to carry out on sheets.

## Maintaining Frame Settings

You can provide a feature for when users reopen an application that causes the frame to appear in the same location and size as when they left the application. This would also happen with an MDI toolbar that would then remember all the settings of when it was last active. The very little code involved in doing this is straightforward. In fact, what I've done in my own framework is place this in a nonvisual user object that I use for all the general application functionality. It's available to each new project with two lines of code (which are themselves inherited, but that's another story).

Four functions within the nonvisual application user object carry out all the work of saving and setting the options for the frame window and associated toolbar.

The first function, `of_SetApplication()`, takes the application object as its only parameter. This is saved into an instance variable for use in other functions. Four toolbar-related attributes are associated with application objects: `ToolbarFrameTitle`, `Toolbar-SheetTitle`, `ToolbarText`, and `ToolbarTips`. This is the code for this function:

```
i_application = a_application

i_application.ToolbarFrameTitle = ProfileString( is_INIFile,"Application", &
                                    "ToolbarFrameTitle","Frame Menu")
i_application.ToolbarSheetTitle = ProfileString( is_INIFile,"Application", &
                                    "ToolbarSheetTitle","Sheet Menu")
i_application.ToolbarText = (Upper( ProfileString( is_INIFile,"Application",&
                                    "ToolbarText","FALSE"))="TRUE")
i_application.ToolbarTips = (Upper( ProfileString( is_INIFile,"Application", &
                                    "ToolbarTips","TRUE"))="TRUE")
```

The `of_SetApplication()` function is called in the application's `Open` event. For example, by using the global variable `gnv_App`, which is defined as type `n_cst_application`, the code in the `Open` event might be the following:

```
// This is required only if the user object isn't set up to be
// auto-instantiating.
gnv_App = Create n_cst_application

// Set some default values
gnv_App.is_INIFile = "PCS.INI"
gnv_App.is_Application = "Order Entry"
gnv_App.is_ApplicationName = "Order Entry - Version 1.1"'

gnv_App.of_SetApplication( This)
```

The next step in setting the environment back to the way users left it is to modify the frame. This is done by using the `of_SetMDIFrame()` function, which takes one parameter— a pointer to a window. Again the object is stored in an instance variable for later use in the object and throughout the application to reference the MDI frame. The frame also holds several properties specific to a toolbar (not just its own toolbar) that can be used in the application for setting global toolbar information. This function is called in the `Open` event of the frame window itself:

```
String ls_Alignment

i_hWndFrame = a_hWnd
```

**10**

Windows and the
Window Painter

```
ls_Alignment = ProfileString( is_INIFile, "Application", &
                             "ToolbarAlignment", "Top!")


Choose Case Upper( ls_Alignment)
 Case "ALIGNATBOTTOM!"
   i_hWndFrame.ToolbarAlignment = AlignAtBottom!
 Case "ALIGNATLEFT!"
   i_hWndFrame.ToolbarAlignment = AlignAtLeft!
 Case "ALIGNATRIGHT!"
   i_hWndFrame.ToolbarAlignment = AlignAtRight!
 Case "ALIGNATTOP!"
   i_hWndFrame.ToolbarAlignment = AlignAtTop!
 Case "FLOATING!"
   i_hWndFrame.ToolbarAlignment = Floating!
End Choose


i_hWndFrame.ToolbarVisible = Upper( ProfileString( is_INIFile,"Application",&
                              "ToolbarVisible", "TRUE")) = "TRUE'"
i_hWndFrame.ToolbarX = ProfileInt( is_INIFile,"Application","ToolbarX",60)
i_hWndFrame.ToolbarY = ProfileInt( is_INIFile,"Application","ToolbarY",60)


Choose Case Upper( ProfileString( is_INIFile,"Application","FrameState","Top!"))
 Case "MAXIMIZED!"
   i_hWndFrame.WindowState = Maximized!
 Case "MINIMIZED!"
   i_hWndFrame.WindowState = Minimized!
   i_hWndFrame.X = ProfileInt( is_INIFile, "Application", "FrameX", 0)
   i_hWndFrame.Y = ProfileInt( is_INIFile, '"Application", "FrameY", 0)
   i_hWndFrame.Height = ProfileInt( is_INIFile,"Application","FrameHeight",600)
   i_hWndFrame.Width = ProfileInt( is_INIFile,"Application","FrameWidth",400)
 Case "NORMAL!"
   i_hWndFrame.WindowState = Normal!
   i_hWndFrame.X = ProfileInt( is_INIFile, "Application", "FrameX", 0)
   i_hWndFrame.Y = ProfileInt( is_INIFile, "Application", "FrameY", 0)
   i_hWndFrame.Height = ProfileInt( is_INIFile,"Application","FrameHeight",600)
   i_hWndFrame.Width = ProfileInt( is_INIFile,"Application","FrameWidth",400)
End Choose
```

To capture the relevant information from the MDI frame as it closes, of_ClosingMDI-Frame() is called in the frame's Close event. All you do is capture the same information that you load in using the previous function, making the appropriate data type changes. This is the code:

```
Choose Case i_hWndFrame.ToolbarAlignment
   Case AlignAtBottom!
      SetProfileString( is_INIFile, "Application", "ToolbarAlignment", &
                        "AlignAtBottom!")
   Case AlignAtLeft!
      SetProfileString( is_INIFile, "Application", "ToolbarAlignment", &
                        "AlignAtLeft!")
   Case AlignAtRight!
      SetProfileString( is_INIFile, "Application", "ToolbarAlignment", &
                        "AlignAtRight!")
   Case AlignAtTop!
      SetProfileString( is_INIFile, "Application", "ToolbarAlignment", &
                        "AlignAtTop!")
   Case Floating!
      SetProfileString( is_INIFile, "Application", "ToolbarAlignment", &
                        "Floating!")
End Choose

If i_hWndFrame.ToolbarVisible Then
   SetProfileString( is_INIFile, "Application", "ToolbarVisible", "TRUE")
Else
   SetProfileString( is_INIFile, "Application", "ToolbarVisible", "FALSE")
End If

SetProfileString( is_INIFile, "Application", "ToolbarX", &
         String( i_hWndFrame.ToolbarX))
SetProfileString( is_INIFile, "Application", "ToolbarY", &
         String( i_hWndFrame.ToolbarY))

Choose Case i_hWndFrame.WindowState
   Case Maximized!
      SetProfileString( is_INIFile, "Application", "FrameState", "Maximized!")
   Case Minimized!
      SetProfileString( is_INIFile, "Application", "FrameState", "Minimized!")
      SetProfileString( is_INIFile, "Application", "FrameX", &
                        String( i_hWndFrame.X))
      SetProfileString( is_INIFile, "Application", "FrameY", &
                        String( i_hWndFrame.Y))
      SetProfileString( is_INIFile, "Application", "FrameHeight", &
                        String( i_hWndFrame.Height))
      SetProfileString( is_INIFile, "Application", "FrameWidth", &
                        String( i_hWndFrame.Width))
   Case Normal!
```

**10**

Windows and the
Window Painter

```
SetProfileString( is_INIFile, "Application", "FrameState", "Normal!")
SetProfileString( is_INIFile, "Application", "FrameX", &
                String( i_hWndFrame.X))
SetProfileString( is_INIFile, "Application", "FrameY", &
                String( i_hWndFrame.Y))
SetProfileString( is_INIFile, "Application", "FrameHeight", &
                String(i_hWndFrame.Height))
SetProfileString( is_INIFile, "Application", "FrameWidth", &
                String( i_hWndFrame.Width))
End Choose
```

The last function called in the application's `Close` event is `of_CloseApplication()`, which captures the current state of the relevant application object attributes and stores it in the INI file. This is the code for this function:

```
If i_application.ToolbarText Then
    SetProfileString( is_INIFile, "Application", "ToolbarText", "TRUE")
Else
    SetProfileString( is_INIFile, "Application", "ToolbarText", "FALSE")
End If

If i_application.ToolbarTips Then
    SetProfileString( is_INIFile, "Application", "ToolbarTips", '"TRUE")
Else
    SetProfileString( is_INIFile, "Application", "ToolbarTips", "FALSE")
End If
```

Consider using the Windows Registry instead of an INI file to store this information (you could use `HKEY_CURRENT_USER` so that each user has different settings).

---

**Tip**

If you're looking at developing applications across platforms, consider constructing a custom class user object that handles making the appropriate access to an INI file or the Registry. This object can sense which operating system it's running in (by using the `GetEnvironment()` function) and makes the appropriate choice.

---

To explore the PFC's equivalent service for handling window settings, look at `n_cst_winsrv_preference`.

# Window Attributes

Some more useful window attributes not yet covered are `Control[]`, `MenuID`, and `WindowState`.

`Control[]` is an array of the controls defined for a window, and you use it in a purely read-only manner. This attribute is useful when you're trying to make widespread changes to a window's controls. A common function is to reset the controls on a window when, for example, users need to enter fresh data. With the `Control[]` array, you can use the code in Listing 10.1 to reset the controls. You need to declare an argument for the function that receives the window to act on.

**LISTING 10.1** Using the `Control[]` Attribute to Reset Window Controls

```
Integer li_Count, li_TotalControls
DataWindow ldw_reset
DropDownListBox lddlb_reset
RadioButton lrb_reset

li_TotalControls = UpperBound( wParent.Control[])

For li_Count = 1 To li_TotalControls
   Choose Case wParent.Control[ li_Count].TypeOf()
      Case DataWindow!
         ldw_reset = wParent.Control[ li_Count]
         ldw_reset.Reset()
      Case DropDownListBox!
         lddlb_reset = wParent.Control[ li_Count]
         lddlb_reset.SelectItem (0)
      Case RadioButton!
         lrb_reset = wParent.Control[ li_Count]
         lrb_reset.Checked = FALSE

         .
         // Any other controls you wish to affect
         .

      Case Else
         // An object we can't or don't need to affect
   End Choose
Next
```

You can make this more object-oriented by sending a message or calling a method in the object to be executed instead of doing it directly from this function. This would also allow the object to carry out more specific processing and is more inherently service based.

The MenuID attribute is the window's pointer to its associated menu. In an MDI application, multiple sheets can cause a menu's class pointer to reference other instances of the menu and even to become a NULL object pointer. This attribute as well as solutions to this problem are discussed in Chapter 12, "Menus and the Menu Painter."

The WindowState attribute is an enumerated data type that can take the following values: Maximized!, Minimized!, and Normal!. This attribute tells you what the current state of the window is; you can also use it to set a new window state.

# Window Events

Window events are where you trap and process user and system actions that affect the whole window. Many window events are discussed in other chapters or other sections of this chapter; the more important ones not covered elsewhere are discussed in this section.

The Activate event is triggered just before a window becomes active and receives focus. This event is often used to update a sheet manager as to which sheet is the current one in use. A corresponding Deactivate event is triggered when the window loses focus and becomes inactive.

The Clicked event is triggered whenever a visible area of the window not covered by a control is clicked. There's also a DoubleClicked event for when users double-click the primary mouse button. If you want to trap when the mouse button is clicked and held down, you need to use MouseDown and the corresponding MouseUp events.

In a window, the following three events (nearly) always have code in them, unless you're inheriting:

- Open is triggered when the window is first opened and after all controls' Constructor events are finished. The script you write in the Open event is usually for the initialization of window attributes, variables, and controls.

- CloseQuery is triggered just before the Close event and is often used as a safety net to check that users are absolutely certain they want to close the window. In this event, you can check the status of DataWindows to ensure that their data is saved and to prompt users with a message box to check that they want to close the window, possibly with unsaved data. PowerBuilder checks the value of Message.ReturnValue to determine whether the close has been aborted (a value of 1) or whether it should continue and trigger the `Close` event (a value of 0).

- Just before a window is closed, `Close` is the last event to occur before each control's `Destructor` events execute. The `Close` event is used for destroying any objects the window has created. You can *still* access all the window's controls, properties, and variables within the `Close` event.

> **Note**
>
> When you close a parent window for another window, the other window (the child) is closed with the parent. Any such child window can halt the entire process with a value of 1 in its `CloseQuery` event.

The final event to be introduced in this section is `SystemKey`. This event is triggered when the Alt key is pressed and the current focus isn't in an edit field.

Sometimes you might want to control precisely the method with which users close an application's windows. To enforce this, you must first disable the appropriate menu item from the system menu. This requires two Windows API calls (see Chapter 36, "API Calls"): `GetSystemMenu()` and `ModifyMenuA()`. These functions are declared in Power-Builder as

```
Function uInt GetSystemMenu( uInt hWindow, boolean bResetFlag) &
                      Library "user32.dll"
Subroutine ModifyMenuA( uInt hMenu, uInt unItem, uInt Flags, uInt unId, &
                      string szText) Library "user32.dll"
```

Then in the window's `Open` event, use the following code directly or as a function:

```
// Declare the handle for the system menu
Uint hMenu
// Define the constant values
Integer MF_BYCOMMAND = 0, MF_GRAYED = 1
Long SC_CLOSE = 61536
// Declare the text for the menu item we are affecting
String ls_MenuItem = "Close~tAlt+F4"

// Get the handle to the windows system menu
hMenu = GetSystemMenu( Handle( This), FALSE)
```

```
// Carry out the modification using the handle
ModifyMenuA( hMenu, SC_CLOSE, MF_BYCOMMAND + MF_GRAYED, 0, ls_MenuItem)
```

In Windows, the main windows use Alt+F4 as the shortcut to close, and sheet windows use Ctrl+F4. However, some Windows applications (such as Word and Excel) seem to be setting a new standard with Ctrl+W for sheets.

The code required for the SystemKey event in the frame window is short:

```
If KeyDown( KeyF4!) Then
    Message.Processed = TRUE
End If
```

This event checks whether Alt+F4 has been pressed and, if so, tells the window that the keys are processed already. This prevents Windows from even realizing that the key combination has occurred. This code must be placed in the frame and all sheet windows; otherwise, Alt+F4 can be used in a sheet to close the frame.

To prevent a sheet window from closing (for example, prevent users from closing the last sheet), place the following code in the sheet's CloseQuery event:

```
Long ll_Return


If KeyDown( keyf4!) Then
    ll_Return = 1
End If


Return ll_Return
```

You also need to use the same code as in the frame window's Open event to disable the menu option. Just remember to change the menu text to reflect Ctrl+F4, not the frame's Alt+F4.

You can place additional control or behavior around the window's minimize and maximize events by mapping a user event to the pbm_syscommand event identifier. In this script, you can then trap various events:

```
If Message.WordParm = 61472 Then
    // Trap the minimize event
    Message.Processed = True
    // Carry out some alternative processing
ElseIf Message.WordParm = 61488 Then
    // Trap the maximize event
    Message.Processed = True
    // Carry out some alternative processing
End If
```

The "Window Manipulation Techniques" section later in this chapter introduces a situation that requires this functionality.

# PowerScript Window Functions

Many PowerScript functions can be used to manipulate windows, and the following sections introduce the more important and commonly used ones.

## Opening and Closing Windows

PowerBuilder provides several functions to create and destroy window objects.

A window's parent can be defined explicitly or implicitly when the window is opened and is dependent on the window type. If the parent window isn't named when a dependent window (pop-up, child, or response) opens, the last active window becomes the parent.

> **Note**
>
> Remember that MDI sheet windows are never considered to be active windows, and the parent in these cases will be the MDI frame window.

In the following sections on the functions for opening windows, you see how to specify the parent window.

## The `Open()` Function

The `Open()` function loads and displays a window and its associated controls. The window's controls, along with its own attributes, functions, and variables, aren't accessible until it is open. There are four versions for the `Open()` function.

The first two versions of `Open()` are defined with this syntax:

```
Open( WindowVariable {, Parent})
```

The *WindowVariable* parameter can be a window object or a variable of the desired window class. In the latter, PowerBuilder places a reference to the opened window in *WindowVariable*. The optional *Parent* parameter lets you specify the opened window's parent if you don't want the open window to be the currently active window. The *Parent* parameter can be used only for pop-up and child windows. The `Open()` function returns -1 if the call fails, and 1 if it succeeds.

*PowerBuilder 7.0*

**372**

**UNLEASHED**

An example of each type of call is shown here:

```
w_edit lw_Instance

// Open the window object class w_edit
Open( w_edit)
//
// Notice the difference between these two...the first
// opens the class the second an instance of the class.
//
// Open an instance of the window object class w_edit
Open( lw_Instance)

// Open an instance of window object class w_edit and make w_frame the parent
Open( lw_Instance, w_frame)
```

> **Note**
>
> To understand how PowerBuilder manages the class and instance pools, see Chapter 24, "Frameworks and Class Libraries."

The last two versions of Open() are defined by using this syntax:

```
Open( WindowVariable, WindowType {, Parent})
```

> **Tip**
>
> This is the syntax to use if you're dynamically creating a window. The window class might be from an array or even the database. The instance variable you use as the instance pointer needs to be of type Window or of a base class for the windows you will create. In the former, you can use only regular events and window-specific methods specifically through the use of the Dynamic keyword.

*WindowVariable* and *Parent* are the same as in the first versions of the Open() function. *WindowType* is a string that's the window object class you want to open. *WindowType*'s data type must be an equal or descendant member of the inheritance tree of the *WindowVariable* class.

An example of each type of call is shown here:

```
String ls_WindowType = "w_single_edit"
w_edit lw_Child


// Opening the window instance wChild with a string, szWindowType, indicating
// the window data type
Open( lw_Child, ls_WindowType)


// Opening the window instance wChild with a string, szWindowType, indicating
// the window data type and a parent window, wParent
Open( lw_Child, ls_WindowType, w_frame)
```

These last two versions require you to ensure that the window object class specified in the *WindowType* parameter is included in the compiled version of the application, either in a PowerBuilder dynamic library (PBD) or listed in a PowerBuilder resource file (PBR).

If you use the *Parent* parameter with the Open() function and specify a child or sheet window as the parent, PowerBuilder searches up the open window hierarchy from the current window until it finds a window that can be a parent.

## The OpenSheet() Function

Like the Open()function, OpenSheet() loads and displays a window; in this case, it's specifically an MDI sheet. Also like the Open() function, an optional parameter lets you specify the window class of which you want to open an instance by string. This is the syntax for this function:

```
OpenSheet(SheetReference {, WindowType},MDIFrame {, MenuPosition {, ArrangeOpen}})
```

The *SheetReference* and *WindowType* parameters carry out the same function as the *WindowVariable* and *WindowType* parameters in the Open() function. The *MDIFrame* parameter is the name of the application's MDI frame window and is required in the same way *Parent* is used for Open(). *MenuPosition* is used to add the sheet's name onto an open sheet list, usually on the Window menu. The default behavior is to list the sheet names under the next-to-last menu. This also occurs if you pass a value greater than the number of menu titles or a zero. The *ArrangeOpen* parameter forces the sheet to display in a certain way. The value is of the *ArrangeOrder* enumerated data type and be one of these values:

| *Value* | *Description* |
|---|---|
| Cascaded! | Opens the sheet so that the other open sheet title bars are still visible (the default). All sheets are sized the same. |
| Layered! | Opens the sheet so that it overlays previous sheets and fills the client area of the frame. |
| Original! | Allows the sheet to open to its original size and cascade it. |

Some examples of calls to OpenSheet() are as follows:

```
String ls_WindowType = "w_special_sheet"
w_sheet lw_Instance

// Open a cascaded instance of the class w_sheet as a sheet in the MDI w_frame
OpenSheet( lw_Instance, w_frame)

// Open an instance of the class w_sheet in MDI w_frame with its original size
OpenSheet( lw_Instance, w_frame, 0, Original!)

// Open an instance of class w_special_sheet in MDI w_frame with original size
OpenSheet( lw_Instance, ls_WindowType, w_frame, 0, Original!)
```

> **Tip**
>
> Rather than hard-code a particular window class name throughout your code, you can use a variable that's part of an NVO application object of type Window. Then the window's class (its name) doesn't matter. For example, the NVO n_cst_applications is created globally as gnv_App and has the instance variable i_hWndFrame declared of type Window. OpenSheet() calls can be coded as
>
> ```
> OpenSheet( lw_Instance, gnv_App.i_hWndFrame)
> ```

## The `Close()` Function

To shut down a window and free all the resources that it's using, use the Close() function. As discussed earlier in the "Window Events" section, this function triggers the CloseQuery and Close events. This is the syntax:

```
Close( WindowObject)
```

# Passing Parameters to Windows

The Open(), OpenSheet(), and Close() functions all have modified versions that allow parameters to be passed between windows. These functions use the Message object to hold the passed information. Three of the Message object's attributes hold the data being passed from an object to the opening window:

| Attribute | Description |
|---|---|
| Message.DoubleParm | Passes Numeric values |
| Message.StringParm | Used for String values |
| Message.PowerObjectParm | Passes PowerBuilder objects |

You can send additional data types by converting them to a String or Numeric value first, and you can send structures or user objects via the PowerObjectParm attribute.

**Note**

Several other methods for passing information to a window are covered later in the section "Other Parameter Mechanisms."

The window being opened that will receive the parameter needs to retrieve the value from the Message object in its Open event before it carries out any additional processing. This is because Message is a globally used object and is used every time an event is triggered or posted; therefore, it runs the risk of being overwritten.

**Note**

The only way to pass multiple parameters is to use structures or user objects and pass that via the PowerObjectParm attribute.

Always validate the parameter attribute of the Message object you're using to make sure that a value was passed.

## The OpenWithParm() Function

The OpenWithParm() function is identical to the Open() function, with the exception of an additional parameter:

```
OpenWithParm( WindowVariable , ValueToPass{, WindowType} {, Parent})
```

The *ValueToPass* parameter passes the data value as a parameter to the window being opened. The appropriate attribute in the Message object is set.

**10**

**Windows and the Window Painter**

An example of the two scripts that you would use to pass a structure to a window follows. Within the calling script, you'd use this:

```
s_character lstr_Character


lstr_Character.Name = "Ulric Von Raven"
lstr_Character.Age = 32
lstr_Character.Profession ="Templar"


OpenWithParm( w_character_detail, lstr_Character)
```

Then within the Open event of the opened window, w_character_detail, the script to retrieve the structure would be this:

```
s_character lstr_ACharacter


If IsValid (Message.PowerObjectParm) Then
   lstr_ACharacter = Message.PowerObjectParm
End If
```

## The OpenSheetWithParm() Function

OpenSheetWithParm(), like the two Open() functions, is similar to the OpenSheet() function, again with only an additional parameter:

```
OpenSheet( SheetReference, ValueToPass {, WindowType}, MDIFrame {, &
          MenuPosition {, ArrangeOpen}})
```

The same statements that are valid for OpenWithParm() are valid for this function.

## The CloseWithReturn() Function

The Close() function's twin is CloseWithReturn(), which can be used only with response windows. CloseWithReturn() can pass a value or, by using the Message object's PowerObjectParm attribute, multiple values, and pass the values back to the script that opened the response window. This is the syntax:

```
CloseWithReturn( WindowObject, ValueToReturn)
```

This function closes the response window and places the return value in the Message object, from where the calling script should immediately remove it.

> **Note**
>
> Remember that response windows are modal. This is what allows you to return a value to a calling script.

Be careful not to return an object that exists in the response window because these are always passed by reference, and the object that they referenced has been destroyed. Attributes or variables can be returned because these are passed by value.

The execution sequence with `CloseWithReturn()` is shown in the following example:

```
String ls_Name

// Open a response window that will return a customer name
Open( w_select_customer)
//
// Once the response window closes execution returns to this
// point and we can retrieve the value from the Message object.
ls_Name = Message.StringParm
```

The script in the method used for closing w_select_customer would be this:

```
CloseWithReturn( Parent, is_CustomerName)
```

In this case, the script is in an object other than the window, and the value being returned is a window instance variable, is_CustomerName. Because the variable will be passed back by value, you don't care that the actual variable is destroyed with the window.

# Other Parameter Mechanisms

You can use several other options if you're passing more complex pieces of data (ones that can't be adequately described in a structure). Generally, though, you will use structures or custom class objects to pass your data to a window.

The obvious solution is to use global variables or publicly accessible window instance variables and to set these immediately after you open the window. You must of course make the opened window carry out a post-event retrieval of the data because the controlling window will not have assigned the values yet. The other issue is that it's difficult to control access to the global variables.

Another parameter-passing mechanism is to call a function on the window, passing the parameters you need. You can also use parameterized events for the same purpose. (For more information on parameterized events, see Chapter 7, "The PowerScript Language.")

These mechanisms should rarely, if ever, be used. They are unreliable and depend completely on certain events occurring in a certain order. Using a custom class user object to pass information is well defined, and the data is immediately accessible in the Open event of the window.

## Printing Windows

You can print a window's contents by using the Print() function's second format. Three other formats deal with specific objects. This is the syntax for this format:

```
ObjectName.Print( PrintJobNumber, X, Y {, Width, Height})
```

*ObjectName* can be an object that's descended from the DragObject class type, which includes windows and window controls. The *X*, *Y*, *Width*, and *Height* parameters are all used to specify a starting location and scaling factor to apply to the printed image.

The call to Print() must be encompassed by a valid PrintOpen() and PrintClose() function pairing. Here's an example of printing the w_about window:

```
Long ll_JobNo

ll_JobNo = PrintOpen()
If ll_JobNo <> -1 Then
   w_about.Print( ll_JobNo, 1, 1)
   PrintClose( ll_JobNo)
End If
```

To print an entire screen, you would use the PrintScreen() function, which takes identical parameters as the Print() function. The only difference between them is that you don't specify an object name to print. Here's an example of using this function:

```
Long ll_JobNo

ll_JobNo = PrintOpen()
If ll_JobNo <> -1 Then
   PrintScreen( ll_JobNo, 1, 1)
   PrintClose( ll_JobNo)
End If
```

# The Window Painter

In PowerBuilder 7.0, to create a new window, click the New icon on the PowerBar, select the Object tab and the Window icon, and click OK. To open an existing window object, click the Open icon on the PowerBar and select Windows from the Object Type drop-down list. All available window objects for the PBL selected in the Application Libraries list will appear; simply select the desired window from the list and click OK.

After you make your selection (or create a new window), the Window painter workspace is opened (see Figure 10.2), which shows the different window views and associated toolbars.

**FIGURE 10.2**
*The Window painter.*

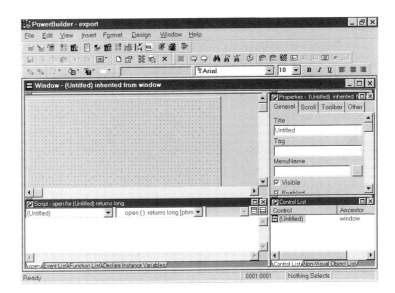

The Window painter has the following views in PowerBuilder 7.0:

| | |
|---|---|
| Layout | Function List |
| Control List | Script |
| Nonvisual Object List | Structure List |
| Properties | Structure |
| Event | List |

These views are common to all painters that allow you to edit objects and are detailed in Chapter 2, "PowerBuilder 7.0 Development Environment."

> **Tip**
>
> With all the information displayed for windows in PowerBuilder 7.0, you might want to customize the PainterBar and views to display only the information that you use regularly.

## Accessing Properties

Because one of the most common things you need to do in the Window painter is set properties of the window and the controls, this section discusses some things you can do with the new Properties view. You access the properties for the window and any of its controls in the Properties view. If it's not displayed (it shows by default), you can be display it from the Properties toolbar button, the Properties option on the pop-up menu, or by choosing Properties from the View menu.

One comment that PowerBuilder developers have made about the last couple of versions is the difficulty in changing the properties of multiple controls at the same time. PowerBuilder 7.0 enables you to change the properties of multiple controls (regardless of the control type) at the same time.

To change the properties of multiple controls, use the mouse to drag a rectangle (known as a *rubberband* or *lasso*) over the controls you want to affect. Each selected control then displays the modification handles in the corners. You can individually add or remove controls from the selected group by Ctrl+clicking. Some properties such as font settings (size, bold, alignment, and so on), text and background colors, and border styles for a group of controls can be modified by using the Window painter's StyleBar and PainterBar.

For properties not on a toolbar, use PowerBuilder 7.0's Properties view. When multiple controls are selected, the Properties view displays all properties common to the selected controls. Any changes you make on the Properties view are then applied to all the selected controls.

The Properties view for a window or control uses the tab metaphor to allow access to different related settings. The window's property sheet (see Figure 10.3) provides all the settings that were previously scattered across a couple of different dialogs and pop-up menu settings.

The General tab page allows you to change the window type, colors, window style, and the associated menu. With the Icon property, you can also specify the mouse pointer graphic when the mouse is over the window and the window's icon when minimized, respectively.

**FIGURE 10.3**

*A window's property sheet.*

Three properties new to PowerBuilder 7.0 that you will find on the General tab of the window Properties view are as follows:

| Property | Description |
| --- | --- |
| Clientedge | A Boolean value used to create a sunken effect of a window's client area. |
| ContextHelp | A Boolean value used with response windows. When set to TRUE, a small question mark appears on the title bar. When the question mark is clicked, the next clicked control has its Help event triggered. |
| PaletteWindow | A Boolean value used with pop-up windows that makes the window the topmost window and have only a Close button in the title bar. |

**Tip**

PowerBuilder 7.0 has changed the location of many properties on the different tabs. Just because you can't find a property where it was located in prior releases doesn't mean that you should give up hope. Keep looking, and you'll soon be comfortable with the new layout.

**10**

**Windows and the Window Painter**

**Note**

The Position tab in prior versions of PowerBuilder is no longer. You have access to the X, Y, Width, and Height properties on the Other tab but don't have a mini-preview area as in the past. To preview the window, click the Preview toolbar button or choose Preview from the Design menu. Doing this displays the window as a standalone and does not execute any application logic.

The Pointer property is also available on the Other tab just below the Position information. The Scroll tab page allows you to customize the way the window is scrolled and whether it has scrollbars. The ToolBar tab page allows you easy access to the window's toolbar-related properties.

The property sheets for controls are similar to each other, with only the General tab page being different for each. Some of the more complex controls (for example, rich text edit) also insert an additional tab page after General. Figure 10.4 shows the General tab page for a command button.

**FIGURE 10.4**
*The General tab page for a command button.*

The Other tab page allows you to specify the Position, Pointer, and Drag & Drop properties. The Position properties provide four edit fields for you to manually change the control's X, Y, Width, and Height properties. You usually do this from within the painter with the mouse. The Pointer drop-down list allows you to set the pointer graphic as it passes over the control. The Drag & Drop section lets you set the drag icon for the control and whether it should be set to automatic drag (see Chapter 34, "Drag-and-Drop").

# Manipulating Controls

You can use three options from the Format menu to control the size and placement of controls with respect to other controls in the window.

## Align Controls

To align a number of controls with a base position, first select the control you want to align with, and then select the others (by using a rubberband or by Ctrl+clicking). After you select all the controls you want to affect, choose Align from the Format menu. The pictures used in past versions of PowerBuilder have been replaced with straight text options of Left, Horizontal Center, Right, Top, Vertical Center, and Bottom. These same options are available on the PainterBar but require that you learn the different icons (see Figure 10.5).

**FIGURE 10.5**
*The Align, Space, and Size controls from the Painter-Bar drop-down.*

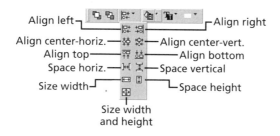

Align left
Align center-horiz.
Align top
Space horiz.
Size width
Align right
Align center-vert.
Align bottom
Space vertical
Space height
Size width and height

**Note**

There is an important consideration when spacing, aligning, or sizing controls: The appropriate value is taken from the first (or first two, in the case of spacing) control selected and then applied to the second control, third control, and so on. You will get unpredictable results if you use the rubberband/lasso method of selecting controls and then carry out one of these operations.

**Note**

One PowerBuilder 7.0 feature is a true multilevel Undo. That means if you make a several changes to your window (such as move several controls), you can undo more than the most recent change. With PowerBuilder 7.0, you also can do multilevel Redo.

NEW in PowerBuilder

10
Windows and the
Window Painter

## Space Controls

To produce uniform spacing between controls horizontally or vertically, choose Space from the Format menu. This allows you to duplicate the spacing (horizontally or vertically) between the first two controls selected. These options are also available on the drop-down toolbar shown in Figure 10.5.

## Size Controls

To resize a control or group of controls to a uniform width and/or height, choose Size from the Format menu. This method works in the same manner as the align option and can also be accessed from the drop-down toolbar.

With PowerBuilder 7.0, you no longer need to adjust the height and width of the same control as separate steps. PowerBuilder offers a new feature that lets you size the height and width at the same time.

## Duplicating Controls

To easily duplicate a control within the Window painter, select the control and press Ctrl+T. This places a new control under the selected one. You can press Ctrl+T as many times as you want to continue stacking the controls under each other.

> **Note**
>
> This operation retains the formatting (height, width, font, text) of the control being copied, so make sure that you've formatted the control to be copied as you want it. Otherwise, you could end up having to do more work than you planned.

## Setting the Tab Order

You set the tab order for controls by choosing Tab Order from the Format menu or the appropriate toolbar button. This disables all other options and control access while you are in tab sequence mode (see Figure 10.6). The current tab sequence order of the controls is shown as a red number by the upper-right corner of each control.

You can change the value by clicking it and entering a new number. When you leave Tab Sequence mode (by selecting the menu option again), PowerBuilder resequences the values in increments of 10.

FIGURE **10.6**
*A window in Tab*
*Sequence mode.*

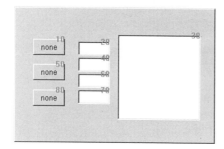

## Showing Invisible Controls

You might want certain controls to be invisible when the window is first displayed. Based on certain user actions or security, the controls will become visible during the course of the application. By default, when a control's Visible property is set to False, it's no longer viewable in the window's Layout view. Choosing Show Invisibles from the Design menu displays controls that have been made invisible so that you can make changes to them.

## Testing the Window

You can preview the window by choosing Preview from the Design menu or by using the PainterBar's Preview button. This shows the window as it will appear at runtime, and you can check the control's tab orders and initial styles. In PowerBuilder 7.0, the development environment is minimized while you view the window.

To test the window without running the whole application, choose Run/Preview from the File menu. In the Run/Preview dialog (see Figure 10.7), you can select the object to be run. This option causes the execution of scripts and controls on the window.

> **Note**
>
> Use Preview mode only for checking simple changes you make. During a normal run, the window may act differently.

FIGURE **10.7**
*The Run/Preview dialog.*

# Controls

Controls are the components of an application that end users interact with to perform desired activities. PowerBuilder provides a range of controls that exist in the operating system, plus a few additional ones such as DataWindows. There are five types of controls:

- Controls that initiate actions (for example, command buttons)

- Controls that indicate states (for example, radio buttons)

- Controls that display and allow manipulation of data (for example, DataWindows)

- Controls that enhance a window's appearance (for example, lines)

- User object controls that can combine all of these controls

You should make appropriate use of each, and use a control only for the task for which it's intuitively meant. For example, don't use a command button to toggle the state of something—use a check box or radio button instead.

To create a control on the window, simply select it from the control list and click the window area. PowerBuilder will draw the control and give it a default name.

# Control Names

It's important to maintain standards not only within your code, but also with control names and even labels. Most developers stick with the default PowerBuilder control type prefixes, but usually little attention is given to the rest of the identifier. By setting a standard (for example, placing underscores between each logical word of the identifier), you can help a team of developers considerably.

> **Note**
>
> The prefixes for controls can be set in the Options dialog, which is opened from the Design menu in the Window painter. If you decide to change the defaults, make sure that all developers do the same so that controls are consistently named across your applications.

The labels you use should be end-user–accepted names and descriptions. This makes end users' tasks easier because they know what the field should be used for, and makes your task easier when describing the system to end users and other developers. This may force you to "write the manual" on the names used, but it's a worthy exercise.

Where possible, avoid using abbreviations. In fact, in one case, a client had a big book of abbreviations used on the mainframe. This was enforced on the client/server pilot project much to the dismay of the PC development team because the developers had to use three- and four-letter words where they would normally have used the full word. There are extremes, and where possible you should make a system intuitive for not only the existing end users but also for future end users who will be using the system with possibly no background knowledge of how the system really works.

> **Note**
>
> Although this chapter should get you started with some of the more intuitive controls, not all of them are covered here. Due to the complexity of many controls, you should read Chapter 11, "Advanced Controls." Sybase has also provided some excellent and well-thought-out examples that demonstrate the use of the events, functions, and properties.

# Tag Values

Each control on a window contains an attribute known as the tag value, `ObjectName.Tag`. Developers frequently use the tag value to store an object description that's displayed in the MicroHelp area of an MDI frame using the `GetFocus` event. The tag value is set in an object's properties dialog. Several developers have extended the use of the tag value from just containing a description to holding additional style information. This is usually the case when general-purpose objects have been built that can be told to act in different ways depending on certain settings.

Take a DataWindow user object called u_dw. There's a requirement to allow for a single row to be selected or, in some cases, multiple rows. Along with this behavior, you also want to sometimes allow the DataWindow to be drag-and-drop enabled. There are three solutions to this problem, and the choice between them depends on your programming philosophy, knowledge background, and ultimately how the object(s) will be used. These solutions are presented in no particular order as to which is the best solution, although the last is probably the most widely adapted these days. The first involves setting up an inheritance chain (see Figure 10.8).

**FIGURE 10.8**
*A DataWindow
inheritance
solution.*

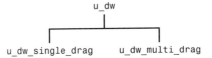

As you can see from Figure 10.8, the code between the objects u_dw_single_drag and u_dw_multi_drag was duplicated to incorporate the capability for drag-and-drop.

The second solution, often called the *Big Object* approach, is to place the functionality for single selects, multiselects, and drag-and-drop functionality in one object (in this case u_dw), and then use switches to turn the appropriate behavior on and off. Obviously, this second approach allows complete encapsulation of the code.

For both approaches that use the object's tag value, you can use the following scripts to turn behavior on and off.

First, define a tag value delimiter standard that you can use to separate the individual pieces of the tag. A good one is the back quote or accent mark character ( ` ). For example, this tag value has a MicroHelp description, allows multirow selections, and can participate in drag-and-drop:

```
Enter customer information here`MULTISELECTABLE`DRAGGABLE`
```

In the object's `Constructor` event, you would then code the following to disassemble the tag string into the component parts:

```
Integer li_Count, li_TotalValues
String ls_Values[]

li_TotalValues = f_tokenize_to_string_array (This.Tag, ` ` ` , ls_Values)

For li_Count = 1 To li_TotalValues
    Choose Case ls_Values[ li_Count]
        Case "SINGLESELECTABLE"
            ib_SingleSelectable = TRUE
        Case "MULTISELECTABLE"
            ib_MultiSelectable = TRUE
        Case "DRAGGABLE"
            ib_Draggable = TRUE
        Case Else
            // It is the MicroHelp description
            This.Tag = ls_Values[ li_Count]
    End Choose
Next
```

You also have two choices with the MicroHelp value: You can assign it to an object-level instance variable or assign it back to the `Tag` attribute, where most developers would expect to find it.

The function `f_tokenize_to_string_array()` breaks the tag value into the respective tokens (see Listing 10.2).

**LISTING 10.2** The `f_tokenize_to_string_array()` Function

```
Integer li_Count = 0
String ls_Misc

Do
    ls_Misc = f_get_token (as_ToSearch, as_Delimiters)
    If ls_Misc <> "" Then
        li_Count = li_Count + 1
        as_Return[ li_Count] = ls_Misc
    End If
Loop Until ls_Misc = ""

Return li_Count
```

**10**

**Windows and the Window Painter**

This function takes three parameters: as_ToSearch, as_Delimiters, and as_Return. All three are strings, with the last being declared as a string array passed by reference. The function returns the number of values stored in the string array as_Return.

The f_get_tokenfunction called by f_tokenize_to_string_array() is as straightforward (see Listing 10.3).

**LISTING 10.3** The **f_get_token()** Function

```
Integer li_Position
String  ls_Return


li_Position = Pos( as_Source, as_Separator)

If li_Position = 0 Then                     // if no separator,
   ls_Return = as_Source                    // return whole source string
   as_Source = ''''                         // and original as 0 length
Else
   ls_Return = Mid( as_Source, 1, li_Position - 1) //o/w, return just the token
   as_Source = Right( as_Source,Len (as_Source) - li_Position)  // strip it and
                                                               // separator

End If


Return ls_Return
```

This function takes two string parameters ( as_Source and as_Separator) and returns a string that's the value found in as_Source. The as_Source parameter is passed by reference and is updated to contain only the remaining part of the string after the value and separator are removed.

By using these functions, you can extensively use the tag value for many purposes.

The third approach uses service-based architecture (SBA), and you create an appropriate service object for the desired object functionality. This can be used by independent objects sometimes of varying classes. The service object is usually explicitly created within the Constructor event of the requesting object, and you won't use tag values.

# Window Manipulation Techniques

You can use several tricks and techniques to manipulate or control your windows. Some have been introduced in other areas of this chapter, and in the following sections, you see how to control windows with no title bar and automatic scrollbars, and how to repaint windows correctly.

# Moving a Window Without a Title Bar

You may require a window in your application to not have a title bar (for example, some form of menu or pop-up window). This of course means that you can't move it around the screen by the normal method of picking it up and dragging it. To allow users to move this kind of window around, you need to use one line of code:

```
Send( Handle( This), 274, 61458, 0)
```

The code is placed in the `MouseDown` event. In this event, you need to send the window a message, `WM_SYSCOMMAND (274)`, with `WordParm` set to `SC_MOVE + 1 (61457)`. This informs the window that the mouse is being moved and to move with the mouse.

# Scrolling Within Sheets

You may have already noticed that when a DataWindow is dynamically resized within a window at runtime, it automatically turns vertical and horizontal scrollbars on as required, provided of course that you've set those particular style attributes. You might further have observed that MDI sheets don't exhibit the same behavior, but it would be great if they did. Well, by using two API calls and a little creativity, you can get your sheets to act as they should. These are the two API function declarations:

```
Subroutine GetScrollRange( uint hWnd, int iScrollBarFlag, ref int iMin, &
                         ref int iMax) Library "user32.dll"
Function int GetScrollPos( uint hWnd, int iScrollBarFlag) Library "user32.dll"
```

These APIs are used to find the range that a scrollbar is operating over and the exact position in that range where the scroll box (thumb) is located. This little bit of API "magic" is required in case users have scrolled the region of a window before resizing it back to an area that can fully display the window's controls.

You also use two window instance variables and a few constants for the API calls:

```
Integer ii_MinWidth, ii_MinHeight

// CONSTANTS:
Constant Integer SB_HORZ = 0
Constant Integer SB_VERT = 1
Constant Integer SB_TOP = 6
Constant Integer WM_HSCROLL = 276
Constant Integer WM_VSCROLL = 277
Constant Long SC_MINIMIZE = 61472
```

These two instance variables are set in the Open event of the window, and set the minimum allowable width and height of the window before scrollbars are required. The code for this is

```
ii_MinWidth = This.Width
ii_MinHeight = This.Height
```

The actual code is split between two functions, with most of it in the Resize event. This event is triggered as soon as users resize the window, whether it's using the window edges or control options (such as minimize). At this point, you need to check the new window width and height against the minimum values you've previously set.

If the width is below the minimum allowed value and the relevant scrollbar isn't already showing, turn on the scrollbar attribute. Note the first If statement, which traps when the user minimizes the window (in this case, you don't want to carry out any processing). In fact, the scrollbars have already been turned off in the SysCommand event, which you see a little later.

The code for the Resize event is

```
UInt hWnd
Integer li_ScrollPos, li_MinPos, li_MaxPos

If This.WindowState = Minimized! Then
    Return
End If

This.SetRedraw( FALSE)

// Store the window handle so we don't have to keep calling Handle()
hWnd = Handle( This)

// Is the current window width less than the allowable width?
If This.Width < ii_MinWidth Then
    // Turn on the horizontal scrollbar
    This.HScrollBar = TRUE
    // Is the horizontal scroll bar currently on?
ElseIf This.HScrollBar Then
    // Get the current position of the thumb within the scrollbar
    li_ScrollPos = GetScrollPos( hWnd, SB_HORZ)

    // Get the range of the scrollbar
    GetScrollRange( hWnd, SB_HORZ, li_MinPos, li_MaxPos)
```

```
   // Has the user scrolled the window horizontally?
   If li_ScrollPos > li_MinPos Then
      // Tell the window to scroll back to the far left edge
      Post( hWnd, WM_HSCROLL, SB_TOP, 0)
   End If
   // Turn the scrollbar off
   This.HScrollBar = FALSE
End If


// Is the current window height less than the allowable height?
If This.Height < ii_MinHeight Then
   // Turn on the vertical scrollbar
   This.VScrollBar = TRUE
   // Is the vertical scrollbar currently on?
ElseIf This.VScrollBar Then
   // Get the current position of the thumb within the scrollbar
   li_ScrollPos = GetScrollPos( hWnd, SB_VERT)

   // Get the range of the scrollbar
   GetScrollRange( hWnd, SB_VERT, li_MinPos, li_MaxPos)

   // Has the user scrolled the window vertically?
   If li_ScrollPos > li_MinPos Then
      // Tell the window to scroll back to the top edge
      Post( hWnd, WM_VSCROLL, SB_TOP, 0)
   End If
   // Turn the scrollbar off
   This.VScrollBar = FALSE
End If


This.Post Function SetRedraw( TRUE)
```

As mentioned earlier, you need to trap the point at which users minimize the window and turn off the scrollbars. This is done in user event SysCommand, which is mapped to pbm_syscommand. The code is

```
If Message.WordParm = SC_MINIMIZE Then
   This.VScrollBar = FALSE
   This.HScrollBar = FALSE
   Return
End If
```

With these two simple scripts, you can provide some missing functionality to your MDI sheet windows.

## Painting Problems

Whenever you resize a control or a window, you should turn off the screen redraw for the appropriate object by using the SetRedraw() function. Passing a FALSE value as an argument turns the screen paint off for the object; TRUE causes the object to be immediately painted and repainted every time a change is made.

A window's Control[] array property holds references to the controls defined in the window and processes the order of the screen paints. If you leave the redraw on for a window, you can sometimes see the controls as they paint on the window. The order of the painting can be altered by sending controls to the background. This change in the control's Z-order (front-to-back ordering) also corresponds to a movement within the Control[] array.

If you have problems with controls flickering or leaving odd pieces of graphics on the window, check how you have the screen painting set up during the operation. It also makes an operation—especially successive visual changes—much faster because the operating system has to draw the screen only once (when you've finished) instead of with each change.

For example, if you need to change the size or position of a window's controls when the window is resized, use this script in the Resize event:

```
This.SetRedraw( FALSE)
//
// Call an application level function that broadcasts the message
// to each control on the window.
gnv_App.BroadCast( "ParentResize")
//
This.SetRedraw( TRUE)
```

# Object Orientation in Windows

The following sections show how windows conform to the big three object-oriented terms: encapsulation, inheritance, and polymorphism.

## Encapsulation

Windows are naturally *encapsulated*. They contain the controls and objects to achieve their processing purposes. Windows and their controls encapsulate their functionality within the scripts that you write for events and window-level functions. Window instance variables and functions can be made as accessible or inaccessible as you want using the protection statements introduced in Chapter 7, "The PowerScript Language."

# Inheritance

*Inheritance* of a window makes the ancestor controls, events, and public or protected instance variables and functions available to a descendant. You can inherit from a previously constructed window by selecting the Inherit button from the PowerBar.

An ancestor window can have an unlimited number of descendants, but a descendant window can have only one ancestor; this is called *single inheritance*. PowerBuilder provides the Object Browser to view the ancestor and descendant windows in your application in a hierarchical display (you need to have Show Hierarchy turned on through the pop-up menu; otherwise, you get an alphabetical list of the objects).

Descendant windows can be modified to fit specific functional requirements, and the attributes of the inherited controls can be overridden. Additional controls can be added to descendants, but you can't remove ancestor controls from the descendant—you can only hide unwanted controls from view (set the Visible attribute to FALSE). The control is still created and takes up resources, which is an important reason you should set up an efficient inheritance structure.

Changes you make to inherited controls don't have to be permanent. In prior versions of PowerBuilder, you could reset the inherited properties by choosing Reset Attributes from the Edit menu. This option resets the attributes of the selected object to be those defined in the ancestor. In PowerBuilder 7.0, you have to do this process manually.

After making any modifications to an ancestor, it's a good idea to regenerate the descendants in case the modifications adversely affect a descendant.

# Polymorphism

*Polymorphism* is the capability of different objects to react to the same request, usually in different ways. Requests are made on windows using functions or events. Which mechanism you use depends on whether you want loose or tight coupling:

- Loose coupling uses nonparameterized events and allows the window to respond to the request if it has an event declared for it. If no event is defined, no error is generated.

- For tight coupling, use window-level functions or parameterized events, which must exist for the call to be made.

# Summary

This chapter showed you the available window types and styles, as well as some techniques for using each type. The properties and events covered should help you determine which type of window best matches the functionality you want to provide in your user interface. The techniques learned for controlling and manipulating windows combined with the controls will allow you to provide strong user interfaces for end users.

# Advanced Controls

In Chapter 10, "Windows and the Window Painter," you learned how to work with the basic PowerBuilder controls in the Window painter. This chapter examines why you would use the more advanced controls and how to use them.

# The Tab Control

The use of a *tab control* is commonly compared to that of a file cabinet. File cabinets consists of several drawers used to contain a large amount of related data. Imagine if all file cabinets were made with just one drawer. You would have an awful lot of file cabinets in your office, and it would be difficult to determine which cabinet contained information related to another cabinet. By combining the drawers in one cabinet, you have a centralized location for all related data, which makes access and control of the data much easier. The tab control provides the same functionality for those times when you have too much information to be displayed all at once on the face of a window.

The tab control uses a file cabinet metaphor: It's a collection of tab pages (similar to a cabinet drawer) that are the basis of all interactions with the tab control itself (see Figure 11.1). Each tab page is effectively a container for other types of controls; user objects can also be included using a different process.

**FIGURE 11.1**
*A basic tab control.*

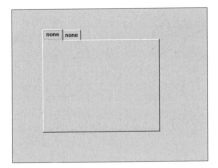

# Creating Tab Controls

To create a tab control, click the tab control icon on the toolbar and then click the window; this creates a tab control with one tab page. If you right-click near the top of the control, you see a list of the available actions, as well as the Properties option. One action option is Insert TabPage, which you use to add tabs to the control.

One thing that can be confusing about the tab control is that you have properties for the tab control itself and properties for each individual tab page. Figure 11.2 displays the property sheets for a tab control and a tab page.

FIGURE 11.2
*The tab control
and tab page
property sheets.*

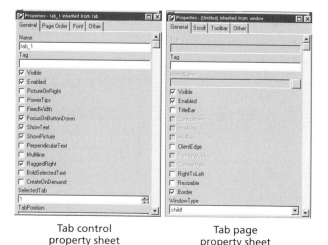

Tab control
property sheet

Tab page
property sheet

Tab pages share the same font settings and all the properties that can be set in the property sheet for the tab control. Some properties you can set on the tab control's property sheet include the following, which are available in the Window painter and also at runtime for modification:

- Alignment (Alignment) is an enumerated value that specifies the text label alignment on the tab pages. Possible values are Left!, Center!, and Right!.

- BoldSelectedText (Boolean) indicates whether to boldface the text for the currently selected tab page. Possible values are TRUE (bold the text) and FALSE (text is the same as other tab pages).

- CreateOnDemand (Boolean) determines whether the objects that exist in the tab pages are instantiated when the tab control is created (FALSE) or when the tab page is first selected (TRUE).

- FixedWidth (Boolean) indicates whether the tab label has a fixed width or shrinks to the length of the text label. When TRUE, all tab label widths are determined by the longest text label; when FALSE, the tab label width adjusts to fit the length of its own text.

- FocusOnButtonDown (Boolean) determines whether the current tab page has a dotted focus rectangle when selected.

- MultiLine (Boolean) specifies whether the tab control can show the tab labels in more than one row. If there's not enough room to display all the tab labels in one row and this property is TRUE, the tabs will be arranged in multiple rows. If there's not enough room for all the tab labels and this property is FALSE, a double-arrow control will be displayed to allow users to scroll the tab labels.

- PerpendicularText (Boolean), when set to TRUE, displays narrow perpendicular tab labels on the tab page; otherwise, the tab labels run along the edge of the tab pages.

- PictureOnRight (Boolean) specifies the position of the picture for the tab pages. When TRUE, the picture is on the right; otherwise, it appears on the left (FALSE).

- PowerTips (Boolean) indicates whether a PowerTip will display when the mouse pointer pauses over a tab label. You can specify PowerTipText values for each individual tab page. These are useful if you're using only pictures for labels.

- RaggedRight (Boolean) determines whether the tab labels are stretched to fill the whole space along the edge of the control (FALSE) or if they remain the size determined by the label text and FixedWidth property (FALSE).

- SelectedTab (Integer) sets the index number of the selected tab page shown when the tab control is created.

- ShowPicture (Boolean) indicates whether the tab label's pictures are displayed.

- ShowText (Boolean) indicates whether the text for each tab label is displayed.

- TabPosition (TabPosition) determines which edges of the tabs are displayed on the control. Table 11.1 shows the values for this property.

**TABLE 11.1** Values for the TabPosition Enumerated Data Type

| Enumerated Value | Resulting Effect |
| --- | --- |
| TabsOnBottom! | Tabs are at the bottom. |
| TabsOnBottomAndTop! | The selected tab and those after it are displayed along the bottom. Tabs before the selected tab are arranged along the top. |
| TabsOnLeft! | Tabs are on the left. |
| TabsOnLeftAndRight! | The selected tab and those before it are displayed on the left. Tabs after the selected tab are on the right. |
| TabsOnRight! | Tabs are on the right. |
| TabsOnRightAndLeft! | The selected tab and those before it are displayed on the right. Tabs after the selected tab are on the left. |
| TabsOnTop! | Tabs are on top. |
| TabsOnTopAndBottom! | The selected tab and those after it are displayed along the top. Tabs before the selected tab are arranged along the bottom. |

Each tab page also has its own property sheet and properties used to individually customize its appearance. These properties can be accessed from the tab page property sheet and at runtime. Some of these properties are as follows:

- `Name` (String) is the PowerBuilder object name for the tab page.

- `Text` (String) specifies the text to be displayed as the tab page's label.

- `Tag` (String) is a tag value to be used for whatever purposes you want.

- `PowerTipText` (String) specifies the text to be displayed in a PowerTip box when the tab control's `PowerTip` property is `TRUE`.

- `BackColor` (Long) is the background color of the tab page.

- `TabBackColor` (Long) is the color of the tab label background.

- `TabTextColor` (Long) is the color of the tab label text.

- `PictureName` (String) is the picture to use in the tab label.

Each tab page also has a couple of properties that you can access at runtime:

- `ObjectType` (UserObjects) is a read-only reference to the user object used for the tab page.

- `Control[]` (WindowObject) is a read-only array of the controls within the tab page. The `Control[]` and `ObjectType` properties are mutually exclusive.

After you create the tab pages and set the properties for each, you are ready to place controls on the tab pages. One way to accomplish this is to place controls directly on each tab page. If you do this, you can customize each tab page with its own look and feel. If each tab page has the same controls and look to it, it seems like a lot of work to re-create the same interface over and over for each tab page, though. To avoid this, you have two options.

The first option is for when you're doing something simple, such as just placing a DataWindow control on each tab page. Consider this situation: If you have six tab pages in your tab control, you would have six DataWindow controls, of which only one is visible at a time. The application has to pay the price of each hidden control in terms of resources. Also, depending on how you've written your application, users might have to wait for all six DataWindows to finish retrieving before they see the window. One solution is to place a DataWindow control outside the tab control and then drag it on top of the tab control. The result is that the DataWindow control always displays regardless of which tab page is selected. You then can write code to change the DataWindow object associated with the single DataWindow control. This cuts down on the number of controls and the number of retrieves performed at startup.

The next option down on the pop-up menu is Insert User Object, which allows you to add a custom visual user object as a new tab page to the control. This allows you to build an interface complete with code (just like any custom visual user object) and to create a tab page with it. Tab pages created from a user object can't have additional controls placed on them. You get a warning if you attempt to drop a control on a tab page created from a user object.

The tab pages you create in the User Object painter can have the following attributes set in the TabPage tab page of the object's properties dialog box:

| Attribute | Description |
| --- | --- |
| Tab Text | The text to be displayed on the tab |
| Tab Picture | The picture for the tab with or instead of the text |
| PowerTipText | Text for the PowerTip message window |
| Tab Background | Color of the tab's background |
| Tab Text Color | Color of the tab's text |
| Picture Mask | Color of the picture's mask |

You can't alter the attributes of any controls on the user object tab page from within the Window painter; you must use the User Object painter for these tasks.

Within your tab control, you can move between the different tab pages by clicking the tab label. This causes the tab page to be brought to the front. Note that the tab labels are rearranged according to the settings you've made for the tab control. This behavior is exactly what users see during runtime execution.

Click the tab labels to activate the tab control's properties in the Properties pane. To alter the properties for a tab page, click the tab page area.

To remove a tab page from the control, right-click to bring up the context-sensitive menu for the tab page (and not the control!) and select Cut or Delete.

You can place and move controls in tab pages as you would in a window, and you can use the pop-up menu to cut, copy, and paste the controls between tab controls and tab pages.

### Caution

Remember that this will change the control's parent, and any script you've written for that control might be made invalid. This is one reason for you to try to write generic code by using the This and Parent pronouns. It's also worth noting that placing a new control onto a tab control's active page and dropping a control onto the window and then moving it to the tab control are subtly different. The first operation assigns the control's parent to be the tab control, and with the second the window remains the parent.

# Tab Control Guidelines

Because a tab control displays only a single row of tabs by default (you must set the MultiLine property if you want more), try to avoid multiple-row and scrolling tab styles because they add complexity to the interface and can be confusing to work with. As an alternative to using multiple lines or scrolling, you might want to consider breaking the tab pages into groups and providing a means to toggle between them.

# Writing Scripts for Tab Controls

After you design your tab pages on your control, you are ready to begin writing code. There are some differences between writing code for controls on a window and for those on a tab page; the following sections look at some of those nuances.

## Accessing Tab Pages

Accessing a tab control, the associated tab pages, and each respective control isn't as complex as you might first think. Using dot notation, you refer to the tab control, then the tab page, and then the control on the page. Here's an example:

```
TabControl.TabPageName.ControlName
```

For example, to access the text of a pushbutton cb_choice that sits on the tabpage_-configuration tab page of the tab control, tab_selection, would be coded as

```
tab_selection.tabpage_configuration.cb_choice.text = "Push Me!"
```

Using the same notation, you can access tab control- or tab page-specific attributes. For example, to change the enabled state of a tab page, you would use the following:

```
tab_selection.tabpage_configuration.Enabled = FALSE
```

The hierarchy used to access objects in the preceding code line doesn't need to be used if you're referencing objects on the same tab page. Within a tab page, you can just reference each individual control name.

## Tab Control Functions

The tab control has a number of specific functions that you will use to control the tabs' behavior and to dynamically add tab pages at runtime. These functions are as follows:

- `CloseTab(`*`UserObjectReference`*`)` removes a tab page from the control, but only if the tab page was added by using the `OpenTab()` or `OpenTabWithParm()` function. This function triggers the `Destructor` event for the user object. After a tab page is closed, all resources associated with it are released. If you attempt to reference the object or any of its attributes, you get an error.

- `MoveTab(`*`nSourceIndex`*`,`*`nDestinationIndex`*`)` moves a tab page with the specified index, *nSourceIndex*, to a new position and changes its index value. The *nDestinationIndex* argument specifies the index before which the tab page will be moved. If this value is 0 or greater than the total number of pages, the tab page is moved to the end.

- `OpenTab(`*`UserObjectReference`*`,`*`nIndex`*`)` creates a new page using a user object of a known class type, *UserObjectReference*. You can use a user object name or a variable of the required data type. This function places a reference to the opened user object into *UserObjectReference*, similarly to other PowerScript `Open()` functions. However, using the `OpenTab()` function, you can specify that the same user object be opened again and again, and each is opened as a new page. The new tab pages don't become selected, and the `Constructor` events for the controls in the user object aren't triggered until the tab page is selected.

- `OpenTab(`*`UserObjectReference`*`,`*`szUserObjectType`*`,`*`nIndex`*`)` is the second format for the `OpenTab()` function, which you use when you need to dynamically determine the type of user object to open.

- `OpenTabWithParm()`comes in a number of flavors that allow either of the two previously described `OpenTab()` methods to pass an argument (a Numeric, a String, or a PowerObject parameter) to the new tab page.

- `SelectTab( DragObject ¦ nIndex ¦ szUserObject)` selects the specified tab page and displays it in the tab control.

- `TabPostEvent( szEvent {, lwParm, llParm ¦ szValue})` posts the *szEvent* message to each tab page in a tab control. You can also specify an enumerated value as the only argument; you can't specify additional arguments. This is similar to the `PostEvent()` function, which is covered in Chapter 7, "The PowerScript Language."

- `TabTriggerEvent( szEvent {, lwParm, llParm ¦ szValue})` triggers the *szEvent* message for each tab page (in index order) in a tab control. You can also specify an enumerated value as the only argument; you can't specify the additional arguments in this case.

# Tab Control Events

As you've seen, the list of functions and properties for a tab control is lengthy. There are fewer unique events for a tab control. The two main events that vary from most other controls are SelectionChanging and SelectionChanged.

The SelectionChanging event is triggered when users select a different tab page but occurs before the new tab page is selected. This event takes two arguments: oldindex and newindex. Both arguments are integers, where oldindex represents the index number of the currently selected tab and newindex represents the index number of the tab page to be selected. The SelectionChanging event can be used to check whether all required values are specified on the current tab page before moving to the new tab page. To specify whether users can move to the new tab page, specify a return value of 1 to prevent them from moving and a 0 to let them move.

The SelectionChanged event triggers after the new tab page is selected. It has the same arguments as the SelectionChanging event, but its purpose is to initialize the newly selected tab. You might place code that refreshes the tab page or performs data retrieval.

Using the SelectionChanged event to perform data retrieval is a convenient means of staging database access. If your tab control contains several DataWindows and you perform your retrieve processing while the window is opening, your users might be waiting for a long while. Also, your users might not even look at all the tab pages, and then the data retrieval was performed for no reason. By retrieving data only as users move to a tab, you can prevent unnecessary retrieval and shorten the open time for the window.

In conjunction with staging your retrieval, you can set the tab control property CreateOnDemand to TRUE. What this accomplishes is that the tab page and the controls on it are created only when the tab page is selected. This helps to cut down on the initial open time of the window and the resources consumed by having all controls instantiated even when not needed.

## Note

One question you might ask is, "What happens if I set a property of a control on a tab page that hasn't yet been instantiated?" The possible answers that jump to mind are a system error with a Null object reference, a GPF, creation of the tab page, or nothing. The answer is none of these. What happens is that all the controls across the tab pages are instantiated when the tab control is created. When your users select the tab page at runtime, PowerBuilder then creates the graphical component of the controls and executes their Constructor events.

A code example using tab pages is shown later in the section "Advanced Controls in Action."

# The Picture List Box and Drop-Down Picture List Box Controls

The list box and drop-down list box visual controls (see Figure 11.3) were made into ancestor objects in the PowerBuilder object hierarchy because each has a corresponding picture-enabled descendant. The plus of having the pictures is that it's easier for users to identify and remember graphics than it is to recall straight textual information. When you are familiar with the standard list box and drop-down list box, the basic behavior for the picture list box and the drop-down picture list box is the same for their nonpicture relatives. The properties and functions for each control that differentiate them from a standard list box and drop-down list box are all related to pictures.

**FIGURE 11.3**

*The picture list box and drop-down picture list box controls.*

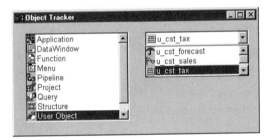

The following are the picture properties for these controls:

- ItemPictureIndex[] (Integer) is a read-only array that holds the picture index for each item in the item list. It's modified through the AddItem() and DeleteItem() functions.

- PictureHeight (Integer) specifies the height at which the pictures appear in the control. This can be set only when there are no items now in the controls list.

- PictureWidth (Integer) specifies the width at which the pictures appear in the control. If this property is 0 (the default), the size of the first image added with the AddPicture() function is used; otherwise, the image is scaled to the specified size. This property has an effect only if it's set before the first picture is added using AddPicture() or after a call to DeletePictures().

- PictureMaskColor (Long) allows you to specify the mask color (which makes the specified color transparent on the bitmap) for a picture. This attribute is used when a bitmap is added and can be changed between AddPicture() calls.

- PictureName[] (String) is a read-only array that corresponds to the values in the ItemPictureIndex array. You can modify this array only through the use of the AddPicture(), DeletePicture(), and DeletePictures() functions.

The following functions have been added to handle these properties:

- AddItem( *szValue, nPictureIndex*) is similar to the AddItem()function for normal list boxes, except that you specify the index of the picture in the PictureName[] array using the *nPictureIndex* argument.

- AddPicture( *szPictureName*) adds a bitmap to the main image list and returns the index at which it was added.

- DeletePicture( *nPictureIndex*) removes the bitmap at the specified index from the image list.

> **Caution**
>
> You will experience strange repaint problems if you delete a picture already in use by the list box.

- DeletePictures() deletes all the pictures in the image list.

- InsertItem( *szValue, nPictureIndex, nIndex*) allows you to specify the index at which you want to add a new item and associated picture to the list.

A code example using a picture list box is examined later in the section "Advanced Controls in Action."

# The ListView Control

Added to the collection of controls that allow you to list information is the ListView control. If you consider the picture list box control as just a list box control that added an array of pictures, you can think of the ListView as a picture list box with a couple more arrays of pictures. You use the ListView control when you need to show a collection of items consisting of a label and an icon. This control allows you to present a set of information in one of four ways:

| Large icon | Items appear as icons, each with a label below it. Users can drag icons within the view. |
|---|---|
| Small icon | Itemsappears as small icons, each with the label to the right. Users can also drag these icons within the view. |
| List | Items appear as small icons, each with the label to the right, in a columnar and sorted presentation. |
| Report | Items appear in a multicolumn list, with the leftmost column displaying the icon and label. You can define as many additional columns as you need and specify the corresponding data to appear in each column. |

These presentations look the same as they do when you select them from the View menu for a Windows 95 drive window. Figure 11.4 shows an example of each.

**FIGURE 11.4A**

*Large icons.*

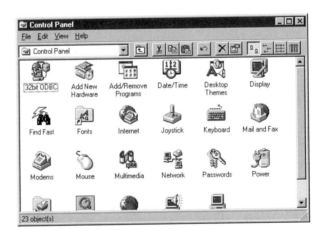

**FIGURE 11.4B**

*Small icons.*

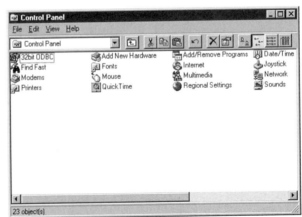

FIGURE **11.4C**
*List.*

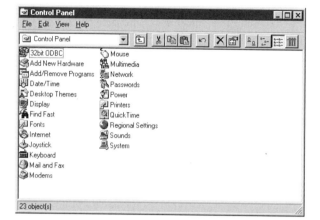

FIGURE **11.4D**
*Report.*

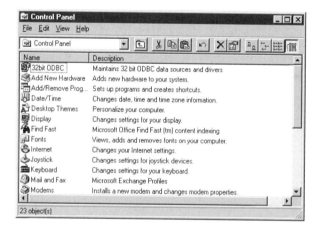

---

**Note**

To use the Report view of this control, you must specify at least one column. This can be done only through a PowerScript function, AddColumn(). Otherwise, nothing will display.

---

# ListView Properties

The properties for a ListView are numerous, as you might expect. When you open the property sheet for a ListView control (see Figure 11.5), you are presented with a variety of tab pages that allow you to customize the control.

**FIGURE 11.5**

*The ListView
property sheet
(the General tab
page).*

On the General tab page, you can specify the following properties:

- `AutoArrange` (Boolean) automatically arranges icons in Large/Small Icon view.

- `ButtonHeader` (Boolean) causes the header in the Report view to appear as buttons instead of just labels.

- `CheckBoxes` (Boolean), when set to TRUE, causes the state images to be replaced by checkboxes.

- `DeleteItems` (Boolean) allows users to delete items from the list by pressing Delete.

- `EditLabels` (Boolean) allows users to modify the item labels.

- `ExtendedSelect` (Boolean) allows users to select multiple list items.

- `FixedLocations` (Boolean) stops users from dragging large/small icons to new positions.

- `FullRowSelect` (Boolean) indicates whether users can select an entire row or just the first column when in Report view.

- `GridLines` (Boolean) specifies whether gridlines are displayed in Report view.

- `HeaderDragDrop` (Boolean), when set to TRUE, allows users to move column headers by dragging them in Report view.

- `LabelWrap` (Boolean) specifies whether the item text is word wrapped or displayed as a single line.

- `OneClickActivate` (Boolean) specifies that a single click triggers the `ItemActivate` event.

- Scrolling (Boolean) specifies whether the control can be scrolled.

- ShowHeader (Boolean) specifies whether the header should appear in the Report view.

- SortType (grSortType) specifies the sort order for the list items. If SortType is UserDefinedSort!, the Sort event will be triggered.

- TrackSelect (Boolean) enables or disables hot tracking (the item color changes when the mouse moves over it).

- TwoClickActivate (Boolean) specifies that two clicks trigger the ItemActivate event.

**Note**

Double-clicking an item still causes the ItemActivate event to fire even if both OneClickActivate and TwoClickActivate are set to FALSE.

- UnderlineCold (Boolean) specifies whether hot tracking is turned on and whether non-highlighted items are underlined when the mouse moves over them.

- UnderlineHot (Boolean) specifies whether hot tracking is turned on and whether highlighted items are underlined when the mouse moves over them.

- View (ListViewView) changes the display type among the four styles.

In addition to specifying how you the want the ListView to appear and behave, you can specify the data and pictures used to create the appearance of the control. Several tab pages help you do this: Large Picture, Small Picture, State, and Items. The first three help you specify the pictures (icons) used for the various views in which the ListView can be displayed. The pictures are usually established in the painter and assigned to the items at runtime, although they can also be assigned at design time if the item information is static. On each picture tab page (see Figure 11.6), you can specify the pictures to be used, the pictures' mask color, and their height and width.

The State pictures are used in the control to indicate that an action has been, or is about to be, performed on the item. The state picture appears in the bottom-left corner of the main icon (like the shortcut designation icon in Windows 95/98). For example, the currently selected item can have a state picture associated with it that appears to the left of the item's picture and indicates that the current item will be part of a group deletion.

**FIGURE 11.6**

*The Large Picture tab page, displaying the different picture properties.*

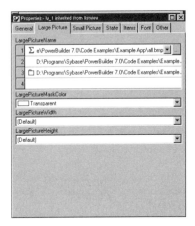

The ListView control also uses *overlay pictures*, which appear over the top of the item's picture and relay additional information about the item's status. Overlay pictures are discussed more in the next section.

## ListView Functions

Now that you've examined the available properties to use when developing a ListView control, it's time to explore the associated functions and how they interact with the properties.

Before you do that, the ListViewItem data type needs to be introduced. This structure is used to hold information on each item in the ListView control. It has the following properties:

- CutHighLighted (Boolean), when set to TRUE, indicates that the highlighted item is the target of a cut operation.

- Data (Any) is the data value you want to associate with the item.

- DropHighLighted (Boolean), when set to TRUE, indicates that the highlighted item is the target of a drag-and-drop operation.

- HasFocus (Boolean) indicates that the item now has the focus.

- ItemX (Integer) is the item's X coordinate in the ListView control.

- ItemY (Integer) is the item's Y coordinate in the ListView control.

- Label (String) specifies the text label of the item.

- OverlayPictureIndex (Integer) indicates the index number of the picture in the overlaying image list.

- `PictureIndex` (Integer) specifies the index within the control's image list to use as the item's icon.

- `Selected` (Boolean) indicates that the item has been selected.

- `StatePictureIndex` (Integer) specifies the index in the control's state image list.

Because the structure of the ListView can be somewhat complex, the `ListViewItem` data type helps to simplify the process. Rather than make you create complex function calls with numerous optional arguments, the `ListViewItem` data type allows you to specify the information you need, which can then be inserted into the ListView control. These are some ListView-specific functions:

- `AddColumn( szLabel, Alignment, nWidth)`adds a new column with the specified label, alignment, and width.

- `AddItem( lviItem)` adds an item of type `ListViewItem` to the ListView control. Returns the index at which the item was added.

- `AddItem( szLabel, nPictureIndex)` is used only to set the label and picture for the item. To specify more information, use the preceding `AddItem()` syntax. This function also returns the index at which the item was added.

- `AddLargePicture( szPicture)`, `AddSmallPicture( szPicture)`, and `AddStatePicture( szPicture)` add the specified picture into the appropriate image list.

- `Arrange()` arranges the icons in rows and is effective in Large Icon and Small Icon views only.

- `DeleteColum( nIndex)` deletes the column at the specified index.

- `DeleteColumns()` deletes all the columns.

- `DeleteItem( nIndex)` deletes the item at the specified index. This function doesn't cause the other items to change index.

- `DeleteItems()` deletes all items from a ListView control.

- `DeleteLargePicture( nIndex)`, `DeleteSmallPicture( nIndex)`, and `DeleteStatePicture( nIndex)` delete the specified picture from the appropriate image list.

- `DeleteLargePictures()`, `DeleteSmallPictures()`, and `DeleteStatePictures()` delete all the pictures from the appropriate image list.

- `EditLabel( nIndex)` places the specified item in edit mode. The ListView control also has a Boolean property (`EditLabel`) that enables all items to be editable. By setting this property to FALSE, you can use the EditLabel() function to isolate certain labels for editing or for editing at controlled points.

- FindItem( *nIndex*, *Direction*, *bFocused*, *bSelected*, *bCutHighlighted*, *bDrophighlighted*) searches for the next item that matches the criteria you specify using the four Boolean parameters. You can specify the direction of the search relative to the index by setting *Direction* to one of the following: DirectionAll!, DirectionUp!, DirectionDown!, DirectionLeft!, or DirectionRight!. The search criteria are the following: Does the item have focus (*bFocused*)? Is the item selected (*bSelected*)? Is the item the target of a cut operation (*bCutHighLighted*)? Is the item the target of a drag-and-drop operation (*bDropHighlighted*)? Like other PowerScript search functions, this one starts at the specified index plus 1, so to start from the beginning, the index needs to be 0.

- FindItem( *nIndex*, *szSearchLabel*, *bPartial*, *bWrap*) is used to search for the next item that has the same label as *szSearchLabel*. *bPartial* allows the search to perform a partial match, and *bWrap* makes the index return to the first item after the function call. *nIndex* is the index after which to start searching (remember to set to 0 to include the first item in the search). The function returns the index of the item if one is found, and -1 if an error occurs.

- GetColumn( *nIndex*, *szLabel*, *Alignment*, *nWidth*) extracts information about the column at the specified index.

- GetItem( *nIndex*, *nColumn*, *szValue*) is used when the ListView control is set to the Report view style. *nColumn* represents the report column index and, together with *nIndex*, provides a cross-reference in the control to extract the value into *szValue*.

- GetItem( *nIndex*, *lviItem*) retrieves a complete ListViewItem object into *lviItem* from the specified index in the control.

- GetOrigin( *nX*, *nY*) finds the X and Y coordinates of the upper-left corner of the ListView item. The parameters *nX* and *nY* are used to receive the coordinates.

- InsertColumn( *nIndex*, *szLabel*, *Alignment*, *nWidth*) inserts a new column at the requested index, with the label, alignment, and width specified.

- InsertItem( *nIndex*, *lviItem*) allows you to specify a complete ListViewItem structure to be inserted at the index specified.

- InsertItem( *nIndex*, *szLabel*, *nPictureIndex*) allows you to just specify a label and picture for the item that you want to insert at the index specified.

- SetItem( *nIndex*, *nColumn*, *szValue*)is used when the ListView control is set to the Report view style. *nColumn* represents the report column index and, with *nIndex*, provides a cross-reference in the control to set the value to *szValue*.

- SetItem( *nIndex*, *lviItem*) sets the item at the index with the values from a ListViewItem structure.

- Sort( *SortType*) sorts the items in the ListView control using an enumerated value of type grSortType: Ascending!, Descending!, Unsorted!, or UserDefinedSort!.

- Sort( *SortType*, *nColumn*) allows you to sort on the specified column.

- SelectedIndex() returns the index of the selected item in the ListView control. If more than one item is now selected, the function returns the index of the first item. Otherwise, it returns -1 on an error or when no items are selected.

---

**Note**

The SelectedIndex() function is intended only for controls allowing single selections, and you should write your own loop to individually check the State property of each item.

---

- SetColumn( *nIndex*, *szLabel*, *Alignment*, *nWidth*) sets the label, alignment, and width values for the specified column. The columns display only in the Report view style for the control.

- SetOverLayPicture( *nOverlayIndex*, *nImageIndex*) is used to map an overlay picture to a large or small image list index. Rather than maintain an additional image list, the overlays are mapped into the control's main image list.

- TotalColumns() returns the number of columns in the control.

- TotalItems() returns the total number of items in the control.

- TotalSelected() returns the total number of selected items in the control.

# Populating a ListView Control

Based on all the properties and functions of the ListView control and the ListViewItem structure, the next question is, how do you assemble all these pieces into a usable control? Although on the surface this might seem complex, it's fairly straightforward. The following code from the Constructor event displays how you would populate a ListView control from a datastore:

```
listviewitem llvi_cust
int li_numrows, i
datastore lds_cust

SetPointer(HourGlass!)

lds_cust = CREATE datastore

//Clear the listview of any prior items
this.DeleteItems()

//Establish the columns for the report view
this.AddColumn("Company", Left!, 700)
this.AddColumn("Contact", Left!, 500)
this.AddColumn("Phone", Left!, 400)

//Retrieve the customers
lds_cust.dataobject = "d_customer"
lds_cust.SetTransObject(SQLCA)
li_numrows = lds_cust.Retrieve()

//If there are any rows retrieved, cycle through all rows
If li_numrows > 0 Then
   //Populate the listview
   For i=1 to li_numrows
      llvi_cust.label = lds_cust.object.company_name[i] + "~t" +&
            lds_cust.object.contact[i] + "~t" + &
            String(lds_cust.object.phone[i], "(@@@)@@@-@@@@")
      llvi_cust.data =  lds_cust.object.id[i]
      llvi_cust.PictureIndex =
      this.AddItem (llvi_cust)
   Next
End If

Destroy lds_cust
```

This code first clears the ListView control of any prior items by using the `DeleteItems()` function. If you want to allow users to display the ListView control using the four different views, you need to specify how the control will appear when in Report view. The first three views (Large Icon, Small Icon, and List) all use the text supplied for the `Label` property and the pictures specified for the various icons (refer to Figure 11.6).

The AddColumn() function defines each column that will appear in the ListView control. In this code, three columns are created displaying the company name, contact name, and phone number. Each column is specified as left aligned, and the last argument indicates the size of each column. The columns need to be defined before you can use the Report view of the ListView.

After retrieving the data into the datastore, you need to circle through all rows retrieved because each one will be a new item in the ListView. To add an item into the ListView control, define a variable of type ListViewItem and assign values for its properties.

The first property is Label, which is the text that displays in the ListView control for each item. In this case, the Label property for llvi_cust is being populated with a tab-delimited string containing the company name, contact name, and phone number. In Large Icon, Small Icon, and List views, the company name is the only information to display. The rest of the information is used when the ListView displays are specified in Report view.

**Note**

The order of the values placed in the Label property should match the order in which you defined the columns using the AddColumns() function.

The Data property stores underlying information that's not displayed to users but can be used in your code. In this example, the customer ID is being stored so that it can be used as a key in any other data retrievals you might need to perform. The PictureIndex property indicates the large and small icons used for the icons (pulled from the icons specified in the Window painter). After all the properties are set for ListViewItem, insert the ListViewItem variable into the ListView control. This is done using the AddItem() function, passing it the ListViewItem structure llvi_cust.

From this point, you can perform whatever other actions you want, whether it be to use the ListView as a selection list or as a means to edit data. If you want to change the view of the ListView, specify an enumerated data type for the control's View property, such as

```
this.View = ListViewReport!
```

## ListView Events

In addition to the aforementioned functions and properties, you might need to use one of the many ListView control–specific events:

- `BeginDrag` is triggered when users use the left mouse button and start dragging. The handle of the ListViewItem users are trying to drag is available as an event argument.

- `BeginLabelEdit` is triggered when users begin to edit an item label. The edit can be prevented by returning a value of 1 from this event. The index of the item is available as an argument.

- `BeginRightDrag` is triggered when users use the right mouse button and start dragging. The handle of the ListViewItem users are trying to drag is available as an event argument.

- `ColumnClick` is triggered when users click a column. The column is passed as a parameter.

- `DeleteAllItems` is triggered when all items in the list are deleted.

- `DeleteItem` is triggered when users delete an item by using a PowerScript function.

- `EndLabelEdit` is triggered when users finish editing a label. You can return 1 to discard the change. The item index and the new label are available as parameters.

- `InsertItem` is triggered when an item is added. The new index is available as a parameter.

- `ItemChanged` is triggered when something in the item has changed. These are the available parameters to determine the change:

| | |
|---|---|
| `Index` | The item that's changing |
| `FocusChange` | The focus state that's changing |
| `HasFocus` | The new focus state |
| `SelectionChange` | The item selection that's changing |
| `Selected` | The new selection state |
| `OtherChange` | Some other change that's affecting the item |

- `ItemChanging` is triggered when something in the item is in the process of changing. You can return 1 to prevent the change. The same parameters as the `ItemChanged` event are available.

- `RightClicked` is triggered when the control is right-clicked.

- `RightDoubleClicked` is triggered when the control is double-right-clicked.

- Sort is triggered when the Sort() function is called using an argument of UserDefinedSort!. To define your own sort order for the items, set the SortType property to UserDefinedSort! and then return the following return value for the two parameters:

| -1 | Index1 is less than Index2. |
| 0 | Index1 is equal to Index2. |
| 1 | Index1 is greater than Index2. |

A code example using a ListView control is shown later in the section "Advanced Controls in Action."

# The TreeView Control

Along with the tab control, the TreeView control (see Figure 11.7), also known as an *outline control*, has been the focus of many third-party controls. The benefits of the TreeView control are that you can display large amounts of hierarchical data in a small amount of space and that you can retrieve data only as you require it.

**FIGURE 11.7**
*The TreeView control.*

The TreeView control has some of the following functionality:

- Traversing data via tree nodes that can be expanded or collapsed

- Graphical and textual node representation

- Drag-and-drop manipulation

- Node manipulation that includes cut, copy, and paste

## TreeView Properties

Similarly to the ListView, the TreeView has many properties. The property sheet for a TreeView control (see Figure 11.8) displays a variety of tab pages that allow you to customize the control.

**FIGURE 11.8**

*The TreeView property sheet.*

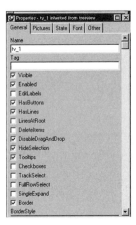

The TreeView and ListView controls do have some properties in common, and the means to select a picture in the painter is the same (see the preceding section, "The ListView Control," for how to specify a picture). Some properties that you can set on the TreeView's property sheet are as follows:

- `DeleteItems` (Boolean) allows items to be deleted from the list using the Delete key.

- `DisableDragDrop` (Boolean) prevents items from being dragged.

- `EditLabels` (Boolean) allows users to edit an item's text.

- `HasButtons` (Boolean) shows the + and - buttons next to parents.

- `HasLines` (Boolean) shows connecting lines between related items.

- `Indent` (Integer) specifies the number of units to indent child items (in PBUs).

- `LinesAtRoot` (Boolean) shows lines connecting all root items.

- `PictureHeight` (Integer) specifies the height of the images. This property, along with the width, can be set only if there are no images now in `PictureName[]`. If this value is 0 when the first image is added, the size of that image is used to set the height and width properties.

- `PictureWidth` (Integer) specifies the width of the images.

- `PictureMaskColor` (Long) indicates the masking color to use with nonsystem bitmaps.

- `PictureName[]` (String) specifies the images to be used at the nodes.

- `SortType` (grSortType) indicates the sort order for the list items. If `SortType` is `UserDefinedSort!`, the `Sort` event is triggered.

- `StatePictureHeight` (Integer) specifies the height of the state icons.

- `StatePictureWidth` (Integer) specifies the width of the state icons.

- `StatePictureMaskColor` (Long) indicates the masking color to use with nonsystem bitmaps.

- `StatePictureName[]` (String) specifies the images to be used for the state icons.

# The TreeViewItem Data Type

After you set up how you want the TreeView control to appear, you then need to be able to populate it. Unlike the other list controls, you can't populate the TreeView control at design time. Because the TreeView control is so complex, each item in the control has numerous properties in addition to those that affect the whole control. The TreeViewItem data type is a structure used to hold information on each item in the TreeView control and has the following properties:

- `Bold` (Boolean) indicates whether the label text should be bold.

- `Children` (Boolean) indicates whether the item has any child items.

- `CutHighLighted` (Boolean) indicates whether the item is highlighted when it's part of a cut operation.

- `Data` (Any) is the data value you want to associate with the item.

- `DropHighLighted` (Boolean) indicates whether the item is highlighted when it's part of a drag-and-drop operation.

- `Expanded` (Boolean) indicates whether the item is now expanded. If the node has visible items below it, this property is TRUE; otherwise, it's FALSE.

- `ExpandedOnce` (Boolean) indicates whether the item has been expanded at least once during the current execution.

- HasFocus (Boolean) indicates whether the item now has the focus.

- ItemHandle (Long)is a unique reference to the item.

- Label (String) specifies the text label of the item.

- Level (Integer) specifies the level of the item within the hierarchy.

- OverlayPictureIndex (Integer) specifies the picture index from the overlay image list.

- PictureIndex (Integer) specifies the index within the control's image list to use as the item's icon.

- Selected (Boolean) indicates whether the item is now selected.

- SelectedPictureIndex (Integer) specifies the picture index to use to indicate that the item is selected.

- StatePictureIndex (Integer) specifies the picture index from the state image list.

To insert an item into the TreeView, define a variable of type TreeViewItem, specify values for the different properties, and then insert the TreeViewItem variable into the control (similar to the ListViewItem and the ListView control). This is done by using some TreeView control functions.

# TreeView Functions

Many functions for the TreeView hinge around the TreeViewItem data type. The first thing you will want to do with your TreeView is to populate it. You can use four functions to insert a variable of type TreeViewItem into the control:

- InsertItem( *lParentHandle*, *lAfterHandle*, [ *szLabel*, *nPictureIndex*] ¦ [ *tviItem*]) inserts the specified item into the TreeView control after the item specified by *lAfterHandle*, and makes the item with *lParentHAndle* the parent. You can specify either the label and the picture or a whole TreeViewItem structure for the item.

- InsertItemFirst( *lParentHandle*, [ *szLabel*, *nPictureIndex*] ¦ [ *tviItem*]) makes the specified item the first child of its parent. You can specify either a label and a picture or a complete item using the TreeViewItem structure. The function returns the handle of the item if it succeeds. If *lParentHandle* is 0, the item is added at the root level.

- InsertItemLast( *lParentHandle*, [ *szLabel, nPictureIndex*] ¦ [ *tviItem*]) is similar to InsertItemFirst(), except that the item is added as the last child item to the parent.

- InsertItemSort( *lParentHandle*, [ *szLabel, nPictureIndex*] ¦ [ *tviItem*]) inserts an item as a child of a parent item in sorted order.

To use these functions, you first need to understand the structure of the items in the TreeView control. Because the data is displayed hierarchically, each level or tier in the hierarchy has an integer value. The root level is 0, and each level is numbered sequentially after that. In the example shown earlier in Figure 11.7, the departments are on level 1, and the employees are on level 2.

Each level is composed of one or more items, and each item is identified using a unique handle (the ItemHandle property). Although you can specify a value for this property, it's typically generated by PowerBuilder when you use an InsertItem() function. The following code populates the first level of the TreeView in Figure 11.9 from a datastore:

```
treeviewitem ltvi_data
datastore lds_dept
int i, li_numdepts

//Initialize the datastore for the list of departments
lds_dept = CREATE datastore
lds_dept.dataobject = "d_department"
lds_dept.SetTransObject(SQLCA)

//Retrieve the data into the department datastore
li_numdepts = lds_dept.Retrieve()

For i=1 to li_numdepts              //create a treeviewitem for each department
   ltvi_data.label = lds_dept.GetItemString( i, "dept_name")
   ltvi_data.data = lds_dept.GetItemNumber( i, "dept_id")
   ltvi_data.pictureindex = i
   ltvi_data.selectedpictureindex =
   ltvi_data.children = True
   tv_emp.InsertItemLast(0, ltvi_data)
Next

Destroy lds_dept
```

After retrieving the data into the datastore, you then need to grab the values from each row and insert an item into the TreeView. The Label property is the text that displays to users (in this case, the department name). The Data property is any information your application needs but users don't. The department ID is used to retrieve the data for the employee level in the TreeView. The PictureIndex and SelectedPictureIndex properties pull the specified pictures from the Pictures tab page that were set in the Window painter. The Children property is extremely important because it indicates to PowerBuilder that the specific item has items under it on the next level (for example, employees).

After the TreeViewItem variable is populated, you are ready to insert it into the TreeView control. You can use any of the four InsertItem() functions depending on where in the TreeView you want the new item to appear. All the insert functions require that you specify the handle of the parent TreeViewItem. Because this is the first level in the TreeView, the parent for all these items is the root level, which has a handle of 0.

The preceding code populates the first level of the TreeView control. You could populate all levels of the control at this point, but one benefit of the TreeView is that you can stage the data retrieval. This is done by retrieving data only when users request that a level be expanded. To accomplish this, you need to know about some additional TreeView functions and events.

The following are some functions that can be used for a TreeView control:

- AddPicture( *szPictureName*) adds the picture (icon, cursor, or bitmap) to the main image list.

- AddStatePicture( *szPictureName*)adds the picture to the state image list.

- CollapseItem( *lHandle*)collapses the item specified by the handle lHandle.

- DeleteItem( *lHandle*) deletes the item specified by the handle lHandle.

- DeletePicture( *nIndex*) deletes the picture from the main image list at the specified index.

- DeletePictures() deletes all the pictures from the main image list.

- DeleteStatePicture( *nIndex*) deletes the picture from the state image list at the specified index.

- DeleteStatePictures()deletes all pictures from the state image list.

- EditLabel( *lHandle*)places the item specified by lHandle in edit mode.

- ExpandAll( *lHandle*) expands all the specified item's child items recursively.

- ExpandItem( *lHandle*) expands just the specified item to show its child items.

- FindItem( *treenavigation*, *lHandle*) finds a matching item using a navigation code of the enumerated type TreeNavigation: ChildTreeItem!, CurrentTreeItem!, DropHighLightTreeItem!, FirstVisibleTreeItem!,

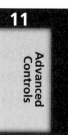

NextTreeItem!, NextVisibleTreeItem!, ParentTreeItem!, PreviousTreeItem!, or PreviousVisibleTreeItem!.

- GetItem( *lHandle*, *tviItem*) retrieves the data for the specified item into a TreeViewItem structure.

- SelectItem( *lHandle*) selects the specified item and makes it the current item.

- SetDropHighLight( *lHandle*)highlights the specified item as the drop target.

- SetFirstVisible( *lHandle*)sets the specified item to be the first visible item in the control.

- SetItem( *lHandle*, *tviItem*) sets the information for an item using the values from a TreeViewItem structure.

- SetLevelPictures( *nLevel*, *nPictureIndex*, *nSelectedPictureIndex*, nStatePictureIndex, *nOverlayPictureIndex*) sets the picture indexes used by all items at a specified level.

- SetOverlayPicture( *nOverlayIndex*, *nImageIndex*) maps an overlaying picture to a large or small image list index.

- Sort( *lHandle*, *grSortType*)sorts the children of the item specified by *lHandle*. *grSortType* specifies the sort method you want to use: Ascending! or Descending!. This function sorts only the level immediately beneath the specified item. If you want to sort multiple levels, use the SortAll() function.

- SortAll( *lHandle*, *grSortType*) recursively sorts all the child items under the specified item using the grSortType method.

## TreeView Events

When you know how to populate and navigate with the TreeView control, you definitely need to understand what several of the different TreeView events are and when they're triggered. Some events for a TreeView control include the following:

- BeginDrag is triggered when users use the left mouse button to start dragging. The index user's attempt to drag is available as an event argument.

- BeginLabelEdit is triggered when users begin to edit an item label. The edit can be prevented by returning 1. The index of the item is available as an argument.

- BeginRightDrag is triggered when users use the right mouse button to start dragging. The index user's attempt to drag is available as an event argument.

- `DeleteItem` is triggered when an item is deleted by a PowerScript function or a user action.

- `EndLabelEdit` is triggered when users finish editing a label. You can return 1 to discard the change. The item index and the new label are available as parameters.

- `ItemCollapsed` is triggered when users collapse an item.

- `ItemCollapsing` is triggered when users attempt to collapse an item. You can return 1 to prevent the collapse from occurring or 0 to allow it to continue.

- `ItemExpanded` is triggered when users expand an item.

- `ItemExpanding` is triggered when an item is expanding. If you need to populate the child items each time the item is expanded, this is the event where you specify it to happen. If no child items are created during the `ItemPopulate` event or this one, the item won't expand. You can prevent the item from expanding by returning 1.

- `ItemPopulate` is triggered the first time an item is expanded. This event or `ItemExpanding` should be used to populate the child items.

- `SelectionChanged` is triggered when users have changed the currently selected item.

- `SelectionChanging` is triggered when the selection is changing between items. You can return 1 for this event to prevent the selection from changing.

- `Sort` is triggered when the `Sort()` function is called using an argument of `UserDefinedSort!`. To define your own sort order for the items, set the `SortType` property to `UserDefinedSort!`, and then return one of the following return values for the two parameters:

| | |
|---|---|
| -1 | Index1 is less than Index2. |
| 0 | Index1 is equal to Index2. |
| 1 | Index1 is greater than Index2. |

To stage the retrieval of the TreeView so that only the expanded item is retrieved, use the `ItemPopulate` event. This event fires the first time users try to expand an item that has the `Children` property set to `True`. (If the value is `False`, the event won't execute). The following code for the `ItemPopulate` event retrieves the employees for a specific department:

```
int li_numrows, i
treeviewitem ltvi_dept, ltvi_emp

If this.GetItem( handle, ltvi_dept) = -1 Then Return
```

```
//Reset the datastore
ids_source.Reset()

//Retrieve the employees for the selected department
li_numrows = ids_source.Retrieve(Integer(ltvi_dept.data))

//Specify the picture and no children for the employee item
ltvi_emp.pictureindex =
ltvi_emp.selectedpictureindex =
ltvi_emp.children = false

//Cycle through retrieved rows
For i=1 To li_numrows
   ltvi_emp.label = ids_Source.GetItemString( i, "emp_name")
   ltvi_emp.data = ids_Source.GetItemNumber( i, "emp_id")
   this.InsertItemSort( handle, ltvi_emp)
Next
```

You first need to populate a `TreeViewItem` variable with the information from the selected department. You do this using the `GetItem()` function, which takes the handle of the item being expanded and a `TreeViewItem` variable to populate. The handle passed in this case is an event argument for the `ItemPopulate` event that indicates the item being expanded.

## Note

Many TreeView control events pass the handle of the item being acted on.

If the `GetItem()` function is successful, the employees are retrieved using a datastore by passing the department ID. The department ID is stored in the `Data` property of the item being expanded  (`ltvi_dept`). The picture properties are set for the new child TreeViewItem, `ltvi_emp`, and the `Children` property is set to `False` because you don't want the employee items to be expanded.

By cycling through the datastore, the `Label` and `Data` properties are assigned values retrieved from the database. The `InsertItemSort()` function inserts the new TreeViewItem under the expanded department.

> **Tip**
>
> The `Label` property displayed to users is often a combination of values from the database. To combine several fields for the label, create a computed field on your DataWindow object, specify a name, and use that for the `Label` value.

If you need to populate more than the two levels discussed previously, check the `Level` property of the item being expanded to determine what the child items will be. After the TreeView population, you can allow the users to modify the information, delete items, or drag and drop items between the levels. To see an example of drag-and-drop using a TreeView control, see Chapter 34, "Drag-and-Drop."

# The Rich Text Edit Control

A rich text edit (RTE) control (see Figure 11.9) is an extension of the single- and multiline edit controls and supports font properties (typeface, size, bold, italic, and so on); character and paragraph formatting (alignment, indents, and so on); and printing of its contents. In effect, it's a simple word processor.

**FIGURE 11.9**

*A rich text edit control.*

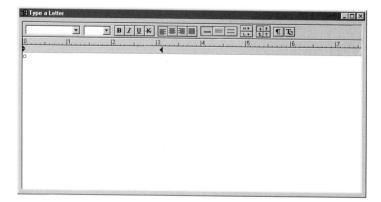

## Rich Text Edit Properties

You can control initial settings for the control using the Document tab page (see Figure 11.10) of the RichTextEdit property sheet.

**FIGURE 11.10**
*The Document
tab page.*

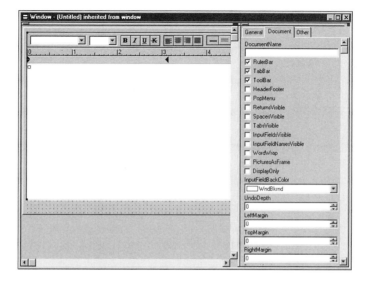

The properties on the Document tab page can also be modified at runtime, either by direct user interaction or programmatically by using PowerScript functions or direct property alterations. These are the properties specific to the rich text edit control:

- HeaderFooter (Boolean) specifies whether header and footer areas are displayed.

- InputFieldNamesVisible and InputFieldsVisible (Boolean) are used when data is being supplied from a DataWindow. They control whether users can see the data fields and names.

- InputFieldBackColor (Long) specifies the background color for input fields.

- Modified (Boolean) specifies whether the control has been edited since it was last saved. As soon as the first change is made, this property is set to TRUE, and the Modified event is triggered.

- PicturesAsFrame (Boolean) controls whether graphics are displayed as frames.

- Resizable (Boolean) indicates whether the RTE control itself can be resized.

- ReturnsVisible, SpacesVisible, and TabsVisible (Boolean) determine whether the three types of nonvisible control characters are shown.

- RulerBar, TabBar, ToolBar, and PopMenu (Boolean) control whether certain features are visible to users.

- WordWrap (Boolean) indicates whether text wraps automatically when the end of a line is reached.

- `BottomMargin`, `LeftMargin`, `RightMargin`, and `TopMargin` (Long) specify and control the positions of the margins for the document when printed.

- `DocumentName` (String) is the name that displays in the print queue when the control's contents are printed.

- `UndoDepth` (Integer) indicates the maximum number of undoable operations.

Many properties can be set at design time, but if you want to provide your users with a flexible environment, they can be modified at runtime.

## Rich Text Edit Functions

After specifying how you want the rich text edit control to appear, use some of the control's functions to populate and modify the rich text capabilities. The rich text edit control uses many specialized functions, such as

- `CopyRTF( {`*`bSelected`*`})` returns the text, pictures, and input fields from an RTE control. The *`bSelected`* argument determines whether only selected text is copied. The default is `TRUE` (only selected text); otherwise, the function copies all the control's text. If no text is currently selected, the function returns an empty string.

- `DataSource(`*`DataStore`* ¦ *`DataWindow`* ¦ *`DataWindowChild`*`)` specifies that the document displayed in the rich text edit control can include input fields linked to a datastore, a DataWindow, or a DataWindow child. In this case, there's an instance of the document in the control for each row in the DataWindow. If the name of an input field matches that of a column in the DataWindow, it's filled with data from the current row.

- `GetAlignment()` returns the alignment of the paragraph at the insertion cursor position.

- `GetSpacing()` returns the line spacing of the paragraph at the insertion cursor position.

- `GetTextColor()` returns the numeric value of the selected text's color.

- `GetTextStyle(`*`tsStyle`*`)` is used to find out what styles are set within the selected text. You query the text by passing in different text styles. The function returns a Boolean value depending on whether the text has that style. For example, to determine whether the currently selected text is bold and italic, the code would be this:

```
Boolean bBoldItalic

bBoldItalic = rte_1.GetTextStyle( Italic!)
bBoldItalic = rte_1.GetTextStyle( Bold!) And bBoldItalic
```

- `InsertDocument( szFileName, bClear, { ftFileType})` is used to insert or replace text in the control with text from a file (.RTF or .TXT). The *bClear* argument controls whether the text is inserted (FALSE) at the current insertion point or replaces the existing contents (TRUE). The optional argument *ftFileType* indicates what type of file is being opened: FileTypeRichText! or FileTypeText!. If you don't specify the type, PowerBuilder tries to determine the type from the file's extension, and defaults to trying to read it as rich text.

- `InsertPicture( szFileName)` places the specified picture into the RTF document at the current insertion point.

- `PageCount()` returns the total number of pages in the document for the control. If the control contains no text, it returns 1. The number of pages in the control is determined by the amount of text and the layout specifications (margins, page size, and so on).

- `PasteRTF( szString {, Band})`is used to paste rich text data into the control. The *Band* argument is used when the RTF string is being pasted into a rich text edit DataWindow and can be Detail!, Header!, or Footer!. (Note that this style of DataWindow doesn't contain summary, trailer, group header, or group footer bands.) The return value of this function indicates the number of characters pasted on success or -1 if an error occurs.

- `Preview( bSetting)` toggles the display of the RTE control contents between Print Preview (TRUE) and Edit view (FALSE). In Preview mode, the page is sized to fit within the control and also provides edit fields for users to enter paper dimensions and margins. Users can't directly modify the text, but they can affect the text using any of the control's functions. Make sure that the RTE control is large enough to handle the Preview mode's additional controls. You can use the IsPreview() function to see whether the RTE control is in Preview mode.

- `Print ( nCopies, szPageRange, bCollate, bCancelDialog)` is used to print the contents of an RTE control. You can specify the number of pages, the page range, whether to collate the copies, and whether the Print Cancel dialog should display.

  You can control the page numbers printed by adding an input field to the footer or header and then using the InputFieldChangeData() function in the PrintHeader or PrintFooter event, you can set whatever value you want.

> **Note**
>
> If the RTE control is sharing data with a DataWindow, the total number of pages is the page count per row times the number of DataWindow rows.

- SaveDocument( *szFileName* {, *FileType*}) saves the contents of the control to a specified file in RTF or ASCII text format. The format is FileTypeRichText! (the default) or FileTypeText! (or the filename extension is .TXT). If the file already exists, the RTE control's FileExists event is triggered.

- SelectedColumn() and SelectedPage() indicate the currently selected column and page number, respectively.

- SelectText( *lFromLine*, *lFromChar*, *lToLine*, *lToChar*) selects the text between two specified lines and two specified character positions. *lToChar* specifies the character before which the selection ends. The return of this function is the number of characters selected.

- SelectTextAll() selects all the RTE control's contents. Returns the number of characters selected.

- SelectTextLine() selects the line containing the insertion point and returns the number of characters selected. If the control has a multiline text selection, the line selected is the bottom line of the selection. This function doesn't select line-ending characters.

- SelectTextWord() selects the word containing the insertion point. If there's white space after the selection point, nothing is selected and the function returns -1.

- SetAlignment( *Alignment*) sets the alignment (Left!, Right!, Center!, or Justify!) for the selected paragraphs.

- SetSpacing( *Spacing*) indicates the line spacing for the selected paragraphs or the paragraph at the current insertion point: Spacing1! (single spacing), Spacing15! (one-and-a-half spacing), or Spacing2! (double spacing).

- SetTextColor( *lColorNo*) sets the color of the selected text in the control.

- SetTextStyle( *bBold*, *bUnderLine*, *bSubScript*, *bSuperScript*, *bItalic*, *bStrikeThrough*) specifies the new text formatting for the selected text in the control through each Boolean argument. If you specify both subscript and superscript, the text will be subscripted.

- `ShowHeadFoot( bEditHeadFoot )` displays (`TRUE`) or hides (`FALSE`) the header and footer panels for editing. If the control is in Preview mode and you call this function, the control returns to Edit mode. You can use the `PrintHeader` and `PrintFooter` events to provide values for header and footer input fields (for page numbers and dates).

PowerBuilder provides five additional functions for the RTE control that allow you to manipulate input fields:

- `InputFieldChangeData( szInputFieldName, szInputFieldValue )` allows you to modify the data value of a specified input field.

- `InputFieldCurrentName()` returns the name of the input field that the insertion point is now in. If the insertion point isn't in an input field, an empty string is returned.

- `InputFieldDeleteCurrent()` deletes the currently selected input field. Although input fields can share the same name (and therefore the same data), you can delete them independently of each other. If you delete all the fields for a given name, the control still retains the data value for future use. If other text is selected along with the input field, the deletion fails.

- `InputFieldGetData( szInputFieldName )` gets the data from the requested input field and returns it as a string.

- `InputFieldInsert( szInputFieldName )` inserts a new input field with the name specified by *szInputFieldName* at the insertion point. If there's currently selected text, the function places the new field at the beginning of the selection.

You use these functions to modify the information retrieved from the data source by adding new input fields that you populate from other controls or dynamically by altering the input fields visible in the control.

The following rich text edit functions operate on or report information about an instance of the document: `LineCount()`, `PageCount()`, `InsertDocument()`, `SaveDocument()`, `SelectedPage()`, `SelectedStart()`, `SelectedLine()`, `SelectText()`, and `SelectTextAll()`. `Print()` is the only function that affects document collection.

# Rich Text Edit Events

The rich text edit control has a number of events unique to it. Some rich text edit events are as follows:

- `FileExists` is triggered if you try to save the contents of the controls to a file and that file already exists. The filename of the file is available as an event parameter.

- `InputFieldSelected` is triggered when users select an input field (by double-clicking or pressing Enter in the field). The field name is available as an event parameter.

- `Modified` is triggered when the first change is made to the contents of the control.

- `PictureSelected` is triggered when users double-click or press Enter on a bitmap.

- `PrintFooter` is triggered when each page's footer is about to be printed. The current page and row, as well as the total number of pages, are available as event parameters.

- `PrintHeader` is triggered when each page's header is about to be printed. The same parameters as for `PrintFooter` are available.

- `RbuttonDown` is triggered when the right mouse button is pressed over the control and the pop-up menu option is disabled.

There are two ways to use rich text capabilities within the PowerBuilder environment: the rich text edit control and the RichText DataWindow presentation style. For database access and ease of use with a specific RTF document, the DataWindow presentation is your best bet. The only downside is that the presentation is limited in terms of the additional functionality you have: It's more difficult to manipulate the document, and you can't save the DataWindow rows to a file in rich text format.

The rich text edit control gives you the extra control and functionality that the DataWindow doesn't provide. The only downside is that the database access is a little more work. The basic process for inserting data from a database into a rich text edit control is as follows:

```
//Insert the document
rte_dso.InsertDocument("reminder.rtf", True)

//Associate the datastore above with the rich text edit control
rte_dso.DataSource( ids_latepay)

//Place insertion points within the document
//and populate them with the total orders and company name
rte_dso.SelectText( 6, 54, 6, 54)
rte_dso.InputFieldInsert ("outstanding_debt")
rte_dso.SelectText( 7, 104, 7, 104)
rte_dso.InputFieldInsert( "day_past_due")
```

The `InsertDocument()` function inserts the specified document into the control and clears the current content of the control. The `DataSource()` function associates the rich text edit

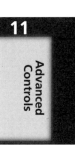
control with a datastore as its data source. The SelectText() function is then used to position the insertion point on a specific line and at a specific location in the document. After the insertion point is in the correct place, the InputFieldInsert() function specifies the name of the field to insert into the rich text edit control. The new input field automatically pulls the value from the datastore as long as the name specified matches exactly the name of a column on the DataWindow object.

A code example using a rich text edit control is shown in the section "Advanced Controls in Action."

# The Progress Bar Controls

PowerBuilder 7.0 introduces two new controls to indicate the progress of a long-running operation, HProgressBar and VProgressBar. These controls allow you to present a more professional look to users (see Figure 11.11). Although using these controls won't speed up the performance of your script, users typically have a better perception of performance when they can see the status of a lengthy process.

**FIGURE 11.11**
*The horizontal progress bar.*

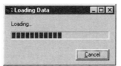

## Progress Bar Properties

The following are the unique properties of the HProgressBar and VProgressBar controls:

- MaxPosition (Unsigned Integer) indicates the value of the position property when the progress bar is all the way to the right (HProgressBar) or at the top (VProgressBar) of the control.

- MinPosition (Unsigned Integer) indicates the value of the position property when the progress bar is all the way at the left (HProgressBar) or bottom (VProgressBar) of the control.

- Position (Integer) specifies the current position of the progress bar.

- SetStep (Integer) is the step increment for the progress bar.

- SmoothScroll (Boolean) specifies that the progress bar should display as smooth instead of segmented.

## Progress Bar Functions

The following new functions allow you to use the progress bar controls in your applications:

- OffsetPos(increment) moves the position of the control by the amount specified.

- SetRange(startpos, endpos) sets the range of the control.

- StepIt() moves the position of the control by the increment specified in the SetStep property.

# The Trackbar Controls

The new Trackbar controls, HTrackBar and VTrackBar, allow users to move a slider to select values in discrete increments. Tick marks are usually displayed along the lower or right edge of the trackbar to help users position the slider. You may have seen trackbars used to control volume or timer properties in Windows (see Figure 11.12).

**FIGURE 11.12**
*The Horizontal Trackbar control.*

## Trackbar Properties

The following are the unique properties of the HTrackBar and VTrackBar controls:

- LineSize (Integer) indicates how far the slider moves when you press an arrow key.

- MaxPosition (Integer) is the value of Position when the slider is at the bottom or right of the control.

- MinPostion (Integer) is the value of Position when the slider is at the left or top of the control.

- PageSize (Integer) indicates the increment between positions when users move the slider with the mouse or keyboard.

- Position (Integer) is a value between MaxPosition and MinPosition that indicates the slider's current location.

- Slider (Boolean) indicates whether a slider is displayed.

- SliderSize (Integer) specifies the size of the slider.

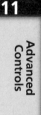

- `TickFrequency` (Integer) indicates the frequency of tick marks for the slider within the range of values.

- `TickMarks` (enumerated) indicates where tick marks should be displayed.

## Trackbar Events

The following events are unique to the Trackbar controls:

- `LineDown` indicates when the down arrow is pressed (VTrackBar only).

- `LineLeft` indicates when the left arrow is pressed (HTrackBar only).

- `LineRight` indicates when the right arrow is pressed (HTrackBar only).

- `LineUp` indicates when the up arrow is pressed (VTrackBar only).

- `Moved` indicates when the slider is moved.

- `PageDown` indicates when the Page Down key is pressed, or when a mouse click occurs below the slider (VTrackBar only).

- `PageLeft` indicates when the Page Up key is pressed, or when a mouse click occurs to the left of the slider (HTrackBar only).

- `PageRight` indicates when the Page Down key is pressed, or when a mouse click occurs to the right of the slider (HTrackBar only).

- `PageUp` indicates when the Page Up key is pressed, or when a mouse click occurs above the slider (VTrackBar only).

## Trackbar Functions

Only one new function has been defined for the Trackbar controls: `SelectionRange()`. Use this function to specify a range of values for the control. A line is drawn in the center of the control, and arrows are placed near the tick marks at the beginning and ending of the selection range.

# The HyperLink Controls

Two new controls have been introduced in PowerBuilder 7.0 to allow developers to easily link their applications to Web sites: StaticHyperLink and PictureHyperLink. Use these controls just as you would a static text or picture control. Use the new URL property to specify the target URL to open in the browser when users click the control. Figure 11.13 shows the StaticHyperLink on an about dialog.

FIGURE **11.13**

*The StaticHyper-Link control.*

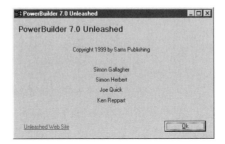

# Advanced Controls in Action

This section presents an example of using several of the advanced controls presented thus far in the chapter. The window in this example contains a tab control with two tab pages. On the first tab page (Customers), a picture list box control displays a list of states and provinces in the United States and Canada. When a state or province is selected in the list, all companies for that state/province are displayed in a ListView control. The ListView control has a pop-up menu that allows you to specify which of the four views you want for the ListView, and the picture list box and ListView controls are populated with datastores. Figure 11.14 shows the Customers tab page.

FIGURE **11.14**

*The Customers tab page.*

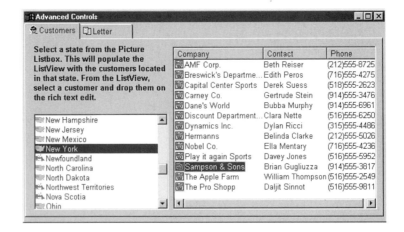

The second tab page (Letter) contains a rich text edit control that inserts a document and is populated with values from a datastore. You also can save the contents of the rich text edit control to a file of your choice and print the document. If a state/province and customer aren't selected prior to moving to the Letter tab page, the tab control stops the users and indicates that a state/province and customer must be selected. Figure 11.15 shows the Letter tab page.

**FIGURE 11.15**
*The Letter tab page.*

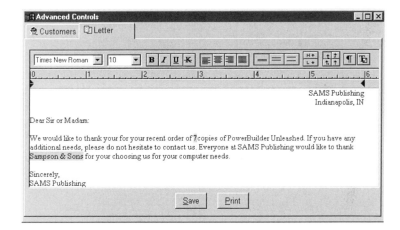

The first event to occur in this window is the Constructor event of the picture list box, plb_states. The code is as follows:

```
datastore lds_states
int li_numrows, i, li_picture

SetPointer(HourGlass!)

lds_states = CREATE datastore

lds_states.dataobject = "d_states"
lds_states.SetTransObject(SQLCA)
li_numrows = lds_states.Retrieve()

For i=1 to li_numrows
   Choose Case lds_states.object.country[i]
      Case "USA"
         li_picture =
      Case "CAN"
         li_picture =
```

```
    Case Else
        li_picture =
    End Choose

    this.AddItem( &
        lds_states.object.state_name[i], li_picture)
Next

Destroy lds_states
```

The states and provinces are retrieved into the datastore, lds_states. The country column is evaluated as to whether it's in the USA, Canada, or somewhere else. Based on the country value, the index number of the picture specified in the Window painter is assigned to li_picture. The AddItem() function is called using the state name from the datastore for the item text and for the picture specified in li_picture.

The Constructor event of the ListView control, lv_customer, is also triggered, which executes the following code:

```
this.AddColumn("Company", Left!, 700)
this.AddColumn("Contact", Left!, 500)
this.AddColumn("Phone", Left!, 400)
```

These three lines of code establish the columns to be used when the ListView control is displayed in the Report view.

After the picture list box is populated, users can then select one of the states. When this occurs, the SelectionChanged event triggers, which is used to populate the ListView control. The code for the SelectionChanged event is as follows:

```
listviewitem llvi_cust
int li_numrows, i

SetPointer(HourGlass!)

//Clear the listview
lv_customer.DeleteItems()

//Retrieve the customers for the selected state
li_numrows = ids_cust.Retrieve(this.Text(index))

If li_numrows > 0 Then
    //Populate the listview
    For i=1 to li_numrows
        llvi_cust.label = ids_cust.object.company_name[i] + "~t" +&
```

```
        ids_cust.object.contact[i] + "~t" + &
           String(ids_cust.object.phone[i], "(@@@)@@@-@@@@")
        llvi_cust.data = ids_cust.object.id[i]
        llvi_cust.PictureIndex =
        lv_customer.AddItem( llvi_cust)
    Next
End If
```

The ListView is cleared using the `DeleteItems()` function. The datastore, `ids_cust` (an instance variable), retrieves data using the selected state from the picture list box. If companies are found for the chosen state, the ListView is populated from the datastore. The `Label` property is assigned a tab-delimited string containing the company name, contact name, and phone number. The company name displays in all four views of the ListView, whereas the contact name and the phone number appear only in Report view. The customer ID is stored in the `Data` property of the ListView for later use. The picture is assigned, and the item is inserted into `lv_customer`.

After the ListView is populated, users can then select the Letter tab page. This fires the `SelectionChanging` event, which checks to see whether users have all the necessary values. The code for the `SelectionChanging` event is

```
//If the user is changing from the customers tab
//to the letter tab, ensure a state and customer are selected
If oldindex = 1 Then
   If tabpage_customer.plb_states.SelectedItem() = "" Then
      //No state is selected, do not allow the user to change tabs
      MessageBox("Required Value", "Please select a state")
      Return
   ElseIf tabpage_customer.lv_customer.SelectedIndex() = -1 then
      //No customer selected, do not allow user to change tabs
      MessageBox( "Required Value", "Please select a customer")
      Return
   End If
End If
```

If the index of the current tab page (specified by the event argument, `oldindex`) is the Customers tab page (a value of 1), a check is performed to see whether users have selected a state in the picture list box. This is done using the `SelectedItem()` function, which returns an empty string if no item is selected. If no state is selected, a message box is displayed informing users, and the event returns a 1, which prevents users from moving to the Letter tab page. The process is repeated for selecting a customer in the ListView using the `SelectedIndex()` function.

After all values are specified on the Customers tab page (thereby passing the SelectionChanging event) and the Letter tab page is selected, the SelectionChanged event fires, which populates the Rich Text Edit control. The code for the Selection-Changed event is

```
int li_selected_item, li_cust_id
listviewitem llvi_cust
datastore lds_orders

//If changing tabs to the Letter tab
If oldindex=1 Then
    //Get the item number for the selected item
    li_selected_item = tabpage_customer.lv_customer.SelectedIndex()
    If li_selected_item > -1 Then
        //Get a reference to the listviewitem
        tabpage_customer.lv_customer.GetItem &
            ( li_selected_item, llvi_cust)

        //Get the customer_id from the listviewitem
        li_cust_id = Integer(llvi_cust.data)

        //create the datastore used to retrieve the total orders
        //for a particular customer
        lds_orders = CREATE datastore
        lds_orders.dataobject = "d_total_orders"
        lds_orders.SetTransObject(SQLCA)
        lds_orders.Retrieve( li_cust_id)

        //Insert the thanks document
        tabpage_letter.rte_letter.InsertDocument("thanks.rtf", True)
        //Associate the datastore above with the rich text edit control
        tabpage_letter.rte_letter.DataSource( lds_orders)

        //Place insertion points within the document
        //and populate them with the total orders and company name
        tabpage_letter.rte_letter.SelectText( 6, 54, 6, 54)
        tabpage_letter.rte_letter.InputFieldInsert( "total_orders")
        tabpage_letter.rte_letter.SelectText( 7, 104, 7, 104)
        tabpage_letter.rte_letter.InputFieldInsert( "company_name")

        Destroy lds_orders
    End If
End If
```

If the previously selected tab (indicated by the event argument, oldindex) is 1 (the Customers tab page), the index number of the selected item in the ListView control is obtained using the SelectedIndex() function. If a valid index is returned, a variable of type ListViewItem is populated using the GetItem() function of the ListView control. The customer ID is then obtained from the Data property of the ListViewItem and used to retrieve data into the datastore, lds_orders. This datastore returns the customer name and the total number of orders for that customer.

The rich text edit control, rte_letter, is then populated with the thanks.rtf document. Rte_letter is associated with lds_orders to obtain the customer name and the number of total orders inserted into the document. The SelectText() function positions the insertion point at the specified location, and the InsertInputField() function identifies a column in the datastore to insert into the Rich Text Edit control at the given location.

The Letter tab page also allows users to save and print the document in the rich text edit control. The code for the save button is

```
string ls_doc, ls_default
int li_rtn

li_rtn = GetFileSaveName("Save Document", ls_default, ls_doc,&
        "RTF", "RichText Format (*.RTF),*.RTF")

If li_rtn = 1 Then
   rte_letter.SaveDocument (ls_doc)
End If
```

This script uses the GetFileSaveName() function to allow users to specify a document name and a location for the saved file. When the filename is obtained, the SaveDocument() function of the rich text edit control is called using the new filename.

The print button's code is even more succinct:

```
//Print one copy of all pages, not collated
//and display the cancel dialog
rte_letter.Print(1, "", False, True)
```

This code uses the Print() function and specifies the following arguments: Print one copy, all pages, not collated, and display the cancel dialog generated by the rich text edit control.

# Summary

As you've seen, the tab control, picture list box, drop-down picture list box, ListView, TreeView, and Rich Text Edit controls are powerful. The new TrackBar, ProgressBar, and HyperLink controls have been added to provide you with even more control over how your application looks and functions. With this power is the additional complexity in each control's use. With a little practice, the advanced controls in PowerBuilder will enhance your application's appearance and functionality.

# Menus and the Menu Painter

**CHAPTER 12**

A menu lists choices or actions that users can choose from to initiate an action. In this chapter, you learn about the Menu painter and the benefits and problems of using menus in an application. Menus can be used in multiple-document interface (MDI) and single-document interface (SDI) applications.

Several concepts, warnings, and terms need to be introduced before you can fully understand the description of the actual Menu painter.

# Menu Types

There are three menu types: drop-down, pop-up, and cascading.

A *drop-down menu* is a menu on a menu bar (see Figure 12.1). Drop-down menus, represented by a title on a window's menu bar, can be accessed by clicking the title or by pressing Alt and the underlined character in the title.

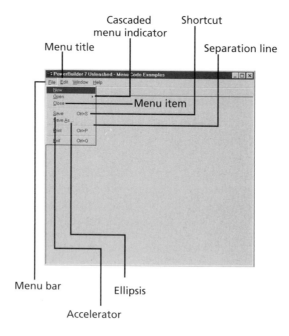

**FIGURE 12.1**
*A drop-down menu.*

A *pop-up menu* appears in relation to an object and is also known as a *contextual menu* (see Figure 12.2). Pop-up menus usually appear at the mouse pointer position and are invoked when the user performs an action such as right-clicking. The menu contains context-sensitive options relating to the object that it was invoked on and provides an efficient means to access methods associated with an object. Pop-up menus should be kept short; there shouldn't be multiple cascading levels.

**FIGURE 12.2**
*A pop-up menu.*

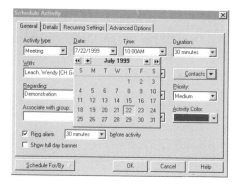

12

Menus and the
Menu Painter

A *cascading menu*, also known as a *submenu*, can appear on drop-down or pop-up menus (see Figure 12.3). Cascading menus are indicated by a right-pointing arrow on the parent menu and are accessed when users select this menu item. A cascading menu is used when you group similar actions together under a heading (for example, the Align Objects menu in the Window painter). By using cascading menus, you can simplify your top-level menus and hide a multitude of options in submenus.

**FIGURE 12.3**
*A cascading menu.*

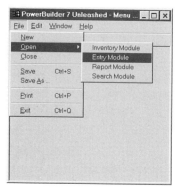

**Tip**

Try to keep the level of cascades to no more than two so that users can see all the options simply by selecting a top-level menu item; otherwise, menus become difficult to navigate.

# Menu Items

A menu's items usually describe actions or commands that are executed when selected, but they also can include open window names or changeable options.

You might have heard the terms *accelerator* and *shortcut key*, and many novice developers confuse the two:

- An *accelerator key* is signified by the underlined letter in a menu item, or even some controls. You select the item by pressing the Alt key (to activates the menu bar) and the underlined character. These can be accessed only if the item is visible. For example, to access the Save As command on the File menu in Figure 12.1, you would press Alt+F (for the menu itself) and then A (for the command).

- A *shortcut key* is always accessible when the window is in focus, no matter where the associated menu item resides in the menu structure. The shortcut key for a menu item appears to the right of the menu item. For example, Ctrl+P is usually used for printing. Shortcut keys directly access the menu item and are used for common actions.

> **Note**
>
> The particular keystrokes for an action are determined by the operating system that the application is being written for, and you should examine the design guide for that system. You can also examine existing commercial applications to see what shortcut keys they use.

If a menu item causes a dialog to be opened, the convention is to use an ellipsis (...) following the item text. This provides a visual cue that the action described won't immediately happen, and that users can modify the behavior or cancel the operation.

As mentioned previously, some menu items indicate settable options for the application, such as a ruler's visibility in a word processor. There's no standard for indicating that a menu item is an option as opposed to an action, unless it's now selected, in which case a check mark appears to the left of the menu item text.

Most options are logically grouped under a particular menu title. You can provide further subdivisions by using separation lines, which appear horizontally in the menu.

# Menu Conventions and Guidelines

When you add a menu to a window, remember that you've just lost some screen real estate; when you add a toolbar (or two), you lose even more. Bear this in mind when creating your application windows and allow sufficient space for menus and toolbars to be accommodated. If you don't, controls will start to disappear from the bottom of the window.

Try to limit the number of items you place in a cascading menu so that you don't overwhelm a user with a multitude of options. As mentioned earlier, also try to keep the number of cascading menus to only one level, or at most two.

Disable (gray out) a menu item, or even a menu title, if users shouldn't have access to it. For example, disable the Save menu item until a change has actually been made.

Keep the text of menu titles and items short and descriptive. Try for just a couple of words—or no more than four—while still fully describing the item. Remember to include the ellipsis (...) if the option opens a dialog.

**12**

Menus and the Menu Painter

### Tip

Avoid changing the text of menu items at runtime because it can be confusing to end users.

If you're developing Windows-based systems, you should purchase *The Windows Interface Guidelines for Software Design: An Application Design Guide,* published by Microsoft Press, which you can use to reference the standard names, positions, and construction of menus. Try to follow these guidelines as much as possible. If you can't get this book, explore other commercial Windows applications, such as Microsoft Word or Excel, and examine their menu structures. This also applies to other development environments; work with an accepted design guide or adopt another widely used application as your template.

If you're going to use a menu item that toggles between one state and another, use a check mark next to the item and also set the associated toolbar button to the appropriate up or down state. A check mark and a button in the down state signify that the option is in effect.

Make sure that each menu item can be reached by the keyboard by using accelerator or shortcut keys. Some people, especially in data-entry applications, hate to move their hands from the keyboard to grab a mouse just to access a menu. Make all key presses unique and consistent within the application, and follow the accepted standards of the operating system being used.

The MDI frame toolbar displays the most common menu items for quick user access. PowerBuilder toolbars conform with those that Microsoft introduced with Office 97. The toolbars now have the following properties:

- Active toolbar items appear two-dimensional until the mouse pointer passes over.

- Disabled toolbar buttons appear as engraved silhouettes.

- Grab bars are used to dock or move toolbars. Toolbars can't be docked outside the frame.

# The Menu Painter

Open the Menu painter by clicking the open button in the PowerBar or PowerPanel or choosing Open from the File menu. In the Open dialog (see Figure 12.4), select Menu from the Object Type drop-down list. When selecting a library, a list of menus in that library appears from which you can select the desired menu. After you select and open the menu, the Menu painter workspace is accessible.

**FIGURE 12.4**

*Selecting a menu through the Open dialog.*

# Menu Views

The Menu painter now utilizes the view concept discussed in Chapter 2, "PowerBuilder 7.0 Development Environment." The available views are as follows:

WYSIWYG Menu view      Function List view

Tree Menu view      Script view

Properties view      Structure List view

Event List view      Structure view

A default layout of the views for the Menu painter (see Figure 12.5) contains the WYSIWYG (What You See Is What You Get) view, which allows you to see the menu as it will pretty much appear at runtime. WYSIWYG view, however, still shows invisible menu items as grayed out; at runtime, these invisible items aren't shown at all.

**12**

Menus and the
Menu Painter

**FIGURE 12.5**
*The Menu painter workspace (default layout).*

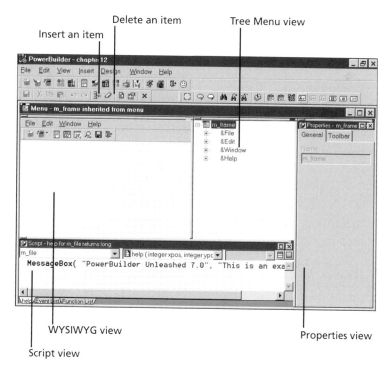

Delete an item

Insert an item

Tree Menu view

WYSIWYG view

Script view

Properties view

The Tree Menu view allows for menu items to be displayed in the standard TreeView style. This view allows you to display all menu items at once, if desired. The default layout also shows the Property and Script views. These views are utilized the same as in all the painters.

## Creating Menu Items

When creating new menu items, you must right-click in WYSIWYG or Tree Menu view and select Insert Submenu Item, or choose Submenu Item from the Insert menu. After the first menu item is created, you can then use the Insert Menu Item toolbar button to create new menu items in the current menu layer.

When you choose to insert a new menu item, the painter places the cursor where the new menu item will be located and allows for typing in that space. Changes won't be reflected in the other views until you commit them by losing focus or pressing Enter.

As soon as you enter the text for each menu title and either focus is lost or Enter is pressed, it's named by PowerBuilder; you will be able to see the assigned name in the Name box on the right side of the window. If you return to the menu item and alter the text, the object's name also changes after the change is committed. This is obviously undesirable when the menu is in use by an application; you need to select the Lock Name check box (below the Name text box) to retain the original name.

To create several menu items quickly, highlight a menu item and press Ctrl+T or select Duplicate from the pop-up menu. This duplicates the highlighted menu in the same layer. You will then want to change the menu item name because the next highest numeric menu item (for example, m_22) will be assigned.

When you're actively working in WYSIWYG or Tree Menu view and choose the Delete button on the toolbar, the selected menu item is deleted.

You can change the order of menu titles and menu items by dragging and dropping the menu items anywhere in the Menu Tree or WYSIWYG view. You aren't restricted to what level you can move the menu items. You can even move menu items between the different drop-downs and within inherited menus.

You assign accelerators for menu items the same way you do for window controls—by using an ampersand (&). A menu item's shortcut key is assigned on the General tab in Properties view. You can assign the key and whether it's associated with the Ctrl, Alt, and/or Shift keys. These options aren't available for menu titles.

> ### Note
>
> If you create a shortcut key for a submenu item, PowerBuilder lets you drag that menu item to the menu title layer and keeps the shortcut key intact. It uses the shortcut key as the menu title at runtime.

To create separator lines in PowerBuilder menus, enter a single hyphen (-) as the item's text (see Figure 12.6). As you can see, the name PowerBuilder constructs is m_-. Because this name clashes every time you create a new separator line, you should number separator lines in increments of 10 so that you can insert new separator lines as required.

**FIGURE 12.6**
*The separator item now highlighted in WYSIWYG and Tree Menu views.*

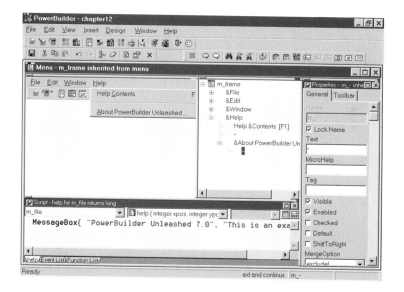

> ### Caution
>
> One option that many developers turn off after they use PowerBuilder for a while is Dashes in Identifiers. This enables you to use hyphens in variable and object names and can be confusing if you actually name objects with hyphens. Inside the Menu painter, PowerBuilder generates names with hyphens in them and even enables you to do the same. However, when you try to save the object with the Dashes in Identifiers option disabled, you get an error detailing some Forward Declarations . The same error appears when you're migrating menus

between versions of PowerBuilder. A useful naming scheme is to number each separator with numbers, the first being the menu title index, and the second some unique number within that index. For instance, in the example in Figure 12.6 the separator would be named m_11.

The Enabled and Visible attributes for each menu title and menu item, in addition to the Checked attribute for menu items, are accessible on the General tab (see Figure 12.7). The other settings in this view are dealt with later in the section "Menu Inheritance."

**FIGURE 12.7**

*The General tab.*

**Caution**

If you delete a submenu title, you aren't warned if items exist in the cascading menu; *everything* is removed.

You can assign a MicroHelp value for each piece of the menu. PowerBuilder uses this value to automatically display in an MDI frame's MicroHelp area (if available) as users traverse the menu. Enter the value in the MicroHelp text box; you can enter quite long descriptions. This saves you from having to write scripts to carry out the same functionality.

When you set the Default attribute for a pop-up menu item, it appears boldfaced on the menu and helps inform users of the menu's default action. This attribute is used with context menus to show which function would be performed if the object were double-clicked. Only one menu item should be chosen as the default.

## Adding Corresponding Toolbar Items

Each menu item can have a corresponding toolbar icon displayed when you create an MDI application. To access these properties, use the Toolbar tab page (see Figure 12.8). You can specify the text displayed with the Show Text toolbar button or with PowerTips. You can also specify the positioning of the button on the toolbar and drop-down toolbar properties.

**FIGURE 12.8**
*The Toolbar tab.*

The ToolbarItemText box enables you to specify the text that displays on the toolbar button and the text that appears in the PowerTip. Button text is displayed when the ToolbarText attribute of the application object is TRUE, and PowerTips are displayed when the ToolbarTips attribute is TRUE. Both properties can be set from within the Application painter. You specify the two pieces of text with a comma-separated string, such as Button Text, PowerTip Text. If you specify only one piece of text, it's used for the button as well as the PowerTip.

### Note

Limit the actual button text to no more than eight or nine characters, because the operating system restricts the button size and will truncate longer text. PowerTip text, however, can be quite extensive.

To separate a toolbar button from the preceding button, you need to enter an integer value into the ToolbarItemSpace text box. This is done to logically group related buttons together. The usual value is 1, and the default (no spacing) is 0. This attribute is ignored when the toolbar is set to display button text.

If, for some reason, you need to change the order of the buttons on the toolbar, use the ToolbarItemOrder text box to set an ordering value. This defaults to 0, and the buttons are displayed in menu order.

> **Note**
>
> Remember that PowerBuilder defaults menu item orders to 0, so you might have to set all the Order values for menu items to get the desired result. Otherwise, all the 0 Order value menu items appear first, and then the menu items with Order values greater than 0. Number each item in increments (5, 10) to give you more flexibility in changing the order or adding new options.

PowerBuilder also can provide drop-down toolbar items (see Figure 12.9). This way, you can make your toolbars shorter so that they can be more easily used and more easily docked (see the later section "Toolbars and PowerTips"). You can provide drop-down toolbar items for menu titles so that all their subordinate menu item toolbar entries appear underneath the parent's drop-down. On the Toolbar tab you must select MenuCascade! for the Object Type drop-down for the parent menu item. When MenuCascade! is chosen, you can specify the number of columns that the drop-down should use when displaying the toolbar pictures by entering a value in the Columns field. The DropDown check box is checked when it becomes visible. If you don't want the subordinate menu item toolbar entries to appear in the drop-down format, uncheck this option. (The Columns field and the DropDown check box don't appear until you select MenuCascade! for the Object Type; see Figure 12.10.)

**Figure 12.9**

*Drop-down toolbar items.*

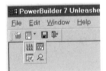

**FIGURE 12.10**

*The Toolbar tab before and after* MenuCascade! *is chosen for Object Type.*

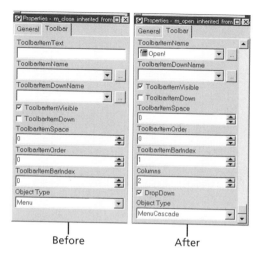

Before                    After

**Note**

The ToolbarItemBarIndex option allows you to open multiple toolbars for the one menu. Each toolbar is independent of the other. You can control which toolbar a menu item appears in by setting this value.

On the Toolbar tab, you can specify the icon displayed on the toolbar button in the ToolbarItemName option. To specify the icon that displays when the button is pressed down, set the ToolbarItemDownName option. You can enter the filename and path of the graphics file (in BMP, GIF, JPEG, or ICO file formats) to be used for the button and down pictures, or click the appropriate button to bring up a file dialog. The stock pictures that come with PowerBuilder are also accessible in this tab by clicking the drop-down arrows.

**Note**

The picture file should be 16 pixels wide by 15 pixels high. Otherwise, PowerBuilder compresses or expands the picture, and you get some ugly results.

If you want the ToolbarItemDownName to remain down when the user releases the mouse button, click the ToolbarItemDown check box. When the button is in the down state, you must use code to alter the menu item's ToolbarItemDown setting to set it back to the normal picture. The value FALSE resets the button. You use this functionality with menu items that can be checked and unchecked.

12

Menus and the
Menu Painter

> **Note**
>
> In WYSIWYG view, any drop-down toolbars that you've specified won't be displayed, and all pictures appear contiguously across the toolbar.

The only step left when you've finished the menu and saved it is to attach it to a window—unless you're dynamically using the menu for creating pop-up menus. Menus are associated with Window objects in the Window painter and are just another property of the window.

# Menu-Specific PowerScript

Several functions, attributes, and events specific to menus are covered in this section. They allow you control where and when a menu is used, how to reference the menu and its parent object, and how to modify the menu's characteristics programmatically.

## Opening a Pop-Up Menu

Now that you can create a menu, two things can be done with it. The menu can be attached to a window, in which case it becomes a drop-down menu and is created and destroyed by PowerBuilder. The menu can also be used as a pop-up menu for which you have control and responsibility. Pop-up menus can also be opened for menu items that exist in the window's current menu.

To create a menu at a certain location, use the `PopMenu()` function:

```
MenuItem.PopMenu( Xlocation, Ylocation)
```

The *MenuItem* argument is a fully qualified name of the desired menu title for the menu and is created at the coordinates (in PowerBuilder units) indicated by the *Xlocation* and *Ylocation* arguments (from the left and top of the window, respectively). Be careful—these coordinates are relative to the currently active window. Also remember that MDI sheets aren't active—only the frame is.

If the menu isn't already open and attached to a window, you must declare and instantiate a variable of the correct menu type before calling the `PopMenu()` function.

> **Note**
>
> If for some reason the menu title you're going to use for a pop-up isn't visible, you must make it visible before it can be displayed as a pop-up.

To understand these concepts, look at some examples.

The first example opens a pop-up menu of a menu title that already exists as part of a window. The two functions that return the current coordinates of the mouse pointer are used to open the pop-up menu at the mouse's position:

```
m_test.m_file.PopMenu( PointerX(), PointerY())
```

The second example opens the same menu that's not currently attached to any open windows:

```
m_sheet lm_PopUp

lm_PopUp = Create m_sheet
lm_PopUp.m_file.PopMenu( PointerX(), PointerY())
```

However, if you're opening the pop-up menu in an MDI sheet, you need to prefix PointerX() and PointerY() with the name of the MDI frame window:

```
lm_PopUp.m_file.PopMenu( w_frame.PointerX(), w_frame.PointerY())
```

After users make a selection, the menu action is carried out, and the pop-up menu is destroyed by PowerBuilder.

### Note

Usually the code for the pop-up menu is placed in the Rbuttondown or the Clicked event of the object. Two arguments for these events are xpos and ypos, which vary from PointerX() and PointerY() because xpos and ypos represent the distance the pointer is from the upper left corner of the window as opposed to the upper left corner of the object that has been clicked. If you use xpos and ypos, the menu won't always appear where you've clicked.

## Menu Attributes

As mentioned earlier in the description of menu items, you can provide items that can be checked and unchecked. This is an attribute of a menu item; it can be accessed either directly by using the dot notation (.Checked) or by using the Check() and UnCheck() functions. You can't check a menu bar item.

PowerBuilder doesn't automatically handle turning the check mark on and off. You must place the following line of code in the Clicked event:

```
this.Checked = Not this.Checked
```

Like other controls, a menu item (and even a menu bar item) can be disabled and enabled at runtime. As before, PowerBuilder provides two ways to alter the state: by using dot notation (`.Enabled`) and by using the `Enable()` and `Disable()` functions.

## The `ParentWindow` Pronoun

Often you need to refer to the window that owns the menu in which you're coding. This special relationship can be written by using the `ParentWindow` pronoun. For example, to code the exit menu item, the code would be

```
Close (ParentWindow)
```

The `ParentWindow` pronoun, however, points only to an object of type window. You can't make specific references to controls or other developer-defined attributes of the menu's parent window.

## Menu Events

Menu items have only three events:

- The `Clicked`event occurs when users click a menu item and release the mouse button.

- The `Selected` event occurs when users browse through the menu and are on the current menu item but have yet to trigger the `Clicked` event. This event is rarely used but is provided if you want to code some specific functionality into your application.

- The `Help` event, new to PowerBuilder 7.0, provides help on a menu item when users press the F1 key.

> **Note**
>
> At the printing of this book, if code has been placed in the `Help` event of the first menu bar item, the event won't be triggered. If any code is in the `Help` events of the first menu bar item's subordinate menu items, the first menu item's code will be triggered.

By placing code in a menu title's `Clicked` event, you can dynamically enable and disable items in the cascading menu every time users select it. You can provide dynamic security based on application parameters or transaction object settings, or more usually a cascading menu that's sensitive to the current state of the window it's associated with. For example, you want to enable an MDI frame menu's Save option only if the current sheet has been modified. The sheet maintains an instance variable `ib_Modified` for this purpose. The code in the `Clicked` event of the File menu title would then be

```
w_sheet lw_Instance

lw_Instance = ParentWindow.GetActiveSheet()

// Disable it for the cases 1) no sheet and 2) no modifications
this.m_save.Enabled = FALSE

If IsValid(lw_Instance) Then
    // Note that these are split into two tests, because PowerBuilder will
    // evaluate both regardless of the success or failure of the first
    // expression. This means that if there was no active sheet, it would
    // still evaluate the 2nd expression and fail with a Null object ref.
If lw_Instance.ib_Modified Then
        this.m_save.Enabled = TRUE
    End If
End If
```

**Note**

This idea works fine but has a subtle problem. If `m_save` has a shortcut key (such as Ctrl+S), users can get to `m_save`'s script without going through `m_file`'s script. In these cases it is best to set a menu item's state from the window rather than trap it in the menu.

## Accessing Menu Items

Accessing a particular menu item can require coding an extensive dot-notation chain, depending on from where you're calling. The format is

```
Window.MenuName.MenuTitle.MenuItem{.MenuItem ...}
```

The chain can be shortened depending on from where you're accessing the menu. For example, a menu function needs to specify only *MenuTitle* and *MenuItem*. You can also use the Object Browser to paste the calling chain for menus.

## Menu Functions and Structures

Menus are one of the four objects (along with applications, windows, and user objects) that can have local functions and structures declared for them. These are created and maintained by using the same views as the other objects, and are covered in Chapter 2, "PowerBuilder 7.0 Development Environment."

# Menu Inheritance

As with other PowerBuilder objects, menus can also be inherited. To do this, click the Inherit toolbar button or choose Inherit from the File menu. This brings up the Inherit dialog, which is similar to the Open dialog. Select Menu from the Object Type drop-down list.

With a descendant menu, you can append items to the end of a cascading menu or modify existing menu items. You can't insert new items between ancestor items or remove ancestor items. As with inherited windows, you can make only the unnecessary menu items invisible.

There is, however, a limited method for inserting new menu items between ancestor menu items. Within the ancestor menu, you must set the `ShiftToRight` attribute for the menu titles you want to move right and for menu items you want to move down. In the descendant menu, any appended menu titles or menu items are placed before the moved ancestor titles and items at runtime. Any changes made are immediately reflected in Tree Menu and WYSIWYG views; the order of the menu items is Ancestor, Descendant, Moved Ancestors.

> **Note**
>
> When working with a descendant, if one of the ancestor's menu items `ShiftToRight` attribute is set, any menu item added in the descendant in the same layer will have the `ShiftToRight` attribute set by default.

Changing the visibility of menu items in inherited and normal menus has performance problems in all the current releases of PowerBuilder (this may be fixed in the next release). This is because every time a menu item is hidden, it's actually destroyed, and the whole menu is re-created and drawn onscreen. Creating a menu at runtime is an expensive operation because each menu item is an individual object within the Windows system. If you start hiding items, you will cause a significant amount of rebuilding and, depending on the machine's speed, might or might not notice the impact.

# Menus and MDIs

When you create an MDI frame in PowerBuilder, you *must* associate a menu with it. This is supposed to lead you into creating a menu that will open sheets and be capable of closing the frame. The sheets in an MDI application don't have to have menus associated with them. If a sheet has its own menu, it displays in the menu bar of the frame window when the sheet is active. The frame's menu, if there is one, is used when a sheet doesn't have its own menu.

PowerBuilder uses two internal window attributes to track which menu is associated with it: `MenuID` and `MenuName`. These attributes can be affected only indirectly by using the `ChangeMenu()` function. `ChangeMenu()` enables you to programmatically change the menu associated with a window:

```
Window.ChangeMenu( Menu {, SheetPosition})
```

The *SheetPosition* argument, used when the window is an MDI frame, indicates the menu title position to which you append the currently open window list. The default is `0`, and all opened sheets appear at the bottom of the second-to-last menu bar item's drop-down menu. If there's only one menu bar item, the opened sheets appear at the bottom of that one.

> **Note**
>
> If a sheet is now open in the MDI frame with its own menu, the new menu associated with the frame isn't visible until the sheet is closed or users activate a sheet without a menu.

Whenever you create or open an object at runtime, PowerBuilder creates a global variable of that type and points it at the instance you just created. However, when you open multiple instances of a window with a menu, PowerBuilder creates a global variable of that menu type and an instance of the menu for each window instance. You might not immediately see a problem with this, but the global variable points to the last created instance. This means that anywhere you specifically code that menu's object name, you're potentially accessing the wrong menu. For example, you have an MDI frame with three open sheets (A, B, and C). Each sheet is an instance of the same window, and all have menus (`m_menu`). If you have the following piece of code in the `Clicked` event of a menu item, it affects the menu pointed to by window C until you close sheet C:

```
m_menu.m_save.Enabled = FALSE
```

You receive a `Null Object Reference` error message the next time you try to access the menu, as the menu instance was released from memory. There are two solutions to this problem:

- Use good coding practices and only pronoun references within your menu scripts. This means using the `Parent` and `ParentWindow` keywords throughout your code, which makes the script work on the current instance rather than the last one created.

- Use the window's `MenuId` property to reference each window's own menu instance. `MenuId` is of type Menu, so you need to cast it to the correct menu object class before making explicit menu item calls or changes. You do this by casting the `MenuId` into another variable:

```
m_mfg_order lm_MyMenu

lm_MyMenu = this.MenuID
lm_MyMenu.m_save.Enabled = FALSE
```

- This example assumes that you know that the window's menu is of a certain class—in this case, `m_mfg_order`. You can of course use the `ClassName()` function to find the value, and then use a case statement to create the correct class type for the variable. Or you can use the `Dynamic` keyword and call the appropriate menu functions straight off the `MenuId` property.

The following list includes some general information and guidelines on using menus within an MDI application:

- If the current sheet doesn't have a menu, the sheet takes the frame's menu.

- To prevent user (and developer) confusion, if you're going to give one sheet a menu, you should provide all sheets with a menu (because the active menu can change depending on the previous sheet).

- If the current sheet's menu doesn't have a toolbar but the previously active sheet did, the menu is the active sheet's. However, the space where the previous sheet's toolbar appeared is still there, although the toolbar itself isn't visible.

- To prevent more confusion, if you code one sheet with a toolbar, code all sheets with a toolbar.

- The open sheet list menu title must have at least one menu item; otherwise, the list won't appear. If you don't intend to place any menu items under this title, you can code a menu item with a single dash, but this causes two lines to appear in the menu when a sheet is opened. You usually include options to arrange the open sheets in some fashion (for example, layered, tiled, and so forth).

# Toolbars and PowerTips

Unique to MDI frames and their sheets is the capability to provide a toolbar based on selected menu items. You read about the rules for specifying a toolbar earlier in the "The Menu Painter" section. In this section, you see how to use toolbars and some restrictions and problems associated with toolbars.

First, understand that toolbars can be used *only* in MDI frames and MDI sheets. If you open a sheet with a menu and toolbar outside the MDI frame, the toolbar doesn't show. Each toolbar button is directly associated with a menu item, and clicking the button simply triggers the Clicked event for that menu item.

You have control over these toolbars only through attributes (see Table 12.1) on the application and on the frame window.

TABLE **12.1**  Toolbar Attributes of an Application Object

| Attribute | Description |
|---|---|
| | *Data Type: String* |
| ToolbarFrameTitle | The title text for a floating FrameBar |
| ToolbarPopMenuText | The text on the pop-up menu for toolbars |
| ToolbarSheetTitle | The title text for a floating SheetBar |
| | *Data Type: Boolean* |
| ToolbarText | Whether the menu item text shows on the button |
| ToolbarTips | Whether PowerTips show when ToolbarText isn't active |
| ToolbarUserControl | Whether the toolbar pop-up menu can be used |

When a user right-clicks the toolbar, PowerBuilder provides a default pop-up menu that provides options to manipulate the toolbar. In fact, it's the same menu you use inside PowerBuilder on the PowerBar and PainterBar. The ToolbarPopMenuText attribute enables you to alter the text on the menu but not the functionality. This attribute is really used only in the construction of multilingual applications. The first two items on the pop-up menu display the titles set for the ToolbarFrameTitle and ToolbarSheetTitle attributes.

You set the ToolbarPopMenuText attribute by using a comma-separated list constructed as follows:

```
&Left, &Top, &Right, &Bottom, &Floating, &Show Text
```

These are the default values for the pop-up menu. For example, the French equivalent, with appropriate accelerators (&), would be

```
a &gauche, en &haut, a &droite, au &fond, f&lottant, montrer le &texte
```

Table 12.2 shows the toolbar properties for window objects.

**TABLE 12.2** Toolbar Properties of MDI Frame and Sheet Window Objects

| Attribute | Data Type | Description |
|---|---|---|
| ToolbarAlignment | ToolbarAlignment | Where the toolbar displays |
| ToolbarHeight | Integer | Height of a floating toolbar |
| ToolbarVisible | Boolean | Whether the toolbar displays |
| ToolbarWidth | Integer | Width of a floating toolbar |
| ToolbarX | Integer | X-coordinate of a floating toolbar |
| ToolbarY | Integer | Y-coordinate of a floating toolbar |

An MDI frame window also has one event associated with toolbars: ToolbarMoved. This event is triggered in an MDI frame window when users move the FrameBar or SheetBar. As shown in Table 12.3, the Message.WordParm and Message.LongParm attributes contain information on what was moved and to where it was moved. (A toolbar control window that demonstrates the use of these attributes is constructed in Chapter 10, "Windows and the Window Painter.")

**TABLE 12.3** Message Control Values

| Value | What It Means |
|---|---|
| | Message.WordParm |
| 0 | The FrameBar has been moved |
| 1 | The SheetBar has been moved |
| | Message.LongParm |
| 0 | Moved to the left |
| 1 | Moved to the top |
| 2 | Moved to the right |
| 3 | Moved to the bottom |
| 4 | Set to be a floating toolbar |

**Note**

Starting with PowerBuilder 5.0, the toolbar picture is grayed out for you when the menu item is disabled. This conforms with the Microsoft Windows 95/98 interface standards.

Hiding a menu item doesn't cause the toolbar button to become disabled or disappear. Again, you must code specifically for this occurrence. However, if you disable a menu title, it disables but doesn't remove the toolbar buttons for all the menu items under it. Both kinds of processing are best encapsulated into the menu itself or into a nonvisual user object built for managing menus.

One of the sometimes annoying toolbar effects in PowerBuilder applications is the double toolbar. When the frame and the sheet both have toolbars, the frame toolbar displays above the sheet toolbar. Both toolbars are active, and options can be selected from either.

A simple way around this is not to construct a toolbar for the sheet menus and have the options you want to make available at the sheet-level part of the frame's menu, but disabled. Obviously, this isn't always practical. With each type of sheet there's usually a different menu; therefore, you can use this method only if the number of types of sheets is small.

Another more complex method requires you to turn off screen redraws while you hide the frame toolbar when a sheet opens. You then have to track when the last sheet is closed to re-enable the frame toolbar. This is best achieved by using a controlling function on the MDI frame window. Within this function, it can update a window instance variable as you open and close sheets. When this counter is decremented back to 0, the function makes the frame toolbar visible again.

Starting with PowerBuilder 5.0, your user can dock these menus together onto one line, thus reclaiming some of the screen space that had been lost (see Figure 12.11).

In the Window painter, you have access to some of the attributes for the initial position of the window's toolbar. This is accessed via the Window properties sheet, under the ToolBar tab (see Figure 12.12). The ToolbarX, ToolbarY, ToolbarWidth, and ToolbarHeight options are enabled only when ToolbarAlignment is set to `floating!`.

# Controlling Toolbars

PowerBuilder provides some functions that allow you to control and query the state of a toolbar for a window. With these functions, you can also dock a toolbar onto the frame window's toolbar.

The `GetToolbar()` function allows you to query a window for basic toolbar information. If the window doesn't have a toolbar, the function returns −1. The function syntax is

```
lw_Window.GetToolbar(li_Index,lb_Visible{,la_Alignment{, ls_Title}})
```

**FIGURE 12.11**

*Two menu tool-bars docked.*

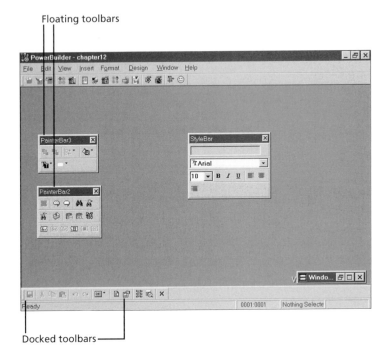

Floating toolbars

Docked toolbars

**FIGURE 12.12**

*The window tool-bar properties.*

Two versions of the `GetToolbarPos()` function let you extract further information about the toolbar:

```
lw_Window.GetToolbarPos(li_Index, li_Row, li_Offset)
lw_Window.GetToolbarPos(li_Index,li_X,li_Y,li_Width,li_Height)
```

The first version returns information about the row the toolbar appears on and the offset from the row's left origin. The second returns the size and position information for a floating toolbar.

The `SetToolbar()` function allows you to set basic toolbar values and has the following syntax:

```
lw_Window.SetToolbar(li_Index,lb_Visible{,la_Alignment{, ls_Title}})
```

Two versions of the `SetToolbarPos()` function allow you to set further information for the toolbar:

```
lw_Window.SetToolbarPos(li_Index, li_Row, li_Offset)
lw_Window.SetToolbarPos(li_Index,li_X, li_Y, li_Width, li_Height)
```

The first version allows you to set the row the toolbar will appear on and the offset from the row's left origin. The second sets the size and position information for floating toolbars.

## Saving and Restoring Toolbar Settings

By using the toolbar functions just described, you can construct generic save and restore functions for preserving the state of a window's toolbars. This information can be written to a number of different places: an INI file, a database table, or (if you are using a Microsoft operating system) the system Registry.

The code in Listing 12.1 uses an INI file, but it should require only minor changes to store the data elsewhere. You might still want to use an INI file instead of the Registry for the same reason that PowerBuilder still uses a PB.INI: cross-platform compatibility. Macintosh and UNIX platforms don't have a corresponding Registry structure, but the PowerBuilder INI access functions work in either case.

> **Note**
>
> So that you can store (Listing 12.1) and restore (Listing 12.2) multiple windows' toolbars, make a new section for each toolbar by using each window's class name. If the section doesn't already exist, the `SetProfileString()` function will create it for you; the only requirement is that the INI file must already exist.

**LISTING 12.1**    `f_save_toolbars (ReadOnly Window aw_Window)`

```
Integer li_Row, li_Offset, li_X, li_Y, li_Width, li_Height
Boolean lb_Visible
ToolbarAlignment la_Alignment
String ls_Title, ls_Alignment, ls_Section

// If the toolbar does not exist, this will return -1
If aw_window.GetToolbar( 1, lb_Visible, la_Alignment, ls_Title) = 1 Then
```

**LISTING 12.1** CONTINUED

```
    // The window's class is the section we will save the toolbar's
    // state under
ls_Section = aw_window.ClassName()

    // Convert the boolean to a string representation
    If lb_Visible Then
        SetProfileString( "ch12.ini", ls_Section, "Visible", "TRUE")
    Else
        SetProfileString( "ch12.ini", ls_Section, "Visible", "FALSE")
    End If

    // Convert the toolbars alignment to a string representation
    Choose Case la_Alignment
        Case AlignAtLeft!
            ls_Alignment = "Left"
        Case AlignAtTop!
            ls_Alignment = "Top"
        Case AlignAtRight!
            ls_Alignment = "Right"
        Case AlignAtBottom!
            ls_Alignment = "Bottom"
        Case Floating!
            ls_Alignment = "Floating"
    End Choose
    SetProfileString( "ch12.ini", ls_Section, "Alignment", ls_Alignment)

    // Extract the row and offset values and save them
    aw_window.GetToolbarPos (1, li_Row, li_Offset)
    SetProfileString( "ch12.ini", ls_Section, "Row", String (li_Row))
    SetProfileString( "ch12.ini", ls_Section, "Offset", String (li_Offset))

    // Extract the size and position values and save them
    aw_window.GetToolbarPos (1, li_X, li_Y, li_Width, li_Height)
    SetProfileString( "ch12.ini", ls_Section, "X", String (li_X))
    SetProfileString( "ch12.ini", ls_Section, "Y", String (li_Y))
    SetProfileString( "ch12.ini", ls_Section, "Width", String (li_Width))
    SetProfileString( "ch12.ini", ls_Section, "Height", String (li_Height))
End If
```

For example, to save the state of a window's toolbar within the CloseQuery event, the code would be

```
g_App.SaveToolbar( this)
```

**Note**

In this case, you are implementing the toolbar save and restore functions in a base class user object. The calls to this and the function in Listing 12.2 can be placed in a base class window object. The information for each window's toolbar is stored under a class name and so won't clash with another.

**LISTING 12.2**   The f_restore_toolbars (ReadOnly Window aw_Window) Function

```
Integer li_Row, li_Offset, li_X, li_Y, li_Width, li_Height
Boolean lb_Visible = FALSE
ToolbarAlignment la_Alignment
String ls_Title, ls_Alignment, ls_Visible, ls_Section

// If the bar does not exist, this will return -1
If aw_window.GetToolbar( 1, lb_Visible, la_Alignment, ls_Title) = 1 Then
   // The window's class is the section that we saved the toolbar's
   // state under
ls_Section = aw_window.ClassName()

   // Try and retrieve the toolbars visiblity
   ls_Visible = ProfileString( "ch12.ini", ls_Section, "Visible", "")
   // If we failed to find the toolbars visible state then do NOT
   // overwrite the current settings of the toolbar.
   If ls_Visible <> "" Then
      ls_Alignment = ProfileString( "ch12.ini", ls_Section, "Alignment", "Top")
ls_Title = ProfileString( "ch12.ini", ls_Section, "Title", "")

      If Upper( ls_Visible) = "TRUE" Then
         lb_Visible = TRUE
      End If

      // Convert the string back into an alignment value
      Choose Case Lower( ls_Alignment)
         Case "left"
            la_Alignment = AlignAtLeft!
```

**LISTING 12.2**  CONTINUED

```
        Case "top"
            la_Alignment = AlignAtTop!
        Case "right"
            la_Alignment = AlignAtRight!
        Case "bottom"
            la_Alignment = AlignAtBottom!
        Case "floating"
            la_Alignment = Floating!
    End Choose
    // Set the base settings for the toolbar
    aw_window.SetToolbar( 1, lb_Visible, la_Alignment, ls_Title)

    // Obtain the other settings for the toolbar ...
    li_Row = ProfileInt( "ch12.ini", ls_Section, "Row", 1)
    li_Offset = ProfileInt( "ch12.ini", ls_Section, "Offset", 0)
    li_X = ProfileInt( "ch12.ini", ls_Section, "X", 0)
    li_Y = ProfileInt( "ch12.ini", ls_Section, "Y", 0)
    li_Width = ProfileInt( "ch12.ini", ls_Section, "Width", 0)
    li_Height = ProfileInt( "ch12.ini", ls_Section, "Height", 0)

    // ... and then set them for the toolbar
    aw_window.SetToolbarPos( 1, li_Row, li_Offset, FALSE)
    aw_window.SetToolbarPos( 1, li_X, li_Y, li_Width, li_Height)
    End If
End If
```

**Note**

The functions in Listings 12.1 and 12.2 have been written so that they save to the Registry through the RegistrySet() and RegistryGet() functions. Aptly named f_save_toolbars_registry() and f_restore_toolbars_registry(), these functions are included on the CD-ROM accompanying this book.

# Tricks with Menus

PowerBuilder functions and attributes offer a number of tricks to using menus. The following sections provide some examples to illustrate these functions and attributes.

# Implementing an Edit Menu

Windows 95/98 already provides a full pop-up edit menu for editable controls. For developers using other operating systems, these features might not be available. A brief description of the code required is given next.

The code listed for each edit action could be incorporated into a base-level menu ancestor or implemented as global or nonvisual object functions.

The standard Edit menu consists of Undo, Copy, Cut, Paste, and Clear. Only the code for the Undo option is shown in detail because the other options require only a function name change. This edit functionality can be applied only to DataWindows, drop-down list boxes, edit masks, multiline edits, single-line edits, and OLE 2.0 controls.

---

**Tip**

You can place a controlling script in the `Clicked` event for the Edit menu title that enables and disables the appropriate menu items, depending on the object that has current focus or whether there's anything to paste. You might expand this menu to include the capability to use the `PasteSpecial()` and `PasteLink()` functions.

---

**Note**

As mentioned earlier, the preceding tip has a problem. Users could press Ctrl+C or Ctrl+V for copy and past, which would bypass the clicked event. This would entail more work to trap each control to verify the whether it is editable.

---

# Undo

An Undo menu option should cancel the last edit made to an editable control; use the PowerBuilder `Undo()` and `CanUndo()` functions.

The `Undo()` function can't be used with drop-down list boxes or OLE 2.0 controls. To see whether the last action can be undone, use the `CanUndo()` function:

```
GraphicObject lgo_Object
DataWindow ldw_Undo
EditMask lem_Undo
```

```
MultiLineEdit lmle_Undo
SingleLineEdit lsle_Undo

Lgo_Object = GetFocus()        // Saves us calling the f() multiple times

If Not IsNull( lgo_Object) Then
   Choose Case TypeOf( lgo_Object)
      Case DataWindow!
         ldw_Undo = lgo_Object
         If ldw_Undo.CanUndo() Then
            ldw_Undo.Undo()
         End If
      Case EditMask!
         lem_Undo = lgo_Object
         If lem_Undo.CanUndo() Then
            lem_Undo.Undo()
         End If
      Case MultiLineEdit!
         lmle_Undo = lgo_Object
If lmle_Undo.CanUndo() Then
            lmle_Undo.Undo()
         End If
      Case SingleLineEdit!
         lsle_Undo = lgo_Object
         If lsle_Undo.CanUndo() Then
            Lsle_Undo.Undo()
         End If
   End Choose
End If
```

You have to set a variable of the correct object type to the current object because the `GraphicObject` object doesn't have `Undo()` or `CanUndo()` as object functions.

## Copy

The Copy menu option nondestructively (that is, leaving the highlighted text alone) duplicates the value in the current control into the Windows Clipboard. Only the highlighted part is copied. For this, you use the PowerBuilder `Copy()` function.

If the control is a drop-down list box, the `AllowEdit` attribute must be set to `TRUE`; otherwise, the control is effectively a list box. Here's an example:

```
Case DropDownListBox!
   ddlbCopy = lgo_Object
```

```
If ddlbCopy.AllowEdit = TRUE Then
    ddlbCopy.Copy()
End If
```

For a DataWindow control, the text value is copied from the edit box, not from the column.

If for some reason you need to trap when nothing was copied or trap what happened with an OLE 2.0 control, you can examine the return value of `Copy()`. For the edit controls, the number of characters copied is returned: If the control was empty, the value is 0, and on an error it's -1. If it was an OLE 2.0 control, the return value is 0 for a success, -1 if the control is empty, -2 if the copy fails, and -9 for all other errors.

# Cut

The Cut menu option destructively (that is, removing the highlighted text) moves the value in the current control into the Windows Clipboard. Only the highlighted part is moved. For this, you use the PowerBuilder `Cut()` function.

The same restrictions for the `Copy()` function apply to `Cut()`.

The return value for `Cut()` is identical to that of `Copy()`. The return values, if it was an OLE 2.0 control, are the same except that -2 means the cut failed. Cutting an OLE object breaks any connection between it and the source file or storage.

# Paste

The Paste menu option inserts the Clipboard's contents into the current text, overwrites the highlighted section, or, with OLE controls, completely replaces the object. For this, you use the PowerBuilder `Paste()` function.

For DataWindow controls, the text is pasted into the edit field, not the column. If the value doesn't match the data type of the column, the whole value is truncated so that an empty string is inserted. For all controls, `Paste()` copies only as many characters as will fit in the control; the rest are truncated. When an OLE object is pasted into an OLE 2.0 control, the data is only embedded, not linked.

The return value for `Paste()` is the number of characters pasted. If the Clipboard doesn't contain a textual value, the function does nothing and returns 0. With OLE 2.0 controls, the function returns 0 on success, -1 if the Clipboard contents can't be embedded, and -9 on all other errors.

# Clear

The Clear menu option deletes the selected text or OLE 2.0 control and doesn't place it in the Clipboard. For this, you use the PowerBuilder `Clear()` function. Clearing an OLE 2.0

control's object deletes all references to it, doesn't save any changes made, and breaks any connections.

The return value for Clear() is 0 on success and -1 on an error. For OLE 2.0 controls, 0 also indicates success, but -9 indicates that an error occurred.

## Maintaining the Edit Menu

It's also helpful for end users if you enable and disable the Edit menu options as appropriate (for example, if no sheet window is now open, or when the current control on a sheet is an edit control):

```
GraphicObject lgo_Object
DataWindow ldw_Undo
EditMask lem_Undo
MultiLineEdit lmle_Undo
SingleLineEdit lsle_Undo
Window lw_Instance
Integer li_SelectedLength

m_undo.Enabled = FALSE
 m_copy.Enabled = FALSE
 m_cut.Enabled = FALSE
 m_paste.Enabled = FALSE
 m_clear.Enabled = FALSE


lw_Instance = ParentWindow.GetActiveSheet()

If Not IsValid( lw_Instance) Then
   Return
End If


lgo_Object = GetFocus()      // Saves us calling the f() multiple times

If IsNull( lgo_Object) Then
   Return
Else
   Choose Case TypeOf( lgo_Object)
      Case DataWindow!
         ldw_Undo = lgo_Object
         li_SelectedLength = ldw_Undo.SelectedLength()
      Case EditMask!
         Lem_Undo = lgo_Object
         li_SelectedLength = lem_Undo.SelectedLength()
```

```
      Case MultiLineEdit!
          Lmle_Undo = lgo_Object
          li_SelectedLength = lmle_Undo.SelectedLength()
      Case SingleLineEdit!
          lsle_Undo = lgo_Object
          li_SelectedLength = lsle_Undo.SelectedLength()
   End Choose
End If


If li_SelectedLength > 0 Then
   m_copy.Enabled = TRUE
   m_cut.Enabled = TRUE
   m_clear.Enabled = TRUE
End If


If ( Len( Clipboard()) > 0) Then
    m_paste.Enabled = TRUE
End If
```

# Accessing the Open Sheet Menu

Maybe you're going to track the open sheets by using the dynamic window list menu, or perhaps you need access to other window titles. Whichever it is, the code in Listing 12.3 can be used to traverse a cascaded menu.

These API functions are used and should be declared globally or locally:

```
FUNCTION uInt GetMenu( uInt hWnd) LIBRARY "user32.dll"
FUNCTION uInt GetMenuItemID( uInt hWnd, int nPosition) LIBRARY "user32.dll"
FUNCTION uInt GetMenuItemCount( uInt hWnd) LIBRARY "user32.dll"
FUNCTION uInt GetSubMenu( uInt hWnd, int nPosition) LIBRARY "user32.dll"
FUNCTION uInt GetMenuStringA( uInt hWnd, uInt nItem, REF string szItem, &
                     int nMax, uint nByCommand) LIBRARY "user32.dll"
```

The code that uses these functions would probably be placed in a menu function. Listing 12.3 is an example of a menu function used to traverse an open sheet menu.

**LISTING 12.3**  Code for Traversing the Open Sheet Menu

```
uInt lh_MainMenu, lh_MenuTitle, lh_MenuItem
Integer li_Length, li_MaxSize = 32
Integer li_NoOfMenuItems, li_Item, li_ItemPosition
String  ls_Buffer
```

**LISTING 12.3** CONTINUED

```
ls_Buffer = Space( li_MaxSize)

// Get main menu handle of a window passed as an argument
lh_MainMenu = GetMenu( Handle( ParentWindow))

// GetSubMenu()'s second argument is the position of the menu
// title that you want the handle. Within this menu we maintain
// a menu instance variable that is used in all OpenSheet() calls.
// However, PowerBuilder is based from 1 onwards, Windows is 0 based.
lh_MenuTitle = GetSubMenu( lh_MainMenu, ii_WindowList - 1)

// Get a count of the menu item for the menu title
li_NoOfMenuItems = GetMenuItemCount( lh_MenuTitle)

// We can now loop through the menu and explore each item
Do While li_Item < li_NoOfMenuItems
    // Get the handle of a menu item
    lh_MenuItem = GetMenuItemID( lh_MenuTitle, li_Item)

    // The menu item text is returned into the string szBuffer
    // The last argument is MF_BYCOMMAND (0) so that we can use hMenuItem
    li_Length = GetMenuStringA( lh_MainMenu, lh_MenuItem, ls_Buffer, &
                                li_MaxSize, 0)

    li_Item ++
Loop
```

The value of li_Length is the length of the text copied into ls_Buffer. For menu items that are line separators, li_Length is 0, and ls_Buffer contains an empty string.

---

**Note**

Remember that the text value contains an ellipsis (...) and the accelerator indicator (&). It also contains the number of the sheet (that is, if the menu item is 1 Stock Sheet, the value returned is &1 Stock Sheet ).

---

Similar in concept to the preceding example is the capability to scan through a menu to find a particular menu item. You can do this easily without having to resort to API functions by using the MenuID attribute of a window and its associated array of menu items. For example, the code in Listing 12.4 is built into a window-level function that takes a menu title and item, locates that item, and disables it.

**LISTING 12.4**  Traversing the `MenuID` Attribute

```
Integer li_MenuTitle, li_TotalTitles, li_MenuItem, li_TotalItems

// Get a count of the top level menu titles
li_TotalTitles = UpperBound( this.MenuID.Item)

For li_MenuTitle = 1 To li_TotalTitles
    // Locate the required menu title
    If this.MenuID.Item[li_MenuTitle].Text = as_Title THEN
        li_TotalItems = UpperBound( this.MenuID.Item[li_MenuTitle].Item)
        For li_MenuItem = 1 To li_TotalItems
            // Locate menu item
            If this.MenuID.Item[li_MenuTitle].Item[li_MenuItem].Text = as_Item Then
Disable( this.MenuID.Item[li_MenuTitle].Item[li_MenuItem])
                li_MenuItem = li_TotalItems
                Exit
            End If
        Next
        Exit
    End If
Next
```

You can use this technique when you don't know the name of the menu with which the window is associated. It also prevents the need to hard-code menu names.

# Menus and OLE 2.0

With OLE 2.0 in-place activation, the OLE server's menu becomes the active menu to enable you to work on the object within its own context. The server menu can be merged into the current PowerBuilder application's menu by using the `MergeOption` attribute for each menu title. This attribute can be found in the Menu Merge Option drop-down list in the Property tab page of the Menu painter. Table 12.4 describes these options.

**TABLE 12.4**  Menu Merge Options

| *Enumerated Data Type* | *Description* |
| --- | --- |
| `Exclude!` | Don't include it in the OLE server menu. |
| `Merge!` | Add this menu title and cascading menu into the OLE server menu, appearing after the first menu title of the server. |

TABLE **12.4** Menu Merge Options

| Enumerated Data Type | Description |
| --- | --- |
| FileMenu! | This menu title is leftmost on the menu bar. The server's File menu isn't used. |
| EditMenu! | The server's Edit menu displays in place of this Edit menu title. |
| WindowMenu! | The menu listing the open windows. The server's Window menu isn't used. |
| HelpMenu! | The server's Help menu displays instead of this Help menu title. |

The default value for the MergeOption attribute is Exclude!.

The In-Place settings cause the menu bar to display the PowerBuilder application's File and Window menus and the server's Edit and Help menus. Any menus that you label as Merge are added to the other server menu titles. For more information on OLE, see Chapter 37, "ActiveX and OLE."

# Summary

This chapter explored how to physically create menus and logically create better menus. You examined guidelines that lead to the construction of better menus. You also took a detailed look at the use of menus in an MDI application and some of the tricks and traps of using toolbars.

# The User Object Painter

User objects are one of the most important components PowerBuilder provides for developing object-oriented applications. They are used mainly to carry out commonly used processing or functionality, which allows you to concentrate on integrating objects instead of reconstructing and retesting certain components across an application. A user object can be written to be used as a visual control on a window object or as a nonvisual object that can be used from anywhere in your PowerScript. This chapter explores the different types of user objects PowerBuilder provides, how they're created and used, and what special functions can be used with them.

# Why User Objects?

A *user object* encapsulates a set of related operations and attributes that define a particular functionality. So why use PowerBuilder user objects? Here are some advantages:

- They eliminate the need to code functionality in different places for the same objects in your application. You can place the code in a central location and call it as required.

- You can collect visual controls that are always used together in a particular manner into one visual control that can be reused.

- They provide *the* method for enforcing a standard look and feel to visual controls by providing a user object for each control type with the desired font face and size, object color, and object size.

- You can encapsulate related functionality with the object to which it belongs.

- They allow the extension of some system objects, such as Transaction, to incorporate your own functionality.

The keyword through most of these advantages is *encapsulation* (information hiding), which allows you to hide the actual workings of the user object and provide interaction through a flexible public accessible interface. This is an important concept to remember when constructing user objects. If the user object needs to act on an object that's external to itself, you should provide a way to pass a reference to this other object into the user object. After a user object is heavily used throughout one or even many applications, you will inevitably have to enhance the functionality or even fix some minor problems or undesired characteristics. Because the user object was written to make the best use of encapsulation, this allows modifications to be made without affecting the objects using it.

When you encapsulate this functionality into a user object, it becomes reusable, allowing you to accelerate application development with pretested objects that have a predefined functionality and interface. With reusability, you get the advantages of improved code quality and efficiency.

User objects are also one of the few objects that can be inherited from, which allows you to carry out further encapsulation and implement polymorphism by inheriting an ancestor object to create functionally specific descendants.

It can't be emphasized enough that you should place your own user objects in place of the standard controls available in the Window painter. This allows you to place functionality into your user objects and immediately have it available throughout your application, rather than have to retro-fit each place a certain control is used. Consider a window that uses a number of single-line edit controls that hold a variety of data. After you construct the window, you find that all the fields have to reset themselves to a particular value at some point in the window's life. If you've used a user object for each field, the functionality to achieve this can be coded in one place and become instantly available. If not, you have to visit each single-line edit control and place the same code in each. As you can see, using your own user objects saves time, effort, and frustration later in the development life cycle.

# Types of User Objects

User objects come in two distinct types: visual and class (or nonvisual). As you will see in the next couple of sections, both types encompass a few different styles.

## Visual User Objects

A *visual object* comprises a single control or multiple related controls that define a certain type of functionality. There are three types of visual user objects: custom, external, and standard. Visual user objects can be used only in the Window painter or in a user object of the custom visual type. Visual user objects can be modified only in the User Object painter and not directly through the Window painter.

You can set external properties of the user object that you place in a window object. These vary depending on the type of user object but include position, size, background color, and scrollbars. You also have access to *at least* the following events for the user object, and the events available vary among the different user object types: Constructor, Destructor, DragDrop, DragEnter, DragLeave, DragWithin, Other, and RButtonDown, as well as any user events that you've added to the user object.

> **Note**
>
> In versions of 16-bit PowerBuilder before 6.0, you had access to a fourth visual user object—the VBX. You can no longer add VBXs to your PowerBuilder applications because VBXs are 16-bit, but PowerBuilder is now *only* a 32-bit development environment. Any existing applications that you have that use VBXs can be migrated and used. In the 32-bit environments, VBX controls have been replaced by OCX controls (better known as ActiveX controls). You can place OCX controls directly on windows as you would a standard control, or you can make standard or custom visual user objects out of them. See Chapter 37, "ActiveX and OLE," for more information.

## Standard Visual User Objects

A *standard visual user object* is, in essence, an inherited object from one of the base classes of visual controls supported by PowerBuilder. The definition of the original object is carried down to the user object, which includes all the properties and events. This type of user object is often used to extend the functionality of the normal control, the most common example being DataWindow controls. The standard user object based on a DataWindow usually has default behavior placed in some events (for example, error handling and processing in DBError).

The standard type of visual user object is the most commonly used because it allows access to all the original properties and events of the object while extending it further. The standard visual controls that can be used to build a standard visual user object are CheckBox, CommandButton, DataWindow, DropDownListBox, DropDownPictureListBox, EditMask, Graph, GroupBox, HprogressBar, HScrollBar, HTrackBar, ListBox, ListView, MultiLineEdit, OLEControl, Picture, PictureButton, PictureHyperLink, PictureListBox, RadioButton, RichTextEdit, SingleLineEdit, StaticText, StaticHyperLink, Tab, TreeView, VprogressBar, VScrollBar, and VTrackBar.

## Custom Visual User Objects

*Custom visual user objects* contain multiple related controls that together provide a defined function. The user object area in the painter is akin to a miniature window, and you use it as you would a window in the Window painter. This type of user object is often used when you're repeatedly grouping a number of the same controls in different areas of the same, or even different, applications.

The user object acts as a single unit when placed on a window object and is of class type `UserObject!`. You access the controls in the custom user object through a `Control[]` array in the same manner as you would a window's controls.

The one difference between the custom visual user object and all the other user object types is that you have multiple controls within one package. This introduces some interesting problems regarding communication from the outside in and from the internal controls to outside the parent user object. There are many ways to achieve object communication, and the method you choose depends on a couple factors. Mainly, what's the purpose of the communication? Other factors are based on the object-oriented concepts that the development team is working against. Consider the problem of a command button that inserts a row into a DataWindow control. The desired communication can be achieved in the following ways:

- Specifically name the DataWindow control to be used. Obviously, this is a poor solution because it's not generic anymore. The object relies on the DataWindow to be called a particular name.

- Create a user event for the custom user object that's then triggered by the button. The event is then coded with the specific DataWindow reference after it's placed in a window. If you use the arguments in event messages, you can even customize the row insertion to add the row at a specific position in the DataWindow control. This allows loose coupling of the custom user object to the parent, such that if the user object were used inside a different custom user object, you would still maintain flexibility in your processing.

- You can use an instance variable for the DataWindow control that's set in the `Constructor` event of the custom user object from within the window object that's using it. This has the advantage of providing you with a direct reference to an object that can be used from many other scripts without having to trigger events that require code to be written externally to the user object. Just remember not to use any of these references until all the `Constructor` events are finished executing.

To illustrate the concept of a custom user object, consider a standard selection list that consists of a list to select from; a list to display the selected items; and buttons to add one item, remove one item, add all, and remove all. This can be constructed as two DataWindow controls linked with four buttons. To encapsulate these six controls and the functionality required for reuse, this would be created as a custom visual user object.

## External Visual User Objects

The *external visual user object* allows you to use objects that have been built by third-party companies or that you can create yourself using the operating system Software

Development Kit (SDK). These are usually supplied in the form of DLLs. You must have the required information on the DLL that tells you about the classes, messages, and styles that the DLL understands.

The SDK custom control must contain a registered class and a window procedure. The window class ties instances of an object to a class definition, which includes color information, cursor and icon settings, and a window procedure. The window procedure is the entry point used every time a message is processed by a custom control. The window procedure must be named *classWndFn*, where *class* is the registered class name.

You can interact with a custom control using three methods: Windows messages, style bits that allow access to particular object attributes, and functions that may have been defined for the object and are contained within the DLL.

# Class User Objects

Class user objects allow the encapsulation of logic and functionality that don't have visual components. The two types of class user objects, custom and standard, are used for the declaration of business logic components, specific management functions, calculations, and extending the nonvisual system objects. In PowerBuilder 6.0, a third type of class user object, the C++ one, was available only after installing the Class Builder portion of PowerBuilder Enterprise. The C++ user object has been removed from PowerBuilder 7.0.

The main advantage of a class user object is that it's truly nonvisual. This means that it consumes no GUI resources and only the memory required for the object, its working structures, and other dynamically created class objects. This also means that you use them a little differently than you do the visual user objects just introduced, as explained later in the section "Creating a Custom Class User Object."

## Auto-Instantiate

The class user objects that you create can be made to be auto-instantiating. This is achieved by selecting the Auto-Instantiate option from the pop-up menu in the User Object painter. This means that to use the class, you now have only to declare a variable using that user object class. There's no need to do explicit Create and Destroy calls because PowerBuilder handles the memory management as the object variable comes into and leaves scope.

# Custom Class User Objects

You use custom class user objects for the encapsulation of processing that won't be visible to users. These objects don't inherit any base-level definition from a PowerBuilder object and are shaped completely by the instance variables, functions, and events that you declare. They have two predefined events: `Constructor` and `Destructor`.

# Standard Class User Objects

Standard class user objects take their definition from the standard PowerBuilder object that they're based on, and like standard visual user objects, they allow you to extend the default behavior with your own code to make them specific to your requirements. Table 13.1 shows the standard classes in PowerBuilder for which you can create standard class user objects.

**TABLE 13.1**   PowerBuilder's Standard Classes

| Standard Class | Description |
| --- | --- |
| ADOResultSet* | Returns an ActiveX Distributed Object resultset |
| Connection | Distributed PowerBuilder connection information |
| ContextInformation | Obtains information about the application's current execution context |
| ContextKeyword | Accesses environment information for the current context |
| DataStore | A nonvisual DataWindow object |
| DynamicDescriptionArea | Stores information on the input and output parameters used in type 4 dynamic SQL |
| DynamicStagingArea | Stores information for use in subsequent dynamic SQL statements; is the only connection between the execution of dynamic SQL and a transaction object |
| Error | Stores information on errors and where the errors occurred |
| ErrorLogging* | Allows an object's container to write messages to the log file such as those used by Jaguar CTS and Microsoft MTS |
| Inet | An Internet service object |
| InternetResult | A buffer object for holding data returned via the Internet |
| JaguarORB* | Allows PowerBuilder to talk to Jaguar through CORBA |
| MailSession | The context in which MAPI processing occurs |
| Message | Used during the processing of events |
| OLEObject | A proxy for a remote OLE object |
| OLEStorage | A proxy for an open OLE storage |
| OLEStream | A proxy for an OLE stream |
| OLETXNObject* | Allows PowerBuilder client applications to have explicit control of Microsoft Transaction Server transactions |
| Pipeline | The context in which a data pipeline is executed |
| Profiling* | Inspects a PowerBuilder application's performance |

**13**

The User Object
Painter

TABLE **13.1** PowerBuilder's Standard Classes

| Standard Class | Description |
|---|---|
| Service* | Provides a means to access non-PowerBuilder host services: context information, context keyword, Internet, transaction server, error logging, and Secure Socket Layer |
| SSLCallBack* | Allows PowerBuilder to handle Secure Socket Layer (SSL) callbacks from Jaguar CTS |
| SSLServiceProvider* | Allows PowerBuilder applications to establish SSL connections to Jaguar CTS |
| Timing* | Implements a timer when a window's Timer event isn't available |
| TraceFile* | Gains access to a trace file generated by a PowerBuilder application during performance analysis |
| TraceTree* | Used for analysis of a PowerBuilder application's performance by providing a tree model that contains all nodes logged in a specific trace file |
| Transaction | The communication area between a script or DataWindow and the database |
| TransactionServer* | Provides information about the current transaction context; also allows you to have a component running in a transaction server to control itself and the transaction |
| Transport | Processes client requests to connect to a server application |

 *Objects new to PowerBuilder 7.0.*

Chapter 26, "Building User Objects," shows an example of a standard class user object that's fully fleshed out and is extending the transaction class to incorporate specific transaction management facilities.

One way to use a standard class user object is to declare it in the application object's property sheet on the Variable Types tab page (see Figure 13.1).

## Transaction Objects and RPCFUNC

If you create a transaction user object, you can include a cool trick for use with stored procedures. You can use database stored procedures (which don't produce a resultset) using the same *Object.Function* notation that you use with other PowerScript functions. This syntax performs better than the multitude of dynamic SQL commands that you normally need to issue to carry out the same operation. This is because PowerBuilder prepares the SQL ahead of time.

You can declare database stored procedures to be used in this manner within transaction class user objects only. Within a standard class user object, you can then enter the syntax required for the call in the Declare Local External Functions view. The syntax for declaring a remote procedure call (RPC) is similar to that of a normal external function and conforms to the following:

```
FUNCTION ReturnDataTypeFunctionName({REF}{Datatype1 Arg1,...DatatypeN ArgN}) &
                              RPCFUNC {ALIAS FOR DataBaseProcedureName}
```

If the stored procedure doesn't return a value, you should use the following syntax:

```
SUBROUTINE FunctionName ({REF} { Datatype1 Arg1, ... DatatypeN ArgN}) &
                    RPCFUNC {ALIAS FOR DataBaseProcedureName}
```

FIGURE **13.1**

*The Variable
Types tab page
for an applica-
tion's properties.*

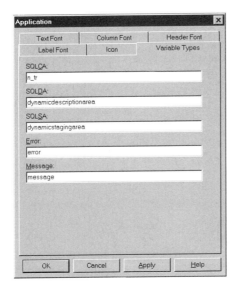

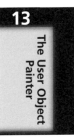

*FunctionName* is the name of the aliased stored procedure that you will use within your PowerScript call. If any arguments are being used as output parameters, prefix them with the REF keyword to indicate that they will be returning a value.

## Note

You should pre-pad string output parameters, just as you would any other external function call that returns values by reference. This is to avoid the value placed in the string parameter from being truncated.

Rather than enter this syntax by hand, use the Paste Special.SQL.Remote Stored Procedures menu to display a list of all currently available stored procedures. When you select one, PowerBuilder automatically generates the RPCFUNC syntax for you.

Remember to change the default global variable type for the SQLCA from `Transaction` to the standard class user object you've created.

### C++ Class User Objects

Although the C++ user object is no longer included in PowerBuilder 7.0, it is mentioned for those of you still using version 6.0 and for migrating existing applications to version 7.0. The C++ class user object allows the construction of fast compiled versions of processor-intensive functions into DLLs that can then be incorporated into your PowerBuilder application in the same way as the other types of class user objects. This object type provides fast execution as well as access to the large library of existing C++ code already in the programming community. The only drawbacks are that you need to know some C++ and the data types of parameters are a little restricting. The user object can accept the common data types (String, Integer, and so on), but it won't handle structures or enumerated data types.

# Using the User Object Painter

To create a new user object, click the PowerBar's New icon and select the Object tab (see Figure 13.2). Then double-click a user object type on the top row of the tab page.

**FIGURE 13.2**

*The New Object tab.*

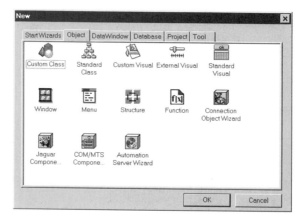

Inheritance in user objects works with the same principles as in windows and menus: You can't directly modify the scripts and controls inherited from the ancestor object. To inherit from an existing user object, click the Inherit button from the PowerBar and select User Objects from the Object Type drop-down list.

# Creating a Standard Visual User Object

To create a standard visual user object, select the Standard Visual icon from the Object tab to open the Select Standard Visual Type dialog (see Figure 13.3), and then select the object type on which you want to base the new user object.

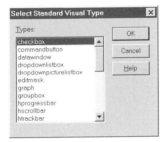

For this example, you create a database-enabled drop-down list box control that populates its list based on a SELECT statement. The drop-down list box control displays in the Layout view and actually defines the area of the user object. As you stretch the user object, you're increasing the size at which the control appears.

By using the Properties view, you can set up the default style of the drop-down list box. In this case, the defaults are exactly what you want. As you explore the user object, notice that it contains the same events that you would see in a drop-down list box control placed on a window. The same is true of the functions that you can use on the user object. The events available for the object are extended with the following custom events:

- DropDown traps when the user clicks the arrow to display the drop-down list of the control.

- Validate is coded in the parent object to allow validation of the control's edit area.

- InvalidEntry is used to provide a custom error message when the validation fails.

- Refresh can be used to refresh the list box control. This would usually be carried out by a broadcast message (see Chapter 26, "Building User Objects," for the code) to reload the list. The actual action is carried out by script written after the user object is placed on a window or custom user object.

- Reset returns the control to some predetermined state. This is also another candidate for a broadcasted message.

The DropDown event is connected to the PowerBuilder pbm_cbndropdown event ID, whereas the remaining events have no event IDs specified.

You should also declare two Boolean instance variables:

- ib_Modified flags that the edit field has been modified. Initially set to FALSE.

- ib_Validated indicates whether the value has been successfully validated. Initially set to FALSE.

The default events and some new ones are coded to handle validation of the data field, as well as some additional tasks.

To provide an auto selection of the edit field, similar to the edit styles in a DataWindow, code the following line in the GetFocus event:

```
This.SelectText( 1, Len (This.Text))
```

When users make a change in the edit field and move the focus (via mouse or Tab key), you want to validate the entry. To do so, place the following code in the Modified event to call the validation code outside the focus change:

```
ib_Modified = TRUE
This.Post Event Validate()
```

When the object is told to reset itself, the object-level variables need to be returned to a FALSE state and the edit field and list need to be emptied. This is done in the Reset event:

```
This.text = ""
This.Reset()
ib_Modified = FALSE
ib_Validated = FALSE
```

You're creating this user object mainly so that it's database aware. For this, you use an additional user event to utilize the parameterized PowerBuilder event style. The event name should be Populate and include an argument. Change the return type to a Long so that this event conforms to the other PowerBuilder events. Specify one argument, as_SQLSelect, of type String. Listing 13.1 shows the code for this event.

**LISTING 13.1** The Populate Event for u_ddlb_from_database

```
Integer li_SQLCode
String ls_SQLText, ls_Value

If as_SQLSelect = "" Then
   Return -1
Else
   PREPARE SQLSA FROM :as_SQLSelect;

   DECLARE dynamic_cursor DYNAMIC CURSOR FOR SQLSA;
```

**LISTING 13.1** CONTINUED

```
    OPEN DYNAMIC dynamic_cursor;

    If SQLCA.SQLCode < 0 Then
        MessageBox( "Unable to open dynamic cursor in Populate event code", &
SQLCA.SQLErrText)
        Return SQLCA.SQLCode
    End If

    This.SetRedraw (FALSE)
    This.Reset()

    Do While SQLCA.SQLCode = 0
        FETCH dynamic_cursor INTO :ls_Value;

        If SQLCA.SQLCode = 0 Then
            This.AddItem( ls_Value)
        ElseIf SQLCA.SQLCode < 0 Then
            li_SQLCode = SQLCA.SQLCode
            ls_SQLText = SQLCA.SQLErrText

            CLOSE dynamic_cursor;
            MessageBox( "Unable to fetch row from table specified", ls_SQLText)

            This.SetRedraw( TRUE)
            Return li_SQLCode
        Else
            Exit
        End If
    Loop

    This.SetRedraw( TRUE)

    CLOSE dynamic_cursor;

    Return 0
End If
```

The same population technique could be used to create a list box user object that could then replace the standard list box you used in the scrolling lookup custom user object.

You can now save this user object and use it in windows and custom user objects to provide a list populated from the database. Obviously, you can achieve the same results by using a drop-down DataWindow within a DataWindow. One advantage to using PowerBuilder is the different ways to achieve the same goal. This user object is useful for providing a simple lookup without requiring you to create two DataWindow objects and a DataWindow control that retrieves the data.

To cause the user object to populate, you could use the following code, possibly executed from a post-open event of the window, another control, or the user object's own `Constructor` event:

```
This.Trigger Event Populate( "SELECT name FROM employee")
```

Unlike in a drop-down DataWindow, you can supply only one column with this user object. You can, of course, concatenate multiple columns and place a known separator between them, which then allows you to extract the various components of the list item if you need to.

## Creating a Custom Visual User Object

To create a custom visual user object, select the Custom Visual icon from the Object Tab, which opens the User Object painter with an empty canvas in the Layout tab (an untitled custom visual user object). For this example, you create a scrolling lookup control.

Have you ever used the search function in a Windows help index and thought, hey, that's just the kind of scrolling lookup I need in my application? PowerBuilder's solution is to create a custom user object that contains a standard single-line edit object and a standard list box object. To do this, just select the appropriate items from the control list on the toolbar. These controls are called `sle_lookup` and `lb_lookup`. The first piece of code traps user keystrokes in the single-line edit. For this, you need to add a user event `EditChange` for the PowerBuilder event ID `pbm_enchange` to the single-line edit. This PowerBuilder-defined event message is fired every time a change is made in a single-line edit. On each keypress, you need to use the current string in a search of the items in the list box. The function `SelectItem( ItemText, StartIndex)` is used for this, with the starting index always being zero. This allows you to search the list from the beginning in case the users backspaced or deleted the previously entered letters.

To make the custom user object a little more open to the outside environment, you should also add a line of code to provide a message to indicate that a key was pressed. So this is the code for `EditChange`:

```
lb_lookup.SelectItem( This.Text, 0)


Parent.TriggerEvent( "sle_keypress")
```

If users are to tab away after entering a partial string, you copy the current selection from the list box into the single-line edit. The following line of code is placed in the `LoseFocus` event of `sle_lookup`:

```
This.text = lb_lookup.SelectedItem()
```

Now, to prevent a tab away from the single-line edit going to the list box, you need to set the tab order of the list box to zero.

Whenever users select an item in the list box, you need to move this to the single-line edit. This provides object interaction in the reverse direction and requires only the following line of code in the `SelectionChanged` event of `lb_lookup`:

```
sle_lookup.Text = This.SelectedItem()
```

To put the finishing touches on this user object, you need to cause the single-line edit and list box to resize themselves so that the size of the custom user object is stretched when placed in a window or other custom user object. The resize code is placed in the `Constructor` events for `sle_lookup` and `lb_lookup`. For `sle_lookup` the code is

```
This.Width = Parent.Width - 10
```

This makes the single-line edit the same width as the user object. The `-10` brings the right edge of the single-line edit to the left of the user object border; otherwise, the single-line edit becomes clipped.

For `lb_lookup`, you must deal with its location below the single-line edit, so the code is

```
This.Width = Parent.Width  - This.X
This.Height = Parent.Height - This.Y - 10
```

Again, you have a `-10` factor to bring the bottom edge inside the border of the parent.

The attributes and related functions of `sle_lookup` and `lb_lookup` can be manipulated from outside the custom user object. The syntax is

```
userobjectname.sle_lookup.attribute.
```

Similarly, each control's functions can also be accessed externally. For example, to populate the list box with items you want to search, you would use this:

```
u_lookup.lb_list box.AddItem( "Albion")
```

The attributes for the controls are accessed in the same way. Suppose that you want to change the three-dimensional borders to a regular border. This would be the code:

```
u_lookup.sle_lookup.BorderStyle = StyleBox!
u_lookup.lb_lookup.BorderStyle = StyleBox!
```

**13**

The User Object Painter

This provides a reasonably encapsulated visual user object that you can place on a window or other user object to provide scrolling lookup functionality.

# Creating an External Visual User Object

To create an external visual user object, select the External Visual icon from the Object Tab, which takes you to the User Object Painter with an empty rectangle in the Layout view. To specify the DLL that contains the external control, select the General Tab on the Properties View and click the button next to the `LibraryName` property. Clicking this button opens the Select Custom Control DLL dialog (see Figure 13.4), where you select the file that contains the object you want to use.

**FIGURE 13.4**

*The Select Custom Control DLL dialog.*

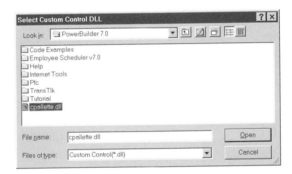

To illustrate this type of user object, use the CPALETTE.DLL that came with the PowerBuilder 5.0 examples directory. The DLL name and default class name are populated in the External User Object Properties General tab (see Figure 13.5).

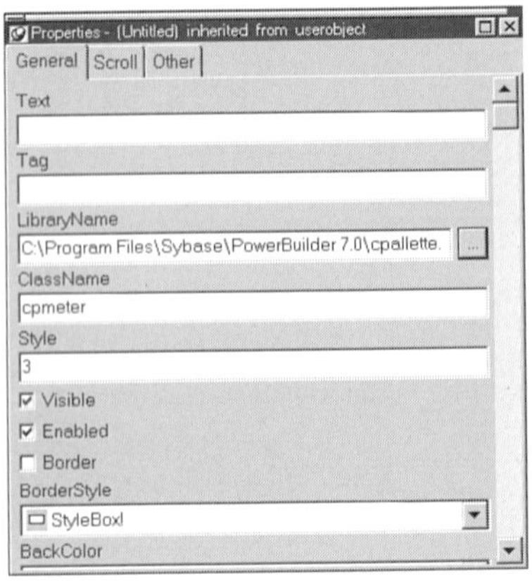

**FIGURE 13.5**

*The External User Object Properties General tab.*

In this example, you use the progress meter control that's part of this DLL. Although PowerBuilder 7.0 now comes with its own progress meter control, the one demonstrated here has a slightly different look and feel. One advantage of external visual user objects is that you can provide a standard Windows control with some enhanced functionality.

After selecting the DLL, you need to change the class name to `cpmeter` and the style to 3 (which changes the border). You can play around with different values for the style to change the border used by the control; when you buy a commercial DLL, you are provided with documentation on the various style settings. You can think of the style bits as attributes for the object, and for some settings you may be required to add style bits together. The untitled user object should now be shown in the painter in the Layout view.

The only functionality you add to this user object is to set the progress bar's position. This is achieved by passing an integer value that indicates the new increment to be made on the bar. The method of passing is by message, and the `cpmeter` object responds to a message ID of `4042`. Thus, the code would be coded into a user object function, `of_IncProgress()`, in this way:

```
Send( Handle( This), 4042, ai_Increment, 0)
```

This function could then be used to indicate how far along a process is. For example, if the saving of some information involved a number of integrated pieces that took more than a few seconds, you could use the progress bar within a status window and place calls to it using the following code:

```
w_status.u_rogress.of_IncProgress( 10)
```

This would allow you to place this same code in nine other locations to indicate 10 percent increment steps in the save process.

Some user objects trigger notification events that are sent in the `wParm` parameter of the `WM_COMMAND` event to the parent of the external object. PowerBuilder intercepts these and translates them to event IDs `pbm_uonexternal01` through `pbm_uonexternal25` for notification messages 0 through 24.

## VBX Visual User Objects

Although you can't create VBX-based user objects within PowerBuilder 7.0, you can still interact with existing ones that have been migrated from previous versions of PowerBuilder. So this section is included as reference only.

Some VBX events pass parameters to the control, and you need to use two VBX-specific functions to retrieve them: `EventParmDouble()` and `EventParmString()`. This is the syntax for these two functions:

**13**

The User Object Painter

```
VBXUserObject.EventParmDouble( Parameter, ParmVariable)
```

```
VBXUserObject.EventParmString( Parameter, ParmVariable)
```

The *Parameter* argument indicates the number of the parameter for which you want the value; *ParmVariable* is a variable of the appropriate data type used to store the value.

For example, in the VBClicked event for the Diamond VBX that came with older versions of PowerBuilder, you need to determine which of the four buttons was pressed:

```
Double ldb_ButtonNo
Integer li_Return

// 0 Up Arrow
// 1 Right Arrow
// 2 Down Arrow
// 3 Left Arrow

li_Return = EventParmDouble( 1, ldb_ButtonNo)

If li_Return <> -1 Then
    // Process button press
Else
    // Error retrieving event parameter
End If
```

The VBX controls gave developers a nice insight into the potential of external controls and objects that could be integrated with PowerBuilder. Now, with 32-bit PowerBuilder, you have access to OCXs and all that they provide.

## Creating a Custom Class User Object

To create a custom class user object, select the Custom Class icon on the Object tab, which opens the User Object painter with an empty canvas. Because this is a nonvisual object, the standard controls are disabled, and you create this type of object using events, variables, structures, and functions.

To demonstrate this type of user object, you will be encapsulating all the rules required to create and manage an order number for an order entry system. This sample user object illustrates the use of events, variables, and object-level functions within a class object.

Before starting, we have to define what an order number is for this object. The *order number* is made up of a two-digit plant number (where the order was entered into the system), followed by a one-digit year representation, a one-character product code, and a four-digit sequence number.

To start, declare three instance variables for the object:

| Scope | Data Type | Variable Name |
|---|---|---|
| Public | Boolean | ib_MaintainConnection |
| Protected | String | is_PlantNo |
| Protected | n_tr_sqlserver | itr_OrderNo |

The is_PlantNo variable is used during the generation of the order number and can be set from outside using a provided method, which you see later. Because this object carries out database access, you want to create and maintain your own connection. You do this in case a script that already has a cursor open using the SQLCA calls this object, and the database access carried out by this object would cause problems in the caller. The itr_OrderNo variable is provided to maintain connection information for the object. Because keeping a connection open to the DBMS can itself cause problems, allow the parent application to cause the object to make and break its connection as required using the ib_MaintainConnection variable.

> **Note**
>
> For the functionality demonstrated in the following code using the transaction object, refer to Chapter 26, "Building User Objects."

The real content of the class user object is contained in object-level functions. The first function (see Listing 13.2) creates a new order number and is based on a key index table.

**LISTING 13.2** Public Function String of_GetNextOrderNo()

```
String ls_OrderNo
Long ll_NextOrderSeqId

If Not ib_MaintainConnection Then
    itr_OrderNo.of_MakeConnection()
End If

UPDATE next_order_seq_id
SET order_seq_id = order_seq_id + 1
USING itr_OrderNo;

If itr_OrderNo.SQLCode <> 0 Then
    Return ""
```

**LISTING 13.2**   CONTINUED

```
End If

SELECT order_seq_id
INTO :ll_NextOrderSeqId
FROM next_order_seq_id
USING itr_OrderNo;

If ll_NextOrderSeqId > 99999 Then
    Error.Text = "Out of sequence numbers - report this to your supervisor!"
Open( w_error)
    Return ""
End If

ls_OrderNo = is_PlantNo + String( Today(), "yy") + String (ll_NextOrderSeqId)

If Not ib_MaintainConnection Then
    Itr_OrderNo.of_CloseConnection()
End If

If Len( ls_OrderNo) <> 8 Then
    Return ""
End If

Return ls_OrderNo
```

The next three functions, in Listings 13.3-13.5, are provided to break down the order number into the encoded pieces.

**LISTING 13.3**   Public Function String of_ExtractPlantNo **(String as_OrderNo)**

```
Return Right( as_OrderNo, 2)
```

**LISTING 13.4**   Public Function String of_ExtractProductClass **(String as_OrderNo)**

```
Return Mid( as_OrderNo, 4, 1)
```

**LISTING 13.5**   Public Function String of_ExtractYear **(String as_OrderNo)**

```
String ls_Today, ls_OrderYear, ls_Partial

ls_Today = String( Today(), "yyyy")
```

**LISTING 13.5** CONTINUED

```
ls_Partial = Mid( as_OrderNo, 3, 1)
ls_OrderYear = Right( ls_Today, 3) + ls_Partial
If ls_OrderYear > ls_Today Then
   ls_OrderYear = String( Integer( Left( ls_Today, 3)) - 1) + ls_Partial
End If


If Len( ls_OrderYear) <> 4 Then
   ls_OrderYear = ""
End If


Return ls_OrderYear
```

To allow external scripts to change the protected is_PlantNo variable, provide an access function (see Listing 13.6), which validates the new value before assigning it.

**LISTING 13.6** Public Function Boolean of_SetPlantNo (String as_NewPlantNo)

```
If Len( as_NewPlantNo) = 2 And IsNumber( as_NewPlantNo) Then
   is_PlantNo = as_NewPlantNo
   Return TRUE
Else
   Return FALSE
End If
```

Another piece of business logic states that "each order may be based on another order," which means that you have a one-to-many self relationship on the order table. To validate an order number that's about to be used as a parent identifier, provide an additional function (see Listing 13.7).

**LISTING 13.7** Public Function Boolean of_ValidateOrderNo (String as_OrderNo)

```
String ls_OrderNo
Boolean lb_Return = FALSE


If Not ib_MaintainConnection Then
   itr_OrderNo.of_MakeConnection()
End If


SELECT order_no
INTO :ls_OrderNo
FROM order_header
WHERE order_no = :as_OrderNo
```

**13**

**The User Object Painter**

**LISTING 13.7**   CONTINUED

```
USING itr_OrderNo;
If itr_OrderNo.SQLCode = 0 Then
    lb_Return = TRUE
End If


If Not ib_MaintainConnection Then
    itr_OrderNo.of_CloseConnection()
End If


Return lb_Return
```

Class user objects start with only two events: Constructor and Destructor. You won't be adding any additional events but will be placing code in both of these.

Within the Constructor event, you set a default value for the plant number variable, using one of the methods that you just created, and clone the default transaction object, SQLCA, for use with the object:

```
This.of_SetPlantNo( "10")


itr_OrderNo = SQLCA.of_CloneObject()
```

The Destructorevent carries out cleanup of the database connection object created in the Constructor event:

```
If itr_OrderNo.of_IsConnected() Then
    Itr_OrderNo.of_CloseConnection()
End If


DESTROY itr_OrderNo
```

This completes the functionality for the class object. To actually use it, you need to place the following code in the application:

```
n_cst_orders inv_Orders


// Instantiate an instance of the class
inv_Orders = CREATE n_cst_orders


// Get a new order number
inv_Orders.of_GetNextOrderNo()


// Destroy what we create
DESTROY inv_Orders
```

The declaration, creation, and destruction of the object can occur anywhere throughout your application, maybe within the application object or a specific window.

# Creating a Standard Class User Object

To create a standard class user object, select the Standard Class icon on the Object tab, which opens the Select Standard Class Type dialog (see Figure 13.6), where you select the class object that you want to extend.

FIGURE **13.6**
*The Select Standard Class Type dialog.*

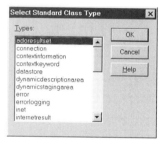

To see this type of user object in action, you extend the `Error` object, so select it from the list. The empty canvas in the User Object painter appears next, and you can begin to build your extensions. Each standard type has a different number of events predefined for it, and the `Error` object just has the basic two: `Constructor` and `Destructor`. Table 13.2 shows the attributes the standard error object contains.

TABLE **13.2**   Attributes of the Standard `Error` Object

| Attribute | Data Type | Description |
| --- | --- | --- |
| Line | Integer | The script line number in which the error occurred |
| Number | Integer | The PowerBuilder error number |
| ClassDefinition | PowerObject | Access to the definition of the class |
| Object | String | The object name in which the error occurred |
| ObjectEvent | String | The event within the object |
| Text | String | The PowerBuilder error text |
| WindowMenu | dString | The window or menu name in which the error occurred |

To further enhance the `Error` object, add four new attributes (public instance variables).

**Tip**

When modifying any standard class objects, consider leaving off prefixes on the variables or the new functions so that they look like part of the original object.

The variables are declared as follows:

| Data Type | Variable Name | Description |
|-----------|---------------|-------------|
| Boolean | AllowHalt | Indicates whether users should be given the option to halt the application from the error window |
| Boolean | SeriousError | Indicates whether to use a "friendly" message window or a full-blown system error window |
| String | SpecialEmail | Additional email requirements for certain error messages (for example, to a DBA for serious database errors) |
| String | UserMessage | The error message text retrieved from the database |

A common method of providing user-friendly messages to error conditions is to store the actual messages in a database table. Of course, this means that you need to check whether the error is a serious database error, which you would handle differently.

The method you provide to fetch the message from the database is RetrieveError() (see Listing 13.8) and takes a numeric error code as its single parameter.

**LISTING 13.8**  Public Function RetrieveError (Long al_Error)

```
SELECT error_message, special_email, serious_error, allow_halt
INTO :This.UserMessage,:This.SpecialEmail,:This.SeriousError,:This.AllowHalt
FROM error_messages
WHERE error_id = :al_Error
USING SQLCA;

If SQLCA.SQLcode = 100 Then
   This.UserMessage = "Unable to find the message for " + String( al_Error)
ElseIf SQLCA.SQLcode = -1 Then
   This.UserMessage = "SQL Error getting " + String( al_Error) + &
                      "~r~n~nSQL Error: " + SQLCA.SQLErrText
End If
```

Depending on the type of error that the object is now processing, you may want it to open one of two different message windows: a comprehensive error reporting window for system type errors or a less intimidating message box-style window. To handle this, provide the OpenErrorWindow() method in Listing 13.9.

**LISTING 13.9**  Public Function OpenErrorWindow()

```
If This.SeriousError Then
   Open( w_error)
Else
   MessageBox( "Error", This.UserMessage, StopSign!, Ok!)
End If


If This.SpecialEmail <> "" Then
   This.MailError()
End If
```

To provide direct, full, and detailed information on an error condition, provide the MailError() method (see Listing 13.10) to allow developers to post the message into the email system. The message recipient could be someone in QA (quality assurance), technical support, or the developers themselves. See Chapter 33, "Mail-Enabling PowerBuilder Applications," for more information on the MAPI functions used in this code example.

**LISTING 13.10**  Public Function MailError()

```
MailSession PBmailSession
MailMessage PBmailMessage
MailReturnCode PBmailReturn
String ls_Recipient, ls_System, ls_User, ls_PhoneBook, ls_Title

//
// Find out who the current user of the system is, and who should be
// notified
//
ls_User = ProfileString( gnv_App.is_INIFile, "Database", "UserId", "")

If This.SpecialEMail <> "" Then
   ls_Recipient = This.SpecialEmail
Else
   ls_Recipient = ProfileString( gnv_App.is_INIFile, gnv_App.is_Application, &
"MailRecipient", "")
End If

ls_System = gnv_App.is_ApplicationName
ls_PhoneBook = ProfileString(gnv_App.is_INIFile, "Errors", &
               "PhoneBook", "FALSE")

If Trim( ls_Recipient) = "" Or IsNull( ls_Recipient) Then
```

**LISTING 13.10**   CONTINUED

```
    //
    // No-one has been specified to receive the mail - error out.
    //
    Return
End If
//
// Create and log into a mail session
//
PBmailSession = Create MailSession

PBmailReturn = PBmailSession.MailLogon()

If PBmailReturn <> mailReturnSuccess! Then
    ls_Title = "Error - " + f_mail_error_to_string( PBmailReturn)
    MessageBox( ls_Title, "Unable to notify administrator by specified mail " &
+ "address. Please notify the system administrator " + &
                        "of this problem.")

    Return
Else
    //
    // Setup the contents of the mail message
    //
    PBmailMessage.Subject = "An error has occurred within " + ls_System
    PBmailMessage.NoteText ="System User: " + ls_User + "~n~n" + &
                            "Window Name: " + This.WindowMenu + "~n" + &
                            "Object Name: " + This.Object + "~n" + &
                            "Object Event:" + This.ObjectEvent + "~n" + &
                            "Line Number: " + String (This.Line) + "~n" + &
                            "Error Number:" + String (This.Number) + "~n~n" + &
This.Text
    //
    // Should the address "phone book" be opened for user to specify
    // recipient
    //
    If Upper( ls_PhoneBook) = "TRUE" Then
        PBmailReturn = PBmailSession.mailAddress( PBmailMessage)
        If PBmailReturn <> mailReturnSuccess! Then
            ls_Title = "Error - " + f_mail_error_to_string( PBmailReturn)

            MessageBox( "Error", "Unable to open the mail list. " + &
                        "Please notify the system administrator of " + &
                        "this problem.")
```

**LISTING 13.11**   CONTINUED

```
}
#endif // PowerBuilder code, do not remove
```

To make this into a DLL that you can access from PowerBuilder, select the Make option from the Targets menu. This invokes the necessary compiler (and appropriate switches) and linker to create the DLL. The status of the compilation is shown in a window on the lower half of the screen. If you see an `Execution Successful` message at the bottom of this window, you can return to PowerBuilder and use this new user object.

The following code creates an instance of the object and passes in a string to be encrypted:

```
String szPassword = "Gallagher", szEncrypted, szDecrypted

u_cpp_security ucppSecurity
ucppSecurity = create u_cpp_security

szEncrypted = ucppSecurity.cf_encrypt( Left (szPassword, 8))
szDecrypted = ucppSecurity.cf_decrypt( szEncrypted)

Destroy ucppSecurity
```

As you can see from this code, you instantiate and access the user object as you would any other user object. A number of pitfalls and restrictions are associated with creating C++ class user objects, but they are beyond the scope of this introductory text.

# Summary

This chapter provides some insight into how easy it can be to code outwardly complex functionality (visual or nonvisual) into manageable objects. Some techniques you need to use to create easily reusable objects are discussed, as is how each user object type should be used.

**13**

The User Object Painter

# DataWindow Scripting

After you place a DataWindow control onto a window or a user object, you need to interact with it. PowerBuilder provides many PowerScript functions that act only on DataWindows.

Commonly misunderstood by anyone new to PowerBuilder is the difference between a DataWindow object and a DataWindow control. The DataWindow *object* is what you create in the DataWindow painter and store in your libraries. The DataWindow *control* is a control, just as a command button is a control placed in a window or a user object. The DataWindow control acts as a container for a DataWindow object, which is an attribute of the control. This is called the `DataObject` attribute.

# The DataWindow Control

Throughout this chapter you encounter code that you can place in a DataWindow control user object, or even in a base DataWindow control user object. Special-purpose DataWindows can then inherit from such user objects—for example, DataWindows that enable multiple selections with drag-and-drop. For more information about DataWindow control user objects, see Chapter 26, "Building User Objects."

## Buffers

You can directly access all four DataWindow control buffers:

- The most important buffer, the *Primary* buffer, holds all the currently available rows (displayed in the DataWindow control), as well as the status of these rows and individual columns. These statuses are used to generate the appropriate SQL (`INSERT`s and `UPDATE`s) during a DataWindow save.

- The *Delete* buffer holds all the rows that have been deleted from the Primary buffer through the `DeleteRow()` or `RowsMove()` function. You can use the `RowsMove()` function to move rows between DataWindows and/or between the various buffers. The rows from the Delete buffer are used in the generation of `DELETE` statements when the DataWindow data is saved.

- The *Filter* buffer holds all the rows that the current DataWindow filter has removed. These rows are included in a save of the data, generating the appropriate `INSERT` or `UPDATE` statements along with the rows in the Primary buffer.

- PowerBuilder uses the *Original* buffer to store the values of the rows as they were retrieved from the database. These values are then used to build the `WHERE` clause on the SQL modification statements. You can also access a column's original value through the `GetItem`x`()` functions by specifying a `TRUE` value as a fourth parameter or via the DataWindow dot notation.

Many DataWindow control functions can access specific buffers. The enumerated data type for specifying which DataWindow buffer to act on is `dwBuffer`, which has the values `Delete!`, `Filter!`, and `Primary!`.

Within the Primary and Filter buffers, each row and each column in a row maintains an *edit status flag*. This flag indicates whether the row or column is new or has been modified. The DataWindow uses this flag's value to determine what type of SQL statement to generate for a row. This flag is of the `dwItemStatus` enumerated data type and can have the following values:

| Value | Description |
| --- | --- |
| `NotModified!` | The row or column is unchanged from the originally retrieved values. A row with this status doesn't need to be saved. A column with this status isn't included in an UPDATE or INSERT statement. |
| `DataModified!` | The specified column or another of the columns for that row is changed. The row is saved, and the changed columns are made part of the UPDATE statement. If the row has this status in the Delete buffer, a DELETE statement is generated. |
| `New!` | The row is inserted into the DataWindow after a retrieve, but no values are specified for any columns. This status applies only to rows. If the row is flagged for deletion with the `DeleteRow()` function, PowerBuilder discards the row rather than move it to the Delete buffer. |
| `NewModified!` | This status applies only to rows. It indicates that the row is inserted into the DataWindow after a retrieve, and values are assigned to some of its columns. A new row also gets this status if one of its columns has a default value. The row generates an INSERT statement that includes all the columns with `DataModified!` status. If the row is flagged for deletion with the `DeleteRow()` function, PowerBuilder discards the row rather than move it to the Delete buffer. |

The `GetItemStatus()` function determines the current status of a row or column. Its syntax is

```
DataWindowControl.GetItemStatus( Row, Column, DWBuffer)
```

The *Row* parameter identifies the row from which the status will be obtained. *Column* specifies the column (by number or name) for which you want the status; if this is a 0, it returns the row's status. The *DWBuffer* parameter identifies the DataWindow buffer you want to check. The function returns a value of type dwItemStatus.

The SetItemStatus() function changes a row or column's modification status to a different value. Use this function to influence the type of SQL statements generated for a row. The syntax is

```
DataWindowControl.SetItemStatus( Row, Column, DWBuffer, Status)
```

The *Row* parameter identifies the row for which the status will be changed. *Column* specifies the column (by number or name) whose status you want to change; if this is a 0, the status of the row is changed. The *DWBuffer* parameter identifies the DataWindow buffer you want to change. The status is of type dwItemStatus.

If you change the status of a row's modification flag, it also affects the flags of all the row's columns and vice versa. That is, setting a row to NotModified! or New! causes all columns to become NotModified!. Be aware that not all status changes are legal; you might have to go through an additional step to set a row or column to a particular status. The status might actually change to a third value that varies from the original and the intended values.

Table 14.1 shows the effect of changing from one status to another. A Yes entry means that the translation is allowed; a No entry means that no change is made. If a specific dwItemStatus value is shown, it's the new status of the row or column rather than the desired one.

**TABLE 14.1**   Valid Item Status Modifications

| Original Status | | Desired Status | | |
|---|---|---|---|---|
| | New! | NewModified! | DataModified! | NotModified! |
| New! | | Yes | Yes | No |
| NewModified! | No | | Yes | New! |
| DataModified! | NewModified! | Yes | | Yes |
| NotModified! | Yes | Yes | Yes | |

You can reach a desired status that's not allowed directly by changing the status to an allowable intermediary one. For example, to change a status of New! to NotModified!, you first must make it DataModified!.

You can encapsulate the information in this table into a function (see Listing 14.1) to be used throughout an application, as a global or DataWindow user object function. This function is useful for controlling DataWindow updates; it can cause some rows not to save or direct others to become updates rather than inserts.

**LISTING 14.1**  `of_ChangeRowStatus()` for the `u_dw` Object

```
// Parameters:
//    dwItemStatus a_state    (The new state)
//    Long al_StartRow        (The start row)
//    Long al_EndRow          (The end row)

Long ll_Row
dwItemStatus dwStatus

If al_StartRow > al_EndRow Then
   Return
End If

For ll_Row = al_StartRow To al_EndRow
   dwStatus = This.GetItemStatus( ll_Row, 0, Primary!)

   Choose Case a_State
     Case New!
       Choose Case dwStatus
         Case NewModified!, DataModified!
            This.SetItemStatus( ll_Row, 0, Primary!, NotModified!)
            This.SetItemStatus( ll_Row, 0, Primary!, New!)
         Case NotModified!
            This.SetItemStatus( ll_Row, 0, Primary!, New!)
       End Choose
     Case NewModified!
       Choose Case dwStatus
         Case New!, DataModified!, NotModified!
            This.SetItemStatus( ll_Row, 0, Primary!, NewModified!)
       End Choose
     Case DataModified!
       Choose Case dwStatus
         Case New!, NewModified!, NotModified!
            This.SetItemStatus( ll_Row, 0, Primary!, DataModified!)
       End Choose
     Case NotModified!
       Choose Case dwStatus
         Case New!, NewModified!
            This.SetItemStatus( ll_Row, 0, Primary!, DataModified!)
            This.SetItemStatus( ll_Row, 0, Primary!, NotModified!)
         Case DataModified!
```

**14**

DataWindow
Scripting

**LISTING 14.1** CONTINUED

```
                This.SetItemStatus( ll_Row, 0, Primary!, NotModified!)
        End Choose
    End Choose
Next
```

You could use this function, for example, if you were saving the data outside the DataWindow and then wanted to carry out a normal DataWindow update. In this case, you would want to alter any INSERT statements to UPDATEs instead. This is sometimes a business requirement and can't always be achieved by using separate DataWindows.

PowerBuilder includes several functions for use with Distributed PowerBuilder and remote datastores that allow you to get and set the complete modification status of all column and row flags: GetFullState(), SetFullState(), GetChanges(), SetChanges(), and GetStateStatus(). For more on distributed PowerBuilder, see Chapter 28, "Developing Distributed PowerBuilder Applications."

The GetNextModified() function lets you find the rows that have been modified in a specific buffer. The syntax is

*DataWindowControl*.GetNextModified( *Row, DWBuffer*)

*Row* is the row number after which to start searching; *DWBuffer* indicates which DataWindow buffer is to be examined. To search from the beginning and include the first row, set *Row* to 0. The function returns a Long value for the first modified row found and 0 if no modified rows are found after the start row. A row is considered modified if it has a status of NewModified! or DataModified!.

> **Note**
>
> Remember that GetNextModified() begins searching after the row you specify, whereas most other DataWindow functions begin at the specified row.

## Accessing the Data

In earlier versions of PowerBuilder, interaction with the data could be achieved only through SetItem() and various GetItem*x*() functions. Starting with version 5.0, PowerBuilder provided direct access to all DataWindow data via PowerScript. Now you can access all the buffers and operate on the entire DataWindow, single rows, or arrays of rows. This is the syntax for this type of access:

```
dw_control.Object.Data[.Buffer[.WhichValue]][Range]
dw_control.Object.Data[Range]
dw_control.Object.Column[RowRange]
```

In this code

- *Buffer* is Primary (the default), Filter, or Delete.

- *WhichValue* is Current (the default) or Original. This allows you to access the original value of a column as it comes in from the database.

- *Range* can be any of the following: 0 for all rows, >0 for a specific row, [Row, Column] for a specific column, [Row1, Column1, Row2, Column2] for a range of rows and columns, or .Selected for all selected rows.

- *RowRange* can be any of the following: 0 for all rows, >0 for a specific row, [Row1, Row2] for a range of rows, or .Selected for all selected rows.

---

**Note**

Some forms of syntax that you might expect to work are in fact invalid. For example, you can't use the syntax dw_1.Data.Buffer.ColumnName[ Row] .

---

A DataWindow's Object property allows direct data manipulation using dot notation. There are a number of forms depending on what data you're trying to extract.

Don't confuse building expressions that act on the data with those that act on the DWObject. If you don't specify at least one optional parameter, the buffer, or the data source, you're accessing the column object and not its data. For example, to access the country column's properties, you use

```
dw_1.Object.country.property
```

Otherwise, to access the data, use one of the forms in the following sections.

## Data by Column Name

When you know the name of the column from which you want to access data, use the following syntax:

```
dwControl.Object.ColumnName{.Buffer}{.DataSource}{[StartRow {, EndRow}]}
```

This returns the specified row or an array of values if the row number isn't specified. You can optionally specify an *EndRow* value to provide a specific range of rows to operate on. If you don't specify a row value, you *must* specify a *Buffer* or *DataSource*. You can also make assignments in this manner.

> **Tip**
>
> To refer to objects/columns in the header, footer, or summary bands, specify a row number of 1. For objects in a group header or trailer, specify the group number as the row number.

Some examples of this call are

```
// Get the country column value for the 6th row
ls_Country = dw_1.Object.country[6]


// Buffer = Delete, DataSource = Original. Pull all of the
// original values for the deleted rows.
String ls_Countries[]
ls_Countries = dw_1.Object.country.Delete.Original


// Set the value for the country column for rows 6 thru 13
String ls_Countries[8] = { "Scotland","England","Brazil","Italy", &
                    "France","Cameroon","Argentina","Germany" }

dw_1.Object.country[6, 13] = ls_Countries

// Pull all the current country values into an array
String ls_Countries[]

ls_Countries = dw_1.Object.country.Current
```

Notice in the previous examples that when the expression returns an array, because no row number was specified, you must assign the result to an array. You *must* do this, even if you know there's only one row as the result.

> **Tip**
>
> If you want to get all the values for a computed column, specify the buffer or data source instead of the row number, just as for columns.

## Selected Data

To pull the selected rows within the DataWindow, use the following syntax:

```
dwControl.Object.ColumnName{.Primary}{.DataSource}.Selected
```

This syntax *always* returns an array. You should assign it to an appropriate data-typed array, even if only one row is returned. You can also make assignments with this syntax, but the same restriction applies: You must supply an array. Some examples of this syntax are as follows:

```
String ls_Countries[]


// Get the Original country values of the rows selected
ls_Countries = dw_1.Object.country.Original.Selected


// Get the Current country values of the rows selected
ls_Countries = dw_1.Object.country.Primary.Current.Selected
```

## Data by Column Number

If you don't know or want to specify the column name at scripting time, you can use numbers to identify the column(s) and row(s) you want to operate on. The syntax is as follows:

```
dwControl.Object.Data{.Buffer}{.DataSource}[StartRow, StartColumn &
                                    {, EndRow, EndColumn}]
```

You can capture the returned information into an array of structures (because we are returning more than one column's worth of data) or an array of user objects. Each row generates one element in the array.

Some examples of this syntax are

```
// Get row ones column one information
ls_AuthorName = dw_1.Object.Data[1,1]


// Capture the deleted author information
ls_AuthorName = dw_1.Object.Data.Delete[1,1]
```

**14**

DataWindow
Scripting

---

**Note**

These are the direct relations to the GetItemx() and SetItem() functions. Just as the function calls accept a string for the column name or a number for the column position, so do the direct syntax's. With the direct syntax, you explicitly state the column name or use this function to specify the column number. Both of the by-column number syntaxes are flexible and reusable, whereas only the `Get/SetItem()` by column name is flexible. The direct syntax that specifies the column name can't be dynamic at runtime.

## Complete Rows of Data

To access a complete row's worth of data from the DataWindow, use the following syntax:

```
dwControl.Object.Data{.Buffer}{.DataSource}{[Row]}
```

This also returns an array of structures or user objects—one array element per row.

> **Note**
>
> To use a user object as the destination of your data, the object needs to be constructed with the same number of instance variables with the correct data type and order as the DataWindow columns.

To access a complete row of information for the selected rows, use the following syntax:

```
dwControl.Object.Data{.Primary}{.DataSource}.Selected
```

This again returns an array of structures or user objects with one array element per row.

Some examples of these versions of the syntax are

```
// Get row ones information
s_authors lstr_Authors[1]
lstr_Authors = dw_1.Object.Data.Primary[1]

// Capture the deleted author information
s_authors lstr_Authors[]
lstr_Authors = dw_1.Object.Data.Delete
```

If you specify just up to the Data part of the syntax, you can access the whole buffer of the DataWindow. This way, you can take the whole buffer from a datastore within a distributed PowerBuilder application and pass it back to the client. See Chapter 28 for more information on this syntax.

You can use the dot notation just introduced to read and write data in a DataWindow control. Here's an example:

```
Real lr_Raise = 1.05
Long ll_Count, ll_Rows, ll_Salary

ll_Rows = dw_1.RowCount()

For ll_Count = 1 To ll_Rows
   // GetItem method: ll_Salary = dw_1.GetItemNumber( ll_Count, "emp_salary")
   ll_Salary = dw_1.Object.Data.emp_salary[ ll_Count]
   ll_Salary = ll_Salary * lr_Raise
   // SetItem method: dw_1.SetItem ( ll_Count, "emp_salary", ll_Salary)
   dw_1.Object.Data.emp_salary[ ll_Count] = ll_Salary
Next
```

The SetItem() function and the GetItem*x*() functions are still available, but as you will see later in this section, there's little purpose in continuing to use them. The only time you will want to fall back on these two functions is when you don't know the column name at the time the code is written (for example, a generic function that acts on data in a particular way). You can't use dot notation for accessing the data because it requires the column to be specified (or accessed through the array index using the column number). Unlike with the SetItem() function, PowerBuilder steps away from a true object-oriented implementation when you have to access data with the GetItem*x*() functions because it forces you to explicitly state the data type of the value. Rather than issue a simple GetItem*x*() function call, you have to use one of the functions in Table 14.2.

TABLE **14.2**  The GetItem*x*() Functions

| Function | Description |
|----------|-------------|
| GetItemDate | Gets a value from a Date column |
| GetItemTime | Gets a value from a Time column |
| GetItemDateTime | Gets a value from a DateTime column |
| GetItemNumber | Gets a value from a Number column (Decimal, Double, Integer, Long, Real, or ULong) |
| GetItemDecimal | Gets a value from a Decimal column |
| GetItemString | Gets a value from a String column |

**14**

DataWindow Scripting

Although PowerBuilder provides numerous functions for taking data out of a DataWindow, it provides only one for putting data back in— SetItem(). This function takes a row, column, and data value as parameters:

```
DataWindowControl.SetItem( Row, Column, DataValue)
```

*Column* can be a column number (integer) or a column name (string); *DataValue* must match that of the receiving DataWindow column. The function returns 1 if it's successful, -1 if an error occurs.

> **Note**
>
> A call to SetItem() validates only that the value's data type matches the column. Any validation rules on the column or coded within or called from the ItemChanged event aren't executed.

Here's a useful trick to remember if your DataWindow uses the radio button edit style for a column: After a value is selected for the radio button group, there's no way to deselect the checked value. You need to provide a way for users to deselect the radio button. Use the SetItem() function with a NULL variable as the data value. You need to take this into consideration for the noneditable DropDownListBox edit style as well.

> **Note**
>
> The variable you use in the SetNull() call must match the data type of the column you will be affecting in the SetItem() call; otherwise, it won't work.

To test the speed benefits of the various methods, PowerBuilder includes a test window consisting of four DataWindows and related command buttons as well as single-line edits to control the timing and operations. All the DataWindow controls use an external-source DataWindow object containing a numeric column and two 10-character string columns. Three DataWindows are prefilled with 1,000 rows (ImportString() inserts its own rows). The write operation consists of looping through all 1,000 rows and setting the three columns with dummy values. The read operation again loops through all 1,000 rows and stores the values into dummy variables. Table 14.3 shows the results of the test.

TABLE 14.3  Speed Comparisons of Different Access Methods

| Operation | Get/SetItem | Direct | ImportString | Redraw |
|-----------|-------------|--------------|--------------|--------|
| Writing | 725 (0.7s) | 3741ms (3.7s) | 10387 (10.4s) | On |
| Writing | 373ms (0.4s) | 436ms (0.4s) | 770 (0.8s) | Off |
| Reading | 356ms (0.4s) | 373ms (0.4s) | N/A | N/A |

As you can see from Table 14.3, the state of the redraw option for the DataWindow control dramatically affects the time taken for all write access to the DataWindow. The timings were taken on a 166MHz Pentium with 32MB RAM running Windows 98. With the direct data-manipulation syntax available, a test was also run using a structure from which to read and write. Table 14.4 shows the results of this method.

TABLE **14.4**  Speed Comparisons of Different Direct Access Methods

| Operation | Direct | Using Structure | Redraw |
|-----------|--------|-----------------|--------|
| Writing | 3668ms (3.7s) | 949 (0.9s) | On |
| Writing | 444ms (0.4s) | 259 (0.6s) | Off |
| Reading | 389ms (0.4s) | 255 (0.6s) | N/A |

The conclusion of this test is that the GetItem*x*() and SetItem() functions are almost identical to the direct-access syntax in terms of speed when the Redraw isn't on. The test indicates that using structures with the direct syntax might be the fastest way to move data around.

You can also use the direct-access syntax to manipulate objects in the DataWindow object. This includes column attributes, nested reports, and OLE objects. With nested reports, there's no limit on the number of levels (a nest within a nest) you can refer to, as long as the previous level exists.

Another DataWindow feature is the capability to load DataWindows by assignment to and from structures. The only restriction is that you must have the structure built to the same specifications as the DataWindow (column data types and order). Here's an example of this type of assignment:

```
ws_assign lstr_Assign

// You can assign to existing rows
dw_1.InsertRow( 0)
dw_1.InsertRow( 0)

// Setup the data values
lstr_Assign.value1 = "Malcolm"
lstr_Assign.value2 = "Devon"

// Load row 1 of the DataWindow
dw_1.Object.Data[1] = lstr_Assign

// Setup some more data

lstr_Assign.value1 = "Maria"
```

**14**

DataWindow
Scripting

```
lstr_Assign.value2 = "Brent"

// Load these into row 2 of the DataWindow
dw_1.Object.Data[2] = lstr_Assign

lstr_Assign = dw_1.Object.Data[ 1]
```

From a few simple tests, it looks as though using this method of loading data outperforms any other method by a factor of almost two. It's well worth experimenting with the various methods to find the optimal performer for any heavy DataWindow access code you develop.

## The Edit Control

One of the most important concepts to understand when dealing with DataWindows is the edit control (see Figure 14.1). The DataWindow uses fewer resources than a window with a similar number of controls mainly because the DataWindow is only a graphical representation of data on a single control. Users actually interact with the DataWindow through the edit control, which floats over the window and validates user input before accepting it and moving to the next field.

If you are familiar with Microsoft Excel, you can liken the edit control to each cell in Excel's grid. When you type a formula into the cell, it's not accepted and calculated until you move to a new field or select the check mark button next to the formula. If the formula is wrong, you can't move to a new location. The DataWindow control uses the same concept.

Occasionally, you need to obtain the value that users have just entered before it becomes accepted and is placed into the column and buffer. Use PowerScript's `GetText()` function for this purpose:

`DataWindowControl.GetText()`

The edit control is text-based, and the value returned is the string users entered. If the value is of a different data type, you must convert the returned value yourself. If the DataWindow has no editable columns, the function returns an empty string. This function is usually called in the `ItemChanged` and `ItemError` DataWindow control events (discussed later in the "DataWindow Events" section) and within any validation rules these events might call. A different set of functions (`SetItem()` and the `GetItemx()` functions described earlier) are used after the value leaves the edit control and is placed in the column for the Primary buffer. This transfer occurs when users move from one column to another or when a script calls `AcceptText()`. If users click a control other than the DataWindow, the last value entered remains in the edit control (and isn't validated).

**FIGURE 14.1**
*How a DataWin-
dow handles data
entry and presen-
tation.*

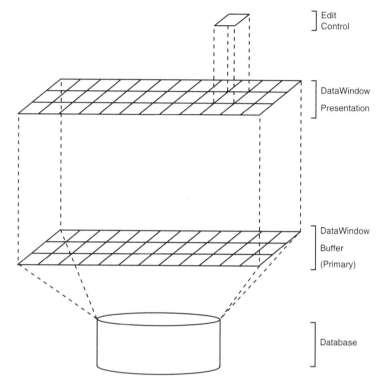

Edit
Control

DataWindow
Presentation

DataWindow
Buffer
(Primary)

Database

If you ask PowerBuilder developers (or Sybase, for that matter) how to ensure that the last column in a DataWindow is accepted when the DataWindow control loses focus, you will receive myriad solutions. Most of these solutions don't work or are so unwieldy they're laughable. This section addresses one correct solution, which doesn't require a lot of coding, is encapsulated, and doesn't cause the double message-box problem that occurs when the value fails a validation check and causes an error message box to appear. When users click OK in the message box, focus flashes back to the DataWindow, and another message box appears. This usually causes another application to be brought in front of the PowerBuilder application. This is because the usual solution is to code an AcceptText() in the LoseFocus event, which causes the following problem: When users leave the DataWindow, the LoseFocus event causes the AcceptText(), which fails and opens the message box. This causes the DataWindow to receive a second LoseFocus because it has now lost the focus to the message box. When users close the message box, the DataWindow processes the new LoseFocus event, which causes the same thing to happen. You might expect this to loop indefinitely, but it doesn't for some unexplainable reason; it possibly has something to do with the way Windows queues events.

14

DataWindow
Scripting

The `AcceptText()` function applies the contents of the DataWindow's edit control to the current column in the Primary buffer, as long as the value passes the validation rules for that column:

```
DataWindowControl.AcceptText()
```

The function returns 1 if it succeeds, -1 if the validation fails. `AcceptText()` can trigger the `ItemChanged` and `ItemError` events and so should never be coded in those locations.

The following code is something you should build into your framework's DataWindow base object. First, declare two Boolean variables:

```
Public:
   Boolean  ib_FailedAccept = FALSE


Private:
   Boolean  ib_InAcceptText = FALSE
```

The `ib_FailedAccept` Boolean is accessible from outside the DataWindow and is used by other scripts to query the DataWindow regarding the success or failure of the last triggered `AcceptText()` function. The `ib_InAcceptText` Boolean is used as a semaphore to indicate whether PowerBuilder is still executing an `AcceptText()`.

A user event, `AcceptText`, is added to the DataWindow, and the following code is placed in the event:

```
If Not ib_InAcceptText Then
   ib_InAcceptText = TRUE
   If This.AcceptText() = -1 Then
      ib_FailedAccept = TRUE
      This.SetFocus()
      This.PostEvent( "PostAccept" )
      Return
   Else
      ib_FailedAccept = FALSE
   End If
End If


ib_InAcceptText = FALSE
```

This code relies on the factor that causes the double message-box problem: the triggering of an additional `LoseFocus` event. The first time into this event, the Boolean `ib_InAcceptText` is FALSE, and the `IF` statement is executed. This immediately sets this Boolean to TRUE to indicate that PowerBuilder is now executing the accept. The `AcceptText()` function is then called, and the return value is checked. This call might invoke an error window if a validation check fails. If this happens, this event is again entered. Because the Boolean `ib_InAcceptText` is now `TRUE`, PowerBuilder drops to the end and resets the Boolean to `FALSE`. Execution then continues in the first called `AcceptText` event, which sets the Boolean `ib_FailedAccept` to `TRUE` and then sets the focus back to the DataWindow control. A custom event, `PostAccept`, is called, which resets the `ib_InAcceptText` flag when you safely finish accepting the text. The additional code is required only when users tab from a column but stay within the DataWindow and the edit value fails a validation check. This particular series of events would cause the double message-box problem. If users moved to another control, the simple (and commonly accepted) way of ensuring that the text is accepted is to post to an event from the `LoseFocus` event, which then carries out the `AcceptText()` call.

The `AcceptText` user event is triggered by posting the message from the `LoseFocus` event:

```
This.PostEvent( "AcceptText")
```

If a validation error occurs, an `ItemError` event is triggered:

```
ib_InAcceptText = TRUE
```

The last event is a user-defined custom event called from the `AcceptText` event. The code simply resets a Boolean flag:

```
ib_InAcceptText = FALSE
```

To complete the family of functions that act on the edit control of a DataWindow, one more function should be mentioned. Sometimes, usually outside the DataWindow, you will want to replace the value of the edit control with a new one. For example, users enter a partial string on which you carry out a lookup, which you then use to replace the value in the DataWindow. `SetText()` is used for this purpose:

```
DataWindowControl.SetText (StringValue)
```

*StringValue* must be in a format compatible with the data type of the column on which the edit control is now located. The function returns 1 if it succeeds, -1 if an error occurs.

Most of the time, you modify data using the `SetItem()` function.

## The Validation Process

When users change a value in a DataWindow column, there are four stages of validation. Two are the responsibility of PowerBuilder (the first and third stages), and two are coded by developers (the second and fourth stages).

- The first check is to see whether the value is of the correct data type for the column. If the data types don't match, an `ItemError` event is triggered and the value is

**14**

**DataWindow Scripting**

rejected. This is needed because the edit control's value is a string, and PowerBuilder must perform an internal conversion to check the original data type of the column.

- The second check tests the value against any validation rules (see Chapter 5, "Databases and the Database Painter," and Chapter 6, "The DataWindow Painter") that might be attached to that DataWindow column. If the rule fails, the value is rejected and an `ItemError` event is triggered.

- The third check is whether the value actually changed from the value that existed before the edit. If the value hasn't changed, validation processing concludes.

- The final check is the script written in the `ItemChanged` event. What occurs depends on the value assigned to something known as an *action code*, which directs what PowerBuilder should do at the end of the DataWindow event. In earlier versions, this was achieved with `SetActionCode()`, but now the preferred method is to use `Return`. If the value is 0, the value is accepted and the focus is allowed to change. If the value assigned is 1, the value is rejected and the `ItemError` event is triggered. If the value is set to 2, the value is rejected, the original value is placed back where it was, and the focus is allowed to change.

The flowchart in Figure 14.2 summarizes the validation process.

Next, look at a validation process in more detail. The last line of defense is the `ItemChanged` event, where you place the validation that can't be carried out within the column validation rule. For example,

```
// Use the event argument dwo to check the column name
// and use the event argument, data, in place of using
// the GetText() function.
Choose Case dwo.Name
    Case "quantity"
        SELECT whs_quantity
        INTO :ll_Quantity
        FROM warehouse
        WHERE whs_no = :li_WhsNo
        USING SQLCA;

        If Long( data) > ll_Quantity Then
            // We need to single this as an error
            Return 1
        End If
    Case "product_class"
        ls_OrderProductClass = dw_order_line_items.Object.product_class[1]
        If data <> ls_OrderProductClass Then
```

```
        // We can let this pass but inform the user of a discrepancy
        Return 2
    End If
End Choose
// Default is a return of 0, which we do not need to code.
```

**FIGURE 14.2**

*Validation process flow.*

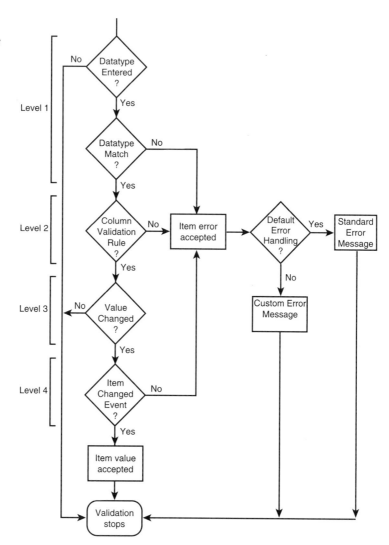

Now you need to trap the error you just caused, which occurs in the `ItemError` event:

```
// Use the event argument dwo to check the column name
Choose Case dwo.Name
  Case "quantity"
    MessageBox("Order Quantity","You have entered a quantity value greater'' + &
              " than the quantity available.", StopSign!, Ok!)
    Return 1
  Case "product_class"
    MessageBox("Product Class","You have entered a different product class" + &
              " to that specified in the order line items.",Information!,Ok!)
    Return 3
End Choose
// Default is a return of 0, which we do not need to code.
```

The next section covers numerous methods of placing data in and removing data from a DataWindow. Accessing data from the database is covered later in the section "Database-Related Functions."

# Adding and Removing Rows

The two functions that add and remove rows from the Primary buffer are `InsertRow()` and `DeleteRow()`. (Three other functions also add and remove rows: `RowsMove()`, `RowsCopy()`, and `RowsDiscard()`. These three are described fully in Chapter 16, "Advanced DataWindow Techniques II.")

## Inserting a Row

The `InsertRow()` function inserts a row into a DataWindow or child DataWindow. As detailed in Chapter 5, PowerBuilder's Extended Attribute Repository can be set up to specify defaults for individual columns. If any columns have such defaults, they're set before the row displays. The syntax for this function is

```
DataWindowControl.InsertRow( Row)
```

The only parameter is the row before which you want the new row to be inserted. To insert a new row at the end of the DataWindow, *Row* needs to be 0. The function returns a Long data type that's the added row number. If an error occurs, -1 is returned.

> **Note**
>
> When a new row is added, the current range of rows displayed in the DataWindow control isn't altered (unless, of course, you add the row after a visible row on the DataWindow, barring the last row). The current row remains unaltered, and the new row isn't made current.

To scroll to the new row and make it current, call the `ScrollToRow()` function. This enables you to show the newly added row to users, especially if it was added out of sight. To make the new row the current row without moving to it, use the `SetRow()` function.

## Deleting a Row

The `DeleteRow()` function deletes a row from a DataWindow or child DataWindow. The syntax for this function is

```
DataWindowControl.DeleteRow( Row)
```

The only parameter is the row you want to delete. To delete the current row, *Row* needs to be 0. The function returns 1 if the row was removed, -1 if an error occurred.

When a row is deleted, it's moved from the Primary buffer into the Delete buffer. The DataWindow row isn't deleted from the database table until the `Update()` function is called and the database transaction is committed.

> **Note**
>
> If the DataWindow object is set up as not updatable, all storage (the memory used by the buffers) associated with the row is cleared when a `DeleteRow()` is issued.

The Delete buffer is emptied, and any associated storage resources are released only after a successful update and reset of the update flags.

## Saving Data

The `Update()` function makes the actual changes in the database to reflect the changes made in the DataWindow object. The syntax is

```
DataWindowControl.Update( { AcceptText {, ResetFlag}})
```

Update() takes two optional parameters. The first enables you to force an AcceptText() to occur and the validation to be passed successfully before the DataWindow can save. *AcceptText* needs to be TRUE to force this. The second parameter is a Boolean value that lets you control the updating of the modification flags. If *ResetFlag* is TRUE, the modification flags (covered earlier in the "Buffers" section) for each row are reset. TRUE is the default for both parameters.

Sometimes you will need to control the status of the modification flags. For instance, during multiple DataWindow updates you need to leave everything in the state it was in before the update in case an error occurs. By default, Update() resets the flag after a successful save.

> **Note**
>
> Remember that if SetTrans(), rather than SetTransObject(), has been used, you can't carry out synchronized DataWindow updates, and *ResetFlag* isn't used in this case.

The Update() function returns 1 if it succeeds, -1 if an error occurs. Calling Update() might trigger the events DBError, SQLPreview, UpdateEnd, and UpdateStart. Also, if *AcceptText* is TRUE, ItemChanged and ItemError might also be triggered.

> **Note**
>
> If for some reason you need to call Update() in an ItemChanged event, you must set *AcceptText* to FALSE to avoid stack faulting the application. *Stack faulting* occurs when code goes into an infinite loop and fills the system-maintained function call stack. Also, because the current edit hasn't been validated yet, you must use SetItem() to place the value in the DataWindow before calling Update().

In some cases, you will want to synchronize the update of DataWindows with the database. The first case occurs when you want to update multiple tables from one DataWindow. This is achieved by using the Describe() and Modify() functions (discussed in Chapter 15, "Advanced DataWindow Techniques I") to change the Update attribute of the columns for each table.

You need to preserve the status of the modification flags between each Update() call by using the optional flags for the function. The code in Listing 14.2 shows a DataWindow object-level function that performs an update to a multitable DataWindow. The function takes two parameters: a table to update and the key fields for the table.

> **Note**
>
> In Listing 14.2, notice the syntax uses for direct access and the appropriate uses of `Describe()` and `Modify()`.

**LISTING 14.2**  o f_UpdateTable() for Object u_dw

```
// Function takes:
//     String as_TableName - the table to be updated
//     String as_KeyFields - a concatenated list of key fields for the table
Integer li_Columns, li_Count
String ls_DBName, ls_TableName, ls_ColumnName, ls_Modify

li_Columns = Integer( This.Object.DataWindow.Column.Count)
as_TableName = Lower( as_TableName)
as_KeyFields = Lower( as_KeyFields)

For li_Count = 1 To li_Columns
   ls_DBName = This.Describe( "#" + String( li_Count) + ".DBName")
   ls_ColumnName = This.Describe( "#" + String( li_Count) + ".Name")
   ls_TableName = Lower( Left( ls_DBName, Pos( ls_DBName, ".") - 1))

   If ls_TableName = as_TableName Then
      ls_Modify = ls_ColumnName + ".Update = Yes"
      If Pos(as_KeyFields, ls_ColumnName) > 0 Then
         ls_Modify = ls_Modify + " " + ls_ColumnName + ".Key = Yes"
      Else
         ls_Modify = ls_Modify + " " + ls_ColumnName + ".Key = No"
      End If
   Else
      ls_Modify = ls_ColumnName + ".Update = No " + ls_ColumnName + ".Key = No"
   End If

   If This.Modify( ls_Modify) <> "" Then
      Return FALSE
   End If
Next
```

**LISTING 14.2**   CONTINUED

```
This.Object.DataWindow.Table.UpdateTable = as_TableName

If This.Update( TRUE, FALSE) > 0 Then
   Return TRUE
Else
   Return FALSE
End If
```

There's only one caveat: The database column names must be prefixed with the table name they relate to. For example, a DataWindow object created with the following syntax

```
SELECT "product"."id", "product"."name", "sales_order_items"."id",
       "sales_order_items"."line_id", "sales_order_items"."prod_id",
       "sales_order_items"."quantity"
FROM "product", "sales_order_items"
WHERE ( "sales_order_items"."prod_id" = "product"."id" )
```

can update itself by using the following code lines:

```
If This.of_UpdateTable( "product", "product_id") Then
   If This.of_UpdateTable( "sales_order_items", "id, line_id") Then
      This.ResetUpdate()
   End If
End If
```

The column names you pass in as the key fields are the names as they appear in the DataWindow and not the database version. The only statement you must remember to add is to the ResetUpdate() function (see next case) to place the DataWindow back into an unmodified state because the Update() didn't do this for you.

In the second case, you're updating multiple DataWindow controls that need to be completed as one transaction. For this reason, the modification flags for each DataWindow control need to be left until all DataWindows are successfully concluded. If any update fails, the DataWindows are left in such a state that users can fix the problem and try again.

> **Tip**
>
> If you have access to or are using the PFC, check out the n_cst_dwsrv_multitable object. This DataWindow service object carries out multitable updates.

In both cases, when the updates are successfully completed, you need to reset the modification flags. For this task, use the `ResetUpdate()` function:

*DataWindowControl*`.ResetUpdate()`

This function resets the modification flags in the Primary and Filter buffers and clears all rows in a DataWindow control's Delete buffer. After calling this function, the flags are all reset to the status `NotModified!` or `New!`. Rows that already have the `New!` status retain the same status, but the status of all other rows is changed to `NotModified!`. This is because all modifications made to `DataModified!` and `NewModified!` will be handled successfully. However, a `New!` status hasn't been saved because there's nothing to save. In the event of future updates where PowerBuilder needs to generate an `INSERT`, the row maintains the `New!` status.

If you call `Update()` with the `ResetFlag` parameter set to `FALSE` and haven't called the `ResetUpdate()` function, the DataWindow issues the same SQL statements the next time you call `Update()`, which will most likely produce numerous errors.

The following code shows an example of coordinated DataWindow updates, which ensures the success of the updates to `dw_customer_dimensions` and `dw_customer_dimensions_wall`. Note that it uses a custom transaction object that's introduced in Chapter 4, "SQL and PowerBuilder," and is further discussed in Chapter 26.

```
Integer li_UpdateStatus
Boolean ib_Success = FALSE

SQLCA.BeginTran()

li_UpdateStatus = dw_customer_dimensions.Update( TRUE, FALSE)

If li_UpdateStatus = 1 Then
   //
   // If this update fails the flags will automatically be left alone
   //
   li_UpdateStatus = dw_customer_dimensions_wall.Update()
   If li_UpdateStatus = 1 Then
     SQLCA.CommitTran()

     dw_customer_dimensions.ResetUpdate()
     dw_customer_dimensions_wall.ResetUpdate()

     ib_Success = TRUE
   End If
End If
```

**14**

DataWindow
Scripting

```
If Not ib_Success Then
   SQLCA.RollbackTran()
End If

Return ib_Success
```

The final piece of the data-saving mechanism is seldom of interest and is thus often overlooked, but it involves the order in which the DataWindow control buffers are saved. Occasionally, you might need to sequence the order in which rows are being saved, and a useful technique is to filter out the subset of the rows you are interested in so that their data modifications occur last. The sequence of the buffers is Delete, Primary, and then Filter. An example of this requirement is if you undertake sequencing or resequencing of row keys that reuse values from deleted rows. In this particular case, you will want to let the deleted and existing rows be updated first, followed by any new rows saved from the Filter buffer.

## NULL values

One feature of PowerBuilder DataWindows you will want to consider when updating your database is the capability to set an empty string to NULL. This prevents wasting space when you save the data back into the database because most databases have a special representation for a NULL that takes up a minimal amount of space.

> **Note**
>
> You might think that a NULL is a NULL is a NULL, but because PowerBuilder distinguishes between data types, you must declare a variable for each data type that you will be setting to NULL. This is one little idiosyncrasy of PowerBuilder that makes it so beloved.

# Update Events

The UpdateStart event is triggered before any changes are sent to the database but after you issue an Update() function call for a DataWindow object. You can control whether the update proceeds or stops without doing any processing by setting the return value. The return values for this event are 0, continue with the update (the default), and 1, don't perform the update.

The UpdateEnd event occurs after all updates for a DataWindow object are completed in the database.

You can use both events to place additional control on an update. For example, if the DataWindow can be updated only if certain fields or options are set, you can encapsulate these checks into a place that will always be executed rather than code them at every point where you do an update.

# Scrolling in the Primary Buffer

Six PowerScript functions allow you to scroll around a DataWindow control. Each scroll function can trigger any of the following events: ItemChanged, ItemError, ItemFocus-Changed, or RowFocusChanged. Also, two scroll-specific events— ScrollVertical and ScrollHorizontal—are triggered whenever the DataWindow scrolls in the appropriate direction.

The Scroll() and ScrollToRow() functions enable relative and direct movement, respectively. The syntax for these functions is

```
DataWindowControl.Scroll( lNumberRows )
```

The only parameter is the number of lines to scroll. The direction of the scroll is specified by using a positive integer to scroll down and a negative integer to scroll up. This function returns the line number of the top line displayed, or returns -1 on an error. If you specify a value that would put the scroll past the beginning or end of the control, the function stops at that boundary. The current row isn't affected by this function.

To scroll to a specific row rather than to a relative row, use the ScrollToRow() function:

```
DataWindowControl.ScrollToRow( lRow )
```

The parameter specifies the row to which you want to scroll. As with Scroll(), if the row value is outside the boundaries, the function stops on the boundary. The function returns 1 on a successful scroll, -1 on an error.

> **Note**
>
> ScrollToRow() affects only the current row, not the current column. This function also doesn't highlight the row. To indicate the current row, use the SelectRow() or SetRowFocusIndicator() function.

If the row scrolled to is already visible, the display doesn't change. If the row wasn't visible, the displayed rows change to display the row at the top unless the row is the next one after the bottom row displayed, in which case PowerBuilder simply scrolls down one row to display the required line.

**14**

DataWindow
Scripting

The functions `ScrollNextPage()` and `ScrollPriorPage()` work similarly, except that they display the next or previous page of rows. (A *page* is the number of rows that can display in the control at one time.) These functions change the current row, but not the current column:

```
DataWindowControl.ScrollNextPage()
```

```
DataWindowControl.ScrollPriorPage()
```

Both functions return the number of the topmost row displayed after scrolling; -1 is returned on an error.

The functions `ScrollNextRow()` and `ScrollPriorRow()` work similarly to `ScrollNextPage()` and `ScrollPriorPage()`. They scroll only one row forward or backward, changing the current row each time. These are the functions' syntax:

```
DataWindowControl.ScrollNextRow()
```

```
DataWindowControl.ScrollPriorRow()
```

Both functions return a Long data type that is the number of the topmost row displayed. If the new current row isn't visible, the display is moved up to show the current row. If an error occurs, -1 is returned.

> **Note**
>
> Support for the Intellimouse device was added to PowerBuilder 6.0 DataWindows. The Intellimouse has an additional wheel that allows easy scrolling from the mouse. You can use the Ctrl key with the wheel for zoom capability also. This functionality is built into the PowerBuilder DataWindow technology and requires no programming effort except for purchasing the Intellimouse.

## Changing the Current Edit Focus

Because a DataWindow is essentially a spreadsheet, an individual field is referenced by a row and column pairing known as an *item*. The DataWindow control maintains knowledge of the current column and the current row. These are changed every time users press Tab or Enter, click another field, or use the up- and down-arrow keys or the Page Up and Page Down keys. The current row and column can also be changed by some DataWindow functions and explicitly by using `SetRow()` and `SetColumn()`. If there's at least one editable column, a DataWindow will always have a current column, even when the DataWindow control isn't active.

## SetColumn()

The SetColumn() function sets the current column of a DataWindow control:

*DataWindowControl*.SetColumn( *Column*)

The *Column* parameter can be the number of the column or a string containing the column name. The function returns 1 if it succeeds, -1 if an error occurs. If the column number is outside the valid range of columns or the column name doesn't exist, the call fails.

SetColumn() moves the cursor to the specified column but doesn't scroll the DataWindow control to that column if it's not visible. You can set only an editable column to be current.

If you try to set a column to be current and none of the columns in the DataWindow object are editable (have a tab value), SetColumn() returns a value of 1. Any subsequent calls to GetColumn() return 0, and GetColumnName() returns the empty string (""). If you try to set an uneditable column and other editable columns are in the DataWindow object, SetColumn() returns -1, and GetColumn() and GetColumnName() return the previously current column.

A call to SetColumn() can trigger the ItemChanged, ItemError, and ItemFocusChanged events. Avoid coding a call to SetColumn() in these events because it will cause a stack fault due to the iterative calls.

## SetRow()

The SetRow() function sets the current row for a DataWindow control:

*DataWindowControl*.SetRow( *Row*)

The *Row* parameter is a Long data type that's the row number to set as current. The function returns 1 if it succeeds, -1 if an error occurs. If the row is outside the valid range of row numbers, the call fails.

SetRow() moves the cursor to the current row but doesn't scroll the DataWindow control if the row isn't visible. You must use the scroll functions described earlier.

A call to SetRow() might trigger the same three events as SetColumn(), as well as a fourth: RowFocusChanged. As with SetColumn(), avoid calling SetRow() from within these events.

## GetRow(), GetColumn(), and GetColumnName()

The SetColumn() and SetRow() functions have reciprocals that return the current row and column: GetRow(), GetColumn(), and GetColumnName(). The GetRow() function returns the row number of the current row in a DataWindow control:

*DataWindowControl*.GetRow()

The function returns the number of the current row in the DataWindow, 0 if no row is current, and -1 if an error occurs. The current row isn't always visible in the DataWindow.

GetColumn() returns the number of the column that has focus. The syntax is

*DataWindowControl*.GetColumn()

If no column is current, the function returns 0, or -1 if an error occurs. A 0 return value can happen only if all the columns have a tab value of 0.

The GetColumnName() function returns the name of the column that has focus. The syntax is

*DataWindowControl*.GetColumnName()

If no column is current or an error occurs, an empty string is returned.

## SetRowFocusIndicator()

To indicate the current row, rather than rely on users to spot the focus rectangle in a field (also optional for DataWindow columns), you can specify a pointer or indicator to appear in the DataWindow pointing at the current row. You can achieve this by using the SetRowFocusIndicator() function:

*DataWindowControl*.SetRowFocusIndicator( *Indicator* {, *Xlocation* {, *Ylocation* }})

The *Indicator* parameter can be of the RowFocusInd enumerated type or the name of a picture control. RowFocusInd can be of the following types: Off! (no indicator), FocusRect! (a dotted-line rectangle around the row), or Hand! (the PowerBuilder pointing hand).

Frequently the indicator is customized, and a picture control is used instead. This control is made invisible after placement on the same object (window or user object) as the DataWindow control.

The *Xlocation* and *Ylocation* parameters enable you to set the position (in PowerBuilder units) of the pointer relative to the upper-left corner of the current row. The indicator position defaults to (0,0).

**Note**

If the DataObject attribute is modified for a DataWindow control, the row focus indicator will be turned off. You have to reissue a SetRowFocusIndicator() call after changing this attribute. If the connection between the DataWindow control and a transaction is broken, the row indicator will remain; it gets turned off only when the DataWindow object is swapped out.

# Selecting by Mouse

A DataWindow is a kind of mini-window, having some but not all of the same behaviors as a window. One similar behavior is the capability to react to users clicking an area of the object—in this case, the DataWindow. PowerBuilder provides numerous functions you can use to react to a user's mouse movements and actions.

## GetClickedColumn()

The GetClickedColumn() function returns the column number that users clicked or double-clicked in a DataWindow control and is used in the Clicked and DoubleClicked events:

*DataWindowControl*.GetClickedColumn()

The function returns 0 if users didn't click or double-click a column. The clicked column becomes the current column after the Clicked or DoubleClicked event finishes. Therefore, the return values of GetClickedColumn() and GetColumn() are different within these events.

## GetClickedRow()

GetClickedRow() is similar to GetClickedColumn() except that it determines the row the user has just clicked. This function is used less frequently because the row is passed as an argument to Clicked and DoubleClicked events. The syntax is

*DataWindowControl*.GetClickedRow()

As with the GetClickedColumn() function, this also returns 0 if users click outside the data area—that is, outside the detail band. The selected row becomes the current row after the Clicked or DoubleClicked event. As before, the GetRow() and GetClickedRow() functions return different values during these scripts.

## SelectRow()

The `SelectRow()` function is used to select and deselect a row or multiple rows of a DataWindow control. It has no further action except to make the rows stand out in the control, and it doesn't affect the current row:

*DataWindowControl*.SelectRow( *Row*, *Boolean*)

The *Row* parameter is a Long data type signifying the number of the row on which you want to change the highlighting. To select or deselect all rows, set *Row* to 0. The *Boolean* parameter determines whether the row is to be selected (TRUE) or deselected (FALSE). Any rows that are already selected and are selected again don't change; similarly, an unselected row remains unselected.

## IsSelected()

The `IsSelected()` function checks whether a particular row is selected. The syntax is

*DataWindowControl*.IsSelected( *Row*)

The function returns a Boolean value that's TRUE if the row is selected, FALSE if it's not. If the specified row is outside the valid range of rows, the function returns FALSE.

## GetSelectedRow()

Whereas the `IsSelected()` function is used to check a particular row, the `GetSelectedRow()` function is usually used in a loop and returns the number of the first row selected after a given row. Rows are selected only with the `SelectRow()` function:

*DataWindowControl*.GetSelectedRow( *StartRow*)

The function returns 0 if no row is selected after *StartRow*.

## GetBandAtPointer()

The `GetBandAtPointer()` function finds out which band the mouse pointer is now within and is usually placed in the `Clicked` event of a DataWindow (Chapter 5 discusses the bands of a DataWindow):

*DataWindowControl*.GetBandAtPointer()

The function returns a string that consists of the band, a tab character, and the number of the row associated with the band. The empty string ("") is returned if an error occurs. The string can consist of the information shown in Table 14.5.

**TABLE 14.5** `GetBandAtPointer` Return Values

| Band | Pointer Location | Associated Row |
|---|---|---|
| detail | Body of the DataWindow | Row at pointer |
| header | Header of the DataWindow | The first row visible in the body |
| header.*n* | Header of group level *n* | The first row of the group |
| trailer.*n* | Trailer of group level *n* | The last row of the group |
| footer | Footer of the DataWindow | The last row visible in the body |
| summary | Summary of the DataWindow | The last row before the summary |

The row value within the string when the pointer is in the detail band depends on the number of rows filling the body. If there aren't enough rows to fill the body because of a group with a page break, the first row of the next group is the value returned. If the body isn't completely filled because there are no more rows, the last row is returned.

## GetObjectAtPointer()

A DataWindow includes a number of objects that consist mostly of columns and labels but also include graphic objects such as lines and pictures. The `GetObjectAtPointer()` function returns the name and row number of the object now under the mouse pointer in a DataWindow:

```
DataWindowControl.GetObjectAtPointer()
```

The returned string contains the name of the object, a tab character, and the row number. The empty string is returned if an error occurs or the object doesn't have a name.

# Putting These Functions to Work

The following code uses most of the functions just described. This example allows users to click individual rows in one DataWindow, click a copy button, and have these rows appear in another DataWindow. This code is placed in the `Clicked` event of the primary DataWindow:

```
// Make use of the event parameter: Row
//
This.SelectRow( Row, TRUE)
```

The code behind the button to copy the rows is as follows:

```
Long ll_Row = 0

dw_1.SetRedraw( FALSE)
dw_2.SetRedraw( FALSE)

Do
```

**14**

**DataWindow Scripting**

```
    ll_Row = dw_2.GetSelectedRow( ll_Row)
    If ll_Row <> 0 Then
        dw_2.RowsCopy( ll_Row, ll_Row, Primary!, dw_1, 1, Primary!)
    End If
Loop While ll_Row <> 0


dw_1.SetRedraw( TRUE)
dw_2.SetRedraw( TRUE)
```

As you can see, this code isn't very sophisticated and can be greatly enhanced. The copy code could, in fact, be placed in a `DragDrop` event to remove the need for a button completely.

The following is a more sophisticated version of the `Clicked` event script that enables users to use the Ctrl key to select individual rows and the Shift key to select ranges:

```
Long ll_Row, ll_StartRow, ll_EndRow


If KeyDown( KeyControl!) Then
    If Row > 0 Then
        This.SelectRow( Row, TRUE)
    Else
        Return
    End If
ElseIf KeyDown( KeyShift!) Then
    This.SetRedraw( FALSE)
    ll_StartRow = This.GetRow()
    ll_EndRow = Row
    //Be able to range select backward as well as forward
    If ll_StartRow > ll_EndRow Then
        For ll_Row = ll_StartRow To ll_EndRow Step -1
            This.SelectRow( ll_Row, TRUE)
        Next
    Else
        For ll_Row = ll_StartRow To ll_EndRow
            This.SelectRow( ll_Row, TRUE)
        Next
    End If
    This.SetRedraw( TRUE)
Else
    //If the user simply clicks on a row - deselect any selected row(s)
    This.SelectRow( 0, FALSE)
    // and highlight the clicked row
```

```
    This.SelectRow( Row, TRUE)
End If
```

# DataWindow Events

A DataWindow control has several events in common with other controls. In addition to these are a few unique events, as defined in the following sections.

## The ButtonClicked Event

ButtonClicked is where you can gather information about the action of the DataWindow button object. This event has the following arguments: row indicates the row that holds the button, actionreturncode has a different meaning for each action, and dwo gives access to the DataWindow object.

Table 14.6 shows the meanings of the actionreturncode argument.

TABLE **14.6**   Action-Dependent Meanings of actionreturncode

| Button Action | Meaning |
| --- | --- |
| User-defined | 0 (default) |
| Retrieve (Yield) | Number of rows retrieved, or -1 if an error occurs. (Yield allows for the retrieval to be canceled.) |
| Retrieve | Number of rows retrieved or -1 if an error occurs |
| Cancel | 0 |
| Page Next | Top row displayed in DataWindow or -1 if an error occurs |
| Page Prior | Top row displayed in DataWindow or -1 if an error occurs |
| Page First | 1 if successful or -1 if an error occurs |
| Page Last | Top row displayed in DataWindow or -1 if an error occurs |
| Sort | 1 if successful or -1 if an error occurs |
| Filter | Number of filtered rows or negative number on an error |
| Delete Row | 1 if successful or -1 if an error occurs |
| Append Row | Row number of new row |
| Insert Row | Row number of new row |
| Update | 1 if successful or -1 if an error occurs |
| Save Rows As | Number of rows saved or a negative number if an error occurs |
| Print | 0 |
| Preview | 0 |
| Preview With | 0, Rulers |
| Query Mode | 0 |
| Query Sort | 0 |
| Query Clear | 0 |

**14**

DataWindow
Scripting

The `ButtonClickedevent` lets you trap when the button action fails and take possible corrective action (or at least advise users). This is also the event where you code a button's user-defined action. By using the `dwo` argument, you can extract the actual button clicked. The following example has several DataWindow buttons, and selective processing is carried out for each:

```
Choose Case dwo.Name
   Case "cb_retrieve"
      If actionreturncode = -1 Then
         MessageBox( "Ooops", "Unable to retrieve rows requested!")
      End If
   Case "cb_my_custom"
      // Populate a user object with current row data
      // and then call processing function.
      lnv_DataManip = This.Object.Data.Primary[row]
      lnv_DataManip.of_ProcessData()
   Case Else
      // Do nothing, some other button!
End Choose
```

A good reason to name your button objects within the DataWindow is because PowerBuilder assigns a name such as `obj_123456`.

## The `ButtonClicking` Event

The `ButtonClicking` event is fired before the `ButtonClicked` event and has the event arguments `row` and `dwo`. You can use this event to trap button clicks and control whether the action assigned to the button is executed. Returning a value of 1 prevents the default action from happening; to allow processing, you should return a `0`. After the default action is executed (if any), the `ButtonClicked` event is fired.

> **Note**
>
> The `Clicked` event is fired before the `ButtonClicking` event.

## The `RowFocusChanging` Event

The `RowFocusChanging` event was a recent enhancement (version 6.0) to the DataWindow control and allows the trapping and control of row focus changes. This event occurs as the DataWindow's current row is about to be changed and before the `RowFocusChanged` event, which is fired after the row is changed.

The two event arguments are `currentrow` (the current row number) and `newrow` (the row that's about to become current). If `RowFocusChanging` is being triggered because of a new row being inserted, `newrow` will be `0`.

You can control whether you want the row to change by using the return code of the event: `0`, continue to set the new current row, or `1`, prevent the current row from changing.

Users usually trigger this event by using the mouse or keyboard to move between rows, but they can also trigger it with the functions `SetRow()`, `Retrieve()`, `RowsCopy()`, `RowsMove()`, `DeleteRow()`, and `RowsDiscard()`.

The event can be useful for situations such as the following:

- Refreshing information in other areas of the DataWindow or window.

- Cleaning up or allocating additional resources.

- Preventing row changes from occurring in a detail window that shows only a limited number of rows. Usually controlled via filtering, the new event makes a much cleaner mechanism.

## The `ItemChanged` and `ItemError` Events

The `ItemChanged` event is the last level of edit validation. It's triggered whenever users modify a field and try to enter another field, and the value entered has passed the previous three levels of validation.

---

**Note**

The only variation on this is when the field is of the `DropDownListBox`, `DropDownDataWindow`, `CheckBox`, and `RadioButton` edit styles. `ItemChanged` is triggered when an item is selected.

---

Both the row and the data value are available as parameters of the `ItemChanged` event, which saves you from having to call the appropriate PowerScript functions to obtain these commonly used values.

As with many DataWindow events, you can set the return value to control what happens when the event's execution finishes. The valid return codes for `ItemChanged` are `0`, accept the data value (the default); `1`, reject the data value and trigger the `ItemError` event; and `2`, reject the data value but allow the focus to change (the value in the column is replaced with the original value).

The `ItemErrorevent` is triggered whenever a field is modified and any validation steps fail. The return codes for this event are 0, reject the data value and show an error message (the default); 1, reject the data value and display no error message; 2, accept the data value; and 3, reject the data value but allow the focus to change (the original value of the column is replaced). As with `ItemChanged`, both the row and the data value are available as parameters of the `ItemError` event.

Some sample code (actually from a production application) for `ItemChanged` (see Listing 14.3) and `ItemError` (see Listing 14.4) shows you how to use both events and how they interrelate. Examine the `print_loc_code` case closely because it triggers the `ItemError` event.

**LISTING 14.3** The `ItemChanged` Event

```
Boolean lb_Process = FALSE
String ls_Value


ls_Value = data


Choose Case dwo.Name
Case "use_increments"
    inv_BagWizard.istr_BagParms.b_UseIncrements = ( ls_Value = "1" )
    lb_Process = TRUE
Case "print_loc_code"
    If dw_extruding_spec_header.GetItemString( 1, "film_type") = "JS" And &
        ls_Value = "2" And Not m_mfg_order.m_activities.m_keyedentry.Checked Then
        Return 1
    End If
    inv_BagWizard.istr_BagParms.i_SidesPrinted = Integer( ls_Value)
    lb_Process = TRUE
Case "figure_unwind_pattern_num"
    If IsNumber( ls_Value) Then
        dw_customer_dimensions.SetItem(1,"figure_unwind_pattern", &
                                    Integer( ls_Value))
    End If
Case "press_cylinder_circumference"
    inv_BagWizard.istr_BagParms.dc_CylinderSize = Real( ls_Value)
    lb_Process = TRUE
Case "color_1", "color_2", "color_3", "color_4", "color_5", "color_6"
    inv_BagWizard.istr_BagParms.i_NoOfColors = of_CountPrintColours()
    lb_Process = TRUE
End Choose
```

**LISTING 14.3** CONTINUED

```
If lb_Process Then
   This.PostEvent( "bagcalculate")
End If
```

**LISTING 14.4** The `ItemError` Event

```
// Check the current column - the one that caused the error
//
If dwo.Name = "print_loc_code" Then
   MessageBox( "Print Location Error", "You cannot have
                                 2-S print for J-Sheeting.")
   // We have handled the error message
   Return 1
Else
   // Open the default message box
   Return 0
End If
```

# The `SQLPreview` Event

The `SQLPreview` event is triggered after a call to `Retrieve()`, `Update()`, or `ReselectRow()` but immediately before those functions carry out any processing. This event is triggered every time a SQL statement is sent to the database, which means that it's triggered for each row updated via the `Update()` function.

By using the return value from this event, you can control what action takes place following the `SQLPreview` event for an `Update()` function call. The return codes are `0`, continue (the default); `1`, stop processing; and `2`, skip this request and execute the next request.

Inside this event, you can capture the SQL about to be submitted. Before version 5.0, you had to use the `GetSQLPreview()` function, but the event now supplies the following parameters:

| Parameter (Type) | Description |
| --- | --- |
| *request*<br>(SqlPreviewFunction) | The type of function requesting database access—for example, `PreviewFunctionReselectRow!`, `PreviewFunctionRetrieve!`, or `PreviewFunctionUpdate!` |

14

DataWindow
Scripting

| Parameter (Type) | Description |
| --- | --- |
| *sqltype* (SqlPreviewType) | The type of SQL statement that's about to be submitted—for example, `PreviewDelete!`, `PreviewInsert!`, `PreviewSelect!`, or `PreviewUpdate!` |
| *sqlsyntax* (String) | The actual SQL statement being submitted |
| *buffer* (dwBuffer) | The DataWindow control buffer to be used in the request—for example, `Delete!`, `Filter!`, or `Primary!` |
| *row* (Long) | The row in the DataWindow to be used in the SQL statement |

The `GetSQLPreview()` function can be called only in the `DBError` and `SQLPreview` events. The syntax is

*DataWindowControl*.GetSQLPreview()

This function returns the current SQL statement string or an empty string if an error occurs.

When a DataWindow generates SQL and binding is enabled for the database being used, the syntax might not be complete. The bind variables haven't yet been replaced with the actual values and will appear as question marks. If you need to see the complete SQL statement, disable binding for the DBMS being used by setting the `DBParm` variable `DisableBind` to 1.

In the `SQLPreview` event, you can also modify the SQL statement returned by `GetSQLPreview()` and then call `SetSQLPreview()` to place the updated SQL statement into the DataWindow control.

The `SetSQLPreview()` function specifies new SQL syntax for the DataWindow control that's about to execute a SQL statement. The syntax is

*DataWindowControl*.SetSQLPreview( *SQLSyntax*)

The string specifying the *SQLSyntax* must contain a valid statement. This function can be called only in the `SQLPreview` event.

> **Note**
>
> If the data source is a stored procedure, you will see the EXECUTE command in the previewed SQL.

# The DBError Event

The DBError event is triggered whenever a database error occurs because of a DataWindow action. By default, this event displays an error message window, but by setting the return code to 1, you can disable this feature and carry out other processing.

Inside the DBError event, you can obtain the database-specific error code and error text from the event parameters:

| Parameter | (Type) | Description |
| --- | --- | --- |
| sqldbcode | (Long) | The DBMS vendor's specific error code |
| sqlerrtext | (String) | The DBMS vendor's error message |
| sqlsyntax | (String) | The SQL statement that caused the error |
| buffer | (dwBuffer) | The DataWindow control buffer being used at the time of the error |
| row | (Long) | The row within the DataWindow that caused the error |

In earlier PowerBuilder versions, you had to use the DBErrorCode() and DBErrorMessage() functions. The syntax for the DBErrorCode() function is

```
DataWindowControl.DBErrorCode()
```

The syntax for the DBErrorMessage() function is

```
DataWindowControl.DBErrorMessage()
```

Both functions should be called only from the DBError event because this is the only place in which they will return anything meaningful.

> **Note**
>
> DBErrorCode() and DBErrorMessage() are mentioned for understanding legacy PowerBuilder code. The event arguments should be used going forward.

In the SQLPreview and DBError events, you have access to the current row and buffer (in earlier versions of PowerBuilder, you used the GetUpdateStatus() function to find the row number and buffer of the row now being updated to the database). This is obviously useful in the DBError event because you can now point out to end users the line causing the problem and allow them to fix it before trying to save again. Of course, if the problem row is in the Filter buffer, you must first give users access to it.

The previous method using `GetUpdateStatus()` has the syntax

```
DataWindowControl.GetUpdateStatus( Row, DWBuffer)
```

*Row* and *DWBuffer* must be variables of type Long and `dwBuffer`, respectively, so that the function can assign the value of the current row's number and buffer.

The following code is placed in the `DBError` event. It scrolls to the offending row and sets the focus to the DataWindow:

```
If Buffer = Primary! Then
   This.ScrollToRow( Row)
   This.SetFocus()
End If


Return 1
```

You also could use the `ReselectRow()` function to re-retrieve the row from the database if the error so requires. You would trap on a per-DBMS error code for this case.

## The `Error` Event

The `Error` event traps runtime errors that occur as a result of using the direct-access syntax and allows you to handle them gracefully. The event provides access to the following information as parameters:

| Parameter (Type) | Description |
| --- | --- |
| *ErrorNumber* (uInt) | The PowerBuilder error number. |
| *ErrorText* (String) | The PowerBuilder message describing the error. |
| *ErrorWindowMenu* (String) | The window or menu that caused the error. |
| *ErrorObject* (String) | The object that caused the error. |
| *ErrorScript* (String) | The event within the object causing the error. |
| *ErrorLine* (uInt) | The line within the event causing the error. |

| Parameter (Type) | Description |
| --- | --- |
| *Action* (ExceptionAction) | What the application will attempt to do after your Error script finishes. This can be one of the following:<br><br>ExceptionFail!,<br>ExceptionIgnore!,<br>ExceptionRetry!, and<br>ExceptionSubstitute-<br>ReturnValue!. |
| *ReturnValue* (Any) | A return value used with the ExceptionSub-stituteReturnValue! action. |

For DataWindows, when an error occurs while evaluating a data or property expression, error processing occurs in the following order:

1. The Error event is triggered.

2. If the Error event doesn't contain any script or the *Action* argument is set to ExceptionFail!, the SystemError event is triggered.

3. If the SystemError event doesn't contain any code, an application error occurs, and the application is terminated.

# DataWindow Functions

As with other controls, the functions available for the DataWindow control can be broken into three major groups: database, information acquisition, and modification.

> **Note**
>
> Some functions that generated an informational message in previous versions now generate a warning in PowerBuilder: DBErrorCode(), DBErrorMessage(), GetMessageText(), GetSQLPreview(), GetUpdateStatus(), and SetActionCode(). These have been flagged as warnings in the last two versions and should be removed from your code.

**14**

DataWindow
Scripting

## Database-Related Functions

These functions direct the DataWindow control to carry out a specific task: connect the control to the database.

## Connecting to the Database

Most DataWindows are attached to some form of database and therefore require a connection to be made between them. This is done through the SetTrans() or SetTransObject() function. If you are unfamiliar with the concept of database transactions, read Chapter 4 before continuing with this section.

These two functions have one distinct difference. With SetTrans(), you don't have to carry out any database initialization or transaction management. You just fill in a transaction object, which doesn't need to be currently connected, and then inform the DataWindow about it. SetTrans() copies the information in the transaction object into a transaction object internal to the DataWindow. The syntax is

*DataWindowControl*.SetTrans( *TransactionObject*)

This syntax means that the DataWindow issues a CONNECT each time a database request is carried out, an automatic ROLLBACK on any error, and a DISCONNECT at the end of the transaction. Remember that Sybase now does a COMMIT after a disconnection. Because database connections are generally expensive operations (in terms of time and resources) to execute, you can see that if you will be making numerous calls, this function will give the worst performance. However, sometimes you might need to use this function rather than SetTransObject()—usually when you have a limited number of available connections to the database or when the application is being used from a remote location.

> **Note**
>
> If you use SetTrans(), remember that you can't coordinate multiple DataWindow updates because the data has already been committed at the end of the update for each DataWindow.

The most commonly used version of the two database connection methods is SetTransObject() because it maintains an open connection to the database and therefore is far more efficient. There's a one-time connection and disconnection, and the developer controls the transaction and can commit or roll back the DataWindow's save. This gives you optimal performance when carrying out any database operations on the DataWindow. The syntax is

*DataWindowControl*.SetTransObject( *TransactionObject*)

As with SetTrans(), you must supply a transaction object. SetTransObject(), however, must have the transaction object connected to the database before the function call or before any DataWindow database operations are executed.

Also unique to SetTransObject() is that if you change the DataWindow control's data object or disconnect and reconnect to a database, the connection between the DataWindow control and the transaction object is broken. You must call SetTransObject() again to rebuild the association.

Both functions return 1 if they succeed, -1 if an error occurs.

---

**Note**

You will receive an error if the DataWindow control hasn't had a DataWindow object assigned to it before calling either SetTrans function.

---

Two little-used functions are mentioned here for completeness. The first, GetTrans(), enables you to access the DataWindow's internal transaction object and copy it into another transaction object. The syntax is

```
DataWindowControl.GetTrans( TransactionObject)
```

If SetTrans() hasn't been called for the DataWindow, GetTrans() will fail. If the DataWindow has been connected via SetTransObject(), GetTrans() won't report any information.

The second little-used function is ResetTransObject(), which terminates a DataWindow connection to a programmer-defined transaction object set up via SetTransObject(). After a call to ResetTransObject(), the DataWindow reverts to using its internal transaction object. The syntax is

```
DataWindowControl.ResetTransObject()
```

SetTrans() must then be called before any database activities can begin. This function is rarely used because you are unlikely to mix the connection types in a single execution of the application.

## Retrieving Data

The Retrieve() function requests rows from the database and places them in a DataWindow control. If the DataWindow object is set up to use retrieval arguments, you must specify them as parameters of the call or, if the arguments aren't specified, PowerBuilder will open a window for users to enter them at runtime. The syntax is

```
DataWindowControl.Retrieve( { Argument, ...})
```

**14**

DataWindow
Scripting

The arguments must appear in the same order in which they were defined for the DataWindow object. You can specify more parameters in your call to `Retrieve()` than the DataWindow object expects. This lets you write a generic retrieval script. You can't specify fewer parameters than are expected because this is still an error. The function returns a Long data type that's the total number of rows retrieved into the Primary buffer and returns -1 if it fails. If the DataWindow has a filter specified, this is applied after the rows are retrieved, and these rows aren't included in the return count.

A call to `Retrieve()` might trigger the following events: `DBError`, `RetrieveEnd`, `RetrieveRow`, `RetrieveStart`, and `RowFocusChanged`.

## Retrieve Events

The `RetrieveStart` event is triggered after a call to `Retrieve()` but before any database actions have been taken. You can control whether the retrieve can proceed, whether it stops without doing any processing, or whether it appends the new rows to the existing ones by setting the return value of the event. The return codes for this event are `0`, continue with the retrieve (the default); `1`, don't perform the retrieve; and `2`, don't reset the rows and buffers before retrieving data.

The `RetrieveRow` event is triggered every time a row is retrieved and after the row is added into the DataWindow. Coding anything in this event can adversely affect the performance of a data retrieval. You can stop the retrieval by setting the return code to `1`; the default, `0`, continues with the retrieve.

The `RetrieveEnd` event is triggered when the retrieval has ended.

## Canceling a Retrieve

One of the most common end-user solutions to an application that doesn't seem to be progressing anymore and is thought to be hung is to use Ctrl+Alt+Delete to kill the process. This might, however, still tie up several server and network resources while the query continues to run. To prevent this from happening, you should provide end users with a way to cancel long-running queries or—even better—provide them with an estimate of the time or records remaining.

### Note

If the `DBParm` parameter `Async` is set to allow asynchronous database operations (1), you can halt the query before the first row is returned. Only some databases support this capability, and you should refer to the database-specific documentation in PowerBuilder. If the DBMS doesn't support `Async`, you can't cancel a retrieval before the database finishes building the resultset.

PowerBuilder provides a PowerScript function, DBCancel(), to halt the row retrieval now being processed by a DataWindow. This function must be called from the RetrieveRow event to interrupt the retrieval. The syntax is

```
DataWindowControl.DBCancel()
```

DBCancel() returns 1 if it succeeds, -1 if an error occurs.

The most common method of providing a way to cancel a retrieval operation is to give users a dialog or pop-up window that displays a row indicator and a Cancel pushbutton.

This pop-up-style window has two static text controls (st_percent and st_rows_ retrieved), one pushbutton (cb_cancel), and two rectangular drawing controls (r_total_percent and r_percent_done). The window also has three private instance variables:

```
Private:
Long il_TotalRows, il_CurrentRow
Boolean ib_Cancel = FALSE
```

The Open event for this window extracts information from the message object that influences the type of cancel window to display (see Listing 14.5).

**LISTING 14.5**   The Open Event for w_retrieve_cancel

```
il_TotalRows = Message.DoubleParm

If IsNull( il_TotalRows) Then
   r_total_percent.visible = FALSE
   r_percent_done.visible = FALSE
   st_percent.visible = FALSE
Else
   st_rows_retrieved.visible = FALSE
   r_percent_done.width = 0
End If

Timer (1)
```

**14**

DataWindow
Scripting

If the script that opens the retrieve's cancel window specifies the total number of rows to be retrieved (which is sometimes possible by running a SELECT COUNT(*) statement), the window sets itself up to display a percentage bar using the rectangle controls. Usually this value is NULL to indicate that the window should just display the number of rows retrieved so far in the operation. A 1-second timer starts up to make the cancel window update its display (see Listing 14.6).

**LISTING 14.6** The `Timer` Event for `w_retrieve_cancel`

```
Double ldb_Percent

If Not IsNull( il_TotalRows) Then
    ldb_Percent = il_CurrentRow / il_TotalRows
    st_percent.text = String( Truncate( ldb_Percent * 100,0)) + "%"
    If ( ldb_Percent * 100) <= 100 Then
        r_percent_done.width = 700 * ldb_Percent
    End If
Else
    st_rows_retrieved.text = "Rows: " + String( il_CurrentRow)
End If
```

The `Timer` event inspects its instance variable, `il_CurrentRow`, which is updated from the calling window's DataWindow. Depending on the display type, this value calculates the new width of the percentage rectangle or displays with the `"Rows: "` text string.

The Cancel button simply closes the retrieve window:

```
Close( Parent)
```

The only thing remaining for the retrieve window to do is shut down the timer resource in the `Close` event using `Timer(0)`.

The retrieve cancel window also has several simple window functions defined; they act on the instance variables. The `of_UpdateRowCount()` function takes a single numeric argument, which is the current total number of rows:

```
If al_CurrentRows > il_CurrentRow Then
    Il_CurrentRow = al_CurrentRows
End If
```

The DataWindow using this retrieve cancel window requires code in two of the three retrieve events: `RetrieveRow` and `RetrieveEnd` (see Listings 14.7 and 14.8).

**LISTING 14.7** The `RetrieveRow` Event of the Retrieve Cancel DataWindow

```
If Not IsValid( w_retrieve_cancel) Then
    // Stop - user wants to cancel
    This.DBCancel()
Else
    // Continue - increment row counter in retrieve cancel window
    w_retrieve_cancel.of_UpdateRowCount( row)
End If
```

**LISTING 14.8**  The `RetrieveEnd` Event of the Retrieve Cancel DataWindow

```
If IsValid( w_retrieve_cancel) Then
   Close( w_retrieve_cancel)
End If
```

Use the `RetrieveRow`event to check whether users have clicked the Cancel button on the pop-up window by seeing whether the retrieve cancel window is still open. If the retrieve hasn't been canceled, the pop-up window variable `il_CurrentRow` is incremented by the current row count by calling the `of_UpdateRowCount()` and passing the event parameter row. If users want to cancel, the `DBCancel()` function is called to tell PowerBuilder to stop the retrieve.

The `RetrieveEnd` event closes the pop-up window. The `IsValid()` function is used to make sure that the window is still open before closing to prevent a runtime error.

Place the following code wherever the retrieve should start. As mentioned earlier, to display a percentage bar, the total number of rows to be returned should first be determined. It would then be passed as the parameter instead of `ll_Null`:

```
Long ll_Null

SetNull( ll_Null)
OpenWithParm( w_retrieve_cancel, ll_Null)
dw_1.Retrieve()
```

> **Note**
>
> This example uses a rectangle control to display the retrieval's progress. PowerBuilder 7.0 introduces the vertical and horizontal progress meter controls to display progress completed. For more information on the controls, see Chapter 11, "Advanced Controls."

14

DataWindow Scripting

## Refreshing Data Rows

If your DBMS and DataWindow object use time stamp data types, the time stamp value occasionally needs to be refreshed from the database. This might be required if the data is retrieved a long time before any changes are made. If the data fails to save and you want to give users the opportunity to view the new information and possibly update it, you can use the `ReselectRow()` function.

This function retrieves values from the database for all updatable and time stamp columns for a specified row in a DataWindow control. The old values are then replaced with the newly retrieved ones:

```
DataWindowControl.ReselectRow( lRow)
```

The function returns 1 if it's successful, -1 if the row can't be reselected. The row can't be reselected if it has been deleted from the database or if the DataWindow isn't updatable.

This function is used most often when a DataWindow update fails because of a changed time stamp, which occurs when the row has been changed between the times of its retrieval and its attempted update.

> **Tip**
>
> You don't need to use this function to access Identity column values after the save of a DataWindow. PowerBuilder automatically fills these values back into the DataWindow column for you.

# Informational Functions

Informational functions are used specifically to obtain information about the DataWindow and DataWindow objects. `Describe()` is an important and useful function covered in detail in Chapter 15.

## Data Extraction

If you need to access all data in the DataWindow, you can use the `SaveAs()` function to avoid having to go through repeated calls to the appropriate `GetItemx()` functions or directly accessing the data.

`SaveAs()` allows you to save the contents of not only a DataWindow but also graphs, OLE controls, and OLE storage. For DataWindows and graphs, the data can be saved in a number of formats, from tab- and comma-delimited to Excel files and even SQL statements. To save the data from a DataWindow or child DataWindow, the syntax is

```
DataWindowControl.SaveAs( { FileName, SaveAsType, ColumnHeadings})
```

If the `FileName` parameter of the output file is omitted, PowerBuilder prompts users for it at runtime. The `SaveAsType` parameter is of the `SaveAsType` enumerated data type and can take one of the following values (if none is specified, `Text!` is taken as the default):

| SaveAsType | Description |
| --- | --- |
| Clipboard! | Save to the Clipboard |
| CSV! | Comma-separated values, terminated with a carriage return |
| dBASE2! | dBASE II format |
| dBASE3! | dBASE III format |
| DIF! | Data Interchange Format |
| Excel!, Excel5! | Microsoft Excel format |
| HTMLTable! | Using HTML tags to create a table |
| PSReport! | PowerSoft report format |
| SQLInsert! | SQL INSERT statements |
| SYLK! | Microsoft Multiplan format |
| Text! | Tab-separated values, terminated with a carriage return |
| WK1!, WKS! | Lotus 1-2-3 format |
| WMF! | Windows MetaFile format |

The `ColumnHeadings` parameter is a Boolean that specifies whether the DataWindow column names should be included at the beginning of the file.

> **Note**
>
> Some formats are platform-specific. The Macintosh (version 6.0 and earlier) doesn't support `PSReport!` and `WMF!`, and doesn't allow the `Clipboard!` format to save graphs to the Clipboard. UNIX doesn't support the `WMF!` format.

**14**

**DataWindow Scripting**

To save the data from graph controls in windows, user objects, or DataWindow controls, the syntax is

```
ControlName.SaveAs( { GraphControl} {, FileName, SaveAsType, ColumnHeadings})
```

`ControlName` is the name of the actual graph control or the name of the DataWindow that contains the graph. The `GraphControl` optional parameter is used only for DataWindow controls and specifies the name of the graph.

If no parameters are specified for the SaveAs() function, at least for these two syntaxes, PowerBuilder displays the Save As dialog (see Figure 14.3), which enables users to specify values for each parameter.

For example, to save the data from the DataWindow dw_employees to the file C:\DATA\EMP.SQL in a SQL syntax format that can be loaded into another database, the call would be

```
dw_employees.SaveAs( "C:\DATAEMP.SQL", SQLInsert!, FALSE)
```

To save the contents of a graph object sitting within this same DataWindow, the syntax might be

```
dw_employees.SaveAs( "dept_graph", "C:\DATAEMP.CSV", CSV!, TRUE)
```

The SaveAs() function has a number of other formats that all relate to OLE controls; see Chapter 38, "ActiveX and OLE," for more information.

**FIGURE 14.3**

*The Save As dialog.*

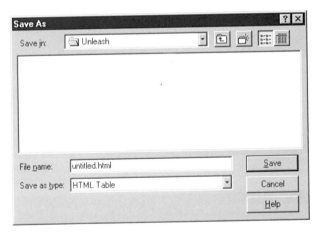

Introduced in PowerBuilder 6.0 was the SaveAsAscii() function, which lets you save the contents of a DataWindow or datastore to an ASCII text file. The syntax for this function is

```
DWControl.SaveAsAscii(FileName {, Delimiter {, QuoteCharacter {, Terminator}}})
```

*Delimiter* is the character used to delimit values. The default is a tab. If you need to enclose your values with a certain character, such as quotation marks, you can specify this with the *QuoteCharacter* parameter. Use the *Terminator* character to specify the row/record terminator; the default is a carriage return and new line (~r~n). PowerBuilder creates

**a value in the text file for each DataWindow object, including computed columns and group totals.**

The following example saves the contents of the DataWindow to the file C:\DEPTS.TXT, which is comma-separated and enclosed in single quotes, with each record terminated with a carriage return and new line:

```
dw_departments.SaveAsAscii( "C:\DEPTS.TXT", ",", "'")
```

PowerBuilder recently added the capability to create an HTML Form containing columns and rows from a DataWindow together with HTML Style information:

```
DataWindowControl.GenerateHTMLForm(Syntax, Style, Action {, StartRow, EndRow, &
                             StartColumn, EndColumn {, Buffer}})
```

The first two parameters, *Syntax* and *Style*, are strings passed by reference and receive the HTML Form syntax and Style Sheet syntax, respectively. The *Action* parameter is a string that defines the ACTION property of the FORM. *StartRow* and *EndRow* specify the range of rows in the DataWindow to include in the syntax. The default is all rows. *StartColumn* and *EndColumn* specify the subset of columns you want; again, the default is all columns. The *Buffer* parameter lets you choose which DataWindow buffer to extract the data from. The return value for this function is a -1 on error, or the number of bytes in the syntax.

The syntax returned from this function needs to be combined with the appropriate HTML tags to construct a complete HTML page. For example

```
String ls_Syntax, ls_Style, ls_Action
String ls_Page
Integer li_Return

ls_Action = "/cgi-bin/pbcgi70.exe/orderentry/uo_order/f_placeorder"
li_Return = dw_1.GenerateHTMLForm( ls_Syntax, ls_Style, ls_Action)

If li_Return = -1 Then
   ls_Page = "Unable to create HTML form."
Else
   ls_Page = "<HTML>"
   ls_Page += ls_Style
   ls_Page += "<BODY>"
   ls_Page += "<H1>Order Information</H1>"
   ls_Page += ls_Syntax
ls_Page += "</BODY></HTML>"
End If
```

## Counting Rows

Four functions return the number of rows in each buffer, or a count of rows with a modified status. The first two functions usually appear in a CloseQuery event of a window to inform users that there are modified records in the DataWindow that haven't yet been saved.

The DeletedCount() function returns the number of rows that have been deleted from the DataWindow but haven't been deleted from the database. This is the number of rows in the Delete buffer. The syntax is

```
DataWindowControl.DeletedCount()
```

This function returns a Long data type of the number of rows, 0 if none are waiting for deletion from the database, or -1 if the function fails.

The ModifiedCount() function returns the number of rows that have been changed in the DataWindow but haven't been updated in the database. The syntax is

```
DataWindowControl.ModifiedCount()
```

This function returns a Long data type of the number of rows, 0 if none are waiting for updating in the database, or -1 if the function fails. The function counts the rows in the Primary and Filter buffers.

The FilteredCount() function returns the number of rows placed into the DataWindow's Filter buffer. The syntax is

```
DataWindowControl.FilteredCount()
```

This function returns a Long data type of the number of rows in the Filter buffer, 0 if all rows are now displayed, or -1 if the function fails.

The most common row-counting function is RowCount(), which can be found in most DataWindow scripts and object scripts operating on the DataWindow. The syntax is

```
DataWindowControl.RowCount()
```

This function returns a Long data type of the number of rows now in the Primary buffer, 0 if no rows are now available, or -1 if an error occurs.

## Crosstab Messages

Unique to crosstab-style DataWindow objects is the generation of messages that detail what the DataWindow is doing. The GetMessageText() function can be used to capture these processing messages as a string, which can then be redisplayed to users to inform them of what actions the DataWindow is now making. The syntax is

```
DataWindowControl.GetMessageText()
```

> **Caution**
>
> This function is now flagged as obsolete in PowerBuilder because the message text is now available as an argument in the event `pbm_dwnmessagetext`. The argument name is `text`.

If there's no text or if an error occurs, the function returns an empty string. This function can be used only in a user-defined event for the PowerBuilder event ID of `pbm_dwnmessagetext` for the DataWindow. The most common messages are `Retrieving data` and `Building crosstab`, and these are usually redisplayed in the MicroHelp area of an MDI frame. Here's an example:

```
w_frame.SetMicroHelp (text)
```

# Modification Functions

An often-used function is `Modify()`, which is covered in detail in Chapter 15. The next few sections describe some of the other DataWindow modification functions.

## Code Table Functions

DataWindow columns that have edit styles of `CheckBox`, `RadioButton`, `DropDownListBox`, `EditMask`, and `Edit` can have associated value lists or code tables. A *value list* is simply a list of constants. A *code table* provides a translation between a visible display value and an invisible data value. Users see and enter display values, and the DataWindow acts on and saves data values. This kind of validation can be called *proactive validation* because it undertakes validation at the time of entry instead of when the data is saved, which is reactive. PowerBuilder provides extraction and modification functions that act on the column's code values.

The `GetValue()` function extracts the value from a column's code table at a specified index:

```
DataWindowControl.GetValue (Column, ValueIndex)
```

`Column` is the name or number of the column that has the code table.

This function returns a string that contains the item at the specified index of the code table. If the value has an associated display value, it's appended to the beginning of the return string with a tab-character separator and then the code value. If the index is invalid or the column has no code table, an empty string is returned. This function can't be used to obtain values from a `DropDownDataWindow` code table.

> **Note**
>
> The following direct-access syntax to access a column's code table returns you to the complete code table, not to specific indexes:
>
> ```
> dwControl.Object.ColumnName.Values
> ```

The SetValue() function allows you to programmatically affect the values of a code table or ListBox edit style. The syntax is

```
DataWindowControl.SetValue( Column, ValueIndex, Value)
```

The *Value* parameter is a string that contains the new value for the item specified by *ValueIndex*. To specify a display value, you must separate the display value and data value with a tab in the same manner as detailed in the GetValue() function. The data value must be converted from a data type that matches the column's data type to a string; this ensures that when PowerBuilder has to convert back within the DataWindow, it won't fail.

The SetValue() function can be used inside a cursor loop to fill a code table from the values returned by a SELECT. You can use drop-down DataWindows to achieve the same effect. The following is a combined example of calls to the GetValue() and SetValue() functions that retrieve a value from a code table, modify it, and place it back:

```
String ls_Status

// Extract the code value
ls_Status = dw_employee.GetValue( "status", 2)
// Find the status data value
ls_Status = Mid( ls_Status, Pos( ls_Status, "~t") + 1)
// Set the 'Newly Employed' display value to the status data value
ls_Status = "Newly Employed~t" + ls_Status
// Place it back into the DataWindow
dw_employee.SetValue( "status", 2, ls_Status)
```

The ClearValues() function removes all the items from a value list:

```
DataWindowControl.ClearValues( Column)
```

A call to this function doesn't affect the data of the associated column in any way other than removing the value list.

# Column Format Functions

You can use the `GetFormat()` function to extract the display format for a DataWindow column:

```
DataWindowControl.GetFormat( Column)
```

This function returns a string containing the display format and an empty string if an error occurs. This value is usually stored during a temporary modification of the format by using the `SetFormat()` function:

```
DataWindowControl.SetFormat( Column, NewFormat)
```

> **Note**
>
> When a column's new format is for a number, the format must be constructed by using the U.S. number notation (that is, using a comma as a thousands separator and a period for decimals). When the application is running, the U.S. delimiters and symbols are replaced by the local symbols as required. This is true of the `SetFormat()` and `GetFormat()` functions.

For example, to save the format of a unit price column and change it to display cents, the code would be as follows:

```
String ls_OldFormat, ls_NewFormat = "$#,###.00"

ls_OldFormat = dw_product_item.GetFormat( "unit_price")
dw_product_item.SetFormat( "unit_price", ls_NewFormat)
```

The old format would have to be stored in an instance variable or some other variable to allow it to exist outside this script. It appears here as a local variable simply to avoid confusion.

# Column Validation Rule Functions

Validation rules can be defined in the Database painter or the DataWindow painter (discussed in Chapters 5 and 6). PowerBuilder provides two functions to enable the modification of existing validation rules or the specification of a validation rule where one didn't previously exist.

`GetValidate()` extracts the validation rule for a column, and its behavior is similar to that of `GetFormat()`:

```
DataWindowControl.GetValidate( Column)
```

In dot notation, it can be rewritten as follows:

```
DataWindowControl.Object.ColumnName.Validation
```

The function returns a string containing the validation rule and an empty string if there's no validation rule. This value is usually stored during a temporary modification of the input rule by using the `SetValidate()` function:

```
DataWindowControl.SetValidate( Column, NewRule)
```

This is useful when you have to deal with exception validation (where only one business unit requires special processing). For example, to save the current validation rule of the unit price column and modify it to accept only values between 0 and 100, the code would be

```
String ls_OldRule, &
       ls_NewRule = "Long(GetText()) >= 0 And Long(GetText()) <= 100"


ls_OldRule = dw_product_item.GetValidate( "unit_price")
dw_product_item.SetValidate( "unit_price", ls_NewRule)
```

# Setting Tab Orders Programmatically

Most applications are used by multiple user groups, and users usually have different security access to different parts of a DataWindow. You sometimes have to turn off a column's edit capabilities at runtime, depending on the current user. You can protect a column in one of two ways: by modifying the `Protect` attribute of the column or by setting the column's tab order to 0.

The `SetTabOrder()` function changes the tab sequence value of a specified column in a DataWindow control:

```
DataWindowControl.SetTabOrder( Column, NewTabValue)
```

or with the dot-notation syntax:

```
DataWindowControl.Object.ColumnName.TabSequence = NewValue
```

The `NewTabValue` parameter is the new tab sequence number for the column and can range from 0 to 9,999. Remember, if you want to disable a column so that users can't enter data into it, set the tab value to 0. The function returns the column's original tab value if it succeeds, -1 if an error occurs. You can use this original tab value to reset the column so that it will be editable or appear in the original tab order again.

You can set the `Protect` attribute of a DataWindow column to override any tab order settings. Although a column is protected, users can't edit it even when the tab order of the column is greater than 0. Here's an example:

```
DataWindowControl.Object.ColumnName.Protect = 1
```

This is the preferred method for disabling a DataWindow column because the tab value isn't destroyed.

## Column Border Style Functions

To provide a more proactive user interface, use the `SetBorderStyle()` function to indicate certain conditions for columns, such as being required or having a bad value. You might not know the conditions at design time, but you can program them into the application by using the functions described in this section. For example, if a particular department is allowed read-only access to a column, you could turn off the border for that column.

Use the `GetBorderStyle()` function to extract the current style of a column's border:

`DataWindowControl.GetBorderStyle( Column)`

The return value is of the Border enumerated data type, and it can have the following values: `Box!`, `NoBorder!`, `ShadowBox!`, or `Underline!`. The function returns a `NULL` if it fails.

You can use the `SetBorderStyle()` function to change a column's border style:

`DataWindowControl.SetBorderStyle( Column, NewBorderStyle)`

You can replace both functions with the following direct-access syntax:

`DataWindowControl.Object.ColumnName.Border`

The border style is an integer value representation: None (`0`), Shadow (`1`), Rectangle (`2`), Resize (`3`), Line (`4`), 3D Lowered (`5`), and 3D Raised (`6`).

## Changing the Height of Detail Rows

To change the height of an individual detail row or a range of detail rows, use the `SetDetailHeight()` function:

`DataWindowControl.SetDetailHeight( StartRow, EndRow, NewHeight)`

The `StartRow` and `EndRow` parameters define an inclusive range of row numbers for which you want to change the height to the `NewHeight` value. The `NewHeight` value is specified in the units of the DataWindow object.

The most common use of this function is to hide certain rows from view by setting their height to `0`.

## Resetting a DataWindow

To throw away all the data from a DataWindow or child DataWindow, use the `Reset()` function, which has three forms. The form for a DataWindow has the following syntax:

```
DataWindowControl.Reset()
```

Reset() doesn't merely transfer rows to a different buffer; it completely and irrecoverably clears out all the DataWindow's buffers. It won't make any changes to the database, regardless of row and column update status flags.

# DataWindow Performance

You can realize a number of performance gains from using a DataWindow; most of these are covered in Chapter 23, "Configuring and Tuning." However, you must still consider the script that you write for DataWindow events. For three groups of DataWindow events, you need to carefully consider not only what you code but also how much you code:

- Anything coded in the RetrieveRow event is executed every time a row is retrieved. Depending on the amount of code, this could dramatically increase the time to retrieve data. Avoid coding anything in this event—even a comment—if at all possible. If you need to code anything in this event, try to keep it as succinct and optimal as possible. If you put any code in this event, PowerBuilder does an asynchronous retrieval, which you can cancel and keep working through.

- If you place any code in the Clicked event, try to make it as short as possible because a second click might be missed and the DoubleClicked event might never get fired.

- The performance of RowFocusChanged and ItemChanged events also suffers more as the length of their scripts increases. This is important because they're triggered far more frequently by users entering data.

If you won't be using all the columns retrieved into a DataWindow, eliminate them from the DataWindow SELECT to increase the retrieval performance.

Don't code redundant error checking. If a check is carried out at one level of the validation sequence, don't repeat it at a lower level.

With each release of PowerBuilder, the developers at Sybase continue to enhance the performance and behind-the-scenes functionality of DataWindows. For example,

- DataWindows use *describeless* retrieves by constructing column lists from the DataWindow structure instead of going to the database interface. This feature is available when you're using Oracle, ODBC, and Sybase interfaces.

- A *rows-to-disk* option allows the retrieved rows to be written to a temporary file for faster subsequent access.

# Summary

This chapter introduced numerous functions and events specific to the DataWindow control and the DataWindow object. You should now understand the difference between the control and the object and how they interact. This chapter also covered the different components of the control: the buffers, events, and functions. You now have a grounding in the functionality of DataWindows, which Chapter 15, "Advanced DataWindow Techniques I," and Chapter 16, "Advanced DataWindow Techniques II," will expand.

**14**

DataWindow
Scripting

# Advanced DataWindow Techniques I

This chapter explores the basic syntax and functions used to query and modify a DataWindow object, and gives some examples of how and where these techniques are used. Chapter 14, "DataWindow Scripting," discusses the direct-access syntax. Some examples in this chapter and in Chapter 16, "Advanced DataWindow Techniques II," show you how to use this access method and how this is used to work as a team with the `Modify()` and `Describe()` functions. Some of your existing calls to `Describe()` and `Modify()` can easily be transformed to the direct-access syntax, often requiring you only to replace the function name with the `.Object` attribute reference and reorganize the quotation marks to convert between the two forms.

# The DataWindow Object

The DataWindow object contains attributes comparable to the DataWindow control's attributes; it also contains objects similar to the controls you place in a window. Before PowerBuilder 5.0, the manner in which these were accessed was a little different, and you may still want to use some of these old functions in the new versions of PowerBuilder. The main reason is that you can bundle multiple attribute changes into one statement, which is more efficiently executed. Some expressions just can't be expressed in the new direct-access format, and you still need to use the `Modify()` and `Describe()` functions that you now have coded.

A specific syntax language is used with the three DataWindow object-description and modification functions: `Describe()`, `Create()`, and `Modify()`. The syntax is usually simple and obvious, but it can border on the stupefying. The `Describe()` function returns strings that consist of this syntax as well as the values of DataWindow object attributes. The `Create()` and `Modify()` functions require only the DataWindow object's attributes as the function's parameters.

---

**Tip**

To obtain a list of the attributes and objects that can be retrieved with `Describe()`, refer to the PowerBuilder help under Properties for the DataWindow Object. Two other great places for finding DataWindow attributes are the Object Browser and the utility tool, DWSyntax, that ships with PowerBuilder.

> **Note**
>
> The DWSyntax utility tool is now located and run within the PowerBuilder 7.0 application. To open it, select the Open toolbar button. You will find the DWSyntax tool on the Tool tab page.

Most actions concentrate on columns in a DataWindow object. This is why giving all columns, especially computed columns, meaningful names is a good practice. Occasionally, the text label associated with a column is acted on; remember that for regular columns, the text label is the same name with a _t appended to the end.

In PowerBuilder, DataWindow functions are generally poor performers. To improve execution speed, you can collect actions into a single string by using a tab character (~t) as a separator for some functions. For example, to hide a column and its associated text, this would be the string:

```
"ss_number.Visible=0 ~t ss_number_t.Visible=0"
```

Any number of actions can be concatenated into one string.

If the value in the assignment is a string rather than a number, you need to embed the quotes to denote a string value. You can do this in a couple of ways, the simplest of which is to use the single quote ('):

```
"start_date.Format='mm/dd/yyyy'"
```

Alternatively, the double quote (") can be used if you first prefix it with an escape character (~) so that it isn't taken as the end of the string:

```
"start_date.Format=~"mm/dd/yyy~""
```

The syntax becomes more convoluted when you need to embed more quotes inside the modification string:

```
"start_date.Format='mm/dd/yy;~~~"None Specified~~~"'"
```

The ~~~" has become something of a legend in PowerBuilder circles. When the concept is understood, there is little mystery. First, you need to think of the whole string as two smaller strings, like this:

```
"start_date.Format="
"mm/dd/yy;~"None Specified~""
```

At this level of quote embedding, you need to use ~" only around None Specified, as you did in the first examples. Now, when you take the second string and embed it into the first, all quotes need to be taken down a level. This means that the string is now enclosed in quotes, either ~" or ' (the two are equivalent). The embedded string needs to become an embedded string. This is where the ~~~" is used. The ~~~" breaks down to a ~~ and a ~", which at the next level up gives a ~ and a ". Then, at the top level, you arrive at the lone quote ("). The escape sequence ~~~" can also be written as ~~'.

Fortunately, there is little need to embed to a level below this, but if you do require such a string, just add ~~ for each level. This equates to the ~ required to escape the following tildes and quote to the next level.

# Using `Describe()` to Find DataWindow Information

To query the DataWindow object for information about itself, use the `Describe()` function (previously known as `dwDescribe()`). The syntax for this function is

`DataWindowName.Describe( AttributeEvaluationList )`

*DataWindowName* can be a DataWindow control or a child DataWindow. The space-separated *AttributeEvaluationList* of attributes or evaluation expressions reports the attribute values of columns and graphic objects. Expressions can be evaluated by using values of a particular row and column.

`Describe()` returns a string containing the values of the attributes and expression results in a newline-separated (~n) list. If an expression or attribute returns more than one item, it does so in a tab-separated (~t) list.

If the attribute list contains an invalid item, `Describe()` returns the results up to that item position and then an exclamation point (!). The rest of the attribute list is ignored. `Describe()` returns a question mark (?) if there's no value for an attribute.

Table 15.1 gives some examples of the `Describe()` function and the result string.

**TABLE 15.1** Examples of `Describe()` Expressions for a DataWindow

| `Describe()` *Expression* | *Result String* |
| --- | --- |
| `"DataWindow.Bands DataWindow.Objects"` | `"header~tdetail~tummary~t footer~nemp_id~temp_id_t"` |
| `"DataWindow.Band DataWindow.Objects"` | `"!"` |
| `"DataWindow Object DataWindow.Bands"` | `"header~tdetail~tsummary~t footer~n!"` |

If an attribute's value would be ambiguous (for example, a string value with an exclamation point, question mark, tab, or newline), it's enclosed in quotes.

The following line returns the string `""Name?""` if the label is `Name?` (note that the quotes aren't `~"` but straight quotes):

```
dw_1.Describe( "l_name_t.Text")
```

When the first value in a list is enclosed in quotation marks, the rest of the list for that attribute is also enclosed in quotes.

An alternative syntax to specifying the column name is to use the column number. Be careful when using this, however, and try to avoid it if possible because the column's number may change on you if you alter the data source. For example, if `l_name` were column six, the `Describe()` function syntax could be

```
dw_1.Describe("#6.ColType")
```

This syntax is more often used with the `GetColumn()` function to retrieve the current column's number, or when you want to step through each column in the DataWindow. For example, the following code could be used to capture each column's data type:

```
Integer li_Column, li_TotalColumns
String ls_Type[]

li_TotalColumns = Integer( dw_1.Object.DataWindow.Column.Count)
ls_Type[ li_TotalColumns] = ""

For li_Column = 1 To li_TotalColumns
   ls_Type[ li_Column] = dw_1.Describe( "#" + String( li_Column) + ".ColType")
Next
```

This particular loop is used in one of the code listings in Chapter 16, "Advanced DataWindow Techniques II."

# Evaluation Expressions

You use the `Evaluate()` function from within your PowerScript to carry out the evaluation of a DataWindow expression by using data from the DataWindow. The syntax for this function is

```
Evaluate( 'Expression', li_RowNumber )
```

`Evaluate()` is placed in the attribute evaluation list of `Describe()`. *Expression* is a DataWindow function or logical operation to be evaluated, and *li_RowNumber* indicates the row within the DataWindow on which to evaluate the expression. For example, to evaluate an `If` statement that checks the field `print_upside_down` for row two and returns 1 or 0, the code is

```
ls_Return = dw_1.Describe("Evaluate('If(print_upside_down = ~"T~", 1, 0)', 2)")
```

`Evaluate()` executes functions unique to the DataWindow painter and can't otherwise be accessed from PowerScript.

## Obtaining the Display Value from a Code Table

One function that can't be called directly from PowerScript but can be included in an `Evaluate()` expression is `LookUpDisplay()`. With this function, you can obtain the display value from a code table or a drop-down DataWindow. If the column uses a code table, users see the value from the display column, and `GetItem` functions (or direct-access syntax) return the data value. The syntax is

```
LookUpDisplay( Column)
```

`Column` used in the `LookUpDisplay()` expression is the actual column name, not a string containing the column name. The function returns the display value or an empty string if an error occurs.

A drop-down DataWindow maintains a code table similar to a developer-generated code table attached to a simple edit. The following example queries a drop-down DataWindow column, `service_rep`, on row one of the control `dw_header`, for the name (display value) associated with the code (data value):

```
ls_ServiceRep = dw_header.Describe( "Evaluate ('LookUpDisplay( serv_rep)', 1)")
```

> **Tip**
>
> The `LookUpDisplay()` function is useful not only in your code but also in computed columns on your DataWindow object. If you want the display value of a column referenced in a computed column rather than the data value, just use `LookUpDisplay()`.

# Using `Modify()` to Modify DataWindow Information

One way to make runtime modifications to DataWindow object attributes is to use the `Modify()` function rather than the direct-access syntax. This is the syntax for the function:

```
DataWindowControl.Modify( ModificationString )
```

DataWindow objects can have their appearance, behavior, and database information changed at runtime by using the appropriate syntax. You can even create and destroy objects within the DataWindow object by providing the complete specifications for the objects. `DataWindowControl` can be a DataWindow control or a child DataWindow object.

`Modify()` returns an empty string if the modifications were successful. If an error was encountered in the modification syntax you tried to use, the return value will be in the form `"Line n Column n incorrect syntax"` , where column *n* is the position of the error counted from the beginning of *ModificationString*.

You can specify three types of statements by using the *ModificationString* parameter: CREATE, DESTROY, and attribute alteration. These formats are addressed in the following sections.

## Using `Modify()` to Create Objects

To add an object (such as text, computed fields, and bitmaps), use this syntax:

```
CREATE Object (Settings)
```

*Settings* defines a list of attributes and values for the object to be created; you must provide enough information to define the object.

The best way to get the correct syntax for an object is to export a simple DataWindow containing the object. You can then cut and paste the object's syntax into your application. Another way is to use Sybase's DWSyntax tool, which displays the syntax for specific objects in a DataWindow.

Assume that you've just dynamically created a completely new DataWindow from scratch (how to do this is covered later in this chapter) and you now want to place a corporate logo in the header band. This would be the syntax:

```
String ls_Modify, ls_Return

ls_Modify = "CREATE bitmap(band=background filename='c:\logo.bmp' " &
+ " x='60' y='8' width='1308' height='513' border='0' name=logo)"

ls_Return = dw_1.Modify( ls_Modify)

If ls_Return <> "" Then
   MessageBox( "Logo Creation Failure", ls_Return)
End If
```

This code creates the logo in just the right position for the report DataWindow you just created. Figure 15.1 shows the DataWindow before you create the logo object, and Figure 15.2 shows the final state of the DataWindow.

**FIGURE 15.1**
*The DataWindow before the logo is created.*

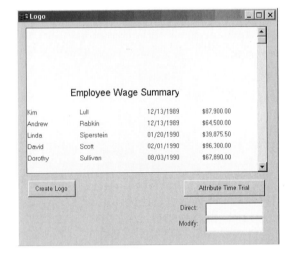

**FIGURE 15.2**
*The dynamically created logo.*

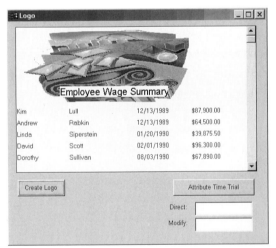

# Using `Modify()` to Destroy Objects

As well as create objects within a DataWindow, you can also destroy objects using the following syntax:

```
DESTROY [COLUMN] Object
```

*Object* is the name of the object in the DataWindow object to destroy. To remove a column and the column's data from the buffer, you need to specify the `COLUMN` keyword. For example, in the preceding section you added a logo to the dynamically created reports. If you provide this as a runtime option—say, via a check box—you need to be able to create and destroy the picture object. This would be the code for the destroy:

```
String ls_Return

ls_Return = dw_1.Modify( "DESTROY logo")

If ls_Return <> "" Then
   MessageBox( "Logo Removal Failure", ls_Return)
End If
```

Here's an example of removing a column and its associated label with this `Modify()` format:

```
String ls_Return

ls_Return = dw_1.Modify( "DESTROY COLUMN salary DESTROY salary_t")

If ls_Return <> "" Then
   MessageBox( "Column Removal Failure", ls_Return)
End If
```

# Attribute Alteration

The last format is probably the most commonly used of the three, but it most likely will be superseded for simple operations by the direct-access syntax. This is the syntax for this format:

```
ObjectName.Attribute=Value
```

Depending on the *Attribute* being affected, the value can be any of the following types:

- Constants are simple value changes of attributes that don't use expressions:

  ```
  ColumnName.Band = Footer
  ```

- Quoted constants are also simple attribute value changes, but for attributes that require expressions:

```
ColumnName.Height = '65'
```

- An expression consists of a default value followed by an expression. It returns values of the same data type as the attribute. Here's an example:

```
ColumnName.Protect='1~tIf(IsRowNew(),0,1)'
```

Note the format of this expression. The whole expression is enclosed in single quotes, and a default value (1) is required and is separated by a tab (~t) from the rest of the expression. The expression returns 0 or 1, which are the valid values for the attribute.

Check online help to determine whether the object's attribute requires a constant or quoted constant; this is indicated by (exp) in the attribute description.

## Using Expressions

As you just saw, one method of changing or even setting a default value in the DataWindow painter is to use an expression. This is the syntax:

```
ColumnName.Attribute='DefaultValue~tExpression'
```

*Expression* can use any DataWindow function and must evaluate to the appropriate data type for the attribute.

When you're setting an attribute using an expression, it's important that the expression be evaluated for each row in the DataWindow. This allows you to set properties for one row without affecting those settings for any other row.

Most expressions that you will build are based on the evaluation of a true/false statement. This is implemented using the DataWindow If function (not to be confused with the PowerScript If...Then construct), which has this format:

```
If( BooleanExpression, TrueValue, FalseValue)
```

*BooleanExpression* can be evaluated to TRUE or FALSE. When the expression evaluates to TRUE, *TrueValue* is returned; when FALSE, *FalseValue* is returned. The return type of If() is whatever the data type of *TrueValue* is, and *TrueValue* and *FalseValue* have to be of the same data type.

*TrueValue* and *FalseValue* can themselves be If() expressions, thus allowing you to nest successive expression evaluations. Here's an example:

```
If (object_color='Red', 1, If( object_color='White', 2, 3))
```

This expression returns 1, 2, or 3, depending on the current value of the column `object_color`.

Boolean expressions also can be constructed by using AND, OR, and NOT operators to provide for elaborate evaluations.

The following are some examples of expressions using the techniques and syntax that have just been introduced:

- Set the salary of a person to red if the person earns more than $80,000; otherwise, leave it black:

  ```
  salary.Color='0~tIf( salary > 80000, 255, 0)'
  ```

- Hide the termination date for the rows that have an active or on-leave status:

  ```
  termination_date.Visible='1~tIf (status = ~~~'T~~~', 0, 1)'
  ```

- Flag a person on his or her birthday if the person's status is active by turning the last name column blue:

  ```
  lname.Color='0~tIf(birth_date=Today() And Status = ~~~'A~~~',16711680,0)'
  ```

An alternative method to evaluating an expression is to use the `Case` DataWindow function. The earlier example to demonstrate the `If` function would be rewritten as

```
Case( object_color When 'Red' Then 1 When 'White' Then 2
     When 'Blue' Then 3 Else 0)
```

# Referencing Relative Rows in Expressions

Occasionally, you will need to build an expression that uses information from another row for an action on the current row. To do this, use a relative position syntax:

```
ColumnName [RelativePosition] RestOfExpression
```

The relative position can be any positive or negative integer. For example, if you wanted to find duplicate customers in your customer table, you could use the following expression for the color attribute of a name field:

```
'0~tIf( GetRow() <> 1 AND lname = lname[-1], 255, 0))'
```

Notice the use of the -1 relative position combined with the GetRow() <> 1 condition. This saves you from having to execute a RowCount() call for each row while checking for the special condition of the last row.

**15**

Advanced
DataWindow
Techniques I

> **Note**
>
> For this example, as for most other applications of the relative row syntax, you will want to sort the data; in this case, you'll sort by the `lname` column.

## Direct-Data Access Versus PowerBuilder Functions

Since the introduction to direct data access, developers have questioned which method is the most efficient. The following time trial was set up to benchmark the two methods. A DataWindow containing a bitmap object was created and placed on a window with a controlling command button and display fields. When clicked, the button executed a 100-iteration loop for the direct access method and then the modify. The bitmap object had the `X`, `Y`, `Width`, and `Height` attributes modified to new values and then back to their original ones. These values were all hard-coded. The time with the redraw left on was approximately 10.7 seconds for the direct access, 3.5 seconds for the modify. Of course, when the screen redraw for the DataWindow was turned off, the efficiency of each method was optimal, and the timing for direct access was .4 seconds and the modify .2 seconds. So don't throw away all your code just yet!

The prior test raises an important issue for developing PowerBuilder applications. The direct-access dot notation is more intuitive and easier to maintain. The DataWindow functions such as `Modify` are more efficient but more cumbersome to write. One approach is to write your initial code by using the more intuitive dot notation. When the code works, convert it to single-line `Modify` statements. After the conversion is tested, you can then create a compound `Modify` statement to get the most efficient process in your application. As you move from one coding technique to the next, comment out the prior code and leave it in the script. This provides an easier mechanism for someone else to maintain your code because he or she can look at the dot notation but still provide the needed speed.

# Filtering Data

To restrict the data displayed in a DataWindow, you can use three methods individually or together:

- You can specify a `WHERE` clause for the DataWindow SQL `SELECT` statement to restrict the rows that the DBMS returns. This is covered in Chapter 4, "SQL and PowerBuilder," and Chapter 6, "The DataWindow Painter."

- You can specify a filter condition by using the `DataWindow.Table.Filter` attribute to restrict the rows placed in the DataWindow buffers. This is covered later in the section "DataWindow SQL Properties."

- You can specify a DataWindow filter expression within the DataWindow or by using the `SetFilter()` and `Filter()` functions to restrict the view of data already in the DataWindow buffer.

The `SetFilter()` function takes a valid string expression that defines the desired filtering:

```
DataWindow.SetFilter( Expression)
```

*DataWindow* can be a DataWindow control, a child DataWindow, or a DataStore object. *Expression* is constructed of columns and DataWindow functions to produce a Boolean value.

`SetFilter()` by itself doesn't cause any action other than setting the new filter for the DataWindow. To actually carry out the filtration, you have to call the `Filter()` function:

```
DataWindow.Filter()
```

When you call this function, the rows not matching the filter expression are transferred from the Primary to the Filter buffer of the DataWindow control. For example, to show only the customers who are in Colorado, you would specify and execute the filter with the following code:

```
dw_1.SetFilter( "state = 'CO'" )
```

```
dw_1.Filter()
```

The filter expression is constructed by using columns, relational operators, functions, and values; you may want to use parentheses to control the evaluation order. For example, to extend the previous filter to include the customer PDD no matter what state in which it appears, this would be the `SetFilter()` expression:

```
"state = 'CO' OR fname = 'PDD'"
```

To reset the filter and return all the rows in the Filter buffer to the Primary, simply call the `SetFilter()` function with an empty string (`""`) and then call `Filter()`.

If you specify the *Expression* argument of the `SetFilter()` function as a string with a NULL value using the `SetNull()` function, PowerBuilder opens the Specify Filter dialog (see Figure 15.3) for users to enter the expression at runtime. The dialog is opened when the `Filter()` function is called.

**FIGURE 15.3**

*The Specify Filter dialog.*

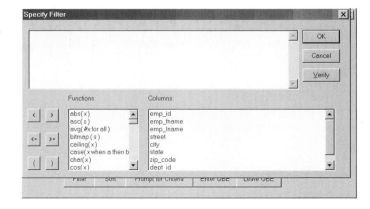

# Sorting Data

To sort the DataWindow data into a certain order, you can also use three methods, again individually or together. They're applied in the following order:

1. Specify an ORDER BY clause for the DataWindow SQL SELECT statement to sort the rows that the DBMS returns.

2. Specify sort criteria by using the DataWindow.Table.Sort attribute to sort the rows placed in the DataWindow buffers. This is covered later in the section "DataWindow SQL Properties."

3. Specify a DataWindow sort expression in the DataWindow or by using the SetSort() and Sort() functions. This sorts the data in the DataWindow Primary buffer.

The SetSort() function takes a string expression that defines the sort criteria desired and has this syntax:

*DataWindow*.SetSort( *Expression*)

*DataWindow* can be a DataWindow control, a child DataWindow, or a DataStore object. *Expression* is constructed of column names with the desired order. If you use SetNull() to create a string with a NULL value and pass that as the *Expression*, PowerBuilder opens the Specify Sort Columns dialog (see Figure 15.4) for users to enter the expression at runtime. Like the filter process, the dialog appears when the Sort() function is called.

Like the filter functions, SetSort() doesn't cause any action to occur other than setting the new sort criteria for the DataWindow. To actually carry out the sort, you have to call the Sort() function:

*DataWindow*.Sort()

This function reorders the rows in the DataWindow to match the sort criteria.

**FIGURE 15.4**

*The Specify Sort Columns dialog.*

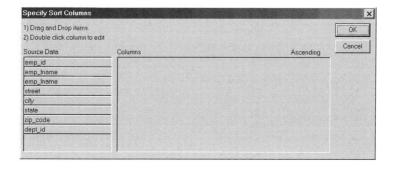

For example, to sort on the employee's last name and then first name, you would specify and execute the sort with the following code:

```
dw_1.SetSort( "emp_lname A, emp_fname A")
```

```
dw_1.Sort()
```

To sort in ascending order, specify A after the column name; for a descending-order sort, specify D (not case-sensitive).

You need to call the Sort() function to place the rows in a sorted order before you use the GroupCalc() function. This function forces a recalculation of the breaks in the grouping levels after you modify a DataWindow's rows. This is the syntax for GroupCalc():

```
DataWindow.GroupCalc()
```

*DataWindow* is a DataWindow control or a child DataWindow. For more on creating group reports, see Chapter 5, "Databases and the Database Painter."

# DataWindow SQL Code

SQL code is the driving force behind most DataWindows, and sometimes you'll need to extract and modify the SQL code that the DataWindow uses as part of its data retrieval and update. In the next few sections, you learn about methods to obtain and alter a DataWindow's SQL code.

## Obtaining the DataWindow SQL Code

One of the most common uses of the Describe() function is to extract the SELECT syntax from a DataWindow so that it can be modified to add or remove conditions from the WHERE clause. The DataWindow stores the SELECT in a special format (called a PBSELECT). You can see this syntax if you export a DataWindow from the Library painter. This is important because if the application isn't connected to a database when the `Describe()` function is executed, the `PBSELECT` statement is returned instead of the true `SELECT`.

The syntax for extracting the SQL `SELECT` can be done one of four ways. You can access the first three directly by using the data-access syntax:

```
ls_Select = dw_1.Describe("DataWindow.Table.Select")

ls_Select = dw_1.Describe("DataWindow.Table.SQLSelect")

ls_Select = dw_1.Describe("DataWindow.Table.Select.Attribute")

ls_Select = dw_1.GetSQLSelect()
```

The value returned for each varies a little (see Figure 15.5). When the DataWindow isn't connected to the database, the first two statements return column names and embedded quotes in tilde quotes. The last two statements return only embedded quotes in tilde quotes. All four display the `SELECT` as a `PBSELECT`. When connected, the first two statements return the true `SELECT`, with embedded quotes in tilde quotes. If the DBMS requires quotes, these are placed in `~"`. The last statement returns the quotes without any tildes, and the third statement still returns the `PBSELECT`.

**FIGURE 15.5**

*DataWindow SQL* `SELECT`*s extracted using the* `Describe()` *function.*

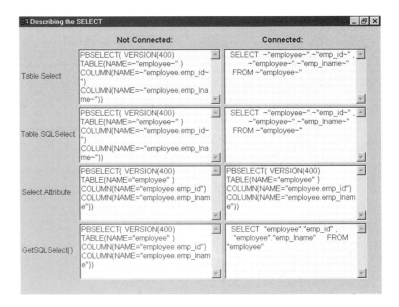

The `Select.Attribute` syntax, used only with `Describe()`, returns a string containing the `PBSELECT` statement for the DataWindow. This is formatted logically with the table name and columns broken out, along with the `WHERE` clause and sorting criteria. You might want to use this if you want to reconstruct the SQL code for some reason. The `SQLSelect` syntax returns the most recently executed `SELECT` statement and can't be set. Most often, the `GetSQLSelect()` function is used to capture the `SELECT` syntax.

# Modifying DataWindow SQL Code

The SQL code obtained by using the methods introduced in the preceding section can then be modified and reapplied to the DataWindow object. As with syntax extraction, a few methods are available for placing the SQL back into the DataWindow: direct syntax, `Modify()`, and `SetSQLSelect()`.

This is the syntax for the `SetSQLSelect()` function:

`DataWindow.SetSQLSelect( SQLStatement)`

`DataWindow` is the DataWindow control or child DataWindow to be modified. `SQLStatement` is a string that defines a valid SQL `SELECT` statement that must structurally match that of the original `SELECT` statement. This means that the same number of columns must be retrieved, with the same data type and in the same order. `SQLStatement` is validated when you call `SetSQLSelect()` only if the DataWindow is updatable. The function returns `-1` if the `SELECT` statement can't be changed and `1` if it succeeds.

If the DataWindow object is updatable and the new `SELECT` statement uses a different table name in the `FROM` clause, PowerBuilder attempts to modify the update settings. PowerBuilder assumes that the key columns are still in the same positions as the original `SELECT`, and it makes the DataWindow not updatable if it runs into the following conditions:

- More than one table is specified in the `FROM` clause.

- A DataWindow update column is a database computed value.

This prevents you from executing an `Update()` function call for this DataWindow object, and you get a runtime `DataWindow Not Updateable` error.

> **Note**
>
> Remember to associate the DataWindow control with a transaction object after calling `SetSQLSelect()` because it loses its reference when executing this function.

The `SetSQLSelect()` function's limitation is that can't be used to modify a DataWindow object's SQL `SELECT` if it has retrieval arguments specified.

You can use the direct syntax to also change the SELECT statement. Here's an example:

```
dw_1.DataWindow.Table.Select="SelectStatement"
```

Using this method (and the corresponding Modify() call) won't cause the SELECT statement to be validated, however, and it won't modify the update properties of the DataWindow. This makes it fast, but you must be careful that the syntax is perfect. You must use either method when the DataWindow has defined arguments.

> **Tip**
>
> Modifying the WHERE clause can be hard enough sometimes, so it's generally a good idea not to specify any additional SQL clauses (such as ORDER BY). This functionality can be implemented within the DataWindow on the client (SetSort() and Sort()).

## DataWindow SQL Properties

As previously mentioned, several SQL properties are associated with a DataWindow and its columns. This section explores each one in turn, and shows you what it is and how to use it:

- DataWindow.Retrieve.AsNeeded determines whether the rows are retrieved into the DataWindow buffer as users scroll the visible portion of the DataWindow downward. This allows users to access the first records of information before PowerBuilder finishes retrieving them all. The value is Yes or No. Here's an example:

    ```
    dw_1.Object.DataWindow.Retrieve.AsNeeded='Yes'
    ```

- DataWindow.Storage reports the amount of virtual storage (in bytes) used by the DataWindow object. This is a property to check whether you allow your users to retrieve large volumes of data (within the RetrieveRow event). Here's an example:

    ```
    Long ll_Storage

    ll_Storage = Long (This.Object.DataWindow.Storage)

    If ll_Storage > 50000 Then This.DBCancel()
    ```

- DataWindow.Table.CrosstabData specifies a tab-separated list of expressions used to calculate the column values for a crosstab DataWindow.

- DataWindow.Table.Filter is the filter expression used by the DataWindow. This filters out records before they reach the DataWindow buffers, whereas SetFilter()

and `Filter()` filter data already in the DataWindow. The filter expression must evaluate to `TRUE` or `FALSE`. For example, you'd use the following to retrieve only items where the state field is set to `'IN'`:

```
dw_1.Object.DataWindow.Table.Filter = "state = 'IN'"
```

- Remember that this applies only to data before it reaches the DataWindow, so if you change this property, you need to retrieve the data afterward for it to take effect.

- `DataWindow.Table.Procedure` changes which stored procedure is used by the DataWindow or the data source to use a stored procedure. For example, you have a stored procedure that selects the same data but from a different database (possibly using different table columns and selection criteria). It could be swapped in using this code:

```
dw_1.Object.DataWindow.Table.Procedure = "EXECUTE sp_customers;0"
```

- `DataWindow.Table.Select`, the SQL `SELECT` statement used as the data source for the DataWindow, is covered earlier in the section "Obtaining the DataWindow SQL Code."

- `DataWindow.Table.Select.Attribute` is a read-only version of the `SELECT` statement and was covered in the section "Obtaining the DataWindow SQL Code."

- `DataWindow.Table.Sort` specifies the sort order of the data before it's loaded into the DataWindow. You use `SetSort()` and `Sort()` to sort data already in the DataWindow. The sort string is specified by column name and direction in a comma-separated list. For example, to sort in ascending order of last name and descending order of state, this would be the expression:

```
dw_1.Object.DataWindow.Table.Sort = "emp_lname A, state D"
```

- `DataWindow.Table.SQLSelect` is a read-only property that returns the most recently executed `SELECT` statement for the DataWindow.

- `DataWindow.Table.UpdateKeyInPlace` specifies the type of SQL update Power-Builder generates if a key column is modified. If the property is `'Yes'`, an `UPDATE` statement is generated to modify the key in place; if it's `'No'`, `DELETE` and `INSERT` statements are generated.

- `DataWindow.Table.UpdateTable` is the name of the table in the `FROM` clause used when PowerBuilder generates data modification statements. You use this property with `ColumnName.Update` to allow updates to multiple tables from a single DataWindow. This is covered in Chapter 10, "Windows and the Window Painter."

- `DataWindow.Table.UpdateWhere` specifies which columns are included in the `WHERE` clause of data modification SQL (see Chapter 9, "Application Objects and the Application Painter," for more information on the settings). The values for this property are Key Columns (0), Key and Updatable Columns (1), and Key and Modified Columns (2). For example, to set the update characteristics to Key and Updatable columns, you use this code:

```
dw_1.Object.DataWindow.Table.UpdateWhere=1
```

As well as DataWindow-wide database requirements and settings, there are also three properties for individual columns:

- `ColumnName.Criteria.Dialog` determines whether PowerBuilder opens the Specify Retrieval Criteria dialog (see Figure 15.6) when the `Retrieve()` function is called. If the column property is `"Yes"`, the column is included in the dialog. `"No"` is the default. For example, to allow specification of the employee's last name, use this code:

```
dw_1.Object.emp_lname.Criteria.Dialog = "Yes"
```

At least one column must be specified with `"Yes"` for the dialog to open.

**FIGURE 15.6**

*The Specify Retrieval Criteria dialog.*

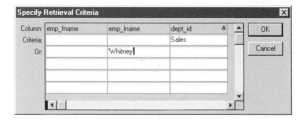

By specifying the criteria users are appending to the end of any existing `WHERE` clause that might be specified for the DataWindow, you might cause conflicts with the conditions already specified, so you will want to provide a DataWindow without an existing `WHERE` clause.

- `ColumnName.Criteria.Override_Edit` controls whether the column edit style should be used for entering data in the Specify Retrieval Criteria dialog. It's also used when the DataWindow is in query mode. If the value is `"Yes"`, the user enters data in a standard edit box. The default is `"No"`, which restricts entry to that edit style. For example, to allow entry in a normal box, this is the code:

```
dw_1.Object.emp_lname.Criteria.Override_Edit = "Yes"
```

- `ColumnName.Criteria.Required` prevents users from specifying operators for a column other than equality (=) and inequality (<>) in the Specify Retrieval Criteria dialog. It's also used when the DataWindow is in query mode. The default (`"No"`) allows users to specify a relational operator in the dialog.

- `ColumnName.Update` governs whether the column is included in the SQL data modification statements. All updatable columns should be in the same table. The value is `"Yes"` for inclusion, `"No"` for exclusion.

The Crosstab presentation style for a DataWindow has some of its own properties that can be looked at and modified:

- `DataWindow.Crosstab.Columns` is a string expression (tab- or comma-separated list) of the column names for the crosstab columns.

- `DataWindow.Crosstab.Rows` is a string expression (tab- or comma-separated list) of the columns to be used as row names in a crosstab.

- `DataWindow.Crosstab.SourceNames` is a string expression (tab- or comma-separated list) of the column names displayed in the Crosstab Definition dialog. This defaults to the column names from the database.

- `DataWindow.Crosstab.Values` is a string (tab- or comma-separated list) that details the expressions used to calculate the values of the crosstab.

DataWindows can be placed in query by example (QBE) mode (see Figures 15.7 and 15.8), which allows users to specify the retrieval criteria by using the DataWindow to enter conditions and values for columns, much like specifying a QuickSelect.

Two DataWindow properties are used to control this behavior:

- `DataWindow.QueryMode` turns QBE mode on or off. When users specify criteria during query mode, this will be used in all future retrievals. The value is either `"Yes"` to place the DataWindow into query mode or `"No"` to disable the query mode. If the query mode is disabled, the user-specified criterion is saved for use in the retrieve. For example, to enter query mode, this would be the code:

```
dw_1.Object.DataWindow.QueryMode = "Yes"
```

- `DataWindow.QuerySort` turns the first line of the DataWindow into a sort specification. Users can specify sorting criteria for the DataWindow if the value is `"Yes"`. If the DataWindow isn't already in query mode, setting `QuerySort` to `"Yes"`

**FIGURE 15.8**
*A DataWindow in query mode.*

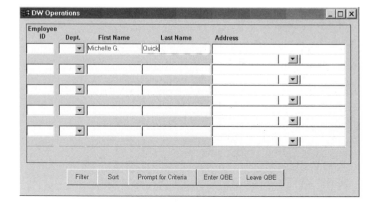

also sets `QueryMode` to `"Yes"`. However, turning off `QuerySort` doesn't turn off `QueryMode`—that must be done as a separate step.

**FIGURE 15.7**
*A DataWindow in normal edit mode.*

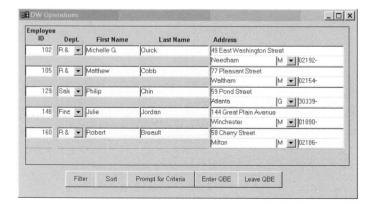

## Note

If you use Query Mode in your application, make sure that it's well documented or that your users are trained on the process because it's not the most intuitive interface.

# DataWindow Stored Procedure Properties

With the support of stored procedures to perform updates in PowerBuilder 7.0, several new properties have been added. This section lists these properties and how they can be used.

Because a DataWindow update can generate an UPDATE, DELETE, or INSERT statement to the database, each might need to associate a different stored procedure to carry out the desired task. In all the following properties, the *action* value will be UDPATE, DELETE, or INSERT:

- *DataWindow*.table.*action*.type is the key to using stored procedures for updating DataWindows:

    dw_1.Object.table.update.type = SP

    The property consists of two possible values:

    | Property | Description |
    | --- | --- |
    | SP | The update, insert, or delete will be carried out via stored procedure. |
    | SQL | The update, insert, or delete will be carried out by using the SQL syntax defined for the DataWindow. |

- *DataWindow*.table.*action*.Method allows users to assign a string that's the name of the stored procedure that should be used with the specified *action*. This procedure is used only if the type property is set to SP.

    dw_1.Object.table.update.method = "sp_update_customer_accounts"

- *DataWindow*.table.*action*.Arguments specifies the values to be passed to the stored procedure as arguments. The following is an example of the format string:

    ("*argname*", *valuetype* { =(" *valuesrc*" {, *datasrc*, *paramtype*})

    *argname* is the stored procedure parameter. *valuetype* contains one of the following values:

    | Property | Description |
    | --- | --- |
    | COLUMN | The argument value taken from the value of *valuesr*. |
    | COMPUTE | The computed field from the value of *valuesrc*. |
    | EXPRESSION | The expression specified in the value of *valuesrc*. |
    | UNUSED | No value is passed to the stored procedure. |

If the *valuetype* was specified as COLUMN, you can specify the values of the *datasrc* and *paramtype*. For *datasrc*, the value NEW is used if you want to use the current value of the column; ORIG is used if you want use the original value retrieved from the database.

**15**

**Advanced
DataWindow
Techniques I**

For *paramtype*, IN (the default) states that the value is being passed in. OUT represents that the stored procedure will return a value and will be stored in the specified column in *valuesrc*. Finally, INOUT represents that the argument will be an input and output parameter.

The following examples illustrate some of the different options:

```
dw_1.Object.Table.Delete.Arguments = ("as_deptid", &
        COLUMN=("dept_id", NEW, OUT))

dw_1.Object.Table.Update.Arguments = ("as_custdisc", &
        COMPUTE=("customer_discount"))
```

# Swapping DataWindows

Often you will want to use a single DataWindow control for many different DataWindow objects—for example, a reporting window, a generic maintenance window, or a DataWindow control placed on top of a tab control that's then used by each tab page. This is achieved by changing the DataObject attribute of the DataWindow control. After you change this attribute, the DataWindow control no longer has a transaction object associated with it; you must issue a new SetTransObject() or SetTrans() call.

> **Note**
>
> If you have a row focus indicator set for the DataWindow, you have to call SetRowFocusIndicator() again after the attribute modification.

If you will be swapping DataWindows and retrieving data into them, it's a good idea to turn off the redraw for the DataWindow control until you have finished. This prevents a lot of messy screen repaints.

In the ancestor DataWindow control, swapping has been built into an object-level method, which handles reconnecting the transaction and resetting the row indicator.

A good use of a generic DataWindow control that's associated with several different DataWindow objects is a reporting window. This window displays a drop-down list of reports from which users can select. When a report is selected, the report displays in a DataWindow control on the window. If you consider some problems of reporting applications, this style application can be useful. With reports, you can easily end up with a different window for each report, adding new reports often results in a redistribution of the whole application, and users have to learn the nuances of different windows to view their reports. The implementation discussed here eliminates these problems by using a single window to populate the report selection list from a database table. The window can be as simple or as complex as you want.

The basic components of the report viewer are two DataWindow controls. The first DataWindow control, `dw_report_list`, contains a DataWindow object (`d_report_list`) displaying one column with a drop-down DataWindow edit style defined for it. This DataWindow is populated from a table containing three columns: `report_id` (a unique sequence number), `report_object` (the name of a DataWindow object), and `report_desc` (a meaningful description of the DataWindow object specified for the `report_object` column). The DataWindow object, `d_report_list`, retrieves the column, `report_object`, and has the drop-down DataWindow object edit style that displays the `report_desc` column and has `report_object` as the data column. By creating `dw_report_list`, you provide your clients with a meaningful list of report names that can be modified and extended simply by accessing a table on your database.

> **Tip**
>
> You can modify the retrieval of the report names based on user security so that users see only the reports that they need.

Now that you have a DataWindow that displays all the necessary reports, you are ready to populate the main DataWindow control, `dw_report_view`. The easiest way to populate this DataWindow is by coding the `ItemChanged` event of `dw_report_list`. The code for the `ItemChanged` event would be

```
dw_report_view.dataobject = data
dw_report_view.SetTransObject(SQLCA)
dw_report_view.Retrieve()
```

This approach assumes that none of the reports has retrieval arguments. All you need to do is populate the `DataObject` property of `dw_report_view`, call `SetTransObject()`, and `Retrieve()`. If you do have retrieval arguments, by default your users will be prompted with the Retrieval Arguments dialog like you find in the DataWindow painter—functional, but not pretty.

To get around this problem isn't really that difficult if you're using the PFC (see Chapter 25, "The PowerBuilder Foundation Class"). The approach I took was to determine whether the selected DataWindow object from `dw_report_list` had any retrieval arguments defined for it. To do this, you need to search the DataWindow object syntax for the retrieval arguments parameter (or `args` parameter if the data source is a stored procedure). Although this is basic string manipulation, it's not the most fun thing to code. The PFC gives you a function (of_DWArguments()) as part of the base DataWindow service that returns two arrays: one with all the retrieval argument names and one with each argument's data types. From these arrays, you can build a SQL statement of computed columns and then generate a DataWindow object dynamically by using `SyntaxFromSQL()`.

# Dynamically Creating DataWindows

To provide ultimate flexibility for your end users, you may want to consider allowing them to create a DataWindow object at runtime. This could be a DataWindow for reporting or even data modification. You can still maintain control over what users create by limiting the tables and columns that can be used.

To dynamically create a DataWindow, you need to use the `Create()` function:

```
DataWindow.Create( Syntax {, ErrorBuffer})
```

`DataWindow` is a control to be associated with the new DataWindow object. `Syntax` is a string that describes the exact syntax (DataWindow source code) to create a DataWindow. `ErrorBuffer` is optionally used to hold any error messages that occur during creation. If you don't specify an `ErrorBuffer`, a message box opens to display the error. The function returns 1 if it succeeds, -1 if an error occurs.

> **Note**
>
> If either argument is NULL, the Create() function returns a NULL.

Because `Create()` replaces the `DataObject` attribute of the control, you need to carry out a `SetTransObject()` or `SetTrans()` call (as you saw in the preceding section).

The first step is the creation of the `Syntax` argument used in the `Create()` call. The source code syntax of a DataWindow is complex and isn't something that you want to try to enter by hand. PowerBuilder provides two functions that create the syntax for you: `LibraryExport()` and `SyntaxFromSQL()`.

# Using Exported Syntax

The LibraryExport() function lets you export a DataWindow object to a textual representation that you can capture. This can then be used as the necessary argument for Create(). This is the syntax for the function:

```
LibraryExport( LibraryName, ObjectName, ObjectType )
```

*LibraryName* is the name of the PowerBuilder library that contains the object to be exported. If the full path isn't specified, the file is searched for, using the system's standard search order. *ObjectName* is the name of the object to be exported, and *ObjectType* is the type of that object. *ObjectType* is a value of the LibExportType enumerated data type. The function returns the object's syntax. It's for use with DataWindows, and a sample call would look like this:

```
String ls_DWSynt, ls_Error

ls_DWSynt = LibraryExport("C:\PB7\UNLEASH.PBL", "d_emp", ExportDataWindow!)

dw_1.Create( ls_DWSyntax, ls_Error)
```

The syntax returned by the LibraryExport() function is the same as that generated in the Library painter, except that it doesn't include an export header. If any argument is NULL, the function also returns a NULL.

> **Tip**
>
> When you have a DataWindow's syntax, you can use the LibraryImport() function and other associated library functions to save the DataWindow to a library for future use. This allows users to create and store DataWindows on-the-fly if you provide the interface to do so.

# Syntax from SQL Code

The other method for generating syntax is the SyntaxFromSQL() function:

```
TransactionObject.SyntaxFromSQL( SQLSelect, Presentation, ErrorBuffer)
```

This function generates the source code required to create a DataWindow based on a SQL SELECT statement. *TransactionObject* is a connected transaction object. *SQLSelect* is a valid SQL SELECT statement string that the DataWindow syntax will be based on.

**15**

**Advanced
DataWindow
Techniques I**

*Presentation* defines the presentation style for the DataWindow, and this is its simplest form:

```
Style( Type = PresentationStyle)
```

*PresentationStyle* can be Tabular (default), Grid, Form (for free-form), Crosstab, Graph, Group, Label, and N-up. *ErrorBuffer* collects any error messages that occur during the function call.

As with `LibraryExport()`, the returned string from `SyntaxFromSQL()` can also be directly passed into a call to the `Create()` function. Here's an example:

```
String ls_SQLSelect, ls_Error, ls_Error2, ls_Syntax
ls_SQLSelect = "SELECT emp_id, emp_lname, emp_fname FROM employee"
ls_Syntax = SQLCA.SyntaxFromSQL( ls_SQLSelect, "Style (Type = Form)", ls_Error)
dw_1.Create( ls_Syntax, ls_Error2)
```

This sample code creates a DataWindow object that uses the FreeForm presentation style to display the `emp_id`, `emp_lname`, and `emp_fname` columns from the `employee` table.

> **Caution**
>
> If the DBMS you use is SQL Server, PowerBuilder can't determine whether the columns are updatable if transaction processing is on. It's assumed that the columns aren't updatable in this case. You should therefore set the `AutoCommit` attribute to TRUE before calling `SyntaxFromSQL()`.

The *Presentation* argument for `SyntaxFromSQL()` can be extended to define other attributes and objects for the DataWindow than just the presentation style. The full format is this:

```
"Style( Type = Value Property = Value ...) &
DataWindow( Property = Value ...) &
Column( Property = Value ...) &
Group( GroupBy_Column1 GroupBy_Column2 ... Property ...) &
Text( Property = Value ...) &
Title('TitleString')"
```

As you can see, you can specify the styles of individual columns, the whole DataWindow, specific areas of the DataWindow, and the text used in the DataWindow.

Table 15.2 shows the properties for the `Style` parameter.

TABLE 15.2 The Properties for the `Style` Parameter

| Property | Description |
| --- | --- |
| Detail_Bottom_Margin | Bottom margin of the detail area |
| Detail_Top_Margin | Top margin of the detail area |
| Header_Bottom_Margin | Bottom margin of the header area |
| Header_Top_Margin | Top margin of the header area |
| Horizontal_Spread | Horizontal space between columns in the detail area |
| Left_Margin | The left margin of the DataWindow |
| Report | Defines whether the DataWindow is a read-only report |
| Type | The presentation style |
| Vertical_Size | The height of the columns in the detail area |
| Vertical_Spread | The vertical space between columns in the detail area |

The properties for the `Group` parameter are as follows:

- `NewPage` indicates whether a change in a group column's value causes a page break to occur.

- `ResetPageCount` indicates whether a new value in a group column causes the page numbering to reset.

The `Title` keyword assigns *TitleString* as the title of the DataWindow object. The properties for the keywords `DataWindow`, `Column`, and `Text` are the standard properties that you would use directly or with the `Describe()` and `Modify()` functions.

To illustrate how all these properties work, the following example builds a free-form DataWindow with a black background, with columns that have green labels (with a transparent background), and data with three-dimensional lowered borders. The top border of the detail band was also modified to give more space:

```
String ls_SQLSelect, ls_Syntax, ls_Style, ls_Error, ls_Error2
ls_Style = "Style(Type=Form Detail_Top_Margin = 100) DataWindow(Color = 0) &
        Column(Border =5) Text (Color = 32768 BackGround.Mode = 1)"
ls_SQLSelect = "SELECT emp_id, emp_lname, emp_fname FROM employee"
ls_Syntax = SQLCA.SyntaxFromSQL (ls_SQLSelect, ls_Style, ls_Error)
dw_1.Create (ls_Syntax, ls_Error2)
```

The resulting window might be familiar to some end users because it looks a lot like a 3270 screen!

You can also use the `Describe()` function or the direct access of DataWindow object attributes to get information that you can then use to reconstruct a DataWindow.

# Sharing DataWindows

Data can be shared between two or more DataWindow controls via the `ShareData()` function. This allows you to use the same data in a different DataWindow without having to duplicate the data and worry how to update from both DataWindows.

There are three categories of data:

- *Static data* is often implemented by hard-coding values into your application as constants, predefined list box values, check box state values, and so on.

- *Occasionally modified data* encompasses system codes (for example, product codes) and is usually associated with database lookup tables.

- With *volatile data*, the values change or are added to multiple times a day (for example, order numbers).

The second and third categories of data are ideal candidates for a drop-down DataWindow, but only the second is truly worth sharing. This is because the volatile data might already have changed by the time users use a secondary DataWindow that has been shared. This is especially so if the data has been cached for applicationwide use and the application is kept open for long periods of time.

There are two types of DataWindow controls in a sharing relationship: primary and secondary. The primary DataWindow actually contains the data within its buffers. Secondary DataWindows are granted access to the data of a primary DataWindow.

Only the data is shared between the DataWindows. This encompasses each buffer as well as the current filter and sort order. Formatting, column placement, and so on are independent for each DataWindow. Because the data itself is shared, modification using any of these functions (or appropriate direct-access syntax) affects the primary and all related secondary DataWindows: `DeleteRow()`, `Filter()`, `ImportClipBoard()`, `Import-File()`, `ImportString()`, `InsertRow()`, `Retrieve()`, `Reset()`, `RowsCopy()`, `Rows-Discrd()`, `RowsMove()`, `SetFilter()`, `SetSort()`, `Sort()`, and `Update()`. In other words, these functions are redirected to the primary DataWindow. This also means that all events associated with these functions are triggered in only the primary DataWindow.

You must make one important consideration before trying to share data between DataWindows. The primary and secondary DataWindows must have the exact same resultset description. This means that they must have the same data types, column names, and column order. `SELECT` statements can vary in the tables and `WHERE` clauses and still be sharable. You can even share with an external data source DataWindow, as long as the columns are defined to be like the expected results.

> **Note**
>
> You need to use the appropriate numeric data type for external source DataWindows. Otherwise, the share will fail.

To turn on data sharing, use the `ShareData()` function:

`PrimaryDataWindow.ShareData( SecondaryDataWindow)`

Call this function for each share you want to make. Neither DataWindow can be a crosstab DataWindow but can be a child DataWindow.

To turn off the sharing between a primary and secondary DataWindow, call the `ShareDataOff()` function:

`DataWindow.ShareDataOff()`

The results of calling this function depend on whether `DataWindow` is a primary or secondary DataWindow. If `DataWindow` is a primary DataWindow, all the related secondary DataWindow controls have their association dropped and are reset. When `DataWindow` is a secondary DataWindow, only its association is dropped and its data cleared.

> **Note**
>
> If you use `ShareData()` from a secondary DataWindow to a new DataWindow, the new DataWindow is then based on the original primary DataWindow. Therefore, when you issue a `ShareDataOff()` for the secondary DataWindow, the new secondary DataWindow doesn't become reset.

# The `DataStore` Object

The `DataStore` object is the nonvisual DataWindow that PowerBuilder developers have been praying for. In earlier versions of PowerBuilder, data stores (more commonly known as *data caches*) were implemented using hidden windows with user objects and DataWindow controls. These data stores were used to cache code tables and lookups and to hold resultsets to allow different presentation styles of the same data. Now when using the `DataStore`, you get not only a nonvisual object but also one that you can extend with variables, events, and functions and even inherit from.

> **Note**
>
> Using datastores is the only way to really make distributed PowerBuilder work by allowing you to easily control and transmit large amounts of data across distributed applications.

The DataStore has only three attributes (all serving the same purpose for the DataStore as they do for a DataWindow):

| | |
|---|---|
| DataObject (String) | The name of the PowerBuilder DataWindow object (for example, d_order_header). |
| Object (dwObject) | The DataWindow object and all its attributes and objects. |
| ClassDefinition (PowerObject) | Specific information about the class definition of the DataStore. |

The DataStore object lets you cache data for your application without consuming any graphics resources. You use the DataStore object much as you would a normal DataWindow, only the setup and initialization are different. Your first step is to declare a variable at the scope at which you want the DataStore to exist (global, shared, instance, local). For example, in the instance variables section of a window, you'd use this:

```
DataStore ids_Departments
```

Then, in the appropriate event, you need to instantiate the object (in this case, the window's Open event) and assign the DataWindow object that you want to associate it with:

```
ids_Departments = CREATE DataStore

ids_Departments.DataObject = "d_departments"
```

You can now do anything (except graphics operations) to ids_Departments that you would to a DataWindow. Here's an example:

```
// Insert a new row into the data store
//
ids_Departments.InsertRow( 0)
//
// Set the dept id of the new row
//
ids_Departments.Object.Data.dept_id[ 1] = li_DeptId
//
// Delete the second row in the DataWindow
```

```
//
ids_Departments.DeleteRow( 2)
//
// Set the sort order to dept_name and sort
//
ids_Departments.SetSort( "dept_name D")
ids_Departments.Sort()
```

The DataStore object provides a useful addition to your data processing tools. An important feature for DataWindows is the capability to cache data to disk, which you can also use with your DataStore objects as well. You may want to consider making an ancestor user object of type DataStore and incorporating many of the same methods you have for your DataWindow ancestor for this.

**Note**

If you want to code any events for a DataStore such as the DBError, you have to create a user object to code the events.

# Summary

This chapter looked at many advanced DataWindow programming techniques that you will need in day-to-day DataWindow development. The Describe() and Modify() functions were introduced, as were the new direct access syntax. With these, you have access to almost any DataWindow attribute. If you aren't sure how to access a specific attribute, consult the PowerBuilder online help under "Attributes for the DataWindow Object" or check the DWSyntax utility.

# Advanced DataWindow Techniques II

This chapter explores some additional advanced DataWindow techniques you can use in your applications. You learn about carrying out data searches, extract object information from DataWindows, and look at a number of reusable and useful functions. DataWindow printing and all the relevant functions are described in depth. Data transfer, the how-tos of drop-down DataWindows, and master/detail relationships round out the chapter.

> **Note**
>
> The examples in this chapter, like those in Chapter 15, "Advanced DataWindow Techniques I," show how direct syntax works with the `Describe()` and `Modify()` functions.

# Finding Data in a DataWindow

A common requirement of end users is the capability to search through large amounts of newly retrieved data. You could give users a way to restrict the data being retrieved, but this can be almost as complex as enabling them to retrieve the data and then providing search capabilities. Restricting data retrieval is covered in other areas of this book; in the following sections, you examine searching based on various criteria and the way in which you can provide end users with a search function.

## The `Find()` Function

The `Find()` function will be at the heart of any search functionality you build for a DataWindow. This function locates the next row, after a given starting row, that matches the specified criteria. You use this syntax with `Find()`:

```
DataWindow.Find( Expression, StartRow, EndRow)
```

You can search on DataWindow controls and child DataWindows by specifying a valid search *Expression* and a *StartRow* and *EndRow*. You can make `Find()` search backward by specifying an *EndRow* that's less than the *StartRow*. The function returns the first row that matches the criteria, or `0` if no rows are found.

*Expression* must evaluate to a Boolean result and is constructed by using column names, data type comparison operators, and Boolean operators. The search is case-sensitive, so you must code your own case-insensitivity into the expression. All DataWindow expressions are constructed in the same manner and follow the same rules. The following code shows some examples of using `Find()` expressions:

```
// Search for an employee without a last name
dw_1.Find( "IsNull( emp_lname)", 1, dw_1.RowCount())
//
// Find any employees who earn more than $50k in department 501
dw_1.Find( "emp_salary > 50000 AND dept_id = 501", 1, dw_1.RowCount())
//
// Find an employee with a last name of O'Connor who starts on 1/1/94
// Notice that we use ~ to escape the following ' so it is placed in the string.
dw_1.Find( "emp_lname='O~'Connor' AND start_date='1/1/94'", 1, dw_1.RowCount())
```

# A Data Search Window

You can use a couple of methods for supplying a scrolling lookup for DataWindows. One method you might have seen is having a series of edit fields appear above the DataWindow for each column you want to search on. Another, and probably the more elegant, method is to use a pop-up window similar to the Find windows of most Windows applications. The advantage of the window over the other methods is that you don't lose any screen space to other controls, the window floats over the DataWindow, and users can move it around as needed. This section describes the latter method in detail.

Figure 16.1 shows the finished dialog window. Table 16.1 lists the controls for the Find dialog. The control property settings in this table refer to the actual properties for the control type listed and the associated value assigned to the control's property.

FIGURE 16.1
*The Find dialog.*

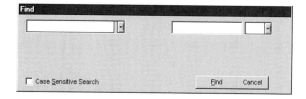

TABLE 16.1   Controls for the Find Dialog

| Control Name | Control Type | Control Properties |
|---|---|---|
| cb_find | CommandButton | Text = "&Find" |
| cb_cancel | CommandButton | Text = "Cancel<br>Cancel = TRUE |
| cbx_case_sensitive | CheckBox | Text = "Case &Sensitive Search" |
| dw_criteria | DataWindow | DataObject = "d_find" VScrollBar = Yes |

The pop-up dialog is called `w_datawindow_find`. It has the following instance variables declared:

| | |
|---|---|
| `il_Row` | A Long value that holds the current position in the DataWindow being searched and is used to continue searches from the previously located value. |
| `is_Types[]` | An array of strings that holds the data types of the columns in the searched DataWindow. |
| `idw_ToActOn` | The DataWindow being searched. |

There will be two main areas of code: in the `Open` event for the dialog and in the `of_Find()` window function. The other pieces of code are quite short and are reactions to user interaction or supporting functionality.

The `Open` event first extracts the DataWindow argument from the `Message` object and assigns it to the instance variable `idw_ToActOn` (see Listing 16.1). The total number of columns in the DataWindow to be searched is ascertained and used to set an upper boundary for the column data type array, `is_Types`. The child drop-down DataWindow for the `column_number` column is captured into a local variable, so you can insert rows for the searchable column information.

**LISTING 16.1** The `Open` Event for `w_find`

```
Integer li_ColumnCount, li_ColumnIndex
String  ls_Column
Long ll_Row
DataWindowChild ldwc_Columns

idw_ToActOn = Message.PowerObjectParm
il_Row = 0

li_ColumnCount = Integer( idw_ToActOn.Object.DataWindow.Column.Count)

dw_criteria.GetChild( "column_number", ldwc_Columns)

is_Types[ li_ColumnCount] = ""

For li_ColumnIndex = 1 To li_ColumnCount
    ls_Column = f_strip( idw_ToActOn.Describe (idw_ToActOn.Describe( "#" + &
             String(li_ColumnIndex) + ".Name") + "_t.Text"))
If ls_Column <> "!" Then
        ll_Row = ldwc_Columns.InsertRow( 0)
        ldwc_Columns.SetItem( ll_Row, "column_name", ls_Column)
```

**LISTING 16.1** CONTINUED

```
        ldwc_Columns.SetItem( ll_Row, "column_number", li_ColumnIndex)
        is_Types[ li_ColumnIndex] = idw_ToActOn.Describe( "#" + &
            String(li_ColumnIndex) + ".ColType")
End If
Next


dw_criteria.TriggerEvent( "NewRow")
```

For each column in the search DataWindow, you need to determine whether it has a label (the only criterion for making a DataWindow searchable), which helps eliminate all those hidden ID and work fields of a DataWindow. When you find a valid column, a row is added to the drop-down DataWindow, and the column's name and number are saved. The column data type is stored in the instance variable array is_Types, using the column number as the index. You then add a row to the main DataWindow, dw_criteria, and await user interaction.

The Clicked events for the check box and the Cancel button are simple. The event for cbx_case_sensitive is of_ResetFind(), and for cb_cancel it's Close (Parent).

The Find dialog's main DataWindow contains only two event scripts: ItemChanged (see Listing 16.2) and NewRow (a user event detailed in Chapter 26, "Building User Objects").

**LISTING 16.2** The ItemChanged Event for dw_criteria

```
Long ll_TotalRows, ll_Index, ll_Return = 0

ll_TotalRows = This.RowCount()

Choose Case dwo.Name
  Case "column_number"
    ll_Index = Long( data)
    If ll_Index > 0 Then
      If is_Types[ ll_Index] <> "" Then
        This.Object.column_datatype[ row] = is_types[ ll_index]
      End If
    End If
  Case "value"
    If Trim( data) <> "" Then
      CHOOSE CASE This.object.column_datatype[ row]
      Case "date"
        If Not IsDate( data) Then
          ll_Return = 1
```

**LISTING 16.2** CONTINUED

```
          End If
      Case "time"
        If Not IsTime( data) Then
          ll_Return = 1
        End If
      Case "long", "ulong", "real"
        If Not IsNumber( data) Then
          ll_Return = 1
        End If
      End Choose
    End If
  Case "join_operator"
    If row = ll_totalRows and Not IsNull( This.Object.column_number[ row] ) Then
      this.TriggerEvent( "NewRow")
    ElseIf Trim( data) = "" And ll_TotalRows > 1 And Row <> ll_TotalRows Then
      dw_criteria.SetRow( Row + 1)
      dw_criteria.TriggerEvent( "DeleteRow")
    End If
End Choose

of_ResetFind()

Return ll_Return
```

The DataWindow's ItemChanged event detects two types of user interaction: a change in the column choice and the addition or subtraction of additional expressions. The first case is trapped to provide feedback to the DataWindow so that the operator drop-down list box can be switched to the correct list for the column's data type. This is achieved by defining three fields: one for numeric operators, another for date and time operators, and the last for string operators. The Visible attribute of each field then is set to display those fields only when the appropriate data type value is in the column_datatype column. The join_operator column controls whether a new expression should be added (if the current row is the last in the DataWindow) or removed (the blank operator was selected). This provides all the control scripts except the actual code that carries out and manages the find—the Clicked event for cb_find (see Listing 16.3).

**LISTING 16.3** The `Clicked` Event for `cb_find`

```
If dw_criteria.RowCount() < 1 Then RETURN

If IsNull( dw_criteria.Object.column_number[1]) Then
    Return
End If

il_Row ++

il_Row = of_Find( il_Row)

If il_Row = 0 Then
    MessageBox( "Data Search", "Unable to find any data matching criteria.")
of_ResetFind()
ElseIf il_Row > 0 Then
    This.Text = "&Find Next"
    idw_ToActOn.SetColumn( Integer( dw_criteria.Object.column_number[1]))
    idw_ToActOn.SetRow( il_Row)
    idw_ToActOn.ScrollToRow( il_Row)
    idw_ToActOn.SetFocus()
End If
```

This script controls the continuation of a search by passing the `il_Row` variable to the `of_Find()` function (covered next). Depending on this function's return value, the script can determine whether a row was found. After a row is found that matches the user criteria, the DataWindow searched is set to the column in the first expression and scrolls to the row so that users are immediately presented with the data requested. The Find button changes its name to Find Next so that users can continue to search for other matches.

The whole search process is achieved by one main and two supporting functions. The `of_Find()` function (see Listing 16.4) generates the expressions that then are used in a call to the PowerScript `Find()` function.

**LISTING 16.4** The `of_Find()` Function for the `w_find` Dialog

```
// private function long of_Find( Long al_StartRow)
//
Long ll_NoOfCriteria, ll_Row, ll_ColumnNo
Integer li_Pos
String ls_Find, ls_Column, ls_Operator, &
    ls_Value, ls_Expression, ls_Join, &
    ls_Format, ls_Value1, ls_Value2, ls_Value3
```

**LISTING 16.4** CONTINUED

```
ll_NoOfCriteria = dw_criteria.RowCount()

For ll_Row = 1 To ll_NoOfCriteria
  ll_ColumnNo = dw_criteria.Object.column_number[ ll_row]

  ls_Column = idw_ToActOn.Describe( "#" + String( ll_ColumnNo) + ".Name")
  ls_Join = dw_criteria.GetItemString( ll_Row, "join_operator")
  If IsNull( ls_Join) Then ls_Join = ""
  ls_Value = ofescapechars( dw_criteria.Object.value[ ll_Row] )

  Choose Case Left( is_Types[ ll_ColumnNo], 5)
  Case "char("
    If IsNull( ls_Value) Then
      ls_Expression = ls_Column
    Else
      ls_Operator = Upper( dw_criteria.object.string_operators[ ll_Row] )
      If Right( ls_Operator, 4) = "LIKE" Then
        If Pos( ls_Value, "%") = 0 Then
          ls_Value = ls_Value + "%"
        End If
      End If
      ls_Expression = ls_Operator + " '" + ls_Value + "' "

      If cbx_case_sensitive.Checked Then
        ls_Expression = ls_Column + " " + ls_Expression
      Else
        ls_Expression = "LOWER( " + ls_Column + ") " + Lower( ls_Expression)
      End If
    End If
  Case "date", "time"
    If IsNull( ls_Value) Then
      ls_Expression = ls_Column
    Else
      ls_Operator = Upper(  dw_criteria.Object. datetime_operators[ ll_row] )
      If Right( ls_Operator, 7) = "BETWEEN" Then
        li_Pos = Pos( Upper( ls_Value), " AND ")
        If li_Pos > 0 Then
          ls_Value1 = Left( ls_Value, li_Pos - 1)
          ls_Value2 = Mid( ls_Value, li_pos + 5)
        End If
      Else
        li_pos = 0
```

**LISTING 16.4** CONTINUED

```
      End If

      If is_Types[ ll_ColumnNo] = "date" Then
        ls_Format = '"yyyymmdd"
        ls_Value = String( Date( ls_Value), ls_Format)
        ls_Value1 = String( Date( ls_Value1), ls_Format)
        ls_Value2 = String( Date( ls_Value2), ls_Format)
      ElseIf is_Types[ ll_ColumnNo] = "time" Then
        ls_Format = "hhmmss"
        ls_Value = String( Time( ls_Value), ls_Format)
        ls_Value1 = String( Time( ls_Value1), ls_Format)
        ls_Value2 = String( Time( ls_Value2), ls_Format)
      End If

      If li_pos = 0 Then
        ls_Expression = "Long( String( " + ls_Column + ", '" + &
                        ls_Format + "')) " + ls_Operator + ls_Value
Else
        ls_Expression = "Long (String (" + ls_Column + ", '" + &
                        ls_Format + "')) " + ls_Operator + &
" " + ls_Value1 + " AND " + ls_Value2
      End If
    End If
  Case Else
    If IsNull( ls_Value) Then
      ls_Expression = ls_Column
    Else
      ls_Operator = Upper( dw_criteria.Object.numeric_operators[ ll_row] )
      If ls_Operator = "IN" Or ls_Operator = "NOT IN" Then
        ls_Expression = ls_Column + " " + ls_Operator + " (" + ls_Value + ") "
      Else
        ls_Expression = ls_Column + " " + ls_Operator + " " + ls_Value + " "
      End If
    End If
  End Choose

  ls_Find = ls_Find + " ( " + Trim( ls_Expression) + ") " + ls_Join
Next

ll_Row = idw_ToActOn.Find( ls_Find, al_StartRow, idw_ToActOn.RowCount())

Return ll_Row
```

This function might seem a little overwhelming at first, but it can be broken down logically into two main parts: the acquisition of an expression's worth of information, and the construction of a numeric, string, or date and time expression from those component pieces.

The first step is to determine whether you can use a cached expression rather than rebuild it each time. If this expression has been reset, you need to create a new Find expression. In this case, for each row in the Find dialog's criteria DataWindow, you need to generate row expressions and then join them.

With each row, you extract the column's name (the name of the column in the DataWindow); the join condition, if any (if there's no join condition, make it an empty string so that you don't create a NULL final expression); and the value users entered for searching. If users don't enter a search value, assume that they enter a function expression for the column name. An example is IsNull (emp_lname), although this obviously requires users to have prior knowledge of the database structure and names, as well as an understanding of PowerScript functions. This is kind of a hidden feature for power users.

Each expression then is constructed based on the requirements of the data type and special operators that can be used. String values must be enclosed in quotation marks, for example, and the LIKE operator uses a percent sign. The date and time expressions are converted into Long values to make the comparison of the values easier.

At the bottom of the For...Next loop, the whole expression is joined to the overall Find string, and each new expression is enclosed in parentheses. After each expression row is analyzed and the Find expression is complete, the actual call to the Find() function is made, starting from the current row in the DataWindow. The returned value then is passed back to the script that called the of_Find() function.

The of_EscapeChars() function (see Listing 16.5) is called from of_Find() to place the PowerBuilder escape character ( ~ ) in front of any characters that would cause a problem in a string.

**LISTING 16.5**   The of_EscapeChars() Function for w_find

```
// Private Function String of_EscapeChars( String as_Value)

Char lc_Char
Integer li_Length, li_Pos

li_Length = Len( as_Value)

For li_Pos = li_Length To 1 Step -1
    lc_Char = Mid( as_Value, li_Pos, 1)
    Choose Case lc_Char
```

*Advanced DataWindow Techniques II*

CHAPTER **16**

621

16

Advanced
DataWindow
Techniques II

**LISTING 16.5** CONTINUED

```
        Case "~t", "~r", "~n", '"', "'", "~~"
            as_Value = Replace( as_Value, li_Pos, 1, "~~" + lc_Char)
    End Choose
Next

Return Trim( as_Value)
```

The `of_EscapeChars()` function is straightforward and should require no commentary, except that the string is parsed backward (enabling you to add to the string without having to alter your position in it), and the escape character `~~` is inserted into the string.

The `of_ResetFind()` function is used in a couple of scripts and simply resets the Find dialog, so it has to generate a completely new expression and search from the start of the DataWindow:

```
// private subroutine of_ResetFind();
//
il_Row = 0
cb_find.Text = "&Find"
```

These lines of code that have been introduced for the various events and functions provide a completely flexible method for providing end-user search capabilities for large resultsets.

# Drop-Down DataWindow Scrolling Lookup

The list box controls available in a window provide the standard behavior of scrolling to the first occurrence within the list in which the first letter matches a typed letter. This section explores the simple code required to provide full word matching, as well as suggestions of the complete value for a DataWindow.

The complete functionality is contained in a single DataWindow event, `LookupDDDW` (see Listing 16.6), which is a custom user event. This function handles only string values because it's unlikely that you'll want to carry out scrolling lookups on any other data type. You easily can expand it for numeric columns if you need that capability.

**LISTING 16.6** The `LookupDDDW` Event

```
String ls_Value, ls_FoundValue, ls_ColumnName, ls_DDDWColumnName, ls_ColumnType
Long ll_Row
DataWindowChild ldwc_Search

ls_ColumnName = this.GetColumnName()
```

**LISTING 16.6** CONTINUED

```
If this.GetChild( ls_ColumnName, ldwc_Search) = 1 Then
  ls_DDDWColumnName = this.Describe( ls_ColumnName + ".dddw.DisplayColumn")
  ls_ColumnType = ldwc_Search.Describe( ls_DDDWColumnName + ".ColType")
  If Left( ls_ColumnType, 4) = "char" Then
    ls_Value = Trim( This.GetText())

    If ls_Value = "" Then
      Return
    End If

    ls_Value = Left( ls_Value, Len( ls_Value) - This.SelectedLength())

    // Case-insensitive search
    ll_Row = ldwc_Search.Find( "Upper( " + ls_DDDWColumnName + ") &
            LIKE Upper( '" + ls_Value + "%')", 1, ldwc_Search.RowCount())

    If ll_Row > 0 Then
      ls_FoundValue = ldwc_Search.GetItemString( ll_Row, ls_DDDWColumnName)
      This.SetText( ls_FoundValue)
      This.SelectText( Len( ls_Value) + 1, Len( ls_FoundValue))

      ldwc_Search.ScrollToRow( ll_Row)
      ldwc_Search.SelectRow( ll_Row, TRUE)
    End If
  End If
End If
```

The script starts by ascertaining several facts about the drop-down DataWindow (initially, that the column is indeed a drop-down DataWindow). The current value of the DataWindow's edit field is captured. Because you will be providing a scrolling lookup that replaces the value being typed, you also will highlight the untyped portion of the value. This enables users to keep typing to replace the value with additional letters, which are, in turn, searched on.

The actual search is carried out by using the unselected part of the value, which already has been passed through the Upper() function to provide a non-case-sensitive search. The column name then is built into the construction with the Like operator and a percent (%) wildcard indicator. If a matching value is found, the edit control is set to this value, and the untyped part is highlighted. The DataWindow child then is scrolled to the appropriate row, and the row is highlighted.

The `LookupDDDW` event is called from within another user event, `Key`, which is mapped to the PowerBuilder `pbm_dwnkey` message ID:

```
If Key <> KeyBack! And Key <> KeyEnter! Then
   This.PostEvent( "LookupDDDW" )
End If
```

This event then posts a message to `LookupDDDW`, which gives PowerBuilder time to process the keystroke. You don't want to perform a search on two special conditions: when the key is a backspace and when users accept the value by pressing Enter. You probably will want to build this event into an ancestor DataWindow object for reuse throughout your application development.

PowerBuilder also lets you search for other conditions within a DataWindow instead of just on the data within it.

# Autoscrolling DataWindow Drag-and-Drop

A nice little feature to give users is the capability to scroll automatically within a DataWindow while carrying out a drag-and-drop operation. This task is fairly simple and requires a timer to check where users place the pointer.

Within the window, you need to turn off the timer by placing a `Timer(0)` statement in the `DragDrop` event. This is when users actually release the dragged object. The only other code required in the window is within the actual `Timer` event, which you use to trigger the custom event `ScrollOnDrag` of the DataWindow control. The code for this follows:

```
dw_1.Trigger Event ScrollOnDrag()
```

The workhorse of this functionality is in the DataWindow control's `ScrollOnDrag` event (see Listing 16.7). This event checks the current position of the mouse pointer against the DataWindow control's boundaries and scrolls the DataWindow one page in the desired direction.

**LISTING 16.7**   The `ScrollOnDrag` Event

```
jmqInteger li_Y

li_Y = PointerY()

If li_Y < This.Y Then
   This.ScrollPriorPage()
End If

// Fudge factor of 150! This allows for the cursor
```

**LISTING 16.7**  CONTINUED

```
// height to be taken into consideration when it
// leaves the dw - otherwise we won't detect it!

If li_Y > This.Y + This.Height - 150 Then
   This.ScrollNextPage()
End If

Timer( 0.1)
```

Two other events require code: the DragDrop event, which turns off the timer because users have stopped the operation, and the DragLeave event, which makes the initial call to the ScrollOnDrag event (this is at the start of the drag-and-drop operation).

# Required Fields

Before you enable users to save the data from a DataWindow, you need to check whether all the required fields have data entered in them. Checking this prevents the database from rejecting an attempted save, especially when you've matched your required fields with the table's NOT NULL columns. By forcing users to enter these values, you don't generate unnecessary network or database management system (DBMS) use. You also don't have to trap the error message from the DBMS for this case; thus, you get a much cleaner and friendlier user interface.

PowerBuilder provides the FindRequired() function to help you carry out this check. This function has the following syntax:

```
DataWindow.FindRequired( dwBuffer, Row, ColumnNumber, ColumnName, UpdateOnly)
```

*dwBuffer* specifies which of the DataWindow's buffers you want to check; it can be Primary! or Filter!. *Row* and *ColumnNumber* specify the first row and column to start searching on. These two arguments, along with *ColumnName*, are passed by reference to the function; the function then uses these arguments to return information on the first required field that has a NULL value. The *UpdateOnly* parameter enables you to boost the performance of the function by requiring it to check only modified columns and inserted rows (TRUE) instead of every row and column (FALSE). This function can be used only with DataWindow controls.

---

**Note**

You can make a column required by using the DataWindow Painter. Just bring up the column's properties and go to the Edit tab page.

---

The code shown in Listing 16.8 is built as a DataWindow object-level function; it returns TRUE or FALSE to indicate whether all the required columns have values.

**LISTING 16.8**  The `CheckRequiredFields()` Object-Level Function

```
Integer li_Column = 1
Long ll_Row = 1
String ls_Column


// Ensure that the last data entry has been accepted into the DataWindow
If This.AcceptText() = -1 Then
   // Problem on the last edit-return focus to the DataWindow so the user
   // can fix it.
   This.SetFocus()
   Return FALSE
End If


// Find the first empty row and column
If This.FindRequired( Primary!, ll_Row, li_Column, ls_Column, TRUE) < 0 Then
   // Search error
   Return FALSE
End If


// Was a row found with a missing value?
If ll_Row <> 0 Then
   // Get the label for the column
   ls_Column = This.Describe( ls_Column + "_t.Text")

   // Indicate problem field
   MessageBox( "Required Value Missing", &
             "You must enter a value for '" + ls_Column + ".", StopSign!, OK!)

   // Make the problem field the current one
   This.SetColumn( li_Column)
   This.ScrollToRow( ll_Row)
   This.SetFocus()
   Return FALSE
End If


// Return success if all rows and columns have data
Return TRUE
```

The `CheckRequiredFields()` function would be called from within the save event script for the DataWindow. Here's an example:

```
If This.CheckRequiredFields() Then
   This.Update()
End If
```

By using the `CheckRequiredFields()` function, you avoid any DBMS-generated errors for columns that have to be NOT NULL. By also providing this function in an ancestor DataWindow object, you need to code it only once.

> **Tip**
>
> The PowerBuilder Foundation Class (PFC) includes a required column DataWindow service in the `n_cst_dwsrv_reqcolumn` object that you might want to explore. Chapter 25, "The PowerBuilder Foundation Class," covers the PFC in more detail.

> **Note**
>
> You easily can extend the `CheckRequiredFields()` function to search the Filter buffer also. Of course, you must provide a means to display any problem rows to users by moving or copying them out of the Filter buffer.

## Group Changes

If you have a DataWindow that uses required fields groups, you can search the groups by using `FindGroupChange()`. This function enables you to locate rows within the DataWindow—possibly for additional processing or focus. The syntax for this function follows:

```
DataWindow.FindGroupChange( Row, Level)
```

*DataWindow* can be a DataWindow control or child DataWindow that you want to search. *Row* specifies in which row to start searching for the break (a group break occurs when the value of a column defined for a group changes from one row to the next). The *Level* argument specifies the group-level number you want to search within (groups are numbered in the order in which you defined them).

FindGroupChange() returns the number of the row in which the change occurred and 0 if no value in the group changed. The return value also conforms to the following rules:

- If *Row* is the first row of a group, the returned row is *Row*.

- If *Row* is a row within a group (other than the last), the returned row is the first row of the next group.

- If *Row* is within the last group, the returned row is 0.

To use the FindGroupChange() function, you need to set *Row* to 0 and then continue to increment this value to find subsequent groups until you find the one you want. To find an inclusive range of rows that match a certain criterion, for example, you could use the code in Listing 16.9. This simple example illustrates using FindGroupChange() within a loop and capturing the group's start and end row numbers.

**LISTING 16.9**  The Use of the FindGroupChange() DataWindow Function

```
Boolean lb_Found = FALSE
Long ll_Row, ll_StartRow = -1, ll_EndRow

Do While Not lb_Found
    ll_Row = dw_1.FindGroupChange( ll_Row, 1)

    // If no breaks are found or error then exit the loop
    If ll_Row <= 0 Then Exit

        // Group break found-is it the one we are looking for?
        If dw_1.GetItemNumber( ll_Row, "manager_id") = 1293 Then
        ll_StartRow = ll_Row
    ElseIf ll_StartRow <> -1 Then
        ll_EndRow = ll_Row - 1
        lb_Found = TRUE
    End If

    // Increment row to find next group break
    ll_Row ++
Loop

If lb_Found Then
    // Processing for Manager 1293 occurs here based on the rows ll_StartRow to
    // ll_EndRow inclusive
Else
    MessageBox( "Data Not Found", "The requested manager was not found!")
End If
```

# Printing DataWindows

PowerBuilder provides two functions to print a DataWindow. There are actually three ways to print, but the third method requires you to code your own `print` function that uses PowerBuilder's low-level `print` functions. Of course, you don't use that approach except in rare cases. You have access to composite reports that remove almost all need to resort to these functions.

Before venturing into the PowerBuilder `print` functions, you need to understand the following terms:

- Similar to a screen cursor, a *print cursor* is used when you open a print job to keep track of the current print location. The print cursor points to the top-left corner of the location where the next object will be printed on the page.

- The *print area* is the available space on the printer's page, not counting the margins. The margins can be altered for DataWindows, but you have to use the `PrintSend()` function to send printer-defined escape sequences to alter the margins for any other print job.

## Starting a Print Job

The `PrintOpen()` function opens a print job and assigns it a unique number that's used as an argument to other print functions. When you call `PrintOpen()`, the currently active window in the application is disabled. This is done so that Windows can handle the printing request because the currently active window is assigned as the parent of a new window. This means that if you try to open a window—for example, a message box—after calling `PrintOpen()`, another application is assigned as the parent of the message box and becomes active. This can cause some confusing behavior for end users. The syntax for `PrintOpen()` follows:

```
PrintOpen( { JobName})
```

`PrintOpen()` returns a Long value for the job number and `-1` if an error occurs. You have the option of naming the print job; this is the name that appears in the print queue.

When a new print job is started, the font is set to the printer's default, and the print cursor is positioned at the top-left corner of the print area.

At the end of the print job, you must close the job and allow PowerBuilder and Windows to clean up the resources used. It's therefore advisable to close the print job in the same event in which you open it.

# Closing a Print Job

You can use two functions to close a print job. The `PrintClose()` function sends the current page to the print spool and closes the job:

```
PrintClose( PrintJobNumber)
```

The `PrintCancel()` function cancels the print job and causes the spool file to be deleted. You can use this function with the `PrintDataWindow()` or `Print()` function. The syntax for use with `PrintDataWindow()` follows:

```
DataWindowControl.PrintCancel()
```

The syntax for use with `Print()` follows:

```
PrintCancel( PrintJobNumber)
```

> **Caution**
>
> `PrintClose()` and `PrintCancel()` are mutually exclusive. You can't and shouldn't call one after the other.

# The `PrintDataWindow()` Function

The `PrintDataWindow()` function prints the contents of a DataWindow control as a single print job. PowerBuilder uses the fonts and layout as they appear in the `DataWindow` object. You can use this function to print multiple DataWindows in one print job. Unfortunately, each `DataWindow` control starts printing on a new page, so if you require a sequence of DataWindows to print on one page, you need to use the low-level print functions or the new composite DataWindow presentation style. The syntax for the `PrintDataWindow()` function follows:

```
PrintDataWindow( PrintJobNumber, DataWindow)
```

*PrintJobNumber* is the Long data type returned by the `PrintOpen()` function that's used to identify a particular print job. *DataWindow* can be a DataWindow control or a child DataWindow. The `PrintDataWindow()` function can't be used with any functions other than `PrintOpen()` and `PrintClose()`.

> **Note**
>
> The `PrintDataWindow()` function is a little unstable and doesn't work well with the `DataStore` object or when screen redraws have been turned off.

This code uses these functions to print four DataWindows as a single print job:

```
Long ll_JobNumber

ll_JobNumber = PrintOpen( "Example Print-4 DataWindows")

// Remember-Each DataWindow will print on separate pages
PrintDataWindow( ll_JobNumber, dw_1)
PrintDataWindow( ll_JobNumber, dw_2)
PrintDataWindow( ll_JobNumber, dw_3)
PrintDataWindow( ll_JobNumber, dw_4)

PrintClose( ll_JobNumber)
```

Occasionally, you will need to make the page numbering between these DataWindows contiguous—unless, of course, you're using PowerBuilder's composite reports. Use a DataWindow expression with access to global functions to accomplish this task. First, declare a global Long (or Integer) variable for the application. Next, write a one-line function that returns this global variable. Then, for each computed field, in each DataWindow that calculates the current page number, add the value returned from the global function:

```
page() + f_global_page_no()
```

Finally, in the `PrintEnd` event of each DataWindow, increment the global variable by the amount in the computed column for the last row.

## The `Print` Function

The other function you can use to print a DataWindow is `Print()`. You can use this general-purpose function to print a wide variety of objects in addition to DataWindows.

The first syntax is used with DataWindows:

```
DataWindowControl.Print( { DisplayCancelDialog})
```

The DataWindow to be printed can be a DataWindow control or a child DataWindow. *DisplayCancelDialog* is an optional Boolean that, if TRUE, causes a nonmodal Print Cancel dialog to appear that enables users to stop the print job. This version of the function

*Advanced DataWindow Techniques II*

CHAPTER 16

631

16

Advanced
DataWindow
Techniques II

handles the creation and destruction of a print job and doesn't require the use of `PrintOpen()` and `PrintClose()`. For this reason, you can't batch multiple DataWindows into one print job unless you're using PowerBuilder's composite report style. The other versions of the `Print()` function require you to manage the print job programmatically.

> **Note**
>
> There's another subtle difference between `Print()` and `PrintDataWindow()`. `PrintDataWindow()` uses the current printer defaults as it prints and not, like `Print()`, the print specifications you set within the DataWindow object. If you have the DataWindow set up to print in landscape mode, for example, and use `PrintDataWindow()` when the current printer is set up for portrait mode, your DataWindow will print in portrait mode.

The second syntax is used to print a particular object—a window or any control you can place on a window—to a specific region of the print area:

```
ObjectName.Print( PrintJobNumber, XLocation, YLocation {, Width, Height})
```

*XLocation* and *YLocation* control the coordinates of the object's left corner and are measured in thousandths of an inch. You can use the optional parameters *Width* and *Height* to resize the object in the print area; they also are measured in thousandths of an inch.

When a new line is started, the X coordinate is reset to 0, and the Y coordinate is incremented by 1.2 times the character height by default. You can modify the line spacing by using the `PrintSetSpacing()` function, which enables you to set a new multiplication factor:

```
PrintSetSpacing( PrintJobNumber, SpacingFactor)
```

The third syntax is used to print lines of text to the print job. With this syntax, you can control the starting horizontal position of each line as well as the horizontal position of the following line:

```
Print( PrintJobNumber, { Position1, } Text {, Position2})
```

*Position1* specifies, in thousandths of an inch, the distance from the left edge of the print area where the text should start. If this value isn't greater than the current position, the text is printed from the current position. *Position2* specifies the position to which the print cursor should move after printing the text. The print cursor moves only if it's not already beyond this point. If *Position2* is omitted from the syntax, the print cursor moves to the start of the next line. If the text contains carriage returns and newlines, the string is printed on multiple lines, but the positioning values are ignored.

> **Note**
>
> Because this syntax automatically increments the position down the page each time a line is created, it also handles all page breaks automatically.

You can use two additional print functions with `Print()`'s third syntax to specify the font to be used when printing a string: `PrintDefineFont()` and `PrintSetFont()`.

`PrintDefineFont()` creates a new font definition for an existing printer font, which then can be used in calls to the `PrintSetFont()` and `PrintText()` functions. Its syntax follows:

```
PrintDefineFont( PrintJobNo, FontNo, FaceName, Height, Weight, FontPitch, &
                 FontFamily, Italic, Underline)
```

*FontNo* can be a number from 1 to 8 that uniquely identifies the font. *FaceName* is a string that contains the name of a printer-supported typeface (for example, Prestige 20Cpi). The *Height* of the font is specified in thousandths of an inch. *Weight* is the *stroke weight* (how thick the characters are) of the type—bold is 700, and normal is 400. *FontPitch* and *FontFamily* are enumerated types that further define the font styling. *FontPitch* can be `Default!`, `Fixed!`, or `Variable!`. *FontFamily* can be `AnyFont!`, `Decorative!`, `Modern!`, `Roman!`, `Script!`, or `Swiss!`. *Italic* and *Underline* are Booleans that specify whether the font should be italicized or underlined, respectively.

> **Note**
>
> Microsoft Windows uses the *FontFamily* parameter of `PrintDefineFont()`, with the font name, to identify the desired font or to substitute a similar font if it's not found.

You can use the `PrintSetFont()` function to make a previously defined font number the current font for the open print job:

```
PrintSetFont( PrintJobNumber, FontNo)
```

The following code shows an example of creating and using a font based on the Prestige 20Cpi font, 10-point, bold, and underlined specifications.

*Advanced DataWindow Techniques II*

CHAPTER 16

633

16

Advanced
DataWindow
Techniques II

```
Long ll_Job

ll_Job = PrintOpen( "A test")
PrintDefineFont( ll_Job, 1, "Prestige 20Cpi", -10, 700, Default!, AnyFont!, &
                 FALSE, TRUE)
PrintSetFont( ll_Job, 1)
```

## DataWindow Print Events

When the Print() function is used on a DataWindow, a PrintStart event is triggered. This event occurs before anything is sent to the print spool.

A PrintPage event is triggered before each page is formatted and sent to the print spool. Within this event, you can force the page to be skipped by setting the return code to the following:

| | |
|---|---|
| 0 | Processes the page normally (the default) |
| 1 | Skips the current page |

The PrintEnd event is triggered at the end of the print job.

These events enable you to carry out specific printing requirements that can't be addressed from the Printer Setup dialog or through the DataWindow objects.

## Building a DataWindow Print Preview Dialog

The Print dialog has become common across most commercial applications, and most such dialogs have many similar features and settings. PowerBuilder is no exception and provides a nice Print dialog (see Figure 16.2).

**FIGURE 16.2**
*The Print dialog.*

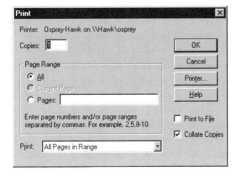

Table 16.2 lists all the available print attributes.

**TABLE 16.2** print Attributes for DataWindow Objects

| Attribute | Value | Specifies |
|---|---|---|
| Collate | Yes<br>No (default) | Whether printing is collated |
| Color | 1 (Color)<br>2 (Monochrome) | Whether the printed output will be color or monochrome |
| Columns | 1 (Default) | The number of newspaper-style columns the DataWindow will print on a page |
| Columns.Width | | The width of the newspaper-style columns in DataWindow units |
| Copies | | The number of copies to print |
| DocumentName | | The name to appear in the print queue |
| Duplex | 1 (Simplex)<br>2 (Horizontal)<br>3 (Vertical) | The orientation of the printed output |
| FileName | | The name of the file to which you want to print the report |
| Margin.Bottom | | The width, as an integer, of the bottom margin on the printed page in DataWindow units |
| Margin.Left | | The width, as an integer, of the left margin on the printed page in DataWindow units |
| Margin.Right | | The width, as an integer, of the right margin on the printed page in DataWindow units |
| Margin.Top | | The width, as an integer, of the top margin on the printed page in the units specified for the DataWindow |
| Orientation | 1 (Landscape)<br>2 (Portrait)<br>0 (Use Default) | The print orientation |
| Page.Range | | The numbers of the pages you want to print (as a string separated by commas); you also can specify a range with a dash |
| Page.RangeInclude | 0 (Print All)<br>1 (Print Even Pages)<br>2 (Print Odd Pages) | As an integer, which pages to print within the desired range |
| Paper.Size | 0 (Default)<br>1 (Letter)<br>(more values exist than listed here; the range is 0 to 41) | The size of the paper to be used for output |

TABLE **16.2**   print Attributes for DataWindow Objects

| Attribute | Value | Specifies |
|---|---|---|
| Paper.Source | 0 (Default)<br>1 (Upper)<br>2 (Lower)<br>3 (Middle)<br>4 (Manual)<br>5 (Envelope)<br>6 (Envelope Manual)<br>7 (Auto)<br>8 (Tractor)<br>9 (Smallfmt)<br>10 (Largefmt)<br>11 (Largecapacity)<br>14 (Cassette) | The paper bin to use |
| Preview | Yes<br>No (default) | Whether the DataWindow object is displayed in preview mode |
| Preview.Rulers | Yes<br>No (default) | Whether rulers are displayed when the DataWindow object is displayed in preview mode |
| Preview.Zoom | 100 (default) | The zoom factor, as an integer, of the print preview |
| Prompt | Yes (default)<br>No | Whether a prompt appears before the job prints so that users can cancel the print job |
| Quality | 0 (Default)<br>1 (High)<br>2 (Medium)<br>3 (Low)<br>4 (Draft) | Quality of the print job Specifies the scale of the printed output as a percentage |

Be aware of some additional considerations when printing:

| Collate | Collating is usually slower than the regular print operation because the print is repeated to produce collated sets. |
|---|---|
| FileName | An empty string means send to the printer. |
| Page.Range | An empty string means to print all pages. |

Emulating the Print dialog requires only a few of the attributes shown in Table 16.2. Some are directly influenced by the Printer Setup dialog, to which you will provide access from your dialog. Also, a smaller group of attributes will be used in a Print Preview dialog (which you will create later in this chapter).

The first step is to lay out the dialog window (see Figure 16.3) with the controls shown in Table 16.3. The attribute settings in Table 16.3 refer to the actual attribute for the control type listed and the associated value assigned to the control's attribute.

**FIGURE 16.3**

*The control layout for the Print specification dialog.*

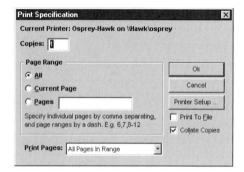

**TABLE 16.3**   Controls for the Print Dialog

| Control Name | Control Type | Control Attribute Settings |
|---|---|---|
| st_current_printer | StaticText | Text = "Current Printer:" |
| st_1 | StaticText | Text = "Copies:" |
| st_2 | StaticText | Text = "Specify individual pages by comma separating, and page ranges by a dash. For example: 6,7,8-12" |
| st_3 | StaticText | Text = "Print Pages:" |
| em_copies | EditMask | Mask = "###" |
| cb_ok | CommandButton | Text = "OK"<br>Default = TRUE |
| cb_cancel | CommandButton | Text = "Cancel"<br>Cancel = TRUE |
| cb_printer_setup | CommandButton | Text = "Printer Setup..." |
| cbx_collate | CheckBox | Text = "Collate Copies" |
| cbx_print_to_file | CheckBox | Text = "Print To File" |
| gb_1 | GroupBox | Text = "Page Range" |
| rb_all_pages | RadioButton | Text = "All"<br>Checked = TRUE |
| rb_current_page | RadioButton | Text = "Current Page" |
| rb_pages | RadioButton | Text = "Pages" |
| sle_page_range | SingleLineEdit | |
| ddlb_range_include | DropdownListBox | Item = {"All Pages In Range", "Even Pages", "Odd Pages"} |

The window is of type Response, is called w_dw_print_dialog, and has two instance variables declared in it. idw_ToActOn of data type DataWindow holds the DataWindow that's passed to the dialog as a parameter. is_FileName of data type String holds the filename if users specify the Print to File option.

There are two main areas of code: in the Open event for the window and the Clicked event of the OK button. The rest of the code is short and results from user interaction or initial setup.

The Open event first extracts the argument from the Message object and assigns it to the instance variable idw_ToActOn (see Listing 16.10). The current default printer is extracted from the DataWindow with a Describe() call on the DataWindow.Printer attribute. The DataWindow current copy count is extracted, and if this is now empty or 0, 1 is assigned to the edit field. The current state of the Collate attribute is extracted and compared inline with the string YES to produce a Boolean value that can be used in the assignment of the Checked attribute. A similar statement is used on the Print to File filename, except that a copy is kept in the instance variable is_FileName.

**LISTING 16.10**  The Open Event for w_dw_print_dialog

```
String ls_Copies

idw_ToActOn = Message.PowerObjectParm

st_current_printer.text = "Current Printer: " + &
                          String( idw_ToActOn.Object.DataWindow.Printer)

ls_Copies = String( idw_ToActOn.Object.DataWindow.Print.Copies)
If ls_Copies <> "" And ls_Copies <> "0" Then
   em_copies.Text = ls_Copies
Else
   em_copies.Text = "1"
End If

cbx_collate.Checked =( Upper(String( &
      idw_ToActOn.Object.DataWindow.Print.Collate)) = "YES")
is_FileName = Trim( String( idw_ToActOn.Object.DataWindow.Print.FileName))
cbx_print_to_file.Checked = ( is_FileName <> "")
```

After users click the Print to File check box, you need to display a dialog in which they can specify the filename and path (see Listing 16.11). The GetFileOpenName() function is used to enable the specification of the print file. (See Chapter 7, "The PowerScript Language," for more information.) A dummy value, ls_File, accepts the filename because you want only the full path and filename. The full path is stored in the instance variable is_FileName, which is blanked out if users uncheck the box.

**LISTING 16.11**  The Clicked Event for cbx_print_to_file

```
String ls_File

If This.Checked Then
   GetFileSaveName("Select Print File", is_FileName, ls_File, &
```

**LISTING 16.11** CONTINUED

```
                    "PRN", "Print Files (*.PRN),*.PRN")

Else
    is_FileName = ""
End If
```

In case users want to specify a page range for the print job, the window automatically sets the focus to the edit field:

```
If This.Checked Then
    sle_page_range.SetFocus()
End If
```

To automatically select the first item in the drop-down list, you need to code a line in the Constructor event, as in this example:

```
This.SelectItem( 1)
```

If users cancel the dialog, you need to close the window and make no other changes. Do this by coding the following in the Clicked event of cb_cancel:

```
Close( Parent)
```

If users want to change the current printer or other, more specific options for the current printer, open the Windows Print dialog. In this dialog, users can change other DataWindow.Print attributes, such as orientation and margins. Users also can change the printer. To catch this, you need to repopulate the static text st_current_printer:

```
PrintSetup()
st_current_printer.text = "Current Printer: " + &
                    String( idw_ToActOn.Object.DataWindow.Printer)
```

All modifications to the DataWindow are made after users click OK (see Listing 16.12). A string, ls_Modify, is built on through the code before being used in a Modify() call. The first part of the string takes the current value from the Copies edit field and concatenates it with the necessary syntax. The Collate check box then is queried, and the value of Print.Collate is set appropriately. The same happens for the Print to File check box. Setting the page range gets a little more involved. To print all pages, the attribute is set to the empty string, and for a specific page range, the value easily is concatenated. To print just the current page, you must execute a call to the Describe() function to evaluate an expression that returns a page number. The Page() DataWindow painter function is used in the expression for the current row and returns the desired page number. The drop-down list box is searched to find the appropriate index, which is decremented by 1 to give the value needed for the RangeInclude attribute. When the modification string is constructed, it's

*Advanced DataWindow Techniques II*

CHAPTER  16

639

16

Advanced
DataWindow
Techniques II

passed into Modify(), and the return value is checked. If Modify() fails, an error window is opened to display the reason. The dialog then closes.

**LISTING 16.12**  The Clicked Event for cb_ok

```
Integer li_Index
String ls_Modify, ls_Page, ls_Return

ls_Modify = "DataWindow.Print.Copies=" + em_copies.text

If cbx_collate.Checked Then
    ls_Modify = ls_Modify + " DataWindow.Print.Collate=Yes"
Else
    ls_Modify = ls_Modify + " DataWindow.Print.Collate=No"
End If

If cbx_print_to_file.Checked Then
    ls_Modify = ls_Modify + " DataWindow.Print.FileName='" + is_FileName + "'"
Else
    ls_Modify = ls_Modify + " DataWindow.Print.FileName=''"
End If

If rb_all_pages.Checked Then
    ls_Modify = ls_Modify + " DataWindow.Print.Page.Range=''"
ElseIf rb_current_page.Checked Then
    ls_Page = idw_ToActOn.Describe( "Evaluate( 'Page()', " + &
            String( idw_ToActOn.GetRow()) + ")")
ls_Modify = ls_Modify + " DataWindow.Print.Page.Range='" + ls_Page + "'"
Else
    ls_Modify = ls_Modify + " DataWindow.Print.Page.Range='" + &
            sle_page_range.text + "'"
End If

li_Index = ddlb_range_include.FindItem( ddlb_range_include.Text, 0)
ls_Modify = ls_Modify + " DataWindow.Print.Page.RangeInclude=" + &
            String( li_Index - 1)

ls_Return = idw_ToActOn.Modify( ls_Modify)

If ls_Return <> "" Then
    MessageBox( "cb_ok", ls_Return)
End If
```

**LISTING 16.12**   CONTINUED

```
Parent.Visible = FALSE

idw_ToActOn.Print( TRUE)

This.SetFocus()

Close( Parent)
```

The dialog is called by using the OpenWithParm() function syntax and takes the DataWindow as the second argument. You also can modify this so that when the dialog is closed, it returns a string with the button's name indicating whether it was closed from the OK or the Cancel button. The calling script then can decide what it wants to do to handle the error.

## Building a DataWindow Print Zoom Dialog

Two of the many nice features of PowerBuilder DataWindows are the print-preview and zoom modes. You access this functionality through some of the DataWindow attributes previously mentioned. To provide a consistent user interface to zoom and preview, you create a reusable window that can be called from any DataWindow-bearing window.

To enable users to specify a zoom value, provide four standard settings—200%, 100%, 50%, and 33%—as well as an area for users to specify an exact value. The interface for this is a group of radio buttons. To the right of the Custom option, an edit mask field with spin-control styling enables users to set a specific value. The spin range is from 1 to 999, with a spin increment of 10. The mask is ### and restricts users to the 1 to 999 range if they enter the zoom value by keyboard instead of by the spin control.

Another feature is the capability to show and hide rulers during preview. The rulers allow users to interactively change the margins for the DataWindow. To turn this feature on and off, use a check box.

The buttons help users make their selections and leave or cancel the window, returning the DataWindow to its original state.

The dialog acts on a DataWindow passed in as a parameter via the OpenWithParm() function, so the DataWindow needs to be retrieved from Message.PowerObjectParm and placed into a window instance variable, idw_ToActOn. In the Open event for the dialog, the Describe() function is used to extract the DataWindow's current state of preview, ruler visibility, and zoom:

```
ls_Describe = idw_ToActOn.Describe( "DataWindow.Print.Preview " + &
```

```
"DataWindow.Print.Preview.Rulers " + &
"DataWindow.Print.Preview.Zoom")
```

By using the string returned, you can set initial states for the radio buttons and the ruler check box. This is done by using a global function, `f_get_token()`, that extracts tokens (see Listing 16.13). This function takes the `ls_Describe` string by reference and returns a string that's the token for which users are searching.

> **Note**
>
> *Token*, a term carried over from compilers, refers to the individual elements of a larger object. In this case, the tokens are the string values separated by spaces.

**LISTING 16.13**  The `f_get_token()` Function

```
// ARGUMENTS:

//    as_Source    (a string passed by reference-tokenized string)

//    as_Separator (a string passed by value-separator between tokens)

// RETURNS:

//    ls_Return    (a string-first token)

Integer    li_Position
String     ls_Return


li_Position = Pos (as_Source, as_Separator)

If li_Position = 0 Then    // if no separator,
    ls_Return = as_Source  // return the whole source string and
    as_Source = ""          // make the original source of zero length
Else
    // otherwise, return just the token and strip it & the separator
    ls_Return = Mid( as_Source, 1, li_Position - 1)
    as_Source = Right( as_Source, Len( as_Source) - li_Position)
End If


Return ls_Return
```

By using the previous trick from the Print dialog, you can compare two strings and return a Boolean for assignment:

```
cb_cancel.Enabled = ( Upper( f_get_token( ls_Describe, "~n")) = "YES")
```

By passing the rest of `ls_Describe` back into the `f_get_token()` function, you get the ruler status:

```
cbx_rulers.checked =( Upper(f_get_token( ls_Describe, "~n")) = "YES")
```

The remaining value is a number representing the current zoom level, which you use in a `Choose...Case` statement to determine the initial state of the radio buttons:

```
Choose Case ls_Describe
   Case "200"
      rb_200.Checked = TRUE
   Case "100"
      rb_100.Checked = TRUE
   Case "50"
      rb_50.Checked = TRUE
   Case "33"
      rb_33.Checked = TRUE
   Case Else
      rb_custom.Checked = TRUE
End Choose


em_custom.Text = ls_Describe
```

The initial value also is set in the edit mask field as a starting point for user modification. The value of the edit mask is set to the appropriate value so that whenever users click a radio button, you have a central location from which the final value can be extracted. The only exception is the custom radio button. Here, you want to move the focus to the edit mask field:

```
em_custom.SetFocus()
```

The Preview button does all the modifications to the DataWindow. In this button's `Clicked` event, a modification string is built to set the values for preview, ruler, and zoom. For optimal performance, all three attributes are built into one string, and `Modify()` is called just once. The value for the zoom level is extracted from the `em_custom` control. The preview state is `Yes`, and the ruler visibility is concatenated onto the end with an `If` statement:

```
ls_Describe = "DataWindow.Print.Preview.Zoom=" + &
em_custom.Text + " DataWindow.Print.Preview=Yes " + &
"DataWindow.Print.Preview.Rulers="
```

```
If cbx_rulers.checked Then
   ls_Describe = ls_Describe + "Yes"
Else
   ls_Describe = ls_Describe + "No"
End If
```

The constructed string then is passed into `Modify()`, and the return value is checked for an error, which then is displayed:

```
ls_Return = idw_ToActOn.Modify( ls_Describe)

If ls_Return <> "" Then
   MessageBox( "Modify() Error", ls_Return)
End If
```

The response window then is closed so that users can see the DataWindow in preview mode. To cancel preview mode, users simply need to reopen this window and select the Cancel Preview button. This sets the preview state to `No`:

```
idw_ToActOn.Modify( "DataWindow.Print.Preview=No")
```

To give access to this window, you can place a command button on the window or run it via a menu option.

# Copying and Moving Data

PowerBuilder provides a set of functions to move or copy DataWindow rows, either within the same DataWindow or to another. These functions, unfortunately, aren't very intelligent and therefore copy a row only if the receiving row's columns exactly match those of the source. The syntax for these functions follows:

```
DataWindow.RowsMove( StartRow, EndRow, SourceBuffer, TargetDW, BeforeRow, &
                     TargetBuffer)
DataWindow.RowsCopy( StartRow, EndRow, SourceBuffer, TargetDW, BeforeRow, &
                     TargetBuffer)
DataWindow.RowsDiscard( StartRow, EndRow, Buffer)
```

The functions `RowsMove()` and `RowsCopy()` act similarly. The only difference is that `RowsMove()` copies rows to the destination DataWindow and then discards (deletes) them from the source DataWindow, and `RowsCopy()` leaves the source rows alone. The *StartRow* and *EndRow* values specify the inclusive range the operation affects in the source DataWindow's buffer, indicated by *SourceBuffer*. The *BeforeRow* value specifies the row before which the new rows appear. Or, if the value is greater than the number of rows now in the target DataWindow, the rows are appended. Rows being moved to a different

DataWindow take on the `NewModified!` status. If the rows stay within the same DataWindow (even if in a different buffer), they retain their status. Here are some examples:

```
// Straight move of all rows from dw_1 to a mirror DataWindow dw_2
dw_1.RowsMove( 1, dw_1.RowCount(), Primary!, dw_2, 1, Primary!)
//
// Then append the rows that have been deleted
dw_1.RowsCopy( 1, dw_1.DeletedCount(), Delete!, dw_2, dw_2.RowCount() + 1, &
               Primary!)
```

### Note

If the same DataWindow is used in a `RowsMove()` or `RowsCopy()` and the value of `BeforeRow` is less than (that is, `RowsMove()` does nothing) or equal to the number of rows in the buffer, you get some strange results. Be careful when moving rows within the same DataWindow.

The `RowsDiscard()` function completely and irrecoverably removes the rows in the inclusive *StartRow* and *EndRow* range from the DataWindow. To enable any row changes to generate INSERTs or UPDATEs but stop any DELETEs, for example, you would use this code:

```
dw_1.RowsDiscard( 1, dw_1.DeletedCount(), Delete!)
```

### Note

`SaveAs()` and `ImportClipboard()` also can be used to move data around, but they provide little benefit over the three functions just introduced.

As mentioned earlier, the copy and move functions just introduced require an exact column match between the source and target DataWindows. With most copy and move operations, this usually isn't the case, and a more intelligent transfer method is required. The function to be built in this section does a "best guess" on the intended column, based solely on the column name (see Listing 16.14).

*Advanced DataWindow Techniques II*

CHAPTER 16

645

16

Advanced
DataWindow
Techniques II

**LISTING 16.14** The `f_transfer_rows()` Function

```
// f_transfer_rows
//
// Parameters:
//     adw_Primary        -the DataWindow to copy data from
//     al_PrimaryStart    -the row to start copying from
//     al_PrimaryEnd      -the row to finish copying from
//     adw_Secondary      -the DataWindow to copy data to
//     al_SecondaryStart  -the row to start copying to
//     ab_CreateNewRows   -whether new rows should be added to the Secondary
//


Long ll_RowCount, ll_PrimaryRows, ll_Difference
Integer li_ObjectCount, li_Count
String ls_Objects[]
dwItemStatus ldw_Status


adw_Secondary.SetRedraw( FALSE)

ll_PrimaryRows = al_PrimaryEnd - al_PrimaryStart

If ab_CreateNewRows Then
  // The +1 is for the correction of the total of the primary rows, ie.
  // al_PrimaryStart = 1 and al_PrimaryEnd = 6, then
  // al_PrimaryEnd - al_PrimaryStart = 5 should be 6, but we use this
  // lesser value later so add the 1 here.
  If adw_Secondary.RowCount() = 0 Then
    ll_Difference = ll_PrimaryRows + 1
  Else
    ll_Difference = ll_PrimaryRows - adw_Secondary.RowCount() + &
                    al_SecondaryStart + 1
End If

  For ll_RowCount = 1 To ll_Difference
    adw_Secondary.InsertRow( 0)
  Next
End If


li_ObjectCount = f_list_objects( adw_Primary, ls_Objects, "column", "*", "*")

For li_Count = 1 To li_ObjectCount
//
// Check there is a 'bucket' to dump data into
```

**LISTING 16.14**   CONTINUED

```
If adw_Secondary.Describe( ls_Objects[ li_Count] + ".type") <> "!" Then
//
// Set data to the first row in the Secondary - Print datawindow
Choose Case Lower( Left (adw_Secondary.Describe( ls_Objects[ li_Count] + &
        ".coltype"), 5))
    Case "char("
      For ll_RowCount = 0 To ll_PrimaryRows
        adw_Secondary.SetItem( al_SecondaryStart + ll_RowCount, &
            ls_Objects[ li_Count], adw_Primary.GetItemString( &
            al_PrimaryStart + ll_RowCount, ls_Objects[ li_Count]))
      Next
    Case "numbe", "long"
      For ll_RowCount = 0 To ll_PrimaryRows
        adw_Secondary.SetItem( al_SecondaryStart + ll_RowCount, &
            ls_Objects[ li_Count], adw_Primary.GetItemNumber( &
            al_PrimaryStart + ll_RowCount, ls_Objects[ li_Count]))
      Next
    Case "decim"
      For ll_RowCount = 0 To ll_PrimaryRows
        adw_Secondary.SetItem( al_SecondaryStart + ll_RowCount, &
            ls_Objects[ li_Count], &
          adw_Primary.GetItemDecimal( al_PrimaryStart + ll_RowCount, &
            ls_Objects[ li_Count]))
      Next
    Case "datet"
      For ll_RowCount = 0 To ll_PrimaryRows
        adw_Secondary.SetItem( al_SecondaryStart + ll_RowCount, &
            ls_Objects[ li_Count], adw_Primary.GetItemDateTime( &
            al_PrimaryStart + ll_RowCount, ls_Objects[ li_Count]))
      Next
  End Choose
End If
Next

adw_Secondary.SetRedraw( TRUE)

Return ll_PrimaryRows + 1
```

Note these points from the function in Listing 16.14:

- The `Describe()` function is used to retrieve the corresponding column position within the secondary DataWindow. The column value then is stored in an array for use in the `copy` loop.

- Direct syntax is used in the actual `copy` loop to transfer between the two DataWindows. The `If` expression ensures that there's a column to copy to from the primary DataWindow.

- By placing a row loop outside the object loop, you get better performance when copying only a few rows.

- If the source and destination DataWindows have exactly matched columns, use the PowerScript functions `RowsMove()` and `RowsCopy()`. They are significantly faster.

- The function took a half second to transfer 76 rows of six columns from one DataWindow to another. `RowsCopy()` and `RowsMove()` each take approximately 40 milliseconds. Half the function's time can be contributed to the `InsertRow()` loop because it's a slow function to execute.

- If you want to use this function to carry out a move, you can achieve the fastest performance by using `RowsDiscard()` to throw away the source rows instead of coding `DeleteRow()` calls.

You can further enhance this function to transfer the edit status of each column and/or row from the source DataWindow to the target DataWindow.

# Drop-Down DataWindow Techniques

Using drop-down DataWindows (DDDWs) can greatly reduce the clutter with a DataWindow. This column edit style provides the functionality of a drop-down list box while being dynamically populated from a relational database. A drop-down DataWindow is simply a DataWindow, usually with the Grid or Tabular presentation style, used as a drop-down list within another DataWindow. It's populated automatically with data when you issue a retrieve or insert a new row into the parent DataWindow, and then it acts just like a drop-down list control.

# Synchronizing Column Values

One trick I learned by accident while helping with another PowerBuilder project is the capability to display and synchronize multiple fields by using a single drop-down DataWindow. You first create the drop-down DataWindow with one visible column and as many other invisible data columns as you want. Then, within the parent DataWindow, place multiple copies of the same column (name them differently so that you can refer to them within your PowerScript) and set all their edit styles to `DropDownDataWindow` with the same data value and the display value you want for each column.

This method provides a quick and easy way for users to select numerous default values in one selection. Be aware, however, that because each column is a drop-down DataWindow, PowerBuilder retrieves data for each. These are good candidates for setting up data sharing.

> **Note**
>
> If this concept seems a little alien, explore the `d_customer2` DataWindow that's part of this chapter's code. It's located on the CD-ROM accompanying this book.

# Problems and Solutions

Drop-down DataWindows do have some pitfalls and issues of which you should be aware and for which you should be able to provide solutions.

One undesirable behavior is when a drop-down DataWindow is populated through a parameter, and you initially retrieve data or insert a row. If you don't specify the necessary arguments for the drop-down DataWindow's retrieval, PowerBuilder prompts you for them. To avoid having to answer these prompts, you can fool the drop-down DataWindow into thinking that it already has data; just insert a blank row into the child DataWindow. The DataWindow `d_order_product`, for example, uses a `DropDownDataWindow` edit style for the retrieved warehouse depending on the value of the `product_id` column; this means that you display only warehouse IDs that stock this particular product item.

To prevent PowerBuilder from prompting you for a `product_id` value when you initially set up the parent DataWindow, you can use two methods. Set up the first method by using the following code:

```
DataWindowChild ldwc_Warehouse

dw_order_product.GetChild( "warehouse_no", ldwc_Warehouse)
//
```

*Advanced DataWindow Techniques II*

CHAPTER **16**

649

16

Advanced
DataWindow
Techniques II

```
ldwc_Warehouse.InsertRow( 0)
//
dw_order_product.Retrieve()
```

You then can continue the script and base the drop-down DataWindow's retrieval on some value pulled back from the parent DataWindow, dw_order_product. For example, this code continues where the previous code leaves off:

```
ls_ProductId = dw_order_product.Object.product_id[ This.GetRow()]
//
ldwc_Warehouse.Retrieve( ls_ProductId)
```

The second method requires you to set up a "dummy" value from within the DataWindow painter by using the Rows menu's Data option. This method has the disadvantage of having the blank row in the child DataWindow until you carry out the child retrieve. The first method enables you to insert the dummy row and then retrieve over it or delete it when you finish with the parent retrieve.

Another problem is that as soon as a drop-down DataWindow is populated, PowerBuilder basically forgets all about having populated it, and further uses of the same drop-down DataWindow or even within the same parent DataWindow cause individual retrievals to occur. You can solve many data-retrieval performance problems by caching the data with the new DataStore object and then using the ShareData() function to connect each use of the drop-down DataWindow to this object. Just remember that when using the cached data, any filtering, sorting, or other manipulation you do with DataStore's data is reflected in all other drop-down DataWindows that are using it.

Editable drop-down DataWindows also can cause some problems for the unwary. Because PowerBuilder attempts to match what users type with an entry in the list, you will run into a problem if the data value of the drop-down DataWindow isn't a string. This problem occurs because of the four levels of validation (see Chapter 14, "DataWindow Scripting"). The second level checks the column's data type and will fail before you can even begin to process it in the ItemChanged event. This requires you to carry out some special processing in ItemError if you want to provide a more friendly user interface. This processing requires you to check the column in error and the data now in the edit control of the DataWindow; from this, you should be able to ascertain whether it's some other type of DataWindow error or one caused by the mismatch of data types for a drop-down DataWindow.

At times, the number of rows retrieved into a drop-down DataWindow becomes excessively large. You should try to alleviate this problem by using retrieval arguments for the child DataWindow to restrict the resultset. This may not always be possible, and you might want to investigate a method that enables users to enter a partial string before carrying out a lookup. You could accomplish this within a user event defined for the pbm_dwndropdown event ID that traps after users click the drop-down arrow of a drop-down DataWindow. The event script then could take a partially entered value and look it up, or it could open a dialog that queries users for additional criteria that limits the resultset. If you create a good user interface, you should be able to remove any need to bring back a list of hundreds or even thousands of rows into the drop-down DataWindow.

# Master/Detail Relationships

A commonly used association between DataWindows is master/detail, where one DataWindow is used as the main interface with one or more other DataWindows displaying supporting and related data. The master DataWindow is usually in a list format, and as users scroll and select rows within it, the detail for the record is shown in a secondary (the detail) DataWindow.

> **Tip**
>
> The PFC comes with a DataWindow linkage service contained in the n_cst_dwsrv_linkage object. You might want to explore this.

You can achieve synchronization between the two DataWindows by using two different techniques: *manual copy* and *sharing*. The manual copy method is really useful only if the detail DataWindow is noneditable and there are only a few columns. You use a call to the RowsCopy() function within the master RowFocusChanged event to copy the new current row to the detail DataWindow.

More often, you will use PowerBuilder's capability to share data between DataWindows with the ShareData() function (covered in Chapter 15. Because two or more DataWindows are sharing data, you have to issue only a single update to save any modified data. Other DataWindow management issues (such as filtering and sorting) also are much easier to handle.

The following sections look at ensuring that the current master row also is displayed in the detail DataWindows and preventing a detail DataWindow from being scrolled.

## Keeping the Detail DataWindow in Sync

To keep the detail DataWindows synchronized with the master, you need to trap two events: RowFocusChanged and ScrollVertical. These events are used to spot row-by-row changes and scrollbar manipulations, respectively.

The code for `RowFocusChanged` checks what row is current in the detail DataWindow against the new current row in the master by using the `CurrentRow` event parameter. This is done because the `ScrollVertical` event may have been triggered first and may have already updated the detail. This is the code for `RowFocusChanged`:

```
If dw_2.GetRow() <> CurrentRow Then
    dw_2.ScrollToRow( CurrentRow)
End If
```

The `ScrollVertical` event also is simple. By determining the row number that appears on the page after the scroll occurs, this event sets the detail DataWindow to the same value. The code for `ScrollVertical` follows:

```
dw_2.ScrollToRow( Long( dw_1.Object.DataWindow.FirstRowOnPage))
```

# Preventing Detail DataWindow Scrolling

Most often, the detail DataWindow is just that—details of the master record. You display only one record's data at a time. Unfortunately, because the data is actually being shared with the master, the detail also has access to the other rows of the data. This capability enables users to scroll through the detail DataWindow by using Tab, Enter, Page Up, Page Down, and the arrow keys.

The method introduced next uses just two events to prevent users from scrolling the detail DataWindow: a user event `KeyPressed` and `RowFocusChanged`. The `KeyPressed` event (see Listing 16.15) uses the `pbm_dwnkey` PowerBuilder event ID and is triggered every time users press a key while in the detail DataWindow.

**LISTING 16.15** The `KeyPressed` Event for a Master/Detail DataWindow

```
Choose Case Key
    Case KeyEnter!, KeyDownArrow!, KeyUpArrow!, KeyPageDown!, KeyPageUp!
        this.AcceptText()
        Return 1
    Case KeyTab!
        This.SetRedraw( FALSE)

        This.Post Function ScrollToRow( This.GetRow())

        If keyflags = 1 Then
            dw_1.SetRedraw( FALSE)
            This.Post Function SetFocus()
            dw_1.Post Function SetRedraw( TRUE)
        End If
```

# Application Development and PowerBuilder

When PowerBuilder was first released, it was designed as a client/server application development tool. Over PowerBuilder's last few releases, the computer industry has been evolving rapidly. The Internet, Java, components, and distributed computing are all making headlines within businesses, as well as in trade publications. PowerBuilder has continued to evolve with the industry while still providing the same great environment for developing client/server applications.

# Client/Server Overview

Client/server is still the predominant architecture used for downsizing or rightsizing projects. The term actually covers a wide range of different methods, not all of which adhere strictly to the client/server paradigm. This architecture is one of many being used by the software engineering community.

The simplest architecture, two-tier, involves a single client machine, a single server machine, and a network connection between the two. The client machine carries out independent processing from the server and uses the server as a source of information as the end user requires it. Obviously, as you extend this definition to include multiple clients and servers, you increase the number of places from which information can be gathered.

Even with the huge interest in the Internet at present and the switch from traditional client/server applications to intranet- or Internet-based ones, the concepts remain the same. With an intranet or the Internet, you still have a client machine, a server machine, and a network, albeit a much larger one, linking the two machines together.

## Servers

A server involves a piece of hardware that provides services (whether that is data or business logic) to a client PC. This isn't unlike a waiter (server) in a restaurant serving you what you request. In fact, within a client/server environment, a client may request files and data from multiple servers. This is also true of servers operating in a multitier computing environment (see Part V, "Application Partitioning and the Internet," for a discussion of *n*-tier computing and its relationship with PowerBuilder) and of servers within the Internet/intranet realm that serve HTML pages, or Java applets.

Many organizations caught up in the downsizing hype of the late 1980s and early 1990s allowed business units to dictate their hardware and software requirements to MIS (also now known as Information Technology or IT) departments. Some departments even maintained servers and client machines outside the control, or at least direct control, of the

MIS departments. This permitted the department to benefit from using computing resources appropriate to its problem domain. However, it also introduced other problems, not the least of which was the difficulty of maintaining controllable standards for software purchasing and development.

This caused information management problems in the late 1980s. Recently, however, numerous software solutions allowing access to heterogeneous data sources and file systems have become available. Now a knowledgeable worker using a PC or Apple Macintosh has access to mainframe data—from the other side of the world, if necessary—at the touch of a button.

Choosing hardware for a server requires careful planning to provide secure, reliable service. The specific task that the server is being acquired for influences the vendor choices somewhat. For example, if you want a high-performance database server that's readily upgradable, you might consider a UNIX box from Hewlett Packard or Sun Microsystems. Communication, file, database, and even the more recent entries into this fold, such as online analytical processing (OLAP) and Web services, require different considerations in their hardware requirements.

## Clients

The real workhorses of traditional client/server systems are the client machines (PCs). This piece of hardware has enabled the explosion of graphics tools and utilities that enhance end-user productivity. The intense computing power required to drive a graphical user interface (GUI) would choke most mainframes if they had to provide this service for a typical organization. Not only does the client machine carry out the data processing within the original problem domain, but it also can be exploited for additional uses, such as word processing, spreadsheets, and email. All this and a friendly graphical user interface—surely this is heaven?

The exact requirements for a desktop client machine have changed considerably in only a few years. It used to be acceptable to place a 386-processor PC on an end user's desk and expect him or her to be content with the performance. But not today. The end-user community has demanded increased performance from machines and software to the point where, in some organizations, the end user works with machines that are superior to those of the developers. That some machines used by developers are lower-powered than the intended end-user machines is actually the intention of some organizations. If the developers can make the application work at an acceptable level on these lower-powered machines, the deployment to the end users can be achieved more easily. Upgrading a department of PCs can be expensive and time consuming. Was it worth the migration from the mainframe? The answer is usually yes, but not from a price perspective. The increased productivity and improved tools for accessing data justify the cost, and this has enabled improved customer responsiveness. Communication between employees and departments is usually higher, due to application and data sharing. This can lead to some interesting partnerships that might never have been thought of within the confines of the old mainframe system.

Some businesses are looking at Net computers (NC) to solve some ownership, maintenance, and administration costs involved with PCs. A Net computer receives all its software and data over the network from servers and uses only minimal hardware. Whenever an application or data is required, it's downloaded from the server to the network computer. This has the added advantage in that users always receive the updated and most recent version of the software or data they're accessing. Of course, the big disadvantage is the additional network infrastructure that has to be in place. Consider that every time any kind of file is required, be that data or application, it has to be downloaded over the network.

The most common complaints from end users seem to be about the responsiveness of the display and the speed of obtaining data from the server. You can increase application graphics speed by purchasing a relatively inexpensive Windows accelerator card or by altering your application code so that end users perceive that the window is opening faster than it actually is.

## The Network

Network throughput greatly influences client/server performance. Some factors affecting throughput include the physical distance over which the network extends (network segments and nodes per segment), the type of cabling used, the client and server network protocols, network topology, bridging versus routing, and overall network loading.

The physical cable distance that separates a client machine from a server might be greater than the actual distance from box to box. The distances the two machines may communicate over can vary between local area networks (LANs), metropolitan area networks (MANs), and wide area networks (WANs). As the network grows, additional pieces of specialized hardware are needed to expand the network (repeaters, routers, bridges, and so on). These can introduce their own performance problems, which may require the whole network to be re-architected. This doesn't even focus on the unique performance problems that come into play when looking at running Internet applications.

If applications will be developed using a MAN or WAN, you might want to consider special versions of the software to provide additional caching or simpler functionality because there's a great difference in communication rates between these and LANs.

One factor not often given serious consideration is the physical cabling. A number of different grades of cable give better performance at greater cost. You may even consider fiber-optic cabling as a solution. Always try to purchase the grade of cable that you can envision using more than a few years into the future, and keep network expansion foremost in mind.

The network protocol used by the client and server can affect the rate at which data can be transferred. Some protocols carry greater overhead than others but are less error prone and can be used to carry larger packet sizes. The protocol you decide on will be influenced by the types of applications that will be using the network.

The type of network technology used can also affect communication rates and is, again, a trade-off between cost and performance. For example, Ethernet technology exhibits a performance drop-off as bandwidth usage approaches 50 percent but is very fast under light to medium loading. Token Ring, on the other hand, has a fixed response time to client requests and doesn't experience the same performance degradation at higher usage. However, there's an associated implementation cost, as well as problems such as a failure at a point in the ring that will cause the whole network to fail.

# Why Client/Server Systems?

Client/server is well suited to the implementation of decision support systems (DSSs) used to access legacy data. *Legacy data* is usually business-critical data used by older, back-office types of applications on the mainframe. The use of those costly mainframe cycles can be greatly reduced with a PC-based DSS. Mainframe data is downloaded to a server once and then updated periodically; this is the only cost incurred on the mainframe. This data can then be loaded into a PC-based database server for access by any number of clients at a significant cost saving.

Sounds simple, doesn't it? It usually isn't. What wasn't taken into consideration in the previous paragraph is that a cost is involved in writing the mainframe export program, having it run periodically, buying and administering the server, buying the client machines, possibly training the users on their new machines, writing the DSS program, and writing the data import program. Did I miss anything? Probably. There's certainly more to it than the simple statements suggest, and you should be prepared to tackle each issue before you start.

Client/server application development is still the primary area of development for MIS departments, even with the pressures to create "something Internet-based" by CEOs, CIOs, and other department heads. Large amounts of money have already been plowed into the creation of such client/server applications, and those that have been successful solve the business needs for which they were intended. With products such as PowerBuilder, it's becoming increasingly easier to Web-enable traditional applications.

Each client/server application must be carefully analyzed before development starts. Will there be cost savings? Wouldn't it be simpler to give each end user a PC and a terminal emulator so that he or she can still access the mainframe data directly? This would provide end users with a powerful workstation to use for word processing, perform spreadsheet calculations, use email, and so on, but still have access to the central data store on the mainframe.

As you start looking at client/server systems in detail, you will have more questions. Carefully consider each step you make into this brave new world.

# Implementing Client/Server Systems

Most companies start with small pilot projects to examine aspects of client/server systems before fully committing time and resources to larger projects. The common structured approach in the mainframe world is sometimes abandoned as developers embrace new development tools that allow rapid changes to be made. This often leads to several false starts and different teams heading off in new directions.

You can't use the same procedures you would use to develop mainframe applications, but some of these procedures can be reworked for client/server systems. Maintaining a structured approach to application design is still paramount within this new technology, and ensuring that you have the right components helps your projects get off to the right start.

The choice of different components can be a predominant factor in the success of any project. Hardware for the three main components has been previously discussed for two-tier client/server, but this is only one part of the puzzle. The other part, the software, can be much harder to decide.

Decisions regarding what to include in a project toolset are often considered after the system requirements stage. The findings in this stage are a driving factor in which tools are chosen. Some organizations might not have an option, and you must use the corporate standard tools. In this case, you might have to be ingenious with the application of these tools rather than use the tools you would have chosen. A good place to start exploring the available tools is with the people you have access to from other projects. They can explain to you their hands-on experience with a range of products and give you their relative strengths and weaknesses. Of course, nothing beats trying it yourself. So after you isolate a couple contenders for the tool of choice, start to experiment with them yourself. Vendors are usually more than happy to provide evaluation versions of their products. Sometimes important questions are left unanswered: What's the market direction and trend? What's the latest and greatest? In what direction is a particular tool market heading? Be careful buying into technology on the trailing or bleeding edge; keeping up with the rest of the industry is usually a strong position to be in.

We hope you've already decided what development tool to use, and we hope it's PowerBuilder. Although we might be biased toward PowerBuilder, we always consider what other tools or development languages might be better for the task. Indeed, a combination of tools and languages often provides an optimal solution.

After you decide on the components to use for each facet of implementing a client/server system, your next step is to build a team of designers, developers, and engineers. When building your team, look for people who have an underlying understanding of what's going on and not just that they can produce PowerBuilder code. The team members should consider concepts before syntax. This allows the team to tackle various projects, whether they are PC-, Macintosh-, or UNIX-based. Enlist original systems staff and incorporate them into teams, because these people often have an in-depth knowledge of not just the systems you're replacing, but of the underlying business concepts. Some may resist change, and you should try to ease their way into a team by placing them in advisory positions, usually with some sort of stake in the success of the system. Others may try to take on development, even though they are ill-equipped at this time to take on the new challenges that new tools bring. Encourage them to experiment with the tools. Provide training and allow them to work on less critical components as they learn.

Often companies don't have the special skills required for their first client/server projects, and they'll look for outside help. Consulting firms can provide several benefits. One benefit is knowledge transfer from these firms to your project members. You will have gained nothing but a client/server system that you can't support if you don't get your company's employees involved in all stages of a project.

The techniques to develop client/server applications are covered in Chapter 18, "Analysis, Design, and Implementation."

# Client/Server Case Studies

The next two sections describe actual accounts from two large corporations that moved to a client/server architecture, the methods chosen to tackle each individual business problem, and their reasons behind the move to client/server.

## Case Study 1: Health-Care Company Moves to Client/Server

In an attempt to curtail expensive, resource-intensive mainframe processing, a Fortune 500 health-care corporation decided to migrate several key application systems to a client/server environment. The hope was to cut costs, provide the user community with a more flexible interface, and integrate new technology into all facets of the work force.

In the process of determining which systems would be migrated, the company decided that it would avoid mission-critical applications and opt for several smaller subsystems. Because the company didn't have any client/server applications yet, it made sense to test the process on one or more small systems that wouldn't affect crucial day-to-day business activities. This would allow for any difficulties encountered in a technology switch and extra time needed to establish standards. Therefore, the first systems chosen were used for reporting purposes. It also was agreed that after the client/server applications were in place, the mainframe equivalent would continue to operate for at least one month.

A high-level timetable was implemented using recommended schedules determined by benchmarking other companies attempting to move to client/server systems. Because the data to be used by the new applications was generated from other applications on the mainframe, the development team needed to create a method to extract the data from the necessary mainframe files and databases. The data was then downloaded to a network server from which the users could run an application for ad hoc queries and the generation of reports. The mainframe extract program was easily implemented, as was the automated download process from the mainframe because this functionality had been used in other projects. After it was sent down to the communications server, how was the data going to be queried and from what application?

The choice was to purchase a server-based relational database management system (RDBMS) and access the data in the tables from a Windows-based application. Several prewritten application software packages were evaluated for the front end. It was decided that the best direction to take was to purchase a Windows development tool and create a custom application that could access the RDBMS and its corresponding tables. By developing an in-house application, MIS determined that it was laying the groundwork for future applications and giving employees exposure to new technology.

After the tools were decided on and the development team was trained in using the products, two issues remained: how to populate the relational database with the downloaded mainframe files and how to create an interface that wouldn't frighten users unfamiliar with Windows. In addition to populating the database, a process needed to be developed for daily and weekly updates of static data, such as code tables. Time and budget dictated that the solution the development team adapted was based on batch files executed using the network operating system's scheduler. These batch files started a copy routine from the communication server to the SQL server and then populated the appropriate tables.

Whereas the table population proved trying, the creation of a Windows interface was even more frustrating. The initial pass-through had an uncanny resemblance to the existing mainframe system that the team wanted to move away from. This was because the project team focused on the functionality of the system (retrieving the data and providing queries) before they designed the interface. To assist in this process, the project team decided to incorporate techniques from other Windows applications and bring in a consultant to review the system and make suggestions on the interface and coding techniques. This combination of recommendations and examination of other applications resulted in a non-MDI interface that gave users a Windows application but still guided them through the system so as not to intimidate them in a new environment.

The application was tested by other MIS employees, not on the immediate project team, to determine ease of use and to find unexpected problems. The application was then demonstrated to several key users, who gave recommendations on functionality and the interface. The changes were reworked and shown to the users again for a final sign-off. To distribute the application, developers installed it from disk one machine at a time. The response from the users was positive, and overall the project was viewed as a success.

The company's plan succeeded for several reasons. The initial decision to start with a small part of the business removed considerable stress and extra work from the development team. It gave the team the ability to focus on learning the technology necessary for the client/server environment. The company was willing to provide training for the development team and the cost of a consultant, if needed. Finally, the project team made sure that other MIS members, as well as the users, were involved and had input in the application's development. The procedures determined by these first applications became the standard for other applications and proved a good foundation for later, more complex applications.

**17**

**Application
Development and
PowerBuilder**

Although this was a success story, the company encountered some problems:

- The project ran over budget due to the cost of new equipment, software, training, double processing on the server and mainframe, consulting fees, and downtime due to unexpected errors.

- The process wasn't particularly efficient on the client, server, or network, and resulted in an application that didn't meet users' speed expectations.

- The system wasn't well documented, and not many standards were in place between developers.

- No process was established to handle problem resolution.

- Bad feelings were created between the new client/server team and the old mainframe support teams because the client/server team could learn and use new technology.

These problems are not uncommon in many companies and often result in an unsuccessful client/server migration. Companies must be committed to the process and have realistic expectations of the new system and their development teams. Also, because the technology and standards are continually evolving, a company must keep an eye on the future and what it may bring.

## Case Study 2: Use of Client/Server by a Fortune 500 Manufacturing Company

In 1991, the Bemis Company, a major supplier of flexible packaging and pressure-sensitive materials, with annual sales of $1.4 billion, realized that its information systems were becoming antiquated. Its mainframe-based business systems, some of which were more than 20 years old, were becoming increasingly difficult to enhance and maintain. These systems, used at four divisional headquarters and more than 40 plant locations throughout the United States, were a major source of dissatisfaction among users throughout the company.

The corporate officers decided to change how information systems were delivered. A strategy was set to replace the central information systems staff with development groups at each division and to make a major investment to replace the aging business systems. Financial and technical committees from the corporate offices and each division were established to set hardware and software standards and to coordinate the effort. These committees agreed on a number of principles:

- The company will implement PC-based client/server systems rather than mini-mainframe applications.

- The company will prefer purchasing packaged applications over developing custom applications.

- The company will use PCs on the desktop and prefer PCs as back-end servers.

- The company will use Microsoft's SQL Server database.

- Custom applications will be developed with Sybase's PowerBuilder.

Selecting PowerBuilder over C or other procedural languages was a strategic decision. PowerBuilder, with its painter-based, event-driven model, allowed Bemis to employ developers with primarily analyst skills who could also operate as programmers, rather than employ dedicated programmers. This was done with the knowledge that the resulting programs would require additional PC hardware resources. PowerBuilder was chosen specifically as the development suite because PowerBuilder has a strong development toolset and Sybase has a dominant position in the marketplace.

With these principles established, each division began to staff its information systems group and set a strategy for the implementation. Some divisions purchased an integrated package and then internally modified it to their specifications; others contracted with a software company to incorporate unique requirements into existing packages.

One division had a large plant with 700 to 800 employees, two smaller 100-employee plants, and a medium-sized plant of 400 employees in Pennsylvania. The Pennsylvania plant was using custom-developed mainframe-based systems outsourced to a large systems house.

The division hired an information systems manager from another division in the company. After much discussion, the division set a strategy to develop its own applications for its order and production control systems (that is, order entry, inventory management, and production control). This decision was made due to the uniqueness of its business and because virtually no applications were being marketed in the chosen environment. The division also hired two developers, both skilled in procedural languages but without knowledge of PowerBuilder or SQL-based databases.

The first project was to eliminate the outsourcing contract for the Pennsylvania plant. This required that the division train its staff while developing four major applications over a six-month period, as well as transferring the financial systems and other supporting systems to the corporate mainframe. These tasks employed two four-person development teams: one at the corporate headquarters and one made up of the two newly hired developers and two contractors. Both teams used training contractors to train the company's developers and to help develop the applications. The division constructed its own application framework (discussed more in Chapter 24, "Frameworks and Class Libraries"), set a number of development standards, and began developing. The headquarters-based team developed an order-entry system and a pricing system. The team at the divisional headquarters developed a production reporting system and a raw materials inventory system for the Pennsylvania plant. A version of the production reporting system was also installed at the large divisional plant.

The newly developed systems were implemented, and the financial and other systems were migrated from the outsourced mainframe to the corporate mainframe. During this project, a number of smaller applications were also developed to transfer information between the corporate mainframe and the new PowerBuilder systems. This amount of development could never have been accomplished in such a short time with a procedural language. Although the toolset and hardware platform was somewhat immature, it proved to be sufficiently stable to accomplish the team's objectives.

Soon after the division had implemented an order-costing system at the Pennsylvania plant and the divisional headquarters, an order-entry system at the divisional headquarters, and a number of smaller applications. In the division's migration from the mainframe, the next goal was to develop a finished goods application, an invoicing application, and a sales reporting application. These applications would be bolted onto both of the existing order-entry systems.

A third project was completed that established a divisional server containing customer and order information used for reporting. The division purchased an information transfer program to assist in transferring the data between the plant servers onto the divisional server.

A number of projects still must be completed before Bemis completely frees itself of the mainframe. After the finished goods application and invoicing application are running at the divisional headquarters, they will be implemented at the Pennsylvania plant. The final step will be to install the entire order-control system at the two smaller plants.

With some help from corporate headquarters with the financial systems, the division should be finished with the migration, just over three years from the beginning of the first project.

## Case Study Conclusions

Both case studies show that as a company starts to investigate client/server systems as an alternative, the system is implemented in carefully phased stages. The remaining sections of this chapter introduce PowerBuilder as a client/server tool and explain why you will want to use its powerful features in your development efforts.

# PowerBuilder as a Client/Server Tool

PowerBuilder provides a graphical user interface development tool. In fact, it offers much more than just the capability to paint GUIs. Developers use a visual integrated development environment (IDE) to produce GUI applications. PowerBuilder uses a painter paradigm to tackle each object and development requirement. Painters provide a point-and-click environment where objects can be built, modified, and managed.

The "glue" used to do the actual work within objects is written in PowerScript, an enhanced version of BASIC. PowerScript is similar to Visual Basic, SQL Windows (now called Centura) Application Language (SAL), or any other of the myriad GUI development environments. The "bonus" to using PowerBuilder to any of the aforementioned development tools is the DataWindow. This unique and patented technology saves developers from writing complex code to carry out data management (see Chapter 6, "The DataWindow Painter," for more information).

However, PowerBuilder provides only one piece of the client/server puzzle. You can develop only client applications. There's no direct access or support for network components, and only limited access to database server structures. There's a good reason for this—such a wide variety of networks and databases can be used that PowerBuilder would have to be huge to cope with only a fraction of them. Instead, developers use database-specific tools (for example, SQL Enterprise Manager for Microsoft SQL Server).

Sybase has designed PowerBuilder as an open system and has built some strategic partnerships through its client/server open development environment (CODE) partners. This is an agreement between Sybase and its partners to establish and maintain a transfer of technical information and work toward tighter integration of products.

Sybase has continually enhanced its product line of tools. Its development tools such as PowerJ, PowerBuilder, and Jaguar CTS have been bundled into an integrated suite called Enterprise Application Studio (EAS). Sybase is positioning itself to provide solutions to all phases of the software development life cycle with what it calls *best-of-breed products*.

PowerBuilder lends itself to cooperative teamwork within a corporate environment, provided that someone can direct and control the effort. PowerBuilder also lends itself to the development of component and solution products. This makes it a powerful tool that can produce low-cost, efficient applications in short periods of time.

**17**

**Application
Development and
PowerBuilder**

# Why Use PowerBuilder?

Developers can become productive in a short time period with PowerBuilder. It requires less training to produce a finished product than is required with some other development tools. This doesn't mean that the best solution will be found or that the developer's knowledge is complete because numerous advanced topics in PowerBuilder come only with experience (and reading this book!).

PowerBuilder enables developers to write event-driven applications in an object-oriented manner or to produce procedural applications. PowerBuilder can be used for "good" or for "evil"—it's the developer's choice. If you delve a little under the surface of PowerBuilder, you will find a world of classes, inheritance, ancestors, descendants, encapsulation, polymorphism, overloading, and overriding. Purists will argue that PowerBuilder isn't a true object-oriented tool. They have a valid case in some areas. However, PowerBuilder does use object-oriented techniques and technology and allows developers to be as object-oriented as they want to be.

Experienced developers can develop applications rapidly. By taking advantage of PowerBuilder's intuitive environment, developers can participate in rapid application development (RAD) sessions to quickly produce functioning prototypes that end users can touch and feel. This is further aided by the use of numerous reusable objects that can be built with PowerBuilder.

Probably one of PowerBuilder's biggest selling points is the DataWindow. This object is the focal point of data interaction in PowerBuilder and is used for reporting as well as data-entry tasks. DataWindows have numerous built-in functions, such as handling communication with the database server, data validation, and complex report presentations. Integral with the database communication is submission of SELECT statements (which are graphically painted by the developer) to retrieve data and the appropriate generation of database UPDATE, INSERT, and DELETE statements to reflect the data changes made by an end user. This might be reason enough to use a DataWindow, but it also offers numerous other advantages. With other development tools, a number of controls must be used to construct a data-entry screen, whereas the DataWindow is actually one control with simply a graphical representation of the desired controls. This places fewer demands on the graphic resources of the operating system and is faster to render onscreen.

Another attractive feature of PowerBuilder is Sybase's commitment to provide a multiplatform tool that requires little or no additional code to run. PowerBuilder 7.0 is available for Windows 95/98, Windows NT, and several UNIX flavors. Objects in library files can be accessed directly by PowerBuilder running on each platform without any migration.

PowerBuilder supports object linking and embedding (OLE), dynamic data exchange (DDE), access to external functions and objects, VBX support, and standard file I/O operations. All these features make PowerBuilder a scalable product, more so than most other client/server tools available.

# Beyond Client/Server

Although the client/server architecture is still the meat and potatoes of PowerBuilder, recent advances in technology by Sybase leave the development possibilities wide open. You can use PowerBuilder as an internet/intranet development tool to build components such as JavaBeans and COM objects (see Chapter 20, "Application and Component Implementation, Creation, and Distribution"), Internet solutions (see Chapter 30, "Developing Internet Applications with PowerBuilder"), and distributed or *n*-tier applications (see Chapter 28, "Developing Distributed PowerBuilder Applications"). The new functionality that PowerBuilder provides allows you to leverage the knowledge you already have and take it to a whole new development level.

# Summary

This chapter described client/server technology and its components. The necessary resource considerations in terms of people, money, and tools were introduced, and you were warned that client/server isn't the solution to every problem.

You learned a little about PowerBuilder and the components that make up the painters. This chapter described the major features in PowerBuilder and why you would want to consider PowerBuilder the development tool of choice for all your client/server applications.

# Analysis, Design, and Implementation

**CHAPTER 18**

The development of successful business applications requires you to create an entire development process that you will use throughout the life of the project. Developers creating applications for a distributed environment, such as a n-tier client/server application, use cyclic development to create, maintain, or improve the solutions they provide.

# Application Development Methodologies

The application development cycle is only a small piece of a larger methodology that encompasses every aspect of a project, including such pieces as quality management and quality assurance. The application development methodology has three main pieces:

- *Process reengineering* is in part the identification and definition of existing problems and their solutions. The basis of the reengineering is to capture the current process and to determine where and if any computer-based solutions can be applied to improve the process. As part of this process, you gather information about the current situational application problems and determine optimal solutions for those problems. It involves incorporating those solutions into the system and continually monitoring and improving the system through problem identification, definition, and solution processes.

- *Architectural foundations* identify the tools used to implement the solution defined during process reengineering. This involves defining the application's packaging, including the interaction among the application, data sources, and external interfaces. This phase is also responsible for monitoring and optimizing database performance and application resource usage.

- *System development* is the phase during which you construct solutions that you further develop to provide an optimal solution. This includes defining a plan and requirements that will be used in the design, creation, and implementation of a system. The system to be implemented is continually monitored and enhanced through maintenance and development.

Although these pieces interact, each has its own development life cycle that allows for discovery, creation, and enhancement. They are circular in nature so that you can start at whatever point in the methodology makes sense for the system (see Figure 18.1). You might be going from paper-based to computer-based, or reengineering an existing computer system.

**Figure 18.1**

*The application development methodology with the individual life cycles.*

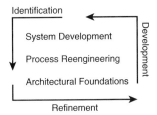

There are many types of analysis and design approaches. Some are tried and tested, mature approaches; others are much newer, radical approaches. Some work better for a given situation and design team, so it's worth doing some research. Some of the most common approaches are waterfall, object-orientation analysis and design, joint application development (JAD), rapid application development (RAD), rapid iterative prototyping (RIP), and business process engineering.

Numerous tools, such as computer-assisted software engineering (CASE), are available to assist development teams with the implementation of these processes. This chapter briefly overviews some of these approaches and then discusses the procedure of matching the analysis and design phases with PowerBuilder functionality and characteristics. It also explores the cornerstone of all successful data-based applications—the database design.

# The Waterfall Development Methodology

The *waterfall* methodology, commonly thought of as the "classic" software life cycle, follows a structured analysis and structured design approach in development. Figure 18.2 shows a model of the waterfall methodology.

The first area , of the model is the analysis and identification of user requirements. Software requirements are then specified in a requirement specifications document, which is a complete description of system external behavior. (Note that this doesn't describe how the system works internally.) An important factor at this point in the design is the behavioral aspect of the system. The detailed design is done in a *Program Design Language* (PDL) notation, also referred to as *Structured English* or *pseudo-code*, and is used to impart intent and structure rather than the actual implementation details.

Two focal points of the waterfall approach are testing and documentation. Throughout the software process, testing is performed continuously. Documentation is also continuously created and updated throughout each phase. As a result, the waterfall model produces a number of documents: a specifications document; a design document; a code document; and many others, including the database, user, and operations manuals. These documents are essential for system maintenance and updating.

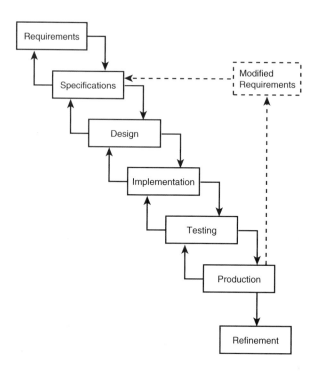

**FIGURE 18.2**
*The waterfall
development
methodology
model.*

This approach to the development life cycle has some inherent problems, the most important being that the project requirements can't be properly tested until a working system is created, and only at that time can a match-up of the requirements to the functionality be made. Obviously, at this point in the project, the current solution might not meet end users' expectations or needs. Problems in the requirement specifications document can't be found until this point and are therefore costly to fix because the cycle has to begin again. Because the working model comes late in the development life cycle, design and performance concerns aren't encountered until the system is almost finished.

In today's businesses, users are looking for systems that can be produced quickly and effectively, and with the production of a working model so late in the life cycle, developers are discovering that the waterfall method doesn't fit into the new application development methodology requirements. One solution to the problems of using the waterfall model is the prototyping approach.

# The Prototyping Methodology

The *prototyping* methodology is more heavily based on design, with system architects working closely with a select group of end users. The team works together in interactive meetings during which they design versions of the system that are then modeled, modified, and updated until there's a complete understanding of the system's requirements.

The obvious advantage of this approach is that users get to work closely with the system architect and get to see and give immediate feedback on the functioning of the system. They can provide insights about the system that the system architect would have been hard-pressed to discover during a classic end-user interview. The end product of this approach is a working prototype that accurately reflects the end users' needs and requirements. This prototype can sometimes be enhanced to produce the final product, but more often it's scrapped so that actual coding frameworks can be put in place.

Documentation is also a part of this approach; with user-generated feedback, a revised requirement specifications document is created along with the prototype.

## Rapid Iterative Prototyping

*Rapid iterative prototyping* (RIP) makes full use of the waterfall methodology model, with the addition of the prototype iteration. At the end of the prototype iteration cycle, an end requirement specification and a final prototype are agreed on by the development and end-user teams, and the analysis phase is considered complete. Figure 18.3 gives an idea of the RIP methodology.

**18**

**Analysis, Design, and Implementation**

FIGURE **18.3**

*The rapid iterative prototype development methodology model.*

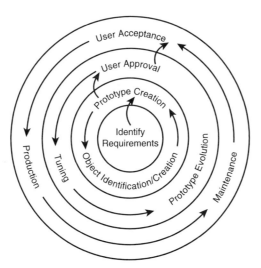

With the obvious high degree of end-user involvement, this approach works well only in organizations where end users can allocate sufficient time to work with the development team. One bonus that might justify this time investment is that the amount of training required on the new system is minimized because many users are already familiar with the application.

## Joint Application Development

An extension of rapid iterative prototyping is *joint application development* (JAD), in which a joint development team comprises the development and end-user teams. Ideally, the team leader should be someone outside either group, without a vested interest in the outcome of the project, and should act purely as a facilitator and mediator.

The joint team actively approaches the needs of the end-user group and develops system screens and reports through the use of rapid prototypes. One goal of the team is to create the requirement specifications document.

It's obvious that this approach requires a great deal of commitment from the development and end-user groups, but the rewards of a successful team are shared by all, and as such there's a vested interest in the project and its success.

## Rapid Application Development

*Rapid application development* (RAD) is an integration of several techniques with the aim of speeding up the development of high-quality systems. Some components of RAD are project scheduling, requirement planning and development, prototyping, and reusable code.

The concept behind *project scheduling* is to use the fewest people possible for the project. The idea is to staff the project so that you maximize the use of developers. Scheduling also allows you to make a determination of a project's duration based on the system interdependencies and time commitments of the development team brought to light through the schedule. The interdependencies can make a project last longer than it might originally appear. These critical steps can hold up further development until they have been successfully completed.

*Requirement planning and development* consists of the combined effort of the end-user and development teams to carry out the structured analysis and application design phase.

*Prototyping* is a central theme to RAD. Prototyping aids in the construction of the final system because the prototype will be used as the application's foundation.

CASE tools are used in RAD because they can integrate existing code in reusable modules. These tools help capture business rules and functional requirements into an electronic format that can have relationships assigned and maintained and also can be presented quickly and in various formats depending on the audience, such as end users and senior management.

# Object-Oriented Analysis and Design

*Object-oriented analysis and design* (OOA and OOD) emphasizes object development, de-emphasizes procedure development, and is based on the concept of modularity. *Modularity* allows system designers to decompose a system into smaller, more manageable pieces that have well-defined interfaces among them.

Using the idea of modularity, the object-oriented approach encapsulates information into separate modules for easier definition and manageability. Encapsulating the information helps implement the concept of *information hiding*, the technique of preventing the use of globally accessible information. This makes these modules (or objects) self-contained, more manageable, modifiable, and—most importantly—reusable.

The object-oriented approach involves three concepts: objects, classes, and inheritance. With this approach, objects become a generic implementation of the encapsulated functionality and information. An *object* is a thing that you can do actions on and interact with, and that has a state and behavior. Objects communicate via messages rather than by direct access or calls. *Classes* are collections of objects that share common behavior and common functionality. You can specialize classes by using *inheritance*, which is a mechanism for sharing and reusing attributes and code between classes. A *child class* adapts the encapsulated attributes and behavior of its parent class by adding new or redefining existing attributes and behavior.

This method allows for the gathering of information for problem definition and solution. With the emergence of more object-oriented programming and development environments and tools, this appears to be the most viable approach to analysis and design for most organizations. For further study in this topic, the book *Object-Oriented Analysis and Design*, by Grady Booch, is an excellent starting point.

## Object-Oriented Analysis and Design with UML

In 1997, the Object Management Group officially accepted the Unified Modeling Language (UML) version 1.0, which was conceived by Grady Booch, Jim Rumbaugh, and Ivar Jacobson (also known as the "Three Amigos"). The creation of the UML stemmed from the desire to standardize many modeling approaches used throughout the world. The UML consists of a rich set of modeling semantics (that is, notations and meta-models) and remains process independent. Not coupling a process with the UML allows its usage to span many different organizations with standard processes that have evolved over the years.

**18**

**Analysis, Design, and Implementation**

**Note**

Companies are beginning to create their development processes around the usage of the UML. For example, Rational Software has created the Rational Unified Process (RUP) product, which fully integrates the UML.

The following sections discuss the highlights of the UML. Many books and training resources are now available. To find more information on training and modeling facilitation, visit `www.ebgconsulting.com`, the Web site for EBG Consulting. This Indianapolis-based firm specializes in OOA&D using UML, software development processes, and training in these areas.

## Use Case Analysis

Use Cases are an integral part of the UML. Use Cases are used to begin the requirements gathering of a proposed system. They define the actors, triggers, goals, and failures. *Actors* are roles, human or nonhuman, with goals fulfilled by the system. *Triggers* are the actions that trigger the Use Case. *Goals* define the desired outcome of the system.

Use Cases help define functional requirements of the proposed system. They're gathered in formal Use Case sessions, which should be attended by members of the systems staff, business customer representatives, a facilitator, and (if possible) a technical writer. The sessions have members play the roles of the Actor and the System. The Actor has needs to which the System responds. The information captured for both roles needs to be at a simplistic level and stay away from any GUI references. The first pass through the system is considered the Main Sequence, the most common requirement usage of the Use Case. The two roles then need to replay the sequence, identify any variations, and capture those variations. Variations are considered any unusual, alternative, or error uses of the system.

When Use Cases are completed, they feed into every phase of the design process. They are first used to create the requirements document, which should be signed off by the customer. When this is done, they are used by the design team and developers to begin to create the diagrams that will be carried into the construction. These diagrams are discussed in detail in the following section.

Scenarios need to be written for each Use Case main sequence and Variation. The scenarios are real-world situations that require the Use Cases. Try to create a minimum of two and as many as five scenarios for each main sequence and variation. These scenarios are used in many stages of the process. They first enable you to walk the customer group through the Use Cases, using rough screen designs with the scenarios driving the flow. By using real-world situations, customers can see the Use Cases flow in a context that they can understand. The scenarios also provide developers with ways of performing unit testing before sending their modules to beta or final testing. Finally, the testing team can use the scenarios to write the scripts to be used in unit, system, and integration testing.

# Diagrams

The UML consists of many diagrams that can be used throughout the analysis and design process. The more you get involved in the UML, the more comfortable you will become with the various diagrams and the best way they can be used. In my experience with the UML, I have found a couple of diagrams necessary in producing high-quality code: interaction diagrams and the Class Model.

Interaction diagrams consist of two types: sequence and collaboration, both showing the relationships between the classes and how the classes will communicate with each other. The sequence diagram is the more favorable of the two because it quickly shows you the order in which these communications take place in a time-ordered sequence and seems to be easier to map from the Use Cases. Figure 18.4 shows an example of a sequence diagram. You need to investigate both interaction diagram styles to find the one that best fits your needs.

**FIGURE 18.4**
*An example of a sequence diagram.*

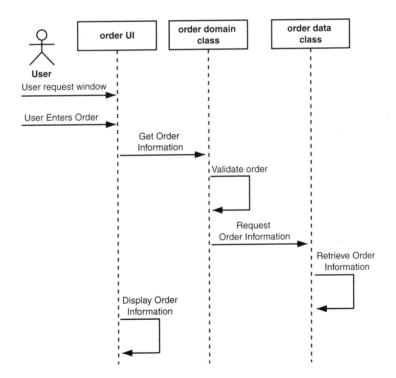

The Class Model is the most important model from a developer's standpoint. The Class Model evolves over the life of the process and, in its complete state, gives the developer a "blueprint" that can be used to build the objects. This approach is different from what many developers are used to because, if done correctly, the coding should consist of only about 30 percent of the system development life cycle. By the time the Class Model is completed, all the operations (functions and events in PowerBuilder) and attributes (user-defined and system-generated instance variables) are defined. Developers will have to physically create the objects and write code that will carry out the desired functionality. Figure 18.5 shows an example of a simple Class Model and some of its notation.

As Figure 18.5 outlines, the control buttons (`cb_ok` and `cb_cancel`) and the DataWindow control (`dw_display`) have aggregate relationships with the window (`w_order_display`). An aggregate relationship can be described as a "part of" relationship (that is, `cb_ok` is part of `w_order_display`). The Class Model also outlines the concept of Generalization, the UML's way of stating inheritance. Having said this, you can see that the diagram shows `dw_display` is inherited from the `u_dw` class.

The diagrams discussed here can be as simple or detailed as you want them to be. When you begin to use and work with the diagrams, you will see your coding time decrease and the accuracy of your work improve immensely.

## CRC Sessions

A Class-Responsibility-Collaboration (CRC) session is a technique that asks developers to "become" an object for a scenario. When I say "become," I'm really saying that, through role playing, the developers take on the responsibilities of a class, and all those involved in the session have to interact with the appropriate class/developer to get the information they need. The sessions have many benefits for developers. First, it helps define the responsibilities (hence the R in CRC) each class has to itself and the other classes. The other classes that use its responsibilities become Collaborators (the last C in CRC). The sequence diagrams discussed earlier as well as the Use Cases are great inputs to these sessions. On completion of the CRC session, developers should have a much better understanding of the class they have responsibility for as well as how the other developers' classes work. Because there is a better understanding, the developers' sequence or collaboration diagram and the Class Model should be able to be filled in with greater detail.

# Analysis

This section covers the analysis phase of the application development life cycle, when you analyze the data and match the system requirements with PowerBuilder's functionality.

**FIGURE 18.5**

*An example of a Class Model.*

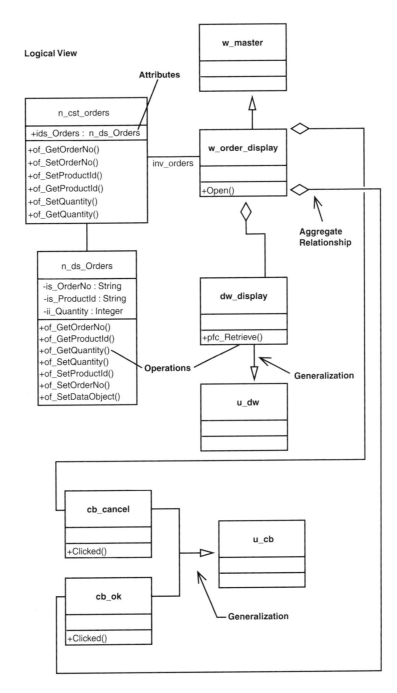

The analysis phase of a project consists of gathering information about the existing system as well as the desired one. This involves working with the system's users to determine the application components, which provides information from different views on the flows, processes, and data of the application.

One way of organizing the data collected during analysis is to address the following categories:

- The *input* category consists of all input the application receives, whether end-user or system generated. User data is generated and modified through the user interface, whereas system-generated data covers additional data sources accessed by the application or created as part of some internal process.

- The *output* category details the information the application produces and includes reports (hard copy or screen based) and modifications to data sources.

- The *processing* category examines the flow of control of the system and details operations such as the manipulation and display of data. This category can also include the interaction of this system with other separate or external systems that provide access to their data or functions.

The first two categories help you determine the data that needs to be tracked by the system and are useful during the data-modeling phase, as discussed later in this section. The section "Programming PowerBuilder" discusses matching all three categories to PowerBuilder components.

The data analysisprocess deals with the construction of logical and physical database models. This process identifies and organizes the information required by the system, and helps capture all user information in a way that enables easy analyzing and classification. This results in a logical model that can be transformed into a functional physical database schema.

The information in the logical model is described by using three concepts: entity, attribute, and relationship. An *entity* is a collection of related characteristics that you need to maintain and use as a unit. An *attribute* is a quality, feature, or characteristic of an entity. A *relationship* is an associative link between two entities. The relationship models an association between records (instances) of one or more entities. An example of this type of modeling is the entity relationship diagram shown in Figure 18.6.

FIGURE **18.6**

*An entity relationship diagram.*

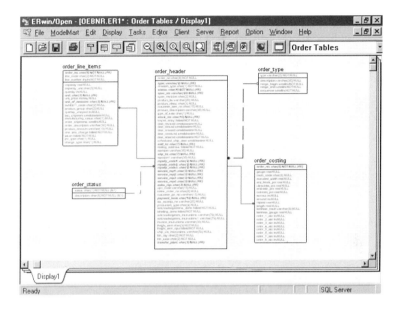

A number of development tools exist for creating such models, such as ERwin/ERX for PowerBuilder by LogicWorks, System Architect, PowerDesigner, and LBMS. Whereas LBMS is a full-scale CASE tool, ERwin/ERX, System Architect, and PowerDesigner are intended more for data modeling, design, and implementation. However, the new versions of these tools can now be used to prototype simple windows and DataWindows and are incorporating more pieces of the development cycle.

A relationship diagram, such as the one in Figure 18.6, helps data modelers visualize the database schema that they are creating. Information gathered during the identification and classification of data elements helps determine the model's entities, attributes, and relationships.

To determine whether an object is an entity, attribute, or relationship, examine the object's properties. Following are some guidelines based on Figure 18.6 for making these classifications:

- If the object has multiple characteristics or values, it's probably an entity. For example, Order has such attributes as status, an identifier (to whom the order was sold), and the ordered date. This makes Order an entity.

- If the object has just one characteristic or value, it's probably an attribute. For example, Order Number is the identifying number of an order, and that's all.

- If the object description contains a verb phrase, it's probably a relationship. For example, the phrase Customer Requests Order describes a relationship between a Customer entity and an Order entity.

During your determination of the attributes associated with an entity, you also want to determine keys of the entities and how you will be organizing the attributes in each entity. You also need to determine the attribute's data type and whether it can be a null value. At an advanced level of the attribute-describing process, you might also want to identify all the extended attribute information, including length, format, edit style, validation rules, and initial values, that can be stored in the PowerBuilder repository tables (see Chapter 5, "Databases and the Database Painter").

After you determine the attributes for the individual entities, you can begin classifying the entities. Group the entities based on their associations with each other. This is the initial phase of *abstraction*, or hiding obscure information to heighten understanding of the analysis. By classifying the data in groups, you produce types of classes for the associated groups (see Figure 18.7), which are more easily viewed and analyzed.

**FIGURE 18.7**

*Grouping related entities for classification.*

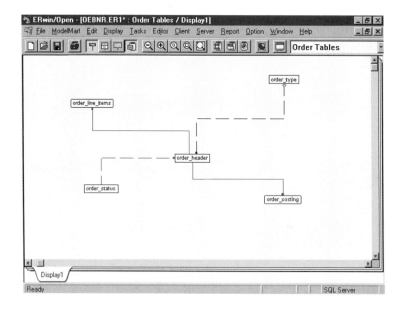

Next, you can generalize multiple entities into single classifications. If you can identify any similarities in their functionality and attribution, you can classify them into a single common entity without losing any of the entities' individual meanings. This phase of classification and generalization of the entities takes you through to the design phase in which you use additional methods, such as normalization (described later in the section "Normalization"), to complete the data analysis to produce a functional database model.

After you collect and model the functionality and data, you are ready to start the design phase of the database and the application.

# Database Design

The database is the central point of any data-based system, and the amount of time invested in the creation of a quality database design greatly determines the quality and success of the system as a whole. Database design can be broken down into four steps:

1. Normalize and finalize table relationships.
2. Identify entity, data, and relational integrity.
3. Create the data's physical schema.
4. Create database objects (triggers, stored procedures, and indexes).

Developing the physical schema uses the products of the data analysis to indicate the tables, columns, and relationships among tables. Columns are assigned data types and possibly even extended attributes, such as the edit style, initial value, validation, display format, and so on. For a more complete description of the extended attributes, refer to Chapter 5.

Table relationships as well as the primary and foreign keys are also defined, and the data analysis will determine most of the table relationships and how they are to be implemented. You can, and should, use a normalization technique to optimize the entities and the relationships between them.

## Normalization

During the data-modeling phase, you use a formal technique known as *normalization* to eliminate certain types of undesirable dependencies among entities. This technique also highlights the constraints and dependencies in the data and aids the data modelers in understanding the actual nature of the data.

By normalizing the database design, you can reduce the amount of stored redundant data, thus easing data maintenance, reducing storage requirements, and dramatically improving data integrity. With normalization, data integrity is easier to enforce because the data resides in only one place in the database. As you see in the examples used to illustrate the normal forms later in this chapter, the size of the records for entities is reduced with normalization as well. For such DBMSs as Sybase's or Microsoft's SQL Server, the smaller the row size, the more data that can be stored per data page, again improving storage requirements and I/O processing because fewer pages need to be read.

But this process has some drawbacks. Because you're breaking up attributes and placing them into separate entities, you have to perform joins between those entities to access a complete record of information. As such, you're accessing data pages for multiple entities and receive a hit in your I/O activities as well as CPU resources because the server has to determine the best method of retrieving the requested information. Techniques to address each performance issue are beyond the scope of this book but can be found in any DBMS-specific book.

> **Note**
>
> Sams Publishing offers a number of books in its *Unleashed* series that address individual DBMSs that provide this kind of information (for example, *Microsoft SQL Server 7.0 Unleashed*, *Oracle Unleashed*, and *SQL Unleashed*).

The higher normal forms that can be reached, typically 3NF and higher, produce well-designed databases with high levels of data independence. Entities in the database model are described as having a certain normal form if they satisfy particular criteria. Each level of the normal forms builds on the previous level.

To aid your understanding of the normalization techniques, each normalization step is followed by a visual example.

The five levels of data normalization are as follows:

- Eliminate repeating groups (1NF, or first normal form)
- Eliminate redundant data (2NF, or second normal form)
- Eliminate columns not dependent on a key (3NF, or third normal form)
- Isolate independent multiple relationships (4NF, or fourth normal form)
- Isolate semantically-related multiple relationships (5NF, or fifth normal form)

The example used in this chapter to illustrate the normalization method consists of the following information:

| Unnormalized attributes for an order-entry system | |
|---|---|
| Order number | Invoice Number |
| Order create date | Invoice Address |
| Customer name | Product description 1 to $n$ |
| Customer address | Product quantity 1 to $n$ |
| | Product discount 1 to $n$ |

# First Normal Form

To eliminate repeating groups, create a separate entity for each group of related attributes and assign to this new entity a primary key and a foreign key to link it back to the parent entity.

In the sample unnormalized attributes, each order can have multiple products but only one customer, so an order could have, for example, five different products going to one customer. If you move these Order Line Item attributes into a separate entity, the other information doesn't need to be repeated for each product (see Table 18.1). At this point, these entities are in the first normal form. You can now use Order Number to easily access both entities: Order and Order Line Item. Order Number acts as a primary key in the Order entity and a foreign key in the Order Line Item entity.

**TABLE 18.1** The Order and Order Line Item Entities and Relationship Between Them

| Order *Entity* | Order Line Item *Entity* |
|---|---|
| Order Number | Order Number |
| Order Create Date | Line Number |
| Customer Name | Product Description |
| Customer Address | Product Quantity |
| Invoice Number | Product Discount |
| Invoice Address | |

**Note**

Sometimes you *won't* want to eliminate a repeating group, which can make this rule difficult to apply. If you have a finite number (usually small) of repeating values that you need to access as side-by-side columns rather than as rows, leave them in the parent. For example, consider that for each order you track up to four service representatives. How those pieces of data are entered and reported would determine whether they stay in the parent or receive their own entity.

## Second Normal Form

To eliminate redundant data, create separate entities for attributes that don't fully depend on the entire primary key of the entity.

In the example, the `Order` entity attributes `Customer Name` and `Customer Address` depend on only the `Customer Number`, whereas the remaining columns depend completely on the `Order Number`. Therefore, you can remove the `Customer Name` and `Customer Address` and create their own entity, such as the one in Table 18.2. These entities are in second normal form.

**TABLE 18.2**  The Addition of the `Customer` Entity to the Entity Pool

| *Order* Entity | *Customer* Entity |
| --- | --- |
| Order Number | Customer Number |
| Order Create Date | Customer Name |
| Customer Number | Customer Address |
| Invoice Number | |
| Invoice Address | |

Further examination also leads you to modify the `Order Line Item` entity because the attributes `Product Description` and `Product Discount` depend on only a `Product Number`, whereas `Order Quantity` depends on both the `Order Number` and a `Product Number`. Therefore, you can remove `Product Description` and `Product Discount` and create their own entity, such as the one in Table 18.3. These entities are in second normal form.

**TABLE 18.3**  The Addition of the `Product` Entity to the Entity Pool

| *Order Line Item* Entity | *Product* Entity |
| --- | --- |
| Order Number | Product Number |
| Line Number | Product Description |
| Product Number | Product Discount |
| Order Quantity | |

## Third Normal Form

You eliminate non-key columns that aren't mutually independent by creating separate entities for these attributes. The `Invoice Address` depends not only on the `Order Number` key but also on the `Invoice Number`. You therefore need to create a new entity, `Invoice` (see Table 18.4), to hold this attribute and remove it from the `Order` entity. The entities are now in third normal form.

**TABLE 18.4** The Addition of the `Invoice` Entity to the Entity Pool

| `Order` *Entity* | `Invoice` *Entity* |
|---|---|
| Order Number | Invoice Number |
| Order Create Date | Invoice Address |
| Customer Number | |
| Invoice Number | |

Third normal form is adequate for most database situations but can't adequately handle the case in which an entity has two or more candidate keys that are composite and have at least one attribute in common. To compensate for this situation, a modified form of third normal form was introduced by two well-known database theorists and is known as *Boyce-Codd Normal Form* (BCNF).

---

**Tip**

To arrive at a 3NF database design, a simple rule is, "Each attribute must be a fact about the key, the whole key, and nothing but the key." (Wiorkowski and Kull, *DB2 Design & Development Guide*.)

---

At this point in the normalization process, you have a functioning database schema; all you need is a system to access it.

Although third normal form is adequate for most databases, some require further normalization. There are also two additional, higher normal forms; some data models might require use of these additional normal forms to produce a better-designed database model.

## Fourth Normal Form

The fourth normal form is concerned with isolating independent multiple relationships. Basically, an entity can't have more than one one-to-many ($1:n$) or many-to-many ($n:m$) relationship that's not directly related to another relationship.

## Fifth Normal Form

Fifth normal form concentrates on isolating semantically-related multiple relationships. You might want to separate many-to-many logically-related relationships; you would use fifth normal form to do so.

# Denormalization

Now use the requirements gathered in the analysis phase to create a design that can be developed for implementation. This additional step creates a database design that's usually one step back from the final level of normalization. This process, called *denormalization*, takes the actual use of the tables and data into consideration to break some normalization rules to provide for duplicate or unrelated attributes in some entities.

This has the advantage of minimizing joins and helping resolve some aggregate values that incur a large penalty to calculate. It also might require less storage space when you compare the additional column sizes against the overhead of a separate table and associated indexes.

> **Note**
>
> Consider this scenario: If you take Sybase/Microsoft SQL Server and repeat three four-character columns in one table, the amount of additional storage required is 12 bytes. However, if the columns were in their own tables, you would have the storage requirements of a primary key, part of which would be a foreign key to the parent table, together with the four-character column for each row. For example, if the primary key of the parent were an eight-character column, the overall storage requirements to store the three rows would be 36 bytes.

Because denormalization is usually done for data-access reasons and not for data modifications, you should weigh the pros and cons for the level of normalization against what the focus of the database is to be—query or data entry.

# Ensuring Data Integrity

It would be a shame to go through all the effort of analysis, design, and even implementation only to have the crux of the whole system, the data, become corrupted over time. Various techniques help ensure the data's integrity, but first the different areas of data integrity need to be defined:

- *Entity integrity* is the characteristic of each row being a unique instance of the entity that contains it. This type of integrity is usually enforced with a unique index being created on the primary-key fields.

- *Domain integrity* ensures the correctness of the actual data values. This type of integrity is enforced by specifying data types, nullability, and database rules and defaults.

- *Referential integrity* is used to ensure that foreign-key values correctly match up to primary-key values in the parent tables. This type of integrity is also used to restrict or cascade changes from parent entities to child entities and is usually implemented using triggers or other declarative referential integrity constraints.

# Creating Triggers, Stored Procedures, and Indexes

Triggers, stored procedures, and indexes enable the database to maintain referential integrity, easy accessibility, and adaptability. *Triggers* can be used to maintain data integrity, parent-child table relationships, and column validations, among other things. *Stored procedures* are used as a repetitive mechanism for working behind the scenes of an application and provide precompiled forms of often-used SQL. *Indexes* are used to promote fast access to data via an ordering scheme.

Triggers are designed for individual tables for three types of operations: deleting, inserting, and updating. These operations can be represented in one trigger, two triggers, or more (trigger implementation is DBMS specific). The appropriate trigger is fired when one of these operations is performed on a table.

Stored procedures are used for repetitive tasks such as pulling down data from one database to update another database, data massaging, and complex queries, to name a few.

Indexes are used to access data more quickly and easily. When you create a table, you will want to set up a primary key. There might be one or more columns that provide a unique value or set of values that identify a single record of information. Creating an index on that primary key enforces entity integrity.

Indexes can also be created on columns other than the primary key. For example, if you wanted to access in alphabetical order all customer names in a customer table where the customer ID is the primary key, you would place an index on the customer name column. This would decrease the time to display those names in order or to access an individual record. Foreign keys (the primary keys from other tables) are also good candidates for indexes because they are used frequently in joins between the tables.

Of course, be selective about what columns should or should not be indexed. As with everything, too much indexing will adversely affect performance, especially when it comes to data updates because the DBMS must make changes to each affected index as well as to the actual data page.

**18**

Analysis, Design, and Implementation

## Documenting the Database Design

Always use some form of documentation for the database design. As stated earlier, many tools and methods—such as ERwin/ERX, PowerDesigner, and Data Description Languages (DDLs) generated straight from the database—capture all this information for you. These types of tools usually provide several report formats that you can use to view the database design in various ways. Doing this allows you to easily maintain the design and make changes in an informed manner.

# Programming PowerBuilder

The processes discussed earlier in the "Object-Oriented Analysis and Design" section are only part of the system development life cycle, which is the inner piece of the client/server application development methodology. The analysis and design phases concentrate on creating a database schema, designing and determining system requirements, and matching those requirements to PowerBuilder functionality. The result is a design of the database and system requirements that can be used to develop and implement a client/server application.

So now that you've learned about the analysis and design phases of a successful client/server application, it's time to focus on the system development phase of the system development life cycle. You use the end product of the system design phase of the life cycle as a building block for the development process. The database design and the designed system requirements are the basis for the development of the application.

The system development phase consists of molding the designed system requirements categories (input, output, and processing) into a working PowerBuilder application. The design provides the indicators of the necessary PowerBuilder functionality for each category. Now you must develop these application-required features using objects and scripts. Two different methods of developing are described here: rapid application development and object-oriented programming. The latter usually follows a successful cycle of the former.

## Using Rapid Application Development (RAD)

RAD is a technique for creating, as quickly as possible, a working application that requires minor testing and can then be shown to users. Updates and revisions, as well as testing, are commonly done in front of end users to get immediate feedback on the changes and the application's functionality. PowerBuilder lends itself to this approach of development because its painters enable you to rapidly create and modify objects used in the application.

A typical rapid application development workflow follows a pattern similar to that shown in Figure 18.8.

**FIGURE 18.8**
*A rapid applica-
tion development
workflow
diagram.*

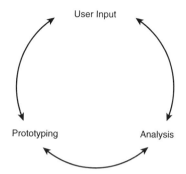

User Input

Prototyping                  Analysis

In PowerBuilder, the major concentration of work is in the development of the user interface portion of the input category of the designed system requirements. The RAD approach enables you to construct the user interface in a way that enables users to interact with it and quickly provide feedback on the updates or revisions they require.

At this point, you basically have a working prototype that users can manipulate. Not only does this expedite the development of the user interface, but it also enables users to visualize and interact with the interface. This visualization and interaction contribute to the users' understanding of the application functionality and acceptance of the application itself. In the RAD process, users directly affect the development and appearance of the user interface by being a part of the initial design and testing phases.

RAD is an excellent way to continue the prototype design method. Because the skeleton of the system already exists in the prototype, you can just add the necessary objects and scripts to move the prototype to a first version of the final application. Often, though, the mistakes and pitfalls of the prototype require that you start from a solid base and that the prototype be used just as a model with only core functionality that will move into the new generation of the application.

Because PowerBuilder provides the means to quickly create and modify objects and scripts in a working application, RAD is the preferred method of development for modules and small systems. The analysts involved during this stage must be aware of end-user-influenced "scope creep." As end users experience and experiment with the prototype, they will consider "What if?" and "How about?" scenarios. This might lead to a more useful final application, but the time and monetary costs should be considered and relayed to end users. This allows you to prioritize modules and features within the scope of the project budget.

**18**

*Analysis, Design,
and
Implementation*

# Object-Oriented Programming

Object orientation is an extensive subject that can't be totally covered in this book. You can find many books completely dedicated to the topic in any good technical bookstore. Probably one of the best-known and most well-respected books is *Object-Oriented Analysis and Design with Applications* by Grady Booch.

Object orientation is an extension of the information modeling techniques discussed in this chapter. It further defines the entities that have been identified to include outside processes that act on these entities. These entities, along with services and data, become objects that are the basis for the program's functionality. The application is created and defined from the interaction of these objects. These interactions can be message- or function-call–based and are requests to the object to carry out a particular task.

This type of programming uses three basic principles. As discussed previously, *abstraction* is the hiding of detail. It allows you to view the problem or process as a black box so that the solution can be arrived at in a nonimplementation-specific manner. *Encapsulation* is the grouping together of related ideas, characteristics, and operations into a single conceptual unit. It allows the hiding of object attributes and characteristics from other objects. *Inheritance* is the development of a hierarchy in related objects so that a child uses the characteristics of its parents.

In PowerBuilder, you encapsulate an object's functionality mainly through the object's events but also through the use of functions and the keywords `Private` and `Protected`. As you construct objects for your application, build each with an eye on where it will exist within the overall object hierarchy. This enables the creation of child objects that can use the scripts and functionality of their parents.

System requirements dictate what you must develop. An important development practice is to decide what should *not* be developed. In other words, some of these matched functionalities are repetitive or unnecessary. You must decide which objects can be grouped together and developed into a hierarchy, thus ensuring that the objects can share functionality and scripts, using a parent or ancestor as the base for their functionality.

# HOW 2.1 Learning Edition

One product growing in popularity among PowerBuilder developers is HOW by Riverton Software. HOW is a business object modeling tool that allows you to design and generate components for use with n-tier PowerBuilder application development. HOW comes equipped with various analysis and design tools that allow you to build and reuse objects in such areas of your application as business processes, data access, and user interface. HOW also comes equipped with a centralized object repository that integrates with ObjectCycle or PVCS for version control for use with multideveloper projects.

HOW allows you to perform Use Case analysis for logically gathering your user's requirements using the Use Case View Builder. From the various Use Case scenarios, you can derive your business rules, which can then be created using hypertext links. The business rules you generate can then be classified by type and used to create your application's business objects. After you define your Use Cases, you can then identify the application's workflow and assemble the application components with storyboards. HOW now includes a UML-compliant Interaction Builder that allows you to create interaction diagrams like the ones discussed in earlier sections.

The Workflow Builder in HOW allows you to visually design your application's business processes using a standard workflow notation. The workflow is used to display how all your previously designed Use Cases fit together in the process flow of the application. After you determine the system flow and identify any potential holes, you can begin the generation of your application components. The Domain Builder allows you to generate the actual business objects from the business rules you've developed. HOW lets you create two kinds of business objects: *persistent objects* that correlate to your database tables and *nonpersistent business objects* that are your PowerBuilder nonvisual user objects (NVOs). The persistent objects (database tables) can be used to generate your data models using ERwin or PowerDesigner.

HOW's Task Storyboard allows you to build your application's interface and the flow graphically. This includes defining window navigation, using business object attributes to populate interface objects such as DataWindows, specifying the links between application components, and creating PowerBuilder controls. After defining the application's appearance and behavior using the Task Storyboard, you are then ready to generate your PowerBuilder objects. The objects that are built, by default, are PowerBuilder PCF-based, but you can configure them to use other frameworks.

In addition to supporting the PFC, HOW uses its own framework built on the PFC. Called the PowerBuilder OpenFrame Reference, it consists of eight PBLs. OpenFrame partitions the application into the interface, business logic, and data access for you. HOW also fully integrates with Sybase's distributed technology.

As you can see, HOW provides a tool that helps you not only in the analysis and design of your application, but also in the initial generation of your PowerBuilder objects. The Learning Edition of HOW, which can be downloaded from Riverton's Web site at www.riverton.com, varies from the HOW Enterprise Edition in that the Learning Edition limits the number of objects you can create and store in the object model. HOW runs in Windows 95/98/NT and is compatible with Platinum ERwin versions 3.0 and 3.5.*x* and PowerDesigner versions through 6.1.1. As with PowerBuilder, HOW 2.1 now supports Java and Microsoft Visual Basic.

**18**

*Analysis, Design, and Implementation*

# Matching Categories to PowerBuilder Functionality

From the design system requirements, you match the three categories of input, output, and processing with PowerBuilder functionality. From here, you can develop the actual functionality of the application. The input and output categories were determined in the database schema. This schema was constructed in the system design phase and must be synchronized into the chosen data sources before development of any of these three categories can occur. After the data source definitions and descriptions are implemented, the development of the application can proceed. Of course, some modification of the database schema will occur during development, but it should always be documented and approved before any changes occur. This gives you the opportunity to verify the impact of such changes throughout the application.

To build the components of the application for the input, output, and processing categories, you use different PowerBuilder painters. These painters provide the tools for creating and modifying objects.

## Developing the Input Category

The input category consists of the user interface and data source access and is directly associated with windows, window controls, and DataWindows.

When you create a window in the Window painter, you define the attributes and properties of that window and add window controls for user interaction. Window controls such as command buttons, radio buttons, edit boxes, and list boxes enable users to perform actions on the window.

There are different types of windows (refer to Chapter 10, "Windows and the Window Painter," for a further description of the window types), but two useful window types are the MDI frame and main windows. The *multiple-document interface* (MDI) enables users to interact with multiple sheets (windows) within the frame. Users can perform different tasks on multiple windows at the same time. The other type of interface is a *single-document interface* (SDI), which provides users with a single, main window to perform a specific task. If users require a different task, a different main window must be accessed. The method of designing and developing the application depends solely on the type of application required and is driven by the system requirements previously defined.

One important fact that you will pull from the design is whether the PowerBuilder application will be constructed using a multiple- or single-document interface. This decision will be based on the perceived flow of information through the system as you defined it in the system design phase. To do this, decide how the data will be organized and presented, and how users will move around in the application. This will dictate how the application's user interface should be designed.

Within these different types of windows, you can map desired functionality to controls. Event-driven processing puts users in control of how an application operates and uses controls to display and interact with the data. (See Chapter 10 and Chapter 11, "Advanced Controls," for further descriptions of the types of controls for windows.)

Menus provide another way of manipulating data or interacting with the application. Users selects menu items to initiate an action. Menus can be accessed from a menu bar, an MDI Frame toolbar, or a pop-up menu. (For a more complete description of menus, see Chapter 12, "Menus and the Menu Painter.")

For example, you might want to create an order-entry application that allows users to have more than one order open at the same time. Users might want to compare multiple orders or create a repeat order, for example. The MDI style easily provides this functionality, but additional code would be required in an SDI application.

The basic techniques employed in developing a user interface require you to know how to display a dialog box or message box, hide and show a window, open multiple instances of a window, enable and disable window controls, and perform drag-and-drop in a window.

For accessing data, you should develop retrieval techniques that can prompt users to enter the selection criteria, retrieve multiple rows of information, and perform retrievals from multiple databases. This information should then be presented to users consistently so that they can perform data-entry-type actions or suitable formatting and printing functions for reports.

You can develop windows and user objects that can be used to pass on functionality through inheritance to other windows and controls. This condenses future programming time and enables you to reuse code by inheriting the scripts and attributes from these objects.

As part of your initial foray into prototyping windows, carefully consider mapping business transactions or processes to individual windows. This worthwhile step can save considerable time in the prototyping stage. Other benefits of considering these relationships are that you will refine task-time estimates, improve task assignment and ordering, and ensure that the design document encompasses all the perceived requirements.

**18**

Analysis, Design,
and
Implementation

# Developing the Output Category

The *output category* consistsof the information produced by the application. The system requirements have already defined the appropriate reports, the data to be written to data sinks, and the external files to be created. You need to consider by what method you will implement these requirements in the application.

PowerBuilder provides DataWindows as an excellent way of reporting and saving information. A DataWindow can be specifically designed to accommodate an online, printed, or file-written report. For a further explanation of the development of the DataWindow as a reporting device, see Chapter 6, "The DataWindow Painter."

By using a similar concept of mapping business transactions/processes to windows, also consider mapping database tables to DataWindows. As with windows, this might not be a one-to-one relationship; more than one DataWindow might retrieve and save data from the same table. If there's considerable overlap of columns between DataWindows, the DataWindows might become candidates for data sharing, or you might need to reexamine the underlying database structure to determine whether the most optimal design has been achieved.

When dealing with data from a data source, you must determine whether you want to use a DataWindow or an embedded SQL statement to create, update, delete, and retrieve the data. For further information on developing the DataWindow for updating database information, see Chapter 14, "DataWindow Scripting." For more information on developing the SQL statements for updating database information, see Chapter 4, "SQL and PowerBuilder."

For updating data and managing DataWindows, you should develop objects that can update multiple rows, update multiple databases, manage master and detail DataWindow controls, accept the data from a user's last entry, work with the current and/or displayed row, share data with other DataWindows, dynamically change a DataWindow, and perform validation in the DataWindow. For example, if a DataWindow will be used to display one or more rows of information, consider from what source the data will be retrieved or entered, what validation will need to occur, what additional processing needs to be carried out, and where the data will be saved when users are finished.

PowerBuilder also enables you to generate external files such as Excel spreadsheets and text files. You dictate which columns of data will be included and the order in which they will appear as the PowerBuilder application writes them out.

Using a DataWindow control to satisfy the input and output design system requirements can sometimes be overkill, and edit fields and other controls should be used instead. For example, a connect window is designed to gather user information for the purpose of connecting to a database. The only required window controls are four single-line edits, two command buttons, and a check box. The window is gathering the user ID, password, database name, and server name through the four single-line edits. This input and output information could use a DataWindow, but you're performing no validation, formatting, data retrieval, or updates. Therefore, a DataWindow provides little more than a slight reduction in the use of Windows resources during the lifetime of the window, which in this case is very short-lived.

> **Note**
>
> Carefully consider the uses of each control and which one of the many provided will give you the desired functionality with the minimum of implementation and maintenance.

## Developing the Processing Category

The processing category handles all internal and external system processing. For the most part, PowerBuilder applications are event driven, and the flow and logic of processing must be controlled and manipulated inside object events. Obviously, you can also write procedural applications with PowerBuilder as you may have done in a more traditional language, but you will soon find end users returning with additional requirements and needed flexibility. You write scripts using PowerScript to specify the processing that occurs when an event is triggered. (For more explanation of object events, see Chapter 2, "PowerBuilder 7.0 Development Environment," and Chapter 7, "The PowerScript Language.")

For example, windows have Open and Close events, window control buttons have Clicked events, edit boxes have Modified events, and DataWindow controls have ItemChanged events. All these events are commonly used to house the application processing logic for these objects.

The Open and Close events are used to perform initialization and cleanup for a window object and its related controls and instance variables. Clicked events are scripted to perform a specific action such as a retrieve, an update, or a delete of data. When users change a value, the Modified event in an edit box and the ItemChanged in a DataWindow are fired. This can be used to verify the new user value, trigger another event, or just enable other controls in the window or DataWindow object.

In any of these situations, you decide how to program the processing logic determined in the system design requirements. You can also define user events for specific processing of an object. (For further explanation of the development of user events, see Chapter 2.)

You can also move or perform certain parts of the processing by interacting with DLL functions, communicating via dynamic data exchange or object linking and embedding, or sending electronic mail (to name just a few ways). From the system requirements, you should be able to identify specific requirements that you know PowerBuilder won't be able to solve directly. This might require the use or access of external controls or software packages, some of which might directly integrate with PowerBuilder—for example, to perform imaging or special graphics tasks.

The scripts you write will reflect the application control flow and the additional services requested from other programs. This includes the process of connecting to other programs to access their data and functions.

The processing category exists as encapsulated code in appropriate objects. Business objects should be constructed for the encapsulation of specific functionality and implemented using class user objects.

### Code and Validation Tables

Depending on the requirements of the supporting code and validation tables in your database schema, you need to decide whether you can construct a generic table maintenance window and runtime-constructed DataWindow or a specific window and individual DataWindows that carry out additional checks or processing on the data entered. Often the access to these types of code-maintenance windows is restricted to a particular subset of the end-user community, and you also need to consider the relevant security.

## Ensuring Application Security

The security of certain application functions and the validity and security of the data is an often-forgotten or even a post-development consideration. As part of the design of input, output, and processing, the necessary security and access privileges also need to be gathered and implemented into the basic framework of the application.

Several third-party add-on packages enable you to control user access to particular functions, objects, and even DataWindow columns. These products might be overkill in some applications, especially those with only a small number of user groups. In those cases, simple restrictions based on SQL group IDs can be used to disable menu options and controls in menu title Clicked events or window Open events, respectively.

> **Note**
>
> The PowerBuilder Foundation Class offers a robust security solution. Even if it's too robust to implement in your project, it's a good place to begin and possibly scale down to fit your needs.

# Starting the Project

Construct your project team to give yourself a good cross-section of the program development knowledge that exists in your department or company. Early definition of each project member's role helps develop a cohesive team and application. Technical leader, technical writer, and tester are some roles to which you should allocate people. Project members can cover more than one of these positions, depending on resources and skill sets.

One of the most important roles that can be filled is that of a change controller. A smoothly running development process can be quickly derailed without some kind of change control. Especially during RAD sessions, users will try to make considerable changes to the system specifications that might have already been signed off on by an end-user representative. The change controller collates the required changes and assigns the priority and scheduling for them.

If other PowerBuilder or GUI projects have been completed successfully, you should hold a debriefing to examine their structure and approach. Even unsuccessful projects can provide valuable insight into the approaches you should take, what to avoid, and what should be done that wasn't done before. Don't be afraid to make mistakes when starting your first client/server application. Learn from the problems you encounter and grow stronger in your processes and knowledge. It's a mistake only if it occurs a second time.

While you're investigating other projects, look for naming conventions and GUI standards that have been used. You don't have to follow these blindly, but you should gauge the effects that any changes you make will have on future development efforts or on prospective end-user groups. End users hate having to learn vastly different application interfaces, and developers hate having to alter the way they code. The following section looks at some standards and conventions.

Before any coding is even started on a production version of the application, you should have identified any frameworks or class libraries that will be used. This will affect the method by which you identify ancestor objects—especially candidates for abstract and concrete class objects. For a full discussion of frameworks and class libraries, see Chapter 24, "Frameworks and Class Libraries."

**18**

Analysis, Design, and Implementation

If you are uncertain about any stage of the project—from starting it to carrying it through development or implementing and distributing the solution—look for outside help. This help can come from other areas of your company or from a recognized consulting firm that can show you a solid history of implemented client/server applications.

# Standards and Naming Conventions

Having standards for coding and conventions for naming objects and variables is as important for individual developers as it is for team projects. Standards and naming conventions provide the following benefits:

- Objects and variables have consistent names.

- You can easily determine what an object is or where a variable is defined.

- Scripts have the same look.

- Scripts are easily maintainable.

- Objects and applications are easily maintainable.

The learning time required for a set of standards is short when you consider the advantages of their application over the life of the application and future applications.

PowerBuilder allows up to 40 characters for an identifier (an object or a variable name).

> **Note**
>
> The 40-character limit on identifiers is the value stated in the PowerBuilder online help, but you can declare an identifier of 99 characters before you get a compile error. Of course, it's unlikely that you would ever use 40 characters, let alone 99.

The following section illustrates various types of standards and conventions. The first type is from the Sybase manuals, and the next is from an actual client project that we have worked on. Each has something to add to the arguments about naming conventions, and you can pull a little from each and decide on your own.

The most common technique used in naming items is to use a prefix in the names of objects and variables that varies depending on the type of object, access level, and scope.

# Sybase Conventions

Sybase has declared a set of standards and conventions, and whereas it used to completely fail to follow them in code examples and online help, the same can't be said now. Sybase has finally delivered on its promise of a clear set of conventions that it will use in all its sample code and in future PowerBuilder releases.

With the introduction of the PowerBuilder Foundation Class (PFC), a set of naming standards was put together and made available for your use. Tables 18.5, 18.6, and 18.7 detail the Sybase-suggested naming guidelines and are taken from the online help available for the PFC.

TABLE **18.5**   Object Naming in the PFC

| Class | Prefix | Example |
|-------|--------|---------|
| Application | (none) | quickstart |
| DataWindow | d_ | d_authors |
| Function | f_ | f_get_symbol |
| Menu | m_ | m_system |
| NonVisualObject | n_ | n_book |
| Pipeline | pl_ | pl_finance_refresh |
| Project | pr_ | pr_quickstart |
| Query | q_ | q_delivery_codes |
| Structure | s_ | s_person |
| UserObject | u_ | u_security |
| Window | w_ | w_library |

TABLE **18.6**   Data Type Naming in the PFC

| Data Type | Prefix | Example |
|-----------|--------|---------|
| Application | app_ | app_myapp |
| Connection | cn_ | cn_orders |
| ConnectionInfo | cninfo_ | cninfo_orderusers |
| ConnectObject | cno_ | cno_orders |
| DataStore | ds_ | ds_servicereplist |
| DataWindow | dw_ | dw_orders |
| DataWindowChild | dwc_ | dwc_ordertype |
| DragObject | drg_ | drg_anorder |
| DrawObject | drw_ | drw_object |
| Dwobject | dwo_ | dwo_dynamic |
| DynamicDescriptionArea | dda_ | dda_mine |
| DynamicStagingArea | dsa_ | dsa_mine |
| Environment | env_ | env_mine |
| Error | err_ | err_mine |
| ExtObject | ext_ | ext_object |

**TABLE 18.6** Data Type Naming in the PFC

| Data Type | Prefix | Example |
|---|---|---|
| GraphicObject | go_ | go_current |
| GrAxis | grax_ | grax_x |
| GrDispAttr | grda_ | grda_attribute1 |
| HorizontalProgressBar | hpb | hpb_install |
| HorizontalTrackBar | htb | htb_rating |
| ListViewItem | lvi_ | lvi_item |
| MailFileDescription | mfd_ | mfd_attach1 |
| MailMessage | mm_ | mm_memo |
| MailRecipient | mr_ | mr_to |
| MailSession | ms_ | ms_error |
| MdiClient | mdi_ | mdi_1 |
| Menu | m_ | m_frame |
| MenuCascade | mc_ | mc_edit |
| Message | msg_ | msg_mine |
| NonVisualObject | nv_ | nv_controller |
| OleControl | oc_ | oc_clip |
| OleObject | oo_ | oo_clip |
| OleStorage | ostg_ | ostg_1 |
| OleStream | ostm_ | ostm_1 |
| OmControl | omc_ | omc_1 |
| OmCustomControl | omcc_ | omcc_1 |
| OmEmbedded control | omec_ | omec_1 |
| OmObject | omo_ | omo_1 |
| OmStream | omstm_ | omstm_1 |
| OmStorage | omstg_ | omstg_1 |
| PictureHyperLink | phl | phl_newquery |
| Pipeline | pl_ | pl_transfer |
| PowerObject | po_ | po_object |
| RemoteObject | rem_ | rem_object |
| RteObject | rteo_ | rteo_memo |
| StaticTextHyperlink | sth | sth_home |
| Structure | str_ | str_bagvalues |
| TabPage | tabpg_ | tabpg_1 |
| Transaction | tr_ | tr_ordercursor |
| Transport | trp_ | trp_mine |
| TreeViewItem | tvi_ | tvi_item |
| UserObject | uo_ | uo_object |
| WindowObject | wo_ | wo_object |
| Window | w_ | w_frame |
| VerticalProgressBar | vpb | vpb_upload |
| VerticalTrackBar | vtb | vtb_confidence |
| Any | a_ | a_current |

TABLE **18.6** Data Type Naming in the PFC

| Data Type | Prefix | Example |
| --- | --- | --- |
| Blob | blb_ | blb_word_doc |
| Boolean | b_ | b_isselected |
| Character | ch_ | ch_gender |
| Date | d_ | d_payday |
| DateTime | dtm_ | dt_logged_at |
| Decimal | dec_ | dec_pi |
| Double | dbl_ | dbl_result |
| Enumerated (any type) | enum_ | enum_alignment |
| Integer | i_ | i_count |
| Long | l_ | l_row |
| Real | r_ | r_fudge |
| String | s_ | s_name |
| Time | tm_ | tm_now |
| UnsignedInteger | ui_ | ui_count |
| UnsignedLong | ul_ | ul_count |
| Custom | cst_ | cst_object |
| External | ext_ | ext_object |
| C++ | cpp_ | cpp_object |

TABLE **18.7** Variable Scope in the PFC

| Variable Type | Scope Qualifier | Example |
| --- | --- | --- |
| Argument | a | as_title |
| Global | g | gnv_app |
| Instance | i | ii_count |
| Local | l | ll_row |
| Shared/Class | s | si_height |

Object-level functions in the PFC are all prefixed with of_ regardless of what type of object they are defined in. This is also true of structures prefixed with os_. User-defined events are prefixed with pfc_.

Single spaces are placed before and after all operators and the assignment verb (=), and after each comma in a function parameter list. Use tabs rather than spaces, however, to indent code to show inclusion in loops and other compound statements.

Function  calls are coded in upper- and lowercase. Variables are all lowercase.

# Alternate Project Conventions

As you can see from the previous section, Sybase didn't go to any great lengths to detail standard naming or coding conventions. Tables 18.8, 18.9, and 18.10 show the conventions used on a real-life project and provide a different set of standards that you can follow.

**TABLE 18.8** Alternate Object Naming Conventions

| Type | Prefix | Example |
|------|--------|---------|
| Application | (none) | order_entry |
| Application function | af_ | af_CloseDown() |
| Application structure | as_ | as_OpenWindows |
| Window | w_ | w_frame |
| Window function | wf_ | wf_SaveOrder() |
| Window structure | ws_ | ws_order |
| Menu | m_ | m_frame |
| Menu function | mf_ | mf_CloseSheet() |
| Menu structure | ms_ | ms_sheets |
| User object | u_ | u_dw |
| Class user object | u_n_ | u_n_transaction |
| C++ user object | u_cc_ | u_cc_encryption |
| Visual external user object | u_vx_ | u_vx_status |
| Visual VBX user object | u_vbx_ | u_vbx_counter |
| User object function | uf_ | uf_ChangeDataObject() |
| User object structure | us_ | us_pointers |
| DataWindow object | d_ | d_order_header |
| DataWindow control | dw_ | dw_HeaderEdit |
| Query | q_ | q_order_summary |
| Project | same as application | order_entry |
| Pipeline | p_ | p_watcom_to_sybase |
| Structure object | s_ | s_keys |
| Function object | f_ | f_GenerateNumber() |
| Function object structure | fs_ | fs_PriorNumbers |

**TABLE 18.9** Alternate Data Type Naming Conventions

| Data Type | Prefix Qualifier | Example |
|-----------|-----------------|---------|
| Blob | bb | bbWordDoc |
| Window | w | wParent |
| MenuItem | m | mFrame |
| DataWindow | dw | dwOrderHeader |
| DataWindowChild | dwc | dwcServiceRep1 |
| ListViewItem | lvi_ | lvi_file |
| TreeViewItem | tvi_ | tvi_file |
| User object | uo | uoButton |
| Integer | n | nCount |
| Unsigned integer | un | unCount |
| Long | l | lRow |
| Unsigned long | ul | ulRow |
| Boolean | b | bFlag |

TABLE 18.9  Alternate Data Type Naming Conventions

| Data Type | Prefix Qualifier | Example |
|---|---|---|
| String | sz | szName |
| Character | c | cInitial |
| Double | d | dCost |
| Real | r | rCost |
| Decimal | dec | decCost |
| Date | dt | dtToday |
| Structure | s | sKeys |
| MailSession | Pbmail | PBmailSession |
| Transaction | tr | trServiceReps |
| Time | t | tNow |
| DateTime | dtm | dtmCreated |

TABLE 18.10  Alternate Variable Scope Conventions

| Scope | Prefix Qualifier | Example |
|---|---|---|
| Global | g_ | g_szID |
| Shared | sh_ | sh_nSheetNo |
| Instance | i_ | i_nThisSheetNo |
| Argument | a_ | a_wParent |

Local variables don't have a scope prefix because they are by far the most commonly used. Therefore, any variable you see without a prefix is a local variable. You also use the argument prefix when specifying arguments within the DataWindow and Custom Event painters.

Single spaces are placed before and after all operators and the assignment verb (=), and before each argument in a function parameter list.

Use tabs rather than spaces to indent code to show inclusion in loops and other compound statements.

Function calls and variables are coded in upper- and lowercase.

Database commands (such as INSERT, SELECT, and DECLARE CURSOR ) should be all uppercase, with field names in lowercase, and PowerBuilder bind variables should use the same convention as normal PowerBuilder variables. PowerScript functions and commands should be coded with the first letter of each word capitalized (such as If and RightTrim()). User-defined objects should be in all lowercase (for example, f_clear_mdi_children()).

Line continuation should leave connecting tokens (for example, AND or +) at the end of the line rather than at the beginning of the next line.

One-line structures should be broken into multiple lines:

```
If nRows > 6 Then
    dw_report.Retrieve()
EndIf
```

rather than appear like this:

```
If nRows > 6 Then dw_report.Retrieve()
```

The interpreter (and now compiler) doesn't differentiate between these formats, and the suggested format removes any unnecessary errors when you want to actually include the next line in the `If` clause but forget to expand the control structure.

## Inheritance

All objects used on a window or in construction of a user object are ideally inherited. This ensures consistency throughout development of the application and of future applications. Ideally, all windows are also inherited.

## Application Objects

The application object is located in its own library. One individual controls this object. Developers should make copies into their private PBLs if they need to make local changes. Any permanent changes must be coordinated through the authorized developer. Because global variables and global external functions are a part of the application object, the authorized developer must make modifications to these functions.

## Library Naming

PBL names conform to the format *AAA_EEEE*, where *AAA* is the project abbreviation (it can be just one or two characters if you want), and *EEEE* is the object type or business function abbreviation (for example, `OE_MAIN.PBL`, `PRS_DWIN.PBL`).

In addition to these libraries are three more types:

- The extension for application-independent objects or framework libraries, which uses the abbreviation `SH_` for shared

- The application-specific ancestor objects, which uses the prefix `ANC_`

- A library for each developer, which should uniquely identify that person (The person's logon should be sufficient if it's eight or fewer characters.)

## The Library Search Path

In the library earch path, the developer's private PBL comes first, followed by shared PBLs, then ancestor PBLs, and finally application-specific PBLs. The order of each section should be as follows: structures, functions, menus, DataWindows, user objects, and then windows.

Developers should check out objects into their private work libraries. All object modifications occur there, and when finished and tested, the objects are checked back into the originating library. See Chapter 22, "Application Maintenance and Upgrades," for more information on object check-in and checkout.

## Control Names

The prefix for controls is rarely changed from the PowerBuilder defaults displayed in the Preferences painter. Table 18.11 lists each control and its default prefix.

TABLE **18.11** Default Control Prefixes

| Control | Prefix | Control | Prefix |
|---------|--------|---------|--------|
| CheckBox | cbx_ | Oval | oval_ |
| CommandButton | cb_ | Picture | p_ |
| DataWindow | dw_ | PictureButton | pb_ |
| DropDownListBox | ddlb_ | PictureListBox | plb_ |
| RadioButton | rb_ | PictureHyperlink | phl |
| DropDownPictureListBox | ddplb_ | Rectangle | r_ |
| EditMask | em_ | RoundRectangle | rr_ |
| Graph | gr_ | RichTextEdit | rte_ |
| GroupBox | gb_ | SingleLineEdit | sle_ |
| HscrollBar | hsb_ | StaticText | st_ |
| HProgressBar | hpb | StaticTextHyperlink | shl |
| HTrackBar | htb | Tab | tab_ |
| Line | ln_ | Tab Page | tabpage_ |
| ListBox | lb_ | TreeView | tv_ |
| ListView | lv_ | User object | uo_ |
| MultiLineEdit | mle_ | VProgressBar | vpb |
| OleControl | ole_ | VScrollBar | vsb_ |

**18**

Analysis, Design, and Implementation

> **Note**
>
> In the PowerBuilder Foundation Class, the following objects have different prefixes:
>
> | Object | Prefix |
> | --- | --- |
> | OleControl | oc |
> | Rectangle | rec |
> | RoundRectangle | rrec |

## Other Standards

The standards described so far are used only within the PowerBuilder development environment; you also need to consider what the front end will look like. For this, you need to set some GUI guidelines. Remember that these are only guidelines. They aren't meant to be all-encompassing or too restricting but to show what colors, 2D or 3D effects, and fonts to use.

An excellent reference for these kinds of guidelines is *The Windows Interface—An Application Design Guide*, published by Microsoft Press. This book, relevant mostly to Microsoft Windows applications, covers the principles of user interface design, the keyboard, windows, menus, dialog boxes, and even OLE and pen computing.

By specifying GUI guidelines, you can eliminate randomly designed GUIs with inconsistent menus, dialog boxes, and buttons.

Several companies are starting to sell GUI and naming guidelines, usually in an online format that you might want to examine. If you buy one of the commercial frameworks available, you will also be buying the GUI and naming standards that have been used in its development.

# Summary

This chapter briefly covered system analysis, design, and development. These processes are only a part of the system development life cycle, which is the inner piece of the client/server application development methodology. The design and analysis phases concentrate on creating a database schema, designing and determining system requirements, and matching those requirements to PowerBuilder functionality. The system development phase is concerned with creating a working application from the system design requirements.

Using PowerBuilder objects and the PowerScript language, you can transform the input, output, and processing design system requirements into the desired client/server application. The ease with which you can design and implement applications using PowerBuilder will improve with experience.

This chapter also looked at some different naming and coding conventions. What you decide to use might be forced on you by a class library or framework, or you might stick with Sybase's conventions or define your own, drawing on various areas of the conventions detailed. If you do create your own, you need to be aware of the many areas that require definition of a standard or convention, such as GUI guidelines.

**18**

Analysis, Design, and Implementation

# Documentation and Online Help

Just as there are many ways to code functionality into your application, there are myriad ways to document a client/server application. This problem isn't a concern just for PowerBuilder development teams, but for all team members involved with client/server technology. This chapter explores some possibilities for documenting your system. You will also look at providing online help for end users through MicroHelp cues or full-blown Windows Help pages.

# System Documentation

Probably the worst moment in the development cycle for developers is when someone says, "Okay, now we need to document the system!" If you can build enough discipline into your developers, you may have some of the system already documented, as they will have been commenting their code as they go. If you have document templates and a procedure for creating the documentation, you can make life easier for all those involved and end up with a better written and more organized piece of work. You should also try to make it as interesting and as varied as possible so that developers can maintain at least some interest in the task.

System documentation should exist not only on paper but also within the application itself. You should use the comment entries available in the Library painter to label each object—and even each library—with a short description. PowerScript functions and events should ideally have a comment block (or code header) at the start, and then short one- or two-line descriptions with logical blocks of code. (See Chapter 7, "The PowerScript Language," for details on comment syntax.)

The following is an example of a code header:

```
/*****************************************************************
   Function/Event Name: wf_SaveHeader()
   Date Created: 04/20/99 by Simon Herbert
   Functional Description:
      This function saves all the relevant header information
      for an order.
   Modifications made:
      08/22/97 by Simon Gallagher
            Added the validation check added for product_code
   *****************************************************************/
```

This theme obviously has many variations, and you will want to track several different pieces of information (such as name, creation date, description, parameters, and modifications made). Make sure that all team members create this kind of comment block; it will be a valuable source of information when someone develops new versions of the software. Any inline comments should be meaningful, not simply restatements of the obvious because that just creates unnecessary clutter in your script. Comments should be short and concise but should provide high-level information about the code.

---

**Note**

With the PowerScript painter, you can set the color of comments to a light gray, which causes comments to fade into the background. This allows you to focus on the code and not be confused with what's code and what's a comment.

---

On the network file server, some development teams provide a file that can be imported into the Script painter that defines a standard comment block.

The actual system document should be structured to include an object's events, functions, variables, and even inheritance. If you're using a framework, the details of which ancestor objects are used can be especially helpful. In fact, documenting inheritance chains is all-around beneficial. If you're constructing your own framework or expanding on a framework, this kind of information can prove invaluable to a development team.

As with most other parts of a system's documentation, there are different styles of detailing PowerBuilder components. You might end up using different styles for different areas of your documentation. The most common style of system documentation is *breakdown*, otherwise known as *drill down*. With this style, you take all the high-level objects (such as global functions, top-level windows, and user objects) and detail all their attributes, events, and object functions. You should collect these top-level objects into groups based on the object type, and then arrange them alphabetically. When the topmost layer has been defined, go down to the next level, and so on, until you reach the actual windows used in the system. At this level, you should detail each control on the window with a brief description.

The following sections show examples of object-level and window-level system documentation using this style.

## u_ddlb

The u_ddlb is a standard drop-down list user object that has been modified to provide additional trappable events. Table 19.1 lists the variables and events used in u_ddlb.

**TABLE 19.1**   u_ddlb's Variables and Events

| Variable/Event | Description |
|---|---|
| *Instance Variables* | |
| Boolean i_bModified | Tracks whether the edit field has been modified. This variable is initialized in the Constructor event. |
| Boolean i_bValidated | Tracks whether the value in the edit field has passed the validation checks. This variable is initialized in the Constructor event. |
| *Object Events* | |
| Constructor | Initializes the instance variables. |
| Destructor | Clears out the edit field contents, due to the Validate event being triggered after the objects are destroyed. The Validate event should check for an empty field and return immediately. |
| GetFocus | Highlights the field contents on receiving focus. |
| LoseFocus | Trims the field contents on leaving the field. |
| Modified | Sets the modified flag and triggers a Validate event. |
| *User Events* | |
| Other | Checks the message IDs coming from Windows and triggers a Dropdown event if one occurs. |
| Dropdown, Validate, Invalid_entry, and Refresh | Blank, for the child to override with specific code. |
| Reset | Resets the instance variables and clears the edit field. |

## u_ddlb_from_database

The u_ddlb_from_database object is inherited from the u_ddlb user object and provides some additional trappable events. Its user object function uf_Populate (String szSQLSelect) uses the supplied SQL SELECT string to populate the drop-down list box.

# w_import

This window is used to import data from different sources (see Table 19.2).

TABLE 19.2  w_import's Variables and Events

| Item | Description |
|------|-------------|
| *Instance Variables* | |
| DataWindow i_dwImport | The DataWindow to which to import |
| String i_szPath | The file path from which to read the data |
| Long i_lStartRow | The first row from which to start reading |
| Long i_lEndRow | The last row to read |
| Long i_lStartColumn | The first column to use |
| Long i_lEndColumn | The last column to use |
| Long i_lDWStartColumn | The DataWindow column where you want to start inserting |
| *Window Functions* | |
| wf_GetParameters() | Translates the edit field values into the instance variables |
| wf_ImportError() | Takes an integer and opens an error window detailing the error code |
| *Window Events* | |
| Open | Copies the passed DataWindow into the instance variable |
| *Controls* | |
| cbx_header | Header information toggle |
| sle_file | Holds the path and filename from which to read data |
| cb_file | Opens the MS Open File dialog; stores the returned value in sle_file |
| cb_from_file | Reads the data from the specified file |
| cb_from_string | Reads the data from sle_string |
| cb_from_clipboard | Reads the data from the Clipboard |
| cb_cancel | Closes the window |

This information can be arranged in a number of ways; the method selected here uses Microsoft Word's table feature to provide a succinct but informative guide to the system. For a little more in-depth documentation, consider using a bulleted list and real paragraph structures. You also can place any documentation with the object you're documenting. Create a custom user event for the object (for example, a user object) and call it ue_Documentation. Place all your documentation in this event and save your object. The beauty of this method is that the documentation won't get lost because it's stored with the object, and PowerBuilder won't include the information in the executable because it considers comments to be whitespace. If you choose this method, make sure that these comments are maintained as changes are made—outdated comments can be misleading to developers who are charged with maintaining the code.

PowerBuilder can generate simple documentation on any number of application objects. This is done with the Object Browser (see Figure 19.1), which you can access from the Script painter or the Library painter.

**FIGURE 19.1**

*The Object Browser.*

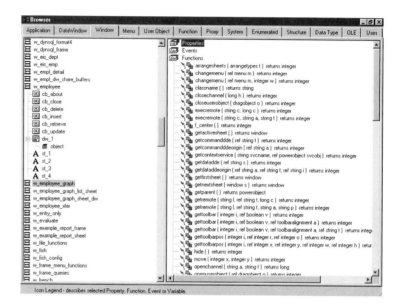

Select the object type you're interested in, expand the category details (Properties, Events, and so on) that you want to document, and then right-click and choose Document from the pop-up menu. By doing this, PowerBuilder creates an RTF (rich text format) document that displays the selected object(s) and the corresponding category details (see Figure 19.2). From this dialog, you can export the RTF document to a file, copy it to the Clipboard, or print it.

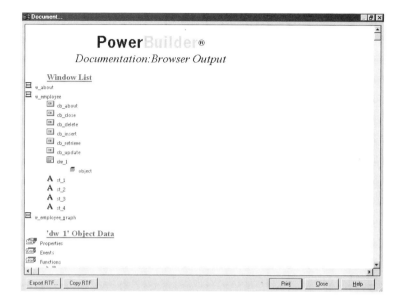

**FIGURE 19.2**
*The Document dialog.*

# User Documentation

End-user documentation should include a brief overview of what the system does and doesn't do, a detailed installation guide, and a detailed guide through the system—possibly with a tutorial.

## Overview

The overview should use simple terms or terms end users can understand and with which they will feel comfortable. You won't provide a good first impression to users if you use a lot of technical jargon. Keep it simple. The most complex ideas can be expressed much more clearly by using examples and graphics. If you make appropriate use of graphics or even a simple flowchart to convey the reason the system has been built, you are much more likely to succeed. The concepts expressed should be based on the business functionality being proposed.

Include brief descriptions of all the major functions that can be carried out in the application. It's not necessary to include pictures because the descriptions are short.

**19**

**Documentation and Online Help**

# System Installation

Depending on how you will deploy your application, you might want to include a system installation guide in the user documentation. This useful source of reference for users and other developers should include step-by-step instructions, making full use of screen shots and window captions to help users through the installation. For example, use bold fonts when describing a button, window title, or menu option, as in the following example:

1. Click the **OK** button.

2. Within the **Choose Printer** window, choose the **Print Preview** menu option.

As this example shows, this technique can really make important information stand out. It can be a great help to more competent users who can just scan through the highlighted text and figure out what to do without having to read all the accompanying text.

Within the guide, you might want to include the files and their locations that will be deployed during installation. This type of information is of more use to other developers, network personnel, and computer-knowledgeable end users than to your average end user.

# Detailed Guide

The detailed guide can be broken into two distinct styles:

- With the by-window style, you take a screen shot of each window and then describe it. If you decide to use this style, you should list all the functions available in each window. Include with the functions each control on the window and any menu items with particular relevance. Each window function should detail what it does, what effect it has on the current window, and any effects it has on the whole application. Navigation between the various windows should be stated, as should the relationship between the current window and other windows. That is, you should make it clear which windows you can open from the current window and how you open them.

- A more logical style of presenting a system guide is by business function. With this style, you need to describe the business function and the flow through the major windows—that is, you enter an order in window X and then go into screen Y to assign a sales representative to it. Then, as mentioned before, you can use a screen shot with descriptions to detail the steps users must take to use the function. Unlike before, however, you should ignore controls, fields, and menu items that have no bearing on the business function.

## Problem Resolution

Whichever style you adopt for your application, you should provide a section in the guide that deals with problem resolution. This section should include how to recover from a particular error condition or message, or how to carry out a certain action that the system wasn't initially designed for but can be carried out with some careful interaction. Again, try to keep any error-message descriptions oriented toward end users as much as possible because users probably don't care much about time stamps or other database-specific jargon.

When an error occurs, you probably will want to detail how to report the situation and possibly to whom it should be reported. See Chapter 33, "Mail-Enabling PowerBuilder Applications," for a way to automate error reporting and make sure that it gets reported to the right person.

# Online Help

Online help that's accessible from within an application or development environment can save time spent chasing down the appropriate manual (and then making sure that the information in it is up-to-date). Such help provides the latest information on the application to the user in an easily browsed format. The next couple of sections look at the different ways you can provide information to an application's users.

## MicroHelp

The MicroHelp area resides along the bottom edge of an MDI frame window. It's also known as a *status bar* within Microsoft circles. (Or should that be outside Sybase circles?) This area is used to display useful information on the current state of the application and system. Most Windows applications use this area extensively to tell users anything from the current mode of the application to the time—even what system resources are free. The most frequent use is to display short messages about what an object is (see Chapter 12, "Menus and the Menu Painter," for an example) or what processing is now occurring.

PowerBuilder provides the `SetMicroHelp()` function to specify text to be displayed in the MicroHelp area on the MDI frame window (the text will be left justified). The syntax is

```
MDIWindow.SetMicroHelp( TextToDisplay)
```

As mentioned earlier, you can build menus to provide a short description of each menu item in the MicroHelp as you change focus between the items. You can provide the same functionality for the controls on a window by using the much-used and overworked `Tag` attribute, or by declaring an instance variable for the ancestor object for each control (assuming that you've constructed a foundation class of all objects). Whichever method

**19**

Documentation
and Online Help

you choose, place a `SetMicroHelp()` call in the `GetFocus` and `LoseFocus` events for each control; or, if you're using inherited controls, just place the code once at the ancestor level.

For example, in the `GetFocus` event of the command button `cb_connect`, the script might be

```
g_App.i_wFrame.SetMicroHelp( "Use this to open the database connect window." )
```

Then within the `LoseFocus` event, it would be

```
g_App.i_wFrame.SetMicroHelp( "Ready" )
```

The `g_App` variable is a nonvisual user object that has been instantiated at the global level and contains all the important information for the application.

> **Note**
>
> In addition to this technique, you can modify the default MicroHelp message (`Ready`) with your own message. This is done by using the application object attribute `MicroHelpDefault`.

## Windows Help Pages

A standard method of providing information to users is via online help, which almost all Windows applications provide. Help is commonly accessible under the rightmost menu item or by pressing the F1 key, either of which tells Windows to load the help file supplied by the application.

In late 1996, Microsoft began moving toward HTML-based help by using Internet Explorer and the HTML Help ActiveX control (see Figure 19.3). The company since then has made this the standard method of providing help in all Windows applications. The WINHELP.EXE is still provided to allow access to existing Windows 3.x help content, but new help files should be developed in the HTML format. Microsoft provides an excellent overview of the HTML help authoring process on the MSDN Web site (`http://msdn.microsoft.com`).

Windows help is based on the hypertext language, which enables the linkage of text, graphics, and sound into a rich multimedia document. A hypertext document is set up with a vast number of links that enable users to jump from topic to topic with ease, while following a particular train of thought or examining side issues. Before tackling the creation of a help file, you need to learn some terms integral to a help file's creation.

**FIGURE 19.3**

*The HTML Help Viewer.*

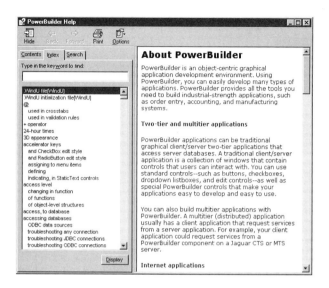

A *help file* is a collection of topics (individual informational screens) interconnected via hypertext jumps. A *jump* is a word, phrase, or graphic that when clicked takes users to another topic. Also defined within each topic are *keywords*, a series of words that point to one or more help topics. Keywords are used when users click the Search button and a keyword is entered, displaying all related topics. In addition to keywords, help files should provide definitions for commonly used terms. This typically is done with *pop-ups*, which appear as temporary windows when users click a particular word. A pop-up is different from a jump in that a pop-up doesn't change the current topic. Pop-ups should be accessible as a glossary via the online help engine.

The information used for building online help can be drawn from parts of previous documents (for example, design specs) or even from documents converted in their entirety. The opposite is also true; some help file generators can use a help file to produce polished documents with indexes and a table of contents.

Internet Explorer and the HTML Help ActiveX control are required to display help files with the .CHM extension, whereas the WINHELP.EXE program is used to display help files with the .HLP extension. Many commercial and shareware help compilers are available to assist in the generation of Windows 3.x or HTML help files.

The types of help file–generation applications can be divided into two main categories: word processor-based and standalone tools. The word processor-based tools are typically written as templates that add to the functionality of an existing word processing application, such as Microsoft Word. The advantage of these programs is that they extend an

**19**

**Documentation and Online Help**

environment with which the developer of the help file is already familiar. The downside of these tools is that they depend on additional software. The obvious benefit of the standalone help generators is that they run independently of any other software. Standalone help generators provide more flexibility, but the intricacy of their help files is limited.

Another tool you can use in help file creation is the Microsoft HTML Help Image Editor. This tool is used to create *hypergraphics*, which are simply bitmaps with hot spots defined for them. A *hot spot* is an area of a graphic that executes a jump, pop-up, or help macro. The hypergraphic can then be placed in a help file.

After you decide on the tool to use to create your help file, you need to design the layout of the help file. This process is often taken lightly and results in a poorly written and laid out help file. After deciding what the individual topics will be, you need to know how they will be linked (which jumps are available), what words are keywords, and what words or phrases need to have pop-ups created. After deciding on the help file structure, use the help tool of choice to develop the topic documents.

The topic documents are added to a help project file and compiled to create the help file you distribute with your application. You should break up your help into topics. For each topic, you might want to create a separate file, depending on the size of each topic and the help tool chosen.

The HTML Help Workshop (see Figure 19.4) allows you to easily create your help project file, add your HTML topic files, create indexes, and build your table of contents.

After you learn the intricacies of the help compiler that you've chosen to use and have a CHM file, how do you use it in PowerBuilder?

Help is usually accessed several different ways in a Windows application. It's standard for an application to have a Help button on each window or a Help menu option. Within the Help menu should at least be a Contents menu item that takes you to the main topic of the help file and a Search menu item that opens the Search tab (or dialog) of the help file. Help can also be activated by pressing the F1 key. Depending on the application's sophistication, pressing F1 might open context-sensitive help or open just the Contents topic.

PowerBuilder provides a ShowHelp() function that you use to launch the Windows 3.x-based Help system and display the specified help file. The syntax is

```
ShowHelp( HelpFile, HelpCommand {, TypeID})
```

**FIGURE 19.4**

*The HTML Help Workshop.*

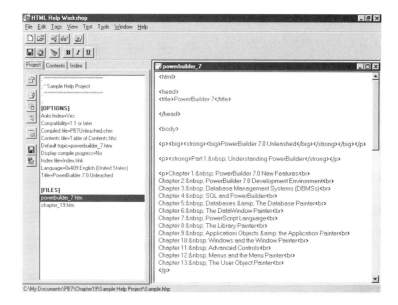

---

### Note

PowerBuilder doesn't provide a function to display HTML help files. To display HTML help, you must use the HTML Help API or a standard URL reference. The following instructions on using ShowHelp and the WinHelpA API call apply only to Windows 3.x-based help. For a sample on how to open an URL from within PowerBuilder, see Chapter 29, "PowerBuilder and the Internet." For information on the HTML Help API, see the documentation that accompanies the HTML Help Workshop.

**19**

**Documentation and Online Help**

The *HelpFile* argument is the filename (optionally with a full path) of the HLP file to be displayed. The *HelpCommand* argument is of the HelpCommand enumerated data type, with the following values:

| Value | Description |
| --- | --- |
| Index! | Displays the top-level Contents topic in the help file |
| KeyWord! | Goes to the topic identified by the keyword in *TypeID* |
| Topic! | Displays the topic identified by the number in *TypeID* |

The *TypeID* is an optional argument that identifies a numeric topic (if the *HelpCommand* argument is Topic!) or a string keyword (if the *HelpCommand* argument is KeyWord!).

To provide access to the help file in the Help menu item, you would code something like the following. This opens the help program and displays the index for the help file OE_010.HLP that's in the current directory or on the system path.

```
ShowHelp( "OE_010.HLP,", Index!)
```

## Context-Sensitive Help

You can provide context-sensitive help by using the other two *HelpCommand* values, Topic! and KeyWord!.

When you build the help project file, you will want to define unique topic identifiers. This way, you can open the help to a particular topic by passing in the numeric identifier:

```
ShowHelp( "OE_010.HLP", Topic!, 94)
```

The KeyWord! value can be used to go straight to a topic associated with the string value or, if the string isn't unique, to open the Search window (or in Windows 95/98, it opens the Index tab, as shown in Figure 19.5).

**FIGURE 19.5**

*The Windows Help Index tab.*

The big question is how to open this dialog in a window with a number of different controls and get the help for the object on which the user is now focused. Actually, it's not too difficult. You use the Key event trapped inside a window. The Key event is fired in a window whenever a key (except Alt) is pressed and the control with focus isn't a line edit control.

> **Note**
>
> The PowerBuilder help page for the Key event really means that this event won't fire when the focus is in a DataWindow. The Key event will be triggered when you are in a single- or multiline edit control or drop-down list box.

Inside this event, you can place a call to ShowHelp() with a topic identifier. The only problem now is to determine which topic to display. This information is set when the control first gains focus and can be placed globally, locally at the window level, within a global user object, or even in the window's Tag attribute. The following example uses a global application object with an i_nHelpTopic variable. An example of the code that might be placed in a command button, check box, or other online edit control's GetFocus event is

```
g_App.i_nHelpTopic = 20    // Display the help topic for the cb_connect button
```

Then, within the Key event, the code would be

```
If KeyDown( KeyF1!) Then
   ShowHelp( g_App.is_HelpFileName, Topic!, g_App.i_nHelpTopic)
End If
```

For DataWindow controls, you need to capture the Key event yourself and then carry out the processing. This is only a matter of declaring a user event for the PowerBuilder message pbm_dwnkey. You can then use the same code that you used for the window Key event.

So that a help topic doesn't appear for objects on which you haven't defined a specific help, you can code a statement in the LoseFocus that sets g_App.i_nHelpTopic = 0. Then in the Key event, you can use the KeyDown() function to check whether F1 was pressed and open the help index instead. Here's an example:

```
If KeyDown( KeyF1!) Then
   If g_App.i_nHelpTopic > 0 Then
      ShowHelp( g_App.is_HelpFileName, Topic!, g_App.i_nHelpTopic)
   Else
      ShowHelp( g_App.is_HelpFileName, Index!)
   End If
End If
```

**19**

Documentation
and Online Help

You can implement the DataWindow's context sensitivity by using the column's name as a KeyWord! search, as in this example:

```
String ls_ColumnName
If KeyDown( KeyF1!) Then
   ls_ColumnName = This.GetColumnName()
   If ls_ColumnName = "" Then
      ShowHelp( g_App.is_HelpFileName, Index!)
   Else
      ShowHelp (g_App.is_HelpFileName, KeyWord!, ls_ColumnName)
   End If
End If
```

An alternative to this is to enter a Choose...Case statement to generate a specific topic identifier column by column, and then perform a topic lookup.

## The WinHelpA() API Function

As with some other API functions provided in PowerBuilder, Sybase has managed to hide the complexities of the call, but in the process has lost some functionality. This is certainly the case with the ShowHelp() function, which is the wrapper around the 32-bit Windows API function WinHelpA():

```
Integer WinHelpA( hWnd, lpszHelpFile, unCommand, lData)
```

The *hWnd* parameter specifies the window that's requesting that the help program be started and is used to keep track of which applications have requested help. *lpszHelpFile* is a string that contains the path and filename of the help file, with the *unCommand* parameter indicating the type of help required. The *lData* parameter is used by some of the help types specified by *unCommand* to supply additional information.

---

**Note**

The filename specified in *lpszHelpFile* can be followed by an angle bracket (>) with the name of a secondary window (rather than the primary window) to be used to display the topic. Secondary windows are used to present information without the full menus and all the buttons of the regular Windows help window.

---

It's also important to note that although the API help files state that WinHelpA() returns a Boolean, it in fact returns an Integer value that's a non-zero value if it's successful; otherwise, it returns zero. This is the same as the PowerBuilder ShowHelp() function return value.

Table 19.3 shows the possible values for the *unCommand* and *lData* parameters. The value in parentheses for each *unCommand* parameter is the numeric value for the constant. For all N/A entries in the *lData* column, you should pass a zero value.

**TABLE 19.3** **VALUES** for *unCommand* and *lData*

| unCommand | lData | Description |
| --- | --- | --- |
| HELP_CONTEXT (1) | Context numberfor a topic | Displays help for the specified topic with a context number defined in the help file. |
| HELP_CONTENTS (3) | N/A | Displays the contents topic. |
| HELP_SETCONTENTS (5) | Context number for the topic to be designated on the contents page | Determines whichcontents topic is displayed when userspress F1. |
| HELP_CONTEXTPOPUP (8) | Context number for a topic | Displays the topic in a pop-up window. |
| HELP_KEY (257) | A string containing a keyword for a topic | Displays the topic found on an exact match of the keyword. If there's more than than one match per search, a dialog is opened, with the topics in the Go To area. |
| HELP_PARTIALKEY (261) | A string containing a keyword for a topic | Displays the topic found on an exact match of the keyword. If there's more than one match or no matches, a search dialog appears with the topics displayed in the Go To area. |
| HELP_MULTIKEY (513) | A pointer to a MULTIKEYHELP structure | Displays the topic identified by the keyword from the alternate keyword table. |
| HELP_COMMAND (258) | A string defining the help macro to execute | Executes a help macro. |
| HELP_SETWINPOS (515) | A pointer to a HELPWININFO structure | Positions the already open help window to the coordinates passed. |
| HELP_FORCEFILE (9) | N/A | The correct help file is opened if the current isn't the default. |
| HELP_HELPONHELP (4) | N/A | Shows the contents topic of a Using Help file. |
| HELP_QUIT (2) | N/A | Tells help to close down if no applications are now using it. |

> **Note**
>
> From Table 19.3 you can see that lData can be used to pass a Numeric, String, or Structure data type. In PowerBuilder, this means that you must declare four external function declarations, one with each different data type, for lData.

Only the HELP_CONTEXT, HELP_INDEX, HELP_CONTENTS, HELP_KEY, and HELP_PARTIALKEY functionality is accessible through the PowerBuilder ShowHelp() function.

> **Note**
>
> To bring up the Search dialog without starting the search with the keyword passed, send an empty string.

To conform with accepted Windows programming practices, before closing the requesting window, send the HELP_QUIT message to WinHelpA() to allow help to close down when all applications are finished with it.

The MULTIKEYHELP structure is used to define a keyword table and an associated keyword to be used by WinHelpA(). The MULTIKEYHELP is defined in PowerBuilder as a regular structure with the following attributes:

| Attribute Name | Data Type | Description |
| --- | --- | --- |
| unSize | UnsignedInteger | The size of the structure |
| cKeylist | Char | Identifies the keyword table to search |
| szKeyphrase | String | The keyword to find in the keyword table |

The HELPWININFO structure is used to specify the size and position of a secondary help window for use with the HELP_SETWINPOS value for the unCommand parameter. Table 19.4 defines the HELPWININFO structure.

**TABLE 19.4**   The HELPWININFO Structure Definition

| Attribute Name | Data Type | Description |
| --- | --- | --- |
| i_StructSize | Integer | The size of the structure |
| i_X | Integer | The X coordinate of window's upper-left corner |

TABLE **19.4**   The HELPWININFO Structure Definition

| Attribute Name | Data Type | Description |
|---|---|---|
| i_Y | Integer | The Y coordinate of window's upper-left corner |
| i_DX | Integer | The width of the window |
| i_DY | Integer | The height of the window |
| i_Max | Integer | Set to 1, it maximizes the window; set to 0, it uses the previous attributes |
| s_WindowName | String | The window name |

**Note**

The display is divided into 1,024 units in X and Y directions. Therefore, to fill the top half of the display, i_X and i_Y should be 0, i_DX should be 1024, and i_DY should be 512.

To declare the WinHelpA() function in PowerBuilder, you need to use the following:

```
Function Integer WinHelpA( uInt hWnd, String szHelpFile, uInt unCmd, &
                          Long lData)  Library "user32.dll"
Function Integer WinHelpA( uInt hWnd, String szHelpFile, uInt unCmd, &
                          String szData) Library "user32.dll"
Function Integer WinHelpA( uInt hWnd, String szHelpFile, uInt unCmd, &
                          s_multikeyhelp sData)  Library "user32.dll"
Function Integer WinHelpA( uInt hWnd, String szHelpFile, uInt unCmd, &
                          s_helpwininfo sData)  Library "user32.dll"
```

With the function defined, you can now call WinHelpA() anywhere you would have called the ShowHelp() function, and you'll get the same results. For example, to open the help window and directly open the Search dialog, you would use the following call:

```
WinHelpA( Handle( Parent), "pbhlp060.hlp", 261, "")
```

# DataWindow Help Special Handling

At runtime, you can customize the help topics related to any DataWindow dialogs that you've made accessible to end users. The help can be altered by using the Help attribute of a DataWindow object in a Modify() call. The syntax required in the Modify() call (or a Describe() call) is

```
"DataWindow.Help.Attribute { = Value }"
```

Table 19.5 shows the attributes of the Help attribute.

**19**

**Documentation
and Online Help**

**TABLE 19.5**   Help Attribute Descriptions

| Attribute | Description |
|---|---|
| Command | Type of help command specified in `TypeID` attributes. Values are `0` (Index), `1` (TopicID), and `2` (Search KeyWord). |
| File | The fully qualified name of the compiled help file; when a value is specified, the help buttons display in DataWindow dialogs. |
| TypeID | The default help command to be used when a help topic isn't specified for the dialog. |
| TypeID.SetCrosstab | The help topic for the Crosstab Definition dialog (opened using `CrossTabDialog()`). |
| TypeID.ImportFile | The help topic for the Import File dialog (opened using `Import-File()`). |
| TypeID.Retrieve.Argument | The help topic for the Retrieval Arguments dialog (opened when a `SELECT` statement is expecting arguments and none are given). |
| TypeID.Retrieve.Criteria | The help topic for the Prompt for Criteria dialog (opened when the Criteria attribute is specified for a column and a retrieve is executed). |
| TypeID.SaveAs | The help topic for the Save As dialog (opened using `SaveAs()`). |
| TypeID.SetFilter | The help topic for the Set Filter dialog (opened using `SetFilter()` and `Filter()`). |
| TypeID.SetSort | The help topic for the Set Sort dialog (opened using `SetSort()` and `Sort()`). |
| TypeID.SetSortExpr | The help topic for the Modify Expression dialog (opened when users double-click a column in the Set Sort dialog). |

Some examples of these attributes used in `Modify()` expressions are

```
dw_1.Modify("DataWindow.Help.File='oe_010.hlp'")
dw_1.Modify( "DataWindow.Help.Command=1")
dw_1.Modify( "DataWindow.Help.TypeID.SetFilter='sort_topic'")
dw_1.Modify( "DataWindow.Help.TypeID.Retrieve.Argument='criteria_topic'")
```

**Note**

These DataWindow attributes can also be modified via the direct object syntax by just dropping `Modify()` and rearranging the quotation marks. For more information on the dot notation syntax, see Chapter 14, "DataWindow Scripting."

## Documentation for Developers

One often-missed area of PowerBuilder online help is the capability to expand the available help to include application- (or, more often, framework-) specific functions, events, and objects. This enables the original writers to provide professional-quality help on their application/framework for developers who will be following in their footsteps or using the existing code.

The online help in PowerBuilder contains a User button. This is where you can extend the PowerBuilder help to include your own. When you create your new help file, you must name a topic with the `index_user_help` identifier, which indicates the topic to access when the button is clicked. This gives the same functionality as pressing F1 and then searching.

To provide context-sensitive help for your application/framework functions, you need to create a help topic that uses a single prefix (for example, `uf_`) and assign a search keyword that matches the function name. For example, the function `uf_SaveHeader()` would have the keyword `uf_SaveHeader`.

You can specify a single prefix for the functions that can have help topics using the `UserHelpPrefix` entry in the PB.INI file. The only requirement is that the prefix must end with an underscore character (for example, `wf_`).

When users (developers) press Shift+F1 on a user-defined function, PowerBuilder checks the prefix against the entry in the PB.INI and, if they match, opens the Help file specified by the `UserHelpFile` entry in the PB.INI file. PowerBuilder then does a keyword search using the function's name.

The `UserHelpFile` entry in the PB.INI file enables you to specify the Help file to be used in a user-function context-sensitive search, and it's set to only the filename and not the full path. If there's no value for this entry, the PBUSR070.HLP file is loaded and searched instead.

# Intranet Help

HTML-based help has been rapidly gaining popularity for several years as a way of displaying user and developer help. Now that Microsoft has made HTML-based help the standard, consider using it for your new applications. The basic concepts are the same for Windows 3.x and HTML-based help. Both types of help consist of text and graphics connected via hypertext links. The primary advantages of HTML-based help are ease of deployment, platform independence, and a richer set of tools to display information with. HTML-based help isn't limited to simple text and graphics; it can contain animations, Java applets, plug-ins, or anything else that can be displayed in a Web browser.

**19**

Documentation and Online Help

Although Microsoft provides the HTML Help Workshop to create compiled .CHM help files, many developers are simply creating standard Web sites and linking their applications directly to them. This eliminates the compilation process and the need to distribute help files to each user. The Web site can then be processed through a Web index engine to provide search capabilities.

In addition to creating user help on an intranet, developer help files can also be created. The intranet help file could be used as mentioned earlier in the section "Documentation for Developers" to describe an application framework. The intranet help files can also be used as a means to view the definition of an application's objects. The only problem with this type of documentation is that the help file quickly becomes outdated as the objects change. You can create a PowerBuilder application that generates intranet help files with up-to-the-minute application information. You can then schedule the application to update and build the Web pages automatically.

The main idea of these quick application intranet help files is to provide a Web page containing an index of all objects in a PowerBuilder library. This index of objects contains hypertext links to the exported syntax of each object. This can be useful to see code, object declarations, inheritance declaration, and much more. An application can be created by using the `Libraryx` functions (discussed in Chapter 8, "The Library Painter") with some string manipulation to generate the HTML tags. This results in a process that can be run at any time to provide online documentation of an application for all developers.

> **Note**
>
> A simple intranet help file generator written in PowerBuilder by Ken Reppart can be found on the *PowerBuilder 7.0 Unleashed* Web site at
> `http://members.iquest.net/~raven/pb7.html`.

After the intranet help file is created, you can view the page with your favorite Web browser. Starting with PowerBuilder 6.0, Sybase provided the capability to add links to your help Web pages in the PowerBuilder development environment. To do this, edit your PB.INI file in the [PB] section. There are four keys labeled WebLink1, WebLink2, and so on. The values for each key is a menu item name and the name of a URL. All you need to do is replace one of Sybase's existing values with your own menu name and URL. An example would be

```
WebLink1=&RUSS Help, http://mercury/russ/index.html
```

This would display RUSS Help under the PowerBuilder Help menu and link you to the specified Web page.

# Summary

In this chapter, you learned not only about the types of documents that could be produced during or at the end of an application's development cycle but also how to incorporate the documents you create into online help that can be accessed at runtime and during development. By fully documenting your applications, you're providing an environment to make maintenance easier and help users learn the application.

# 20

# Application and Component Implementation

CHAPTER

Up to this point in this book, we have concerned ourselves only with the development environment. Obviously, end users won't be running the development environment—well, not quite anyway—but they will use some of the same DLLs. This chapter discusses the various component parts that you need to create and distribute for the successful deployment of a production copy of an application. In addition to the traditional PowerBuilder application deployment, PowerBuilder 7.0 expands your options by allowing you to generate several different components from your PowerBuilder code. The process to create these new components also is outlined in this chapter.

# Creating a Standard PowerBuilder Application

PowerBuilder enables you to build an executable file in one of three ways. The first method is the production of a single, all-inclusive executable file that users can run. The second method uses files called *PowerBuilder dynamic libraries* (PBDs) and a smaller executable file. PBDs are similar to DLLs; they enable demand loading of objects within the file to provide more control of memory consumption by the application. The third method allows you to compile to 32-bit machine code, for the executable and PBDs; a PBL file can now directly be compiled into a DLL rather than a PBD. The remainder of this chapter refers to situations in which you can use a PBD or DLL version of a PBL as a dynamic library.

> **Note**
>
> Although the compiled machine code EXE is a true executable, the compiled DLL isn't intended to be used by other applications. You are still required to also distribute a runtime environment (the PowerBuilder Deployment Kit) with the EXE and DLL files. This is because, as with the previous versions of PowerBuilder, large portions of PowerBuilder's functionality are contained in the DLLs and not directly in your application.

The PowerBuilder native executable file (not the machine code version) that's created actually contains a small bootstrap at the front of it that causes the PowerBuilder DLLs to be loaded. The code PowerBuilder has placed in the native EXE file, and optionally in the PBDs, is PowerBuilder-compiled code, not Windows-compiled code. The bootstrap causes the runtime PowerBuilder DLLs to interpret the compiled code in the remainder of the EXE file and PBDs.

# The Executable File

When the native executable file is created, PowerBuilder copies the compiled code, called *pseudocode* (or, more commonly, *p-code*), into the EXE file in the order of the library search path specified for the application. P-code is the intermediate code that PowerBuilder compiles and stores with the objects in a library. This is the code interpreted by the runtime PowerBuilder DLLs—or, more accurately, the virtual machine that interprets the byte codes. P-code instructions break down to a number of machine code instructions, which is where the interpretation comes in. Think of native PowerBuilder code as parallel to Java: Both use byte codes and a virtual engine/machine to execute.

For a machine code executable, PowerBuilder actually generates a true binary file that causes the runtime DLLs (PowerBuilder or your own) to be loaded as they're used; this is exactly like any other machine-native application.

The key difference is that the p-code has to be interpreted before it can perform an operation, whereas the machine code just performs the operation. P-code is, however, more compact, and PowerScript function calls are made into optimized PowerBuilder runtime DLLs.

As PowerBuilder is traversing the library search path, it copies only the objects that are explicitly referenced and not in libraries that will be made into dynamic libraries (PBDs or DLLs). This means that dynamically referenced graphics objects (bitmaps, icons, and pointers), windows, data pipelines, and DataWindows aren't copied. Many of these can be compiled by explicitly listing them in a resource file (detailed in the next section).

The finished executable file contains the Windows bootstrap code, followed by the p-code versions of the objects, and then any dynamically assigned resources. In the case of a machine-code version, you have just the executable and the dynamically assigned resources. The p-code and machine code executables store an *execution library list*, which is used by the PowerBuilder execution system to find objects and resources in any dynamic libraries you've created along with the executable. This list is the same as the library search path you created within the PowerBuilder development environment.

To create a standard PowerBuilder executable, you must create a new Application Project Object or open an existing one. To create a new executable, click the New toolbar button on the PowerBar and select the Application object on the Project tab. The Project painter is described further in the section "The Project Painter."

# Creating a Resource File

You create the *resource file*, or *PBR file* as it's more commonly known, in any ASCII text editor. As mentioned earlier, objects (graphics or otherwise) not explicitly referenced in an application (except the application icon) aren't included in the EXE file. All objects other than graphics objects are compiled into dynamic library files if you specify that compile option. This includes dynamically assigned DataWindows, windows, and so on. You still have to specify the graphics objects (bitmaps, icons, and so on) in a resource file.

The PBR file contains the name of each bitmap, icon, pointer, and DataWindow to be included in the executable or dynamic library. Depending on the project restrictions placed on you, you have two options: fully qualify the path of the resources, or specify no path and place the objects in the same directory as that from which the executable file is constructed. If you fully qualify the path to the graphic objects, you must also fully qualify the path and library for DataWindows. If you choose not to specify the path, you might have to go through some extra steps when assigning bitmaps, drag/drop icons, and mouse pointers. An example of two resource files follows:

```
q:\projects\prs\prs_rept.pbl(d_stk199)
q:\projects\prs\prs_rept.pbl(d_stk430)
q:\projects\prs\prs_rept.pbl(d_stk754a)
q:\projects\prs\prs_rept.pbl(d_stk763)

q:\projects\shared\ptr.bmp
q:\projects\shared\logo.bmp
q:\projects\shared\next.bmp
q:\projects\shared\prev.bmp
q:\projects\shared\maint.ico
q:\projects\shared\entry.ico
q:\projects\shared\reports.ico
```

The first file contains dynamically assigned DataWindows; this resource file would be associated with the executable file. The second file contains bitmaps and icons to be stored in a dynamic library file. This file is associated with the dynamic library at the time of the file's creation. The complete path and name are stored in the EXE or dynamic library file. The reason for this is discussed next.

### Note

You can associate a resource file with each dynamic library that you create, but that can become a management nightmare. One solution is to collect all application-specific dynamic resources into one PBR and associate that with the executable. All shared/common dynamic resources that are used across applications should be collected into another PBR, which is then associated with the dynamic library that contains the shared/common objects.

If you place the resource file into the EXE file or a dynamic library, PowerBuilder searches for the exact name of the resource. For example, if you have a picture button with the path C:\PBSTUFF\ULRIC.BMP, PowerBuilder attempts to match on the fully qualified path and name within the EXE or dynamic library files. That's why it's recommended that you fully qualify all references. It also prevents you from inadvertently picking up resources from other than the intended location.

At runtime, if PowerBuilder can't find the resource within the EXE or dynamic libraries, it attempts to find the resource files using the Windows search path: the current directory, \WINDOWS, \WINDOWS\SYSTEM, and then the system search path. If the resource can't be found, one of two things can happen depending on the type of resource. For graphics objects, PowerBuilder uses a default or shows nothing. For DataWindow objects, the DataWindow control appears but has no assigned DataWindow object.

# Creating Dynamic Libraries

A PBD, or a generated DLL, is similar in concept to Windows DLLs and contains all the compiled code for one *PowerBuilder library* (PBL) file. The PBD file can be used only with a PowerBuilder-compiled executable file and must be part of the application's library search path to be accessed. Placing code in dynamic libraries enables you to partition your application into smaller, related segments. By skillful consideration of which objects are placed in a PBL, you can speed up object load times and better economize resources when that PBL is made into a dynamic library. Like a DLL, only the code from a required PBD is loaded, which is different from an EXE file, where everything is loaded at once. See the later section "Performance of EXEs Versus Dynamic Library Files" for a discussion of the trade-offs between EXE files and dynamic libraries.

> **Note**
>
> Remember, the whole PBD isn't loaded into memory—only the required object is. Sybase has stated, "PowerBuilder doesn't load an entire PBD file into memory at once. Instead, it loads individual objects from the PBD file only when needed." As previously stated, this is the mechanism also used by DLL files.

By using a dynamic library, you can share some code between multiple applications, and it saves you from distributing redundant copies of the code if it was compiled into the EXE file each time. This also enables you to update the functionality of your application without having to distribute a new EXE file or other files.

**20**

Application and
Component
Implementation

> **Caution**
>
> If you intend to share a dynamic library among different applications or even to replace one for an existing application, it's possible only if *all* the objects are self-contained. By this I mean that objects within the library cannot reference any objects outside the library or use any global variables or constants. This is because during compilation substitutions are made for object, variable, and constant references, and among applications the substituted values will likely be different.

PowerBuilder includes a copy of the library search path in the executable file and uses that copy to search for objects in the same manner that it does during development. If PowerBuilder can't find an object in the EXE file at runtime, it searches through any available dynamic library files in the order of the library search path. For this reason, you should store commonly used objects in the executable file or in a PBL (and therefore PBD/DLL) positioned early in the search path.

Dynamic libraries have a number of advantages:

- Reusability—The dynamic library file is accessible by multiple applications.

- Maintainability—You can individually upgrade application component pieces rather than redistribute the complete application.

- Completeness—Because a dynamic library contains all objects in the PBL file, you can use dynamic referencing more easily. In fact, the only dynamically created PowerBuilder objects that can be placed in the executable file are DataWindows, so you are required to place dynamically created windows, user objects, and so forth in PBDs/DLLs.

- Efficiency—Better use can be made of the operating system memory. Only the object is loaded into memory, rather than the entire PBD. The executable stub will therefore be smaller, making it less intrusive on the OS resources and much faster to load.

- Modularity—Because each dynamic library corresponds to a PBL file, they enable easy partitioning of the application, which leads to better management of the application as well as all the benefits listed in the preceding points.

You can create dynamic library files in the Library painter or in the Project painter by using an Application Project object.

The Build Runtime Library option is available under the pop-up context menu for a library or from the Library painter menu.

When you select this menu item, the Build Runtime Library dialog (see Figure 20.1) opens. The library name is the currently selected name in the Library painter or the first library in your library search path. Be sure to select the right one before continuing.

**Figure 20.1**

*The Build Runtime Library dialog.*

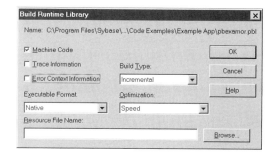

You can select a resource file to be compiled into the PBD or DLL by typing directly into the field provided or clicking the Browse button. You then have the option of choosing between a PowerBuilder native PBD or a machine code DLL. See the next section, "The Project Painter," for more information on the various options. After specifying the dynamic library options, click OK to create a PBD or DLL file in the same directory as the PBL file.

# The Project Painter

The Project painter creates a project object that stores all the information required to create an application. You access the Project painter from the PowerBar by clicking the New button and selecting the Application icon from the Project tab. The other option to create a standard PowerBuilder executable, new to PowerBuilder 7.0, is to use the Application Wizard on the Project tab.

The Application Wizard simplifies the creation of a project object as it walks you through the appropriate steps. The different wizard windows ask you to specify the following:

- The library in which the new project object is to be stored

- The name of the new project object

- The name of the executable and PBR if you have one for the executable

- The rebuild options (Full or Incremental) and whether you want to be prompted to overwrite any existing files

- The compile option (machine code or p-code)

- The option to create all PBLs as dynamic libraries (PBDs/DLLs)

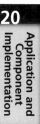

The last window of the Application Wizard presents a list asking you to verify the information selected in the prior steps. You also can have PowerBuilder create a To-Do List for you with the final steps needed to complete the application build.

After you finish creating your new project object or choose an existing application project, the Application Project painter is displayed (see Figure 20.2). The painter provides an Edit menu that enables you to paste in values via a dialog rather than type them into the three edit fields: executable filename, resource filename, and library resource filename.

**FIGURE 20.2**

*The Application Project painter.*

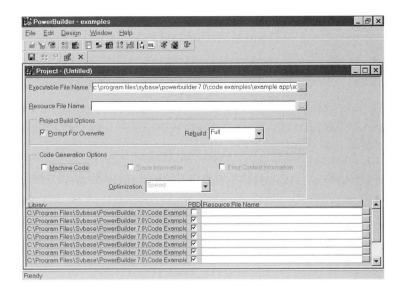

From the Design menu, you can build the project or open a list of the objects used in the creation of the last executable (see Figure 20.3). This list details the library name, object name, and object type. The list can be sorted on any of these fields.

Within the Project painter, you can tell the painter to prompt you before it overwrites the EXE and dynamic library files. You can also specify whether to regenerate all the objects in the listed libraries before compilation begins or carry out an incremental rebuild of only the libraries that have changed. The incremental option is useful when you're creating an executable with dynamic libraries. This is because it allows you to check off the PBD box in the Project painter, which tells PowerBuilder to not rebuild the dynamic library unless the date of the PBL file is greater than the PBD/DLL date.

**FIGURE 20.3**

*The object list.*

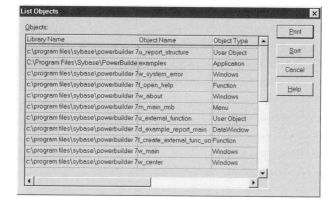

The capability to generate machine code is specified in the Code Generation Options area of the Project painter (or the dialog called in the Library painter for creating runtime libraries). To turn on machine code generation, make sure that the Machine Code check box is checked; this allows you to toggle between native PowerBuilder code for the executable and dynamic libraries and the machine code versions.

> **Note**
>
> PowerBuilder 7.0 allows you to create executables for only the 32-bit environment. Before version 7.0, you could create 16-bit and 32-bit executables, but this version dropped 16-bit support.

The other options in this area relate only to machine code generation:

- Trace Information allows you to use the /PBDEBUG feature that you can use on PowerBuilder native executables and works in the same manner. It slows performance of the code and should be used for debugging purposes only.

- In p-code, the line number and script information are easily obtainable; in machine code, this isn't the case. When Error Context Information is used, information about each executed line is captured. This slows the performance of the application and should be used for debugging purposes only.

- With the Optimization option, you can tune the generation of your final machine code by having the compiler undertake optimization for size and speed. You can use the third optimization option to turn off optimization if you want to.

**20**

**Application and Component Implementation**

> **Note**
>
> When Powersoft (PRE-Sybase) bought Watcom, it also acquired one of the most highly regarded compilers on the market. This is the workhorse used by this compilation process to provide the most optimized code possible.

If you're going to be creating machine-code executables of any sizable application, be aware that the process can take a while and will run best on a high-powered machine. The C compiler and optimizer has been stated by Sybase to be "very aggressive about using memory," but you can reduce your compile times by significantly increasing the physical memory available on the machine doing the compilation. P-code executables are much faster to create because compilation uses simple copy routines that take the compiled versions of the objects from the PBL files and place them into the EXE or PBD files.

In the Project painter, you can build an executable file that incorporates all the libraries, or you can make an executable stub by selecting all the libraries (except the library containing the application object) and specifying them as dynamic libraries.

> **Caution**
>
> If you're going to use dynamic libraries, you should place the application object in a library by itself. This is because of the inheritance chains in your application. If ancestor and descendant objects are spread across the executable file and a dynamic library, you can get unexpected compiler errors or even Page Faults. Therefore, the ideal situation is to create a small executable file from the library containing just the application object and create dynamic libraries out of the remainder (see the later section "Library Partitioning" for more information).

You specify which libraries will be made into PBD/DLL files by checking the box by the library's name and specifying any associated resource files.

Select Options under the Design menu to access the Options dialog, where you can specify to ignore informational and obsolete warnings generated during the compilation process.

When you are ready to build, you can select Build Project from the Design menu or click the Build button in the painter. The Project painter regenerates the objects you requested and then builds the executable file and any dynamic libraries. If any problems occur during the compilation or regeneration process, an error window (see Figure 20.4) appears, showing the error, line number, event, and object where the error occurred.

**FIGURE 20.4**
*Compiler errors appear in a window so that you can see what happened.*

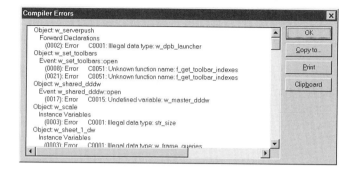

When you make a successful compilation, or if you are just giving up for the moment, you are prompted to save the project when you leave the painter. The project object is then stored in the appropriate library.

## Deploying a Standard PowerBuilder Application

Now that you've compiled your PowerBuilder code into executable files and dynamic libraries, you need to distribute it. Because the code uses much of the functionality available in the development environment, you also need to distribute the runtime version of PowerBuilder with the EXE and PBD files. This is the *PowerBuilder Deployment Kit* (PBDK); it's provided with all product versions of PowerBuilder. If your application accesses a database (and most of them do), you need to distribute the necessary files from the database deployment kit as well. For more information on deploying your PowerBuilder application, see the later section "Deployment of the Application."

# Library Partitioning

You can use one of two philosophies when partitioning your objects into libraries: doing it by object or by function. Collecting objects into libraries by object type might provide an easy means to navigate and find objects during development, but when building an application, unless you're going for one big executable file, this provides an inefficient split of objects. When the application is run using PBDs, you will probably force most of the PBDs into memory. Although this doesn't take up a great deal of actual memory (remember, only the currently used objects are loaded), Windows resources are still consumed. The biggest hit to performance is that PowerBuilder now has to search through a number of PBDs to find the required object.

**20**

**Application and Component Implementation**

When you partition by function, the majority of the objects to be used in any one business function are located together. More common objects should be placed at a higher level in the library search path.

> **Note**
>
> Sybase demonstrates both approaches; look at the sample application (by object) and the PFC (by function) libraries. Notice which approach is used by the one designed for real development use.

# Performance of EXEs Versus Dynamic Library Files

Placing every object into one big executable file gives you a small performance gain during execution, provided that the whole application can sit in memory at once and isn't swapped out because of other Windows applications. There is, however, a big initial speed penalty while the executable file is loaded into memory. During execution, the location of objects occurs entirely in memory (again not considering Windows swapping issues), unlike with dynamic libraries. With dynamic libraries, when PowerBuilder has determined where the object is located, it will more than likely have to load it from disk. As mentioned earlier, it's rarely practical to make a single EXE file, unless the application is small or the end users have high-performance machines.

> **Caution**
>
> By creating everything in one executable, you will almost definitely have to use a resource file to specify DataWindow objects. This file requires a lot more work to create than if you use dynamic libraries that would automatically have included these objects.

As previously mentioned, you have to consider several other issues. The main one is that any modifications to the system require you to redistribute your entire executable file, whereas an application that uses dynamic libraries allows you to replace just the necessary files. The main benefit of using dynamic libraries is that they enable the modularization of the application and all the benefits that entails, such as added security, cacheable small files, and responsibility assignment. Placing all the most frequently accessed objects (ancestors, functions, and so on) at the top of the library list can offset some of the speed loss of using dynamic libraries.

> **Tip**
>
> See Chapter 9, "Application Objects and the Application Painter," for a useful trick concerning the runtime alteration of the library search path.

The Sybase recommended size for an executable file is between 1.2MB and 1.5MB, after which you should consider breaking it down to use dynamic libraries. You might want to set the upper limit to 1.44MB so that you can get it onto a disk without having to compress it.

# Performance of Machine Versus Native Code

Some questions that many developers ask are: What's the performance gain in speed for my application? Does my application now run lightning fast? The answers are: A little faster and Quite a bit faster. The speed difference you will see depends entirely on what operations your application carries out.

The greatest benefit is provided within PowerScript execution because the other areas of an application are already using compiled code, as shown in the following table:

| Script Area | PowerBuilder 7.0 |
| --- | --- |
| Database Access | Compiled |
| DataWindows | Compiled |
| PowerBuilder System Functions | Compiled |
| PowerScript | Interpreted or Compiled |

If your application is computationally intensive, you will see marked improvements in the execution of this type of code. Other areas of improvement are looping constructs, floating-point arithmetic, and function calls. For example, the following code took about four times longer to run as native PowerBuilder than as 32-bit machine code compiled for speed:

```
Decimal {3} ldc_Value1, ldc_Value2, ldc_Value3
Integer li_Count
```

```
For li_Count = 1 To 1000
    ldc_Value1 = ldc_Value1 * 2
    ldc_Value2 = ldc_Value2 * ldc_Value2
    ldc_Value3 = Sqrt (ldc_Value1)
Next
```

**Tip**

There has been a lot of discussion over just how much faster an application is when compiled to machine code versus being left as p-code. You might want to consider other factors when making the decision:

- Consider the time taken to compile large applications to machine code. P-code applications take little time to compile in comparison.

- Some applications work fine when compiled to p-code but have unexplainable crashes and other strange behavior when made into machine code.

What works best for you will require your own investigation and can't be answered by anyone else.

To get the best performance out of your application, you should still rely on the developers' experience to write the best code they can. Try to optimize your own code as much as possible and use the best syntax or function for the job. Throughout this book are many hints and tips that point out which syntax or method of coding provides the best results.

To examine the differences in build time and final binary size, we built an application using the PowerBuilder Application Template that was created using the Template Application Wizard. In this test, no additional code was added to the template application, although there is more functionality in the PowerBuilder 7.0 template application than in prior releases. The timings and sizes shown in Table 20.1 indicate the differences you might expect in larger applications.

**TABLE 20.1**  Comparison of Build Types

| Build Type | Time to Build | Size |
| --- | --- | --- |
| PowerBuilder PBL (code size) | n/a | 215KB |
| PowerBuilder native (p-code) | 33s | 168KB |
| Machine code (No optimization) | 96s | 486KB |
| Machine code (Speed) | 99s | 3744KB |
| Machine code (Space) | 117s | 334KB |
| Machine code (No optimization, full debug) | 137s | 672KB |
| Machine code (Speed, full debug) | 153s | 529KB |

TABLE **20.1** Comparison of Build Types

| Build Type | Time to Build | Size |
|---|---|---|
| Machine code (Space, full debug) | 183s | 491KB |

The times in Table 20.1 were taken using a Pentium 233 with 32MB RAM, running Windows 98. The amount of time to compile varies from machine to machine. The final size of the application also varies greatly, and you might want to consider different compilation options for each application you distribute. This is a good reason for maintaining project objects for each application.

# Accessing Executable File Command-Line Parameters

A useful feature available with most Windows programs is the capability to specify a parameter when you run the executable file and have it carry out some operation automatically, such as opening a particular file. PowerBuilder provides the `CommandParm()` function for this purpose. An example of a command-line parameter is `NOTEPAD C:\TODO.LST`, where C:\TODO.LST is the filename to open when the NOTEPAD.EXE file executes.

> **Note**
>
> If you're extracting the command-line parameters from the `Open` event of the application object, you can instead use the `CommandLine` event parameter.

The `CommandParm()` function extracts the parameter string that occurs after the program name when the executable file is executed. The syntax is simply

```
CommandParm()
```

An empty string is returned if the call fails for some reason or if there was no parameter. In the previous example, the function would return the string `C:\TODO.LST`. The function returns a single string even if there were multiple parameters, and you need to parse out the separate parts. The most common method of specifying multiple parameters (across multiple platforms) is to separate them with a space and prefix each switch with a dash ( - ). This enables you to build a loop that breaks down the returned string using the `Pos()` function to search for a space:

```
String ls_Command, ls_Arguments[]
Integer li_Pos, li_NextPos
```

```
// Get a white space trimmed command-line
ls_Command = Trim( CommandParm())

Do While Len( ls_Command) > 0
   li_NextPos = Pos( ls_Command, " -", li_Pos + 1)
   // Unable to find a token, set position to end of string
   If li_NextPos = 0 Then li_NextPos = Len( ls_Command) + 1

   ii_Argc ++

   // Extract the component parts of the argument and store
   // them in string instance arrays
   ls_Argument = Trim( Left( ls_Command, li_NextPos-1))
   is_Switches[ ii_Argc] = Left( ls_Argument, 2)
   is_Parameters[ ii_Argc] = Mid( ls_Argument, 3)

   ls_Command = Replace( ls_Command, 1, li_NextPos-1, "")
   li_Pos = Pos( ls_Command, " -")
Loop
```

# Deployment of the Application

Just as there are numerous ways to partition and build the runtime files for your application, so are there many methods of deploying those same files and their supporting files.

Probably one of the biggest decisions is determining which parts of the system should reside locally on a user's machine and which should be globally accessible from a network file server. The decision on how this partitioning occurs (local, network, or sometimes even both) depends highly on the size and intended audience of the application; the hardware available for the client, network, and servers; the total number of users; and the number of concurrent users. Another big influence is how frequently you anticipate having to distribute not only application enhancements and fixes but also PowerBuilder DLL fixes, or even version migrations.

Methods for the distribution of maintenance and upgrade files are discussed in Chapter 22, "Application Maintenance and Upgrades."

For the best performance, place the executable and deployment kit files locally for every user. Obviously, this is feasible only if you have a small, easily accessible user group or some method of distributing files. There might even be a corporate security policy that prevents you from doing this.

As for deploying the new components available in PowerBuilder 7.0, most of the work is handled for you by the Project painter. This is covered later in the section "The Component Factory."

# Application Execution Management

When an executable file is first run, PowerBuilder starts the Object Manager, which finds and loads the application object, stores the class definition, makes an instance (and global pointer), and then triggers that object's Open event. The Object Manager is used to locate and load all objects and, more importantly, to track which objects are already loaded and which objects have been instantiated.

When you make a request of the Object Manager by using an Open() function or by declaring a variable of an object type, it retrieves the class definition for the object from the EXE or dynamic library file and then creates an instance of that object in memory. Only one copy of the class definition is made in the class definition pool held in memory. Therefore, when you open or create a variable of a definition already in memory, the Object Manager uses that rather than accesses the EXE or dynamic library file again.

When you instantiate a class definition and create an actual instance of that definition, the Object Manager makes a copy of the class-definition attributes that depend on that instance—for example, instance variables. It keeps object functions and shared variables with the class definition. The class definition isn't released until the application is terminated (but Sybase has indicated this might change in future versions of Power-Builder).

DataWindows are handled separately from all other objects and are serviced by a DataWindow engine. This engine loads a template of the DataWindow into memory when a DataWindow is instantiated. If another instance of the same DataWindow is issued, a new template and instance are created. There are no class definitions, and the engine doesn't use a pool for the templates; storage is allocated on an as-needed basis.

# Distribution

As mentioned earlier, several other files have to be deployed along with your EXE and dynamic library files.

# Installing the PowerBuilder Runtime Kit

PowerBuilder comes with a separate installation that contains the runtime DLLs (the PowerBuilder Deployment Kit). These often don't include any of the maintenance fixes you're running in your development environment. You must ensure that you also deploy any maintenance releases. Otherwise, your users might run into bugs that you didn't find during testing but that Sybase has fixed in a maintenance release. Occasionally, your executable file can act unpredictably and cause a GPF if you provide different DLLs than the ones used during compilation.

The list of the runtime DLLs appears later in the section "The PowerBuilder Runtime Files."

# Installing the Database Interface

If your application uses a database (and most of them do), you also must set up the appropriate database interface files. This includes not only the PowerBuilder native or ODBC drivers but also the drivers supplied by the individual DBMS vendors.

The native files required are listed later in the section "PowerBuilder Database Interface Files."

## Configuring ODBC Data Sources

If you use an ODBC data source, you must also install and configure the appropriate ODBC drivers and set up the data source.

The base ODBC files are listed later in the section "The Microsoft ODBC Driver Files."

## Installing Special Network Drivers

If the DBMS is located on a server that runs a different network protocol than is on an end user's machine, you have to install the appropriate network transport protocols. An example of this would be if a department used a Novell NetWare file server running IPX/SPX, and the division located the DBMS on a UNIX box that used TCP/IP.

## Modifying the Operating System

Depending on the application, you might also need to distribute specific DLLs, such as for mapping or enhanced graphing capabilities. Depending on what other applications are running on an end user's machine, you might also make other adjustments to the system, such as adjusting disk caches, swap files, or video drivers. Most importantly, ensure that the machine's search path is properly configured.

## Installing the Application

Remember to include all the necessary files for your application: EXE files, PBD/DLLs, initialization (.INI) files, help (.HLP) files, icons (.ICO), graphics (.BMP, .RLE, .WMF, .GIF, .JPG), cursors (.CUR), and sound (.WAV) files. You won't have to distribute any of the resources you stated in a PBR file when creating the executable file or dynamic libraries.

If you used a local database solution for your application, remember to distribute copies of the databases.

> **Tip**
>
> Some sites have placed these files into BLOB columns in a central database, which can then be downloaded when versions change. Another solution is to use the company's FTP server with the Synchronizer tool.

As a final step, make an entry into the Start menu, the Program Manager group, or another desktop area that enables these files to start up your application.

# The Component Factory

The Component Factory was created to be an extensible architecture that can support component-based development. It was initially released in PowerBuilder 6.0 with generators for an application, proxy library, and C++ object. This has been expanded in PowerBuilder 7.0 to include additional components such as Jaguar, COM/MTS, and Java proxies. Each generator provides the capability to take PowerBuilder objects and compile them into a component of the specified target generator. These generators can be made available outside major version releases due to the re-architecture that Sybase has made with the new project options.

## The Proxy Library

If you choose to create a new proxy library target (see Chapter 29, "PowerBuilder and the Internet," for a discussion of proxy objects) or choose an existing proxy library project, the Proxy Library Project painter opens (see Figure 20.5).

The painter provides the same Edit menu as the Application painter, except that the Select Objects and Properties entries are now enabled.

**FIGURE 20.5**

*The Proxy
Library Project
painter.*

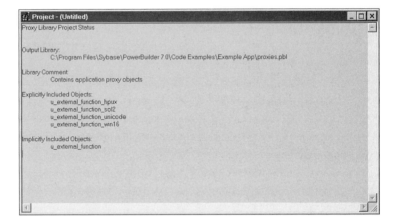

To select the user objects you want to make into proxies, choose Select Objects from the Edit menu or the painter toolbar. This opens the Select Objects dialog (see Figure 20.6), where you can choose the libraries and user objects contained within those libraries.

**FIGURE 20.6**

*The Select
Objects dialog.*

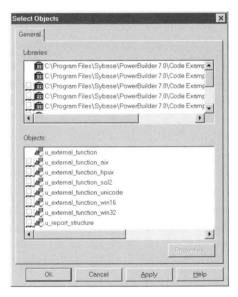

As you select a library, the user objects contained in it are added to the list in the bottom part of the dialog. The user objects you choose in this bottom part of the dialog will be made into proxies. When you've made all your choices, click OK to return to the painter, where you see the selected user objects listed under the Explicitly Included Objects section. If any selected objects are descendant objects, their ancestors are included automatically in the Implicitly Included Objects section. PowerBuilder then creates proxies for these objects as well.

You now *must* select the output library name. You do this by choosing Properties from the Edit menu or the toolbar, which opens the Properties for Proxy Library dialog (see Figure 20.7).

**FIGURE 20.7**
*The Properties for Proxy Library dialog.*

From this dialog, you can specify an existing library or, by using the ellipsis ( ... ) button, create a new library. New to PowerBuilder 7.0 are two options in the Properties dialog:

- The option to be prompted if you're going to overwrite an output file that already exists.

- The option to have the output library deleted and re-created. If this option, Clear Output Library for Each Build, isn't checked, the new proxies are added to the output library (assuming that it already exists). If the object already exists, it is overridden.

From the Design menu, you can now select to build the project or click the PainterBar icon. The other options don't make sense for a proxy library and are disabled.

**20**

Application and Component Implementation

This new generator that Sybase has created makes it easy to create a library of proxy objects that you can then provide to the client-application development teams. In earlier releases, you had to individually generate proxy objects and manually gather them together; this is a much more elegant solution.

# Working with Jaguar

As previously mentioned, one of PowerBuilder 7.0's strengths is its integrated application environment. Sybase has been successful with the new development environment by allowing you to access Sybase's transaction server, Jaguar. This allows you to create a PowerBuilder nonvisual object to use as a Jaguar component and deploy it to the Jaguar transaction server from within PowerBuilder. The next two sections discuss how to deploy the Jaguar component and the corresponding Jaguar proxy.

## Jaguar Components

Jaguar components can be easily built using the new Jaguar Component Start Wizard. The wizard asks you several questions:

- The application and library for the new component

- The component object's name

- The Jaguar server information and your login information

- The name for the Jaguar package to deploy

- The component type (whether it's a Standard, Shared, or Service component)

- The component's Instance Pooling options (for reuse of component instances and therefore, better performance)

- The Transaction Support options (for indicating how the component fits into Jaguar's database transaction handling)

- The component's Interface options as specified by the CORBA 2.0 Interface Definition Language (IDL)

- Additional component options (such as debugging and live editing)

- The PowerBuilder project name that will build and deploy your Jaguar component

After going through the wizard, PowerBuilder creates your Jaguar component. You can then access it using the User Object painter and add your specific application business functionality. The benefit of building your Jaguar component using the wizard is that it not only builds the component (a custom class user object) for you, but also a project object to deploy your component. If you choose not to use the Jaguar Component Start Wizard, you can go directly into the User Object painter and create a custom class user object.

After you finish your new component, you are ready to deploy it to Jaguar. If you used the wizard to create you component, you already have a project object created. You can open this object and click the Build icon on the PainterBar. If you didn't use the Start Wizard, you can create your project object by clicking New on the PowerBar and selecting the Project Tab. Within this tab are two options: the Jaguar Component Wizard or just Jaguar Component. Both options result in creating and deploying the component to Jaguar. Depending on your comfort level with build process, you can choose to bypass the wizard and go directly to the Jaguar Project painter. When building the project, you have to specify most of the information listed previously for the Jaguar Component Start Wizard.

After a successful build, the following occurs:

- The appropriate CORBA IDL for the new components is created and then stored in Jaguar's repository.

- At least one PBD file for the new components is created and stored in Jaguar's repository.

- A property file for the new components is created and stored in Jaguar's repository.

Now that you've built and deployed your components to Jaguar, you are ready to build the client application, which accesses the component via Jaguar proxies.

## Jaguar Proxies

If you want to use the new Jaguar component that you've built from a PowerBuilder application, you need to construct a Jaguar proxy object. The proxy object defines the Jaguar server component's public interface to your PowerBuilder application. In addition to creating a proxy object, you also need to have a connection object, which connects your application to the Jaguar server.

To build the connection object, you can use the Connection Object Wizard found by clicking New from the PowerBar and selecting the Object tab.

**20**

**Application and Component Implementation**

> **Tip**
>
> The Connection Object Wizard can also be used to easily create a connection object to your database.

When asked, select the Jaguar connection as your Connectivity Option. The wizard then prompts you to specify your Jaguar server name, port number, and login information. You are asked to specify the Jaguar package name, the new connection object name, and where the connection information comes from (INI file, Registry, or script). When the wizard is complete, a standard class user object inherited from the system class of `connection` has been created for you with all the Jaguar server connection information, which can be retrieved by your application by calling the new object's function, `of_GetConnectionInfo()`.

Your Jaguar proxy object can be built manually or by using the Jaguar Proxy wizard. Either way you choose to build it, you need to specify the following:

- The library to contain the new proxy object

- The name of the new project object

- The Jaguar Server connection and login information

PowerBuilder connects to Jaguar and displays the available components for your application to use. You then can select the component that you want to create the proxy for. From this point on, you can build your other application objects (windows, user objects, and so on) and access the functionality of the Jaguar component by calling the methods of the proxy object.

## The COM/MTS Component

With the previous release of PowerBuilder, you could take a custom class user object and build an OLE automation server and a COM in-process server. If you wanted to deploy your COM server to Microsoft Transaction Server (MTS), you were required to go through several steps outside PowerBuilder. Although PowerBuilder 7.0 still allows you to create OLE automation servers and COM in-process servers, Sybase has simplified the process of deploying your COM server to MTS.

To create your COM component, you have a several options:

- Create a custom class user object manually. When you are ready to deploy, create your project object by using the COM/MTS Component Wizard or manually by using the COM/MTS Component option on the Project tab.

- Use the COM/MTS Component option on the Start Wizard tab, which creates a brand-new application, a custom class user object, and a new project object.

- Use the COM/MTS Component Wizard option on the Object tab, which creates a custom class user object and a new project object in one of your existing libraries.

Whichever method you choose, you need to specify the following when creating the project object:

- The components to be deployed to MTS

- The component Interface Options (Type, Name, and ID)

- The component Class Options (Program ID, Class Name, Class ID, and the version information)

- The COM server information (the component's filename and server AppID)

- The component Type Library information (the type library ID, help string, and version)

- The component Build Options (any PBR used, whether to register the component after the build successfully completes, and whether to deploy to MTS)

If you choose to deploy the component to MTS, you are asked to specify the following:

- The MTS package name, description, and protection options

- The MTS export package information, if used

- The component Transaction and Security options

If you have the MTS administration objects installed local to your machine, PowerBuilder automatically deploys the component to MTS. If you don't, you can use the export package options, which create a PAK file that can then be imported into MTS from another machine.

After you successfully create and test your COM component, you can build your client application in PowerBuilder, Visual Basic, or any other COM compliant application. For more information on COM, see Chapter 37, "ActiveX and OLE."

# The Java Proxy

The Java proxy object allows you to build a Java client application that accesses a distributed PowerBuilder server application. Your PowerBuilder server application will consist of mainly custom class user objects containing your application business logic (for more information on distributed PowerBuilder, see Chapter 28, "Developing Distributed PowerBuilder Applications," and Chapter 29, "PowerBuilder and the Internet").

20

Application and Component Implementation

After you build your distributed PowerBuilder application, create a proxy object that exposes the public interfaces of your custom class user objects to the Java client application. To do this, use the Java proxy on the Project tab. This takes you into the Project painter. To specify how the proxy will be built, select the Properties icon from the PainterBar. On the ensuing property sheet, specify the Deployment Path Name, the Package Name, and the compile options (such as whether to use bytecode, the compile type, and so on).

After setting up the project generation properties, select the objects that need to be accessed by your Java client. To do this, click the Select Objects icon on the PainterBar. This opens a dialog that allows you to select the libraries the desired objects reside in and the objects themselves. After you select all objects that require Java proxies and return to the main project painter, you are ready to build the proxies. Like all the other project objects discussed, click the Build toolbar icon and sit back and let PowerBuilder 7.0 work its magic.

After your Java proxies are created, include the new Java classes containing the proxy objects in your Java client application. You then can code your Java application to access the functions in the distributed PowerBuilder server application.

## Additional Project Options

PowerBuilder 7.0 also includes two more project objects: the OLE Automation Server (also in wizard format) and Web.PB. The OLE Automation Server allows you to take your custom class user objects and convert them to an in-process OLE server, which can then be accessed by any COM-compliant client application. For more information on OLE Automation Servers, see Chapter 37, "ActiveX and OLE."

The Web.PB project object allows you to build an HTML form that calls functions in a distributed PowerBuilder server application. The form can be created using CGI, ISAPI (Microsoft), or NSAPI (Netscape). For more information on Web.PB see Chapter 29, "PowerBuilder and the Internet," and Chapter 30, "Developing Internet Applications with PowerBuilder."

# The Actual PowerBuilder Deployment Files

As you might have gathered from the previous sections, a number of files must be deployed. I've broken them down into component parts and listed them in the following sections.

Due to much prompting by the PowerBuilder development community, Sybase has introduced different naming schemes for the different versions of PowerBuilder (where the *xxx* is replaced with a file type identifier):

| PowerBuilder Version | DLL Naming |
|---|---|
| Standard PB*xxx* | 70.DLL |
| Hebrew PB*xxx* | 70H.DLL |
| Arabic PB*xxx* | 70A.DLL |

# The PowerBuilder Runtime Files

Place the PowerBuilder runtime DLLs in the same directory as the application or in a directory mentioned in the search path. Table 20.2 lists the files.

TABLE 20.2   The PowerBuilder Runtime DLLs

| Filename | Required? |
|---|---|
| PBVM70.DLL | Yes |
| LIBJCC.DLL | Yes |
| PBDWE70.DLL | If DataWindows or DataStores are used |
| PBRTC70.DLL | If RichText controls or DataWindows are used |
| PBAEN70.TLB | If PowerBuilder.Application is used for an OLE Automation Server |
| PBFNT70.INI | For unavailable mapping fonts |
| PBLAB70.INI | For DataWindow labels with predefined formats |
| PBTRA70.DLL | For tracing database connections |

# The PowerBuilder Database Interface Files

The files for the Sybase database interfaces that your application uses belong in the application directory or in a directory that appears on the system path.

The following interface files are required under Windows:

| DBMS | File |
|---|---|
| INFORMIX I-Net 7 | PBIN770.DLL |
| INFORMIX I-Net 9 | PBIN970.DLL |
| Microsoft SQL Server | PBMSS70.DLL |
| Oracle 7.3 | PBO7370.DLL |
| Oracle 8.0 | PBOR870.DLL |
| Oracle 8.0.4 or later | PBO8470.DLL |

| *DBMS* | *File* |
|--------|--------|
| Sybase DirectConnect | PBDIR70.DLL |
| Sybase Adaptive Enterprise CT-LIB | ServerPBSYC70.DLL |
| Sybase Adaptive Server Enterprise CT-LIB for Jaguar deployment only | PBSYJ70.DLL |

## The Microsoft ODBC Driver Files

If your application uses ODBC, you need PowerBuilder's database driver and INI file for ODBC (PBODB70.DLL and PBODB070.INI—these are usually in the Windows System directory, but you might want to keep them in the deployment directory to make upgrades easier). The only constraint is that these files must be in the client machine's path. You also need two ODBC INI files (ODBCINST.INI and ODBC.INI), which are found in the Windows directory and, if they already exist, must be updated during deployment.

For Win32, the following files need to be in the Windows system directory:

| | |
|---|---|
| ODBC32.DLL | ODBCCP32.CPL |
| DS16GT.DLL | ODBCCR32.DLL |
| ODBC32GT.DLL | ODBCINST.CNT |
| DS32GT.DLL | ODBCINST.HLP |
| ODBCAD32.EXE | ODBCINT.DLL |
| ODBCCP32.DLL | ODBCTRAC.DLL |

In Windows 95, the ODBC INI settings are stored in the Registry as well.

## Additional Installation Files

The previously listed files are the most commonly used files when installing a standard PowerBuilder application setup. What happens if you're installing an application using OLE DB, JDBC, Jaguar, or any other of the possible PowerBuilder generated components? Several files need to be distributed with each deployment. The details for each deployment file can be found in a technical document on the Sybase Developer Network (`http://sdn.sybase.com`).

# InstallShield

The de facto standard installation program for Windows 95/98/NT is InstallShield. This is a commercially available product that provides easy-to-use wizards and an integrated environment to aid in the creation of an application installation.

InstallShield allows you to create file groupings and control where the files are installed. The actual setup program that users run when installing the software can be customized by you to include any of the following:

| | |
|---|---|
| Welcome Bitmap | Custom Setup |
| Welcome Message | Select Program Folder |
| Software License | Agreement  Start Copying Files |
| Readme Information | Progress Indicator |
| User Information | Billboards |
| Choose Destination Location | Setup Complete |
| Setup | Type |

The choices you make here allow you to construct the flow of the setup that users go through. Depending on the target operating system, you can make file-based application modifications or Registry-based ones.

For system file changes, you have the choice of a custom INI, WIN.INI, SYSTEM.INI, PROTOCOL.INI, AUTOEXEC.BAT, or CONFIG.SYS files. The dialog provided allows you to create new sections, keywords, and values. You also have control over entry positioning, environment variables, and path changes within the AUTOEXEC.BAT file.

If you will be using the Registry for your application, you can specify new keys and values, or even specify a REG file to be used to merge in with the user's own Registry. The interface provided, like so many others, is intuitive and visually reflective of changes you make.

InstallShield allows you to specify the application's icon and where the entry appears in the user's Start menu/Program Manager. You can also specify the application run command and optional run parameters; the description that appears for the application; and whether it runs initially in a normal, maximized, or minimized state.

InstallShield allows you to create a variety of target installation mediums. You have default choices of floppy sizes 720KB through 120MB. You can also choose CD-ROM, a Web install, or a custom size. With the CD-ROM option, you can also have InstallShield create an AUTORUN.INF file for auto-running the setup program when users insert CD-ROMs containing your install.

**20**

Application and
Component
Implementation

InstallShield Express has full install and uninstall support for Windows 95/98/NT, automated file compression and library splitting, automatic registration of standard OLE controls, automatic Registry entries, language support, and Microsoft SMS support.

# Guidelines for Application Installation

Try to follow several guidelines when installing your application on another person's machine—most of them are common sense. They allow you to maintain your applications more easily and will result in fewer duplicate files (some of which may cause problems because of their versions). These are just a few of the many points that deserve consideration during the deployment of your application:

- Avoid copying any files into system directories unless you're upgrading a common file used by applications outside PowerBuilder (for example, the ODBC or native database drivers). This helps prevent operating system degradation by reducing the number of files within these areas. Any files that you place in a Windows 95/98/NT system directory should be registered in the SharedDLL subkey of HKEY_LOCAL_MACHINE.

- If the file is a common file shared only among your own applications, create a subdirectory in the Common Files subdirectory of the Program Files directory. An alternative is to make an entry under Program Files itself for the shared files. Whichever method you use, the path should be registered with the Path subkey of the App Paths subkey of HKEY_LOCAL_MACHINE.

- Always check that you're not replacing a newer version of the file with one of your own. This is true of your own files as well as shared system ones.

- In Windows 95/98/NT, place your application in its own directory under the Program Files directory. You can locate the appropriate directory by checking the ProgramFilesDir value in the CurrentVersion subkey of HKEY_LOCAL_MACHINE\Software\Microsoft\Windows.

- It's recommended for Windows 95/98/NT (and you might want to adopt this for other operating systems) that you partition supporting files (HLP, DLL, WAV, and so on) in a subdirectory of your application directory called System. You would then register its location in the Registry in the App Paths subkey of HKEY_LOCAL_MACHINE\Software entry for your application.

- Use the Registry to store all the necessary information about your application, and don't alter the AUTOEXEC.BAT, CONFIG.SYS, WIN.INI, or your own application INI file.

- Provide access to your application by making an entry in the appropriate launch engine of the operating system. For Windows 95/98/NT, place a shortcut icon for the application in the `Programs` folder (found by checking the `Shell Folders` subkey of `HKEY_CURRENT_USER\Software\Microsoft\Windows\CurrentVersion\Explorer`.

- Numerous commercial installation programs are available for your use. If you want to design your own, provide sufficient setup options for users, as well as constant feedback on such things as percentage complete, disk space available, disk space used, and the capability to cancel the install. Remember that one logo compliance requirement for Windows 95/98/NT is the capability to uninstall an application; this might be a useful feature to add because it will allow you to back out changes you make to a user's existing system.

Although most of these are directly related to Windows 95/98/NT and their interrelation with the Registry, the naming and hierarchy structure can be adapted for other operating systems.

# Summary

In this chapter, you saw how to create the individual components of an application, how to create the executable file and dynamic libraries, what occurs during runtime, and how you can use a project object to collect information on building the application together. The files required for the deployment of PowerBuilder and its database interfaces were listed in this chapter, and different ways to package your application were explained.

# Testing and Debugging

Testing is integral to every application development process. Without it, you can't be sure that a quality application will be produced and provide end users with the necessary functionality to perform their jobs. In this chapter, you learn about a standard approach to testing, as well as techniques that will assist you in that process.

PowerBuilder comes equipped with several tools, such as the Debugger and the PBDEBUG option, that you can use to test and identify problem areas. Many developers use additional methods of testing logic and functionality within their applications; you will learn about these as well. Although PowerBuilder contains several different means to test and debug, a suite of third-party products is available that complements the PowerBuilder application development process.

# The Testing Process

Before exploring the steps to successful application testing, you should review the goal of testing and the steps to get started.

## The Goal of Testing

The most common misconception about testing is that its intention is to prove that developers have created an application with no errors. Because creating an application with no errors is an improbability, you must approach testing with a slightly different mindset. Testing should mean running an application with the intent of finding errors. You probably haven't had a successful test until you've found several errors.

The process of finding errors in an application is referred to as *quality assurance*. This means that your application and its documentation are correct, complete, reliable, and easy to maintain in addition to meeting all the specifications and requirements laid out by users.

## Getting Started

One of the most difficult aspects of the testing process is creating a test plan. Many people don't have the slightest clue about where to begin and panic at the thought of testing and ensuring that a quality product is delivered. Formulate a test plan based on the functional design specifications of your application. You then can break down the testing process into small, manageable groups. Standard approaches to testing follow:

- The *unit test* tests each low-level (primitive) business process.

- The *system test* tests each unit together as a whole entity/object.

- The *integration test* tests whether the whole application runs with all components of the application (network, server, and so on) and with other applications.

- The *volume test* tests whether the application can maintain production volume of data and stay within acceptable time limits.

- The *acceptance test* tests continuously throughout all stages of the testing process to determine whether end users approve of the system's design and functionality.

In a perfect world, each component would be completed before the next phase of testing began. More often than not, however, there are gray areas and overlap between each different test mode. Now look at each test phase and some common practices.

# Unit Testing

The unit test tests the basic functionality of each low-level process of your system. Consider this example: A basic requirement of a system is to calculate the net accounts receivable amount for specific customers based on the days of sales outstanding (DSO). This process was implemented by using a DataWindow that retrieves totals for all unpaid invoices and displays information based on each DSO total (for example, 30 to 60 days). The test scenario asks whether the DataWindow correctly calculates the net accounts receivable.

This information can be validated in several ways. If developers have the appropriate business knowledge, they can manually determine what the correct amount will be for customer ABC for 30 to 60 DSO. A better approach would be to obtain a copy of an existing report that calculates the figures for a given period of time (preferably, a minimum of three months). The DataWindow then could be run against the data for the same time frame, and results from the application could be validated against the existing report.

With this scenario in mind, the goal of the unit test is to tell developers which scripts need to be corrected or better understood. This is done by using two approaches: testing the code logic and examining the functional specifications. By testing the code logic, testers should develop test cases that attempt to execute every line of code in the application component being tested. Code testing can be time-consuming and, on a large system, difficult to formulate for all test cases. Even if all lines of code are executed, a bug-free application isn't guaranteed because the overall functionality isn't tested. Testing whether an application component meets the desired functional specifications also must be a part of unit testing. This is done by treating the component as a black box. This approach means that you don't care about what line of code is being executed when; instead, you are concerned with whether all aspects of the application perform as requested under different conditions.

As soon as a section of the application is completed, begin testing it to ensure that it provides all the necessary behavior. The initial test should be completed by the developer and subsequently by other individual team members. It's particularly useful if a team member is an end user or has business experience similar to that of an end user. One of the most important reasons to get others involved as early as possible is that, as the developer, you have a tendency to try the same, tired routine each time. If you always use the same test scenario, you'll make sure that scenario works in those circumstances but potentially will miss testing other key areas. Each unit also should be constructed to include the appropriate error-handling tests to ensure that the system won't crash.

Getting end users involved in this early stage is important for several other reasons. They know what they need to do and can immediately tell you whether something looks strange or acts incorrectly. If the interface isn't what they want or the functionality isn't completely there, wouldn't you rather know now instead of a week before implementation? By involving users from the beginning, you ensure that they will be happy with the application (they have only themselves to blame) and happy because they're contributing to the development process. Also, the users now have a stake in the application because their names and reputations are associated with it.

After all low-level units are identified, tested, and approved by several members of the project team, it's time to assemble all pieces of the application and begin the next phase of testing: the system test.

# System Testing

The system test combines all application units to ensure that the application flows smoothly and that there's compatibility between the individual components. By this time, each unit should correctly provide the necessary business requirements. The system test ensures that navigation through the system is consistent, a common look and feel is maintained (good GUI), and the application provides the flexibility and components users have requested. It's essential that at least one or two end users be involved in the system test to ensure that no requirement is left out of the application.

Also included in the system test is a process some people refer to as *idiot testing*. This is often one of the more fun parts of the testing process. Ask a developer from another project to take a few minutes to test your application. The developer's goal should be to try to break your application. In essence, the other developer should approach the application as though he is an idiot and try to do things that don't make sense, click everywhere, and question everything. You will be surprised at the number of unexpected results, potential pitfalls, and general protection faults (GPFs) or page faults this testing approach uncovers. If you skip this type of testing, you may also be surprised at how quickly end users can break your code!

After everyone signs off on the application as it now exists, you are ready to begin the later phases of the testing process: integration and volume testing.

# Integration Testing

The integration test takes the completed business application and places it in a mock production environment. The goal of the integration test is to make sure that the application functions properly with the network, database, hardware, and any other platforms or environmental factors specific to the company.

An important part of the integration test is running the application on a user's workstation. This can uncover multiple problems. If all testing has been done on a Pentium 366 with 128MB of RAM, for example, and the client workstation is a Pentium 166 with 32MB, you'll likely notice some performance degradation. The resolution of the end user's monitor also is important because many developers run $800 \times 600$ or higher, whereas it is common for end users to run standard $640 \times 480$. Application windows might be too large or have too-fancy color schemes, or graphical effects might be lost or look poor. The minimum resolution requirements should be determined before coding begins; consider using $640 \times 480$ if the minimum resolution cannot be determined. Also check to see how the application looks with your user's Windows color scheme. You might be surprised at the results (for example, black text on a black background).

Another portion of the integration test is to ensure that the application executes and integrates with other company systems. Many times, new software releases or patches to existing software are required. It's tempting to install the latest and greatest versions of the software. This can lead to problems if existing applications are on an earlier release that's not compatible with the new version, such as updates to dynamic link libraries (DLLs). It's a good idea to find this out before the application is deployed into the production environment. A problem such as this also leads to another important aspect of the integration test: recovery. You should implement and test a procedure to back out of your application and recover the previously existing application with minimal effort.

Integration testing identifies many unforeseen and previously untestable conditions: network traffic delays, long-running processing times (resulting in timeouts or missed availability time), data integrity and user concurrency issues, and the need for additional error handling. Pinpointing problems during integration testing can be challenging because many components are operating simultaneously. If a problem is encountered, determine what the problem is first and then try to nail down the component that's causing the problem. The integration test works hand in hand with the last phase: volume testing.

## Volume Testing

Volume testing (also called *load testing*) ensures that all application components can handle the production volume of data being processed. Typically during application construction developers use a scaled-down model of the production database. For applications dealing with small amounts of data, the volume test might not even be an issue, but for larger databases it's crucial.

The volume test determines whether the application can handle the data without crashing or timing out and whether the current hardware configuration is robust enough to support the company's needs. Although testing the data volume is important to the application's front-end developers, this test will greatly help the individuals in charge of the servers, databases, and networks.

In addition to testing high volumes of data, be aware of the issue of user concurrency. Do users have sufficient data access? You must ensure that while using your application, users can retrieve and modify data without holding large numbers of locks on data or erroring out because of a timing or deadlock issue. You might find that your application can handle large amounts of data but can't handle the number of users concurrently accessing the data.

## User Testing

As emphasized in the previous sections, user participation in the testing process is essential for successful client/server application deployment. Users find problems not only with the functionality of the system, but also with the interface. Users typically respond to the system in ways you never would have considered. They can tell you whether the application process is natural to their way of thinking and approaching problems. By involving your users, you can maintain credibility, keep user expectations on track, and ensure that they have an application that suits their needs.

# Identifying Problem Areas

One of the most difficult aspects about testing client/server applications is the involvement of multiple layers and components. It's important to determine which component is breaking down to identify and correct the problem. You can break down the components of a client/server application into three main groups: client, network, and server.

The client group includes the following:

- The client operating system

- Your application executable

- Optional initialization (INI) files

- Optional help files

- A database library for database communication

- The PowerBuilder DLLs found in the Database Distribution and Deployment Kit

- The PowerBuilder database interface DLLs

Each component is crucial to your application functioning correctly. Misplacing or mismatching versions of any of these files can result in your application behaving unpredictably or incorrectly. All these components, including their distribution and setup, usually are left as the application developer's responsibility.

The network and server typically are out of the developer's control in the production environment. Some common components that make up the network are access and permissions (security), resource dedication, and general processing and data-transfer times. The server contains the relational database management system (RDBMS) software that manages table structures, triggers, rules, stored procedures, and backup and recovery procedures, just to name a few operations. It's important to familiarize yourself with the network and the server to help identify where certain problems can occur.

Now that you have a general framework to use in an approach to the testing phase of your application development, it's time to examine some methods, tools, and techniques you can use to maximize your test cases and minimize your testing time.

# Testing Tools and Techniques

PowerBuilder comes equipped with several features to assist in the testing process. In addition to these features are some extra tips and techniques to use when testing a PowerBuilder application.

## The Debugger

PowerBuilder comes with a built-in debugging tool that helps you find errors in any of your application's scripts. The Debugger was completely rewritten in PowerBuilder 6.0 to provide a more flexible and powerful environment than was previously available. The Debugger enables you to set stops (or *breakpoints*) within the different scripts you want to debug. When you execute your application in Debug mode, PowerBuilder suspends processing right before it executes the PowerScript statement containing the breakpoint. At that point, you can step through each line of code and observe what code is executed, view what objects are loaded into memory, and examine variables now in scope. Debugging also enables you to watch variable values during breakpoints and to change variable values.

To enter the Debugger, click the PowerBar icon with the slashed-through bug on it. The Debugger opens and displays the source, source browser, local, and call stack panes in the default configuration (see Figure 21.1). Each pane enables you to view a different component of your application during execution.

**FIGURE 21.1**

*The Debugger.*

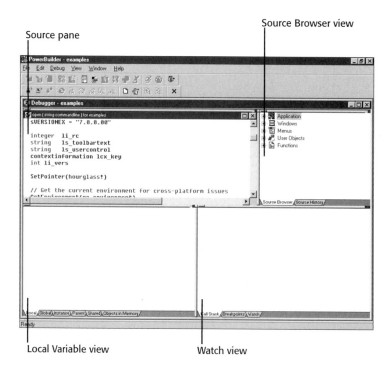

Source pane

Source Browser view

Local Variable view

Watch view

Before you specify the script you want to debug, take a few minutes to familiarize yourself with the way in which you can configure the Debugger to your liking. The Debugger gives you full control over what information is displayed and the way it's presented.

## What You Can View

Each pane within the Debugger displays different information that you can use to track program execution and determine logic errors. A major advantage of the Debugger is that it is fully customizable. You can choose to display information in various configurations—just choose the following options from the View menu:

- Source Browser displays a tree-view control that lists objects in your application.

- Source History lists scripts that have been displayed in the Source pane.

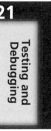

- Source displays the source code for a specified object's functions or events.

- Object in Memory lists objects that have been loaded into memory during the execution of your application.

- Variables displays global, shared, instance, and local variables during a particular breakpoint in your application code. It also displays any variables defined for the current object's parent (if applicable).

- Call Stack displays the events/functions executed before the existing script being viewed.

- Breakpoints lists all the breakpoints set for the application.

- Instances lists instances of a remote component that's being debugged using the new remote debugging capability.

- Watch Variables lists all variables that you want to view constantly.

After you choose one of these options, the Debugger opens a separate pane in which to display that information.

## Starting Debug Mode

To start debugging an application, first specify where in your application's code you want to halt execution and begin to step through your code. You accomplish this by setting a breakpoint. To set a breakpoint, locate the object you want to debug in the Source Browser view. The Source Browser lists all five PowerBuilder objects that can contain scripts: Application, Windows, Menus, User Objects, and Functions. Select the type of object for which you want to set a breakpoint; it then expands to show all the objects of the object type.

After you select a particular object name (such as w_about), all controls or objects that have a script written for them appear in the list. Continue to expand the tree view until the script name you want to debug is displayed. After you locate the desired script, double-click the script's name or right-click and choose Open Source to view the script's source code in the Source pane.

In the Source pane, double-click each PowerScript statement on which you want to set a breakpoint. A red dot appears next to the lines with breakpoints specified (see Figure 21.2). Remember that processing stops before executing the line with the breakpoint. It also is important to note that comments, variable declarations, and empty lines can't contain breakpoints.

**FIGURE 21.2**
*A script with
Debugger break-
points specified.*

Breakpoint indicator

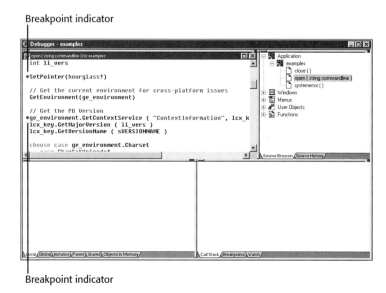

Breakpoint indicator

If you have limited display space and choose not to use the Source Browser pane,
PowerBuilder provides an alternative method for script selection. From the Edit menu,
choose Select Script. Or, click the Select Script icon (it looks like a sheet of paper) on the
PainterBar to open the Select Script dialog (see Figure 21.3).

**FIGURE 21.3**
*The Select Script
dialog.*

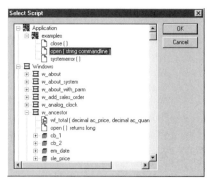

The Select Script dialog provides the same tree-view interface as the Source Browser.
Although the approach mentioned for setting breakpoints is the most common debugging
approach, four additional alternatives are available for launching your application into
Debug mode.

The first alternative uses the Edit Breakpoints dialog (see Figure 21.4). You can access this dialog from the Edit menu, from many of the Debugger view's pop-up menus, or by clicking the Edit Stop icon (a hand with a pencil in it) on the PainterBar.

**FIGURE 21.4**
*The Edit Break-points dialog.*

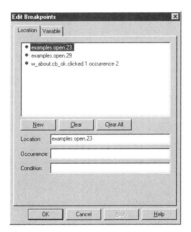

The Location tab displays all the breakpoints now set for your application. You can use this tab to create new breakpoints, clear the breakpoint selected in the list, and clear all breakpoints. The bottom section of the tab displays information about each breakpoint. The Location text box displays the location of the breakpoint and has this format:

```
FullyQualified_ScriptName.LineNumber
```

`FullyQualified_ScriptName` is the method name plus the full qualification of the method, and `LineNumber` is the line at which the breakpoint should be set. A breakpoint set on line 12 in the `Clicked` event of command button `cb_ok` on window `w_orders`, for example, would appear as this:

```
w_about.cb_ok.clicked.12
```

The Occurrence text box contains an integer value. When PowerBuilder executes the statement specified in the Location text box the specified number of times, it enters Break mode. Use the Condition text box to enter a Boolean expression that's evaluated each time the script in the Location text box is executed. If the expression evaluates to TRUE, PowerBuilder enters Break mode. The Occurrence and Condition text boxes are useful in debugging repetitive processes and loops in your code.

The other tab page on the Edit Breakpoints dialog, Variable, allows you to specify a breakpoint that depends on the value of the changing variable. You can also clear any or all existing variable breakpoints from this tab page. To create a new variable breakpoint, click the New button on the page, enter the variable's name, and then click Apply. The variable is then placed in the list box at the top of the tab. If, for example, you wanted to check whenever the value of a long variable, ll_rows, changes, you would enter ll_rows and click Apply. This would then create the following entry in the list box:

```
when ll_rows changes
```

During execution of your application, if ll_rows is modified, you enter the Debugger automatically.

At any point after the Edit Breakpoints dialog is closed, if you want to view the breakpoints you've set for your application, select the Breakpoints pane. This lists all the breakpoints set and gives you some additional functionality via the view's pop-up menu. You can perform these tasks:

- Enable and disable breakpoints (noted by the circle next to a breakpoint being filled in or not)

- Clear breakpoints

- Enable, disable, or clear all breakpoints

- Open the corresponding script in the Source pane

- Open the Edit Breakpoints dialog

The other three methods for starting Debug mode don't require you to enter the Debugger and set breakpoints. One method for starting Debug mode is to place a debug statement directly in your code. The function that triggers Debug mode is DebugBreak(). Start your application testing by clicking the PowerBar's Run icon. When this line of code is executed during Run mode in the development environment, PowerBuilder halts execution and opens the Debugger.

The other two methods are what Sybase refers to as *just-in-time* debugging. One way to start Debug mode is to choose System Options from the Window menu. In the System Options dialog (see Figure 21.5), enable the Just In Time Debugging check box. Now, when you run your application in regular Run mode and experience a runtime error, PowerBuilder automatically takes you into the Debugger.

FIGURE **21.5**

*The System
Options dialog.*

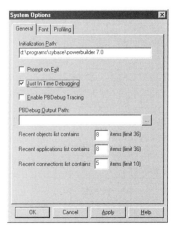

You can use the last method while you're running your application by clicking the PowerBuilder 7.0 icon on the taskbar or desktop. In earlier versions of PowerBuilder, after you clicked the PowerBuilder icon, you saw a prompt telling you that your application was still running and asking whether you wanted to terminate it. In version 7.0, you can choose to terminate the application, continue execution (by clicking Cancel), or go into Debug mode (if Just In Time Debugging is enabled).

After you establish a breakpoint, you can view your application in Debug mode.

## Running in Debug Mode

One of the most important scripts in any PowerBuilder application that uses a relational database as its source of information is the script that connects that application to the database. Not only is it important, but if an error occurs, it also can be one of the trickier problems to solve. The problem could be caused by the script, communication on the network, or communication with the database.

Consider this scenario: For some reason, an application won't connect to the database. The application object Open event opens the first window, w_login. The logon window contains the script to populate the default transaction object, SQLCA, and contains two fields. Users type their user ID and password in these fields and click OK to connect to the database.

With this scenario in mind, try to figure out the cause of this problem.

In the Debugger, select the Window object type and choose w_login on the Source Browser pane and cb_ok (the OK command button) from the list of controls. Because you aren't sure where the problem is occurring, place a breakpoint on the first line of code in the Clicked event script. To get to this code, double-click this event in the Source Browser pane (see Figure 21.6).

FIGURE **21.6**

*Selecting* cb_ok*'s* Clicked *event in the Source Browser pane.*

To start the application in Debug mode, click the icon with a bug next to a green arrow on the PainterBar or choose Start from the Debug menu. The application runs as it normally would until the OK button on w_login is clicked. After you trigger the script for the Clicked event for cb_ok and hit the specified breakpoint, PowerBuilder goes into Debug mode.

To find out what's wrong with the application, you need to step through each code line and ensure that the attributes of the SQLCA object are being populated correctly. To execute your application code, you have one of three options that you can access from the PainterBar or the Debug menu:

- Step In executes one line at a time. The first time you click the Step In icon, PowerBuilder executes the code marked with the breakpoint. If the line of code you're executing is a user-defined method, choosing Step In displays the method's script and enables you to execute one line at a time.

- Step Over treats a line with a user-defined method as one line of code and doesn't take you into the method's script. This is useful if you've already confirmed that a script works and you don't want to have to step through it.

> **Tip**
>
> You'll want to use the Step Over option often when using a class library, such as the PFC, because Step Over allows you to bypass checking all the library's functions.

- Step Out is useful if you find yourself in a function and want to execute it without having to step through each line. Step Out allows you to execute the rest of a method script and return to the calling script.

In addition to stepping through your script, you can specify the next line of code to be executed by using the Set Next Statement option, available on the PainterBar, the Debug menu, or the Source pane's pop-up menu. Set Next Statement bypasses all code between the current line and the specified statement. This option can be useful for testing code execution for which runtime conditions can't easily be created (such as certain errors) and for bypassing erroneous code while still executing cleanup code.

> **Caution**
>
> Although the Set Next Statement option can be powerful, you easily might bypass important code, which could result in runtime errors.

As you debug your code, you might find that you want to continue executing it until you reach a specific line that doesn't contain a breakpoint. You can add a breakpoint and click the Continue icon, or you can use the Run to Cursor option. This option executes all code between the current line being executed to the location of your cursor.

In the SQLCA example, you need to validate that SQLCA is being populated correctly by viewing each attribute as it's being assigned a value. Because SQLCA is a global variable, you need to look for it with the global variables. To do this, click the Global tab on the Variables pane (see Figure 21.7).

In the variable list, look at the transaction object SQLCA. Click SQLCA to list all its attributes and their current values (see Figure 21.8).

Because you are at the beginning of the script, only the default values are in SQLCA. To see what values the script is assigning to SQLCA, click the Step In PainterBar icon. The first two steps populate the DBMS and DBParm attributes from the fields in w_login. Both values were assigned properly, although viewing the code might make you think there should be some

**FIGURE 21.7**

*The Global Variables pane.*

Variable pane,
Global tab

**FIGURE 21.8**

*A list of attributes for SQLCA in the Global Variables pane.*

validation when users enter their user IDs and passwords before doing any more processing. If you need to stop debugging to code this script, click the PainterBar's Close icon.

Another way to exit Debug mode is to click the Continue PainterBar icon (with the circle consisting of two arrows) or choose Continue from the Run menu. This takes you out of stepping through code and forces PowerBuilder to continue processing. Processing stops, however, if PowerBuilder encounters another breakpoint. After the application continues, exit the application normally (which returns you to PowerBuilder's Debugger). Close the Debugger and add the password and user ID validation checks.

After making the changes, start debugging again and see whether you can find the problem. When the Debugger reaches the condition check for the SQLCode property of SQLCA, the value is 0; this is correct, although my application generates an error message. By looking at the Source pane, you can see that the condition check for SQLCode is incorrect (see Figure 21.9).

**FIGURE 21.9**

*The SQLCA's attribute values in Debug mode and the Source Browser pane.*

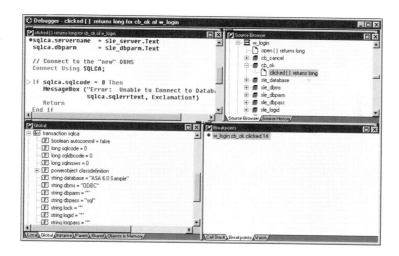

In this case, if you want to continue processing and fix the error later, click a line after the error check and use the Set Next Statement option. If the problem is that SQLCA's properties have been set incorrectly, you can right-click the property and choose Edit Variable to access the Modify Variable dialog (see Figure 21.10). With this dialog, you can modify the value of any variable. This allows you to force PowerBuilder to test certain lines of code by mimicking test conditions.

## Watching Variables

When debugging, it's easy to find the values of global, shared, and local variables because a view is specified for each scope. You also can view variables in the Debugger by using the Objects in Memory and Watch views.

**FIGURE 21.10**

*The Modify Variable dialog.*

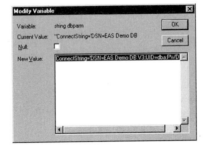

The Objects in Memory view shows you copies of all objects loaded into memory. It contains a tree-view control that lists all the objects and allows you to expand each object to see the properties of that object and any secondary objects. This tree view is particularly useful when looking for window instance variables declared on windows opened with a local reference variable.

To locate one of these instance variables, locate the object's class name in the Objects in Memory view and expand it in the tree view. In the tree view, you should find an equal number of references for instances of the particular window class. In Figure 21.11, the window w_orders has three instances open. Each instance reference then contains its own instance variables and their corresponding values. The only difficult part of tracking instance variables in this situation is keeping track of which instance was opened first.

**FIGURE 21.11**

*Viewing multiple instances of the w_orders window.*

A second way to find an instance variable involves the Parent tab. Here, *parent* has the same meaning in the Debugger as it does in any of your scripts. The parent designation depends on the object you're debugging. For controls on windows, *parent* refers to the window on which the controls are placed. For controls placed in a custom visual user object, *parent* refers to the user object. For menu options, *parent* refers to the menu on which the options are located. As you can imagine, the use of pronouns considerably simplifies locating variables in the Debugger.

---

**Tip**

To track objects created by using local reference variables, you also could create a global reference variable and assign it to the local reference variable. This way, you always would have a reference to the object via the global variable. The only downside is you then have to remove the code after you are done testing.

---

With the Watch pane, you can specify an expression that you can view as the program executes. To specify an expression, right-click the pane and choose Insert to open the New Expression dialog (see Figure 21.12). The expression can be any valid PowerScript statement that you then can view the result of in the Watch pane. The expressions give you command-line accessibility and enable you to track the commands you executed for that debug session.

**FIGURE 21.12**
*The New Expression dialog.*

The simplest expression you can add to the Watch pane is a single variable. You can add a variable to the Watch pane in several ways:

- Type the variable name directly into the New Expressions dialog.

- Right-click a variable in the local, global, parent, shared, or instance panes, and choose Add Watch from the pop-up menu.

- Use the mouse to drag a variable from one of the variable panes to the Watch pane. When you release the mouse button, PowerBuilder automatically creates the watch for you.

The Call Stack and Source History panes can also help you debug your application. Use the Call Stack pane to track the history of the way in which one method called another method. In Figure 21.13, the `Open` event of the `examples` application called the `uf_get_pb_ini()` function on the `u_external_function_win32` object .

**FIGURE 21.13**

*The Call Stack pane shows how a method called another method.*

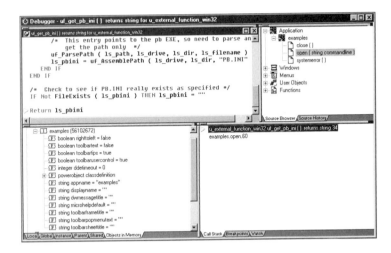

The Call Stack pane displays the current script on top and works its way down the list to the initiating script. This list is useful when stepping through code in a class library to determine the application's execution process. If you want to view the script of an entry in the Call Stack list, right-click the entry and choose Set Context to display the code in the Source pane. The Source History pane is useful for displaying which scripts you've viewed in the Source pane (see Figure 21.14). You can use the Source pane to recall the name of a script you viewed earlier in your debugging process.

**FIGURE 21.14**

*The Source History pane, displaying scripts you've viewed.*

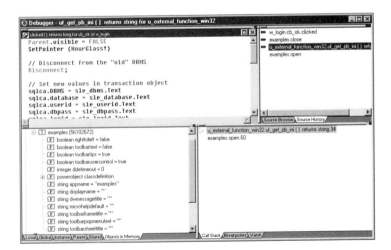

To view the code of a previously viewed script in the Source pane, right-click the entry in the Source History pane and choose Open Source. If the list gets too lengthy, you can right-click the pane and choose Clear from the menu.

Although the Debugger is powerful, it has its limitations. You often need to make slight modifications to your code to display the information you need. When you're assigning a return value from a function in an expression with other values, for example, you need to assign the return value to a new variable to view or modify it. So the code

```
Choose Case dw_1.Retrieve()
```

would become this:

```
long ll_rtn
```

```
ll_rtn = dw_1.Retrieve()
CHOOSE CASE ll_rtn
```

It's difficult to use the Debugger and breakpoints to track down focus change and timer problems. The Debugger can trap you in an infinite loop, and you will have to close PowerBuilder (press Ctrl+Alt+Delete) or remove your breakpoints. Some testing techniques you can use to test these types of problems are covered later in the section "Additional PowerBuilder Testing Techniques."

## Remote Debugging

PowerBuilder 7.0 adds the capability to debug PowerBuilder objects deployed on a Jaguar 3.0 server. To use the new remote debugging features, you must install the PowerBuilder remote debugging package on the Jaguar server and select the Component Is Debuggable option in the Project painter when you build the components you want to debug. Open the project used to generate the Jaguar components, start the Debugger, and click choose Start Remote Debugging from the Debug menu. Finally, run the application that uses the components you want to debug. You can then use the new Instance pane in the Debugger to view state information about the components you're debugging and can set breakpoints in the component code just as you would when debugging locally.

## The PBDEBUG Utility

In addition to the Debugger, PowerBuilder comes equipped with another utility to assist in the testing and debugging process. PBDEBUG traces object creation and destruction and the execution of scripts, system functions, global functions, object-level functions, and external functions.

Your application must be made into an executable before you can use PBDEBUG. When you create your executable, you must enable the Trace Information and Error Context Information check boxes (for machine-code executables) in the Code Generation Options section of the Project painter (see Figure 21.15).

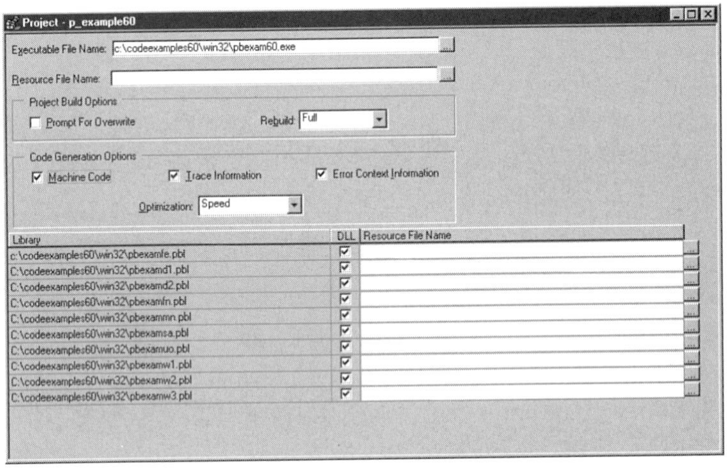

**FIGURE 21.15**

*The Code Generation Options section in the Project painter.*

**Note**

If you disable Trace Information and Error Context Information when you create a machine-code executable, the DBG file won't be created. If you create an executable that's not machine code (in other words, p-code), the trace information still is automatically placed in the executable.

After you have an executable, choose Run from the Start menu and enter the following:

```
C:\application_path\appname.exe /PBDEBUG
```

In this line, *application_path* is the location of the executable, and *appname.exe* is the name of your application executable. The application will run as it normally does, but when you are finished, a new file is created in the executable's directory. The new file is named *appname.dbg*, where *appname* is the name of your executable file.

This approach is compatible with prior versions. PowerBuilder 6.0 simplified this process via the System Options dialog (refer to Figure 21.5), in which you can specify whether you want to enable the PBDEBUG trace option and the name of the output file. Listing 21.1 shows a sample of what PBDEBUG generates.

**LISTING 21.1** A PBDEBUG File

```
Executing object function +CREATE for class UNLEASH, lib entry UNLEASH
  Executing instruction at line 2
  Executing instruction at line 3
  Executing object function +CREATE for class MESSAGE, lib entry _TYPEDEF
  End object function +CREATE for class MESSAGE, lib entry _TYPEDEF
  Executing instruction at line 4
  Executing object function +CREATE for class TRANSACTION, lib entry _TYPEDEF
  End object function +CREATE for class TRANSACTION, lib entry _TYPEDEF
  Executing instruction at line 5
  Executing object function +CREATE for class DYNAMICDESCRIPTIONAREA,
         lib entry _TYPEDEF
  End object function +CREATE for class DYNAMICDESCRIPTIONAREA,
         lib entry _TYPEDEF
  Executing instruction at line 6
  Executing object function +CREATE for class DYNAMICSTAGINGAREA,
         lib entry _TYPEDEF
  End object function +CREATE for class DYNAMICSTAGINGAREA, lib entry _TYPEDEF
  Executing instruction at line 7
  Executing object function +CREATE for class ERROR, lib entry _TYPEDEF
  End object function +CREATE for class ERROR, lib entry _TYPEDEF
End object function +CREATE for class UNLEASH, lib entry UNLEASH
Executing event +OPEN for class UNLEASH, lib entry UNLEASH
  Executing instruction at line 1
  Executing class function OPEN for class SYSTEMFUNCTIONS, lib entry _TYPEDEF
    Executing system dll function
    Executing object function +CREATE for class W_LOGIN, lib entry W_LOGIN
      Executing instruction at line 2
      Executing object function +CREATE for class P_1, lib entry W_LOGIN
      End object function +CREATE for class P_1, lib entry W_LOGIN
      Executing instruction at line 3
      Executing object function +CREATE for class ST_4, lib entry W_LOGIN
      End object function +CREATE for class ST_4, lib entry W_LOGIN
      Executing instruction at line 4
      Executing object function +CREATE for class ST_3, lib entry W_LOGIN
      End object function +CREATE for class ST_3, lib entry W_LOGIN
      Executing instruction at line 5
```

**LISTING 21.1**   CONTINUED

```
      Executing object function +CREATE for class ST_2, lib entry W_LOGIN
      End object function +CREATE for class ST_2, lib entry W_LOGIN
      Executing instruction at line 6
      Executing object function +CREATE for class ST_1, lib entry W_LOGIN
      End object function +CREATE for class ST_1, lib entry W_LOGIN
      Executing instruction at line 7
      Executing object function +CREATE for class DDLB_VENDOR,
          lib entry W_LOGIN
      End object function +CREATE for class DDLB_VENDOR, lib entry W_LOGIN
      Executing instruction at line 8
      Executing object function +CREATE for class SLE_DATABASE,
          lib entry W_LOGIN
      End object function +CREATE for class SLE_DATABASE, lib entry W_LOGIN
      Executing instruction at line 9
      Executing object function +CREATE for class SLE_PASSWORD,
          lib entry W_LOGIN
      End object function +CREATE for class SLE_PASSWORD, lib entry W_LOGIN
      Executing instruction at line 10
      Executing object function +CREATE for class SLE_USER_ID,
          lib entry W_LOGIN
      End object function +CREATE for class SLE_USER_ID, lib entry W_LOGIN
      Executing instruction at line 11
      Executing object function +CREATE for class CB_CANCEL, lib entry W_LOGIN
      End object function +CREATE for class CB_CANCEL, lib entry W_LOGIN
      Executing instruction at line 12
      Executing object function +CREATE for class CB_OK, lib entry W_LOGIN
      End object function +CREATE for class CB_OK, lib entry W_LOGIN
      Executing instruction at line 13
      Executing object function +CREATE for class GB_LOGIN, lib entry W_LOGIN
      End object function +CREATE for class GB_LOGIN, lib entry W_LOGIN
      Executing instruction at line 14
   End object function +CREATE for class W_LOGIN, lib entry W_LOGIN
  End class function OPEN for class SYSTEMFUNCTIONS, lib entry _TYPEDEF
  Executing instruction at line 1
End event +OPEN for class UNLEASH, lib entry UNLEASH
```

The text file generated by running PBDEBUG shows the order of each object as it's created (W_LOGIN), the events executed (OPEN for class UNLEASH), the numbers of the lines of code executed for a particular event script (Executing instruction at line 2 ), and the destruction of each object. The PBDEBUG file can tell you much about what events and code are being run at what time. It also helps you see how many times script/functions are executed. This can help identify areas for improving performance.

PBDEBUG allows you to track down focus and, to some degree, timer problems. The output file generated quickly can become very large, and it's advisable to get to the area of interest in the application as quickly as possible. Remember that when you create your executable to go into production, you shouldn't use trace execution because it increases the size of the executable and decreases performance.

> **Note**
>
> Removing the debug options applies only when you're creating a machine-code executable. A nonmachine-code executable will include the debug information anyway.

## Database Tracing

Another technique useful in determining PowerBuilder and database connectivity is the trace facility. In the code in which you assign attributes to your transaction object, place the word TRACE before the DBMS attribute value (for example, Trace ODBC for Adaptive Server Anywhere or Trace SYB for Sybase). PowerBuilder then generates a trace log text file that displays what SQL processing occurred during the execution of the code.

> **Note**
>
> If you're using an ODBC data source, you also can generate a log file to track the ODBC processing. You set this option via the Windows Control Panel under the ODBC option.

For more information on database tracing, see Chapter 4, "SQL and PowerBuilder."

# Additional PowerBuilder Testing Techniques

In addition to using the Debugger and PBDEBUG to find errors, you can use a number of other common techniques to pinpoint problems in a PowerBuilder application.

# Embedded SQL

If your application uses complex, embedded SQL statements, it's a good idea to test the SQL statements outside the Script painter before including them in the application. After you write the SQL statements, you first need to test them in the database administrator. (See Chapter 5, "Databases and the Database Painter," for more about this painter.) Run the SQL to ensure that you have no syntax errors and to validate any resultsets to remove logic errors. After the SQL is tested, copy it into the appropriate script and compile the script.

> **Note**
>
> Just because the database administrator properly executed your SQL doesn't automatically mean that the SQL will require no changes when placed into a script. PowerBuilder accepts many standard data-manipulation language statements as they are, but for more complex dynamic SQL and data-definition statements, you must incorporate additional code. (See Chapter 4 for more information on coding embedded SQL in PowerBuilder.)

# The `SQLPreview` Event

Earlier in this chapter, you looked at ensuring that your embedded SQL statements perform as desired. That discussion, however, didn't address the SQL statements generated when you're retrieving and updating data through a DataWindow. If you are unsure that the SQL being generated is correct, you can use the `SQLPreview` event of a DataWindow control to view the SQL before it's sent to the database.

The `SQLPreview` event is triggered after a `Retrieve()`, `Update()`, or `ReselectRow()` function is called but before the SQL is sent to the database. For `Retrieve()` and `ReselectRow()`, the `SQLPreview` event obviously is executed only once. For the `Update()` function, `SQLPreview` is triggered for each row being updated.

The method used to capture the SQL statements is the `SQLPreview` event argument `SqlSyntax`, which is a string containing the SQL statement generated by the DataWindow. Rather than use the Debugger to watch the value, place a multiline edit on the window with the DataWindow control in question and assign `SqlSyntax` to the text attribute. The `SqlSyntax` argument replaces the need for using the `GetSQLPreview()` function.

> **Note**
>
> If your database engine uses bind variables (as do Watcom, Oracle, and Gupta), you might see several question marks in your SQL statement. If you want to get rid of these for testing purposes, use the `DisableBind` option in `DBParm` when you connect:
>
> `SQLCA.DBParm = 'DisableBind=1'`

# The `DBError` Event

You can use `DBError` to determine the row in error when `Update()` is called for a DataWindow control and a SQL error triggers this event. The `Row` and `Buffer` arguments indicate the row number in error and the DataWindow buffer (Primary, Delete, or Filter) in which the row exists. You then can look at the values being sent to the database and the SQL statement generated by the `Update()` function.

# The `GetItemStatus()` Function

`GetItemStatus()` often is useful with the `DBError` and `SQLPreview` events. `GetItemStatus()` returns the modification status of a row or column (`New!`, `NewModified!`, `NotModified!`, or `DataModified!`). This status identifies what type of SQL statement the `Update()` function will generate. When you know the status, you can determine whether PowerBuilder is generating the desired SQL statement for your application.

# Displaying Messages to the Screen

Rather than use the Debugger, you can display a message in a window to indicate PowerBuilder's position within a script or the value of certain key variables. Two common places to display these messages are to a single- or multiline edit control and to MicroHelp (for MDI applications). The messages can consist of just about anything—for example, variable values or the function name now being called.

The `MessageBox()` function can also be called to tell developers when a certain point in the script has been reached. Although displaying messages on a single-line edit might be quicker and easier to code, the `MessageBox()` function stops the script it's in (because a message box is modal) and doesn't continue until you click one of the buttons.

> **Note**
>
> The `MessageBox()` function can alter the normal sequence of focus in your application.

## The `Beep()` Function

The `Beep()` function indicates that a predetermined point in a script has been reached. `Beep()` brings additional attention to the point in the script because of the sound aspect. This technique is useful particularly in testing for focus events (`GetFocus`, `Activate`, and `Deactivate`), where a message box causes only additional focus changes.

# Rational TeamTest

One of the more popular third-party products is Rational TeamTest (formerly called SQA Suite) from Rational Software Corporation. Rational TeamTest lets you test and track your application development process. One main reason this product is doing well is that it's tightly integrated with PowerBuilder objects, particularly DataWindows. You can use Rational TeamTest to plan test strategies and development, track test execution and results, track defects, and generate a multitude of reports. The engine for Rational TeamTest uses a Visual Basic-compatible script language to create the test scenarios.

Many testing tools just track keystrokes and mouse movements. Rational TeamTest is a little different because it tracks your application on an object level and therefore doesn't depend on extraneous information, such as a window's appearance or location. For this reason, Rational TeamTest works well across different versions of the same application.

Although setting up the test procedures might not seem worthwhile to smaller companies, many components can be particularly useful. The Rational Robot allows you to record and play back various test scenarios. In Playback mode, Rational TeamTest indicates whether an object's state has changed from the recorded scenario (perhaps a command button is now disabled that was previously enabled). For DataWindows, TeamTest captures not only the DataWindow's format but also the columns and data retrieved for a particular test case. Rational TeamTest flags changes in the data as well, so that you can notify your DBA that there could be a potential problem on the database.

In addition to the Rational Robot for supplying test scripts, TeamTest comes equipped with an excellent defect tracker-and-reporting facility. Manually keeping tabs on defects and their status can be an exhausting and complex ordeal. TeamTest does a good job of simplifying this process.

Also part of the Rational family is the Performance Studio product. Performance Studio helps you with volume testing and user concurrency testing. Traditionally, to simulate 50 users running your application at the same time, you had to have 50 people involved in your testing or do an inadequate test. Performance Studio allows you to automate this process. All you need to do is run the 50 machines with predefined scripts for your application without involving a large number of testers.

# Additional Third-Party Tools

The list of tools you can use to assist you with debugging and testing is lengthy. Many applications are available as freeware products or can be purchased for a nominal fee. Some common examples of these are WPS, DDE Spy, WinSnoop, and Rbrand. The following are some tools we have become familiar with and have used (other utilities are available that perform the same or similar tasks):

- You can find WPS on the Microsoft tech net CD-ROM. It provides a memory dump of EXE, DLL, and DRV files that now are loaded.

- DDE Spy enables you to watch DDE conversations taking place between two applications and is available on the Microsoft tech net CD-ROM.

- WinSnoop provides various information on a window, from its handle to its parent. This program is freeware and is available almost anywhere.

- Sybase provides Rbrand for checking the time stamps on PowerBuilder DLLs.

# Summary

In this chapter, you looked at some standard approaches to the testing process. The methodologies for testing an application vary from project to project, but one key component—user involvement—should be maintained in all test procedures. After a test strategy is agreed on, you can use numerous tools and tricks within PowerBuilder to ensure that the application fulfills all business requirements. The Debugger and PBDEBUG option are two of the PowerBuilder utilities that assist in identifying problem areas. In addition to these tools, several third-party tools are available for purchase or as freeware.

The testing and debugging process can be long and complicated. It's important to always identify where the process is breaking down (client, network, or server) and which component is causing the problem. Never jump to conclusions. By developing a detailed test strategy, you're ensuring the delivery of a quality application of which you can be proud.

# Application Maintenance and Upgrades

An important part of a project's life cycle is maintaining and upgrading the application code and runtime environment. As application components are enhanced or have bugs fixed, a properly controlled rollout of the new code is essential. This should include a plan for recovery to the previously known working version if problems arise with the new code. This is true not only of upgraded application code but also of PowerBuilder runtime files and other supporting files (including network and database drivers). The iterative model used for software development allows the rapid release of application versions. This allows several teams to work concurrently, which makes managing these releases more important than ever.

One word that hasn't been mentioned yet is *quality*. One big reason for release management and version control is to enforce *quality assurance*. This ensures the product's completeness, correctness, reliability, and maintainability, and ensures that it meets the design specifications and requirements with acceptable performance. (For a detailed discussion on producing quality products, see Chapter 21, "Testing and Debugging.") Another reason for release management is to provide an audit trail of the changes made to an application, and by whom.

# Team Management

An integral part of release management and version control is the procedures set in place for team members. These procedures should include the formalization of a directory structure to hold the various project files—from ER diagrams, SQL scripts, bitmaps, sound files, and documents to the actual PowerBuilder libraries.

Members of the team, or possibly from various teams, need to be assigned certain management responsibilities pertinent to the control and upkeep of object libraries, source code, and standards. Such titles as source librarian and object custodian are frequently used to describe the job functions.

With such procedures in place, release management and version control can be introduced and used with minimal fuss and problems.

# Release Management

Before a version of a software product is sent out for use by end users, it usually passes through a set of release steps (if it doesn't, maybe the following sections can persuade you that it should). In fact, before even reaching a release status, the code passes through numerous tests, such as unit testing and integration testing. (See Chapter 21 for information on these methods.)

The release steps use two distinct types of testing:

- The process of *verification* is to find errors within the code by executing it within a simulated/controlled environment. This process, more commonly known as *alpha testing*, can also be broken down into three areas of testing: unit, module, and integration. Unit testing allows testers to focus on each visual and nonvisual object and make sure that the objects perform all the tasks they were intended to. Module testing ensures that communication between the objects with in a module performs properly. Finally, integration testing verifies that all modules and the application's infrastructure work together seamlessly and efficiently.

- The process of *validation* is to find errors using real data in a live environment. This step is more commonly known as *beta testing*. The code is used to enter real transactions, but users know that the system could fail at any point and that they are to report any problems to the developers in as detailed description as they can.

Figure 22.1 shows numerous steps and areas of potential management restrictions. The time that the whole process takes is unique for each individual project. As you can see from some of the larger software houses, such as Microsoft, the arrival of an actual version can take many months and many beta releases. One important aspect is compatibility with existing applications. For example, everyone has his or her own version of the OLE DLLs that aren't always compatible with the ones you need to install.

# Version Control

After you have a release of your application that's a candidate for a version number and deployment, consider at least the following questions:

- Does the application require upgrades of other software?

- Are additional files required to support the new version?

- Have the end users signed off on this version?

Version control software can be used to control the use and migration of all of an application's objects. However, the application is only the beginning of the problem, and, as in performance and design phases, you need to consider all other contributing factors. To this end, you should make full use of your version-control software to maintain versions of the following:

- Database objects (stored procedures, triggers, views, and so on)

- Database drivers (server and client)

- Network drivers (server and client)

- Printer drivers

- Project documentation

**FIGURE 22.1**

*The software release process.*

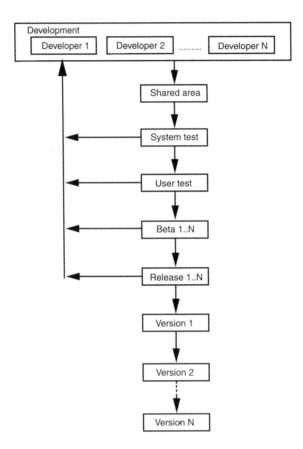

You might think that printer drivers are an odd addition to the list, but this one comes from experience. A client suddenly ran into some problems when printing a complex report. A structured troubleshooting session (these really pay off) led to the conclusion that an updated printer driver was the problem, and after *much* searching, the original drivers were found and installed. The problem was fixed by the simple regression of the printer drivers. How much simpler it would have been to pull up a report of changes to the complete client/server system and pinpoint the problems, as well as have immediate access to the appropriate files.

When PowerBuilder or any other development tool moves to a new version, carefully consider the impact on your existing applications and development efforts. You may not have the resources or time to migrate every application to the latest PowerBuilder version. In fact, some corporate departments were still using PowerBuilder 4.0 applications after Version 6.5 was released, which is purely a team resource problem. This can lead to various application and runtime environment files that need to be tracked and maintained.

Each version of a piece of software that's released for use is denoted by using a numbering scheme based on major and minor changes to the software. Software vendors all seem to have their own ideas about what the numbers mean and how the numbers are incremented. For example, Microsoft recently went from version 4.21 of the SQL Server product to 6.0, whereas Sybase numbers its maintenance releases at the third position (for example, 5.0.03).

These numbering schemes are based on the type of changes made to the software. A significant change is indicated by incrementing the first number by one. Incrementing the second number indicates minor software changes—generally bug fixes and some additional functionality. Occasionally, developers use the third number internally for bug fixes, which are then rolled up until a released version and indicated by the second number.

A detailed log (*audit trail*) of the changes made between releases is usually kept and maintained. This can be done manually or, preferably, by a software package; version-control software is the usual location of this functionality.

The most common terms in version control are *check in* and *check out*, the basic procedures that make version control work. Before you start any work on an existing object, it must first be checked out to a work area. This process makes a copy of the object and locks the original so that no one else can work on it at the same time. After you finish making changes to the object, test it, and are ready to resubmit it for use in the application, you check the object back in. Depending on the software you're using, a copy of the original object (a *delta*) is usually kept.

# Version Control in PowerBuilder

PowerBuilder provides limited version control in the Library painter's check-in and check-out facilities. This paradigm is borrowed straight from real libraries and the book control mechanism they use. By using a good directory structure judiciously, you can isolate and maintain major version releases of an application, but if you're tackling any sort of large-scale application development, a proper version-control tool (such as ObjectCycle) should be used.

> **Note**
>
> PowerBuilder doesn't maintain previous versions of the object for you; you must do this yourself.

Using PowerBuilder's check-in and check-out facilities doesn't prevent other developers from opening the original object, but it does prevent them from overwriting it until the modified object is checked back in or the status is cleared.

The first time you check out an object in PowerBuilder, you are prompted to set the user ID to be used for the process. The mechanics of the various methods to use the check-in and check-out functions are discussed in Chapter 8, "The Library Painter."

> **Caution**
>
> Choose an ID not already in use by another developer; otherwise, you can access each other's checked-out objects. This ID is best set to your logon name to prevent duplication.

This ID is accessible from the PB.INI file using a text editor. This means that you can alter your ID and assume someone else's identity to check an object back in; you should, however, do this with caution and remember to immediately reset your ID.

The next (or first, if you've already been registered) dialog to appear is the Check Out Library Entries dialog (see Figure 22.2), which shows all the library files in the current working directory.

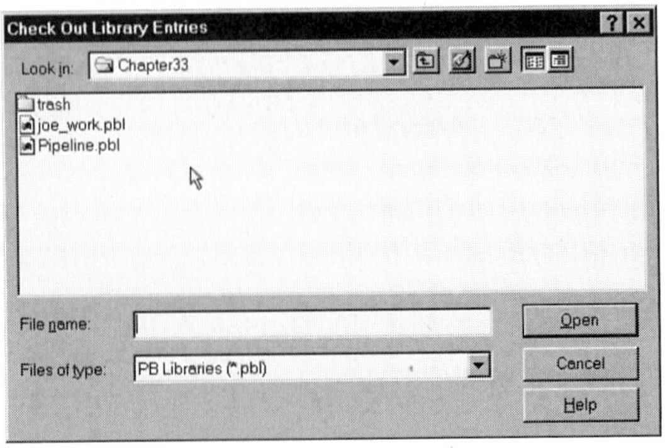

**FIGURE 22.2**
*The Check Out Library Entries dialog.*

After you select a PBL, PowerBuilder does one of two things:

- Normally, it copies the object to the indicated PBL and marks both objects with a checked-out status. PowerBuilder puts one of two icons (see Figure 22.3) next to the object name in the Library painter to indicate that an object is checked out.

- If the selected object is already checked out, PowerBuilder tells you (see Figure 22.4). (Of course, this never happens because we all carefully look for an object's check-out icon in the Library painter—right?)

**FIGURE 22.3**

*One icon indicates the working copy of the checked-out object; the other icon indicates the original version of a checked-out object.*

Working copy

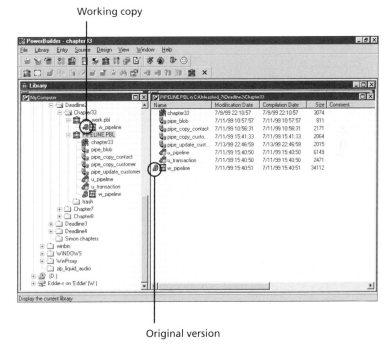

Original version

**FIGURE 22.4**

*The object-already-checked-out warning.*

The object copied to your working area is accessible only by you and will remain in that library until you check it back in or clear its checked-out status. You can also copy the object if you want, but you may not delete or move it.

When you check an object back in, the original version of the object is overwritten, the working copy is deleted from your work area, and the check-out status is reset. The object can now be checked out by other developers. The new object is known as a *revision*.

If you want to remove an object's checked-out status and leave the original version, select the Clear Check Out Status option from the Source menu. A dialog asks you whether PowerBuilder should delete your working copy at the same time (see Figure 22.5). You can clear the check-out status of an object from the working library or the originating library. Recovering the original object can be useful if the working PBL is accidentally deleted.

**FIGURE 22.5**
*The clear check out status dialog.*

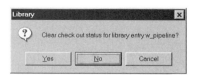

A problematic issue in earlier versions of PowerBuilder is that while you're checking in an object, for some reason it fails. The reasons seem to be based on the server's file system and how many people are accessing the library and its objects concurrently. Whatever the reason, the result is the same: The original object maintains a checked-out status, and the working copy remains in your working PBL but is no longer considered to be checked out. Sybase seems to have made some changes to PowerBuilder in this area because this now occurs a lot less frequently.

Recovery from this situation isn't as bad as you might think and requires you to follow these steps:

1. Check all other objects into the original PBL.
2. Within the operating system, rename the original PBL file.
3. Create a new PBL with the same name as the original.
4. Move all the objects (except the checked-out one) from the old original to the new.
5. Move the modified object from your work PBL to the new original PBL.
6. Delete the original PBL file.

# Version-Control Interfaces

As you can see, PowerBuilder provides only the barest means of version control—it protects against multiple overwriting of updates to the same object. To provide a means of full version control with the capability to provide phased implementations, auditing, and version back-out, you need to turn to a third-party tool vendor.

PowerBuilder's version-control facilities are limited. Several third-party tool vendors provide full version-control products that tightly integrate with PowerBuilder through the ORCA interface.

Before using a version-control product, you must first register all your objects with the tool—this effectively checks them all out into the control system. You now check in and check out against this system through a vendor-supplied interface accessed from the Library painter.

These tools track every change made to a registered object in an archive that can be reported against, and old versions of an object can be opened.

The following sections provide a concise breakdown of the major features for four of the most common version-control products that integrate directly with PowerBuilder. These vendors, and their competitors, are always updating their product features; one may have a more appealing feature set that fits your development requirements and budget than another.

# ObjectCycle

ObjectCycle is Sybase's network-based source-management and version-control software for PowerBuilder applications. ObjectCycle varies from many existing file-based version-control packages in that it uses Sybase SQL Anywhere to store all its information. Registered versions of your application's objects are stored in the Sybase SQL Anywhere database. ObjectCycle's last release is version 2.0, and Sybase has stated that it won't continue to be developed further.

ObjectCycle can be networked or run on a standalone machine, as long as Windows NT 3.51 or higher or Windows 95/98 are used for the server components. The ObjectCycle Client Utilities can be installed on Windows NT 3.51 or Windows 95/98. The client utilities consist of the ObjectCycle Manager and help files. ObjectCycle Manager lets you manage projects, objects, and users by accessing the Sybase SQL Anywhere database.

In addition to the client and server software, ObjectCycle 2.0 ships with a Software Development Kit, which allows you to write code that accesses ObjectCycle and extends ObjectCycle to support the Microsoft Interactive Development Environments (IDE) for use with ObjectCycle.

ObjectCycle's objects equate to the PowerBuilder objects that comprise your application. If your application is large enough to be dispersed across multiple library files, you can keep track of the object placement within ObjectCycle. Because this is a Sybase product, it has a strong integration with PowerBuilder, and much of ObjectCycle's functionality can be managed through PowerBuilder's Library painter.

After you register all your objects with ObjectCycle, it allows you to check objects out, version your objects, provide logical labels for groups of objects, and generate several reports to track version history. If you are the administrator, you also can freeze an object (as well as a folder) so that it can no longer be modified.

ObjectCycle 2.0 provides a tight and robust interface into PowerBuilder via the Library painter and uses a different approach than many other version-control software products by using a centralized database to store your application's objects.

# The Endevor Interface

The Endevor product by Computer Associates controls PowerBuilder objects within a repository controlled by Endevor Workstation. Endevor's interface requires the following software versions and disk space:

- Endevor Workstation release 7.0

- PowerBuilder 3.0 or greater

- At least 850KB available disk space

Endevor 7.0 now supports full-name-length support through its Common Source Code Control (CSCC) interface. You now can choose to use this interface or PowerBuilder's source control interface.

Endevor offers the following features:

- Automatic inventory

- Change and configuration management

- Release management for development and maintenance

- Compression of versions

- Source code merging with conflict notification

- Comprehensive reporting

- Security classes for users to manage developer privileges to code

> **Caution**
>
> Don't make any changes to PowerBuilder objects in the Endevor Workstation program because this will corrupt the information being maintained.

# PVCS Version Manager

PVCS Version Manager from Merant has gained a large share of the version-control market within the PC environment and is one of the most commonly used interfaces in PowerBuilder. The PVCS interface has the following functionality:

- Registering objects

- Checking objects in and out

- Retrieving earlier revisions of objects

- Running reports

- Rebuilding earlier releases of your application

- Assigning version labels to your objects

- Creating a new release of your application

- Synchronizing your objects with PVCS archives

- Clearing object-registration status

- Clearing an object's checked-out status

- Viewing a list of checked-out objects

PVCS tracks your changes within its archive and lets you recover PowerBuilder objects from disasters. Each time an object is checked into PVCS, it's assigned a new revision level. Version labels are assigned to object groups to indicate a particular phase in your project's life cycle.

# ClearCase

ClearCase by Rational Software provides a robust source-management tool for not only your PowerBuilder objects but also all documents produced throughout the software's life. Because of the tight integration and popularity of the Rational tool suite, which includes Rose, SQA TeamTest, Requisite Pro, and ClearCase, it becomes a staple for developers wanting complete and seamless project life-cycle management. ClearCase has the following functionality:

- Check-in and check-out functionality

- Automatic file compression

- Unlimited development branching

- Use of triggers

- Ability to version directories, subdirectories, and all files

- Rule-based version selection

ClearCase versions objects at the operating system file level; PowerBuilder doesn't manage its objects at this level. You might think that causes issues. Well, ClearCase manages this by seamlessly and efficiently exporting the PowerBuilder objects and versioning the source files. ClearCase requires only that you regularly resynchronize your objects to ensure that you have the most recent versions of the objects.

You can use ClearCase to manage multiple development efforts to the same application by creating views. Several views may be created for the same application, allowing for the different development teams to access, modify, save, and compile the same object at the same time. The developers will see only the objects and any changes made in their view. An example of this would be if one group was working on maintenance to the existing system and another group was working on Y2K changes. More than likely both teams need to access the same objects. By creating views for each team, the developers can work more efficiently without the waiting for the other team to finish.

Because development efforts vary from release to release, the views will ultimately need to be merged, reflecting all the changes made. ClearCase lets you do this through *Visual Differencing*, which helps you combine changes in all the objects in all the views by going through each object, comparing any changes made in any views, and merging those changes. If during the merging process there are multiple changes and ClearCase can't determine which change to implement, it will bring up a text-editor-style viewer for the original version of the object's source code and the source code of the objects being merged. It will then allow you to step through the code and manually select which change you want to implement.

# Carrying Out Application Upgrades

Upgrading an existing system can be an involved process, and a sound plan is a definite requirement. You need to address the following in your planned upgrade:

- Is the target group relatively small?

- Do you have physical access to the machines?

- Is the application run from a LAN, a WAN, or locally?

- How frequently will you be updating files?

- Where are the various files located?

For small user groups with physically accessible machines, not much can stop you from carrying out an upgrade by using a floppy disk carried to each machine. The drawbacks are if the machines are "diskless" workstations, if there's a corporate antivirus policy, or if you're updating many files.

For large user groups or large updates, consider an automated approach to file distribution. Also consider several factors with this approach:

- The network connection is lost during an upgrade.
- The client or server machine fails during upgrade.
- The destination drive runs out of space.
- A file is already in use on the client machine.
- Your automated distribution program fails.

> **Caution**
>
> If the application is now running, the EXE and PBD files are in use by the operating system and can't be replaced. Be careful that you don't get a partial upgrade of only some PBD or DLL files.

## Auto-Update at Logon

The first thing most users do when arriving at work in the morning is turn on their computers and log on to the file server. This provides an ideal opportunity to copy new files to the desired location because users will rarely have any of the files being upgraded in use. The automation is simply an extension to the file server login batch file—to call a batch file or DOS program that you supply to make the copy. This is usually transparent to users, who often won't mind if logging on takes a little longer.

This approach has some drawbacks, though. For example, not all users log on and off each day. Also, most users log on only once a day, which prevents you from carrying out incremental upgrades during the day.

# Manual Update by User

With this method, you provide users a desktop icon or toolbar button that sits right next to the one the users use to start the PowerBuilder applications you've deployed. This method causes a custom program to copy all updated files to the client area. This has the advantage of being accessible all day to users. Update notices can be emailed or broadcast from a file server. You could even make your PowerBuilder applications sensitive to an update situation and display a message box during an application `Idle` event.

# Auto-Sensing by Application

During an application's `Open` event, the application checks for the existence of a program file or records in a certain database table. When the application detects that an update is pending, it can then carry out one of three options:

- Tell users to carry out a manual requested upgrade.

- Auto-load another program to carry out the operation.

- Auto-generate a BAT file that can be executed or used the next time users log on.

If you want to use the second method, be careful not to have any of the files that will be replaced in use at the time. If you plan to distribute any PowerBuilder runtime DLLs, use a different method.

# Third-Party Tools

You can use a third-party tool to take away the strain of upgrades. The most obvious choice at the moment is Microsoft's System Management Server (SMS). This allows you to carry out maintenance releases of your PowerBuilder application along with releases of other commercial packages, drivers, and so on.

# Synchronizer

Sybase addressed some issues of distributing application updates and code to end users with the Synchronizer tool, formerly known as PBSync. Sybase no longer distributes this product with the PowerBuilder software; however, it's available for download on the Sybase Web site (www.sybase.com/sdn). Synchronizer can be used in three ways: as the Synchronizer application (SYNC.EXE), as a runtime executable (SYNCRT.EXE), or as an ActiveX control (SYNC.OCX).

Two ways in which you can create a synchronization data file are by using a text-based editor or, even better, by using the Synchronizer editor (SYNC.EXE). Within the editor, you can open an existing data file or start creating a new one. Some options let you set up process-level settings such as logging, runtime variables, the display of the status window, and start and end options.

Synchronizer can use the following sources to copy files for synchronization:

| *Source* | *Example* |
|----------|-----------|
| FTP | FTP://FTP.RAVENSOFT.COM |
| Local drive | C:\ARTIST\CYRIL.DLL |
| Server on the network | \\RAVEN\COMMON\ULRIC.EXE |

The PBSync runtime executable (SYNCRT.EXE) is an end-user deployable executable that carries out the actual synchronization. When the executable is run, the instructions in the indicated synchronization data file are executed, and a status screen indicates that file transfers are occurring. When the synchronization process is complete, the status screen closes.

For greater flexibility, Sybase also provides Synchronizer in ActiveX form. This allows the ActiveX control to be placed into a PowerBuilder-created window, an application built via some other development tool, or even an HTML page.

# Upgrading PowerBuilder Itself

With each PowerBuilder maintenance release, Sybase generally changes many of the DLLs, and with each new version number, all the DLLs are released with new names. As your development team starts to use the new DLLs, you need to start planning for end-user deployment of the same DLLs.

PowerBuilder DLLs are generally upwardly compatible, which means that your existing EXE and PBD files will work with the new DLLs. Don't totally rely on this, however; recompiling EXE and PBD files is always a wise precaution.

Files generated using new DLLs are nearly never backward compatible. As soon as your development team produces a release using upgraded DLLs, you should upgrade the end users' DLLs in one fell swoop.

# Summary

This chapter showed why version control and release management need to be an integral part of a serious development effort. The four main version control products available for direct use with PowerBuilder were briefly introduced, along with suggested methods of application upgrade deployment.

# Configuring and Tuning

Many factors can affect the performance of a client/server-based application. You must consider the configuration of the server, the network, and the client, and each area can be broken down further into hardware and software pieces. The often-forgotten piece is the human factor—in other words, the end users or people for whom the system is being constructed in the first place.

This chapter covers some areas you need to examine when tuning your application, as well as some PowerBuilder-specific coding traps into which you might have fallen. A number of factors can affect performance:

- Server configuration

- Database structure

- Type and configuration of network

- Network load

- Environment parameters on servers and clients

- Capability of the development team

- Perception of the users

As well as discussing tuning techniques and overall performance enhancement, this chapter also looks at PowerBuilder's profiling tool.

# The Server

The database server or database management system (DBMS) is the obvious place to look for performance degradation. Optimally, the database server will be only that and won't be used to provide additional file or print services. The more memory the DBMS has, the more data and code (triggers and stored procedures) it can place into memory cache and the less it has to share with the host operating system. The usual bottlenecks on database servers are the I/O channels and the network interface. Both can become clogged with multiple user requests, so it's well worth the extra money to purchase a high-performance network card and disk subsystem.

The disk subsystem increases performance because the I/O requests are spread across multiple disk controllers and multiple disks. *Redundant array of inexpensive disks* (RAID) drive arrays can provide additional performance and security. Some operating systems, notably Windows NT, provide duplexing at the software level, but you should always do this at the hardware level or you will take a performance hit.

After you have your high-performance hardware solution in place, you need to configure the software (operating system and DBMS) to best use it. This involves two steps: optimizing the number of drivers and other miscellaneous programs loaded by the server, and attempting to get the smallest memory footprint possible for the operating system. Also, some databases frequently run faster on certain operating systems (for example, MS SQL Server is specially optimized for Windows NT).

# The Database

The way in which a database is physically and logically structured can profoundly affect the performance of queries and data entry. The performance of a particular database is a function of the data structure and the size of the data sets. The development team should spend the necessary time and effort to complete all data-modeling stages to arrive at an optimized third normal form entity-relationship diagram (which sometimes is called BNF, or *best normal form*).

During the modeling stage, you determine whether the database is to be used for a *decision support system* (DSS), an *executive information system* (EIS), or data entry. Actually, it's not recommended that you write a reporting system against a database already involved in data entry because of the performance degradation and data locking a report can have on data-entry processes. A database designed for DSS or EIS will use summarized data and can be populated at off-peak times from a data-entry database. This requires normalization techniques that produce data models that don't conform with the accepted normal forms, which is acceptable if it yields higher performance and remains manageable.

Using indexes can increase or decrease the performance of data access to a table. The benefit of indexes is that they provide quicker data access. Indexes can cause problems with concurrency by causing pages or rows to become locked, so you should use the number and type of column indexes judiciously.

Some DBMSs, notably SQL Server, carry out what are known as *deferred updates* when the table's columns accept NULLs or variable-length data types. Rather than have the DBMS make the necessary changes to the data in the table's columns during an UPDATE command, these updates cause the record to be deleted and then reinserted into the table. When possible, use NOT NULL columns and column defaults to solve this problem.

During the data-analysis phase of data modeling, you should define each entity attribute's data type and its valid range of values. Ideally, try to avoid variable-length data types in favor of fixed-length ones. This requires some extra space to achieve, but it can be well worth the expense to gain better performance than you would have attained because of the problem with deferred updates.

**23**

Configuring and Tuning

A number of classes, books, and database-proficient consultants can provide tuning techniques for your particular database and operating system setup, but it's beyond the scope of this book to delve into any specifics of this field. Usually, the best place to start looking is the documentation that comes with the DBMS itself.

# The Network

The network is another of the forgotten, or not closely examined, areas of a client/server application that can profoundly affect performance. The network's physical wiring restricts the amount of information that can pass along it because of its power rating. The faster a network cable, the more power required to transmit data through it and the higher the cost.

This type of network topology can cause bottlenecks or degradation as load increases. An Ethernet network might provide satisfactory performance for a small departmentwide system, but when you attach it to a companywide network, an increased number of data clashes occurs and everyone's performance drops. A token-ring topology, although more expensive, guarantees network performance with increasing load.

High-performance network cards are really worth getting for machines that are servers of one kind or another; they usually don't provide a noticeable performance gain for individual client machines. Setting up the network cards and drivers with optimal settings can help solve numerous performance and error issues.

# The Human Factor

The human factor of a client/server project can be the make-or-break point, and it includes not only end users but also project team members.

The development team must be highly motivated and technically minded to bring a client/ server project to fruition. Management and technical staff must have a partnership to ensure that all the necessary pieces of the project come together. If the team members are motivated and energetic in their approach, it will rub off on the end users during interviews and prototyping. If project team members are new to client/server, they should be provided with internal or external courses to bring them up to speed on the technology and development environment.

Unfortunately, regardless of the development team, the system's performance ultimately is only as good as the end users' expectations. If end users are given the misconception that the system will be much faster or contain more features than the existing one, they usually are in for a surprise. That's because most client/server systems being installed are replacing mainframe sessions; also, because the old programs are text-based and centrally run, it's more than likely that there will be a speed difference. The reverse is also true: If end users are told by a project member that the system will be much slower, they will form a hasty misconception that probably will be worse than the truth.

# Before the Development Process

Because much of the configuration and tuning affects the development and testing process, you must make several decisions before you begin the development stage. These include programming standards, PowerBuilder library organization, source code and version control, and client setup, to name a few. Some decisions directly affect performance; all lead to more solid code being produced.

## Programming Standards

One of the first things you must consider is the coding standards that you and your project team will follow. These include naming standards for your objects and variables (see Chapter 18, "Analysis, Design, and Implementation," for common naming conventions). When you are consistent across the application, it's much easier for other developers to assist each other with problem areas, maintenance is considerably less cumbersome, and it's easy to determine which object is which.

You also must decide what approach to take in creating the application. Will you develop a class library or use an existing framework? What objects can you borrow from other development teams at your company? Will you use PowerBuilder's object-oriented capabilities (such as inheritance, polymorphism, and encapsulation)?

All these questions must be considered—if possible, before development—to make the process as smooth as possible. For a first application, these types of questions can be difficult to answer because the answers often come from experience. Try to decide what objects can be used in all aspects of the application and start from there. Don't be discouraged if you find yourself knee-deep in code before you realize that the object would have been a good candidate for inheritance; you always can go back later. Development with a particular product becomes fine-tuned only with practice and experience.

**23**

Configuring and
Tuning

# Managing Your PowerBuilder Libraries

When creating your application, decide where the PowerBuilder library files should reside for performance reasons and source management. The following sections cover some guidelines that can help increase the performance and ease of use of your library files.

## Library Guidelines

Before you begin any development, it's recommended that you use several guidelines with PowerBuilder library files for tuning and ease of use. These guidelines include library location, organization, size, and optimization.

It's important to decide where you will store the actual PowerBuilder library files (PBLs)—that is, on what drive and in which directory. There are some special considerations when several developers are creating an application versus when a single developer is creating an application. The way in which the objects are distributed within your PBLs is important for ease of access and ease of use.

The library search path also is important in the performance tuning of your PowerBuilder application. Frequently used objects should be placed near the top so that PowerBuilder doesn't have to search through multiple PBLs to find the requested object. The library search path can be modified at runtime by using the SetLibraryList() function to get the optimal configuration for each user. After you organize your PBLs, it's important that your library files be optimized to prevent fragmentation of your objects. For a discussion of library file maintenance, see Chapter 8, "The Library Painter."

## Configuring the Client

Another area that can greatly affect the performance of any application is the configuration of the machine on which it's running. Before implementing your application, consider that it might run fine on your Pentium/233 with 64MB of RAM, but it's just a little bit slower on a user's Pentium/120 with 32MB of RAM. Although it might not be in the budget to upgrade user workstations, you can do some things to get better performance from user machines.

A simple change is to make sure that the machine is using a permanent swap file residing on a local drive, which ensures that Windows knows where the swap file is located and its size. If you use a temporary swap file, don't place it on the network or have a TEMP directory on the network because access time will increase dramatically. Windows 95/98 enables the use of 32-bit disk- and file-access features, and you will see a performance gain with local disk access.

Memory also is an area you can tune to improve performance. Depending on what else needs to be done on your user's workstation, consider using extended memory and loading drivers into high memory. Wallpaper used as a background in Windows often is popular with users but is a resource hog. If you can convince users to get rid of their wallpaper, do so. Similar to the way in which wallpaper takes up resources, higher resolutions slow your application. The last thing to remember with memory is the more, the merrier! If you can't purchase new machines for users, see whether you can get more memory for them. Memory is relatively inexpensive and can greatly affect an application's performance.

Many decisions that need to be considered before development begins don't take much time. Pull from the experience of other development teams to see what worked for them. Remember that these are guidelines, not hard-and-fast rules.

# The Development Process

The following sections provide tips that you can use to improve your application's performance through your scripts, event use, and implementation of object-oriented programming. The tips combine techniques that actually decrease process time and hints to give users the appearance that the application is running faster. It's surprising how a few seemingly simple modifications can dramatically affect your application's actual and perceived speed.

## PowerScript

PowerBuilder lets you create machine-code executables and runtime libraries. This PowerBuilder feature will have the greatest effect on PowerScript speed. To see a comparison of an application using p-code versus machine code, see Chapter 20, "Application and Component Implementation, Creation, and Distribution." The following sections look at commonly misused PowerScript statements that lead to decreased performance.

**23**

Configuring and Tuning

## Calling Functions

A frequent area of abuse concerns how various functions in PowerBuilder are used. You would be surprised at the amount of time some developers devote to creating a function that the PowerScript language already provides. PowerScript has more than 400 functions available; chances are that what you want to do is incorporated into those functions.

If PowerScript doesn't provide the functionality you need (for example, calculating current inventory), there are a couple of ways to go. If you plan to use the functionality more than once, create a user-defined function. If the function is applicable only to a specific object class, create an object-level function so that it's stored with the object it references. If the function will be called by multiple objects, create a global function or a nonvisual user object (especially if there are related functions or variables).

Intuition would tell you that the object-level function would be accessed more quickly than a corresponding global function. Depending on the way it's coded, this might not be true. If you fully qualify the function name within your scripts with the object name, the object-level function will run faster than if you just state the function name. In the Clicked event of a Save command button, compare line 1 to line 2:

```
wf_update()
```

```
w_parts.wf_update()
```

Line 2 will run faster than line 1 because of the hierarchy PowerBuilder uses to execute functions that aren't fully qualified. This is the order in which PowerBuilder searches for an unqualified function:

- A global external function
- A global function
- An object function
- A local external function
- A system function

The first function found with the specified name is executed. As you can see, if you don't fully qualify an object-level function, PowerBuilder searches through the global functions first, which could adversely affect performance.

**Note**

Object-level functions execute faster than globals for machine-code executables. Global functions run faster than object-level functions for p-code executables.

When you're using inheritance, PowerBuilder begins at the bottom descendant and searches upward for object and local external functions through the inheritance hierarchy until it finds a match. Event order also must be considered when using inheritance. PowerBuilder starts at the bottom descendant and looks up through the inheritance hierarchy until it reaches the topmost ancestor script or it finds an event script that overrides the ancestor. Depending on the inheritance levels and extension of events, PowerBuilder might have to traverse multiple inheritance layers.

Similar to the function and event hierarchy is the precedence of variable scope for variables with the same name. PowerBuilder's order of precedence is local, shared, global, and then instance. Because everyone should use a naming standard that incorporates scope into the variable names, this shouldn't be an issue.

> **Note**
>
> You will see a small performance degradation when using dynamically bound methods rather than statically bound methods because the dynamic reference must be resolved at runtime.

## Choose...Case

If you're moving from a mainframe environment to PowerBuilder, you're probably a big fan of the If...Then statement. Although this statement is more familiar to most programmers, consider using Choose...Case instead. You will find that reading a Choose...Case is much easier than reading an If...Then, and it's much easier to maintain, as you can see in this example:

```
If li_division_code = 10 Or li_division_code = 40 Then
    //Division 10 and 40 processing
ElseIf li_division_code = 20 Or li_division_code = 21 &
or li_division_code = 22 Then
    //Division 20 , 21, and 22 processing
ElseIf li_division_code >= 50 Then
    //Division 50 and greater processing
Else
    //Default division processing
End If
```

Here's another example:

```
Choose Case li_division_code
```

```
  Case 10, 20
     //Division 10 and 20 processing
  Case 20 To 22
     //Division 20, 21, and 22 processing
  Case Is >= 50
     //Division 50 and greater processing
  Case Else
     //Default division processing
End Choose
```

With the second example, it's easier to determine which values are being evaluated and what logic is executed when. Regardless of which method you use to evaluate an expression, remember that the values that occur most often should be placed first, and the least common values should be placed last in the test case list. This is true of the Choose...Case and If...Then statements.

## Loops

A mistake commonly made by beginners is to use a function that always returns the same value in a loop control statement (for example, Do...While). Look at the following code:

```
long ll_row, ll_cust_id

//Loop through the DataWindow looking for required customer id
Do Until ll_cust_id = Long( sle_cust_id.text)
   ll_row = ll_row + 1
   If ll_row > dw_customer.RowCount() Then
      MessageBox( "Customer Not Found", "Could not locate customer")
      Return
   End If
   ll_cust_id = dw_customer.GetItemNumber( ll_row, "customer_id")
Loop
```

The function RowCount(), which returns the number of rows in the DataWindow Primary buffer, is executed inside the loop until the desired customer ID is found (also using the Long() function within the Do...Loop). Instead, the code should be written as follows (the changes appear in bold):

```
long ll_row, ll_row_count, ll_cust_id, ll_req_cust

ll_row_count = dw_customer.RowCount()

//Grab the desired customer id entered by the user
ll_req_cust = Long( sle_cust_id.text)
```

```
//Loop through the DataWindow looking for required customer id
DO UNTIL ll_cust_id = ll_req_cust
   ll_row = ll_row + 1
   If ll_row > ll_row_count Then
      MessageBox( "Customer Not Found", "Could not locate customer")
      Return
   End If
   ll_cust_id = dw_customer.GetItemNumber( ll_row, "customer_id")
Loop
```

With this code, RowCount() is executed once and then stored in a variable, reducing the overhead of multiple function calls.

## Modify()

Several functions, such as Modify() and Describe(), can be easy targets for tuning. During development, you might typically have the following script:

```
dw_order.Modify( "received_date.background.color='9477526'")
dw_order.Modify( "received_date.border='5'")
dw_order.Modify( "ship_date.background.color='9477526'")
dw_order.Modify( "ship_date.border='5'")
```

This code would be desirable during development because you want to ensure that each modification to the DataWindow object is correct and occurs as coded. After the syntax is correct for these statements, the application should be modified (and, of course, retested) to the following:

```
dw_order.Modify( "received_date.background.color='9477526' &
~treceived_date.border='5'~tship_date.background.color='9477526' &
~tship_date.border='5'")
```

This reduces the script from four function calls to one. Also, with multiple commands being sent to one call of Modify(), Windows repaints the screen only once.

You also can directly reference the attributes of your DataWindow object. Just like each Modify() call, directly manipulating an attribute causes the DataWindow to repaint. To minimize the number of screen repaints, use the SetRedraw() function. The syntax follows:

```
ObjectName.SetRedraw( Flag)
```

*ObjectName* is the desired object (in this case, a DataWindow control), and *Flag* is a Boolean value. A value of TRUE ensures a screen repaint after an attribute is modified; a FALSE value specifies that the object shouldn't be repainted. With this in mind, the previous Modify() statement can be written as this:

```
dw_order.SetRedraw(False)
dw_order.object.received_date.background.color='9477526'
dw_order.object.received_date.border='5'
dw_order.object.ship_date.background.color='9477526'
dw_order.object.ship_date.border='5'
dw_order.SetRedraw(True)
```

Although you have the option of using the `Modify()` function or the DataWindow dot notation, there's a difference between the performance of the two. The fastest option for changing DataWindow properties is a compound `Modify()` call. The second-fastest method consists of individual `Modify()` calls, and the slowest method uses individual dot notation. These processing times also hold true for the `Describe()` function, the `GetItemx()` functions, and the `SetItem()` function.

> **Note**
>
> `GetItemx()` and `SetItem()` are faster than dot notation only when you access a single value. Dot notation outperforms the functions when you need to access multiple values at once.

> **Tip**
>
> Unless performance is the most important issue, data expressions are easier to code and maintain than the dot-notation equivalents.

## Array Processing

If you're using arrays in your application, you might want to review your code to make sure that it's functioning as efficiently as it can. This is particularly important if you're using dynamic arrays. Every time the dynamic array grows, PowerBuilder requests a new memory block from Windows that's the same size as the existing array plus the new elements to be added. The data from the old array then is copied to the new array in memory before the memory of the old array is released. Therefore, you use memory equal to at least double the size of the existing array. Although this method makes dynamic arrays easier to program, it decreases efficiency considerably (because of the processing overhead of maintaining and copying between two arrays and memory fragmentation).

You can use a few techniques to reduce the effects of this problem. The easiest and most efficient technique is to not use dynamic arrays. But because static arrays aren't always flexible enough, consider allocating more memory for the array than is first needed. If you need 100 elements, for example, specify 110 elements. This way, you have 10 more elements available to you, and PowerBuilder doesn't have to request more memory for the next 10 elements added.

Another method is to step backward through the elements in the array to populate it. The first element should be high (100, for example), which causes PowerBuilder to request the memory for 100 elements. Any access between 1 and 100 won't require Windows to allocate more memory. You then can work backward through the array, decreasing the index by 1, to assign the elements. This is particularly useful in loops that create and fill dynamic arrays, as shown in the following code:

```
Integer li_index, li_array_size
Decimal{2} lc_price[]

li_array_size = Integer( sle_max.text)

FOR li_index = li_array_size TO 1 STEP -1
   lc_price[li_index] = gc_original_price * .20
NEXT
```

When using a dynamic array, it's often necessary to find the lower or upper bound of an array. You can do this by using the functions LowerBound() and UpperBound(), respectively. Both functions are expensive in terms of processing time, so use them sparingly.

## Caution

Absolute care should be taken to not use the LowerBound() and UpperBound() functions inside a loop construct.

If you're using a global dynamic array (to track references to instances of a particular window class in a MDI application, for example) or a shared dynamic array, PowerBuilder doesn't release the memory until the application is terminated. This is a problem if you are finished using the array, and you need the memory for other processing.

You need to return the dynamic array to an empty state. To accomplish this, declare another array of the same type and set the original array equal to the new array. This method clears out the original array. Calling the `UpperBound()` function after completing the processing returns a value of 0. Here's an example of resetting an array to an empty state:

```
Long ll_order_no[]


//Empty out global array
gl_order_no[] = ll_order_no[]
```

Similar to the problem of memory allocation of dynamic arrays is that of passing arrays as arguments to a function. As you know, you can pass arguments by reference or by value. If you pass by reference, you pass the memory location of the array, and the function can modify the array. If you pass by value, you copy the array and pass it to the function. If you have a large array and pass it by value to a function, you could consume quite a bit of memory. If your function doesn't need to modify the array, be sure to pass the array by reference.

## The Control Array

If you need to track the controls placed in a window, consider creating an array. PowerBuilder already takes care of this, however, and enables you to access it in your code.

PowerBuilder uses the control array to paint the window. The order in which the controls appear in the array is important in producing an even painting effect. Your application will look better if it paints across and down the screen rather than jumps to different locations. The control array's default order is the order in which the controls were placed onscreen. If you want to change the order, send the controls to the back and then bring them to the front in the order in which you want them to be painted.

The control array also can be used in your code. You might find the array to be useful if you have a window with a Reset button that restores all controls to their initial states, as in this code:

```
Integer li_index, li_count
SingleLineEdit lsle_generic
DropDownListBox lddlb_generic
DataWindow ldw_generic
CheckBox lcbx_generic

li_count = UpperBound( parent.Control)

For li_index=1 to li_count
   Choose Case TypeOf( parent.Control[ li_index])
      Case SingleLineEdit!  //Clear text
         lsle_generic = parent.Control[li_index]
         lsle_generic.text = ""
```

```
    Case DropDownListBox! //Clear drop-down listbox
        lddlb_generic = parent.Control[li_index]
        lddlb_generic.SelectItem(0)
    Case DataWindow!        //Reset DataWindow and insert new row
        ldw_generic = parent.Control[li_index]
        ldw_generic.Reset()
        ldw_generic.InsertRow(0)
    Case CheckBox!          //Uncheck all checkboxes
        lcbx_generic = parent.Control[li_index]
        lcbx_generic.checked = FALSE
  End Choose
Next
```

By using the `TypeOf()` function, you can determine the type of control the array element is referencing and provide the appropriate code to the object type.

## Miscellaneous Scripting Techniques

When you are finished with a window and users no longer need to access data from it, close it. Not only does leaving unneeded windows open create a sloppy interface, but these windows also consume resources that could be used more effectively by other parts of your application. The same is true of windows for which the `Visible` attribute is `FALSE`.

Finally, any object that you create also should be destroyed. If you create any nonvisual user objects in your application via the `CREATE` statement, ensure that the object is removed properly from memory by using the `DESTROY` statement when you are finished with the object.

23

Configuring and Tuning

> **Note**
>
> PowerBuilder gives you some help in ensuring that objects are destroyed properly with the `AutoInstantiate` property for custom class user objects. If you set this property to on, PowerBuilder creates and destroys the objects for you.

Although the use of `CREATE` and `DESTROY` as a matched pair is a sign of well-written code, PowerBuilder assists you in resolving any objects you forget to destroy. PowerBuilder's garbage-collection process cleans up any objects that lose their references. For more information on garbage collection, see Chapter 7, "The PowerScript Language."

# Event Use

You easily can tune the use of functions to increase efficiency in your application, and the same technique applies to events.

A window's Open event is an excellent target for improving your application's performance and perceived performance. Many beginning PowerBuilder developers place a great deal of code in this event, which means that the window takes a while to open and become visible to users.

If you need to populate a DataWindow or a drop-down list box for your users, for example, you might think that the Open event is the perfect place to perform this logic. But if either script runs long, users must wait to see the window. To get around this delay, create a user event (with no event ID) and place the retrieval or population logic there. Then, from the Open event, use the PostEvent() function to call the new user event. The message then is placed at the bottom of the Windows message queue and permits the window to appear before the code finishes executing. This way, users see the window but probably won't be quick enough to do anything before the posted event finishes executing. If the script does take longer, use a status window indicating that initialization still is occurring so that users won't feel as though they're waiting.

Keep the amount of code written in the Open event script to a minimum, but the Open event is a good candidate for manipulating graphics. The objects in the window already have been constructed but not yet displayed, so they can be manipulated. By performing this manipulation before the window opens, Windows must paint the window only once. This increases performance and doesn't cause the screen to flicker, which is an unattractive user-interface feature. Avoid long-running scripts for the Activate event so that users don't have to wait for the event to finish before using the window.

Also avoid the Other event because it's used to trap all Windows messages not associated with a specific object. If you want to trap a particular Windows message, create a user-defined event tied to the appropriate event ID. If PowerBuilder doesn't trap that message with a corresponding event ID, you can't capture the message via a custom event.

# Object-Oriented Programming

PowerBuilder, unlike many front-end development tools, incorporates many object-oriented features that help streamline the development process. By providing an object-based approach to development, you easily can reuse objects and create an easier-to-maintain application.

> **Note**
>
> For first-time PowerBuilder developers, the object-oriented features of Power-Builder actually can increase the length of development. This is because first-time developers won't know what objects work well and can be reused; this knowledge comes with experience and a strong design.

The object-oriented features are inheritance, encapsulation, and polymorphism. For in-depth coverage of these topics, see Chapter 18, "Analysis, Design, and Implementation."

## Inheritance and Encapsulation

Inheritance and encapsulation enable you to create an application with cleaner code and objects that can be reused repeatedly. Code is located in one place and isn't duplicated throughout the application, making maintenance much simpler.

Inheritance, in addition to providing reusable objects, can give you a performance gain at execution time. When an inherited object is loaded into memory at runtime, all its ancestors also are loaded. If several objects are inherited from the same ancestors, the ancestor definitions already are loaded into memory, so each subsequent descendant object's load time is faster.

For example, an application requires the development of three windows: `w_product_sales`, `w_sales_rep`, and `w_regional_sales`, which all contain Data-Windows that retrieve data to display overall weekly sales figures, sales representative sales, and regional sales, respectively. If each window is created as a separate entity (no inheritance), the time taken to open each window is 10 seconds.

As the development of all windows nears completion, you realize that you've just written the same code for each window (updates, insert, deletes, error handling, and sales calculations). You decide that the common DataWindow processing (updates, insert, deletes, and error handling) can be placed in an ancestor window: `w_ancestor`. This window can be used by other applications, so you decide to inherit a new window from `w_ancestor` that contains the specific sales calculations: `w_sales_ancestor`. After you build the two ancestor windows, `w_product_sales`, `w_sales_rep`, and `w_regional_sales` are inherited from `w_sales_ancestor` and modified to perform their own specific processing. Figure 23.1 shows the resulting inheritance chain.

When users specify that they want to open `w_product_sales`, the class definitions for `w_ancestor` and `w_sales_ancestor` must be loaded into memory before `w_product_sales` can be loaded. The time taken to load `w_product_sales` is 15 seconds—an increase of 5 seconds from the standalone version of the same window. When `w_sales_rep` is opened,

**23**

Configuring and Tuning

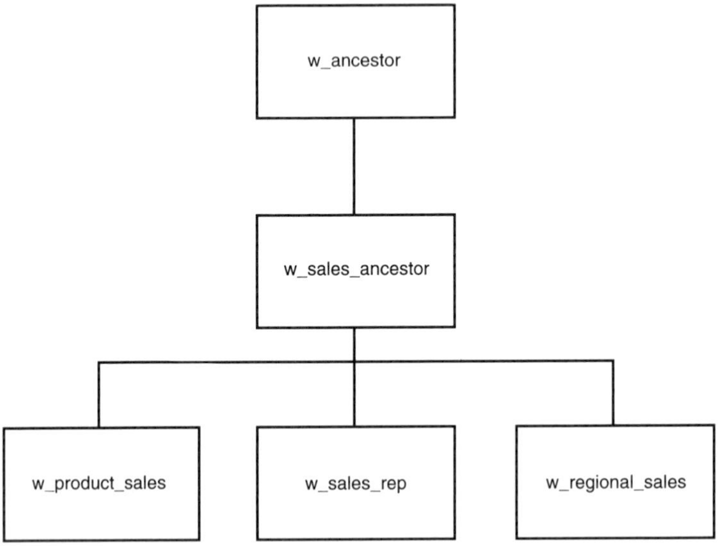

**FIGURE 23.1**
*A window inheri-
tance tree.*

its ancestors— w_ancestor and w_sales_ancestor—already are loaded into memory, so
only w_sales_rep's definition needs to be loaded. The open time necessary for the
inherited windows w_sales_rep and w_regional_sales is only 5 seconds. This also
means that each subsequent descendant window takes less time to load. For the three
windows, you went from a combined open time of 30 seconds to 20 seconds by using
inheritance. Of course, this example is greatly simplified, but you can begin to see some
performance benefits of inheritance.

## Polymorphism

Another object-oriented technique incorporated with inheritance is *polymorphism*, which
enables you to define a series of operations for different objects even if they behave
differently. Consider this: A function is defined for a set of objects but acts differently
based on the referenced object type. An update function might update a database for one
window, for example, and save to a file for another window. Using polymorphism can
speed up your code by reducing the amount of code needed.

Suppose that you have two sheets (w_order_detail and w_customer) open in an MDI
application that update different tables. You could create a function in each sheet to perform
the update. In the Clicked event for a Save menu item, you could place the following code:

```
window lw_sheet
w_order_detail lw_order
w_customer lw_customer
```

```
lw_sheet = w_mdiFrame.GetActiveSheet()

If IsValid(lw_sheet) Then
    Choose Case ClassName(lw_sheet)
        Case "w_order_detail"
            lw_order = lw_sheet
            lw_order.wf_UpdateOrderTable()
        Case "w_customer"
            lw_customer = lw_sheet
            lw_customer.wf_UpdateCustTable()
    End Choose
End If
```

If another window is added that uses this menu, you must add that window to the code. Unfortunately, this addition requires hard-coding values into your script, which you should avoid. The polymorphic solution is to create an ancestor window (w_ancestor) containing an object-level function named wf_Update() with no script in it. The Save menu item's Clicked script then would be much simpler:

```
w_ancestor lw_sheet

lw_sheet = w_mdiFrame.GetActiveSheet()

If IsValid (lw_sheet) Then
    lw_sheet.wf_Update()
End If
```

As you can see, the code is much easier to read. PowerBuilder doesn't have to evaluate multiple arguments, which makes the script process faster, and you don't have to modify the code if all new windows use w_ancestor through inheritance. Each descendant window then would override the ancestor function with its own specific update processing.

Another way to achieve the same functionality is to use the TriggerEvent() function, which immediately executes an event for a specified object. From the Clicked event of the Save menu, you could code

```
ParentWindow.TriggerEvent("ue_filesave")
```

This code would attempt to execute the user-defined event ue_filesave in the menu's associated window. The beauty of doing this is that the event doesn't have to be defined for all windows for two reasons:

- Because the event-name argument for `TriggerEvent()` is just a string, PowerBuilder can't validate at compile time that the event exists.

- If the event doesn't exist, `TriggerEvent()` doesn't cause an application-terminating runtime error; instead, it simply returns `-1`. This method should be used as a workaround for those occasions when you don't have the time to implement a polymorphic solution.

# DataWindows

As if you didn't already know, the DataWindow is the main reason PowerBuilder is the popular application-development tool it is today. The DataWindow incorporates much of the functionality developers need with minimum code. The DataWindow has many strengths:

- Various display formats

- Several edit styles (for example, edit masks and radio buttons)

- An easy method for laying out a data-entry screen

- Built-in scrolling

- Multiple reporting techniques (graphing, crosstabs, groups, and layers)

- Data validation by PowerBuilder and developers

- Less resource-intensive than conventional controls

- Minimal script requirement to retrieve data

- Update of databases handled internally by the DataWindow object

- Increased performance

Obviously, by providing a control that requires minimal script to retrieve data, handle updates, scroll, and validate data, the performance of the application will increase as development time decreases. One reason performance increases is that to build the functionality of a DataWindow with standard controls would result in a considerable amount of code on the developer's behalf. The interpreted code won't be as fast (and potentially not as well structured) as the same compiled code built into PowerBuilder.

The DataWindow also is more efficient in terms of controls on a window and screen painting. Suppose that you have an application that displays 10 columns and 10 rows from a database at one time and doesn't have the DataWindow available. You would have to use 100 single-line edits and a lot of code. Imagine populating each control every time the user scrolls down. Even worse, if users want to update the database, you have to track what has been changed and generate the appropriate SQL statement.

Not only would this be tedious to code, but the amount of memory consumed by the 100 single-line edits also would have an adverse effect on your application's performance. The DataWindow, on the other hand, tracks changes, generates the SQL statements, and is considered one control that consumes significantly less memory. That the DataWindow is considered to be only one control also means that when Windows repaints the screen, the DataWindow control is painted all at once, which increases the repainting speed.

Although the DataWindow is a powerful object that can increase your application's efficiency, don't abuse it. If you don't need to access a database, for example, it might make more sense and provide better performance to use the standard PowerBuilder controls.

# DataWindow Tuning

Avoid using the `RetrieveRow` event of the DataWindow control. `RetrieveRow` is triggered every time a row is retrieved from the database into the DataWindow (after a `Retrieve()` function call). PowerBuilder performs a `Yield` after each row, which slows down the retrieval process.

**Note**

Even if you code only a comment line in the `RetrieveRow` event, performance is still affected.

**Tip**

Although the `RetrieveRow` event affects your application's performance, using it may be a trade-off you're willing to make. By using `RetrieveRow`, you can display a counter of the number of rows retrieved to give your users constant feedback.

Also limit the amount of code placed in the `ItemChanged`, `ItemFocusChanged`, and `RowFocusChanged` events. Your application retrieves a product description from a database every time the product code changes (using the `ItemChanged` event), for example. If users have to wait more than a second for a response, you're guaranteed to get a phone call.

In addition to keeping the scripts short in the aforementioned events, keep the script brief in the `Clicked` event if you plan to use the `DoubleClicked` event also. If you have too much code in the `Clicked` event, the script still might be running when users click a second time. The second click won't be recognized and therefore the `DoubleClicked` event won't be triggered.

# Data Retrieval

Although a DataWindow is an efficient way to retrieve data, even it can produce long-running queries and use memory poorly. One way to improve application performance is to minimize the number of rows and columns returned to the client by making your queries as specific as possible. By bringing back unnecessary data (rows or columns), you're tying up resources on the server, the network, and the client. You can use several additional techniques to minimize the amount of data returned to the client.

## Limit the User

The easiest way to limit what's retrieved is to make users define the queries they will need and to implement only those queries (you might have to force users to choose a "Top 10" list). By specifying the queries up front, you know exactly what will be retrieved and approximately the time needed. This information then can be shown to users.

Although you won't get any surprises in what data is retrieved via this method, this approach does have some serious disadvantages. Limiting your users to specific queries isn't flexible, and users invariably want more functionality. Plus, when you implement the specific queries, you can ensure that the data retrieved isn't too large, but the database might grow and then the queries will begin to take longer.

## SQL `Count()`

Because limiting your users to a specific query eventually can result in a lot of data being retrieved, it would be nice to know how many rows will be returned and to ask users whether they want to continue. You can accomplish this task by using the `Count()` function in a SQL statement.

Suppose that your DataWindow were to execute this SQL statement:

```
SELECT order_num, customer_name, item_no, quantity, ship_date
FROM order_detail od, customer cs
WHERE od.cust_id = cs.cust_id
```

```
AND cs.cust_id = :a_cust_id
AND od.ship_date BETWEEN "07/11/93" AND GetDate()
```

You probably would want to know whether the selected customer was going to retrieve many orders. You could run the following code first to find out the exact number of rows returned:

```
SELECT Count(*)
FROM order_detail od, customer cs
WHERE od.cust_id = cs.cust_id
AND cs.cust_id = :a_cust_id
AND od.ship_date BETWEEN "07/11/93" AND GetDate()
```

The Count() statement tells you exactly how many rows match the criteria specified in the WHERE clause. You then can display a message box telling users how much data will be retrieved and asking whether they want to continue.

The disadvantage of this approach is that you're executing the SQL statement twice. Although you don't have the overhead of bringing data across the network into memory, you still have a performance hit. Depending on the query, this is a common method of limiting the data retrieved.

## The RetrieveRow Event

If performing a count takes too long, you can use the DataWindow control's RetrieveRow event to count the number of rows returned from the database. Increment a counter every time a row is retrieved. After it reaches a certain number of rows (for example, 100), ask your users whether they want to continue to query or cancel the retrieval.

This approach seems good, but it does negatively affect performance. The RetrieveRow event is executed each time a row is retrieved from the database; this slows down all retrievals, including the small ones.

## Database Cursors

If you want the ultimate in control, consider using a *database cursor*, which enables you to manipulate one row at a time in a resultset. By using a cursor, you can ask users whether they want to continue after a certain number of rows is reached. If users choose Yes, you can continue the retrieval where you left off.

The downside to using a cursor is that you're bypassing most of the power given to you by the DataWindow. You have to manually place the data into the DataWindow by using SetItem() or the corresponding direct-access syntax.

## Retrieve As Needed

The Retrieve As Needed option is found on the Rows menu in the DataWindow painter. PowerBuilder retrieves as many rows as it takes to fill the DataWindow and presents the data to users while the query still is returning data from the server. As users scroll or move to see additional data, PowerBuilder continues to retrieve more data from the server. Retrieve As Needed gives users immediate access to the data for even long-running queries.

> **Note**
>
> If you specify any client-side sorting, grouping, averages, or any other functions that act on the resultset as a whole, Retrieve As Needed is overridden.

The query has effectively finished! The database server now is just waiting on requests to send data to the client.

The downside of the Retrieve As Needed option is that users must wait as they scroll down because PowerBuilder is retrieving additional data. PowerBuilder also is maintaining an open connection (by using an internal cursor) to the server. Maintaining this connection is dangerous because locks are being held. You also can't commit to free these locks, or the cursor closes and no more data is returned. After presenting the data to users following the initial retrieve, you might consider turning off Retrieve As Needed by using the following syntax:

```
dw_1.Object.DataWindow.Retrieve.AsNeeded = 'NO'
```

This code enables PowerBuilder to return the remaining data to the DataWindow.

> **Note**
>
> Another option is the capability to specify that retrieved rows are saved to disk, which frees memory to your application. Use this option (choose Retrieve Rows to Disk from the Rows menu) in cases when users don't require constant access to the retrieved data. Otherwise, performance decreases due to the extra disk access.

# Query Mode

You can set the DataWindow to Query mode, which enables users to specify data-retrieval criteria for the WHERE clause in the DataWindow's SQL SELECT statement. This mode enables users to tune queries to their precise requirements. Query mode is activated at runtime by using this code:

```
dw_1.Object.DataWindow.QueryMode='Yes'
```

The interface is the same query-by-example look, as shown in the Quick Select data source option (see Figure 23.2).

**FIGURE 23.2**

*Query mode for a DataWindow.*

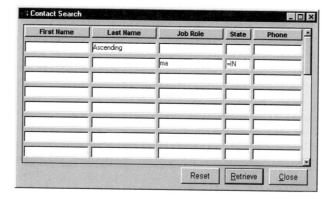

PowerBuilder clears the DataWindow object and enables users to type criteria on any lines. If you also want users to be able to specify sort criteria, code a line like this:

```
dw_1.Object.DataWindow.QuerySort='Yes'
```

In Query mode, it's important that you initially create your DataWindow object with no WHERE clause. Otherwise, you might have information from an existing WHERE clause that conflicts with information from the user specifications.

# Prompt for Criteria

Prompt for Criteria is similar to Query mode, with a few minor differences. You can turn on Prompt for Criteria from the Rows menu in the DataWindow painter, or you can use Modify() or the appropriate direct object syntax. When you use Prompt for Criteria, you specify in which columns you want users to be able to specify their criteria (see Figure 23.3), whereas Query mode enables users to specify criteria for all visible columns.

You can't specify a sort criteria with Prompt for Criteria, however. Also note that if users don't specify any criteria, the SQL still is executed but with no WHERE clause. The downside

**FIGURE 23.3**

*The Specify Retrieval Criteria dialog.*

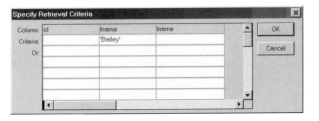

to using Query mode and the Prompt for Criteria option is that PowerBuilder is required to compile the SQL for each DataWindow retrieval.

## Additional DataWindow Considerations

The previous techniques to control the amount of data returned to the client are important. You can apply several additional techniques to the client to help increase your application's performance. Perform data validation on the client to prevent bad data being sent across the network to the database, only to be rejected. Data formatting also should be done by the client to provide interface consistency and to keep unnecessary formatting characters from being stored in the database.

The client also should manage database connections and transaction processing. Keep to a minimum the number of times you connect and the number of connections to a database. Issuing a CONNECT is an expensive operation and ties up resources on the server and client. To manage connections effectively, use the SetTransObject() function instead of SetTrans(). SetTrans() manages the database connections for you, going so far as to connect and disconnect after every Retrieve() and Update() function call. The application, with SetTransObject(), should perform COMMITs after a logical unit of work processes on the database to remove database locks and free memory on the server.

Although the client has numerous responsibilities, the server also has its share. Aggregation should be performed on the server because it's most likely a more powerful machine than the client. If the SQL needed to retrieve data is too complex for a DataWindow or a script to handle, consider using stored procedures (if supported by your DBMS) to execute the SQL. Stored procedures are useful particularly if you have complex multiple joins that the DataWindow can't handle and when you want to use temporary tables to fine-tune your SQL.

When minimizing the number of times data is retrieved, you might want to consider one of the following options. You can capture often-used static data in one of two ways: by caching it using arrays or by using a DataStore object. If you're using a DataStore, after the data is retrieved, you can use the ShareData() function so that the same data doesn't have to be maintained multiple times in memory for different DataWindows.

Two other areas for review when using DataWindows are the use of images and nested DataWindows. Images are resource intensive and add to the files that need to be tracked for the application. One way to cut down on image use is to use a corresponding Symbol font in the image's place. Nested DataWindows also can severely affect performance because the number of retrieves for a nested report is equal to the number of detail rows plus one. Caching data, using SQL tuning, and using bind variables can help speed up the retrieval.

# The User Interface

As mentioned earlier, the human factor can make or break any project. This is true of the development team, but also—more importantly—of the users. If your users don't like the application, you'll have nothing but headaches. For that reason, get your users involved in every facet of the development and testing process. Users then can't complain about the end product and also have their reputations at stake if the application doesn't perform well.

The user interface has a huge impact on the application's perceived performance. If the interface isn't intuitive and users have to spend time figuring out what they need to do, it matters little whether the application runs at lightning speed. Therefore, it's important to spend time developing and enforcing good GUI standards across your company's applications.

The number of menu items and objects on a window shouldn't be excessive, or users won't know what to do. Also, people can't comprehend as much on a computer screen as they can on a printed page (up to 50 percent less, in some cases).

The density of items on a window is as important as the placement of the controls. Microsoft publishes a list of common user access (CUA) practices and GUI guidelines that you should review before and after the development process. For more details on the guidelines for the Windows environment and other platforms, see Appendix E, "Cross-Platform PowerBuilder."

# Application Profiling

You can analyze just how your applications are working by using enhanced tracing with PowerBuilder's profiling feature. The tracing and profiling features help you identify areas that require rewriting to improve performance and identify errors in the application's logic.

> **Note**
>
> The tracing and profiling features are available only in the Enterprise Edition of PowerBuilder. All editions of PowerBuilder let you generate a text trace file without timer values by using the PBDebug option (for more information, see Chapter 21, "Testing and Debugging").

When you run an application with tracing turned on, a log file is generated with entries for specific activities as well as a timer value. You control which activities you want to capture and when logging starts and stops. You can collect profile data in three ways:

- Enable tracing on the Profiling tab of the System Options dialog.

- Place TraceX() PowerScript functions in your application scripts. These functions control what is traced and when.

- Use a window to control tracing from within your application. Sybase supplies w_starttrace in PROFILE.PBL as a basis from which to build.

> **Note**
>
> Trace files can be created from within the PowerBuilder development environment or from executables running outside PowerBuilder. For machine-code executables, tracing is enabled only if you enable the Trace Information check box when the executable is compiled.

After you create a trace file (using a .pbp extension), you can use the Application Profiler that Sybase provides to analyze the data. The Application Profiler enables you to view the application in different ways by extracting specific types of information from the trace file. You can explore how often routines are called and what's calling them, for example. The Application Profiler can be accessed by selecting New and using the Tools tab on the New dialog. The Profiler provides three views:

- *Class view* is extracted from a call graph model and shows calls, hits, and timing information for each class in the application.

- *Routine view* is extracted from a call graph model and shows calls, hits, and timing information for each routine in the application.

- *Trace view* is extracted from a trace tree model and shows the elapsed time taken by each activity in chronological order.

> **Note**
>
> When this chapter refers to *routines*, it actually means both functions and events.

> **Tip**
>
> The profiling tool provided by Sybase has most of the functionality you need and has a friendly interface. When you're looking at a particular view in the profiler, remember that you can drill down to the lowest code level by double-clicking objects.

Sybase keeps your options open by providing a number of objects and functions for you to create your own analysis tools:

- Performance-analysis objects and functions enable you to construct a call graph model from the trace file. A *call graph model* contains information about all the routines in the trace file—for example, routine call count, which routines called it and which routines it called, and the execution times taken.

- Trace tree objects and functions enable you to construct a nested trace tree model. A *trace tree model* lists, in chronological order, all recorded activities in the trace file and the elapsed time for each activity.

- Trace file objects and functions enable you to access the data in the trace file sequentially.

The Application Profiler is a good place to start learning about profiling with PowerBuilder if you want to develop your own analysis tools.

## Analyzing Trace Information

PowerBuilder provides three ways to analyze trace information:

- Construct a call graph model to analyze performance by extracting information about specific classes and routines.

- Construct a trace-tree model showing the execution sequence of activities and the time elapsed for each activity.

- Access the data in the trace file directly to perform custom processing.

**23**

**Configuring and Tuning**

You can use the Application Profiler to perform the first two types of analysis.

Trace files aren't portable across platforms because they are compressed and rely on information from within the executable file that created them. The creation time stamp and the path to the executable file must match those recorded in the trace file.

The following sections look at the objects and functions for generating and using each model type.

# Types of Timers

You have the choice, depending on your platform, of what kind of timer the trace functions use to measure time values. By default, timer values on Windows 95/98/NT use the clock timer. This measures an absolute time, in microseconds, with reference to the machine's startup time.

> **Note**
>
> The clock timer may be able to offer a resolution of less than 1 microsecond. This resolution is the smallest unit of time the timer can measure and is dictated by the speed of the machine's CPU.

You also have the choice of process or thread timers, which measure time in microseconds in reference to the starting point of the process's or thread's execution. These two timer types are more accurate but have a lower resolution than the clock timer.

The time values written to the trace file don't include the time taken to collect the trace data. You also can choose to carry out logging without timer information.

# Trace Functions

The following functions are available to collect data into a trace file:

- TraceOpen( *TraceFileName*, *TimerKind*) opens a trace file with the specified filename and enables the logging of application activities. *TimerKind* is an enumerated value that indicates the type of timer. When the trace file is opened, the current application and library list are written to it. After TraceOpen is called, you can select activities to be logged by using TraceEnableActivity() and then start the trace with TraceBegin(). To stop logging, you call TraceEnd() followed by TraceClose().

**Caution**

If the trace file grows so much that it runs out of disk space, no error is generated and logging stops. This means that the trace file can't be used for analysis.

- `TraceEnableActivity( ActivityType)` turns on logging of the specified activity. By default, when `TraceOpen()` is called, only developer-specified activity is logged. You must enable the desired activities *before* calling `TraceBegin()`. The valid `ActivityType` values are

| | |
|---|---|
| `ActBegin!` | Always enabled; indicates the start and finish of logging |
| `ActError!` | Any system errors and warnings |
| `ActESQL!` | Embedded SQL statement entry and exit |
| `ActGarbageCollect!` | Start and finish of garbage collection |
| `ActLine!` | Routine line hits (if this is enabled, `ActRoutine!` is enabled automatically) |
| `ActObjectCreate!` | Object creation entry and exit |
| `ActObjectDestroy!` | Object destruction entry and exit |
| `ActProfile!` | Meta tag for enabling `ActRoutine!`, `ActESQL!`, `ActObjectCreate!`, `ActObjectDestroy!`, and `ActGarbageCollect!` with a single call |
| `ActRoutine!` | Routine entry and exit |
| `ActTrace!` | Meta tag to enable all activities except `ActLine!` |
| `ActUser!` | Activity you indicate; always enabled by `TraceOpen()` |

PowerBuilder automatically logs all activities except `ActError!` and `ActUser!` during a trace. Both activity types require the passing of strings to the trace file, and you must call the `TraceError()` and `TraceUser()` functions to log this information.

- `TraceDisableActivity( ActivityType)`, the counterpart to `TraceEnableActivity()`, is used outside active logging (before a `TraceBegin()` call) to disable the logging of specified activities.

- `TraceBegin( Identifier)` makes an entry in the trace file to indicate that logging has begun. You pass a string argument to this function that's used to write an identifier for the tracing block in the file. You can use `TraceBegin()` and `TraceEnd()` to record multiple tracing blocks to a single trace file if you want to capture different areas of an application execution.

23

Configuring and Tuning

- TraceError( *Severity, Message*) enables you to log custom error messages and severity levels to the trace file. *Severity* is a long value for the severity of the error to record, and *Message* is the error text to log.

### Note

Remember to turn on ActError! to log any error activities.

- TraceUser( *ReferenceNumber, Message*) enables you to log any activity you want in the trace file. You specify a numeric value, *ReferenceNumber*, and a text message, *Message*.

- TraceEnd() writes an entry to the trace file to indicate that logging has ended and stops logging application trace activities.

- TraceClose() closes the trace file.

## A Trace Example

Now that you've met the functions, it's time to look at incorporating these into an application that you want to trace. Listing 23.1 opens a trace file called TEST.PBP that has all object-creation and destruction activities written to it.

**LISTING 23.1**  Logging Some Simple Activity

```
If TraceOpen( "TEST.PBP", Clock!) <> Success! Then
    Return -1
End If


TraceEnableActivity(ActObjectCreate!)
TraceEnableActivity(ActObjectDestroy!)

TraceBegin( "Starting Trace - Section 1")
//
// Use an ObjectArray we have previously populated with user objects
// to cause initialization and subsequent additional internal create
// and destroys.
//
For nCount = 1 To 10
    TraceUser( 0, "Initializing " + ObjectArray[ nCount].ClassName())

    If Not ObjectArray[ nCount].uf_Initialize() Then
```

**LISTING 23.1**   CONTINUED

```
        TraceError( -1, "Failed to init. " + ObjectArray[ nCount].ClassName())
    End If
Next

TraceEnd()
//
// Change logging characteristics
//
TraceEnableActivity(ActTrace!)

TraceBegin( "Starting Trace - Section 2")
//
// Do some more work...
//
TraceEnd()

TraceClose()
```

# Profile Object and Functions

PowerBuilder supplies a number of new objects and functions that support tracing and profiling. The next few sections look briefly at each and provide a few consolidated examples of how to use them.

> **Note**
>
> The entire contents of PowerBuilder's online help file won't be rehashed here. Instead, explore PowerBuilder's online help for more information on each object mentioned in these sections.

## Performance-Analysis Objects

The objects listed in Table 23.1 provide the functionality—through functions and properties—to create performance-analysis models from your trace files.

23
Configuring and Tuning

TABLE 23.1 Performance-Analysis Objects

| Object | Description |
|--------|-------------|
| Profiling | Provides a performance-analysis model that lists all the routines logged in a given trace file. This object analyzes a PowerBuilder application's performance and has a number of functions that enable you to build the model and list the classes and routines included in the model. The Profiling object is used with all the following objects. |
| ProfileCall | Provides information about the calls in the performance-analysis model. This information includes the calling routine, the number of times the call was made, and the elapsed time. ProfileCall is used with the ProfileRoutine and Profiling objects. |
| ProfileClass | Provides information about the classes, such as the class routines, in the performance-analysis model. ProfileClass also is used with the Profiling object. |
| ProfileLine | Provides information about the lines in each routine. This information includes the number of times the line was executed, any calls made from the line, and the time spent on the line. ProfileLine is used with the ProfileRoutine and Profiling objects. |
| ProfileRoutine | Provides information about the routines in the performance-analysis model. This information includes the time spent in the routine, the routines called, the number of times each routine was called, and the class to which the routine belongs. ProfileRoutine is used with the Profiling and ProfileCall or ProfileLine objects. |

# Nested Tree-Model Objects

Nested tree-model objects provide the functionality to create a nested tree model from your trace file and to extract information from that model. Table 23.2 lists these objects.

TABLE 23.2 Nested Tree-Model Objects

| Object | Description |
|--------|-------------|
| TraceTree | Provides a way to analyze a PowerBuilder application's performance by creating a tree model. The tree model lists all the nodes logged in a trace file. You use the TraceTree object with the following objects. |
| TraceTreeNode | Provides information about the individual nodes in the tree model. |
| TraceTreeObject | Provides information about a tree-model node that has been identified as an occurrence of an object. This object is assigned a TraceTreeNode object that has the activity type ActObjectCreate! or ActObjectDestroy!. This object enables you to access additional information, such as timer values and the object's class. |

TABLE 23.2    Nested Tree-Model Objects

| Object | Description |
| --- | --- |
| `TraceTreeRoutine` | Provides information about a tree-model node that has been identified as an occurrence of a routine. This object is assigned a `TraceTreeNode` object that has the activity type `ActRoutine!`. This object enables you to access additional information, such as timer values and the object's class. |
| `TraceTreeLine` | Provides information about a tree-model node that has been identified as an occurrence of a routine line hit. This object is assigned a `TraceTreeNode` object that has the activity type `ActLine!`. This object enables you to access additional information, such as timer values and the line number. |
| `TraceTreeESQL` | Provides information about a tree-model node that has been identified as an occurrence of an Embedded SQL statement. This object is assigned a `TraceTreeNode` object that has the activity type `ActESQL!`. This object enables you to access additional information, such as timer values. |
| `TraceTreeUser` | Provides information about a tree-model node that has been identified as an occurrence of a user-selected logging activity. This object is assigned a `TraceTree-Node` object that has the activity type `ActUser!`. This object enables you to access additional information, such as a message you defined when making the logging entry. |
| `TraceTreeGarbageCollect` | Provides information about a tree-model node that has been identified as an occurrence of garbage collection. This object is assigned a `TraceTreeNode` object that has the activity type `ActGarbageCollection!`. This object enables you to access additional timer information. |
| `TraceTreeError` | Provides information about a tree-model node that has been identified as an occurrence of a system error or warning. This object is assigned a `TraceTreeNode` object that has the activity type `ActError!`. This object enables you to access additional information, such as the error message and severity level. |

**23**

Configuring and
Tuning

# Sequential Trace-File Objects

Sequential trace-file objects provide the functionality to read the data sequentially from a trace file. Table 23.3 lists these objects.

**TABLE 23.3** Sequential Trace-File Objects

| Object | Description |
| --- | --- |
| TraceFile | Accesses the contents of a trace file. This and its associated objects don't provide you with the means to create an analysis model like the Profiling and TraceTree objects. Instead, they enable you to step through the file. You use the TraceFile object with the following objects. |
| TraceActivityNode | Provides activity information about the nodes in a trace file. |
| TraceBeginEnd | Provides information about a node in a trace file that has been identified as an occurrence of a logging start or finish. This object is assigned a TraceActivityNode object that has the activity type ActBegin!. This object enables you to access additional information, such as a message you defined when logging started or stopped. |
| TraceObject | Provides information about a node in a trace file that has been identified as the creation or destruction of an object. This object is assigned a TraceActivityNode object that has the activity type ActObjectCreate! or ActObject-Destroy!. This object enables you to access additional information about the object's class. |
| TraceRoutine | Provides information about a node in a trace file that has been identified as an occurrence of a routine. This object is assigned a TraceActivityNode object that has the activity type ActRoutine! to access additional information. |
| TraceLine | Provides information about a node in a trace file that has been identified as an occurrence of a routine line hit. This object is assigned a TraceActivityNode object that has the activity type ActLine! to access additional information. |
| TraceESQL | Provides information about a node in a trace file that has been identified as an occurrence of an Embedded SQL statement hit. This object is assigned a TraceActivityNode object that has the activity type ActESQL! to access additional information. |
| TraceUser | Provides information about a node in a trace file that has been identified as an occurrence of a logging activity you selected. This object is assigned a TraceActivityNode object that has the activity type ActUser! to access additional information. |
| TraceGarbageCollect | Provides information about a node in a trace file that has been identified as an occurrence of garbage collection. This object is assigned a TraceActivityNode object that has the activity type ActGarbageCollect! to access additional information. |
| TraceError | Provides information about a node in a trace file that has been identified as an occurrence of a system error or warning. This object is assigned a TraceActivityNode object that has the activity type ActError! to access additional information. |

# An Analysis Example

As you might have noticed, the objects listed in Tables 23.1 through 23.3 have a lot in common and are used depending on what type of analysis you're attempting. Listing 23.2 shows some sample code that uses these types of objects by writing output into a DataWindow as a trace file is read. Notice that this example also introduces some of the trace functions: `Open()`, `Close()`, and `NextActivity()`.

**LISTING 23.2**   Interpreting a Trace File

```
TraceFile ltf_Trace
TraceActivityNode ltan_Node
ErrorReturn ler_Return


ltf_Trace = Create TraceFile


ler_Return = tfTrace.Open( "c:\run.pbp")


If ler_Return <> Success! Then
   MessageBox( "Trace File Open", "Unable to open the trace file!", &
            StopSign!, OK!)
   Return
End If


// Collection Time
sle_collection_time.text = String(ltf_Trace.CollectionTime)
// Num Activities
sle_no_of_activities.text = String(ltf_Trace.NumberOfActivities)


ltan_Node = ltf_Trace.NextActivity()


Do While IsValid (ltan_Node)
   lRow = dw_1.InsertRow(0)

   Choose Case ltan_Node.ActivityType
      Case ActBegin!
         TraceBeginEnd tbeNode

         tbeNode = ltan_Node
         dw_1.Object.string1[lrow] = "Begin"
         dw_1.Object.string2[lrow] = tbeNode.Message
         dw_1.Object.long1[lrow] = tbeNode.TimerValue
```

**LISTING 23.2**   CONTINUED

```
      Case ActError!
         TraceError teNode

         teNode = ltan_Node
         dw_1.Object.string1[lrow] = "Error"
         dw_1.Object.string2[lrow] = teNode.Message
         dw_1.Object.long1[lrow] = teNode.TimerValue
         dw_1.Object.long2[lrow] = teNode.Severity
      Case ActESQL!
         // MessageBox( "", "ESQL")
      Case ActGarbageCollect!
         // MessageBox( "", "GarbageCollect")
      Case ActLine!
         //MessageBox( "", "Line")
      Case ActObjectCreate!
         //MessageBox( "", ""Create")
      Case ActObjectDestroy!
         //MessageBox( "", "Destroy")
      Case ActProfile!
         //MessageBox( "", "Profile")
      Case ActRoutine!
         TraceRoutine trNode

         trNode = ltan_Node
         dw_1.Object.string1[lrow] = "Routine"
         dw_1.Object.string2[lrow] = trNode.ClassName
         dw_1.Object.long1[lrow] = trNode.TimerValue
      Case ActTrace!
         //MessageBox( "", "Trace")
      Case ActUser!
         //MessageBox( "", "User")
   End Choose

   ltan_Node = ltf_Trace.NextActivity()
Loop

ltf_Trace.Close()
```

# Modeling Functions

To supplement the functions that extract the data from a trace file, you can use a number of functions to build and modify models. These functions operate on the `Profiling` or `TraceTree` objects.

Use the `BuildModel()` function to build a performance-analysis or trace-tree model from a trace file. By using optional parameters to the function, you can monitor the progress of the build or even interrupt it. The syntax follows:

```
BuildModel( { ProgressObject, EventName, TriggerPercent})
```

`ProgressObject` is a PowerObject that contains the `EventName` to be used to communicate process progress. `TriggerPercent` specifies the number of activities that should be processed before triggering the `EventName` event of the `ProgressObject` object. These optional arguments are necessary only if you want to monitor the building of the model and then interrupt it if the process is taking too long.

The event `EventName` must be defined as taking two Long data type parameters. The first parameter accepts the number of the current activity; the second parameter accepts the total number of activities recorded in the trace file. If you want the event to fire for every activity, set `TriggerPercent` to `0`; if you never want the event to fire, set the value higher than `100`. You can cancel the build by returning a `FALSE` value from this event.

Before you can call the `BuildModel()` function, you must indicate the trace file to be modeled by using the `SetTraceFileName()` function:

```
SetTraceFileName( FileName)
```

This function returns a `Success!` value if it opened the trace file for reading.

Following along with the credo that whatever you create you also must destroy, after you finish with the model constructed by `BuildModel()`, use the `DestroyModel()` function to clean up any resources used.

`SystemRoutine( RefRoutine)` returns by reference the routine node that is the system root of the model. This function is used with the `Profiling` object.

A number of functions provide information about the analysis or trace-tree models in the form of lists:

- `ClassList( RefList[])` returns, by reference, a list of the classes in the analysis model. You should call this `Profiling` object function with an unbounded array of type `ProfileClass`. Each array element is a `ProfileClass` object that provides class information, and the elements are stored in the array in no particular order. The following code extracts a list of the classes from a model:

**23**

Configuring and
Tuning

```
ProfileClass lpc_ClassList[]
Profiling lp_Model

lp_Model = Create Profiling
lp_Model.BuildModel()

lp_Model.ClassList(lpc_ClassList)
```

- RoutineList( *RefList*[]) returns, by reference, a list of the routines in the analysis model and can be called on the Profiling or ProfileClass objects. The array must be declared as an unbounded array of type ProfileRoutine. The class objects' creation and destruction are indicated by a routine in this list, as are Embedded SQL statements.

- IncomingCallList( *RefList*[], *AggregateDupes*) returns, by reference, a list of the callers of a routine in the model and is used with the ProfileRoutine object. The array must be declared as an unbounded array of type ProfileCall. The second argument, *AggregateDupes*, is a Boolean that controls whether duplicate routine calls are entered into the array once (TRUE) or multiple times (FALSE). *Aggregate-Dupes* has no effect if line tracing wasn't enabled during the trace.

```
Long ll_Routine, ll_TotalRoutines
ProfileCall lpc_Calls[]
ProfileRoutine lpr_List[]
Profiling lp_Model

lp_Model.BuildModel( )
lp_Model.RoutineList (lpr_List)
ll_TotalRoutines = UpperBound (lpr_List)

For ll_Routine = 1 To ll_TotalRoutines
  prList[ll_Routine].IncomingCallList (lpc_Calls, TRUE)
  // Process the entries in prCalls[]
Next
```

- LineList( *RefList*[]) returns, by reference, a list of the lines in a routine in the model and is used with the ProfileRoutine object. The array must be declared as an unbounded array of type ProfileLine. This array, unlike the others, is in actual line order of the routine.

> **Caution**
>
> Lines aren't returned for database statements and objects, or if line information wasn't logged in the trace file.

- OutgoingCallList( *RefList*[], *AggregateDupes*) returns, by reference, a list of the calls to other routines in a routine in the analysis model and is used with the ProfileRoutine or ProfileLine objects. The array must be declared as an unbounded array of type ProfileCall. The *AggregateDupes* argument works in the same manner as for the IncomingCallList() function.

- EntryList( *RefList*[]) returns, by reference, a list of the top-level entries in a trace-tree model and is used with the TraceTree object. The array must be declared as unbounded and of type TraceTreeNode. The following example extracts a top-level list of nodes in a trace tree:

```
TraceTree ttModel
TraceTreeNode ttnList[]

ttModel = Create TraceTree
ttModel.BuildModel()

ttModel.EntryList (ttnList)
```

- GetChildrenList (*RefList*[]) returns, by reference, a list of the children of a routine in a trace-tree model. This function can be used with the TraceTreeObject, TraceTreeRoutine, and TraceTreeGarbageCollect objects. The array must be declared as unbounded and of type TraceTreeNode. When GetChildrenList() is called for TraceTreeGarbageCollect objects, each array element usually signifies the destruction of a garbage-collected object.

**23**

Configuring and Tuning

# Summary

Numerous places can be focal points for tuning. This chapter pointed out some techniques to help make your PowerBuilder application run more smoothly. It also introduced PowerBuilder's profiling tool for tracking application performance. Make sure that you and other project team members configure all the components (that is, server, network, client, software, and hardware) in your client/server application. By doing so, you will provide a product that you can be proud of and your users will love.

# CHAPTER 24

# Frameworks and Class Libraries

Whether you build your own, work from someone else's, or purchase a commercial package, frameworks and class libraries can accelerate your development and reduce your debugging and maintenance time. Frameworks and class libraries are completely different animals; you might be working with what you think is a framework without realizing that it is, in fact, a class library. You need to decide which approach will work best for the project you're developing because each has advantages and disadvantages. Frameworks, however, provide many more advantages, so most of this chapter deals with that subject.

Before you start, consider that a true object incorporates attributes, services, and methods, and it can be inherited. Some PowerBuilder "objects" don't conform to this definition. When you see the word *object*, though, you should interpret it as a general description that encompasses windows, structures, functions, and the rest of PowerBuilder's objects and controls.

# A New Philosophy

Most developers must adjust their perspective on design and implementation methods; they must switch from having a project view to having a component (object) view. This is an important change for developers to make and will be what drives and directs the effort put into building and maintaining an organizationwide framework.

A developer's focus shifts slightly away from the department and now considers how an object might be constructed to benefit development work on an organization level. The time taken to create a department-level application also includes time invested in the modification and refinement of the framework used. This is when you really start to reuse objects rather than simply copy "good" objects from one project to the next.

The following sections discuss spotting and creating objects that should be part of your framework, as well as what methods and mechanisms are available to develop these objects in an object-oriented manner.

## Class Libraries

A *class library* is a collection of objects independent of each other that usually can be used without any other object in the library. Each object is essentially a black box with defined inputs and known outputs or effects, which allows you to plug and play easily. Because the objects in the class library are black boxes, you must code as much functionality and flexibility into them as possible. This means that the objects generally are much larger than they would be in a framework because you have to provide additional parameters to switch functionality on and off.

Class libraries rarely, if at all, impose any kind of interface standards on developers. Each object might have an interface consistent with the others, but there is little or no method for enforcing these standards.

The objects in a class library usually consist of the following:

- General-purpose functions, such as for string handling and conversion

- A concrete level of standard controls, most of them containing general-purpose code

- Standalone windows, such as Print and Import/Export dialogs

- An abstract level of windows, such as frames, dialogs, and sheets (but these libraries start to become hybrids, as discussed later in the "Hybrids" section)

Throughout this book, you've learned about windows, objects, and functions that you easily can add to a class library. Each element is independent of the others and has no external requirements on an application.

# Frameworks

*Frameworks* also are collections of objects, but because of their tight coupling, they can't be used outside the framework. *Coupling* describes the relationships between objects. Tight coupling usually is due to global and object instance variables, object-level functions, and object attributes. Developers construct each object with the intention of inheriting and expanding the functionality. In contrast to class libraries, a framework object is a white box; developers have access to the internal workings and can modify them if necessary.

By using a framework, you provide a foundation for all developers to work from; this usually leads to a consistent interface for applications built from the same framework.

Objects within a framework are built on specific application tasks—for example, managing the application object, database connections, and business rules. A framework is built to use explicit references to other objects. Therefore, the code will be much tighter and faster because you won't provide for all cases developers might require (which you would have to do if the object were in a class library).

Frameworks can provide too much functionality, and you end up hiding controls and overriding excessive numbers of scripts to carry out simple tasks. On certain occasions, it's more appropriate to copy and override some code rather than inherit and extend it. The point at which you need to do this depends on the functionality you want and the way in which you can achieve that from the framework with a minimum of code. The advantages of frameworks generally outweigh these factors, and with careful and considered design, you can minimize these effects.

With a framework, you can tackle a system by breaking down the areas into problem domains:

- The *user-interface*domain deals with the look and feel of the application by providing standard controls in a consistent way.

- The *business* domain encompasses the business rules and logic required for the system.

- The *system* domain provides the management of the application, including object communication, database access and processing, and other system tasks and processing.

As you already might have realized, probably only the user and system domains are reusable parts of the framework. Business domains generally are application-specific and provide some reusability only if you're constructing an application suite within the same problem domain.

## Hybrids

Hybrids of class libraries and frameworks also exist. These hybrids provide for your application's loosely coupled, standalone objects, in addition to some objects that require tight coupling. These kinds of tools tend to be homegrown affairs built to tackle a particular type of project or to fit a certain type of development group. Most often, these tools start out as a sharable library of objects, and as the project progresses, existing objects start to be coupled, and new ones are added.

Many experienced PowerBuilder developers find commercial frameworks to be restrictive and to carry too much overhead. These developers use a solid class library and build a framework based on that library per the requirements of the problem domain. This approach has a number of obvious advantages:

- Developers have a deep understanding of the objects available and the ways in which they're used.

- The framework easily can be extended. With commercial frameworks, you often are left wondering how future releases of the product will affect existing development work.

- Developers have a stake in providing the most optimal and useful objects—they will be the users of them.

- The framework doesn't carry the unused components that most frameworks do.

So how can you tell what you have? If you can take an object and use it by itself in another application, you might have a class library. If you can do this with all the objects, you definitely have a class library. Otherwise, you have a hybrid. Don't include global functions in this testing process, because they will mostly be transportable between applications regardless of their origins.

---

**Note**

Since the introduction of the PowerBuilder Foundation Class (PFC), the service-based architecture (SBA) has become *the* way to construct PowerBuilder applications. An SBA is constructed around a number of class objects that define specific classes that can be defined and used by visual objects and other class objects. This way, you can create thin objects and use only the functionality you need and nothing more. Chapter 25, "The PowerBuilder Foundation Class," includes a full discussion and description of this architecture.

---

# Building a Framework

Now that you understand what frameworks and class libraries are, you probably can see the benefits of building or purchasing a framework. In the following sections, you see some of the requirements and structures involved in building a framework. You can use the same information in your evaluation and determination of which commercial framework to buy.

## Classes

A *class* can be considered a template from which other objects are created. In fact, it can be a collection of objects that share similar attributes and behaviors. Every PowerBuilder object is based on a class (for example, all user objects are of the class UserObject).

According to Grady Booch, of the five types of classes, two are appropriate for use with PowerBuilder: abstract and concrete. The *abstract* class is purely a definition and is never instantiated and used. A *concrete* class object usually is inherited from an abstract class object. The concrete class is an instantiation of an abstract class and provides the objects that actually will be used in an application. In your libraries, try to differentiate between abstract and concrete classes by their placement in different PBL files or by their names.

An *instance* is an embodiment or one representation of a class, and the class is said to be *instantiated*. Depending on the method that instantiated a class, you can create multiple instances of the same class. The following code, for example, shows both methods of instantiating a window class:

24

Frameworks and
Class Libraries

```
w_sheet lw_Instance, lw_Instance2
//
// Open one instance of the class w_sheet
OpenSheet( lw_Instance, w_frame)
//
// Open a second instance of the class w_sheet
OpenSheet( lw_Instance2, w_frame)
//
// Open the one and only one direct instance of class w_report. Note: we can
// still declare a variable of type w_report and open the window as we do above
OpenSheet( w_report, w_frame)
```

A class definition incorporates attributes, services, and methods, which are all properties you uncover during an object-oriented design and analysis phase. *Attributes* contain information about the class and its current state; you add to the attributes predefined by PowerBuilder by using object-level instance variables. Controls placed in another object also become attributes of the parent object. The *services* of a class provide a defined functionality available to objects external to the class. *Methods* are provided to implement the services provided by the class; in PowerBuilder, this is achieved through events and functions.

# Abstraction

*Abstraction* is the process of designing and implementing high-level objects. This removes the complexities of the exact way in which the functionality is implemented and allows you to define the interface components of the object to be used in performing the function. This process helps you create more stable and flexible abstract class objects that use polymorphism, encapsulation, and inheritance.

# Polymorphism

*Polymorphism* is a technique that enables a single operation to have different effects on different objects. You also could look at polymorphism as objects reacting differently to the same message. This technique is an important part of building a framework; it's usually implemented by using functions, but you can get a form of polymorphism by using message events.

At the abstract class level, the function might contain code, but usually it is a virtual function. A *virtual function* means that the function is named and the parameters are specified, as is the return data type. The function does nothing except return a default value, if one is required. The concrete classes provide the actual code and also can redefine the input or output parameters. You write virtual functions in an abstract object so that other objects can make calls to methods for any concrete classes based on that abstract class.

The calling object uses the abstract object as a data type and then can reference the method for any derived concrete classes. All the MDI sheets for an application (suppose that there are two types: w_mfg_sheet and w_stock_sheet), for example, are inherited from an abstract class, w_sheet. In the application, you can find the active sheet and assign it to a variable of type w_sheet and then make calls to methods that were prototyped in the abstract class and coded in the concrete classes.

## Function Overriding

After you define a virtual function, you redeclare the same function at the descendant levels with the same name, parameters, and return type. Within this descendant-level function, you actually carry out the required functionality. This is known as *function overriding*.

## Function Overloading

Another alternative is to overload the function. You can overload functions in two ways:

- Use inheritance. At each level, the function can be redeclared with the same name but different parameters. The function then can be called for an object, and the parameters passed will determine which function is to be executed.

- Overload at the same level, to save from resorting to multiple inheritance levels. TriggerEvent() is an example of an overloaded PowerBuilder function.

Another form of polymorphism is class-based, with a number of different abstract classes defining the same function. Examples of this exist throughout the PowerBuilder object structure; for example, the Paste() function is defined for DataWindow and SingleLineEdit (among others) but not at the next level up (DragObject), which is the ancestor to both. This form forces you to repeat your code for each class, which certainly is less desirable.

## Encapsulation

*Encapsulation* is the process of hiding the workings of an object. It's implemented by using the Private and Protected keywords in variable and function declarations. Objects contain all the information they need to know about themselves and how other objects will interact with them, which enables the object to become independent of other objects. All an object's variables should be declared as one of these two types. No Public variables should be declared. To provide access to a variable, code Get() and Set() functions so that you can validate the value being set and to carry out additional actions if required after changing the variable. As you might have already guessed, this also helps you debug your code because you can place a breakpoint in the Set() function and trace back to each caller to see which one is affecting the variable.

# Inheritance

*Inheritance* is the mechanism that makes a framework operate and uses previously defined qualities. Inheritance enables an object to incorporate the definition of another object into its own definition. PowerBuilder enables you to inherit from windows, menus, and user objects. As you saw earlier, when you construct a window/menu/user object, you're inheriting from the appropriate abstract class. There must also be a determination of what type of inheritance tree you will build for each class (see Figure 24.1).

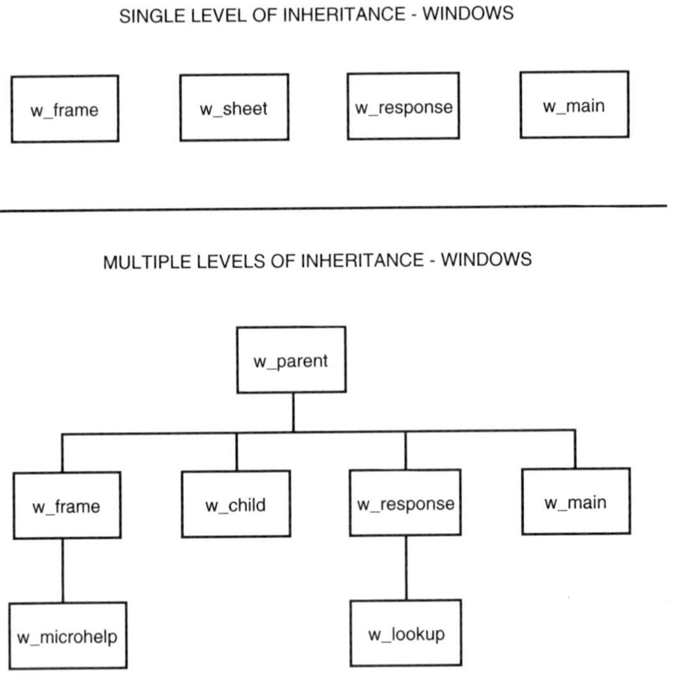

**FIGURE 24.1**

*The levels of inheritance for windows.*

SINGLE LEVEL OF INHERITANCE - WINDOWS

| w_frame | w_sheet | w_response | w_main |
| --- | --- | --- | --- |

MULTIPLE LEVELS OF INHERITANCE - WINDOWS

w_parent

w_frame    w_child    w_response    w_main

w_microhelp    w_lookup

With a single chain of inheritance, it's easy to construct an insulation layer (see "Insulation Layers" later in this chapter) and indicate from which class object an object should inherit. However, because of the object's single-mindedness, functionality that might not be required will be present. This redundant code will need to be maintained between the related classes. The objects are coded as solving all problems but being masters of none.

With multiple inheritance levels, the objects are more specific to a task and methods. With a single chain of inheritance, you can place attributes and events at the correct level in the inheritance tree instead of at inopportune or duplicate levels.

Suppose that you need to add a new function or attribute to all related objects. You would have to tackle it in different ways, depending on the inheritance type. With a single level, you would have to code the same modification in each object of the related classes (the class-based polymorphism discussed earlier). For multiple inheritance levels, you can truly use the inheritance and code it at the ancestor level, which was the first type of polymorphism discussed (it's known as *inclusion polymorphism*).

So far, this chapter hasn't addressed inheritance in PowerBuilder object terms. In PowerBuilder, only windows, user objects, and menus can be inherited. Menus can provide some performance problems when placed on windows within an inheritance chain, or if they're inherited from classes and used. Try to keep menu inheritance to no more than two levels at most, and be wary of defining menus for abstract classes or concrete classes from which you're inheriting.

You've just seen single and multiple levels of inheritance for windows. Next, you see how menus fit into this scheme (see Figure 24.2).

**FIGURE 24.2**
*The levels of inheritance for menus.*

ONE LEVEL OF INHERITANCE - MENUS

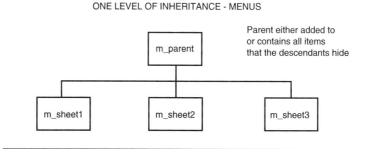

MULTIPLE LEVELS OF INHERITANCE - MENUS

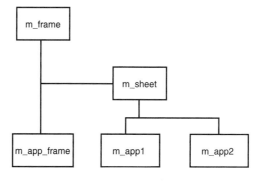

> **Note**
>
> Remember this one piece of information: When a menu item is made invisible at runtime, the whole menu is destroyed and reconstructed. Thus, if you make numerous changes to a menu, you will take some performance hits. Keep it simple or keep it visible! Although PowerBuilder's more recent versions have made some significant performance gains in the area of menus, it's still something to keep in mind.

The diagram in Figure 24.2 doesn't conform with the ideas of the object-oriented approach. Menus can be considered to be window attributes; if you look at some existing menus, notice that they usually are tied closely with one particular window class. Therefore, your framework's menu hierarchies should closely match those of the windows they operate against (see Figure 24.3).

**FIGURE 24.3**
*The levels of inheritance for menus as they relate to windows.*

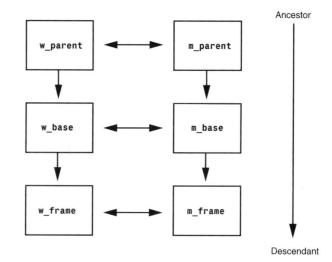

## Memory Management

Classes, instances, and inheritance all profoundly affect the way available memory is used. It's important to understand how PowerBuilder manages memory when allocating resources for objects.

When a request is made to create a class instance, PowerBuilder allocates memory to hold the class definition (only on the first instance of the class to be created) and then allocates the memory for the instance to use. The memory used by the instance is for its instance variables and objects. On subsequent requests to create a class instance, only the memory required for the instance needs to be allocated. When an instance is destroyed, the memory allocated for just the instance is released.

Consider what happens when you start an application. First, PowerBuilder must load the application object, which is a descendant of the PowerObject class. This means that PowerBuilder must load the PowerObject class and allocate memory for it before loading the application object. The first window or menu created causes the GraphicObject class to be loaded, followed by the Window or Menu class, respectively, then the window or menu object class, and finally the instance of the class. Consider the example in Figure 24.4, which creates an instance of the window w_connect (in this example, the first window to be opened in the application).

**FIGURE 24.4**
*Memory alloca-tions during a window's creation.*

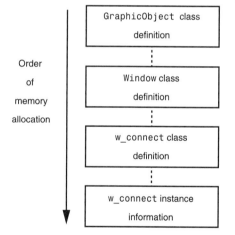

By carefully considering your framework's hierarchy tree and applications, you can anticipate memory requirements and class use. Plan on loading heavily-used class hierarchies as soon as you can to improve performance as the application is used.

# Object Relationships

*Object relationships* are the particular properties that set frameworks apart from class libraries. The relationship can be based on association or ownership.

24

Frameworks and
Class Libraries

With an *associative* relationship, either object can exist without the other, and the actual relationship is achieved by using reference variables (a pointer). This type of relationship can be constructed as one-way or two-way, with one object or both maintaining a pointer to the other. When you open two different windows, for example, such as w_mfg_sheet and w_stock_sheet, PowerBuilder creates a global variable for each. This enables w_stock_sheet to reference w_mfg_sheet and vice versa. Within a framework, however, you must code this kind of behavior yourself and not rely on PowerBuilder's global help. This type of relationship enables many different objects to access one another.

An *ownership-based* (or aggregate) relationship is one in which an object can't exist without another object. The second object is the owner object. As with the associative relationship, this type of relationship also is usually implemented with reference variables. The best example is a control on a window; the window can exist without the control, but the control requires the window for its existence. The control is placed in the Control[] array attribute of the window, and this array provides the reference variable to the control. The owning object then is obligated to create and destroy the dependent object.

## Making Sense of It All

You've been given many definitions and much advice in the past few sections, but how does this help you construct your application?

Your first step is to explore any accessible existing systems or prototypes. By extracting common functionality and requirements from these, you begin the process of building an abstraction or an abstract class layer. This is where you impose a consistent look and feel to all objects, especially if you've pulled code from various applications. Usually, when different project teams have created the applications, various coding and notation standards exist. Extracting common functionality into an abstract class gives you an ideal opportunity to standardize the code and carry out a code walkthrough at the same time. This code walkthrough gives you a chance to look at any optimizations or improvements in encapsulation that can be made.

The abstract class should include an MDI frame, a main window and a sheet window, menus for the MDI frame and sheet windows, and all the controls as standard user objects. Probably the most important of all is the DataWindow user object.

I can't stress enough how important it is to provide standard user objects for all the controls and to use those instead of the controls directly available in the Window painter. This way, you can extend your objects' functionality easily and with minimal changes to existing objects and code. This capability is important when you don't initially know what functionality belongs in the ancestor object, and it enables you to include and extend the object at a later date.

From this stage on, you should have a firm idea of who will be using the framework—whether it will be a single team, the whole department, or the whole enterprise. This will affect the type of code placed at each level of the object inheritance tree. For single teams or departments, redundant code easily can be moved higher up the inheritance tree and more often than not will be used. At the Enterprise level, however, keep the upper levels of the inheritance tree as generic as possible. You also might provide a slightly different inheritance tree because the additional abstract classes (mentioned in the next section) can't be department-specific. The investment in time and effort will be much greater to provide a good framework that everyone can use effectively. You might have come across the object-oriented term *thin objects*—this is what the term means.

From the abstract class windows, you also might want to inherit additional function- or type-based abstract class windows. This could be a window that does master/detail browsing, for example, or a window that defines the way in which all response windows will appear. Don't produce type-based abstract class objects just for the sake of doing it. If you're going to make an abstract `w_response` window for all dialogs, add something more to it than just setting the `WindowType` attribute to `Response`. With each abstract object, try to encapsulate as much as possible. An ideal way to do this is to set up messages on the window that its controls can call to carry out communication between this window and other windows or objects.

## Insulation Layers

For enterprise-level frameworks, the additional abstract classes may contain an extra layer that provides a buffer between the top-level object and a department's object (see Figure 24.5). Insulation layers also are used often as a buffer between a purchased framework and departmental objects.

The objects in the insulation layer are part of an *insulation class*, which also is an abstract class. This class effectively provides a department-level version of the master abstract class so that department-specific code can be added and other scripts can inherit from it.

As mentioned earlier, you should provide a standard class user object for each control type and must impress on the development team that it should use these objects instead of the normal controls accessible in the painter. These user objects provide a consistent 2D or 3D look and the same font, font size, coloring, and labeling. Internally, these objects contain common code that you always will add, such as a `SetTransObject()` call in the `Constructor` event for a DataWindow.

Insulation layers are important and are an integral method you should use to create a flexible framework. Consider the additional code and/or development group control that would be required to implement the departmental solutions shown in Figure 24.5.

**FIGURE 24.5**
*An enterprise-wide framework.*

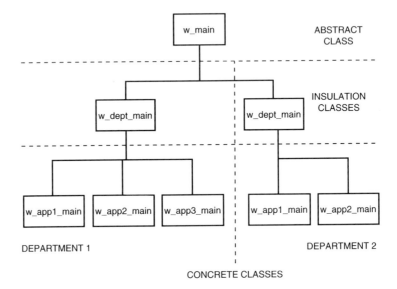

## Object Coupling

The method used for communicating between objects can profoundly affect the framework and the way in which it's used. For tightly coupled objects, use direct referencing and functions; for loosely coupled objects, use indirect referencing, pronouns, PowerBuilder functions, and messages. There is a trade-off between having objects loosely coupled, which enables them to be more easily dropped in place, and the performance gains that come from direct references between objects.

Whether the referencing is direct or indirect, the pointer created by PowerBuilder takes up four words of memory (a *word* is the number of bits treated as a unit by the computer hardware). This occurs whether the pointer is to a window, a DataWindow, or simply a command button. The pointer retains information about the class to which it's pointing, which PowerBuilder relies on during compilation within the Script painter. If you try to access an attribute of the object that doesn't belong to that class, the compilation fails.

## Direct Referencing

*Direct referencing* uses the actual name of the object to carry out some processing involving the object—for example, `Open (w_mfg_sheet)`. After this particular operation is done, the object `w_mfg_sheet` can be used anywhere in the application. This obviously works only if the object is opened once; you will run into problems if you try to open additional instances of the window because the global pointer points at the last instance opened. This kind of behavior is undesirable in a framework and can lead to problems.

# Indirect Referencing

Frameworks use *indirect referencing* to operate generically on an arbitrary object as directed by the application. These reference variables can be assigned from the pronoun keywords or other reference variables that usually are passed as parameters to the object.

When using reference variables, you must make sure that the variable is declared of the expected type. If you execute the following code, for example, you get a compilation error:

```
Window lw_MfgSheet

lw_MfgSheet = w_mfg_sheet

lw_MfgSheet.of_SaveOrder()
```

This happens because PowerBuilder has used the class definition of the variable and not the class referenced by the variable. To fix this, you would use this code:

```
w_mfg_sheet lw_MfgSheet

lw_MfgSheet = w_mfg_sheet

lw_MfgSheet.of_SaveOrder()
```

Look at the second line of both pieces of code. Until the variable is referenced to an object, it points at nothing, and you get `Null Object` error messages.

As long as you have a way to get to a created object, you don't need to maintain a pointer to it. You can reach MDI sheets through `GetSheet()` and `GetNextSheet()`, for example. Within objects, you can use the pronouns `This`, `Parent`, `Super`, and `ParentWindow`. This is the preferred way to reference all objects, and you can use the pronouns to pass reference pointers to other objects. The function declaration must be set to pass by value because you can't use pronouns when the parameter is by reference. For more information on how to use pronouns, see Chapter 7, "The PowerScript Language."

Remember that object types other than windows also can be used as reference variables, but they require that you use the `Create` command to instantiate the object. Also remember that you can't make object assignments directly from one reference variable to another if the objects come from different levels of the inheritance chain. If the object `n_transaction_oe` is inherited from `n_transaction`, for example, the following compiles but produces a `cannot assign` error at runtime:

```
n_transaction trCustomers
n_transaction_oe trSoldTo
```

```
trCustomers = Create n_transaction
trSoldTo = trCustomers
```

The statement made in the preceding paragraph isn't strictly true. You can make assignments within the inheritance chain if they occur going back up the tree, as in this example:

```
n_transaction trCustomers
n_transaction_oe trSoldTo


trCustomers = Create n_transaction_oe
trSoldTo = trCustomers
```

## Object Communication

Now that you know how to obtain references to other objects, how do you communicate requests between the objects? You can use messages or direct function calls. Again, this gets back into loose and tight coupling. Of course, you can use a message to request that the receiving object execute one of its own functions.

Events execute from the topmost ancestor on down the inheritance chain to the descendant, unless you've set Event Override to On. If you send a message to an object that's not set up to receive it, you won't get a runtime error, and the object will do nothing.

Object-level functions are used to *strongly type* the request (ensure that the correct function is called). If the function's *signature* (function name and arguments) doesn't match that of the called function, the ancestor chain is traversed from the descendant up until it's matched.

You can specify functions that override or overload at each level of the inheritance chain (starting at the first inherited level). Overriding a function requires you to define a function with the same name, arguments, and return value. You then code the function to carry out some behavior different from that of the ancestor. With function overloading, you call the function the same name, but you alter the number and type of arguments.

> **Note**
>
> You can't overload the return type of a function.

Using functions or events provides the initiation of a conversation, but the whole idea is to pass information to, and sometimes from, the other object.

> **Tip**
>
> Remember that you can use the keyword `Dynamic` to allow looser coupling at development time, but it will be checked at runtime.

Functions, as you already know, can receive and return values during a call. Access to functions (except global functions) can be as open or as restricted as you want, using the `Public`, `Protected`, and `Private` declarations. Events, on the other hand, are always `Public`.

You will use events and functions in your framework, but you should choose the correct candidate for the job. Here are some tips for selecting the method to use:

| *Requirement* | *Method* |
| --- | --- |
| Strong data typing | Function or parameterized events |
| Passing values back and forth | Function or parameterized events |
| Controlling access | Function |
| Loose coupling | Event (not parameterized) |
| Extendibility lower | Event in inheritance chain |

When you use an event or a function and want to pass a number of values, there are many different ways to do it:

- Parameters to the event/function

- Global variables or application instance variables

- Single or multiple global structures

- A hidden window used only for communication purposes

- A class (nonvisual) user object

Obviously, the first and the last methods are more object-oriented, because control can be placed on the modification and retrieval of values.

## What Does Object Coupling Provide?

What does all this mean for your framework? If you've declared attributes at a high enough level, you can use a base class as the reference variable data type instead of a specific object. This enables you to use generic data type reference variables to affect a wider range of objects than if the variable has to be declared using a set class.

Remember one more thing before you continue to the next section. The `PowerObject` data type is the ancestor of all objects; when you use loose coupling, you can use `TriggerEvent()` and related functions to cause actions to be performed easily when using control or object arrays.

# Including Objects in a Framework

Not all objects or functions belong in a framework. Some that you already may have included may themselves have missing links in their own class structures. The following questions can be broken into two areas: Is the object complete? Is the object necessary?

| Question | Solution |
|----------|----------|
| Does the object share the same or similar functionality with another object? | Create a superclass object that you can use to inherit this and other objects from that contains the duplicate functionality. |
| Does the object fail to carry out a well-defined function? Is it trying to perform more than one role? | Determine whether the object can be broken into more distinct pieces. Revisiting the abstraction design for this object also might be worthwhile to see whether you can clean up the object's definition. |
| Does the object rely on many other objects to complete its own task? Are these supporting objects used by other objects? | Determine whether these objects can or should be combined into one object. This will be determined by the functionality being implemented. If the objects are self-contained and reusable, they can be left alone. |
| Does the object have more than a few attributes and methods? | Consider whether the object is actually necessary. |
| Does the object contain redundant functionality? Is the same functionality available in other objects? | Consider whether the object is actually necessary. |

The careful analysis of a problem domain and the design of object-oriented solutions will help you create and include good objects into your framework.

# Maintaining a Framework

When the framework is in use, you must treat any enhancements and additions to it with the greatest of care. Although adding a new function or other attribute to an object is easy, when you're modifying existing code and attributes, you must ensure that any changes appear seamless to inherited objects and developers.

Don't feel that it's dangerous or unnecessary to examine and update the framework objects, however, because this step is necessary in ongoing framework support and maintenance. Consider all the requests that come back from the development teams, but carefully consider the modifications and their implications before making a change.

Although a number of people might have been involved in writing the framework initially, the task of maintaining and modifying the code should be restricted to a single person: the framework guardian (*object administrator* and *reuse coordinator* are just two other titles for the same duty). The original members of the framework-development team will return to specific projects and can't be relied on to give subjective views of the needs of a framework, and they rarely will have the time to spend making carefully considered changes. The guardian also will be responsible for maintaining versions of the framework so that if a disastrous change is made, it can be quickly and painlessly reversed, and the old copy can be reinstated. The guardian's other duties include keeping good communications channels open between the various development teams, informing the teams of changes and additions to the objects, making modifications to objects, removing old code and objects, and reviewing and updating object code.

Having a guardian in place shouldn't exclude the original developers or other project members from contributing to the framework. Indeed, you ideally will set up regular meetings for discussion of problems, missing functionality, or enhancements that the project teams actually using the framework in their developing have come across. These items then can be discussed in a cross-team effort.

# Other Considerations

Whatever methods you use to construct your framework, keep in mind that simple structures can lead to elegant products. Try to keep your inheritance trees under control and not too deep (around five or six levels is manageable). This will help your development teams in the long run and will make their debugging exercises that much easier.

**24**

**Frameworks and Class Libraries**

Documentation can't be stressed enough. If you construct your own objects, document them with the intention of making it easy for developers to pick up an object and drop it into an application with a minimum of fuss.

> **Tip**
>
> To incorporate the documentation for a window or user object into the object itself, declare a `ue_Documentation` user event and place the text there. Now that's true encapsulation!

The hierarchy of the PowerBuilder objects themselves provides a good base of investigation and learning. You can view this hierarchy in the PowerBuilder Object Browser by selecting the System tab page and enabling the Hierarchy check box. From this list, you can see how and why objects are inherited and superclassed; it provides good indicators for your own framework.

> **Note**
>
> Even commercial frameworks aren't above changing the hierarchy structure. For example, PowerBuilder at one point moved `DynamicDescriptionArea`, `DynamicStagingArea`, `Error`, `MailSession`, and `Message` under a new superclass, `NonVisualObject`.

Your framework will be only as good as the time and resources you devote to it.

# Commercial Products

If the previous sections have been sufficient to dissuade you from constructing your own framework, you probably are thinking about buying a commercial framework. The advantages of commercial products are that they are prebuilt and include pretested code. You get full documentation, tutorials, usually technical support, and even training if you require it. Sybase provides its own framework, the PowerBuilder Foundation Class (PFC). This framework has become the de facto standard in creating framework-based PowerBuilder applications. Even so, several commercial frameworks and class libraries are in the marketplace from Sybase partners such as ServerLogic and Greenbriar & Russell.

You can use your knowledge from the previous sections to help you determine the worth that one of these frameworks or class libraries can add to your development effort. A number of framework and class library vendors now are producing PFC extension libraries instead of or in addition to their own products. A list of these vendors and their products can be found on the Sybase Web site (www.sybase.com).

# PowerBuilder Foundation Class Library

The PowerBuilder Foundation Class Library is from Sybase Corporation. The Application Library is provided as part of the Professional and Enterprise Editions of PowerBuilder and consists of software and a reference book/tutorial.

The PowerBuilder Foundation Class is written in PowerBuilder using all the same objects and PowerScript to which every developer has access. The product draws on the many object-oriented coding techniques that apply to PowerBuilder and features a thorough service-oriented architecture. Service-based architectures enable applications to use only the necessary amount of computer resources and provide an as-needed functionality model for developers to code against.

PFC isolates related types of processing into groups that it calls *services*. Most services are implemented as custom class user objects and include the following:

| | |
|---|---|
| Window services | DBMS services |
| DataWindow services | Date and time services |
| File services | String services |

The major advantage of this approach is that you control which services you load and use, thus minimizing application overhead. Development is easier for using and extending the services and enables you to build simple as well as complex applications using the same techniques. PFC uses the auto-instantiating feature for custom class user objects, so you don't even have to worry about cleaning up services after you finish with them and the service leaves scope.

The PFC consists of a set of five main PBLs, which you must include in any PFC-based application's search path. These PBLs contain ancestor objects and other important objects used by PFC:

| | |
|---|---|
| PFCMAIN.PBL | Basic PFC services |
| PFCAPSRV.PBL | Application manager and application services |
| PFCDWSRV.PBL | DataWindow services |

| PFCUTIL.PBL | Utility services |
| PFCWNSRV.PBL | Window services |

These libraries aren't intended to be modified by anyone but Sybase, and you have to use extension-level libraries.

Because no class library can meet your development needs straight out of the box, Sybase has designed an extension layer. If you modify the top-level objects to integrate some applicationwide functionality, for example, when Sybase releases the next version of PFC, all your changes will be gone. This would force you to manually reapply your changes.

Objects in the extension level are unmodified descendants of the corresponding objects in the ancestor library. You customize your application to use PFC by modifying objects at this extension level, as well as by inheriting from such objects. Sybase provides five extension-level libraries that match the ancestor libraries: PFEMAIN.PBL, PFEAPSRV.PBL, PFEDWSRV.PBL, PFEUTIL.PBL, and PFEWNSRV.PBL.

All in all, the PowerBuilder Foundation Class appears to be a well-thought-out and well-constructed framework, and its use should become second nature to many PowerBuilder developers. For more information, see Chapter 25, "The PowerBuilder Foundation Class."

# Summary

By using a framework or a class library, you can increase the end-user community's involvement in the prototyping stages of an application because of the rapid development and changes that can be made. Frameworks and class libraries provide increased quality and more reliable applications that are much easier to maintain.

# The PowerBuilder Foundation Class

Chapter 24, "Frameworks and Class Libraries," explained the service-based architecture. This method of developing a framework provides many benefits: rapid application development (RAD), code reuse, interface and coding standardization and consistency, and a structured methodology. Sybase provides its own service-based GUI application framework: the PowerBuilder Foundation Class (PFC). With the PFC, in addition to the benefits of a service-based architecture, you have faster object instantiation, can extend noninheritable objects, and can delegate processing as needed.

This chapter looks at the numerous objects that comprise the PFC. You examine the structure of the inheritance hierarchy and its interrelationships. After you understand the PFC's structure, you examine many of the commonly used services and objects that help you quickly develop a quality PowerBuilder application.

# The PFC Components

The PFC consists of several object categories. As with most frameworks, you have a category of windows, menus, DataWindows, and user objects that form the structure of your framework. The second object category in the PFC is the custom class user objects (NVOs or *nonvisual objects*), which are used to create the application services. Similar to the service objects are standalone utility objects. The last group of objects is the extension layer for all your class objects.

## The PFC Libraries

The PFC objects are spread across a number of PowerBuilder library files that can be split into two groups: ancestor libraries and extension libraries.

The ancestor libraries all begin with the PFC prefix. Five libraries contain all the methods, properties, and code that make up the PFC's functionality. The objects contained in these libraries are the ancestors to all other objects in the PFC and eventually in your application:

- PFCMAIN.PBL contains the standard class user objects, window objects, menus, and standard visual user objects.

- PFCAPSRV.PBL contains custom class user objects that provide the application services.

- PFCDWSRV.PBL contains custom class user objects that provide the DataWindow services.

- PFCWNSRV.PBL contains custom class user objects that provide Window services and menu objects.

- PFCUTIL.PBL contains utility services such as `pfc_n_cst_debug` and `pfc_n_cst_sqlspy`, to name a few.

Two other ancestor libraries pertain to the PFC security service. These libraries set up and manage the security for each object. They aren't required to be included in the library search path or distributed with the application to the client machines. The PFC security allows for the implementation of security from window level all the way down to DataWindow column level. Each library is installed in a separate directory:

- PFCSECAD.PBL contains objects necessary to implement security administration services.

- PFCSECSC.PBL contains objects necessary to implement the security scanner.

The extension libraries correspond to the first five ancestor libraries discussed and also can be referred to as the *descendant libraries*. These libraries maintain untouched descendants of the objects in the corresponding ancestor libraries. The five extension libraries begin with PFE: PFEMAIN.PBL, PFEAPSRV.PBL, PFEDWSRV.PBL, PFEWNSRV.PBL, and PFEUTIL.PBL. These libraries provide a layer so that you can customize the objects for your own application processing. The extension library objects can be modified directly or can be used as ancestors for new objects.

> **Note**
>
> Don't modify any objects in the ancestor libraries. Any changes made here won't be reflected in any upgrades made to the PFC by Sybase unless done manually. This is one of the pluses of using an extension layer because your changes are retained in the extension layer while allowing you to replace the PFC libraries at will.

In addition to these PowerBuilder libraries, the PFC also uses pfccom32.dll for additional functionality and speed.

# Naming Conventions

The PFC uses its own object-naming conventions, similar to the standard PowerBuilder conventions:

| Prefix | Description | Prefix | Description |
|--------|-------------|--------|-------------|
| w_ | Window | u_ | Visual user object |
| m_ | Menu | n_ | Standard class user object |
| s_ | Global structure | n_cst | Custom class user object |

All objects in the ancestor libraries, which may be inherited, prefix these naming conventions with pfc_.

## Custom Class User Objects

The PFC provides many custom class user objects. These are the meat of the PFC because they encapsulate the many services the PFC provides. These services can be categorized as follows:

- *Application services* provide functionality such as error handling, DataWindow caching, security, debugging, and transaction registration via service objects.

- *DataWindow services* provide functionality for data processing by using the DataWindow control via service objects.

- *Menu services* provide common menu processing via functions, menu items, and events.

- *Utility services* provide functionality to extend the PowerScript language.

- *Window services* provide common window processing via functions and events.

Each service is examined in its own section later in this chapter.

# The PFC Architecture

Before looking at the individual services and what they can provide, you need to understand the PFC's implementation using the service-based architecture. This relatively straightforward architecture follows the basic client/server model with which you already are familiar.

As you know, in the client/server model, the client application connects to a server and makes a request to the database management system (DBMS) residing on the server. The request can consist of a simple SQL statement, a complex calculation, or a data modification. The server processes the request and then sends a message back to the client in response to the request. The message can be data or a success/failure code. In a service-based architecture, the client is referred to as the *requestor class*, and the server is called the *service class*.

As you would expect, the requestor needs to know what the individual service classes are and how to get to them. This is done by creating the requestor with references to the server (in the form of instance variables) and methods that enable you to activate the individual services. The requestor's job is to create a service, issue a request for processing, and destroy the service when it's no longer needed.

The service class's job is to receive requests from the requestor, perform the required task, and send a response back to the requestor. The benefit of the service class is that it can encapsulate functionality and control modifications to properties.

In the PFC, the best example of a requestor/service model is the DataWindow control user object, u_dw, and the DataWindow services. Figure 25.1 shows the relationship between the DataWindow control user object and

**FIGURE 25.1**

*The DataWindow control user object and the DataWindow services architecture.*

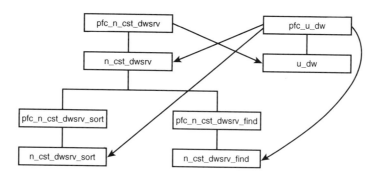

The service classes are all custom class user objects inherited from a base service class (pfc_n_cst_dwsrv). Because the service classes have to know who the requestor is, pfc_n_cst_dwsrv has defined a protected instance variable of type u_dw that holds a reference to the DataWindow control that requested the service.

**Note**

The instance variable defined in the base service is defined by using the extension layer object, u_dw, and not the ancestor, pfc_u_dw. This is because all the DataWindow controls on your application windows will be inherited from u_dw and allow you to make modifications to u_dw without affecting the ancestor object.

In addition to the reference variable (idw_requestor) pointing to the object that requested it, the service must have a method to populate that reference variable. In the PFC, the common function to this is of_SetRequestor(), which takes an argument of the class type of the requestor object (in this example, the argument would be of type u_dw). All this function does is populate the instance reference variable, idw_requestor, with the argument passed.

From the requestor object's viewpoint, it needs a reference variable pointing to the service object and a method that instantiates the service and populates the requestor's reference variable. This process is the same for all services, regardless of the requestor. Continuing with the base DataWindow service as an example, the requestor object, pfc_u_dw, has an instance variable (inv_base) that points to the extension service class, n_cst_dwsrv.

> **Note**
>
> The reference to the extension layer object follows the same logic as the reference variable to the requestor from the service object, as discussed earlier.

To instantiate the service, each requestor object has a corresponding of_Set*Service*() function, where *Service* is replaced by the name of the service class. These functions take a Boolean argument that determines whether the function should be instantiated or destroyed. To instantiate the base DataWindow service in the Constructor event of an instance of u_dw, the code would be

```
this.of_SetBase(True)
```

The of_SetBase() function mainly consists of the following code:

```
IF IsNull(inv_base) Or Not IsValid (inv_base) THEN
    inv_base = Create n_cst_dwsrv
    inv_base.of_SetRequestor ( this)
    Return 1
END IF
```

You first should make sure that the service hasn't already been instantiated by using the IsValid() function. If it hasn't, the service is instantiated with the CREATE statement. The requestor object then registers itself with the service by calling the of_SetRequestor() function.

Because the requestor created the service, it also has the responsibility to destroy the service. This is built into the PFC in the Destructor or Close events of the requestor objects. When an instance of u_dw has its Destructor event triggered, for example, `of_SetBase()` is called and passed a value of `FALSE`, which causes the requestor to destroy the service.

As you can see, creating a service is easy to do with the PFC, and the underlying code is straightforward. Now that you have the service instantiated, how do you use it? In the object-oriented spirit, the PFC tries to keep each object as encapsulated as possible. This means that you typically don't have direct access to any service class variables and have to redirect your events from the requestor to the service.

To access a service's instance variable, the PFC has implemented `of_Set`*x*`()` and `of_Get`*x*`()`, where *x* is the variable name. This gives PowerBuilder control over who has access to the variables and how they're changed.

Because one of the main uses of a service is to provide the functionality typically coded into events for an object, the service class has defined a number of events complete with code that correspond to the events of the requestor object. The requestor then must redirect its events to the service class's events. If you were using the row selection service for u_dw, for example, the `Clicked` event of `pfc_u_dw` would need to redirect the process to the service, which is done with this code:

```
If IsValid( inv_RowSelect) Then
   inv_RowSelect.Event pfc_clicked ( xpos, ypos, row, dwo )
END IF
```

The instance variable, `inv_RowSelect` (type `n_cst_dwsrv_RowSelection`), has an event called `pfc_clicked` that takes the exact same arguments as the DataWindow control `Clicked` event. The requestor needs only to redirect the event to the service that performs the task specific to the service. In addition to the standard PowerBuilder events, the service object also has PFC specifically defined events. Some of these events are precoded in the PFC and are triggered by other objects in the class library. The rest of the events are triggered by the PFC but are placeholders for you to write your own specific code.

The PFC also provides numerous functions for use with the different services. To call a function for a service, you must qualify it by using the service reference variable. All object functions in the PFC begin with the naming convention `of_`.

# Application Services

One of the first services you have to learn to use is the application service. This service provides common applicationwide processing and allows you to use inheritance in an "application object-like" manner. Because PowerBuilder's application object can't be inherited, the application service allows you to create reusable applicationwide processes.

# Setting Up the Application Manager

The Application Manager service is the one global variable that must be created in your application. In your global variable declarations, declare a reference variable used to point to the Application Manager service. You could use the extension layer service, n_cst_appmanager, but because you likely will want to extend the functionality with application-specific processing, you should inherit your own Application Manager from n_cst_appmanager. After you create your descendant Application Manager (for example, named n_cst_menace_appmanager), declare a global reference variable, gnv_app, to store the address of the service instance, which would appear as this:

```
n_cst_menace_appmanager gnv_app
```

> **Note**
>
> You must declare the variable as gnv_app because it is referenced in the PFC framework.

After you create the Application Manager reference variable, create the instance and redirect your application object's events to the Application Manager service. The Open event of your application should be written as this:

```
gnv_app = CREATE n_cst_menace_appmanager
gnv_app.Event pfc_Open( commandline)
```

For each of the other events you plan to use, redirect them to your Application Manager (be sure to pass any event arguments).

> **Note**
>
> Application initialization code normally coded in the application object's Open event now should be placed in the pfc_Open event of the Application Manager.

Because the Open event created the Application Manager, the Close event of the application object should destroy it. The Close event would be written as the following:

```
gnv_app.Event pfc_Close()
DESTROY gnv_app
```

While you are in the Application painter specifying the creation of the Application Manager service and redirecting the events, bring up the property sheet for the application object. On the Variable Types tab, change the data SQLCA type from transaction to the PFC transaction object n_tr. This ensures that SQLCA is created by using the PFC transaction user object. n_tr also provides several functions that eliminate repetitive tasks, such as connecting and disconnecting (of_Connect() and of_Disconnect()) and transaction management (of_Commit() and of_Rollback()), to name a few.

> **Note**
>
> You also can use any of the other PFC-created user objects to replace the class data types for the PowerBuilder global objects. You could replace message with n_msg for the Message object, for example.

After the Application Manager is created, it holds all your applicationwide variables. The Application Manager has a number of Get and Set functions that provide access to common global data, such as the following:

- The application .INI filename

- The user .INI filename

- The help filename

- The application's Registry key

- The application's MDI frame window

- The user's ID

- The application logo

- The application's copyright information and version

To specify the application copyright information, for example, you could use this code:

```
gnv_app.of_SetCopyright("PowerBuilder Unleashed 7.0, 2000")
```

The Application Manager also enables you to instantiate two windows— w_splash and w_logon—commonly associated with application startup:

**25**

**The PowerBuilder Foundation Class**

- The splash window displays using some of the global data you set for the application (such as the copyright statement). To open the splash window, use the of_Splash() function and specify the number of seconds you want the splash window to display.

- To display the logon window and extract the user's ID and password, just call the of_LogonDlg() function, which invokes a series of steps that hinges around opening the w_logon window. Before the window opening, the pfc_PreLogonDlg event for the Application Manager is triggered, which initializes the values used to display in the logon window. The logon window then is displayed; when it's closed by clicking OK, it sends information back to the Application Manager via the pfc_Logon event. The event arguments as_userid and as_password then can be used to populate your transaction object and connect to the database.

In addition to setting the global data values and the creation of the splash and logon windows, the Application Manager enables you to instantiate the services.

# Application Manager Services

The Application Manager services provided by the PFC follow:

- *Application Manager* provides access to application-level variables and all other application services.

- *Application Preferences* provides a means to save application and user data to an INI file or the Windows Registry.

- *DataWindow caching* provides a means of storing data of frequently accessed DataWindow objects.

- *Debugging* provides a development tool to track errors.

- *Error handling* provides a way to display and log errors for various PowerBuilder actions.

- *Security* provides the means to administer and secure objects in your application.

- *Transaction object* provides standard database processing, such as managing connections and transactions.

- *Transaction registration* provides a way to track all transaction objects used in your application.

The Application Manager is the gatekeeper that allows you access to all the other application services; it must be used to have access to much of the PFC's functionality. The next two subsections examine a couple of the application services in greater depth.

# DataWindow Cache Service

The DataWindow caching service gives you a method for caching the data from commonly used DataWindow objects. This reduces the need for repetitive database calls and duplicated data on the client. Anytime you need to access the same data in several locations in your application, the DataWindow Cache service provides you with the answer.

---

**Tip**

Use the DataWindow Cache service for drop-down DataWindows used throughout your application.

---

The DataWindow Cache service, `n_cst_dwcache`, is declared in the Application Manager via the instance variable `inv_dwcache`. To instantiate the service, code the following in the `pfc_Open` event in the Application Manager:

```
this.of_SetDWCache(True)
```

The next step is to register a DataWindow with the service by using the `of_Register()` function. Three types of syntax exist for the DataWindow Cache service. The most useful of the three follows:

```
gnv_app.inv_dwcache.of_Register( id, dwobject, trans {, arguments })
```

Here, *id* is a string value used to uniquely identify the cached data. *dwobject* is a string containing the name of the DataWindow object you want to cache. *trans* is the name of a transaction object of type `n_tr` that retrieves the rows for the DataWindow object specified in *dwobject*. Optionally, you may need to pass one or more values for *arguments* that retrieve the data for the DataWindow object. *arguments* is any data type array of up to 20 elements. When the function is called for a DataWindow object, the data is retrieved for the object and stored with the DataWindow Cache service. For example, to cache the data in DataWindow `d_customer`, code the following:

```
gnv_app.inv_dwcache.of_Register( "Customer Listing", "d_customer", SQLCA)
```

To access the data elsewhere in your application, call the function `of_GetRegistered()`:

```
gnv_app.inv_dwcache.of_GetRegistered( id, datastore)
```

Here, *id* is the string value specified in the `of_Register()` function that identifies the cached data, and *datastore* is a variable of type `n_ds` that's populated with the cached data. After you call this function, you can do a `ShareData()` to the desired DataWindow

**25**

The PowerBuilder
Foundation Class

object. To retrieve the customer data from the DataWindow cache stored in the previous example, you would code the following:

```
//Instance variable datastore declaration: n_ds ids_data
DataWindowChild ldwc_child

gnv_app.inv_dwcache.of_GetRegistered( "Customer Listing", ids_data)
dw_custlist.GetChild( "customer", ldwc_child)
ids_data.ShareData( ldwc_child)
```

> **Tip**
>
> Create a function in `n_cst_dwcache` that calls `of_GetRegistered()` and then performs the `ShareData()`, thus eliminating an extra step.

## Error-Handling Service

The error-handling service enables you to display error messages for multiple error types: SQL, DataWindows, application (for example, validation), and system. The errors can be displayed in message boxes or the PFC's error window and can be generated from a table on your database. The error-handling service also lets you log errors and send emails automatically.

To enable the error-handling service, call `of_SetError()` in the Application Manager `pfc_Open` event. If you want to keep all your error messages centralized in a table on your database, copy the Messages table and the existing rows from the PFC demo database to your application database. You then can add your own application-specific messages to the Messages table. To have your application use the table, use this code:

```
gnv_app.inv_error.of_SetPredefinedSource( trans)
```

Here, *trans* is the name of a transaction object of type n_tr that points to the database containing the Messages table. Calling this function populates a datastore (`ids_messages`) in the service with all the error messages. You then can choose whether you want to have any error message displayed with a standard PowerBuilder message box or by using the PFC's w_message window. To do this, use this code:

```
gnv_app.inv_error.of_SetStyle( style)
```

Here, *style* is 0 for a message box or 1 for the PFC message window. When an error is encountered, use this code to display the error message:

```
gnv_app.inv_error.of_Message( MessageID, Parameters)
```

Here, *MessageID* is a string that identifies the message to be displayed (corresponding with the `msgnumber` column in `ids_messages`). *Parameters* is an optional string array containing values that can be placed into the error message at specified placeholders. In the text of an error message that you create, you might specify the following:

```
Value Required! Please enter a value for %s.
```

Because you can reuse this message for multiple fields, the `%s` indicates a placeholder for which a value will be specified when `of_Message()` is called. The code then would look like this:

```
string ls_error[]

ls_error[1] = "Customer Name"
gnv_app.inv_error.of_Message( "VAL122", ls_error)
```

The error-handling service enables you to define severity levels and email notification lists for specific errors.

## Standard Class User Objects

As you saw with the Application Manager services, the PFC subclasses many standard PowerBuilder nonvisual classes in the extension layer. You can use these in place of the standard PowerBuilder class objects:

| | |
|---|---|
| n_cn | Connection object descendant |
| n_ds | Datastore object descendant |
| n_err | Error object descendant |
| n_ms | Mail Session object descendant |
| n_msg | Message object descendant |
| n_pl | Pipeline object descendant |
| n_tr | Transaction object descendant |
| n_trp | Transport object descendant |

Use these nonvisual classes whenever you need an instance of the standard PowerBuilder classes.

# Menus

The PFC provides two menu types: main application menus (used for drop-down menus) and pop-up menus. The Most Recently Used (MRU) object service lists the five last used windows under the File menu in an MDI application. Like the PFC windows, the menus also provide a class hierarchy (see Figure 25.2).

**FIGURE 25.2**
*The PFC menu hierarchy.*

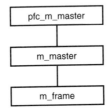

As you can see, the menu hierarchy isn't very deep, which is consistent with the known performance issues with menus. Keeping this in mind, you can use m_frame directly for your application's MDI frame menu, or inherit your frame menu from m_master and customize the descendant. All sheet menus should be inherited from m_master as well.

> **Note**
>
> The general rule is that when using the PFC, you should stay within the PFC (meaning that you should use all PFC objects). This rule often is broken when evaluating the PFC menus, however. The menus contain a considerable amount of useful code, but much of it may not apply to your application. Therefore, you can choose to create a scaled-down version of the PFC menus or implement your existing menu framework into the PFC.

The menu inheritance in the PFC uses the ShiftToRight menu property to control menu-item placement. The PFC menu uses a message router to communicate with the PFC windows, which provides considerable functionality while minimizing the code in the menus.

The other types of menus in the PFC are the pop-up or context menus:

| | |
|---|---|
| m_dw | Pop-up menu for DataWindow controls inherited from u_dw |
| m_edit | Pop-up menu with standard edit options used for specific standard visual user objects |
| m_oc | Pop-up menu with OLE control functionality for controls inherited from u_oc |
| m_view | Pop-up menu for controls inherited from u_lv |
| m_lvs | Pop-up menu for controls inherited from u_lvs |
| m_tvs | Pop-up menu for controls inherited from u_tvs |

These menus are available automatically when the appropriate user object is used on a window.

## The Menu Message Router

The message router implemented in the PFC menus allows you to send a message to perform a specific process to a window. The plus is that the menu needs to know only the event name to execute. The message router searches for the appropriate object to receive the message by using the function of_SendMessage().

The message router function of_SendMessage() is called from each item in the PFC menus and is passed the event name to execute. The router, in turn, calls its corresponding window's pfc_MessageRouter event. pfc_MessageRouter then tries to invoke the event passed from the menu in the following order: to the window, to the current control, and to the last active DataWindow.

> **Note**
>
> If you don't want to use the PFC menus but still want to implement a message router, simply move of_Message() and any menu item code you might need to your own menus.

# Windows and Window Services

The PFC contains several base-class windows that should be used as the ancestors for all your application-specific windows. Several services also are specific to windows that provide additional functionality.

The window class hierarchy in the PFC is often an area of confusion at first glance. The base class for all PFC windows is pfc_w_master. Figure 25.3 shows the window hierarchy.

**FIGURE 25.3**
*The PFC window class hierarchy.*

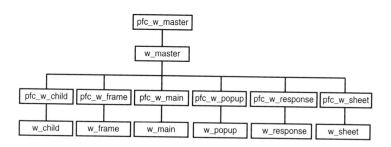

As you would expect, all objects that begin with `pfc` are contained in the ancestor libraries, and the rest exist in the extension libraries. This means that the hierarchy from `pfc_w_master` to `w_master` to `pfc_w_main` spans from the ancestor libraries to the descendant libraries back to the ancestor libraries. Although this might seem strange at first glance, this hierarchy is used for good reason. As was mentioned earlier, you don't want to change any objects in the ancestor libraries. What happens if you want to change your window hierarchy so that all window descendants see the modification? If `pfc_w_main` and all other window classes were inherited directly from `pfc_w_master`, you would have to make the same modification in all descendant windows in the extension libraries (for example, `w_main` and `w_sheet`). By inserting `w_master` in the hierarchy, you have a common ancestor you can modify without having to touch the ancestor libraries.

The rest of the windows in the hierarchy are designed with specific functionality for each window type. When you begin creating your application windows, they should be inherited from the corresponding window ancestor in the extension libraries.

## Base Window Service

You would expect the Base Window service to be a full-featured service, considering that windows are such a large component in a GUI environment. When you look at the PFC's Window service (`pfc_n_cst_winsrv`), though, it appears to be missing much of the processing you would expect. The main function in the Base Window service is `of_Center()`, which is used to center a window in the middle of the user's screen. To use the Base Window service, you can code the following in your window's Open event:

```
//Instantiate the base window service
this.of_SetBase( True)
//Center the window
this.inv_base.of_Center()
```

> **Tip**
>
> Add this code to your response window ancestor class so that it will always be centered.

You might be wondering whether anything else is provided on a window level besides the capability to center a window. Most of the additional functionality is provided in the window base class `pfc_w_master`.

# pfc_w_master

The PFC base class window, `pfc_w_master`, can create and destroy the different window services. It also contains the processing for the menu message router, in-depth `CloseQuery` event processing, coordination of the save process via the `pfc_Save` event, and empty user events for your application code that are triggered by the PFC.

Remember that the menu message-routing function `of_SendMessage()` passes the name of an event from a menu item to the `pfc_MessageRouter` event, which is defined in `pfc_w_master`. In turn, this event takes the passed event name and tries to execute it first for the window, followed by the active control. Finally, it tries to execute the passed event in the last active DataWindow control.

The `CloseQuery` event provides considerable power to PowerBuilder applications that use DataWindows with a minimal amount of code needed by developers. The `CloseQuery` event calls the event `pfc_PreClose`, which is a placeholder that enables you to write any application-specific code needed before the window closes. If `pfc_PreClose` returns 1 (the default), `CloseQuery` calls a function of `pfc_w_master` called `of_UpdateChecks()`.

> **Note**
>
> If you don't want the `CloseQuery` processing to occur, code `ib_DisableCloseQuery = True` in your window's `Open` event.

You use `of_UpdateChecks()` to determine whether any DataWindows on the window have unsaved data. It also ensures that any validation logic has been processed successfully for each DataWindow. This function calls three additional events, in this order: `pfc_AcceptText`, `pfc_UpdatesPending`, and `pfc_Validation`. Each event loops through all the controls (including those on tab controls and custom visual user objects) on the window to perform its checks.

`pfc_AcceptText` uses the Logical Unit of Work service, `n_cst_luw`. The `pfc_AcceptText` event calls the method `of_AcceptText()` of `n_cst_luw`, which ensures that all changes have been processed on the controls on the window. `pfc_UpdatesPending` calls `pfc_UpdatesPendingRef`, which calls the `of_UpdatesPending` function of `n_cst_luw`. This function returns whether any changes have occurred that have yet to be saved.

If any changes are pending, the validation process occurs via `pfc_Validation`, which kicks off the `of_Validation()` process of `n_cst_luw`. This function calls the `of_Validation()` function for the various objects on the window, and with DataWindow controls, this eventually results in the `pfc_Validation` event being triggered. In this event, you can write your own specific processing.

If the pending changes make it through this entire process called from `of_UpdateChecks()`, a 1 is returned from the function back to the `CloseQuery` event. The `CloseQuery` event then prompts users to see if the save should be performed; if users choose to save, the `pfc_Save` event is called, which kicks off numerous events that enable you to interact with DataWindow update processes at different times in the process. The PFC calls `pfc_PreUpdate`, `pfc_BeginTran`, `pfc_Update`, `pfc_EndTran`, and `pfc_PostUpdate`. Generally, these events can be allowed to process without modification. The `pfc_EndTran` event is the one exception because it should be coded to perform a `COMMIT` pending the success of `pfc_Update`.

> **Note**
>
> You can call `of_SetUpdateObjects()` in `pfc_w_master` to specify the order in which you want the DataWindows to be updated if the order is other than what's in the control array.

As you saw with the `CloseQuery` event, the PFC has created several empty user-defined events that it triggers as part of its standard processes. These events allow you to place your application-specific logic into the logical flow of the PFC's processing (for example, `pfc_validate`).

## Self-Updating Objects

As discussed earlier, the `n_cst_luw` service makes all the necessary calls to perform the save. One cornerstone of this process is the implementation of Self Updating Objects (SUO). When the Logical Unit of Work service carries out the update process, it looks for six functions, most of which are described in the earlier section. These functions are redirected to six matching events, which enable you to override or extend. These functions and events are as follows:

| Function | Matching Event |
|---|---|
| of_AcceptText | pfc_AcceptText |
| of_UpdatesPending | pfc_UpdatesPending |
| of_Validation | pfc_Validation |
| of_UpdatePrep | pfc_UpdatePrep |

```
of_Update                    pfc_Update
of_PostUpdate                pfc_PostUpdate
```

The PFC provides several objects already created as SUOs, but that doesn't mean that they are the only objects that can be used as such. Any object can become an SUO by having the previously defined functions and events placed in it. When the functions and events are defined, the PFC detects them and makes the appropriate call, using the metaclass service described later.

The concept of the SUO is a powerful and flexible way to handle updates within PowerBuilder. The PFC already has integrated this into its update process, so it's a concept you need to grasp to successfully use all its benefits.

## pfc_n_cst_metaclass

The n_cst_metaclass service is important to creating your own SUOs. As mentioned, the PFC already has several objects in which it has defined the necessary functions and events, which will make these objects SUOs. The PFC has also coded into its update process the capability to detect whether you've created your own SUOs. It has done this by using the n_cst_metaclass service.

The metaclass service allows you to call functions, which provide information about variables, functions, and events of a particular object. The LUW service uses this service by calling the of_IsFunctionDefined() function for each object not determined to be predefined PFC SUOs. This returns a Boolean that indicates whether the function in question has been defined on the object in question. If it has, the function is dynamically called. The following is an excerpt from the LUW service's of_AcceptText() function:

```
// Check/Perform for SelfUpdatingObject Functionality.
lb_defined = inv_metaclass.of_isFunctionDefined &
   (lpo_tocheck.ClassDefinition, "of_AcceptText", ls_args)
If lb_defined Then
   li_rc = lpo_tocheck.Function Dynamic of_AcceptText (ab_focusonerror)
   If li_rc < 0 Then Return -1
   Continue
End If
```

As you can see, this service is important to the way in which the PFC can flexibly handle updates, but this service transcends just the update process. As you get deeper into the PFC and your quest for true object-oriented development, it can and will become a valuable tool in your toolbox.

# Other Window Services

In addition to the Base Window service and `pfc_w_master`, the PFC implements additional window services:

- *Preference* stores users' window settings to an INI file or the Registry.

- *Most Recently Used* registers the last used windows for quick reopening.

- *Split Bar* provides a vertical or horizontal split bar (like the Windows Explorer) between adjacent controls.

- *Resize* provides a mechanism so that controls are resized automatically with the window.

- *Sheet Manager* provides a mechanism for managing sheets in an MDI application.

- *Status Bar* displays additional information in the bottom right of the status bar in an MDI application.

The following sections examine the Preference, Status Bar, and Resize services.

## Preference Service

The window Preference service allows you to save and read values containing each user's window settings from an INI file or the Windows Registry. The service saves information such as the window size, toolbar settings, and window position. To start the service, use this code in the window's `Open` event:

```
this.of_SetPreference(True)
```

By default, the Preference service saves all the window settings. Although this ensures that any customization to a user's window is saved, it also can slow application performance. Therefore, avoid saving the information you don't want to capture. The following functions enable you to specify what's saved:

| | |
|---|---|
| `of_SetMenuItems()` | Tracks menu settings |
| `of_SetToolbars()` | Tracks toolbar positions |
| `of_SetToolbarTitles()` | Tracks toolbar titles |
| `of_SetToolbarItemOrder()` | Tracks the order of toolbar items |
| `of_SetToolbarItemSpace()` | Tracks spacing between toolbar items |
| `of_SetToolbarItemVisible()` | Tracks the visibility of toolbar items |
| `of_SetWindow()` | Tracks window properties |

Each function takes a Boolean argument indicating whether you want the data saved. You might want to consider turning off `of_SetToolbarItemOrder()`, `of_SetToolbarItemSpace()`, `of_SetToolbarTitles()`, and `of_SetMenuItems()`; these functions typically cannot be modified by users, and turning them off increases performance. To cause the window to save the desired information, call the `of_Save()` function:

```
this.inv_preference.of_Save( IniFileorReg, {Section})
```

Here, `IniFileorReg` is the name of the application's INI file (remember, this is available as part of the Application Manager) or the name of a Registry key. If you've specified an INI file, `Section` refers to the section in which you want the settings stored. To retrieve the values for the window, call `of_Restore()` with the same arguments shown in the code line.

## Status Bar and Toolbar Service

If you're creating an MDI application, you should be using an MDI frame inherited from `w_frame`. The PFC has built into `pfc_w_frame` two processes that can enhance the presentation of your application.

The Status Bar service enables you to specify multiple panels of information in the status bar of your MDI frame. This includes the current date and time and memory information. To start the service, use this code in your MDI frame `Open` event:

```
this.of_SetStatusBar(True)
```

The other enhancement that can be used with an MDI frame descendant of `w_frame` is the Toolbar Control dialog. This dialog enables you to manipulate common toolbar properties, such as the position of the toolbars and whether PowerTips and ShowText are on or off. To open the toolbar window `w_toolbars`, use this code:

```
gnv_app.of_GetFrame().Event pfc_Toolbars()
```

This code gets a reference to the MDI frame for the application and triggers the `pfc_Toolbars` event to open the Toolbar Control dialog.

## Resize Service

The Resize service automatically sizes and moves the controls on a window or tab when the window or tab is resized. After instantiating the service with `of_SetResize()`, specify which controls you want to have resized. Use this code:

```
this.inv_resize.of_Register( ControlName, ResizeMethod)
```

`ControlName` is the name of the control you want resized; `ResizeMethod` is a string indicating how you want the control to respond when the window is resized. The options are

```
FixedToBottom                    Scale
FixedToRight                     ScaleToBottom
FixedToRight&Bottom              ScaleToRight
FixedToBottom&ScaleToRight       ScaleToRight&Bottom
FixedToRight&ScaleToBottom
```

The best way to view what each option does is to run the PFC sample application and to toggle the different options on to see how the controls react.

By default, the Resize service enables you to shrink the window and its control to an indecipherable display. To prevent this from occurring, call of_SetMinSize() and specify the minimum width and height for the window.

# u_dw and the DataWindow Services

As a PowerBuilder developer, you know that the DataWindow is one of the product's most powerful features. It then makes sense that the DataWindow user object u_dw and the DataWindow services are a central part of the PFC's functionality. If you recall from Figure 25.1, all the DataWindow services are inherited from the base class pfc_n_cst_dwsrv. To use the DataWindow services, the DataWindow controls in your application must be descendants of the DataWindow control user object u_dw.

In addition to the base DataWindow service, the following services are provided for DataWindows in the PFC:

- *Drop-Down Search* provides automatic scrolling through a drop-down DataWindow based on one or more letters entered.

- *Filter* provides three ways to filter DataWindow data.

- *Find and Replace* provides an easy-to-use mechanism to find and replace data in your DataWindow.

- *Linkage* establishes a relationship between DataWindows, such as a master/detail structure.

- *Multitable Update* manages the update of two or more tables in a single DataWindow object.

- *Print Preview* provides common print-preview functionality.

- *QueryMode* provides the capability to implement Query mode for ad-hoc queries.

- *Reporting* provides enhanced reporting features, such as adding items, zooming, and printing.

- *Required Column* provides an automatic check for values for all required DataWindow columns.

- *Resize* resizes DataWindow objects when the DataWindow control is resized (like the Window Resize service).

- *Row Management* provides common row handling, such as inserts, deletes, and undeletes.

- *Row Selection* gives you single, multi-, and extended select capabilities.

- *Sort* provides different mechanisms for sorting your DataWindow data.

In addition to all the DataWindow services, u_dw also has considerable functionality, including the capability to create a drop-down calendar for easy date selection for any date column in your DataWindow and a drop-down calculator for computing values for a column in a DataWindow.

The ancestor of all the other DataWindow services is the base DataWindow service, which contains references to all the other DataWindow services. The base service also provides several alternatives to using the standard PowerScript functions, such as `Modify()` and `Describe()`, and a number of functions for accessing DataWindow object values.

Although the base DataWindow service is straightforward to use, this not true of all the services. Now look at a few of the DataWindow services so that you can get a feel for what's in store.

## Sort Service

The DataWindow Sort service allows your users to sort their data in several ways. Users can employ four dialogs and can click a column heading. To instantiate the Sort service, use the `of_SetSort (True)` function of your DataWindow control. To turn on the capability to have a column sorted when its header is clicked, call `of_SetColumnHeader()`, passing it a value of `TRUE`.

---

**Note**

When using the column headers to sort the data, name the column header with a `t` suffix in the DataWindow object. If you choose a different suffix, you must call `of_SetDefaultHeaderSuffix()` to set the suffix.

---

To have one of the four dialogs appear, use this code:

```
this.inv_sort.of_SetStyle( SortDialog)
```

Here, *SortDialog* is an integer that specifies one of the following dialogs:

| | |
|---|---|
| 0 | The PowerBuilder Sort dialog |
| 1 | Drag-and-drop sorting using w_sortdragdrop |
| 2 | Single sorting using w_sortsingle |
| 3 | Multiple sorting using w_sortmulti |

> **Note**
>
> For option 3, each data column in the DataWindow object must have a corresponding text object. The text object's name must be the same as the column, with a _t appended to the name.

To specify what values appear in the Sort dialogs (by default, the column names on the DataWindow object appear), call of_SetColumnDisplayNameStyle(). The values that can be passed are 0 to show DataWindow column names, 1 to show database column names, and 2 to show DataWindow column header names (usually the most meaningful to users). If one or more columns have edit styles with code tables, you can specify whether the sorting is done on the data value or the display value using of_SetUseDisplay() passing TRUE to sort on the display values.

After you set up the way in which you want the Sort dialogs to appear and behave, use this code:

```
dwControl.Event pfc_SortDlg()
```

Here, *dwControl* is the name of your DataWindow control. If you're using the PFC menus, this is built into the menu and doesn't need to be coded.

## Find and Replace Service

If you need to provide a Find dialog and a Find and Replace dialog for your DataWindows, the Find and Replace DataWindow service gives you this capability. For the functionality this provides, the coding is minor. To instantiate the service, call of_SetFind (True). If you're using the PFC menu, you don't have to write any additional code as the menus of the appropriate windows. If you want to invoke the process yourself, use this code to open the Find dialog:

```
dwControl.Event pfc_FindDlg()
```

For the Replace dialog, use this code:

```
dwControl.Event pfc_ReplaceDlg()
```

Again, *dwControl* is the name of your DataWindow control.

# Drop-Down Search Service

The Drop-Down Search service implements into your application the capability to type multiple letters in a drop-down DataWindow and have it search to find the matching entity. By default, the drop-down DataWindow enables you to type a letter, and PowerBuilder moves you to the first row that begins with the typed letter. Unfortunately, you can't type a letter and then a second letter to qualify the item for which you want to search.

To use the Drop-Down Search service, call of_SetDropDownSearch( True). You then need to specify for which columns in your DataWindow you want to have the search capabilities turned on by using this code:

```
dwControl.inv_dropdownsearch.of_AddColumn({Column})
```

Here, *dwControl* is your DataWindow control, and *Column* is a string with the name of the column with a drop-down DataWindow edit style for which you want to have the search enabled. If you don't specify a value of *Column*, all drop-down DataWindow columns will have the functionality.

The last step is to redirect your DataWindow control's EditChanged and ItemFocus-Changed events to their corresponding PFC events, pfc_EditChanged and pfc_ItemFo-cusChanged. For example, in the EditChangedevent, use this code:

```
inv_dropdownsearch.Event pfc_EditChanged( row, dwo, data)
```

# Required Column Service

A common requirement for a database application is to ensure that all necessary column values have been entered. If you've ever used the Required Column option on a DataWindow column edit style, you know that the concept is nice, but the constant dialogs prompting for values are annoying. This often encourages users to enter any data just to bypass the message. A solution many developers have implemented is to have a process that searches for all required values before performing an update to the database. The Required Column service provides that functionality for you.

To use the service, call of_SetReqColumn( True). On each DataWindow column for which you want to require the columns be entered, enable the Required Column check box on the column's edit style.

> **Note**
>
> The Required Column service works only on columns that use the `nilisnull` property. Edit masks don't have this property, so they aren't included in this service.

When the window invokes the `pfc_Save` event processing, the PFC automatically checks to make sure that all required fields are specified.

# Linkage Service

The DataWindow Linkage service is useful for coordinating processing between two or more DataWindows. The most common use of the Linkage service is implementing a master/detail window. To instantiate the service for each DataWindow to be linked, use the `of_SetLinkage()` function:

```
dw_order_header.of_SetLinkage( True)
dw_order_detail.of_SetLinkage( True)
```

You then need to indicate the transaction object for the DataWindow that will be the master in the relationship by using this code:

```
dw_order_header.of_SetTransObject( SQLCA)
```

The specified transaction object is used for all DataWindows in the linkage chain. To form the association between the DataWindows, you need to establish the master/detail relationship and the columns the service uses to synchronize the DataWindows.

To establish the relationship between the DataWindows, call `of_SetMaster()` for the detail DataWindow(s):

```
dw_order_detail.inv_linkage.of_SetMaster( dw_order_header)
```

You then must relate the DataWindows via common columns for synchronization. You do this by using the `of_Register()` function for the detail DataWindow(s). The syntax for this function follows:

```
dwDetailControl.inv_linkage.of_Register( MasterColumn, DetailColumn)
```

Here, *dwDetailControl* is the name of your detail DataWindow control. *MasterColumn* is a string containing the name of a column in the master DataWindow that's the linkage argument for the detail DataWindows. *DetailColumn* is a string containing the name of the column in the detail DataWindow that relates to the column specified by *MasterColumn*.

The next step in using the Linkage service is to specify what happens to the detail DataWindow(s) when the master DataWindow row changes. The of_SetStyle() function takes three possible values:

| | |
|---|---|
| 1 | Uses the master DataWindow columns as filter criteria for the detail DataWindow(s) |
| 2 | Uses the master DataWindow columns as retrieval arguments for the detail DataWindow(s) |
| 3 | Uses the master DataWindow columns to control scrolling in the detail DataWindow(s); uses ShareData() |

> **Note**
>
> The arguments for the of_SetStyle() function are also defined as CONSTANT instance variables in the pfc_n_dwsrv_linkage service. You can substitute the argument values mentioned previously with FILTER, RETRIEVE, and SCROLL, respectively.

The last step is to retrieve the data for the DataWindows. You do this by calling of_Retrieve() for the master DataWindow control, which starts with the retrieval of the data in the master and works its way down for each detail DataWindow.

> **Note**
>
> The master DataWindow control must have the Retrieve() function coded in its pfc_Retrieve event.

If you're using the linked DataWindows for updating, you can specify whether the update process starts with the master DataWindow and works down or updates from the bottom up. You do this by using the function of_SetUpdateStyle(), which takes a numeric argument or a constant instance variable defined in the pfc_n_dwsrv_linkage object, similar to the of_SetStyle() example discussed previously.

# Multitable Update Service

The Multitable Update service allows you to update two or more tables from within one DataWindow object. Rather than call the individual Modify() statements yourself, the PFC provides an easy-to-use mechanism that requires very little coding on the developer's part.

To instantiate the service, call of_SetMultiTable (True) . For each table in the DataWindow object, call of_Register(), which specifies the information that's usually set in the Update Characteristics dialog in the DataWindow painter. The syntax follows:

```
dwControl.inv_multitable.of_Register( Table, KeyCols, {UpdateCols, KeyMod, Where})
```

Here, *dwControl* is the DataWindow control, *Table* is a string containing the table to update, *KeyCols* is a string array containing the key column(s) used for updating, *UpdateCols* is an optional string array containing all updatable column names (the default is all columns), *KeyMod* is a Boolean that indicates whether the row is deleted and then inserted or just updated in place when the primary key changes, and *Where* is an integer that indicates how to build the WHERE clause for UPDATE and DELETE statements (0 indicates key columns, 1 indicates key and updatable columns, and 2 indicates key and modified columns).

Then, to invoke the update process for the DataWindow, call the pfc_Update event for the DataWindow control.

# Standard Visual User Objects

The DataWindow control is the most used standard visual user object, and the PFC has subclassed all the standard PowerBuilder controls. Most of the controls have built-in editing pop-up menus, automatic MicroHelp text for MDI applications, integration with other PFC objects, and simplification of complex tasks. You can see the power of the PFC when using the TreeView user object u_tv and the ListView control user object u_lv. These controls greatly simplify the amount of necessary code and the learning curve needed to implement basic functionality. The PFC has even created relationships between controls, such as the Explorer interface.

Several added objects mirror the new objects in PowerBuilder 7.0. The new PFC objects are as follows:

| | |
|---|---|
| u_hpb | The Horizontal Progress Bar object |
| u_vpb | The Vertical Progress Bar object |
| u_htb | The Horizontal Track Bar object |
| u_vtb | The Vertical Track Bar object |
| u_phl | The Picture Hyperlink object |
| u_sth | The Text Hyperlink object |

Although many controls have additional processes incorporated into their corresponding user object, this isn't true of all controls. Although it might seem unnecessary to use a control such as the static text user object u_st, it can be useful for providing visual standardization (such as fonts, colors, and so on).

# Utility Services

The PFC contains many standalone services you can use independent of any other PFC objects. To use a Utility service, all you need to do is create it, use its functions, and destroy it (some Utility services use the auto-instantiate feature, whereas others don't). Some common Utility services follow:

- *Conversion* provides various data-type conversions.

- *Date/Time* provides numerous date-calculation functions.

- *File* provides common file-management processing.

- *INI File* provides read and write capabilities for an INI file.

- *Numerical* provides support for accessing binary data.

- *Platform* provides platform-specific processing, such as free memory and system resources.

- *Selection* provides an interface that allows users to retrieve one or more rows from the database.

- *SQL Parsing* provides the means to parse and assemble SQL statements.

- *String Handling* provides common string processes, such as global replace, array conversions, and case conversions.

# Adding Services

After you are comfortable with the services available in the PFC and its architecture, you might see areas in which you can provide enhancements in the form of a new service. When you understand the object relationships, adding a service to the PFC is easy.

If you want to add a new DataWindow service, inherit your new service from n_cst_dwsrv. In u_dw, add an instance reference variable for your service. In the same object, declare an object-level function called of_Set*AAA*(), where *AAA* is the name of your service. This function should look like all the existing of_Set functions for instantiating services. Add the destruction of the service to the Destructor event of the u_dw. If necessary, add any event redirection to the service in u_dw.

# Extending the PFC

Depending on your company's size, whether to extend the PFC might be a hot topic. Extension layers allow you to reuse code while insulating separate business units' specific application processing. In a large company, you might need a corporate layer for high-level business rules, a division layer, and even a departmental layer. Each layer allows you to place reusable code without affecting other business units. The PFC gets you started by providing one extension layer in the form of the PFE libraries. You need to consider up front whether you will need additional extension layers.

The steps for inserting an extension layer begin with creating one or more PBLs to contain the extension objects. Inherit the desired objects from the PFC libraries and save them to the new extension library (use meaningful naming conventions for this layer). After making any modifications to the new extension layer, change the PFE objects' inheritance hierarchy by inheriting them from the new extension layer instead of directly from the PFC objects. For example, `pfc_u_dw` would have a descendant of `corp_u_dw`, which would have a descendant of `u_dw`.

# Summary

As you can see, the PowerBuilder Foundation Class library is a flexible and powerful development tool. By following the service-based architecture, Sybase gives you a framework for using multiple inheritance and instantiating only the functionality needed.

# 26

# Building User Objects

This chapter introduces PowerScript's user-object–specific functions and some of the most common user objects you will find in a framework. You will find some similar objects within the PFC, and although some of the functionality is similar to that found in the PFC, this chapter addresses other functionality and approaches as well. The appropriate PFC service object is mentioned, if applicable.

# Creating User Objects at Runtime

You can place visual user objects on a window by using two different methods. You can paint them on the window during development as you would any other control, or dynamically create them during execution by using the functions outlined in the following sections. The following sections introduce the relevant functions and give you examples of how and where to use them.

## The `OpenUserObject()` Function

To create and display a user object on a window, use the `OpenUserObject()` function. It makes the attributes, controls, functions, and events available for use within the window.

The user object is drawn onscreen when the display is next updated; this can occur because of another function call or a display attribute change that causes the screen to be repainted, or because of a function call at the end of the script. This feature is useful if you're creating many objects because it won't cause a lot of screen flicker.

This function has two syntaxes, which parallel the `Open()` function used with windows. The first syntax opens an instance of a particular user object; the second lets you specify the class of the object to open. The first syntax is as follows:

```
WindowName.OpenUserObject( UserObjectVariable {, X, Y})
```

The `UserObjectVariable` parameter specifies the user object data type or a variable declared of the desired user object data type. The function returns a reference to the opened user object and stores it in the variable used in the argument or as the instance pool entry for that object class. The `X` and `Y` parameters are optional positions in the window to open the user object. If you call this function a second time with the same user object or variable, the user object is activated twice, and you won't have two instances appearing. For example, to dynamically open an instance of a single-line edit user object at coordinate `300,200` on the window, this would be the code:

```
u_sle lsle_dynamic1

OpenUserObject( lsle_dynamic1, 300, 200)
```

With the second syntax you can open a user object by specifying the class type as an additional parameter:

```
WindowName.OpenUserObject( UserObjectVariable, UserObjectClass {, X, Y})
```

The parameter *User ObjectVariable* must be a variable, and it can be declared as an ancestor class for all user objects you will be opening or be of type `DragObject`. The function places a reference to the opened user object in this variable. The *UserObjectClass* parameter is a string that specifies the name of the user object to display, which must be a descendant of the class *UserObjectVariable*. Just remember that you can't access attributes, functions, or structures that belong to the class *UserObjectVariable*.

Use the second syntax of `OpenUserObject()` when you don't know the user object that will be opened when the script is executed. For example, if a function will be used to open several different classes of user objects, you would pass a string representing the class:

```
// String as_ClassName
DragObject doNewUO

OpenUserObject( doNewUO, as_ClassName)
```

Or, if you knew that the user objects were all inherited from a base class, such as u_sle, you could use that as the variable data type:

```
// String as_ClassName
// which might contain "u_sle_numeric" or "u_sle_required"
u_sle lsle_NewUO

OpenUserObject( lsle_NewUO, as_ClassName)
```

This has the advantage of allowing you to access ancestor-level functions and attributes that you couldn't use with the first example that used `DragObject` as the variable data type.

### Note

Using these functions adds the new user object to the control property arrays of windows and tab controls. In versions before PowerBuilder 6.0, these functions didn't add the new user object to the window's control array.

**Note**

PowerBuilder doesn't include the object specified by `UserObjectClass` in an executable, so you must use a PBD to incorporate it into your finished application.

## The `OpenUserObjectWithParm()` Function

The `OpenUserObjectWithParm()` function is similar in purpose to the `OpenWithParm()` function used with windows. By using `OpenUserObjectWithParm()`, not only can you carry out the same functionality as detailed in the preceding section, but you also can pass parameters to the user object. As with `OpenWithParm()`, the parameter(s) are stored in the `Message` object.

Again, two syntaxes mirror those available for `OpenUserObject()`. The following syntax creates a user object of the specified class and passes a parameter value to it:

*WindowName*.`OpenUserObjectWithParm(` *UserObjectVariable*, *Parameter* {, *X*, *Y*})

The alternative syntax requires you to also specify the user objects class:

*WindowName*.`OpenUserObjectWithParm(` *UserObjectVariable*,*Parameter*,*UserObjectClass*
➥{, *X*,*Y*})

Chapter 10, "Windows and the Window Painter," covers the use of the `Message` object and retrieving information from it.

The same warnings that apply for opening windows with parameters and user objects hold:

- Access the `Message` object immediately in the user object in case the `Message` object is inadvertently used by another event.

- Check the `PowerObject` value for a `NULL` object reference before trying to use it.

## The `CloseUserObject()` Function

By using the `CloseUserObject()` function, you can close down and free up the resources of user objects you've opened. This causes the user object to be removed from the display and the `Destructor` event to be triggered in the user object. This is the syntax for this function:

*WindowName*.`CloseUserObject(` *UserObjectName*)

*UserObjectName* is the object name or instance to be closed.

**Note**

Remember to destroy all objects that you create. This should be part of your credo while developing PowerBuilder applications. This clears the memory that has been used by your created objects before your object pointers leave scope, without relying on PowerBuilder's garbage collection feature.

# A Dynamic User Object Example: An MDI Status Bar

The PowerBuilder sample libraries include a useful window that allows you to create a status bar similar to the ones found in most commercial Windows applications. This effect is achieved by using a window and dynamically creating user objects for different areas of the bar.

**Tip**

The comparable PFC object is `pfc_n_cst_winsrv_statusbar`.

## The Status User Object

The actual status area is a custom visual user object, `u_mdi_microhelp_item`, that contains a single static text control that's stretched to fill the user object area, along with one gray and one white line graphic controls. The lines are placed at the far left of the user object area to form a 3D-looking separator.

The user object has a single instance variable, as follows, and five functions that provide an interface to the attributes of the user object.

```
Private:
// Specifies the action that the user object is to display, ie. Date and time
Integer ii_Action
```

To change the object's width, provide a `of_SetWidth()` function that's called with the new width and a text alignment enumerated type (see Listing 26.1). When the user object is resized, the static text control is also resized.

**LISTING 26.1**    The Public Subroutine `of_SetWidth()`

```
//Parameters:
//    Integer ai_Width
//    Alignment aa_Align

this.Width = ai_Width
st_1.Width = ai_Width - st_1.X
st_1.Alignment = aa_align
```

To maintain the total encapsulation of the user object, also provide the `of_SetText()` function to set the `Text` attribute of the static text object:

```
//Parameters:
//    String as_Text

st_1.text = as_Text
```

To alter the color of the text displayed in the static text object, use the `of_SetColour()` function:

```
//Parameters:
//    Long al_Colour

st_1.TextColor = al_Colour
```

The following two functions provide set and get access to the private instance variable of the user object. The set function, `of_SetAction()`, is as follows:

```
//Parameters:
//    Integer ai_Action

ii_Action = ai_Action
```

This is the get function:

```
Return ii_Action
```

This user object provides the basis of all status items to be displayed on the window attached to the frame.

# The Frame Parasite Window

The window object `w_frame_system_data` is of type Popup and is initially declared as invisible, disabled, and without a border. Listing 26.2 shows the private instance variables declared for this window.

**LISTING 26.2** The Private Instance Variables for `w_frame_system_data`

```
Window iw_Parent
Integer ii_Items, ii_WinHeight, ii_Offset
Integer ii_BorderHeight, ii_BorderWidth, ii_ResizeableOffset
u_mdi_microhelp_item iuo_Items[]


// Constants
Integer SYS_TIME = 1, USER_HEAP = 2, GDI_HEAP = 3, SYS_MEMORY = 4, DB_SERVER = 5
Integer TOTAL_ITEMS = 5
```

The window is based on three event scripts: Open, Close, and Timer.

The Open event sets up the required pieces of the status bar. The window is opened with a numeric parameter, which is a bit representation (see Table 26.1) of the desired styles to add to the status bar.

**TABLE 26.1** Bit Styles for `w_frame_system_data`

| Bit Value | Decimal Value | Description |
|-----------|---------------|-------------|
| 00001 | 1 | Time |
| 00010 | 2 | User heap |
| 00100 | 4 | GDI heap |
| 01000 | 8 | Memory |
| 10000 | 16 | Database server and database (current) |

To add a style to the list, simply add the decimal values. For example, to display just the time and memory items, you would open `w_frame_system_data` with the value 9.

**Note**

This method of passing style bits around is useful if you don't want to deal with structures and the associated overheads.

Within the Open event (see Listing 26.3), the style bits are converted from a numeric representation into separate Boolean equality tests. As you can see in Table 26.1, each style overlays (without overwriting) the other styles, so you can determine each individual setting by successively dividing by 2, taking the result away from the total value, and checking for a remainder.

**LISTING 26.3** The Open Event for w_frame_system_data

```
Integer li_Count, li_Work, li_Previous, li_Border

// Hold for later
li_Work = message.Doubleparm

// Initialize and determine environment information
iw_Parent = ParentWindow()

// This assumes standard PC screen dimensions
Choose Case g_App.i_Environment.ScreenHeight
   Case 480
      ii_WinHeight = 57
      ii_Offset = 16
   Case 600
      ii_WinHeight= 54
      ii_Offset = 18
   Case Else
      ii_WinHeight= 57
      ii_Offset = 10
End Choose
this.Height = ii_WinHeight

li_Border = ProfileInt( "win.ini", "windows", "borderwidth", 2)
ii_BorderHeight = 4 * li_Border
ii_BorderWidth = PixelsToUnits(li_Border, XPixelsToUnits!)

// If the window that was passed is resizable include additional border
// thickness
If Not iw_Parent.Resizable Then
   ii_ResizeableOffset = 8 * (li_Border + 2)
End If

// Break out the bit pattern of the passed parm
li_Previous = li_Work
For li_Count = 1 to TOTAL_ITEMS
 li_Work /= 2
   If ((li_Previous - (li_Work * 2)) = 1) Then
      If li_Count = 1 Then of_AddItem( Center!, SYS_TIME, FALSE)
      If li_Count = 2 Then of_AddItem( Center!, USER_HEAP, FALSE)
      If li_Count = 3 Then of_AddItem( Center!, GDI_HEAP, FALSE)
      If li_Count = 4 Then of_AddItem( Center!, SYS_MEMORY, FALSE)
      If li_Count = 5 Then of_AddItem( Center!, DB_SERVER, FALSE)
```

**26**

**LISTING 26.3** CONTINUED

```
   End If
 li_Previous = li_Work
Next


of_ParentResized()


this.TriggerEvent( Timer!)


// Every 30 seconds refresh the item text
Timer( 30, this)
```

Information about the environment in which the window will appear is gathered by using the Environment object: screen height, window height, offset within window, and window border (and whether this border is resizable). The window function of_AddItem() is called for each status item requested to be displayed. After all the status items are created, the window is resized to show just these items and then positions itself over the correct area of the parent. A 30-second timer is then set to cause the status items to be refreshed regularly.

The initial setting and subsequent refreshing of the status items is carried out in the Timer event (see Listing 26.4). Five status types can be displayed: SYS_TIME, USER_HEAP, GDI_HEAP, SYS_MEMORY, and DB_SERVER. Two user object functions, of_SetText() and of_SetColour(), are used to set each item's text and appropriate color.

**LISTING 26.4** The Timer Event for w_frame_system_data

```
Uint lui_Resource
Ulong lul_Mem
Integer li_Count
String ls_ServerName

For li_Count = 1 To ii_Items
  Choose Case iuo_Items[li_Count].of_GetAction()
  Case DB_SERVER
   ls_ServerName=Upper(Left(SQLCA.ServerName,1)) + Mid(SQLCA.ServerName,2)
   iuo_Items[ li_Count].of_SetText(ls_ServerName + " (" + SQLCA.Database+")")
  Case SYS_TIME
   iuo_Items[ li_Count].of_SetText (String (Today(), "m/dd/yyyy") + " " + &
   String( Now(), "h:mm am/pm"))
   iuo_Items[ li_Count].of_SetColour( RGB (0, 0, 128))
  Case GDI_HEAP
   lui_Resource = gnv_App.inv_Externals.of_GetFreeSystemResources(1)
   If lui_Resource < 20 Then
```

**LISTING 26.4**    CONTINUED

```
      // Set the colour to red - indicate potential problem
      iuo_Items[ li_Count].of_SetColour( 255)
   Else
      // Normal black text colour
      iuo_Items[ li_Count].of_SetColour (0)
   End If
   iuo_Items[li_Count].of_SetText("GDI: " + String( lui_Resource,"###")+" %")
 Case USER_HEAP
   lui_Resource = gnv_App.inv_Externals.of_GetFreeSystemResources(2)
   If lui_Resource < 20 Then
      // Set the colour to red - indicate potential problem
      iuo_Items[li_Count].of_SetColour( 255)
   Else
      // Normal black text colour
      iuo_Items[li_Count].of_SetColour( 0)
   End If
   iuo_Items[li_Count].of_SetText("User: "+ String(lui_Resource,"###") +" %")
 Case SYS_MEMORY
   lul_Mem = gnv_App.inv_Externals.of_GetFreememory()
   If lul_Mem < 2 Then
      iuo_Items[ li_Count].of_SetColour( 255)
   Else
      iuo_Items[ li_Count].of_SetColour( 0)
   End If
   // Divide the value by 1024 * 1024 to convert from bytes to MB
   iuo_Items[li_Count].of_SetText("Mem: "+String(lul_Mem/1048576,"#.0")+" Mb")
 End Choose
Next
```

At the start of this chapter, we added a phrase to the developers' credo: destroy all objects that you create. The Close event in Listing 26.5 puts this into practice. Each user object that was opened is now closed, and the associated resources are recovered.

**LISTING 26.5**    The Close Event for w_frame_system_data

```
Integer li_Count

For li_Count = 1 To ii_Items
   CloseUserObject( iuo_Items[li_Count])
Next
```

Next, explore four supporting window functions that undertake various tasks.

The of_ParentResized() function in Listing 26.6 is called by the parent window whenever a Resize event occurs. The width and height of w_frame_system_data must be calculated to display the requested status areas. The height and width of the user objects are taken into consideration when calculating the new width, height, and position of the window in the parent frame.

**LISTING 26.6** The Public Subroutine of_ParentResized()

```
// Position window so it is over lower right hand portion of MicroHelp bar
Integer li_WindowHeight, li_WindowWidth, li_Temp
Boolean lb_Visible

lb_Visible = this.Visible
this.Visible = FALSE

If iw_Parent.WindowState = Minimized! Then
   Return
End If

of_CalculateItemSizes()

li_WindowHeight = iw_Parent.Y + iw_Parent.Height - &
                ( this.Height + ii_Offset + ii_BorderHeight)
li_WindowWidth = iw_Parent.X + iw_Parent.WorkSpaceWidth() + &
            ii_BorderWidth - ( this.Width + 12)
If gnv_App.i_Environment.OSMajorRevision = 4 Then
   // Move the parasite more to the left because of the resize box in Win95
 li_WindowWidth -= 45
End If

// Calculate smallest possible distance in from left edge of frame
li_Temp = iw_Parent.X + 2 * ii_BorderWidth + 16

// Is the window width less than the smallest possible frame size?
If li_WindowWidth < li_Temp Then
   // Then move the window to the left most edge of the frame.
 li_WindowWidth = li_Temp
   this.Width = iw_Parent.WorkSpaceWidth() - ( ii_BorderWidth + 32)
End If
```

**LISTING 26.6**   CONTINUED

```
this.Move(li_WindowWidth, li_WindowHeight)
this.Visible = lb_Visible
iw_Parent.SetFocus()
```

The function of_CalculateItemSizes() in Listing 26.7 is called to calculate the overall width of the visible status items and to adjust the spacing of the objects in case a status object has been created or destroyed since the last call. The window's width is then adjusted to allow the status objects to be displayed.

**LISTING 26.7**   The Private Subroutine of_CalculateItemSizes()

```
// Determine the overall window width and reposition the items themselves
Integer li_Count, li_TotalWidth

If ii_Items <= 0 Then Return

iuo_Items[ ii_Items].X = 0
li_TotalWidth = iuo_Items[ ii_Items].Width

For li_Count = (ii_Items - 1) To 1 Step -1
    iuo_Items[li_Count].X = iuo_Items[li_Count + 1].X + &
                            iuo_Items[li_Count + 1].Width
li_TotalWidth += iuo_Items[li_Count].Width
Next

this.width = li_TotalWidth
```

The of_AddItem() function in Listing 26.8 demonstrates the OpenUserObject() function in use. The second format is used to open each instance of the u_mdi_microhelp_item class. The object reference is stored in the instance array iuo_Items. The attributes of the object instance are then set using the access functions provided. Finally, because you just altered the number of visible status items, of_ParentResized() is called to resize the window, and then a Timer event is caused to set the initial value of the new item.

**LISTING 26.8**   The Public Function of_AddItem()

```
//Parameters:
//      Alignment aa_Alignment
//      Integer ai_Code
//      Boolean ab_Update

Integer li_ItemWidth
```

**LISTING 26.8** CONTINUED

```
// Add an item to the list of items, and appear to the left of the last
ii_Items ++

Choose Case ai_Code
   Case DB_SERVER
 li_ItemWidth = 450
   Case SYS_TIME
 li_ItemWidth = 450
   Case GDI_HEAP
 li_ItemWidth = 260
   Case USER_HEAP
 li_ItemWidth = 260
   Case SYS_MEMORY
 li_ItemWidth = 360
End Choose


OpenUserObject( iuo_Items[ ii_Items], "u_mdi_microhelp_item")

iuo_Items[ ii_Items].Height = ii_WinHeight
iuo_Items[ ii_Items].of_SetAction (ai_Code)
iuo_Items[ ii_Items].of_SetWidth(li_ItemWidth, aa_Alignment)

If ab_Update Then
   of_ParentResized()
   PostEvent( Timer!)
End If

Return ii_Items
```

The function of_DeleteItem() in Listing 26.9 is called to selectively remove status items from w_frame_system_data. The CloseUserObject() function destroys the storage associated with the item, and the iuo_Items array is shuffled to fill the remaining hole. The of_ParentResized() function is called to resize the window to the smaller number of visible status items.

**LISTING 26.9** The Public Function of_DeleteItem()

```
//Parameters:
//    Integer ai_Position
//Returns:
//    Boolean
```

**LISTING 26.9** CONTINUED

```
// Delete the item at the passed position
Integer li_Count

If ( ( ai_Position > ii_Items) Or ( ai_Position <= 0)) Then
    Return FALSE
End If

CloseUserObject( iuo_Items[ ai_Position])

ii_Items --
// Remove the deleted item from the array of items
If ii_Items > 0 Then
    For li_Count = ai_Position To ii_Items
        iuo_Items[li_Count] = iuo_Items[li_Count + 1]
    Next
End If

of_ParentResized()
Return TRUE
```

You can add many access functions to allow the frame window to query, and maybe set, some private instance variables, if you want. Figure 26.1 shows the finished MDI frame status bar.

**Figure 26.1**
*The MDI frame status bar.*

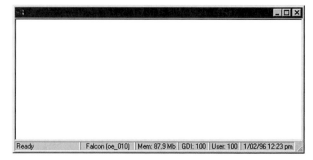

# Inserting Dynamic User Objects Tab Pages

With the expanding popularity of tab controls in applications, users continue to push for different and more creative ways to implement these controls. The next few sections discuss how to create tab page user objects and maximize their functionality with your tab controls.

## The `OpenTab()` Function

PowerBuilder's `OpenTab()` function has enabled developers to implement the tab control more effectively and easily. This function allows developers to create tab pages dynamically at runtime by using a prebuilt custom visual user object. This technique is useful for displaying different modules based on the current user's requirements, allowing users to select modules they want to see at runtime, or displaying a tab page for each row retrieved from the database. The last usage is the type explained in the section "A Dynamic Tab Page Example: Viewing Employee Information."

This function has two syntaxes that again parallel the `Open()` function used with windows. The first syntax opens an instance of a particular user object as a tab page on the tab control. The second lets you specify the desired class in a string argument.

The first syntax is as follows:

```
tabcontrol.OpenTab( UserObjectVariable, index)
```

The *UserObjectVariable* parameter is the user object data type or a variable declared of the desired user object data type. The function returns a `1` if successful, `-1` if there's an error. A reference to the opened tab page is placed in the *UserObjectVariable*.

The *index* parameter indicates the tab page index after which you want to open the specified user object. An *index* value of `0` or a number greater than the number of tab pages in the tab control opens the user object as the last tab page.

If users chose to look at two different modules—say, the Invoicing and the Commission modules—the following code would allow this implementation:

```
u_tabpg_invoicing ltp_invoicing
u_tabpg_commission ltp_commission

tab_1.OpenTab( ltp_invoicing, 0)
tab_1.OpenTab( ltp_commission, 0)
```

The second syntax requires users to open a tab page more generically by allowing for the user object type to be declared with a string variable. Its syntax is as follows:

```
tabcontrol.OpenTab( UserObjectVariable, UserObjectType, index)
```

The *UserObjectVariable* must be a declared as a variable of data type UserObject or a descendant of type UserObject. The *UserObjectType* argument is a string containing the name of the user object class you want to open. The *index* parameter works just as it did in the previous explanation.

For the same scenario described before, the following syntax could be used:

```
UserObject luo_dynamic

Tab_1.OpenTab( luo_dynamic, "u_tabpg_invoicing", 0)
Tab_1.OpenTab( luo_dynamic, "u_tabpg_commission", 0)
```

> **Note**
>
> Unlike the OpenUserObject() function, you can call OpenTab() and use the same user object multiple times; a new tab page will be opened each time.

## The OpenTabWithParm() Function

The OpenTabWithParm() function is also similar to the OpenWithParm() function used with windows. Using OpenTabWithParm() allows you to carry out the same functionality as the OpenTab() function but also allows you to pass an argument to the user object through the Message object. Two syntaxes mimic those used for OpenTab(). The following creates a user object tab page of a specified class and passes a parameter to it:

```
tabcontrol.OpenTabWithParm( UserObjectVariable, parm, index)
```

The other syntax opens a user object tab page and passes a parameter; however, the user object class is specified in the string variable contained in the *UserObjectType* argument.

```
tabcontrol.OpenTabWithParm( UserObjectVariable, parm, UserObjectType, index)
```

The same rules around the use of the Message object discussed earlier in the OpenUserObjectWithParm() section apply here.

# A Dynamic Tab Page Example: Viewing Employee Information

One use discussed earlier is opening tab pages based on information retrieved from the database. In this example, you see a simple implementation that uses a custom visual user object containing a DataWindow control, a window with an empty tab control, and the first syntax for the `OpenTab()` function.

## The Custom Visual User Object

The user object actually inserted into the tab control via the `OpenTab()` function is `u_tabpg_employees`. The only object on the user object is a DataWindow control. The user object contains three functions and the following instance variable:

```
Private:
// Specifies the employee Id to be viewed on the instance of this object
integer ii_empid
```

To set the value of `ii_empid` by other objects, the `of_SetEmpId()` function is created. It accepts one argument of type integer whose value is set to the instance variable:

```
//set the value of the argument to the ii_empid variable
ii_empid = ai_empid
```

Because the tab pages are created dynamically based on the number of employees retrieved, the data used in that process needs to be shared with all its tab pages. To enable this, a function called `of_Share()` is created to accept a datastore and uses that argument to share the data with the DataWindow:

```
// This will share the data contained in the argument with the datawindow on
// this object.

RETURN ads_source.ShareData( dw_1)
```

In this example, each tab page displays one employee's information. Because of the dynamics behind sharing data (see Chapter 15, "Advanced DataWindow Techniques I"), a function called `of_FilterData()` is created for the filtering of the DataWindow based on the value of the `ii_empid` instance variable:

```
// Filter the data with the employee id assigned to this page
dw_1.SetFilter( "emp_id = " + String (ii_empid))
RETURN dw_1.Filter()
```

The u_tabpg_employees object encapsulates all the functionality it needs to display the appropriate information. The next section discusses the window that implements this functionality.

## The Employee Window

The w_employee_tabs window implements the dynamic tab page functionality. It contains one tab control with no tab pages. The SelectionChanged event (see Listing 26.10) of the tab control is coded to call the of_FilterData() function on the tab page when a new tab page is selected.

**LISTING 26.10**  The SelectionChanged Event of tab_1

```
u_tabpg_employee ltp_emp

// Get the object in the control array for the newly
// selected tab page and set it to a variable of the
// user object type so the functions can be referenced
ltp_emp = control[ newindex]

// The data will be filtered to the employee id set to
// the tab
ltp_emp.of_FilterData()
```

The window's Open event is the last bit of code needed for this example. It creates an instance-level datastore that contains all the employee information. Tab pages are created based on the number of rows retrieved, and the data from the datastore is shared with the tab pages for the displaying of the employee information. Listing 26.11 shows the code used to pull all the functionality together.

**LISTING 26.11**  The Open Event of w_employee_tabs

```
Long ll_RowCount, ll_Cnt, ll_emp
Integer li_rc
u_tabpg_employee u_tp_emp

// create the datastore
ids_Employee = CREATE datastore

// Initialize SQLCA
SQLCA.DBMS = "ODBC"
SQLCA.Database = "EAS Demo DB V3"
SQLCA.AutoCommit = False
```

**LISTING 26.11** CONTINUED

```
SQLCA.DBParm = "ConnectString='DSN=EAS Demo DB V3;UID=dba;PWD=sql'"
//Connect to the database
Connect Using SQLCA;

If SQLCA.SQLCode <> 0 Then
    MessageBox("Connect Problem", "Could not connect!~r~n" + &
                    "DBMessage: " + SQLCA.SQLErrText, StopSign!)
    Halt
End If


// Set the datawindow object for the datastore
ids_employee.DataObject = "d_employee_filtered"


// Set the transaction object for the datastore
ids_Employee.SetTransObject(SQLCA)


// Retrieve the Employee data
ll_RowCount = ids_Employee.Retrieve()

//loop through all of the records and open a tabpage for each
FOR ll_cnt = 1 to ll_RowCount
    ll_emp = ids_employee.Object.emp_id[ ll_cnt]
    // Open the user object after the last tabpg
    tab_1.OpenTab( u_tp_emp, 0)
    // Set the employee id with the current rows id
    u_tp_emp.of_SetEmpId( ll_emp)
    // Share the data with the tabpage
    u_tp_emp.of_Share( ids_employee)
    // Make the tab name to be the employee id
    u_tp_emp.Text = String( ll_emp)
NEXT
```

All the preceding code produces a tab control that contains several tab pages, each displaying the information about the employee displayed on the tab (see Figure 26.2). This demonstrates an implementation of the OpenTab() function, which can be enhanced to contain more functionality as your application expands.

FIGURE **26.2**
*Dynamic tab
pages created
on the*
w_employee_-
tabs
*window.*

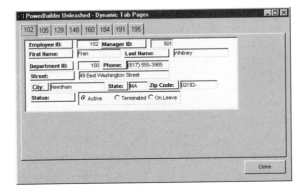

---

**Tip**

When using the rows retrieved from the database, remember to make sure that a reasonable number of rows are being dealt with. Too many rows cause the tab control to lose its usefulness and become too cumbersome for users.

# Transaction Class Objects

Along with the DataWindow standard visual user object, one of the most important user objects you can create is a standard class user object based on the Transaction system class. This allows you to encapsulate basic functionality into one object, rather than repeatedly code the same statements (for example, starting a transaction). The transaction object that you build in this section incorporates the transaction-management practices introduced in Chapter 4, "SQL and PowerBuilder," as well as some additional object-management functions.

---

**Tip**

The comparable PFC object is n_tr.

The user object u_n_transaction is written as an abstract class, and you will inherit concrete class objects for each database-management systems you will be using. A few instance variables are declared for the object:

```
Protected:
   Error i_Error
   Integer ii_OpenTransactions = 0
   Boolean ib_Connected = FALSE, ib_BeginTran = FALSE, ib_SaveTran = FALSE
```

In the abstract class, five functions are prototyped (as follows) and are all set to return a 0 value. These will be overridden in each concrete class for DBMS-specific transaction management.

```
public function integer SaveTran( String as_TranName)
public function integer CommitTran()
public function integer BeginTran()
public function integer RollbackToSave( String as_TranName)
public function integer RollbackTran()
```

## Transaction Class Events

Within the Constructor event, shown in the following code, you create the error object to be used by this object's functions for error reporting. The private Error object allows you to set persistent values and make additional assignments without affecting the calling script's error object that's held by the application.

```
i_Error = Create Error
i_Error.Object = this.ClassName()
```

Before the object is destroyed, ensure that the current connection has closed down correctly. Then the private error object must be destroyed, along with its parent:

```
If ib_Connected Then
   this.CloseConnection()
End If

Destroy i_Error
```

## Transaction Class Methods

A function that you will use throughout the transaction object being created is CheckForError() (see Listing 26.12), which is called to check the SQLCode object property and open the standard error window if requested to. The SQLCode is returned by the function for additional processing in the calling function (see the MakeConnection() function in Listing 26.14 for an example).

**LISTING 26.12**   The Public Function CheckForError()

```
//Parameters:
//    Error a_Error
//    Boolean ab_DisplayError
//Returns:
//    Integer

If this.SQLCode = -1 And ab_DisplayError Then
   error.WindowMenu = a_Error.WindowMenu
   error.Object = a_Error.Object
   error.ObjectEvent = a_Error.ObjectEvent
   error.Line = a_Error.Line
   error.Number = this.SQLDBCode
   error.Text = this.SQLErrText
   open( w_error)
   Return this.SQLCode
Else
   Return this.SQLCode
End If
```

IsConnected() is an access function that returns the current status of the connection:

```
Return ib_Connected
```

InTransaction() is an access function that returns whether the connection is now in the midst of a transaction:

```
Return ib_BeginTran
```

OpenTransactions() is an access function that returns the current level of transaction nesting:

```
Return ii_OpenTransactions
```

The ExecuteSQL() function (see Listing 26.13) provides a controlled point to execute SQL code that's outside the commands PowerBuilder recognizes.

**LISTING 26.13**   The Public Function ExecuteSQL() for u_n_transaction

```
//Parameters:
//    String as_Statement
//    Boolean ab_ShowError
//Return:
//    Integer

EXECUTE IMMEDIATE :as_Statement USING this;
```

**LISTING 26.13** CONTINUED

```
If ab_ShowError Then
    i_Error.ObjectEvent = "ExecuteSQL()"
    i_Error.line = 1
    Return CheckForError( i_Error, TRUE)
Else
    Return this.SQLCode
End If
```

The MakeConnection()function (see Listing 26.14) issues the CONNECT statement and carries out error processing for you.

**LISTING 26.14** The Public Function MakeConnection() for u_n_transaction

```
//Returns:
//      Integer

i_Error.ObjectEvent = "MakeConnection()"
i_Error.Line = 4

If ib_Connected Then
    // Already connected!
    Return -1
End If

CONNECT USING this;

If CheckForError( i_Error, FALSE) = 0 Then
    ib_Connected = TRUE
End If

Return this.SQLCode
```

Listing 26.15 shows the CloseConnection() function, which issues the DISCONNECT statement and carries out any error processing for you. Also, rather than have to rely on PowerBuilder to carry out an implicit transaction rollback or commit, you know for certain that an explicit rollback of an open transaction will occur.

**LISTING 26.15**  The Public Function `CloseConnection()`

```
//Returns:
//       Integer

If Not ib_Connected Then
    // Already disconnected!
    Return -1
End If

i_Error.ObjectEvent = "CloseConnection()"

// Currently have an open transaction roll it back.
If this.AutoCommit Then
    If ib_BeginTran Then
        this.RollbackTran()
        i_Error.Line = 10
        CheckForError( i_Error, TRUE)
    End If
Else
    ROLLBACK USING this;
    i_Error.Line = 15
    CheckForError( i_Error, TRUE)
End If

DISCONNECT USING this;
i_Error.Line = 17

If CheckForError( i_Error, TRUE) = 0 Then
    ib_Connected = FALSE
    ii_OpenTransactions = 0
End If

Return this.SQLCode
```

# The Concrete Transaction Class SQL Server

In each concrete class object inherited from `u_n_transaction`, the methods outlined in this section should be defined. The sample code shown in Listing 26.16 is for a Microsoft or Sybase SQL Server transaction object.

**LISTING 26.16** The Public Function `u_n_sqlserver_transaction CloneObject()`

```
u_n_sqlserver_transaction ltr_ChildTransaction

ltr_ChildTransaction = create u_n_sqlserver_transaction

ltr_ChildTransaction.DBMS = this.DBMS
ltr_ChildTransaction.database = this.database
ltr_ChildTransaction.servername = this.servername
ltr_ChildTransaction.logid = this.logid
ltr_ChildTransaction.logpass = this.logpass
ltr_ChildTransaction.userid = this.userid
ltr_ChildTransaction.dbparm = this.dbparm
ltr_ChildTransaction.dbpass = this.dbpass
ltr_ChildTransaction.lock = this.lock
ltr_ChildTransaction.autocommit = this.autocommit

Return ltr_ChildTransaction
```

The first function in Listing 26.16 wasn't prototyped in `u_n_transaction` because it would have served no purpose; the function isn't used in the object itself, and the variable it uses is particular to each concrete class. The `CloneObject()` function creates and returns a new unconnected transaction object based on the current transaction object.

The remaining methods for this object are discussed in Chapter 4, "SQL and PowerBuilder," but are shown in their completed form here.

The `BeginTran()` function (see Listing 26.17) starts a database transaction based on the current value of the transaction's `AutoCommit` attribute, starting a true transaction if it's set to `TRUE`, and a PowerBuilder transaction if it's set to `FALSE`.

**LISTING 26.17** The Public Function `BeginTran()`

```
//Returns:
//      Integer

i_Error.ObjectEvent = "BeginTran()"

If this.AutoCommit Then
   EXECUTE IMMEDIATE "BEGIN TRANSACTION" USING this;
   i_Error.Line = 4
Else
   // There is no BEGIN TRANSACTION for PB with no AutoCommit
   COMMIT USING this;
```

**LISTING 26.17**   CONTINUED

```
    i_Error.Line = 8
End If

ii_OpenTransactions ++
ib_BeginTran = TRUE

Return CheckForError( i_Error, TRUE)
```

The `CommitTran()` function in Listing 26.18 completes an open database transaction and causes the changes to be committed to the database. The method used depends on the current value of the transaction's `AutoCommit` attribute.

**LISTING 26.18**   The Public Function `CommitTran()`

```
//Returns:
//      Integer

i_Error.ObjectEvent = "CommitTran()"

If this.AutoCommit Then
   If ib_BeginTran Then
      EXECUTE IMMEDIATE "COMMIT TRANSACTION" USING this;
      i_Error.Line = 5
   End If
Else
   COMMIT USING this;
   i_Error.Line = 9
End If

ib_BeginTran = FALSE
ib_SaveTran = FALSE
ii_OpenTransactions --

Return CheckForError( i_Error, TRUE)
```

The `RollbackTran()` function in Listing 26.19 completes an open database transaction and causes the changes made in it to be thrown away. The method used depends on the current value of the transaction's `AutoCommit` attribute.

**LISTING 26.19** The Public Function `RollbackTran()`

```
//Returns:
//      Integer

i_Error.ObjectEvent = "ExecuteSQL()"
If this.AutoCommit Then
   If ib_BeginTran Then
      EXECUTE IMMEDIATE "ROLLBACK TRANSACTION" USING this;
      i_Error.Line = 5
   End If
Else
   ROLLBACK USING this;
   i_Error.Line = 9
End If

ib_BeginTran = FALSE
ib_SaveTran = FALSE
ii_OpenTransactions = 0

Return CheckForError( i_Error, FALSE)
```

The next two functions are based on SQL Server's capability to save points in a transaction and allow partial recovery of these points to occur.

The `SaveTran()` function (see Listing 26.20) labels a position in the transaction so that recovery can occur to that point. There's no corresponding save transaction point command in the default PowerBuilder behavior, and everything must be committed or rolled back together.

**LISTING 26.20** The Public Function `SaveTran()`

```
//Parameters:
//     String as_TranName
//Returns:
//      Integer

String ls_Command

ls_Command = "SAVE TRANSACTION " + as_TranName

i_Error.ObjectEvent = "SaveTran()"

If this.AutoCommit Then
```

**LISTING 26.20**   CONTINUED

```
    EXECUTE IMMEDIATE :ls_Command USING this;
    i_Error.Line = 8
Else
    // There is no SAVE TRANSACTION for PB with no AutoCommit
    // continue the existing transaction, and commit or rollback everything.
End If

ib_SaveTran = TRUE
ii_OpenTransactions ++

Return CheckForError( i_Error, TRUE)
```

The `RollbackToSave()`function (see Listing 26.21) carries out a partial rollback of all commands issued since the save transaction label specified. Again, there's no corresponding partial rollback command in the default PowerBuilder behavior, and everything must be committed or rolled back together.

**LISTING 26.21**   The Public Function `RollbackToSave()`

```
//Parameters:
//    String as_TranName
//Returns:
//      Integer

String ls_Command

ls_Command = "ROLLBACK TRANSACTION " + as_TranName

i_Error.ObjectEvent = "ExecuteSQL()"

If this.AutoCommit Then
   If ib_BeginTran Then
      EXECUTE IMMEDIATE :ls_Command USING this;
      i_Error.Line = 9
   End If
Else
   ROLLBACK USING this;
   i_Error.Line = 13
End If

ii_OpenTransactions --
```

**LISTING 26.21** CONTINUED

```
If as_TranName = "" Then
    ib_BeginTran = FALSE
    ii_OpenTransactions = 0
End If
ib_SaveTran = FALSE

Return CheckForError( i_Error, TRUE) ()
```

# Application Class Objects

Another useful addition to any framework or class library is an abstract application class from which you inherit for each application. This allows you to perform generic processing for each application and also provides a location to store global variables. You can provide access functions to them if you want.

> **Tip**
>
> The comparable PFC object is `u_cst_appmanager`.

The application class object uses a custom class user object as the base. The `u_n_application` user object has a number of instance variables declared (as follows), and they are all publicly accessible from within the application.

```
u_n_externals inv_Externals
Environment i_Environment
Application i_Application
Window iw_WndFrame
String is_Application, is_ApplicationName, is_INIFile
```

The first variable, `inv_Externals`, is in fact another custom class user object and is further discussed in Chapter 36, "API Calls." It references the appropriate class user object through which external calls should be made. During the initialization of the application user object, the environment that the application is running in is determined, and `inv_Externals` is instantiated with the appropriate API user object. This is the code:

```
of_SetEnvironment()
```

As important as the Constructor event is the call in the Destructor event used to clean up the resources used by the application. This is the code:

```
of_CleanUp()
```

The complete functionality of this user object is hidden behind object-level functions, and in some function descriptions shown in Listing 26.22, you see comments where code introduced in Chapter 10, "Windows and the Window Painter," goes.

**LISTING 26.22** The Public Subroutine of_SetApplication()

```
//Parameters:
//     application a_application

i_application = a_application
//
// See Chapter 11- set the toolbar startup attributes
//
```

One user object to be introduced later in this chapter is a standard class transaction user object. If you use this user object, it needs to be instantiated with the correct type of transaction object. The function of_SetDBMS() (see Listing 26.23) is used for this purpose. The function would be ideally called in a connection window, but the application Open event would serve just as well.

**LISTING 26.23** The Public Subroutine of_SetDBMS()

```
//Parameters:
//     String as_DBMS
//Returns:
//     Boolean

Boolean lb_Success = TRUE

Choose Case Lower( as_DBMS)
   Case "mss - microsoft 6.x"
      SQLCA = Create u_n_mss_sqlserver_transaction
   Case "in4 - i-net v4.x", "in5 - i-net v5.x"
      SQLCA = Create u_n_informix_transaction
   Case "or6 - oracle v6.x", "or7 - oracle v7.x"
      SQLCA = Create u_n_oracle_transaction
   Case "syb - sql server v4.x"
      SQLCA = Create u_n_sqlserver_transaction
   Case Else
```

**LISTING 26.23**  CONTINUED

```
      // Failed to pick up a specific transaction object
      lb_Success = FALSE
End Choose
Return lb_Success
```

The return from this function should be checked to ensure that the DBMS string passed was
recognized.

When the application is first run, the of_SetEnvironment() function in Listing 26.24 is
called to set up the environment-related variables: the operating environment and the
necessary API object that works in this environment. As you extend your applications
across multiple platforms, you can extend the Choose...Case statement to use the API user
objects that you create. Because of the way you construct the API object and call those
functions, you won't need to change a single line of code elsewhere in your application.

**LISTING 26.24**  The Private Subroutine of_SetEnvironment()

```
GetEnvironment( i_Environment)

Choose Case i_Environment.OSType
   Case Windows!
      If i_Environment.OSMajorRevision = 4 Then
         // Windows 95
inv_Externals = Create u_n_externals_win32


End If
   Case WindowsNT!
      inv_Externals = Create u_n_externals_win32
   Case Else
      SetNull( inv_Externals)
End Choose
```

Just as you'd want an application's toolbar to appear in the exact way that it did last time
you used the application, making a window (well, the main one at least) open with the
previous size and position is also a nice feature. The of_SetMDIFrame() function (see
Listing 26.25) not only sets up the frame and toolbar to the last known settings, but also
keeps a reference to the frame window for use throughout the application.

**LISTING 26.25** The Public Subroutine of_SetMDIFrame()

```
//Parameters:
//      window aw_hWnd

String ls_Alignment
iw_WndFrame = aw_hWnd

//
// See windows chapter - set the toolbar start up attributes
//

Choose Case Upper(ProfileString(is_INIFile,"Application","FrameState","Top!"))
    Case "MAXIMIZED!"
     iw_WndFrame.WindowState = Maximized!
    Case "MINIMIZED!"
     iw_WndFrame.WindowState = Minimized!
     iw_iw_WndFrame.X = ProfileInt( is_INIFile, "Application", "FrameX", 0)
     iw_iw_WndFrame.Y = ProfileInt(is_INIFile, "Application", "FrameY", 0)
iw_iw_WndFrame.Height=ProfileInt(is_INIFile,"Application","FrameHeight",600)
iw_iw_WndFrame.Width=ProfileInt(is_INIFile,"Application","FrameWidth",400)
    Case "NORMAL!'"
     iw_WndFrame.WindowState = Normal!
     iw_WndFrame.X = ProfileInt(is_INIFile, "Application", "FrameX", 0)
     iw_WndFrame.Y = ProfileInt(is_INIFile, "Application", "FrameY", 0)
iw_WndFrame.Height=ProfileInt(is_INIFile,"Application","FrameHeight",600)
iw_WndFrame.Width=ProfileInt(is_INIFile,"Application","FrameWidth",400)
End Choose
```

**Tip**

The Preference service in the PFC allows you to handle many of the same functions such as saving the window's X and Y coordinates, the size, the toolbar size, and the toolbar position, to name a few. It gives you the opportunity to choose the settings to be saved to the Registry or an INI file.

To maintain the last position and settings of toolbars and the frame, of_ClosingMDIFrame() in Listing 26.26 is called to inform the application that the frame is being closed, save the information, and carry out any other shutdown procedures.

**LISTING 26.26** The Public Subroutine of_ClosingMDIFrame()

```
//
// See windows chapter - store the toolbar attributes
//

Choose Case iw_WndFrame.WindowState
 Case Maximized!
    SetProfileString( is_INIFile, "Application", "FrameState", "Maximized!")
 Case Minimized!
    SetProfileString(is_INIFile, "Application", "FrameState", "Minimized!")
    SetProfileString(is_INIFile,"Application","FrameX",String(iw_WndFrame.X))
    SetProfileString(is_INIFile,"Application","FrameY",String(iw_WndFrame.Y))
    SetProfileString(is_INIFile,"Application","FrameHeight", &
                                             String(iw_WndFrame.Height))
    SetProfileString(is_INIFile,"Application","FrameWidth", &
                                             String(iw_WndFrame.Width))
 Case Normal!
    SetProfileString(is_INIFile, "Application", "FrameState", "Normal!")
    SetProfileString(is_INIFile,"Application","FrameX",String(iw_WndFrame.X))
    SetProfileString(is_INIFile,"Application","FrameY",String(iw_WndFrame.Y))
    SetProfileString(is_INIFile,"Application","FrameHeight", &
                                           String(iw_WndFrame.Height))
    SetProfileString(is_INIFile,"Application","FrameWidth", &
                                           String(iw_WndFrame.Width))
End Choose
```

Similar to the previous function (of_ClosingMDIFrame()), of_ClosingApplication() is called as part of the application shutdown process to save settings and perform any further cleanup (see Listing 26.27).

**LISTING 26.27** The Public Subroutine of_ClosingApplication()

```
If i_application.ToolbarText Then
   SetProfileString( is_INIFile, "Application", "ToolbarText", "TRUE")
Else
   SetProfileString( is_INIFile, "Application", "ToolbarText", "FALSE")
End If

If i_application.ToolbarTips Then
   SetProfileString( is_INIFile, "Application", "ToolbarTips", "TRUE")
Else
   SetProfileString( is_INIFile, "Application", "ToolbarTips", "FALSE")
End If
```

When the user object is closed, the cleanup routine, of_CleanUp(), is called to clean up the resources used by any created objects.

# Applicationwide Functionality

The previously detailed functions form the basic functionality you need from the application object. You can add other commonly used functions to the user object as well. The following sections describe some examples of functions you might want to add.

## Centering a Window

Centering a window within the screen requires some simple calculations and conversions (see Listing 26.28), but it's tedious to keep repeating the same code in different places. Therefore, this task is an ideal candidate to add as an object-level function to u_n_application, which allows you to encapsulate this code to just one place in an application.

**LISTING 26.28**  The Public Subroutine of_CenterWindow()

```
//Parameters:
//    window aw_ToActOn

Long ll_ScreenWidth, ll_ScreenHeight

ll_ScreenWidth = PixelsToUnits( i_Environment.ScreenWidth, XPixelsToUnits!)
ll_ScreenHeight = PixelsToUnits( i_Environment.ScreenHeight, YPixelsToUnits!)

// Calculate central position
aw_ToActOn.X = ( ll_ScreenWidth - aw_ToActOn.Width) / 2
aw_ToActOn.Y = ( ll_ScreenHeight - aw_ToActOn.Height) / 2
```

> **Tip**
>
> You can use the of_Center() function of the n_cst_winsrv object when using the PFC to center the window.

# Logging Application Events

Another useful function is to provide the capability to log an event to a database or a flat file. The function in Listing 26.29 uses a stored procedure to make an entry in the appropriate database table. Use this so that you don't have to know anything about the underlying database structure; the only requirement is that a stored procedure called sp_log_event be available in each database. In SQL Server, this would be a simple matter of adding the stored procedure and required tables to the model database so that each database subsequently created automatically has the necessary database objects.

**LISTING 26.29**  The Protected Function of_LogEvent()

```
//Parameters:
//    String as_SystemId
//    String as_EventId
//    String as_Status
//    String as_Description
//
//Returns:
//    Boolean

DateTime ldt_Now
u_n_transaction ltr_EventLog
Boolean lb_Success = TRUE

// Clone the SQLCA settings for our own transaction object
ltr_EventLog = SQLCA.CloneObject()

// Connect the new transaction to the DBMS
ltr_EventLog.MakeConnection()

DECLARE log_event PROCEDURE FOR sp_log_event
@systemid = :as_SystemId, @eventid = :as_EventId,
@eventdt = :ldt_Now, @status = :as_Status, @desc = :as_Description
USING ltr_EventLog;

ldt_Now = DateTime( Today(), Now())

EXECUTE log_event;

If ltr_EventLog.SQLCode <> 0 Then
   lb_Success = FALSE
End If
```

**LISTING 26.29**   CONTINUED

```
// Close the database connection
ltr_EventLog.CloseConnection()

Destroy ltr_EventLog

Return lb_Success
```

## Broadcasting Messages

It's useful to be able to broadcast a message to all a window's or user object's controls. The following three functions (all call of_Broadcast() by using function overloading) are based on making calls to a window object's controls and can be copied directly for the UserObject-based ones. The first version of the of_Broadcast() function, in Listing 26.30, is the simplest; it only triggers the event for each object of the requested type. The other functions are all based on the exact same code with the only difference being the TriggerEvent call and, for the user-object–based functions, the calling parameter.

**LISTING 26.30**   of_Broadcast(), Which Takes a String Message

```
//Parameters:
//    Window aw_WindowParent
//    Object ao_Objects
//    String as_Message

Integer li_NoControls, li_Affected, li_Count

li_NoControls = UpperBound( aw_WindowParent.Control)

For li_Count = 1 To li_NoControls
   If TypeOf( aw_WindowParent.Control[ li_Count]) = ao_Objects Then
      li_Affected ++
      aw_WindowParent.Control[ li_Count].TriggerEvent( as_Message)
   End If
Next

Return li_Affected
```

The next version of the function (see Listing 26.31) allows the WordParm and LongParm attributes of the Message object to be sent as part of the broadcasted message.

**LISTING 26.31**   of_Broadcast(), **Which Takes Additional Numeric Parameters**

```
//Parameters:
//     Window aw_WindowParent
//     Object ao_Objects
//     String as_Message
//     Long al_WordParm
//     Long al_LongParm

Integer li_NoControls, li_Affected, li_Count

li_NoControls = UpperBound (aw_WindowParent.Control)

For li_Count = 1 To li_NoControls
   If TypeOf (aw_WindowParent.Control[ li_Count]) = ao_Objects Then
      li_Affected ++
      aw_WindowParent.Control[ li_Count].TriggerEvent (&
      as_Message, al_WordParm, al_LongParm)
   End If
Next

Return li_Affected
```

As you can see, these functions share the same base code, with minor alterations. You can choose to combine them into one function, but then there are optional parameters that have to be defined by anyone using the function, which you will usually require to be NULL so that you can determine the required functionality. The approach I have shown here may require additional code but is much simpler to call. Listing 26.32 shows the of_Broadcast() function written for broadcasting messages to user object controls. As you can see, it contains only a few minor alterations to the code used for broadcasting to windows.

**LISTING 26.32**   of_Broadcast(), **Which Takes a Numeric and a String Parameter**

```
//Parameters:
//     UserObject auo_UserObjectParent
//     Object ao_Objects
//     String as_Message
//     Long al_WordParm
//     String as_LongParm

Integer li_NoControls, li_Affected, li_Count
```

**LISTING 26.32** CONTINUED

```
li_NoControls = UpperBound( auo_UserObjectParent.Control)

For li_Count = 1 To li_NoControls
   If TypeOf( auo_UserObjectParent.Control[ li_Count]) = ao_Objects Then
      li_Affected ++
      auo_UserObjectParent.Control[ li_Count].TriggerEvent( &
      as_Message, al_WordParm, as_LongParm)
   End If
Next


Return li_Affected
```

The parameter for the parent object must be passed in as type Window or UserObject because these are the only two classes with a `Control[]` array. Of course, it would be helpful if these were both subclassed so that you could use a generic data type in the parameter list and then pass either object type to the same function(s).

Here are two sample calls to these functions:

```
// Tell all window datawindows to refresh their contents
gnv_App.of_Broadcast( this, Datawindow!, "Refresh")


// Tell all user object singlelineedit objects to set their
// values to the passed string
gnv_App.of_Broadcast( uo_lookup, SingleLineEdit!, "Undefined", 0, "")
```

# Using the Application Class Object

At the start of each new application you create, you should inherit from the application class user object to provide a concrete class object that can be modified for the specific processing required. This might include additional functions and most certainly will include globally accessible variables. The `of_LogEvent()` function has been defined as protected, and within each inherited application object you can provide a single access or multiple-point access to this function.

To use this user object, place function calls in specific areas of your application. First, declare a global variable of the application class user object:

```
u_n_oe_application gnv_App
```

Use the same variable name in each application (in this case, gnv_App). In the Open event of the application object, you need to instantiate this variable, assign values to the relevant variables, and then call the `of_SetApplication()` function (see Listing 26.33).

**LISTING 26.33** The Open Event for an Application

```
gnv_App = Create u_n_oe_application

gnv_App.is_Application = "Order Entry"
gnv_App.is_ApplicationName = "Order Entry System - Version 1.3"
gnv_App.is_INIFile = "PCS.INI"

gnv_App.of_SetApplication( this)
```

With these commands issued, you can then use the different functionality of the application object:

```
// Set the DataWindow error message window title to the application name
this.DWMessageTitle = gnv_App.is_ApplicationName

// Make an API call
lw_Wnd = gnv_App.inv_Externals.of_FindWindow( "FNWNS040", ls_Null)
```

In the Open event of your MDI frame window, call of_SetMdiFrame() to register the window with the application:

```
gnv_App.of_SetMdiFrame( this)
```

More importantly, when the MDI frame (and, subsequently, the application) is closed, two important function calls must be made. The first is in the Close event of the frame:

```
gnv_App.of_ClosingMdiFrame()
```

The second is in the Close event of the application:

```
gnv_App.of_ClosingApplication()
```

# The Message Dispatcher

The previous section introduced a message broadcast object attached to the application object. This section turns that concept into a full-fledged service object. First, you need some instance variables to store the pointers to the objects you want to send messages to:

```
PowerObject ipo_Objects[]
Integer ii_TotalObjects
```

For total flexibility, we provide three different methods, through overloading, for registering objects with this service. The first (see Listing 26.34) just adds the object to the end of the object array.

**LISTING 26.34**   The Public Subroutine `RegisterObject()`

```
//Parameters:
//      apo_Object    of type PowerObject by reference

ii_TotalObjects ++

ipo_Objects[ ii_TotalObjects] = apo_Object
```

The second version (see Listing 26.35) adds the object into the array at the specified location.

**LISTING 26.35**   The Public Subroutine `RegisterObject()`

```
//Parameters:
//      apo_Object    of type PowerObject by reference
//      ai_Index      of type Integer

If ai_Index > ii_TotalObjects Then
   ii_TotalObjects = ai_Index
End If

ipo_Objects[ ai_Index] = apo_Object
```

The final version, in Listing 26.36, takes the previous function one step further and lets you specify whether the index element is to be overridden or an empty element should be found.

**LISTING 26.36**   The Public Subroutine `RegisterObject()`

```
//Parameters:
//      apo_Object    of type PowerObject by reference
//      ai_Index      of type Integer
//      ab_OverWrite of type Boolean

Integer li_Count
Boolean lb_Found = FALSE

If ai_Index > ii_TotalObjects Then
   ii_TotalObjects = ai_Index
End If

If aab_Overwrite Then
   ipo_Objects[ ii_TotalObjects] = apo_Object
```

**LISTING 26.36**  CONTINUED

```
Else
   If Not IsValid( ipo_Objects[ ii_TotalObjects]) Then
      ipo_Objects[ ii_TotalObjects] = apo_Object
Else
      For li_Count = ai_Index To ii_TotalObjects
         If Not IsValid( ipo_Objects[ li_Count]) Then
            lb_Found = TRUE
            Exit
         End If
      Next

      If Not lb_Found Then
         ii_TotalObjects ++
         li_Count = ii_TotalObjects
      End If

      ipo_Objects[ li_Count] = apo_Object
   End If
End If
```

The crux of this service is the actual event dispatch method that I will again overload here to provide two different ways to call it. The first version of this method, in Listing 26.37, simply takes a string that is the message to trigger and calls it for every object the service knows about.

**LISTING 26.37**  The Public Function `DispatchMessage()`

```
//Parameters:
//      as_Message  of type String
//Returns:
//      Integer

Integer li_Count, li_Called = 0

For li_Count = 1 To ii_TotalObjects
   If IsValid( ipo_Objects[ li_Count]) Then
      ipo_Objects[ li_Count].TriggerEvent( as_Message)
      li_Called ++
   End If
Next

Return li_Called
```

The second version of the `DispatchMessage()` function (see Listing 26.38) also takes parameters for a parent object to check whether a stop condition is met. This allows you to dispatch a save message to all the registered objects, specify a stop condition (for example, -1), and then check back with the parent window of the data to see whether any object indicated a failure.

**LISTING 26.38**  The Public Function `DispatchMessage()`

```
//Parameters:
//        as_Message  of type String (ReadOnly)
//        apo_Parent     of type PowerObject (ReadOnly)
//        al_StopCondition of type Long
//Returns:
//        Integer

Integer li_Count, li_Called = 0

For li_Count = 1 To ii_TotalObjects
   If IsValid( ipo_Objects[ li_Count]) Then
      ipo_Objects[ li_Count].TriggerEvent( as_Message)
      //
      // The parents CatchException event must take a boolean argument
      // so that we can do a non-destructive read of the value.
      //
      If apo_Parent.Dynamic Trigger Event CatchException( FALSE) = &
                                            al_StopCondition Then

         Return li_Called
      End If

      li_Called ++
   End If
Next

Return li_Called
```

The event declared for the parent object called by the `DispatchMessage()` function needs to be called `CatchException` (see Listing 26.39). The parent object tracks an instance-level variable that's updated by the objects being called.

26

**LISTING 26.39**  The `CatchException` Event

```
Long ll_Exception

ll_Exception = il_Exception

If ab_DestructiveRead Then
    //
    // This is a destructive read of the exception value. Need to
    // reset for future usage, this should be the NORMAL operation
    // of this code...be VERY careful about doing no destructive
    // reads.
    //
    il_Exception = 0
End If


Return ll_Exception
```

To use the dispatch service, call the `RegisterObject()` method for each object and then call the `DispatchMessage()` method. For example, to register three DataWindows and then cause a save to occur, the code would be as in Listing 26.40.

**LISTING 26.40**  Registering DataWindows and Issuing a Request to Save

```
u_n_dispatch lnv_Dispatch
//
// Note: u_n_dispatch is an auto-instantiator!
lnv_Dispatch.RegisterObject (DataWindow_1)
lnv_Dispatch.RegisterObject (DataWindow_2)
lnv_Dispatch.RegisterObject (DataWindow_3)
//
// Some work is done...the following code carries out the save!
//
SQLCA.BeginTran()

lnv_Dispatch.DispatchMessage( "SaveData", this, -1)
//
If this.Trigger Event CatchException( TRUE) = -1 Then
    SQLCA.RollbackTran()
Else
    SQLCA.CommitTran()
End If
```

# Standard DataWindow Control Objects

Probably the most important user object you will create or use is a standard visual user object based on the DataWindow control. In this user object, you can encapsulate frequently used functionality. Any operation on, or action required by, a DataWindow should be done through an associated event or function that you've created in your standard DataWindow user object.

> **Tip**
>
> The comparable PFC object is u_dw. This is one of most highly extended objects in the PFC.

The user object u_dw is declared with a number of instance variables for use in the various event and function scripts (see Listing 26.41).

**LISTING 26.41**  Instance Variables for u_dw

```
Public:
Boolean lb_FailedAccept = FALSE, ib_FailedSave = FALSE
Boolean ib_AutoResizeHorizontal = FALSE, ib_AutoResizeVertical = FALSE
Integer ii_BottomGap, ii_RightGap
Integer ii_MinWidth, ii_MaxWidth = -1, ii_MinHeight, ii_MaxHeight = -1
Window iw_Parent


Private:
Boolean ib_InAcceptText = FALSE
```

Whenever you change the `DataObject` attribute of a `DataWindow` object, the associated transaction object is disconnected and the row focus indicator is lost. `of_ChangeDataObject()` provides a central point to change the value of this attribute, reconnect the transaction, and reset the row pointer (see Listing 26.42). You can overload the function so that a picture object or a pointer type can be passed in.

**LISTING 26.42**  The Public Subroutine of_ChangeDataObject()

```
//Parameters:
//    String as_DataObject
//    Version 1 of the function: RowFocusInd arfi_PointerType
//    Version 2 of the function: Picture aptr_Pointer
//    Integer ai_XLocation
//    Integer ai_YLocation
//    Transaction atr_Transaction

this.DataObject = as_DataObject

If IsValid( aptr_Pointer) Then
   this.SetRowFocusIndicator( aptr_Pointer, ai_XLocation, ai_YLocation)
Else
   this.SetRowFocusIndicator( arfi_PointerType, ai_XLocation, ai_YLocation)
End If

this.SetTransObject( atr_Transaction)
```

Here are examples of a call to this function for both overloaded versions:

```
// Version 1 of the function - uses the pointer type as the 2nd argument
dw_1.of_ChangeDataObject( "d_shipping_list", Hand!, pNull, 0, 0, SQLCA)
dw_1.TriggerEvent( "RetrieveData")

// Version 2 of the function - uses a picture object as the 2nd argument
dw_1.of_ChangeDataObject( "d_shipping_list", p_pointer, pNull, 0, 0, SQLCA)
dw_1.TriggerEvent( "RetrieveData")
```

# Customizing with DataWindow Events

Where better than the Constructor event (see Listing 26.43) of a DataWindow control to set up the transaction object? It's a task you perform for every DataWindow control, so code it once and forget about it. If for some reason you don't require a transaction object to be set for the DataWindow, it is an external, or has a dynamically set DataWindow object, simply override the Constructor event.

**LISTING 26.43**  The Constructor Event for u_dw

```
If this.SetTransObject (SQLCA) <> 1 Then
   PopulateError(SQLCA.SQLDBCode, SQLCA.SQLErrText)
   // Open a standard error window
   open( w_error)
End If
```

Most DataWindows use the SQLCA as their transaction object. If you need alternative processing, you can override this script and copy the code to the descendant level.

Errors are a fact of life, and the DBError event (see Listing 26.44) is written to make handling DataWindow errors a little less painful. With this event, the standard error window is displayed with the error code and text supplied by the DataWindow. The GetUpdateStatus() function is used to find the row that caused the error, which is then scrolled into view and has the focus set to it.

**LISTING 26.44** The DBError Event for u_dw

```
Long ll_Row
dwBuffer lptr_Buffer
// Open the standard error window, no values can be passed from this level
// any information displayed apart from error text will have to be defined
// at the child level

error.text = SQLErrorText
error.number = SQLDBCode

Open (w_error)
//
// Scroll to the row causing the error, if it is in the visible, PRIMARY!,
// buffer

ll_Row = row
lptr_buffer = buffer
If lptr_Buffer = PRIMARY! Then
   this.ScrollToRow( ll_Row)
   this.SetFocus()
End If

// Do Not process message any further
RETURN 1
```

## Resizing the DataWindow

Some windows are laid out in such a manner that it makes sense to allow the controls within them to be resized to use additional window space if the window is itself resized.

By using two attributes of the attributes you added to u_dw, you can tell the DataWindow control to resize with its parent; then use some additional instance variables to finely control the resizing operation (see Listing 26.45). If you turn on the vertical and horizontal scrollbars of a DataWindow control, they will display if there's not enough space to show the whole DataWindow object.

**LISTING 26.45** The `ParentResize` Event for `u_dw`

```
Integer li_NewWidth, li_NewHeight

this.SetRedraw( FALSE)

If ib_AutoResizeHorizontal Then
    li_NewWidth = iw_Parent.Width - this.X - ii_RightGap
    If li_NewWidth >= ii_MinWidth And &
        ((this.X + li_NewWidth) <= ii_MaxWidth Or ii_MaxWidth = -1) Then
        this.Width = li_NewWidth
        this.HScrollBar = TRUE
    ElseIf li_NewWidth < ii_MinWidth Then
        this.Width = ii_MinWidth
    End If
End If

If ib_AutoResizeVertical Then
    li_NewHeight = iw_Parent.Height - this.Y - ii_BottomGap
    If li_NewHeight >=ii_MinHeight And &
        ((this.Y + li_NewHeight) <= ii_MaxHeight Or ii_MaxHeight=-1) Then
        this.Height = li_NewHeight
        this.VScrollBar = TRUE
    ElseIf li_NewHeight < ii_MinHeight Then
        this.Height = ii_MinHeight
    End If
End If

this.SetRedraw( TRUE)
```

Two steps must be carried out to make this functionality active. The first is coded in the DataWindow `Constructor` event and sets the values `iw_Parent`, `ii_RightGap`, and `ii_BottomGap`. For example, in the `Constructor` event of a DataWindow, the code might be this:

```
this.iw_Parent = Parent
this.ii_RightGap = Parent.Width - this.X - this.Width
this.ii_BottomGap = Parent.Height - this.Y - this.Height
this.ii_MinWidth = this.width
this.ii_MaxWidth = dw_2.x - 20
```

```
this.ii_MinHeight = this.Height
this.ii_MaxHeight = dw_3.y - 20
this.ib_AutoResizeHorizontal = TRUE
this.ib_AutoResizeVertical = TRUE
```

The second requirement is that a parent (which could be Window or UserObject) inform the DataWindow of a resize. This simply requires you to use the application custom class object and its associated methods. Here's an example:

```
this.SetRedraw( FALSE)
gnv_App.of_Broadcast( this, DataWindow!, "ParentResize")
this.SetRedraw( TRUE)
```

This is the only code required in the Resize event. It allows you to add, delete, and rename the DataWindows to your heart's desire, and they will all still receive the message with no further coding or modification to code. The calls to SetRedraw() allow the window to paint correctly after all the object resizing occurs.

## Modifying DataWindow Rows

One common operation on a DataWindow is the deletion of a row. To do this, use the code in Listing 26.46, which can also be encapsulated in the object. This allows you to carry out extensive error checking and friendlier post scrolling without having to repeat a lot of code.

**LISTING 26.46**   The DeleteRow Event for u_dw

```
// Argument passed al_row of type long
Long ll_Row


ll_row = al_row

If ll_Row = 0 Then
    // Row NOT sent as parameter - get current row
    ll_Row = this.GetRow()
End If

If ll_Row = -1 Then
    PopulateError(-1, "Error getting row information from the datawindow.")
    open( w_error)
Else
    If this.DeleteRow (ll_Row) <> 1 Then
        PopulateError(-1, "Unable to Delete a new row into the datawindow.")
        open( w_error)
    Else
        this.ScrollToRow( ll_Row - 1)
```

**LISTING 26.46** CONTINUED

```
      this.SetFocus()
   End If
End If
```

Notice that you can delete a specified or current row. To delete a particular row—in this case, the fourth—use the following code:

```
dw_1.Event DeleteRow (4)
```

Another common operation on a DataWindow is the addition of a row. By using the code in Listing 26.47, you can encapsulate the whole operation in the object. When defining the NewRow event, define an argument of type long so that the row can be passed in which you want to insert before or after. Define a second argument of type Boolean, which will be TRUE if you want insert after the row, or FALSE if you want to insert before.

**LISTING 26.47** The NewRow Event for u_dw

```
// an argument al_row of type long is passed in
// ab_position boolean value stating whether to place before or after passed row
Long ll_Row

ll_Row = al_row

If ab_position = TRUE  Then
// Insert after the current row
ll_Row = ll_Row  + 1
End If

If ll_Row = -1 Then
   PopulateError(-1, "Error get row information from the datawindow.")
   open( w_error)
Else
   ll_Row = this.InsertRow (ll_Row)
   If ll_Row = -1 Then
      PopulateError(-1, "Unable to insert a new row into the datawindow.")
      open(w_error)
   Else
      this.SetColumn (1)
      this.ScrollToRow (ll_Row)
      this.SetFocus()
   End If
End If
```

Here's the code to call this event for the various insert row configurations:

```
// New first row
dw_1.Event NewRow( 1, FALSE) //
// New last row
dw_1.Event NewRow( dw_1.RowCount(), TRUE)
//
// New row after current
dw_1.Event NewRow( ( dw_1.GetRow(), TRUE)
//
// New row before current
dw_1.Event( dw_1.GetRow(), FALSE)
```

## Data Retrieval Events

For generic retrieval calls, the following user-defined event provides the necessary functionality. For most calls, you will be passing only a few arguments to the DataWindow, so we will be declaring a total of 10 Any data type parameters for the event (see Listing 26.48). The DataWindow doesn't care whether it's passed more arguments than it requires; this allows you to implement the retrieval function of many a PowerBuilder developer's dreams!

**LISTING 26.48**   The `RetrieveData` Event for `u_dw`

```
//Parameters:
//     aa_Arg[10]  of type Any


Long ll_Row


this.SetRedraw (FALSE)


SQLCA.BeginTran()


ll_Row = this.Retrieve( aa_Arg[1], aa_Arg[2], aa_Arg[3], aa_Arg[4], aa_Arg[5], &
                        aa_Arg[6], aa_Arg[7], sa_Arg[8], aa_Arg[9], aa_Arg[10])


SQLCA.CommitTran()


If ll_Row = -1 Then
   PopulateError(-1, "Unable to retrieve data into the datawindow.")
   Open( w_error)
End If
```

**LISTING 26.48** CONTINUED

```
this.Title = String( this.RowCount()) + " records"

this.SetRedraw( TRUE)
```

You can then call this event with up to 10 different arguments. For example, to pass an integer ID, a string name, and a date of birth, this would be the call:

```
Any args[10]

args[1] = 10
args[2] = "Vedder"
args[3] = Date("6/12/1969")

dw_employee.Trigger Event RetrieveData( args)
```

## Saving Data

To save a DataWindow control's data to the database or elsewhere, use the `SaveData` event (see Listing 26.49). A call to this event should be enclosed in a transaction begin and end, and the `ib_FailedSave` is provided for examination by the calling script. If you're saving the data somewhere other than a database, you can extend or override this event in the descendant and provide your own functionality.

**LISTING 26.49** The `SaveData` Event for `u_dw`

```
Long ll_Row

ll_Row = this.Update()
If ll_Row <> 1 Then
   ib_FailedSave = TRUE
   PopulateError(-1, "Unable to save data from the datawindow.")
   open( w_error)
Else
   ib_FailedSave = FALSE
End If
```

## Accepting the Last Edit

Chapter 14, "DataWindow Scripting," discusses the process of detecting when a call to the `AcceptText()` function is required. The code required for the detection and execution of this functionality is detailed in the code in Listings 26.50 to 26.53.

**LISTING 26.50**   The AcceptText Event for u_dw

```
If Not ib_InAcceptText Then
    ib_InAcceptText = TRUE
    If this.AcceptText() = -1 Then
        lb_FailedAccept = TRUE
        this.SetFocus()
        this.PostEvent( "PostAcceptText")
        Return
    Else
        lb_FailedAccept = FALSE
    End If
End If

ib_InAcceptText = FALSE
```

**LISTING 26.51**   The LoseFocus Event for u_dw

```
this.PostEvent( "accepttext")
```

**LISTING 26.52**   The ItemError Event for u_dw

```
ib_InAcceptText = TRUE
```

**LISTING 26.53**   PostAcceptText for u_dw

```
ib_InAcceptText = FALSE
```

# Object Documentation

A useful user event to add to each of your user objects is one to document what the object is and how certain tasks are accomplished, possibly with required external calls and sample code (see Listing 26.54). When you compile the object, this event's contents are considered white space and won't be included in your final executable. By using this method, you've encapsulated the object's documentation as part of the object itself.

**LISTING 26.54**   A Documentation User Event for any Object

```
// This DataWindow object contains the following functionality:
//
// Events:
//      DeleteRow - Handles deleting the current row
//      Yatta yatta yatta
```

The DataWindow user object introduced here is a good starting point from which you can add or inherit for additional functionality.

# Summary

This chapter explored the functions that allow you to dynamically create visual user objects at runtime or tab pages, and it gave examples of their use. It also explored some standard user objects found in frameworks and the functionality you would expect to be contained in them. You should make extensive use of user objects in your PowerBuilder applications to encapsulate the functionality that PowerBuilder doesn't provide and that you find yourself duplicating as you program your application.

# Distributed Processing and Application Partitioning

Distributed processing provides a means to decentralize the processing and location of business functions and the data they act on in such a way that it's transparent to the client. Applications automatically use the best resources available from the network to complete their processing. Applications also can use parallel processing to achieve greater performance by issuing multiple service requests to distributed servers.

The most commonly implemented computing architecture now is *client/server*, which is actually a form of distributed processing in which the client and server cooperate in their processing. This chapter explores what distributed processing provides for a computing environment and how PowerBuilder fits into this architecture.

# Buzzword Definitions

As the world of distributed computing rapidly expands, protocols and specifications are constantly being upgraded, replaced, and reworked. The following are explanations of some common buzzwords, current and historical, in the world of distributed computing and computer communications:

- *Advanced program-to-program communications* (APPC) provides peer-to-peer communication support and a generic API.

- The Open Software Foundation (OSF), now known as simply the Open Group, developed the *distributed computing environment* (DCE) to provide a standards-based environment for heterogeneous platform portability and interoperability.

- *Distributed data management* (DDM) is an architecture that provides access to data stored on remote systems.

- The OSF developed the *distributed management environment* (DME) to provide a distributed management solution for DCE.

- IBM developed the *distributed relational database architecture* (DRDA) as a connection architecture that provides access to distributed relational databases.

- *Distributed transaction processing* (DTP) is transaction processing accomplished using LU6.2 protocols with synchronous communication. LU6.2 protocols include peer-to-peer communications, end-to-end error processing, and a generic API.

- A *distributed request* is a single SQL statement that requests data distributed over several DBMSs.

- A *distributed unit of work* (DUW) is a period of time from the start of a piece of work to the end and spans several distributed DBMSs.

- *Remote data access* (RDA) is an ANSI standard (proposal) for accessing remote DBMSs.

- A *remote procedure call* (RPC) is a method of communication between a client (requester) and a server (remote service provider) that causes the execution of a procedure on the server.

- A *remote request* is a SQL statement that requests data from a single remote system.

- A *remote unit of work* (RUW) is similar to a DUW except that the data is requested from a single remote server.

- *Systems application architecture* (SAA) is a framework used for the design and development of consistent and portable applications in different environments.

- *Systems network architecture* (SNA) provides standards for the configuration and operation of networks that incorporate structures, formats, and protocols.

# Open Systems

The preeminent goal of a computing architecture is to provide an open computing environment. This allows for the selection of the correct tools (hardware or software) for a given task, without having to be too concerned about the impact on existing systems and implementations.

Open systems allow the realization of distributed computing's potential by making possible the following:

- True application scalability.

- Transparent data access and processing over networks.

- Seamless resource sharing.

- Speedy development by providing prebuilt components for programmers to build faster solutions through assembly.

- Lowering integration costs by providing a common set of interfaces; this means less customization is required to integrate components from different vendors into complete solutions.

- Improving deployment flexibility by customizing the software solution for individual departments of a company by just changing the components used by the overall application.

- Lowering maintenance costs by isolating functionality into encapsulated components; this allows easy upgrades of functionality without having to rework the entire application.

They also offer the benefit of lower costs for hardware and software vendors, who can develop from a firm base design rather than start from scratch and build a proprietary product. This also opens the global marketplace for these and other products built on them because of the numerous countries that participate in an open system standard.

The true winners are, of course, the end users, who can pick the best hardware and software solution for their problem domain, budget, and overall requirements without being forced into buying a proprietary system for compatibility reasons.

This vision is still just that—a vision. The rise of Linux and the open source movement in general have helped attract renewed attention to open systems. The Open Group has designed and encouraged the use of an open distributed computing environment. This chapter examines the Open Group's DCE architecture.

Numerous types of distributed systems all compete and interoperate with one another:

- CORBA (Common Object Request Broker Architecture)

- DCOM (Distributed Component Object Model)

- DCE (Distributed Computing Environment)

- RPC (Remote Procedure Calls)

- Shared-memory–based interaction

- Named Pipe communication

- Socket-level programming

- Message Queuing

- Other IPC (interprocess communication) mechanisms

The following sections explore some of these.

# CORBA

CORBA is one standard for distributed objects that supports many existing languages that can make implementation both distributed and object-oriented. CORBA describes a specification for distributed object computing that's implemented through Object Request Brokers (ORBs). Because CORBA is a recognized industry standard, numerous vendors are creating implementations that allow developers a comfortable degree of portability between different CORBA products. With this high level of interoperability between CORBA products, companies can build solutions on top of different implementations and have them communicate.

The implementation is done by using CORBA IDL (Interface Description Language), which defines the server component by using IDL structures, sequences, and other syntax to describe the data passing mechanism. A server implements a specific interface, and this implementation is the distributed object. Clients communicate with this object through a reference, passing parameters over the network to the server. The distributed object within the server then executes the desired operation and returns the data. CORBA supports a synchronous request/response mechanism as well as dynamic invocations.

With the CORBA 2.0 specification comes a new protocol for ORB interoperability, Internet Inter-ORB Protocol (IIOP). Sybase's Jaguar CTS product fully supports CORBA 2.0 IIOP.

# DCOM

DCOM is a distributed component architecture that extends Microsoft's object technology COM (Component Object Model). Microsoft calls DCOM "COM with a longer wire." COM is the core technology within ActiveX. Numerous development tool vendors— among them Sybase—allow you to create ActiveX components.

Being based on ActiveX allows DCOM to act as the glue between objects such as Java and the HTTP network protocol. To keep its technology open, Microsoft has open licensing allowing companies to create implementations running on all major operating systems. The company also is trying to get DCOM accepted as the standard for the Internet as well. DCOM is actually layered on the Open Group Distributed Computing Environment RPC mechanism—an open and widely deployed communications technology.

DCOM is one of a string of Microsoft object technologies: DDE (Dynamic Data Exchange—messaging between Windows applications), OLE (Object Linking and Embedding—embedding visual links between programs within an application), COM (Component Object Model—used for object binding), and ActiveX (COM enabled for the Internet). DCOM also integrates Internet certificate-based security with Windows NT-based security.

DCOM is now available on all major platforms including Windows, Macintosh, and several versions of UNIX.

## The Distributed Computing Environment

In 1990, the Open Software Foundation announced a suite of technologies that comprise the distributed computing environment. These technologies provided a foundation on which distributed applications could be built regardless of the underlying complexity of the computing network.

The distributed computing environment (see Figure 27.1) provides an integrated environment that's based on the Distributed File Services (DFS) component. Further components include a directory service, thread service, time service, and remote procedure calls. Figure 27.1 is simplified to show just the main components, which are explained in greater detail in the following sections.

**FIGURE 27.1**

*DCE's architecture.*

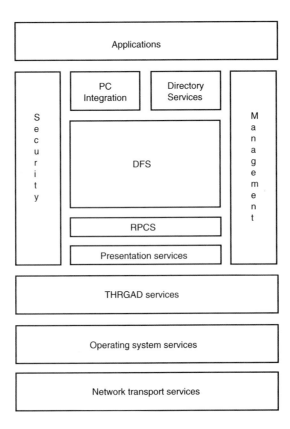

# The Distributed File System

A DFS allows clients to access and modify files or data from systems attached to a network. The system providing the file is the server; it controls access to concurrent clients by means of a token system. Clients can request the same file, which is cached at the client, for their own use. When one client requires modification rights, the server grants a write token and informs the file's other clients that the status has changed and that their data is now out of date; the server might even revoke clients' existing tokens.

As you can imagine, this requires some extra features not usually inherent in a normal file system. File security access is provided in the form of user authentication (using security tickets) and an access list mechanism, and is assigned for clients and servers. So that files/data have high availability and integrity, a replication service is used. This allows for the failure or maintenance of an area of the network without affecting the overall operation. Some slowdown will occur, but processing can continue uninterrupted. To track and manage all the DFS's operations, DCE uses distributed databases that hold file locations and security information.

# Directory Services

The directory service provides information on objects in the network that are accessed by a name and address, and is central to the DCE. The service provides information on an object so that the object can be moved or reconfigured without affecting how a client accesses it. The DCE directory service has been designed to interoperate with the X.500 worldwide directory service using global directory agents (naming gateways) that allow clients to look up names on the worldwide service. Access to this service is based on the X/Open Directory Services (XDS) API.

# Remote Procedure Calls

The RPC mechanism is *the* means of access for all DCE components and allows the execution of code on physically remote processors transparent to an application. DCE RPCs are designed to allow transparent access to various network architectures and to support threads. (Remote procedure calls are covered in more detail later in the section "Understanding Remote Procedure Calls.")

# Thread Services

Threads are used in parallel processing architectures to describe subprocesses of a single program that concurrently use a processor. The thread service for the DCE is based on Digital Equipment's Concert Multithread Architecture (CMA), which is highly portable and is also POSIX 1003 compliant.

The other main components of the DCE architecture undertake services that you will find in most other computing architectures and provide the wraparound functionality to the core services. These components of the DCE model are placed between applications and the network layer at the client and the server. This molds easily into the existing client/server paradigm, in which the service provider is considered a DCE server and the service requester the DCE client.

# Distributed Systems

As you've just seen with the DCE, distributed systems consist of many components that interact to provide an environment for applications to be executed. Applications can be themselves broken down into components, which can then also be distributed across a network. These are the main components of an application:

- *Presentation logic* is the graphical user interface (GUI) component of the application that manages keyboard and mouse input, screen drawing, and window management. These are the services offered by the operating system. Presentation logic can also include the character-based world of CICS and other mainframe presentation facilities.

- *Business logic* embodies the business processes and functionality into a computerized form. The code is written using third- or fourth-generation languages such as COBOL and PowerBuilder.

- *Database logic* encompasses two parts of the application: the code used to manipulate data within the application and the actual processing of the data by a DBMS.

Where these components reside dictates the type of computing environment. For example, the traditional host-based system runs all the components on the mainframe. The architecture of client/server, as has been stated, is a form of distributed computing and provides a launching point for further distribution of services.

Distributed systems require additional planning and design to implement because you need to decide where to divide the processing and then where to place each component object. This is also true to some degree with areas of client/server, particularly the business logic.

# Client/Server Architecture

With client/server architecture, also known as *two-tier architecture*, applications are split into two components: data and presentation (see Figure 27.2). These two areas can become indistinct when you consider the logic component that's split across them. The data component, the RDBMS, contains parts of the business logic in the form of defaults, rules, triggers, and stored procedures. The presentation also contains business logic in the form of functions and events, and additional presentation logic in windows and other visual objects.

**FIGURE 27.2**
*The two-tier architecture.*

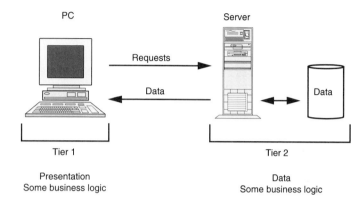

27

Distributed Processing and Application Partitioning

This blurring of the two components leads to the duplication of effort with some inherent problems, such as who is maintaining the server-based version and who the client-based. Which object should developers use in a new application or when upgrading an existing one? What happens when a piece of the business logic changes—how many places now need to be updated with that information? This obviously results in an architecture that can be more difficult to maintain and in which to troubleshoot problems.

# Advantages of Client/Server Computing

The client/server model has several inherent advantages over its predecessors, and even over the current n-tier architectures that might eventually completely replace it:

- The use of desktop computing power and technology, which was previously centralized on mainframes.

- The implementation of GUI applications that use the PC hardware and software to provide easier navigation, multitasking, and enhanced visualization of data and reports.

- Client/server computing provides an introduction to the concepts behind open systems to end users and IT departments. End users can be using a mix of PC hardware and software to access various file and database servers that also exist on various hardware types.

- Many people work in this area, and you can hire them to help with projects or bring them in for consulting help.

- Considerable knowledge within the computing industry now exists to provide the right help and proven tools as they are required.

## Problems with Client/Server Computing

Of course, there are disadvantages to everything, and client/server architecture has the following:

- The architecture is only as good as its design. A client/server system can be configured similarly to a mainframe master/slave relationship, with a lot of the business logic embodied in the server. This can cause the server to become processor-bound while it handles multiple client requests.

- You must invest resources into hardware and software acquisition for PC-based implementations, and you must incur the associated costs of training for end users, support staff, and development teams.

- You must invest in the construction or upgrade of a network that will support a wide bandwidth. Client/server applications generally send a lot of information back and forth over networks to accomplish their tasks, whether they're transaction processing or reporting.

# The N-Tier Architecture

The current cutting-edge architecture to be investing in is n-tier architecture (see Figure 27.3), which defines an application architecture that's separated into three logical components: presentation, logic, and data. It's called *n-tier* because there's no limit to the number of application servers you can use.

An exciting development in n-tier architectures is the use of a Web browser for the presentation layer. This allows for true thin-client computing because only limited code can be run in the browser. Also, the application is transmitted to the client (in the form of HTML) along with the data, eliminating deployment and installation overhead.

## Advantages of N-Tier Architectures

Using a tiered approach to an application's architecture has many inherent benefits, as discussed in the following sections.

**FIGURE 27.3**

*The n-tier archi-tecture.*

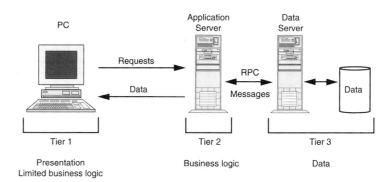

# Defined Division of Logic

The addition of a third tier to the architecture allows you to move all logic functions out of the other two components into a defined component. This allows the standardization of logic functions, with a defined set of standards and implementers. Modularization and encapsulation are the ultimate goal of any object-oriented system design, and logic division allows this to be attained with greater ease.

# Resource Optimization

With the functionality of an application broken down into three areas, sometimes with different project teams addressing each component, the componentization when carrying out implementation allows for the production of more optimized code. High-performance processors can be used for processing logic, and different processors used for the retrieval of data. With these servers spread through an organization, access as well as installation and maintenance costs can be shared across departments.

As just mentioned, separate teams commonly attack the problems of each component. This allows the construction of teams that use the specific aptitudes of your developers with GUI design, data modeling, or business process acumen. Team members with good understanding of all the areas should be used to direct the component interfaces between the tiers.

Not only is there an optimization of team resources, but there's also a reduction in the hardware requirements for client machines. Client/server applications are no longer overly large, requiring fast CPUs and large amounts of memory. You can now optimize and slim the application down to a more acceptable size using distributed objects that are used as they are required. A smaller client application places less demand on the client-side operating system.

## Minimal Change Impact

Distinctly isolated tiers allow modifications to be made within one that don't affect the others. Each tier is effectively a black box to the others, providing a set of interface functionality that can be used without an understanding of how the task is accomplished. For example, if a distributed object is used by multiple client applications, you have to update the object at only one location: on the application server on which the object is located.

## Heterogeneous Data Sources

The presentation tier makes requests to the logic tier, which then decides which data source to use to satisfy the request. By using a calling interface similar to that used by the presentation layer, the logic tier can make requests against any available data sources.

## Increased and Improved Security

Access privileges can be assigned or built in at each tier to provide three levels of security. Security can now be centralized to specific business logic objects.

# Problems with Tier Architectures

As with the client/server architecture, multiple-tier architectures have inherent problems, as discussed in the following sections.

## Increased Network Traffic

Now that you have distributed business and data-processing logic around the network, clients need to make numerous calls to achieve the required processing. This doesn't necessarily mean that the network will be brought down, but you should be aware of the potential increase in traffic. Any problems can usually be solved by updating the network's design.

## Immature Technology

Compared to the history of host-based and now client/server systems, n-tier architectures and the tools required to implement them are newcomers. The tools now available have some incompatibilities and don't yet provide the true openness of the ideal distributed system.

## Increased Price

Additional software and hardware costs are incurred as part of a tiered architecture. These costs include the distributed system software for servers and clients, and the necessary upgrades in hardware (disk, memory, processor, and so on) to support it. The cost of hiring or training personnel who have expertise in the distributed system arena also needs to be considered.

## Implementation Complexity

Obviously, as you increase the number of components and access paths, the implementation and management complexities also increase. OSF is now working on a proposed distributed management environment to offset some of these issues.

# Transaction Monitors

The two-tier approach lacks the features needed to provide large-scale, industrial-strength, business-critical applications. These applications can be characterized by the following:

- Many users

- Business-critical data and processing

- High availability (24 hours a day, 365 days a year)

- Heterogeneous computing environments (UNIX, IBM, Macintosh, and so on)

- Heterogeneous database environments (Oracle, Sybase, DB2, and so on)

- Use of LANs, MANs, and WANs

This class of application (often known as *online transaction processing*, or OLTP) is ideally suited to the n-tier architecture and is often implemented with a transaction monitor middleware component as the second tier. Transaction monitors provide control and management of transaction execution, synchronization, and integrity. They also provide the following benefits:

- High transaction throughput

- Load balancing

- Support for many users

- Transaction management and routing

# Understanding Remote Procedure Calls

Remote procedure calls are one method now used to implement three-tier architecture and allow applications to access services from remote systems. Services offered by a remote system can provide access to different communication protocols such as MAPI and TAPI, perform a business function, or access data. An RPC can be compared with the call and execution of a database stored procedure. Both are called from the client, which then optionally waits for results, and both are executed on a remote system without further interaction by the client machine (see Figure 27.4).

**FIGURE 27.4**
*Remote proce-*
*dure calls.*

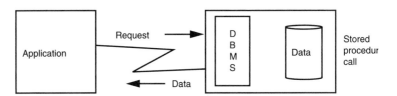

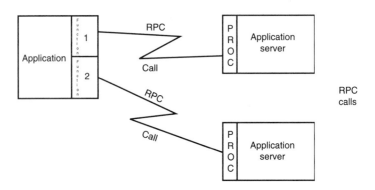

When using RPCs, you don't have to concern yourself with the underlying network protocols, data translation, and host languages because these are hidden by the RPC tool used. Specific RPC tools may support different network protocols. The only requirement for their use is the capability to locate a server that the procedure exists on, and this is achieved by using the directory services of a distributed system.

RPCs are especially suited to client/server applications, and developers usually have access to tools for use in the construction of RPC-enabled applications.

The DCE implementation of RPC is one of the more commonly accepted and used. To create a DCE-compliant application, use an Interface Definition Language (IDL) file. The syntax for IDL looks like a form of C that has been enhanced with networking functionality. IDL files are passed through a compilation stage that turns them into *stubs* bound to server and client. The stub is used as a simulation of the missing piece—for example, on a client it would be the server-based functionality—and is similar to function/procedure stubs used in structured programming within a team environment. Many tools (such as PowerBuilder) now generate IDL files automatically.

# Application Partitioning

Application partitioning is, as its name suggests, the process of segmenting an application into components that can then be distributed across a network. The concept has been introduced in various ways in the preceding sections, but this section examines some methods that can be used to decide where an application can, or should, be partitioned. The process of determining the application's architecture is separate from the design of the deployment architecture already discussed.

You have to tackle the problem of partitioning in the same manner that you would any other problem: with analysis, design, and implementation.

The first step is to look at the system you're trying to build and begin collecting related data and functions. These different elements form the basis of modules, which you will continue to refine throughout the analysis and design stages. To help organize and identify the elements, use *domain analysis*, which collects elements into one of three domains:

- The *user interface* (or presentation) domain collects all the elements and specifications that detail what the interface looks like to end users and other systems. This covers graphical elements as well as the methods available to other systems to interact with it. Prototyping is the preferred method for capturing graphical elements.

- The *problem* (or business) domain contains the processes, concepts, and characteristics of the business functions that the application is being designed to implement.

- The elements in the *system* (or management) domain define the system components that interact and manage the other two domains. This domain covers transaction management, error handling, security, and other similar management functions.

This is illustrated in Figure 27.5, which also indicates that elements may lie along the boundary of multiple domains.

**FIGURE 27.5**
*The three domains of analysis.*

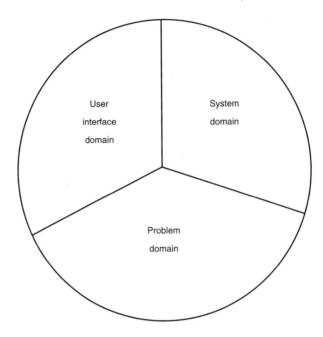

After you define all the elements for each domain, you can start to construct modules from them. From these modules, you can determine the partitions of the application and their possible location within the distributed system. Partitioned applications have more reusable classes that are truly encapsulated and can be easily used in cross-platform deployment.

# Distributed Computing Using PowerBuilder

PowerBuilder 5.0 introduced Distributed PowerBuilder, which allows developers to implement n-tier solutions. Distributed PowerBuilder is based on the use of nonvisual user objects that can execute on a separate machine from the primary application. The advantage is that only one copy of the distributed component exists and can be shared by multiple clients.

With the release of its Enterprise Application Server product, Sybase has abandoned Distributed PowerBuilder in favor of component-based computing using Jaguar CTS or Microsoft's MTS. PowerBuilder 7.0 will be the last release with support for Distributed PowerBuilder.

Using Jaguar or MTS with PowerBuilder 6.0 was a complicated and involved process. PowerBuilder 7.0 has eliminated much of this complexity by providing several wizards, which allow you to create, deploy, and debug your components with Jaguar and MTS. See Chapter 28, "Developing Distributed PowerBuilder Applications," for more information on how to use PowerBuilder with Jaguar and MTS.

# Summary

As always, you have to decide between different methods of achieving the same result, and you need to choose not only the best tools for the job, but also the best architecture. Both client/server and n-tier architectures have benefits over each other, as well as accompanying disadvantages or issues.

Distributed processing is going to force development teams to reexamine their conceptions of how their applications work and interact. This may, in fact, require some additional analysis and design rework to make use of the advantages of the n-tier architecture.

# Developing Distributed PowerBuilder Applications

Distributed PowerBuilder, introduced with PowerBuilder 5.0, allows developers to implement n-tier computing by using a tool they already are familiar with—PowerBuilder itself. PowerBuilder 7.0 introduces several new wizards that make it easy to create and deploy PowerBuilder components to Sybase Enterprise Application Server (Jaguar) and Microsoft Transaction Server (MTS).

> **Note**
>
> Sybase has announced that its long-term plan for distributed computing includes the use of the Sybase Enterprise Application Server (which includes Jaguar) in place of Distributed PowerBuilder. No new functionality was added to Distributed PowerBuilder in the current version, and 7.0 will be the final release to include Distributed PowerBuilder functionality.

The key to using PowerBuilder in a distributed environment is the class user object, which allows you to implement functionality without a visual component. This object can then be reused throughout an application and even across several applications. By using PowerBuilder's distributed features, you can place this object onto an application server so that only one copy exists in a computing environment that can be used by multiple users and applications. After you have a basic knowledge of the construction and use of class user objects, it's a simple extension to make this into a distributable component: a remote object.

# Remote Objects and Proxies

A *remote object* is a special type of class user object that has been saved with a proxy name. Remote objects can reference and accept as arguments only nonvisual data types. These objects can make PowerScript function calls and issue database commands.

*Proxy objects* are created as stubs (see Chapter 27, "Distributed Processing and Application Partitioning") for the client application, and they define the available methods of the server-based remote object. PowerBuilder 7.0 includes several new project types to aid in the creation of proxy objects (see Figure 28.1). You use the proxy objects in your client applications to access the remote methods and data on the server objects.

FIGURE 28.1
*The New window showing proxy objects available on the Project tab.*

# PowerBuilder and Jaguar

With PowerBuilder 6.0 and Jaguar 1.11, deploying your PowerBuilder objects to a Jaguar server took a tremendous amount of effort. PowerBuilder 7.0 introduces a set of wizards and project types that greatly simplify object deployment. Developing a distributed application with PowerBuilder and Jaguar involves three basic steps: creating your server components, creating your client application, and generating the Jaguar proxy objects.

## Create the Remote Components

Begin the creation of your remote component by running the Jaguar Component Start Wizard. Choose New from the File menu. In the PowerBuilder New window, click the Start Wizards tab (see Figure 28.2). Next, double-click the Jaguar Component icon to start the Jaguar Component Start Wizard (see Figure 28.3).

FIGURE 28.2
*The Start Wizards tab page.*

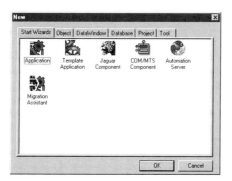

28

Developing
Distributed
PowerBuilder
Applications

FIGURE 28.3
*The Jaguar Component Start Wizard.*

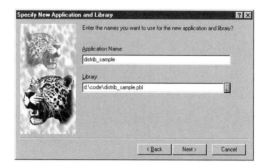

The wizard's first two screens present an overview of the component creation process. The wizard guides you through all the steps necessary to create and deploy your new remote component. It even generates a to-do list outlining the tasks you need to complete as soon as the wizard is finished. The following steps outline the process you will follow to create your remote component.

1. Create the application and library list.
2. Choose a name for your new component.
3. Specify the server and login information.
4. Name the Jaguar Package.
5. Specify the component type.
6. Select Instance Pooling options.
7. Choose transaction support options.
8. Specify interface options.
9. Specify other options.
10. Specify project options.

After you complete all the steps in the wizard, PowerBuilder generates the application, library, and object you specified. Add your methods to the new component, and then compile the component using the project that the wizard created for you.

> **Note**
>
> The Jaguar server must be running for you to compile your remote component. When you compile the project, PowerBuilder automatically deploys the object to the Jaguar server. The server must be stopped and restarted for your new object to appear on the server's list of available objects.

# Create the Client Application

Now that you've created and deployed a component to the Jaguar server, you must build the client application that will use the remote object. Again, PowerBuilder provides a wizard to guide you through the process. In the New window, choose Template Application from the Start Wizards tab page. Specify the desired options for your new application. When you reach the Specify Connectivity dialog, select Requires Jaguar Connection (see Figure 28.4).

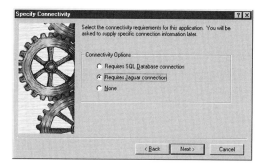

Next, provide the connection information required to log in to the Jaguar server and select the package that you want to connect to. Specify Script as the source for the connection and choose Finish. PowerBuilder generates the application according to the options you selected in the wizard. The Jaguar `Connection` object is also created. If you selected Script as the source for the connection, you can open the `Connection` object and see that the script to set the connection properties is already generated for you.

Finally, create a global or instance variable of the Jaguar connection type that you will use to actually connect to the server.

# Generate Jaguar Proxy Objects

The final step is to generate the proxy objects that your application will use to access the methods available on the remote component. Open the New window and select the Project tab (refer to Figure 28.1). Double-click the Jaguar Proxy Wizard icon to start the wizard, which guides you through the process.

When the wizard asks you for the destination library, specify the client application library that you created in the preceding section. Next, specify a name for the project that will build the proxy object. The wizard then prompts you for the Jaguar connection information required to connect to the server. After you connect to the server, a list of available packages and components are displayed. Select your component from the list, specify any build options, and click Finish. PowerBuilder creates the project that will generate your proxy object. Open this project and compile it to create your proxy object. If the project compiles successfully, your proxy object will display in the Library painter.

The final steps to access your remote object are to declare an instance of the proxy object type, connect to the Jaguar server, and instantiate the remote object.

## Using a Remote Object in PowerScript

Use the `ConnectToServer()` function on your `Connection` object to connect to the Jaguar server at runtime. No parameters are required because PowerBuilder has already generated the connection code for you when you created the remote component in the first step. The `CreateInstance()` function gets a local reference to the remote object running on the Jaguar server. The syntax for `CreateInstance()` is

```
transactionserver.CreateInstance  (remoteobjectvariable {, classname} )
```

You can now reference the methods and properties on your remote object as though it were any other user object.

# PowerBuilder and MTS

In addition to the new wizards for creating and deploying PowerBuilder components with Jaguar, Sybase has created three new wizards to help create COM/DCOM components: the COM/MTS Start Wizard, COM/MTS Object Wizard, and the COM/MTS Project Wizard. All three wizards allow you to automatically register and deploy your COM objects to an MTS server running on your local machine or create a PAK file to assist in installation on another machine.

# Basics of Distributed PowerBuilder

The following sections discuss the components that comprise a distributed application and how to put them together.

## Components of Distributed PowerBuilder

Distributed PowerBuilder uses four class user object types, which follow this hierarchy:

```
NonVisualObject
    ConnectObject
        Connection
        Transport
```

```
   RemoteObject
Structure
   ConnectionInfo
```

Each class and the `ConnectionInfo` structure are introduced in the following sections, and then all the concepts are drawn together into examples of the client and server code required for a Distributed PowerBuilder application. `ConnectObject` is the base class for the `Connection` and `Transport` classes, which are used by the client and server applications, respectively. `ConnectObject` has the following properties:

| | |
|---|---|
| ErrCode (Long) | Error code value for the last error |
| Handle (ObjHandle) | Handle for the object |
| Application (String) | Name of the application |
| Driver (String) | Network driver to use when setting up to connect or listen |
| ErrText (String) | Error-code description for the last error |
| Location (String) | Optional description of the user's location |
| Options (String) | One or more comma-separated options that determine how data will be passed over the network (this property is ignored when the NamedPipes or Local driver is used) |
| Trace (String) | Enables the specification of trace options |

The `ConnectionInfo` structure is used by `GetServerInfo()` for the `Connection` object to retrieve information on the current connections into the server. It has the following structure:

| | |
|---|---|
| Busy (Boolean) | Whether the connection is busy making a request |
| ConnectTime (DateTime) | Date and time the client connected |
| ConnectString (String) | The value of the `ConnectString` property on the `Connection` object |
| ConnectUserID (String) | The value of the `UserID` property on the `Connection` object |
| LastCallTime (DateTime) | Date and time the client last made a request to the server |
| CallCount (Long) | Total number of calls made on the server by the client |
| ClientId (String) | ID of the client on the server |
| Location (String) | Client location |
| UserId (String) | User's ID |

**28**

Developing
Distributed
PowerBuilder
Applications

If a client connects with a connect privilege of ConnectWithAdmin! (see the next section for details on setting this), the client can retrieve information on all clients connected to the server. This functionality is discussed in detail in the sections "Server Applications" and "Server Consoles."

The following sections examine the components of Distributed PowerBuilder and the way in which they integrate.

## Transport Objects

The Transport object is used by PowerBuilder server applications to receive incoming client requests for a particular communications connection type. This object, like the client's connection, is inherited from the ConnectionObject class. Transport has only one property in addition to those inherited from its parent class: TimeOut. This property controls the time interval the server waits before it considers a client connection to have been lost. If the value of the TimeOut property is greater than 0 before a Listen() call is executed, the application starts a timeout thread on the server. The timeout thread examines currently connected clients and terminates their connections (and releases server resources) if they haven't made a call during the time period specified by TimeOut. This value is specified in milliseconds.

> **Tip**
>
> The TimeOut property requires tuning and careful consideration when your users are operating over wide-area networks (WANs) or other slow network connections.

Also, two additional functions are declared for the Transport object:

- After an application executes Listen(), it can accept client requests for the communication protocol for which the transport object was set up.

- StopListening() prevents the application from accepting more client requests for the Transport object.

The Transport object uses the same properties and option settings as the Connection object.

## Connection Objects

The Connection object is used by PowerBuilder applications that need to access remote objects on a server. This object is set up by using a particular communications connection type. The `Connection` object also is inherited from the `ConnectionObject` class. `Connection` defines three properties in addition to those inherited from its parent class:

| | |
|---|---|
| `ConnectString` (String) | Additional information that can be passed to the server application at connection time. The value of this property could include application-specific information, such as database connection parameters. |
| `Password` (String) | Password used to connect to the server. |
| `UserId` (String) | Name or ID of the user connecting to the server. |

Additional functions are declared for the `Connection` object:

- `ConnectToServer()`connects to a remote object server using the communications protocol specified for the `Connection` object.

- `CreateInstance ( NewRemoteObject {, szClassName})` creates an object on a remote server. With a deployed client application, you have the remote object's class definition and can create a reference to a local object (using the `Create` statement) or a reference to a remote object (using this method). The physical location is transparent to the client scripts and is made based on implementation requirements.

- `DisconnectServer()` disconnects from a server after you finish using the requested services and class user objects.

- `GetServerInfo( ciInfo[])` collects the current state of the server.

- `RemoteStopConnection ( szClientId)` is used by a supervisor logon to kill the connection of another remote user.

- `RemoteStopListening()` enables a client application to inform the server to stop listening for further client requests. You must be connected with administrative rights to issue this function call.

`Connection` object use varies by communications driver in the following ways:

- NamedPipes uses the `Application` and `Location` properties to specify the pipe's name:

  `\\Location\PIPE\Application`

- Or, for a local pipe, it's constructed this way:

  `\\.\PIPE\Application`

- WinSock uses the `Application`, `Location`, and `Options` properties to set up a TCP/IP connection.

**28**

Developing
Distributed
PowerBuilder
Applications

- The `Application` property can be set using one of two formats. The first format lets you specify the service name as it appears in the service's file. The second format specifies the actual port number to connect to.

- The `Location` property also can be set using two formats. The first format is the name of the server as it appears in the host's file. The second format is the host's actual IP address.

- The `Options` property allows you to tune the TCP/IP protocol. It has the following available settings:

| | |
|---|---|
| `RawData` | When set to 1, makes the WinSock driver pass raw data over the network. The value has to be set the same on the client and server, or they won't be able to communicate. Setting this to 1 gives you a slight performance increase, but the data is in human-readable form. The default is 0, and the driver encrypts the data as it passes over the network. |
| `BufSize` | Sets the buffer sizes used by WinSock. |
| `NoDelay` | Causes each data packet to be sent without a delay. This setting can have severe performance implications and should be used with care. |
| `TimeOut` | The amount of time PowerBuilder will wait for a synchronous operation to finish before returning an error. |
| `MaxRetry` | Specifies the number of times the client will try to connect to a server if the listening port is busy before reporting a connection error. |

These options should be set before calling `ConnectToServer()` or `Listen()`. Here's a sample option string:

```
"RawData=1, BufSize=4096, NoDelay=0, MaxRetry=10"
```

# Working with Shared Objects

Distributed PowerBuilder provides support for shared objects that enables you to work with persistent, shared data across multiple client connections within a distributed application. The benefits of shared objects follow:

- They can maintain state information for Web.PB applications.

- They provide sharing of recent database accesses, which helps reduce database server load.

- They let you share common information that otherwise must be maintained for each client connection.

To allow client applications to share a single object, the server application carries out the following operations. These calls can be made from within the main thread of the server application or from inside a client session:

- It calls the `SharedObjectRegister()` function to register a named instance of the object.

- It invokes the `SharedObjectGet()` function to get an object instance that's a reference to the shared object.

> **Note**
>
> The server doesn't issue a `Create` call for the shared object created automatically by the `SharedObjectRegister()` function.

The client applications access the shared object wrapper and not the shared object directly. To have access to a shared object, the client application has to communicate with another object that has an instance variable that provides the actual reference to the shared object. This intermediate object can be thought of as a *shared object wrapper.*

Client applications gain indirect access to the shared object's methods by calling methods on the shared object wrapper. The shared object wrapper methods make the actual call and should have the same names as the methods on the actual shared object.

When calling remote methods, you can use only certain data types for the method's arguments. You can pass the standard PowerBuilder data types (for example, Integer, Long, and String), structures and structure arrays, and custom class user objects. The shared object methods can't receive an argument passed by reference.

PowerBuilder creates a separate thread for each shared object instance and its workspace. The workspace includes a copy of the application's global variables and any objects the shared object creates.

As client applications make requests for the services of a shared object, they're queued sequentially to prevent the problems of concurrent access. This means that only one client at a time can modify the properties of a shared object.

> **Note**
>
> All errors, whether fatal or execution time, that occur while accessing a shared object are passed back to the client.

Figure 28.5 shows the shared object mechanism.

**FIGURE 28.5**

*The shared object mechanism.*

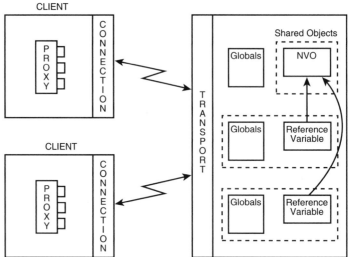

Shared objects are destroyed when any of the following occurs:

- The object instance is unregistered by the server application.

- The server application is shut down.

- The object instance is explicitly destroyed with a Destroy statement.

- A reference to the shared object is explicitly destroyed. This isn't the case, however, if the reference is destroyed by PowerBuilder's garbage collector.

# Making Asynchronous Function Calls

One of the biggest requests for Distributed PowerBuilder was the capability to make asynchronous calls. This feature enables the client to make a call to the remote server and then continue with other work while the server processes the request. The mechanism for making an asynchronous function call is the same as for calling local functions asynchronously: using the Post keyword.

Just as there are restrictions for calling local methods asynchronously, there also are restrictions for asynchronous remote calls:

- The return value of a function is ignored.

- You can't pass parameters by reference in an asynchronous call. If you try to do so, you will get an execution and not a compilation-time error.

- There's no mechanism for the client to poll the server about the state of the asynchronous request. Notification is made from the server to the client by a message.

- Asynchronous calls are executed in the order in which the server receives them.

- With a client crash, there's no guarantee of the queued request completing. If the server crashes, any queued requests are lost.

Asynchronous calls actually are queued local to the client so that the script can continue immediately with its execution. The local queue then is traversed, and each request is sent to the server, where it's added to the client session's asynchronous request queue. However, this doesn't mean that the asynchronous request is executed immediately. A synchronous call is executed as soon as possible, and objects process all synchronous requests made before any asynchronous requests.

# Pushing Messages to the Client

To help implement asynchronous requests, you use a method known as *server push* to enable the server to send messages back to the client. Just like the client, the server also can make synchronous and asynchronous calls to client-side objects. Clients handle server-side requests using the same mechanisms the server uses to handle client-side requests.

To send a message back to a client application, the server acts against a client-side object. This requires the client to have previously passed an object reference to the server for this purpose. Any function calls made against this remote reference are passed back over the network to the object that owns the client. Figure 28.6 shows the asynchronous call with server push.

**FIGURE 28.6**

*Asynchronous
calls and server
push.*

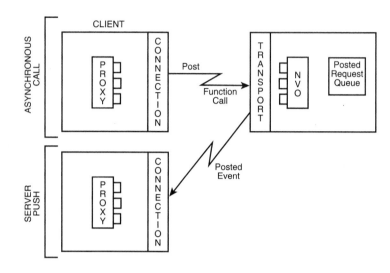

## The Remote Object Reference Mechanism

The server uses remote references just as it does any local object reference because it places the remote reference into an instance variable so that the client doesn't have to continually send the object reference with each request. This method also enables the server application to use the object reference in shared object sessions, if desired.

PowerBuilder attempts to optimize an object reference passed to a server if it is itself a remote reference. This attempt is to make the remote reference point to the actual object that would receive the requests. This method saves additional hops in the number of objects a message has to pass through.

This type of optimization can be made only if the target object is contained in a session that's acting as a server. Otherwise, the reference points to the remote object in the client that passed the reference. This means that multiple hops are necessary to get the request to the target object.

# Distributed Applications

A Distributed PowerBuilder application is constructed around the services of a server application and a client application. The following sections look at building these server- and client-side components.

# Server Applications

PowerBuilder applications can participate in the distributed computing environment as clients and servers. The PowerBuilder server application contains numerous class user objects developed with the intention of allowing them to be invoked by one or more client applications. These types of class user objects, known as *remote objects*, are covered earlier in the section "Remote Objects and Proxies." They may be called from any application in the distributed computing environment, on the same machine, or across a network connection to another physically separate machine. The server piece is implemented by using a Transport object (see "Transport Objects," earlier in this chapter).

When designing an application, remember that it can be made into a server and still be used as a normal PowerBuilder application while serving requests for the class user objects defined for it. It can even be a client of another remote server.

Two events have been added to the application object for use with applications acting as servers for distributed requests:

- ConnectionBegin is triggered when a client makes a connection for services. Information on the client user is made available in this event so that you can carry out authentication if you want. The return value of this event determines a user's level of access as well as whether the user should be rejected. The return data type is of the enumerated value ConnectPrivilege, which can be ConnectPrivilege!, ConnectWithAdminPrivilege!, or NoConnectPrivilege!.

- ConnectionEnd is triggered when the client application requests that the connection be closed and can be used to carry out maintenance tasks for the server application.

As mentioned earlier, a PowerBuilder application that's used as a client in a typical client/server situation also can act as a server for distributed client requests. More often, you will create your application server with no visible component or, more likely, a simple interface that you can use to control the behavior of various settings of the application.

You develop such applications by using the PowerBuilder skills you've already acquired. Remote object construction and distribution to development teams are contained in the familiar PBL library file. The remote objects can be inherited from existing class user objects or created, stored in a PBL for compilation into a server application, and distributed to development teams for use in their application construction. The following PowerScript is required to set up an application to be a server for a remote request:

```
// Declaration at a global or instance level would look like the following:
//    Transport g_DPBTransport

//Create the server transport object
```

28

Developing
Distributed
PowerBuilder
Applications

```
g_DPBTransport = Create Transport

// Set the communications driver.
// This can be NamedPipes, Sockets, or Local.
g_DPBTransport.Driver = "NamedPipes"

// Set the application server name.
g_DPBTransport.Application = "Test1"

// Listen out for clients on the selected communication protocol.
g_DPBTransport.Listen()

If g_DPBTransport.ErrCode <> 0 Then
   Messagebox( "DPB Server Test1", "Failed to start!")
End If
```

As you can see from this example, the server application uses only the Transport object to accept requests for its services. Place this code in the Open event of the application or one of the application's windows.

## Server Consoles

When creating your server application, you can choose whether to have any visual interface. If you create an interface for your server, you can make it simple (a window with one button to start the server and one to stop it) or more complex (so that you can trace and administer the server's performance). If you choose not to have an interface to start and stop the server, you still will most likely want a means to access the server and determine its current status. To accomplish this for either scenario, you need to create a server console. The console is used to check existing client connections, display the server's current status, and terminate client connections.

The basic idea of a server console is to create a client that connects to the server with administrative privileges. The client can be created as a separate application that connects to the server or as a window in the existing server application. First, look at a remote server console because this lets you administer the server application without actually having to be running from the server machine.

The client application containing the server console should connect to the server using the same process as any other client. The difference is that this client connects to the server with administrative privileges. To do so, the client needs to pass the server an ID and password. These are sent from the client to the server using the values placed in the UserId and Password properties of the client's Connection object.

When the client application calls ConnectToServer() to connect to the server application, the ConnectionBegin event is fired in the server application object. This event has three event arguments passed to it:

- UserId contains a user ID populated from the UserId property of the client's connection object.

- Password contains a password populated from the Password property of the client's connection object.

- ConnectString contains additional connection information populated from the ConnectString property of the client's connection object.

In the ConnectionBegin event, UserId and Password should be evaluated to determine the client application's privileges. The client's privileges are determined by the return value of the ConnectionBegin event. This event returns a value using the enumerated data type ConnectPrivilege. It has the following values:

| | |
|---|---|
| ConnectPrivilege! | Client can connect without administrative privileges. |
| ConnectWithAdminPrivilege! | Client can connect with administrative privileges. |
| NoConnectPrivilege! | Client can't connect to the server application. |

**28**

Developing
Distributed
PowerBuilder
Applications

**Note**

To determine whether the client connecting to the server has administration authority, you can have the server connect to a database containing a security table that specifies the authority level of the user ID.

After checking the UserId property and determining that the user has administration authority, the ConnectionBegin event returns a value of ConnectWithAdminPrivileges!.

After the client is established as an administrator of the server application, call the Connection object's GetServerInfo() method. If the client is connected without administration privileges, the function returns the connection information for the client calling the function. If the client is connected with administration privileges, GetServer-Info() returns an array of ConnectionInfo structures (the number of elements in the array matches the number of all clients connected to the server). This structure array contains all the information the console needs to determine the current status of the server application.

The only question to be answered is how to display all the information in the
ConnectionInfo array in a meaningful manner. The easiest way to use the data in your
array is to populate an external source DataWindow for which the data source matches the
layout of the ConnectionInfo structure. This then would display the current connection
information for all clients of the server. Listing 28.1 shows the code to accomplish this task.

**LISTING 28.1**  Populating the Server Console DataWindow

```
ConnectionInfo lcni_console[]
long ll_numconnect, i

//Reset the DataWindow console
dw_console.Reset()

//Turn off the redraw
dw_console.SetRedraw(False)

//Populate the ConnectionInfo array from the server
ll_numconnect = in_connection.GetServerInfo ( lcni_console)

//Loop through the number of clients connected and
//populate the console DataWindow
For i=1 to ll_numconnect
   dw_console.InsertRow(0)

   If lcni_console[i].busy Then
      dw_console.SetItem( i, "Busy", "True")
   Else
      dw_console.SetItem( i, "Busy", "False")
   End If

   dw_console.SetItem( i, "ConnectTime", lcni_console[i].ConnectTime)
   dw_console.SetItem( i, "LastCallTime", lcni_console[i].LastCallTime)
   dw_console.SetItem( i, "CallCount", lcni_console[i].CallCount)
   dw_console.SetItem( i, "ClientID", lcni_console[i].ClientID)
   dw_console.SetItem( i, "Location", lcni_console[i].Location)
   dw_console.SetItem( i, "UserId", lcni_console[i].UserId)
Next

//Turn on the redraw
dw_console.SetRedraw(True)
```

> **Note**
>
> Because the Busy property of the ConnectionInfo structure is a Boolean value and the external DataWindow data types don't include a Boolean, it must be converted to something else.

Now you have a console that can view the existing client connections but nothing else. If this is all you require, you might want to add a Print button for the DataWindow console. A more full-featured option would be to allow the administrator to kill client connections or stop the server from allowing additional connections.

To disconnect a client, select the desired client from the DataWindow and pass the user ID value to the RemoteStopConnection()method of the connection object. This would be implemented as follows:

```
long ll_row
string ls_userid

//Get the currently selected row
ll_row = dw_console.GetSelectedRow (0)

//Make sure a row was selected
If ll_row = 0 Then
    MessageBox( "Disconnect error", "Please select a client!")
    Return
End If

ls_userid = dw_console.GetItemString( ll_row, "UserId")

If MessageBox( "Disconnnect confirmation", "Are you sure you" + &
            " want to disconnect " + ls_userid + "?", &
            Question!, YesNo!, 2) = 1 Then
    in_connection.RemoteStopConnection( ls_userid)
End If
```

To stop the () server from listening, call the RemoteStopListening() function of the Connection object to stop the server from processing any more client requests. You can use this function to update the server or perform any maintenance.

**28**

Developing
Distributed
PowerBuilder
Applications

> **Note**
>
> By using `RemoteStopListening()`, you can stop the server from listening for new client requests, but it doesn't terminate the server. This can't be done with a remote console.

As mentioned earlier, the server console can be implemented as a separate application or within the server application. The process to create a console within your server application is the same as that for a remote console. The server application now contains `Connection` and `Transport` objects and connects to itself. This method, unlike a remote console, enables you to terminate and start the server application.

## Transaction Pooling

Transaction pooling enables a Distributed PowerBuilder server to manage the number of database connections open at one time. By default, for each client that connects to a server application, the server opens a new connection to the database and disconnects when the client is finished. If the application doesn't constantly request database connections or isn't used by many users, this is a satisfactory situation.

If your application services many users with a high volume of transactions, the constant connecting and disconnecting affects your application's performance and that of your database server. By establishing a transaction pool, the server application maintains the physical connections to the database rather than connect to and disconnect from the database for each client. PowerBuilder logically terminates each connection and performs a `Commit` to save any modifications to the database. The actual physical connection remains open so that when another client requests database access, the connection can be used again without the overhead of reconnecting.

In PowerBuilder, to use transaction pooling, you must call the `SetTransPool()` method of the application object in the server application. The syntax follows:

`ApplicationObject.SetTransPool (MinimumNum, MaximumNum, TimeOut)`

Here, `MinimumNum` is the minimum number of transactions that you want to keep open, `MaximumNum` is the maximum number of transactions to keep open, and `TimeOut` is how many seconds a client should wait for a connection to become available. After this function is called, whenever a client connects to the server and requests a database connection, the server application checks to see whether the database parameters coming in match those of the connections held in the transaction pool. The parameters PowerBuilder matches on in the transaction object are `DBMS`, `ServerName`, `LogID`, `LogPass`, `Database`, and `DBParm` values.

The shared object functionality provided initially with PowerBuilder 6.0 allows you to use shared objects to maintain database connections or static data and reuse the connection or information for multiple clients.

## Load Balancing

*Load balancing* is the process of ensuring that the server(s) can handle the expected number of client requests. If a server has too many requests from its clients, performance may suffer and the server may crash. Load balancing analyzes the number of client requests with server resources to identify the need for additional servers and potential server location.

To implement load balancing in a PowerBuilder server, the server application in the `ConnectionBegin` event can do one of two things. The server can call the `Connection` object's `GetServerInfo()` method to determine how many clients are now connected. If the maximum number of connections has been reached, it can terminate an inactive client, refuse the client connection, or delegate the work to additional servers.

The other action the server can take is to determine whether it has adequate resources to accept a new client. This is done by making a call to the operating system (via an external function). If resources are at a certain level, the server can refuse the connection by returning `NoConnectPrivilege!` from the `ConnectionBegin` event.

28

Developing
Distributed
PowerBuilder
Applications

> **Note**
>
> With shared objects, you also can keep a counter of the number of clients now connected to the server application and use that as the basis for allowing a new client request to be serviced.

## Business Objects

So far, the implementation of a Distributed PowerBuilder application has been about implementing a server; you haven't yet looked at the heart of a server application. Because the entire goal of n-tier applications is to partition the business logic from the interface and the data, it makes sense that the business logic is the main component of a server application.

The business logic in a server application created with PowerBuilder is encapsulated into one or more custom class user objects. If you've been building your applications by using *nonvisual objects* (NVOs), moving to a distributed environment should be relatively simple.

The basic process for creating the application logic is to build the NVO, create a proxy object, ensure that the proxy is placed in the client application, and ensure that the NVO is placed in the server application. After all the objects are placed correctly, the client application needs to connect to the server, instantiate the remote object (the NVO), and invoke any needed functionality in the remote object.

An important consideration when creating your remote objects is the expected time of any given process. By default, any request sent to the server is processed synchronously, which means that the client must wait for the server to finish processing the request before returning control back to the client. PowerBuilder lets you implement asynchronous processing so that the client can call a function and have control returned to the client while the server continues to process in the background. After the server finishes the processing, it sends a message to the client indicating its completion and relaying any applicable information. This process can be extremely useful for generating large reports, which can be requested and then relayed back to the client when completed.

## Client Applications

In PowerBuilder, a *client application* requests services from a PowerBuilder server application by invoking remote objects. This task is carried out through the Connection object. You instantiate a client-side proxy of the object and then the object on the server. This method enables you to use the object as though it were local to the application.

Just as PowerBuilder applications easily can be turned into server applications, they can be made into clients that use remote objects in other applications. The actual PowerScript required is as straightforward and easy to set up as it was for the server. It will look similar to Listing 28.2.

**LISTING 28.2**   Connecting a Client to the Server Application

```
// Declared at a global or instance level would be the following:
// The connection object to connect to the app server for accessing
// the remote object
//    Connection g_DPBConnection
// The proxy user object p_service1 is used to declare the client side pointer
//    uo_service1 guo_Service1

g_DPBConnection = Create Connection
guo_Service1 = Create uo_service1

g_DPBConnection.Application = "Test1"

// A server IP address
```

**LISTING 28.2** CONTINUED

```
//    g_DPBConnection.Location = "196.96.166.000"
// or a local test connection
//    g_DPBConnection.Location = "localhost"
// or some other named location.
g_DPBConnection.Location = "AppServer1"

// Change to the network driver you are using.
g_DPBConnection.driver = "NamedPipes"

If g_DPBConnection.ConnectToServer() <> 0 Then
   Messagebox( "Client", "Error Code = " + String (g_DPBConnection.ErrCode) + &
               "~r~nError Text = " + g_DPBConnection.ErrText)
   HALT CLOSE
End If

g_DPBConnection.CreateInstance(guo_Service1)
```

From this point on, within the scope of the remote object variable guo_Service1, you can use any properties and methods that you've defined for this custom class user object.

# Platform and Driver Requirements

Distributed PowerBuilder now is available with the configurations shown in Table 28.1.

**TABLE 28.1** Distributed PowerBuilder Configurations

| Platform | Communications Protocol | As a Server | As a Client |
|---|---|---|---|
| Windows 95 | NamedPipes | No | Yes |
|  | Sockets | Yes | Yes |
| Windows 98 | NamedPipes | No | Yes |
|  | Sockets | Yes | Yes |
| Windows NT 3.51 | NamedPipes | Yes | Yes |
| and 4.0 | Sockets | Yes | Yes |
| PowerBuilder UNIX | NamedPipes | Yes | Yes |
|  | Sockets | Yes | Yes |

Security for Distributed PowerBuilder is handled completely at the network protocol level and doesn't impose any additional checks.

**28**

Developing Distributed PowerBuilder Applications

## WinSock Driver Considerations

You need to make entries into the hosts file for each machine that will use Distributed PowerBuilder objects. You will have an entry for each server used.

You also can specify a loopback address to the local machine for testing purposes. This entry, by convention, is called `localhost` and has the IP address `127.0.0.1`.

> **Note**
>
> Microsoft supplies a hosts.sam file to show how to format the entries for the hosts file. It also supplies the `localhost` entry.

# Debugging Distributed PowerBuilder

As you might expect, debugging a PowerBuilder application that's a client or server in a distributed environment presents some unique difficulties. The main focus of any development work for a server or a client application is to create it independently of the final platform on which it will be deployed. This enables developers to develop and test the code on their own machines without having to worry about loading objects onto other machines. Distributed PowerBuilder provides some debugging and diagnostic tools to help you track down problems with remote calls. The most well-known of these tools is the PowerBuilder debugger. You can use the familiar PowerBuilder debugger to watch the application code and variables in the same way you would use any other PowerBuilder application.

## The "Local" Driver

Because the PowerBuilder debugger can now handle only single-process local debugging, a local loopback driver is available to enable single-process symbolic processing. This driver has the following effects on the client and server sides of an application: The server doesn't create a transport object, and the client uses the connection driver "Local".

The "Local" driver then emulates a remote server locally and within the same process as the client application. The object-reference indirections that normally occur during distributed processing are converted into locally serviced references so that the variables and object data can be seen within the debugger.

> **Note**
>
> This conversion process also means that a single variable and data space are used by client and server applications, which may lead to usage conflicts.

The local driver method won't help you debug actual connection and communications problems; you have to use the methods outlined in the following sections for those.

# Error Processing

Rather than force you to check each call you make to a remote object for possible errors, Sybase implements error processing for Distributed PowerBuilder via the SystemError event.

If an error occurs in the client-request context on the server, it's trapped, and the Error structure is populated for that client thread. This then is sent back to the client side, where an application error is triggered. The developer has two locations that can be used to handle the error condition: the Error event for the Connection object and the SystemError event for the application.

> **Note**
>
> The Error event is modeled on the OLE error-event mechanism.

The Connection object's Error event can be set up to respond to different error conditions by setting the Action parameter to one of the following values:

- ExceptionFail! triggers the SystemError event.

- ExceptionIgnore! ignores the error and attempts to continue processing. Use this value with caution because the error you're processing may cause another error, ad infinitum.

- ExceptionRetry! attempts to reexecute the function or reevaluate the expression.

- ExceptionSubstituteReturnValue! substitutes the return code with that in the ReturnValue event parameter and cancels the error condition. The ReturnValue parameter is a value of the same data type as the value that would have been expected to be returned.

Using these options provides more flexibility than the SystemError event's continue or halt options. If an object or method isn't available on the server you connected to, for example, you can disconnect, reconnect to another server, and then retry the operation that failed.

For more serious errors, such as page faults or other fatal system conditions, Distributed PowerBuilder attempts to save server applications by terminating the offending client thread. If the exception handler determines that the executing client thread caused the exception, it attempts to gracefully kill the thread, release acquired resources, and inform the client side of the problem. The client side then can respond in whatever manner you want; it probably will attempt to reconnect to the server and continue processing. If the server application has a more serious problem, the server may be terminated, and client applications will receive Server no longer responding messages on their next use of a remote object.

## Trace Options

The ConnectionObject class (which encompasses the Transport and Connection objects) contains a Trace property, which you can use to obtain debug information during an application's execution. The following options can be specified for the Trace property:

- Setting All to 1 logs all activity, including internal information on memory usage, as well as the types and values for parameters.

- Level sets the level of information to capture. Setting this option to 1 captures basic information (Console, ObjectLife, ObjectCalls, and ConnectInfo).

- Setting ObjectLife to 1 captures the creation and destruction of objects. It will be written in this format:

  ```
  DSE Create 'object class name' (object id), SUCCEEDED/FAILED
  DSE Destroy (object id), SUCCEEDED/FAILED
  ```

- By setting ObjectCalls to 1, you can capture method calls for the server and client. This is written in the following format for server-method invocation:

  ```
  DSE (context id, object id) Called: Function name, SUCCEEDED/FAILED
  DSE Return (return type)
  Parm# (parm type) by Value/Reference
  ```

- In this format for server-attribute access

  ```
  DSE Get/Set (context id, object id) attribute name, (attribute type)
  ```

- In this format for client-method invocation

  ```
  DSE (object id) Call: object class name.function name
  ```

```
DSE Return (return type), SUCCEEDED/FAILED
Parm# (parm type) by Value/Reference
```

- And in this format for client-attribute access

```
DSE (object id) Get/Set object class name.attribute name
(attribute type), SUCCEEDED/FAILED
```

- `Log` sets the filename and path of the log file. The file is opened in Append mode.

- Set `DumpArgs` to 1 to log the types of parameters and their values.

- Set `WebPB` to 1 to log all WebPB activity.

- Setting `Console` to 1 enables the console window.

You can use these trace options to customize the log file generated. Some sample trace settings follow:

```
DPBConnection.Trace = "Log=c:\pb5i32\debug\app1.log, " + &
                      "ObjectCalls=1, ObjectLife=1"
//
DPBConnection.Trace = "Console=1, ObjectCalls=1, ObjectLife=1"
//
DPBConnection.Trace = "Console=1, Level=1"
```

The task of debugging Distributed PowerBuilder can be complex, but you can use the methods described in this section to make it easier.

# Summary

As you have seen in this chapter, PowerBuilder 7.0 fully supports the development of distributed and n-tier applications. New component wizards make it easy to create distributed components and deploy them to Jaguar and Microsoft Transaction Server. The features of Distributed PowerBuilder have been maintained in this release to allow developers time to migrate to EA Server or MTS. Sybase has clearly demonstrated its commitment to distributed computing by continuing to give PowerBuilder developers new options for creating and working with distributed components.

**28**

Developing
Distributed
PowerBuilder
Applications

# PowerBuilder and the Internet

Sybase has been steadily adding Internet functionality to PowerBuilder since version 5.0. The HTML-generation features, tight integration with the Jaguar component server, and the new Web DataWindow provide a solid platform for Internet-based development within PowerBuilder. This chapter presents a summary of some Internet/intranet concepts and the PowerBuilder features that allow you to access them. Chapter 30, "Developing Internet Applications with PowerBuilder," looks at how you can use PowerBuilder to create applications incorporating Internet functionality.

# The Internet and Intranets

In simple terms, the *Internet* is a large collection of computers all connected to one another in one huge network. Communication over the Internet uses the TCP/IP network protocol, and each computer that's part of the network has a unique IP address.

*Intranets* are miniature versions of the Internet that are private to an organization. Servers perform the same tasks (WWW, FTP, and so on), and TCP/IP is used as the network protocol. Intranets typically provide a secure, high-performance platform to leverage new Internet technologies internally. Because intranets aren't constrained by the same performance and security issues as the Internet, users are better able to share information and find new ways to work.

## World Wide Web

The *World Wide Web*, commonly referred to as *WWW* or simply *the Web*, can be compared to a spider's web, with each strand being a connection between two Web servers. At each node is an HTTP server hosting and providing access to one or many Web sites. Each Web site can be constructed using HTML, CGI scripting, Java, and a host of other languages, tools, and software. The HTML pages that make up the shell of a Web site can have links to other pages, which can be situated local to the server or on the other side of the world.

### URL

A *URL* (uniform resource locator) is used with the Web to specify a resource's location. Here is an example of a URL:

```
http://www.reppart.org/members/kenneth/index.html
```

which breaks down into the following:

```
ServiceType://HostName/Path/FileName
```

*ServiceType* is the service protocol used to access the resource (http in the preceding example). This usually is the Hypertext Transfer Protocol (HTTP) or the File Transfer Protocol (FTP). *HostName* specifies the machine where the resource can be found (www.iquest.net). *Path* is the directory pathname for the resource (~herbs), and *FileName* is the file containing the desired information (sjah.html).

# HTML

*Hypertext Markup Language* (HTML) originated from the *Standard Generalized Markup Language* (SGML) that defines a Web document's structure and content. HTML works by using tags embedded into the document that specify what document contents to display and how to display them. You may have seen something similar if you've ever turned on the codes in your word processor. HTML allows documents to incorporate graphics, video, and sound along with the text.

HTML pages are accessed by using the following steps:

1. A user enters the Web page's URL into his browser.

2. The request is sent from the user's PC through the Internet to the Web server specified, using a fully qualified domain name (see the next section, "Name Servers").

3. The Web server locates the desired Web page and transmits the string syntax back to the browser.

4. The user's machine caches a temporary copy of the file, decodes the HTML tags, and displays the file.

# Name Servers

*Name servers* are used within the network to translate the English address—for example, www.sybase.com—to the computer-understandable IP address. An IP address is composed of four bytes of information that look like a period-delimited number—for example, 255.255.255.0. This actually details a specific computer location, much like a ZIP Code does for postal services around the world.

> **Note**
>
> If you know the IP address of a Web server, you can substitute that address for the text name in the URL. The name portion of the URL must always be resolved into a valid IP address before a connection can be made.

# FTP

*File Transfer Protocol* (FTP) is a method for transmitting and receiving files (text or binary) over a network. As with most Internet software, FTP is based on the client/server architecture. The machine that you connect to in order to copy files from or to is running an

FTP server. This allows connection via a specified port (connection point that the service is listening on) for file transfer. The FTP server might force you to log on, or it might allow an anonymous logon that allows access to anyone.

An FTP server exposed to the Internet or running within a corporate intranet provides a good location for storing the latest PC drivers and software updates to corporate applications. With PowerBuilder's PBSync feature, you can use an FTP site to automatically update users with the latest versions of your PowerBuilder applications.

# Net-Based Applications

As the number of Internet users (particularly Web users) has grown exponentially over the past few years, businesses worldwide have been scrambling to take advantage of the new business models that the Internet makes possible. Many companies have expanded their business onto the Internet in various forms. The three basic types of content that can be provided on a Web site are static, dynamic, or executable.

The most basic implementation is to just display static information with a predefined format. This is commonly referred to as "brochure-ware." The name comes from the fact that the first step most companies take on the Internet is to convert their existing brochures and literature into HTML format and publish it on the Web. Although this approach can provide worldwide visibility to any individual or company, it's usually the least attractive to users.

As Internet technologies matured, it became possible to create dynamic content or Web applications by responding to user actions. On the server, CGI scripts or Active Server Pages (ASP) are commonly used to generate content on-the-fly. On the client side, Java applets, JavaScript, and VBScript can be used to respond to user actions. This model is essentially the same as the client/server model that PowerBuilder was designed for. The primary difference is that with Web applications, no files are deployed to the client machine, and a standard Web browser is all that's needed for access.

The last type of Net-based application is executable content. The information generated by executable content can be dynamic, but most of the processing occurs on the client machine. When the browser makes a request, the Web server sends back a component that then executes on the client (such as a Java program).

**Note**

The PowerBuilder Web Deployment Kit is based on a unique model, which Sybase calls *live client*. This model falls somewhere between dynamic and executable content. With this approach, all the application processing occurs on the server,

> but the power of the client machine is used to draw the interface and trap mouse and keyboard events. See the later section "The PowerBuilder Web Deployment Kit" for more information on this deployment option.

## Java

Java is a programming language created by Sun Microsystems to be a truly cross-platform development language. Developed from the ground up to be object-oriented, the language is a powerful tool for developers creating distributed applications. Java is based loosely on C++ but hides the troublesome pointer mechanisms of that language. It also has many other programmer-friendly features, such as garbage collection, storage management, exception handling, and type-safe references.

Sybase provides access to Java development with its PowerJ tool. PowerJ is part of the Enterprise Application Studio and offers features such as the Java DataWindow and tight integration with EA Server.

# PowerBuilder's Internet Features

Beginning with version 5.0, PowerBuilder has steadily introduced new features that allow developers to move their applications to the Internet. With the new Web DataWindow and tight integration with EA Server, PowerBuilder 7.0 is even more Internet enabled. The following sections briefly overview how PowerBuilder's Internet features enable you to leverage your existing knowledge of PowerBuilder to develop Internet-enabled applications.

## The Web DataWindow

The Web DataWindow (also called the HTML DataWindow) is a new server component that provides DataWindow functionality in pure HTML. Most DataWindow functionality is provided in the browser, without the need for any PowerBuilder runtime DLLs. Some features supported by the Web DataWindow include

- Computed fields (some limitations apply)
- Validation rules
- Display formats
- Updates
- Client-side events

# How the Web DataWindow Works

When users request a page containing a Web DataWindow, the application server calls the `Generate` method on the server component, which generates the HTML for the specified DataWindow. Computed columns, expressions, validation rules, and events are translated to JavaScript and included in the HTML. The application server then combines the HTML with any other elements on the page and returns the results to the browser. For tips on how to control the appearance of the generated HTML, see the later section "DataWindow HTML Generation."

The Web DataWindow server component can be deployed to Jaguar CTS as a Java component using CORBA, or to other application or component servers such as Microsoft IIS or MTS using a COM server object. If you're using EA Studio, the Web DataWindow component will automatically be preinstalled in Jaguar for you.

# Interacting with the Web DataWindow

The easiest way to allow users to interact with the Web DataWindow is to add buttons to the DataWindow object and set the `Action` property to enable the specified processing. Table 29.1 lists the supported DataWindow button actions.

**TABLE 29.1**   Supported Button Actions

| Action | Description |
| --- | --- |
| AppendRow | Adds a row at the end. |
| DeleteRow | Deletes the current row. |
| InsertRow | Inserts a row before the current row. |
| PageFirst | Scrolls to the first page. |
| PageLast | Scrolls to the last page. |
| PageNext | Scrolls to the next page. |
| PagePrior | Scrolls to the previous page. |
| Retrieve | Retrieves rows from the database. |
| Sort | Opens the sort dialog and then sorts the rows in the order specified. |
| Update | Updates the database; a commit is automatically issued if the update is successful. |

You can also call methods on the client control from JavaScript code if you set the `HTMLGen.ClientScriptable` property in the DataWindow painter. When this property is set, JavaScript functions are created for the following methods:

| | | |
| --- | --- | --- |
| AcceptText | GetItem | ScrollNextPage |
| DeletedCount | GetItemStatus | ScrollPriorPage |
| DeleteRow | InsertRow | SetItem |
| GetClickedColumn | ModifiedCount | SetColumn |
| GetClickedRow | Retrieve | SetRow |

| GetColumn | RowCount | SetSort |
| --- | --- | --- |
| GetNextModified | ScrollFirstPage | Sort |
| GetRow | ScrollLastPage | Update |

**Note**

Several of these methods can be called directly by using the button `Action` property. Because client scripting significantly increases the size of the JavaScript that must be downloaded, be sure to turn off this option unless you need it.

The capability to call these methods is useful if you don't want to add buttons to your DataWindow controls, or if you want to provide a more advanced interface.

So now you know how to call methods on the Web DataWindow, but what if you want to respond to the control's events in client script? No problem—just turn on the `HTMLGen.ClientEvents` property and define a JavaScript function on the page with the following syntax:

`WebDWName_eventname(arguments)`

The Web DataWindow automatically calls your function when that event occurs. The following events are supported:

| ButtonClicking | ItemFocusChanged |
| --- | --- |
| ButtonClicked | RowFocusChanged |
| Clicked | RowFocusChanging |
| ItemChanged | UpdateStart |
| ItemError | |

The new Web DataWindow lets you harness the power of the familiar DataWindow control without the baggage of the PowerBuilder deployment DLLs. This gives you the flexibility to serve Web DataWindow-based pages over the Internet without requiring large downloads. Because most of the DataWindow's functionality is available, you can now create advanced Web-based applications by using familiar technologies. Although the plug-in and ActiveX options presented in the following sections can be useful for putting your existing applications online quickly, in the long run, the Web DataWindow is the most flexible and has the fewest limitations on how it can be deployed.

**29**

**PowerBuilder and the Internet**

# Plug-Ins and ActiveX

One of the quickest ways to get your PowerBuilder application onto the Internet is to use a PowerBuilder plug-in or the Window ActiveX control. The DataWindow and Window plug-ins and ActiveX controls provide graphical interfaces inside an HTML Web page. They can be used with any Web browser that supports plug-ins and ActiveX controls.

## The DataWindow Plug-In

The DataWindow plug-in lets you display a Powersoft report file (PSR) in an HTML page. The PSR is a static snapshot of a DataWindow's data and its presentation. It can be created from the DataWindow painter, the Report painter, a DataWindow control, or a DataStore. Because a PSR is a snapshot of the data, a database connection isn't needed. This makes implementing a Web page with the DataWindow plug-in very easy.

After creating a PSR, build an HTML page that contains a reference to the PSR. Use the following HTML tag:

```
<EMBED SRC=PSRName WIDTH=WindowWidth HEIGHT=WindowHeight>
```

*PSRName* is a URL for the PSR object to be viewed, *WindowWidth* is the width of the window area in which the PSR will be displayed, and *WindowHeight* is the height of the window area.

When the browser processes the `<EMBED>` tag, it then requests that the server send it the PSR and locates the appropriate DLL used to handle DataWindow content in the browser's PLUGINS directory. For the DataWindow plug-in, the client machine must contain the DataWindow plug-in DLL, NPDWE70.DLL, and must be registered with the Web server and the browser.

When a PSR is embedded in an HTML page, the first thing the server does is send a header file to the Web browser that gives a description of the embedded object. To send the header file, the resource type (in this case, a PSR) must be registered with the server. When the header is received by the browser, it must determine whether it has the appropriate files to handle the embedded resource. Because each browser checks to see what files it needs for the resource, you can send the same resource from the server and have each browser (regardless of what operating system) respond to it in its own way.

When the Web browser displays the DataWindow in the plug-in, you can scroll through the report, change values (although the changes don't get sent to the database), or right-click the PSR, which displays a pop-up menu, allowing you to save the data in the PSR, print the PSR, or navigate between pages of the PSR.

# The Window Plug-In

The Window plug-in works in much the same way as the DataWindow plug-in. It allows you to display a PowerBuilder window of window type Child in an HTML page for Web browsers that support plug-ins. The window you create can be identical to any window you would deploy in a PowerBuilder application. This means that you can use any of your favorite controls, including the DataWindow control. All scripts for the window will execute as you would expect them to. With the Window plug-in, you can connect to a database for retrieval and update purposes and open secondary windows (pop-up or response) from the child window.

With the Window plug-in, you have all the functionality of a standalone PowerBuilder window, which leaves you asking, "What's the catch?" Although the Window plug-in gives you all the functionality of a standard PowerBuilder window, you also need to deploy all the same runtime files. This means that every client using the Window plug-in must have the plug-in DLL (NPPBA70.DLL) and the PowerBuilder deployment files.

> **Note**
>
> A secure version of the Window plug-in is available in NPPBS70.DLL. This version restricts the activities that the window in the plug-in can perform. The restrictions include no external function calls, no OLE or DDE calls, no email calls, and no database or distributed PowerBuilder access.

When creating the application to be displayed using the plug-in, keep several things in mind. First, the application cannot contain any global variables, including global reference variables, unless you use the <APPLICATION> tag. This includes the reference variable for the window you're displaying in the plug-in. If you have a window named w_customer that you want to display in the plug-in, you couldn't code the following unless you have specified the application in using the <EMBED> tag:

```
w_customer.title = "Please select a customer"
```

This is because w_customer is a globally defined variable (created by PowerBuilder) used to refer to an instance of w_customer. With the plug-in, PowerBuilder never creates the reference variable; you therefore experience a runtime error. The exception to the global variable rule is that the standard PowerBuilder system objects such as SQLCA and Message are created and available for use.

In addition, all code for database connections should be included within the window if you are not planning to use <APPLICATION> because no application object is available to perform any initial setup.

> **Note**
>
> When writing the code for the window, keep in mind the order that events are processed. In particular, remember that the Constructor event for each control on the window processes before the Open event for the window.

Another event to watch for is Activate. Because the window type must be a child window and child windows are never active, any code in the Activate event will never execute. Other nuances of the child window type is that it can be minimized, maximized, and resized. You will probably want to disable these properties for the window.

Any paths specified in file references need to be valid on each client workstation. The easiest solution is to use a mapped network drive or specify the server name in the path. The last consideration when creating your application window is that if the window opens any other windows, it must also close them. The Web browser will make sure that the child window in the plug-in is destroyed when users move to another Web page, but any other opened windows will stay open.

> **Tip**
>
> Use the child window's Close or CloseQuery event to ensure that all secondary windows are closed.

The best way to create an application to be used in the Window plug-in is to test everything within the PowerBuilder development environment. The child window to be displayed in the plug-in initially can be specified as a main window and tested in the PowerBuilder development environment. When the window and any objects it references are working satisfactorily, convert the main window to a child window and generate a PBD (PowerBuilder dynamic library) for the application PBL.

Before you generate the PBD, make sure that any unnecessary objects are removed because PowerBuilder downloads the PBD every time it's run (unless it's now cached). Also, the dynamic library must not be a machine code library because those libraries don't work with the plug-in.

The HTML needed to display your window using the plug-in is

```
<EMBED SRC=PBDName WIDTH=WindowWidth HEIGHT=WindowHeight WINDOW=WindowName>
```

In this syntax, *PBDName* is the URL indicating the location and name of the PBD, *WindowWidth* is the width in pixels of the window in which the PowerBuilder window will be displayed, *WindowHeight* is the height of the window in pixels, in which the PowerBuilder window will be displayed, and *WindowName* is the name of the child window to be displayed. Three optional values can also be included in the `<EMBED>` tag:

- `APPLICATION` specifies the application object in the PBD. Using the `APPLICATION` attribute allows you to access the `Open` and `Close` events on the application object, as well as global variables and functions.

- `LIBRARY` specifies an absolute URL indicating the location and name of an additional PBD needed by the child window in the plug-in. The `LIBRARY` attribute should be repeated for each required PBD.

- `COMMANDPARM` passes an argument to the child window. The value can be retrieved by using the `CommandParm()` function within the child window.

Like the DataWindow plug-in, the Window plug-in must be registered on the Web server and the client browser. The browser must also be able to locate the PowerBuilder runtime DLLs. You can ensure this by including the path to the DLLs in the operating system's search path or by updating the browser application's path key in the Registry.

## The Window ActiveX Control

The Window ActiveX control provides much the same functionality as the Window plug-in. The window displayed in the ActiveX control should be constructed in the same manner as the plug-in window. The ActiveX control can give some additional functionality to your Web page by providing access to the window through JavaScript or VBScript. Also, certain events in the ActiveX control trigger events in the ActiveX container. When one of these events fires, any PowerBuilder code for that event is triggered, and any code written for the ActiveX container is fired (in JavaScript or VBScript).

After building the window to be contained in the ActiveX control (see the preceding section for tips on creating the window), make sure that the ActiveX control is registered for the server and the client. The ActiveX control, like the Window plug-in, is available in a secure-mode version as well as the standard version. The ActiveX control is supported only in Windows 95/98 and Windows NT 4.0 and must be registered before it can be used.

**29**

**PowerBuilder and the Internet**

To use the ActiveX control in a Web page, you must include the following HTML:

```
<OBJECT NAME="ObjectName" WIDTH=WindowWidth HEIGHT= WindowHeight

CLASSID="CLSID:ClassId">
    <PARAM NAME="_Version" VALUE="65536">
    <PARAM NAME="_ExtentX" VALUE="5962">
    <PARAM NAME="_ExtentY" VALUE="2164">
    <PARAM NAME="_StockProps" VALUE="0">
    <PARAM NAME="PBWindow" VALUE=" WindowName">
    <PARAM NAME="LibList" VALUE=" PBDList">
    <PARAM NAME="PBApplication" VALUE=" AppObject">
</OBJECT>
```

The main components that you must be concerned with are as follows:

| Attribute | Description |
|-----------|-------------|
| NAME | Name of the ActiveX object used for reference in code or as part of a form |
| WIDTH | The window width for viewing the child window |
| HEIGHT | The window height for viewing the child window |
| CLASSID | The class ID obtained when the ActiveX control was registered |

You can add the option attribute of CODEBASE, which specifies a URL indicating the location of the ActiveX control to be downloaded if it doesn't exist on the client machine. The PARAM attributes of the <OBJECT> tag are as follows:

| Attribute | Description |
|-----------|-------------|
| PBWINDOW | The name of the PowerBuilder child window to be displayed |
| LIBLIST | A list of PBDs used by the application; multiple libraries must be separated by a semicolon |
| PBAPPLICATION | The name of the PowerBuilder application object |
| DISPLAYERRORS | Specifies whether runtime errors are displayed (optional) |
| COMMANDPARM | A string to be passed to the child window; the value is retrieved by calling the CommandParm() function in the application |

Via the value specified for the NAME attribute, JavaScript and VBScript can interact with the PowerBuilder window in the ActiveX control. This can be done by using the following methods:

- Create an event handler in JavaScript or VBScript to be executed when an event is executed on the PowerBuilder child window.

- Call a PowerScript function from JavaScript or VBScript. The functions you can call are PointerX(), PointerY(), Print(), SetRedraw(), and Timer().

- Use the InvokePBFunction() function to call a user-defined function on the PowerBuilder child window.

- Use the TriggerPBEvent() function to call a user-defined event on the PowerBuilder child window.

As you can see, the Window ActiveX control gives you much of the power of the Window plug-in, plus some additional scripting capability from within the HTML page.

# Web.PB

Web.PB gives you access to distributed PowerBuilder components directly from HTML. With Web.PB, no components need to be installed on the client machine because all the processing occurs on the server. This allows you to have a *thin client*, with your processing occurring on the server. For more information on PowerBuilder's implementation of its distributed architecture, see Chapter 28, "Developing Distributed PowerBuilder Applications."

### Note

Sybase has announced that its long-term plan for Internet-based computing includes the use of the Sybase Enterprise Application Server (which includes PowerDynamo and Jaguar) in place of Distributed PowerBuilder. PowerBuilder 7.0 will be the final release to include Distributed PowerBuilder and Web.PB functionality. No new functionality has been added to Web.PB in PowerBuilder 7.0.

29

**PowerBuilder and the Internet**

Web.PB consists of four main pieces:

- The Web browser on a client, which must support CGI (Common Gateway Interface) calls. The browser calls functions in the server application on the Web server.

- The Web server, which manages requests from the client machines and contains the server application and the Web.PB software.

- The Distributed PowerBuilder application, which runs on the Web server and contains business logic (in the form of custom class user objects) that can be invoked by the Web browsers on the clients.

- The Web.PB interface that corresponds to the program interface you're using for your Web server (for example, standard CGI or ISAPI).

The basic idea of Web.PB is as follows: The Web browser on the client receives an HTML page containing a tag that calls a method on a distributed PowerBuilder application running on the Web server. The Web server calls the appropriate Web.PB interface program, which in turn passes the request to the distributed PowerBuilder server application. The PowerBuilder server application then invokes the method and returns the desired output to the Web browser. The benefit of this method is that all the processing is done on the server with full PowerScript support, and no installation is necessary on the client machines.

To build a Web.PB application, you first need to create and test your distributed PowerBuilder server application. The server application consists of `Transport` and `Application` objects, a console window (if desired), and one or more custom class user objects containing all the necessary business processing in the form of functions.

The methods in the nonvisual objects (NVOs) can receive arguments from the browser. These arguments can be any standard data type except for structures and arrays. If no value is specified for an argument, a `NULL` value is passed to the function.

> **Note**
>
> The functions called from the browser can't be overloaded. Internal private and protected functions can be overloaded.

The method can also return values but is limited to specifying a string or a BLOB. These two return types cover most of the information you would want to return to a browser: text, HTML, graphics, sounds, and PSRs, to name a few. When a browser receives information from a Web server, the server sends a header containing a description of the content being returned to the client.

When a method is invoked that returns a string value, Web.PB calls the method once and returns the string value specifying that the content type being returned is text/html. When a BLOB is returned from a server method, Web.PB calls the method repeatedly until the method returns a NULL BLOB value. Because a BLOB can contain many different content types (images, WAVs, AVIs), the server application must also generate a header indicating the content type being returned.

After you create the server application, install it on the Web server. The PBWEB.INI file determines how a Web.PB application runs on the server. It contains the connection properties for each installed server application. The information contained for each server is used just like the properties of a Connection object are used. There are three main sections to PBWEB.INI:

| Section | Description |
| --- | --- |
| Web.PB | Contains systemwide settings for Web.PB |
| Default | Specifies the default values for the server application and user objects |
| Server | Contains the connection values that Web.PB uses to connect to a specific server application (each server application will have its own entry) |

The [Web.PB] section consists of the following four keywords:

| Keyword | Description |
| --- | --- |
| errormessage | An HTML string returned by Web.PB when an error occurs |
| ISAPIKeywords | CGI environment variables used for Microsoft IIS |
| CGIKeywords | CGI environment variables used for any Web server that supports the Common Gateway Interface |
| NSAPIKeywords | CGI environment variables used for Netscape Commerce Server |

The [Default] section consists of the following two keys:

| Keyword | Description |
| --- | --- |
| Serveralias | Specifies the server alias name that Web.PB should use when a URL reference doesn't specify a server alias; the server alias specified must have a corresponding [Server] entry. |
| Serverobject | Specifies the server object name that Web.PB uses when a URL reference doesn't specify a server alias. |

The [Server] section contains the specific connection information that Web.PB requires to connect to the server application. Common keywords specified are the Application, Location, and Driver, which correspond to the Connection object properties.

> **Note**
>
> If you specify a service name for the Application key in PBWEB.INI, you need to add the service and a port number to the SERVICES file on the Web server. If a hostname is specified for the Location key, the hostname and IP address need to be added to the HOSTS file on the Web server.

The other piece of installing Web.PB on your Web server is to make sure that the appropriate program interface is installed on your Web server. The interfaces are PBCGI70.EXE for standard CGI support, PBISA70.DLL for ISAPI on Microsoft IIS, PBNS170.DLL for NSAPI on Netscape Commerce and Communications servers, PBNS270.DLL for NSAPI on version 2.*x* Netscape FastTrack and Enterprise servers, and PBNS370.DLL for NSAPI on version 3.*x* Netscape FastTrack and Enterprise servers.

The last piece to the puzzle is the actual HTML that specifies which method of which object is to be invoked. The Web.PB HTML tag can be in an <ANCHOR> tag or built with an HTML <FORM> tag. These tags can be created manually or by using the Web.PB Wizard. In addition to the specific HTML that invokes a Web.PB application, you most likely will want to provide additional HTML tags to format and present the generated Web page. The Web.PB class library consists of a number of NVOs that can help you build the necessary HTML for your PowerBuilder Web applications. For more information on the HTML needed to call a Web.PB application and the corresponding Web.PB class library, see Chapter 30, "Developing Internet Applications with PowerBuilder."

# DataWindow HTML Generation

When PowerBuilder introduced the HTML-generation features to the DataWindow in version 5.0, the resulting HTML was rudimentary. PowerBuilder's support for HTML generation has greatly improved in versions 6.0 and 7.0. The following sections examine the HTML-generation capabilities now built into PowerBuilder.

## DataWindows Generating HTML Forms

DataWindows can generate HTML form syntax that displays columns using the appropriate edit control for the specified number of rows. Now you can generate form syntax for the detail band of a DataWindow. The only DataWindow styles that produce usable forms are freeform or tabular.

---

**Note**

Any nested DataWindows will appear as HTML tables.

---

You do, however, need to consider the column edit styles of the DataWindow you want to use as a form. Not all edit styles are converted to a usable form, as shown here:

| Column Edit Style | HTML Form Element |
|---|---|
| CheckBox | CHECKBOX input type |
| DropDownDataWindow | Looks like a SELECT input type but isn't |
| DropDownListBox | SELECT input type |
| Edit | TEXT input type |
| EditMask | N/A |
| RadioButtons | RADIO input type |

You create HTML forms by using the GenerateHTMLForm() function, which takes the following arguments:

```
DWorDS.GenerateHTMLForm( RefSyntax, RefStyle, Action {, StartRow, EndRow, &
                    StartColumn, EndColumn {, Buffer}})
```

This function places the form element syntax in *RefSyntax* and the HTML style sheet in *RefStyle*. Both arguments are passed by reference.

**29**

PowerBuilder and
the Internet

> **Note**
>
> As you can see from the syntax example, you can create a form that spans multiple lines. Whether you have one line or many, PowerBuilder creates a unique name for each element.

Place the style sheet syntax returned from the function between <HTML> and <BODY> tags.

## The `Data.HTML` DataWindow Property

An additional property added to DataWindows, and visible if you export a DataWindow, describes the DataWindow object in an HTML table format.

Just as the edit styles previously mentioned don't translate completely, not all DataWindow presentation styles translate to HTML as well as others. The Crosstab, Freeform, Grid, Group, and Tabular presentation styles produce the best results.

> **Caution**
>
> Be careful how you place objects within a DataWindow. If objects overlap, even by a little bit, you may get some unexpected results in the HTML, such as missing or incorrectly aligned column headers.

If you extract data from the Composite, Graph, OLE 2.0, or RichText presentation styles, you get tables based on the resultset only and not based on the presentation style.

The HTML table syntax is accessed using dot notation from the DataWindow. The syntax is

```
dwControl.Object.DataWindow.Data.HTMLTable
```

The return of this call is the HTML table syntax for the DataWindow layout and data content. Use this value to send back to a client from within a Distributed PowerBuilder server application.

## Enhancements to HTML Generation

To control the compatibility of the HTML stored in the DataWindow's `HTMLTable` property, use the `HTMLTable.GenerateCSS` property. If you set `HTMLTable.GenerateCSS` to `'No'`, no formatting is referenced in the `HTMLTable` property. If you set it to `'Yes'`, cascading style sheet elements are included in the `HTMLTable` property that reference the style sheet stored in HTML.StyleSheet. When you set it to 'Yes', you can also specify the following properties to control table layout:

- NoWrap indicates whether text wraps within a table cell. Values are 'Yes' and 'No'.

- Border specifies the border line width.

- Width specifies the cell width.

- CellPadding specifies the number of pixel spaces within cells.

- CellSpacing specifies the number of pixels between cells.

You can access these properties directly by using dot notation. Let's examine the differences in the HTML with the HTMLTable.GenerateCSS property set each way.

When this property is set to 'Yes', table formatting information and style sheet CLASS references are included in the syntax:

```
<table cellspacing=1 cellpadding=3 border=5 width=10>
<tr>
<td CLASS=0 ALIGN=center>Employee ID
<td CLASS=0 ALIGN=center>Manager ID
<td CLASS=0 ALIGN=center>First Name
<td CLASS=0 ALIGN=center>Last Name
<tr>
<td CLASS=6 ALIGN=right>102
<td CLASS=6 ALIGN=right>501
<td CLASS=7>Fran
<td CLASS=7>Whitney
</table>
```

If HTMLTable.GenerateCSS is set to 'No', no HTMLTable properties are used to create the table elements:

```
<table>
<tr>
<th ALIGN=center>Employee ID
<th ALIGN=center>Manager ID
<th ALIGN=center>First Name
<th ALIGN=center>Last Name
<tr>
<td ALIGN=right>102
<td ALIGN=right>501
<td>Fran
<td>Whitney
</table>
```

**Caution**

This is how the GenerateCSS setting is supposed to work, but as of the publication of this book, the feature is broken. Look for it to be fixed in subsequent maintenance releases.

When this technique is incorporated into a Web.PB application, it allows you to dynamically create HTML on user request and gives you the flexibility to modify the HTML table syntax as you see fit. In the following example, we modified the HTMLTable properties to the settings we wanted and then created the HTML page to send back to the client:

```
String szHTMLPage

ds_1.Modify("datawindow.HTMLTable.GenerateCSS='yes' " + &
            "datawindow.HTMLTable.NoWrap='yes' "        + &
            "datawindow.HTMLTable.width=5 "             + &
            "datawindow.HTMLTable.border=5 "            + &
            "datawindow.HTMLTable.CellSpacing=2 "       + &
            "datawindow.HTMLTable.CellPadding=2")

szHTMLPage = "<HTML>" + &
            ds_1.Object.DataWindow.HTMLTable.StyleSheet + &
            "<BODY>" + ds_1.Object.DataWindow.Data.HTMLTable + "</BODY>" + &
            "</HTML>"

Return szHTMLPage
```

# Context Information

PowerBuilder now includes a context object that allows access to external services. This new feature gives PowerBuilder functionality similar to the COM QueryInterface. The context object provides access to three services:

- *Context information* is based on the ContextInformation type (all platforms).

- *Keyword* is based on the ContextKeyword type (all platforms).

- *ErrorLogging* is based on the ErrorLogging type.

- *SSLServiceProvider* is based on the SSLServiceProvider type.

- *TransactionServer* is based on the `TransactionServer` type.

- *Internet* is based on the `Inet` type (only Windows 95/98/NT).

As you see later in the section "Opening a Web Page," you use the context object to create a service object within the current execution context to take full advantage of that environment. An execution context now can be native PowerBuilder, the Window plug-in (NPPBA70.DLL or NPPBS70.DLL), or the Window ActiveX control (PBRX70.OCX or PBRXS70.OCX).

Being able to act within the context of the environment allows your application to control an Internet Explorer via the ActiveX Automation Service or to access parameters specified in an `<EMBED>` element when working in the context of the Window plug-in.

By using the context object as the basis for further services, Sybase can provide those services without requiring major reworks of the development environment.

The service is created using the `GetContextService()` function, one of whose arguments is the type of service to create. For example,

```
ContextInformation      lcxinfo_Service
ContextKeyword          lcxk_Service
ErrorLogging            lerrlg_Service
SSLServiceProvider      lsslprov_Service
TransactionServer       ltranserv_Service
Inet                    linet_Service
```

```
This.GetContextService( "ContextInformation", lcxinfo_Service)
This.GetContextService( "Keyword", lcxk_Service)
This.GetContectService( "ErrorLogging", lerrlg_Service)
This.GetContextService( "SSLServiceProvider", lsslprov_Service)
This.GetContextService( "TransactionServer", ltranserv_Service)
This.GetContextService( "Internet", linet_Service)
```

## Using the Context Information Service

Use the context service to gather information on the application's current execution context. This allows you to modify the behavior of your application appropriately.

**29**

PowerBuilder and the Internet

> **Note**
>
> The context information service is available on all deployment platforms.

The following methods are available for querying the context information service:

- `GetCompanyName(` *CompanyName* `)`, in which the *CompanyName* argument is a string passed by reference that's the company that created the service. For example: Sybase, Inc.

- `GetFixesVersion (` *FixVersion* `)`, in which the *FixVersion* argument is an integer passed by reference that's the fix version number. For example: 1.

- `GetHostObject(`*HostObject* `)`, in which the *HostObject* argument is a PowerObject passed by reference that's a reference to the context's host object. The only host object now supported is that of the Window ActiveX when running under Internet Explorer. In this case, the function returns a reference to the `IWebBrowserApp` ActiveX Automation Server object.

- `GetMajorVersion(` *MajorVersion* `)`, in which the *MajorVersion* argument is an integer passed by reference that's the major version number. For example: 6.

- `GetMinorVersion(` *MinorVersion* `)`, in which the *MinorVersion* argument is an integer passed by reference that's the minor version number. For example, 0.

- `GetName(` *Name* `)`, in which the *Name* argument is a string reference that's the full context name and can have one of the following values:

  | | |
  |---|---|
  | Default | PowerBuilder Runtime |
  | Window ActiveX | PowerBuilder Runtime ActiveX |
  | Window Plug-in | PowerBuilder Window Plug-in |

- `GetShortName(` *ShortName* `)`, in which the *ShortName* argument is a string reference that's the abbreviated context name and can have one of the following values:

  | | |
  |---|---|
  | PBRUN | PowerBuilder Runtime |
  | PBRTX | PowerBuilder Window ActiveX |
  | PBWinPlugIn | PowerBuilder Window Plug-in |

- `GetVersionName(` *VersionName* `)`, in which the *VersionName* argument is a string reference that's the full version number of the service. For example: 7.0.0.

One of the main uses for these methods and the context information service is to alter the appearance and behavior of your application based on the execution context—for example, hiding a Close button that's part of a Window plug-in. In that case, if the window closes, a blank HTML page is displayed in the browser.

# Accessing the ActiveX Automation Server

As already mentioned, if you're accessing the context information service's `GetHostObject()` method while running the Window ActiveX control under Internet Explorer, you can obtain the ActiveX Automation Server object reference. This is a reference to the `IWebBrowserApp` automation server, which now allows you to access and modify certain browser features:

| | |
|---|---|
| Go home | Refresh current page |
| Go back | Load a specific page |
| Go forward | Exit the browser |

The following is a short example of how to access and interact with the ActiveX automation server:

```
// Declare a variable for the Context information service and
// the automation server reference
ContextInformation ciService
OLEObject oleBrowser
//
// Create the context information service
//
GetContextService( "ContextInformation", ciService)
//
// Get a reference to the ActiveX Automation Server
//
ciService.GetHostObject( oleBrowser)
//
// Open one of the authors web pages
If IsValid( oleBrowser) Then
    oleBrowser.Navigate("http://member.iquest.net/~raven/raven.html", 0, 0, 0)
End If
```

**Tip**

You can find more information on the `IWebBrowserApp` interface in the Internet Explorer documentation available from Microsoft.

## Customizable Web Jumps

You can code your applications to start up a browser and display a Web page. The page is displayed in the default browser and can further interact with it via additional functions. This is all done by using the Internet service object. This service is now available only on the Windows 95/98/NT platforms.

> **Note**
>
> PowerBuilder 7.0 introduces two new controls that allow you to create hyperlinks in your application: `statichyperlink` and `picturehyperlink`. For more information on these controls, see Chapter 11, "Advanced Controls."

## Opening a Web Page

After you create an Internet service instance, you can call the `HyperLinkToURL()` function to start up the browser with the specified URL. To get an instance of the Internet service, first call the `GetContextService()` function. `GetContextService()` creates a reference to a service object, which then allows that service's methods and properties to be used. Its syntax is

```
GetContextService( ServiceName, ServiceReferenceVar)
```

> **Note**
>
> This is the preferred method over creating the service object directly by using the `Create` statement. If you use `Create`, the object is created for the default context regardless of where the application is running, which is a problem with a distributed server application.

Specifying the `"Internet"` value for the *ServiceName* argument tells `GetContextService` to return a reference to the Internet service.

The *ServiceReferenceVar* is a variable passed by reference into which the function places a reference to the service object.

Therefore, the code for opening a Web page is

```
// Declare variable for the service object we will be creating.
Inet linet_Service
```

```
// Get the service object.
GetContextService( "Internet", linet_Service)

// Pass the URL and cause browser to open.
linet_Service.HyperlinkToURL( " http://www.reppart.org/members/kenneth ")
```

## Performing an HTTP Get

By using the previously created Internet service, you can use the `GetURL()` function to perform an *HTTP get*. Doing so provides the raw HTML for the specified URL.

Before you can do an HTTP get, you must inherit the `InternetResult` object and create an `InternetData` function that accepts a BLOB argument by value and returns an integer.

> **Note**
>
> You can't directly use the `InternetResult` object. You must subclass this object and then add the `InternetData` function.

In the following example of an `InternetData` function, the first 2,000 bytes of the returned BLOB are extracted for display:

```
String ls_Syntax

ls_Syntax = String( BlobMid( a_bData, 1, 2000))

MessageBox( "URL HTML", ls_Syntax)

Return 1
```

The code to actually undertake the HTTP get is

```
// Declare variable for the service object we will be creating.
Inet                  linet_Service
u_n_internet_result   lir_Syntax

// Get the service object.
GetContextService( "Internet", linet_Service)

lir_Syntax = Create u_n_internet_result

linet_Service.GetURL( "http://www.sybase.com", lir_Syntax)
```

When the GetURL() function completes, it calls the InternetData() function defined previously, passing the HTML as the BLOB argument.

## Performing an HTTP Post

The flip side of HTTP get is *HTTP post*, which allows you to send data from your PowerBuilder application to a CGI, ISAPI, or NSAPI program. The function, PostURL(), returns the HTML via the InternetResult object, as described in preceding section. This sample code uses PostUrl():

```
// Declare variable for the service object we will be creating.
Inet                    linet_Service
u_n_internet_result     lir_Syntax
Blob                    lblb_Arguments
String                  ls_Header
String                  ls_URL
Long                    ll_Length


// Get the service object.
GetContextService( "Internet", linet_Service)


lir_Syntax = Create u_n_internet_result


ls_URL = "http://members.iquest.net/cgi-bin/pbcgi70.exe/myapp/n_customer/f_add?"
lblb_Arguments = Blob("12345")
ll_Length = Len( lblb_Arguments)
ls_Header = "Content-Length: " + String( ll_Length) + "~0~n~n"


linet_Service.PostURL( ls_Url, lblb_Arguments, ls_Header, lir_Syntax)
```

Just as with the GetURL() function, PostURL() calls the InternetData() function that you defined in your descendant InternetResult object. The InternetResult object is used by the GetURL() and PostURL() functions as a buffer to receive data asynchronously from the Internet. After all the data is received, the InternetData() function is called.

# The PowerBuilder Web Deployment Kit

The PowerBuilder Web Deployment Kit allows unmodified PowerBuilder applications to be run on any platform that supports the Java Virtual Machine. This is done by using Java classes that provide a remote user interface to the PowerBuilder application. The PowerBuilder Program Window is a set of Java classes that allow the client machine to connect to the server and run an application. When the application is run on the client, an instance of that application is started on the server. The PowerBuilder Application Adapter then translates the interface into Java calls and events, which allow the application to be displayed on the client machine. All the mouse and keyboard events that occur on the client are captured by the Java classes and passed back to the server. Although the interface is drawn on the client machine, all the processing occurs on the server.

The advantages of this are obvious: you can provide cross-platform access to your existing PowerBuilder applications with no installation needed (aside from the Java Virtual Machine). The downside is that you must have a fast network to handle the increased traffic. Also, the performance of Java is still poor on many platforms.

The minimum server requirements are

- Windows NT 4.0

- Intel Pentium 200 MHz

- 128MB RAM (plus 4 to 8 MB per client)

- 2GB hard disk space

The minimum network requirements are

- 10Mbit Ethernet or T1 level access

- TCP/IP network transport

The minimum requirements for the client vary according to platform and the Java Virtual Machine implementation.

# Summary

As you've seen, Sybase has provided significant functionality to allow you to develop applications for the Internet, as well as Internet-enabling your existing PowerBuilder applications. The new Web DataWindow control extends the reach of PowerBuilder developers to the Web, and the set of supported Internet features continues to grow. The Web Deployment Kit presents a unique solution to the problem of cross-platform, thin-client computing. With PowerBuilder 7.0, it's easier than ever to integrate Internet functionality into your applications.

# CHAPTER 30

# Developing Internet Applications with PowerBuilder

In the previous three chapters, you've looked at Distributed PowerBuilder and the Internet features available in PowerBuilder 7.0. This chapter examines the tools available in the Enterprise Application Studio suite and how you can use them to develop applications for the Internet or your intranet.

# Enterprise Application Server

Sybase Enterprise Application Server (EA Server) provides several tools that help you develop Internet and distributed applications. Because EA Server supports a wide range of languages, clients, platforms, and component types, you have a great deal of flexibility when you begin developing Internet applications. This chapter starts by looking at EA Server's major components and then shows how you can use the tools together to create an Internet application.

## Jaguar

Sybase has introduced its own contender into the Component Transaction Server (CTS) arena to directly compete with Microsoft's Transaction Server. The Sybase CTS, Jaguar, is designed to provide connection management, session management, database connectivity, and easy administration to help developers create multitier applications such as Distributed PowerBuilder. Jaguar combines the features of a Transaction Processing (TP) monitor and an object request broker (ORB) that can be used to form the basis of transactional applications for WebOLTP. Jaguar is based on open computing standards and provides ISAPI, NSAPI, and CGI Web server interfaces. Object component models that can be brokered include CORBA, JavaBeans, and ActiveX.

By using Jaguar, you can focus on solving business problems because the business logic is isolated from the presentation logic. Jaguar provides the connectivity to the database and access to the business components, whereas the client application can focus on the presentation. Databases can be accessed via ODBC, JDBC, or Open Client Client-Library calls, and support is provided for transaction pooling, which allows for reuse of database connections to provide better response and scalability.

## PowerDynamo

PowerDynamo is an application and HTML page server that includes tools to manage Web content. The PowerDynamo application server bridges the gaps between the client browser, the component server, and the database, allowing development of full-featured Web applications. When users request a page from the PowerDynamo server, the HTML is assembled dynamically by using the powerful DynaScript scripting language. Highlights of PowerDynamo include

- The capability to store Web sites and applications in a database

- Distribution of Web applications and content through database replication tools

- Full compatibility with all components supported by EA Studio, including COM objects, Java applets, JavaBeans, Jaguar components, and MTS components

- Database connection pooling to maximize the use of available connections

- Support for session management to maintain information about the client state

# PowerSite

PowerSite is a tool for creating, managing, and deploying enterprise Web applications. Although technically PowerSite isn't a part of EA Server, it's bundled with PowerBuilder and provides tight integration with the primary components of EA Server, Jaguar, and PowerDynamo. Consistent with Sybase's philosophy of providing open solutions, PowerSite uses a common object model that works with many different Web application servers such as Netscape LiveWire, Microsoft ASP, and Sybase PowerDynamo, as well as supports several Web servers including those from Microsoft and Netscape.

One important aspect of PowerSite is its capability to integrate several different components into the Web page development process. PowerSite supports HTML, ActiveX, JavaBeans, and any other component that EA Studio supports. Development tools include

- An HTML WYSIWYG editor

- Support for various Microsoft ActiveScripts (JavaScript and VBScript) on the client and server sides, script debugging on client and server sides

- Design-time controls (DTCs) for assisting in the generation of HTML and scripts for specific components (for example, the Web DataWindow DTC)

In addition to providing the development tools used to create a Web site, PowerSite also provides the capability to manage the components that make up the Web site. In PowerSite, you can define projects that are composed of different components and tasks. Users and groups can be defined with specific permissions to projects.

Components are stored in a central repository called the PowerSite Development Server (PDS). All Web components, such as HTML pages, images, scripts, JavaBeans, and ActiveX controls, are stored in the PDS. The component manager provides your Web site with version and release control as well as the capability to ensure that all your links are valid. PowerSite also comes with a database that lets you reuse code and database connections as well as maintain a number of different settings.

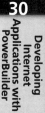

**30**

Developing Internet Applications with PowerBuilder

After setting up the structure of your Web application, PowerSite lets you deploy your application to many different Web servers and Web application servers. In addition to supporting the more common Web application servers, PowerSite gives you the means, via an SDK, to create your own Web application server. PowerSite has built in different deployment engines that take your Web application components and make the necessary changes to deploy them to your specified Web and application server.

As well as support various Web and application servers, PowerSite supports several third-party HTML editors, different component types (scripts, JavaBeans, ActiveX, PB), browsers (Microsoft Internet Explorer, Netscape Navigator), and languages (JavaScript, VBScript, DynaScript, Java).

## Using EA Server and PowerBuilder

Now that you know about the tools, see how you can use PowerSite, PowerDynamo, and Jaguar to deploy a simple Web page with a Web DataWindow. Start by creating your DataWindow in PowerBuilder as you normally would. Use the HTML Table and HTML Generation tabs to specify the HTML properties for your DataWindow. Save your DataWindow.

> **Tip**
>
> If you select the HTML DataWindow check box on the General tab in the DataWindow properties, you can preview the HTML that the Web DataWindow generates. Choose the HTML Preview menu item from the Design menu. Choose View Source in your browser, and you can examine the JavaScript generated for client-side scripting. If you forget to turn on the HTML DataWindow option when you create your DataWindow object, the Web DataWindow server component automatically sets this attribute for you when the Generate method is called.

After you create your DataWindow, start PowerSite and create a new Web page to display it. Add a title, background picture, and any other static content you want to include. Next, from the Insert menu, choose Component and then ActiveX. Select the Web DataWindow DTC from the listed ActiveX components and click OK. PowerSite places the control on your Web page at the cursor, and the DTC properties window automatically opens.

On the General tab, select the PBL where you saved your DataWindow object. Then select your DataWindow from the DataWindow list box. Next, click the Control tab and choose a connection for your Web DataWindow. This connection must already be set up in PowerSite (see the PowerSite documentation for more information on how to set up a connection).

Finally, click the Jaguar tab and select the Enable Jaguar Component check box. Locate your Jaguar server in the tree view and select the HTMLGenerator component. The HTMLGenerator component is installed automatically on the Jaguar server when you install EA Studio. Click the Set button, and then click OK to close the properties window.

Your page is now ready to view, and you haven't written a single line of code! Depending on how you're using PowerSite, you may need to deploy the page to PowerDynamo before you can view it.

> **Note**
>
> If you click the source tab in PowerSite on the page edit window, you can view the HTML script generated by the DTC to call your Web DataWindow.

When you type the URL of your sample page in your browser window, PowerDynamo instantiates an instance of the Web DataWindow component on the Jaguar server using DynaScript. The PBL, DataWindow name, and connection name are passed to the component, and the Generate method is called. The server component then creates a datastore object and retrieves the data. Next, the component creates the HTML presentation using the HTML generation features of the standard datastore control. Any validation rules, computed columns, display formats, or client events are then translated into JavaScript. The HTML and JavaScript are returned to PowerDynamo, where they're merged with the rest of the content and sent to the browser.

With the combined power of PowerBuilder, the Jaguar component server, the Power-Dynamo application server, and the PowerSite development tool, you have everything you need to begin creating dynamic Web applications.

# Web.PB

PowerBuilder provides the Web.PB class library, which includes several functions and user objects that make it easier to generate HTML syntax to send back to the client. The following sections look at the available prebuilt objects and methods and how you use them to construct a Web.PB application.

30

Developing
Internet
Applications with
PowerBuilder

> **Note**
>
> Sybase has announced that PowerBuilder 7.0 will be the last release to support Web.PB and distributed PowerBuilder. It's recommended that you migrate your existing distributed PowerBuilder applications to EA Server.

## Object Types

The Web.PB class library is composed of the following five class user objects:

- Form (u_html_form) gives you methods to create HTML form elements.

- Format (u_html_format) gives you methods for carrying out formatting tasks.

- Template (u_html_template) provides the methods for reading files set up as templates and carrying out substitutions for generic situations.

- Session (u_session) is a session-management service object for maintaining state information.

- Transaction (u_transaction) is a transaction-management service object used by the session service.

In addition to the standard class objects, the following service objects are available:

- u_datetime contains date and time conversion functions.

- u_string contains string functions above what PowerBuilder offers. Now the only function declared is one for carrying out string replacement.

- u_transport provides a starting point for creating a Distributed PowerBuilder application for use with Web.PB.

For a detailed description of the Web.PB class library, look at the corresponding book in the PowerBuilder documentation set.

## Object Methods

The methods you create for the class user objects you will use in your Web.PB application need to conform to the following rules:

- Any standard data type (String, Integer, and so on) can be passed as an argument. Structures and arrays, however, aren't allowed.

- If the request to Web.PB doesn't supply a value for an argument, Web.PB will supply a NULL. This means that at the top of all your methods you will need to check that you have sufficient information to continue processing.

- The object methods can return data in only one of two forms: as a string or as a BLOB. The BLOB return data type allows you to pass back graphics, sound, and other binary files to the user.

- When Web.PB returns a string value from a method, it inserts a content type of TEXT/HTML into the stream before it gets to the user's browser.

- When Web.PB returns a BLOB, the method is repeatedly called to get the complete BLOB. So, for a single request, Web.PB makes multiple method calls to get the BLOB; it stops calling when the return from the method is a NULL. Your method needs to make the appropriate identification of the content type—for example, specifying IMAGE/JPG for a graphic.

Because this last rule can be a little confusing when you first look at it, look at an example of a function returning a BLOB value. The important part to remember is that the HTTP header in the response is made up of the string `Content-type: text/html~r~n~r~n`, where you substitute the correct MIME type for the data. The two sets of carriage returns and line feeds are important and must be included. Listing 30.1 illustrates these requirements in a function that returns an image via HTML for display in a browser.

**LISTING 30.1**  A Function to Return an Image

```
//
// This function is passed a single string argument that is the filename
// of the image to return: as_ImageName
//
// This function also makes use of the following instance variables:
//      ib_EOI    - Boolean - The end-of-image indicator
//      ii_FileNo - Integer - The handle of the image file
//
Blob    lblb_Image
Long    ll_FileLen
String  ls_ImagePiece
String  ls_MIMEType

If ib_EOI Then
    // End Of Image (EOI)
    SetNull (lblb_Image)
    Return lblb_Image
End If
```

**LISTING 30.1**   CONTINUED

```
//
// If this is the first time in this function the file handle will be zero.
//
If ii_FileNo = 0 Then
   // open the image file and generate the HTTP header
   ib_EOI = FALSE

   If Not FileExists(as_ImageName) Then
      // Cannot find the picture. Return informational message.
      lblb_Image = Blob( "content-type: text/plain~r~n~r~n image '" + &
                   as_ImageName + "' does not exist~r~n")
      // Set up the End Of Image indicator ready for following call
      // to this function
      ib_EOI = TRUE
      Return lblb_Image
   End If

   // Get the file length, and open the file
   ll_FileLen = FileLength( as_ImageName)
   ii_FileNo = FileOpen(as_ImageName, StreamMode!, Read!)
   If ii_FileNo = -1 Then
      lblb_Image = Blob( "content-type: text/plain~r~n~r~n image '" + &
                   as_ImageName + "' could not be opened for read~r~n")
      ib_EOI = TRUE
      ii_FileNo = 0
      Return lblb_Image
   End if

   // take the last three characters (should be something like "gif" or "bmp")
   ls_ImagePiece = Right( as_ImageName, 3)
   // Determine the appropriate MIME type based on file extension.
Choose Case Lower( ls_ImagePiece)
      Case "gif"
         ls_MIMEType="image/gif"
      Case "jpg"
         ls_MIMEType="image/jpeg"
      Case "tiff"
         ls_MIMEType="image/tiff"
      Case "bmp"
         ls_MIMEType="image/x-MS-bmp"
      Case Else
         //Unknown type - try appending the file's extension.
```

**LISTING 30.1** CONTINUED

```
        ls_MIMEType="image/" + ls_ImagePiece
    End Choose

    lblb_Image =   Blob( "content-type: " + ls_MIMEType + "~r~n")
    lblb_Image +=  Blob( "content-length: ")
    lblb_Image +=  Blob( String(ll_FileLen))
    lblb_Image +=  Blob( "~r~n~r~n")
    Return lblb_Image
Else
    // We have started reading the file...so let us continue...
    If FileRead( ii_FileNo, lblb_Image) <= 0 Then
        // We didn't find any more data
        FileClose( ii_FileNo)
        SetNull( lblb_Image)
        ii_FileNo = 0
    End If
End If
// Otherwise we drop to here and we return the current image
// piece to Web.PB
Return lblb_Image
```

As you can see from this code example, the user object must maintain information for the function so that it can communicate with itself between successive calls to satisfy the one user request. Returning a string from a method is much simpler and involves only the use of the Return statement.

# CGI Environment Variables

A number of CGI (Common Gateway Interface) variables give you information on the environment the user's browser is operating in. To access their values, create an object method within your Web.PB application that takes string arguments with the same name as the CGI variable you want.

The client-side CGI environment variables are as follows:

- AUTH_TYPE indicates the authentication method used to access the CGI program.

- CONTENT-LENGTH specifies the amount of data occurring after the request header.

- CONTENT-TYPE specifies the type of data occurring after the request header.

- HTTP_REQUEST_METHOD specifies the HTTP method request header.

30

Developing
Internet
Applications with
PowerBuilder

- PATH_INFO is the information that occurs after the CGI program reference and before the start of the query string information.

- PATH_TRANSLATED combines the values of PATH_INFO and DOCUMENT_ROOT. This is the fully qualified path from the root directory of the server to the directory defined by PATH_INFO.

- QUERY_STRING contains everything that occurs after the first question mark in the request header.

- REMOTE_ADDR specifies the IP address of the client.

- REMOTE_HOST specifies the domain name of the client.

- REMOTE_IDENT is set if the user name is retrieved from the server using the CGI IDENTD method.

- REMOTE_USER indicates the caller of the CGI program. This is available only if a challenge/response with the client has occurred.

- SERVER_PORT specifies the TCP port to which the request was sent.

- SERVER_PROTOCOL specifies the protocol and version being used by the server. Now the only protocol in use is HTTP.

If, for example, you need to access the user's IP address and do something extra with the query string in the request, you would add two arguments to the method being accessed: REMOTE_ADDR and QUERY_STRING, both of type String. Within your Web.PB method, you would then have access to those arguments and the values populated by the CGI.

## Invoking a Web.PB Method

You can invoke a Web.PB method in three ways. The first two use the HTML Form syntax, and the third uses a simple anchor tag.

To call a remote method using HTML Forms, use the syntax

```
<FORM METHOD="[GET ¦ POST]"
    ACTION="URLPath/Web.PB/ServerAlias/Object/Method>
    { text<INPUT NAME="ArgumentName"{VALUE=" ArgumentValue"}>
    <INPUT TYPE="SUBMIT" VALUE="ButtonText">
</FORM>
```

The METHOD section of the FORM tag is where you specify either of the following:

- With GET, the arguments are appended to the URL path sent to the server. This method is best suited to a small number of arguments or if you want users to be able to bookmark the call with specific argument values.

- With POST, the arguments are added to the message body. POST is the recommended method for sending large amounts of data.

To get a better idea of a call using the HTML Form syntax, look at an example that calls the f_find_employee() method of the class user object u_n_people that can be accessed through the HR server:

```
<FORM METHOD="GET"
 ACTION="http://members.iquest.net/pbcgi070.exe/HR/u_n_people/f_find_emplyee">
 <INPUT TYPE="SUBMIT" VALUE="Get Employee!">
</FORM>
```

Alternatively, if you needed to collect some information before calling the method, you would use this:

```
<FORM METHOD="GET"
 ACTION="http://members.iquest.net/pbcgi070.exe/HR/u_n_people/f_find_employee2">
 Enter color:<INPUT NAME="Color">
 Enter age:<INPUT NAME="Age" VALUE="6">
 <INPUT TYPE="SUBMIT" VALUE="Get Employee!">
</FORM>
```

You probably would want to clean up the user interface with a <PRE> tag to allow you to space and lay out the entry fields like you want.

The third method uses the HTML anchor tag <A>, which has the syntax

```
<A HREF="URLPath/Web.PB/ServerAlias/Object/Method?ArgumentValues>Text</A>
```

This, however, can be used only if the method doesn't take any arguments, or if you know them ahead of time and hard-code them into the HTML anchor tag. A call to the same method used in the Form examples would be coded as

```
<A HREF="http://members.iquest.net/pbcgi070.exe/HR/u_n_people/f_find_employee">
Find the Employee!</A>
```

or, for the version that required arguments, as

```
<A HREF="http://members.iquest.net/pbcgi070.exe/HR/u_n_people/f_find_employee?
Black+6">Find the Employee!</A>
```

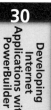

**30**

Developing Internet Applications with PowerBuilder

These are the mechanisms you will use to call your Web.PB application methods and also how you can build HTML pages created dynamically by those object methods to call other methods.

## Maintaining State Information

One characteristic you will quickly notice when dealing with HTML pages is that one page doesn't inherently know anything about the page that came before it, or what users did before they arrived at that page. As developer of the Web.PB application, you have to manage the state information about users and the information they've entered that needs to be available to future pages they might travel through.

There are two ways to maintain state information using a Web.PB application: using the Web.PB session service object or using cookies.

The Web.PB session service creates an entry that's stored in a database table to which the application is connected. You then pass the ID for this table entry back to the browser as part of the Web page. The Web page then passes it back to Web.PB as an argument on any call it makes. The Web.PB application can then access the database table to look up necessary information users have previously entered, and also to store new information. This session ID is again sent back with the newly requested page, and so on.

> **Tip**
>
> Use the `f_MakeHidden()` function that's part of the Web.PB class library object `u_html_form` to maintain state information within the HTML page.

The second method uses another CGI environment variable, `HTTP-COOKIE`, which makes the client's browser responsible for remembering who users are and what they were doing rather than require the server to remember. This also allows users to connect to the same server the next day and still have state information available for use.

The cookie information is created on each user's machine through the use of the `Set-Cookie` response header. Within this header, you can use several fields, but you can use each key field only once. If you need to set the same field with multiple values, you can pass back multiple `Set-Cookie` response headers in a single response header chain. The fields are

- `Name`, the only required field, which you can call whatever you want. This uniquely identifies the cookie to the browser.

- `Expires`, which instructs the browser to retain the information only until the specified date.

- `Domain`, which sets the domain name of the server being accessed.

- `Path`, which restricts the URIs (uniform resource indicators) that can be used with the cookie.

An example of a `Set-Cookie` call that sets the domain to be `www.unleashed.com` with an expiration date of Friday, December 31, just before midnight and a session identifier of 12345678 is as follows:

```
Set-Cookie: sessiond_id=12345678; domain=www.unleashed.com;
            expires=Friday, 31-Dec-1999 11:59:59 GMT;
```

Notice that the fields are separated by a semicolon (;).

Rather than specify a particular date and time, you can make further use of CGI programming and make a cookie that expires after an hour like this:

```
Set-Cookie: sessiond_id=12345678; expires=$ENV{'DATE'} + 1 HOURS;
```

PowerBuilder provides two service objects that help you deal with cookies:

- `u_cookie` details an individual cookie and the methods needed to interact and manage it.

- `u_cookie_jar` is a container class for managing a number of cookies within a server-based application.

With these concepts and methods firmly under your belt, now turn your attention to using them to construct a small application.

# An Outline of the Sample Application

Throughout the rest of this chapter, you construct components of an order system based around the PowerBuilder sample database. You use the Window plug-in and the HTML Form syntax for capturing data from users and adding it into the server-side database tables.

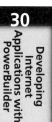

**30**

Developing
Internet
Applications with
PowerBuilder

> **Note**
>
> You can't use the DataWindow plug-in for capturing data entry. It's purely for displaying pregenerated reports.

For the reporting features of the example Internet-enabled application, use the DataWindow plug-in and the DataWindow `HTMLTable` property.

# Data Entry

One way to perform data entry is to use the Window plug-in. This is the easiest method because it doesn't require much modification to an existing PowerBuilder application window used for data entry.

The most important thing to remember is that the window used in the plug-in is standalone and doesn't have any other processing occur before the standard window open processing (for example, `Open` and `Constructor` events). In the `Open` event for your window, you would code the connection to your database and then retrieve any necessary data.

> **Note**
>
> You can still use SQLCA for your transaction object. You must also remember that if the database connection is in the `Open` event, you shouldn't have any retrieval processing in your window control's `Constructor` events because they happen first.

The rest of your window, if encapsulated, can remain the same as though it were in PowerBuilder. The DataWindow `Update()` function and all others can be called and used within the plug-in. The window can open other windows (pop-up and response types) as well. The only thing to remember is to close any open secondary windows and disconnect from the database in the `Close` event of the window. After the window is coded and tested in the PowerBuilder environment, create a PBD and the corresponding HTML to insert the Window plug-in into the Web page, like this:

```
<EMBED SRC="weboe.pbd" WIDTH=500 HEIGHT=300 WINDOW=w_customer>
```

> **Note**
>
> Each user must have the plug-in and the PowerBuilder deployment kit (PBDK) installed on his machine. Because most people on the Internet don't have the PBDK and don't want to sit and wait for it to download, the Window plug-in should, therefore, be considered as an option only when creating an intranet application.

An alternative means to creating a data-entry screen is to use Web.PB to build an HTML form that accepts user input and sends it to a distributed PowerBuilder application that then inserts data into the database. First create a custom class user object containing an object-level function to be used to insert customer data into the database. The function, f_InsertCust(), receives arguments that match each column in the customer table and return a string. The code would be as shown in Listing 30.2.

**LISTING 30.2** The Function `f_InsertCust()`, to Insert a Customer

```
INSERT INTO "customer"
("id", "fname","lname","address","city","state","zip","phone","company_name")
VALUES
(:id,:firstname,:lastname,:address,:city,:state,:zip,:phone,:company);

If SQLCA.SQLCode = 0 Then
   Commit Using SQLCA;
   RETURN "Insert successful!"
Else
   Rollback Using SQLCA;
   RETURN "No data was saved!" + &
          "<P>" + SQLCA.SQLErrText
End If
```

The user object is built into a distributed PowerBuilder application that runs on the server. Next, create the HTML that will create the form. This can be easily done by using the Web.PB Wizard, which walks you through the HTML creation based on selections you make. This generates the code shown in Listing 30.3.

**LISTING 30.3** The HTML Used to Create the Customer Addition Web Page

```
<html>
<head>
   <title>Customer Order Entry</title>
```

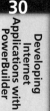

**30**

Developing
Internet
Applications with
PowerBuilder

**LISTING 30.3**   CONTINUED

```
<h1>Customer Order Entry</h1>
</head>
<IMG SRC="unleashed.jpg">
<body>
<p><FORM METHOD="Post" ACTION="/cgi-shl/pbcgi050.exe/order_entry/
                    u_n_cust/f_insertcust/">
<PRE>
Enter ID: <input name = "id"  type = "TEXT"
                    value = "" ALIGN=right>  <br>
Enter first name: <input name = "firstname"  type = "TEXT"
                    value = "" ALIGN=right>  <br>
Enter last name: <input name = "lastname"  type = "TEXT"
                    value = "" ALIGN=right>  <br>
Enter address: <input name = "address"  type = "TEXT"
                    value = "" ALIGN=right>  <br>
Enter city: <input name = "city"  type = "TEXT"
                    value = "" ALIGN=right>  <br>
Enter state: <input name = "state"  type = "TEXT"
                    value = "" ALIGN=right>  <br>
Enter zip code: <input name = "zip"  type = "TEXT"
                    value = "" ALIGN=right>  <br>
Enter phone number: <input name = "phone"  type = "TEXT"
                    value = "" ALIGN=right>  <br>
Enter company name: <input name = "company"  type = "TEXT"
                    value = "" ALIGN=right>  <br>
<input type = "submit" value = "Submit">
<input type = "reset" value = "  Clear   ">
</PRE>
 </form>
<p>
<hr>
</body>
</html>
```

**Note**

The values specified in the `name` attribute of the `input` tag must match the names of the arguments specified for the user object function, `f_InsertCust()`.

When this Web page is displayed to users, they can enter data into the form and click the Submit button, which sends the data to the user object function. This function takes the values, generates a SQL INSERT statement, and sends it to the database. If the new row is inserted successfully, the function returns a message indicating success to the user.

## Validation

The validation that you carry out within a Web.PB application is simply functions and events that you code within the class user objects that you make part of the application. These methods are called from within the user-initiated functions of the application, in the exact same manner as a user with a traditional Windows-based PowerBuilder application.

Your validation methods can use any PowerScript function as well as database connectivity to validate particular values users have entered.

# Reports

Reports provided via Web pages can be created in one of two ways: as pure HTML through the SaveAs() function or HTMLTable DataWindow property, or via the DataWindow plug-in. The method you choose depends on what the target client will have loaded and what sort of information you need to show. The DataWindow plug-in obviously requires users to have the plug-in set up or to have it set up for them; the HTML method requires only the use of a browser but limits the presentation styles you can use.

## Creating an HTML Table Report

For the simplest data reporting, you can use the DataWindow-generated HTML Table syntax. By combining this with the appropriate HTML formatting tags, you can return the information easily (see Listing 30.4).

**LISTING 30.4**   Creating a Report Using a DataWindow

```
String      ls_Page
DataStore   lds_Table

lds_Table = Create DataStore

lds_Table.DataObject = "d_employee_table"

lds_Table.SetTransObject( SQLCA)

lds_Table.Retrieve()
```

**LISTING 30.4** CONTINUED

```
lds_Table.Modify("datawindow.HTMLTable.GenerateCSS='yes' " + &
                "datawindow.HTMLTable.NoWrap='yes' "      + &
                "datawindow.HTMLTable.width=5 "           + &
                "datawindow.HTMLTable.border=5 "          + &
                "datawindow.HTMLTable.CellSpacing=2 "     + &
                "datawindow.HTMLTable.CellPadding=2")


ls_Page = "<HTML>" + &
        lds_Table.Object.DataWindow.HTMLTable.StyleSheet + &
        "<BODY>" + lds_Table.Object.DataWindow.Data.HTMLTable + "</BODY>" + &
        "</HTML>"


Destroy lds_Table


Return ls_Page
```

Calling this reporting function couldn't be easier; it requires a single HTML tag:

```
<A HREF="/scripts/pbisa050.dll/Order System/u_n_reports/uf_employee_table?">
Employee Listing</A>
```

This is the simplest form of reporting information back to users, and in most cases it's adequate. You control the look of the table with wrapping, border sizes, cell widths, and so on.

# Creating a DataWindow Plug-In Report

You have to fall back on the DataWindow plug-in when you want to show users the more complex DataWindow display styles. For example, allow users to call up a product sales report in graph format.

The report is requested from within a Distributed PowerBuilder application running on the Web server. The report is created through a request to uf_sales_graph() and the passing of two date arguments. The function is defined as shown in Listing 30.5.

**LISTING 30.5** A Function that Returns a DataWindow for Viewing with the DataWindow Plug-In

```
// uf_sales_graph()
//
// Arguments: ad_BeginDate    Date
//            ad_EndDate      Date
// Returns: String
```

**LISTING 30.5** CONTINUED

```
//
String          ls_Page
String          ls_FileName
DataStore       lds_Graph


lds_Graph = Create DataStore


lds_Graph.DataObject = "d_sales_graph"


lds_Graph.SetTransObject( SQLCA)


lds_Graph.Retrieve( ad_BeginDate, ad_EndDate)
//
// Create a random filename to allow for multi-user access.
//
ls_FileName = "SALES" + String(Rand(999)) + ".PSR"


lds_Graph.SaveAs( ls_FileName, PSReport!, FALSE)


ls_Page = "<HTML><BODY BGCOLOR=~"#FFFFFF~"><P>"
ls_Page = ls_Page + "<EMBED SRC=~"" + ls_FileName + "~" WIDTH=550 HEIGHT=300>"
ls_Page = ls_Page + "</BODY></HTML>"


Return ls_Page
```

At the WWW root on the server, place the HTML page that is the user interface to this function. By using HTML Form syntax, you need to collect the two date arguments and pass them to the function (see Listing 30.6).

**LISTING 30.6** The Web Page to Access the Report Function

```
<html>
<head>
<title>Product Sales</title>
<h1>Product Sales</h1>
</head>
<body>
<p><FORM METHOD="Post"
    ACTION="/scripts/pbisa60.dll/Order System/u_n_reports/uf_sales_graph/">
<PRE>
Enter Starting Date <input name="ad_BeginDate" type="TEXT"
                    value="1/1/95" ALIGN=right><br>
```

**LISTING 30.6**    CONTINUED

```
Enter Ending Date <input name="ad_EndDate" type="TEXT"
                    value="12/12/95" ALIGN=right><br>
      <input type="submit" value="Report"> <input type="reset" value="Clear">
</PRE>
</form>
<p>
</body>
</html>
```

The code in Listing 30.6 uses the `<PRE>` tag to indicate that what comes after that tag is preformatted. Notice that the strings are laid out in a particular way with spaces and an empty line  (`<p>`). This is how the fields will appear within the browser. `<PRE>` is a useful tag for laying out HTML elements.

# Summary

This chapter looked at each Enterprise Application Server component and how you can use them to create full-featured Web applications. You learned how to quickly create a Web page containing the new Web DataWindow. You also looked at several other methods of providing Web functionality from within PowerBuilder and its related tools. The Internet capabilities of PowerBuilder 7.0 combined with the new tools from Sybase allow you to use your existing PowerBuilder knowledge to develop Web applications using the latest technologies.

# Graphing

**31**

**CHAPTER**

Graphs provide a means of visually presenting large amounts of data to provide summaries or overviews. Humans can better assess information if they're presented with a graphical representation rather than the individual pieces of data. In PowerBuilder, a graph can be used in three ways: as a DataWindow style, a separate object in a DataWindow, or a control in a window. Graphs can also be built as user objects but are accessed and controlled as they would be in a window (and, for the purposes of this discussion, they're considered the same). The definition of a graph is the same regardless of how you're using it; only the population and runtime manipulation of the graph are different.

This chapter examines the components that make up a graph and the process to build one. After you create a graph (via a DataWindow or a graph control), you look at some coding techniques that can be used with graphs.

# Principles of Graphing

Before you build a graph, be aware of some limitations. Graphs can be built only around certain data types. Each axis has different constraints. The data types are as follows:

| Axis | Possible Data Types |
|---|---|
| Series | String |
| Value | Number, Date, DateTime, Time |
| Category | String, Number, Date, DateTime, Time |

After you determine what values you want to incorporate into your graph, you are ready to build your graph.

## Components of a Graph

A PowerBuilder graph consists of three parts: categories, values, and series. A *category* is the major division of the data, the *values* are the data values, and a *series* is a set of data. Figure 31.1 shows these components, along with corresponding labels and text.

The category axis corresponds to the X axis in normal XYZ geometry. The value axis corresponds to the Y axis, and the series axis corresponds to the Z axis. Optionally, you can also specify a title and legend.

**FIGURE 31.1**
*Components of a graph.*

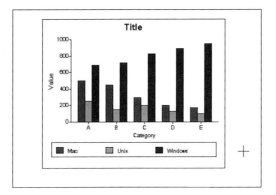

# Types of Graphs

PowerBuilder provides a wide variety of graph types, each of which can have multiple styles. The graph types can be broken down into three main groups.

The first group includes area, bar, column, and line graphs. The properties among these types are common, and they vary only in the method of presentation. The typical use for area and line graphs is for displaying continuous data. Bar and column graphs are used for noncontinuous data. This group of styles can be displayed in two or three dimensions. Rather than appear along the category axis, series now use the extra dimension as the series axis (see Figure 31.2).

**FIGURE 31.2**
*A three-dimensional graph.*

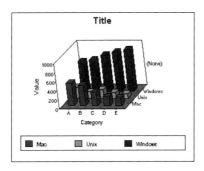

Bar and column graphs can also be presented in a stacked format (see Figure 31.3); another option is a solid, stacked style that looks three-dimensional. Each category is represented as one bar for all series, rather than as separate bars for each individual series.

The second group consists of pie graphs (see Figure 31.4), which show data as a percentage of the whole. Multiseries pie graphs (see Figure 31.5) display the series as concentric circles and are usually used in the comparison of data series.

**FIGURE 31.3**

*A stacked graph.*

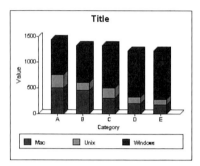

**FIGURE 31.4**

*A three-dimensional pie graph.*

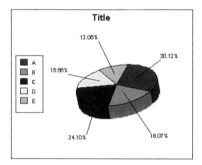

**FIGURE 31.5**

*A multiseries pie graph.*

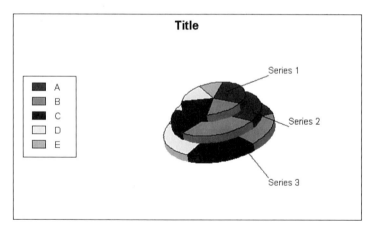

Scatter graphs make up the last group and are used to display X,Y data (see Figure 31.6). For this reason, scatter graphs don't use categories. This type of graph is usually used in the comparison of two or more sets of numerical data.

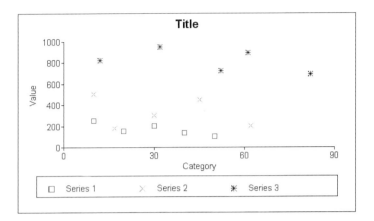

FIGURE **31.6**

*A scatter graph.*

# Defining a Graph's Attributes

After you decide on the type of graph presentation you want, you can enhance its presentation by changing the graph's attributes.

Recall the three ways a graph can be created: as a DataWindow presentation, an object in a DataWindow, or a control (within a window or user object). When a graph is placed in a DataWindow, it can be positioned in the foreground to enable users to move and resize it during execution. If the graph is placed in a band, movement can be prevented. In windows, graphs are placed in the same way as other window controls. Regardless of how the graph is implemented, the interface for defining the graph is the same.

All graphs use the Graph properties tab pages (see Figure 31.7). As you modify the graph's attributes, the changes are reflected in the Design or Preview windows. The labels you entered are used, and sample data is shown (the Design window doesn't display actual data from the DataWindow) to represent series, categories, and values. For the most part, most tab pages are the same for the DataWindow graph and the graph control.

## Text Attributes

Several text objects are connected with a graph, from the title to the axis labels. The attributes of each text element can be specified by using the Text tab page (see Figure 31.8).

**FIGURE 31.7**

*The General tab page of the Graph properties pane.*

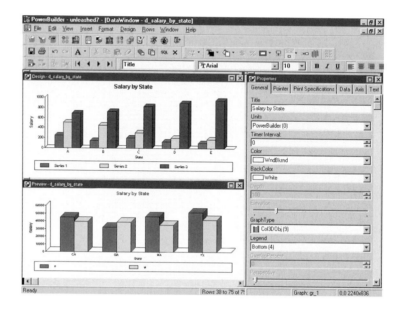

**FIGURE 31.8**

*The Text tab page.*

You can specify what text object you want to modify in the Text Object drop-down list box. The text's rotation, font, size, and color can be changed. The label can also be set to Autosize (autoscale) itself to be in step with the overall graph size. In addition to using just a string literal, you can use an expression by clicking the ... button next to the Display Expression text box. Clicking this button opens the familiar Modify Expression dialog. Because you can build an expression that returns a Numeric data type, a display format can also be specified using the Format drop-down list box.

**Note**

To create text that spans multiple lines in a text expression, use ~n at the position where you require the line break.

# Axes

Use the Axis tab page to modify axis attributes (see Figure 31.9). Select the axis you want to modify by using the Axis drop-down list box. You can define the scaling required for a numeric axis, the major and minor divisions, and the line styles for each axis. Table 31.1 describes the scaling attributes that you can specify for your axes.

**FIGURE 31.9**
*The tab page for specifying axis attributes.*

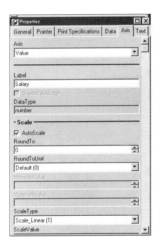

**TABLE 31.1** Scaling Attributes

| Attribute | Description |
| --- | --- |
| DataType | Specifies the axis data type. |
| AutoScale | PowerBuilder automatically scales the numbers along the axis based on the data values. |
| RoundTo | The value to which you want to round the axis values. |
| MinimumValue | The smallest number to be used on the axis (used only if AutoScale isn't set). |
| MaximumValue | The largest number to be used on the axis (used only if AutoScale isn't set). |
| ScaleType | Linear (`linear!`), Log10 (`log10`), or LogE (`loge`) scaling |

Axes are divided into divisions. The larger, *major divisions* are supplied by default; smaller breakdowns within each major division are called *minor divisions* (see Figure 31.10).

FIGURE **31.10**

*Major and minor divisions.*

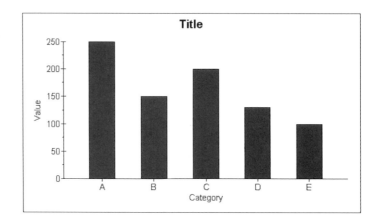

> ### Caution
>
> The interface for specifying divisions can be confusing the first time through. If you want a major tick mark at every 200 and minor tick marks at each 50, intuition tells you to set major at 200 and minor at 50. If you do this, you will sit and watch PowerBuilder struggle and grind away for minutes trying to draw 200 major divisions, with each broken down further into 50 minor divisions. The number you specify is the number of divisions, not the value where the division will appear.

To specify frequency of minor tick marks, you need to enter a value in the `MinorDivisions` field (set to 5 in Figure 31.10). You can also specify where the tick marks appear in reference to the axis: outside, inside, straddle, and none.

Grid lines can be added for major and minor divisions, with various line styles. For the major divisions, drop lines can also be specified that display a line from the point to the opposing axis. These are useful for complex graphs where your users may need to line up different values for comparison (see Figure 31.11).

FIGURE 31.11

*A graph containing drop lines.*

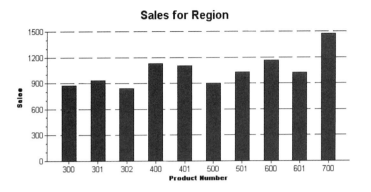

**Note**

The items in the MajorGridLine drop-down list box are off by one item. For example, when you select the first item, None, you see Solid lines (the second item) instead. Sybase will likely fix this bug in a maintenance release.

# Overlays

An *overlay* helps you call attention to the trend of a particular series in a graph. Overlays are usually used in the bar and column graph types and can provide information similar to that of the stacked style. The overlay is shown as a line passing through the column for each series.

If you're using a column for the overlay, use the following format in the Series text box:

```
"@overlay~t" + ColumnName
```

When you're specifying a label for the series, this is the format:

```
"@overlay~tSeriesLabel"
```

For example, to show the total salary for each department and the average salary within that range, the axes would be set up as follows:

| Axis | Value |
| --- | --- |
| Category | dept_id, dept_id |
| Value | sum(salary for graph), avg(salary for graph) |
| Series | "Total Salary" , "@overlay~tAverage Salary" |

The resulting graph (see Figure 31.12) shows the total salaries as a green bar with the highest salary appearing as the line overlay.

**FIGURE 31.12**

*A graph containing an overlay.*

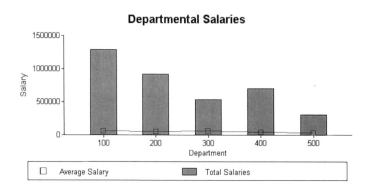

## Overlapping Bars and Columns

You also can set up bar and column graphs to overlap the bars or columns, or to space them apart (see Figure 31.13). The overlap attribute is the percentage of the current bar that's drawn over by the following bars. The default is no overlap. The spacing attribute is a percentage of the bar's width that appears as space between each group of bars. The width of the bars also changes to use the extra space or to make room for the spacing. As you change both attributes on the General tab page in the Graph properties, the model graph reflects the new settings.

**FIGURE 31.13**

*A graph with overlapping bars.*

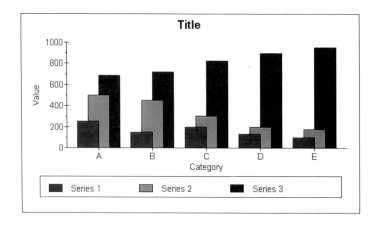

# DataWindow Graphs

Graphs can be used in DataWindows in one of two ways: as the presentation style for the DataWindow or as an object with a DataWindow of any other style. In the first case, users won't see the underlying data. The second method is used to provide enhancements to the information display.

## Creating a DataWindow Graph

To add a graph to a pre-existing DataWindow, click the Graph button in the PainterBar, and then click the area where you want the graph. PowerBuilder then displays the Graph Data dialog (see Figure 31.14) for you to specify the graph's data properties. If you want to change the data properties after you close the Graph Data dialog, you must use the Data tab page. The default is for the graph to be in the foreground and appear in front of retrieved data. It's also movable and resizable and will remain so at runtime unless you turn off the appropriate attributes.

FIGURE **31.14**
*The Graph Data dialog.*

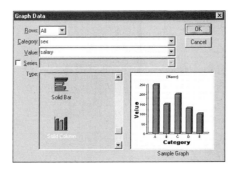

To create a DataWindow with the graph presentation style, select the graph option in the DataWindow tab page on the New dialog.

## Populating a DataWindow Graph

The axes are associated with columns from the DataWindow or expressions involving columns. Changes to data within the DataWindow are reflected in the graph.

For the graph object, the range of rows for which the graph will display can be specified:

| Value | Description |
| --- | --- |
| All | All rows of data in the primary buffer |
| Page | Only data now onscreen |
| Group *n* | Only data from the specified group *n* |

For multiple groups, the graph should be moved to the appropriate group band with which the data is to be related.

If the categories column is based on a code table (such as a drop-down DataWindow), the graph will use the column's data values by default. To use the display values, define the column with the LookUpDisplay() function. For example, the dept_id column has a code table that you want to use as a category for a graph. To display the department name instead of the data values in the categories, enter the following into the Category box in the Graph Data dialog:

```
LookUpDisplay( dept_id)
```

The drop-down list for the value axis shows all available columns, as well as Count() entries for all non-numeric columns and Sum() entries for all numeric columns. You can build any valid expression, such as Sum(salary * 0.9 for graph).

For a single-series graph, leave the Series box empty. For multiple series, you need to check the box to the left of the field. You can select column names from the list box or enter them as an expression, or you can separate multiple entries with commas.

To see this in action, create a graph displaying the category LookUpDisplay(sex), having the value Avg(salary for graph) (see Figure 31.15). Figure 31.16 shows the resulting graph.

By using the same graph, add a series by state (see Figure 31.17). Figure 31.18 shows the resulting graph.

**FIGURE 31.15**
*The* LookUp-
Display() *graph*
*definition.*

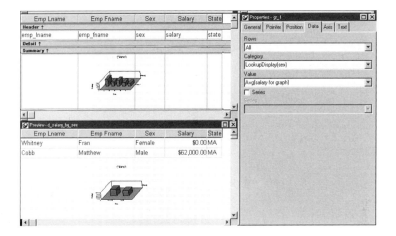

**FIGURE 31.16**
*A Graph*
*demonstrating*
LookUp-
Display().

**Salary by Sex**

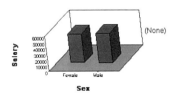

**FIGURE 31.17**
*A graph with*
*state series*
*definition.*

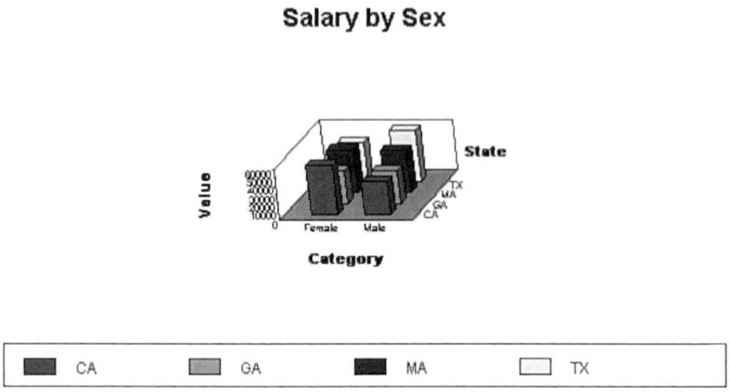

**FIGURE 31.18**
*A graph demon-
strating the added
state series.*

# Graph Controls

In addition to specifying a graph using DataWindows, you can create a graph on a window using a graph control.

## Creating a Graph Control

To create a graph control, click the Graph Control icon on the PainterBar, or from the Insert menu choose Control, Graph. You then add the control as you would any other window control—by clicking the desired window location.

## Populating a Graph Control

Graph controls have one main difference from their DataWindow counterpart. DataWindow graphs are populated by the specified data source (typically a SQL SELECT statement). Graph controls don't have this underlying set of data to rely on, so they must be manually populated.

You can use numerous PowerScript functions specifically for graph controls to manipulate the data in the graph. How you want your graph to appear dictates which functions you use. The first functions needed are those that populate the graph with data.

The AddSeries() function adds a new series to a graph. The series is assigned a sequential number that can be used for reference later on. This is the syntax:

```
graph_control.AddSeries( SeriesName )
```

The string argument *SeriesName* contains the name of the series you want to add to the graph control. The function returns an integer, which is the sequential number assigned to the series or -1 for failure.

After creating a series, you need to add the actual data values by using the AddData() function. This is the syntax for all graph styles except scatter graphs:

```
graph_control.AddData( SeriesNumber, DataValue, {CategoryName})
```

The *SeriesNumber* argument is the sequential number of the series in which the data is to be inserted. *DataValue* is the actual data to appear on the graph, and the last argument is the name of the category for the data value being inserted. Although *CategoryName* is optional, it's a good idea to specify a value; otherwise, the value will be added to the graph without a corresponding category. AddData() returns a Long data type containing the position of the new data value or -1 for failure. If *CategoryName* doesn't already exist, the data is placed at the end of the series unless the axis is sorted. With sorting specified, the new category is placed in the appropriate location in the sort order. If *CategoryName* does exist, the data replaces the existing information.

---

**Note**

For scatter graphs, the syntax for AddData() varies in the last two arguments. This is the syntax for a scatter graph:

```
graph_control.AddData( SeriesName, XValue, YValue)
```

The two arguments, *XValue* and *YValue*, are the data values for the corresponding X and Y values you want to plot on the graph.

---

The code in Listing 31.1 uses the AddSeries() and AddData() functions to populate a graph.

**LISTING 31.1** Graph Control Population

```
Integer li_Series_No
//Add first region
li_Series_No = gr_1.AddSeries("Northeast")
If li_Series_No <> -1 Then
    //Add sales and reps for series
    gr_1.AddData(li_Series_No, 201, "Carrie")
    gr_1.AddData(li_Series_No, 318, "Kurt")
    gr_1.AddData(li_Series_No, 420, "Cliff")
End If
```

This creates three categories containing the sales reps' names and plots their sales for that region. The script would add more regions/reps in much the same manner. Of course, this example was simplified to demonstrate the functions. Most likely, you wouldn't hard-code the values in your script but would retrieve the values from some other source (for example, a database, remote object, or user entry).

If you want to define the category values before placing the data values, use the AddCategory() function. This function takes a String value containing the name of the new category. Category names must be unique. Keep in mind that the category names are case-sensitive; the same category name with different capitalization is considered two unique names.

To add to the functions already discussed, Table 31.2 describes some common graph functions for insertion, deletion, and modification of graph data. The functions work much the same way as the addition functions.

**TABLE 31.2** Graph Control Functions

| Graph Function | Description |
| --- | --- |
| InsertCategory() | Inserts a new category on the graph. All existing series are renumbered to remain sequential. |
| InsertData() | Inserts a data point in a series of a graph. This isn't used for scatter graphs. |
| InsertSeries() | Inserts a series in a graph. All existing series are renumbered to remain sequential. |
| ImportClipboard() | Inserts data into a graph control from tab-delimited data on the Clipboard. |
| ImportFile() | Inserts data into a graph control from data in a file. |
| ImportString() | Inserts data points into a graph from tab-delimited data in a string. |
| DeleteCategory() | Deletes a category and associated data values from the category axis of a graph. |
| DeleteData() | Deletes a data point from a series. The remaining data in the series is shifted left. |
| DeleteSeries() | Deletes a series and its data values from a graph. |

TABLE **31.2**  Graph Control Functions

| Graph Function | Description |
|---|---|
| ModifyData() | Modifies a data point value. Syntax is different for scatter graphs (must specify X and Y values). |
| Reset() | Clears the graph's contents. You can specify All!, Category!, Data!, and Series!. |

# Dynamic Graphs

The preceding sections focus on the graph's design and populating it with data. You can dynamically modify almost any component of your graph via PowerScript. The type of graph you're using dictates how you interface with the graph. For a graph control, the attributes are accessed as with any other control:

```
gr_1.Title = "Regional Sales"
```

For DataWindows, you need to reference the Object attribute (for details on dynamically referencing a DataWindow object's attributes, see Chapter 14, "DataWindow Scripting"):

```
dw_1.Object.Title = "Regional Sales"
```

**Note**

Remember that you can achieve the same results by using the Modify() function.

In addition to manipulating the graph via its attributes, you can use several functions. The graph functions can be grouped into three types of functionality—information, extraction, and modification—as shown in Table 31.3.

TABLE **31.3**  Graph Functions

| Function | Description |
|---|---|
| | *Information* |
| CategoryCount() | Number of categories in a graph |
| CategoryName() | Name of a category number |
| DataCount() | Number of data points in a series |
| FindCategory() | Number of a category for a given name |
| FindSeries() | Number of a series for a given name |
| GetData() | Value of data at a given series and position |
| GetDataPieExplode() | Percentage of slice exploded |
| GetDataStyle() | The visual property of a data point |
| GetDataValue() | A more flexible GetData() |

TABLE **31.3**  Graph Functions

| Function | Description |
|---|---|
| | *Information* |
| GetSeriesStyle() | Visual property of a series |
| ObjectAtPointer() | Graph element clicked |
| SeriesCount() | Number of series in graph |
| SeriesName() | Name of a series number |
| | *Extraction* |
| Clipboard() | Copies image of graph to Clipboard (not data) |
| SaveAs() | Saves underlying data in one of a number of formats |
| | *Modification* |
| ResetDataColors() | Resets colors of a data point |
| SetDataPieExplode() | Explodes a pie slice |
| SetDataStyle() | Sets visual properties of a data point |
| SetSeriesStyle() | Sets visual properties for a series |

Look at an example that uses several of these functions. The application's business functionality is to create a graph displaying each region's sales as a percentage of the overall sales. When users double-click a region, they want to see what products are selling well for the selected region. Now create this application (one window) using two DataWindow graphs.

You first need to create the DataWindow graph that displays each region's overall sales percentage. For this, create a three-dimensional pie graph with a data source of the following Sybase SQL Anywhere statement:

```
SELECT "sales_order"."region",
   SUM("sales_order_items"."quantity")
FROM "sales_order",
   "sales_order_items"
WHERE  ("sales_order_items"."id" = "sales_order"."id" )
GROUP BY "sales_order"."region"
```

The category is the region, and the value is the computed sum field. After specifying the axis's labels and title, you get the graph in Figure 31.19. The name of this DataWindow is d_regional_sales.

Next, create the second DataWindow graph that displays the detail for a specified region. The SQL for this DataWindow is as follows:

```
SELECT "sales_order_items"."prod_id",
   sum("sales_order_items"."quantity")
```

**FIGURE 31.19**
*The Sales by
Region pie graph.*

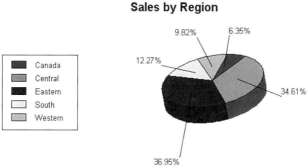

**Sales by Region**

**FROM** "sales_order",
    "sales_order_items"
**WHERE**  ("sales_order_items"."id" = "sales_order"."id" ) and
    ( ("sales_order"."region" = :arg_region ) )
**GROUP BY** "sales_order_items"."prod_id''·

Notice that the SQL statement contains a retrieval argument for the region name. The graph
type initially is a column graph (see Figure 31.20). The category is prod_id, and the value
is the computed column. The graph also has drop lines specified for the major divisions.
The name of this DataWindow is d_sales_for_region.

**FIGURE 31.20**
*Product sales
details for a
specified region.*

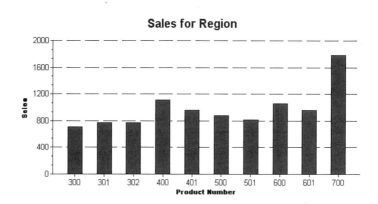

**Sales for Region**

Now that the two graphs are created, you can synchronize the two graphs on the window.
The window w_graphing contains two DataWindow controls: the top control (dw_Total)

is associated with d_regional_sales, and the bottom control (dw_Detail) is associated with d_sales_for_region. dw_Detail's Visible attribute is set to FALSE.

For the Constructor events for both DataWindow controls, the transaction object is set and the Open event of the window performs a Retrieve() for dw_Total. Most of the code is located in the DoubleClicked event for dw_Total. Users can double-click a piece of the pie graph to reveal the second graph, displaying the detail for the clicked region.

First, you need to find out where on the graph users double-clicked. This can be done by using the ObjectAtPointer() function:

```
ControlName.ObjectAtPointer ( {GraphControl,} SeriesNumber, DataPoint)
```

*ControlName* is the name of the graph control or the DataWindow control containing the graph. *GraphControl* is used when dealing with a DataWindow graph. It's a String containing the name of the graph as it's defined on the DataWindow object. *SeriesNumber* is an Integer used to store the number of the series users clicked. *DataPoint* is an Integer that stores the number of the data point clicked.

The return value of the ObjectAtPointer() function is of the grObjectType enumerated data type. A value of grObjectType is returned if users click anywhere in the graph, including an empty area, and a NULL value is returned if users click outside the graph. Table 31.4 defines the return values of the enumerated data type grObjectType.

**TABLE 31.4** Return Values for the Function ObjectAtPointer()

| Enumerated Data Type | Description |
| --- | --- |
| TypeCategory! | A label for a category |
| TypeCategoryAxis! | The category axis or between the category labels |
| TypeCategoryLabel! | The label of the category axis |
| TypeData! | A data point or other data marker |
| TypeGraph! | Any place within the graph control that's not another grObjectType |
| TypeLegend! | Within the legend box but not on a series label |
| TypeSeries! | The line connecting the data points of a series when the graph's type is a line or on the series label in the legend box |
| TypeSeriesAxis! | The series axis of a three-dimensional graph |
| TypeSeriesLabel! | The label of the series axis of a three-dimensional graph |
| TypeTitle! | The title of the graph |
| TypeValueAxis! | The value axis, including on the value labels |
| TypeValueLabel! | Users clicked the label of the value axis |

ObjectAtPointer() should be called first in the Clicked or DoubleClicked event for your graph to ensure that the proper value is captured. The graph control also must be enabled, or the Clicked event script won't be executed.

If users click a valid data point on `dw_Total` (indicating a region), you want to extract the data value and use the region name as the argument value for `dw_Detail`. On its own, this would provide the necessary functionality for your users, but with a little extra effort, you can make the presentation something the users won't soon forget. Users will easily remember what region was clicked if the clicked piece of the graph exploded out from the rest of the pie. This can easily be implemented by using the functions `SetDataPieExplode()` and `GetDataPieExplode()`.

`SetDataPieExplode()` causes a specified pie slice to be separated from the rest of the pie graph. This is the syntax:

*ControlName*`.SetDataPieExplode(`{*GraphControl,*`}` *SeriesNumber, DataPoint, Percent*`)`

*ControlName* is a graph control or a DataWindow control name. If you're using a DataWindow control graph, you must specify the *GraphControl* argument, which is a string indicating the name of the graph object. *SeriesNumber* is the number identifying the series. *DataPoint* is the number of the desired data point (or pie slice) that you want to have exploded out. The last argument, *Percent*, is the percentage of the pie's radius at which the pie slice is to be moved away from the center. The valid values are from 0 to 100. `SetDataPieExplode()` returns an Integer, with 1 being a success and -1 a failure.

`GetDataPieExplode()` is used to find out whether a particular pie slice is exploded and at what percentage it's exploded from the center. This function has the exact same arguments as `SetDataPieExplode()`, except that the *Percent* argument is an integer variable used to return the percent that the pie slice is exploded.

Listing 31.2 shows the script for the `DoubleClicked` event of `dw_Total`. This code results in an easy-to-use drill-down graph (see Figure 31.21).

**LISTING 31.2**   The `DoubleClicked` Event of `dw_Total`

```
Integer      li_Series, li_Data, li_Percent
String       ls_Region
GrObjectType clicked_object

//Determine what part of the graph was clicked
clicked_object = This.ObjectAtPointer("gr_1", li_Series, li_Data)

//Turn the redraw off
This.SetRedraw(FALSE)

//Determine if pie was clicked before
If ii_Series <> 0 and ii_Data <> 0 then
   If li_Series = ii_Series and ii_Data = li_Data then
```

**LISTING 31.2**    CONTINUED

```
      //Same object was clicked, so do nothing
      This.SetRedraw(TRUE)
      Return
   Else
      //Reset previous pie explosion
      This.SetDataPieExplode("gr_1", ii_Series, ii_Data, 0)
   End If
End If

//Determine if the clicked object was a data point
If clicked_object = TypeData! then
   //Find out if current object is exploded
   This.GetDataPieExplode("gr_1", li_Series, li_Data, li_Percent)
   // If Not exploded
   If li_Percent = 0 Then
      //Explode 50 percent
      This.SetDataPieExplode("gr_1", li_Series, li_Data, 50)
      //Set instance variable to remember series and data
      ii_Series  = li_Series
      ii_Data    = li_Data
      //Get the region
      ls_Region = This.CategoryName("gr_1", li_Data)
      //Retrieve data
      dw_Detail.SetRedraw(FALSE)
      dw_Detail.Retrieve(ls_region)
      //Set the title of the second datawindow
      dw_Detail.object.gr_1.Title="Sales for the " + ls_Region + " Region"
      dw_Detail.Show()
   Else
      //Pie already exploded, reset
      This.SetDataPieExplode("gr_1", li_Series, li_Data, 0)
      dw_Detail.Hide()
      dw_Detail.Reset()
      ii_Series  = 0
      ii_Data    = 0
   End If
Else //Clicked on anything else
   dw_Detail.Hide()
   MessageBox("Not a Region", "Please click on a region")
End If
This.SetRedraw(TRUE)
dw_Detail.SetRedraw(TRUE)
```

FIGURE **31.21**

*Graph drill-down
for regional sales.*

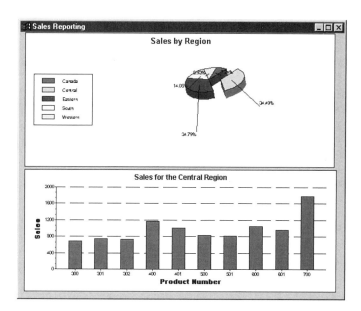

A couple of features were added to enhance the presentation even more. The two integer instance variables for w_graphing (ii_Series and ii_Data) remember what pie slice was exploded last so that if the same pie slice is clicked, it's not reset and then exploded again. Also notice that the title of dw_Detail is modified to reflect the clicked region name.

Keep in mind that in DataWindows, PowerBuilder creates and destroys graphs internally as users page through the data. This means that any changes you've made to your graph's appearance are continually lost. To avoid this, trap the graph creation event as a DataWindow user event mapped to the event ID, pbm_dwngraphcreate, and reissue all necessary changes. This event is triggered after the graph is created and populated with data but before the graph is displayed.

**Tip**

As you probably noticed in Listing 31.2, you can improve performance and the user presentation by using the SetRedraw() method. This allows you to make numerous modifications to your graph without continuously repainting the graph. The other option is to toggle the Visible attribute on and off.

Some other examples of how to modify a DataWindow graph at runtime are to change the type of graph being displayed, change the color of a column in a graph when it's clicked, and rotate the graph. First, to change the graph type, you change the GraphType property of the graph object on your DataWindow object. The syntax is

```
Control_Name.Object.GraphName.GraphType = Value
```

where *Control_Name* is the name of your DataWindow control, *GraphName* is the name of the graph object in your DataWindow object (defaults to "gr_1"), and *Value* is an integer value representing the type of graph you want to display.

> **Tip**
>
> A great way to determine the correct syntax and property values is to use the DWSyntax tool that comes with PowerBuilder.

In this example, you want to change the graph from a two-dimensional column graph (*Value* equal to 7) to a three-dimensional column graph (*Value* equal to 8).

```
dw_graph.object.gr_1.GraphType = 8
```

To change the graph back to the two-dimensional graph, just change the GraphType:

```
dw_graph.object.gr_1.GraphType = 7
```

Next, you need to change a column's color when it's clicked. For this example, you have a two-dimensional column graph in which all columns begin as red. To display emphasis, a column changes to blue when clicked. To accomplish this, use some of the functions listed in Table 31.3 in a DataWindow control's Clicked event, as shown in Listing 31.3.

**LISTING 31.3** Processing to Change the Color of a Series

```
Integer li_Series, li_Data
//Determine if the clicked object is a data point
If This.ObjectAtPointer("gr_1", li_Series, li_Data) = TypeData! Then
    //Turn off the redraw for the DataWindow
    dw_Graph.SetRedraw(FALSE)
    //Reset the graph to its original color for the previously modified column
    dw_Graph.ResetDataColors("gr_1", ii_Prior_Series, ii_Prior_Data)
    //Change the foreground color of the clicked data point
    dw_Graph.SetDataStyle("gr_1", li_Series, li_Data, ForeGround!, 16711680)
    //Store the values of the selected data point and series in the instance
    //variables in order to change the color back for the next clicked column
```

**LISTING 31.3**   CONTINUED

```
    ii_Prior_Data    = li_Data
    ii_Prior_Series  = li_Series
    //Refresh the DataWindow with the new changes
    dw_Graph.SetRedraw(TRUE)
End If
```

ObjectAtPointer() is called to determine where users clicked. If users clicked a column (a return value of TypeData!), SetRedraw() is called to ensure that the DataWindow control's display isn't refreshed until all changes are made to the graph. Because users may already have clicked a column (which would change the column's color from red to blue), you want to make sure that the blue column is reset to its original red color. This is done by the ResetDataColors() function, which resets the specified data point to the original series color. The color change for a specific column is done using SetDataStyle(). Its syntax is

*ControlName*.SetDataSyle( *GraphName, SeriesNum, DataPointNum, ColorType, Color*)

where *ControlName* is the name of the DataWindow control, *GraphName* is the name of the graph object in your DataWindow object, *SeriesNum* is an integer containing the series number that contains the data point you want to change, and *DataPointNum* is an integer containing the data point number you want to modify. *ColorType* is an enumerated data type of grObjectType for which the valid values are ForeGround!, BackGround!, LineColor!, and Shade!. The last argument, *Color*, is a Long containing the new color value. This changes the color of the clicked column to blue. The last two steps are to store the series number and data point number into two instance variables to be used in the ResetDataColors() call the next time the script is executed.

Your users now can change the graph type at runtime and modify the graph's colors. The last requirement you have is to allow users to rotate the graph if it's a three-dimensional style. This process is surprisingly easy in PowerBuilder. All you need is to reference the Rotation property of the DataWindow graph object. The code to rotate the graph up to 90 degrees to the right is

```
String   ls_Rotate, ls_Mod
Integer  li_Rotate
li_Rotate = Integer(dw_graph.Describe("gr_1.Rotation"))
If li_Rotate >= 90 Then
   Beep(1)
   Return
Else
   ls_Mod = "gr_1.Rotation=" + "'" + String(li_Rotate + 10) + "'"
   dw_Graph.Modify(ls_Mod)
End If
```

The Describe() function returns the current rotation of the graph so that you can check to see whether the rotation is greater than or equal to 90 degrees. If it is, you want to stop the rotation process. Otherwise, you need to change the rotation property to the current rotation of the graph plus 10. To rotate the graph to left, the code is

```
String   ls_rotate, ls_mod
Integer  li_rotate
li_Rotate = Integer(dw_graph.Describe("gr_1.Rotation"))
If li_Rotate <= -90 Then
   Beep(1)
   Return
Else
   ls_Mod = "gr_1.Rotation=" + "'" + String(li_Rotate - 10) + "'"
   dw_graph.Modify(ls_Mod)
End If
```

The only difference between this and the prior code is that you need to check for a rotation of negative 90 degrees or less to stop the rotation, and when changing the rotation, you now need to subtract 10 degrees rather than add. With all these different graphing techniques, you can create an application that gives your clients a rich presentation combined with additional functionality.

# Summary

This chapter demonstrated how to provide a graphical representation of data within a DataWindow and a window using a graph control. Although much of the functionality that your clients require may be specified at design time, you can use PowerBuilder to dynamically create and modify different components of your graph to give your clients a flexible environment.

# Data Pipelining

A common problem among developers is the task of moving data and data structures from one database to another. In the client/server environment, the need to copy tables and their data from a test database to a development database or from the server to a local database is constant unless the project happens to have a full-time DBA to facilitate this task. When a DBA is a luxury that's not at your disposal, depending on the tools available, data and data structure moving can be a fairly easy task or result in a lot of manual work that takes away from valuable development time.

The same problem occurs in the business community. With more people relying on computers to perform their day-to-day business activities, managing data is a serious concern. As a growing number of business people use laptops and dial in to access remote information, IT professionals must find easier ways to move data from a centralized server to locally maintained machines. The solution to both development and runtime transfer of data and data structures is PowerBuilder's data pipeline object. It provides an easy method to transfer data from one database to another regardless of the DBMS.

This chapter examines how to transfer (or *pipe*) data and data structures from one database to another. Information piping can be done during development by using the Data Pipeline painter or can be implemented in your application for your users to use at runtime. After defining a pipeline object in the Data Pipeline painter, you see how to use the pipeline object in your application.

# The Pipeline Object

As just mentioned, the data pipeline can be used to transfer data for developers or users. This is a general definition of what a pipeline object can do for you. The data pipeline can perform three main groups of tasks that result in great time and effort savings for you: transfer data, copy an entire database from one DBMS to another, and perform maintenance on an existing table structure.

The most obvious reason to use a pipeline object is to transfer data from one database to another. These databases can be the same DBMS or different DBMSs. Data transfer can consist of inserts into an existing table or updates of existing data. The data in the source database remains the same and is reproduced only in the destination database. Although it's most common for the source and destination databases to be different databases, they can be the same one.

The entire database can be moved from one DBMS to another, one table at a time. This way, you can create a copy of an existing database in another location (for example, if you wanted to replicate a SQL Server database to an Adaptive Server Anywhere database for local access). All extended attributes (such as edit styles, displays formats, and labels) for a table can be chosen to be migrated for the whole table, as can just the table and its data.

The last task you can use the data pipeline for is to make changes to a table that aren't allowed through the Database painter. For example, you might want to change the primary key definition or even allow certain columns to contain NULLs when they didn't previously.

Whatever purpose you have for using the data pipeline, you must specify several options when creating a pipeline object:

- The source database

- The destination database

- The source tables from which to move data

- The destination table to which the data will be moved

- The piping operation to be performed

- The frequency with which commits are performed

- The maximum number of errors allowed

- The extended attributes that need to be included

All this information is combined to form your data pipeline or pipeline object. When the definition of the pipeline object is complete, it can be run in PowerBuilder or used in an application. Either way, you can save the definition to your library file and reuse it repeatedly. The pipeline object is created in the Data Pipeline painter, as discussed in the next section.

# The Data Pipeline Painter

You access an existing pipeline object by clicking the Open toolbar button or by choosing Open from the File menu. In the Open dialog, select Pipelines from the Object Type drop-down at the bottom (see Figure 32.1).

To create a new pipeline object, click the New toolbar button or choose New from the File menu to open the new object window discussed in Chapter 2, "PowerBuilder 7.0 Development Environment." Select the Database tab page and then the Data Pipeline icon (see Figure 32.2).

After you choose to create a new data pipeline, PowerBuilder prompts you with the New Data Pipeline dialog (see Figure 32.3). In this dialog, you must choose the database profile from which you want to migrate data, the source connection, and the database profile to which you want the data migrated (or the destination connection). If you've already connected to a database in the Database painter, it will be your default source database. If a desired database doesn't appear in either Database Connections list, you must define the database profiles. For more information about database profiles, refer to Chapter 3, "Database Management Systems."

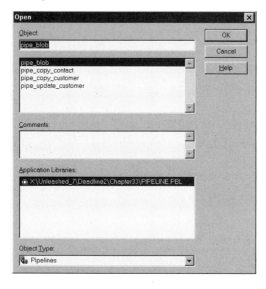

**FIGURE 32.1**
*The Open Object dialog used to open the data pipeline object.*

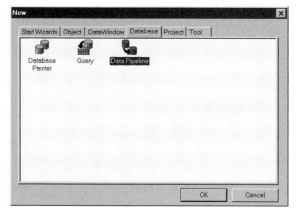

**FIGURE 32.2**
*The New dialog used to create a new data pipeline object.*

You also can select the type of data source to use: Quick Select, SQL Select, Query, or Stored Procedure. All four options are different ways to generate the SQL SELECT statement needed to pipe your data. The different data sources behave exactly as they do in the DataWindow painter. (For more information on the how to use the data sources, see Chapter 6, "The DataWindow Painter.") After you click OK, a dialog for the chosen data source appears, allowing you to specify the data you want to migrate. To access a different database in the Pipeline painter, you must enter the Database painter and point to a different data source.

FIGURE 32.3

*The New Data Pipeline dialog.*

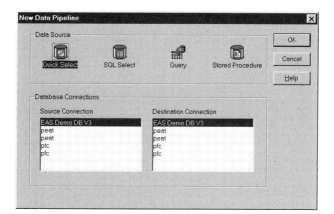

> **Note**
>
> The SQL Select painter functions exactly the same as it does in the DataWindow painter. It even can create retrieval arguments, which lets you narrow the scope of migrated data.

The SELECTstatement you generate should specify the data you want to migrate from the source database. The SELECT statement can be an entire table or a subset of one or more tables. When you're satisfied with your SELECT statement, click the Return icon on the PainterBar to return to the pipeline definition window (see Figure 32.4).

Other ways to access the Data Pipeline painter are to right-click a table title in the Database painter and then select Data Pipeline from the pop-up menu, or click the Pipeline icon on the PainterBar. With this method, PowerBuilder defaults the source and destination database to your current connection. The generated SELECT statement retrieves all columns for the table chosen in the Database painter and automatically takes you into the pipeline definition window.

The Data Pipeline painter is divided into several different sections: the source table, the destination table, and the pipeline options. Figure 32.5 shows the PainterBar for the Data Pipeline painter.

**FIGURE 32.4**

*The pipeline definition window.*

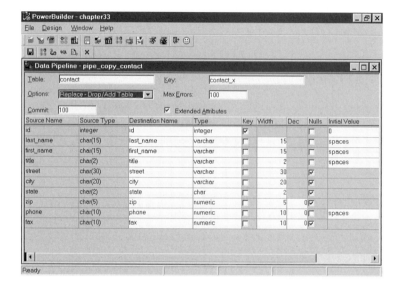

**FIGURE 32.5**

*The Data Pipeline PainterBar.*

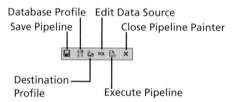

## The Source Data Section

The source section of the Data Pipeline painter displays the information about the tables to be piped:

- The name of the source column

- The data type (source type) of the column that has the current size—the total number of significant digits—of the column specified in parentheses

The source data columns can't be modified in the pipeline definition window. The only way to modify the source data information is to choose Edit Data Source from the Design menu or click the corresponding PainterBar icon (refer to Figure 32.5). Clicking the icon takes you back into the SQL Select painter.

After you finish modifying the SELECT statement and return to the pipeline definition window, PowerBuilder notifies you that the pipeline definition will change.

After specifying all the source information, you need to define how the destination columns should appear.

# The Destination Table

The destination data section of the pipeline definition is used to indicate where the data will be migrated. By using the destination columns, you can specify the new column names, the appropriate data types, and primary key information. The destination data section includes the following:

- The name of the destination column

- The data type of the destination column

- Whether each column should be included as part of the primary key

- If applicable, the column width (the total number of significant digits)

- The number of decimal (DEC) places, if applicable

- Whether the column can have a NULL value

- An initial value for the column

- A default value for the column, such as auto-incremented, current date or time, time stamp, NULL, or the user

You can modify all this information to suit your needs. The Type column provides a drop-down list displaying the valid data types for the destination database (because it can be a different DBMS with different data type definitions). If you choose that a column can contain NULL values, you can't specify an initial value.

The data pipeline supports BLOB (binary large object) columns. Select Database Blob from the Design menu, which opens the Database Binary/Text Large Object dialog (see Figure 32.6). In this dialog, specify the name of the destination column, the source table, and the name of the BLOB column. After this information is specified, the BLOB column is added to the list of columns in the pipeline definition window, and a different data type and default value can be specified (all other columns are disabled).

> **Note**
>
> To edit the definition of the BLOB column, double-click the newly added row in the pipeline definition window or right-click the row and select Properties.
> To remove the BLOB column, right-click the row and select Clear from the pop-up menu.

**32**

**Data Pipelining**

**FIGURE 32.6**

*The Database
Binary/Text Large
Object dialog.*

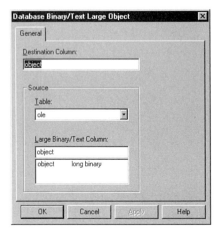

An additional feature of the Data Pipeline painter is that you can change the destination database at any time. This way, you can pipe data to one database and then modify the destination database profile and pipe the identical data to another database. To change the destination database, click the Destination Profile icon on the PainterBar, which opens the Database Profiles dialog (see Figure 32.7).

**FIGURE 32.7**

*The Database
Profiles dialog.*

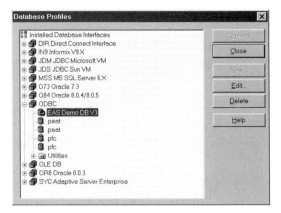

You can now select a new destination database, and PowerBuilder will try to connect to the newly specified database. An alternative method of changing the destination database is to choose Destination Connect from the File menu and select one of the database profiles listed in the cascading menu. After you settle on a destination database, you can specify some pipeline options that further define how the pipeline object will perform.

# Pipeline Options

Above the source and destination column specifications are options that indicate how you want the piping to occur:

- The destination table name

- The name of the primary key for the destination table

- The piping options

- The maximum number of errors allowed

- The number of committed rows in a transaction

- Whether extended attributes are piped

The destination table name can be changed at any time. The primary-key name can be modified if the piping option is either Create - Add Table or Replace - Drop/Add Table.

The piping options have the greatest effect on how you interact with the pipeline definition. Five options affect how you pipe your data. The first two allow you to modify the data structures; the last three affect the actual data maintained in the tables:

- Create - Add Table creates the specified destination table in the destination database. If the table already exists in the destination database, PowerBuilder notifies you that the table exists. To continue, you must rename the destination table or select another piping option. If the table doesn't already exist, PowerBuilder creates the new table and inserts the source rows into the destination table.

- Replace - Drop/Add Table also creates the specified destination table in the destination database and inserts the source rows into the new table. The difference between the Create and Replace options is that if the destination table already exists in the destination database, PowerBuilder will drop the existing table and create the new table.

**Caution**

Because the Replace option will drop the existing table, use this option with caution.

**32**

*Data Pipelining*

- Refresh - Delete/Insert Rows deletes all rows in the destination table and then inserts the rows from the specified source. The difference between Refresh and Replace is that Refresh requires that the destination table exist and just deletes existing rows, whereas Replace drops and then re-creates the destination table.

- Append - Insert Rows generates INSERT SQL statements for all source rows and inserts them into the destination table. Unlike Replace and Refresh, this option retains the existing rows.

- Update - Update/Insert Rows generates an UPDATE SQL statement for a source row whose key matches the key of a row in the destination database. The source rows that don't find a key match with the destination database generate INSERT SQL statements. The only option you can change in the destination table section is the key field check boxes. The primary key columns must be selected and must match the primary key in the destination table or uniquely identify each source row in case the destination table has no primary key.

**Note**

The last three piping options require that the destination table already exist in the destination database. If you specify a table name that doesn't exist, the Destination Table section of the painter is disabled.

After you decide on the piping options, you need to specify the maximum number of errors that you will allow, the number of rows processed before a commit is performed on the destination database, and whether you want to copy extended attributes to the destination database:

- Set the Max Errors value to the number of errors that can occur during execution of the pipeline object. When the specified value is reached, the pipeline is halted. Depending on the number of anticipated errors, you might want to set a higher value—or even No Limit—for the Max Errors value.

- Set the Commit value to the number of rows that make up one transaction. When the number count specified is reached, a commit is performed on the destination database. The Commit value should reflect how often you want the data to be written to disk. If you specify a Commit value of All, a commit will be performed only after all source rows are piped. If an error occurs during a transaction, all changes after the last commit are rolled back. You also can specify a value of None for a Commit value, which indicates that no commit will be performed after the data is migrated.

- Select the Extended Attributes check box if you want to copy any of the extended attributes associated with the specified source columns. If an extended attribute definition already exists in the destination table with the same name as a source column, the source's extended attribute definition isn't copied. The column in the destination table then uses the existing extended attribute definition.

# Executing the Pipeline

When the definition of the pipeline object is complete, you can click the Execute icon in the PainterBar (refer to Figure 32.5) or choose Execute from the Design menu. If you've specified any retrieval arguments in the SQL SELECT statement, PowerBuilder prompts you for values when you try to execute the pipeline. PowerBuilder then generates the necessary SQL statements to migrate the data as specified by the piping options. PowerBuilder also indicates the number of rows read, the number of rows written, and the time elapsed in the MicroHelp.

After execution of the pipeline object begins, you can cancel the processing. After you click the Execute icon, the icon changes to a red hand that, when clicked, stops the pipeline processing. If you reach the maximum number of errors specified for your pipeline, PowerBuilder halts processing and then displays the erroneous rows. (For more information on handling pipeline errors, see the next section.)

> **Note**
>
> Remember that because you're performing database processing, the database will ensure any integrity constraints via foreign keys or triggers. These can be the cause of errors in the data pipeline process.

# Pipeline Errors

When PowerBuilder detects any pipeline errors, it displays them in a standard pipeline error DataWindow (see Figure 32.8). The DataWindow displays all columns for each failed row and an error message indicating what the problem was. This DataWindow allows you to either correct the errors by editing each problem column or ignore the errors.

FIGURE **32.8**

*The pipeline error DataWindow.*

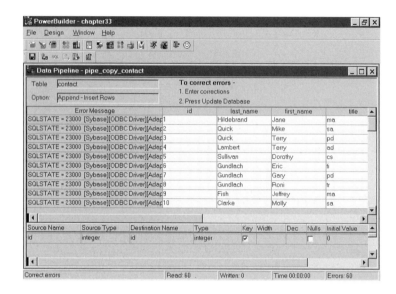

If you want to ignore the errors, click the Design icon on the PainterBar or choose Design from the Design menu, either of which returns you to the pipeline definition window. You can't return to the error DataWindow after you return to the pipeline definition.

If you want to correct pipeline errors, review each error message and make the appropriate modifications to the problem columns. Because the error DataWindow is a grid presentation, you can resize the columns to view more or less of the column's value. After correcting the errors, click the Update Database icon or choose Update Database from the Design menu. PowerBuilder tries to repipe these rows to the destination database and displays any new or remaining errors after the process completes. Although the other PainterBar icons appear, only the Update Database and Design icons are enabled when you're correcting errors.

### Note

If you reach the maximum error limit, you can't continue the pipeline even after fixing the errors. To get around this problem, you must fix the pipeline object's definition or the source data. You can then execute the pipeline again.

The rest of the information on the window indicates the pipeline object's definition. This information can't be modified.

## Saving a Pipeline Object

A pipeline object is saved the same way as any other PowerBuilder object. Choose Save from the File menu or click the Save icon on the PainterBar to open the Save Data Pipeline dialog (see Figure 32.9). By saving the pipeline object to a PowerBuilder library, you can reuse it later or incorporate the pipeline into any of your applications.

**FIGURE 32.9**
*The Save Data Pipeline dialog.*

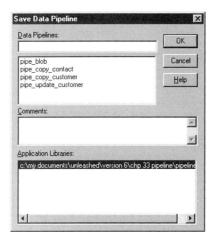

# Using a Pipeline in Your Application

To implement a pipeline in any of your applications, you must create several objects. The first (and most obvious) is the pipeline object created in the Data Pipeline painter. The other components are a standard class user object of type Pipeline and a window containing a DataWindow control. Depending on your approach, runtime pipelines can be simple; with a little more effort, a pipeline can be a reusable object that many applications can use.

## The Pipeline User Object

You create the pipeline user object by using the User Object painter and selecting a standard class of type pipeline. For a simple application, all you need to do is save the user object and continue to create your window and pipeline object. This, of course, would be the easy way out and would force you to create a non-object-oriented solution as well as rework the code if you implement any additional pipelines in the application.

## Pipeline Properties

The pipeline user object has six properties: ClassDefinition, DataObject, RowsInError, RowsRead, RowsWritten, and Syntax.

### The `ClassDefinition` Property

The ClassDefinition property gives information about the Pipeline class. This property contains such information as the name of the class, the library that it resides in, and its ancestor.

### The `DataObject` Property

The DataObject property works in much the same way as the DataWindow control property of the same name. This property specifies the name of the pipeline object created in the Data Pipeline painter that you want to execute in your application. Unlike the DataWindow control property, this value may be set only at runtime by using dot notation, as in this example:

```
iu_pipeline.DataObject = "pipe_copy_contact"
```

iu_pipeline is the instance of the pipeline user object; pipe_copy_contact is the name of the pipeline object.

> **Caution**
>
> Because DataObject can be assigned only at runtime (unless you create a pipeline standard class user object), the pipeline object won't be included in your executable. Pipeline objects therefore must be distributed through PowerBuilder dynamic libraries (PBDs or DLLs) because they can't be specified in a PBR either.

### The `RowsInError`, `RowsRead`, and `RowsWritten` Properties

These Long properties provide information about the number and status of the rows being processed by the pipeline. These values are typically displayed to users via your application's pipeline window to indicate the pipeline's current status.

RowsInError indicates the number of rows the pipeline found in error. For example, if your pipeline processed 100 rows and seven of them weren't accepted due to a duplicate key error, RowsInError would have a value of 7.

RowsRead indicates the number of rows that the pipeline has read. In the previous example, RowsRead would be 100.

RowsWritten specifies the number of rows that have been written to the database (although not necessarily committed). Following the same example, RowsWritten would contain a value of 93.

### The syntax Property

The Syntax property is a string that contains the syntax used to create the pipeline object. When you create a pipeline object in the Data Pipeline painter, this syntax is generated and assigned for you. By using a series of string-manipulation functions (for example, Mid(), Pos(), and Len()), you can allow users to query information about the pipeline's setup and modify its definition (such as the Commit and Max Errors values).

## Pipeline Events

In addition to the two standard events, Constructor and Destructor, are three events specific to the pipeline user object:

- The PipeStart event is triggered after the pipeline Start() or Repair() function is called.

- PipeMeter is triggered after a transaction (determined by the value of the Commit option in the Data Pipeline painter) is committed.

- PipeEnd is triggered when the process executed by Start() or Repair() has terminated.

You can use these events for several reasons. The most common use of these events is to provide users with the status of the pipeline's processing, in rows processed or time taken.

## Pipeline Methods

The pipeline user object also has several unique methods or functions that apply to it: Start(), Repair(), and Cancel(). The following sections examine the syntax for each function and then incorporate the functionality into the pipeline user object.

### The start() Function

The Start() function begins execution of the pipeline object. Its syntax is

```
pipeline_user_object.Start( source_trans, dest_trans, dw_error, &
{arg1, arg2,..., argn})
```

The first three arguments are required; every additional argument is optional, depending on the data pipeline object's retrieval arguments. The *source_trans* argument is the name of the transaction object that's connected to the database containing the source tables. The *dest_trans* argument identifies the name of the transaction object that's connected to the destination database. The third required argument is the name of the DataWindow control that will contain any rows in error during the pipeline process. PowerBuilder generates a DataWindow object and assigns it to the DataWindow control passed to the `Start()` function. Each additional argument identifies any retrieval arguments defined in the data pipeline object's SELECT statement.

The `Start()` function returns an integer of one of the following values:

| Value | Meaning | Value | Meaning |
| --- | --- | --- | --- |
| 1 | Function executed successfully | -9 | Fatal SQL error in destination |
| -1 | Pipeline open failed | -10 | Maximum number of errors exceeded |
| -2 | Too many columns | -12 | Bad table syntax |
| -3 | Table already exists | -13 | Key required but not supplied |
| -4 | Table doesn't exist | -15 | Pipeline already in progress |
| -5 | Missing connection | -16 | Error in source database |
| -6 | Wrong retrieval | -17 | Error in destination arguments |
| -7 | Column mismatch | -18 | Destination database is read-only |
| -8 | Fatal SQL error in source | | |

The error checking for a call to the `Start()` function is implemented as another function in the pipeline user object, as detailed in the section "Building a Pipeline in an Application."

## The `Cancel()` Function

The `Cancel()` function is executed when you need to stop a pipeline already in progress. It returns an integer with a value of 1 for success and -1 for a failure. Its syntax is

```
pipeline_user_object.Cancel()
```

## The `Repair()` Function

The `Repair()` function is used after your application executes a pipeline that has had some rows error out. The rows in error are displayed in the DataWindow control that's passed as an argument to the `Start()` function. The user can correct the problems and reapply the fixes to the database by using the `Repair()` function. `Repair()`'s syntax is

```
pipeline_user_object.Repair( dest_trans )
```

The *dest_trans* argument passed is the name of the transaction object connected to the destination database. Repair() returns the following values:

| Value | Meaning |
| --- | --- |
| 1 | Function executed successfully |
| -5 | Missing connection |
| -9 | Fatal SQL error in destination |
| -10 | Maximum number of errors exceeded |
| -11 | Invalid window handle |
| -12 | Bad table syntax |
| -15 | Pipeline already in progress |
| -17 | Error in destination database |
| -18 | Destination database is read-only |

The error checking for Repair() is combined with the error processing for the Start() function in the pipeline user object.

## Building a Pipeline in an Application

This section discusses some basic functionality you should implement in your pipeline user object so that you can reuse it in multiple applications. In addition to the pipeline user object, you will use a window with a DataWindow control (required) and several other controls (see Figure 32.10).

**FIGURE 32.10**
*The contact pipeline window*
w_pipeline.

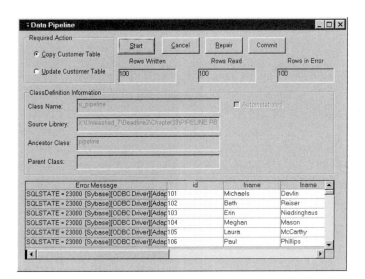

You first must do some initialization before you execute the pipeline. In the window's Open event, you need to create instances of the transaction objects and user object (defined as window instance variables), connect to the appropriate databases, and initialize several key variables. Listing 32.1 shows the script for the window's Open event.

**LISTING 32.1**  The Open Event for w_pipeline

```
SetPointer(HourGlass!)

//Instantiate instance variables
iu_pipeline = CREATE u_pipeline
itr_sourcetrans = CREATE u_transaction
itr_desttrans = CREATE u_transaction

//Connect to databases
If wf_connect() <> 0 Then
   Close(this)
End If
//PostEvent to initialize pipeline user object
this.PostEvent("PostOpen")
```

The window function wf_connect() connects your application to the source and destination databases. Listing 32.2 shows the code.

**LISTING 32.2**  The Public Function wf_connect() in w_pipeline

```
// This script will read all the database values from PB.INI
//    and store them in itr_sourcetrans.

itr_sourcetrans.DBMS        = "ODBC"
itr_sourcetrans.Database    = "EAS Demo DB V3"
itr_sourcetrans.DbParm  = "ConnectString='DSN=EAS Demo DB V3;UID=dba;PWD=sql'"

Connect Using itr_sourcetrans;

If itr_sourcetrans.SqlCode < 0 then
    MessageBox("Connect error","Could not connect to source db")
    Return -1
End If

// This script will read all the database values from PB.INI
// and store them in itr_desttrans.
itr_desttrans.DBMS        = "ODBC"
```

**LISTING 32.2**  CONTINUED

```
itr_desttrans.Database   = "EAS Demo DB V3"
itr_desttrans.DbParm     = "ConnectString='DSN=EAS Demo DB V3;UID=dba;PWD=sql'"

Connect Using itr_desttrans;

If itr_desttrans.SqlCode < 0 then
    MessageBox("Connect error","Could not connect to destination db")
    Return -1
End If

Return 0
```

**32**

Data Pipelining

The function takes no arguments and returns an integer. If an error is encountered while connecting, a message box is displayed and -1 is returned, causing the window to close. If the connection is successful, a custom event (PostOpen) is posted to, which initializes the pipeline user object's variables. Listing 32.3 shows the script for this.

**LISTING 32.3**  The PostOpen Event for w_pipeline

```
ClassDefinition lpo_PipeClass, lpo_ParentClass, lpo_AncestorClass

iu_pipeline.uf_init (itr_sourcetrans,itr_desttrans,dw_error)

iu_pipeline.ist_read = st_read
iu_pipeline.ist_written = st_written
iu_pipeline.ist_error = st_error

// Input the ClassDefinition Information
lpo_PipeClass = iu_pipeline.ClassDefinition
lpo_ParentClass = lpo_PipeClass.ParentClass
lpo_AncestorClass = lpo_PipeClass.Ancestor

sle_name.text = lpo_PipeClass.Name
sle_library.text = lpo_PipeClass.LibraryName
sle_ancestor.text = lpo_AncestorClass.Name
// Make sure that there is a parent class
If IsValid (lpo_ParentClass) then sle_parent.text = lpo_ParentClass.Name
cbx_1.Checked = lpo_PipeClass.IsAutoinstantiate

iu_pipeline.dataobject = "pipe_copy_customer"
```

To make the pipeline user object as reusable as possible, you define a user object function that initializes all required variables. The internal instance variables for the pipeline user object are

```
transaction   itr_sourcetrans, itr_desttrans
datawindow    idw_error
statictext    ist_read, ist_written, ist_error
```

After each instance variable is declared, you must create the user object function uf_Init() to assign values to some of these variables:

```
//Initialize the instance variables used in the pipeline
itr_sourcetrans = atr_sourcetrans
itr_desttrans = atr_desttrans
idw_error = adw_dwerror
```

The static text instance variables aren't required to perform the basic pipeline processing and therefore aren't included in the initialization function, but they're assigned in the PostOpen to allow for use later.

After setup is complete, the window is displayed to users. The window contains two radio buttons that allow users to specify what action to perform (in this example, users can copy or update the contact table). In the Clicked events of the two radio buttons, the DataObject attribute of iu_pipeline is assigned to a data pipeline object. Here's an example:

```
iu_pipeline.DataObject = "pipe_copy_contact"
```

Users can then click the Start button to begin the pipeline processing. Listing 32.4 shows the Clicked event for the Start button.

**LISTING 32.4**  The Clicked Event for cb_start on w_pipeline

```
Integer li_rtn
li_rtn = iu_pipeline.uf_Start()
//Check the value of the return code from Start()
If li_rtn <> 1 Then
   iu_pipeline.uf_error (li_rtn)
   cb_Repair.Enabled = TRUE
End If
```

The user object function uf_Start() starts the pipeline processing with the following code:

```
//Execute the pipeline and return the value
Return this.Start( itr_sourcetrans, itr_desttrans, idw_error)
```

The function returns an integer that can be used to perform the standard error processing incorporated into the pipeline user object subroutine uf_error(). The repair command button, cb_Repair, is enabled so that the errors can be fixed. The function uf_error() is defined as shown in Listing 32.5.

**LISTING 32.5**  The Public Function uf_error() for u_pipeline

```
string ls_msg
Choose Case a_rtn_code
   Case -1
      ls_msg = "Pipe open failed"
   Case -2
      ls_msg = "Too many columns"
   Case -3
      ls_msg = "Table already exists"
   Case -4
      ls_msg = "Table does not exist"
   Case -5
      ls_msg = "Missing connection"
   Case -6
      ls_msg = "Wrong arguments"
   Case -7
      ls_msg = "Column mismatch"
   Case -8
      ls_msg = "Fatal SQL error in source"
   Case -9
      ls_msg = "Fatal SQL error in destination"
   Case -10
      ls_msg = "Maximum number of errors exceeded"
   Case -12
      ls_msg = "Bad table syntax"
   Case -13
      ls_msg = "Key required but not supplied"
   Case -15
      ls_msg = "Pipe already in progress"
   Case -16
      ls_msg = "Error in source database"
   Case -17
      ls_msg = "Error in destination database"
   Case -18
      ls_msg = "Destination database is read-only"
End Choose
If a_rtn_code <> 1 Then
```

**LISTING 32.5**   CONTINUED

```
   MessageBox("Pipeline Error", ls_msg, StopSign!, Ok!)
Else
   MessageBox("Pipeline Successful", "Operation completed")
End If
```

The subroutine takes one argument: the return value from uf_Start().

If users decide to cancel the pipeline processing at any time, they only need to click the cancel command button, which executes the following code:

```
If iu_pipeline.uf_cancel() < 0 Then
   MessageBox("Cancel","Cancel Failed")
End If
```

The function uf_Cancel() is declared in the user object and returns an integer indicating the function's success or failure:

```
Return this.Cancel()
```

In the PipeMeter event of the pipeline user object, use the following code to display status information to users every time a transaction is committed to the database:

```
ist_error.text = String(this.RowsInError)
ist_read.text = String(this.RowsRead)
ist_written.text = String(this.RowsWritten)
```

Finally, if any errors are encountered during the pipeline execution, they're displayed in the DataWindow control dw_error. Users can make changes to the data in error and then click the Repair button, which contains the code in Listing 32.6.

**LISTING 32.6**   The Clicked Event for cb_repair on w_pipeline

```
integer li_rtn
li_rtn = iu_pipeline.uf_Repair()
//Check the value of the return code from Repair()
If li_rtn <> 1 Then
   iu_pipeline.uf_error(li_rtn)
End If
```

The subroutine uf_Repair() is defined as follows:

```
Return this.Repair(itr_desttrans)
```

Notice that the same error processing  (uf_Error) is used for uf_Repair() as for uf_Start().

This makes up most of the application. The only other processing that needs to be built into the window is one additional function that performs the disconnect from the databases and destroys the transaction objects and user object. This is implemented in `wf_Disconnect()` (see Listing 32.7), which is called from the window's `CloseQuery` event.

**LISTING 32.7**  The Public Function `wf_Disconnect()` for `w_pipeline`

```
Disconnect Using itr_desttrans;
If itr_desttrans.SQLCode <> 0 Then
    MessageBox("Database Error","Could not disconnect from the destination")
Return -1
End If
Disconnect Using itr_sourcetrans;
If itr_sourcetrans.SQLCode <> 0 Then
    MessageBox("Database Error","Could not disconnect from the source")
    Return -1
End If
//Destroy instance variables
Destroy itr_desttrans
Destroy itr_sourcetrans
Destroy iu_pipeline
Return 0
```

The `CloseQuery` event has the following code:

```
If wf_Disconnect() = -1 Then
    Return 1
End If
```

This processing lays most of the foundation for creating a reusable pipeline object. In addition to the processing found here, some functionality can be incorporated into your user object if deemed necessary. This includes creating a series of user object functions that use string functions to manipulate the `Syntax` attribute of the pipeline user object. Information can be displayed to users for any of the data pipeline object's definition (for example, the current value for `commit` or `errors`). Listing 32.8 shows an example of a function to return the pipeline object's commit setting.

**LISTING 32.8**  The `uf_GetCommit` Function for `u_pipeline`

```
//Return the set commit value for a pipeline object
string ls_pipe_def, ls_commit
long ll_pos_commit, ll_pos_errors

//Get the pipeline object's syntax
```

**LISTING 32.8** CONTINUED

```
ls_pipe_def = this.Syntax

//Find the position of the commit value in the syntax string
ll_pos_commit = Pos( ls_pipe_def, "commit")
//Find the position of the errors value in the syntax string
ll_pos_errors = Pos( ls_pipe_def, "errors")

//Subtract the difference between the commit and errors
//pipeline value and grab the commit value from the syntax
ls_commit = Mid ( ls_pipe_def, ll_pos_commit + 7, &
                    (ll_pos_errors - 1)- (ll_pos_commit + 7))

Return ls_commit
```

You can modify this process for each value of the pipeline object to extract values and to modify the pipeline definition.

# Summary

As you've seen in this chapter, the data pipeline can be useful for both developers and end users. By using a data pipeline, you can move data and data structures across databases with a minimal amount of work. The pipeline is useful at any time to developers using PowerBuilder for working with relational databases. It can also be implemented into an application using a pipeline user object, which allows for easy reuse of a pipeline in multiple applications.

# Mail Enabling PowerBuilder Applications

The point of the client/server paradigm is to make data more available and accessible for end users. By mail enabling your application, users can communicate the results of their work to others. There are a number of reasons for mail enabling your application, however—sharing data is just one. Another reason is the ability to create a standard error-message window so that when errors occur, they're relayed directly to a development coordinator. This is an attempt to ensure that problems are collated and can be acted on properly, because you can't always rely on end users to give correct or accurate accounts of application or system errors.

# The Microsoft Messaging Application Programming Interface

Microsoft defined a standard *Messaging Application Programming Interface* (MAPI) in the early 1990s, in collaboration with a number of application and messaging service vendors, and included it in the Windows API set. Before MAPI was available, developers had to write source code for each proprietary mail system's API. MAPI now provides a layer between the client application and the messaging service, enabling total independence. Messaging services are connected to a subsystem by using the MAPI service provider interface as service provider drivers.

PowerBuilder provides an interface to MAPI through a number of functions, structures, and enumerated data types. No PowerBuilder-provided mail functions work on the Macintosh platform. The code listings introduced in this chapter were coded and tested against Microsoft Exchange but should work with other mail systems that support MAPI without any changes.

The other common messaging API is VIM. Apple, Borland, Lotus, and Novell developed VIM (vendor independent messaging) to provide a common set of functions across multiple platforms. Now, the VIM API talks only to Lotus cc:Mail and Notes, and isn't directly supported by PowerBuilder. To carry out mail operations using VIM, you need to use external function calls to the appropriate VIM DLLs.

> **Note**
>
> For further information, explore the PowerBuilder Library for Lotus Notes Reference, available on the Sybase Developer's Network Web site (http:\\sdn.sybase.com). You need to migrate this to version 7.0 because support for the library was stopped with version 6.5.

All PowerBuilder interaction with the mail system is done through a single object, `mailSession`.

## The `mailSession` Object

The main mail object, `mailSession`, consists of only two primary attributes: `SessionID` and `MessageID[]`. `SessionID` is a protected Long data type used for holding the handle of the mail session used in calls to external functions; `MessageID[]` is an array of strings. This array holds message identities, which are used in arguments to mail functions. Before making any calls to mail functions, however, the `mailSession` object must be declared, created, and then connected by using the `mailLogon()` function.

## The `mailLogon()` Function

The `mailLogon()` function makes the connection between the PowerBuilder application and the mail system by creating a new session or using an already existing session. The syntax is

`mailSession.mailLogon ({ UserId, Password} {, LogonOption})`

*UserId* and *Password* are the user's ID and password for the mail system. *LogonOption* is an enumerated value of the `mailLogonOption` data type (see Table 33.1) and specifies whether a new session should be started and whether new messages should be downloaded on connection. These three parameters are all optional, but if a user ID is specified, the password must also be included.

**TABLE 33.1** `mailLogonOption` Enumerated Data Types

| Enumerated Data Type | Description |
| --- | --- |
| `mailNewSession!` | Starts a new mail session, regardless of any current connections. |
| `mailDownLoad!` | Starts a new mail session only if the mail application isn't already running. Forces the download of any new messages from the server to the user's inbox. |
| `mailNewSessionWithDownLoad!` | Starts a new mail session. Forces the download of any new messages from the server to the user's inbox. |

The default action of `mailLogon()` is to use an existing session and not to force new messages to be downloaded.

`MailLogon()` returns a value of the `mailReturnCode` enumerated data type. This function's value can be any of the following: `mailReturnSuccess!`, `mailReturnLoginFailure!`, `mailReturnInsufficientMemory!`, `mailReturnTooManySessions!`, or `mailReturnUserAbort!`. `mailReturnCode` has a number of other values that other mail functions use.

To display the error code after failing an error check, it's useful to have a function that converts a `mailReturnCode` to a string message that can be shown to the user. This function is detailed later in this chapter.

If a new session isn't started, the PowerBuilder mail session uses the existing session and doesn't require a user ID and password. If a new session needs to be established, however, the mail system's login dialog opens if the user ID and password aren't supplied.

In the following example, a series of `mailLogon()` calls are made. Note that this is simply to illustrate the various manners of calling and that code wouldn't look like this:

```
mailSession PBmailSession
PBmailSession = CREATE mailSession
//
// Try to connect to an existing session, o/w create a new one
PBmailSession.mailLogon()
//
// Create a new session - do NOT download new mail
PBmailSession.mailLogon (mailNewSession!)
//
// Create a new session and download new mail
PBmailSession.mailLogon( "Devon", "secret7", mailNewSessionWithDownLoad!)
```

## The `mailLogoff()` Function

The `mailLogoff()` function breaks the connection between the PowerBuilder application and the mail system. The syntax is

```
mailSession.mailLogoff()
```

If the mail application was running before PowerBuilder began its mail session, the mail system is left in the state in which it was found.

`mailLogoff()` also returns a value of the `mailReturnCode` enumerated data type, which for this function can be one of the following: `mailReturnSuccess!`, `mailReturnLoginFailure!`, or `mailReturnInsufficientMemory!`.

After you finish with and close the mail session, you need to release the memory used by the `mailSession` object. For example, to close the mail session started by the previous examples, the code is

```
PBmailSession.mailLogOff()
DESTROY PBmailSession
```

# The `mailHandle()` Function

Although PowerBuilder provides a basic set of functions you can use with the mail system, you might need to make calls to external functions that carry out a certain unprovided functionality. As with some other API function calls, you need to pass a handle to the object on which you want to act. The `mailHandle()` function provides the handle of the mail object. Its syntax is

```
mailsession.mailHandle()
```

The handle returned is of type `unsigned long`.

# The `mailAddress()` Function

The `mailAddress()` function is used to check the validity of the recipients of a mail message. If there's an invalid entry in the `mailRecipient` array of the `mailMessage` object, `mailAddress()` opens the Address Book dialog (see Figure 33.1) so the user can fix the problem address.

**33**

Mail Enabling
PowerBuilder
Applications

**FIGURE 33.1**
*The Address Book dialog.*

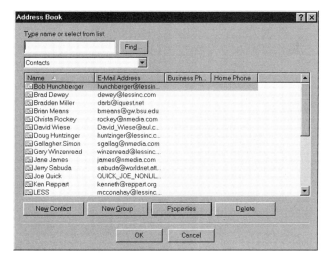

The `mailRecipient` array for the mail message is then updated. The syntax is

```
mailSession.mailAddress( {MailMessage})
```

If no *MailMessage* is specified, the Address Book dialog is opened for the user to look for addresses and maintain his personal address lists. When this happens, the dialog doesn't return addresses for use in addressing a message.

> **Note**
>
> The `mailRecipient` array contains information about recipients of a mail message or the originator of a message. The originator field isn't used when you send a message.

`mailAddress()` returns a value of the `mailReturnCode` enumerated data type and takes one of the following values: `mailReturnSuccess!`, `mailReturnFailure!`, `mailReturnInsufficientMemory!`, or `mailReturnUserAbort!`.

To check that the address is valid for a previously constructed mail message, the code would be

```
If PBmailSession.mailAddress( PBmailMessage) <> mailReturnSuccess! Then
   MessageBox( "Sending Mail", "The addressing for this Message failed.")
   Return
End If
```

## The `mailResolveRecipient()` Function

To enable the entry of partial names as addresses, the `mailResolveRecipient()` function validates them and retrieves the full address. The syntax is

```
mailSession.mailResolveRecipient( Recipient {, AllowUpdates})
```

The *Recipient* parameter is a string variable or a `mailRecipient` structure. `mailResolveRecipient()` sets the string or the structure to the resolved address information. A string address variable is sufficient for users in a local mail system, but if the mail will be sent through mail gateways, the full address details should be obtained in a `mailRecipient` structure. The *AllowUpdates* Boolean indicates whether the mail system updates the address list with the recipient's name; the default is FALSE. If the user doesn't have update privileges, *AllowUpdates* is ignored.

`mailResolveRecipient()` returns a value of the `mailReturnCode` enumerated data type and takes one of the following values: `mailReturnSuccess!`, `mailReturnFailure!`, `mailReturnInsufficientMemory!`, or `mailReturnUserAbort!`. If the name isn't found, the function returns `mailReturnFailure!`.

If the partial address matches multiple addresses, the mail system opens a dialog to enable users to select the correct name. This is system dependent, however. Figure 33.2 shows the MS Exchange Check Names dialog.

FIGURE **33.2**

*The MS Exchange dialog to resolve a mail address.*

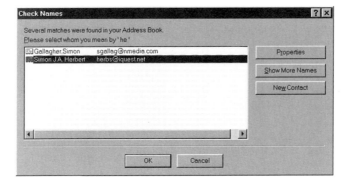

In the following example, the single-line edit `sle_address` contains a full or partial recipient name. The value is assigned to a `mailRecipient` structure, and the function `mailResolveRecipient()` is called to find the address details. The resolved address is then placed back into the edit field:

```
mailRecipient PbmailRecipient

PBmailRecipient.Name = sle_address.Text

If PBmailSession.mailResolveRecipient( PBmailRecipient) &
                        <> mailReturnSuccess! Then
MessageBox( "Address Resolution", sle_address.Text + " not found.")
Else
   sle_address.Text = PBmailRecipient.Name
End If
```

## The `mailRecipientDetails()` Function

To display a dialog with the specified recipient's address information, use the `mailRecipientDetails()` function (see Figure 33.3). The syntax is

*mailSession*`.mailRecipientDetails(` *MailRecipient* `{,` *AllowUpdates*`})`

The *MailRecipient* structure contains a valid address recipient identifier returned by `mailAddress()`, `mailResolveRecipient()`, or `mailReadMessage()`. The *AllowUpdates* Boolean indicates whether the recipient's name can be modified, but only if the user has update privileges for the mail system.

`mailRecipientDetails()` returns a value of the `mailReturnCode` enumerated data type and takes one of the following values: `mailReturnSuccess!`, `mailReturnFailure!`, `mailReturnInsufficientMemory!`, `mailUnknownReturnRecipient!`, or `mailReturnUserAbort!`.

**FIGURE 33.3**

*The recipient information dialog.*

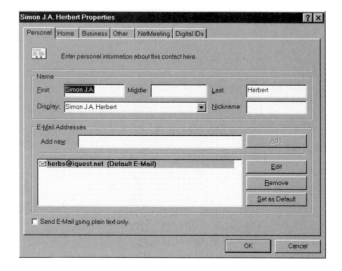

The following example builds on the example started in the `mailResolveRecipient()` function description. On a successful resolution, it displays the address details by calling `mailRecipientDetails()`:

```
mailRecipient PBmailRecipient

PBmailRecipient.Name = sle_address.Text

If PBmailSession.mailResolveRecipient( PBmailRecipient) &
                        <> mailReturnSuccess! Then
MessageBox("Address Resolution", sle_address.Text + " not found.")
Else
    PBmailSession.mailRecipientDetails( PBmailRecipient)
End If
```

## The `mailGetMessages()` Function

Use the `mailGetMessages()` function to populate the `messageID` array of the `mailSession` object with the message IDs found in the user's inbox. The syntax is

*mailSession*.mailGetMessages( { *MessageType*,} { *UnreadOnly* })

*MessageType* is a string that identifies the type of a message. The default type is InterPersonal Messages (IPM); use `"IPM"` or the empty string (`""`). Mail system interprocess messages can be accessed by using `"IPC"`, as can other message types defined by the mail administrator. The *UnreadOnly* parameter is a Boolean that indicates whether only the IDs of unread messages (`TRUE`) or all messages (`FALSE`) are to be returned.

`mailGetMessages()` returns a value of the `mailReturnCode` enumerated data type and takes one of the following values: `mailReturnSuccess!`, `mailReturnFailure!`, `mailReturnInsufficientMemory!`, `mailReturnNoMessages!`, or `mailReturnUserAbort!`. The returned message IDs are used as arguments to other mail functions to indicate which message should be acted on.

To retrieve the actual contents of a message specified by the ID held in the message ID array of a session object, the `mailReadMessage()` function is used. The syntax is

`mailSession.mailReadMessage( MessageID, MailMessage, ReadOption, Mark)`

The `MailMessage` parameter is a variable declared of type `mailMessage`. `mailMessage` is a MAPI structure that holds the fields listed in Table 33.2.

**TABLE 33.2**   Attributes of the `mailMessage` MAPI Structure

| Attribute | Data Type | Attribute | Data Type |
|---|---|---|---|
| ReceiptRequested | Boolean | MessageType | String |
| MessageSent | Boolean | DateReceived | String |
| Unread | Boolean | ConversationID | String |
| Subject | String | Recipient[] | mailRecipient array |
| NoteText | String | AttachmentFile[] | mailFileDescription array |

This structure's fields are populated depending on the `ReadOption` parameter, which uses the `mailReadOption` enumerated data type to control which parts of the message are retrieved. `ReadOption` can take the following values:

| Enumerated Data Type | Description |
|---|---|
| mailEntireMessage! | Obtain header, text, and attachments. |
| mailEnvelopeOnly! | Obtain header information only. |
| mailBodyAsFile! | Obtain header, text, and attachments. Treat the message text as the first attachment and store it in a temporary file. |
| mailSuppressAttach! | Obtain only the header and text. |

The `Mark` parameter is a Boolean that indicates whether the message should be marked as read (`TRUE`) in the user's inbox, or unmarked (`FALSE`).

`mailReadMessage()` returns a value of the `mailReturnCode` enumerated data type and takes one of the following values: `mailReturnSuccess!`, `mailReturnFailure!`, or `mailReturnInsufficientMemory!`.

Attachment information is stored in the `AttachmentFile` attribute of the `mailMessage` object. The `AttachmentFile` attribute is itself an object of type `mailFileDescription`, which is structured as follows:

| Attribute | Data Type |
|-----------|-----------|
| FileName | String |
| PathName | String |
| FileType | mailFileType |
| Position | Unsigned Long |

The PathName attribute holds the location of the temporary file created for the attachment. This file is created in the directory specified by the environment variable TEMP.

The FileType attribute is of the mailFileType enumerated type. The values for this enumerated type are mailAttach!, mailOLE!, and mailOLEStatic!.

If the Position attribute is 1, the attachment is placed at the beginning of the note, prefixed and suffixed by spaces. If the value of Position is greater than 1 or equal to 0, the attachment replaces the character at that position in the note.

Recipient information is stored in the Recipient attribute of the mailMessage object. The structure identifies senders and receivers. The Recipient attribute is itself an object of type mailRecipient, which is structured as follows:

| Attribute | Data Type |
|-----------|-----------|
| Name | String |
| Address | String |
| RecipientType | mailRecipientType |
| EntryID | Protected BLOB |

The RecipientType attribute is of the mailRecipientType enumerated type. The values for this enumerated type are mailTo!, mailCC!, mailOriginator!, and mailBCC!. The suffixes stand for the following:

| | |
|---|---|
| To | The recipient of the message |
| CC | The addressees receiving carbon copies of the message |
| Originator | The message sender (used only with received messages) |
| BCC (blind carbon copy) | Recipients not shown to CC and To recipients |

An example using the two functions introduced so far, mailGetMessages() and mailReadMessage(), populates a DataWindow (the control is named dw_mail) with a list of all message headers now in the user's inbox:

```
mailSession PBmailSession
mailMessage PBmailMessage
Integer li_Count, li_TotalMsgs
Long ll_Row

PBmailSession = CREATE mailSession

If PBmailSession.mailLogon() <> mailReturnSuccess! Then
   Return
End If

PBmailSession.mailGetMessages()

li_TotalMsgs = UpperBound( PBmailSession.MessageID[])

For li_Count = 1 To li_TotalMsgs
   PBmailSession.mailReadMessage( PBmailSession.MessageID[ li_Count], &
            PBmailMessage, mailEnvelopeOnly!, FALSE)
   ll_Row = dw_mail.InsertRow( 0)
" "
   dw_mail.object.message_id[ ll_Row] = PBmailSession.MessageID[ li_Count]
" "
   dw_mail.object.message_date[ ll_Row] = PBmailMessage.DateReceived""
   dw_mail.object.message_subject[ ll_Row] = Left (PBmailMessage.Subject, 40)
Next
```

## The `mailDeleteMessage()` Function

To delete a mail message from a user's inbox, use the `mailDeleteMessage()` function. The syntax is

*mailSession*`.mailDeleteMessage(` *MessageID*`)`

*MessageID* is the string value ID of the message that was previously retrieved with a call to `mailGetMessages()`.

`MailDeleteMessage()` returns a value of the `mailReturnCode` enumerated data type and takes one of the following values: `mailReturnSuccess!`, `mailReturnFailure!`, `mailReturnInsufficientMemory!`, `mailReturnInvalidMessage!`, or `mailReturnUserAbort!`.

33

Mail Enabling
PowerBuilder
Applications

# The `mailSaveMessage()` Function

If you need to save a new message or replace an existing message in the user's inbox, use the `mailSaveMessage()` function. The syntax is

*mailSession*.`mailSaveMessage(` *MessageID*, *MailMessage*)

*MessageID* is the string ID of the message to be replaced, or an empty string (`""`) if the message is to be a new one. *MailMessage* is a variable of the `mailMessage` type that has had its structure filled with the information to be saved. The message must be correctly addressed, even if it's replacing an existing message.

`mailSaveMessage()` returns a value of the `mailReturnCode` enumerated data type and takes one of the following values: `mailReturnSuccess!`, `mailReturnFailure!`, `mailReturnInsufficientMemory!`, `mailReturnInvalidMessage!`, `mailReturnUserAbort!`, or `mailReturnDiskFull!`.

In the following example, a new message is being created and addressed. This message will be sent the next time the mail system checks for messages to send:

```
mailSession PBmailSession
mailRecipient PBmailRecipient
mailMessage PbmailMessage

PBmailSession = CREATE mailSession

If PBmailSession.mailLogon() <> mailReturnSuccess! Then
   // Error Handling - unable to startup
   Return
End If


PBmailRecipient.Name = "Herbert, Malcolm"

If PBmailSession.mailResolveRecipient( PBmailRecipient) &
                        <> mailReturnSuccess! Then
MessageBox( "Address Resolution", "The address specified is invalid!.")
   Return
End If


PBmailMessage.Subject = sle_subject.Text
PBmailMessage.NoteText = mle_message.Text


PBmailMessage.Recipient[ 1] = PBmailRecipient
```

```
If PBmailSession.mailSaveMessage( "", PBmailMessage) &
                        <> mailReturnSuccess! Then
MessageBox( "New Message Creation", "The Save of the message failed.")
    Return
End If
```

## The `mailSend()` Function

To send a previously created message or to open the mail system message entry dialog, use the `mailSend()` function. The syntax is

```
mailSession.mailSend( { MailMessage})
```

If no message information is supplied, the mail system opens a dialog so that you can enter the information before sending the message.

`mailSend()` returns a value of the `mailReturnCode` enumerated data type, and takes one of the following values: `mailReturnSuccess!`, `mailReturnFailure!`, `mailReturnInsufficientMemory!`, `mailReturnLogFailure!`, `mailReturnUserAbort!`, `mailReturnDiskFull!`, `mailReturnTooManySessions!`, `mailReturnTooManyFiles!`, `mailReturnTooManyRecipients!`, `mailReturnUnknownRecipient!`, or `mailReturnAttachmentNotFound!`.

# Mail Enabling a System Error Window

As mentioned at the beginning of this chapter, one use of mail enabling is the communication of application and system errors to a development team coordinator. In this section, you learn how to build the script that can be used as part of this process.

Listing 33.1 contains a useful function that converts a mail return code, returned by all the mail functions, into a string that can then be used in a message box. This can be written as a global function or as a method for a class user object based on `MailSession`.

**LISTING 33.1.** The `MailErrorToString()` Function

```
// Parameters:
//          a_mailReturnCode      (mailReturnCode)
// Returns:
//          string                (the string representation)


Choose Case a_MailReturnCode
  Case mailReturnAccessDenied!
```

33

Mail Enabling
PowerBuilder
Applications

**LISTING 33.1.** CONTINUED

```
      Return "Access Denied"
   Case mailReturnAttachmentNotFound!
      Return "Attachment Not Found"
   Case mailReturnAttachmentOpenFailure!
      Return "Attachment Open Failure"
   Case mailReturnAttachmentWriteFailure!
      Return "Attachment Write Failure"
   //
   // ...and more and more...all possible returns
   // are not listed for brevity of this listing!
   //
   Case mailReturnUserAbort!
      Return "User Abort"
   Case Else
      Return "Other - Unknown"
End Choose
```

When building or extending your framework, you can include a global object, `gnv_App`, that's a holder for application-related objects. One of these objects contains information about the application INI file. One of the INI file's entries specifies whether the user's address book should be opened (`ls_PhoneBook`) or whether a recipient address is hard-coded (`ls_Recipient`). A number of single- and multiline edit fields are populated with error information in the `Open` event script. A window function `of_Notify()`—or, if you're using the `Error` class user object you built in Chapter 13, "The User Object Painter," the `MailError()` function—is then called to check whether mail notification should be carried out, the condition being an empty mail recipient entry in the INI file. The function is shown in Chapter 13, and as you can see, most mail functions and a few of the structures and objects are used. The only thing worthy to note is that new lines can be embedded into the note field by using the escape character (`~n`).

# Mailing a DataWindow Object

A neat little feature to add to your application is the capability to email a report or DataWindow to someone else. This is, in fact, straightforward and uses the `SaveAs()` DataWindow function.

The first step is to save the DataWindow in a Powersoft Report (PSR) file format by using the `SaveAs()` function with the `PSReport!` enumerated type, as follows:

```
dw_report.SaveAs( "datadump.psr", PSReport!, FALSE)
```

This saves a description of the DataWindow and the currently retrieved data into a file in the first directory in the path list. The third parameter (include column headings) can be TRUE or FALSE—it makes no difference to the PSR format.

When you've created the mail session and logged on, the following code is issued:

```
mailFileDescription PbmailAttachment


PBmailAttachment.FileType = mailAttach!
PBmailAttachment.PathName = "q:\reports"
PBmailAttachment.FileName = "datadump.psr"
PBmailAttachment.Position = -1


PBmailMessage.AttachmentFile[ 1] = PbmailAttachment
```

A variable of type `mailFileDescription` is created to hold the attachment file information. The type of file to be attached is normal (`mailAttach!`), and the filename used in `SaveAs()` is assigned to the `PathName` and `FileName` attributes. The attachment is in the first position (`-1` is your best bet). The file description is then assigned to the first element of the `AttachmentFile` array, after which the message is ready for transmittal.

The only step left is to tidy up the temporary file used. This needs to be done on any error conditions as well as at the end of the script:

```
FileDelete( "datadump.psr")
```

When the recipients of the message open it (providing they have set up the association in File Manager), they can simply double-click the attachment and have PowerBuilder or InfoMaker launch the Report painter and display the DataWindow pretty much as it was saved.

**33**

**Mail Enabling
PowerBuilder
Applications**

---

**Note**

You can easily add multiple attachments to a message by populating the `PBmailAttachment` structure with the next file's details and then assigning it to the next position in the `AttachmentFile[]` array.

# Summary

The MAPI functions, structures, and enumerated data types available from within PowerBuilder enable you to create mail-enabled applications to better serve end users. They can also be used to aid in the process of application deployment, tuning, and debugging by use of a mail-enabled error window. PowerBuilder doesn't tie your development to just MAPI but allows you access to other messaging providers through external functions.

# Drag-and-Drop

**34**

**CHAPTER**

Drag-and-drop is a useful technique for moving, copying, and linking objects in your application. Clicking an object and holding down the mouse button down while moving the mouse is referred to as *dragging*. When the object is moved to a specified object and the mouse button is released, that's referred to as *dropping* the object. Drag-and-drop is therefore a method of directly manipulating an object and its data using a mouse.

The most familiar example of drag-and-drop is the operating system's file management tool. In this case, you will look at the Windows Explorer in Windows 98. Explorer allows you to click a file or directory and drag it to a new location. The default behavior is to move the file/directory to a new directory location (see Figure 34.1). As you can see, the destination object (in this case, the directory) defines the action to take place. This technique can be implemented in different places in your application, such as copying information between DataWindows or providing a color palette for changing object colors.

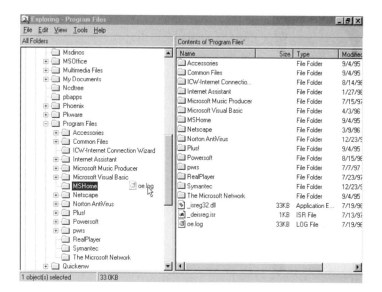

**FIGURE 34.1**
*Dragging a file in the Windows Explorer.*

# Drag-and-Drop Terminology

Before looking at how to implement drag-and-drop, you need to understand all the components that make up drag-and-drop. The two main components are the object being dragged and the target object. The object being dragged is the object on which you want to perform an action. The target object is the object on which the object being dragged is dropped and defines what processing will occur. When an object that can be dragged has been clicked and the mouse button is held, you are said to be in *drag mode*.

Just about any PowerBuilder control can be used as the dragged or target objects. The only requirement is that they must be inherited from the system class `DragObject`. To determine whether a control is derived from this class, click the System tab in the Object Browser. Right-click an entry and make sure that the Show Hierarchy option is selected. The entry for `DragObject` can be found under the `PowerObject\GraphicObject\WindowObject` hierarchy path (see Figure 34.2).

**FIGURE 34.2**

*The Object Browser system class hierarchy.*

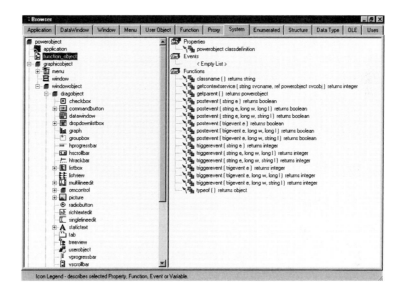

The only objects not inherited that can't be involved in the drag-and-drop process are drawing objects: lines, ovals, rectangles, and round rectangles. Because they're derived from the system class `PowerObject\GraphicObject\WindowObject\DrawObject` and not under `DragObject`, they are rendered them undraggable.

# Drag-and-Drop Guidelines

Now that you know what objects can be dragged and can be targets, it's important that you use the drag-and-drop paradigm with moderation. Drag-and-drop can be an obvious method to carry out a task in your application, but you should follow some rules to ensure its success.

It's tempting to overuse drag-and-drop in your application. Keep in mind that drag-and-drop represents an action being performed on a particular object. The correlation between the source object and the action performed by the target should be intuitive and meaningful.

**34**

**Drag-and-Drop**

After you decide on a useful purpose for implementing drag-and-drop, identify which objects will be used for the dragged object and the target. Some good candidates for a dragged object are

- A DataWindow row or column

- A Picture control representing data

- An item in a TreeView or ListView control

- An item in a list box

> **Note**
>
> Drag-and-drop shouldn't interfere with the control's normal usage. For example, a command button would be a poor choice for a dragged object because you usually click the button to start some process, not to begin a drag-and-drop session.

For the target objects, good choices might be

- A DataWindow

- A list box or drop-down list

- A Picture control representing an action

- A command button

- An item in a TreeView or ListView control

- Any object whose attributes you want to modify

If you're using pictures on the dragged or target objects, be sure to use meaningful pictures, to provide a more intuitive interface for users. Also, when you're dragging between two objects, a *drag icon* indicates that the object is in drag mode. Use a meaningful drag icon so that users know exactly what's being dragged and where it's going to be dragged to.

Finally, drag-and-drop should never be the only method to accomplish a task. A keyboard or menu option should always be provided to allow users to perform the same functionality. This way, they have more flexibility and aren't tied to a particular input device.

# Implementing Drag-and-Drop

Objects derived from the system class DragObject have several attributes, events, and functions available to them to implement drag-and-drop.

## Attributes

Two important attributes are needed in the drag-and-drop process: DragAuto and DragIcon. DragAuto indicates whether the selected control is automatically placed in drag mode when clicked. Drag mode, as discussed earlier, occurs when users click the dragged object and continue to hold down the mouse button (almost always the primary mouse button).

DragAuto is a Boolean attribute, where a value of TRUE indicates that the control is placed in drag mode when clicked. A FALSE value means that drag mode must be started through PowerScript code. Therefore, drag mode has two options: automatic and manual. When a control is specified with DragAuto set to TRUE, the control no longer responds to any Click events. More often than not, drag-and-drop is implemented with manual drag mode so that the Click events can still be used.

DragIcon is the icon used to indicate that an object is in drag mode. If no icon is specified, the default is a transparent rectangle the same size as the dragged object (DragIcon has a value of None!). Because the transparent rectangle doesn't look very professional (imagine a rectangle the size of a large DataWindow), an icon should always be specified.

> **Tip**
>
> Remember to include the icons you use in a PBR file for distribution with your executable. Otherwise, users will run into the transparent rectangles.

To specify DragAuto and DragIcon, select the object to be dragged and then select the Other tab in the Property view. The properties for Drag & Drop are located on the bottom of the Other tab (see Figure 34.3). To set drag mode to automatic, make sure that the DragAuto check box is selected. For DragIcon, you can choose from the stock icon pictures in the drop-down or specify your own ICO file.

The DragAuto property usually retains the value set at design time, but DragIcon is typically changed at runtime from within the drag-and-drop events.

**34**

Drag-and-Drop

**FIGURE 34.3**
*The drag-and-drop settings on the Other tab page.*

# Events

A `DragObject` control has defined for it four basic events: `DragDrop`, `DragEnter`, `DragLeave`, and `DragWithin`.

The most important event is `DragDrop`, which is triggered when your application is in drag mode and the primary mouse button is released when the mouse pointer is over the target object. In this event, you place the code for the target object's response to the dragged object being dropped on it.

The other three events are triggered when the application is in drag mode and the dragged object is being moved over the target object. The movement and position of the dragged object determine which event is fired:

| | |
|---|---|
| `DragEnter` | The center (also referred to as the *hot spot*) of the dragged object crosses the edge into the target object. |
| `DragLeave` | The center of the dragged object exits the target object. |
| `DragWithin` | The center of the dragged object is within the target object. |

These three events are typically used to change the dragged object's `DragIcon` attribute. If the target is a picture, it too can be changed to indicate that users can now release the mouse button.

# Functions

You need to use several functions when building a drag-and-drop application.

## Drag()

Drag() manually places an object in drag mode (in other words, DragAuto is set to FALSE). The syntax is

`control.Drag (DragMode)`

In this case, `control` is the name of the dragged object, and `DragMode` is one of the following values:

| | |
|---|---|
| Begin! | Place `control` in drag mode. |
| Cancel! | Stop drag mode but don't cause a DragDrop event. |
| End! | Stop drag mode and, if `control` is above a target object, trigger a DragDrop event. |

Drag() returns an integer, with 1 indicating success and -1 indicating a failure. This is true of all controls except for OLE controls, such as ActiveX controls, which return the following:

| Return Value | Description |
|---|---|
| 0 | Drag was successful. |
| 1 | Drag was canceled. |
| 2 | Object was moved. |
| -1 | Control was empty. |
| -9 | Unspecified error. |

Of the arguments passed to Drag(), Begin! is the most common. Typically, clicking a control and holding down the mouse button starts drag mode. It's possible to implement drag-and-drop by having users click an object, release the mouse button, and click the target object to *drag* an object. In this case, Cancel! and End! are used to end drag mode without requiring users to hold down the mouse button. Although this is possible, it's not the standard method of implementing drag-and-drop.

The Drag() function can be called from several events, the most common being Clicked and MouseMove. If the Clicked event isn't being used, simply use `control.Drag (Begin!)` to start `control` dragging. If you're using the Clicked event to perform some other type of processing, MouseMove is your best alternative.

For the selected dragged object, define a user event mapped to event ID pbm_mousemove (for more information on creating user events, see Chapter 2, "PowerBuilder 7.0 Development Environment"). Before you exit the User Events view, look at the parameters defined for MouseMove (see Figure 34.4).

**FIGURE 34.4**

*Parameters for*
pbm_mousemove.

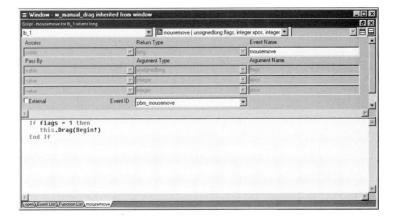

The flags parameter indicates the state of the primary mouse button when the event is triggered. A value of 1 indicates that the primary mouse button is being held down. This means that the user is moving the mouse and holding down the primary mouse button—in other words, the user is attempting to drag the object. The basic code for starting drag mode from the MouseMove event is

```
//Check to see if mouse button is down
If flags = 1 Then
   This.Drag( Begin!)
End If
```

After drag mode begins, the icon specified for the DragIcon property appears. This is all that's required for the dragged object. The rest of the processing is done in the drag events for the target object.

## DraggedObject()

DraggedObject() can be called from any drag event and returns a value indicating the control that triggered the event. The return value is of type DragObject and is actually a reference to the dragged object.

A common use of the function when called from DragEnter, DragLeave, or DragWithin is to change the DragIcon attribute. The code for the DragEnter event would be this:

```
DragObject ado_dragged

ado_dragged = source
Source.DragIcon = "openfile.ico"
```

This code is insensitive to the type of dragged object (for example, a DataWindow versus a list box) and changes the DragIcon appropriately. Coding all your drag-and-drop events like this can be dangerous because you might want to take different actions depending on the object type or particular class. The next two sections examine some functions that can be used to refer to a specific object in drag-and-drop.

## TypeOf()

This function determines the system class that a control was inherited from. In drag-and-drop, this function can be used to provide processing based on a particular object type as opposed to a specific object. The syntax is

```
ObjectName.TypeOf()
```

*ObjectName* is the object or control for which you want to know the object type. The return value is of the enumerated data type Object. An example of using TypeOf() in the DragDrop event would be to reset any object to its original values if it's dropped on the target (see Listing 34.1).

**LISTING 34.1**   Generic Control Reset Processing Using the TypeOf() Function

```
SingleLineEdit lsle_drag
DataWindow ldw_drag
DropDownListBox lddlb_drag

Choose Case source.Typeof()
   Case SingleLineEdit!
      sle_drag = source
      sle_drag.text = ""
   Case DataWindow!
      dw_drag = source
      dw_drag.Reset()
      dw_drag.InsertRow(1)
   Case DropDownListBox!
      ddlb_drag = source
      ddlb_drag.SelectItem(1)
End Choose
```

In Listing 34.1, the object type is determined and then the dragged object is set equal to a variable of the appropriate object type. This is done so that you have full access to the dragged object's attributes and functions. Otherwise, you're limited to the attributes and properties common to DragObject (such as X, Y, Width, and Height).

TypeOf() is useful when you're just concerned with receiving a generic reference to identify a particular system class. In the next section, you see how to directly reference a specific class instance.

34

Drag-and-Drop

## ClassName()

The function ClassName() retrieves the class (the name) of the object specified. Its syntax is

```
ControlName.ClassName()
```

*ControlName* is the control you want to know the class for—in this case, the dragged object. ClassName() returns a string with the name of the control or an empty string to indicate that an error occurred. The function could be used this way:

```
Choose Case source.ClassName()
    Case "dw_customer_list"
       //Do something
    Case "dw_customer_detail"
       //Do something else
    Case "sle_id"
       //Do this
End Choose
```

An alternative method of direct reference can be written like this:

```
Choose Case Source
    Case dw_customer_list
       //Delete a customer
    Case dw_customer_detail
       //Add new data
    Case sle_id
       //reset value
End Choose
```

The benefit of these two methods is that you don't have to declare separate object variables to access the control's attributes and functions. The downside is that you're hard-coding the control name into your script, which makes maintenance more involved.

Depending on the application's complexity and the extent to which object-oriented development is adhered to, you might consider using a nonvisual user object. If you're dragging between DataWindows, the business object can be structured to include instance variables for each column, array of column values, and function used to set and extract the column data. Although this would follow a more object-oriented approach by encapsulating the drag-and-drop functionality within the user object, it often overcomplicates the process and has unnecessary overhead. Also, in most drag-and-drop implementations, the target object is either directly related to the dragged object or the script is generic enough that it cares only about the object's type.

# Drag-and-Drop Examples

The rest of this chapter looks at examples of implementing drag-and-drop in your application.

## The Trash Can

Implementing a trash can for data deletion is one of the most common uses of drag-and-drop. In this section, you create a trash can similar to the Windows 95/98 Recycle Bin or the Macintosh trash can. The w_delete_contacts window contains three controls: a DataWindow displaying a list of contacts, a picture control displaying the trash can, and a command button for closing the window (see Figure 34.5).

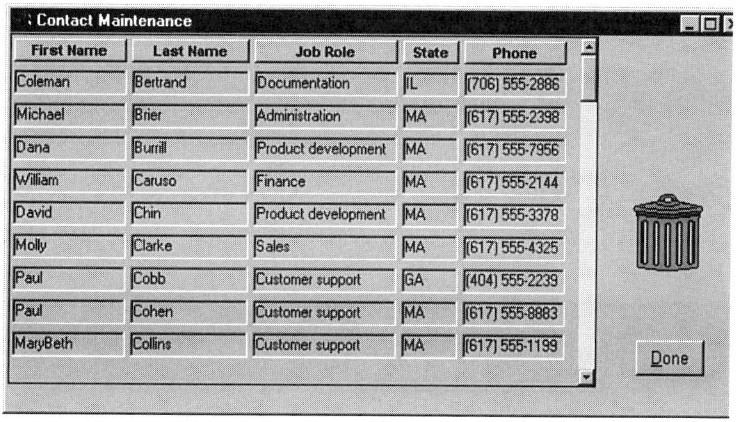

FIGURE 34.5

*The trash can window.*

FIGURE 34.5

*The trash can window.*

The purpose of the window is to display all contacts and allow users to delete a customer by dragging a row to the trash can. The DataWindow is the object being dragged, and the picture control is the target. The window has one instance string variable defined, is_dragicon, which holds the value of the DragIcon attribute of the DataWindow. Drag mode is started in the MouseMove event of the DataWindow using the Drag() function.

The picture control, p_trash, has scripts coded for the DragEnter, DragLeave, DragDrop, and RButtonDown events.

The DragEnter event for p_trash (see Listing 34.2) captures the initial value of the DragIcon. This is done in case users drag back outside the trash can, and DragIcon needs to be reset. The icon is then changed to an open folder to indicate that the trash can is the target object.

**LISTING 34.2** The `DragEnter` Event for the Picture Control `p_trash`

```
//Capture the initial value for the DragIcon
is_dragicon = source.DragIcon
//Change the icon to an open folder
source.DragIcon = "folder.ico"
```

Figure 34.6 shows the effect on the mouse pointer due to the `DragEnter` event.

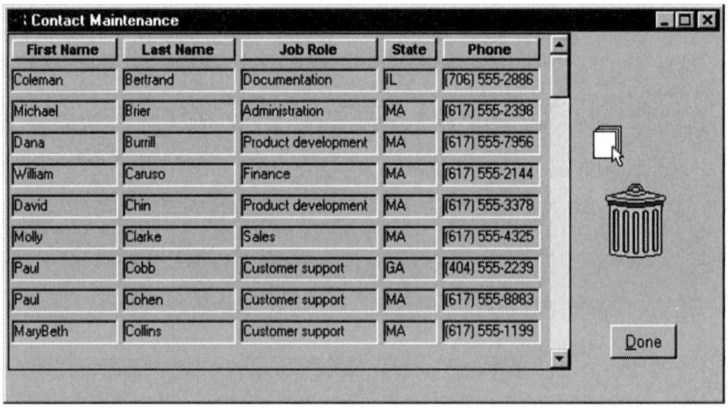

**FIGURE 34.6**

*Dragging a row to the trash can.*

The `DragLeave` event for `p_trash` in the following code resets `DragIcon` back to the initial icon displayed before dragging over the trash can:

```
//Change the DragIcon property back to initial value
source.DragIcon = is_dragicon
```

When the dragged DataWindow is dropped on the trash can (see Listing 34.3), the `DragDrop` event is triggered. In this event, the dragged object is identified; if it is the DataWindow d_contacts, the current row is deleted. The trash can picture is changed to indicate that at least one row is flagged for deletion. Figure 34.7 shows the enlarged trash can indicating a deleted row.

**LISTING 34.3** `DragDrop` for `p_trash`

```
If source = dw_contacts then
    //Delete the current row
    dw_contacts.DeleteRow(0)
    //Change the picture to a full trash can
    this.PictureName = "fatcan.bmp"
    //Change the DragIcon back to the initial value
```

**LISTING 34.3** CONTINUED

```
    source.DragIcon = is_dragicon
End If
```

**FIGURE 34.7**

*A row dropped in the trash can.*

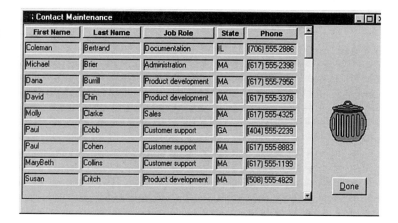

As a final touch, right-clicking the trash can displays a pop-up menu giving the options to empty the trash can (update the database) or undo the changes (restore deleted row). This is implemented with the RButtonDown event, as shown in Listing 34.4. Figure 34.8 shows the pop-up menu.

**LISTING 34.4** RButtonDown for p_trash

```
m_drag_trash lm_popup
//Create a popup menu for clearing trash and undoing deletions
lm_popup = Create m_drag_trash
lm_popup.m_edit.PopMenu( Parent.PointerX(), Parent.PointerY())
```

The DragEnter and DragLeave events are used to toggle DragIcon to indicate that the picture control is the target object. The DragDrop event determines whether the drag object is the DataWindow, dw_contacts. If it is, the current row is deleted, the trash can is made wider to indicate that it contains data, and DragIcon is reset for the next time drag mode is started. The last event, RButtonDown, captures a right-click on p_trash and displays a pop-up menu, allowing users to delete all data in the trash can or undo all changes.

In addition to the scripts written for p_trash, the DragEnter and DragLeave events were coded for the command button cb_close to indicate that it's not a valid target. The code is identical to that for p_trash, except that a different icon is specified. Figure 34.9 shows the result.

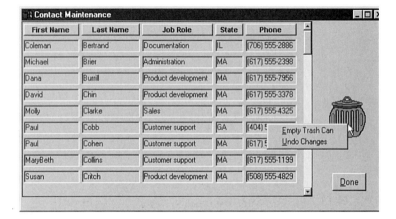

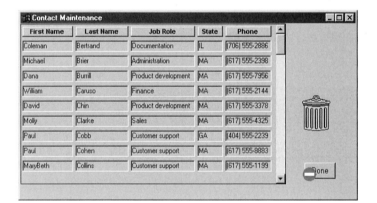

# The Color Palette

The trash can drag-and-drop example provides a means of modifying data. In another
example, you use drag-and-drop to modify an object's attributes. The color palette is used
to modify an object's color attributes (see Figure 34.10). The color palette allows you to
change an object's foreground and/or background color.

The color palette is composed of two PowerBuilder objects: a standard static text user
object, u_colour_square, and a window, w_colour_pallet. The window contains 16
instances of the user object, each with a different background color. DragAuto is set to TRUE
on all user objects, and DragIcon is the same for each user object. The name of each user
object is st_color_##, where ## is a sequential number from 1 to 16. w_colour_pallet
has a private instance Boolean variable defined for it (ib_FG) that has an initial value of

TRUE. This variable indicates whether the background or foreground will change on the target.

**FIGURE 34.10**
*The color palette.*

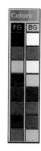

The window also contains two additional static text boxes. One is clicked to indicate that you want to change the object's foreground color; the other is clicked to indicate a change in the background color. The Clicked events for these static texts are in Listings 34.5 and 34.6.

**LISTING 34.5**  The Clicked Event for the Foreground Static Text

```
this.BackColor = RGB( 0, 0, 0)// Black
this.TextColor = RGB( 255, 255, 255)// White
st_bg.BackColor = RGB( 192, 192, 192)// Light Gray
st_bg.TextColor = RGB( 0, 0, 0)// Black
ib_FG = TRUE
```

**LISTING 34.6**  The Clicked Event for the Background Static Text

```
this.BackColor = RGB( 0, 0, 0)// Black
this.TextColor = RGB( 255, 255, 255)// White
st_fg.BackColor = RGB( 192, 192, 192)// Light Gray
st_fg.TextColor = RGB( 0, 0, 0)// Black
ib_FG = FALSE
```

This code indicates whether you want to change the target's foreground or background color. Whichever is selected will have a black background with white lettering, whereas the other static text will have a light gray background with black lettering. As well as visually indicate to users which option is selected, the value of ib_FG is changed.

Because ib_FG is a private variable, w_colour_pallet must provide a means for developers to access its value to determine whether to change the target object's foreground or background color. This is done by declaring a window function called wf_textcolor() and is defined as

**34**

**Drag-and-Drop**

```
//No arguments
//Returns integer
Return ib_FG
```

When this is defined, you can code the DragDrop event for the target object. If the target object is a window, the event should be coded, as in Listing 34.7.

**LISTING 34.7**   The DragDrop Event for a Window

```
statictext drag_text
//Determine if the dragged object is one of the color pallet static texts
If Left(Lower(source.ClassName()),8) = "st_color" then
   drag_text = source
   //Change the windows backcolor
   this.BackColor = drag_text.BackColor
End If
```

If you're changing the color scheme of a control, you must differentiate between changing the foreground and the background colors according to the value of ib_FG. Listing 34.8 shows the code needed to change the colors for a single-line edit.

**LISTING 34.8**   The DragDrop Event for a Single-Line Edit

```
statictext drag_text
// Determine if the dragged object is one of the color pallet static texts
If Left(Lower(source.ClassName()),8) = "st_color" then
   drag_text = source
   //Check the status of ib_FG to determine whether to change foreground
   // or background
   If w_colour_pallet.wf_textcolor() Then
      //Change the foreground color
      this.TextColor = drag_text.BackColor
   Else
      //Change the background color
      this.BackColor = drag_text.BackColor
   End If
End If
```

The same code can be used for most other standard PowerBuilder controls, with the only modification being the assignment of the dragged object. The only control that must be addressed differently is the DataWindow. Changing the background changes the whole background color of the DataWindow. Changing the foreground changes all objects' color attributes. The background modification is relatively simple, but changing all objects' foreground colors requires that you know the names of all the objects in the DataWindow. To accomplish this, create a global function to allow interrogation of a DataWindow (see Listing 34.9).

**LISTING 34.9**  DataWindow Object Interrogation Using the `f_list_objects()` Function

```
//ARGUMENTS:
// adw_ToActOn      (the datawindow control passed by value)
// as_ObjectList    (a string array passed by reference)
// as_ObjectType    (a string passed by value)
// as_ColumnType    (a string passed by value)
// as_Band          (a string passed by value)

String ls_Objects, ls_AnObject
Boolean lb_NotEOS = TRUE, lb_FoundEOS = FALSE // EOS = End Of String
Integer li_ObjectCount, li_StartPos=1, li_TabPos, li_Count = 0

ls_Objects = adw_ToActOn.Describe( "datawindow.objects")

li_TabPos = Pos( ls_Objects, "~t", li_StartPos)

Do While lb_NotEOS
   ls_AnObject = Mid( ls_Objects, li_StartPos,( li_TabPos - li_StartPos))
   If ( adw_ToActOn.Describe( ls_AnObject + ".type") = as_ObjectType Or &
         as_ObjectType = "*") And &
         ( adw_ToActOn.Describe (ls_AnObject + ".band") = as_Band &
         Or as_Band = "*") And &
         ( Left( adw_ToActOn.Describe( ls_AnObject + ".coltype"), 5) &
         = Left( as_ColumnType, 5) Or as_ColumnType = "*") Then
      li_Count ++
      as_ObjectList[li_Count] = ls_AnObject
   End If
   li_StartPos = li_TabPos + 1
   li_TabPos = Pos (ls_Objects, "~t", li_StartPos)
   If li_TabPos = 0 And Not lb_FoundEOS Then
      li_TabPos = Len (ls_Objects) + 1
      lb_FoundEOS = TRUE
   ElseIf lb_FoundEOS Then
      lb_NotEOS = FALSE
```

**34**

**Drag-and-Drop**

**LISTING 34.9**   CONTINUED

```
   End If
Loop

Return li_Count
```

This function returns a list of the DataWindow objects using the `Describe()` function. You can specify which objects you want to filter, thus removing unwanted object types from the final list. If you want all objects returned, you must pass an asterisk (*) to the function. After an object passes through the filter (the first `If` statement), it's placed into a string array that's returned from the function.

After you create the means to retrieve all the DataWindow's objects, you are ready to code the `DragDrop` event for the DataWindow (see Listing 34.10).

**LISTING 34.10**   `DragDrop` for a `DataWindow Control`

```
statictext drag_text
string ls_PrimaryObjects[]
integer li_PrimaryObjects, li_count
If Left(Lower(source.ClassName()),8) = "st_color" then
   drag_text = source
   If w_colour_pallet.wf_textcolor() Then
      //Fill array with all objects on the DW
      li_PrimaryObjects = f_list_objects( this, ls_PrimaryObjects, "*","*","*")
      //Change the foreground color
      For li_count = 1 to li_PrimaryObjects
         this.Modify( ls_PrimaryObjects [li_count] + ".Color = " + &
         String( drag_text.BackColor))
      Next
   Else
      //Change the background color
      this.object.datawindow.color = drag_text.BackColor
   End If
End If
```

An alternative placement of this code would be in the user object as a function that accepts the object type as an argument.

# Drag-and-Drop in a TreeView Control

The introduction of the TreeView in PowerBuilder opened up some new options for when you're developing applications. Because users are familiar with the uses and functionality of TreeViews, they quickly became highly desired controls in applications. TreeViews display data in a hierarchical or outline format (see Figure 34.11).

**FIGURE 34.11**

*An example of a TreeView control.*

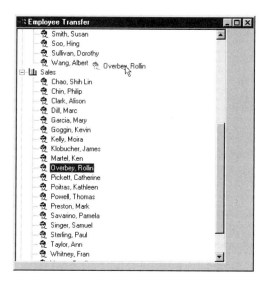

A common request with this interface is to have the capability to move or transfer information from one branch in the TreeView to another. One way to implement this functionality is to use drag-and-drop.

After the TreeView control is populated (see Chapter 11, "Advanced Controls," for more information on how to do this), you need to code a few events and set some properties to implement drag-and-drop.

One property that you need to be sure to set when using drag-and-drop on a TreeView control is DisableDragDrop. When you initially place a TreeView on a window, this property is initially set to TRUE, which means that you can't perform drag-and-drop. The easiest way to change this value is to bring up the properties for the TreeView control and uncheck the Disable Drag Drop check box.

> **Note**
>
> In most cases, PowerBuilder 7.0 labels the properties for objects in the Property view to reflect the actual property name that can be referenced in PowerScript. In the case of the `DisableDragDrop` property, the property view labels this as `DisableDragAndDrop`. In lieu of this, remember to continue to reference the `DisableDragDrop` property in your code.

After you enable drag-and-drop, you might want to specify the `DragIcon` and whether you want the TreeView's `DragAuto` property to be `TRUE` on the Drag & Drop section of the Other tab page (refer to Figure 34.3).

As with most controls, most processing occurs in the `DragDrop` event. The difference is that, in this case, the TreeView control is the source *and* the target object. The other difference is that the TreeView control provides two additional events for use with drag-and-drop (these events are also used with the ListView control):

- `BeginDrag` occurs at the start of the actual dragging process. This event lets you provide up-front process checking before you allow users to move any `TreeViewItem`. Uses would include restricting access to drag data based on security, allowing only certain items to be moved, and providing visual feedback to users indicating drag-and-drop is in progress (for example, displaying a message to the MicroHelp).

- `BeginRightDrag` is triggered at the start of the drag process when using the right mouse button.

In this example, users can transfer employees from one department to another. In the `BeginDrag` event (see Listing 34.11), a check is performed to ensure that only employees are being dragged. If users try to drag a department, the drag process is canceled.

**LISTING 34.11**  The `BeginDrag` Event for `tv_emp`

```
treeviewitem ltvi_data
this.GetItem (handle, ltvi_data)
// check that only employees (level 2) are being dragged
If ltvi_data.Level <> 2 Then
   This.Drag(Cancel!)
Else
   // Save the handle of the item being dragged
   il_DragSource = handle
End If
```

`BeginDrag` has one event argument, `handle`, which is a Long data type that contains a reference to the item a user is trying to drag. After calling the `GetItem()` function to populate a variable of type `TreeViewItem`, you need to check the level in the TreeView hierarchy to see whether the item being dragged is a department (`Level` = 1) or an employee (`Level` = 2). If the dragged `TreeViewItem` isn't an employee, cancel the drag process. If it's an employee, save the item handle in an instance variable, `il_DragSource`, which will be used in the `DragDrop` event.

The `DragDrop` event of the TreeView control performs the deletion of the dragged item and reinserts it under the new department (see Listing 34.12).

**LISTING 34.12**   The `DragDrop` Event of `tv_emp`

```
long ll_newitem, ll_parent
treeviewitem ltvi_target, ltvi_source
//Make sure all handles are valid
If this.GetItem(handle, ltvi_target) = -1 Then Return
If this.GetItem(il_dragsource, ltvi_source) = -1 Then Return
// First delete the first item from the TreeView
this.DeleteItem(il_dragsource)
//check to see what level got dropped on
Choose Case ltvi_target.Level
   Case 1 //dropped on a department
      // Insert the item under the department
      ll_newitem = this.InsertItemSort( handle, ltvi_source)
   Case 2 //dropped on an employee
      //Get a reference to the parent
      ll_parent = this.FindItem( ParentTreeItem!, handle)
      ll_newitem = this.InsertItemSort( ll_parent, ltvi_source)
End Choose
// Select the new item
this.SelectItem(ll_newitem)
```

The `GetItem()` functions ensure that the references to the target item, `handle`, and the source item, `il_DragSource`, are both valid. After populating `TreeViewItems` from the target and source handles, delete the dragged item by using the `DeleteItem()` function. To insert the item in its new location, you first need to figure out which level in the TreeView (1=department, 2=employee) the item was dropped on. If the item was dropped on level 1, insert it directly under the target item. If the dragged item was dropped on an employee, you don't want to insert under the employee, but rather the employee's parent (in other words, the department). To do this, use the `FindItem()` function to get a reference to the target object's parent and then insert the item there. The last step is just for user convenience—selecting the newly inserted item.

# Dragging Between DataWindows

A useful implementation of drag-and-drop is moving data from one DataWindow to another. Imagine how easy it would be for your users to click a row in one DataWindow, drag the data, and have it inserted into another DataWindow.

The window w_orders contains two DataWindows: a list of products and a sales order form. The product list, d_products, is populated with all valid company products by retrieving data from a table. The sales order form DataWindow, d_sales_order, initially has no rows in it. When users want to order a particular product, they click the product description and drag the product over to the sales order form. When the product is dropped on the order form, a new line is inserted into d_sales_order, and the product ID, description, and unit price are filled in. Users can then enter a quantity, which is summed into the total cost (see Figure 34.12).

**FIGURE 34.12**
*Sales order form insertion.*

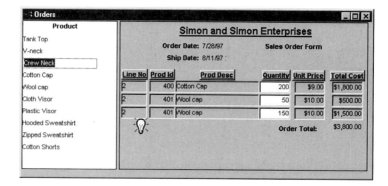

The code follows the same pattern as many of the other examples in this chapter. Listing 34.13 shows the DragDrop event.

**LISTING 34.13**   The DragDrop Event for d_sales_order

```
long newnum, currow
//Make sure the products DataWindow is being dragged
If source = dw_product Then
    //Insert a new row
    newnum = this.InsertRow(0)
    currow = dw_product.GetRow()
    //Copy the information from the product DataWindow
```

**LISTING 34.13** CONTINUED

```
    this.SetItem(newnum,"prod_id",dw_product.GetItemNumber&
    (currow, "id"))
    this.SetItem(newnum,"prod_desc",dw_product.GetItemString&
    (currow, "description"))
    this.SetItem(newnum,"unit_price",dw_product.GetItemNumber&
    (currow, "unit_price"))
End If
```

An alternative method of moving data from one DataWindow to another is by using the RowsCopy() and RowsMove() functions, but only if they share the same resultset.

# Dragging the Current Date and Time

Requirements vary from application to application, and a constant challenge for developers is to implement the various requirements in unique, intuitive, and efficient ways. One requirement frequently requested in applications is to capture the current date or date and time for a particular data capture record. One implementation of drag-and-drop can help streamline this task.

This particular implementation, included in the w_drag_time window in the code examples, consists of a picture object and a DataWindow (see Figure 34.13). During runtime, rather than have users type the date or date and time, they can just drag the picture object to the DataWindow and drop it on the column and row desired. If the column is of type date or date/time, it will be populated with the current date or date and time.

**FIGURE 34.13**

*Current date and time drag.*

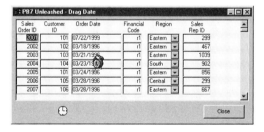

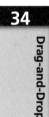

One benefit of this implementation is that it requires the coding of only the DataWindow's DragDrop event. Another required step is to set the DragAuto property of picture object to TRUE. The example of the DragDrop code is in Listing 34.14.

**LISTING 34.14** The `DragDrop` **Event for** `dw_orders`

```
string ls_Class, ls_ColType, ls_ColName
DateTime ldtm_CurrDate


ls_Class = source.ClassName()

CHOOSE CASE Left( ls_Class, 2)
   CASE "p_"
   // Get the current column Name
ls_ColName = dwo.name

   // set the current datetime
   ldtm_CurrDate = DateTime( Today(), Now())

   // If the object is not on a column, then just return
   If ls_ColName = "datawindow" then RETURN

   // Get the column type
   ls_ColType = dwo.ColType
   // if the type is date or datetime, then get the system time and
   // place it in the current column
   CHOOSE CASE ls_ColType
      CASE "datetime"
         This.SetItem( row, ls_ColName, ldtm_CurrDate)
      CASE "date"
         this.SetItem( row, ls_ColName, Date (ldtm_CurrDate))
      CASE ELSE
         RETURN
   END CHOOSE

END CHOOSE
```

This useful implementation of drag-and-drop would give your users immediate gratification by combining intuitive functionality with a time-saving feature.

# Summary

Drag-and-drop is an application development technique that follows the object-to-action metaphor. In this chapter, you learned about the components needed to implement drag-and-drop and some guidelines about when and where to use it. By using the examples provided, you have a basis for developing sophisticated drag-and-drop-enabled applications.

# 35

# Animation, Sound, and Multimedia

## CHAPTER

When an application is near completion, developers commonly spend a little time adding some interesting features. This can include the construction of some type of hidden "signature," such as displaying the developer's name in a fireworks presentation. A standard and fun way to accomplish this in an application is to use some sort of animation. Animation consists of changing pictures, moving objects, or any other type of visual treat that goes beyond the functionality of the base system. Not only is this typically fun for developers to create, but end users also often enjoy discovering and playing with the different features. Animation can also add value to your application by drawing attention to an object on a window, and it's useful with drag-and-drop.

Using sound in an application can be fun as well as informative for users. Only a few years ago, animation and sound were about as complex as Windows applications got. With the ever-growing speed of processors, the rise of the Internet, and increasing support for multimedia in hardware and software, that's no longer the case. Users today expect a sophisticated interface that seamlessly provides visual and audio cues to aid them in their work.

This chapter shows several different techniques for creating animation, enabling sound, and implementing multimedia in your PowerBuilder applications.

# Picture Animation

Probably the most common use of animation in an application is to make a picture seem to come to life to indicate that processing is taking place. This can be accomplished in several different ways, depending on where you want the picture to be changing (such as a toolbar icon, picture control, or mouse pointer). The basic concept of picture animation is to use an object that contains a picture, and then at runtime change the `Picture` attribute of that object. Before you get too far into planning your picture animation, you must decide what pictures you are going to use.

PowerBuilder 7.0 now allows GIF and JPEG files to be displayed anywhere a bitmap can be displayed. The picture and picture button controls can also display animated GIF files.

If you aren't sure what picture to use in your application, you can look for one in several places. PowerBuilder comes with a series of stock icons for toolbars (available through the Menu painter) and images with its sample applications. If you can't find what you want there, explore the directories of other Windows applications and see whether you can find some (for instance, \Windows\MORICONS.DLL). You can also purchase icon and bitmap libraries or use a third-party tool such as Snag-It to perform screen captures.

The last option for determining a picture for animation is to design and create your own. As with the icon and bitmap libraries, you can use a number of tools to create pictures. The most accessible tool for a PowerBuilder developer is the Microsoft Paint image editor that ships with Windows (MSPAINT.EXE). Also, a large number of freeware and shareware image editors are available on the Internet. You can use these to manipulate an existing picture to suit your needs (which is especially useful if you aren't artistically inclined or are just impatient), or you can create a brand-new one (see Figure 35.1).

**FIGURE 35.1**
*The Microsoft Paint image editor.*

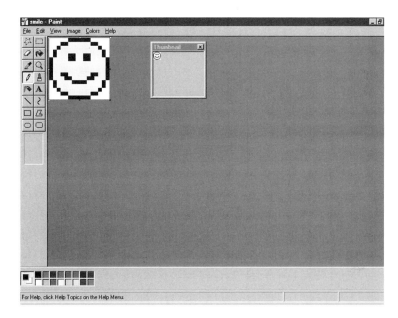

Typically, you need a series of different pictures with subtle differences in each picture to give the appearance that the picture is animated. Determine the initial picture and then use an editor (such as Microsoft Paint) to change the picture and save it to a new picture file. After you do this, you can begin to implement the picture animation.

## Toolbar Icons

You can use a couple of methods to manipulate the pictures in the toolbars associated with an MDI application. The easiest method is to specify a Picture and a Down Picture (when the button appears pressed) for the toolbar icon in the Menu painter (see Figure 35.2). At runtime, whenever users click the toolbar icon, the picture changes from the up icon to the down icon and then back again (see Figure 35.3).

**FIGURE 35.2**

*Using the Toolbar tab page to specify different pictures for an icon's up and down states.*

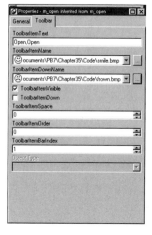

**FIGURE 35.3**

*The up and down pictures in the toolbar.*

**Note**

Unfortunately, if your users decide that they want the Show Text option on, PowerBuilder won't display the down picture.

This is the easiest way to incorporate animation into your application because everything is done during design time. The only limitation to this method is that it's initiated by user interaction. Users must click the toolbar icon to see anything happen. It's even more interesting to have the toolbar change without users doing anything. To implement this type of functionality, you need to change the `ToolbarItemName` attribute of the associated menu object via your code. This requires no user interaction.

For example, you can display a face on the toolbar that's cycled through to show a smile, no expression, and a frown. The first thing you need is a face bitmap. The bitmap (SMILE.BMP) in this example was created by using the Microsoft Paint image editor (16 × 16 pixels) with two additional bitmaps (NONE.BMP and FROWN.BMP). You first associate these pictures with the menu toolbar (SMILE.BMP will be the default), and then you're ready to write the code.

# Timers

Another key ingredient to make the application animation work effectively is to use the `Timer` event. With PowerBuilder and animation, you will need to rely extensively on a window's `Timer` event and the `Timer()` function. The `Timer()` function triggers a window's `Timer` event at the interval specified. The `Timer()` function takes the number of seconds you want between `Timer` events, and optionally the window name (the current window by default). The number of seconds that can be specified ranges from 0 to 65. A zero interval turns off the timer so that `Timer` events are no longer executed.

> **Note**
>
> The smallest time frame between time events is .055 ($\frac{1}{18}$) seconds, which is a Windows limitation.

When the `Timer()` function is called, PowerBuilder triggers the `Timer` event for the specified window and resets the timer. When the timer interval is reached, PowerBuilder again executes the `Timer` event. This continues to occur until `Timer(0)` is coded to turn off the timer.

The timer is useful with animation because it lets you change the attributes of an object constantly (in this case, the object is the picture on the toolbar). See how you can use the timer with changing the toolbar icon.

## The Timer and the Toolbar

Because the `Timer` event is the heart of the code, look at the code you need here. Remember that the toolbar works only for MDI applications, so this code is in the MDI frame's `Timer` event. Declare an integer instance variable (`ii_toolbar`) with an initial value of 1. This is used to determine which picture is now displayed and which picture will be displayed next. Each of the three bitmaps is associated with a value of `ii_toolbar`. Use a `Choose...Case` statement to determine the value and swap the pictures in and out:

```
Choose Case ii_Toolbar
   Case 1
      m_frame.m_file.m_open.m_report.toolbaritemname = "none.bmp"
      ii_Toolbar = 2
   Case 2
      m_frame.m_file.m_open.m_report.toolbaritemname = "frown.bmp"
      ii_Toolbar = 3
```

```
   Case 3
      m_frame.m_file.m_open.m_report.toolbaritemname = "smile.bmp"
      ii_Toolbar = 1
End Choose
```

To reference the `ToolbarItemName` attribute for the menu, you must fully qualify the menu name. The bitmap must also be in the directory from which the application is being run or in your search path. At runtime, you can include these in your EXE or PBD/DLLs via a PBR. By changing the value of `ii_toolbar`, you change the picture displayed to users.

The only other code necessary is in the `Open` event of the MDI frame window. In that event, you need to trigger the `Timer` event using the `Timer()` function. For example, the following code triggers the `Timer` event for the MDI frame window every half-second:

```
Timer(0.5, This)
```

Although animation can be fun, not all users are amused by icons changing onscreen. Some find it distracting; as a result, always provide a menu item to turn off the animation. The following code stops the `Timer` event from being executed:

```
Timer( 0)
```

## Picture Controls and Picture Buttons

Many times you don't want to change the icon on a toolbar. Using picture controls and picture buttons provides an alternative. Of the two controls, the picture control is more prevalent in animated applications. The same logic used with the toolbars is used for both controls. The only difference is that the attribute to change for the picture control and picture button is `PictureName`. Using a picture control on an About box is common, and having a changing picture adds a little extra excitement.

## Window Icon Animation

If you don't want to place any potentially distracting animation in the application workspace, consider animating the window's icon when it's minimized to the Windows desktop.

As for toolbars and picture controls, the basic premise of swapping pictures and using timers holds true. The code for the window `Timer` event would be as follows:

```
Choose Case ii_Picture
   Case 1
      This.Icon = "face1.ico"
      ii_Picture = 2
   Case 2
```

```
      This.Icon = "face2.ico"
      ii_Picture = 3
   Case 3
      This.Icon = "face3.ico"
      ii_Picture = 4
   Case 4
      This.Icon = "face0.ico"
      ii_Picture = 1
End Choose
```

The variable `ii_Picture` is again an instance integer variable initialized to a value of 1. The main difference between the previous examples and this one is in how the `Timer` event is triggered. Because you want the picture to change only when the window is minimized to the desktop, you need to find out when users have minimized the current window. This is accomplished through the window's `Resize` event:

```
If This.WindowState = Minimized! Then
   Timer(1)
Else
   Timer(0)
End If
```

When users change the window's size, this code checks to see whether they chose to minimize the window. The valid values for the window attribute `WindowState` are `Maximized!`, `Minimized!`, and `Normal!`. When `WindowState` is equal to `Minimized!`, the `Timer` event is triggered every second. If users set the window to anything but minimized, the timer is turned off until the next time the window is minimized.

# Drag-and-Drop

The capability to drag an object (such as a filename or a record in a DataWindow) and drop it on a picture of a trash can is common in many applications. When the dragged object is released on the trash can, fire shoots out of the top of the trash can and the dragged object is consumed (which translates into a deleted record or file). Although this technique might be disheartening for many, it isn't magic—it's a simple case of animation combined with drag-and-drop techniques. For more in-depth coverage of drag-and-drop, see Chapter 34, "Drag-and-Drop."

# Object Movement

All the previously discussed examples use an object or control that has a constant location onscreen. All you've done is change the picture being viewed. In addition to providing this functionality, you can code additional scripts to manipulate the location/size of objects to give the appearance that the objects themselves are moving across a window.

## Moving Pictures

A fun way to use animation in your application is to write a script that's triggered only when a specific series of events occurs (usually something that's not a common functionality in the system). For example, double-clicking a static text control in an About box or on the window itself could be the event that triggers the animation. This is a good choice because users might accidentally stumble across this hidden functionality and not be sure exactly what they did. When users figure out what they did to activate your script, they will probably tell other users. It seems like an easy way to get your name out in a positive light with users if you include it in your application. (First make sure that your company doesn't frown on such things before you implement this!)

Place a picture control on your window and associate the desired picture. Because you don't want users to see the picture until they trigger the event with the animation script (such as DoubleClicked), set the Visible attribute to FALSE at design time. Access the script for which you want the animation to be triggered and decide what you want the script to do.

You probably want the picture to move around the window and then display a message (maybe your name). Your initial thought on how to accomplish this is probably to change the picture's X and Y attributes to move the picture in increments across the screen. You can do it that way, but the results might be less than satisfactory. To demonstrate this for yourself, create a window with a picture control and a static text control. Place the static text control in the middle to top half of the window and the picture control on the top left. To have the picture control move around the static text control, write the following script for the DoubleClicked event of the window:

```
Integer li_x,li_y
li_x = p_1.X
li_y = p_1.Y


Do While p_1.X < (This.Width - 250)
   p_1.X = p_1.X + 1
Loop
```

```
Do While p_1.Y < (This.Height / 2)
   p_1.Y = p_1.Y + 1
Loop

Do While p_1.X > li_x
   p_1.x = p_1.X - 1
Loop

Do While p_1.Y > li_y
   p_1.y = p_1.Y - 1
Loop
```

## Note

The same thing can be accomplished with the Move() function to specify the X and Y coordinates. When you run the window by using the Move() function, the picture doesn't paint crisply across the window. This is because the window must be repainted every time the picture control is moved. PowerBuilder actually re-creates a small window with the picture in it for each successive change.

To avoid the flickering encountered with the Move() function, use the PowerScript Draw() function. This function takes two arguments: the X and Y coordinates of where the image is to be drawn. The Draw() function moves the picture much more quickly and cleanly by drawing directly on the window. The Draw() doesn't change the actual position of the picture control; rather, it just displays the control's picture at the position specified in the function. The function does, however, leave the image at the specified location. To avoid leaving trailing pieces of different images across the screen, move the image in small increments so that the next image covers up the prior image.

## Tip

Make the background of your picture image the same color as the background of the window; otherwise, you will leave a trail across the window. You can also avoid this by having a second picture control the same color as the window background moving after the first picture control. Any color trail left by the first picture control will be overlaid by the second control.

**35**

Animation,
Sound, and
Multimedia

A common example of this sort of animation that you've probably seen is a starship that flies across the window (see Figure 35.4). Now incorporate the starship example in PowerBuilder and add some enhancements.

**FIGURE 35.4**

*The flying starship.*

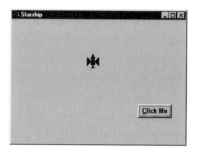

At design time, the actual location of the picture control is with the top of the control aligned with the top of the window. (This is where you want the picture control at the end.) The picture control and a static text control both have their Visible attributes set to FALSE. The Click Me command button contains the first part of the code that moves the picture control:

```
Long ll_Vertical = 880
Do Until ll_Vertical = 0
   ll_Vertical = ll_Vertical - 1
   p_starship.Draw( 750, ll_Vertical)
Loop
p_starship.PictureName = "destroy.bmp"
p_starship.Visible = TRUE
```

The variable ll_Vertical is the Y coordinate if the bottom of the picture control is aligned at the bottom of the window. When you specify this as the starting position, the starship begins at the bottom of the window; through each pass of the Do...Until loop, the vertical position decreases by one. The starship will fly to the top of the screen until its Y coordinate equals zero (aligned with the top of the window).

After the starship moves to the top of the screen, the picture is changed from the original, STARSHIP.BMP, to DESTROY.BMP. This picture shows the starship bursting into flames, and then the picture control is made visible.

To add extra functionality, add the following code to the Clicked event of the command button:

```
Integer li_Count, li_Index
```

```
// Flash the window's background colors
For li_Count = 1 To 30
   Parent.BackColor = RGB( 46, 46, 46)
   Parent.BackColor = RGB( 0, 0, 0)
   li_Index = li_Index + 1
Next

p_starship.PictureName = "rubble.bmp"
st_unleashed.Visible   = TRUE

For li_Index = 1 To 200
   FlashWindow( Handle( Parent), TRUE)
Next
```

The background color of the window is flashed by cycling through a loop 30 times, and then the picture control image is changed to RUBBLE.BMP to show the destroyed starship. After the rubble is displayed, a static text control shows the message underneath the destroyed starship (see Figure 35.5).

**FIGURE 35.5**
*The final effect after the starship crashes.*

The Windows API function FlashWindow() flashes the window's title, using the following declaration:

```
Function Boolean FlashWindow(int hWnd, Boolean bInvert) Library "user32.dll"
```

The starship example demonstrates some different ideas you can use in application animation. Not only can you move a picture, but you also can hide and display different controls. Changing the colors (particularly the window's background color) can add some flair to your application.

**35**

**Animation, Sound, and Multimedia**

## External Function Calls

In addition to using the PowerScript functions and changing the viewed image, you can use several Windows API functions in your application. You just saw an example of this usage when the `FlashWindow()` function in USER32.DLL was used to make the window title bar flash on and off. You can use any applicable function in the Windows SDK (look at the library GDI32.DLL) or any third-party function library, or you can write your own DLLs. You learn about using an external function call to enable sound for your application later in the section "Sound Enabling." For more information on using external function calls, see Chapter 36, "API Calls."

## Moving Windows

The way a window is opened or closed can also add some interesting effects to your application. For example, an opening window can start small and expand to its normal size. This exploding technique is fairly simple to implement; all you must do is change four attributes of the window: `X`, `Y`, `Height`, and `Width`. The only difficulty is determining how fast you want the window to open and the size to which you want the window opened.

For this example, the window is created small and then made to explode to fill most of the screen when it's opened. Most of the code needed to make the window expand is in a user-defined window event named `ue_explode`. (See Chapter 2, "PowerBuilder 7.0 Development Environment," on how to create user events.) In the window's `Open` event, the `PostEvent()` function triggers `ue_explode` so that the resizing of the window occurs after the window is displayed. The `ue_explode` event contains the following code:

```
Do Until This.Height >= 1650
   This.Width  = This.Width + 35
   This.Height = This.Height + 25
   This.X      = This.X - 10
   This.Y      = This.Y - 10
Loop
```

The window's height and width are incremented, while at the same time the X and Y coordinates of the window's upper-left corner are moved. Both must be done; otherwise, your window will disappear off the right side and bottom of the screen. The only negative parts about making the window explode are controlling how the window's controls look while the window is exploding and determining the incremental and decremental values of the `X`, `Y`, `Height`, and `Width` attributes. These values vary depending on the size you want to make your window and how quickly you want it to open. You might have to try several different values until you find what you like.

**Tip**

Don't increment the height and width by a number less than 10; otherwise, it takes too long for the window to open.

The other downside is how controls appear, due to the window being repainted each time you resize it. Because the window is constantly being repainted, PowerBuilder doesn't have time to paint the controls, so they end up looking like splotches on the window as it opens. To avoid this, make all controls invisible initially and make them visible after the window explodes to its desired size.

The same code, except in reverse, can be implemented to shrink a window when it's closed. Although this can be fun to play with, it would probably be suitable only for an unimportant window such as an About box. Due to the time taken to draw this, you might consider creating a special window that has no controls, use it just for the purpose of exploding/imploding, and then hide it and show the intended window.

# Sound Enabling

You can easily use Windows API calls to add sound to PowerBuilder applications. Chapter 36 discusses the actual mechanics of making API calls, so you might want to explore that chapter first.

You can use sound to provide an audio cue along with the visual cues you've already used within your application. Imagine in the drag-and-drop example that you not only drag a file to a trash can, which animates burning the trash, but you also play a sound clip at the same time to make even more of an impression. Granted, these are embellishments, but they can make the difference between an average application and one that captures users' attention.

**Note**

The API call used to play sound requires you to have installed specific drivers for a sound card or a generic sound driver that uses the computer's internal speaker.

**35**

**Animation, Sound, and Multimedia**

The external function declaration for the Windows API function that plays a WAV file is

```
Function Boolean sndPlaySoundA( String szSound, uLong Flags) &
                                Library "winmm.dll"
```

This function plays a sound specified in one of three ways: by filename, by resource, or by system event. A system event can be associated with a sound in the Registry or in the WIN.INI file.

The *szSound* specifies the sound to play. If this parameter is NULL, any currently playing waveform sound is stopped. Three flags (SND_ALIAS, SND_FILENAME, and SND_RESOURCE) determine whether *szSound* is interpreted as an alias for a system event, a filename, or a resource identifier. If none of these flags is specified, sndPlaySoundA() searches the Registry or the WIN.INI file for an association with the specified sound name. If no association is found in the Registry, the name is interpreted as a filename.

The *Flags* indicates the flags that, when combined, give the desired method for playing the sound. The values shown in Table 35.1 can be combined with OR (by adding the decimal values) to carry out multiple functions during the same call.

**TABLE 35.1**   Valid Values for the Flags Argument

| Constant Name | Hex Value | Decimal Value | Description |
|---|---|---|---|
| SND_ALIAS | 0x10000 | 65536 | The *szSound* is a system-event alias in the Registry or the WIN.INI file. |
| SND_ALIAS_ID | 0x110000 | 1114112 | The *szSound* is a predefined sound identifier. |
| SND_ASYNC | 0x00001 | 1 | The sound is played asynchronously. sndPlaySoundA() returns immediately after beginning the sound. |
| SND_FILENAME | 0x20000 | 131072 | The *szSound* parameter is a filename of a sound file. |
| SND_LOOP | 0x00008 | 8 | Plays repeatedly until sndPlaySoundA() is called again with *szSound* set to NULL. |
| SND_MEMORY | 0x00004 | 4 | The *szSound* points to an image of a sound in memory. |
| SND_NODEFAULT | 0x00002 | 2 | If the sound can't be found, returns without playing the default sound. |
| SND_NOSTOP | 0x00010 | 16 | Yields to another sound event that's already playing. |

TABLE 35.1    Valid Values for the `Flags` Argument

| Constant Name | Hex Value | Decimal Value | Description |
|---|---|---|---|
| SND_NOWAIT | 0x02000 | 8192 | If the driver is busy, returns immediately without playing the sound. |
| SND_SYNC | 0x00000 | 0 | Synchronous playback of a sound event; returns after the sound event completes. |

The SND_ASYNC option plays the sound asynchronously until it finishes or you call sndPlaySoundA() with *szSound* set to NULL. You must use the SND_ASYNC flag when using SND_LOOP to indicate that the sound event can be eventually stopped.

---

**Note**

The sndPlaySoundA() searches for the sound file to play in the following order:

- It searches the Registry for a keyname matching the *szSound* argument before attempting to load a file with this name. The application sound event entries belong at the same position in the Registry hierarchy as the rest of the sound events.

- It looks in the current directory, the Windows directory, the Windows system directory, directories listed in the PATH environment variable, and the list of directories mapped in a network.

Thus, packaging any sound files with your application when you distribute it is a good idea. If the sound file isn't found in any of these locations, the default sound is played or, if no default sound is specified, the function makes no sound.

---

If sndPlaySoundA()can't find the specified sound, the default system event sound entry is played instead. If the system default entry or default sound can't be found, sndPlaySoundA() makes no sound and returns FALSE.

By using the SND_ALIAS flag, you can make sndPlaySoundA() play sounds referred to by a keyname in the Registry. This way, end users can customize the system alerts and warnings with their own sounds. (Sounds associated with system alerts and warnings are called *sound events*.) For example, to play the sound associated with the SystemExclamation entry and to wait for the sound to complete before returning, this would be the call:

```
Ulong SND_SYNC = 0

sndPlaySoundA( "SystemExclamation", SND_SYNC)
```

The predefined sound events vary with the Windows platform you're using. The following sound events are defined for all Windows implementations:

| | |
|---|---|
| SystemAsterisk | SystemHand |
| SystemExclamation | SystemQuestion |
| SystemExit | SystemStart |

To provide complete customization for end users, you should have your application register its own sound events. This allows users to configure the sound event by using the standard Control Panel interface.

To check the Windows system to make sure that you can play sound files, a second function is used. Its declaration is

```
Function uInt waveOutGetNumDevs() Library "winmm.dll"
```

The two functions are used in the following code in a call to play the Windows TADA.WAV file continuously and synchronously:

```
uInt ui_NoOfDevices

ui_NoOfDevices = WaveOutGetNumDevs()

If ui_NoOfDevices > 0 Then
    sndPlaySoundA ("TADA.WAV", 0+2+8+16)
End If
```

Note the 2 (indicating the SND_NODEFAULT flag) to ensure that the WAV file exists before you try to play it. If you don't specify this flag, the application will make the default beep, indicating an error (but application processing continues unless you terminate it).

A great touch to add to your application is to play a welcome sound when your user starts the application. This can be made sensitive to the time of day and say "Good morning" or "Good afternoon." Similarly, when the application closes, a voice saying "Goodbye" or "Good night" is a nice touch. A voice saying "Error" is another one you could incorporate easily.

> **Tip**
>
> Keep sound bites short; users will often tire of hearing them and will become irritated at having to sit through 20 seconds of musical fanfare when they leave the application.

# Multimedia

PowerBuilder can write scripts for some Windows multimedia events. PowerBuilder supports joystick input, enhanced timer services, multimedia file input and output, and audio control.

To interface with the multimedia capabilities of Windows, you need to have already installed the driver for the particular multimedia device you want to use (such as CD audio or a joystick). Also, you must have the Windows translation file for multimedia, WINMM.DLL.

You use the Media Control Interface (MCI) to perform Windows multimedia application development. The MCI gives access to media devices with high-level methods that use standard human-language commands and a lower-level method that consists of parameters. The high-level approach is easy to implement in your applications by using such commands as `Play welcome.avi`. The low-level method would be necessary for complex multimedia device communication, which requires you to detail specific operations and parameters.

PowerBuilder traps Windows multimedia messages in a series of events that you can add as user-defined events, as shown in Table 35.2.

**TABLE 35.2**  PowerBuilder Event IDs for Windows Multimedia Messages

*Joystick*

| | |
|---|---|
| pbm_mmjoy1move | pbm_mmjoy1buttondown |
| pbm_mmjoy2move | pbm_mmjoy2buttondown |
| pbm_mmjoy1zmove | pbm_mmjoy1buttonup |
| pbm_mmjoy2zmove | pbm_mmjoy2buttonup |

*MCI*

pbm_mmmcinotify

*Waveform Output*

pbm_mmwom_open
pbm_mmwom_close
pbm_mmwom_done

*Waveform Input*

pbm_mmwim_open
pbm_mmwim_close
pbm_mmwim_data

**35**

Animation,
Sound, and
Multimedia

**TABLE 35.2**   PowerBuilder Event IDs for Windows Multimedia Messages

### MIDI Input

| | |
|---|---|
| pbm_mmmim_open | pbm_mmmim_longdata |
| pbm_mmmim_close | pbm_mmmim_error |
| pbm_mmmim_data | pbm_mmmim_longerror |

### MIDI Output

pbm_mmmom_open
pbm_mmmom_close
pbm_mmmom_done

For example, if you want your application to access a CD audio player, you might add the event ID pbm_mmmcinotify. Windows uses this event to notify a window that an MCI device has completed a particular task. In PowerBuilder, the WordParm attribute of the Message object is used to return those values, as follows:

| *Value* | *Meaning* |
|---|---|
| 1 | Task aborted |
| 2 | Task successful |
| 4 | Task superseded |
| 8 | Task failed |

Along with declaring the user event, you also need to declare two external functions, mciSendStringA and mciGetErrorStringA. These Windows function declarations are shown in Listing 35.1.

**LISTING 35.1**   MCI Function Declarations

```
FUNCTION Long mciSendStringA( string lpstrCommand, &
ref string lpstrRtnString, int wRtnLength, uint hCallBack) LIBRARY "WINMM.DLL"
FUNCTION Boolean mciGetErrorStringA( long dwError, &
ref string lpstrBuffer, int wLength) LIBRARY "WINMM.DLL"
```

The mciSendStringA() function passes a string request to the Windows multimedia translation layer (WINMM.DLL), which interprets it and sends the request to the appropriate device drivers. The following is coded in a window function:

```
Long ll_Return
String ls_Return, ls_Message = "play_cdaudio_notify"
ls_Return = Fill( Char(0), 255)
```

```
ll_Return = mciSendStringA( ls_Message, ls_Return, 255, Handle( this))
If ll_Return <> 0 Then
    mciGetErrorStringA( ll_Return, ls_Return, 255)
    MessageBox( "CD Audio Error", ls_Return)
End If
```

The return value (`ll_Return`) from the `mciSendStringA()` function can be used to pass to `mciGetErrorStringA()` (if not equal to zero), which returns the MCI error message as a string.

Because the CD will now be playing, you must trigger the user event assigned to `pbm_mmmcinotify`; it won't be triggered until after the CD is done playing. You don't need any code in the `pbm_mmmcinotify` event, but you could check `Message.WordParm` for returned information. Instead, code a `Timer` event that triggers every half-second and calls `mciSendStringA()` using the message `status cdaudio mode wait`. The function returns the status of the CD player as a String value that can be displayed in the window title (such as `"Playing"`). When you use the `Timer` event, you're constantly checking to see what the status of the CD player is.

# Playing Windows AVI Files

Now that you've been introduced to the basics of the MCI high-level method of multimedia programming, you can see how to write an application that plays Windows AVI (Audio Video Interleave) files. Incorporating a Windows video clip into your application uses the same MCI high-level method you saw in the CD example. You need to declare two functions, `mciSendStringA()` and `mciGetErrorStringA()` (refer to Listing 35.1). After you declare them, you can use the code in Listing 35.2 to run your video file.

The video file can be run one of two ways: in a separate window or in a DataWindow control. In Listing 35.2, you implement the second method. After placing a DataWindow control on your window, declare a window function that calls `mciSendStringA()`. The function receives a String variable containing the command that you want to process.

**LISTING 35.2** The Public Subroutine `wf_SendStringA()`, Calling External Function `mciSendStringA()`

```
//Argument:
//   String arg_message
//Returns Long
Long ll_rtn
String ls_error, ls_string

//Initialize the return strings
ls_error  = Space(128)
```

**LISTING 35.2** CONTINUED

```
ls_string = Space(128)


//Execute the argument message
ll_Rtn = mciSendStringA( arg_message, ls_string, 127, 0)


//Check to see if execution was successful
If ll_rtn <> 0 then
   mciGetErrorStringA(ll_rtn, ls_error, Len(ls_error) - 1)
   MessageBox("Media error","Error message: ~r~n" + ls_error)
   return ll_rtn
End If
Return 1
```

The window, thus far, could be used as an ancestor window from which all multimedia application windows could be inherited. Then, depending on the type of multimedia application you were building, the framework would be in place. In this case, you create a series of command buttons that control the play of the AVI file.

If the AVI file will be constant, the filename can be hard-coded into the application code. If the DataWindow will be used as a viewer for potentially several different AVI files, you give users a way to select the desired file. This can be done by using `GetFileOpenName()`. After the file is determined, you need to send a series of commands calling the window function `wf_SendStringA()`. This is implemented in the `Clicked` event of an Open command button on the window (see Listing 35.3).

**LISTING 35.3** The `Clicked` Event of the Command Button `cb_Open`

```
String ls_handle, ls_named
Long    ll_rtn_code

//Get the desired AVI file and store it in
//an instance variable, is_file_name
ll_rtn_code = GetFileOpenName("Select File", &
   is_file_name, ls_named, "DOC",&
   "AVI Files (*.AVI), *.AVI")

If ll_rtn_code = -1 Or Upper(Right(Trim(is_file_name), 3)) <> "AVI" Then
   MessageBox("Selection Error", "You must select an AVI file!")
   is_file_name = ""
   Return
End If
//Open the media device
```

**LISTING 35.3** CONTINUED

```
ll_rtn_code = wf_SendStringA("Open " + is_file_name)
If ll_rtn_code <> 1 Then Return
ls_handle = String(handle(dw_1))
//Send the handle of the DataWindow Control
//To indicate where the AVI file will be displayed
wf_SendStringA("Window " + is_file_name + " Handle " + ls_handle)
//Expands the AVI display to fit the DataWindow Control
wf_SendStringA("Put " + is_file_name + " destination")
//Specify that the AVI display intervals is frames
wf_SendStringA("Set " + is_file_name + " time format frames")
```

The default frame to start with is the first frame. If all is successful, you are now ready for users to interact with the AVI file. The window can also contain several other buttons, such as one to play the AVI file, one to pause execution, one to rewind to the beginning, one to stop playing, and one to close the file. The code for the Clicked event for each button varies only slightly. This would be the script for the Play button:

```
If wf_SendStringA("Play " + is_file_name) <> 1 Then
   MessageBox("Play Failed", "Could not play " + is_file_name)
End If
```

Table 35.4 shows the commands sent to wf_SendStringA() to perform the rest of the processing.

**TABLE 35.4** The AVI Command Set for wf_SendStringA()

| Desired Functionality | Commands |
|---|---|
| Pause execution | "Pause " + is_file_name |
| Rewind to beginning | "Seek " + is_file_name + " to 1" |
| Stop execution | "Stop " + is_file_name |
| Close file | "Close " + is_file_name |

Your users might not understand why they need to close a file, and they shouldn't have to worry about consciously closing a file. Therefore, perform the Close command from the window's CloseQuery event to ensure that the file is properly closed and that all resources are released.

For more information about all the possible string values that can be sent to the Windows multimedia translation layer (WINMM.DLL), look in the Windows SDK documentation.

**35**

Animation,
Sound, and
Multimedia

# Summary

The use of animation and multimedia can make one application stand head and shoulders above another. Not only is it fun to write these parts of an application, but users also enjoy discovering and playing with the different components. Several techniques can be used: pictures toggling in toolbars, picture controls, and picture buttons; object movement; sound; and external function calls. Unless animation is specifically requested, however, it's probably a good idea to minimize its use because it can be distracting and resource intensive. If you do animate the application, let your users shut it off if they want to.

In addition to animation, PowerBuilder now provides the capability to implement an application that uses multimedia features to display a rich environment to users. You can access a number of external devices and receive input from such devices as joysticks and CDs. Although many companies haven't moved into multimedia application development, users' expectations are increasing, and implementation is becoming easier. As time goes by, the topics discussed in this chapter will become more and more frequently used.

# 36

# API Calls

CHAPTER

PowerBuilder, like many other GUI development languages, allows you to extend outside the constraints of the host language and use functionality inherent in the operating system and in third-party controls and functions. This process is referred to as making an API (Application Programming Interface) call.

In PowerBuilder, a common use of API calls occurs when the application undertakes a math-intensive task; due to the slowness of PowerBuilder's interpreted runtime code, this time-consuming processing is moved into a dynamic link library (DLL). You can write DLLs using any language that supports the Pascal calling sequence, but often you write them in C or Pascal. No matter which language is used or what the requirements of using an API call are, you need to know how PowerBuilder provides an interface to the outside environment. The most common use of these calls is to the operating system API for carrying out tasks that PowerBuilder doesn't give developers direct access to. In this chapter, you look at examples of these.

# Declaring an External Function

There are two types of external functions: *global* and *local*. Global external functions can be declared and are available anywhere in the application. They're stored in the application object with the other global variables. Local external functions can be defined for a window, menu, user object, or global function and become part of that object's definition. These functions can be made accessible or inaccessible to other objects by using the `Public`, `Private`, and `Protected` keywords in the same manner as object instance variables.

You can access local external functions only by prefixing the external function name with the object's name by using dot notation, as follows:

```
ObjectName.ExternalFunction( Arguments)
```

For example, if you declared the local external function `FlashWindow()` for the window `w_connect`, you would call the function like this:

```
w_connect.FlashWindow()
```

As with PowerBuilder functions, there are two types of code blocks: *functions*, which return a value, and *subroutines*, which carry out specific processing and return no value (a return value of the `Void` data type). However, PowerBuilder makes a distinction with the external code blocks and provides two different syntaxes:

```
{Access} FUNCTION ReturnDataTypeFunctionName({REF}{DataType1 Arg1,...}) &
LIBRARY LibraryName {ALIAS FOR ExternalName}
```

```
{Access} SUBROUTINE SubroutineName({REF}{DataType1 Arg1, ... } ) &
                    LIBRARY LibraryName {ALIAS FOR ExternalName}
```

The *Access* declaration is valid only for local external functions. The *ReturnDataType* must be a supported PowerBuilder data type that matches the return data type of the external function (see Table 36.1 in the following section for the PowerBuilder-supported data types). The *FunctionName/SubroutineName* is the name of the function as it appears in the DLL/EXE file; *LibraryName* is the name of the DLL or EXE file in which the function is stored.

> **Note**
>
> If you want to use a different name for the function in your PowerScript for the external function, or if the name of the function contains invalid characters, you must specify an alias. This is done by using the ALIAS FOR keywords followed by a string containing the real name. This establishes the association between the PowerScript name and the external name.

> **Tip**
>
> If you're migrating an application originally written under the 16-bit version of Windows, you can use ALIAS FOR in your declaration lines to avoid having to change all the places you make external function calls. Of course, if you're using an API manager class, like the one detailed later in the "Building an API Controller User Object" section, this won't be a problem for you.

The library must be accessible to the application at runtime (in the DOS path); PowerBuilder doesn't parcel it with the application or ensure that you distribute it with the EXE.

> **Note**
>
> If you create your own external function libraries for use with PowerBuilder, you must declare them by using FAR PASCAL (see the next section for an example). Or, if you're using Microsoft Visual C++, use the following:
>
> ```
> #define DllExport __declspec( dllexport)
> ```

and then your function declarations are of the form

```
DllExport int APIENTRY MyFunction();
```

The function name within the DLL is a little mangled because Visual C++ places extra characters in the name. You should use the Windows 95/98/NT quick view program to find out what it is. You can also use ALIAS FOR to provide a better name for use within your PowerBuilder application.

External functions are declared from within most objects' Script View. Choose Declare from the first drop-down and then Local or Global External Functions from the second drop-down menu. This will open an area at the top of the Script View where you can type the function declaration by using one of the previous syntaxes. When you move away from this area, by switching to an event or other declaration area, PowerBuilder compiles the declaration and checks for syntax errors. You must fix any errors before you can save the function declaration.

**Note**

PowerBuilder *won't* tell you that the function doesn't exist in the DLL, or that the call arguments are incorrect during the statement's compilation. Instead, you get runtime errors.

# Data Type Translation

Table 36.1 lists the PowerBuilder-supported C data types and their PowerBuilder equivalents. PowerBuilder supports only passing FAR pointers, and the external function must have the FAR qualifier in its declaration. This table is from Watcom C++ Class Builder documentation.

**T**ABLE **36.1**   PowerBuilder-Supported Data Types for External Functions

| C++ Data Type | PowerBuilder Data Type | Data Type Description |
|---|---|---|
| BOOL | Boolean | 2-byte signed integer |
| WORD | uInt | 2-byte unsigned integer |
| DWORD | uLong | 4-byte unsigned integer |
| HANDLE | uInt | 2-byte unsigned integer |
| HWND | uInt | 2-byte unsigned integer |
| LPINT | String | 4-byte FAR pointer |
| LPWORD | String | 4-byte FAR pointer |

With the
function

FUNCTION

The only
This, ho
PowerB

**Caut**

Be ca
size.
string

If the ex
an array

## Pass

Some W
know th
PowerB
to do th

For exa
API. Th
paramet
s_syst

**TABLE 3**

| Var |
| --- |
| ulOE |
| ulPa |
| szMi |
| szMa |
| ulAc |
| ulNo |
| ulPr |
| ulRe |
| ulRe |

**TABLE 36.1** PowerBuilder-Supported Data Types for External Functions

| C++ Data Type | PowerBuilder Data Type | Data Type Description |
| --- | --- | --- |
| LPLONG | String | 4-byte FAR pointer |
| LPDWORD | String | 4-byte FAR pointer |
| LPVOID | String | 4-byte FAR pointer |
| LPVOID | Char | 4-byte HUGE pointer |
| BYTE | Char | 1 byte |
| CHAR | Char | 1 byte |
| CHAR CHARARRAY[10] | Char CHARARRAY[10] | 10 bytes |
| INT | Int | 2-byte signed integer |
| UNSIGNED INT | uInt | 2-byte unsigned integer |
| LONG | Long | 4-byte signed integer |
| UNSIGNED LONG | uLong | 4-byte unsigned integer |
| DOUBLE | Double | 8-byte double-precision floating-point number |
| DOUBLE | Decimal | 8-byte double-precision floating-point number |
| FLOAT | Real | 4-byte single-precision floating-point number |
| N/A | Time | Date and time structure |
| N/A | Date | Date and time structure |
| N/A | DateTime | Date and time structure |

PowerBuilder doesn't support the C NEAR pointer data type (that is, PSTR and NPSTR), and the keyword REF must be used to provide a 32-bit FAR pointer to a PowerBuilder variable. For example, the API function is declared as follows:

```
BOOL FAR PASCAL VerQueryValue(..., UINT FAR *lpBuffSize);
```

This would be declared in PowerBuilder as

```
FUNCTION Boolean VerQueryValue(..., REF UINT lpBuffSize) LIBRARY "VER.DLL"
```

The following code could then be used to call the function:

```
// A pointer to a buffer
UINT lui_BuffSize
// Other processing
If VerQueryValue( ...., lui_BuffSize) THEN
    // Some processing
ELSE
    // Some other processing, function failed
END IF
```

The external function declaration would be

```
SUBROUTINE GetSystemInfo(REF s_system_info sSystemInfo ) &
                         LIBRARY "kernel32.dll"
```

First, you need a declaration at a global or an instance level:

```
s_system_info istr_SystemInfo
```

The actual call would be something like this:

```
GetSystemInfo( istr_SystemInfo)
MessageBox( "Processor Type", String( istr_SystemInfo.ul_ProcessorType))
```

# Where to Find Further Information

The source of information you use depends on the kind of information you want to obtain. You can find information on function names, the value of constants, and the construction of window structures by opening the windows.h file in a text editor. This file is included as part of any C/C++ compiler for Windows (for example, Visual C++). It's the file that contains all the prototype information for the Windows API. You use this with a grep-like utility to find pattern matches to a certain word. For example, if you were searching for a function to flash a window, you could easily find all references to the word *flash*.

Actually finding the DLL or EXE file where the function is located takes a little more effort. With Windows 3.x, your best bet is to start with USER.EXE, KRNL386.EXE, and GDI.EXE, and then any other DLL that looks like it might have a name similar to the function's. In the Win32 API, the corresponding DLLs are USER32.DLL, KERNEL32.DLL, and GDI32.DLL, respectively. A few tools can be used to dissect a Windows binary file and return the functions stored within it (for example, EXEHDR from Microsoft Visual C++, or TDUMP from Borland's C++ Windows compiler).

A more user-friendly, but not as easily searched, reference is the WIN31API.HLP, WIN31WH.HLP, and API32.HLP files that come with Windows C/C++ compilers and some other GUI development tools. These Windows help files provide the same sort of limited searching as the PowerBuilder help pages. You usually use these with the output from one of the disassemblers mentioned, to provide further information after a function or structure is found.

> **Tip**
>
> If you're using the Windows 95/98 operating system, you can use the quick view program (QUIKVIEW.EXE) to look at the functions available in DLL files. You can add this optional component if it isn't already installed.

You can find a number of books that deal with the Windows API. Some are good, but some are poorly written. A helpful book is Schildt, Pappas, and Murray's *Osborne Windows Programming Series Vol. 2, General Purpose API Functions*, which includes many of the general API functions, structures, data types, and constants.

> **Note**
>
> In the Win32 API, be aware that some functions may have different names from those shown in the API documentation you are using. Some function calls are suffixed with an A or a W to indicate whether the function is Unicode, wide character (W) enabled, or an ANSI-type function (A).

# Building an API Controller User Object

Because PowerBuilder is a multiplatform development tool, you need to make your applications environment-aware and environment-independent. To do this, you need to build and use class user objects—that is, build an ancestor user object that prototypes all the functions that can be defined for each environment. These functions are user-object functions and not the external declarations. The environment specifics (the actual external function declarations) are attached to descendant user objects of the main user object. Within an application or application object, you would declare an instance variable of the following type:

```
n_cst_externals inv_externals
```

> **Note**
>
> Sybase supplies a version of the externals object with 32-bit descendants in its sample application. There's also a similar type object in the PFC Framework.

In the `Constructor` event (shown in the following code) for the application user object, or in the `Open` event of the application object, you need to call an initialization function. This function is coded as follows:

```
private subroutine of_initialize()
GetEnvironment( i_Environment)
//
// Instantiate the appropriate API object for the environment
//

Choose Case i_Environment.OSType
    Case Windows!
        // Windows 95
        inv_externals = Create n_cst_externals_win32_win95
    Case WindowsNT!
        inv_externals = Create n_cst_externals_win32_nt
    Case Else
        SetNull (externals)
End Choose
```

This function uses `GetEnvironment()` to query the application's environment and determine under which operating system it's running. In a `Case` statement, the `inv_externals` instance variable previously declared is assigned an instantiation of a descendant user object class that provides API calls specific to the current operating system.

To access the user object functions for an application user object `gnv_App`, using the instance variable `inv_externals`, the code from anywhere within an application would be

```
gnv_App.inv_externals.of_FlashWindow( This)
```

This ensures that no matter what the actual API function call is, the application is written to a consistent interface.

The base object of `n_cst_externals` would contain a prototype function for `of_FlashWindow()` that does nothing. The inherited objects `n_cst_externals_winapi` and `n_cst_externals_win32` would also declare the same function and provide the appropriate calls to the local declared external functions.

# Sample Code

The easiest way to relay information is to provide examples, so the following sections describe a number of the most common uses for API functions.

# Determining Whether an Application Is Already Open

A common requirement is for an application to query the other open applications running on the host machine, usually to determine whether another application needs to be opened first. You can accomplish this task in the following way, using the `FindWindow()` API function:

```
HWND FindWindow( LPCSTR lpszClassName, LPCSTR lpszTitle)
```

This translates to a PowerBuilder external function declaration of

```
// Win32
Function uInt FindWindowA( String szClass, String szName) Library "user32.dll"
```

Either parameter can be `NULL`, in which case the function matches on all classes and/or titles (you learn later in this section how to determine an application's class and title). The function returns the window handle of the window, if it can be found, or `0` if no match is found.

For example, to see whether the Windows Calculator application is already open, the code would be as follows:

```
uInt hWnd

hWnd = gnv_App.inv_externals.of_FindWindow( "scicalc","calculator")

If hWnd = 0 Then
   Run( "calc")
Else
   gnv_App.inv_externals.of_SetFocus( hWnd)
End If
```

Note the use of another API call to `SetFocus()` that enables you to bring an already open window to the front. The `SetFocus()` function takes a Windows handle and is defined inside PowerBuilder as

```
// Win32
Function uInt SetFocus( uInt hWnd ) Library "user32.dll"
```

To find whether a DOS prompt window has been opened, set the class name parameter to tty. To find the DOS prompt window in particular, you look for a window by the name of MS-DOS Prompt. The case, spaces, and characters must match exactly with those of the window.

Determining a window's class can be a little tricky. WinSnoop by D.T. Hamilton is a freeware program that gives you valuable information about windows. WinSnoop displays the window's handle, title, creator, parent, class, and owner. A number of other programs (for example, SPY.EXE and WSPY.EXE) return the same information. A good place for finding these types of utilities is http:\\www.shareware.com.

Another method that works is to use the GetWindow() function (described at the end of this chapter) to step through each window and then, using the GetWindowTextA() function, compare each window's title text with the current application's main window title. The GetWindowTextA() function is defined as follows:

```
// Win32
Function int GetWindowTextA( Long hWindow, ref string windowtext, &
                             int length) &
Library "USER32.DLL"
```

You call the function with the following code:

```
uInt lui_Window, lui_NextWindow
String ls_Text

ls_Text = Space (80)

// Obtain handle of the main window...in this example we use This
lui_Window = Handle (This)

// Loop through each window
lui_NextWindow = GetWindow( lui_Window, 0)

Do While lui_NextWindow > 0
   If lui_NextWindow <> lui_Window Then
      GetWindowTextA( lui_NextWindow, ls_Text, 80)
      If ls_Text = This.Title Then
         MessageBox( "Application", "App already running")
         HALT CLOSE
      End If
   End If
   lui_NextWindow = GetWindow( lui_NextWindow, 2)
Loop
```

This is a little crude because it relies on checking window titles, just like the FindWindow() example.

# Attracting Attention

Occasionally, you need to draw the user's attention to a particular window in an application, when it's either open or iconized. The accepted GUI standard is to cause the window title (or icon, if the window is iconized) to flash. You do this with the FlashWindow() function:

```
// Win32
Function Boolean FlashWindow( uInt handle, Boolean bFlash) Library "user32.dll"
```

The Boolean *bFlash* should be TRUE to cause the window to flash from one state to another, FALSE to return the window to its original state (active or inactive). For example, to attract attention to an error window, you first need to obtain the Windows handle for the window w_error and pass it to the external function as follows:

```
uInt hWnd

hWnd = Handle( w_error)
gnv_App.inv_externals.of_FlashWindow( hWnd, TRUE)
```

The call to FlashWindow() usually appears in a Timer event so that you get the window to truly flash. A timer interval of about half to a quarter of a second seems about right.

# Centering a Window

A common requirement when you open a window is to have it centered onscreen. Although PowerBuilder gives you access to the window's X and Y coordinates, you need to know the current screen resolution to set these values. The width and height of the screen varies between resolutions, so Microsoft provides a function, GetSystemMetrics(), that you can use to access these values, among others. Its syntax is

```
Function int GetSystemMetrics( int nIndex) Library "user32.dll"
```

The nIndex parameter provides access to a number of different system constants (see Table 36.3). Note that all SM_CX* values are widths, and all SM_CY* values are heights.

**TABLE 36.3** GetSystemMetrics Parameter Constants

| Value | Meaning |
| --- | --- |
| SM_CMOUSEBUTTONS | Number of mouse buttons, or zero if no installed mouse |
| SM_CXBORDER, SM_CYBORDER | Width and height of window border |
| SM_CXCURSOR, SM_CYCURSOR | Width and height of cursor |
| SM_CXDLGFRAME, SM_CYDLGFRAME | Width and height of frame for dialog |
| SM_CXFRAME, SM_CYFRAME | Width and height of frame for a resizable window |

**TABLE 36.3** `GetSystemMetrics` Parameter Constants

| Value | Meaning |
| --- | --- |
| SM_CXFULLSCREEN, SM_CYFULLSCREEN | Width and height of the client area for a full-screen window |
| SM_CXHSCROLL, SM_CYHSCROLL | Width and height of arrow bitmap on horizontal scrollbar |
| SM_CXHTHUMB | Width of horizontal scrollbar thumb box |
| SM_CXICON, SM_CYICON | Width and height of an icon |
| SM_CXICONSPACING, SM_CYICONSPACING | Width and height of cell used in tiling icons |
| SM_CXMIN, SM_CYMIN | Minimum width and height of a window |
| SM_CXSCREEN, SM_CYSCREEN | Width and height of the screen |
| SM_CXSIZE, SM_CYSIZE | Width and height of bitmaps contained in the title bar |
| SM_CXVSCROLL, SM_CYVSCROLL | Width and height of arrow bitmap on vertical scrollbar |
| SM_CYVTHUMB | Height of vertical scrollbar thumb box |
| SM_CYCAPTION | Height of normal caption area |
| SM_CYMENU | Height of single-line menu bar |
| SM_MOUSEPRESENT | Zero if a mouse isn't installed; non-zero otherwise |
| SM_SWAPBUTTON | Non-zero if the left and right mouse buttons are swapped |

The `GetSystemMetrics()` function can be added to the external call controller user object previously mentioned with the following syntax in the `n_cst_externals` object:

```
public function integer of_GetSystemMetrics (integer ai_Index);
    Return GetSystemMetrics( ai_Index)
end function
```

You could then write a global function or application function to use one or all three functions, as follows:

```
// The window to center is passed in as an argument to the function.
// Window aw_ToActOn
//
Long ll_Width, ll_Height

// Query the system for the desktop size, and then convert to the
// PB unit system.
ll_Width = This.inv_externals.of_GetSystemMetrics(0) * (686/150)
ll_Height = This.inv_externals.of_GetSystemMetrics(1) * (801/200)

// Calculate central position
aw_ToActOn.X =(  ll_Width - aw_ToActOn.Width) / 2
aw_ToActOn.Y =(  ll_Height - aw_ToActOn.Height) / 2
```

The return value from GetSystemMetrics() is modified by using a conversion factor that takes pixels and converts them to PowerBuilder units.

> **Note**
>
> This example only illustrates the use of the function. You would, of course, use the GetEnvironment() function and the ScreenHeight and ScreenWidth properties from the returned structure. Therefore, the two lines would be
>
> ```
> ll_Width = PixelsToUnits( i_Environment.ScreenWidth, XPixelsToUnits!)
> ```
>
> ```
> ll_Height = PixelsToUnits( i_Environment.ScreenHeight, YPixelsToUnits!)
> ```

When all the code is in place, each window can then make a single call in the Open event. The following example uses an application user object and center function:

```
gnv_App.of_CenterWindow( This)
```

It should be obvious that this code can't be used to center a sheet within an MDI application but will work on all other window types. To center a sheet, you have only to reference the client area of the MDI frame; remember, however, that the sheet will always open according to the ArrangeOrder argument value and will automatically be visible.

# Modifying a Window's Style

Whenever youopen a sheet in an MDI frame, regardless of the window type and style bits you've set, PowerBuilder overrides them. This is done to produce a window that can be resized, minimized, and maximized with a system menu. Sometimes you might want to provide slightly different behavior, which requires you to use the SetWindowLongA() function. The definition of this function is

```
Function Long SetWindowLongA( uInt hWindow, Integer unIndex, Long lNewValue) &
Library "user32.dll"
```

The window to act on is passed as a handle through *hWindow*. The *unIndex* argument is used to specify what area of the window you will be changing; for the style changes that you might possibly want to make, this value will always be GWL_STYLE (-16) . The *lNewValue* argument is a bit representation of the new styles (see Table 36.4).

**TABLE 36.4**    Values for the `lNewValue` Argument

| *Window Constant* | *NumericValue* | *Window Description* |
| --- | --- | --- |
| WS_BORDER | 8388608 | Has a normal border. |
| WS_CAPTION | 12582912 | Has a title bar (implies the WS_BORDER style). |
| WS_DLGFRAME | 4194304 | A modal dialog (no title). |
| WS_EX_TOPMOST | 8 | Appears above all non-topmost windows and stays above them even when window is deactivated. |
| WS_EX_TRANSPARENT | 32 | Any windows beneath the window aren't obscured by the window. |
| WS_HSCROLL | 1048576 | Has a horizontal scrollbar. |
| WS_MAXIMIZE | 16777216 | Has a maximized state. |
| WS_MAXIMIZEBOX | 65536 | Has a maximize button. |
| WS_MINIMIZE | 536870912 | Has a minimized state. |
| WS_MINIMIZEBOX | 131072 | Has a minimize button. |
| WS_OVERLAPPED | 0 | Has a caption and a border. |
| WS_POPUP | 2147483648 | Created as a pop-up. |
| WS_SYSMENU | 524288 | Has a System menu box on its title bar. |
| WS_THICKFRAME | 262144 | Has a thick resizable border. |
| WS_VSCROLL | 2097152 | Has a vertical scrollbar. |

The constants listed in Table 36.4 can be combined by adding the numeric values, although not all combinations are allowed, and some require other specific constants to also be listed.

> **Caution**
>
> Before you start altering a window's style, you first need to capture the current settings. Otherwise, you need to specify all the style bits required to make the window function correctly.

The current style is captured by using the `GetWindowLongA()` function, which is defined as

```
Function Long GetWindowLongA( uInt hWindow, Integer unIndex) &
Library "user32.dll"
```

The following alters the existing window by adding the minimize button and removing (disabling) the maximize button:

```
uInt hWindow
Integer GWL_STYLE = -16
Long WS_MAXIMIZEBOX = 65536, WS_MINIMIZEBOX = 131072, ll_OldStyle
```

```
hWindow = Handle (This)

ll_OldStyle = GetWindowLongA( hWindow, GWL_STYLE)
SetWindowLongA( hWindow, GWL_STYLE, ll_OldStyle + &
                WS_MINIMIZEBOX - WS_MAXIMIZEBOX)
```

Notice that it's simply a matter of adding or subtracting the style value from the current window style setting.

# Obtaining System Resource Information

Resources are handled in the 32-bit Windows environments a little differently than those of the old 16-bit world, but anyone who has worked just a little with Windows 95/98 knows that resources still get consumed and aren't always released. First, a little background on how the different memory management systems work.

Within Windows 3.x are two 64KB heaps from which resources are allocated. The user and menu heaps are both limited to 64KB of data, which limits the maximum number of windows and menus to about 200.

Windows 95/98 naturally enhances this method, and adds an additional 32-bit heap, which can grow as large as available memory; the 16-bit heap is still limited to 64KB. Windows 95/98 stores data structures within the 16-bit heap and physical objects such as fonts and bitmaps in the 32-bit heap. GDI regions have also been moved to the 32-bit, freeing up the 16-bit heap's responsibilities. When a process terminates, the GDI resources used in Windows 95/98/NT are freed immediately, unless the application was a 16-bit application, in which case the resources are held until the last 16-bit application is closed. The user and menu heaps with Windows 95/98 have been increased to 2MB each, and the previous limit of 200 windows/menus is effectively eliminated.

You can check on Windows 95/98 memory usage with the API function, GlobalMemoryStatus(), which has this definition:

```
// Win32
Subroutine GlobalMemoryStatus( s_memory_status lpBuffer) Library "kernel32.dll"
```

This uses a single parameter, a pointer to a _MEMORYSTATUS structure, which was re-created in PowerBuilder, as shown in Table 36.5.

**TABLE 36.5**  The s_memory_status Structure

| Variable Name | Variable Data Type | Description |
| --- | --- | --- |
| ulLength | uLong | Length of the structure, which you should set before using. |
| ulMemoryLoad | uLong | A general idea of current memory utilization. Between 0 (no memory use) and 100 (full memory use). |
| ulTotalPhys | uLong | Total number of bytes of physical memory. |
| ulAvailPhys | uLong | Number of bytes of physical memory available. |
| ulTotalPageFile | uLong | Total number of bytes that can be stored in the paging file. |
| ulAvailPageFile | uLong | Number of bytes available in the paging file. |
| ulTotalVirtual | uLong | Total number of bytes in the virtual address space. |
| ulAvailVitrual | uLong | Number of bytes of unreserved and uncommitted memory in the virtual address space. |

You can then call the GlobalMemoryStatus() function by using the following code:

```
uLong lul_PhysicalFree, lul_PagingFree, lul_VirtualFree
s_memory_status lstr_SystemInfo

lstr_SystemInfo.ulLength = 32
GlobalMemoryStatus( lstr_SystemInfo)

// Calculate percentage free of each memory resource
lul_PhysicalFree =( lstr_SystemInfo.ulAvailPhys / &
                    lstr_SystemInfo.ulTotalPhys) * 100
lul_PagingFree=( lstr_SystemInfo.ulAvailPageFile / &
                    lstr_SystemInfo.ulTotalPageFile) * 100
lul_VirtualFree= (lstr_SystemInfo.ulAvailVirtual / &
                    lstr_SystemInfo.ulTotalVirtual) * 100
```

These values provide little meaningful information for average users, though, because they provide only an indicator of the current state of memory available. In Windows 95/98/NT, there's little reason to track heaps anyway, so this is a moot point.

# Copying a File

To copy a file in 16-bit Windows was a real strain. With the 32-bit API, you can relax and let a single function call take all the strain. The one function is CopyFileA(), which is declared as

```
Function Boolean CopyFileA( String szExistingFile, String szNewFile, &
                     Boolean bFail) Library "kernel32.dll"
```

The code to use this function is this:

```
String ls_Source = "c:\temp\unleash", &
       Ls_Destination = "c:\temp\unleash.cpy"
Boolean lb_Fail = TRUE

// Make the copy fail if the file already exists
CopyFileA( ls_Source, ls_Destination, lb_Fail)
```

The *lb_Fail* argument is used to prevent an existing destination file from being overwritten. If the value is TRUE, the function fails; otherwise, it continues and overwrites the file.

Also, the MoveFileA() move function allows you to move a file or directory (including all child objects) instead. The function definition is

```
Function Boolean MoveFileA (String szExistingFile, String szNewFile) &
                     Library "kernel32.dll"
```

The only restrictions on this function are that the new name can't already exist and a new directory must be on the same drive.

# Capturing Associated Windows

You can capturewindows that are associated in some manner to another window. Remember that a window even includes controls such as command buttons. The external function GetWindow() obtains the handle of the window that has the defined relationship of a desired window. This is the external function:

```
HWND GetWindow( HWND hWindow, UINT fuRelationship)
```

The GetWindow() function can be directed to retrieve a window's handle, depending on the relationship between it and the window that the call is issued with using the *hWindow* parameter. The function can be used to search the system's list of top-level windows, associated child windows, child windows of child windows, and siblings of a window.

The PowerBuilder declaration for Win32 is as follows, and the Win16 function can be found in USER.EXE:

```
FUNCTION uInt GetWindow( uInt hWindow, Int nRelationShip) Library "user32.dll"
```

The *hWindow* parameter specifies the window to use as the base to search from. The *nRelationShip* parameter specifies the relationship between the original window and the window to be returned. Table 36.6 lists its possible values.

**TABLE 36.6**  Relationship Constants for `GetWindow()`

| Relationship | Value | Meaning |
|---|---|---|
| GW_CHILD | 5 | The window's first child window" |
| GW_HWNDFIRST | 0 | The first sibling window for a child window; otherwise, the first top-level window in the list |
| GW_HWNDLAST | 1 | The last sibling window for a child window; otherwise, the last top-level window in the list |
| GW_HWNDNEXT | 2 | The sibling window that follows the given window in the window manager's list |
| GW_HWNDPREV | 3 | The previous sibling window in the window manager's list |
| GW_OWNER | 4 | Identifies the window's owner |

The function returns the handle of the window if the function is successful. If it's not, a NULL is returned.

# Summary

In this chapter, you were introduced to external functions, why you would use them, and where you need to declare them. The chapter listed PowerBuilder-supported data types and gave examples that use several external functions. The Win32 API has introduced many new functions that range from file operations to date and time manipulators. By using this new functionality, tasks that seemed extremely difficult and involved—even impossible —are now possible with a few API calls.

# ActiveX and OLE

In this chapter, you learn about a couple of different methods and techniques that you can use for interprocess communication and application integration in the Windows environment. Although there are several ways to exchange information between Windows applications, this chapter focuses mainly on Microsoft's ActiveX and OLE. Start by looking at the concepts behind ActiveX and OLE, and then see how PowerBuilder lets you take advantage of these technologies.

# Interprocess Communication

The term *interprocess communication* (IPC) is defined as the process used by two or more Windows applications running at the same time to send messages and data to one another. The most common methods of IPC are DDE, OLE, external function calls to dynamic link libraries (DLLs), file access, and the Windows Clipboard.

All these methods enable different Windows applications to have conversations with one another. In PowerBuilder, you can build applications implementing all these techniques, but the most prevalent methods to communicate are DDE and OLE.

## DDE

The first form of interprocess communication available to Windows developers was dynamic data exchange, or DDE. DDE was first implemented in Windows (pre-3.*x*) as a message-based protocol used to exchange data between different Windows applications. Although OLE and ActiveX have replaced DDE as the preferred means of interprocess communication, PowerBuilder 7.0 maintains support for DDE as a client and a server. For more information on how to use DDE in your applications, see Chapter 16 in the Application Techniques section of the PowerBuilder HTML books.

## OLE Overview

Object linking and embedding, or OLE (pronounced "o-lay"), is a set of standardized interfaces that enable you to integrate multiple applications in the Windows environment. Through these standard interfaces, OLE permits applications to use each other's data or objects and call each other's services.

An OLE object can be any number of different types: a document, spreadsheet, graphical image, or user control, to name just a few. OLE communication occurs between a client and a server. The server creates and maintains one or more OLE objects. A common example is embedding a graph created with Microsoft Excel in a Word document. In this example, Excel acts as the OLE server, and Word acts as the client. The Word document can *embed* the graph or *link* to it. If the graph is embedded, the data is physically stored in the Word document. The graph can also be linked to a file, in which case Word stores a reference to the original Excel document.

In addition to linking or embedding documents, PowerBuilder lets you use ActiveX controls (also known as OLE Custom Controls) in your applications. ActiveX controls are a special type of OLE server designed in part for use in Web pages. You now can use hundreds of ActiveX controls in your PowerBuilder applications.

# OLE and ActiveX Terminology

Because the computer industry is scattered with TLAs (three-letter abbreviations!), it's difficult enough to keep track of what the abbreviations stand for, let alone understand what they mean. This section defines what OLE really means.

OLE 1.0 was first introduced in Windows 3.0. This limited version was introduced to get the Windows community familiar with the concepts. OLE 1.0 was built on DDE and used Windows messages and callbacks to pass information between applications. All that it gave you was a fancy method to shell out to another application from your PowerBuilder application.

OLE 2 was released with Windows 3.1 to address some limitations of OLE 1. OLE 2 is based on the COM (Component Object Model) architecture rather than DDE. It's implemented by using lightweight remote procedure calls (LRPC), which are similar to RPCs in the UNIX environment. Remote procedure calls enable applications to pass data to one another (not just messages). The *lightweight* adjective indicates that unlike UNIX RPCs, the COM calls are limited to passing information within the same machine. COM specifies the minimum interfaces for an object, as well as a reference counting mechanism that controls object creation and destruction. COM is now available for the Windows product line, Macintosh, and several versions of UNIX.

COM defines the sharing of information using a defined set of interfaces referred to as Uniform Data Transfer (UDT). UDT enables the exchange of data by having the client application grab a pointer to the OLE interface of the server application and then execute the functions incorporated into the server's OLE interface.

Microsoft introduced ActiveX controls as a replacement for the earlier OLE Custom Controls (OCX) made popular with Visual Basic 4. ActiveX controls added some features to make them more Internet friendly, such as smaller code sizes and security enhancements. ActiveX controls are based on the OLE and COM technologies.

> **Note**
>
> The terms *ActiveX control*, *OLE Custom Control*, and *OCX* are typically used interchangeably. I have tried to use the term *ActiveX control* in this chapter to conform with Microsoft's latest conventions. The PowerBuilder documentation still refers to ActiveX controls as OLE Custom Controls.

OLE maintains a method for storing objects known as *structured storage*. Structured storage can be thought of in terms of the DOS file structure concept of files and directories. These files (called *streams*) and directories (called *storages*) can be moved and copied just like their DOS counterparts. Using OLE streams and storages allows you to construct a compound document. A *compound document* is simply a collection of objects (for example, a Word document and an Excel graph) within one container application.

Integral to understanding OLE is that one application (typically your PowerBuilder application) is a client that shares data and functionality with a server application. The client application is more commonly known as the container application.

The most common question about OLE concerns the difference between an object being embedded and an object being linked. An embedded object is stored in your application. The OLE data object maintains the original OLE server application's full functionality, but the document physically resides in the container application. Embedding is useful for data that doesn't need to change, such as a letter template. Although your users can edit the data in the embedded object, their changes can't be saved because the object is physically part of your EXE (or PBD/DLL). If the embedded object needs to be updated, you must re-create the application. Note that users still can make changes and save them with a new filename.

If you need the capability to update the data of an OLE object and have the document retain the changes, you must link the document. When you link an object, the object physically resides outside your application. Your application maintains a reference to the data but doesn't contain the actual data. PowerBuilder provides a visual presentation of the OLE object only for display purposes. The advantage of this is that if any application changes the data of the OLE object, the changes are reflected in all documents maintaining a link to the document.

OLE 2.0 enables users to activate the control and edit the OLE object by using the server application's built-in functionality. For example, a PowerBuilder application has a window with an OLE 2.0 control containing an Excel spreadsheet. When the control is activated, the application has Excel's full functionality available to it (menus and all) without having to jump to Excel. This capability is called *in-place activation*. You also can open the server application (as in OLE 1.0) and edit the document directly in the server application (which is called *offsite activation*). OLE standards state that linked objects are to be activated offsite, and embedded objects are handled in place.

You can also programmatically create an OLE object, manipulate it, and use the server application's capabilities without the visual component. This capability to use the server's commands to modify an object is referred to as *OLE Automation*.

# OLE in the DataWindow Painter

OLE 2.0 support in the DataWindow painter was introduced in PowerBuilder 5.0 and is available through a database column, as a presentation style, and as an OLE object on the DataWindow. In a database column, you can add an OLE column to a DataWindow to store and retrieve binary large object (BLOB) data in your database. BLOB data could include a spreadsheet from Microsoft Excel or a document from Word. The OLE presentation style leaves the choices for a DataWindow presentation wide open. Any OLE 2.0 server that supports UDT can be used as a presentation for the DataWindow object. The OLE object is similar to the OLE 2.0 container used in the Window painter and can be used to manipulate data in an OLE server application.

## BLOB Columns

To create an OLE column in the DataWindow painter, you first must have a table in your database that has a BLOB data type. The data type name will vary from one DBMS to another. Adaptive Server Anywhere and SQL Server use the Image data type. A common table structure for OLE objects is a numeric primary-key column (id), the BLOB column containing the OLE object (object), and a text description of the BLOB column. The table with the OLE object must contain at least one additional field other than the OLE object to uniquely identify a row in the table. Also, the BLOB column should accept NULL values.

After the table is created, specify SQL or Quick Selects and select a presentation style for your new DataWindow object. In your Selection List, specify the key columns for the table, but don't select the BLOB column as part of the data source (PowerBuilder won't let you anyway). The BLOB column will be added later in an additional step. The DataWindow object is displayed in Design mode showing just the primary-key columns.

To add the BLOB column to your DataWindow object, click the OLE Database Blob menu item in the Objects menu. Click the DataWindow where you want to place the BLOB object. This opens the Database Binary/Text Large Object dialog (see Figure 37.1).

**FIGURE 37.1**

*The Database
Binary/Text Large
Object dialog.*

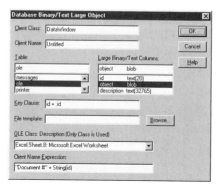

The optional Client Class defaults to the DataWindow value and is used by some OLE server applications to create the title displayed at the top of the server's window. The Client Name (also optional) defaults to Untitled and also is used by some OLE servers to create the title displayed at the top of the server application's window.

The Table list box contains a list of all tables contained in the current database. Scroll through the list to locate the table containing the BLOB column and click the table name. The Large Binary/Text Columns list box displays all the columns for the selected table and indicates the BLOB column (object). Use the Key Clause to build the WHERE clause for the SELECT statement and to update the DataWindow to the database.

The next two text boxes, File Template and OLE Class Description, are used to specify the OLE server application that will generate the files for storage in the BLOB column. If you always want to open the same file in the OLE server, type the name into the File Template text box. (Make sure that the file is in the current DOS path; if it's not, fully qualify the filename.) If you don't know the exact location or filename, click the Browse button to open the Select a File Name dialog. Locate the file and click Open to place the filename and path in the File Template text box.

If you want to open a different file each time, leave the File Template box empty and specify an OLE Class Description. The drop-down list shows the valid server applications registered on your system. If your application doesn't appear, you must run the Registry Editor (REGEDIT.EXE) and merge the server application's registration file.

The last item to specify in this dialog is an expression that displays in the OLE server application's title and can be used to specify the current row you are on in the DataWindow. The Client Name Expression must evaluate to a string. It's a good idea to create a unique name for each column (such as 'Excel Worksheet ' + String(id) ).

Just like most objects in the DataWindow painter, you can change the pointer on the Pointer tab; specify the object's position on the Position tab; and specify name, tag value, and some formatting options on the General tab. On the General tab, a name is optional for your OLE object. A name is required if you're going to refer to the object in any of your scripts.

After specifying all the necessary information, click OK to display the DataWindow design with the new BLOB column. The column is displayed as a box with the label Blob on it. The BLOB column is often invisible to users until the server application is started. To accommodate this, be sure to set the border so that users know where to double-click to activate the server application.

The Preview window in the DataWindow painter allows you to view how the OLE column works in PowerBuilder. Insert a new row and enter a value for the ID column (see Figure 37.2). The OLE column data is still edited using offsite activation. Therefore, when you double-click the BLOB column (where the drawing object is) to activate the OLE server application, the server application opens as a separate window. This window displays the file you specified in the File Template box or an empty workspace if you chose an OLE Class Description (see Figure 37.3).

**FIGURE 37.2**

*A DataWindow object preview with OLE column.*

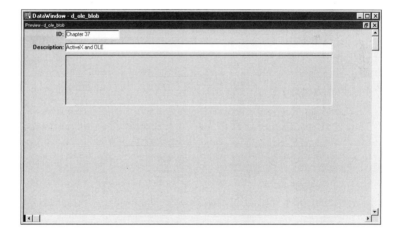

Make any changes you want in the OLE server application. When you are finished, the File menu's Update item will update the data in the server and in the client applications. After you select Update, the new information is sent back to the DataWindow. Close the server file (or close the server) to return to the DataWindow painter. Notice that the BLOB column now displays the information you typed into the server application (if there's a significant amount of information, the data may be unreadable), as shown in Figure 37.4.

**FIGURE 37.3**
*An OLE object in the server application.*

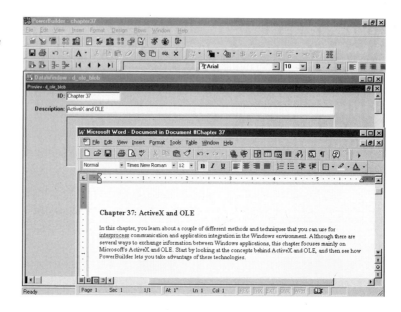

**FIGURE 37.4**
*An OLE column with updated data.*

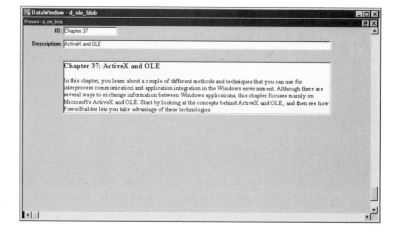

You can now save your changes back to the database. The BLOB column will be retrieved any subsequent time you use Preview, or at runtime when the DataWindow object is associated with a DataWindow control and the `Retrieve()` function is specified. At runtime, after the data is retrieved from the database, users can interact with the data by double-clicking just as in Preview mode.

If you prefer to provide your users with a way to open the OLE server application other than double-clicking, use the `OLEActivate()` function. This function is a method of a DataWindow control and takes three arguments:

- A Long that identifies the row in the DataWindow of the desired OLE column.

- The OLE column itself—the column number (an integer) or, preferably, the column name (a string).

- The action to pass to the OLE server application (commonly referred to as a *verb* in Windows). Most of the time, your users will want to edit the document in the server, which is typically a value of `0`. To find out which verbs a specific OLE server application supports, run the Registry Editor and look at the verbs defined under `HKEY_LOCAL_MACHINE\SOFTWARE\Classes\ClassName\Protocol\StdFileEditing\Verb`, where *ClassName* is the object class of the server application (for example, `Excel.Sheet.5`). The following is an example:

  ```
  dw_Budget.OLEActivate(dw_Budget.GetRow(), "object", 0)
  ```

  You can place this in the script you want to use to activate the OLE object (for example, a command button `Clicked` event or the `Clicked` event of the DataWindow control).

In addition to placing a database BLOB column on your DataWindow, you now can create an OLE presentation style.

## OLE DataWindow Presentation Style

The OLE 2.0 DataWindow presentation allows you to combine data retrieved via SQL with an OLE server. This has opened the presentation of the DataWindow to anything OLE developers can imagine—they can transform it into an OLE 2.0-compatible application. After you specify the data source for the DataWindow, the Insert Object property sheet appears (see Figure 37.5), asking you to specify the type of OLE object you want to create.

At this point, you have several options. You can choose a specific server application, a specific object or file, an ActiveX control, or nothing for the control. To create an empty OLE control, click the Cancel button.

To create a new OLE object in a server application, select the Create New tab page in the property sheet. The Object Type list box lists the OLE server applications that have been registered with Windows. Select a server application from the list, indicate whether you want it displayed as the server application's icon, and click OK. PowerBuilder activates the server application, enabling you to edit the new OLE object. By default, a new object is specified as embedded.

**FIGURE 37.5**

*The Insert Object property sheet.*

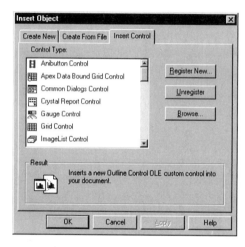

To create an OLE object from an existing file, click the Create From File tab page (see Figure 37.6).

**FIGURE 37.6**

*The Create From File tab page.*

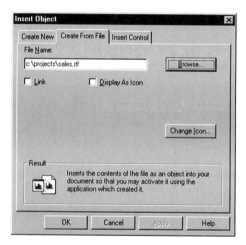

The DataWindow now becomes tied to a specific file. You can type the name into the File Name text box; or, if you don't know the path or filename, click the Browse button. If you want the OLE object to be linked instead of embedded, click the Link check box. You can also specify whether the object should be displayed as an icon. The default icon is the server application's icon, but you can specify another by using the Change Icon button and choosing a new icon. You can also specify an ActiveX control on the Insert Control tab page, but these typically don't form the basis for a presentation style.

After you specify the OLE server, PowerBuilder activates the server application, allowing you to make any changes you require. When you are finished, close the server application to return to the DataWindow Design mode.

You now can preview the DataWindow, which retrieves the data specified but doesn't automatically activate the OLE server. To view the data in the OLE server, double-click the DataWindow to activate the server in place. You can then implement and access the DataWindow just like any other DataWindow object.

If you want to integrate an existing DataWindow with an OLE server, you can do so by using the new OLE object. To place an OLE object on your DataWindow, click the OLE icon from the control drop-down toolbar. This opens the Insert Object property sheet (refer to Figure 37.5). After you choose the object type to insert and click OK, click the Data tab page in the painter properties tab to make the data specifications. The main difference between the OLE control and the OLE presentation style is that the OLE control doesn't consume the whole DataWindow. For example, you could have a tabular presentation with an OLE object on it using an MS Graph to summarize the data.

If you want to access an OLE server without accessing a database, you can do so by using the OLE 2.0 control.

## The OLE 2.0 Container

OLE 2.0 is available in the Window and User Object painters as a container control. This chapter discusses a window OLE control that can be manipulated the same way as an OLE user object.

To place an OLE control on a window, click the PainterBar icon that says OLE. PowerBuilder places an empty container (a rectangle) on the window and opens the Insert Object dialog (refer to Figure 37.5).

Just as with the DataWindow presentation style, you can choose a specific server application, a specific object or file, an ActiveX control, or nothing for the control.

After you make the association between the OLE control and the OLE server, you can specify the rest of the attributes of the OLE control on the property sheets (see Figure 37.7).

The OLE control has several standard attributes on the General tab page, such as `Name`, `Visible`, `Enabled`, `FocusRectangle`, `Border`, `Color`, and `Resizable`. In addition to these common control attributes, several other attributes are specific to the OLE 2.0 control.

The ContentsAllowed drop-down list lets you specify whether the control is linked, embedded, or any (the default). If you choose any, the object can be linked or embedded.

**37**

**ActiveX and OLE**

The DisplayType drop-down list box specifies what's displayed in the OLE 2.0 control: the contents, an ActiveX document, or just the icon. If you want to display a physical representation of the OLE object, choose the `displayascontent!` option.

**FIGURE 37.7**
*The OLE 2.0 control General property sheet.*

---

**Note**

The size of the OLE object is usually reduced so that it fits into the size of the OLE 2.0 control and, therefore, can be unreadable. Using Word as your OLE server increases the control to the size of the document page.

---

PowerBuilder 7.0 now supports the display of ActiveX documents in the OLE control. The main difference is that rather than show the hatched border, the document fills the container. To display an ActiveX document in the OLE control, select `displayasactivexdocument!` from the DisplayType drop-down list.

The other DisplayType option is `displayasicon!`. The icon associated with the data contained in the OLE 2.0 control is displayed in the window. The icon is typically the one used to represent the server application.

The LinkUpdateOptions drop-down list specifies how an object is updated if the server object is specified as linked. If the link is broken and PowerBuilder can't find the file that was linked, the `linkupdateautomatic!` option opens a dialog so that users can specify the file. When you're using `linkupdatemanual!`, if the link is broken, you can't activate the OLE object. To reestablish the link to the file, you must code some script with the `LinkTo()` function.

The Activation drop-down list box determines how the OLE control is activated. The `activateondoubleclick!` and `activateongetfocus!` options correspond to the OLE 2.0 control events `DoubleClick` and `GetFocus`. Whenever users double-click the OLE control or click or tab to the control, the respective event triggers and activates the OLE object. The third option, `activatemanually!`, requires that the control be activated using the `Activate()` function via a script.

> **Note**
>
> Even if you use one of the events for activation, you can still use the `Activate()` function.

If you decide that you want to change the object associated with the OLE 2.0 control, right-click the OLE 2.0 control to bring up the pop-up menu. The Object cascading menu lists the options you have to manipulate the OLE connection. If a server application isn't specified, the Insert menu item is the only one available. Clicking Insert opens the Insert Object property sheet. To activate the object from the Window painter, select Open, which starts the server application and activates the OLE object offsite. Clear removes the connection to a server application. Paste Special allows you to paste the current information from the Clipboard into your OLE control.

# Using the OLE 2.0 Control

After you decide how you want the OLE object set up (Linked, Embedded, Any, or No Object Specified Yet) in the DataWindow painter, you need to consider a few other items:

- How will the object be activated: in place or offsite?
- How will the menus behave if the object is activated in place?
- How will users activate the OLE object?

All these questions revolve around how users will interact with the OLE 2.0 control.

## In-Place Versus Offsite Activation

Do you want your users to be able to invoke the server application's full functionality without leaving the current window (in-place activation)? Or do you want users to open the server application and edit the data in the native server environment before returning to your application (offsite activation)? As mentioned previously, a linked object must be activated offsite.

With in-place activation, the control is activated by the value specified for the OLE 2.0 control's Activation attribute (in the Control Style dialog). When the control is activated in place and the display type is set to `displayascontent!`, the control has a wide, hatched border. If display type is set to `displayasactivexdocument!` and the control is activated in place, the document will fill the container. You can also change the menus, as you see later in this chapter.

> **Note**
>
> OLE 1.0 servers can be attached to OLE 2.0 controls, but they can't have in-place activation.

Offsite activation opens the server and allows users to edit the object in the server application window. The menus are the standard server application's menus, with some additional menu items such as Update. The OLE control also appears with a shaded border to indicate that the object is open.

## How Is the Control Activated?

The default method for activating an OLE object, whether activated in place or offsite, is to double-click the control. You can change this to the `GetFocus` event or to Manual at design time (in the control style dialog). If you choose the Manual option, you can specify when the OLE object is activated programmatically by using the `Activate()` function. This function takes one argument of data type `ActivationType`. The enumerated values are `InPlace!` and `OffSite!`. `Activate()` returns the following integer values:

| Value | Meaning |
| --- | --- |
| -1 | Control is empty. |
| -2 | Invalid verb for object. |
| -3 | Verb not implemented by object. |
| -4 | No verbs supported by object. |
| -5 | Object can't execute verb. |
| -9 | Other error. |

`Activate()` can be coded anywhere, but some common places are in the `Clicked` event of the OLE 2.0 control, the `Clicked` event of a command button, and the `Clicked` event of a menu item.

As you can see, the `Activate()` function will fail and return -1 if no object is specified for the control. You must assign an object before it can be activated. To do this programmatically, look at the `InsertObject()` function (discussed later in the "OLE Automation" section). `Activate()` will also fail if you have a linked object and the corresponding linked file isn't found (for instance, if the network crashed and the drive is no longer available). Depending on how the `Link Update` attribute is set (Automatic or Manual), PowerBuilder prompts you with a dialog (Automatic) or forces you to catch the error with PowerScript (Manual).

## Menus and In-Place Activation

If you decide you allow users to activate the OLE object in place, you also need to consider how the server's menus will interact or merge with your application's existing menus. To specify how the two menus will merge, you need to become familiar with the MergeOption drop-down list box in the Menu painter (see Figure 37.8).

**FIGURE 37.8**
*The MergeOption menu attribute in the Menu painter.*

The MergeOption drop-down list is activated only when you are positioned on a menu title (such as File, Edit, or Help). You can't combine individual menu titles from the different applications, but you can specify which menu displays. Table 37.1 shows menu settings and their uses.

**TABLE 37.1** MergeOption Activation Options in the Menu Painter

| Menu Setting | How It's Used |
|---|---|
| exclude! | The menu won't display when the OLE object is activated. |
| merge! | The menu from the container to be displayed after the first menu of the OLE server application. |

TABLE **37.1**   MergeOption Activation Options in the Menu Painter

| Menu Setting | How It's Used |
|---|---|
| filemenu! | The menu from the container application to be placed first (farthest to the left) on the menu bar. (The File menu from the OLE server won't display.) |
| editmenu! | The menu from the container specified as Edit won't display. The Edit menu from the OLE server application will display. |
| windowmenu! | The menu from the container displaying the list of open sheets will display. The OLE server's Window menu won't display. |
| helpmenu! | The menu from the container specified as Help won't display. The Help menu from the OLE server application will display. |

Any menus specified as Merge are included. The menu bar also includes additional menus that the server application has deemed appropriate. Figure 37.9 shows the PowerBuilder application's menus. Figure 37.10 shows Word's menus. Both menu sets are in their natural states. In Figure 37.11, you see the result of the menu merge when the OLE 2.0 control was activated in place.

**FIGURE 37.9**

*A PowerBuilder application's menus.*

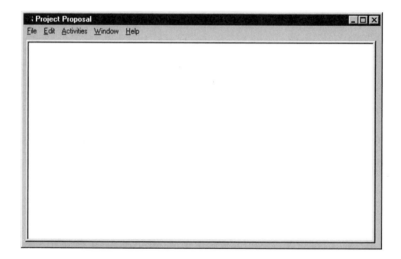

The aforementioned properties of an OLE object enable you to use the OLE server application without having to generate much code (with the exception of `Activate()`). Part of the beauty of OLE 2.0 is its capability to access the server application in your code.

**FIGURE 37.10**
*An OLE server's menus (Word).*

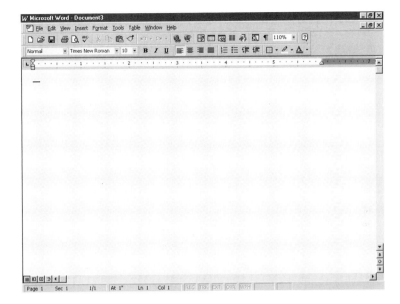

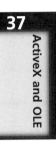

**FIGURE 37.11**
*A PowerBuilder application's menus with in-place activation.*

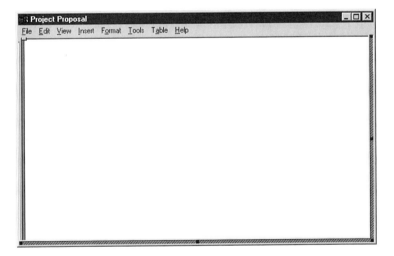

# OLE 2.0 Control Events

Table 37.2 shows several events specific to the OLE 2.0 control. These events all notify PowerBuilder when some action has occurred or is going to occur in the server application that affects the OLE object. The changes that trigger these events are automatically reflected in the OLE 2.0 control. They are made available in case you need to perform additional processing in response to a server action.

**TABLE 37.2**   Unique OLE 2.0 Control Events

| Event | Occurs When |
|---|---|
| DataChange | Data has changed in the server application. |
| Error | Dot notation specified to access properties or data is invalid at runtime. |
| ExternalException | Dot notation specified to access properties or data is invalid at runtime. Occurs before the Error event. |
| PropertyChanged | A property of the object has been changed by the server (server specific). |
| PropertyRequestEdit | A property of the object is about to be changed, and the server sends a notification (server specific). |
| Rename | The object is renamed in the server application. |
| Save | The data is saved from the server application. |
| ViewChange | The view shown to users has changed. |

If an error occurs in an OLE server call, the OLE control executes several levels of error handling. The first event triggered is ExternalException. The server application provides information about the error code and even passes the help topic context ID that documents the error. The event parameter, Action, indicates how the OLE control responds to the error. Action is of the enumerated data type ExceptionAction and has the following values:

| Value | Description |
|---|---|
| ExceptionFail! | Error isn't fixed, and processing continues to the Error event. |
| ExceptionIgnore! | Ignore the error and continue processing. |
| ExceptionRetry! | Execute the last command again to ensure server readiness. |
| ExceptionSubstituteReturn Value! | Use the ReturnValue argument of the event instead of the value passed by the OLE server and stop the error processing. |

If the ExternalException script sets the Action argument to ExceptionFail! or no script is written for the event, the Error event occurs. The Error event works similarly to ExternalException but with not as much detail. The Error event also allows you to set a default return value in response to an error. If the Error event is triggered and doesn't have a script or sets the Action argument to ExceptionFail!, the SystemError event is triggered as your last line of defense before the application terminates.

These events are triggered not only for the OLE control but also for the OLEObject standard class user object. To use the OLEObject or OLE control in your application, you usually need to write some script. This scripting capability is referred to as *OLE Automation*.

# OLE Automation

OLE Automation allows you to use the OLE server application's command set within the context of your application. You can use this with an object in an OLE 2.0 control or by defining an OLEObject variable in your script without actually displaying the OLE object to users.

## Manipulating the OLE Control

You've seen that activation of the OLE object can be done by double-clicking, by the control receiving focus, or by manually coding the Activate() function. You also can use the DoVerb() function to initiate OLE actions. A *verb* is defined as an integer value used to specify the action to be performed, as defined by the server application. The default action for most servers is 0, which means edit and also activates the OLE object:

```
ole_1.DoVerb(0)
```

You can find more information about a server's verbs in each server application's documentation and in the Windows Registry.

If you create an OLE 2.0 control and don't assign an object to the control at design time, you must assign the object at runtime. You can use several different functions to do this. The first function is olecontrol.InsertObject(), which opens the Insert Object dialog and allows users to specify a new or existing OLE object to be inserted into the OLE control. If the Contents attribute of the OLE 2.0 control is set to Any, users can also specify whether the object is embedded or linked. The return codes are 0 if successful, -1 if users clicked Cancel, and -9 for all other errors.

If you have a specific file that you want to embed into an existing OLE control, use the function olecontrol.InsertFile(). The argument for the function is a string containing the name and location of the file to be embedded in the OLE control; 0 means success, -1 means that the file wasn't found, and -9 is for all other errors.

A more specific case of InsertFile() is LinkTo(). This function also specifies a particular filename, but it enables you to link to a specific item within the file (such as a range of cells in an Excel spreadsheet). If an item name isn't specified, the link is established with the whole file. The return codes are 0 for success, -1 if the file wasn't found, -2 if the item wasn't found, and -9 for all other errors.

A function similar to InsertFile() is olecontrol.InsertClass(), which embeds a new object of the chosen OLE server into the OLE control. If you don't know the names of the registered OLE server applications installed, open the Object Browser from within the

PowerScript painter and select the OLE tab page to list all OLE server applications (see Figure 37.12).

**FIGURE 37.12**

*The Object Browser OLE tab page.*

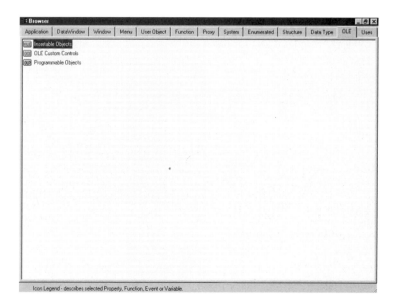

The OLE tab page has three headings: Insertable Objects, OLE Custom Controls (ActiveX controls), and Programmable Objects. You can expand each heading by double-clicking it. The insertable objects are the different application servers you can connect to. Some objects can be expanded to display the methods and properties available for you to access via your script. If you select a listed insertable object and click the Paste button, the object's class is pasted into your script. The object class can then be used for the `InsertClass()` function. Common examples of insertable objects are `Word.Document.8` and `Excel.Sheet.8` for Word and Excel, respectively. The `InsertClass()` function also returns 0 and -9, just like `InsertFile()`, and -1 when an invalid class name is specified.

You can also specify an OLE object stored as a BLOB variable to be assigned to the OLE control by referencing the `ObjectData` attribute, as follows:

```
Blob sales_blob
```

```
ole_1.ObjectData = sales_blob
```

You can cut, copy, or paste data into the OLE control via the Windows Clipboard. The functions used to paste Clipboard data into an OLE object or control are `Paste()`, `PasteLink()`, and `PasteSpecial()`. The difference between the functions, respectively, is how the object is placed in the OLE control: embedded, linked, or allowing users to embed or link the data via a dialog. Chapter 12, "Menus and the Menu Painter," outlines the code necessary to implement standard Cut, Copy, and Paste menu items.

Whether you assign the OLE object at design time or at runtime, in most cases users will want to edit the data. If the object is embedded, users can't save the changes back to the file because it's part of your EXE or PBD. If you want to save changes, you must save them to a database or another file.

To save the OLE object to a database, reference the ObjectData attribute of the OLE control and store the value in a BLOB variable. To update the database, you must use a special SQL statement, UPDATEBLOB.

> **Note**
>
> PowerBuilder writes BLOBs in 32KB chunks. If the last update isn't a full 32KB, PowerBuilder appends NULL values at the end. When retrieving the data, be sure to remember that the NULLs must be stripped off programmatically so that garbage isn't displayed in the server application.

To save the OLE object as a file, use the GetFileSaveName() function as follows to open the Save common dialog and the SaveAs() function:

```
String    ls_FileName, ls_PathName
Integer   li_rtn

li_rtn = GetFileSaveName("File Select", ls_PathName, ls_FileName, "OLE", &
 "OLE Files (*.OLE),*.OLE")

If li_rtn <> -1 then
   li_rtn = ole_1.SaveAs(ls_FileName)
End If
```

Users can specify the filenames they want the objects to have when saved.

> **Note**
>
> An OLE file can't be opened by using the server application; it can be opened only by using the OLE control in PowerBuilder and activating the server application.

# Manipulating the OLE Object

Everything discussed so far has dealt with manipulating the OLE control and its assignment with an OLE object. Now you get to see how to manipulate the OLE object. With DDE, you needed to issue functions such as `ExecRemote()` and `SetRemote()` that specified tasks for the server to perform. With OLE 2.0, you can explicitly call server commands in your scripts by referencing the `Object` attribute of the OLE 2.0 control. The syntax is as follows:

```
oleObjectName.Object.Method  (Arguments)
oleObjectName.Object.Attribute = Value
```

An easy example is assigning a bookmark value in a Word document, as follows:

```
ole_1.InsertFile("c:\msoffice\winword\unleash\cover.doc")
ole_1.Activate(InPlace!)
ole_1.Object.application.editgoto("last_name")
ole_1.Object.application.insert ("Reppart")
```

PowerBuilder doesn't do syntax checking on any statements after the OLE control's `Object` attribute. The obvious reason for this is that PowerBuilder doesn't know the valid syntax for the server application. It's a good idea to test the script in the server application before placing it in PowerBuilder.

What if you don't know the server's command language (for example, VBA with Microsoft Office)? Two methods are common and are usually used together to generate the commands to use in a PowerBuilder application. The easiest method is to buy a book that details the server application's native script or macro language. In addition to this reference material, most server applications enable you to record actions as you perform them. Record your movements and edit the recorded script (which is usually referred to as a *macro*). Sometimes you can copy the script verbatim, but it might need some additional tweaking to get it to work in your application's script.

In PowerBuilder, you can access information about a server's methods, properties, and events via the Object Browser. As shown earlier in Figure 37.12, the OLE tab page of the Object Browser displays all the registered OLE servers in Windows. Depending on the server, you can drill down via the OLE tree and view the accessible methods, properties, and events for that object and paste them into your script (see Figure 37.13).

For Excel's `Delete` method, clicking the Paste button would place the following in your script:

```
OLEControl.Object.Delete()
```

**FIGURE 37.13**

*Insertable object syntax in the Object Browser.*

The same process is also true of any ActiveX control you might use in your application. If the ActiveX control has been registered with Windows, it will appear in the OLE Custom Controls section of the Object Browser. You can then expand the tree view to see the class information as well as the different events, methods, and properties of the control (see Figure 37.14).

When the desired value is located, clicking the Paste button places the following in your script:

```
OLECustomControl.object.Enabled
```

PowerBuilder works with OLE Automation by executing one function at a time. This means that you can't access the server's control statements (such as `If...Then` and `For...Next`). You must add this kind of logic into your PowerBuilder application.

> **Tip**
>
> You could execute a server macro from PowerBuilder with the control statements written in the server application. The only negative is that now you're maintaining code in multiple locations.

**FIGURE 37.14**

*ActiveX controls
in the Object
Browser.*

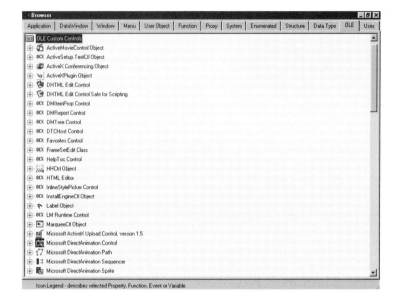

One thing to be careful of is how you qualify the server command—for instance, whether you use the application's name. This depends on the server application and how the object is connected. The object hierarchy varies from one application to another and needs to be considered when writing your OLE commands. For example, in Excel, seemingly identical commands in PowerBuilder produce different results:

```
ole_1.Object.cells(5,5).value = dw_1.GetItemNumber(1, "unit_price")
```

This statement modifies the cell in an Excel spreadsheet located in the PowerBuilder OLE control. However, an error will occur if the document isn't activated first:

```
ole_1.Object.cells(5,5).application.value = dw_1.GetItemNumber(1, "unit_price")
```

Although this statement appears to do exactly the same thing as the previous example, it doesn't. By referencing the application, the specified cell (row 5, column 5) will be changed in the active document whether or not the active document is the same one specified in your OLE control. Because you might be updating the wrong spreadsheet, it's best to use the first method with Excel.

## OLEObject

If you just want to use the functionality of a particular application and never let users see the server application, create an OLE object in your script that's independent of an OLE 2.0 control. You can create an OLE object with the data type OLEObject and connect your application to the server; then you have exactly the same capabilities to call functions and set attributes in the server application. You can also create a standard class user object with standardized processing. For some OLE server applications, you can even specify whether users can see that the server application is open.

The following lines declare and instantiate an OLE object:

```
OLEObject ole_letter
```

```
ole_letter = CREATE OLEObject
```

This allocates memory for the OLE object, which is actually quite small because UDT ensures that the variable contains only a reference to the actual object. The object itself is stored with the server application. Depending on the kind of processing you will be doing in your application, you might declare the OLE object as an instance variable rather than a local one.

After creating your OLE object, establish a connection with a server application before doing any other processing. Two functions accomplish this: `oleobject.ConnectTo`
`NewObject()` and `oleobject.ConnectToObject()`.

Use `ConnectToNewObject()` like the `InsertClass()` function to create a brand-new object for an OLE server. Use `ConnectToObject()` to connect to an OLE object using an existing file. With `ConnectToObject()`, you specify the filename and optionally the class name (`ConnectToNewObject()` just needs the class name). If you don't specify a class name, PowerBuilder uses the filename's extension to determine which server application to start.

When the connection is established, you can continue and use the server's commands to do your processing, as in this example, which you saw earlier:

```
ole_letter.ConnectToNewObject("word.basic")
ole_letter.EditGoto("last_name")
ole_letter.Insert ("Puckett")
```

Notice that you don't need to include the application qualifier for the commands (`application` no longer needs to be added). It was already specified when connecting to the server.

PowerBuilder provides two functions for use with `OLEObject` variables: `SetAutomation-Pointer()` and `SetAutomationTimeout()`. `SetAutomationPointer()` is used with a standard class user object of `OLEObject`. You would create a user object to extend the functionality of the PowerBuilder class of `OLEObject` (for example, to write a script for the `ExternalException` event). You can now pass an OLE Automation pointer from a variable of type `OLEObject`, which you used to establish a connection to an OLE server, to your `OLEObject` user object. Do this by using the following syntax:

```
OLE_UserObjectVar.SetAutomationPointer(OLEObjectVar)
```

where *OLE_UserObjectVar* is a variable defined from your user object, and *OLEObjectVar* is a variable of type OLEObject. This provides a clean mechanism for passing the OLE Automation pointer.

Use the second function, SetAutomationTimeout(), to specify how long your Power-Builder application waits before canceling a call to the OLE server. The syntax is as follows:

```
OLEObjectVar.SetAutomationTimeout(WaitTime)
```

where *OLEObjectVar* is the variable name of your OLEObject, and *WaitTime* is the number of milliseconds you want your application to wait before canceling the process. The default time is 300,000 milliseconds (5 minutes).

After all processing is completed, disconnect from the server application and release the memory that the OLE object is using (just like disconnecting from a database), as follows:

```
ole_letter.DisconnectOjbect()
DESTROY ole_letter
```

> **Note**
>
> Be sure to disconnect before your OLEObject variable goes out of scope; otherwise, there's no means to programmatically close the server application. If the server is visible, users can close it, but that would be sloppy programming.

## The Any Data Type

Because PowerBuilder doesn't know the syntax of the server's command language, it also makes sense that it knows nothing of the data types returned from any commands executed. To handle this situation, PowerBuilder has a generic data type called Any, which can handle assignments from the server regardless of the data type. At runtime, when the Any data type is assigned a value, it becomes a variable of the appropriate data type (such as string or integer). To determine the true data type of the any variable, use the function ClassName() as follows:

```
OLEObject  ole_Excel
String     ls_String
Integer    li_Integer
Any        la_Any
```

```
ole_Excel = CREATE OLEObject
ole_Excel.ConnectToObject("budget.xls")

la_Any = ole_Excel.application.cells(10,5).value

Choose Case ClassName(la_Any)
   Case "string"
      ls_String = la_Any
   Case "int"
      ls_Integer = la_Any
   Case Else
      MessageBox("Retrieve Error","Unknown data type returned")
      Return
End Choose
```

Although the Any data type definitely has its use with OLE applications, it's not wise to use it regularly because of its high overhead.

## OLEStorage and OLEStream

As defined earlier, OLE storages and streams make up the underlying structures of OLE and are how OLE objects are stored. Recall that OLE storages equate to DOS directories, and streams equate to the files within a storage. For the most part, you can work with OLE objects and never have to worry about managing OLE storages. If you need to perform some complex OLE functionality, such as combining multiple OLE objects into one structure, PowerBuilder allows you to manipulate OLE data.

PowerBuilder supplies two standard class user objects: OLEStorage and OLEStream. These objects are treated like any other nonvisual user objects in that they must be declared, instantiated, and destroyed. You also need to open and close the storages by using the Open() and Save() or SaveAs() methods. Because streams are contained within a storage, you must remember to open the storage first.

In most cases, if you need to store OLE data, you can by using a BLOB column from the database. If you aren't using a database or your DBMS doesn't support BLOBs, consider using storages as an alternative.

# DCOM

PowerBuilder 6.0 added support for Microsoft's Distributed Component Object Model (DCOM) for use with remote server activation. Rather than connect to an OLE server on the client machine, your application uses a COM application located on a networked server machine.

To attach to a DCOM application, use `ConnectToRemoteObject()` or `ConnectToNew-RemoteObject()`. These functions are used in much the same way as their `Connect-ToObject()` and `ConnectToNewObject()` counterparts discussed earlier in the section "OLEObject." The only difference in using these functions is that an additional string argument now identifies the location of the remote server application. This argument is the first passed in both functions. The remaining arguments are the same as `ConnectToObject()` and `ConnectToNewObject()`.

> **Note**
>
> To use a DCOM server application, the application must be registered on the server and client machines. DCOM is available for Windows, Macintosh, and several versions of UNIX.

# ActiveX Controls

PowerBuilder supports the use of ActiveX technology via the OLE 2.0 control. ActiveX controls are OLE-based components that became available when Microsoft released Visual Basic 5. Before that, they were referred to as OLE Custom Controls and were most commonly known by their file extension, OCX. After placing an OLE control on your window, user object, or DataWindow, select the Insert Control tab page on the Insert Object property sheet (see Figure 37.15).

**FIGURE 37.15**
*The Insert Control tab page.*

This tab page displays all the ActiveX controls registered with Windows. If you have an ActiveX control that doesn't appear, you can register via the Register New button, which opens a Browse dialog allowing you to indicate the ActiveX file. You can also remove an ActiveX control via the Unregister button.

Clicking the Browse button opens the OLE Object Browser (see Figure 37.16). This browser lets you view the methods, events, and properties for the selected control. After specifying the desired control, click OK to return to the Window painter and place the OLE control.

**FIGURE 37.16**

*The OLE Object Browser.*

Right-clicking the control lets you set the standard control properties and gives you a menu option of setting the OLE Control (ActiveX) properties. This menu item opens the property sheet for the specified ActiveX control (see Figure 37.17). Here you can specify the desired settings for the control as detailed in the ActiveX control's documentation. The control's events are then accessible from the Script painter in the Select Event drop-down list box.

**FIGURE 37.17**

*The OLE Control Properties sheet (for the* Active-MovieControl*).*

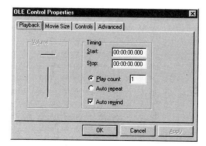

To access an ActiveX control's properties or methods, this is the syntax:

```
OLEControl.Object.PropertyOrMethodName
```

*OLEControl* is the name of the OLE 2.0 control, and *PropertyOrMethodName* is the desired property or method. You can find these in the control documentation, or you can use the Object Browser. From the PowerScript painter, open the Object Browser and click the OLE tab page. Double-click the OLE Custom Controls entry to display a list of all the registered ActiveX controls. Each control can be expanded to show its methods, events, and properties. Each can be expanded in turn and then pasted into your script (see Figure 37.18).

**FIGURE 37.18**

*The expanded control in the Object Browser.*

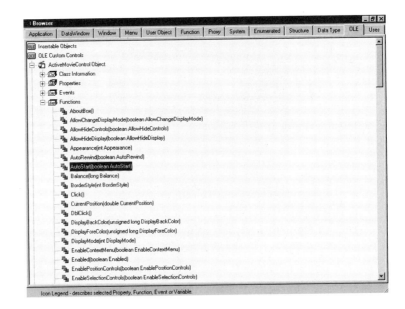

Select the desired category and click the Paste button to place the necessary syntax in your script, including placeholders for any arguments. Pasting the function selected in Figure 37.18 would produce this:

```
CustomControl.object.AutoStart(boolean AutoStart)
```

PowerBuilder has made ActiveX implementation a relatively seamless process by allowing ActiveX controls to be accessed like any other control. PowerBuilder includes several lightweight controls in its Component Gallery, and additional controls can be purchased in the Component Pack.

# PowerBuilder as an OLE Server

Many people wonder whether PowerBuilder can be a server application for another Windows application. PowerBuilder can act as an OLE server via a nonvisual user object. The Sybase product InfoMaker also can be a server. InfoMaker generates Powersoft reports (PSRs), which are embedded or linked to the OLE client application. These reports can be added to an application supporting OLE 2.0. When the OLE PSR is activated, InfoMaker is started, and its full functionality can be used. On the other hand, unlike PowerBuilder, InfoMaker can't be an OLE client or contain OLE objects in its reports. PSR files can also be generated from within PowerBuilder through the DataWindow painter or by using the SaveAs() function.

You first need to create the custom class user object with all attributes and functions you want to access via OLE Automation defined as public. The user object needs to be compiled into a dynamic library (machine code or p-code) from within PowerBuilder. If you use the COM/MTS Component Wizard, PowerBuilder guides you through all the steps necessary to create and register your custom component; otherwise, you need to register the control manually.

You can manually register your new component in two ways:

- Create a Registry entry that helps OLE locate the user object. The entry takes the program identifier (the user object class name) and translates it into a global unique identifier. After the global identifier is created, additional entries are defined in the Registry to set the library list indicating the PowerBuilder dynamic library containing the user object and the executable type (machine code or p-code). When this is done, each OLE client application can create an instance of the object in its application (in PowerBuilder, this is accomplished via ConnectToNewObject()). The only problem with this approach is that translation information must be predefined in the Registry.

- The other method doesn't require predefining the Registry entries and allows you to generate the Registry file via the OLE Automation object PowerBuilder .Application. This object has four methods— GenerateGUID(), GenerateRegFile(), CreateObject(), and GenerateTypeLib()—that you can use to create a global unique identifier (GUID) and then create the Registry file to update the client machine's Registry. The optional GenerateTypeLib() function is used to create a type library so that other OLE browsers can display the properties and methods of your OLE object.

Before you can access any properties or methods, create an instance of `PowerBuilder.`‑`Application` by using the `ConnectToObject()` function. Here's the syntax:

```
OLEObject  PBObject
Long       ll_rtn


PBObject = CREATE OLEObject


ll_rtn = PBObject.ConnectToObject("PowerBuilder.Application")
```

In addition to the three methods there are two properties of `PowerBuilder.Application` that must be set after the OLE Automation object is instantiated. The `LibraryList` property is a string that contains a list of dynamic libraries that are searched to locate object classes when creating instances. The list must be set before the creation of the first object because it's fixed after the first object is instantiated. The second property, `MachineCode`, is a Boolean value (the default is `TRUE`) used to indicate the library code type (machine code or p-code). Both properties are ignored after the first object is created.

`GenerateGUID()` creates the GUID and returns a string representing the identifier in a reference parameter. The return values are as follows:

| Value | Description |
| --- | --- |
| 0 | GUID successfully generated. |
| -1 | Couldn't load required DLL to generate GUID. |
| -2 | No network card found; GUID not generated. |
| -3 | Create failed. |
| -9 | Unknown error. |

The string reference returned is passed to the `GenerateRegFile()` function to create the registration file. This is the syntax:

```
GenerateRegFile(GUID, ClassName, ProgId, MajorVersion, MinorVersion, &
                Description, TargetFile)
```

*GUID* is the string reference generated by `GenerateGUID()`. *ClassName* is a string containing the class name of the user object. *ProgId* is a string containing the OLE programmatic identifier (such as `Tax.Object`). *MajorVersion* and *MinorVersion* are used to indicate the major and minor releases of the OLE object. *Description* is a descriptive name displayed by OLE. *TargetFile* is a string specifying the name of the text registration file to create. GenerateRegFile() returns one of the following Long values:

| Value | Description |
| --- | --- |
| 0 | Registry file created |
| -1 | Memory allocation error |
| -2 | No target file name specified |
| -3 | Can't open target file |
| -9 | Unknown error |

Listing 37.1 shows the whole process to create a registration file.

**LISTING 37.1**    Registration File Generation

```
OLEObject    PBObject
String       GUID
Long         ll_rtn


PBObject = CREATE OLEObject


ll_rtn = PBObject.ConnectToNewObject("PowerBuilder.Application")
If ll_rtn < 0 Then
  MessageBox("Connect Error", "Could not connect to OLE Automation object")
  Return
Else
  //Set the library list
  PBObject.LibraryList = "c:\projects\tax\tax.dll"
  //Specify the library compilation type
  PBObject.MachineCode = True
  //Generate the GUID
  ll_rtn = PBObject.GenerateGUID(REF GUID)
  If ll_rtn < 0 Then
    MessageBox ("Generation Error", "Could not generate GUID.")
    Return
  Else
    //Generate the registration file
    ll_rtn = PBObject.GenerateRegFile(GUID, "u_tax_calc", "Tax.Object", 1, 0, &
    "Tax calculations", "c:\projects\tax\tax.reg")
    If ll_rtn < 0 Then
      MessageBox("Generation Error", "Could not generate registration file")
    End If
  End If
End If
End If
```

After you successfully create the registration file, you can merge it into the Registry by using the Registry Editor. This results in entries under the key HKEY_CLASSES_ROOT\CLSID. The registration file for the tax application generates the registration file shown in Listing 37.2.

**LISTING 37.2**   The tax.reg File

```
REGEDIT
;;;;;;;;;;;;;;;;;
;
; Registry entries for tax.object
;
; CLSID = {9FE589C8-5587-11CF-B5DC-E44A01C10079}
;
;;;;;;;;;;;;;;;;

; Version independent entries:
HKEY_CLASSES_ROOT\tax.object = tax application
HKEY_CLASSES_ROOT\tax.object\CLSID = {9FE589C8-5587-11CF-B5DC-E44A01C10079}
HKEY_CLASSES_ROOT\tax.object\CurVer = tax.object.1
HKEY_CLASSES_ROOT\tax.object\NotInsertable

; Version specific entries:
HKEY_CLASSES_ROOT\tax.object.1 = tax application
HKEY_CLASSES_ROOT\tax.object.1\CLSID = {9FE589C8-5587-11CF-B5DC-E44A01C10079}
HKEY_CLASSES_ROOT\tax.object.1\NotInsertable

; CLSID entries:
HKEY_CLASSES_ROOT\CLSID\{9FE589C8-5587-11CF-B5DC-E44A01C10079} =
                            ➥tax application
HKEY_CLASSES_ROOT\CLSID\{9FE589C8-5587-11CF-B5DC-E44A01C10079}\ProgID =
                            ➥tax.object.1
HKEY_CLASSES_ROOT\CLSID\{9FE589C8-5587-11CF-B5DC-E44A01C10079}\
                            ➥VersionIndependentProgID = tax.object
HKEY_CLASSES_ROOT\CLSID\{9FE589C8-5587-11CF-B5DC-E44A01C10079}\
                            ➥InProcServer32 = PBROI050.DLL
HKEY_CLASSES_ROOT\CLSID\{9FE589C8-5587-11CF-B5DC-E44A01C10079}\NotInsertable
HKEY_CLASSES_ROOT\CLSID\{9FE589C8-5587-11CF-B5DC-E44A01C10079}\Programmable
HKEY_CLASSES_ROOT\CLSID\{9FE589C8-5587-11CF-B5DC-E44A01C10079}\PowerBuilder\
                            ➥ClassName = u_tax
HKEY_CLASSES_ROOT\CLSID\{9FE589C8-5587-11CF-B5DC-E44A01C10079}\PowerBuilder\
                            ➥LibraryList =
```

**LISTING 37.2**  CONTINUED

```
HKEY_CLASSES_ROOT\CLSID\{9FE589C8-5587-11CF-B5DC-E44A01C10079}\PowerBuilder\
                          ➥BinaryType = PCODE
```

When this is finished, you are ready to access the OLE object from your client automation application. For example, to call the tax object u_tax_calc from Visual Basic, you'd use this code:

```
Dim PBObject As Object
Dim Taxuo As Object
Dim GrossPay as Integer
Dim TaxRate as Integer

 'Connect to the tax object
Set PBObject = CreateObject("PowerBuilder.Application")
If pbobject Is Nothing Then
   MsgBox "Create of PB object failed"
   End Sub
Else
   PBObject.LibraryList = "c:\pbi32\tax.pbd"
   Set Taxuo = PBObject.CreateObject("u_tax_calc")
   If Taxuo Is Nothing Then
      MsgBox "tax uo failed"
      End Sub
   Else
      'Call the tax bracket function
      TaxRate = Taxuo.uf_Tax (GrossPay)
      Set Taxuo = Nothing
   End If
   Set pbobject = Nothing
End If
```

So that you can create PowerBuilder OLE servers, you need to merge PBAPPL.REG into the Windows Registry and update the path for PBVM70.DLL and PBAEN70.TLB to point to the installed directory. After you complete the registration, your component is displayed in the Object Browser's OLE tab.

**37**

*ActiveX and OLE*

# Summary

In this chapter, you saw several ways that you can use OLE and ActiveX in your PowerBuilder applications. Microsoft is committed to making OLE and ActiveX the standard way of building component software. Although the technology has been plagued with problems in the past, support for OLE has improved dramatically over the past several years.

# PowerBuilder Resources

Many PowerBuilder resources are available, such as training partners, CODE partners, user groups, and so on. This appendix lists the resources available as of the writing of this book. Sybase's Web site or the Infobase CD contains up-to-date information of each.

# Training Partners

Training partners are companies that teach the certified Sybase/Powersoft courses. All instructors on staff must obtain at least CPD Associate-level status and pass the Sybase Instructor certification. Each company is a value-added reseller, having achieved success in selling, consulting, training, and developing applications using PowerBuilder.

# Business Solutions Alliance Partner

Sybase's newest partner program is extended to value-added companies that have achieved success in developing applications using Sybase products. For more information on Sybase partnerships, see `http://www.sybase.com/partners/`.

# CODE Partners

CODE stands for *Client/server Open Development Environment*. These companies offer third-party software that increases PowerBuilder's product capabilities. These include the ongoing development of vendor partnerships that cover the entire enterprise computing environment as well as the expansion of the company's training, consulting, and product support services and alliances.

# PowerBuilder User Groups

Many PowerBuilder User Groups are available, and you should search the Web or Sybase's Web site for information on your local group. Sybase is also willing to help in the setting up of user groups and can provide speakers.

# Technical Support

Technical support services offered by Sybase and the PowerBuilder community range from telephone support to electronic services.

# Fee-Based Support Options

As you might expect, you have to pay for most telephone assistance from Sybase. The support-line technical engineer assists you in diagnosing problems, solving product-related technical issues, and understanding platform-specific issues.

If the technical issue or question requires more than a limited amount of programming assistance, call 1-800-8SYBASE so that Sybase can direct you to one of its many consulting and training partners. Before you call Sybase technical support, however, it's highly recommended that you follow these steps:

1. Read the relevant Sybase documentation.
2. Check the Web to make sure that you are running the latest product fixes.
3. Check the PowerBuilder Infobase CD-ROM and Web for information that may solve or help isolate the problem, or to determine whether you've encountered a known bug.
4. Check one of the many Sybase newsgroups listed on `http://support.sybase.com`.

If these simple steps don't produce an answer or you are experiencing a known bug, you need to call technical support. Before you call, first try to isolate the problem. If you call support before completely isolating the problem, you will face considerably longer delays in solving your problem. Follow these steps:

1. Determine the precise steps required to consistently reproduce the problem.
2. Create a new library and copy the application and its objects into the new library.
3. Reconstruct the application to use only the problem windows. Change the script to open the windows from the application. Remove all variables and unnecessary external functions.
4. Reproduce the problem with this small library.
5. Document in a text file the steps needed to reproduce the problem.
6. If you still encounter the problem, call technical support and be prepared to create a zip file of the small library and the text file and email it to Sybase.

To save yourself and the engineer time, have the following information at hand:

- Your registration card number or support ID
- The exact error message
- The product and version number you're using
- Your DBMS, including version number

- Your network protocol

- Your local system, including specific PC components, RAM, hard disk space (both available and total), add-ons, peripherals, and network information

## Annual Support

The annual support option provides ongoing support during your project development cycle and entitles you to support for Sybase products and unlimited technical calls from designated primary contacts at your site. The support-line technical engineers are typically available from 8 a.m. to 8 p.m. EST Monday through Friday, but bonus plans can be purchased to extend those hours. You also receive the server edition of the Sybase Infobase CD-ROM. You can purchase an annual support agreement by calling your local Sybase/ Powersoft office.

## Pay Per Issue

By using your American Express, VISA, or MasterCard, you can receive technical support on a pay-per-call basis. Sybase will follow up on all unresolved issues at no additional charge to you and won't charge you if it determines that your problem is the result of a software bug. Calls are limited to one issue per call and can be purchased in multiples of ten.

## Bug Reporting

The best bet for submitting bugs is on the Sybase Web site at `http://casexpress.sybase.com`. If you do not have Internet access, you can call 1-800-8SYBASE and they will direct your call.

## Enhancement Requests

The process to request an enhancement is much the same as reporting a bug. You can manually fill out the Enhancement Request form (PBNHANCE.TXT) from the BBS or faxline document, or you can fill out a form on the Sybase Web site at `http://casexpress.sybase.com`.

## InfoBase CD-ROM

Sybase's CD-ROM is available through an annual subscription, or free to customers who subscribe to the Sybase annual support program. There's also now a Web-based version of this on the Sybase site.

Infobase includes access to thousands of technical tips from Sybase's own technical engineers, questions and answers, problem reports and workarounds, how-to videos, all the faxline documents, and maintenance releases.

Within the Infobase, you can carry out keyword searches to quickly find the information you want, or all related articles.

# Online Sources

By using a modem, you can access many other resources for technical support and sample code.

## Web Pages

Sybase's Web page is accessible at `www.sybase.com` and provides access to

- Company overview—A message from the CEO, a Sybase company overview, and press releases.

- Product information—PowerBuilder, InfoMaker, and Sybase companion products, as well as PowerBuilder third-party books and magazines. You can even order Sybase products via this Internet resource.

- Employment opportunities—At Sybase.

- Training—Information on self-paced training, course descriptions, Certified Power-Builder Developer (CPD) program, and Sybase training schedule (Adobe .PDF format).

- Consulting—Description of Sybase Consulting Services and Sybase Best Practices.

- International offerings—Local Sybase offices and subsidiaries.

- Customer service and support—Faxline documents, FTP, complete product documentation, white papers, online magazines, and emailed newsletters.

- What's new—Covers the latest-breaking news concerning PowerBuilder.

- Events—PowerBuilder user groups, trade shows, seminars and speaking engagements.

- Partners—Partner programs, North American partner listings, and international partner listings.

The number of PowerBuilder Web sites created by the PowerBuilder development community is growing. It's recommended that you either use a search engine to find them, or start at one of the authors' Web pages (see the authors section at the front of the book), which have links to a number of resources.

The Macmillan site, `www.mcp.com`, provides up-to-the-minute information on the publication of books such as *PowerBuilder 7.0 Unleashed* and feature releases.

## Newsgroup

A Usenet newsgroup, `comp.soft-sys.powerbuilder`, is for the discussion of Sybase-related subjects. This is an ideal place to exchange advice and information with other developers using PowerBuilder. The preferred newsgroups are now under `powersoft.-public.powersoft.*` (where the * is an area such as `datawindow`, `powerscript`, `pfc`, or `general`).

# Other Sources on Sybase Products

Several of the more specialized computer magazines, such as *Intelligent Enterprise* (formerly *DBMS*), *Data Based Advisor*, and *Database Programming & Design*, contain articles on PowerBuilder topics as well as product reviews. PowerBuilder journals also are available; the most well known is *PowerBuilder Developers Journal*.

# PowerBuilder
# Data Types

## IN THIS APPENDIX

- **PowerBuilder Standard Data Types    1232**
- **PowerBuilder Enumerated Data Types    1232**

PowerBuilder data types are broken into two distinct types: standard data types and enumerated data types.

# PowerBuilder Standard Data Types

The standard data types are used in most programming languages and include Char, Integer, Decimal, Long, and String.

TABLE B.1. PowerBuilder Standard Data Types

| Data Type | Description |
| --- | --- |
| Any | Undeclared data type. You must use the `ClassName()` function to determine the actual data type. |
| Blob | Binary large object. |
| Boolean | A Boolean value (`TRUE` or `FALSE`). |
| Character | A single character. Abbreviated to Char. |
| Date | Dates in the *yyyy-mm-dd* or *yyyy/mm/dd* format. Hyphens (or forward slashes) and leading zeros are required, and blanks aren't allowed. |
| DateTime | Date and time combined into a single value. |
| Decimal | Signed decimal numbers with up to 18 digits of precision. Often abbreviated to Dec. |
| Double | Signed floating-point numbers with 15 digits of precision. The actual range varies between platforms. |
| Integer | 16-bit signed whole numbers with a range of -32768 to +32767. Sometimes abbreviated Int. |
| Long | 32-bit signed whole numbers with a range of -2,147,483,648 to +2,147,483,647. |
| Real | Signed floating-point numbers with six digits of precision. The actual range varies between platforms. |
| String | Strings of 0 to 2,147483,647 ASCII characters. |
| Time | Times in 24-hour format (*hh:mm:ss:ffffff*). Colons and leading zeros are required, and blanks aren't allowed. |
| UnsignedInteger | 16-bit unsigned whole numbers with a range of 0 to 65535. Often abbreviated UnsignedInt or Uint. |
| UnsignedLong | 32-bit unsigned whole numbers with a range of 0 to 4,294,967,295. Often abbreviated Ulong. |

# PowerBuilder Enumerated Data Types

Enumerated data types have predefined sets of values. These data types can be used either as arguments in function calls or in the assignment of a value to an object attribute. The values of an enumerated data type always end with an exclamation point (!). To see the full list, open the Object Browser and select the Enumerated Data Types page.

# Investigating Exported Code

Few novice (or even intermediate) programmers delve into the mysteries of export object definitions. Sometimes, however, it's necessary to be able to export an object, make a modification, and re-import it. Understanding exported code can also provide experienced developers with insight into how PowerBuilder creates the various objects in your applications.

# Exporting

You export the code from within the Library painter by using either the pop-up menu on an object or the PainterBar button. This prompts you for the destination filename, to which PowerBuilder assigns a three-character file extension based on the object type.

| Object Type | File Extension |
| --- | --- |
| Window | .srw |
| DataWindow | .srd |
| Menu | .srm |
| Structure | .srs |
| Application | .sra |
| Function | .srf |
| Project | .srj |
| User object | .sru |

PowerBuilder supports long filenames and creates the files with the exact name of the object with the appropriate extension from the preceding list.

# Making Modifications to Different Areas of the File

The two most common modifications made to an object when it has been exported are global string replacement and the changing of the ancestor object. To illustrate the syntax of the exported file and what it means for inherited objects, this appendix illustrates the areas of the exported object using the exported code of a window with nine controls. The exported window file shown in Listing C.1 provides a good basis to start with; a number of the other object types share a similar structure.

> **Note**
>
> Some listings in this appendix contain line numbers to provide reference points to the text and are not created or generated as part of the export process.

**LISTING C.1**　An Export of a Window with Nine Controls

```
 1: $PBExportHeader$w_error.srw
 2: forward
 3: global type w_error from window
 4: end type
 5: type mle_error from multilineedit within w_error
 6: end type
 7: type st_event from statictext within w_error
 8: end type
 9: type st_name from statictext within w_error
10: end type
11: type sle_object_name from singlelineedit within w_error
12: end type
13: type sle_object_event from singlelineedit within w_error
14: end type
15: type cb_quit from u_cb within w_error
16: end type
17: type sle_error_number from singlelineedit within w_error
18: end type
19: type cb_print_report from u_cb within w_error
20: end type
21: type ws_error from structure within w_error
22: end type
23: end forward
24:
25: type ws_error from structure
26: string    s_error
27: string    i_error
28: end type
29:
30: shared variables
31: Integer si_Count
32: end variables
33:
34: global type w_error from window
```

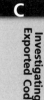

**LISTING C.1** CONTINUED

```
35: integer x = 595
36: integer y = 485
37: integer width = 2460
38: integer height = 1425
39: boolean titlebar = true
40: string title = "Application Error"
41: boolean controlmenu = true
42: windowtype windowtype = response!
43: long backcolor = 67108864
44: event playsound ()
45: mle_error mle_error
46: st_event st_event
47: st_name st_name
48: sle_object_name sle_object_name
49: sle_object_event sle_object_event
50: cb_quit cb_quit
51: sle_error_number sle_error_number
52: cb_print_report cb_print_report
53: end type
54: global w_error w_error
55:
56: type prototypes
57:   Function UInt FindWindow( string sCls, string sNme) Library "user32.dll"
58: end prototypes
59:
60: type variables
61:   Integer ii_Count
62: end variables
63:
64: forward prototypes
65:   public subroutine of_Notify ()
66: end prototypes
67:
68: public subroutine of_Notify ();MailSession  PBmailSession
69:   // Code removed for brevity
70: end subroutine
71:
72: event open;//gnv_app.of_CenterWindow( This)
73:   // Code removed for brevity
74: end event
75:
76: event playsound;If FileExists( "error.wav") Then
```

**LISTING C.1** CONTINUED

```
77:     //   gnv_App.inv_Externals.of_PlaySound ("error.wav", 0)
78:   End If
79: end event
80:
81: on w_error.create
82: this.mle_error=create mle_error
83: this.st_event=create st_event
84: this.st_name=create st_name
85: this.sle_object_name=create sle_object_name
86: this.sle_object_event=create sle_object_event
87: this.cb_quit=create cb_quit
88: this.sle_error_number=create sle_error_number
89: this.cb_print_report=create cb_print_report
90: this.Control[]={this.mle_error,&
91: this.st_event,&
92: this.st_name,&
93: this.sle_object_name,&
94: this.sle_object_event,&
95: this.cb_quit,&
96: this.sle_error_number,&
97: this.cb_print_report}
98: end on
99:
100: on w_error.destroy
101: destroy(this.mle_error)
102: destroy(this.st_event)
103: destroy(this.st_name)
104: destroy(this.sle_object_name)
105: destroy(this.sle_object_event)
106: destroy(this.cb_quit)
107: destroy(this.sle_error_number)
108: destroy(this.cb_print_report)
109: end on
110:
111: type sle_error_number from singlelineedit within w_error
112: integer x = 449
113: integer y = 493
114: integer width = 311
115: integer height = 89
116: integer taborder = 10
117: integer textsize = -8
118: integer weight = 400
```

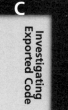

**LISTING C.1**    CONTINUED

```
119: fontcharset fontcharset = ansi!
120: fontpitch fontpitch = variable!
121: fontfamily fontfamily = swiss!
122: string facename = "Arial"
123: long textcolor = 33554432
124: borderstyle borderstyle = stylelowered!
125: end type
126:
127: type cb_quit from u_cb within w_error
128: integer x = 1399
129: integer y = 248
130: integer width = 617
131: integer taborder = 20
132: string text = "&Quit the Application"
133: end type
134:
135: event clicked;call super::clicked;If FileExists( "rusure.wav") Then
136:     //   gnv_App.inv_Externals.of_PlaySound( "rusure.wav", 0)
137:     End If
138:
139:     If MessageBox("Caution", "Are you sure you wish to quit?", &
140:                     StopSign!, YesNo!) = 1 Then
141:         Halt Close
142:     End If
143: end event
```

Lines 1–23 contain the export header declaration. There's no need to ever touch line 1. The remaining lines declare all the controls used in the window. Line 3 is the type declaration for the actual window; in this listing, it is of type Window. Note that the window is a *global* type declaration. This is used at runtime to direct PowerBuilder to declare a global variable to point at this window. The remaining controls are declared from either PowerBuilder standard control types (singlelineedit, statictext, and multilineedit) or user objects (in this case, just u_cb).

Lines 25–32 show window structures and shared variables that have been defined for the window.

Lines 34–54 show the declaration of the windows' attributes; only attributes with assigned values are listed. Notice that user events and window controls are listed as attributes of the window.

Lines 56–66 are the prototypes for window-level functions, instance variables, and local external functions that are declared in the following section

Lines 72–79 detail window events that have script associated with them (at this level and not at the ancestor level) and take the following form:

```
event EventName;
  // Here is your event PowerScript
end event
```

Lines 81–109 show the window's event section, which always contains two important events: on `create` and on `destroy`. The first event is where each object is instantiated when the window is created at runtime. Notice that the objects are instantiated into the variables defined in lines 45-52 and are added into the control array attribute. During window destruction, all controls are destroyed as well.

Lines 111–143 of the export file contain the definitions, attributes, and event code for each control. This export has been shortened to save space, but you should get the idea from the two controls displayed.

The layout of the export file varies among the different types of objects, as you will see next. User objects are the exception and are identical to windows except in the global type definition, where they are naturally inherited from `UserObject` rather than from `Window`. Of course, this doesn't apply if they're inherited, as you will see later in the section "Object Inheritance," which uses a window as an example.

# Application Objects

Application objects (see Listing C.2) naturally contain the definitions of global variables and the global variable data types (such as `SQLCA` and `error`).

**LISTING C.2**   An Export of an Application Object

```
$PBExportHeader$export.sra
$PBExportComments$Generated Application Object
forward
global type export from application
end type
global n_tr sqlca
global dynamicdescriptionarea sqlda
global dynamicstagingarea sqlsa
global error error
global message message
end forward
```

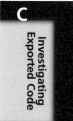

**LISTING C.2** CONTINUED

```
global variables
exp_n_cst_appmanager gnv_app
end variables

global type export from application
string appname = "export"
end type
global export export

on export.create
appname="export"
message=create message
sqlca=create n_tr
sqlda=create dynamicdescriptionarea
sqlsa=create dynamicstagingarea
error=create error
end on

on export.destroy
destroy(sqlca)
destroy(sqlda)
destroy(sqlsa)
destroy(error)
destroy(message)
end on

event open;gnv_app.Event pfc_Open( commandline)
end event
event close;gnv_app.Event pfc_Close()
end event
event idle;gnv_app.Event pfc_Idle()
end event
event systemerror;gnv_app.Event pfc_SystemError()
end event
```

Note that PowerBuilder creates and destroys the default global variable data types for you.

# Functions

Functions are easy to understand, but you will rarely export one because you have access to everything about the object in the Function painter. As you will notice, the example in Listing C.3 follows much the same structure as a window, except (of course) it doesn't contain any controls or the code to declare, create, and destroy them.

**LISTING C.3** An Export of a Function

```
$PBExportHeader$f_boolean_to_number.srf
global type f_boolean_to_number from function_object
end type


forward prototypes
global function int f_boolean_to_number (boolean bvalue)
end prototypes


global function int f_boolean_to_number (boolean bvalue);Integer nReturn
// Code removed for brevity
end function
```

# Structures

Structures (see Listing C.4) are even simpler than functions. Again, you will only modify this object from within the Structure painter.

**LISTING C.4** An Export of a Structure

```
$PBExportHeader$s_outline.srs
global type s_outline from structure
    string   s_entrytext
    integer  i_level
    integer  i_children
    integer  i_parentindex
    string   s_expanded
end type
```

# Menus

Menus are a little more involved but are still similar to window objects. As you can see from Listing E.5, when a menu is created at runtime, each individual menu item is also created; this is the performance degradation hinted at in areas of this book. This should be obvious from the number of Create and Destroy events in the export in Listing C.5.

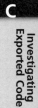

**LISTING C.5**  An Export of a Menu

```
$PBExportHeader$m_frame.srm
forward
global type m_frame from menu
end type
type m_file from menu within m_frame
end type
type m_newmfgorder from menu within m_file
end type
type m_2 from menu within m_file
end type
type m_exit from menu within m_file
end type
type m_file from menu within m_frame
m_newmfgorder m_newmfgorder
m_2 m_2
m_exit m_exit
end type
type m_help from menu within m_frame
end type
type m_about from menu within m_help
end type
type m_help from menu within m_frame
m_about m_about
end type
end forward

global type m_frame from menu
m_file m_file
m_help m_help
end type
global m_frame m_frame

type variables
Integer        i_nWindowListPosition = 6
String         i_szMRU1, i_szMRU2, i_szMRU3
end variables

forward prototypes
public subroutine mf_setmaintenancepermissions ()
public subroutine mf_openmru (string a_szorderno, integer a_nposition)
end prototypes
```

**LISTING C.5** CONTINUED

```
public subroutine mf_setmaintenancepermissions ();
//Code removed for brevity
end subroutine

public subroutine mf_openmru (string a_szorderno, integer a_nposition);
//Code removed for brevity
end subroutine

on m_frame.create
m_frame=this
this.m_file=create m_file
this.m_help=create m_help
this.Item[]={this.m_file, &
this.m_help}
end on

on m_frame.destroy
destroy(this.m_file)
destroy(this.m_help)
end on

type m_file from menu within m_frame
m_newmfgorder m_newmfgorder
m_2 m_2
m_exit m_exit
end type

on clicked;//Code removed for brevity
end on

on m_file.create
this.Text="&File"
this.m_newmfgorder=create m_newmfgorder
this.m_2=create m_2
this.m_exit=create m_exit
this.Item[]={this.m_newmfgorder, &
this.m_2, &
this.m_exit}
end on

on m_file.destroy
destroy(this.m_newmfgorder)
```

**LISTING C.5**   CONTINUED

```
destroy(this.m_2)
destroy(this.m_exit)
end on


type m_newmfgorder from menu within m_file
end type


on clicked;//Code removed for brevity
end on


on m_newmfgorder.create
this.Text="&New Mfg. Order~tCtrl+N"
this.ToolBarItemName="q:\projects\oe\oe_010\mfgsheet.bmp"
this.ToolBarItemText="New Mfg. Sheet"
this.Enabled=false
this.Shortcut=334
end on


type m_2 from menu within m_file
end type


on m_2.create
this.Text="-"
end on


type m_exit from menu within m_file
end type


on clicked;//Code removed for brevity
end on


on m_exit.create
this.Text="E&xit~tCtrl+X"
this.Microhelp="Leave application"
this.Shortcut=344
end on


type m_help from menu within m_frame
m_about m_about
end type


on m_help.create
```

**LISTING C.5** CONTINUED

```
this.Text="&Help"
this.m_about=create m_about
this.Item[]={this.m_about}
end on

on m_help.destroy
destroy(this.m_about)
end on

type m_about from menu within m_help
end type

on clicked;open(w_about)
end on

on m_about.create
this.Text="&About..."
this.Microhelp="About the application"
end on
```

# DataWindows

DataWindows (see Listing C.6) are different in their exported format from any of the objects discussed to this point. You might expect this from the range of special commands used with them within your PowerScript.

**LISTING C.6** An Export of a DataWindow

```
 1: $PBExportHeader$d_cust.srd
 2: release 7;
 3: datawindow(units=0 timer_interval=0 color=79416533 processing=0
 4: HTMLDW=no print.documentname="" print.orientation = 0
 5: print.margin.left = 110 print.margin.right = 110 print.margin.top = 96
 6: print.margin.bottom = 96 print.paper.source = 0 print.paper.size = 0
 7: print.prompt=no print.buttons=no print.preview.buttons=no )
 8: header(height=136 color="536870912" )
 9: summary(height=0 color="536870912" )
10: footer(height=0 color="536870912" )
11: detail(height=96 color="536870912" )
12: table(column=(type=long update=yes updatewhereclause=yes key=yes
13: name=id dbname="customer.id" )
14: column=(type=char(15) update=yes updatewhereclause=yes name=fname
```

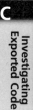

**LISTING C.6**    CONTINUED

```
15: dbname="customer.fname" )
16: column=(type=char(20) update=yes updatewhereclause=yes name=lname
17: dbname="customer.lname" )
18: column=(type=char(35) update=yes updatewhereclause=yes name=address
19: dbname="customer.address" )
20: column=(type=char(20) update=yes updatewhereclause=yes name=city
21: dbname="customer.city" )
22: column=(type=char(2) update=yes updatewhereclause=yes name=state
23: dbname="customer.state" )
24: column=(type=char(10) update=yes updatewhereclause=yes name=zip
25: dbname="customer.zip" )
26: column=(type=char(12) update=yes updatewhereclause=yes name=phone
27: dbname="customer.phone" )
28: column=(type=char(35) update=yes updatewhereclause=yes
29: name=company_name dbname="customer.company_name" )
30: retrieve="PBSELECT(TABLE(NAME=~"customer~")
31: COLUMN(NAME=~"customer.id~") COLUMN(NAME=~"customer.fname~")
32: COLUMN(NAME=~"customer.lname~") COLUMN(NAME=~"customer.address~")
33: COLUMN(NAME=~"customer.city~") COLUMN(NAME=~"customer.state~")
34: COLUMN(NAME=~"customer.zip~") COLUMN(NAME=~"customer.phone~")
35: COLUMN(NAME=~"customer.company_name~"))"
36: update="customer" updatewhere=1 updatekeyinplace=no )
37: text(band=header alignment="2" text="Customer ID" border="6"
38: color="0" x="18" y="16" height="104"' width="274"  name=id_t
39: font.face="MS Sans Serif" font.height="-8" font.weight="700"
40: font.family="2" font.pitch="2" font.charset="0" background.mode="1"
41: background.color="536870912" )
42: text(band=header alignment="2" text="First Name" border="6"
43: color="0" x="311" y="16" height="52" width="411"  name=fname_t
44: font.face="MS Sans Serif" font.height="-8" font.weight="700"
45: font.family="2" font.pitch="2" font.charset="0" background.mode="1"
46: background.color="536870912'' )
47: //
48: // Repeated for each text object, and other objects within the DataWindow
49: //
50: column(band=detail id=1 alignment="1" tabsequence=10 border="5"
51: color="0" x="18" y="16" height="60" width="206" format="[general]"
52: name=id  tag="Unique Identification number of the customer"
53: edit.limit=0 edit.case=any edit.autoselect=yes edit.autohscroll=yes
54: font.face="MS Sans Serif" font.height="-8" font.weight="400"
55: font.family="2" font.pitch="2" font.charset="0" background.mode="1"
56: background.color="536870912" )
```

**LISTING C.6**    CONTINUED

```
57: column(band=detail id=2 alignment="0" tabsequence=20 border="5"
58: color="0" x="311" y="16" height="60" width="411" format="[general]"
59: name=fname  tag="First name of the customer" edit.limit=15
60: edit.case=any edit.autoselect=yes edit.autohscroll=yes
61: font.face="MS Sans Serif" font.height="-8" font.weight="400"
62: font.family="2" font.pitch="2" font.charset="0" background.mode="1"
63: background.color="536870912" )
64: //
65: // Repeated for each column
66: //
67: htmltable(border="1" )
68: htmlgen(clientevents="1" clientvalidation="1" clientcomputedfields="1"
69: clientformatting="0" clientscriptable="0" generatejavascript="1" )
```

Lines 1–7 include the source header information and define the specifications for printing the DataWindow, from the margins to the paper orientation.

Lines 8–11 state the height of the different bands and the different colors for each band in the DataWindow.

Each database column and database-computed value is listed in lines 12–29 with its data type, update information, DataWindow name, and database name. Any database computed values will show up as compute_000 and higher if you didn't name them. That's why it's advisable to name all your database computed fields.

Lines 30–35 show the actual retrieval statement for the DataWindow (if it has one). As you can see, it's stored in PowerBuilder's own internal format (called the PB Select), which makes it transportable between different databases.

Additional update information is stated in line 36. The columns to include in the update are specified in lines 12–29.

Each static text object, along with other drawing objects, is listed with each of its settings in lines 37–49.

Lines 50–66 list each column placed on the DataWindow along with the settings of all its attributes, which are accessible at runtime through the Describe() and Modify() functions (as are the text objects' properties).

Lines 67–69 maintain information on generating the DataWindow as HTML.

**C**

Investigating
Exported Code

## Projects

Exporting a project yields the same information that's available through the Object-Browsing menu item in the Project painter because all the objects for the libraries of a project are listed. Listing C.7 shows a shortened list of objects.

**LISTING C.7**  An Export of a Project

```
$PBExportHeader$order_entry.srj
EXE:q:\projects\oe\oe_010\oe_010.exe,q:\projects\oe\oe_010\oe_010.pbr,0,1
CMP:1,0,0,0,2,0
PBD:q:\projects\shared\sh_uobj.pbl,,1
PBD:q:\projects\shared\sh_func.pbl,q:\shared\shared.pbr,1
PBD:q:\projects\shared\sh_wind.pbl,,1
PBD:q:\projects\oe\oe_010\oe_010.pbl,,0
PBD:q:\projects\oe\oe_010\oe_main.pbl,,1
PBD:q:\projects\oe\oe_010\oe_mfg.pbl,,1
PBD:q:\projects\oe\oe_010\oe_mnt.pbl,,1
PBD:q:\projects\oe\oe_010\oe_rept.pbl,,1
PBD:q:\projects\oe\oe_010\oe_stock.pbl,,1
OBJ:q:\projects\oe\oe_010\oe_main.pbl,f_transfer_line_to_line,f
OBJ:q:\projects\shared\sh_func.pbl,f_close_all_mdi_children,f
OBJ:q:\projects\oe\oe_010\oe_mfg.pbl,d_converting_spec_entry,d
OBJ:q:\projects\oe\oe_010\oe_main.pbl,f_convert_decimal_to_fraction,f
OBJ:q:\projects\shared\sh_func.pbl,f_print_multi_lines,f
OBJ:q:\projects\shared\sh_wind.pbl,w_change_password,w
OBJ:q:\projects\oe\oe_010\oe_main.pbl,d_line_items_entry,d
OBJ:q:\projects\shared\sh_func.pbl,f_boolean_to_string,f
OBJ:q:\projects\oe\oe_010\oe_mnt.pbl,w_maintenance,w
OBJ:q:\projects\shared\sh_uobj.pbl,u_n_externals_win32,u
```

The EXE line states the filename and path of the executable that will be created, the resource file (if any), whether the Project painter should prompt for overwrite (0=FALSE, 1=TRUE), and whether the libraries in the search path should be regenerated (0=FALSE, 1=TRUE).

The PBD lines state each library in the search path, the resource file (if any), and whether the library should be made into a PBD file (0=FALSE, 1=TRUE).

The OBJ lines list the objects used by the application, along with the library in which they reside. The last character is the object type, which is used in the Object Browser accessible in the Project painter.

The CMP line indicates the set compilation options: machine code, error context, and so on.

# Pipelines

The export of a pipeline object (in Listing C.8) shows the settings for the pipeline, a definition of the source tables and columns, the retrieve statement to get the data from those tables and columns, and a definition of the destination table and columns.

**LISTING C.8**  An Export of a Pipeline

```
$PBExportHeader$p_emp_master_create.srp
$PBExportComments$Creates a copy of the employee table to emp_pipe_master
PIPELINE(source_connect=EAS Demo DB V3,destination_connect=EAS Demo DB V3,type=-
replace,commit=100,errors=10,keyname="emp_pipe_master_x")
SOURCE(name="employee",COLUMN(type=long,name="emp_id",dbtype="integer",
      key=yes,nulls_allowed=no)
 COLUMN(type=varchar,name="emp_fname",dbtype="char(20)",nulls_allowed=no)
 COLUMN(type=varchar,name="emp_lname",dbtype="char(20)",nulls_allowed=no)
 COLUMN(type=long,name="dept_id",dbtype="integer",nulls_allowed=no)
 COLUMN(type=varchar,name="bene_health_ins",dbtype="char(1)",nulls_allowed=yes)
 COLUMN(type=varchar,name="bene_life_ins",dbtype="char(1)",nulls_allowed=yes)
 COLUMN(type=varchar,name="bene_day_care",dbtype="char(1)",nulls_allowed=yes))
RETRIEVE(statement="PBSELECT(TABLE(NAME=~"employee~")
 COLUMN(NAME=~"employee.emp_id~")
 COLUMN(NAME=~"employee.emp_fname~")
 COLUMN(NAME=~"employee.emp_lname~")
 COLUMN(NAME=~"employee.dept_id~")
 COLUMN(NAME=~"employee.bene_health_ins~")
 COLUMN(NAME=~"employee.bene_life_ins~")
 COLUMN(NAME=~"employee.bene_day_care~"))")
DESTINATION(name="emp_pipe_master",
 COLUMN(type=long,name="emp_id",dbtype="integer",key=yes,nulls_allowed=yes)
 COLUMN(type=varchar,name="emp_fname",dbtype="char(20)",nulls_allowed=yes)
 COLUMN(type=varchar,name="emp_lname",dbtype="char(20)",nulls_allowed=yes)
 COLUMN(type=long,name="dept_id",dbtype="integer",nulls_allowed=yes)
 COLUMN(type=varchar,name="bene_health_ins",dbtype="char(1)",
      nulls_allowed=no,initial_value="spaces")
 COLUMN(type=varchar,name="bene_life_ins",dbtype="char(1)",
      nulls_allowed=no,initial_value="spaces")
 COLUMN(type=varchar,name="bene_day_care",dbtype="char(1)",
      nulls_allowed=no,initial_value="spaces"))
```

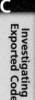

# Searching and Replacing

You can use any text editor's search-and-replace feature to make global name—or even code—changes. A word of warning, however: Be very careful of replacing small words because you might clobber other statements in a way you didn't intend. Although the object might import correctly, you will either get strange runtime errors or a general protection fault when you try to open it in a painter.

There should be little or no need to change any of the PowerBuilder object-specific code unless you are making inheritance changes.

# Object Inheritance

The other most common reason for exporting an object is to make a change to the inheritance chain. By careful manipulation of the export code, you can reattach an object at any level of the inheritance chain.

For a demonstration of this technique, look at this simple window called w_oe_error, which is initially inherited from w_error. You will change the ancestor object to be w_dialog_for_errors.

The initial export code looks like this:

```
$PBExportHeader$w_oe_error.srw
forward
global type w_oe_error from w_error
end type
end forward


global type w_oe_error from w_error
end type
global w_oe_error w_oe_error


on timer;call w_error::timer;Timer (0)


cb_recover.TriggerEvent( Clicked!)
end on


on open;call w_error::open;Timer( 30, this)
end on


on w_oe_error.create
call w_error::create
end on
```

```
on w_oe_error.destroy
call w_error::destroy
end on
```

This is actually a simple case of text replacement from `w_error` to `w_dialog_for_errors`, which covers all the simple code changes. However, you must be aware that some of the controls inherited from the original ancestor might not be available in the new ancestor, and you should remove all references to them. Otherwise, you can't import the modified window into PowerBuilder.

# Importing

You import the code back into PowerBuilder through the Library painter, either with the menu option or the PainterBar button. This prompts you for the source filename and then lists the libraries in the current search path. When you select a library, the file is imported. Any errors are displayed in a dialog, and the object won't be created in the destination library.

# Getting Certified in PowerBuilder

**APPENDIX**

**D**

Sybase's Certified PowerBuilder Developer (CPD) program is designed to recognize individuals as skilled PowerBuilder developers. To find the latest certification requirements for PowerBuilder, check out the Sybase Learning Connection on the Web at http://slc.sybase.com/certification.

# Key Benefits of Certification

The CPD program provides a number of benefits that range from being recognized within your own company to being recognized throughout the PowerBuilder community:

- *External and Internal company recognition.* Consulting companies are often gauged by how many PowerBuilder CPDs they employ, and often become preferred vendors because of their acknowledged expertise. Your company's employees also will recognize you as a source of answers to PowerBuilder questions.

- *Industry recognition and leadership.* Clients can feel confident in the PowerBuilder applications that you develop for them. Other developers will look to you for leadership and knowledge based on your certification.

- *Official certification kit.* Sybase provides a certification kit that includes a business card carrier, card, certificate, and CPD logo sheet.

- *Use of the CPD logo.* As a CPD, you are permitted to include the CPD logo on all your business literature.

- *Listing in the CPD directory.* Sybase places your name in the CPD directory as a qualified resource to provide design and implementation services for PowerBuilder solutions. This directory is available through all the media Sybase provides.

- *Technical support.* As a CPD, you receive a preferred rate when you sign up for Sybase's technical support.

- *Sybase communication.* Sybase informs you of all opportunities to keep your PowerBuilder skills up-to-date.

# Levels of Certification

Currently, two levels of certification are available: Associate and Professional. To attain certification, you must pass Sybase's rigorous tests that have been constructed around real-world use of PowerBuilder. They test your ability to apply PowerBuilder in real-world situations.

# CPD Associate Certification

To become an Associate-level CPD, you must pass the CPD Associate computer-based test. The test covers PowerBuilder fundamentals and some advanced PowerBuilder concepts. The test has questions in the forms of multiple choice, short answer, and true/false.

The fundamentals portion of the Associate test assesses your basic knowledge of PowerBuilder concepts. It includes topics such as the development environment, transaction management, PowerBuilder painters, the PowerScript language, and Data-Window concepts. General questions also cover client/server computing, object-oriented programming, event-driven processing, graphical user interfaces, relational databases, and basic SQL.

The advanced concepts part of the Associate test assesses your ability to use advanced concepts and techniques to develop complex applications. This test covers understanding the development environment, transaction management, PowerBuilder painters, the PowerScript language, advanced DataWindow techniques, distributed PowerBuilder, PowerBuilder and the Internet, and object-oriented programming.

The CPD Associate test is based, for the most part, on the available PowerBuilder training courses. See the Sybase Web site (`slc.sybase.com`) for a list of Sybase training partners near you. To prepare for these tests, the following training courses are recommended:

- Fast Track to PowerBuilder
- Mastering DataWindows
- Advanced PowerBuilder Controls
- Building Object-Oriented Applications with PowerBuilder

It's also recommended that you have at least six months of PowerBuilder experience.

# CPD Professional Certification

To get the Professional level of certification, you must first have obtained an Associate-level CPD certification. You are then required to pass the PowerBuilder application test.

The PowerBuilder application test takes approximately $2\frac{1}{2}$ hours and is designed to test your PowerBuilder expertise. You're required to build a small application that solves a series of problems. Your grade is based on your ability to solve problems, how well you follow directions, and how clean and effective your code is.

The CPD Professional test is based entirely on your real-world experience with PowerBuilder. The best way to prepare for this test is to have been using PowerBuilder for a while and to have developed a number of systems. Sybase recommends a minimum of 12 months of PowerBuilder experience.

# Maintaining Certification

CPD certifications are no longer tied to a period of time; they are now version specific. This policy, introduced by Sybase in version 5.0, addresses what developers are doing in practice. CPD Associates or Professionals currently qualified on the 6.0 tests are considered certified in version 6.0.

Version certifications now expire only when Sybase no longer officially supports a version. Generally, Sybase supports only two versions at any one time; therefore, version 5.0 of PowerBuilder is now unsupported with the release of 7.0. This means that any CPDs certified in 5.0 who haven't passed the maintenance test for 6.0 have a three-month grace period to become certified in either 6.0 or 7.0. CPD Professionals are given a six-month grace period to become re-certified by taking the Professional maintenance test.

The beta 7.0 Associate maintenance test should be available after one month of version 7.0 being publicly released, and the beta 7.0 Professional maintenance test will be available after two months of version 7.0's release. Final versions of both tests will be made available six months after the release of version 7.0.

# Registering for Certification Tests

All Sybase certification tests are administrated by Sylvan Prometric and VUE and are given at authorized Sylvan and VUE testing centers. Contact the regional Sylvan testing centers for more information at (800) 792-EXAM or (612) 820-5747 or register online at http://www.2test.com/register. To register for with a VUE testing center, call (800) 243-7184 or register online at http://www.vue.com/sybase.

# Cross-Platform PowerBuilder

APPENDIX

E

Today's businesses have many hardware options. Thus, many MIS departments must create applications that run on multiple platforms. Because most software is created specifically for a particular environment (for example, UNIX or Windows), MIS must build multiple applications using different software for each required platform. Another alternative is to convert all users to the same hardware system. Either resolution results in considerable hardware or software costs for the company. The need for development to occur across multiple platforms is usually a difficult undertaking that requires you to fall back to a language such as C++ and the cross-platform libraries available for it.

With the release of PowerBuilder version 4.0, Powersoft allowed developers to create PowerBuilder applications on multiple platforms. PowerBuilder can now run on Windows 95, Windows 98, Windows NT, and UNIX Motif, giving developers a great deal of flexibility. Developers need to learn only one tool (PowerBuilder), which they can use to develop applications for multiple environments.

> **Note**
>
> PowerBuilder 7.0 no longer supports the Windows 3. *x* or Macintosh environ-ments. If you need to support either of these platforms, the PowerBuilder Web Deployment kit allows PowerBuilder applications to be deployed on any machine with a Java virtual machine. See Chapter 29, "PowerBuilder and the Internet," for more details on the Web Deployment Kit. Sybase's vision for cross-platform computing involves HTML-based applications using EA Server.

In addition to multiple-platform support, another requirement for many business applications is deployment in multiple countries and multiple languages. Sybase has been striving to address this issue and has added features to enable international deployment of PowerBuilder applications.

This appendix looks at PowerBuilder's cross-platform capabilities and addresses some unique aspects of cross-platform development. The appendix also looks at PowerBuilder's support for international languages and gives examples of some coding techniques you can use to develop code that can be used across platforms.

# PowerBuilder Platforms

The idea behind PowerBuilder's cross-platform functionality is so that you can create applications in one environment (for example, Windows 98) and deploy them to all users, regardless of the operating system in use. PowerBuilder allows two or more developers to work on the same library files (PBLs), even if they're developing on different platforms (for example, one AIX and one Windows developer). After the application is developed, the executable must be created in its planned runtime environment (for example, HP-UX).

PowerBuilder's advanced object library and source manager provide binary-format compatibility across multiple operating platforms. This allows teams of developers to share PowerBuilder objects and libraries with other PowerBuilder applications in a multiplatform environment that includes Intel-based Windows 95/98/NT; DEC Alpha Windows NT; and UNIX for Sun Solaris, HP-UX, and IBM AIX. Developers can build a single application, deploy it across a heterogeneous environment, and provide users with a look and feel consistent with their native OS environment.

## Microsoft Windows

The Microsoft Windows platform now consists of Windows NT, Windows 95, and Windows 98. All three share the same user interface and the same 32-bit API. The underlying code has significant differences, but most of these have little impact on PowerBuilder developers.

Windows NT is Microsoft's server and high-powered workstation operating system. It provides multitasking, robust security features, and greater stability than the desktop operating systems, all of which are requirements for success in the server market.

Windows 95 and Windows 98, Microsoft's desktop operating systems, are typically deployed on user desktops, where performance, stability, and security features are less critical.

> **Note**
>
> With the upcoming release of Windows 2000 (originally Windows NT 5.0), Microsoft plans to incorporate the Windows NT kernel into the entire Windows product line. Enterprise versions of Windows 2000 will be available for use as servers, whereas the typical user will run a scaled-down desktop version.

The Microsoft product line design guide recommended reading is *The Windows Interface Guidelines for Software Design*, by Microsoft Press.

## UNIX Motif

PowerBuilder for UNIX was created to exploit the raw processing power of RISC technology that gives you extremely high throughput of data from server to client. PowerBuilder for UNIX provides a 32-bit development platform. It provides scalability and security often needed in a large, complex, and computation-intensive application. PowerBuilder for UNIX uses an extended Motif GUI environment including multiple screen displays. The minimum system requirements are

- Sun Solaris, HP-UX, or IBM AIX

- 32MB RAM

- 96MB swap space

- 100MB hard disk space

A good source for more information on UNIX Motif design is the *Motif Style Guide* by Open Software Foundation.

PowerBuilder 6.0 introduced the `Timing` object, primarily for use with the UNIX platform as well as distributed PowerBuilder. The `Timing` object is needed within the UNIX environment because window objects don't have a `Timer` event on that platform. To use the `Timing` object, create a standard class user object of type `Timing` and write your code for the `Timer` event, which is located in the `Timing` object. To use it in your application, instantiate the user object and call the `Timing` object's `Start()` method, which takes a double as an argument to indicate the number of seconds between execution of the `Timer` event. To terminate the execution of the `Timing` object, call the object's `Stop()` method.

# Internationalization

To support the growing need to create applications that can service multiple countries, Sybase has added several Internationalization capabilities to PowerBuilder. These include support for applications in Arabic and Hebrew, Double Byte Character Set (DBCS), and a Unicode version of PowerBuilder. PowerBuilder can now produce 32-bit executables in Arabic, Hebrew, Japanese, and Unicode.

PowerBuilder's DBCS version is used for Japanese development. DBCS supports the Japanese character set, setting it apart from the ANSI and Unicode versions of PowerBuilder.

In addition to the DBCS and ANSI versions of PowerBuilder, PowerBuilder 7.0 is available in a Unicode version (under Windows NT 4 *.x* only). Unicode is being embraced because it surpasses ASCII's limitation to encode information using only the Latin alphabet. Unicode introduces a new character code that gives the capability to encode all characters used for written languages across the world. This is done by using a 16-bit code set versus ASCII, which uses a 7-bit code set. Unicode can, therefore, create codes for 65,000 characters as opposed to ASCII's 128 characters. Each character in the Unicode version is assigned a unique 16-bit character that makes the processing for software much easier to encode.

Applications created by using PowerBuilder's Unicode version need to be deployed with the Unicode deployment DLLs on a Unicode-compliant operating system. The PowerBuilder library files will be saved with the extension .PUL (for PowerBuilder Unicode Library).

PowerBuilder applications can be migrated from ANSI to Unicode and back. This is done through the Library painter in the Unicode version. The PowerScript language also supports two new functions, `ToAnsi()` and `ToUnicode()`, to aid in the conversion of characters.

> **Caution**
>
> If an application in Unicode adds a character not supported in the ANSI version, the Unicode version can't be migrated back to the ANSI version. (This is also true of ANSI to DBCS.)

To aid in the process of translating an application from one language to another, Sybase has released a translation toolkit to help translate phrases in your application to the necessary languages. After the translation is complete using the toolkit, the application only needs to be compiled and deployed to the appropriate platforms.

> **Note**
>
> In addition to the features built into the PowerBuilder development environment for use with international applications, PowerBuilder has numerous language-specific runtime DLLs that aid international deployment.

# Building Cross-Platform Applications

Before you can create an application, you need to identify which platforms users and developers will have access to. The difficulty in writing a cross-platform application is designing it so that it takes advantage of the different platforms and complies to the standard behavior of the common applications for that environment.

Because your interface should comply with the standards for each environment, you will have to keep these in mind as you build the application. Subtle differences such as menu-naming conventions must be considered because they will be immediately obvious (and possibly confusing) to end users.

Because each environment has its own special behavior and coding techniques, you might be tempted to create several different applications and deploy a different version of the same application to each platform. This would defeat the whole purpose of PowerBuilder's cross-platform capability. The following sections address how to control the fonts used and how to code one application so that it can dynamically incorporate the functionality required for each platform.

## Font Specifications

One consideration for cross-platform development is the font selections for your application. You are relatively safe if you stick to a TrueType font. To assist you with the problem of a font not existing, PowerBuilder 6.0 introduced the capability to map fonts by using initialization files.

When PowerBuilder is started, it reads and stores what fonts are available on a user's system. You can now have PowerBuilder read an initialization file containing font mapping and then map the application fonts as specified in the application. To do this, create a file as specified by your deployment platform as follows:

| *Platform* | *Initialization File* |
|---|---|
| Windows | C:\windows\pbfont70.ini |
| UNIX | ~user/.pbfont70.ini |

Within each file, create the following:

```
[FontSubstitution]
original_font=mapped_font
```

where *original_font* is the specified font in the application and *mapped_font* is the font you want the original mapped to.

# The Environment Object

Coding a multiplatform application depends on a PowerBuilder structure that lets you get information about the platform your application is running on. Table E.1 shows the properties defined for the Environment object.

**TABLE E.1**   Environment Object Properties

| Property | Data Type | Values | Description |
|---|---|---|---|
| PBType | PbTypes | Desktop! Enterprise! | Version of PowerBuilder product |
| PBMajorRevision | Int | | Major version of PB |
| PBMinorRevision | Int | | Minor version of PB |
| PBFixesRevision | Int | | Maintenance version of PB |
| OSType | OsTypes | AIX!, HPUX!, OSF1!, SOL2! Windows!, WindowsNT! | Operating system or environment |
| OSMajorRevision | Int | | Major version of operating system |
| OSMinorRevision | Int | | Minor version of operating system |
| OSFixesRevision | Int | | Maintenance version of operating system |
| CPUType | CpuTypes | Alpha!, Hppa!, I286!, I386!, I486!, M68000!, M68020!, M68030!, M68040!, Mips!, Pentium!, Powerpc! Powerrrs!, ppc601!, ppc603!, ppc604!, Sparc!UltraSparc! | CPU |
| ScreenWidth | Long | | Width of the screen in pixels |
| ScreenHeight | Long | | Height of the screen in pixels |
| NumberOfColors | Long | | Number of colors onscreen (for example, 16 or 256) |

After an Environment object is declared, you need to populate the structure with values. This is done by using the GetEnvironment() function. GetEnvironment() takes the name of your newly declared Environment object as an argument. The function returns an integer, 1 for success and -1 for failure. After the function is called successfully, evaluate the Environment object's attributes to determine what processing you want to occur.

# Screen Width and Height

One problem of moving across platforms and even within the same platform is the resolution of the user's monitor. Applications should be developed using the least common denominator in terms of the resolution. If one of your users is running $640 \times 480$, the application should be developed for a $640 \times 480$ environment. If this isn't done (for example, the application is developed for $800 \times 600$), objects may be too large and therefore cut off in a $640 \times 480$ display. The problem is that applications developed in lower resolutions will have windows appear in the upper-left corner of any higher-resolution environments. This produces a strange-looking application.

For the code that can be used to center a window for different resolutions, see Chapter 36, "API Calls."

# The System Registry

The Windows operating systems maintain a hierarchical database to store application information such as file associations and hardware and software configurations. This database is referred to as the Windows Registry and is accessed by the Registration Editor.

In the Windows 3.*x* environment, many applications used INI files to store system and user configurations. INI files can still be accessed in PowerBuilder 7.0 via several PowerScript functions, such as `ProfileString()`. In the 32-bit Windows environments, the information previously stored in INI files should be maintained in the Registry.

The Registry database organizes information in a hierarchical format that's composed of keys. A *key* is an element within the Registry, and each key is a subkey of the parent key above it in the database hierarchy. Several predefined root keys are supplied, such as `HKEY_CLASSES_ROOT`, `HKEY_CURRENT_USER`, `HKEY_LOCAL_MACHINE`, and `HKEY_USERS`. Each key is separated by slashes. The key to a field within the Registry database looks like a DOS pathname and can be treated as a path to a particular database entry. For example, the connection information for the Sybase Demo database might be stored in `HKEY_CURRENT_USER\Software\Sybase\PowerBuilder\Code Examples\sqlca` .

For a specific key, typically one or more entries are referred to as value names (such as database or DBMS in the previous example). Two types of value names can be specified: one unnamed value name and multiple named value names. A value can be associated with each value name or with just the key.

**Note**

Although the Registry is recommended for the 32-bit environment, it's not required. Many applications, including PowerBuilder, use the Registry and INI files for backward compatibility and for UNIX, which doesn't support the 32-bit Registry.

# INDEX

# C

## FROM KNOWLEDGE TO MASTERY

**Unleashed** *takes you beyond the average technology discussions. It's the best resource for practical advice from experts and the most in-depth coverage of the latest information.* **Unleashed**—*the necessary tool for serious users.*

**Microsoft SQL Server 7.0 Programming Unleashed**
*Matthew Shepker, John Papa*
ISBN: 0-672-31293-X
$49.99 US/
$74.95 CAN

# Other Unleashed Titles

**Microsoft SQL Server 7.0 Unleashed**
*Simon Gallagher, Sharon Bjeletich, Vipul Minocha, Greg Mable, et al.*
ISBN: 0-672-31227-1
$49.99 US/$74.95 CAN

**TCP/IP Unleashed**
*Mark A. Sportack, et al.*
ISBN: 0-672-31690-0
$49.99 US/$59.95 CAN

**Red Hat Linux 6 Unleashed, Third Edition**
*Bill Ball, David Pitts*
ISBN: 0-672-31689-7
$39.99 US/$59.95 CAN

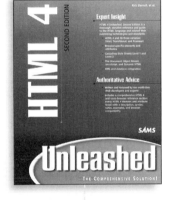

**HTML 4 Unleashed, Second Edition**
*Rick Darnell*
ISBN: 0-672-31347-2
$39.99 US/
$57.95 CAN

**Active Server Pages 2.0 Unleashed**
*Stephen Walther*
ISBN: 0-672-31613-7
$49.99 US/
$74.95 CAN

*www.samspublishing.com*

All prices are subject to change.

# Other Related Titles

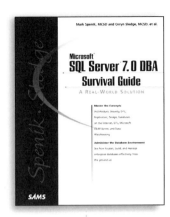

**Microsoft SQL Server 7 DBA Survival Guide**
*Mark Spenik, Orryn Sledge*
ISBN: 0-672-31226-3
$49.99 US/
$74.95 CAN

**Sams Teach Yourself HTML 4 in 24 Hours, Fourth Edition**
*Dick Oliver*
ISBN: 0-672-31724-9
$19.99 US/$29.95 CAN

**Roger Jennings' Database Developer's Guide with Visual Basic 6**
*Roger Jennings*
ISBN: 0-672-31063-5
$59.99 US/$89.95

**Peter Norton's Guide to Access 2000 Programming**
*Peter Norton, Virginia Andersen*
ISBN: 0-672-31760-5
$34.99 US/$49.95 CAN

**Bob Lewis's IS Survival Guide**
*Bob Lewis*
ISBN: 0-672-31437-1
$24.99 US/$37.95 CAN

**Sams Teach Yourself SQL Server 7 in 10 Minutes**
*Bill Robison*
ISBN: 0-672-31663-3
$12.99 US/
$19.95 CAN

**Sams Teach Yourself Active Server Pages in 24 Hours**
*Christoph Wille*
ISBN: 0-672-31612-9
$19.99 US/
$29.95 CAN

**SAMS**

*www.samspublishing.com*

All prices are subject to change.

# What's on the CD-ROM

The companion CD-ROM contains some full versions of various software products and several demo or tryout versions from third-party vendors.

## Windows 95 Installation Instructions

1. Insert the CD-ROM into your CD-ROM drive.

2. From the Windows desktop, double-click the My Computer icon.

3. Double-click the icon representing your CD-ROM drive.

4. Double-click the START.EXE icon to run the CD-ROM interface. You can install any or all of the software from the interface or by exploring the folders and selecting the .EXE file.

> **NOTE**
>
> If Windows 95/98 is installed on your computer and you have the AutoPlay feature enabled, the START.EXE program starts automatically whenever you insert the disc into your CD-ROM drive. You also might be able to double-click your My Computer icon and right-click the CD to perform various tasks, such as installing the author code.

## Windows NT Installation Instructions

1. Insert the CD-ROM into your CD-ROM drive.

2. From File Manager or Program Manager, choose Run from the File menu.

3. Type *drive*:\START.EXE and press Enter, where *drive* corresponds to the drive letter of your CD-ROM. For example, if your CD-ROM is drive D:, type D:\START.EXE and press Enter to run the CD-ROM interface. You can install any or all of the software from the interface.